MW01174421

FOOTBALL IN

ENGLAND

a statistical record

1950 to 2005

Alexander Graham

INTRODUCTION

This book features a statistical history of football in England from 1950 to 2005. For these years, this book contains the results of all League matches, Final League tables and F.A. Cup results from the Quarter-final stages onwards. This book also lists the top goal-scorers for each season.

The Origins of the F.A. Cup and Football League

The F.A. Cup (or The Football Association Challenge Cup to give the full title) was the first major competition but the roots of organised English football predate this by almost 10 years. Organised football as we know it began with the formation of the Football Association in a meeting in the Freemason's Tavern in Great Queen Street, London on 26th October 1863. At that time there were no universally accepted rules for the playing of the game of football with a number of variations used in different areas of the country. The first revision of the rules for the modern game was drawn up during a series of six meetings held in the social room of this public house between October and December of 1863 and, with relatively minor alterations, these rules are used worldwide to this day!

The F.A. Cup itself was first suggested by C.W. Alcock, then Secretary of the Football Association, at a meeting on 20th July 1871 and the competition was embodied at a later meeting on 16th October 1871. The F.A. Cup remains the oldest and most prestigious domestic cup competition in the world and the 12 clubs who entered in 1872 could scarcely have believed that the Cup would grow to a record entry of 660 clubs for the 2004-2005 competition. The Cup is still played as a strict knock-out competition with no seeding of clubs and this book lists the F.A. Cup results from the Quarter-Final stage onwards including full line-ups and goalscorers for the Final matches themselves.

After the great success of the F.A. Cup, it was inevitable that a League competition would eventually begin and to this end William McGregor, a director of Aston Villa FC, arranged a preliminary meeting on 22nd March 1888 at Anderton's Hotel in Fleet Street. The Football League officially came into existence at a subsequent meeting on 17th April 1888 with 12 members. The Football League is, unsurprisingly, the oldest domestic League competition in the world. Since the first game was played on 8th September 1888, the League has expanded considerably and at it's height consisted of 4 separate divisions containing a total of 92 professional clubs. When the top division of clubs split off to form an independent F.A. Premier League in 1992, the remaining 3 divisions of the Football League continued to run as before and it is still commonplace to refer to the clubs in these two competitions as the "92 League Clubs."

This Book

Most of the information in this book is taken from the now defunct "Statistical History of Football" series which were published by Skye Soccer Books. As in the original series, the full names of clubs are used whenever possible with name-changes, mergers etc. shown as and when they occur. The club names are listed in the following format: Club Name (Home Town/City/Village).

The information contained in this book has been gathered over a number of years and has come from myriad sources although most was collected through personal contacts. Other sources of information include newspapers, magazines, books etc. and in more recent times the internet. I would like to extend my thanks to all those who helped with the collection of this information. In an attempt to ensure accuracy, the information has been checked and collated. However, if any errors are found, readers are invited to notify the author care of the address below and if possible provide the corrected information.

Alex Graham

British Library Cataloguing in Publication Data

A catalogue record for this book is available from the British Library

ISBN 1-86223-134-6

Copyright © 2005, SOCCER BOOKS LIMITED. (01472 696226)   www.soccer-books.co.uk

72 St. Peter's Avenue, Cleethorpes, N.E. Lincolnshire, DN35 8HU, England

All rights are reserved. No part of this publication may be reproduced, stored in a retrieval system or transmitted, in any form or by any means, electronic, mechanical, photocopying, recording, or otherwise, without the prior written permission of Soccer Books Limited.

Printed by 4edge Limited.

1950-51

Football League Division 1 1950-51 Season	Arsenal	Aston Villa	Blackpool	Bolton Wands.	Burnley	Charlton Ath	Chelsea	Derby County	Everton	Fulham	Huddersfield T.	Liverpool	Man. United	Middlesbrough	Newcastle Utd.	Portsmouth	Sheffield Wed.	Stoke City	Sunderland	Tottenham H.	W.B.A.	Wolves
Arsenal FC	■	2-1	4-4	1-1	0-1	2-5	0-0	3-1	2-1	5-1	6-2	1-2	3-0	3-1	0-0	0-1	3-0	0-3	5-1	2-2	3-0	2-1
Aston Villa FC	1-1	■	0-3	0-1	3-2	0-0	4-2	1-1	3-3	3-0	0-1	1-1	1-3	0-1	3-0	3-3	2-1	6-2	3-1	2-3	2-0	1-0
Blackpool FC	0-1	1-1	■	2-0	1-2	0-0	3-2	3-1	4-0	4-0	3-1	3-0	1-1	2-1	2-2	3-0	3-2	3-0	2-2	0-1	2-1	1-1
Bolton Wanderers FC	3-0	1-0	1-2	■	1-1	3-0	1-0	3-0	2-0	0-1	4-0	2-1	1-0	0-2	0-2	4-0	0-1	1-1	1-2	1-4	0-2	2-1
Burnley FC	0-1	2-0	0-0	2-0	■	5-1	2-1	1-0	1-1	0-2	0-1	1-1	1-2	3-1	1-1	1-1	1-0	1-1	1-1	2-0	0-1	2-0
Charlton Athletic FC	1-3	2-2	2-3	4-3	0-0	■	1-2	1-2	2-1	0-0	3-2	1-0	1-2	3-0	1-3	0-1	2-1	2-0	3-0	1-1	2-3	3-2
Chelsea FC	0-1	1-1	0-2	4-0	0-2	2-3	■	1-2	2-1	2-0	1-2	1-0	1-0	1-1	3-1	1-4	4-0	1-1	3-0	0-2	1-1	2-1
Derby County FC	4-2	4-2	4-1	2-2	1-1	5-0	1-0	■	0-1	3-2	3-0	1-2	2-4	6-0	1-2	2-3	4-1	1-1	6-5	1-1	1-1	1-2
Everton FC	1-1	1-2	0-2	1-1	1-0	0-0	3-0	1-2	■	1-0	3-2	1-3	1-4	32	3-1	1-5	0-0	0-3	3-1	1-2	0-3	1-1
Fulham FC	3-2	2-1	2-2	0-1	4-1	1-3	1-2	3-5	1-5	■	1-1	2-1	2-2	2-0	1-1	1-4	4-2	2-0	1-1	0-1	0-1	2-1
Huddersfield Town AFC	2-2	4-2	2-1	0-4	3-1	1-1	2-1	2-0	1-2	1-2	■	2-2	2-3	2-3	0-0	3-4	3-1	3-4	3-2	1-2	1-2	1-2
Liverpool FC	1-3	0-0	1-0	3-3	1-0	1-0	1-0	1-0	0-2	2-0	1-4	■	2-1	0-0	2-4	2-1	2-1	0-0	4-0	2-1	1-1	1-4
Manchester United FC	3-1	0-0	1-0	2-3	1-1	3-0	4-1	2-0	3-0	1-0	6-0	1-0	■	1-0	1-2	0-0	3-1	0-0	3-5	2-1	3-0	2-1
Middlesbrough FC	2-1	2-1	4-3	1-1	3-3	7-3	3-0	1-1	4-0	1-1	8-0	1-1	1-2	■	2-1	3-1	2-1	1-0	1-1	1-1	2-1	1-2
Newcastle United FC	2-1	0-1	4-2	0-1	2-1	3-2	3-1	3-1	1-1	1-2	6-0	1-1	0-2	1-0	■	0-0	2-0	3-1	2-2	0-1	1-1	1-1
Portsmouth FC	1-1	3-3	2-0	2-1	2-1	3-3	1-3	2-2	6-3	1-0	1-0	1-3	0-0	1-1	0-0	■	4-1	5-1	0-0	1-1	2-2	1-4
Sheffield Wednesday FC	0-2	3-2	3-1	3-4	0-1	1-2	2-2	4-3	6-0	2-2	3-2	4-1	0-4	0-1	0-0	2-1	■	1-1	3-0	1-1	3-0	2-2
Stoke City FC	1-0	1-0	1-0	2-1	0-0	2-0	4-1	2-0	1-0	2-3	2-0	2-0	1-2	1-2	1-1	1-2	1-1	■	2-4	0-0	1-1	0-1
Sunderland AFC	0-2	3-3	0-2	1-2	1-1	4-2	1-1	1-0	4-0	0-1	0-0	2-1	2-1	2-1	2-1	0-0	5-1	1-1	■	0-0	1-1	0-0
Tottenham Hotspur FC	1-0	3-2	1-4	4-2	1-0	1-1	2-1	2-1	3-0	2-1	0-2	3-1	1-0	3-3	7-0	5-1	1-0	6-1	1-1	■	5-0	2-1
West Bromwich Albion FC	2-0	2-0	1-3	0-1	2-1	3-0	1-1	1-2	0-1	0-2	1-1	0-1	2-3	1-2	5-0	1-3	1-1	3-1	1-2	■		3-2
Wolverhampton Wanderers FC	0-1	2-3	1-1	7-1	0-1	2-3	2-1	2-3	4-0	1-1	3-1	2-0	0-0	3-4	0-1	2-3	4-0	2-3	2-1	2-1	3-1	■

Division 1

#	Team	Pd	Wn	Dw	Ls	GF	GA	Pts	
1.	TOTTENHAM HOTSPUR FC (LONDON)	42	25	10	7	82	44	60	
2.	Manchester United FC (Manchester)	42	24	8	10	74	40	56	
3.	Blackpool FC (Blackpool)	42	20	10	12	79	53	50	
4.	Newcastle United FC (Newcastle-upon-Tyne)	42	18	13	11	62	53	49	
5.	Arsenal FC (London)	42	19	9	14	73	56	47	
6.	Middlesbrough FC (Middlesbrough)	42	18	11	13	76	65	47	
7.	Portsmouth FC (Portsmouth)	42	16	15	11	71	68	47	
8.	Bolton Wanderers FC (Bolton)	42	19	7	16	64	61	45	
9.	Liverpool FC (Liverpool)	42	16	11	15	53	59	43	
10.	Burnley FC (Burnley)	42	14	14	14	48	43	42	
11.	Derby County FC (Derby)	42	16	8	18	81	75	40	
12.	Sunderland AFC (Sunderland)	42	12	16	14	63	73	40	
13.	Stoke City FC (Stoke-on-Trent)	42	13	14	15	50	59	40	
14.	Wolverhampton Wanderers FC (Wolverhampton)	42	15	8	19	74	61	38	
15.	Aston Villa FC (Birmingham)	42	12	13	17	66	68	37	
16.	West Bromwich Albion FC (West Bromwich)	42	13	11	18	53	61	37	
17.	Charlton Athletic FC (London)	42	14	9	19	63	80	37	
18.	Fulham FC (London)	42	13	11	18	52	68	37	
19.	Huddersfield Town AFC (Huddersfield)	42	15	6	21	64	92	36	
20.	Chelsea FC (London)	42	13	8	22	53	65	32	
21.	Sheffield Wednesday FC (Sheffield)	42	12	8	22	64	83	32	R
22.	Everton FC (Liverpool)	42	12	8	22	48	86	32	R
		924	348	228	348	1413	1413	924	

Top Goalscorer

1) Stanley MORTENSEN (Blackpool FC) 30

Football League Division 2 1950-51 Season	Barnsley	Birmingham City	Blackburn Rovers	Brentford	Bury	Cardiff City	Chesterfield	Coventry City	Doncaster Rovers	Grimsby Town	Hull City	Leeds United	Leicester City	Luton Town	Manchester City	Notts County	Preston North End	Q.P.R.	Sheffield United	Southampton	Swansea Town	West Ham United
Barnsley FC	■	0-2	3-0	2-3	2-3	0-0	0-0	3-0	0-1	3-1	4-2	1-2	0-0	6-1	1-1	2-0	4-1	7-0	1-1	1-2	1-0	1-2
Birmingham City FC	2-0	■	3-2	1-1	3-3	0-0	2-1	1-1	0-2	1-1	2-1	0-1	2-0	3-0	1-0	1-4	1-0	1-1	3-0	2-1	5-0	3-1
Blackburn Rovers FC	3-4	2-3	■	3-2	2-4	2-0	1-1	1-0	4-2	2-0	2-2	2-1	1-0	1-0	4-1	0-0	2-1	2-1	0-2	1-0	3-0	1-3
Brentford FC	0-2	2-1	3-2	■	4-0	4-0	4-0	0-4	1-1	5-1	2-1	1-2	0-0	1-0	2-0	1-3	2-4	2-1	3-1	4-0	1-1	1-1
Bury FC	0-3	4-1	1-3	2-1	■	1-2	2-2	1-0	3-1	2-3	0-2	0-1	2-3	4-1	2-0	0-0	3-1	0-1	1-1	1-0	1-1	3-0
Cardiff City AFC	1-1	2-1	1-0	1-1	2-2	■	1-0	2-1	0-0	5-2	2-1	1-0	2-2	2-1	1-1	2-0	0-2	4-2	2-0	2-2	1-0	2-1
Chesterfield FC	1-2	1-1	4-1	2-2	3-0	0-3	■	1-1	1-4	2-2	0-0	1-0	1-0	1-1	1-2	0-0	2-0	3-1	0-2	2-3	3-1	1-2
Coventry City FC	3-3	3-1	6-1	3-3	5-2	2-1	1-0	■	3-1	1-0	4-1	1-0	2-1	4-1	0-2	1-2	1-0	3-0	2-3	2-2	3-1	1-0
Doncaster Rovers FC	3-2	0-1	0-1	0-3	1-1	0-0	1-2	2-1	■	3-1	2-4	4-4	2-2	5-2	4-3	3-2	2-0	0-2	1-1	0-0	1-0	3-0
Grimsby Town AFC	3-1	1-1	1-1	7-2	2-1	0-0	1-2	1-2	1-0	■	1-1	2-2	0-2	0-2	4-4	1-4	0-4	2-2	2-2	4-2	4-2	0-1
Hull City AFC	3-3	3-2	2-2	3-0	4-0	2-0	2-1	0-2	1-2	2-1	■	2-0	1-3	5-3	3-3	1-0	0-0	5-1	1-1	4-1	2-1	1-2
Leeds United AFC	2-2	3-0	0-1	1-0	1-1	2-0	2-0	1-0	3-1	1-0	3-0	■	2-1	2-1	1-1	0-1	0-3	2-2	1-0	5-3	2-0	2-0
Leicester City FC	1-2	1-3	2-0	1-2	4-0	1-1	1-0	3-0	2-0	0-0	4-0	1-5	■	3-1	1-2	1-1	2-3	6-2	2-2	3-1	2-3	1-0
Luton Town FC	1-1	1-1	1-1	2-0	4-2	1-1	3-0	1-1	3-1	4-0	1-2	2-3	0-2	■	2-2	1-1	1-2	2-0	0-0	0-1	3-1	1-1
Manchester City FC	6-0	3-1	1-0	4-0	5-1	2-1	5-1	1-0	3-3	2-2	0-0	4-1	1-1	1-1	■	0-0	0-3	5-2	5-3	2-3	1-2	2-0
Notts County FC	2-1	0-1	1-1	2-3	4-2	1-2	0-2	1-2	3-2	2-2	0-0	2-3	2-2	0-0	0-0	■	1-3	3-3	3-0	2-2	3-2	4-1
Preston North End FC	7-0	1-0	3-0	4-2	2-0	1-1	4-1	1-1	6-1	2-0	1-0	2-0	3-2	1-0	2-4	3-1	■	1-0	1-1	3-2	5-1	0-1
Queen's Park Rangers FC	2-1	2-0	3-1	1-1	3-2	3-2	1-1	3-1	1-2	7-1	3-1	3-0	3-0	1-1	1-2	1-0	1-4	■	2-1	2-0	1-1	3-3
Sheffield United FC	0-2	3-2	0-3	5-1	3-0	1-2	4-1	2-0	0-0	4-2	3-1	2-2	2-1	2-1	0-0	1-2	2-3	2-0	■	1-2	6-1	1-1
Southampton FC	1-0	0-2	1-1	2-1	1-0	1-1	1-1	5-4	1-1	5-1	2-3	2-0	2-2	1-1	2-1	1-0	3-3	2-2	1-0	■	2-1	2-2
Swansea Town AFC	1-0	0-1	1-2	2-1	2-0	0-0	2-0	2-1	2-2	1-3	1-0	4-2	2-1	0-2	2-3	2-1	2-1	1-0	1-2	2-1	■	3-2
West Ham United FC	4-2	1-2	2-3	1-2	2-3	0-0	2-0	3-2	0-0	2-1	3-3	3-1	0-0	2-1	2-4	4-2	2-0	4-1	3-5	3-0	1-1	■

	Division 2	Pd	Wn	Dw	Ls	GF	GA	Pts	
1.	Preston North End FC (Preston)	42	26	5	11	91	49	57	P
2.	Manchester City FC (Manchester)	42	19	14	9	89	61	52	P
3.	Cardiff City AFC (Cardiff)	42	17	16	9	53	45	50	
4.	Birmingham City FC (Birmingham)	42	20	9	13	64	53	49	
5.	Leeds United AFC (Leeds)	42	20	8	14	63	55	48	
6.	Blackburn Rovers FC (Blackburn)	42	19	8	15	65	66	46	
7.	Coventry City FC (Coventry)	42	19	7	16	75	59	45	
8.	Sheffield United FC (Sheffield)	42	16	12	14	72	62	44	
9.	Brentford FC (London)	42	18	8	16	75	74	44	
10.	Hull City AFC (Kingston-upon-Hull)	42	16	11	15	74	70	43	
11.	Doncaster Rovers FC (Doncaster)	42	15	13	14	64	68	43	
12.	Southampton FC (Southampton)	42	15	13	14	66	73	43	
13.	West Ham United FC (London)	42	16	10	16	68	69	42	
14.	Leicester City FC (Leicester)	42	15	11	16	68	58	41	
15.	Barnsley FC (Barnsley)	42	15	10	17	74	68	40	
16.	Queen's Park Rangers FC (London)	42	15	10	17	71	82	40	
17.	Notts County FC (Nottingham)	42	13	13	16	61	60	39	
18.	Swansea Town AFC (Swansea)	42	16	4	22	54	77	36	
19.	Luton Town FC (Luton)	42	9	14	19	57	70	32	
20.	Bury FC (Bury)	42	12	8	22	60	86	32	
21.	Chesterfield FC (Chesterfield)	42	9	12	21	44	69	30	R
22.	Grimsby Town FC (Cleethorpes)	42	8	12	22	61	95	28	R
		924	348	228	348	1469	1469	924	

Football League Division 3 (N) 1950-51 Season

	Accrington St.	Barrow	Bradford City	Bradford P.A.	Carlisle United	Chester	Crewe Alex.	Darlington	Gateshead	Halifax Town	Hartlepools	Lincoln City	Mansfield T.	New Brighton	Oldham Ath.	Rochdale	Rotherham U.	Scunthorpe U.	Shrewsbury T.	Southport	Stockport Co.	Tranmere R.	Wrexham	York City
Accrington Stanley		1-0	0-2	3-3	0-4	1-2	1-0	1-0	2-2	1-0	2-0	3-1	0-2	1-1	1-2	1-2	0-2	0-0	2-0	3-1	2-3	0-2	1-0	2-0
Barrow AFC	4-0		1-3	2-3	1-2	2-0	0-1	0-3	1-1	2-0	3-0	3-1	2-3	1-1	2-1	4-3	0-2	1-0	0-0	3-1	1-0	1-2	2-0	2-0
Bradford City AFC	7-0	5-1		4-1	2-4	0-1	1-1	0-3	2-2	2-0	3-1	0-0	2-3	3-0	1-0	2-1	3-4	2-0	1-0	3-0	0-1	2-2	5-3	5-2
Bradford Park Ave.	3-0	5-0	3-1		0-2	2-0	1-1	2-1	2-0	2-1	1-1	2-1	1-0	2-1	3-1	0-1	0-4	2-2	2-4	2-0	3-0	4-1	0-1	4-0
Carlisle United FC	3-1	1-1	2-1	1-0		2-1	2-1	2-1	3-0	1-0	1-0	2-0	2-0	1-0	1-0	4-0	0-0	3-1	2-2	3-1	2-2	3-1	0-2	3-2
Chester FC	2-2	1-2	2-2	2-0	1-1		1-1	3-1	2-2	2-1	2-1	2-1	0-1	3-1	3-1	1-3	1-2	4-1	3-1	0-2	3-0	1-3	0-0	3-1
Crewe Alexandra FC	3-0	2-0	1-1	2-4	1-1	3-0		5-0	0-1	0-0	3-1	0-4	2-0	2-0	2-1	3-1	1-2	2-0	1-2	1-0	0-2	1-1	1-1	2-4
Darlington FC	3-0	1-1	2-1	1-4	1-0	0-0	2-0		4-2	2-0	0-1	1-1	1-2	5-3	0-0	0-2	2-2	3-2	2-1	1-1	2-1	1-1	1-1	0-3
Gateshead FC	7-0	1-0	2-0	5-0	4-3	2-1	4-0	5-2		5-0	0-1	1-2	1-3	4-0	3-2	4-1	0-3	1-0	3-0	1-3	2-0	2-0	0-0	3-0
Halifax Town AFC	2-2	0-0	1-2	2-2	1-0	3-1	1-0	2-2	1-0		1-0	4-1	0-1	0-2	3-0	1-1	1-3	3-3	1-1	4-0	1-0	0-1	1-0	1-3
Hartlepools United	1-0	6-1	1-1	3-1	3-3	1-2	0-2	6-1	3-0	5-2		2-2	1-1	0-1	0-1	0-0	3-1	4-2	1-0	3-2	2-0	2-1	4-1	4-1
Lincoln City FC	9-1	3-0	1-4	1-3	1-1	2-1	4-1	3-0	2-1	3-1	1-0		3-0	3-0	2-0	4-2	0-2	2-1	5-0	1-2	6-0	2-1	2-1	2-1
Mansfield Town FC	5-0	4-0	1-1	3-2	2-1	2-1	4-1	2-1	2-1	1-0	1-1	4-0		3-1	1-0	1-1	1-1	4-0	2-2	2-1	2-1	1-1	1-1	3-1
New Brighton FC	1-1	1-2	0-6	3-3	0-1	1-0	0-2	2-2	0-1	1-0	1-0	0-1	0-1		2-0	1-5	2-4	1-2	0-0	1-0	1-0	1-1	3-0	0-0
Oldham Athletic AFC	2-1	0-1	2-2	2-3	1-1	1-0	0-2	2-3	2-0	5-1	0-0	2-0	3-1			2-0	4-5	3-4	2-1	4-0	1-3	3-4	2-2	2-2
Rochdale AFC	3-1	1-0	4-0	1-2	4-1	2-3	1-1	0-0	2-0	3-1	3-0	0-0	1-0	0-1			0-2	2-0	5-0	1-1	1-1	2-3	2-0	0-1
Rotherham United FC	6-2	3-0	1-0	2-1	3-0	0-0	2-3	0-1	1-2	2-1	2-1	3-0	3-0	5-3	3-0	3-0		4-1	2-0	1-1	0-0	1-2	5-0	3-1
Scunthorpe United	3-0	1-0	0-0	1-1	1-1	2-0	1-1	2-0	2-1	2-2	0-0	1-1	0-0	6-0	1-0	3-0	0-0		0-0	3-0	1-1	2-0	1-1	0-1
Shrewsbury Town FC	0-1	1-0	2-0	1-0	0-3	1-0	2-2	1-0	2-0	1-0	1-2	1-1	4-2	2-2	0-2	1-2	3-1	1-56		0-3	1-2	2-1	1-0	
Southport FC	3-0	4-1	0-1	2-4	1-0	0-1	2-0	1-0	1-0	1-1	0-2	0-1	1-4	1-1	0-1	2-2	1-2				2-0	0-1	3-1	1-1
Stockport County FC	0-0	4-1	3-1	2-1	1-2	0-3	3-0	1-0	5-2	2-1	2-0	2-0	3-1	4-0	2-2	1-3	1-2	2-0	3-2			0-0	2-1	1-1
Tranmere Rovers FC	1-1	3-0	3-1	2-2	2-2	3-1	3-0	3-2	2-2	3-2	1-0	0-1	2-1	4-3	1-0	2-1	2-1	1-0	0-1	4-0	1-1		1-2	7-2
Wrexham AFC	1-1	1-0	0-3	3-1	2-1	2-0	0-2	3-1	0-0	2-2	1-0	2-3	2-2	0-1	0-2	3-1	0-0	3-1	1-0	3-3	2-0	2-1		4-3
York City FC	3-0	0-2	1-2	1-3	1-1	2-2	1-2	1-1	1-1	0-0	3-0	2-2	1-1	2-0	2-2	2-2	3-3	0-0	2-0	2-0	0-0	4-0	3-0	

Division 3 (North)

		Pd	Wn	Dw	Ls	GF	GA	Pts	
1.	Rotherham United FC (Rotherham)	46	31	9	6	103	41	71	P
2.	Mansfield Town FC (Mansfield)	46	26	12	8	78	48	64	
3.	Carlisle United FC (Carlisle)	46	25	12	9	79	50	62	
4.	Tranmere Rovers FC (Birkenhead)	46	24	11	11	83	62	59	
5.	Lincoln City FC (Lincoln)	46	25	8	13	89	58	58	
6.	Bradford Park Avenue FC (Bradford)	46	23	8	15	90	72	54	
7.	Bradford City AFC (Bradford)	46	21	10	15	90	63	52	
8.	Gateshead FC (Gateshead)	46	21	8	17	84	62	50	
9.	Crewe Alexandra FC (Crewe)	46	19	10	17	61	60	48	
10.	Stockport County FC (Stockport)	46	20	8	18	63	63	48	
11.	Rochdale AFC (Rochdale)	46	17	11	18	69	62	45	
12.	Scunthorpe & Lindsey United FC (Scunthorpe)	46	13	18	15	58	57	44	
13.	Chester FC (Chester)	46	17	9	20	62	64	43	
14.	Wrexham AFC (Wrexham)	46	15	12	19	55	71	42	
15.	Oldham Athletic AFC (Oldham)	46	16	8	22	73	73	40	
16.	Hartlepools United FC (Hartlepool)	46	16	7	23	64	66	39	
17.	York City FC (York)	46	12	15	19	66	77	39	
18.	Darlington FC (Darlington)	46	13	13	20	59	77	39	
19.	Barrow AFC (Barrow-in-Furness)	46	16	6	24	51	76	38	
20.	Shrewsbury Town FC (Shrewsbury)	46	15	7	24	43	74	37	T
21.	Southport FC (Southport)	46	13	10	23	56	72	36	
22.	Halifax Town AFC (Halifax)	46	11	12	23	50	69	34	
23.	Accrington Stanley FC (Accrington)	46	11	10	25	42	101	32	
24.	New Brighton FC (Wallasey)	46	11	8	27	40	90	30	#
		1104	431	242	431	1608	1608	1104	

T: Shrewsbury Town FC (Shrewsbury) were transferred to Division 3 (South) for next season.

\# New Brighton FC (Wallasey) were not re-elected and were replaced by Workington AFC (Workington) for next season.

Football League Division 3 (S) 1950-51 Season

	Aldershot Town	Bournemouth	Brighton & H.A.	Bristol City	Bristol Rovers	Colchester United	Crystal Palace	Exeter City	Gillingham	Ipswich Town	Leyton Orient	Millwall	Newport County	Northampton Town	Norwich City	Nottingham Forest	Plymouth Argyle	Port Vale	Reading	Southend United	Swindon Town	Torquay United	Walsall	Watford
Aldershot Town FC	▓	0-1	0-0	0-0	1-1	2-0	3-0	4-2	2-4	0-1	3-1	2-1	3-1	3-0	1-1	1-0	2-2	2-0	1-1	2-2	0-1	1-0	3-0	1-1
Bournemouth & Bos.	4-0	▓	2-2	1-0	2-0	2-0	5-0	1-1	3-1	2-1	5-0	1-0	2-0	1-0	0-0	3-2	0-2	3-1	1-0	3-1	2-1	0-0	3-1	3-3
Brighton & Hove Alb.	1-2	2-1	▓	1-1	2-2	3-1	1-0	4-1	2-2	4-0	3-0	2-3	9-1	5-1	1-1	1-2	0-6	2-2	1-1	2-1	1-0	2-2	1-0	1-1
Bristol City FC	1-1	2-0	2-0	▓	1-0	0-2	2-0	3-1	2-0	2-1	4-1	2-1	2-1	2-2	0-3	1-0	3-1	3-3	0-3	2-0	0-2	3-3	3-1	3-0
Bristol Rovers FC	3-0	2-0	3-2	2-1	▓	1-1	1-1	3-1	3-0	1-1	2-1	1-0	1-0	1-1	3-3	0-2	3-1	2-0	4-0	4-1	1-0	1-1	1-1	3-0
Colchester United FC	1-0	4-1	4-1	1-1	0-0	▓	1-0	0-1	4-2	2-3	1-0	3-0	1-1	2-1	2-3	0-2	3-0	1-1	1-1	1-3	4-1	3-1	0-1	4-1
Crystal Palace FC	0-2	0-1	0-2	1-0	1-0	1-3	▓	0-1	4-3	1-3	1-1	1-1	0-0	0-5	1-6	0-1	0-2	0-3	0-2	2-0	2-1	1-0	1-1	1-1
Exeter City FC	3-0	2-1	4-2	1-0	0-2	5-0	1-2	▓	1-2	2-0	0-0	0-1	2-2	1-0	1-2	0-5	3-2	0-3	1-3	1-0	1-0	0-0	0-0	3-3
Gillingham FC	3-0	2-2	1-1	1-2	1-0	0-0	0-0	9-4	▓	0-1	1-0	4-3	0-1	3-1	2-2	1-4	1-2	1-1	0-3	0-0	2-1	2-0	4-1	3-1
Ipswich Town FC	5-2	1-0	3-0	2-0	2-3	3-0	1-1	1-0	5-1	▓	2-2	2-1	2-1	1-1	0-1	1-3	2-0	2-2	0-2	1-0	4-1	3-1	3-1	2-1
Leyton Orient FC	1-0	2-0	1-1	0-2	1-0	1-1	2-0	1-3	4-0	2-0	▓	0-2	0-3	1-0	3-1	0-4	1-2	2-3	2-0	1-1	1-1	5-1	2-1	1-2
Millwall FC	1-0	3-0	1-1	5-3	1-0	2-0	1-0	5-0	4-3	4-0	3-1	▓	2-4	2-1	1-1	1-1	2-2	1-3	1-1	1-0	4-1	4-1	2-0	4-1
Newport County AFC	7-0	1-0	3-0	0-1	2-1	2-0	2-4	0-3	1-0	1-2	0-0	2-3	▓	2-2	1-1	0-2	1-2	5-0	6-1	2-1	2-1	2-1	3-0	2-2
Northampton Town	1-0	0-1	0-0	2-2	1-1	2-1	2-0	4-1	4-1	2-1	3-3	1-2	1-4	▓	1-2	2-2	1-3	1-1	1-1	1-1	1-2	1-0	1-1	6-0
Norwich City FC	2-2	3-0	1-1	0-0	2-0	1-1	3-1	3-0	2-0	1-3	3-1	2-1	2-1	0-0	▓	2-0	1-0	2-0	2-1	3-0	2-0	1-1	1-0	3-1
Nottingham Forest	7-0	1-0	4-0	0-0	2-1	0-0	1-0	2-2	9-2	0-0	2-0	2-1	2-2	4-2	1-1	▓	4-1	2-1	1-1	3-0	2-1	3-1	4-0	2-1
Plymouth Argyle FC	5-1	3-1	3-3	2-0	0-0	7-1	4-0	1-0	2-0	2-1	2-2	1-1	4-1	2-1	0-2	1-0	▓	1-0	2-0	2-0	5-1	1-1	1-1	3-1
Port Vale FC	3-1	3-1	0-1	1-3	0-0	1-1	2-2	2-0	4-3	1-0	3-1	0-1	1-0	0-3	2-1	1-1	2-1	▓	0-0	3-1	2-1	1-0	1-1	2-1
Reading FC	7-1	0-0	7-0	4-2	0-0	3-2	1-1	4-2	1-1	2-0	4-0	1-1	5-0	2-0	3-1	0-2	4-0	3-0	▓	0-2	3-1	0-0	2-1	1-0
Southend United FC	4-2	6-1	3-1	1-1	1-1	4-2	5-2	5-1	4-0	1-0	0-1	3-0	3-0	0-2	3-2	1-0	1-1	3-3	3-1	▓	8-2	3-0	0-1	5-1
Swindon Town FC	4-0	2-1	0-0	1-0	1-2	1-0	2-0	1-0	2-0	0-2	0-1	2-0	1-0	2-3	1-2	2-1	1-1	4-1	1-0	1-1	▓	2-1	1-1	3-2
Torquay United FC	1-2	0-2	3-1	4-1	1-2	4-1	4-1	2-0	1-2	0-1	2-1	2-1	3-4	1-1	1-5	3-2	1-3	3-2	2-1	2-2	1-0	▓	3-2	3-2
Walsall FC	3-1	0-1	1-0	3-1	1-2	4-2	0-0	0-2	2-1	2-0	1-1	4-0	0-0	1-0	0-1	0-2	1-1	2-0	1-2	1-2	1-0	3-1	▓	1-0
Watford FC	1-2	2-1	1-1	1-2	1-0	2-0	1-0	1-2	5-0	0-2	2-0	0-0	0-2	0-1	0-2	1-1	1-1	2-0	3-1	1-3	1-2	2-2	1-3	▓

Division 3 (South)

	Team	Pd	Wn	Dw	Ls	GF	GA	Pts	
1.	Nottingham Forest FC (Nottingham)	46	30	10	6	110	40	70	P
2.	Norwich City FC (Norwich)	46	25	14	7	82	45	64	
3.	Reading FC (Reading)	46	21	15	10	88	53	57	
4.	Plymouth Argyle FC (Plymouth)	46	24	9	13	85	55	57	
5.	Millwall FC (London)	46	23	10	13	80	57	56	
6.	Bristol Rovers FC (Bristol)	46	20	15	11	64	42	55	
7.	Southend United FC (Southend-on-Sea)	46	21	10	15	92	69	52	
8.	Ipswich Town FC (Ipswich)	46	23	6	17	69	58	52	
9.	Bournemouth & Boscombe Athletic FC (Bournemouth)	46	22	7	17	65	57	51	
10.	Bristol City FC (Bristol)	46	20	11	15	64	59	51	
11.	Newport County AFC (Newport)	46	19	9	18	77	70	47	
12.	Port Vale FC (Stoke-on-Trent)	46	16	13	17	60	65	45	
13.	Brighton & Hove Albion FC (Hove)	46	13	17	16	71	79	43	
14.	Exeter City FC (Exeter)	46	18	6	22	62	85	42	
15.	Walsall FC (Walsall)	46	15	10	21	52	62	40	
16.	Colchester United FC (Colchester)	46	14	12	20	63	76	40	
17.	Swindon Town FC (Swindon)	46	18	4	24	55	67	40	
18.	Aldershot FC (Aldershot)	46	15	10	21	56	88	40	
19.	Leyton Orient FC (London)	46	15	8	23	53	75	38	
20.	Torquay United FC (Torquay)	46	14	9	23	64	81	37	
21.	Northampton Town FC (Northampton)	46	10	16	20	55	67	36	
22.	Gillingham FC (Gillingham)	46	13	9	24	69	101	35	
23.	Watford FC (Watford)	46	9	11	26	54	88	29	
24.	Crystal Palace FC (London)	46	8	11	27	33	84	27	
		1104	426	252	426	1623	1623	1104	

F.A. CUP FINAL (Wembley Stadium, London – 28/04/1951 – 100,000)

NEWCASTLE UNITED FC   2-0   Blackpool FC (Blackpool)
Milburn 2

Newcastle: Fairbrother, Cowell, Corbett, Harvey, Brennan, Crowe, Walker, Taylor, Milburn, G.Robledo, Mitchell.
Blackburn: Farm, Shimwell, Garrett, Johnston, Hayward, Kelly, Matthews, Mudie, Mortensen, Slater, Perry.

Semi-finals

Blackpool FC (Blackpool)   2-1   Tottenham Hotspur FC (London)
Bolton Wanderers FC (Bolton)   4-3   Everton FC (Liverpool)

Quarter-finals

Birmingham City FC (Birmingham)   1-0   Manchester United FC (Manchester)
Blackpool FC (Blackpool)   1-0   Fulham FC (London)
Newcastle United FC (Newcastle-upon-Tyne)   0-0, 3-1   Bristol Rovers FC (Bristol)
Sunderland AFC (Sunderland)   1-1, 1-3 Wolverhampton Wanderers FC (Wolverhampton)

1951-52

Football League Division 1 1951-52 Season	Arsenal	Aston Villa	Blackpool	Bolton Wanderers	Burnley	Charlton Athletic	Chelsea	Derby County	Fulham	Huddersfield Town	Liverpool	Manchester City	Manchester United	Middlesbrough	Newcastle United	Portsmouth	Preston North End	Stoke City	Sunderland	Tottenham Hotspur	W.B.A.	Wolves
Arsenal FC	■	2-1	4-1	4-2	1-0	2-1	2-1	3-1	4-3	2-2	0-0	2-2	1-3	3-1	1-1	4-1	3-3	4-1	3-0	1-1	6-3	2-2
Aston Villa FC	1-0	■	4-0	1-1	4-1	0-2	7-1	4-1	4-1	1-0	2-0	1-2	2-5	2-0	2-2	2-0	3-2	2-3	2-1	0-3	2-0	3-3
Blackpool FC	0-0	0-3	■	1-0	1-0	1-2	1-2	2-1	4-2	3-1	2-0	2-2	2-2	2-2	6-3	0-0	0-3	4-2	3-0	1-0	2-0	3-2
Bolton Wanderers FC	2-1	5-2	1-0	■	1-4	2-1	3-0	1-2	2-1	2-1	1-1	2-1	1-0	3-1	0-0	0-3	1-1	1-1	1-1	1-1	3-2	2-2
Burnley FC	0-1	2-1	2-0	1-3	■	1-0	1-1	0-1	1-0	0-2	0-0	0-0	1-1	7-1	2-1	1-0	0-2	4-0	0-1	1-1	6-1	2-2
Charlton Athletic FC	1-3	0-1	2-0	1-0	1-0	■	1-1	3-3	3-0	4-0	2-0	0-0	2-2	4-3	3-0	0-2	4-2	4-0	2-1	0-3	3-3	1-0
Chelsea FC	1-3	2-2	2-1	1-3	4-1	1-0	■	0-1	2-1	2-1	1-3	0-3	4-2	5-0	1-0	1-1	0-0	1-0	1-0	0-2	1-3	0-1
Derby County FC	1-2	1-1	1-1	5-2	1-0	1-3	1-1	■	5-0	2-1	1-1	1-3	0-3	3-1	1-3	1-0	4-3	4-2	3-4	4-2	2-1	1-3
Fulham FC	0-0	2-2	1-2	1-2	1-2	3-3	1-2	3-0	■	1-0	1-1	1-2	3-3	6-0	1-1	2-3	2-3	5-0	0-1	1-2	1-0	2-2
Huddersfield Town AFC	2-3	3-1	1-3	0-2	1-3	1-0	1-0	1-1	1-0	■	1-2	5-1	3-2	1-0	2-4	0-1	2-0	0-2	2-2	1-1	3-0	1-7
Liverpool FC	0-0	1-2	1-1	1-1	3-1	1-1	1-1	2-0	4-0	2-1	■	1-2	0-0	1-1	3-0	0-2	2-2	2-1	2-2	1-1	2-5	1-1
Manchester City FC	0-2	2-2	0-0	0-3	0-1	4-2	3-1	4-2	1-1	3-0	1-2	■	1-2	2-1	2-3	0-1	1-0	0-1	3-1	1-1	1-2	0-0
Manchester United FC	6-1	1-1	3-1	1-0	6-1	3-2	3-0	2-1	3-2	1-1	4-0	1-1	■	4-2	2-1	1-3	1-2	4-0	0-1	2-0	5-1	2-0
Middlesbrough FC	0-3	2-0	1-0	2-0	5-0	2-1	0-0	0-0	2-0	2-1	3-3	2-2	1-4	■	2-1	2-1	2-5	3-0	0-2	2-1	0-1	4-0
Newcastle United FC	2-0	6-1	1-3	0-1	7-1	6-0	3-1	2-1	0-1	6-2	1-1	1-0	2-2	0-2	■	3-3	3-0	6-0	2-2	7-2	1-4	3-1
Portsmouth FC	1-1	2-0	1-3	3-0	2-2	1-0	1-0	3-1	4-0	3-1	1-3	1-0	1-0	5-4	3-1	■	1-2	4-1	0-2	2-0	1-1	2-3
Preston North End FC	2-0	2-2	3-1	2-2	1-2	3-0	1-0	0-1	0-1	5-2	4-0	1-1	1-2	0-1	1-2	2-2	■	2-0	4-2	1-1	1-0	3-0
Stoke City FC	2-1	4-1	2-3	1-2	2-1	1-2	1-2	3-1	1-1	0-0	1-2	3-1	0-0	3-2	4-5	2-0	0-0	■	1-1	1-6	1-1	1-0
Sunderland AFC	4-1	1-3	1-3	0-2	0-0	1-1	4-1	3-0	2-2	7-1	3-0	3-0	1-2	3-1	1-4	3-1	0-0	0-1	■	0-1	3-3	1-1
Tottenham Hotspur FC	1-2	2-0	2-0	2-1	1-1	2-3	3-2	5-0	1-0	1-0	2-3	1-2	2-0	3-1	2-1	3-1	1-0	2-0	2-0	■	3-1	4-2
West Bromwich Albion FC	3-1	1-2	1-1	3-2	1-1	1-1	0-1	1-0	0-2	0-0	3-3	3-2	3-3	2-3	3-3	5-0	1-1	1-0	1-1	3-1	■	2-1
Wolverhampton Wanderers FC	2-1	1-2	3-0	5-1	1-2	2-2	5-3	1-2	2-2	0-0	2-1	2-2	0-2	4-0	3-0	1-1	1-4	3-0	0-3	1-1	1-4	■

	Division 1	Pd	Wn	Dw	Ls	GF	GA	Pts	
1.	MANCHESTER UNITED FC (MANCHESTER)	42	23	11	8	95	52	57	
2.	Tottenham Hotspur FC (London)	42	22	9	11	76	51	53	
3.	Arsenal FC (London)	42	21	11	10	80	61	53	
4.	Portsmouth FC (Portsmouth)	42	20	8	14	68	58	48	
5.	Bolton Wanderers FC (Bolton)	42	19	10	13	65	61	48	
6.	Aston Villa FC (Birmingham)	42	19	9	14	79	70	47	
7.	Preston North End FC (Preston)	42	17	12	13	74	54	46	
8.	Newcastle United FC (Newcastle-upon-Tyne)	42	18	9	15	98	73	45	
9.	Blackpool FC (Blackpool)	42	18	9	15	64	64	45	
10.	Charlton Athletic FC (London)	42	17	10	15	68	63	44	
11.	Liverpool FC (Liverpool)	42	12	19	11	57	61	43	
12.	Sunderland AFC (Sunderland)	42	15	12	15	70	61	42	
13.	West Bromwich Albion FC (West Bromwich)	42	14	13	15	74	77	41	
14.	Burnley FC (Burnley)	42	15	10	17	56	63	40	
15.	Manchester City FC (Manchester)	42	13	13	16	58	61	39	
16.	Wolverhampton Wanderers FC (Wolverhampton)	42	12	14	16	73	73	38	
17.	Derby County FC (Derby)	42	15	7	20	63	80	37	
18.	Middlesbrough FC (Middlesbrough)	42	15	6	21	64	88	36	
19.	Chelsea FC (London)	42	14	8	20	52	72	36	
20.	Stoke City FC (Stoke-on-Trent)	42	12	7	23	49	88	31	
21.	Huddersfield Town AFC (Huddersfield)	42	10	8	24	49	82	28	R
22.	Fulham FC (London)	42	8	11	23	58	77	27	R
		924	349	126	349	1490	1490	924	

Top Goalscorer

1) George ROBLEDO   (Newcastle United FC)   33

Football League Division 2 — 1951-52 Season

	Barnsley	Birmingham City	Blackburn Rovers	Brentford	Bury	Cardiff City	Coventry City	Doncaster Rovers	Everton	Hull City	Leeds United	Leicester City	Luton Town	Nottingham Forest	Notts County	Q.P.R.	Rotherham United	Sheffield United	Sheffield Wednesday	Southampton	Swansea Town	West Ham United
Barnsley FC	■	1-2	1-2	0-0	3-3	2-0	1-0	1-1	1-0	2-2	3-1	3-3	1-2	1-1	2-1	3-1	0-1	3-4	5-4	3-1	2-3	1-1
Birmingham City FC	2-1	■	0-1	1-2	2-1	3-2	3-1	2-2	1-2	2-2	1-1	2-0	3-1	0-2	2-0	1-0	4-0	3-0	0-0	1-1	1-1	2-1
Blackburn Rovers FC	2-1	1-4	■	3-0	1-2	0-1	0-1	3-3	1-0	1-0	2-3	2-1	2-1	3-2	2-0	4-2	1-1	1-5	0-0	0-1	3-1	3-1
Brentford FC	1-1	1-0	1-1	■	4-0	1-1	1-0	1-0	1-0	2-1	2-1	1-3	3-3	1-1	1-0	0-0	2-0	4-1	2-3	1-2	3-1	1-1
Bury FC	3-0	3-0	0-2	1-0	■	1-1	0-2	1-1	1-0	3-1	1-2	1-4	0-1	2-0	2-1	3-1	3-1	1-0	1-2	8-2	4-1	4-0
Cardiff City AFC	3-0	3-1	3-1	2-0	3-0	■	4-1	2-1	3-1	1-0	3-1	4-0	3-0	4-1	1-0	3-1	2-4	1-1	2-1	1-0	3-0	1-1
Coventry City FC	0-0	1-1	1-2	2-1	3-0	2-1	■	1-2	2-1	1-4	4-2	1-3	5-2	3-3	0-2	0-0	2-1	1-1	0-2	3-1	3-2	1-2
Doncaster Rovers FC	1-2	0-5	1-0	1-2	1-1	1-0	1-0	■	3-1	0-1	2-0	2-2	1-1	0-1	1-5	4-0	0-3	2-1	1-1	0-1	3-0	4-1
Everton FC	1-1	1-3	0-2	1-0	2-2	3-0	4-1	1-1	■	5-0	2-0	2-0	1-3	1-0	1-5	3-0	3-3	1-0	3-3	3-0	2-1	2-0
Hull City AFC	0-0	0-1	3-0	4-1	5-0	0-0	5-0	2-0	1-0	■	3-2	3-1	1-2	1-4	1-3	4-1	3-2	3-1	0-1	0-0	5-2	1-1
Leeds United AFC	1-0	1-1	1-0	1-1	2-1	2-1	3-1	0-0	1-2	2-0	■	2-1	1-1	0-0	1-0	3-0	3-0	3-1	3-2	1-1	1-1	3-1
Leicester City FC	1-2	4-0	2-1	1-1	1-1	3-0	3-1	2-1	1-2	1-0	1-2	■	3-3	3-1	1-1	4-0	2-0	5-5	3-1	3-0	1-1	3-1
Luton Town FC	4-2	2-4	1-1	0-2	2-1	2-2	2-1	1-4	1-1	1-1	2-1	1-2	■	3-3	6-0	0-1	1-1	2-1	5-3	2-1	2-2	6-1
Nottingham Forest FC	3-3	0-1	1-0	2-0	1-0	2-3	3-1	1-1	2-0	4-0	1-1	2-2	2-0	■	3-2	3-1	4-2	0-2	2-1	3-0	2-2	0-0
Notts County FC	4-0	5-0	0-1	5-2	1-1	2-1	1-0	0-0	4-0	1-2	2-3	5-4	2-2		■	0-0	0-3	3-1	2-2	3-4	2-0	1-0
Queen's Park Rangers FC	1-1	0-2	2-1	3-1	3-2	1-1	1-4	0-2	4-4	1-1	0-0	1-0	0-0	4-3	1-4	■	2-3	4-2	2-2	2-1	1-1	2-0
Rotherham United FC	4-0	1-2	3-0	1-1	4-3	2-0	0-1	2-0	1-1	1-1	4-2	0-2	0-1	1-2	2-0	1-0	■	3-1	3-3	4-1	1-3	2-1
Sheffield United FC	1-2	4-2	1-1	1-4	1-0	6-1	1-2	2-1	1-2	4-1	3-0	5-0	3-0	1-4	1-0	1-2	1-0	■	7-3	2-2	5-0	6-1
Sheffield Wednesday FC	2-1	1-1	1-1	2-0	2-1	4-2	3-1	3-1	4-0	6-0	1-2	1-0	4-1	1-1	6-0	2-1	3-5	1-3	■	3-1	1-1	2-2
Southampton FC	1-1	2-0	2-1	2-1	4-2	1-1	2-2	2-0	1-0	1-1	0-0	2-3	5-2	4-0	1-1	3-1	0-1	1-4		■	3-2	1-2
Swansea Town AFC	2-1	4-0	5-1	1-1	0-2	1-1	7-1	1-2	0-2	3-0	4-1	1-0	0-3	1-2	1-1	2-3	1-2	5-0	3-1	1-2	■	2-1
West Ham United FC	2-1	0-1	3-1	1-0	1-1	2-1	3-1	3-3	3-3	2-0	2-0	2-3	3-0	3-1	2-1	4-2	2-1	5-1	0-6	4-0	2-2	■

	Division 2	Pd	Wn	Dw	Ls	GF	GA	Pts	
1.	Sheffield Wednesday FC (Sheffield)	42	21	11	10	100	66	53	P
2.	Cardiff City AFC (Cardiff)	42	20	11	11	72	54	51	P
3.	Birmingham City FC (Birmingham)	42	21	9	12	67	56	51	
4.	Nottingham Forest FC (Nottingham)	42	18	13	11	77	62	49	
5.	Leicester City FC (Leicester)	42	19	9	14	78	64	47	
6.	Leeds United AFC (Leeds)	42	18	11	13	59	57	47	
7.	Everton FC (Liverpool)	42	17	10	15	64	58	44	
8.	Luton Town FC (Luton)	42	16	12	14	77	78	44	
9.	Rotherham United FC (Rotherham)	42	17	8	17	73	71	42	
10.	Brentford FC (London)	42	15	12	15	54	55	42	
11.	Sheffield United FC (Sheffield)	42	18	5	19	90	76	41	
12.	West Ham United FC (London)	42	15	11	16	67	77	41	
13.	Southampton FC (Southampton)	42	15	11	16	61	73	41	
14.	Blackburn Rovers FC (Blackburn)	42	17	6	19	54	63	40	
15.	Notts County FC (Nottingham)	42	16	7	19	71	68	39	
16.	Doncaster Rovers FC (Doncaster)	42	13	12	17	55	60	38	
17.	Bury FC (Bury)	42	15	7	20	67	69	37	
18.	Hull City AFC (Kingston-upon-Hull)	42	13	11	18	60	70	37	
19.	Swansea Town AFC (Swansea)	42	12	12	18	72	76	36	
20.	Barnsley FC (Barnsley)	42	11	14	17	59	72	36	
21.	Coventry City FC (Coventry)	42	14	6	22	59	82	34	R
22.	Queen's Park Rangers FC (London)	42	11	12	19	52	81	34	R
		924	352	220	352	1488	1488	924	

Football League Division 3 (N) 1951-52 Season	Accrington Stanley	Barrow	Bradford City	Bradford Park Avenue	Carlisle United	Chester	Chesterfield	Crewe Alexandra	Darlington	Gateshead	Grimsby Town	Halifax Town	Hartlepools	Lincoln City	Mansfield Town	Oldham Athletic	Rochdale	Scunthorpe United	Southport	Stockport County	Tranmere Rovers	Workington	Wrexham	York City
Accrington Stanley		1-1	0-1	5-1	0-2	4-2	2-0	2-3	1-3	1-2	0-3	2-2	0-0	1-3	1-0	1-2	0-0	2-2	0-0	0-3	1-1	0-0	4-2	2-1
Barrow AFC	3-1		1-0	0-2	0-1	1-0	2-0	2-1	2-2	2-1	3-1	0-0	2-1	1-2	1-1	0-1	4-0	2-1	0-0	1-3	2-0	1-0	3-1	0-0
Bradford City AFC	1-3	2-2		2-2	1-2	1-0	1-0	0-2	3-1	1-1	0-2	3-2	0-2	1-1	2-1	5-2	3-0	1-0	2-1	2-3	2-0	1-0	3-2	3-3
Bradford Park Ave.	1-1	3-1	2-1		0-1	3-0	3-3	3-2	2-0	2-0	3-2	6-1	1-2	1-1	0-1	1-0	1-1	2-2	2-2	4-2	2-3	2-1	5-0	2-1
Carlisle United FC	4-1	0-1	1-0	1-0		0-0	2-3	2-0	1-1	0-0	1-2	2-2	2-1	1-4	0-0	3-3	1-1	3-0	0-2	2-1	1-0	0-1	2-0	2-1
Chester FC	3-1	0-0	1-0	4-2	4-2		3-0	2-0	2-0	0-3	0-3	5-1	3-3	0-1	1-5	1-2	4-0	3-1	2-1	0-0	4-1	2-2	2-1	0-1
Chesterfield FC	2-0	2-0	2-2	0-0	3-0	2-0		0-0	4-2	3-1	3-1	2-2	2-2	1-1	1-0	5-1	3-0	2-0	0-1	1-1	3-1	3-0	2-1	2-1
Crewe Alexandra FC	3-3	1-1	0-1	3-4	1-1	1-2	2-1		3-0	4-2	1-2	4-1	4-2	0-2	1-0	3-1	1-0	2-2	1-0	1-0	2-1	2-0	2-2	0-0
Darlington FC	4-5	1-2	3-1	3-0	1-2	1-1	3-0	0-1		3-2	0-2	0-2	2-1	1-1	2-1	2-2	2-1	2-3	1-1	1-2	2-2	2-1	2-1	1-0
Gateshead FC	1-0	2-0	2-2	0-1	1-1	1-0	1-1	1-0	2-2		1-1	3-0	2-0	3-1	4-1	1-0	2-1	3-0	0-2	4-1	4-1	1-1	1-1	1-1
Grimsby Town FC	2-1	1-0	2-1	1-2	4-1	2-1	2-0	0-1	3-0	2-0		8-1	2-0	2-3	1-1	3-1	4-0	3-2	4-1	4-0	1-0	5-0	1-0	0-1
Halifax Town AFC	0-4	0-1	1-1	0-0	1-2	4-1	0-0	2-3	4-1	0-1	3-0		2-0	1-3	1-0	1-0	2-1	0-1	1-2	1-0	3-1	2-0	1-1	1-1
Hartlepools United	4-2	3-1	2-1	2-1	1-0	2-1	4-1	3-0	2-0	1-0	2-1	6-1		1-1	2-0	1-1	1-1	3-1	3-1	0-1	0-1	0-1	1-0	3-2
Lincoln City FC	2-2	3-0	2-1	2-0	2-2	4-1	5-1	11-1	7-2	1-0	0-2	4-1	4-3		1-2	4-0	2-0	4-1	4-0	2-1	3-0	7-0	3-2	3-1
Mansfield Town FC	3-0	2-1	2-1	1-0	1-2	3-1	2-1	1-2	3-2	2-3	2-2	4-2	0-1	1-0		2-1	1-1	4-1	4-0	1-0	3-0	3-2	3-0	1-1
Oldham Athletic AFC	3-1	3-1	2-1	1-2	2-0	11-2	3-0	5-2	3-2	2-0	1-1	2-0	5-2	4-1	5-3		1-1	2-0	2-1	1-0	3-0	0-1	2-1	2-0
Rochdale AFC	3-1	4-1	1-1	1-1	0-4	0-5	2-0	1-0	6-2	0-3	0-0	0-2	3-0	0-1	1-0	2-2		1-2	1-0	0-0	3-2	2-0	1-5	0-2
Scunthorpe United	3-1	0-0	1-0	0-0	1-1	2-2	1-1	2-0	5-2	1-1	1-3	2-1	2-0	1-3	4-1	2-2	3-1		1-1	1-1	2-0	3-1	0-0	1-1
Southport FC	0-0	2-2	1-1	0-0	2-1	1-0	4-1	1-1	3-0	0-2	2-0	3-2	2-0	0-3	0-1	0-0	1-2	5-1		0-1	1-0	4-2	2-1	2-1
Stockport County FC	6-0	2-2	1-2	1-0	1-1	0-0	2-1	4-2	5-0	0-0	1-1	6-2	0-1	1-1	2-0	0-0	1-0	1-1	3-1		2-0	5-0	0-0	3-1
Tranmere Rovers FC	3-1	3-1	3-1	1-2	3-2	3-1	2-0	1-0	3-0	5-1	2-3	1-2	4-1	2-2	1-1	0-4	4-3	3-1	5-1	2-0		3-1	3-1	2-0
Workington AFC	0-2	3-1	0-1	2-3	1-2	2-2	3-1	3-1	2-1	1-2	2-4	2-1	1-1	0-3	0-1	0-1	1-1	0-0	6-1	0-3	1-2		2-0	1-0
Wrexham AFC	1-0	2-4	3-0	3-2	3-1	3-2	0-3	4-0	1-1	2-1	2-0	2-1	0-0	4-2	3-1	1-0	2-0	1-2	3-0	0-0	0-1	0-0		1-1
York City FC	6-1	2-1	3-1	1-0	0-0	4-2	1-0	3-0	2-1	1-0	1-1	6-2	3-1	1-0	3-0	5-0	1-1	0-1	0-2	0-1	1-1	5-1	4-2	

	Division 3 (North)	Pd	Wn	Dw	Ls	GF	GA	Pts	
1.	Lincoln City FC (Lincoln)	46	30	9	7	121	52	69	P
2.	Grimsby Town FC (Cleethorpes)	46	29	8	9	96	45	66	
3.	Stockport County FC (Stockport)	46	23	13	10	74	40	59	
4.	Oldham Athletic AFC (Oldham)	46	24	9	13	90	61	57	
5.	Gateshead FC (Gateshead)	46	21	11	14	66	49	53	
6.	Mansfield Town FC (Mansfield)	46	22	8	16	73	60	52	
7.	Carlisle United FC (Carlisle)	46	19	13	14	62	57	51	
8.	Bradford Park Avenue FC (Bradford)	46	19	12	15	74	64	50	
9.	Hartlepools United FC (Hartlepool)	46	21	8	17	71	65	50	
10.	York City FC (York)	46	18	13	15	73	52	49	
11.	Tranmere Rovers FC (Birkenhead)	46	21	6	19	76	71	48	
12.	Barrow AFC (Barrow-in-Furness)	46	17	12	17	57	61	46	
13.	Chesterfield FC (Chesterfield)	46	17	11	18	65	66	45	
14.	Scunthorpe & Lindsey United FC (Scunthorpe)	46	14	16	16	65	74	44	
15.	Bradford City AFC (Bradford)	46	16	10	20	61	68	42	
16.	Crewe Alexandra FC (Crewe)	46	17	8	21	63	82	42	
17.	Southport FC (Southport)	46	15	11	20	53	71	41	
18.	Wrexham AFC (Wrexham)	46	15	9	22	63	73	39	
19.	Chester FC (Chester)	46	15	9	22	72	85	39	
20.	Halifax Town AFC (Halifax)	46	14	7	25	61	97	35	
21.	Rochdale AFC (Rochdale)	46	11	13	22	47	79	35	
22.	Accrington Stanley FC (Accrington)	46	10	12	24	61	92	32	
23.	Darlington FC (Darlington)	46	11	9	26	64	103	31	
24.	Workington FC (Workington)	46	11	7	28	50	91	29	
		1104	430	244	430	1658	1658	1104	

Football League Division 3 (S) 1951-52 Season	Aldershot Town	Bournemouth	FC	Bristol City	Bristol Rovers	Colchester Utd.	Crystal Palace	Exeter City	Gillingham	Ipswich Town	Leyton Orient	Millwall	Newport County	Northampton T.	Norwich City	Plymouth Argyle	Port Vale	Reading	Shrewsbury T.	Southend Utd.	Swindon Town	Torquay United	Walsall	Watford
Aldershot Town FC	■	1-3	0-2	1-0	1-3	1-1	3-0	4-1	2-1	1-1	0-1	2-1	4-0	0-1	2-0	1-2	4-1	0-2	1-1	2-2	4-0	1-3	3-1	2-0
Bournemouth & Bos.	0-2	■	3-1	0-0	1-0	5-0	1-2	0-4	3-3	2-2	3-2	0-2	5-1	3-0	1-2	1-2	0-1	1-2	2-0	2-1	4-1	3-1	2-1	0-0
Brighton & Hove Alb.	4-2	0-1	■	1-1	1-1	5-1	4-3	2-1	0-0	5-1	3-1	0-0	1-2	2-0	2-0	2-3	2-1	1-0	1-0	5-0	4-0	3-4	5-1	4-1
Bristol City FC	1-1	1-0	4-1	■	1-1	2-0	2-0	1-1	3-2	0-2	1-1	2-1	3-1	2-0	2-5	1-1	1-0	1-3	3-0	6-0	2-1	2-2	2-0	1-3
Bristol Rovers FC	5-1	1-2	5-0	2-0	■	6-0	4-0	2-2	5-0	1-0	1-0	2-1	1-1	2-2	1-1	1-2	4-1	1-2	3-3	2-0	1-0	5-0	5-1	0-1
Colchester United FC	0-2	1-1	0-0	4-1	2-1	■	1-2	1-0	1-0	0-1	2-2	2-1	2-5	1-1	1-0	0-0	4-1	2-2	1-0	2-0	0-0	3-2	1-0	
Crystal Palace FC	0-2	2-2	1-2	2-1	0-1	2-2	■	2-1	0-2	3-1	2-1	1-1	1-1	3-3	2-0	0-1	3-1	1-2	1-1	1-0	0-1	1-1	2-1	2-0
Exeter City FC	0-4	2-2	2-0	0-0	0-1	0-0	0-1	■	4-2	2-1	6-1	0-3	3-4	0-3	2-4	1-0	2-0	1-4	4-2	2-2	1-2	4-0	1-0	3-0
Gillingham FC	3-3	0-2	2-3	5-0	2-1	1-2	4-4	2-1	■	1-1	1-1	1-1	2-3	2-1	1-2	1-2	4-2	1-1	0-0	2-0	4-0	3-0	4-1	3-0
Ipswich Town FC	2-3	3-1	5-0	1-1	1-2	0-2	1-1	2-4	1-1	■	1-0	3-0	3-1	3-2	0-2	2-2	2-0	4-2	1-0	4-1	1-5	2-0	0-1	2-0
Leyton Orient FC	0-1	1-0	2-3	2-0	3-3	7-0	0-4	3-0	1-0	2-0	■	0-0	1-1	2-1	3-3	1-0	2-0	0-4	4-1	1-4	1-0	3-0	0-0	
Millwall FC	3-2	3-1	0-3	3-2	1-1	1-1	3-1	4-0	3-1	4-0	2-0	■	2-0	2-1	2-1	0-2	1-1	3-2	0-0	2-0	0-0	4-1	2-1	1-0
Newport County AFC	4-2	2-0	1-1	1-0	2-2	0-1	1-0	4-0	1-1	2-1	1-0	2-1	■	2-0	2-2	3-3	1-1	3-1	3-1	3-0	0-0	1-2	4-2	2-5
Northampton Town	6-2	5-3	3-0	1-2	2-0	2-0	5-2	3-1	2-1	1-0	4-0	1-1	5-0	■	1-2	3-1	3-1	0-3	6-0	4-3	1-0	2-4	4-1	1-4
Norwich City FC	1-2	2-0	1-0	1-0	5-2	1-0	1-0	5-0	1-0	0-2	1-0	1-2	2-1	3-0	■		2-3	2-1	3-2	1-0	0-0	7-0	8-0	3-0
Plymouth Argyle FC	2-1	4-1	2-2	2-2	1-2	3-1	5-0	2-1	4-2	2-0	3-0	5-0	5-0	2-0	3-1	■	3-0	3-2	6-1	2-0	3-0	2-2	3-0	3-1
Port Vale FC	4-1	2-2	1-1	1-0	1-1	1-1	2-0	3-0	1-0	0-0	3-0	2-1	4-2	0-0	0-0	1-0	■	0-2	1-0	0-0	2-2	2-2	1-0	1-1
Reading FC	5-1	5-0	1-4	3-0	4-2	4-2	3-1	2-1	2-1	4-0	1-1	2-0	1-2	2-0	1-1	2-0	5-1	■	6-2	5-2	2-0	6-1	3-0	4-1
Shrewsbury Town FC	5-1	2-0	1-1	1-0	2-1	1-2	2-1	2-2	2-2	0-1	4-1	3-1	0-1	1-2	1-3	2-0	2-1		■	0-1	0-1	1-1	1-2	2-3
Southend United FC	7-1	1-0	2-0	5-1	2-1	3-2	4-0	3-1	5-0	0-1	2-1	2-0	2-1	1-1	0-0	2-0	2-2			■	2-2	2-2	3-0	5-1
Swindon Town FC	1-1	2-0	0-2	0-0	0-0	2-1	0-2	3-1	2-1	1-2	2-0	2-2	1-1	1-1	1-1	2-2	2-0	2-0	1-2	1-0	■	2-1	1-1	0-1
Torquay United FC	6-1	2-2	0-1	1-2	4-2	3-1	1-5	5-1	2-1	1-0	1-1	2-5	1-2	1-2	1-2	3-2	2-3	0-3	3-2	1-3	9-0	■	1-1	2-0
Walsall FC	1-0	2-2	1-1	2-0	1-0	1-3	3-0	1-2	1-0	1-3	2-4	1-2	0-1	3-0	4-0	2-5	3-0	2-0	0-4	2-0	0-0	2-3	■	3-1
Watford FC	2-2	1-2	3-1	3-1	0-3	0-1	2-0	1-1	2-2	1-1	0-1	1-2	1-1	2-4	1-1	1-3	2-0	3-1	4-1	0-0	1-7	1-2	2-0	■

Division 3 (South)

	Team		Pd	Wn	Dw	Ls	GF	GA	Pts	
1.	Plymouth Argyle FC (Plymouth)		46	29	8	9	107	53	66	P
2.	Reading FC (Reading)		46	29	3	14	112	60	61	
3.	Norwich City FC (Norwich)		46	26	9	11	89	50	61	
4.	Millwall FC (London)		46	23	12	11	74	53	58	
5.	Brighton & Hove Albion FC (Hove)		46	24	10	12	87	63	58	
6.	Newport County AFC (Newport)		46	21	12	13	77	76	54	
7.	Bristol Rovers FC (Bristol)		46	20	12	14	89	53	52	
8.	Northampton Town FC (Northampton)		46	22	5	19	93	74	49	
9.	Southend United FC (Southend-on-Sea)		46	19	10	17	75	66	48	
10.	Colchester United FC (Colchester)		46	17	12	17	56	77	46	
11.	Torquay United FC (Torquay)		46	17	10	19	86	98	44	
12.	Aldershot FC (Aldershot)		46	18	8	20	78	89	44	
13.	Port Vale FC (Stoke-on-Trent)		46	14	15	17	50	66	43	T
14.	Bournemouth & Boscombe Athletic FC (Bournemouth)		46	16	10	20	69	75	42	
15.	Bristol City FC (Bristol)		46	15	12	19	58	69	42	
16.	Swindon Town FC (Swindon)		46	14	14	18	51	68	42	
17.	Ipswich Town FC (Ipswich)		46	16	9	21	63	74	41	
18.	Leyton Orient FC (London)		46	16	9	21	55	68	41	
19.	Crystal Palace FC (London)		46	15	9	22	61	80	39	
20.	Shrewsbury Town FC (Shrewsbury)		46	13	10	23	62	86	36	
21.	Watford FC (Watford)		46	13	10	23	57	81	36	
22.	Gillingham FC (Gillingham)		46	11	13	22	71	81	35	
23.	Exeter City FC (Exeter)		46	13	9	24	65	86	35	
24.	Walsall FC (Walsall)		46	13	5	28	55	94	31	
			1104	434	236	434	1740	1740	1104	

T: Port Vale FC (Stoke-on-Trent) were transferred to Division 3 (North) for the next season.

F.A. CUP FINAL   (Wembley Stadium, London – 03/05/1952 – 100,000)

NEWCASTLE UNITED FC	1-0	Arsenal FC (London)

G.Robledo

Newcastle: Simpson, Cowell, McMichael, Harvey, Brennan, E.Robledo, Walker, Foulkes, Milburn, G.Robledo, Mitchell.

Arsenal: Swindin, Barnes, L.Smith, Forbes, Daniel, Mercer, Cox, Logie, Holton, Lishman, Roper.

Semi-finals

Arsenal FC (London)	1-1, 3-0	Chelsea FC (London)
Newcastle United FC (Newcastle-upon-Tyne)	0-0, 2-1	Blackburn Rovers FC (Blackburn)

Quarter-finals

Blackburn Rovers FC (Blackburn)	3-1	Burnley FC (Burnley)
Luton Town FC (Luton)	2-3	Arsenal FC (London)
Portsmouth FC (Portsmouth)	2-4	Newcastle United FC (Newcastle-upon-Tyne)
Sheffield United FC (Sheffield)	0-1	Chelsea FC (London)

1952-53

Football League Division 1 1952-53 Season	Arsenal	Aston Villa	Blackpool	Bolton Wanderers	Burnley	Cardiff City	Charlton Athletic	Chelsea	Derby County	Liverpool	Manchester City	Manchester United	Middlesbrough	Newcastle United	Portsmouth	Preston North End	Sheffield Wed.	Stoke City	Sunderland	Tottenham Hotspur	W.B.A.	Wolves
Arsenal FC	■	3-1	3-1	4-1	3-2	0-1	3-4	2-0	6-2	5-3	3-1	2-1	2-1	3-0	3-1	1-1	2-2	3-1	1-2	4-0	2-2	5-3
Aston Villa FC	1-2	■	1-5	1-1	2-0	2-0	1-1	1-1	3-0	4-0	0-0	3-3	1-0	0-1	6-0	1-0	4-3	1-1	3-0	0-3	1-1	0-1
Blackpool FC	3-2	1-1	■	3-0	4-2	0-1	8-4	3-1	2-1	3-1	4-1	0-0	1-1	0-2	3-2	1-1	0-1	1-1	2-0	2-0	2-0	2-0
Bolton Wanderers FC	4-6	0-0	4-0	■	1-2	0-1	1-2	1-1	2-0	2-2	1-0	2-1	5-3	4-2	0-5	0-3	1-1	2-1	5-0	2-3	0-1	2-1
Burnley FC	1-1	1-0	0-1	0-1	■	0-0	2-0	1-1	1-2	2-0	2-1	2-1	0-1	2-1	3-2	2-2	1-1	3-2	5-1	3-2	5-0	0-0
Cardiff City AFC	0-0	1-2	2-2	1-0	0-0	■	0-1	3-3	2-0	4-0	6-0	1-2	1-1	0-0	0-1	0-2	4-0	2-0	4-1	0-0	1-2	0-0
Charlton Athletic FC	2-2	5-1	2-0	2-0	0-0	3-1	■	2-2	3-1	3-2	1-2	2-2	2-0	0-0	2-2	2-1	3-0	5-1	3-1	3-2	0-0	2-2
Chelsea FC	1-1	4-0	4-0	1-0	0-2	0-2	0-1	■	1-1	3-0	3-1	2-3	1-1	1-2	2-0	5-3	1-0	0-0	3-2	2-1	0-2	1-2
Derby County FC	2-0	0-1	1-1	4-3	1-3	1-1	1-1	3-2	■	3-2	5-0	2-3	3-3	0-2	0-1	2-1	4-0	3-1	0-0	1-1	1-1	2-3
Liverpool FC	1-5	0-2	2-2	0-0	1-1	2-1	1-2	1-1	1-1	■	0-1	1-2	4-1	5-3	1-1	2-2	1-0	2-0	2-0	3-0	2-1	2-1
Manchester City FC	2-4	4-1	5-0	1-2	2-0	2-2	5-1	4-0	1-0	0-2	■	2-1	5-1	2-1	2-1	0-2	3-1	2-1	2-5	0-0	0-1	3-1
Manchester United FC	0-0	3-1	2-1	1-0	1-3	1-4	3-2	2-3	3-1	1-1	1-1	■	3-2	2-2	1-0	5-2	1-1	0-2	0-1	3-2	2-2	0-3
Middlesbrough FC	2-0	1-0	5-1	1-2	2-2	3-0	1-0	4-0	1-1	2-3	5-4	5-0	■	2-1	3-2	1-1	2-2	0-0	1-2	0-4	4-2	1-1
Newcastle United FC	2-2	2-1	0-1	2-3	0-0	3-0	3-2	2-1	1-0	1-2	2-0	1-2	1-0	■	1-0	4-3	1-5	1-2	2-2	1-1	3-5	1-1
Portsmouth FC	2-2	1-1	0-2	3-1	2-1	0-2	1-1	2-0	2-1	2-1	2-0	1-4	5-1	1-2	■	2-5	5-2	1-1	5-2	2-1	1-2	2-2
Preston North End FC	2-0	1-3	4-2	2-2	2-1	2-3	2-1	3-0	1-1	6-2	0-5	3-0	2-1	4-0	2-0	■	1-0	3-0	3-2	1-0	1-0	1-1
Sheffield Wednesday FC	1-4	2-2	2-0	1-1	2-4	2-0	0-3	1-0	0-2	1-1	0-0	2-0	2-2	3-4	1-1	0-0	■	1-0	4-0	2-0	4-5	2-3
Stoke City FC	1-1	1-4	4-0	1-2	1-3	0-0	1-0	1-1	1-2	3-1	2-1	3-1	1-0	1-0	2-4	0-0	1-3	■	3-0	2-0	5-1	1-2
Sunderland AFC	3-1	0-0	2-1	2-0	2-1	2-1	2-1	2-1	3-2	3-3	2-2	1-0	0-2	1-1	2-2	2-1	1-1	1-1	■	1-1	1-0	5-2
Tottenham Hotspur FC	1-3	1-1	4-0	1-1	2-1	2-1	2-0	2-3	5-2	3-1	3-3	1-2	7-1	3-2	3-3	4-4	2-1	1-0	2-2	■	3-4	3-2
West Bromwich Albion FC	2-0	3-2	0-1	0-1	1-2	1-0	3-1	0-1	2-2	3-0	2-1	3-1	3-0	1-0	2-0	2-1	0-1	3-2	1-1	2-1	■	1-1
Wolverhampton Wanderers FC	1-1	2-1	2-5	3-1	5-1	1-0	1-2	2-2	3-1	3-0	7-3	6-2	3-3	2-0	4-1	0-2	3-1	3-0	1-1	1-1	0-0	■

	Division 1	Pd	Wn	Dw	Ls	GF	GA	Pts	
1.	ARSENAL FC (LONDON)	42	21	12	9	97	64	54	
2.	Preston North End FC (Preston)	42	21	12	9	85	60	54	
3.	Wolverhampton Wanderers FC (Wolverhampton)	42	19	13	10	86	63	51	
4.	West Bromwich Albion FC (West Bromwich)	42	21	8	13	66	60	50	
5.	Charlton Athletic FC (London)	42	19	11	12	77	63	49	
6.	Burnley FC (Burnley)	42	18	12	12	67	52	48	
7.	Blackpool FC (Blackpool)	42	19	9	14	71	70	47	
8.	Manchester United FC (Manchester)	42	18	10	14	69	72	46	
9.	Sunderland AFC (Sunderland)	42	15	13	14	68	82	43	
10.	Tottenham Hotspur FC (London)	42	15	11	16	78	69	41	
11.	Aston Villa FC (Birmingham)	42	14	13	15	63	61	41	
12.	Cardiff City AFC (Cardiff)	42	14	12	16	54	46	40	
13.	Middlesbrough FC (Middlesbrough)	42	14	11	17	70	77	39	
14.	Bolton Wanderers FC (Bolton)	42	15	9	18	61	69	39	
15.	Portsmouth FC (Portsmouth)	42	14	10	18	74	83	38	
16.	Newcastle United FC (Newcastle-upon-Tyne)	42	14	9	19	59	70	37	
17.	Liverpool FC (Liverpool)	42	14	8	20	61	82	36	
18.	Sheffield Wednesday FC (Sheffield)	42	12	11	19	62	72	35	
19.	Chelsea FC (London)	42	12	11	19	56	66	35	
20.	Manchester City FC (Manchester)	42	14	7	21	72	87	35	
21.	Stoke City FC (Stoke-on-Trent)	42	12	10	20	53	66	34	R
22.	Derby County FC (Derby)	42	11	10	21	59	74	32	R
		924	346	232	346	1508	1508	924	

Top Goalscorer

1)   Charles WAYMAN   (Preston North End FC)   24

Football League — Division 2 — 1952-53 Season

	Barnsley	Birmingham City	Blackburn Rovers	Brentford	Bury	Doncaster Rovers	Everton	Fulham	Huddersfield Town	Hull City	Leeds United	Leicester City	Lincoln City	Luton Town	Nottingham Forest	Notts County	Plymouth Argyle	Rotherham United	Sheffield United	Southampton	Swansea Town	West Ham United
Barnsley FC		1-3	1-4	0-2	3-2	2-2	2-3	1-1	2-4	5-1	2-2	0-3	1-1	2-3	0-2	1-2	0-3	2-3	1-3	0-1	3-1	2-0
Birmingham City FC	3-1		1-2	3-1	0-2	2-1	4-2	1-4	0-2	4-3	2-2	3-1	2-2	2-2	0-5	3-2	4-0	4-0	1-2	2-0	1-4	2-0
Blackburn Rovers FC	2-0	1-2		3-0	4-0	2-1	3-1	2-2	1-1	2-0	1-1	2-0	0-2	1-1	2-1	3-2	1-3	0-1	1-2	3-0	3-0	3-0
Brentford FC	4-0	1-2	3-2		2-2	1-0	2-4	2-2	1-3	1-0	3-3	4-2	1-0	1-1	1-1	5-0	1-2	1-1	0-0	3-0	0-0	1-4
Bury FC	5-2	3-0	1-0	3-0		2-1	0-5	1-1	1-1	2-1	2-2	1-4	2-2	1-0	2-0	0-1	3-2	2-0	0-4	0-0	1-3	1-1
Doncaster Rovers FC	1-1	1-0	3-3	0-2	1-1		3-0	0-0	1-1	3-1	0-0	0-0	2-0	1-0	1-0	2-0	1-1	2-1	0-2	1-0	2-3	1-1
Everton FC	2-1	1-1	0-3	5-0	3-0	7-1		3-3	2-1	0-2	2-2	2-2	0-3	1-1	3-0	1-0	2-0	0-1	0-0	2-2	0-0	2-0
Fulham FC	3-1	3-1	2-1	5-0	2-0	1-3	3-0		0-2	2-1	2-1	4-6	4-2	2-0	0-1	6-0	2-1	4-1	1-2	1-1	3-1	2-3
Huddersfield Town AFC	6-0	1-1	0-3	0-0	2-0	3-1	8-2	4-2		1-1	1-0	1-0	5-0	3-0	1-2	1-0	4-0	1-0	1-1	5-0	3-0	0-1
Hull City AFC	2-2	2-0	3-0	2-2	0-2	1-1	1-0	3-1	0-2		1-0	1-1	1-1	0-2	3-1	6-0	0-1	3-2	4-0	1-0	1-1	1-0
Leeds United AFC	4-1	0-1	0-3	3-2	2-0	1-1	2-0	2-0	2-1	3-1		0-1	2-1	2-2	2-1	3-1	1-1	4-0	0-3	1-1	5-1	3-2
Leicester City FC	2-2	3-4	2-1	2-3	3-2	4-2	4-2	6-1	2-1	5-0	3-3		3-2	1-1	1-1	3-0	2-0	3-2	0-0	4-1	2-1	0-0
Lincoln City FC	1-1	1-1	4-1	0-0	4-0	2-0	1-1	2-2	2-2	2-1	1-1	3-2		1-2	2-3	3-0	0-0	1-3	3-2	2-2	3-1	3-1
Luton Town FC	6-0	0-1	6-0	0-1	4-1	1-2	4-2	2-0	0-2	3-2	2-0	2-0	4-0		3-0	5-1	1-0	2-1	4-1	1-2	3-1	0-0
Nottingham Forest FC	3-0	0-2	1-2	3-0	4-1	2-2	3-3	0-1	1-0	4-1	2-1	1-3	1-1	4-3		1-0	3-1	4-3	1-1	2-3	6-4	0-0
Notts County FC	1-0	2-0	5-0	4-0	2-1	4-3	2-2	1-1	1-0	2-0	3-2	2-2	1-1	3-2	3-2		0-4	2-1	0-3	1-2	3-4	1-1
Plymouth Argyle FC	4-0	2-1	3-1	1-0	0-0	0-0	1-0	3-1	0-2	1-2	0-1	2-1	0-0	2-1	0-3	2-2		4-3	5-2	3-1	3-2	1-1
Rotherham United FC	3-1	1-1	0-0	4-1	6-1	4-2	2-2	1-0	0-0	2-1	3-1	0-0	3-2	1-3	2-3	2-3	2-3		0-2	2-2	2-1	1-1
Sheffield United FC	3-0	2-2	3-0	3-2	3-1	2-2	1-0	2-1	0-2	0-2	2-1	7-2	6-1	1-1	2-0	2-1	5-0	1-4		5-3	7-1	3-1
Southampton FC	1-2	1-1	6-1	0-2	1-2	3-3	1-1	5-3	0-2	5-1	2-2	5-2	1-0	1-3	2-2	1-1	2-3	2-3	4-4		1-4	1-2
Swansea Town AFC	3-0	1-1	1-1	3-2	2-0	2-1	2-2	1-1	3-3	3-0	3-2	1-1	1-1	4-2	2-1	5-1	2-2	0-0	1-2	1-2		4-1
West Ham United FC	3-1	1-2	0-0	3-1	3-2	1-3	3-1	1-2	0-1	0-0	2-2	4-1	5-1	0-1	3-2	2-2	0-1	2-4	1-1	1-0	3-0	

	Division 2	Pd	Wn	Dw	Ls	GF	GA	Pts	
1.	Sheffield United FC (Sheffield)	42	25	10	7	97	55	60	P
2.	Huddersfield Town AFC (Huddersfield)	42	24	10	8	84	33	58	P
3.	Luton Town FC (Luton)	42	22	8	12	84	49	52	
4.	Plymouth Argyle FC (Plymouth)	42	20	9	13	65	60	49	
5.	Leicester City FC (Leicester)	42	18	12	12	89	74	48	
6.	Birmingham City FC (Birmingham)	42	19	10	13	71	66	48	
7.	Nottingham Forest FC (Nottingham)	42	18	8	16	77	67	44	
8.	Fulham FC (London)	42	17	10	15	81	71	44	
9.	Blackburn Rovers FC (Blackburn)	42	18	8	16	68	65	44	
10.	Leeds United AFC (Leeds)	42	14	15	13	71	63	43	
11.	Swansea Town AFC (Swansea)	42	15	12	15	78	81	42	
12.	Rotherham United FC (Rotherham)	42	16	9	17	75	74	41	
13.	Doncaster Rovers FC (Doncaster)	42	12	16	14	58	64	40	
14.	West Ham United FC (London)	42	13	13	16	58	60	39	
15.	Lincoln City FC (Lincoln)	42	11	17	14	64	71	39	
16.	Everton FC (Liverpool)	42	12	14	16	71	75	38	
17.	Brentford FC (London)	42	13	11	18	59	76	37	
18.	Hull City AFC (Kingston-upon-Hull)	42	14	8	20	57	69	36	
19.	Notts County FC (Nottingham)	42	14	8	20	60	88	36	
20.	Bury FC (Bury)	42	13	9	20	53	81	35	
21.	Southampton FC (Southampton)	42	10	13	19	68	85	33	R
22.	Barnsley FC (Barnsley)	42	5	8	29	47	108	18	R
		924	343	238	343	1535	1535	924	

Football League Division 3 (N) — 1952-53 Season

	Accrington Stanley	Barrow	Bradford City	Bradford Park Ave.	Carlisle United	Chester	Chesterfield	Crewe Alexandra	Darlington	Gateshead	Grimsby Town	Halifax Town	Hartlepools	Mansfield Town	Oldham Athletic	Port Vale	Rochdale	Scunthorpe United	Southport	Stockport County	Tranmere Rovers	Workington	Wrexham	York City
Accrington Stanley	■	1-0	1-1	3-2	1-0	1-1	1-1	1-1	1-0	1-1	1-2	1-1	1-1	2-2	0-2	1-1	2-1	2-1	1-2	1-4	0-2	0-1	1-2	1-0
Barrow AFC	2-0	■	5-1	2-0	0-0	3-0	2-1	1-2	2-2	2-2	1-1	5-1	2-1	3-0	4-3	1-2	2-1	2-1	1-1	1-0	2-0	3-0	1-1	1-0
Bradford City AFC	3-2	2-2	■	2-1	7-2	2-2	2-1	1-3	4-3	3-1	1-0	5-0	1-1	2-1	0-0	1-0	0-3	0-0	2-2	3-0	5-3	4-0	3-1	1-1
Bradford Park Ave.	4-0	1-0	2-2	■	2-2	1-0	0-1	1-0	3-0	3-0	0-3	1-2	1-1	1-1	0-0	2-2	2-1	1-1	1-0	1-1	1-0	6-1	1-2	2-3
Carlisle United FC	4-4	0-0	4-4	1-3	■	1-1	3-0	1-2	4-2	2-2	3-0	1-2	4-1	1-0	0-0	2-0	5-0	8-0	2-0	2-1	4-0	3-1	1-0	1-1
Chester FC	2-0	2-1	2-0	0-3	1-2	■	2-0	2-2	6-3	2-0	0-2	2-1	0-1	2-2	0-1	2-2	3-0	1-1	0-0	4-0	3-2	1-1	1-2	1-1
Chesterfield FC	3-0	1-1	1-1	1-1	4-2	2-1	■	1-0	3-0	1-1	3-2	2-1	4-1	1-2	1-0	1-1	1-1	1-2	2-1	1-1	2-1	1-2	2-1	1-2
Crewe Alexandra FC	3-2	1-1	1-1	2-3	2-2	4-1	2-1	■	0-1	4-3	1-2	1-1	2-0	1-0	0-1	1-4	4-2	2-0	2-0	2-0	1-0	4-0	3-3	3-0
Darlington FC	1-0	1-0	4-1	1-3	0-0	3-2	3-1	1-1	■	1-0	1-1	0-2	3-0	2-1	0-5	0-2	3-2	1-0	3-1	1-0	1-2	1-0	2-2	0-1
Gateshead FC	5-0	3-1	2-2	3-2	2-0	4-1	2-4	6-1	5-1	■	2-0	3-1	1-1	1-2	1-1	3-1	1-1	1-2	2-0	0-1	1-1	1-0	1-1	
Grimsby Town FC	3-0	2-1	0-0	2-3	2-3	5-4	0-0	1-0	2-0	0-0	■	2-0	7-0	5-1	1-1	1-1	3-2	1-0	0-1	3-1	2-0	2-0	2-1	
Halifax Town AFC	3-0	1-0	1-1	2-4	2-1	3-1	3-1	1-3	3-2	1-3	3-2	■	3-2	1-2	2-2	1-2	3-1	2-1	4-1	3-0	0-0	5-2	0-0	0-0
Hartlepools United	4-1	2-0	0-0	0-1	1-0	2-2	2-0	2-1	1-0	0-0	2-0	0-0	■	2-0	4-1	2-0	1-1	3-0	0-2	4-1	2-2	1-2	2-1	
Mansfield Town FC	0-0	2-2	3-1	1-1	2-1	2-2	1-4	3-0	3-2	2-0	1-1	2-1	2-0	■	0-2	1-0	1-0	2-2	2-2	1-0	0-0	0-2	1-1	
Oldham Athletic AFC	3-0	3-0	2-0	2-1	2-4	2-1	1-1	0-1	5-0	1-1	1-1	1-0	4-2	1-0	■	0-1	1-0	0-1	3-0	1-1	5-2	4-1	4-2	1-1
Port Vale FC	0-2	3-0	1-0	1-0	0-0	1-1	3-0	3-1	2-1	1-1	4-0	1-1	3-0	1-1	1-1	■	5-2	4-0	0-0	2-0	2-0	2-0	0-0	2-0
Rochdale AFC	1-0	6-2	1-1	1-0	1-2	3-1	0-2	0-1	3-1	2-3	0-2	1-1	3-1	1-0	3-1	1-1	■	2-2	0-0	2-2	3-0	2-0	4-1	0-3
Scunthorpe United	5-2	1-2	4-0	1-2	1-2	1-1	1-0	2-0	2-0	0-0	1-1	0-0	0-1	1-1	1-2	5-1	■	3-0	2-2	2-0	2-1	1-2	2-0	
Southport FC	1-0	3-2	3-0	2-2	2-0	2-0	1-0	3-0	3-2	4-3	1-1	0-0	1-3	1-0	0-0	1-0	2-3	■	3-0	1-2	2-0	1-0	2-0	
Stockport County FC	3-1	6-1	6-1	3-0	3-0	4-1	4-1	2-2	2-2	2-1	1-1	1-1	2-0	0-2	2-0	1-1	3-0	2-0	3-0	■	3-2	6-0	3-1	1-1
Tranmere Rovers FC	2-0	2-0	3-1	4-0	4-1	4-0	3-1	1-0	5-2	2-0	2-1	0-0	0-2	1-0	0-0	1-1	1-0	0-1	1-1	1-0	■	3-0	4-2	1-3
Workington AFC	3-0	3-1	3-2	2-2	1-1	1-2	2-3	4-0	3-1	0-2	3-1	2-0	1-1	0-1	1-1	1-1	1-2	0-3	2-4	0-2	2-0	■	4-0	1-3
Wrexham AFC	3-1	4-0	2-1	0-3	3-0	7-0	2-2	1-0	4-2	1-0	3-1	2-1	3-2	1-0	2-2	3-1	3-0	2-3	3-2	5-2	1-0	3-0	■	1-1
York City FC	2-0	1-1	0-0	3-1	1-0	0-0	0-0	2-1	3-0	1-2	2-0	2-2	1-0	2-0	1-2	1-0	2-0	0-2	3-1	3-0	2-0	1-3	2-1	■

Division 3 (North)

		Pd	Wn	Dw	Ls	GF	GA	Pts	
1.	Oldham Athletic AFC (Oldham)	46	22	15	9	77	45	59	P
2.	Port Vale FC (Stoke-on-Trent)	46	20	18	8	67	35	58	
3.	Wrexham AFC (Wrexham)	46	24	8	14	86	66	56	
4.	York City FC (York)	46	20	13	13	60	45	53	
5.	Grimsby Town FC (Cleethorpes)	46	21	10	15	75	59	52	
6.	Southport FC (Southport)	46	20	11	15	63	60	51	
7.	Bradford Park Avenue FC (Bradford)	46	19	12	15	75	61	50	
8.	Gateshead FC (Gateshead)	46	17	15	14	76	60	49	
9.	Carlisle United FC (Carlisle)	46	18	13	15	82	68	49	
10.	Crewe Alexandra FC (Crewe)	46	20	8	18	70	68	48	
11.	Stockport County FC (Stockport)	46	17	13	16	82	69	47	
12.	Chesterfield FC (Chesterfield)	46	18	11	17	65	63	47	Jt.
12.	Tranmere Rovers FC (Birkenhead)	46	21	5	20	65	63	47	Jt.
14.	Halifax Town AFC (Halifax)	46	16	15	15	68	68	47	
15.	Scunthorpe & Lindsey United FC (Scunthorpe)	46	16	14	16	62	56	46	
16.	Bradford City AFC (Bradford)	46	14	18	14	75	80	46	
17.	Hartlepools United FC (Hartlepool)	46	16	14	16	57	61	46	
18.	Mansfield Town FC (Mansfield)	46	16	14	16	55	62	46	
19.	Barrow AFC (Barrow-in-Furness)	46	16	12	18	66	71	44	
20.	Chester FC (Chester)	46	11	15	20	64	85	37	
21.	Darlington FC (Darlington)	46	14	6	26	58	96	34	
22.	Rochdale AFC (Rochdale)	46	14	5	27	62	83	33	
23.	Workington AFC (Workington)	46	11	10	25	55	91	32	
24.	Accrington Stanley FC (Accrington)	46	8	11	27	39	89	27	
		1104	409	286	409	1604	1604	1104	

Football League Division 3 (S) 1952-53 Season

	Aldershot Town	Bournemouth	Brighton & H.A.	Bristol City	Bristol Rovers	Colchester United	Coventry City	Crystal Palace	Exeter City	Gillingham	Ipswich Town	Leyton Orient	Millwall	Newport County	Northampton Town	Norwich City	Q.P.R.	Reading	Shrewsbury Town	Southend United	Swindon Town	Torquay United	Walsall	Watford
Aldershot Town FC	■	1-0	1-2	1-2	0-0	0-0	4-1	0-1	1-1	3-2	1-1	2-0	1-2	2-2	2-1	1-2	4-1	2-2	4-2	1-1	2-2	0-2	2-0	1-2
Bournemouth & Bos.	0-3	■	2-1	4-1	1-2	1-0	3-0	4-2	2-1	4-2	2-1	4-1	1-1	1-2	0-1	0-0	1-0	2-0	2-0	5-1	1-1	0-1	5-1	4-1
Brighton & Hove Alb.	4-2	2-0	■	0-1	2-1	0-0	1-1	4-1	4-2	5-0	1-4	3-1	1-0	2-2	1-1	2-3	2-0	1-1	3-1	2-2	1-2	2-1	4-2	1-2
Bristol City FC	0-0	1-1	2-2	■	0-0	3-2	1-0	5-0	4-1	4-0	4-2	2-1	0-0	2-0	2-3	0-1	4-4	1-1	3-2	5-0	4-2	4-4	6-1	5-1
Bristol Rovers FC	4-1	2-1	7-0	0-0	■	3-1	5-2	2-0	0-0	3-1	3-0	2-1	1-1	3-1	1-1	3-1	2-1	4-0	2-1	2-1	1-2	3-0	2-0	0-3
Colchester United FC	1-2	1-1	0-0	3-1	0-3	■	0-1	3-0	3-1	1-1	0-0	3-1	0-0	3-3	1-2	0-4	1-1	2-1	1-0	3-3	-1	4-1	6-1	1-1
Coventry City FC	3-0	2-3	3-1	2-2	1-1	2-2	■	4-2	1-0	2-1	2-0	3-0	4-1	0-1	1-1	2-1	2-0	4-0	0-0	2-1	1-2	7-2	3-1	1-0
Crystal Palace FC	3-0	1-0	2-1	1-3	1-0	3-1	2-2	■	2-0	0-0	1-1	2-2	0-1	2-1	4-3	1-1	4-2	0-3	1-2	0-0	3-0	2-2	4-1	1-0
Exeter City FC	2-2	5-1	1-5	1-1	0-0	2-0	1-0	2-0	■	0-0	1-1	0-1	1-0	3-2	2-0	1-0	2-2	2-0	2-2	0-2	1-2	4-1	6-1	1-1
Gillingham FC	2-0	1-2	1-2	0-1	0-4	1-1	0-0	1-0	1-0	■	1-1	3-2	0-1	1-1	1-1	0-3	3-0	1-1	4-2	1-1	0-0	2-1	3-1	2-1
Ipswich Town FC	2-1	2-1	1-0	1-0	1-5	2-2	3-0	2-0	0-1	1-1	■	0-1	1-6	3-0	1-1	2-1	0-1	1-2	2-1	0-0	1-1	2-2	5-0	1-1
Leyton Orient FC	4-1	2-2	3-0	1-3	3-3	5-3	1-2	0-0	2-0	1-1	3-1	■	1-4		0-1	3-1	5-0	1-1	3-0	2-2	4-1	4-1	2-0	
Millwall FC	0-0	3-1	1-1	1-1	3-0	3-1	2-0	0-0	0-0	3-1	3-2	0-0	■	3-0	1-2	2-3	2-1	1-1	4-1	4-1	3-0	3-0	3-0	1-1
Newport County AFC	2-1	2-1	0-3	4-3	2-2	0-1	4-4	3-2	1-0	1-2	1-3	0-1	1-3	■	4-1	1-1	2-0	1-0	4-2	1-1	3-0	3-0	3-2	1-1
Northampton Town	4-0	5-1	5-3	0-2	2-2	2-0	3-1	5-1	3-1	3-1	2-0	3-1	1-1	5-0	■	3-3	4-2	6-1	3-1	4-3	3-1	3-3	2-1	4-1
Norwich City FC	5-0	1-1	3-2	0-0	0-0	3-0	1-1	5-1	2-0	3-2	1-0	5-1	2-2	2-0	1-2	■	2-0	3-0	2-1	3-1	1-1	3-0	3-0	5-2
Queen's Park Rangers	2-2	2-1	3-3	2-1	0-1	1-0	0-4	1-1	1-1	1-1	2-2	0-1	1-3	4-2	2-2	3-1	■	1-0	1-0	3-2	1-1	0-1	4-2	2-2
Reading FC	2-3	1-3	0-0	4-0	2-0	2-0	1-0	4-1	3-1	3-2	1-1	2-0	5-0	2-1	2-0	0-1	2-0	■	5-3	1-0	4-1	4-1	0-0	3-0
Shrewsbury Town FC	2-1	1-0	0-0	0-1	0-1	3-0	1-0	1-1	1-3	3-1	2-2	2-0	2-4	1-1	2-4	1-8	0-3	1-1	■	7-1	2-1	2-1	1-0	3-1
Southend United FC	1-1	0-0	1-2	0-4	2-1	4-0	1-0	2-2	1-1	3-1	2-0	1-0	3-1	1-2	2-0	3-1	2-2		2-2	■	3-0	3-1	2-1	1-0
Swindon Town FC	3-2	1-2	3-0	0-0	1-3	0-1	2-3	3-6	5-2	0-0	2-0	1-1	1-2	2-0	3-0	2-1	1-3	2-0	2-2	1-3	■	2-0	1-2	0-0
Torquay United FC	1-2	5-1	1-2	1-2	1-0	5-1	2-1	1-1	5-2	3-2	4-1	5-0	1-0	3-3	3-0	4-1	1-1	2-0	4-0	4-2	3-1	■	0-3	2-2
Walsall FC	0-0	2-2	3-0	3-3	3-5	0-3	1-1	2-4	2-2	1-3	1-3	1-0	0-2	1-3	1-5	3-2	1-1	2-0	4-4	1-1	1-2	2-0	■	0-0
Watford FC	1-1	3-0	2-3	4-1	2-3	2-0	1-1	2-0	3-1	0-0	1-0	1-0	1-1	0-1	2-1	3-2	1-1	2-1	1-1	1-1	2-1	1-1	3-0	■

Division 3 (South)

		Pd	Wn	Dw	Ls	GF	GA	Pts	
1.	Bristol Rovers FC (Bristol)	46	26	12	8	92	46	64	P
2.	Millwall FC (London)	46	24	14	8	82	44	62	
3.	Northampton Town FC (Northampton)	46	26	10	10	109	70	62	
4.	Norwich City FC (Norwich)	46	25	10	11	99	55	60	
5.	Bristol City FC (Bristol)	46	22	15	9	95	61	59	
6.	Coventry City FC (Coventry)	46	19	12	15	77	62	50	
7.	Brighton & Hove Albion FC (Hove)	46	19	12	15	81	75	50	
8.	Southend United FC (Southend-on-Sea)	46	18	13	15	69	74	49	
9.	Bournemouth & Boscombe Athletic FC (Bournemouth)	46	19	9	18	74	69	47	
10.	Watford FC (Watford)	46	15	17	14	62	63	47	
11.	Reading FC (Reading)	46	19	8	19	69	64	46	
12.	Torquay United FC (Torquay)	46	18	9	19	87	88	45	
13.	Crystal Palace FC (London)	46	15	13	18	66	82	43	
14.	Leyton Orient FC (London)	46	16	10	20	68	73	42	
15.	Newport County AFC (Newport)	46	16	10	20	70	82	42	
16.	Ipswich Town FC (Ipswich)	46	13	15	18	60	69	41	
17.	Exeter City FC (Exeter)	46	13	14	19	61	71	40	
18.	Swindon Town FC (Swindon)	46	14	12	20	64	79	40	
19.	Aldershot FC (Aldershot)	46	12	15	19	61	77	39	
20.	Gillingham FC (Gillingham)	46	12	15	19	55	74	39	
21.	Queen's Park Rangers FC (Glasgow)	46	12	15	19	61	82	39	
22.	Colchester United FC (Colchester)	46	12	14	20	59	76	38	
23.	Shrewsbury Town FC (Shrewsbury)	46	12	12	22	68	91	36	
24.	Walsall FC (Walsall)	46	7	10	29	56	118	24	
		1104	404	296	404	1745	1745	1104	

F.A. CUP FINAL   (Wembley Stadium, London – 02/05/1953 – 100,000)

BLACKPOOL FC (BLACKPOOL)   4-3   Bolton Wanderers FC (Bolton)

Mortensen 3, Perry   *Lofthouse, Moir, Bell*

Blackburn: Farm, Shimwell, Garrett, Fenton, Johnston, Robinson, Matthews, Taylor, Mortensen, Mudie, Perry.

Bolton: Hanson, Ball, R.Banks, Wheeler, Barrass, Bell, Holden, Moir, Lofthouse, Hassall, Langton.

Semi-finals

Blackpool FC (Blackpool)   2-1   Tottenham Hotspur FC (London)
Bolton Wanderers FC (Bolton)   4-3   Everton FC (Liverpool)

Quarter-finals

Arsenal FC (London)   1-2   Blackpool FC (Blackpool)
Aston Villa FC (Birmingham)   0-1   Everton FC (Liverpool)
Birmingham City FC (Birmingham)   1-1, 2-2, 0-1   Tottenham Hotspur FC (London)
Gateshead FC (Gateshead)   0-1   Bolton Wanderers FC (Bolton)

1953-54

Football League Division 1 1953-54 Season	Arsenal	Aston Villa	Blackpool	Bolton Wands.	Burnley	Cardiff City	Charlton Ath.	Chelsea	Huddersfield T.	Liverpool	Manchester City	Man. United	Middlesbrough	Newcastle U.	Portsmouth	Preston N.E.	Sheffield Utd.	Sheffield Wed.	Sunderland	Tottenham H.	W.B.A.	Wolves
Arsenal FC	■	1-1	1-1	4-3	2-5	1-1	3-3	1-2	0-0	3-0	2-2	3-1	3-1	2-1	3-0	3-2	1-1	4-1	1-4	0-3	2-2	2-3
Aston Villa FC	2-1	■	2-1	2-2	5-1	1-2	2-1	2-2	2-2	2-1	3-0	2-2	5-3	1-2	1-1	1-0	4-0	2-1	3-1	1-2	6-1	1-2
Blackpool FC	2-2	3-2	■	0-0	2-0	4-1	3-1	2-1	3-1	3-0	2-0	2-0	0-0	1-3	1-1	4-2	2-2	1-2	3-0	1-0	4-1	0-0
Bolton Wanderers FC	3-1	3-0	3-2	■	0-0	3-0	3-1	2-2	0-0	2-0	3-2	0-0	3-2	2-2	6-1	0-2	2-1	2-1	3-1	2-0	2-1	1-1
Burnley FC	2-1	3-2	2-1	1-1	■	3-0	2-0	1-2	2-1	1-1	3-1	2-0	5-0	1-2	1-0	2-1	2-1	4-1	5-1	4-2	1-4	4-1
Cardiff City AFC	0-3	2-1	0-1	1-1	1-0	■	5-0	0-0	2-1	3-1	0-3	1-6	1-0	2-1	3-2	2-1	2-0	2-2	1-1	1-0	2-0	1-3
Charlton Athletic FC	1-5	1-1	4-2	1-0	3-1	3-2	■	1-1	2-1	6-0	2-1	1-0	8-1	0-0	3-1	2-1	3-0	4-2	5-3	0-1	1-1	0-2
Chelsea FC	0-2	1-2	5-1	2-0	2-1	2-0	3-1	■	2-2	5-2	0-1	3-1	1-1	1-2	4-3	1-0	1-2	0-1	2-2	1-0	5-0	4-2
Huddersfield Town AFC	2-2	4-0	0-0	2-1	3-1	2-0	4-1	3-1	■	2-0	1-1	0-0	2-1	3-2	5-1	2-2	2-2	2-0	1-2	2-5	0-2	2-1
Liverpool FC	1-2	6-1	5-2	1-2	4-0	0-1	2-3	1-1	1-3	■	2-2	4-4	4-1	2-2	3-1	1-5	3-0	2-2	4-3	2-2	0-0	1-1
Manchester City FC	0-0	0-1	1-4	3-0	3-2	1-1	3-0	1-1	0-1	0-2	■	2-0	5-2	0-0	2-1	1-4	2-1	3-2	2-1	4-1	2-3	0-4
Manchester United FC	2-2	1-0	4-1	1-5	1-2	2-3	2-0	1-1	3-1	5-1	1-1	■	2-2	1-1	2-0	1-0	2-2	5-2	1-0	2-0	1-3	1-0
Middlesbrough FC	2-0	2-1	0-1	3-2	1-3	0-0	0-2	3-3	0-3	0-1	0-1	1-4	■	2-3	2-2	0-4	2-0	4-1	0-0	3-0	1-1	3-3
Newcastle United FC	5-2	0-1	2-1	2-3	3-1	4-0	0-2	1-1	0-2	4-0	4-3	1-2	2-3	■	1-1	0-4	4-1	3-0	2-1	1-3	3-7	1-2
Portsmouth FC	1-1	2-1	4-4	3-2	3-2	1-1	3-1	3-2	5-2	5-1	4-1	1-1	0-2	2-0	■	1-3	3-4	2-1	4-1	1-1	3-0	2-0
Preston North End FC	0-1	1-1	2-3	3-1	2-1	1-2	2-0	1-0	1-2	2-1	4-0	1-3	1-0	2-2	4-0	■	2-1	6-0	6-2	2-1	0-2	0-1
Sheffield United FC	1-0	2-1	3-4	3-0	0-1	1-1	1-3	3-6	3-1	2-2	1-3	2-2	3-1	3-1	1-1	1-1	■	2-0	1-3	5-2	1-2	3-3
Sheffield Wednesday FC	2-1	3-1	1-2	2-1	2-0	2-1	1-2	2-0	1-4	1-1	2-0	0-1	4-2	3-0	4-4	4-2	3-2	■	2-2	2-1	2-3	0-0
Sunderland AFC	7-1	2-0	3-2	1-2	2-1	5-0	2-1	1-2	1-1	3-2	4-5	0-2	0-2	1-1	3-1	2-2	2-2	2-4	■	4-3	2-1	3-2
Tottenham Hotspur FC	1-4	1-0	2-2	3-2	2-3	0-1	3-1	2-1	1-0	2-1	3-0	1-1	4-1	3-0	1-1	2-6	2-1	3-1	0-3	■	0-1	2-3
West Bromwich Albion FC	2-0	1-1	2-1	1-1	0-0	6-1	2-3	5-2	4-0	5-2	1-0	2-0	2-1	2-2	2-3	3-2	2-2	4-2	2-0	3-0	■	0-1
Wolverhampton Wanderers FC	0-2	1-2	4-1	1-1	1-2	3-1	5-0	8-1	4-0	2-1	3-1	3-1	2-4	3-2	4-3	1-0	6-1	4-1	3-1	2-0	1-0	■

	Division 1	Pd	Wn	Dw	Ls	GF	GA	Pts	
1.	WOLVERHAMPTON WANDERERS FC (WOLV'N)	42	25	7	10	96	56	57	
2.	West Bromwich Albion FC (West Bromwich)	42	22	9	11	86	63	53	
3.	Huddersfield Town AFC (Huddersfield)	42	20	11	11	78	61	51	
4.	Manchester United FC (Manchester)	42	18	12	12	73	58	48	
5.	Bolton Wanderers FC (Bolton)	42	18	12	12	75	60	48	
6.	Blackpool FC (Blackpool)	42	19	10	13	80	69	48	
7.	Burnley FC (Burnley)	42	21	4	17	78	67	46	
8.	Chelsea FC (London)	42	16	12	14	74	68	44	
9.	Charlton Athletic FC (London)	42	19	6	17	75	77	44	
10.	Cardiff City AFC (Cardiff)	42	18	8	16	51	71	44	
11.	Preston North End FC (Preston)	42	19	5	18	87	58	43	
12.	Arsenal FC (London)	42	15	13	14	75	73	43	
13.	Aston Villa FC (Birmingham)	42	16	9	17	70	68	41	
14.	Portsmouth FC (Portsmouth)	42	14	11	17	81	89	39	
15.	Newcastle United FC (Newcastle-upon-Tyne)	42	14	10	18	72	77	38	
16.	Tottenham Hotspur FC (London)	42	16	5	21	65	76	37	
17.	Manchester City FC (Manchester)	42	14	9	19	62	77	37	
18.	Sunderland AFC (Sunderland)	42	14	8	20	81	89	36	
19.	Sheffield Wednesday FC (Sheffield)	42	15	6	21	70	91	36	
20.	Sheffield United FC (Sheffield)	42	11	11	20	69	90	33	
21.	Middlesbrough FC (Middlesbrough)	42	10	10	22	60	91	30	R
22.	Liverpool FC (Liverpool)	42	9	10	23	68	97	28	R
		924	363	198	363	1626	1626	924	

Top Goalscorers

1)	James GLAZZARD	(Huddersfield Town AFC)	29
	Johnny NICHOLLS	(West Bromwich Albion FC)	29

Football League Division 2 — 1953-54 Season

	Birmingham City	Blackburn Rovers	Brentford	Bristol Rovers	Bury	Derby County	Doncaster Rovers	Everton	Fulham	Hull City	Leeds United	Leicester City	Lincoln City	Luton Town	Nottingham Forest	Notts County	Oldham Athletic	Plymouth Argyle	Rotherham United	Stoke City	Swansea Town	West Ham United
Birmingham City FC	■	0-0	5-1	1-1	0-0	3-0	0-1	5-1	2-2	2-0	3-3	1-2	1-0	5-1	2-2	3-0	2-1	3-0	2-3	1-0	6-0	2-0
Blackburn Rovers FC	3-0	■	2-2	1-1	4-1	0-3	2-0	0-0	5-1	3-1	2-2	3-0	6-0	2-0	2-0	2-0	4-0	2-3	3-0	3-0	1-0	4-1
Brentford FC	2-0	1-4	■	0-3	2-1	0-0	1-4	1-0	2-1	2-2	2-1	1-3	0-1	0-1	1-1	0-0	3-1	1-0	0-1	0-0	3-1	3-1
Bristol Rovers FC	1-1	1-2	0-0	■	2-0	3-0	0-1	0-0	2-1	4-2	1-1	3-0	0-1	3-3	1-0	1-1	1-0	3-1	1-0	3-2	0-1	2-2
Bury FC	1-1	0-0	1-1	3-1	■	4-0	2-1	2-2	1-3	3-0	4-4	2-5	1-1	0-1	2-1	3-3	1-0	3-0	3-0	0-6	1-2	2-0
Derby County FC	2-4	2-2	4-1	0-1	3-1	■	2-0	2-6	3-3	2-0	0-2	2-1	2-0	1-2	1-2	0-0	3-1	1-4	1-1	1-1	4-2	2-1
Doncaster Rovers FC	3-1	0-2	3-0	1-0	0-1	1-3	■	2-2	2-2	4-1	0-0	0-2	1-1	1-3	1-3	4-2	1-0	3-3	1-2	1-0	1-0	2-0
Everton FC	1-0	1-1	6-1	4-0	0-0	3-2	4-1	■	2-2	2-0	2-1	1-2	3-1	2-1	3-3	3-2	3-1	8-4	3-0	1-1	2-2	1-2
Fulham FC	5-2	2-3	4-1	4-4	3-0	5-2	1-2	0-0	■	5-1	1-3	1-1	4-1	5-1	3-1	4-3	3-1	3-1	2-4	0-1	4-3	3-4
Hull City AFC	3-0	0-2	2-0	4-1	3-0	3-0	3-1	1-3	2-1	■	1-1	0-3	3-0	1-2	3-0	0-2	8-0	2-0	1-0	1-2	4-3	2-1
Leeds United AFC	1-1	3-2	4-0	3-3	3-4	3-1	3-1	3-1	1-2	0-0	■	7-1	5-2	2-1	0-2	6-0	2-1	1-1	4-2	1-1	3-2	1-2
Leicester City FC	3-4	4-0	6-0	1-0	2-2	2-0	2-2	2-2	1-3	5-0	3-1	■	9-2	1-1	1-0	2-1	1-0	4-2	4-1	4-0	4-1	2-1
Lincoln City FC	0-1	8-0	2-1	1-2	0-0	2-1	0-2	1-1	4-2	3-0	2-0	3-1	■	1-1	2-2	3-0	3-1	2-0	4-3	1-1	3-1	1-2
Luton Town FC	2-0	2-1	1-1	1-1	3-2	2-1	2-0	1-1	1-2	3-1	1-1	2-2	1-0	■	0-1	2-1	4-4	2-1	1-1	0-1	2-0	3-1
Nottingham Forest FC	1-1	0-1	2-1	3-1	2-2	4-2	2-2	3-3	4-1	2-0	5-2	3-1	4-2	2-1	■	5-0	1-1	3-0	4-1	5-4	2-1	4-0
Notts County FC	2-1	0-5	2-0	1-5	0-0	0-1	1-5	0-2	0-0	1-1	2-0	1-1	1-1	1-2	1-1	■	2-0	2-1	1-2	2-1	3-0	3-1
Oldham Athletic AFC	2-3	1-0	0-0	0-0	0-0	0-0	2-2	0-4	2-3	0-0	4-2	0-2	1-0	1-2	1-3	1-3	■	1-1	2-3	1-0	2-2	3-1
Plymouth Argyle FC	2-2	1-1	3-2	3-3	1-1	3-2	0-0	4-0	2-2	2-2	1-1	0-3	1-2	2-2	1-0	3-3	5-0	■	0-2	1-1	1-1	2-1
Rotherham United FC	1-0	1-4	1-1	1-1	1-0	5-2	4-0	1-2	3-2	3-2	2-4	1-1	4-1	2-1	3-0	0-1	7-0	2-1	■	2-2	2-1	5-0
Stoke City FC	3-2	3-0	1-1	3-2	4-0	2-2	2-2	2-4	1-3	0-1	4-0	2-2	4-1	1-1	1-1	0-1	0-1	3-2	1-1	■	5-0	1-1
Swansea Town AFC	1-3	2-1	1-0	3-1	2-1	2-1	0-1	0-2	2-0	4-3	0-0	4-2	1-1	2-1	2-2	4-0	0-1	0-2	2-2	2-2	■	1-1
West Ham United FC	1-2	2-1	0-1	1-1	5-0	0-0	2-1	1-1	3-1	1-0	5-2	4-1	5-0	1-0	1-1	1-2	0-1	2-2	3-0	2-2	4-1	■

	Division 2	Pd	Wn	Dw	Ls	GF	GA	Pts	
1.	Leicester City FC (Leicester)	42	23	10	9	97	60	56	P
2.	Everton FC (Liverpool)	42	20	16	6	92	58	56	P
3.	Blackburn Rovers FC (Blackburn)	42	23	9	10	86	50	55	
4.	Nottingham Forest FC (Nottingham)	42	20	12	10	86	59	52	
5.	Rotherham United FC (Rotherham)	42	21	7	14	80	67	49	
6.	Luton Town FC (Luton)	42	18	12	12	64	59	48	
7.	Birmingham City FC (Birmingham)	42	18	11	13	78	58	47	
8.	Fulham FC (London)	42	17	10	15	98	85	44	
9.	Bristol Rovers FC (Bristol)	42	14	16	12	64	58	44	
10.	Leeds United AFC (Leeds)	42	15	13	14	89	81	43	
11.	Stoke FC (stoke-on-Trent)	42	12	17	13	71	60	41	
12.	Doncaster Rovers FC (Doncaster)	42	16	9	17	59	63	41	
13.	West Ham United FC (London)	42	15	9	18	67	69	39	
14.	Notts County FC (Nottingham)	42	13	13	16	54	74	39	
15.	Hull City AFC (Kingston-upon-Hull)	42	16	6	20	64	66	38	
16.	Lincoln City FC (Lincoln)	42	14	9	19	65	83	37	
17.	Bury FC (Bury)	42	11	14	17	54	72	36	
18.	Derby County FC (Derby)	42	12	11	19	64	82	35	
19.	Plymouth Argyle FC (Plymouth)	42	9	16	17	65	82	34	
20.	Swansea Town AFC (Swansea)	42	13	8	21	58	82	34	
21.	Brentford FC (London)	42	10	11	21	40	78	31	R
22.	Oldham Athletic AFC (Oldham)	42	8	9	25	40	89	25	R
		924	338	248	338	1535	1535	924	

Football League Division 3 (N) 1953-54 Season	Accrington Stanley	Barnsley	Barrow	Bradford City	Bradford Park Avenue	Carlisle United	Chester	Chesterfield	Crewe Alexandra	Darlington	Gateshead	Grimsby Town	Halifax Town	Hartlepools	Mansfield Town	Port Vale	Rochdale	Scunthorpe United	Southport	Stockport County	Tranmere Rovers	Workington	Wrexham	York City
Accrington Stanley		3-0	3-2	0-1	0-0	2-2	1-0	2-2	2-1	0-0	2-2	3-1	3-0	2-0	5-1	2-2	1-0	0-1	1-1	2-1	0-1	4-2	1-2	2-0
Barnsley FC	5-0		3-2	4-2	2-1	1-1	3-0	4-1	1-1	5-1	0-2	0-0	1-2	3-2	2-1	0-1	2-1	0-1	2-1	4-1	3-0	4-2	3-0	2-1
Barrow AFC	4-3	0-1		3-0	4-1	1-1	2-1	2-2	3-1	2-2	0-0	4-0	1-1	1-1	4-2	0-0	4-2	1-2	2-3	1-0	2-0	0-1	1-0	4-1
Bradford City AFC	1-0	1-0	1-0		3-0	1-0	1-0	2-0	3-0	2-0	2-2	3-0	2-0	1-1	2-2	1-1	4-0	1-3	4-1	1-1	1-0	1-1	1-2	1-0
Bradford Park Ave.	6-4	0-2	2-1	4-0		2-4	5-0	1-1	1-1	2-2	3-1	4-1	4-2	5-0	1-0	1-2	2-2	2-2	1-1	3-2	1-2	3-1	2-0	2-0
Carlisle United FC	2-1	2-4	2-2	2-0	0-1		1-1	2-3	5-0	1-1	1-0	3-3	5-0	2-3	5-0	0-0	7-0	5-1	3-2	2-0	0-2	2-2	0-0	1-1
Chester FC	3-0	1-1	1-1	3-0	2-3	0-1		2-2	2-0	2-2	5-0	1-1	3-1	1-1	0-2	0-1	2-0	0-0	1-0	1-2	3-0	2-1	3-1	
Chesterfield FC	0-0	1-1	1-1	2-3	5-1	5-0	4-0		0-2	1-1	1-1	1-0	1-2	2-1	0-0	1-2	2-1	1-0	2-0	4-0	2-1	1-0	1-0	3-2
Crewe Alexandra FC	0-3	3-2	2-0	1-2	1-1	0-0	1-0	2-0		1-0	3-1	1-1	3-1	3-0	0-0	0-0	2-1	1-1	0-0	1-5	1-2	2-3	1-2	1-1
Darlington FC	4-1	1-1	1-3	1-0	2-1	3-2	1-0	3-2	0-1		0-2	3-0	1-1	0-1	1-2	0-3	0-0	3-0	0-1	1-0	2-1	3-0	0-2	1-3
Gateshead FC	4-0	0-0	1-0	1-0	0-1	2-2	2-1	3-3	2-0	1-2		7-1	4-0	1-3	1-3	1-0	2-1	0-0	1-0	4-2	2-1	4-1	3-1	3-0
Grimsby Town FC	2-0	0-1	1-0	1-0	0-0	3-2	0-0	1-1	3-1	1-0	2-0		2-1	3-0	0-2	2-2	3-2	0-1	1-2	1-0	1-0	1-0	0-0	3-0
Halifax Town AFC	2-0	1-2	2-0	0-1	2-2	2-0	1-1	2-1	1-0	0-0	0-0	2-0		1-0	2-0	0-1	1-1	0-3	1-2	0-1	1-1	3-0	0-2	2-3
Hartlepools United	0-1	0-1	2-2	1-1	0-2	1-1	2-0	0-1	0-0	1-0	1-0	3-0	2-0		3-1	2-1	6-0	3-2	1-1	6-0	1-2	2-2	1-1	2-2
Mansfield Town FC	1-1	2-0	2-3	0-0	1-1	2-1	2-1	2-2	6-0	6-0	1-1	5-1	3-1	1-0		1-2	2-0	2-1	4-2	3-1	2-0	0-2	4-0	7-2
Port Vale FC	1-0	0-0	4-0	3-0	2-0	1-0	1-0	2-2	1-0	1-1	0-0	2-0	2-0	3-1	1-1		6-0	0-0	0-0	7-0	2-0	2-0	2-0	5-0
Rochdale AFC	1-0	1-1	1-0	3-2	0-1	2-1	4-0	0-1	4-1	3-0	0-1	4-1	0-1	2-2	1-0	0-0		1-1	2-0	0-0	0-1	4-2	6-2	1-1
Scunthorpe United	1-2	6-0	3-2	2-1	4-1	2-1	1-0	2-1	2-2	1-1	1-1	2-1	3-2	0-0	2-2	0-2	1-1		1-1	2-0	3-1	4-1	3-1	3-0
Southport FC	5-3	5-2	0-1	0-1	1-0	3-0	0-1	2-1	1-2	3-0	2-4	2-1	1-0	2-1	2-1	0-0	1-1	4-3		1-2	0-0	1-1	4-0	1-1
Stockport County FC	1-1	3-0	5-1	5-0	4-1	3-2	5-0	6-1	1-0	2-0	0-1	3-2	1-1	1-0	3-2	1-1	1-2	1-1	1-1		6-0	2-0	2-2	0-1
Tranmere Rovers FC	1-0	0-1	1-0	0-1	1-1	1-2	2-1	1-2	1-0	1-0	1-4	2-4	1-0	3-2	2-5	1-3	5-1	1-1	2-0	2-2		4-2	6-1	1-1
Workington AFC	3-1	2-0	1-1	2-2	1-1	2-2	2-0	2-1	1-2	1-1	2-0	2-0	3-1	0-0	1-1	2-0	0-1	1-3	0-1	0-0	2-1		1-1	5-2
Wrexham AFC	4-2	1-1	1-2	0-1	2-0	4-2	2-1	1-2	1-1	4-2	5-1	4-0	5-0	2-0	2-0	1-1	2-0	3-1	2-1	1-0	3-0	8-0		1-1
York City FC	1-2	0-2	5-2	3-2	0-0	1-3	2-1	1-3	0-3	3-3	1-1	1-2	1-1	5-0	5-1	0-1	1-2	2-0	2-1	0-0	0-0	0-0	5-2	

Division 3 (North)

		Pd	Wn	Dw	Ls	GF	GA	Pts	
1.	Port Vale FC (Stoke-on-Trent)	46	26	17	3	74	21	69	P
2.	Barnsley FC (Barnsley)	46	24	10	12	77	57	58	
3.	Scunthorpe & Lindsey United FC (Scunthorpe)	46	21	15	10	77	56	57	
4.	Gateshead FC (Gateshead)	46	21	13	12	74	55	55	
5.	Bradford City AFC (Bradford)	46	22	9	15	60	55	53	
6.	Chesterfield FC (Chesterfield)	46	19	14	13	76	64	52	
7.	Mansfield Town FC (Mansfield)	46	20	11	15	88	67	51	
8.	Wrexham AFC (Wrexham)	46	21	9	16	81	68	51	
9.	Bradford Park Avenue FC (Bradford)	46	18	14	14	77	68	50	
10.	Stockport County FC (Stockport)	46	18	11	17	77	67	47	
11.	Southport FC (Southport)	46	17	12	17	63	60	46	
12.	Barrow AFC (Barrow-in-Furness)	46	16	12	18	72	71	44	
13.	Carlisle United FC (Carlisle)	46	14	15	17	83	71	43	
14.	Tranmere Rovers FC (Birkenhead)	46	18	7	21	59	70	43	
15.	Accrington Stanley FC (Accrington)	46	16	10	20	66	74	42	
16.	Crewe Alexandra FC (Crewe)	46	14	13	19	49	67	41	
17.	Grimsby Town FC (Cleethorpes)	46	16	9	21	51	77	41	
18.	Hartlepools United FC (Hartlepool)	46	13	14	19	59	65	40	
19.	Rochdale AFC (Rochdale)	46	15	10	21	59	77	40	
20.	Workington AFC (Workington)	46	13	14	19	59	80	40	
21.	Darlington FC (Darlington)	46	12	14	20	50	71	38	
22.	York City FC (York)	46	12	13	21	64	86	37	
23.	Halifax Town AFC (Halifax)	46	12	10	24	44	73	34	
24.	Chester FC (Chester)	46	11	10	25	48	67	32	
		1104	409	286	409	1587	1587	1104	

Football League Division 3 (S) 1953-54 Season	Aldershot Town	Bournemouth	Brighton & H.A.	Bristol City	Colchester United	Coventry City	Crystal Palace	Exeter City	Gillingham	Ipswich Town	Leyton Orient	Millwall	Newport County	Northampton Town	Norwich City	Q.P.R.	Reading	Shrewsbury Town	Southampton	Southend United	Swindon Town	Torquay United	Walsall	Watford
Aldershot Town FC	■	1-2	2-3	2-5	3-0	4-2	1-2	1-2	1-2	3-0	1-1	1-1	2-0	3-1	0-0	1-4	2-2	1-0	1-1	4-0	1-0	4-1	3-1	3-1
Bournemouth & Bos.	1-1	■	1-1	5-2	4-2	1-0	2-0	4-1	4-1	2-3	1-2	4-1	1-1	2-1	2-0	0-1	1-1	2-1	3-1	0-1	4-0	1-2	1-1	1-3
Brighton & Hove Alb.	3-2	3-0	■	2-1	1-0	3-1	3-0	2-1	3-1	1-2	2-1	4-0	4-2	3-2	0-0	3-1	3-2	2-3	2-1	3-2	1-1	1-2	5-3	3-3
Bristol City FC	4-0	1-1	1-1	■	3-0	1-0	4-0	5-1	1-1	2-3	1-0	2-1	3-0	2-1	3-1	1-2	3-1	3-1	1-0	4-1	5-1	3-0	4-1	2-1
Colchester United FC	3-0	1-1	1-1	0-2	■	0-3	4-1	0-1	0-1	1-2	1-0	3-0	2-2	1-1	0-1	5-0	2-4	3-1	0-1	0-1	2-2	3-1	1-1	2-2
Coventry City FC	2-1	2-0	1-2	3-0	2-1	■	0-0	2-0	2-1	1-3	4-0	0-0	1-2	0-0	1-0	3-1	1-1	2-1	2-1	1-0	0-0	4-0	2-0	0-1
Crystal Palace FC	0-0	3-1	1-1	1-2	0-1	3-1	■	0-0	1-2	1-1	2-2	2-3	3-0	2-2	1-0	0-3	1-0	3-2	4-3	4-2	3-2	4-1	1-0	1-1
Exeter City FC	1-3	1-0	0-1	0-1	1-2	4-0	7-0	■	1-2	1-2	2-1	4-1	1-0	1-0	0-2	0-0	2-0	0-1	4-0	1-1	3-1	1-2	2-1	2-1
Gillingham FC	1-3	1-0	0-0	2-2	2-0	2-0	3-2	0-1	■	1-1	1-2	2-0	0-1	2-1	3-1	1-0	3-0	2-0	2-0	3-1	1-0	0-4	3-0	2-3
Ipswich Town FC	4-0	2-1	2-3	2-1	3-0	4-1	2-0	1-1	6-1	■	3-1	1-1	1-2	2-1	1-1	2-1	0-1	0-0	2-1	1-1	2-0	2-1	3-0	1-0
Leyton Orient FC	1-2	5-0	0-2	4-1	3-1	1-0	2-0	3-1	3-1	1-2	■	2-2	3-0	2-1	3-1	2-2	2-1	2-0	1-4	1-1	1-1	3-2	2-1	1-1
Millwall FC	2-0	2-1	0-2	1-0	0-0	1-2	2-2	2-1	3-1	1-2	0-3	■	3-1	1-0	1-3	4-0	2-0	3-1	2-1	2-1	6-1	2-2	3-0	1-0
Newport County AFC	2-2	4-0	1-0	3-2	1-1	2-1	1-3	0-3	1-0	1-2	1-1	0-0	■	2-0	4-1	2-1	4-1	2-1	0-4	3-2	2-0	2-0	4-2	0-1
Northampton Town	6-2	2-1	4-2	3-0	3-0	0-1	6-0	2-2	1-1	1-0	2-2	4-2	1-0	■	2-0	2-1	1-1	1-0	3-0	5-0	2-0	3-1	5-1	4-1
Norwich City FC	3-3	1-3	1-0	1-1	2-1	2-1	2-1	1-2	0-0	1-2	3-1	4-3	2-0	4-1	■	2-2	2-3	1-0	1-0	2-2	0-1	3-0	4-1	
Queen's Park Rangers	0-2	2-1	1-2	0-1	0-0	0-3	1-1	0-0	3-1	3-1	2-1	4-0	5-1	1-1	0-2	■	2-0	0-0	0-1	1-0	0-2	5-1	2-0	0-4
Reading FC	6-1	0-1	2-1	0-2	2-0	4-3	4-1	4-1	0-1	3-1	1-1	2-4	4-1	2-0	4-4	3-1	■	1-1	4-1	2-0	3-1	2-4	0-2	4-1
Shrewsbury Town FC	0-2	1-1	3-1	4-3	3-1	1-1	1-1	1-1	0-0	1-1	3-3	3-1	2-1	-4	4-0	1-1	0-3	■	3-2	2-1	1-0	2-1	4-1	6-4
Southampton FC	2-0	2-1	1-0	4-2	2-1	2-1	3-1	2-0	1-0	4-1	4-2	4-0	1-0	0-0	3-1	1-1	4-2		■	3-5	3-1	2-2	0-0	2-0
Southend United FC	2-1	2-1	1-0	2-3	2-0	2-2	1-2	0-1	1-1	1-2	1-2	0-1	2-0	5-2	4-1	1-2	3-0	2-1		■	3-1	1-0	3-1	3-0
Swindon Town FC	3-1	2-1	0-1	5-0	3-0	1-1	1-1	2-4	2-1	1-2	2-1	2-1	7-1	0-0	0-0	0-1	1-0	2-1	0-1	3-0	■	6-1	3-0	2-2
Torquay United FC	3-0	2-0	2-3	4-0	3-1	1-1	1-0	3-2	3-3	1-1	2-3	2-2	3-2	1-1	2-4	2-2	2-2	2-0	1-1	1-1	2-1	■	3-1	2-2
Walsall FC	0-2	1-0	3-1	0-0	2-3	1-0	1-0	1-1	1-1	0-2	4-2	0-2	0-1	0-1	1-4	2-0	1-3	0-0	1-0	2-0	0-1	1-3	■	0-0
Watford FC	6-1	2-3	1-1	2-0	3-0	1-0	4-1	0-2	6-1	1-0	3-1	2-1	1-0	1-1	1-3	0-2	3-0	3-1	2-0	2-2	2-1	3-1		■

Division 3 (South)

		Pd	Wn	Dw	Ls	GF	GA	Pts	
1.	Ipswich Town FC (Ipswich)	46	27	10	9	82	51	64	P
2.	Brighton & Hove Albion FC (Hove)	46	26	9	11	86	61	61	
3.	Bristol City FC (Bristol)	46	25	6	15	88	66	56	
4.	Watford FC (Watford)	46	21	10	15	85	69	52	
5.	Northampton Town FC (Northampton)	46	20	11	15	82	55	51	
6.	Southampton FC (Southampton)	46	22	7	17	76	63	51	
7.	Norwich City FC (Norwich)	46	20	11	15	73	66	51	
8.	Reading FC (Reading)	46	20	9	17	86	73	49	
9.	Exeter City FC (Exeter)	46	20	8	18	68	58	48	
10.	Gillingham FC (Gillingham)	46	19	10	17	61	66	48	
11.	Leyton Orient FC (London)	46	18	11	17	79	73	47	
12.	Millwall FC (London)	46	19	9	18	74	77	47	
13.	Torquay United FC (Torquay)	46	17	12	17	81	88	46	
14.	Coventry City FC (Coventry)	46	18	9	19	61	56	45	
15.	Newport County AFC (Newport)	46	19	6	21	61	81	44	
16.	Southend United FC (Southend-on-Sea)	46	18	7	21	69	71	43	
17.	Aldershot FC (Aldershot)	46	17	9	20	74	86	43	
18.	Queen's Park Rangers FC (London)	46	16	10	20	60	68	42	
19.	Bournemouth & Boscombe Athletic FC (Bournemouth)	46	16	8	22	67	70	40	
20.	Swindon Town FC (Swindon)	46	15	10	21	67	70	40	
21.	Shrewsbury Town FC (Shrewsbury)	46	14	12	20	65	76	40	
22.	Crystal Palace FC (London)	46	14	12	20	60	86	40	
23.	Colchester United FC (Colchester)	46	10	10	26	50	78	30	
24.	Walsall FC (Walsall)	46	9	8	29	40	87	26	
		1104	440	224	440	1695	1695	1104	

F.A. CUP FINAL (Wembley Stadium, London – 01/05/1954 – 100,000)

WEST BROMWICH ALBION FC   3-2   Preston North End FC (Preston)

Allen 2 (1 pen.), Griffin   *Morrison, Wayman*

West Bromwich: Sanders, Kennedy, Millard, Dudley, Dugdale, Barlow, Griffin, Ryan, Allen, Nicholls, Lee.
Preston: Thompson, Cunningham, Walton, Docherty, Marston, Forbes, Finney, Foster, Wayman, Baxter, Morrison.

Semi-finals

Preston North End FC (Preston)	2-0	Sheffield Wednesday FC (Sheffield)
West Bromwich Albion FC (West Bromwich)	2-1	Port Vale FC (Stoke-on-Trent)

Quarter-finals

Leicester City FC (Leicester)	1-1, 2-2, 1-3	Preston North End FC (Preston)
Leyton Orient FC (London)	0-1	Port Vale FC (Stoke-on-Trent)
Sheffield Wednesday FC (Sheffield)	1-1, 2-0	Bolton Wanderers FC (Bolton)
West Bromwich Albion FC (West Bromwich)	3-0	Tottenham Hotspur FC (London)

1954-55

Football League Division 1 1954-55 Season	Arsenal	Aston Villa	Blackpool	Bolton Wands.	Burnley	Cardiff City	Charlton Athletic	Chelsea	Everton	Huddersfield T.	Leicester City	Manchester City	Manchester Utd.	Newcastle United	Portsmouth	Preston N.E.	Sheffield United	Sheffield Wed.	Sunderland	Tottenham H.	W.B.A.	Wolves
Arsenal FC	■	2-0	3-0	3-0	4-0	2-0	3-1	1-0	2-0	3-5	1-1	2-3	2-3	1-3	0-1	2-0	4-0	3-2	1-3	2-0	2-2	1-1
Aston Villa FC	2-1	■	3-1	3-0	3-1	0-2	1-2	3-2	0-2	0-0	2-5	2-0	2-1	1-2	1-0	1-3	3-1	0-0	2-2	2-4	3-0	4-2
Blackpool FC	2-2	0-1	■	2-3	1-0	0-0	1-1	1-0	4-0	1-1	2-0	1-3	2-4	2-0	2-2	1-2	1-2	2-1	0-0	5-1	3-1	0-2
Bolton Wanderers FC	2-2	3-3	3-0	■	0-1	0-0	3-2	2-5	2-0	1-0	4-1	2-2	1-1	2-1	3-1	2-1	1-0	2-2	3-0	1-2	2-4	6-1
Burnley FC	3-0	2-0	0-1	2-0	■	1-0	3-0	1-1	0-2	1-1	3-1	2-0	2-4	0-1	1-0	2-2	2-1	2-0	0-1	1-2	0-2	1-0
Cardiff City AFC	1-2	0-1	1-2	2-2	0-3	■	4-3	0-1	4-3	1-1	2-1	3-0	3-0	4-2	1-1	2-5	1-1	5-3	0-1	1-2	3-2	3-2
Charlton Athletic FC	1-1	6-1	3-3	2-0	3-1	4-1	■	0-2	5-0	2-3	1-1	1-1	1-1	2-2	0-4	2-1	3-0	1-3	1-1	2-1	1-3	1-3
Chelsea FC	1-1	4-0	0-0	3-2	1-0	1-1	1-2	■	0-2	4-1	3-1	0-2	5-6	4-3	4-1	0-1	1-1	3-0	2-1	2-1	3-3	1-0
Everton FC	1-0	0-1	0-1	0-0	1-1	1-1	2-2	1-1	■	4-0	2-2	1-0	4-2	1-2	2-3	1-0	2-3	3-1	1-0	1-0	1-2	3-2
Huddersfield Town AFC	0-1	1-2	1-3	2-0	0-1	2-0	0-0	1-0	2-1	■	3-1	0-0	1-3	2-0	2-1	0-4	1-2	3-0	1-1	1-0	3-3	2-0
Leicester City FC	3-3	4-2	2-2	4-0	2-2	2-1	0-1	1-1	2-2	1-3	■	0-2	1-0	3-2	4-0	0-1	0-1	4-3	1-1	2-0	6-3	1-2
Manchester City FC	2-1	2-4	1-6	4-2	0-0	4-1	1-5	1-1	1-0	2-4	2-2	■	3-2	3-1	1-2	3-1	5-2	2-2	1-0	0-0	4-0	3-0
Manchester United FC	2-1	0-1	4-1	1-1	1-0	5-2	3-1	2-1	1-2	1-1	3-1	0-5	■	2-2	1-3	2-1	5-0	2-0	2-2	2-1	3-0	2-4
Newcastle United FC	5-1	5-3	1-1	0-0	2-1	3-0	3-1	1-3	4-0	2-2	2-0	2-0	2-0	■	2-1	3-3	1-2	5-0	1-2	4-4	3-0	2-3
Portsmouth FC	2-1	2-2	3-0	1-0	0-2	1-3	2-0	0-0	5-0	4-2	2-1	1-0	0-0	3-1	■	2-0	6-2	2-1	0-3	6-1	0-0	
Preston North End FC	3-1	0-3	3-1	2-2	0-1	7-1	1-2	1-2	0-0	2-3	2-4	5-0	0-2	3-3	1-1	■	1-2	6-0	3-1	1-0	3-1	3-3
Sheffield United FC	1-1	1-3	2-1	2-0	1-0	1-3	5-0	1-2	2-5	2-2	1-1	0-2	3-0	6-2	5-2	0-5	■	1-0	1-0	4-1	1-2	1-2
Sheffield Wednesday FC	1-2	6-3	2-1	3-2	1-1	1-1	2-2	1-1	2-2	4-1	1-0	2-4	2-4	0-3	1-3	2-0	1-2	■	1-2	2-2	5-0	2-2
Sunderland AFC	0-1	0-0	2-0	1-1	2-2	1-1	1-2	3-3	3-0	1-1	1-1	3-2	4-3	4-2	2-2	2-2	2-0		■	1-1	4-2	0-0
Tottenham Hotspur FC	0-1	1-1	3-2	2-0	0-3	0-2	1-4	2-4	1-3	5-1	2-2	0-2	2-1	1-1	3-1	5-0	7-2	0-1		■	3-1	3-2
West Bromwich Albion FC	3-1	2-3	0-1	0-0	2-2	1-0	2-1	2-4	3-3	2-1	6-4	2-1	2-0	4-2	3-1	2-0	3-3	1-2	2-2	1-2	■	1-0
Wolverhampton Wanderers FC	3-1	1-0	1-0	1-2	5-0	1-1	2-1	3-4	1-3	6-4	5-0	2-2	4-2	2-2	2-2	1-1	4-1	4-2	2-0	4-2	4-0	■

	Division 1	Pd	Wn	Dw	Ls	GF	GA	Pts	
1.	CHELSEA FC (LONDON)	42	20	12	10	81	57	52	
2.	Wolverhampton Wanderers FC (Wolverhampton)	42	19	10	13	89	70	48	
3.	Portsmouth FC (Portsmouth)	42	18	12	12	74	62	48	
4.	Sunderland AFC (Sunderland)	42	15	18	9	64	54	48	
5.	Manchester United FC (Manchester)	42	20	7	15	84	74	47	
6.	Aston Villa FC (Birmingham)	42	20	7	15	72	73	47	
7.	Manchester City FC (Manchester)	42	18	10	14	76	69	46	
8.	Newcastle United FC (Newcastle-upon-Tyne)	42	17	9	16	89	77	43	
9.	Arsenal FC (London)	42	17	9	16	69	63	43	
10.	Burnley FC (Burnley)	42	17	9	16	51	48	43	
11.	Everton FC (Liverpool)	42	16	10	16	62	68	42	
12.	Huddersfield Town AFC (Huddersfield)	42	14	13	15	63	68	41	
13.	Sheffield United FC (Sheffield)	42	17	7	18	70	86	41	
14.	Preston North End FC (Preston)	42	16	8	18	83	64	40	
15.	Charlton Athletic FC (London)	42	15	10	17	76	75	40	
16.	Tottenham Hotspur FC (London)	42	16	8	18	72	73	40	
17.	West Bromwich Albion FC (West Bromwich)	42	16	8	18	76	96	40	
18.	Bolton Wanderers FC (Bolton)	42	13	13	16	62	69	39	
19.	Blackpool FC (Blackpool)	42	14	10	18	60	64	38	
20.	Cardiff City AFC (Cardiff)	42	13	11	18	62	76	37	
21.	Leicester City FC (Leicester)	42	12	11	19	74	86	35	R
22.	Sheffield Wednesday FC (Sheffield)	42	8	10	24	63	100	26	R
		924	351	222	351	1572	1572	924	

Top Goalscorer

1) Ronald ALLEN   (West Bromwich Albion FC)   27

Football League Division 2 1954-55 Season	Birmingham City	Blackburn Rovers	Bristol Rovers	Bury	Derby County	Doncaster Rovers	Fulham	Hull City	Ipswich Town	Leeds United	Lincoln City	Liverpool	Luton Town	Middlesbrough	Nottingham Forest	Notts County	Plymouth Argyle	Port Vale	Rotherham United	Stoke City	Swansea Town	West Ham United
Birmingham City FC	■	3-1	2-1	1-3	1-1	4-1	3-2	0-0	4-0	2-0	3-3	9-1	2-1	3-0	0-1	1-1	3-1	7-2	3-1	2-0	2-0	1-2
Blackburn Rovers FC	3-3	■	8-3	1-1	5-2	7-2	3-1	4-0	4-1	1-2	1-0	4-3	0-0	9-0	0-1	4-5	2-2	2-1	4-1	2-0	4-1	5-2
Bristol Rovers FC	1-1	2-1	■	2-1	4-1	1-0	4-1	1-0	4-0	5-1	2-2	3-0	3-2	2-2	2-1	1-4	3-1	1-0	1-0	1-1	7-0	2-4
Bury FC	0-1	2-1	3-1	■	2-2	1-4	1-3	4-1	2-1	5-3	3-1	3-4	2-1	0-1	1-1	1-2	3-1	2-2	2-2	1-1	2-1	4-1
Derby County FC	0-0	0-3	1-1	2-3	■	5-0	3-4	3-0	2-0	2-4	3-0	3-2	0-0	1-2	1-2	1-1	2-2	6-1	2-3	1-2	1-4	0-0
Doncaster Rovers FC	1-5	1-3	2-2	1-0	2-0	■	4-0	2-2	1-1	0-1	1-1	4-1	0-3	3-1	0-3	4-2	3-2	1-0	0-4	1-1	2-1	2-1
Fulham FC	2-1	5-1	2-3	0-0	2-0	5-2	■	0-1	4-1	1-3	3-2	1-2	3-1	1-2	1-1	3-1	2-3	3-1	1-1	2-2	5-1	0-0
Hull City AFC	0-3	1-4	0-1	1-0	1-1	1-1	0-0	■	4-2	0-2	4-0	2-2	0-4	1-0	2-3	5-2	0-2	2-1	1-2	1-1	4-3	0-1
Ipswich Town FC	1-2	1-1	1-0	2-3	2-1	5-1	2-4	2-0	■	1-2	1-2	2-0	3-1	6-1	2-1	0-1	2-1	1-0	2-2	0-1	1-1	0-3
Leeds United AFC	1-0	2-0	2-0	1-0	1-0	1-0	1-1	3-0	4-1	■	2-3	2-2	4-0	1-1	1-1	2-0	3-2	3-0	2-4	0-1	5-2	2-1
Lincoln City FC	1-1	2-1	0-2	3-2	3-0	5-1	2-2	0-1	1-1	2-0	■	3-3	1-2	3-3	2-1	1-2	3-2	0-1	2-3	1-4	2-2	2-1
Liverpool FC	2-2	4-1	5-3	1-1	2-0	3-2	4-1	2-1	6-2	2-2	2-4	■	4-4	3-1	1-0	3-1	3-3	1-1	3-1	2-4	1-1	1-2
Luton Town FC	1-0	7-3	2-0	3-2	2-0	3-0	3-0	1-1	3-2	0-0	2-1	3-2	■	2-0	3-0	3-1	3-1	4-2	4-0	3-1	1-2	2-0
Middlesbrough FC	2-5	4-3	1-0	1-1	3-1	3-1	4-2	1-2	0-1	1-0	1-2	1-2	0-2	■	1-4	2-0	4-1	2-0	5-1	1-2	4-2	6-0
Nottingham Forest FC	0-2	1-2	1-0	2-3	3-0	3-1	2-0	0-1	2-0	1-1	1-1	3-1	1-5	4-2	■	0-1	2-0	2-3	0-2	0-3	0-0	1-1
Notts County FC	3-2	3-1	2-0	2-1	2-3	4-0	0-0	3-1	2-1	1-2	2-1	0-3	3-3	1-3	4-1	■	2-0	1-1	3-2	1-0	2-1	5-1
Plymouth Argyle FC	1-0	0-2	0-1	2-4	1-0	1-2	3-2	1-2	2-0	3-1	1-0	1-0	2-1	2-2	1-2	1-3	■	0-0	2-1	2-0	2-2	1-1
Port Vale FC	2-0	0-3	1-0	1-0	3-0	1-1	4-0	3-0	3-3	0-1	1-3	4-3	1-1	1-1	1-2	1-1	1-0	■	1-0	0-1	1-0	1-1
Rotherham United FC	0-2	5-1	6-2	4-2	2-1	2-3	2-3	2-0	3-2	3-0	3-0	6-1	2-0	3-0	3-2	2-0	2-0	3-0	■	2-1	2-0	2-2
Stoke City FC	2-1	1-1	2-0	3-2	3-1	3-0	1-1	0-0	3-0	0-1	4-2	2-0	0-0	1-2	2-0	3-0	3-1	0-0	1-2	■	4-1	0-2
Swansea Town AFC	0-3	2-3	1-1	1-1	3-0	3-0	2-2	1-0	6-1	2-0	3-1	3-2	2-1	2-0	3-2	3-0	4-2	7-1	2-1	3-5	■	5-2
West Ham United FC	2-2	2-5	5-2	3-3	1-0	0-1	2-1	1-1	4-0	2-1	0-1	0-3	2-1	2-1	2-0	3-0	6-1	2-0	1-2	3-0	3-3	■

	Division 2	Pd	Wn	Dw	Ls	GF	GA	Pts	
1.	Birmingham City FC (Birmingham)	42	22	10	10	92	47	54	P
2.	Luton Town FC (Luton)	42	23	8	11	88	53	54	P
3.	Rotherham United FC (Rotherham)	42	25	4	13	94	64	54	
4.	Leeds United AFC (Leeds)	42	23	7	12	70	53	53	
5.	Stoke City FC (Stoke-on-Trent)	42	21	10	11	69	46	52	
6.	Blackburn Rovers FC (Blackburn)	42	22	6	14	114	79	50	
7.	Notts County FC (Nottingham)	42	21	6	15	74	71	48	
8.	West Ham United FC (London)	42	18	10	14	74	70	46	
9.	Bristol Rovers FC (Bristol)	42	19	7	16	75	70	45	
10.	Swansea Town AFC (Swansea)	42	17	9	16	86	83	43	
11.	Liverpool FC (Liverpool)	42	16	10	16	92	96	42	
12.	Middlesbrough FC (Middlesbrough)	42	18	6	18	73	82	42	
13.	Bury FC (Bury)	42	15	11	16	77	72	41	
14.	Fulham FC (London)	42	14	11	17	76	79	39	
15.	Nottingham Forest FC (Nottingham)	42	16	7	19	58	62	39	
16.	Lincoln City FC (Lincoln)	42	13	10	19	68	79	36	
17.	Port Vale FC (Stoke-on-Trent)	42	12	11	19	48	71	35	
18.	Doncaster Rovers FC (Doncaster)	42	14	7	21	58	95	35	
19.	Hull City AFC (Kingston-upon-Hull)	42	12	10	20	44	69	34	
20.	Plymouth Argyle FC (Plymouth)	42	12	7	23	57	82	31	
21.	Ipswich Town FC (Ipswich)	42	11	6	25	57	92	28	R
22.	Derby County FC (Derby)	42	7	9	26	53	82	23	R
		924	371	182	371	1597	1597	924	

Football League Division 3 (N) 1954-55 Season

	Accrington Stanley	Barnsley	Barrow	Bradford City	Bradford P.A.	Carlisle United	Chester	Chesterfield	Crewe Alexandra	Darlington	Gateshead	Grimsby Town	Halifax Town	Hartlepools	Mansfield Town	Oldham Athletic	Rochdale	Scunthorpe United	Southport	Stockport County	Tranmere Rovers	Workington	Wrexham	York City
Accrington Stanley	■	2-3	6-3	1-0	4-3	3-2	3-0	4-1	1-0	3-0	6-2	3-0	3-1	2-5	3-2	4-0	5-4	2-1	1-1	0-1	3-1	2-0	2-0	2-2
Barnsley FC	1-2	■	3-0	1-0	2-1	3-1	4-2	3-0	3-1	4-1	3-0	1-3	3-0	0-0	1-0	2-2	2-0	1-0	0-0	2-0	4-1	3-1	4-2	1-0
Barrow AFC	1-2	3-1	■	3-2	3-1	2-1	2-0	2-0	0-3	1-1	0-1	2-0	1-3	0-2	2-2	3-1	4-2	1-3	2-1	2-0	1-0	2-2	1-1	1-5
Bradford City AFC	0-3	0-2	2-1	■	1-1	2-0	0-0	1-1	2-0	3-0	1-1	4-0	2-0	0-1	1-0	0-1	1-0	2-4	0-1	2-3	2-1	0-1	2-2	2-3
Bradford Park Ave.	3-2	1-0	3-0	2-0	■	0-2	3-0	1-3	2-1	1-1	2-2	2-1	0-1	1-0	0-0	0-2	1-1	0-0	1-0	2-1	0-0	3-1	0-0	1-3
Carlisle United FC	1-0	2-4	4-0	1-0	3-2	■	1-2	1-2	4-0	0-1	1-2	3-1	4-0	3-2	1-2	5-2	7-2	1-2	2-1	3-3	1-2	0-4	1-0	4-5
Chester FC	1-1	0-2	3-1	1-0	2-0	1-2	■	1-0	3-1	0-2	1-2	1-3	1-0	1-0	0-1	1-0	2-4	0-0	1-0	0-1	0-1	0-2	1-0	1-1
Chesterfield FC	6-1	3-1	4-1	2-1	1-3	2-1	5-3	■	0-0	2-0	1-3	1-0	2-1	3-0	4-1	1-3	3-1	2-0	2-1	3-7	2-1	2-0	3-1	0-3
Crewe Alexandra FC	0-3	1-2	5-1	1-0	2-1	4-1	1-3	2-2	■	2-2	1-1	2-0	0-0	1-1	2-1	4-1	2-2	1-1	2-3	4-4	3-0	1-1	2-2	2-3
Darlington FC	3-3	0-1	3-2	4-0	3-0	1-1	4-1	0-2	2-1	■	5-1	1-3	1-0	0-1	3-1	0-2	2-2	1-1	2-0	0-0	2-2	1-2	2-2	1-0
Gateshead FC	1-1	0-4	3-1	2-1	3-2	0-0	0-0	1-3	1-0	1-1	■	1-0	4-0	3-0	4-0	2-2	0-1	0-1	1-0	4-4	3-1	3-2	0-1	1-1
Grimsby Town FC	2-1	1-3	1-0	1-4	1-0	2-0	3-1	2-1	2-1	0-2	1-1	■	0-1	3-2	1-1	1-1	1-4	0-1	1-0	2-2	1-1	1-1	1-3	2-1
Halifax Town AFC	1-1	1-1	1-2	0-0	0-0	5-3	3-1	2-0	3-3	4-1	4-0	3-2	■	1-0	1-2	0-0	1-1	3-1	0-1	1-2	0-0	2-2	2-0	3-3
Hartlepools United	1-3	0-3	0-0	0-0	0-1	1-0	3-1	2-0	2-1	1-0	0-0	3-2	1-0	■	1-2	2-0	3-1	4-2	2-1	2-1	4-0	3-2	3-0	1-0
Mansfield Town FC	2-2	1-1	0-5	1-0	2-1	1-1	2-0	4-2	3-1	0-1	3-0	2-1	0-2	1-0	■	1-3	3-2	2-1	3-0	0-0	3-1	2-0	2-1	1-2
Oldham Athletic AFC	0-1	4-1	3-2	1-1	5-0	4-1	4-1	4-0	3-1	1-2	4-0	1-2	0-1	1-1	1-0	■	0-0	1-1	1-0	1-1	2-1	2-1	2-1	3-2
Rochdale AFC	0-0	3-0	4-1	1-2	3-2	1-2	2-0	0-0	1-1	2-2	4-0	0-3	2-2	2-1	2-0	2-1	■	2-0	0-0	1-0	2-0	2-1	2-1	1-1
Scunthorpe United	4-0	1-0	3-0	1-0	1-1	1-1	1-1	2-1	3-1	0-1	0-1	1-0	2-2	5-1	2-0	6-1	2-2	■	2-0	3-0	1-2	1-1	1-0	1-1
Southport FC	1-1	0-2	2-1	1-1	1-0	4-1	1-1	0-0	1-0	0-0	2-2	4-1	1-0	1-0	1-0	1-1	1-1	0-1	■	1-1	0-0	1-2	1-2	2-2
Stockport County FC	0-0	1-0	1-2	1-1	6-0	5-2	3-0	3-2	6-1	3-0	2-1	0-0	0-2	2-2	3-2	1-1	4-2	0-2	3-2	■	4-0	4-1	2-2	1-0
Tranmere Rovers FC	3-1	0-1	0-4	2-0	3-3	6-1	1-1	1-0	1-2	0-1	2-0	1-2	3-1	3-2	2-1	3-1	1-2	2-2	1-1	1-1	■	1-1	1-2	1-0
Workington AFC	0-1	1-0	0-0	1-1	1-3	1-0	1-1	2-3	3-3	6-1	4-0	2-2	1-0	0-1	2-2	3-0	1-0	1-1	0-1	4-1	1-0	■	2-1	2-1
Wrexham AFC	3-1	3-0	3-0	1-3	1-0	1-1	2-1	0-2	5-0	2-2	2-0	5-0	1-1	1-4	1-3	2-1	0-0	0-1	2-2	1-4	1-2	1-1	■	2-6
York City FC	1-1	1-3	1-4	0-1	1-2	2-1	5-0	3-2	3-1	3-1	2-1	0-0	2-1	1-0	3-1	2-1	2-0	2-3	1-1	4-0	1-0	0-0	3-3	■

	Division 3 (North)	Pd	Wn	Dw	Ls	GF	GA	Pts	
1.	Barnsley FC (Barnsley)	46	30	5	11	86	46	65	P
2.	Accrington Stanley FC (Accrington)	46	25	11	10	96	67	61	
3.	Scunthorpe & Lindsey United FC (Scunthorpe)	46	23	12	11	81	53	58	
4.	York City FC (York)	46	24	10	12	92	63	58	
5.	Hartlepools United FC (Hartlepool)	46	25	5	16	64	49	55	
6.	Chesterfield FC (Chesterfield)	46	24	6	16	81	70	54	
7.	Gateshead FC (Gateshead)	46	20	12	14	65	69	52	
8.	Workington AFC (Workington)	46	18	14	14	68	55	50	
9.	Stockport County FC (Stockport)	46	18	12	16	84	70	48	
10.	Oldham Athletic AFC (Oldham)	46	19	10	17	74	68	48	
11.	Southport FC (Southport)	46	16	16	14	47	44	48	
12.	Rochdale AFC (Rochdale)	46	17	14	15	69	66	48	
13.	Mansfield Town FC (Mansfield)	46	18	9	19	65	71	45	
14.	Halifax Town AFC (Halifax)	46	15	13	18	63	67	43	
15.	Darlington FC (Darlington)	46	14	14	18	62	73	42	
16.	Bradford Park Avenue FC (Bradford)	46	15	11	20	56	70	41	
17.	Barrow AFC (Barrow-in-Furness)	46	17	6	23	70	89	40	
18.	Wrexham AFC (Wrexham)	46	13	12	21	65	77	38	
19.	Tranmere Rovers FC (Birkenhead)	46	13	11	22	55	70	37	
20.	Carlisle United FC (Carlisle)	46	15	6	25	78	89	36	
21.	Bradford City AFC (Bradford)	46	13	10	23	47	55	36	
22.	Crewe Alexandra FC (Crewe)	46	10	14	22	68	91	34	
23.	Grimsby Town FC (Cleethorpes)	46	13	8	25	47	78	34	
24.	Chester FC (Chester)	46	12	9	25	44	77	33	
		1104	427	250	427	1627	1627	1104	

Football League Division 3 (S) 1954-55 Season	Aldershot Town	Bournemouth	Brentford	Brighton & H.A.	Bristol City	Colchester United	Coventry City	Crystal Palace	Exeter City	Gillingham	Leyton Orient	Millwall	Newport County	Northampton Town	Norwich City	Q.P.R.	Reading	Shrewsbury Town	Southampton	Southend United	Swindon Town	Torquay United	Walsall	Watford
Aldershot Town FC		1-1	2-3	2-2	0-2	2-2	1-1	3-0	4-2	0-2	0-1	3-0	0-0	3-4	4-1	2-0	3-1	2-0	2-0	1-0	0-0	2-1	4-0	3-0
Bournemouth & Bos.	4-0		1-2	1-1	0-1	2-0	2-1	4-1	2-0	1-2	0-3	0-1	3-3	0-1	1-3	2-2	0-0	3-1	1-1	2-1	1-1	0-2	1-1	1-1
Brentford FC	1-1	1-3		2-3	2-2	3-2	2-3	3-0	1-0	3-0	2-0	3-1	1-0	1-3	1-0	1-1	2-2	2-2	0-3	2-2	4-2	4-2	0-2	3-2
Brighton & Hove Alb.	5-3	1-1	3-4		0-1	1-1	2-0	1-0	5-3	1-0	1-0	1-2	4-1	2-1	0-1	4-1	3-2	0-0	1-2	2-1	3-1	1-1	3-0	3-1
Bristol City FC	6-1	2-2	2-1	3-2		4-0	2-0	3-0	2-0	1-4	5-0	5-1	0-0	5-1	0-1	1-1	2-1	4-1	2-0	3-2	3-0	1-1	5-3	1-0
Colchester United FC	1-1	3-3	3-2	2-4	0-2		0-1	2-0	1-2	2-2	2-2	0-2	1-0	4-1	1-0	1-0	0-2	2-4	3-5	2-0	0-0	0-2	2-2	1-3
Coventry City FC	2-1	1-0	1-0	2-1	1-3	0-0		4-1	1-1	4-1	2-2	4-1	3-2	0-0	4-0	5-1	3-0	1-1	1-4	1-0	0-1	5-3	3-2	
Crystal Palace FC	3-2	2-1	1-1	1-0	1-2	0-0	1-0		1-1	0-2	1-1	1-1	2-1	3-1	2-0	2-1	1-1	2-2	1-2	2-2	0-0	1-1	3-1	1-1
Exeter City FC	0-1	1-1	3-2	3-1	0-1	2-2	0-0	2-0		1-1	1-7	1-4	1-1	3-1	0-1	2-1	3-1	1-0	0-1	2-1	2-1	1-2	1-1	0-0
Gillingham FC	0-2	0-2	2-1	1-1	1-1	2-1	2-1	2-1	1-1		0-0	1-1	4-2	2-2	2-1	3-1	5-1	3-3	1-0	1-1	2-1	3-1	3-2	0-1
Leyton Orient FC	1-5	3-1	0-1	0-0	4-1	2-0	1-0	2-1	5-0	2-2		1-0	1-2	2-1	1-2	3-0	2-0	5-0	4-1	5-1	1-0	2-1	1-0	0-1
Millwall FC	3-1	1-1	2-2	1-3	5-2	3-1	5-2	2-2	3-2	1-0	1-0		1-1	1-0	0-1	2-2	2-0	2-0	1-4	1-0	4-1	1-0	1-1	
Newport County AFC	2-1	1-1	3-1	1-3	2-2	0-0	1-1	0-1	2-1	1-3	1-2	2-1		0-1	1-1	4-0	3-1	1-1	0-1	3-2	2-2	1-1	1-0	0-2
Northampton Town	2-1	5-0	1-2	1-0	2-0	6-1	1-0	1-1	2-0	4-1	2-2	0-1	2-2		1-1	1-3	2-6	3-1	2-1	6-2	1-0	1-0	1-1	0-1
Norwich City FC	4-3	0-1	1-0	0-0	0-1	0-2	1-1	2-0	3-0	1-2	1-1	2-1	2-0	3-2		1-1	2-0	2-0	3-3	2-1	5-1	2-1	3-1	
Queen's Park Rangers	5-0	1-1	1-1	3-2	1-1	4-1	3-2	1-0	1-2	1-0	2-0	1-2	2-0	1-0	2-1		2-3	2-0	2-2	1-1	3-1	4-2	1-1	2-1
Reading FC	2-2	1-0	0-0	0-2	0-2	4-0	2-2	5-0	0-0	2-2	0-2	0-0	2-1	0-1	1-1	3-1		1-2	0-1	1-1	2-1	3-2	2-2	1-1
Shrewsbury Town FC	1-0	3-0	2-2	3-0	0-2	2-0	1-0	1-1	1-1	1-0	0-2	3-2	3-0	4-0	2-1	1-0	2-3		3-1	2-3	7-0	3-2	2-2	2-1
Southampton FC	1-1	0-0	6-4	3-2	2-1	0-1	1-0	2-2	3-0	3-1	1-0	3-0	4-0	3-1	2-2	3-1	2-1			3-0	1-1	0-0	2-1	2-0
Southend United FC	0-1	2-2	3-2	4-0	3-2	4-2	1-0	0-3	1-2	1-0	1-1	4-1	4-1	2-2	0-0	4-1	0-1				4-1	1-2	2-1	1-3
Swindon Town FC	1-0	0-2	1-1	0-2	2-2	1-1	3-0	0-0	2-0	2-1	0-0	1-1	1-3	0-1	1-0	2-0	2-0	2-1	1-0	0-1		0-0	2-2	6-1
Torquay United FC	2-2	0-1	4-2	2-1	2-2	2-1	1-2	2-2	1-0	1-3	2-7	4-2	2-3	5-2	2-0	3-2	3-1	2-0	2-2	4-1	1-1		2-0	2-2
Walsall FC	2-2	6-1	2-2	0-2	1-3	3-1	1-1	1-4	1-0	0-1	1-1	1-4	1-1	3-3	6-1	2-1	4-1	4-0	0-0	4-1	1-2	2-4		0-1
Watford FC	0-0	1-0	2-2	0-0	0-2	2-0	1-0	7-1	1-1	1-1	1-3	5-3	3-2	1-1	2-2	1-1	1-3	2-1	2-1	1-1	3-0	4-1	4-0	

	Division 3 (South)	Pd	Wn	Dw	Ls	GF	GA	Pts	
1.	Bristol City FC (Bristol)	46	30	10	6	101	47	70	P
2.	Leyton Orient FC (London)	46	26	9	11	89	47	61	
3.	Southampton FC (Southampton)	46	24	11	11	75	51	59	
4.	Gillingham FC (Gillingham)	46	20	15	11	77	66	55	
5.	Millwall FC (Millwall)	46	20	11	15	72	68	51	
6.	Brighton & Hove Albion FC (Hove)	46	20	10	16	76	63	50	
7.	Watford FC (Watford)	46	18	14	14	71	62	50	
8.	Torquay United FC (Torquay)	46	18	12	16	82	82	48	
9.	Coventry City FC (Coventry)	46	18	11	17	67	59	47	
10.	Southend United FC (Southend-on-Sea)	46	17	12	17	83	80	46	
11.	Brentford FC (London)	46	16	14	16	82	82	46	
12.	Norwich City FC (Norwich)	46	18	10	18	60	60	46	
13.	Northampton Town FC (Northampton)	46	19	8	19	73	81	46	
14.	Aldershot FC (Aldershot)	46	16	13	17	75	71	45	
15.	Queen's Park Rangers FC (London)	46	15	14	17	69	75	44	
16.	Shrewsbury Town FC (Shrewsbury)	46	16	10	20	70	78	42	
17.	Bournemouth & Boscombe Athletic FC (Bournemouth)	46	12	18	16	57	65	42	
18.	Reading FC (Reading)	46	13	15	18	65	73	41	
19.	Newport County AFC (Newport)	46	11	16	19	60	73	38	
20.	Crystal Palace FC (London)	46	11	16	19	52	80	38	
21.	Swindon Town FC (Swindon)	46	11	15	20	46	64	37	
22.	Exeter City FC (Exeter)	46	11	15	20	47	73	37	
23.	Walsall FC (Walsall)	46	10	14	22	75	86	34	
24.	Colchester United FC (Colchester)	46	9	13	24	53	91	31	
		1104	399	306	399	1677	1677	1104	

F.A. CUP FINAL   (Wembley Stadium, London – 07/05/1955 – 100,000)

NEWCASTLE UNITED FC   3-1   Manchester City FC (Manchester)

Milburn, Mitchell, Hannah   *Johnstone*

Newcastle: Simpson, Cowell, Batty, Scoular, Stokoe, Casey, White, Milburn, Keeble, Hannah, Mitchell.

Man. City: Trautmann, Meadows, Little, Barnes, Ewing, Paul, Spurdle, Hayes, Revie, Johnstone, Fagan.

Semi-finals

Manchester City FC (Manchester)   1-0   Sunderland AFC (Sunderland)

Newcastle United FC (Newcastle-upon-Tyne)   1-1, 2-0   York City FC (York)

Quarter-finals

Birmingham City FC (Birmingham)   0-1   Manchester City FC (Manchester)

Huddersfield Town AFC (Huddersfield)   1-1, 0-2   Newcastle United FC (Newcastle-upon-Tyne)

Notts County FC (Nottingham)   0-1   York City FC (York)

Sunderland AFC (Sunderland)   2-0   Wolverhampton Wanderers FC (Wolverhampton)

1955-56

Football League Division 1 1955-56 Season	Arsenal	Aston Villa	Birmingham City	Blackpool	Bolton Wands.	Burnley	Cardiff City	Charlton Athletic	Chelsea	Everton	Huddersfield T.	Luton Town	Man. City	Man. United	Newcastle United	Portsmouth	Preston N.E.	Sheffield United	Sunderland	Tottenham H.	W.B.A.	Wolves
Arsenal FC		1-0	1-0	4-1	3-1	0-1	3-1	2-4	1-1	3-2	2-0	3-0	0-0	1-1	1-0	1-3	3-2	2-1	3-1	0-1	2-0	2-2
Aston Villa FC	1-1		0-0	1-1	0-2	2-0	2-0	1-1	1-4	2-0	3-0	1-0	0-3	4-4	3-0	1-3	3-2	3-2	1-4	0-2	3-0	0-0
Birmingham City FC	4-0	2-2		1-2	5-1	1-2	2-1	4-0	3-0	6-2	5-0	0-0	4-3	2-2	3-1	3-2	0-3	0-2	1-2	3-0	2-0	0-0
Blackpool FC	3-1	6-0	2-0		0-0	1-1	2-1	5-0	2-1	4-0	4-2	3-2	0-1	0-0	5-1	2-3	2-6	1-1	7-3	0-2	5-1	2-1
Bolton Wanderers FC	4-1	1-0	6-0	1-3		0-1	4-0	1-3	4-0	1-1	2-2	4-0	1-3	3-1	3-2	4-0	0-0	2-1	0-3	3-2	4-0	2-1
Burnley FC	0-1	2-0	3-2	0-2	2-0		0-2	2-1	5-0	0-1	2-0	3-1	2-2	0-0	3-1	3-0	1-2	1-1	4-0	2-0	1-2	1-2
Cardiff City AFC	1-2	1-0	2-1	1-0	1-0	2-2		3-1	1-1	3-1	1-2	2-0	4-1	0-1	1-1	2-3	3-1	3-2	3-1	0-0	1-3	1-9
Charlton Athletic FC	2-0	3-1	2-0	1-2	3-1	2-1	0-0		1-2	0-2	4-1	2-2	5-2	3-0	0-2	6-1	2-1	3-2	2-1	1-2	5-1	0-2
Chelsea FC	2-0	0-0	1-2	2-1	0-2	0-0	2-1	3-1		6-1	0-0	0-0	2-1	2-4	2-1	1-5	0-1	1-0	2-3	2-0	2-0	2-3
Everton FC	1-1	2-1	5-1	1-0	1-0	1-1	2-0	3-2	3-3		5-1	0-1	1-1	4-2	0-0	0-2	0-4	1-4	1-2	2-1	2-0	2-1
Huddersfield Town AFC	0-1	1-1	1-1	3-1	3-1	1-0	1-2	4-0	1-3	1-0		0-2	3-3	0-2	2-6	1-0	2-2	1-2	4-0	1-0	1-0	1-3
Luton Town FC	0-0	2-1	0-1	3-1	0-0	2-3	3-0	2-1	2-2	2-2	1-2		3-2	0-2	4-2	1-0	2-1	2-1	8-2	1-1	0-2	5-1
Manchester City FC	2-2	2-2	1-1	2-0	2-0	1-3	3-1	0-2	2-2	3-0	1-0	3-2		1-0	1-2	4-1	0-2	3-1	4-2	1-2	2-0	2-2
Manchester United FC	1-1	1-0	2-1	2-1	1-0	2-0	1-1	5-1	3-0	2-1	3-0	3-1	2-1		5-2	1-0	3-2	3-1	2-1	2-2	3-1	4-3
Newcastle United FC	2-0	2-3	2-2	1-2	3-0	3-1	4-0	4-1	1-1	1-2	1-1	4-0	3-1	0-0		2-1	5-0	4-2	3-1	1-2	0-3	3-1
Portsmouth FC	5-2	2-2	0-5	3-3	3-3	3-1	1-1	4-0	4-4	1-0	5-2	0-0	2-4	3-2	0-2		0-2	1-1	2-1	4-1	1-1	2-1
Preston North End FC	0-1	0-1	1-1	3-3	0-1	4-2	1-2	2-2	2-3	0-1	1-2	2-1	0-3	3-1	4-3	2-1		0-2	2-2	3-3	0-1	2-0
Sheffield United FC	0-2	2-2	0-3	2-1	1-3	1-2	2-1	0-0	2-1	1-1	3-1	0-4	1-1	1-0	2-1	1-3	3-1		2-3	2-0	2-2	3-3
Sunderland AFC	3-1	5-1	1-0	0-0	0-0	4-4	1-1	3-2	4-3	0-0	4-1	1-2	0-3	2-2	1-6	4-2	2-2	3-2		3-2	2-1	1-1
Tottenham Hotspur FC	3-1	4-3	0-1	1-1	0-3	1-1	1-1	2-3	4-0	1-1	1-2	2-1	1-2	3-1	1-1	0-4	3-1	2-3			4-1	2-1
West Bromwich Albion FC	2-1	1-0	0-2	1-2	2-0	1-0	2-1	3-3	3-0	2-0	1-2	3-1	0-4	1-4	1-1	4-0	3-2	2-1	3-0	1-0		1-1
Wolverhampton Wanderers FC	3-3	0-0	1-0	2-3	4-2	3-1	0-2	2-0	2-1	1-0	4-0	1-2	7-2	0-2	2-1	3-1	2-1	3-2	3-1	5-1	3-2	

	Division 1	Pd	Wn	Dw	Ls	GF	GA	Pts	
1.	MANCHESTER UNITED FC (MANCHESTER)	42	25	10	7	83	51	60	
2.	Blackpool FC (Blackpool)	42	20	9	13	86	62	49	
3.	Wolverhampton Wanderers FC (Wolverhampton)	42	20	9	13	89	65	49	
4.	Manchester City FC (Manchester)	42	18	10	14	82	69	46	
5.	Arsenal FC (London)	42	18	10	14	60	61	46	
6.	Birmingham City FC (Birmingham)	42	18	9	15	75	57	45	
7.	Burnley FC (Burnley)	42	18	8	16	64	54	44	
8.	Bolton Wanderers FC (Bolton)	42	18	7	17	71	58	43	
9.	Sunderland AFC (Sunderland)	42	17	9	16	80	95	43	
10.	Luton Town FC (Luton)	42	17	8	17	66	64	42	
11.	Newcastle United FC (Newcastle-upon-Tyne)	42	17	7	18	85	70	41	
12.	Portsmouth FC (Portsmouth)	42	16	9	17	78	85	41	
13.	West Bromwich Albion FC (West Bromwich)	42	18	5	19	58	70	41	
14.	Charlton Athletic FC (London)	42	17	6	19	75	81	40	
15.	Everton FC (Liverpool)	42	15	10	17	55	69	40	
16.	Chelsea FC (London)	42	14	11	17	64	77	39	
17.	Cardiff City AFC (Cardiff)	42	15	9	18	55	69	39	
18.	Tottenham Hotspur FC (London)	42	15	7	20	61	71	37	
19.	Preston North End FC (Preston)	42	14	8	20	73	72	36	
20.	Aston Villa FC (Birmingham)	42	11	13	18	52	69	35	
21.	Huddersfield Town AFC (Huddersfield)	42	14	7	21	54	83	35	R
22.	Sheffield United FC (Sheffield)	42	12	9	21	63	77	33	R
		924	367	190	367	1529	1529	924	

Top Goalscorer

1) Nat LOFTHOUSE (Bolton Wanderers FC) 33

Football League Division 2 — 1955-56 Season

	Barnsley	Blackburn Rovers	Bristol City	Bristol Rovers	Bury	Doncaster Rovers	Fulham	Hull City	Leeds United	Leicester City	Lincoln City	Liverpool	Middlesbrough	Nottingham Forest	Notts County	Plymouth Argyle	Port Vale	Rotherham United	Sheffield Wednesday	Stoke City	Swansea Town	West Ham United
Barnsley FC	■	2-1	0-0	4-3	3-3	2-2	3-0	2-1	2-1	0-1	1-0	0-5	0-4	1-1	3-1	1-2	1-2	3-2	0-3	1-0	3-2	1-1
Blackburn Rovers FC	5-1	■	4-6	2-0	3-1	1-1	1-0	2-0	2-3	2-3	0-2	3-3	2-1	2-2	2-0	2-1	7-1	3-1	2-2	3-0	3-0	4-1
Bristol City FC	2-0	2-0	■	1-1	3-1	4-1	2-1	5-2	0-1	1-1	5-1	2-1	2-0	0-0	1-3	6-0	0-0	5-2	3-2	0-1	2-1	3-1
Bristol Rovers FC	1-1	1-0	0-3	■	4-2	4-2	2-2	4-2	4-1	2-1	3-0	1-2	7-2	4-1	2-0	1-1	1-2	1-4	4-2	4-2	1-2	1-1
Bury FC	3-0	0-4	1-1	0-1	■	5-1	1-5	3-2	1-0	3-1	3-3	1-4	1-1	1-2	4-0	7-1	2-2	2-1	2-5	1-0	2-4	1-1
Doncaster Rovers FC	1-1	2-2	3-2	2-1	2-3	■	4-2	3-0	1-2	6-2	2-0	1-0	0-1	1-3	1-1	3-1	3-0	1-1	2-2	2-4	3-1	2-1
Fulham FC	5-1	3-0	3-0	3-5	3-1	4-0	■	5-0	1-2	3-2	3-0	3-1	4-1	4-3	1-1	2-1	1-4	1-1	1-2	2-0	4-1	3-1
Hull City AFC	4-1	0-3	1-3	1-2	2-3	1-1	2-2	■	1-4	2-4	2-1	1-2	2-2	0-3	2-0	0-1	2-1	0-3	2-3	3-2	1-4	3-1
Leeds United AFC	3-1	1-2	2-1	2-1	1-0	3-0	6-1	1-0	■	4-0	1-0	4-2	2-0	3-0	1-0	4-2	1-1	4-1	2-1	1-0	2-2	3-3
Leicester City FC	0-0	0-2	2-2	4-2	5-0	2-0	2-1	1-2	5-2	■	4-0	3-1	1-1	5-2	4-0	5-1	4-1	3-1	1-2	3-1	6-1	2-1
Lincoln City FC	4-0	3-0	2-0	2-0	4-2	1-1	6-1	2-0	1-1	7-1	■	2-0	1-2	1-3	2-0	1-0	1-0	1-1	2-2	2-1	3-1	1-1
Liverpool FC	1-1	2-2	2-1	0-2	4-2	1-2	7-0	3-0	1-0	3-1	2-1	■	1-1	5-2	2-1	4-2	2-0	2-0	0-3	2-2	4-1	3-1
Middlesbrough FC	1-1	1-0	2-1	0-1	1-3	4-1	1-1	5-1	5-3	4-3	4-2	1-2	■	3-2	3-0	1-2	1-1	0-1	2-2	1-3	4-1	2-0
Nottingham Forest FC	1-0	1-1	0-2	1-1	0-2	5-0	1-0	2-1	2-0	2-2	1-3	2-4		■	0-2	3-1	2-2	1-0	0-1	2-3	2-1	0-0
Notts County FC	2-2	1-2	3-2	5-2	2-1	3-2	3-4	0-2	2-1	1-1	2-2	2-1	5-0	1-3	■	3-0	0-0	1-2	1-1	1-3	1-5	0-1
Plymouth Argyle FC	3-0	1-0	5-0	0-1	1-4	2-2	0-0	1-1	4-3	0-1	1-4	4-0	4-0	1-2	1-1	■	1-1	3-1	1-1	0-1	0-1	0-1
Port Vale FC	1-2	4-1	2-0	1-1	1-1	2-0	2-1	0-1	2-0	2-3	1-1	1-1	3-2	0-2	3-1	3-1	■	4-1	0-1	1-0	3-0	2-1
Rotherham United FC	0-0	3-2	1-3	1-0	1-3	3-3	2-3	0-2	0-2	3-1	2-2	0-1	2-1	1-1	0-0	1-0		■	2-3	0-1	2-3	3-2
Sheffield Wednesday FC	3-0	5-1	2-1	4-2	3-3	2-3	2-3	4-1	4-0	1-1	5-3	1-1	3-1	1-2	1-0	5-2	4-0	0-2	■	4-0	2-2	1-1
Stoke City FC	2-1	1-2	4-2	1-2	0-2	5-2	1-2	4-1	2-1	2-0	3-0	3-2	2-5	1-1	0-2	4-1	1-1	1-0	2-0	■	5-0	3-0
Swansea Town AFC	3-1	2-1	2-1	1-2	5-3	2-0	2-0	4-1	1-1	6-1	0-2	2-1	2-1	0-1	5-1	2-2	0-0	4-1	2-1	0-0	■	4-2
West Ham United FC	4-0	2-3	3-0	2-1	3-2	6-1	2-1	1-1	1-1	1-3	2-4	2-0	1-0	1-2	6-1	4-0	0-2	1-1	3-3	2-0	5-1	■

	Division 2	Pd	Wn	Dw	Ls	GF	GA	Pts	
1.	Sheffield Wednesday FC (Sheffield)	42	21	13	8	101	62	55	P
2.	Leeds United AFC (Leeds)	42	23	6	13	80	60	52	P
3.	Liverpool FC (Liverpool)	42	21	6	15	85	63	48	
4.	Blackburn Rovers FC (Blackburn)	42	21	6	15	84	65	48	
5.	Leicester City FC (Leicester)	42	21	6	15	94	78	48	
6.	Bristol Rovers FC (Bristol)	42	21	6	15	84	70	48	
7.	Nottingham Forest FC (Nottingham)	42	19	9	14	68	63	47	
8.	Lincoln City FC (Lincoln)	42	18	10	14	79	65	46	
9.	Fulham FC (London)	42	20	6	16	89	79	46	
10.	Swansea Town AFC (Swansea)	42	20	6	16	83	81	46	
11.	Bristol City FC (Bristol)	42	19	7	16	80	64	45	
12.	Port Vale FC (Stoke-on-Trent)	42	16	13	13	60	58	45	
13.	Stoke City FC (Stoke-on-Trent)	42	20	4	18	71	62	44	
14.	Middlesbrough FC (Middlesbrough)	42	16	8	18	76	78	40	
15.	Bury FC (Bury)	42	16	8	18	86	90	40	
16.	West Ham United FC (London)	42	14	11	17	74	69	39	
17.	Doncaster Rovers FC (Doncaster)	42	12	11	19	69	96	35	
18.	Barnsley FC (Barnsley)	42	11	12	19	47	84	34	
19.	Rotherham United FC (Rotherham)	42	12	9	21	56	75	33	
20.	Notts County FC (Nottingham)	42	11	9	22	55	82	31	
21.	Plymouth Argyle FC (Plymouth)	42	10	8	24	54	87	28	R
22.	Hull City AFC (Kingston-upon-Hull)	42	10	6	26	53	97	26	R
		924	372	180	372	1628	1628	924	

Football League Division 3 (N) 1955-56 Season

	ACC	BAR	BDC	BPA	CAR	CHE	CHF	CRE	DAR	DER	GAT	GRI	HAL	HAR	MAN	OLD	ROC	SCU	SOU	STO	TRA	WOR	WRE	YOR
Accrington Stanley		2-0	2-0	7-0	1-0	4-0	5-1	5-1	2-1	2-0	2-2	0-1	2-2	1-0	3-1	2-2	3-0	2-0	4-2	3-1	0-0	5-1	3-1	1-3
Barrow AFC	3-1		3-1	2-2	0-0	1-2	3-1	5-0	0-1	1-2	4-0	0-0	2-2	3-2	4-1	4-1	2-0	2-2	0-2	2-0	1-1	2-0	0-3	0-1
Bradford City AFC	2-1	1-1		5-0	0-0	1-1	3-5	3-1	3-0	2-1	3-1	0-2	2-0	2-0	4-2	0-0	2-2	4-3	2-0	4-1	5-0	2-0	4-3	3-1
Bradford Park Ave.	1-0	3-2	1-1		2-1	1-1	0-5	2-0	3-0	2-4	3-1	2-1	1-1	1-3	0-3	4-1	3-3	2-0	0-3	2-0	4-5	4-0	4-2	2-1
Carlisle United FC	0-4	2-0	0-0	4-1		4-1	1-1	4-1	2-0	0-3	2-1	1-2	2-2	0-3	5-2	3-1	1-2	1-2	4-0	4-1	0-3	2-4	0-1	3-1
Chester FC	1-1	1-0	1-1	0-0	3-3		2-1	0-0	2-1	2-5	3-0	2-0	1-0	0-1	4-3	3-2	0-0	3-5	1-3	1-4	0-0	1-0	2-1	2-2
Chesterfield FC	0-1	2-0	1-1	5-1	2-1	2-1		8-0	2-1	2-0	3-0	1-0	3-0	2-3	2-1	1-0	7-2	2-0	5-1	2-3	2-0	2-4	2-0	3-1
Crewe Alexandra FC	0-3	0-1	1-4	4-2	3-1	0-0	0-3		1-1	2-1	1-0	0-0	1-4	1-3	2-1	1-2	2-1	1-1	3-1	4-0	2-1	1-1	1-1	1-2
Darlington FC	2-0	4-2	1-1	4-1	3-5	0-1	2-1	4-1		1-0	0-0	0-1	1-2	0-0	3-1	2-1	2-0	1-0	0-1	0-0	6-2	2-2	2-2	1-4
Derby County FC	6-2	2-1	4-1	4-0	3-0	3-1	3-0	3-3	6-2		4-1	1-3	4-1	3-2	4-0	2-0	2-0	2-2	2-0	2-0	0-0	2-2	2-0	3-2
Gateshead FC	4-0	3-2	4-1	3-0	2-3	1-1	3-3	4-1	0-1	2-4		2-0	1-1	2-1	3-0	1-3	4-1	1-0	2-0	1-1	3-3	4-3	2-1	3-2
Grimsby Town FC	3-0	3-0	2-0	1-0	2-1	6-1	1-0	5-1	1-0	2-1	3-1		4-0	1-0	2-0	5-1	1-1	0-1	2-0	3-0	1-0	1-0	1-2	1-1
Halifax Town AFC	2-0	1-0	3-2	6-0	2-2	0-1	3-0	2-0	3-0	2-2	3-3	0-1		0-2	1-1	5-1	1-1	0-3	0-1	1-0	0-2	2-0	1-1	2-4
Hartlepools United	0-0	1-0	1-0	3-1	3-0	3-1	3-0	6-1	3-0	2-1	3-1	1-2	3-2		4-2	1-0	0-2	1-0	0-0	4-0	1-0	3-2	0-1	
Mansfield Town FC	3-2	4-0	0-0	5-0	0-1	3-0	0-1	1-1	3-3	1-1	3-1	0-2	3-1	5-1		2-0	6-0	3-2	0-1	1-1	6-0	0-0	6-1	3-1
Oldham Athletic AFC	1-3	6-1	1-1	5-1	2-2	4-1	2-2	1-1	3-3	1-1	1-2	1-1	1-3	3-2	1-1		2-2	2-1	1-1	3-2	4-1	0-1	1-1	1-1
Rochdale AFC	1-1	5-1	3-1	4-2	5-2	4-2	1-5	1-0	1-0	0-5	1-1	2-0	2-1	1-4	1-1	4-4		3-2	1-3	0-0	1-3	1-0	1-0	3-1
Scunthorpe United	2-3	2-0	2-0	4-2	4-0	2-1	2-0	1-1	0-1	0-2	1-1	0-1	1-0	5-1	3-0	2-1	1-2		0-1	1-5	2-1	3-1	1-1	1-1
Southport FC	1-1	2-1	3-1	3-0	3-0	1-0	1-0	5-0	0-1	2-5	2-0	2-0	0-0	1-1	1-1	2-0	2-2	2-0		1-1	1-0	0-0	1-1	3-3
Stockport County FC	1-2	4-1	1-0	0-0	8-1	2-1	2-1	2-1	2-1	2-1	1-2	0-0	3-1	4-0	7-2	0-0	0-0	3-2	4-0		7-0	4-5	4-0	4-1
Tranmere Rovers FC	4-1	1-1	1-1	4-1	0-1	4-0	0-1	2-1	0-1	0-1	1-1	0-1	2-1	2-2	1-0	0-3	2-1	2-1	1-2	2-1		2-0	0-2	2-1
Workington AFC	0-0	6-1	2-1	4-0	4-0	0-0	0-1	1-0	2-0	0-3	6-1	0-0	2-0	5-1	2-1	4-3	0-1	1-2	2-3	0-1	3-0		3-1	0-0
Wrexham AFC	1-4	0-0	2-1	1-0	5-2	0-0	3-0	4-2	2-1	3-1	1-1	1-0	1-2	1-3	2-0	1-1	0-0	0-1	2-1	0-1	3-1	0-1		4-5
York City FC	0-1	3-2	0-2	5-0	3-1	3-0	3-1	1-1	4-0	1-0	1-0	3-4	5-0	3-0	1-1	2-0	1-2	0-0	1-1	1-0	2-4	1-1	1-3	

	Division 3 (North)	Pd	Wn	Dw	Ls	GF	GA	Pts	
1.	Grimsby Town FC (Cleethorpes)	46	31	6	9	76	29	68	P
2.	Derby County FC (Derby)	46	28	7	11	110	55	63	
3.	Accrington Stanley FC (Accrington)	46	25	9	12	92	57	59	
4.	Hartlepools United FC (Hartlepool)	46	26	5	15	81	60	57	
5.	Southport FC (Southport)	46	23	11	12	66	53	57	
6.	Chesterfield FC (Chesterfield)	46	25	4	17	94	66	54	
7.	Stockport County FC (Stockport)	46	21	9	16	90	61	51	
8.	Bradford City AFC (Bradford)	46	18	13	15	78	64	49	
9.	Scunthorpe & Lindsey FC (Scunthorpe)	46	20	8	18	75	63	48	
10.	Workington AFC (Workington)	46	19	9	18	75	63	47	
11.	York City FC (York)	46	19	9	18	85	72	47	
12.	Rochdale AFC (Rochdale)	46	17	13	16	66	84	47	
13.	Gateshead FC (Gateshead)	46	17	11	18	77	84	45	
14.	Wrexham AFC (Wrexham)	46	16	10	20	66	73	42	
15.	Darlington FC (Darlington)	46	16	9	21	60	73	41	
16.	Tranmere Rovers FC (Birkenhead)	46	16	9	21	59	84	41	
17.	Chester FC (Chester)	46	13	14	19	52	82	40	
18.	Mansfield Town FC (Mansfield)	46	14	11	21	84	81	39	
19.	Halifax Town AFC (Halifax)	46	14	11	21	66	76	39	
20.	Oldham Athletic AFC (Oldham)	46	10	18	18	76	86	38	
21.	Carlisle United FC (Carlisle)	46	15	8	23	71	95	38	
22.	Barrow AFC (Barrow-in-Furness)	46	12	9	25	61	83	33	
23.	Bradford Park Avenue FC (Bradford)	46	13	7	26	61	122	33	
24.	Crewe Alexandra FC (Crewe)	46	9	10	27	50	105	28	
		1104	437	230	437	1771	1771	1104	

Football League Division 3 (S) 1955-56 Season

	Aldershot Town	Bournemouth	Brentford	Brighton & H.A.	Colchester United	Coventry City	Crystal Palace	Exeter City	Gillingham	Ipswich Town	Leyton Orient	Millwall	Newport County	Northampton Town	Norwich City	Q.P.R.	Reading	Shrewsbury Town	Southampton	Southend United	Swindon Town	Torquay United	Walsall	Watford
Aldershot Town FC		1-3	4-1	0-3	1-0	2-2	1-1	1-0	2-2	0-3	1-1	2-1	1-0	2-0	0-0	1-2	4-4	2-0	3-2	3-3	1-1	1-2	2-1	1-1
Bournemouth & Bos.	2-2		0-0	2-0	3-1	0-1	1-0	0-0	1-2	1-1	3-1	4-0	0-0	0-0	0-1	1-0	2-1	2-0	1-3	4-1	4-0	2-0	2-0	4-0
Brentford FC	2-0	2-1		4-2	2-2	1-1	3-0	2-0	1-4	3-2	1-0	2-2	1-1	2-1	1-2	2-0	2-2	1-1	2-1	2-1	1-2	1-3	2-2	0-0
Brighton & Hove Alb.	5-2	4-1	3-0		2-0	2-1	5-0	1-0	5-0	3-0	1-1	2-1	4-1	4-0	6-0	1-1	3-1	3-2	5-0	4-0	2-0	3-2	3-0	2-3
Colchester United FC	4-0	1-0	0-3	3-3		2-0	2-4	5-1	1-1	3-3	2-1	1-2	2-1	2-0	3-2	4-1	0-3	2-0	3-2	3-6	5-0	3-2	1-1	4-1
Coventry City FC	1-1	3-1	2-1	3-2	2-0		1-3	2-2	2-0	3-1	3-0	5-1	3-0	0-1	5-3	4-1	0-0	2-1	2-0	0-0	6-0	1-2	1-0	3-0
Crystal Palace FC	1-0	1-3	0-2	1-2	1-1	3-0		0-1	1-3	1-0	2-2	1-0	2-3	2-0	1-1	2-3	0-0	0-2	1-2	0-2	3-0	2-0	1-2	
Exeter City FC	2-1	2-0	2-3	0-5	0-0	2-3	6-1		2-1	2-2	1-1	3-1	2-0	3-1	1-1	2-0	0-2	3-0	3-2	0-1	1-2	0-0	1-1	1-2
Gillingham FC	2-0	2-1	1-2	1-0	2-1	1-1	1-1	2-1		0-0	0-1	4-3	3-2	0-2	3-1	0-2	2-0	3-1	1-2	2-3	4-0	1-3	0-1	3-0
Ipswich Town FC	2-1	1-0	1-1	2-1	3-1	1-0	3-3	2-2	1-1		2-0	6-2	3-2	1-0	4-1	4-1	3-3	2-1	4-2	3-0	6-2	0-2	5-2	0-0
Leyton Orient FC	8-3	3-0	0-1	0-1	6-0	3-1	8-0	1-1	2-0	1-2		2-1	3-1	1-1	2-2	7-1	1-0	5-2	4-0	3-0	4-0	3-2	4-0	3-1
Millwall FC	3-3	4-0	4-0	2-4	0-1	0-2	1-1	5-0	0-5	5-0			2-4	4-1	1-0	2-0	4-1	3-2	5-0	1-1	3-2	3-2	1-1	
Newport County AFC	0-1	1-0	1-2	1-0	0-0	4-2	0-1	1-2	3-2	2-1	3-0	1-4		0-1	2-2	2-1	2-3	1-2	1-0	2-0	1-0	2-1	2-0	0-1
Northampton Town	3-2	2-1	1-0	3-0	0-2	2-1	1-1	3-0	0-2	0-5	0-1	4-0	5-0		1-1	5-2	1-0	3-1	1-1	2-1	2-0	3-1		1-3
Norwich City FC	0-1	0-2	1-0	3-3	1-1	1-0	3-1	2-1	5-1	3-2	2-2	4-1	2-3	4-1		1-0	3-1	1-1		7-2	1-0		0-2	4-1
Queen's Park Rangers	2-2	0-1	1-1	2-1	6-2	1-2	0-3	1-0	2-2	1-1	4-0	0-0	3-2	2-3			3-3	1-1	4-0	1-2	1-0	3-1	3-2	3-2
Reading FC	0-5	0-2	5-2	0-2	1-3	1-0	1-0	1-2	1-2	1-5	0-1	4-1	3-0	4-1	2-2	3-1		0-1	1-1	4-1	0-1	0-3	2-0	6-1
Shrewsbury Town FC	3-3	1-1	1-1	2-1	2-1	3-0	2-0	2-0	3-1	1-1	1-4	3-1	5-0	1-1	6-0	1-1	3-0		2-0	1-1	1-1	1-2	2-1	0-0
Southampton FC	3-1	3-2	1-2	1-2	3-0	3-2	5-0	5-0	2-1	2-2	1-2	3-3	2-3	2-5	4-0	5-2	1-1			0-0	6-2	4-1	1-0	
Southend United FC	3-2	4-1	2-2	1-2	4-0	0-4	4-3	6-2	2-2	0-3	3-1	4-1	2-0	4-1	5-1	0-0	2-1	0-0	2-3		3-2	1-0		
Swindon Town FC	1-1	2-2	0-1	0-0	3-1	1-1	0-0	0-1	0-1	1-2	1-0	1-2	0-1	1-1	0-1	0-0	2-1	1-1	1-1			2-1	1-2	0-0
Torquay United FC	5-0	0-0	3-1	0-0	1-2	0-0	1-1	3-1	1-1	2-2	1-3	3-0	1-1	3-1	1-1	2-0	0-5	3-2	2-2	4-0			3-2	4-1
Walsall FC	4-2	0-0	1-2	2-2	0-0	2-0	4-0	3-1	2-1	1-3	0-2	2-1	3-3	2-0	2-0	2-2	1-0	1-3	3-1	4-0	1-4			2-1
Watford FC	1-1	0-2	0-2	1-3	1-1	2-1	0-2	2-3	0-1	0-2	0-4	4-2	1-1	2-2	1-1	0-1	1-0	3-4	1-0	3-2	2-1	2-1	4-2	

Division 3 (South)

		Pd	Wn	Dw	Ls	GF	GA	Pts	
1.	Leyton Orient FC (London)	46	29	8	9	1065	49	66	P
2.	Brighton & Hove Albion FC (Hove)	46	29	7	10	112	50	65	
3.	Ipswich Town FC (Ipswich)	46	25	14	7	106	60	64	
4.	Southend United FC (Southend-on-Sea)	46	21	11	14	88	80	53	
5.	Torquay United FC (Torquay)	46	20	12	14	86	63	52	
6.	Brentford FC (London)	46	19	14	13	69	66	52	
7.	Norwich City FC (Norwich)	46	19	13	14	86	82	51	
8.	Coventry City FC (Coventry)	46	20	9	17	73	60	49	
9.	Bournemouth & Boscombe Athletic FC (Bournemouth)	46	19	10	17	63	51	48	
10.	Gillingham FC (Gillingham)	46	19	10	17	69	71	48	
11.	Northampton Town FC (Northampton)	46	20	7	19	67	71	47	
12.	Colchester United FC (Colchester)	46	18	11	17	76	81	47	
13.	Shrewsbury Town FC (Shrewsbury)	46	17	12	17	69	66	46	
14.	Southampton FC (Southampton)	46	18	8	20	91	81	44	
15.	Aldershot FC (Aldershot)	46	12	16	18	70	90	40	
16.	Exeter City FC (Exeter)	46	15	10	21	58	77	40	
17.	Reading FC (Reading)	46	15	9	22	70	79	39	
18.	Queen's Park Rangers FC (London)	46	14	11	21	64	86	39	
19.	Newport County AFC (Newport)	46	15	9	22	58	79	39	
20.	Walsall FC (Walsall)	46	15	8	23	68	84	38	
21.	Watford FC (Watford)	46	13	11	22	52	85	37	
22.	Millwall FC (London)	46	15	6	25	83	100	36	
23.	Crystal Palace FC (London)	46	12	10	24	54	83	34	
24.	Swindon Town FC (Swindon)	46	8	14	24	34	78	30	
		1104	427	250	427	1772	1772	1104	

F.A. CUP FINAL   (Wembley Stadium, London – 05/05/1956 – 100,000)

MANCHESTER CITY FC (MANCHESTER)   3-1   Birmingham City FC (Birmingham)
Hayes, Dyson, Johnstone   *Kinsey*

Man. City: Trautmann, Leivers, Little, Barnes, Ewing, Paul, Johnstone, Hayes, Revie, Dyson, Clarke.
Birmingham: Merrick, Hall, Green, Newman, Smith, Boyd, Astall, Kinsey, Brown, Murphy, Govan.

Semi-finals

Birmingham City FC (Birmingham)	3-0	Sunderland AFC (Sunderland)
Manchester City FC (Manchester)	1-0	Tottenham Hotspur FC (London)

Quarter-finals

Arsenal FC (London)	1-3	Birmingham City FC (Birmingham)
Manchester City FC (Manchester)	2-1	Everton FC (Liverpool)
Newcastle United FC (Newcastle-upon-Tyne)	0-2	Sunderland AFC (Sunderland)
Tottenham Hotspur FC (London)	3-3, 2-1	West Ham United FC (London)

1956-57

Football League Division 1 1956-57 Season	Arsenal	Aston Villa	Birmingham City	Blackpool	Bolton Wands.	Burnley	Cardiff City	Charlton Athletic	Chelsea	Everton	Leeds United	Luton Town	Man. City	Man. United	Newcastle United	Portsmouth	Preston N.E.	Sheffield Wed.	Sunderland	Tottenham H.	W.B.A.	Wolves
Arsenal FC		2-1	4-0	1-1	3-0	2-0	0-0	3-1	2-0	2-0	1-0	1-3	7-3	1-2	0-1	1-1	1-2	6-3	1-1	3-1	4-1	0-0
Aston Villa FC	0-0		3-1	3-2	0-0	1-0	4-1	3-1	1-1	5-1	1-1	1-3	2-2	1-3	3-1	2-2	2-0	5-0	2-2	2-4	0-0	4-0
Birmingham City FC	4-2	1-2		2-2	0-0	2-0	2-1	4-2	0-1	1-3	6-2	3-0	3-3	3-1	6-1	3-1	3-0	4-0	1-2	0-0	2-0	2-2
Blackpool FC	2-4	0-0	3-1		4-2	1-0	3-1	3-2	1-0	5-2	1-1	4-0	4-1	2-2	2-3	5-0	4-0	3-1	1-2	4-1	0-1	3-2
Bolton Wanderers FC	2-1	0-0	3-1	4-1		3-0	2-0	2-0	2-2	1-1	5-3	2-2	1-0	2-0	3-1	1-1	2-3	3-2	2-1	1-0	1-1	0-3
Burnley FC	3-1	2-1	2-0	2-2	1-0		6-2	2-1	2-0	2-1	0-0	1-1	0-3	1-3	3-2	1-1	2-2	4-1	2-0	1-0	1-0	3-0
Cardiff City AFC	2-3	1-0	1-2	3-4	2-0	3-3		2-3	1-1	1-0	4-1	0-0	1-1	2-3	5-2	0-2	2-3	2-1	1-0	0-3	0-0	2-2
Charlton Athletic FC	1-3	0-2	1-0	0-4	2-1	1-2	0-2		3-1	1-2	1-2	1-2	1-0	1-5	1-1	1-3	3-4	4-4	3-2	1-1	3-2	2-1
Chelsea FC	1-1	1-1	1-0	2-2	2-2	2-0	1-2	1-3		5-1	1-1	4-1	4-2	1-2	6-2	3-3	1-0	0-0	0-2	2-4	2-4	3-3
Everton FC	4-0	0-4	2-0	2-3	2-2	1-0	0-0	5-0	0-3		2-1	2-1	1-1	1-2	2-1	2-2	1-4	1-0	2-1	1-1	0-1	3-1
Leeds United AFC	3-3	1-0	1-1	5-0	3-2	1-1	3-4	0-0	5-1	1-2		2-0	1-0	2-0	0-0	4-1	1-2	3-1	3-1	1-1	0-0	0-0
Luton Town FC	1-2	0-0	0-0	0-2	1-0	0-2	3-0	4-2	0-4	2-0	2-2		3-2	0-2	4-1	1-0	2-0	6-2	1-3		0-1	1-0
Manchester City FC	2-3	1-1	3-1	0-3	1-3	0-1	4-1	5-1	5-4	2-4	1-0	3-2		2-4	1-2	5-1	0-2	4-2	3-1	2-2	2-1	2-3
Manchester United FC	6-2	1-1	2-2	0-2	0-2	2-0	3-1	4-2	3-0	2-5	3-2	3-1	2-0		6-1	3-0	3-2	4-1	4-0	0-0	1-1	3-0
Newcastle United FC	3-1	1-2	3-2	2-1	4-0	1-1	3-1	1-2	0-0	2-3	2-2	0-3	1-1			2-1	1-2	1-2	6-2	2-2	5-2	1-1
Portsmouth FC	2-3	5-1	3-4	0-0	1-1	1-0	1-0	1-0	2-2	3-2	2-5	2-2	0-1	1-3	2-2		2-2	3-1	3-2	2-3	0-1	1-0
Preston North End FC	3-0	3-3	1-0	0-0	2-2	1-0	6-0	4-3	1-0	0-0	3-0	2-0	3-1	1-3	1-0	7-1		1-0	6-0	1-4	3-2	1-0
Sheffield Wednesday FC	2-4	2-1	3-0	1-2	1-2	0-0	5-3	3-1	4-0	2-2	2-3	3-0	2-2	2-1	4-0	3-1	3-1		3-2	4-1	4-2	2-1
Sunderland AFC	1-0	1-0	0-1	5-2	3-0	2-1	1-1	1-3	1-1	1-1	0-0	2-0	1-0	1-2	3-3	0-0	5-2			0-2	1-4	2-3
Tottenham Hotspur FC	1-3	3-0	5-1	2-1	4-0	1-2	5-1	6-2	3-4	6-0	5-1	5-0	3-2	2-2	3-1	2-0	1-1	1-1	5-2		2-2	4-1
West Bromwich Albion FC	0-2	2-0	0-0	1-3	3-2	2-2	1-2	2-2	2-1	3-0	0-0	4-0	1-1	2-3	1-0	2-1	0-0	1-4	2-0	1-1		1-1
Wolverhampton Wanderers FC	5-2	3-0	3-0	4-1	3-2	1-2	3-1	7-3	3-1	2-1	1-2	5-4	5-1	1-1	2-0	6-0	4-3	2-1	2-2	3-0	5-2	

Division 1

		Pd	Wn	Dw	Ls	GF	GA	Pts	
1.	MANCHESTER UNITED FC (MANCHESTER)	42	28	8	6	103	54	64	
2.	Tottenham Hotspur FC (London)	42	22	12	8	104	56	56	
3.	Preston North End FC (Preston)	42	23	10	9	84	56	56	
4.	Blackpool FC (Blackpool)	42	22	9	11	93	65	53	
5.	Arsenal FC (London)	42	21	8	13	85	69	50	
6.	Wolverhampton Wanderers FC (Wolverhampton)	42	20	8	14	94	70	48	
7.	Burnley FC (Burnley)	42	18	10	14	56	50	46	
8.	Leeds United AFC (Leeds)	42	15	14	13	72	63	44	
9.	Bolton Wanderers FC (Bolton)	42	16	12	14	65	65	44	
10.	Aston Villa FC (Birmingham)	42	14	15	13	65	55	43	
11.	West Bromwich Albion FC (West Bromwich)	42	14	14	14	59	61	42	
12.	Birmingham City FC (Birmingham)	42	15	9	18	69	69	39	Jt.
12.	Chelsea FC (London)	42	13	13	16	73	73	39	Jt.
14.	Sheffield Wednesday FC (Sheffield)	42	16	6	20	82	88	38	
15.	Everton FC (Liverpool)	42	14	10	18	61	79	38	
16.	Luton Town FC (Luton)	42	14	9	19	58	76	37	
17.	Newcastle United FC (Newcastle-upon-Tyne)	42	14	8	20	67	87	36	
18.	Manchester City FC (Manchester)	42	13	9	20	78	88	35	
19.	Portsmouth FC (Portsmouth)	42	10	13	19	62	92	33	
20.	Sunderland AFC (Sunderland)	42	12	8	22	67	88	32	
21.	Cardiff City AFC (Cardiff)	42	10	9	23	53	88	29	R
22.	Charlton Athletic FC (London)	42	9	4	29	62	120	22	R
		924	353	218	353	1612	1612	924	

Top Goalscorer

1) John CHARLES (Leeds United AFC) 38

Football League Division 2 1956-57 Season	Barnsley	Blackburn Rovers	Bristol City	Bristol Rovers	Bury	Doncaster Rovers	Fulham	Grimsby Town	Huddersfield Town	Leicester City	Leyton Orient	Lincoln City	Liverpool	Middlesbrough	Nottingham Forest	Notts County	Port Vale	Rotherham United	Sheffield United	Stoke City	Swansea Town	West Ham United
Barnsley FC	■	3-3	3-0	0-2	1-1	3-1	1-1	2-0	0-5	2-0	3-0	5-2	4-1	1-3	1-1	1-1	2-0	1-1	1-6	2-2	2-3	1-2
Blackburn Rovers FC	2-0	■	3-1	2-0	6-2	2-2	2-0	2-0	3-2	1-1	3-3	3-4	2-2	1-0	2-2	1-1	2-4	3-2	3-1	1-0	5-3	0-2
Bristol City FC	1-2	3-0	■	5-3	2-0	4-0	0-3	0-2	2-1	0-2	4-2	5-1	2-1	2-1	1-5	3-0	3-3	2-1	5-1	1-2	3-1	1-1
Bristol Rovers FC	1-1	0-1	0-0	■	6-1	6-1	4-0	1-0	4-0	1-2	3-2	0-1	0-0	0-2	3-2	3-0	2-1	4-2	3-1	4-0	1-1	1-1
Bury FC	1-2	2-2	2-3	7-2	■	4-4	0-1	2-3	1-3	4-5	1-3	1-0	0-2	3-2	1-2	2-1	1-0	1-4	0-1	0-1	1-3	3-3
Doncaster Rovers FC	5-2	1-1	4-1	2-4	1-1	■	4-0	0-1	4-0	0-2	6-1	3-1	1-1	2-1	1-1	4-2	4-0	1-1	1-0	4-0	0-1	3-0
Fulham FC	2-0	7-2	2-1	3-2	1-3	3-0	■	3-1	1-0	2-2	3-1	0-1	1-2	1-2	0-1	5-1	6-3	3-1	1-2	1-0	7-3	1-4
Grimsby Town FC	4-1	1-3	0-3	3-2	0-1	4-2	3-1	■	1-2	2-2	0-0	2-0	0-0	3-2	0-0	2-1	1-0	3-2	1-2	4-1	5-0	2-1
Huddersfield Town AFC	2-0	0-2	2-1	2-1	1-2	0-1	1-1	2-1	■	1-2	3-0	0-1	0-3	0-1	1-0	3-0	3-1	1-0	1-4	2-2	2-2	6-2
Leicester City FC	5-2	6-0	1-1	7-2	3-0	3-1	1-3	4-3	2-2	■	1-4	4-3	3-2	1-1	0-0	6-3	2-1	5-2	5-0	3-2	1-1	5-3
Leyton Orient FC	2-0	1-1	2-2	1-1	4-3	1-1	0-2	1-1	3-1	1-5	■	2-1	0-4	1-1	1-4	2-2	3-2	2-1	1-2	2-2	3-0	1-2
Lincoln City FC	4-1	1-2	1-1	1-0	2-0	4-1	1-0	1-0	1-2	2-3	0-2	■	3-3	1-1	0-2	1-0	4-0	3-3	4-1	0-1	0-2	0-2
Liverpool FC	2-1	2-3	2-1	4-1	2-0	2-1	4-3	3-2	2-3	2-0	1-0	4-0	■	1-2	3-1	3-3	4-1	4-1	5-1	2-0	2-0	1-0
Middlesbrough FC	1-2	2-1	4-1	3-2	2-2	3-2	3-1	2-1	7-2	1-3	1-2	3-0	1-1	■	2-2	0-0	3-1	0-1	3-1	1-1	6-2	3-1
Nottingham Forest FC	7-1	2-1	2-2	1-1	5-1	2-1	3-1	1-1	0-0	1-2	1-2	1-1	1-0	0-4	■	2-4	4-2	3-1	2-1	4-0	4-3	3-0
Notts County FC	3-2	2-0	1-1	0-2	2-2	1-2	0-0	0-1	1-2	0-0	1-3	3-0	1-1	2-1	1-2	■	3-1	1-5	2-2	5-0	1-4	4-1
Port Vale FC	0-0	0-3	3-1	2-3	3-2	4-1	2-1	3-0	1-2	2-3	1-2	1-1	1-2	2-1	1-7	1-2	■	2-1	0-6	2-2	0-2	0-0
Rotherham United FC	0-0	0-2	6-1	0-0	1-1	0-1	4-3	2-1	3-3	1-1	2-0	3-0	2-2	2-3	3-2	0-0	1-0	■	0-4	1-0	6-1	0-1
Sheffield United FC	5-0	0-2	1-1	0-0	1-1	4-0	5-2	2-0	2-0	1-1	2-3	2-0	3-0	2-1	0-4	5-1	4-2	2-7	■	1-1	2-2	1-0
Stoke City FC	3-0	4-1	0-2	2-1	2-0	1-1	0-2	1-0	5-1	3-1	7-1	8-0	1-0	3-1	2-1	6-0	3-1	6-0	3-3	■	4-1	0-1
Swansea Town AFC	2-3	5-1	5-0	2-3	3-0	4-2	4-5	3-1	4-2	2-3	1-0	1-2	1-1	2-2	1-4	2-1	2-2	1-0	4-1	1-0	■	3-1
West Ham United FC	2-0	1-3	3-1	1-2	1-0	1-1	2-1	0-1	0-2	2-1	2-1	2-1	1-1	1-1	2-1	2-1	2-1	1-1	3-2	1-0	1-2	■

	Division 2	Pd	Wn	Dw	Ls	GF	GA	Pts	
1.	Leicester City FC (Leicester)	42	25	11	6	109	67	61	P
2.	Nottingham Forest FC (Nottingham)	42	22	10	10	94	55	54	P
3.	Liverpool FC (Liverpool)	42	21	11	10	82	54	53	
4.	Blackburn Rovers FC (Blackburn)	42	21	10	11	83	75	52	
5.	Stoke City FC (Stoke-on-Trent)	42	20	8	14	83	58	48	
6.	Middlesbrough FC (Middlesbrough)	42	19	10	13	84	60	48	
7.	Sheffield United FC (Sheffield)	42	19	8	15	87	76	46	
8.	West Ham United FC (London)	42	19	8	15	59	63	46	
9.	Bristol Rovers FC (Bristol)	42	18	9	15	81	67	45	
10.	Swansea Town AFC (Swansea)	42	19	7	16	90	90	45	
11.	Fulham FC (London)	42	19	4	19	84	76	42	
12.	Huddersfield Town AFC (Huddersfield)	42	18	6	18	68	74	42	
13.	Bristol City FC (Bristol)	42	16	9	17	74	79	41	
14.	Doncaster Rovers FC (Doncaster)	42	15	10	17	77	77	40	
15.	Leyton Orient FC (London)	42	15	10	17	66	84	40	
16.	Grimsby Town FC (Cleethorpes)	42	17	5	20	61	62	39	
17.	Rotherham United FC (Rotherham)	42	13	11	18	74	75	37	
18.	Lincoln City FC (Lincoln)	42	14	6	22	54	80	34	
19.	Barnsley FC (Barnsley)	42	12	10	20	59	89	34	
20.	Notts County FC (Nottingham)	42	9	12	21	58	86	30	
21.	Bury FC (Bury)	42	8	9	25	60	96	25	R
22.	Port Vale FC (Stoke-on-Trent)	42	8	6	28	57	101	22	R
		924	367	190	367	1644	1644	924	

Football League Division 3 (N) 1956-57 Season	Accrington Stanley	Barrow	Bradford City	Bradford P.A.	Carlisle United	Chester	Chesterfield	Crewe Alexandra	Darlington	Derby County	Gateshead	Halifax Town	Hartlepools	Hull City	Mansfield Town	Oldham Athletic	Rochdale	Scunthorpe United	Southport	Stockport County	Tranmere Rovers	Workington	Wrexham	York City
Accrington Stanley		4-1	0-2	5-0	1-2	4-0	1-1	5-0	4-2	0-0	2-0	4-0	2-1	0-3	3-3	2-2	2-1	0-1	4-2	4-0	1-0	2-1	1-0	3-0
Barrow AFC	3-1		4-0	1-0	3-0	3-0	2-1	3-0	3-1	2-2	1-2	1-0	3-1	1-2	2-0	2-1	2-0	1-2	1-1	0-3	5-0	5-2	2-1	1-2
Bradford City AFC	1-2	0-2		2-0	3-2	1-0	3-2	5-1	1-2	0-2	3-1	1-0	1-1	4-3	4-1	1-1	3-1	3-1	1-1	4-1	2-3	2-1	2-1	0-2
Bradford Park Ave.	2-0	4-1	2-0		1-3	3-1	2-0	4-3	3-1	3-2	0-1	2-1	0-2	4-1	1-4	2-2	0-0	1-2	2-3	3-2	1-2	1-3	0-4	0-2
Carlisle United FC	2-2	1-1	1-4	2-1		3-0	4-2	2-1	1-2	1-3	3-2	0-0	2-1	1-3	6-1	2-2	1-1	0-0	1-2	3-3	2-2	1-1	2-2	2-0
Chester FC	0-2	2-0	1-2	2-0	1-2		3-4	4-1	0-3	2-2	4-1	1-1	0-1	1-1	6-2	1-0	2-2	2-2	1-4	1-1	1-0	0-0	0-0	3-4
Chesterfield FC	1-0	3-2	1-1	4-1	2-2	3-0		2-0	4-1	2-2	6-0	2-1	5-1	3-1	1-0	1-0	2-1	1-0	6-0	1-1	3-1	2-2	2-1	2-1
Crewe Alexandra FC	3-4	1-1	1-0	2-2	0-0	0-4	0-2		1-3	2-5	0-3	1-3	1-2	2-3	6-4	2-2	1-6	2-1	0-0	0-1	0-0	0-1	3-0	1-1
Darlington FC	0-0	1-1	3-2	0-5	0-1	5-1	4-1	3-0		1-1	7-0	0-1	3-1	1-1	1-3	1-0	4-3	1-2	1-0	3-1	1-1	4-2	1-5	2-4
Derby County FC	2-2	3-3	0-2	6-1	3-0	3-0	7-1	4-0	1-1		5-3	6-0	2-0	1-0	4-0	3-2	4-0	2-0	2-0	4-0	2-3	1-0	1-0	1-0
Gateshead FC	1-1	2-2	1-2	1-3	4-2	4-1	1-3	1-1	1-2	1-1		2-1	4-3	2-0	1-1	2-3	2-1	0-0	3-1	1-5	3-1	1-2	4-2	0-0
Halifax Town AFC	0-1	3-2	1-0	3-1	1-3	2-1	1-1	0-1	3-2	1-0	0-1		2-0	1-1	2-1	1-1	3-1	3-2	4-0	4-2	1-2	0-0	1-2	0-0
Hartlepools United	2-1	2-0	2-0	2-1	2-1	2-2	5-1	2-0	2-1	2-1	4-1	0-1		3-3	2-1	4-1	0-0	5-2	4-1	5-1	2-1	2-1	2-1	2-0
Hull City AFC	2-1	3-0	1-0	2-0	0-0	2-0	3-2	2-0	1-1	3-3	1-1	3-1	2-0		1-2	2-1	2-2	2-1	5-3	4-1	0-2	1-2	1-2	1-1
Mansfield Town FC	1-3	1-3	3-1	2-1	5-1	1-1	3-0	2-1	7-3	1-2	2-4	2-0	4-1	2-1		2-4	2-3	1-1	1-2	4-2	3-0	2-2	3-1	3-1
Oldham Athletic AFC	2-4	0-1	1-1	3-1	2-2	0-0	3-3	2-0	3-2	1-2	1-2	4-3	0-0	1-3	1-1		0-1	1-1	2-0	1-0	1-0	1-0	1-2	3-1
Rochdale AFC	0-2	1-0	4-1	2-1	2-1	2-1	1-0	1-1	3-0	3-1	0-0	1-1	1-0	4-3	0-0	0-2		3-0	6-1	2-2	1-0	0-0	0-2	1-0
Scunthorpe United	2-3	1-1	1-1	2-2	1-2	3-0	5-1	5-1	1-2	1-4	1-2	6-1	1-2	1-1	0-1	1-0	0-0		1-0	2-3	1-4	2-1	4-3	2-1
Southport FC	3-5	0-0	1-5	5-1	4-1	1-1	0-0	0-1	1-0	3-2	2-3	1-1	1-6	1-0	1-1	2-0	0-1	2-2		0-1	3-1	0-1	1-1	1-1
Stockport County FC	2-1	2-1	1-1	4-0	2-0	2-1	2-1	5-2	3-2	2-4	1-2	2-1	2-1	1-3	1-2	2-1	2-1	1-3	2-0		3-1	1-0	3-0	3-0
Tranmere Rovers FC	1-2	0-2	0-0	0-3	0-1	3-1	2-2	3-0	2-2	0-1	0-0	0-2	0-1	2-4	3-1	2-1	2-2	4-2	1-1	2-2		1-1	2-4	3-3
Workington AFC	4-1	0-1	5-1	0-1	2-0	0-1	2-1	4-0	6-2	2-1	2-1	3-1	1-1	4-3	3-3	0-0	5-0	2-2	2-0	4-1	3-2		3-0	3-2
Wrexham AFC	5-2	5-0	1-2	2-0	6-4	2-2	1-3	5-0	5-0	0-2	4-1	3-2	2-2	5-2	0-0	4-4	4-1	1-1	1-1	2-3	1-0	3-0		1-1
York City FC	3-1	1-0	3-1	1-2	2-0	0-1	1-2	2-1	1-0	1-1	1-0	1-2	3-3	2-1	2-0	2-1	4-0	0-2	9-1	0-0	1-0	2-2	1-0	

	Division 3 (North)	Pd	Wn	Dw	Ls	GF	GA	Pts	
1.	Derby County FC (Derby)	46	26	11	9	111	53	63	P
2.	Hartlepools United FC (Hartlepool)	46	25	9	12	90	63	59	
3.	Accrington Stanley FC (Accrington)	46	25	8	13	95	64	58	
4.	Workington AFC (Workington)	46	24	10	12	93	63	58	
5.	Stockport County FC (Stockport)	46	23	8	15	91	75	54	
6.	Chesterfield FC (Chesterfield)	46	22	9	15	96	79	53	
7.	York City FC (York)	46	21	10	15	75	61	52	
8.	Hull City AFC (Kingston-upon-Hull)	46	21	10	15	84	69	52	
9.	Bradford City AFC (Bradford)	46	22	8	16	78	68	52	
10.	Barrow AFC (Barrow-in-Furness)	46	21	9	16	76	62	51	
11.	Halifax Town AFC (Halifax)	46	21	7	18	65	70	49	
12.	Wrexham AFC (Wrexham)	46	19	10	17	97	74	48	
13.	Rochdale AFC (Rochdale)	46	18	12	16	65	65	48	
14.	Scunthorpe & Lindsey FC (Scunthorpe)	46	15	15	16	71	69	45	
15.	Carlisle United FC (Carlisle)	46	16	13	17	76	85	45	
16.	Mansfield Town FC (Mansfield)	46	17	10	19	91	90	44	
17.	Gateshead FC (Gateshead)	46	17	10	19	72	90	44	
18.	Darlington FC (Darlington)	46	17	8	21	82	95	42	
19.	Oldham Athletic AFC (Oldham)	46	12	15	19	66	74	39	
20.	Bradford Park Avenue FC (Bradford)	46	16	3	27	66	93	35	
21.	Chester FC (Chester)	46	10	13	23	55	84	33	
22.	Southport FC (Southport)	46	10	12	24	52	94	32	
23.	Tranmere Rovers FC (Birkenhead)	46	7	13	26	51	91	27	
24.	Crewe Alexandra FC (Crewe)	46	6	9	31	43	110	21	
		1104	431	242	431	1841	1841	1104	

Football League Division 3 (S) 1956-57 Season

	Aldershot Town	Bournemouth	Brentford	Brighton & H.A.	Colchester United	Coventry City	Crystal Palace	Exeter City	Gillingham	Ipswich Town	Millwall	Newport County	Northampton Town	Norwich City	Plymouth Argyle	Q.P.R.	Reading	Shrewsbury Town	Southampton	Southend United	Swindon Town	Torquay United	Walsall	Watford
Aldershot Town FC	▓	3-2	0-2	1-4	2-1	0-1	2-1	1-4	0-0	3-1	3-0	3-1	4-0	0-0	0-2	4-2	1-4	1-1	1-1	5-3	2-2	0-1	4-1	3-1
Bournemouth & Bos.	3-2	▓	3-0	1-1	1-1	1-2	2-2	3-1	3-1	1-0	6-1	2-1	4-1	1-1	2-1	1-0	2-1	6-1	1-0	1-1	7-0	0-0	2-2	4-0
Brentford FC	2-2	2-2	▓	2-5	1-1	1-1	1-1	3-0	3-2	1-1	5-0	0-0	2-1	1-1	4-1	2-0	4-0	3-1	4-0	3-2	4-1	0-0	6-2	1-5
Brighton & Hove Alb.	2-2	2-2	1-2	▓	0-0	2-1	1-1	3-0	3-1	3-2	3-2	2-0	5-0	3-0	3-1	1-0	8-3	4-3	1-0	1-1	2-0	6-0	1-3	2-2
Colchester United FC	1-1	3-0	1-0	0-0	▓	3-2	3-3	4-0	0-0	0-0	2-1	1-0	5-1	1-1	2-1	1-1	3-2	6-0	3-1	3-2	1-1	2-1	2-1	2-0
Coventry City FC	5-1	4-2	1-1	1-2	2-4	▓	3-3	1-0	4-1	1-1	1-2	2-0	3-1	3-2	1-4	5-1	0-1	3-3	2-1	2-0	3-0	3-2	2-2	0-2
Crystal Palace FC	2-1	1-1	0-2	2-2	2-4	1-1	▓	0-0	1-2	1-3	2-2	2-1	1-1	4-1	2-1	2-1	1-1	0-1	1-2	2-0	0-0	1-1	3-0	0-0
Exeter City FC	1-1	1-2	1-1	1-3	0-2	4-2	2-1	▓	4-0	1-2	1-1	2-0	0-0	0-0	2-1	0-0	1-1	5-1	0-4	6-1	3-2	1-1	0-1	1-2
Gillingham FC	6-2	1-0	2-1	0-0	1-2	1-2	4-1	2-1	▓	1-1	1-3	1-1	1-2	1-1	0-3	0-1	0-0	1-1	0-0	0-2	3-0	1-1	2-1	0-3
Ipswich Town FC	4-1	1-0	4-0	4-0	3-1	4-0	4-2	3-0	1-1	▓	0-2	5-0	0-1	3-1	2-1	4-0	4-2	5-1	2-0	3-3	4-1	6-0	2-2	4-1
Millwall FC	1-5	3-4	1-1	4-3	3-1	3-2	3-0	1-3	2-1	2-2	▓	1-0	1-0	5-1	2-2	2-0	1-0	0-0	0-0	0-0	2-1	7-2	1-0	1-1
Newport County AFC	3-0	5-3	3-0	0-1	0-0	1-0	2-2	1-0	1-0	0-0		▓	3-0	4-1	1-1	1-2	2-0	2-3	2-1	2-1	2-1	3-0	2-2	3-0
Northampton Town	4-2	2-2	5-1	1-0	1-0	4-0	1-0	1-1	4-1	2-1	2-1	0-3	▓	1-1	2-0	3-0	3-0	2-1	2-2	2-0	3-0	2-3	1-2	
Norwich City FC	1-1	1-3	1-1	1-1	1-2	3-0	1-0	1-0	1-3	1-2	2-0	1-1	2-1	▓	3-0	1-2	2-5	3-0	0-3	1-2	2-4	1-2	2-2	1-2
Plymouth Argyle FC	2-2	2-0	2-0	2-0	2-2	0-0	0-1	5-0	2-0	1-2	0-0	3-2	4-3	3-2	▓	1-2	0-6	1-1	2-1	0-0	1-0	0-0	2-4	3-3
Queen's Park Rangers	0-1	2-1	2-2	0-0	1-1	1-1	4-2	5-3	5-0	0-2	1-1	1-0	3-0	3-0	1-1	▓	2-1	1-2	3-0	3-0	0-1	1-0	3-1	
Reading FC	2-1	0-4	2-0	2-2	0-3	3-0	1-2	4-0	4-0	1-3	3-0	0-0	1-1	2-1	3-2	1-0	▓	2-2	2-4	3-2	1-0	3-1	3-0	1-2
Shrewsbury Town FC	2-2	0-0	3-2	4-0	1-3	5-0	1-1	1-2	1-0	1-1	2-0	2-0	2-0	4-5	3-1	0-0	1-1	▓	0-0	0-0	7-3	1-1	3-2	1-0
Southampton FC	1-0	3-0	3-3	1-0	2-1	1-1	3-0	2-2	0-1	0-2	4-0	3-0	2-0	2-2	1-2	4-1	4-0		▓	1-2	2-1	1-0	3-1	3-1
Southend United FC	2-4	2-1	1-0	3-1	3-2	1-2	1-1	2-0	5-0	2-0	1-0	3-3	0-0	0-1	3-0	4-0	1-2	1-2		▓	1-0	2-0	2-0	2-0
Swindon Town FC	1-2	2-1	1-3	3-0	4-1	2-2	2-3	3-5	2-3	3-1	1-0	1-0	4-0	1-1	0-3	1-0	3-2	1-2	0-0	3-2	▓	1-2	1-2	2-0
Torquay United FC	4-2	1-0	2-0	1-0	4-2	3-1	3-0	1-0	3-3	4-1	7-2	4-0	2-0	7-1	1-1	3-0	3-1	1-1	2-0	3-3	7-0	▓	2-0	3-0
Walsall FC	5-1	0-0	7-0	3-2	2-1	1-1	1-2	2-0	2-2	2-0	7-1	0-0	2-2	6-3	1-0	0-2	3-2	1-1	1-1	0-1	1-2	0-1	▓	2-0
Watford FC	3-0	1-1	1-1	2-1	0-0	1-0	1-4	1-1	2-3	2-1	1-1	5-0	2-1	3-3	0-1	2-4	1-0	2-3	4-2	1-1	3-4	4-1	1-0	▓

		Pd	Wn	Dw	Ls	GF	GA	Pts	
1.	Ipswich Town FC (Ipswich)	46	25	9	12	101	54	59	P
2.	Torquay United FC (Torquay)	46	24	11	11	89	64	59	
3.	Colchester United FC (Colchester)	46	22	14	10	84	56	58	
4.	Southampton FC (Southampton)	46	22	10	14	76	52	54	
5.	Bournemouth & Boscombe Athletic FC (Bournemouth)	46	19	14	13	88	62	52	
6.	Brighton & Hove Albion FC (Hove)	46	19	14	13	86	65	52	
7.	Southend United FC (Southend-on-Sea)	46	18	12	16	73	65	48	
8.	Brentford FC (London)	46	16	16	14	78	76	48	
9.	Shrewsbury Town FC (Shrewsbury)	46	15	18	13	72	79	48	
10.	Queen's Park Rangers FC (London)	46	18	11	17	61	69	47	
11.	Watford FC (Watford)	46	18	10	18	72	75	46	
12.	Newport County AFC (Newport)	46	16	13	17	65	62	45	
13.	Reading FC (Reading)	46	18	9	19	80	81	45	
14.	Northampton Town FC (Northampton)	46	18	9	19	66	73	45	
15.	Walsall FC (Walsall)	46	16	12	18	80	74	44	
16.	Coventry City FC (Coventry)	46	16	12	18	74	84	44	
17.	Millwall FC (London)	46	16	12	18	64	84	44	
18.	Plymouth Argyle FC (Plymouth)	46	16	11	19	68	73	43	
19.	Aldershot FC (Aldershot)	46	15	12	19	79	92	42	
20.	Crystal Palace FC (London)	46	11	18	17	62	75	40	
21.	Exeter City FC (Exeter)	46	12	13	21	61	79	37	
22.	Gillingham FC (Gillingham)	46	12	13	21	54	85	37	
23.	Swindon Town FC (Swindon)	46	15	6	25	66	96	36	
24.	Norwich City FC (Norwich)	46	8	15	23	61	94	31	
		1104	405	294	405	1760	1760	1104	

Division 3 (South)

F.A. CUP FINAL   (Wembley Stadium, London – 04/05/1957 – 100,000)

ASTON VILLA FC (BIRMINGHAM)   2-1   Manchester United FC (Manchester)
McParland 2   *Taylor*

Aston Villa: Sims, Lynn, Aldiss, Crowther, Dugdale, Saward, Smith, Sewell, Myerscough, Dixon, McParland.

Man. United: Wood, Foulkes, Byrne, Colman, Blanchflower, Edwards, Berry, Whelan, Taylor, R.Charlton, Pegg.

Semi-finals

Aston Villa FC (Birmingham)	2-2, 1-0	West Bromwich Albion FC (West Bromwich)
Manchester United FC (Manchester)	2-0	Birmingham City FC (Birmingham)

Quarter-finals

Birmingham City FC (Birmingham)	0-0, 1-0	Nottingham Forest FC (Nottingham)
Bournemouth & Boscombe Athletic FC (B'mouth)	1-2	Manchester United FC (Manchester)
Burnley FC (Burnley)	1-1, 0-2	Aston Villa FC (Birmingham)
West Bromwich Albion FC (West Bromwich)	2-2, 2-1	Arsenal FC (London)

Football League Division 1 1957-58 Season	Arsenal	Aston Villa	Birmingham City	Blackpool	Bolton Wands.	Burnley	Chelsea	Everton	Leeds United	Leicester City	Luton Town	Man. City	Man. United	Newcastle United	Nottingham F.	Portsmouth	Preston N.E.	Sheffield Wed.	Sunderland	Tottenham H.	W.B.A.	Wolves
Arsenal FC	■	4-0	1-3	2-3	1-2	0-0	5-4	2-3	2-1	3-1	2-0	2-1	4-5	2-3	1-1	3-2	4-2	1-0	3-0	4-4	2-2	0-2
Aston Villa FC	3-0	■	0-2	1-1	4-0	3-0	1-3	0-1	2-0	5-1	2-0	1-2	3-2	4-3	1-1	2-1	2-2	2-0	5-2	1-1	2-1	2-3
Birmingham City FC	4-1	3-1	■	0-0	5-1	2-3	3-3	2-1	1-1	0-1	1-1	4-0	3-3	1-4	0-2	4-1	3-1	1-0	2-3	0-0	3-5	1-5
Blackpool FC	1-0	1-1	4-2	■	2-3	2-4	2-1	0-1	3-0	5-1	1-2	2-5	1-4	3-2	3-0	2-1	1-2	2-2	7-0	0-2	2-0	3-2
Bolton Wanderers FC	0-1	4-0	1-0	3-0	■	2-1	3-3	1-5	0-2	2-3	1-2	0-2	4-0	1-1	2-0	1-0	0-4	5-4	2-2	3-2	2-2	1-1
Burnley FC	2-1	3-0	3-1	2-1	3-1	■	2-1	0-2	3-1	7-3	1-2	2-1	3-0	0-2	3-1	3-1	2-0	2-0	6-0	2-0	2-2	1-1
Chelsea FC	0-0	4-2	5-1	1-4	2-2	6-1	■	3-1	2-1	4-0	1-3	2-3	2-1	2-1	0-0	7-4	0-2	1-0	0-0	2-4	2-2	1-2
Everton FC	2-2	1-2	0-2	0-0	1-1	1-1	3-0	■	0-1	2-2	0-2	2-5	3-3	1-2	1-1	4-2	4-2	1-1	3-1	3-4	1-1	1-0
Leeds United AFC	2-0	4-0	1-1	2-1	2-1	1-0	0-0	1-0	■	2-1	0-2	2-4	1-1	3-0	1-2	2-0	2-3	2-2	2-1	1-2	1-1	1-1
Leicester City FC	0-1	6-1	2-2	2-1	2-3	5-3	3-2	2-2	3-0	■	4-1	8-4	0-3	2-1	3-1	2-2	1-3	4-1	4-1	1-3	3-3	2-3
Luton Town FC	4-0	3-0	3-0	2-0	1-0	3-2	0-2	0-1	1-1	2-1	■	1-2	2-2	0-3	3-1	2-1	1-3	2-0	7-1	0-0	5-1	3-1
Manchester City FC	2-4	1-2	1-1	4-3	2-1	4-1	5-2	6-2	1-0	4-3	2-2	■	2-2	2-1	1-1	2-0	3-1	5-1	4-1	3-4		
Manchester United FC	4-2	4-1	0-2	1-2	7-2	1-0	0-1	3-0	5-0	4-0	3-0	4-1	■	1-1	1-1	0-3	0-0	2-1	2-2	3-4	0-4	0-4
Newcastle United FC	3-3	2-4	1-2	1-2	1-2	1-3	1-3	2-3	1-2	5-3	3-2	4-1	1-2	■	1-4	2-0	0-2	0-0	2-2	3-1	3-0	1-1
Nottingham Forest FC	4-0	4-1	1-1	1-2	0-0	7-0	1-1	0-3	1-1	3-1	1-0	2-1	1-2	2-3	■	2-0	2-1	5-2	2-0	1-2	0-2	1-4
Portsmouth FC	5-4	1-0	3-2	1-2	2-2	0-0	3-0	3-2	1-2	5-0	2-1	3-3	2-2	1-4		■	0-2	3-2	0-2	5-1	2-2	1-1
Preston North End FC	3-0	1-1	8-0	2-1	3-0	2-1	5-2	3-1	3-0	4-1	1-0	6-1	1-1	2-1	2-0	4-0	■	3-0	3-0	3-1	3-1	1-2
Sheffield Wednesday FC	2-0	2-5	5-3	0-3	1-0	1-2	2-3	2-1	3-2	2-1	2-1	4-5	1-0	1-0	1-2	4-2	4-4	■	3-3	2-0	1-2	2-1
Sunderland AFC	0-1	1-1	1-6	1-4	1-2	2-3	2-2	1-1	2-1	3-2	3-0	2-1	1-2	2-0	3-0	1-1	0-0	3-3	■	1-1	2-0	0-2
Tottenham Hotspur FC	3-1	6-2	7-1	2-1	4-1	3-1	1-1	3-1	2-0	1-4	3-1	5-1	1-0	3-3	3-4	3-5	3-3	4-2	0-1	■	0-0	1-0
West Bromwich Albion FC	1-2	3-2	0-0	1-1	2-2	5-1	1-1	4-0	1-0	6-2	4-2	9-2	4-3	2-1	3-2	3-1	4-1	3-1	3-0	0-2	■	0-3
Wolverhampton Wanderers FC	1-2	2-1	5-1	3-1	6-1	2-1	2-1	2-0	3-2	5-1	1-1	3-3	3-1	3-1	2-0	1-0	2-0	4-3	5-0	4-0	1-1	■

Division 1

		Pd	Wn	Dw	Ls	GF	GA	Pts	
1.	WOLVERHAMPTON WANDERERS FC (WOLV.)	42	28	8	6	103	47	64	
2.	Preston North End FC (Preston)	42	26	7	9	100	51	59	
3.	Tottenham Hotspur FC (London)	42	21	9	12	93	77	51	
4.	West Bromwich Albion FC (West Bromwich)	42	18	14	10	92	70	50	
5.	Manchester City FC (Manchester)	42	22	5	15	104	100	49	
6.	Burnley FC (Burnley)	42	21	5	16	80	74	47	
7.	Blackpool FC (Blackpool)	42	19	6	17	80	67	44	
8.	Luton Town FC (Luton)	42	19	6	17	69	63	44	
9.	Manchester United FC (Manchester)	42	16	11	15	85	75	43	
10.	Nottingham Forest FC (Nottingham)	42	16	10	16	69	63	42	
11.	Chelsea FC (London)	42	15	12	15	83	79	42	
12.	Arsenal FC (London)	42	16	7	19	73	85	39	
13.	Birmingham City FC (Birmingham)	42	14	11	17	76	89	39	
14.	Aston Villa FC (Birmingham)	42	16	7	19	73	86	39	
15.	Bolton Wanderers FC (Bolton)	42	14	10	18	65	87	38	
16.	Everton FC (Liverpool)	42	13	11	18	65	75	37	
17.	Leeds United AFC (Leeds)	42	14	9	19	51	63	37	
18.	Leicester City FC (Leicester)	42	14	5	23	91	112	33	
19.	Newcastle United FC (Newcastle-upon-Tyne)	42	12	8	22	73	81	32	
20.	Portsmouth FC (Portsmouth)	42	12	8	22	73	88	32	
21.	Sunderland AFC (Sunderland)	42	10	12	20	54	97	32	R
22.	Sheffield Wednesday FC (Sheffield)	42	12	7	23	69	92	31	R
		924	368	188	368	1721	1721	924	

Top Goalscorer

1)   Robert SMITH   (Tottenham Hotspur FC)   36

Football League Division 2 1957-58 Season	Barnsley	Blackburn Rovers	Bristol City	Bristol Rovers	Cardiff City	Charlton Athletic	Derby County	Doncaster Rovers	Fulham	Grimsby Town	Huddersfield Town	Ipswich Town	Leyton Orient	Lincoln City	Liverpool	Middlesbrough	Notts County	Rotherham United	Sheffield United	Stoke City	Swansea Town	West Ham United
Barnsley FC	■	0-2	4-1	2-2	1-1	4-1	3-0	1-1	1-0	3-3	2-3	5-1	3-0	1-3	2-1	1-1	1-1	3-0	0-2	1-2	1-0	1-0
Blackburn Rovers FC	3-1	■	5-0	2-0	4-0	1-1	3-1	3-2	1-1	3-0	1-1	0-0	4-1	0-1	3-3	3-3	3-0	5-0	1-0	1-0	2-2	2-1
Bristol City FC	5-0	0-0	■	3-2	2-0	1-2	2-1	2-2	0-5	3-2	1-3	1-0	2-2	4-0	1-2	0-0	3-1	0-1	1-4	2-1	1-2	1-1
Bristol Rovers FC	1-1	4-0	3-3	■	0-2	1-0	5-2	2-1	2-2	0-7	1-1	3-1	4-0	3-0	3-1	5-0	5-2	1-3	2-2	2-0	3-0	2-3
Cardiff City AFC	7-0	4-3	2-3	0-2	■	0-3	3-2	3-1	3-0	1-3	1-0	1-1	1-1	3-2	6-1	0-2	2-0	2-2	0-0	5-2	0-0	0-3
Charlton Athletic FC	4-2	3-4	1-0	2-3	3-1	■	2-2	2-0	2-2	2-0	7-6	4-1	3-2	4-1	5-1	6-2	4-1	4-0	3-1	3-0	1-1	0-3
Derby County FC	1-4	0-3	5-2	2-1	0-2	1-3	■	1-0	3-3	1-0	2-4	2-2	2-0	3-2	2-1	2-1	2-1	3-4	2-0	0-0	1-0	1-2
Doncaster Rovers FC	1-1	1-5	2-1	3-2	0-1	1-2	1-2	■	1-6	3-3	0-3	1-1	2-0	1-3	1-1	3-2	4-0	3-2	2-2	0-1	3-0	1-2
Fulham FC	1-1	1-1	3-4	3-0	2-0	3-1	2-0	4-1	■	6-0	2-1	0-0	3-1	4-1	2-2	0-1	1-0	3-1	6-3	3-4	2-0	2-2
Grimsby Town FC	2-1	3-4	1-1	3-2	1-1	4-2	3-2	3-1	3-1	■	4-1	0-2	7-2	4-0	3-1	4-1	2-0	3-1	1-3	0-0	2-2	1-2
Huddersfield Town AFC	0-5	2-1	0-0	0-0	1-1	3-3	0-0	2-2	0-3	1-0	■	3-0	2-0	0-1	2-1	1-0	3-0	1-3	1-1	1-0	2-2	3-1
Ipswich Town FC	3-0	2-1	4-2	3-2	3-1	1-4	2-2	2-0	1-1	3-2	4-0	■	5-3	1-3	1-1	1-1	1-2	1-0	1-3	0-1	2-1	2-1
Leyton Orient FC	2-1	5-1	4-0	1-3	4-2	3-2	1-1	2-0	1-3	5-1	3-1	2-0	■	1-0	1-0	4-0	2-2	6-2	0-1	0-2	5-1	1-4
Lincoln City FC	1-3	1-1	4-0	0-1	3-1	2-3	1-1	1-1	0-1	1-4	1-1	2-1	2-0	■	0-1	2-3	2-2	2-0	2-2	1-3	4-0	1-6
Liverpool FC	1-1	2-0	4-3	2-0	3-0	3-1	2-0	5-0	3-1	3-2	1-1	3-1	3-0	1-0	■	0-2	4-0	2-0	1-0	3-0	4-0	1-1
Middlesbrough FC	3-1	2-3	0-0	4-3	4-1	2-0	3-2	5-0	2-0	5-1	5-2	2-0	3-1	2-2	2-1	■	3-1	2-2	1-2	1-3	2-1	1-3
Notts County FC	2-3	1-1	0-1	0-0	5-2	2-1	1-0	0-5	1-5	2-0	1-1	0-3	0-1	1-0	0-2	2-0	■	1-0	1-0	1-2	2-4	1-0
Rotherham United FC	4-1	1-2	4-1	2-0	3-1	1-5	0-2	2-1	3-1	2-0	1-1	1-4	2-2	1-2	2-2	1-4	1-3	■	1-6	0-2	5-2	1-2
Sheffield United FC	0-0	4-2	0-3	2-0	3-0	0-3	0-1	3-0	1-1	3-1	3-2	1-1	0-2	4-0	1-1	3-2	1-0	2-0	■	3-0	2-2	2-1
Stoke City FC	3-1	2-4	3-0	3-5	3-0	2-2	2-1	0-0	1-2	4-1	1-1	5-1	1-3	1-1	1-2	4-1	0-1	4-1	2-3	■	6-2	1-4
Swansea Town AFC	4-2	0-4	5-1	6-4	0-1	1-3	7-0	4-3	4-4	0-2	1-1	0-0	1-2	5-1	0-2	1-4	1-3	1-3	0-2	4-1	■	3-2
West Ham United FC	1-1	1-1	3-2	6-1	1-1	0-0	2-1	1-1	3-2	2-0	5-2	1-1	3-2	2-2	1-1	2-1	3-1	8-0	0-3	5-0	6-2	■

	Division 2	Pd	Wn	Dw	Ls	GF	GA	Pts	
1.	West Ham United FC (London)	42	23	11	8	101	54	57	P
2.	Blackburn Rovers FC (Blackburn)	42	22	12	8	93	57	56	P
3.	Charlton Athletic FC (London)	42	24	7	11	107	69	55	
4.	Liverpool FC (Liverpool)	42	22	10	10	79	54	54	
5.	Fulham FC (London)	42	20	12	10	97	59	52	
6.	Sheffield United FC (Sheffield)	42	21	10	11	75	50	52	
7.	Middlesbrough FC (Middlesbrough)	42	19	7	16	83	74	45	
8.	Ipswich Town FC (Ipswich)	42	16	12	14	68	69	44	
9.	Huddersfield Town AFC (Huddersfield)	42	14	16	12	63	66	44	
10.	Bristol Rovers FC (Bristol)	42	17	8	17	85	80	42	
11.	Stoke City FC (Stoke-on-Trent)	42	18	6	18	75	73	42	
12.	Leyton Orient FC (London)	42	18	5	19	77	79	41	
13.	Grimsby Town FC (Cleethorpes)	42	17	6	19	86	83	40	
14.	Barnsley FC (Barnsley)	42	14	12	16	70	74	40	
15.	Cardiff City AFC (Cardiff)	42	14	9	19	63	77	37	
16.	Derby County FC (Derby)	42	14	8	20	60	81	36	
17.	Bristol City FC (Bristol)	42	13	9	20	63	88	35	
18.	Rotherham United FC (Rotherham)	42	14	5	23	65	101	33	
19.	Swansea Town AFC (Swansea)	42	11	9	22	72	99	31	
20.	Lincoln City FC (Lincoln)	42	11	9	22	55	82	31	
21.	Notts County FC (Nottingham)	42	12	6	24	44	80	30	R
22.	Doncaster Rovers FC (Doncaster)	42	8	11	23	56	88	27	R
		924	362	200	362	1637	1637	924	

Football League Division 3 (N) 1957-58 Season	Accrington St.	Barrow	Bradford City	Bradford P.A.	Bury	Carlisle United	Chester	Chesterfield	Crewe Alex.	Darlington	Grimsby Town	Halifax Town	Hartlepools	Hull City	Mansfield T.	Oldham Ath.	Rochdale	Scunthorpe U.	Southport	Stockport Co.	Tranmere R.	Workington	Wrexham	York City
Accrington Stanley		3-2	2-2	5-2	3-0	3-2	1-2	0-4	2-0	0-0	3-0	2-1	1-2	3-0	4-1	1-1	3-2	2-1	2-2	3-2	2-1	3-0	2-1	3-0
Barrow AFC	3-1		1-2	0-0	4-2	2-3	4-1	4-1	0-1	2-1	1-2	0-3	3-3	0-0	2-1	2-2	2-1	0-1	1-0	1-1	1-4	0-0	2-2	1-0
Bradford City AFC	1-1	4-1		2-1	3-3	1-1	5-0	0-0	2-1	3-1	0-1	3-0	0-1	1-0	1-1	0-0	1-0	2-3	2-0	2-1	3-0	0-0	3-1	3-2
Bradford Park Ave.	1-3	1-1	0-0		1-4	4-1	3-0	2-0	3-1	4-2	2-2	0-2	2-3	4-4	0-2	1-3	2-2	1-2	3-5	1-0	1-0	3-3	3-0	0-2
Bury FC	1-1	4-1	1-0	1-0		3-0	1-2	1-0	2-0	5-0	4-1	1-0	3-3	1-1	0-2	4-0	4-1	2-1	4-1	1-1	8-2	3-0	3-0	4-1
Carlisle United FC	6-1	2-1	0-3	2-3	0-2		3-2	2-2	2-0	5-2	5-1	2-1	1-2	0-1	3-4	1-1	1-0	3-4	4-0	3-1	3-1	2-2	4-0	2-1
Chester FC	5-1	2-2	0-0	1-2	0-0	0-0		0-0	3-2	0-1	1-1	1-1	2-1	1-1	1-2	0-0	2-0	1-2	1-1	3-0	1-3	4-3	0-1	9-2
Chesterfield FC	1-0	4-3	0-1	1-1	1-1	1-3	2-1		1-1	2-0	5-3	1-1	2-1	0-0	1-4	2-1	2-2	1-1	0-0	2-1	2-1	3-0	3-2	2-0
Crewe Alexandra FC	4-1	1-4	2-2	3-0	0-1	0-0	0-3	1-2		2-2	2-2	1-2	2-1	1-2	1-0	0-2	3-2	1-2	0-4	0-3	2-0			3-4
Darlington FC	0-2	3-0	4-0	4-0	3-2	1-2	2-3	2-0	3-0		2-2	5-0	1-3	2-2	2-0	3-1	4-2	1-2	1-0	2-1	3-1	2-1	2-0	
Gateshead FC	1-3	0-2	0-0	2-4	1-2	3-2	3-2	3-0	3-1	4-0		0-0	0-0	3-1	2-1	1-0	3-2	1-2	2-1	3-0	2-3	3-0	1-1	0-0
Halifax Town AFC	0-2	3-1	3-2	2-0	1-2	5-0	2-1	3-2	2-0	1-0	4-1		3-0	2-2	4-0	4-0	4-1	0-0	4-1	0-0	1-1	2-2	0-0	2-1
Hartlepools United	1-1	4-1	2-0	0-0	2-1	0-1	2-1	0-2	1-1	5-1	2-2	5-0		5-1	2-0	4-1	1-2	1-2	1-1	1-0	1-2	1-1	1-0	2-2
Hull City AFC	1-0	1-1	1-3	3-3	2-1	4-0	3-0	1-0	1-0	2-1	1-1	5-2	1-1		1-1	9-0	2-1	2-0	3-2	1-0	0-0	3-2	2-0	0-1
Mansfield Town FC	0-2	4-2	5-2	2-1	6-4	2-0	3-1	1-1	2-1	4-2	3-0	2-1	5-1	1-3		4-4	2-4	3-5	3-0	2-2	4-1	6-3	2-1	2-1
Oldham Athletic AFC	0-3	1-1	1-1	4-2	1-3	1-0	5-1	2-1	1-0	2-2	0-0	2-4	4-0	1-1	1-1		0-0	3-2	2-4	1-0	4-1	4-1	2-3	
Rochdale AFC	3-0	1-1	0-2	1-2	1-1	1-0	1-1	3-4	3-0	5-4	0-0	5-1	7-0	2-1	3-0	1-3		1-4	2-0	3-0	2-0	1-0	2-0	2-1
Scunthorpe United	1-0	1-0	0-2	6-2	1-0	3-1	2-1	1-1	3-2	5-0	1-1	2-0	2-0	3-3	1-1	2-0	1-4		1-0	4-0	1-1	2-2	1-0	1-2
Southport FC	3-3	0-4	0-2	2-1	2-2	2-0	2-4	5-2	2-0	0-3	1-0	0-3	0-0	1-2	4-1	2-1	0-2	1-2		1-0	0-3	0-1	1-3	0-1
Stockport County FC	0-0	2-0	0-4	3-0	4-0	4-1	2-2	4-1	5-1	4-1	5-1	4-2	2-1	1-0	3-3	3-0	0-3	2-1	1-2		2-1	0-2	1-1	2-1
Tranmere Rovers FC	0-1	1-1	4-1	5-0	1-1	0-1	2-2	1-2	5-2	2-1	2-0	3-2	4-4	1-2	1-1	3-1	1-4	2-1	3-2			1-0	2-1	6-1
Workington AFC	0-1	0-1	1-1	1-2	2-1	5-3	0-2	3-2	2-2	1-1	4-4	1-0	3-2	4-0	4-0	4-2	1-2	3-2	2-0	1-1	1-2		4-2	0-0
Wrexham AFC	1-0	0-0	1-1	1-1	2-0	1-0	1-0	2-2	0-1	2-0	1-2	2-1	3-1	6-0	4-2	2-2	2-0	1-0	1-0	1-0	2-2	1-1		2-2
York City FC	0-3	0-0	2-0	3-0	2-1	0-5	1-2	3-3	3-1	3-0	2-2	1-1	2-2	3-1	3-1	2-2	1-0	0-0	1-0	0-0	4-0	3-0	1-2	

	Division 3 (North)	Pd	Wn	Dw	Ls	GF	GA	Pts	
1.	Scunthorpe & Lindsey United FC (Scunthorpe)	46	29	8	9	88	50	66	P*
2.	Accrington Stanley FC (Accrington)	46	25	9	12	83	61	59	
3.	Bradford City AFC (Bradford)	46	21	15	10	73	49	57	
4.	Bury FC (Bury)	46	23	10	13	94	62	56	
5.	Hull City AFC (Kingston-upon-Hull)	46	19	15	12	78	67	53	
6.	Mansfield Town FC (Mansfield)	46	22	8	16	100	92	52	
7.	Halifax Town AFC (Halifax)	46	20	11	15	83	69	51	
8.	Chesterfield FC (Chesterfield)	46	18	15	13	71	69	51	
9.	Stockport County FC (Stockport)	46	18	11	17	74	67	47	
10.	Rochdale AFC (Rochdale)	46	19	8	19	79	67	46	
11.	Tranmere Rovers FC (Birkenhead)	46	18	10	18	82	76	46	
12.	Wrexham AFC (Wrexham)	46	17	12	17	71	73	46	
13.	York City FC (York)	46	17	12	17	68	76	46	
14.	Gateshead FC (Gateshead)	46	15	15	16	68	76	45	
15.	Oldham Athletic AFC (Oldham)	46	14	17	15	72	84	45	
16.	Carlisle United FC (Carlisle)	46	19	6	21	80	78	44	
17.	Hartlepools United FC (Hartlepool)	46	16	12	18	73	76	44	
18.	Barrow AFC (Barrow-in-Furness)	46	13	14	18	66	74	41	
19.	Workington AFC (Workington)	46	14	13	19	72	81	41	
20.	Darlington FC (Darlington)	46	17	7	22	78	89	41	
21.	Chester FC (Chester)	46	13	13	20	73	81	39	
22.	Bradford Park Avenue FC (Bradford)	46	13	11	22	68	95	37	
23.	Southport FC (Southport)	46	11	6	29	52	88	28	
24.	Crewe Alexandra FC (Crewe)	46	8	7	31	47	93	23	
		1104	419	166	419	1783	1783	1104	

* Scunthorpe & Lindsey United FC (Scunthorpe) changed their name to Scunthorpe United FC for the next season.

Football League Division 3 (S) 1957-58 Season	Aldershot Town	Bournemouth	Brentford	Brighton & H.A.	Colchester United	Coventry City	Crystal Palace	Exeter City	Gillingham	Millwall	Newport County	Northampton T.	Norwich City	Plymouth Argyle	Port Vale	Q.P.R.	Reading	Shrewsbury T.	Southampton	Southend United	Swindon Town	Torquay United	Walsall	Watford
Aldershot Town FC		0-0	0-2	2-3	2-1	1-1	4-1	2-2	2-0	2-2	2-1	0-0	2-1	3-3	0-1	1-1	1-0	0-1	1-5	0-2	2-1	1-1	1-3	2-2
Bournemouth & Bos.	5-1		1-0	1-3	1-1	0-0	3-1	2-1	2-1	4-0	4-3	1-1	3-1	0-0	3-1	4-1	4-1	3-1	5-2	2-1	1-1	2-0	1-2	2-1
Brentford FC	4-2	4-2		1-0	3-3	1-3	0-3	1-0	1-0	4-1	2-1	7-1	7-1	2-0	4-1	1-1	2-0	2-0	0-0	4-2	0-0	0-1	2-1	0-0
Brighton & Hove Alb.	0-1	2-1	1-1		5-2	3-0	3-2	2-2	5-2	4-2	5-3	1-4	0-1	3-2	0-0	1-1	1-2	1-1	2-1	1-1	3-1	1-0	1-1	6-0
Colchester United FC	1-1	3-2	1-1	1-2		4-1	1-1	3-0	3-2	2-1	1-1	1-0	1-2	1-2	2-1	2-1	1-3	3-0	4-2	1-0	1-3	3-0	1-1	4-0
Coventry City FC	6-0	0-3	0-0	2-2	1-0		2-0	2-2	6-1	1-1	1-4	1-2	1-1	2-1	1-1	1-0	1-1	5-0	0-0	1-0	0-1	2-1	4-1	2-2
Crystal Palace FC	1-1	3-0	2-1	2-4	1-1	2-0		2-0	3-0	0-1	2-2	1-3	0-3	3-0	1-0	2-3	2-2	3-1	1-4	2-0	4-1	1-1	4-1	4-2
Exeter City FC	3-0	1-2	3-5	2-0	4-3	1-0	0-1		1-1	1-3	2-0	0-2	0-1	2-2	4-2	1-0	0-0	1-1	2-1	2-2	0-5	5-1	1-1	1-2
Gillingham FC	1-1	1-1	3-2	0-1	2-3	3-2	3-0	1-1		1-0	0-1	1-2	1-0	1-0	0-2	1-1	2-1	1-3	2-1	2-0	2-1	1-0	3-0	1-1
Millwall FC	3-3	0-2	0-1	2-2	1-4	4-1	3-0	3-0	3-1		1-2	0-0	2-2	0-1	2-1	5-0	0-0	1-3	1-2	1-2	1-1	1-2	1-3	2-3
Newport County AFC	3-2	3-1	1-2	1-2	2-2	2-2	0-0	0-0	5-0	1-2		2-1	0-1	1-0	0-2	2-1	4-2	0-0	1-1	1-0	4-1	3-2	2-0	2-1
Northampton Town	0-0	4-1	3-1	2-4	4-1	4-0	1-2	9-0	3-1	7-2	0-3		1-1	0-1	5-0	3-2	1-5	1-2	2-1	1-3	1-3	3-0	1-0	3-3
Norwich City FC	1-3	2-2	3-2	0-0	1-1	1-1	3-2	3-2	2-0	1-1	5-2	2-2		2-1	1-0	3-0	2-0	2-2	0-2	0-0	1-1	3-1	2-1	1-1
Plymouth Argyle FC	4-2	3-1	0-0	2-1	1-1	4-0	1-0	1-0	2-1	1-0	1-0	3-0	0-1		1-0	3-1	1-0	2-2	4-0	2-3	2-2	1-0	2-1	2-1
Port Vale FC	6-1	2-3	0-1	2-2	2-0	0-1	4-0	3-2	2-0	1-1	2-2	3-0	2-2	0-0		2-1	1-2	0-0	4-0	1-3	3-1	2-1	2-1	5-0
Queen's Park Rangers	0-1	3-0	1-0	0-1	1-0	3-0	4-2	1-1	1-1	3-0	1-1	1-0	1-1	2-1	1-0		3-0	3-0	3-2	1-1	2-1	1-1	1-0	3-0
Reading FC	3-0	2-0	1-2	1-1	7-0	3-1	2-2	4-0	4-1	1-0	5-2	1-2	1-3	3-0	3-0	2-0		2-2	1-0	1-1	0-4	1-1	3-1	1-1
Shrewsbury Town FC	5-1	0-4	0-2	1-1	0-0	1-3	0-0	1-0	2-1	0-1	1-1	3-1	0-0	2-1	1-0	2-1	0-2		1-3	1-1	1-3	3-0	2-0	1-1
Southampton FC	2-2	7-0	4-2	5-0	3-2	7-1	2-1	6-0	5-1	3-2	2-1	2-1	7-3	0-1	0-3	5-0	0-1	2-2		2-2	1-3	4-2	4-1	5-0
Southend United FC	1-2	2-0	0-0	0-2	2-3	5-1	2-0	2-0	2-0	2-0	6-3	5-2	2-1	1-1	6-0	2-1	5-1	3-2	2-1		2-3	0-0	4-1	2-1
Swindon Town FC	3-0	1-0	4-1	2-0	4-0	2-1	0-0	5-1	1-1	3-0	4-0	5-1	1-2	1-0	1-1	1-1	1-0	1-0	2-1	1-1		3-1	2-3	0-0
Torquay United FC	2-1	3-1	0-1	2-0	1-3	1-0	1-1	1-3	3-2	2-3	2-2	1-0	1-1	0-2	1-1	3-1	1-4	0-2	1-1	2-2	2-2		2-1	1-0
Walsall FC	0-0	3-1	0-2	2-3	3-0	4-1	2-1	3-0	1-1	4-2	3-0	2-1	2-1	0-2	3-0	1-2	0-0	0-1	1-1	1-1	1-1	0-0		1-3
Watford FC	1-3	1-1	4-1	0-1	1-1	1-0	2-1	5-4	3-0	3-0	2-2	0-2	1-4	0-2	0-2	0-0	1-1	3-0	3-0	1-1	0-0	1-0	1-1	

Division 3 (South)

		Pd	Wn	Dw	Ls	GF	GA	Pts	
1.	Brighton & Hove Albion FC (Hove)	46	24	12	10	88	64	60	P
2.	Brentford FC (London)	46	24	10	12	82	56	58	
3.	Plymouth Argyle FC (Plymouth)	46	25	8	13	67	48	58	
4.	Swindon Town FC (Swindon)	46	21	15	10	79	50	57	
5.	Reading FC (Reading)	46	21	13	12	79	51	55	
6.	Southampton FC (Southampton)	46	22	10	14	112	72	54	
7.	Southend United FC (Southend-on-Sea)	46	21	12	13	90	58	54	
8.	Norwich City FC (Norwich)	46	19	15	12	75	70	53	
9.	Bournemouth & Boscombe Athletic FC (Bournemouth)	46	21	9	16	81	74	51	
10.	Queen's Park Rangers FC (London)	46	18	14	14	64	65	50	
11.	Newport County AFC (Newport)	46	17	14	15	73	67	48	
12.	Colchester United FC (Colchester)	46	17	13	16	77	79	47	
13.	Northampton Town FC (Northampton)	46	19	6	21	87	79	44	
14.	Crystal Palace FC (London)	46	15	13	18	70	72	43	
15.	Port Vale FC (Stoke-on-Trent)	46	16	10	20	67	58	42	
16.	Watford FC (Watford)	46	13	16	17	59	77	42	
17.	Shrewsbury Town FC (Shrewsbury)	46	15	10	21	49	71	40	
18.	Aldershot FC (Aldershot)	46	12	16	18	59	89	40	
19.	Coventry City FC (Coventry)	46	13	13	20	61	81	39	
20.	Walsall FC (Walsall)	46	14	9	23	61	75	37	
21.	Torquay United FC (Torquay)	46	11	13	22	49	74	35	
22.	Gillingham FC (Gillingham)	46	13	9	24	52	81	35	
23.	Millwall FC (London)	46	11	9	26	63	91	31	
24.	Exeter City FC (Exeter)	46	11	9	26	57	99	31	
		1104	413	278	413	1701	1701	1104	

The league was re-structured for the next season with clubs placed 2nd to 12th in Division 3 North and South plus clubs relegated from Division 2 forming a new Division 3. The remaining clubs who finished 13th to 24th in Division 3 North and South formed a new Division 4.

F.A. CUP FINAL   (Wembley Stadium, London – 03/05/1958 – 100,000)

BOLTON WANDERERS FC (BOLTON)   2-0   Manchester United FC (Manchester)

Lofthouse 2

Bolton: Hopkinson, Hartle, Banks, Hennin, Higgins, Edwards, Birch, Stevens, Lofthouse, Parry, Holden.

Man. United: Gregg, Foulkes, Greaves, Goodwin, Cope, Crowther, Dawson, Taylor, R.Charlton, Viollet, Webster.

Semi-finals

Blackburn Rovers FC (Blackburn)	1-2	Bolton Wanderers FC (Bolton)
Manchester United FC (Manchester)	2-2, 5-3	Fulham FC (London)

Quarter-finals

Blackburn Rovers FC (Blackburn)	2-1	Liverpool FC (Liverpool)
Bolton Wanderers FC (Bolton)	2-1	Wolverhampton Wanderers FC (Wolverhampton)
Fulham FC (London)	3-1	Bristol Rovers FC (Bristol)
West Bromwich Albion FC (west Bromwich)	2-2, 0-1	Manchester United FC (Manchester)

1958-59

Football League Division 1 1958-59 Season	Arsenal	Aston Villa	Birmingham C.	Blackburn R.	Blackpool	Bolton Wands.	Burnley	Chelsea	Everton	Leeds United	Leicester City	Luton Town	Manchester City	Man. United	Newcastle Utd.	Nottingham F.	Portsmouth	Preston N.E.	Tottenham H.	W.B.A.	West Ham Utd.	Wolves
Arsenal FC	■	1-2	2-1	1-1	1-4	6-1	3-0	1-1	3-1	1-0	5-1	1-0	4-1	3-2	3-2	3-1	5-2	1-2	3-1	4-3	1-2	1-1
Aston Villa FC	1-2	■	1-1	1-0	1-1	2-1	0-0	3-1	2-4	2-1	1-2	3-1	1-1	0-2	2-1	2-3	3-2	2-0	1-1	1-4	1-2	1-3
Birmingham City FC	4-1	4-1	■	3-0	4-2	1-3	2-1	4-1	2-1	4-1	4-2	0-1	6-1	0-4	1-0	0-3	2-2	5-1	5-1	0-6	3-0	0-3
Blackburn Rovers FC	4-2	2-3	3-2	■	0-0	1-1	4-1	0-3	2-1	2-4	5-0	3-1	2-1	1-3	3-0	3-0	2-1	4-1	5-0	0-0	1-2	1-2
Blackpool FC	1-2	2-1	2-0	1-1	■	4-0	1-1	5-0	1-1	3-0	2-1	3-0	0-0	2-1	3-0	1-0	1-1	4-2	0-0	1-1	2-0	0-1
Bolton Wanderers FC	2-1	1-3	2-0	3-1	4-0	■	1-2	6-0	0-3	4-0	3-3	4-2	4-1	6-3	1-1	3-2	2-1	2-1	4-1	2-1	0-2	2-2
Burnley FC	3-1	3-1	0-1	0-0	3-1	0-1	■	4-0	3-1	3-1	3-3	2-2	3-4	4-2	2-2	0-1	2-1	1-0	3-1	1-3	1-0	0-2
Chelsea FC	0-3	2-1	1-0	0-2	3-1	0-1	1-3	■	3-1	2-0	5-2	3-3	2-0	2-3	6-5	4-1	2-2	3-1	4-2	0-2	3-2	6-2
Everton FC	1-6	2-1	3-1	2-2	3-1	1-0	1-2	3-1	■	3-2	0-1	3-1	3-1	3-2	0-2	1-3	2-1	1-4	2-1	3-3	2-2	0-1
Leeds United AFC	2-1	0-0	0-0	2-1	1-1	3-4	1-1	4-0	1-0	■	1-1	1-1	0-4	1-2	3-2	1-0	1-1	1-3	3-1	0-1	1-0	1-3
Leicester City FC	2-3	6-3	2-4	1-1	0-3	0-1	1-1	0-3	2-0	0-1	■	3-1	3-1	2-1	0-1	0-3	3-1	2-2	3-4	2-2	1-1	1-0
Luton Town FC	6-3	2-1	1-1	1-1	1-1	1-0	6-2	2-1	0-1	1-1	4-3	■	5-1	0-0	4-2	5-1	3-1	4-1	1-2	1-1	4-1	0-1
Manchester City FC	0-0	0-0	4-1	0-1	0-2	3-3	1-4	5-1	1-3	2-1	3-1	1-1	■	1-1	5-1	1-1	3-2	1-1	5-1	0-2	3-1	1-4
Manchester United FC	1-1	1-1	1-0	6-1	3-1	3-0	1-3	5-2	2-1	4-0	4-1	2-1	4-1	■	4-4	1-1	6-1	0-2	2-2	1-2	4-1	2-1
Newcastle United FC	1-0	1-0	1-1	1-5	1-0	2-0	5-2	1-2	4-0	2-2	3-1	1-0	4-1	1-1	■	1-3	2-0	1-2	1-2	1-2	3-1	3-4
Nottingham Forest FC	1-1	2-0	1-7	1-1	2-0	3-0	1-2	1-3	2-1	1-4	3-1	4-0	0-3	3-0		■	5-0	0-1	1-1	1-1	4-0	1-3
Portsmouth FC	0-1	5-2	1-1	2-1	1-2	0-1	4-2	2-2	2-3	2-0	4-1	2-2	3-4	1-3	1-5	0-1	■	1-2	1-1	2-6	1-2	3-5
Preston North End FC	2-1	4-2	3-0	1-2	0-3	0-0	0-4	2-0	3-1	1-2	3-1	0-0	2-0	3-4	3-4	3-5	3-1	■	2-2	2-4	2-1	1-2
Tottenham Hotspur FC	1-4	3-2	0-4	3-1	2-3	1-1	2-2	4-0	10-4	2-3	6-0	3-0	3-1	1-3	1-3	1-0	4-4	1-2	■	5-0	1-4	2-1
West Bromwich Albion FC	1-1	1-1	2-2	2-3	3-1	1-2	2-4	4-0	2-4	2-2	2-0	3-0	1-3	2-2	2-0	1-2	1-1	4-3		■	2-1	2-1
West Ham United FC	0-0	7-2	1-2	6-3	1-0	4-3	1-0	4-2	3-2	2-3	0-3	0-0	5-1	3-2	3-0	5-3	6-0	1-1	2-1	3-1	■	2-0
Wolverhampton Wanderers FC	6-1	4-0	3-1	5-0	2-0	1-2	3-3	1-2	1-0	6-2	3-0	5-2	2-0	4-0	1-3	5-1	7-0	2-0	1-1	5-2	1-1	■

	Division 1	Pd	Wn	Dw	Ls	GF	GA	Pts	
1.	WOLVERHAMPTON WANDERERS FC (WOLV.)	42	28	5	9	110	49	61	
2.	Manchester United FC (Manchester)	42	24	7	11	103	66	55	
3.	Arsenal FC (London)	42	21	8	13	88	68	50	
4.	Bolton Wanderers FC (Bolton)	42	20	10	12	79	66	50	
5.	West Bromwich Albion FC (West Bromwich)	42	18	13	11	88	68	49	
6.	West Ham United FC (London)	42	21	6	15	85	70	48	
7.	Burnley FC (Burnley)	42	19	10	13	81	70	48	
8.	Blackpool FC (Blackpool)	42	18	11	13	66	49	47	
9.	Birmingham City FC (Birmingham)	42	20	6	16	84	68	46	
10.	Blackburn Rovers FC (Blackburn)	42	17	10	15	76	70	44	
11.	Newcastle United FC (Newcastle-upon-Tyne)	42	17	7	18	80	80	41	
12.	Preston North End FC (Preston)	42	17	7	18	70	77	41	
13.	Nottingham Forest FC (Nottingham)	42	17	6	19	71	74	40	
14.	Chelsea FC (London)	42	18	4	20	77	98	40	
15.	Leeds United AFC (Leeds)	42	15	9	18	57	74	39	
16.	Everton FC (Liverpool)	42	17	4	21	71	87	38	
17.	Luton Town FC (Luton)	42	12	13	17	68	71	37	
18.	Tottenham Hotspur FC (London)	42	13	10	19	85	95	36	
19.	Leicester City FC (Leicester)	42	11	10	21	67	98	32	
20.	Manchester City FC (Manchester)	42	11	9	22	64	95	31	
21.	Aston Villa FC (Birmingham)	42	11	8	23	58	87	30	R
22.	Portsmouth FC (Portsmouth)	42	6	9	27	64	112	21	R
		924	371	182	371	1692	1692	924	

Top Goalscorer

1) James GREAVES (Chelsea FC) 33

Football League Division 2 1958-59 Season	Barnsley	Brighton & Hove Albion	Bristol City	Bristol Rovers	Cardiff City	Charlton Athletic	Derby County	Fulham	Grimsby Town	Huddersfield Town	Ipswich Town	Leyton Orient	Lincoln City	Liverpool	Middlesbrough	Rotherham United	Scunthorpe United	Sheffield United	Sheffield Wednesday	Stoke City	Sunderland	Swansea Town
Barnsley FC	■	0-2	4-7	0-0	3-2	7-1	0-0	2-4	3-1	1-0	3-0	1-3	2-2	0-2	1-0	1-1	0-1	1-3	0-1	2-1	0-2	3-1
Brighton & Hove Albion FC	1-1	■	2-2	1-1	2-2	2-2	3-1	3-0	2-0	2-0	4-1	2-2	2-1	2-2	4-6	3-0	2-1	2-0	1-3	2-2	2-0	2-2
Bristol City FC	3-1	3-0	■	1-1	2-3	2-4	1-3	1-1	1-0	2-1	3-0	0-1	1-0	1-3	2-2	6-1	0-1	3-1	1-2	2-1	4-1	4-0
Bristol Rovers FC	0-2	2-0	1-2	■	2-0	2-1	2-1	0-0	7-3	1-1	1-1	1-3	3-0	3-0	3-1	4-1	4-0	1-1	2-1	1-0	2-1	4-4
Cardiff City AFC	0-1	3-1	1-0	2-4	■	1-2	0-0	1-2	4-1	3-2	1-2	2-1	3-0	3-0	3-2	1-0	0-2	3-1	2-2	2-1	2-1	0-1
Charlton Athletic FC	4-0	2-3	4-1	4-3	0-0	■	1-2	2-1	2-1	2-1	5-1	4-1	3-2	2-3	1-0	5-2	2-3	1-1	3-3	1-2	3-2	2-1
Derby County FC	3-0	1-3	4-1	3-2	1-3	3-2	■	2-0	3-0	3-1	3-2	1-2	1-0	3-2	0-3	1-1	3-1	2-1	1-4	3-0	2-0	3-1
Fulham FC	5-2	3-1	1-0	1-0	2-1	2-1	4-2	■	3-0	1-0	3-2	5-2	4-2	0-1	3-2	4-0	1-1	4-2	6-2	6-1	6-2	1-2
Grimsby Town FC	3-3	1-1	2-0	1-2	5-1	1-5	3-0	2-2	■	2-1	2-3	4-1	4-2	2-3	3-2	1-1	1-1	1-2	0-2	2-2	1-1	0-1
Huddersfield Town AFC	2-1	3-2	0-1	1-2	3-0	1-0	1-1	2-1	2-0	■	3-0	0-0	2-1	5-0	5-1	3-0	0-1	0-2	1-2	1-2	1-1	3-2
Ipswich Town FC	3-1	5-3	1-1	0-2	3-3	3-1	1-1	1-2	2-1	0-0	■	2-1	4-1	2-0	2-1	1-0	3-1	1-0	0-2	0-2	0-2	3-2
Leyton Orient FC	5-1	2-2	4-2	1-3	3-0	6-1	1-3	0-2	0-2	2-5	2-0	■	0-0	1-3	5-2	2-0	2-1	1-1	0-2	0-1	6-0	0-0
Lincoln City FC	2-1	4-2	0-2	4-1	4-2	3-3	1-4	2-4	4-4	1-1	3-1	2-0	■	2-1	1-1	1-0	3-3	1-2	0-1	3-1	3-1	1-2
Liverpool FC	3-2	5-0	3-2	2-1	1-2	3-0	3-0	0-0	3-3	2-2	3-1	3-0	3-2	■	1-2	4-0	3-0	2-1	3-2	3-4	3-1	4-0
Middlesbrough FC	3-1	9-0	0-0	2-2	1-1	1-3	5-0	2-3	1-0	3-1	2-3	4-2	1-2	2-1	■	1-2	6-1	0-0	2-2	0-0	0-0	6-2
Rotherham United FC	3-0	0-1	1-2	3-3	1-0	4-3	3-0	4-0	2-1	0-1	1-2	1-1	1-0	0-1	1-4	■	1-0	2-2	1-0	0-0	0-4	3-3
Scunthorpe United FC	1-0	2-3	3-3	0-0	1-0	3-3	2-2	1-2	1-3	0-3	1-1	2-0	3-1	1-2	0-3	2-0	■	1-3	1-4	1-1	3-2	3-1
Sheffield United FC	5-0	3-1	4-0	5-2	1-1	5-0	1-2	2-0	2-1	0-0	2-0	2-3	6-1	2-0	0-1	2-0	4-1	■	1-0	2-1	3-1	2-0
Sheffield Wednesday FC	5-0	2-0	2-3	3-1	3-1	4-1	1-1	2-2	6-0	4-1	3-1	2-0	7-0	1-0	2-0	5-0	2-0	2-0	■	4-1	6-0	2-1
Stoke City FC	2-1	3-0	2-1	2-2	0-1	2-1	2-1	4-1	4-0	5-1	1-0	3-2	1-0	0-2	3-1	3-0	4-3	1-2	3-0	■	0-0	3-0
Sunderland AFC	2-2	4-1	3-1	3-1	0-2	0-3	3-0	1-2	1-0	1-0	0-2	4-0	2-0	2-1	0-0	1-1	3-1	4-1	3-3	3-1	■	2-1
Swansea Town AFC	2-1	4-2	1-0	2-1	1-3	2-2	4-4	1-2	1-1	0-1	4-2	3-3	3-1	3-3	5-2	3-0	3-0	0-2	4-0	1-0	5-0	■

	Division 2	Pd	Wn	Dw	Ls	GF	GA	Pts	
1.	Sheffield Wednesday FC (Sheffield)	42	28	6	8	106	48	62	P
2.	Fulham FC (London)	42	27	6	9	96	61	60	P
3.	Sheffield United FC (Sheffield)	42	23	7	12	82	48	53	
4.	Liverpool FC (Liverpool)	42	24	5	13	87	62	53	
5.	Stoke City FC (Stoke-on-Trent)	42	21	7	14	72	58	49	
6.	Bristol Rovers FC (Bristol)	42	18	12	12	80	64	48	
7.	Derby County FC (Derby)	42	20	8	14	74	71	48	
8.	Charlton Athletic FC (London)	42	18	7	17	92	90	43	
9.	Cardiff City AFC (Cardiff)	42	18	7	17	65	65	43	
10.	Bristol City FC (Bristol)	42	17	7	18	74	70	41	
11.	Swansea Town AFC (Swansea)	42	16	9	17	79	81	41	
12.	Brighton & Hove Albion FC (Brighton)	42	15	11	16	74	90	41	
13.	Middlesbrough FC (Middlesbrough)	42	15	10	17	87	71	40	
14.	Huddersfield Town AFC (Huddersfield)	42	16	8	18	62	55	40	
15.	Sunderland AFC (Sunderland)	42	16	8	18	64	75	40	
16.	Ipswich Town FC (Ipswich)	42	17	6	19	62	77	40	
17.	Leyton Orient FC (London)	42	14	8	20	71	78	36	
18.	Scunthorpe United FC (Scunthorpe)	42	12	9	21	55	84	33	
19.	Lincoln City FC (Lincoln)	42	11	7	24	63	93	29	
20.	Rotherham United FC (Rotherham)	42	10	9	23	42	82	29	
21.	Grimsby Town FC (Cleethorpes)	42	9	10	23	62	90	28	R
22.	Barnsley FC (Barnsley)	42	10	7	25	55	91	27	R
		924	375	174	375	1604	1604	924	

44

Football League Division 3 1958-59 Season

	Accrington Stan.	Bournemouth	Bradford City	Brentford	Bury	Chesterfield	Colchester United	Doncaster Rovers	Halifax Town	Hull City	Mansfield Town	Newport County	Norwich City	Notts County	Plymouth Argyle	Q.P.R.	Reading	Rochdale	Southampton	Southend United	Stockport County	Swindon Town	Tranmere Rovers	Wrexham
Accrington Stanley		3-2	1-3	1-1	0-2	3-1	1-1	2-0	4-2	0-1	2-0	2-2	0-2	3-0	1-1	2-4	4-3	4-2	0-0	3-0	2-2	0-0	3-1	1-1
Bournemouth & Bos.	5-2		4-0	0-0	2-0	2-1	1-1	1-0	3-0	1-0	3-3	1-1	2-0	0-0	1-1	2-0	0-1	0-0	2-1	1-4	2-0	3-3	4-0	0-0
Bradford City AFC	0-0	0-1		3-0	1-0	1-0	1-3	3-0	1-3	2-1	1-1	1-0	2-2	4-1	0-0	1-0	1-2	7-1	2-3	6-1	4-2	1-2	2-0	3-2
Brentford FC	2-1	1-1	4-0		0-0	1-1	2-1	0-1	2-0	1-1	2-0	3-0	0-4	4-0	3-0	1-0	3-1	2-1	2-0	6-1	1-4	2-2	5-2	2-1
Bury FC	3-1	5-1	2-2	1-1		1-0	0-0	5-0	3-1	2-1	2-2	0-0	3-2	0-1	1-1	3-1	1-1	6-1	1-0	2-3	3-3	0-0	4-2	3-1
Chesterfield FC	0-1	1-0	2-0	1-2	3-0		2-2	2-0	2-3	2-1	3-1	3-1	1-1	1-0	1-2	2-3	1-0	0-0	3-3	4-0	1-0	1-3	3-2	1-1
Colchester United FC	1-0	3-1	3-2	0-4	1-3	1-0		1-0	3-1	1-3	1-3	3-2	2-1	4-1	2-0	3-0	3-1	2-1	1-3	0-1	8-2	1-0	1-1	1-0
Doncaster Rovers FC	3-0	5-1	0-3	1-0	0-1	2-1	2-1		1-2	0-2	0-2	1-0	0-1	2-1	4-6	2-0	2-5	1-1	3-2	2-1	4-1	2-0	2-0	1-1
Halifax Town AFC	0-2	0-1	3-3	0-0	4-2	3-2	4-1	5-1		1-2	0-0	3-1	1-1	1-1	0-1	2-1	4-1	2-1	2-0	1-0	4-3	1-0	3-0	4-1
Hull City AFC	4-2	5-3	4-0	3-1	2-0	3-1	3-0	5-1	4-0		5-2	2-3	3-3	5-0	1-0	2-0	2-1	3-0	3-2	3-1	0-0	1-0	1-0	
Mansfield Town FC	3-2	1-4	2-1	1-1	0-2	2-1	3-2	3-1	4-3	1-1		2-1	1-1	3-0	1-4	3-4	1-0	0-0	1-6	1-4	2-1	0-0	0-2	3-1
Newport County AFC	2-1	4-1	3-2	1-0	1-1	0-1	0-1	3-1	0-2	1-3	1-0		2-2	3-1	0-1	3-1	2-1	1-0	4-2	3-1	2-0	3-0	3-0	2-1
Norwich City FC	2-4	2-2	4-2	4-1	3-2	2-1	1-2	3-0	3-1	0-1	1-0	3-0		3-3	1-1	5-1	1-0	2-1	3-1	4-0	1-3	1-1	0-0	2-2
Notts County FC	1-1	4-3	1-3	0-0	1-1	3-1	0-1	2-2	4-4	1-1	3-4	1-1	1-3		1-2	0-1	3-1	1-1	1-2	1-4	0-2	1-0	1-1	2-0
Plymouth Argyle FC	2-4	3-1	1-1	1-1	3-0	2-0	1-1	4-0	1-1	1-1	8-3	3-2	0-1	3-0		3-2	2-2	2-1	1-0	3-1	2-1	3-2	4-0	2-2
Queen's Park Rangers	3-1	0-4	3-0	1-2	2-1	2-2	4-2	3-1	3-1	1-1	1-1	4-2	2-1	2-1	2-1		2-0	3-0	2-2	1-3	0-0	2-1	1-1	5-0
Reading FC	5-0	2-0	3-2	3-1	1-0	1-2	0-0	2-0	3-0	2-0	3-3	1-3	3-1	3-1	0-2	2-2		3-0	4-1	3-0	2-1	3-1	0-0	2-1
Rochdale AFC	1-0	2-1	0-0	1-0	0-0	0-1	1-0	1-0	1-0	2-2	1-1	1-2	1-2	0-2	2-2	1-0			1-0	1-1	1-0	1-4	1-3	1-1
Southampton FC	3-1	0-0	1-2	0-6	4-2	0-0	3-0	1-1	5-0	6-1	3-2	3-3	1-1	3-0	5-1	1-0	3-3	6-1		3-2	2-1	1-1	2-3	1-2
Southend United FC	4-2	2-0	1-1	2-0	1-0	2-5	1-1	5-0	3-2	1-1	5-1	1-0	1-0	5-2	0-0	4-0	2-2	3-1	1-1		3-1	0-2	1-3	4-1
Stockport County FC	0-0	3-1	1-1	1-1	0-1	1-1	0-1	2-0	0-1	2-1	4-1	2-1	2-3	1-1	2-2	2-3	0-1	1-0	4-0	0-1		2-0	1-0	2-2
Swindon Town FC	1-2	0-1	2-2	1-1	0-0	1-2	2-0	0-0	0-2	2-0	2-1	4-3	3-1	3-4	2-0	2-1	3-1	2-1	3-0				1-2	1-0
Tranmere Rovers FC	9-0	4-0	3-1	1-2	4-0	2-0	3-3	3-0	1-2	1-0	2-2	2-1	0-1	0-3	2-0	2-0	2-1	2-1	2-0	1-1	3-1	3-1		1-2
Wrexham AFC	2-2	1-0	3-3	2-1	0-0	3-4	2-0	2-1	1-1	5-1	2-1	0-0	1-2	3-2	1-1	1-0	0-1	1-0	1-3	3-1	3-1	1-0	2-5	

	Division 3		**Pd**	**Wn**	**Dw**	**Ls**	**GF**	**GA**	**Pts**	
1.	Plymouth Argyle FC (Plymouth)		46	23	16	7	89	59	62	P
2.	Hull City AFC (Kingston-upon-Hull)		46	26	9	11	90	55	61	P
3.	Brentford FC (Brentford)		46	21	15	10	76	49	57	
4.	Norwich City FC (Norwich)		46	22	13	11	89	62	57	
5.	Colchester United FC (Colchester)		46	21	10	15	71	67	52	
6.	Reading FC (Reading)		46	21	8	17	78	63	50	
7.	Tranmere Rovers FC (Birkenhead)		46	21	8	17	82	67	50	
8.	Southend United FC (Southend-on-Sea)		46	21	8	17	85	80	50	
9.	Halifax Town AFC (Halifax)		46	21	8	17	80	77	50	
10.	Bury FC (Bury)		46	17	14	15	69	58	48	
11.	Bradford City AFC (Bradford)		46	18	11	17	84	76	47	
12.	Bournemouth & Boscombe Athletic FC (Bournemouth)		46	17	12	17	69	69	46	
13.	Queen's Park Rangers FC (London)		46	19	8	19	74	77	46	
14.	Southampton FC (Southampton)		46	17	11	18	88	80	45	
15.	Swindon Town FC (Swindon)		46	16	13	17	59	57	45	
16.	Chesterfield FC (Chesterfield)		46	17	10	19	67	64	44	
17.	Newport County AFC (Newport)		46	17	9	20	69	68	43	
18.	Wrexham AFC (Wrexham)		46	14	14	18	63	77	42	
19.	Accrington Stanley FC (Accrington)		46	15	12	19	71	87	42	
20.	Mansfield Town FC (Mansfield)		46	14	13	19	73	98	41	
21.	Stockport County FC (Stockport)		46	13	10	23	65	78	36	R
22.	Doncaster Rovers FC (Doncaster)		46	14	5	27	50	90	33	R
23.	Notts County FC (Nottingham)		46	8	13	25	55	96	29	R
24.	Rochdale AFC (Rochdale)		46	8	12	26	37	79	28	R
			1104	421	262	421	1733	1733	1104	

Football League Division 4 1958-59 Season

	Aldershot Town	Barrow	Bradford P.A.	Carlisle United	Chester	Coventry City	Crewe Alexandra	Crystal Palace	Darlington	Exeter City	Gateshead	Gillingham	Hartlepools	Millwall	Northampton Town	Oldham Athletic	Port Vale	Shrewsbury Town	Southport	Torquay United	Walsall	Watford	Workington	York City
Aldershot Town FC		0-1	3-3	4-0	1-0	0-4	0-0	1-2	1-4	1-0	8-1	4-2	2-4	4-2	1-3	1-3	0-4	0-0	3-2	1-4	0-5	0-0	2-0	0-1
Barrow AFC	3-4		2-3	1-3	1-2	0-3	0-2	1-0	2-1	1-0	0-3	2-2	1-1	3-1	2-2	2-1	1-2	3-4	3-0	2-2	0-0	0-4	2-2	2-3
Bradford Park Ave.	5-1	0-2		0-3	3-0	2-0	0-2	5-0	1-2	0-3	4-1	2-0	4-1	4-1	1-2	2-1	0-2	3-1	3-0	3-1	3-2	1-1	3-2	2-1
Carlisle United FC	1-0	1-0	1-1		4-3	1-6	2-0	3-3	1-1	1-2	4-2	1-2	1-0	0-1	2-1	3-0	0-3	0-0	5-0	0-1	1-1	2-0	3-2	0-0
Chester FC	2-2	2-0	2-0	2-1		1-1	0-1	3-2	1-0	4-2	0-1	1-2	1-0	0-0	2-3	5-2	1-2	3-5	2-1	0-2	2-0	2-1	1-2	2-2
Coventry City FC	7-1	2-0	0-0	1-2	5-1		3-2	2-0	0-0	2-0	4-1	1-1	4-1	1-0	2-0	1-0	3-2	1-0	3-0	0-0	1-0	4-0	2-0	
Crewe Alexandra FC	5-0	5-0	4-1	3-1	2-4	1-1		4-1	2-1	0-0	0-0	0-2	0-2	4-1	1-2	5-0	2-0	2-4	1-1	1-1	5-3	1-3	2-0	2-4
Crystal Palace FC	4-1	2-2	2-0	0-2	3-3	1-1	6-2		4-1	1-1	3-1	4-1	2-4	0-1	4-0	1-1	4-3	1-0	3-1	1-3	3-0	1-1	0-0	
Darlington FC	2-3	5-2	1-1	0-1	0-0	1-4	1-1	1-4		1-1	3-2	1-2	3-1	0-2	2-2	1-1	2-1	4-0	3-2	2-3	1-1	1-1	1-1	
Exeter City FC	2-0	4-0	4-0	2-1	1-1	2-1	3-0	3-1	2-2		1-1	3-0	3-0	3-1	3-4	3-2	3-4	1-0	3-2	2-2	3-0	3-0	1-0	0-2
Gateshead FC	1-0	4-0	1-4	4-1	0-1	1-1	0-0	1-3	1-3	1-2		2-0	3-0	1-2	4-1	2-1	0-4	1-2	1-1	1-0	2-1	1-0	0-3	1-0
Gillingham FC	3-0	4-2	1-1	1-1	3-3	2-0	3-0	1-1	0-0	0-2	3-0		4-1	1-2	4-1	3-2	2-1	2-0	3-2	4-2	2-1	5-1	2-2	
Hartlepools United FC	0-3	10-1	3-0	1-2	1-3	2-1	2-1	4-1	1-0	3-3	0-0	3-1		3-0	4-0	1-5	0-2	1-1	2-4	1-1	4-3	0-3		1-5
Millwall FC	4-0	3-0	1-1	1-0	0-1	1-1	2-0	2-1	1-2	1-1	0-2	2-0	3-2		3-0	4-2	4-2	0-0	1-1	2-0	1-3	4-1	1-1	5-2
Northampton Town	1-0	2-0	4-1	0-0	4-0	4-0	3-0	3-0	1-3	1-1	1-0	4-2	2-1	0-1		2-1	2-4	3-3	3-1	1-1	3-2	2-1	1-1	1-2
Oldham Athletic AFC	0-1	2-0	1-0	2-0	3-5	2-0	2-1	3-0	1-3	2-0	3-0	3-1	1-0	1-3	2-1		0-2	3-1	2-0	1-0	1-4	3-5	1-0	0-1
Port Vale FC	3-2	4-1	4-2	1-1	4-0	3-0	1-1	2-3	1-1	5-3	8-0	3-1	1-1	5-2	1-4	0-0		2-0	4-1	3-1	2-1	1-3	2-0	2-2
Shrewsbury Town FC	3-1	1-2	0-1	4-1	3-0	4-1	2-2	2-1	1-0	3-0	1-1	3-2	3-0	1-2	4-0	0-0	4-3		6-2	5-0	2-0	4-2	1-1	2-2
Southport FC	0-1	0-0	1-0	0-1	1-1	1-2	3-0	0-2	2-0	0-1	2-2	2-1	1-1	2-1	1-2	1-1	2-2	0-1		2-2	1-1	0-3	3-0	1-0
Torquay United FC	1-1	1-0	2-1	0-0	4-0	1-1	6-2	0-2	4-1	3-4	0-1	3-1	1-3	2-0	4-2	2-1	1-1	1-4	1-0		1-2	2-3	4-1	1-1
Walsall FC	2-4	3-1	3-2	5-0	2-2	3-0	6-0	0-2	0-0	3-0	1-2	0-0	2-1	2-1	3-0	1-1	2-3	5-1	2-2			3-2	3-0	5-0
Watford FC	2-1	1-1	2-1	2-2	4-2	1-4	0-1	2-2	0-0	2-1	5-1	2-2	4-1	1-1	3-1	2-1	0-2	1-4	5-1	1-2	1-2		3-0	2-3
Workington AFC	1-0	2-2	2-1	0-1	1-0	2-2	1-0	0-4	3-3	2-2	4-2	0-1	3-0	1-1	3-3	2-0	2-2	1-1	2-0	3-3	0-1	3-1		2-2
York City FC	0-0	1-0	4-0	1-1	1-1	0-0	4-0	1-1	2-1	0-2	1-0	3-1	1-1	3-3	2-1	3-1	0-0	2-0	2-0	1-0	3-2	0-0	2-2	

	Division 4	Pd	Wn	Dw	Ls	GF	GA	Pts	
1.	Port Vale FC (Stoke-on-Trent)	46	26	12	8	110	58	64	P
2.	Coventry City FC (Coventry)	46	24	12	10	84	47	60	P
3.	York City FC (York)	46	21	18	7	73	52	60	P
4.	Shrewsbury Town FC (Shrewsbury)	46	24	10	12	101	63	58	P
5.	Exeter City FC (Exeter)	46	23	11	12	87	61	57	
6.	Walsall FC (Walsall)	46	21	10	15	95	64	52	
7.	Crystal Palace FC (London)	46	20	12	14	90	71	52	
8.	Northampton Town FC (Northampton)	46	21	9	16	85	78	51	
9.	Millwall FC (London)	46	20	10	16	76	69	50	
10.	Carlisle United FC (Carlisle)	46	19	12	15	62	65	50	
11.	Gillingham FC (Gillingham)	46	20	9	17	82	77	49	
12.	Torquay United FC (Torquay)	46	16	12	18	78	77	44	
13.	Chester FC (Chester)	46	16	12	18	72	84	44	
14.	Bradford Park Avenue FC (Bradford)	46	18	7	21	75	77	43	
15.	Watford FC (Watford)	46	16	10	20	81	79	42	
16.	Darlington FC (Darlington)	46	13	16	17	66	68	42	
17.	Workington AFC (Workington)	46	12	17	17	63	78	41	
18.	Crewe Alexandra FC (Crewe)	46	15	10	21	70	82	40	
19.	Hartlepools United FC (Hartlepool)	46	15	10	21	74	88	40	
20.	Gateshead FC (Gateshead)	46	16	8	22	56	85	40	
21.	Oldham Athletic AFC (Oldham)	46	16	4	26	59	84	36	
22.	Aldershot FC (Aldershot)	46	14	7	25	63	97	35	
23.	Barrow AFC (Barrow-in-Furness)	46	9	10	27	51	104	28	
24.	Southport FC (Southport)	46	7	12	27	41	86	26	
		1104	422	260	422	1794	1794	1104	

F.A. CUP FINAL   (Wembley Stadium, London – 02/05/1959 – 100,000)

NOTTINGHAM FOREST FC (NOTTINGHAM)   2-1   Luton Town FC (Luton)

Dwight, Wilson   *Pacey*

Forest: Thomson, Whare, McDonald, Whitefoot, McKinlay, Burkitt, Dwight, Quigley, Wilson, Gray, Imlach.
Luton: Baynham, McNally, Hawkes, Groves, Owen, Pacey, Bingham, Brown, Morton, Cummins, Gregory.

Semi-finals

Aston Villa FC (Birmingham)	0-1	Nottingham Forest FC (Nottingham)
Luton Town FC (Luton)	1-1, 1-0	Norwich City FC (Norwich)

Quarter-finals

Aston Villa FC (Birmingham)	0-0, 2-0	Burnley FC (Burnley)
Blackpool FC (Blackpool)	1-1, 0-1	Luton Town FC (Luton)
Nottingham Forest FC (Nottingham)	2-1	Bolton Wanderers FC (Bolton)
Sheffield United FC (Sheffield)	1-1, 2-3	Norwich City FC (Norwich)

1959-60

Football League Division 1 1959-60 Season	Arsenal	Birmingham City	Blackburn Rovers	Blackpool	Bolton Wanderers	Burnley	Chelsea	Everton	Fulham	Leeds United	Leicester City	Luton Town	Manchester City	Manchester United	Newcastle United	Nottingham Forest	Preston N.E.	Sheffield Wed.	Tottenham H.	W.B.A.	West Ham United	Wolves
Arsenal FC		3-0	5-2	2-1	2-1	2-4	1-4	2-1	2-0	1-1	1-1	0-3	3-1	5-2	1-0	1-1	0-3	0-1	1-1	2-4	1-3	4-4
Birmingham City FC	3-0		1-0	2-1	2-5	0-1	1-1	2-2	2-4	2-0	3-4	1-1	4-1	1-1	4-3	4-1	2-1	0-0	0-1	1-7	2-0	0-1
Blackburn Rovers FC	1-1	2-1		1-0	1-0	3-2	1-0	3-1	4-0	3-2	0-1	0-2	2-1	1-1	1-1	1-2	1-4	3-1	1-4	3-2	6-2	0-1
Blackpool FC	2-1	0-1	1-0		3-2	1-1	3-1	0-0	3-1	3-3	3-3	0-0	1-3	0-6	2-0	0-1	0-2	0-2	2-2	2-0	3-2	3-1
Bolton Wanderers FC	0-1	4-1	0-3	0-3		2-1	2-0	2-1	3-2	1-1	3-1	2-2	3-1	1-1	1-4	1-1	2-1	1-0	2-1	0-0	5-1	2-1
Burnley FC	3-2	3-1	1-0	1-4	4-0		2-1	5-2	0-0	0-1	1-0	3-0	4-3	1-4	2-1	8-0	2-1	3-3	2-0	2-1	1-3	4-1
Chelsea FC	1-3	4-2	3-1	2-3	0-2	4-1		1-0	4-2	1-3	2-2	3-0	3-0	3-6	2-2	1-1	4-4	0-4	1-3	2-2	2-4	1-5
Everton FC	3-1	4-0	2-0	4-0	0-1	1-2	6-1		0-0	1-0	6-1	2-2	2-1	2-1	1-2	6-1	4-0	2-1	2-1	2-2	0-1	0-2
Fulham FC	3-0	2-2	0-1	1-0	1-1	1-0	1-3	2-0		5-0	1-1	4-2	5-2	0-5	4-3	3-1	1-2	1-2	1-1	2-1	1-0	3-1
Leeds United AFC	3-2	3-3	0-1	2-4	1-0	2-3	2-1	3-3	1-4		1-1	1-1	4-3	2-2	2-3	1-0	2-1	1-3	2-4	1-4	3-0	0-3
Leicester City FC	2-2	1-3	2-3	1-1	1-2	2-1	3-1	3-3	0-1	3-2		3-3	5-0	3-1	0-2	0-1	2-2	1-1	0-1	2-1	1-2	1-5
Luton Town FC	0-1	1-1	1-1	0-1	0-0	1-1	1-2	2-1	4-1	0-1	2-0		1-2	2-3	3-4	1-0	1-3	0-1	1-0	0-0	3-1	1-5
Manchester City FC	1-2	3-0	2-1	2-3	1-0	1-2	1-1	4-0	3-1	3-3	3-2	1-2		3-0	3-4	2-1	2-1	4-1	1-2	0-1	3-1	4-6
Manchester United FC	4-2	2-1	1-0	3-1	2-0	1-2	0-1	5-0	3-3	6-0	4-1	4-1	0-0		3-2	3-1	1-1	3-1	1-5	2-3	5-3	0-2
Newcastle United FC	4-1	1-0	3-1	1-1	0-1	1-3	1-1	8-2	3-1	2-1	0-2	3-2	0-1	7-3		2-1	1-2	3-3	1-5	0-0	0-0	1-0
Nottingham Forest FC	0-3	0-2	2-2	0-0	2-0	0-1	3-1	1-1	2-2	4-1	1-0	2-0	1-2	1-5	3-0		1-1	2-1	1-3	1-2	3-1	0-0
Preston North End FC	0-3	3-2	5-3	4-1	1-0	1-0	4-5	0-0	4-1	1-1	1-1	2-0	1-5	4-0	1-2	1-0		3-4	1-1	1-1	1-1	4-3
Sheffield Wednesday FC	5-1	2-4	3-0	5-0	1-0	1-1	1-1	2-2	1-1	1-0	2-2	2-0	1-0	4-2	2-0	0-1	2-2		2-1	2-0	7-0	1-5
Tottenham Hotspur FC	3-0	0-0	2-1	4-1	0-2	1-1	0-1	3-0	1-1	1-4	1-2	1-1	0-1	2-1	4-0	2-1	5-1	4-1		2-2	2-2	5-1
West Bromwich Albion FC	1-0	1-1	2-0	2-1	1-1	0-0	1-3	6-2	2-4	3-0	5-0	4-0	2-0	3-2	2-2	2-3	4-0	3-1	1-2		3-2	0-1
West Ham United FC	0-0	3-1	2-1	1-0	1-2	2-5	4-2	2-2	1-2	1-2	3-0	3-1	4-1	2-1	3-5	4-1	2-1	1-1	1-2	4-1		3-2
Wolverhampton Wanderers FC	3-3	2-0	3-1	1-1	0-1	6-1	3-1	2-0	9-0	4-2	0-3	3-2	4-2	3-2	2-0	3-1	3-3	3-1	1-3	3-1	5-0	

	Division 1	Pd	Wn	Dw	Ls	GF	GA	Pts	
1.	BURNLEY FC (BURNLEY)	42	24	7	11	85	61	55	
2.	Wolverhampton Wanderers FC (Wolverhampton)	42	24	6	12	106	67	54	
3.	Tottenham Hotspur FC (London)	42	21	11	10	86	50	53	
4.	West Bromwich Albion FC (West Bromwich)	42	19	11	12	83	57	49	
5.	Sheffield Wednesday FC (Sheffield)	42	19	11	12	80	59	49	
6.	Bolton Wanderers FC (Bolton)	42	20	8	14	59	51	48	
7.	Manchester United FC (Manchester)	42	19	7	16	102	80	45	
8.	Newcastle United FC (Newcastle-upon-Tyne)	42	18	8	16	82	78	44	
9.	Preston North End FC (Preston)	42	16	12	14	79	76	44	
10.	Fulham FC (London)	42	17	10	15	73	80	44	
11.	Blackpool FC (Blackpool)	42	15	10	17	59	71	40	
12.	Leicester City FC (Leicester)	42	13	13	16	66	75	39	
13.	Arsenal FC (London)	42	15	9	18	68	80	39	
14.	West Ham United FC (London)	42	16	6	20	75	91	38	
15.	Manchester City FC (Manchester)	42	17	3	22	78	84	37	
16.	Everton FC (Liverpool)	42	13	11	18	73	78	37	
17.	Blackburn Rovers FC (Blackburn)	42	16	5	21	60	70	37	
18.	Chelsea FC (London)	42	14	9	19	76	91	37	
19.	Birmingham City FC (Birmingham)	42	13	10	19	63	80	36	
20.	Nottingham Forest FC (Nottingham)	42	13	9	20	50	74	35	
21.	Leeds United AFC (Leeds)	42	12	10	20	65	92	34	R
22.	Luton Town FC (Luton)	42	9	12	21	50	73	30	R
		924	363	198	363	1618	1618	924	

Top Goalscorer

1) Dennis VIOLLET   (Manchester United FC)   32

Football League Division 2 — 1959-60 Season

(Home \ Away)	Aston Villa	Brighton & Hove Albion	Bristol City	Bristol Rovers	Cardiff City	Charlton Athletic	Derby County	Huddersfield Town	Hull City	Ipswich Town	Leyton Orient	Lincoln City	Liverpool	Middlesbrough	Plymouth Argyle	Portsmouth	Rotherham United	Scunthorpe United	Sheffield United	Stoke City	Sunderland	Swansea Town
Aston Villa FC	—	3-1	2-1	4-1	2-0	11-1	3-2	4-0	1-1	3-1	1-0	1-1	4-4	1-0	2-0	5-2	3-0	5-0	1-3	2-1	3-0	1-0
Brighton & Hove Albion FC	1-2	—	5-1	2-2	2-2	1-1	2-0	3-2	1-1	1-4	1-1	3-3	1-2	3-2	2-2	3-1	0-0	0-1	0-2	1-0	2-1	1-2
Bristol City FC	0-5	0-1	—	2-1	0-3	1-2	0-1	2-3	0-1	5-1	1-1	1-0	1-0	2-0	2-1	2-0	2-3	0-2	2-2	1-2	1-0	2-2
Bristol Rovers FC	1-1	4-5	2-1	—	1-1	2-2	2-1	2-0	1-0	2-1	2-2	3-3	0-2	0-2	2-0	2-0	3-1	1-1	3-2	3-1	3-1	3-1
Cardiff City AFC	1-0	1-4	4-2	2-2	—	5-1	2-0	2-1	3-2	3-2	5-1	6-2	3-2	2-0	0-1	1-4	1-4	4-2	2-0	4-4	2-1	2-1
Charlton Athletic FC	2-0	3-1	4-2	2-2	2-1	—	6-1	1-1	3-2	1-3	0-0	2-2	3-0	1-0	5-2	6-1	2-2	5-2	1-1	1-2	3-1	2-2
Derby County FC	2-2	0-1	3-0	1-0	1-2	1-2	—	3-2	1-3	3-0	1-1	3-1	1-2	1-7	1-0	1-0	1-1	3-0	1-1	2-0	0-1	1-2
Huddersfield Town AFC	0-1	2-0	6-1	0-1	0-1	4-0	2-2	—	1-0	3-1	1-1	3-0	1-0	2-0	2-0	6-3	2-1	2-0	0-1	2-3	1-1	4-3
Hull City AFC	0-1	3-1	1-1	3-1	0-0	0-4	1-1	1-1	—	2-0	1-2	0-5	0-1	3-3	3-1	1-3	1-0	0-2	0-2	4-0	0-0	3-1
Ipswich Town FC	2-1	3-0	1-3	3-0	1-1	1-1	1-1	1-4	2-0	—	6-3	3-0	0-1	1-0	3-3	1-1	2-3	1-0	2-0	4-0	6-1	4-1
Leyton Orient FC	0-0	3-2	3-1	1-2	3-4	2-0	3-0	2-1	3-1	4-1	—	4-0	2-0	5-0	2-3	1-2	2-3	1-1	1-1	2-1	1-1	2-1
Lincoln City FC	0-0	2-1	3-1	0-1	2-3	5-3	6-2	0-2	3-0	0-1	2-2	—	4-2	5-2	0-1	0-2	0-1	2-1	2-0	3-0	0-0	2-0
Liverpool FC	2-1	2-2	4-2	4-0	0-4	2-0	4-1	2-2	5-3	3-1	4-3	1-3	—	1-2	4-1	1-1	3-0	2-0	3-0	5-1	3-0	4-1
Middlesbrough FC	0-1	4-1	6-3	5-1	1-1	3-0	3-0	1-0	4-0	4-1	2-2	3-2	3-3	—	6-2	0-0	3-0	3-1	1-2	1-0	1-1	2-0
Plymouth Argyle FC	3-0	3-2	1-4	5-3	1-1	6-4	0-5	1-3	3-2	3-1	1-0	0-2	1-1	2-2	—	1-1	1-0	4-0	1-1	2-3	0-0	3-1
Portsmouth FC	1-2	2-2	2-0	4-5	1-1	2-2	2-3	0-2	1-1	0-2	1-1	1-2	1-2	6-3	1-0	—	2-0	4-0	0-2	2-2	1-2	1-3
Rotherham United FC	2-1	1-0	3-1	3-0	2-2	3-3	1-2	1-1	1-0	1-4	1-1	1-0	2-2	0-2	1-1	2-1	—	1-1	0-0	3-0	1-0	1-1
Scunthorpe United FC	1-2	1-2	1-1	3-4	1-2	1-1	3-2	0-2	3-0	2-2	2-1	5-0	1-1	1-1	2-0	1-0	2-1	—	1-1	1-1	3-1	3-1
Sheffield United FC	1-1	4-1	5-2	1-1	2-1	2-0	2-1	2-0	6-0	1-0	0-2	3-2	2-1	0-0	4-0	0-0	2-3	2-1	—	0-1	1-2	3-3
Stoke City FC	3-3	1-3	1-3	0-1	0-1	1-3	2-1	1-1	1-2	2-1	6-1	1-1	2-5	1-0	4-0	2-3	1-3	1-2	1-2	—	3-1	4-2
Sunderland AFC	1-0	0-0	3-2	2-2	1-1	1-3	3-1	0-0	1-3	0-1	1-4	2-4	1-1	2-2	4-0	2-0	1-2	1-0	5-1	0-2	—	4-0
Swansea Town AFC	1-3	2-2	6-1	3-0	3-3	5-2	1-3	3-1	0-0	2-1	1-0	2-1	5-4	3-1	6-1	1-1	2-2	3-1	2-1	2-2	1-2	—

	Division 2	Pd	Wn	Dw	Ls	GF	GA	Pts	
1.	Aston Villa FC (Birmingham)	42	25	9	8	89	43	59	P
2.	Cardiff City AFC (Cardiff)	42	23	12	7	90	62	58	P
3.	Liverpool FC (Liverpool)	42	20	10	12	90	66	50	
4.	Sheffield United FC (Sheffield)	42	19	12	11	68	51	50	
5.	Middlesbrough FC (Middlesbrough)	42	19	10	13	90	64	48	
6.	Huddersfield Town AFC (Huddersfield)	42	19	9	14	73	52	47	
7.	Charlton Athletic FC (London)	42	17	13	12	90	87	47	
8.	Rotherham United FC (Rotherham)	42	17	13	12	61	60	47	
9.	Bristol Rovers FC (Bristol)	42	18	11	13	72	78	47	
10.	Leyton Orient FC (London)	42	15	14	13	76	61	44	
11.	Ipswich Town FC (Ipswich)	42	19	6	17	78	68	44	
12.	Swansea Town AFC (Swansea)	42	15	10	17	82	84	40	
13.	Lincoln City FC (Lincoln)	42	16	7	19	75	78	39	
14.	Brighton & Hove Albion FC (Hove)	42	13	12	17	67	76	38	
15.	Scunthorpe United FC (Scunthorpe)	42	13	10	19	57	71	36	
16.	Sunderland AFC (Sunderland)	42	12	12	18	52	65	36	
17.	Stoke City FC (Stoke-on-Trent)	42	14	7	21	66	83	35	
18.	Derby County FC (Derby)	42	14	7	21	61	77	35	
19.	Plymouth Argyle FC (Plymouth)	42	13	9	20	61	89	35	
20.	Portsmouth FC (Portsmouth)	42	10	12	20	59	77	32	
21.	Hull City AFC (Kingston-upon-Hull)	42	10	10	22	48	76	30	R
22.	Bristol City FC (Bristol)	42	11	5	26	60	97	27	R
		924	352	220	352	1565	1565	924	

Football League Division 3 1959-60 Season	Accrington Stanley	Barnsley	Bournemouth	Bradford City	Brentford	Bury	Chesterfield	Colchester United	Coventry City	Grimsby Town	Halifax Town	Mansfield Town	Newport County	Norwich City	Port Vale	Q.P.R.	Reading	Shrewsbury Town	Southampton	Southend United	Swindon Town	Tranmere Rovers	Wrexham	York City
Accrington Stanley		2-1	2-1	0-4	3-4	1-3	1-3	1-2	0-2	2-4	0-5	0-1	0-0	3-4	1-3	1-2	0-0	2-2	2-2	0-4	3-1	1-3	2-2	4-0
Barnsley FC	5-0		1-0	2-0	1-2	2-2	3-1	2-1	1-0	3-3	1-2	2-2	0-2	2-0	1-0	2-1	3-3	0-0	1-0	4-1	0-3	2-0	6-1	1-1
Bournemouth & Bos.	3-1	1-1		3-2	1-2	2-1	1-1	3-2	2-2	4-2	1-0	6-0	4-1	0-0	3-0	1-1	1-1	2-2	1-3	0-0	3-1	2-1	1-3	2-0
Bradford City AFC	4-5	0-0	0-0		0-2	0-0	1-0	0-0	1-3	2-2	1-2	4-1	6-2	1-1	3-1	3-1	0-2	2-3	2-0	3-1	1-0	1-0	2-2	2-0
Brentford FC	3-0	3-0	1-0	4-0		1-1	3-0	2-0	3-1	0-2	1-1	1-1	1-2	3-4	2-0	1-1	2-2	2-2	3-1	2-1	2-1	3-1	1-2	
Bury FC	0-1	0-2	0-2	0-0	1-0		1-1	3-1	2-1	1-1	2-2	4-1	0-1	1-0	3-1	2-0	1-0	2-1	1-2	3-0	0-3	4-1	3-2	2-0
Chesterfield FC	0-3	4-1	4-0	1-2	1-0	0-2		1-1	0-3	2-2	2-1	0-1	2-0	2-1	4-1	0-4	2-1	2-2	3-2	1-0	1-3	2-0	5-1	2-0
Colchester United FC	5-1	2-2	1-2	2-1	2-1	3-0	1-0		0-0	2-2	1-0	3-0	2-1	3-0	3-1	2-0	4-2	3-2	1-1	2-3	0-0	4-0	3-1	2-0
Coventry City FC	2-1	2-1	4-0	2-2	2-1	0-1	1-0	3-1		0-2	0-1	2-0	1-1	2-1	1-1	0-0	1-1	4-1	2-0	3-1	1-0	5-3	5-2	
Grimsby Town FC	4-0	2-0	1-1	1-3	1-3	2-2	5-1	4-1	3-0		3-2	2-1	0-1	1-1	1-1	3-1	1-1	3-2	1-1	3-0	1-1	3-1	3-1	2-2
Halifax Town AFC	0-2	5-0	1-0	4-0	1-0	1-0	0-1	3-2	2-2	1-2		4-2	2-1	0-1	1-1	3-1	1-2	1-2	3-1	2-1	3-1	0-3	2-0	1-2
Mansfield Town FC	4-1	1-4	3-4	0-0	0-1	1-5	4-1	1-3	2-4	3-2	1-1		3-1	3-2	6-3	4-3	4-4	1-0	4-2	1-1	1-2	0-2	6-2	2-0
Newport County AFC	1-3	4-0	5-2	2-0	4-2	3-1	3-1	3-2	2-0	0-2	5-1	0-1		1-1	4-3	2-3	3-2	1-3	5-1	1-1	1-3	2-1	4-1	3-2
Norwich City FC	4-0	0-0	2-3	0-0	2-1	2-0	3-0	3-2	1-4	1-1	3-0	5-1	1-0		5-1	1-0	4-2	1-1	1-2	4-3	3-2	3-0	3-1	1-0
Port Vale FC	2-0	1-0	1-0	0-2	3-1	3-0	3-1	1-1	0-1	2-1	7-0	4-1	2-1	2-1		0-0	4-1	0-3	1-1	3-1	6-1	1-1	3-1	2-0
Queen's Park Rangers	5-1	1-0	3-0	5-0	2-4	2-3	3-3	3-1	2-1	0-0	3-0	2-0	3-0	0-0	2-2		2-0	1-1	0-1	0-0	2-0	2-1	2-1	0-0
Reading FC	2-0	3-2	2-2	1-0	3-3	0-1	6-3	2-1	4-2	1-2	1-1	3-2	0-1	0-2	2-3	2-0		2-3	2-0	4-1	3-0	5-4	0-1	1-0
Shrewsbury Town FC	5-0	2-2	0-0	3-0	1-1	0-2	2-4	1-1	3-2	5-2	2-2	6-3	6-2	1-3	2-1	1-1	3-2		1-1	1-3	3-0	4-1	3-2	4-0
Southampton FC	5-1	2-1	4-3	2-0	2-0	0-2	4-3	4-2	5-1	1-1	3-2	5-2	2-0	2-2	3-2	2-1	1-0	6-3		3-1	5-1	1-1	3-0	3-1
Southend United FC	6-1	2-2	3-0	2-1	2-0	0-4	1-2	1-0	1-0	3-0	0-2	3-2	1-0	2-1	3-2	2-1	2-1	2-4			1-3	7-1	1-1	1-1
Swindon Town FC	0-1	1-1	2-0	5-3	0-0	1-0	1-1	4-3	2-0	3-2	1-1	2-1	1-0	0-1	2-3	2-1	0-4	4-2	0-3	2-0		1-1	4-1	1-1
Tranmere Rovers FC	5-1	2-0	1-1	2-3	2-1	2-0	3-0	1-1	3-1	2-0	1-1	4-2	2-2	0-0	6-0	0-3	0-1	3-3	2-4	1-0	2-2		4-1	2-2
Wrexham AFC	2-3	1-0	1-2	4-3	3-2	1-1	2-3	1-1	1-3	2-1	2-1	3-0	0-0	1-2	1-0	1-1	2-1	1-1	2-1	3-1	1-2	1-0		3-1
York City FC	3-0	0-0	3-2	1-1	0-1	1-0	1-0	2-3	1-1	3-3	1-2	2-1	2-0	1-2	2-0	2-1	2-3	0-1	2-2	2-3	1-0	3-0	3-0	

	Division 3	Pd	Wn	Dw	Ls	GF	GA	Pts	
1.	Southampton FC (Southampton)	46	26	9	11	106	75	61	P
2.	Norwich City FC (Norwich)	46	24	11	11	82	54	59	P
3.	Shrewsbury Town FC (Shrewsbury)	46	18	16	12	97	75	52	
4.	Coventry City FC (Coventry)	46	21	10	15	78	63	52	
5.	Grimsby Town FC (Cleethorpes)	46	18	16	12	87	70	52	
6.	Brentford FC (London)	46	21	9	16	78	61	51	
7.	Bury FC (Bury)	46	21	9	16	64	51	51	
8.	Queen's Park Rangers FC (London)	46	18	13	15	73	54	49	
9.	Colchester United FC (Colchester)	46	19	11	17	83	74	47	
10.	Bournemouth & Boscombe Athletic FC (Bournemouth)	46	17	13	16	72	72	47	
11.	Reading FC (Reading)	46	18	10	18	84	77	46	
12.	Southend United FC (Southend-on-Sea)	46	19	8	19	76	74	46	
13.	Newport County AFC (Newport)	46	20	6	20	80	79	46	
14.	Port Vale FC (Stoke-on-Trent)	46	19	8	19	80	79	46	
15.	Halifax Town AFC (Halifax)	46	19	10	18	70	72	46	
16.	Swindon Town FC (Swindon)	46	19	8	19	69	78	46	
17.	Barnsley FC (Barnsley)	46	15	14	17	65	66	44	
18.	Chesterfield FC (Chesterfield)	46	18	7	21	71	84	43	
19.	Bradford City AFC (Bradford)	46	15	12	19	66	74	42	
20.	Tranmere Rovers FC (Birkenhead)	46	14	13	19	72	75	41	
21.	York City FC (York)	46	13	12	21	57	73	38	R
22.	Mansfield Town FC (Mansfield)	46	15	6	25	81	112	36	R
23.	Wrexham AFC (Wrexham)	46	14	8	24	68	101	36	R
24.	Accrington Stanley FC (Accrington)	46	11	5	30	57	123	27	R
		1104	430	244	430	1816	1816	1104	

Football League Division 4 — 1959-60 Season

	Aldershot Town	Barrow	Bradford P.A.	Carlisle United	Chester	Crewe Alexandra	Crystal Palace	Darlington	Doncaster Rovers	Exeter City	Gateshead	Gillingham	Hartlepools	Millwall	Northampton Town	Notts County	Oldham Athletic	Rochdale	Southport	Stockport County	Torquay United	Walsall	Watford	Workington
Aldershot Town FC		6-1	6-1	0-2	3-2	6-1	1-0	3-0	1-1	1-0	3-2	3-1	3-0	1-2	3-0	1-1	2-0	0-0	0-0	1-0	1-3	0-2	2-2	3-1
Barrow AFC	3-0		3-3	5-1	3-0	0-0	0-1	4-1	1-1	3-3	2-2	0-1	2-2	2-2	0-1	4-3	2-0	3-0	3-1	5-1	1-1	2-3	2-1	2-1
Bradford Park Ave.	3-2	2-0		1-1	1-1	2-2	3-1	1-0	3-3	1-0	4-2	3-0	6-2	1-1	3-0	1-1	2-0	0-0	3-0	1-1	2-2	1-3	1-1	3-2
Carlisle United FC	0-0	0-1	1-3		2-1	4-1	2-2	1-0	2-0	0-4	4-0	0-1	1-1	3-3	0-2	2-0	0-1	1-1	1-0	0-4	2-0	1-1	1-0	0-1
Chester FC	5-1	3-2	1-1	0-1		0-0	0-1	1-1	2-0	1-0	4-2	4-1	1-1	2-1	1-1	2-1	0-0	2-1	2-2	1-2	1-1	1-3	0-1	3-1
Crewe Alexandra FC	3-2	3-2	4-1	3-0	2-1		1-1	5-0	2-0	1-1	4-1	1-2	1-0	2-0	0-1	2-1	2-2	1-3	5-1	4-2	1-2	1-5	1-3	2-0
Crystal Palace FC	1-1	9-0	1-0	2-1	3-4	4-0		2-0	4-0	1-0	2-2	3-3	5-2	1-2	0-1	1-1	3-2	4-0	2-2	3-1	1-1	1-2	8-1	0-1
Darlington FC	4-0	3-1	4-3	2-1	0-0	1-1	1-1		2-2	0-1	2-1	2-0	1-3	5-2	1-3	0-0	5-0	1-2	1-0	0-2			0-3	0-3
Doncaster Rovers FC	1-2	1-4	2-0	4-1	2-0	4-0	1-2	0-1		0-1	1-0	3-0	5-1	0-0	3-2	0-4	0-0	2-1	5-0	1-0	1-3	1-1	1-0	2-0
Exeter City FC	3-1	2-2	3-1	1-3	2-0	2-4	2-2	0-0	4-2		2-1	2-0	5-0	2-2	1-1	3-3	4-3	4-1	1-1	2-1	1-0	1-2	2-0	1-0
Gateshead FC	4-1	3-1	1-2	1-0	0-1	4-2	0-2	1-3	5-0	1-0		2-2	1-1	1-0	1-3	0-0	2-0	1-2	1-0	2-1	0-2	3-0	1-3	2-1
Gillingham FC	3-1	1-0	2-0	3-1	3-1	1-1	0-0	2-0	2-1	2-1	5-4		3-1	3-1	2-1	0-2	4-1	0-2	1-0	4-0	1-1	3-0	1-2	0-0
Hartlepools United	3-0	0-1	3-0	1-2	2-3	2-0	1-0	1-2	2-6	4-3	3-0	3-1		0-2	1-4	2-4	2-2	0-1	3-2	2-1	4-0	1-2	0-0	1-4
Millwall FC	2-0	3-3	2-0	1-1	7-1	1-4	1-0	5-2	1-1	2-3	4-0	3-3	4-0		2-1	1-1	0-1	2-0	2-2	3-2	2-0	1-1	2-2	3-0
Northampton Town	2-0	6-0	3-1	2-2	1-0	0-0	0-2	3-1	3-1	1-1	2-0	2-1	3-0	0-3		4-2	8-1	3-1	2-2	1-1	3-0	1-0	1-2	0-0
Notts County FC	5-3	1-2	0-1	2-1	2-1	4-1	7-1	5-4	3-4	4-0	3-1	4-0	2-1	2-1			3-1	2-1	4-1	3-0	1-1	2-1	2-1	2-0
Oldham Athletic AFC	0-1	1-0	2-0	0-1	0-0	2-4	1-0	1-3	1-1	1-2	1-1	3-1	1-2	1-1	0-1	0-3		1-0	0-1	0-0	0-2	2-4	0-0	2-2
Rochdale AFC	2-0	4-1	0-1	3-0	0-0	4-2	4-0	2-0	2-0	3-0	2-0	1-0	2-0	0-1	2-2	1-4	2-0		1-0	3-0	4-2	0-2	3-3	1-1
Southport FC	0-4	1-0	1-1	1-1	3-1	0-1	3-1	0-1	1-1	3-2	1-0	1-1	2-1	1-0	0-4	1-2	1-0	2-2		3-0	1-2	1-4	1-1	2-2
Stockport County FC	1-1	1-2	0-0	0-0	3-0	1-0	1-0	1-0	2-0	1-0	1-1	2-2	2-2	3-0	3-1	3-1	2-1	1-0			0-1	2-0	4-0	2-0
Torquay United FC	2-1	3-2	1-1	2-1	1-2	5-2	2-1	1-2	2-1	2-3	1-0	2-0	3-0	2-3	3-1	4-1	1-1	4-0	4-0			2-1	2-1	2-1
Walsall FC	1-0	2-1	2-1	0-1	2-1	3-1	3-0	1-0	5-2	2-2	2-2	2-3	2-2	2-1	1-2	2-2	2-1	4-2	8-0	3-1	3-2		3-4	2-2
Watford FC	1-3	2-0	1-0	3-1	4-2	2-0	4-2	2-1	1-2	5-2	5-0	3-1	7-2	0-2	3-1	4-2	6-0	2-1	2-1	0-0	0-1	2-2		3-2
Workington AFC	3-3	1-1	0-1	1-0	5-0	5-0	1-1	1-1	2-0	2-1	1-1	1-1	3-0	4-0	5-1	0-1	2-0	2-0	1-1	1-1	0-2	0-3	0-1	

Division 4

		Pd	Wn	Dw	Ls	GF	GA	Pts	
1.	Walsall FC (Walsall)	46	28	9	9	102	60	65	P
2.	Notts County FC (Nottingham)	46	26	8	12	107	69	60	P
3.	Torquay United FC (Torquay)	46	26	8	12	84	58	60	P
4.	Watford FC (Watford)	46	24	9	13	92	67	57	P
5.	Millwall FC (London)	46	18	17	11	84	61	53	
6.	Northampton Town FC (Northampton)	46	22	9	15	85	63	53	
7.	Gillingham FC (Gillingham)	46	21	10	15	74	69	52	
8.	Crystal Palace FC (London)	46	19	12	15	84	64	50	
9.	Exeter City FC (Exeter)	46	19	11	16	80	70	49	
10.	Stockport County FC (Stockport)	46	19	11	16	58	54	49	
11.	Bradford Park Avenue FC (Bradford)	46	17	15	14	70	68	49	
12.	Rochdale AFC (Rochdale)	46	18	10	18	65	60	46	
13.	Aldershot FC (Aldershot)	46	18	9	19	77	74	45	
14.	Crewe Alexandra FC (Crewe)	46	18	9	19	79	88	45	
15.	Darlington FC (Darlington)	46	17	9	20	63	73	43	
16.	Workington AFC (Workington)	46	14	14	18	68	60	42	
17.	Doncaster Rovers FC (Doncaster)	46	16	10	20	69	76	42	
18.	Barrow AFC (Barrow-in-Furness)	46	15	11	20	77	87	41	
19.	Carlisle United FC (Carlisle)	46	15	11	20	51	66	41	
20.	Chester FC (Chester)	46	14	12	20	59	77	40	
21.	Southport FC (Southport)	46	10	14	22	48	92	34	
22.	Gateshead FC (Gateshead)	46	12	9	25	58	86	33	#
23.	Oldham Athletic AFC (Oldham)	46	8	12	26	41	83	28	
24.	Hartlepools United FC (Hartlepool)	46	10	7	29	59	109	27	
		1104	424	256	424	1734	1734	1104	

\# Gateshead FC (Gateshead) were not re-elected to the league for the next season and were replaced by Peterborough United FC (Peterborough).

F.A. CUP FINAL   (Wembley Stadium, London – 07/05/1960 – 100,000)

WOLVERHAMPTON WANDERERS FC   3-0   Blackburn Rovers FC (Blackburn)

McGrath o.g., Deeley 2

Wolves: Finlayson, Showell, Harris, Clamp, Slater, Flowers, Deeley, Stobart, Murray, Broadbent, Horne.

Blackburn: Leyland, Bray, Whelan, Clayton, Woods, McGrath, Bimpson, Dobing, Dougan, Douglas, MacLeod.

Semi-finals

| Aston Villa FC (Birmingham) | 0-1 | Wolverhampton Wanderers FC (Wolverhampton) |
| Blackburn Rovers FC (Blackburn) | 2-1 | Sheffield Wednesday FC (Sheffield) |

Quarter-finals

Aston Villa FC (Birmingham)	2-0	Preston North End FC (Preston)
Burnley FC (Burnley)	3-3, 0-2	Blackburn Rovers FC (Blackburn)
Leicester City FC (Leicester)	1-2	Wolverhampton Wanderers FC (Wolverhampton)
Sheffield United FC (Sheffield)	0-2	Sheffield Wednesday FC (Sheffield)

1960-61

Football League Division 1 — 1960-61 Season

	Arsenal	Aston Villa	Birmingham City	Blackburn Rovers	Blackpool	Bolton Wanderers	Burnley	Cardiff City	Chelsea	Everton	Fulham	Leicester City	Manchester City	Manchester United	Newcastle United	Nottingham Forest	Preston North End	Sheffield Wed.	Tottenham Hotspur	W.B.A.	West Ham United	Wolves
Arsenal FC		2-1	2-0	0-0	1-0	5-1	2-5	2-3	1-4	3-2	4-2	1-3	5-4	2-1	5-0	3-0	1-0	1-1	2-3	1-0	0-0	1-5
Aston Villa FC	2-2		6-2	2-2	2-2	4-0	2-0	2-1	3-2	3-2	2-1	1-3	5-1	3-1	2-0	1-2	1-0	4-1	1-2	0-1	2-1	0-2
Birmingham City FC	2-0	1-1		1-1	0-2	2-2	0-1	2-1	1-0	2-4	1-0	0-2	3-2	3-1	2-1	3-1	1-3	1-1	2-3	3-1	4-2	1-2
Blackburn Rovers FC	2-4	4-1	2-0		2-0	3-1	1-4	2-2	3-1	1-3	5-1	1-1	4-1	1-2	2-4	4-1	1-1	1-4	2-1	4-1	2-1	
Blackpool FC	1-1	5-3	1-2	2-0		0-1	0-0	6-1	1-4	1-4	2-5	5-1	3-3	2-0	2-1	4-0	0-1	0-1	1-3	0-1	3-0	5-2
Bolton Wanderers FC	1-1	3-0	2-2	0-0	3-1		3-5	3-0	4-1	3-4	0-3	2-0	3-1	1-1	2-1	3-1	1-1	0-1	1-2	0-1	3-1	0-2
Burnley FC	3-2	1-1	2-1	1-1	1-2	2-0		1-2	4-4	1-3	5-0	3-2	1-3	5-3	5-3	4-1	5-0	3-4	4-2	1-1	2-2	5-3
Cardiff City AFC	1-0	1-1	0-2	1-1	0-2	0-1	2-1		2-1	1-1	2-0	2-1	3-3	3-0	3-2	1-3	2-0	0-1	3-2	1-1	1-1	3-2
Chelsea FC	3-1	2-4	3-2	5-2	2-2	1-1	2-6	6-1		3-3	2-1	1-3	6-3	1-2	4-2	4-3	1-1	0-2	2-3	7-1	3-2	3-3
Everton FC	4-1	1-2	1-0	2-2	1-0	1-2	0-3	5-1	1-1		1-0	3-1	4-2	4-0	5-0	1-0	0-0	4-2	1-3	1-1	4-1	3-1
Fulham FC	2-2	1-1	2-1	1-1	4-3	2-2	0-1	2-2	3-2	2-3		4-2	1-0	4-4	4-3	1-0	2-0	1-6	0-0	1-2	1-1	1-3
Leicester City FC	2-1	3-1	3-2	2-4	1-1	2-0	2-2	3-0	1-3	4-1	1-2		1-2	6-0	5-3	1-1	5-2	2-1	1-2	2-2	5-1	2-0
Manchester City FC	0-0	4-1	2-1	4-0	1-1	0-0	2-1	4-2	2-1	2-1	3-2	3-1		1-3	3-3	1-2	2-3	1-1	0-1	3-0	1-2	2-4
Manchester United FC	1-1	1-1	4-1	1-3	2-0	3-1	6-0	3-3	6-0	4-0	3-1	1-1	5-1		3-2	2-1	1-0	0-0	2-0	3-0	6-1	1-3
Newcastle United FC	3-3	2-1	2-2	3-1	4-3	4-1	0-1	5-0	1-6	0-4	7-2	1-3	1-3	1-1		2-2	0-1	3-4	3-2		5-5	4-4
Nottingham Forest FC	3-5	2-0	1-0	1-1	0-0	2-2	3-1	2-1	2-1	1-2	4-2	2-2	2-2	3-2	0-2		2-0	1-2	0-4	1-2	1-1	1-1
Preston North End FC	2-0	1-1	2-3	2-0	0-0	0-0	2-3	1-1	0-2	1-1	2-0	0-0	1-1	2-4	2-3	0-1		2-2	0-1	2-1	4-0	1-2
Sheffield Wednesday FC	1-1	1-2	2-0	5-4	4-0	2-0	3-1	2-0	1-0	1-2	2-0	2-2	3-1	5-1	1-1	5-1	1-0		2-1	1-0	1-0	0-0
Tottenham Hotspur FC	4-2	6-2	6-0	5-2	3-1	3-1	4-4	3-2	4-2	2-0	5-1	2-3	1-1	4-1	1-2	1-0	5-0	2-1		1-2	2-0	1-1
West Bromwich Albion FC	2-3	0-2	1-2	1-2	3-1	3-2	0-2	1-1	3-0	3-0	2-4	1-0	6-3	1-1	6-0	1-2	3-1	2-2	1-3		1-0	2-1
West Ham United FC	6-0	5-2	4-3	3-2	3-3	2-1	1-2	2-0	3-1	4-0	1-2	1-0	1-1	2-1	1-1	2-4	5-2	1-1	0-3	1-2		5-0
Wolverhampton Wanderers FC	5-3	3-2	5-1	0-0	1-0	3-1	2-1	2-2	6-1	4-1	2-4	3-2	1-0	2-1	5-3	3-0	4-1	0-4	4-2	4-2		

	Division 1	Pd	Wn	Dw	Ls	GF	GA	Pts	
1.	TOTTENHAM HOTSPUR FC (LONDON)	42	31	4	7	115	55	66	
2.	Sheffield Wednesday FC (Sheffield)	42	23	12	7	78	47	58	
3.	Wolverhampton Wanderers FC (Wolverhampton)	42	25	7	10	103	75	57	
4.	Burnley FC (Burnley)	42	22	7	13	102	77	51	
5.	Everton FC (Liverpool)	42	22	6	14	87	69	50	
6.	Leicester City FC (Leicester)	42	18	9	15	87	70	45	
7.	Manchester United FC (Manchester)	42	18	9	15	88	76	45	
8.	Blackburn Rovers FC (Blackburn)	42	15	13	14	77	76	43	
9.	Aston Villa FC (Birmingham)	42	17	9	16	78	77	43	
10.	West Bromwich Albion FC (West Bromwich)	42	18	5	19	67	71	41	
11.	Arsenal FC (London)	42	15	11	16	77	85	41	
12.	Chelsea FC (London)	42	15	7	20	98	100	37	
13.	Manchester City FC (Manchester)	42	13	11	18	79	90	37	
14.	Nottingham Forest FC (Nottingham)	42	14	9	19	62	78	37	
15.	Cardiff City AFC (Cardiff)	42	13	11	18	60	85	37	
16.	West Ham United FC (London)	42	13	10	19	77	88	36	
17.	Fulham FC (London)	42	14	8	20	72	95	36	
18.	Bolton Wanderers FC (Bolton)	42	12	11	19	58	73	35	
19.	Birmingham City FC (Birmingham)	42	14	6	22	62	84	34	
20.	Blackpool FC (Blackpool)	42	12	9	21	68	73	33	
21.	Newcastle United FC (Newcastle-upon-Tyne)	42	11	10	21	86	109	32	R
22.	Preston North End FC (Preston)	42	10	10	22	43	71	30	R
		924	365	194	365	1724	1724	924	

Top Goalscorer

1) James GREAVES (Chelsea FC) 41

Football League Division 2 — 1960-61 Season

	Brighton & Hove Albion	Bristol Rovers	Charlton Athletic	Derby County	Huddersfield Town	Ipswich Town	Leeds United	Leyton Orient	Lincoln City	Liverpool	Luton Town	Middlesbrough	Norwich City	Plymouth Argyle	Portsmouth	Rotherham United	Scunthorpe United	Sheffield United	Southampton	Stoke City	Sunderland	Swansea Town
Brighton & Hove Albion FC		6-1	3-5	3-2	2-1	2-4	2-1	1-1	1-0	3-1	1-0	0-1	2-2	2-0	2-2	1-0	1-1	0-0	0-1	0-1	1-2	0-0
Bristol Rovers FC	0-1		3-1	1-1	1-2	1-1	4-4	4-2	3-1	4-3	4-1	2-3	3-1	2-5	2-0	2-1	3-3	3-1	4-2	1-0	1-0	4-2
Charlton Athletic FC	3-1	2-1		3-1	2-3	0-2	2-0	2-0	3-0	1-3	4-1	6-6	0-1	6-4	7-4	4-3	1-1	2-3	1-3	3-1	2-2	6-2
Derby County FC	4-1	1-1	2-3		1-1	1-4	2-3	3-1	3-1	1-4	4-1	1-0	0-0	4-1	6-2	3-0	2-5	2-0	2-2	1-1	1-1	2-3
Huddersfield Town AFC	0-1	4-0	2-2	1-3		1-3	0-1	1-0	4-1	2-4	1-1	1-0	1-1	1-5	3-3	0-1	1-2	0-1	3-1	0-0	4-2	3-1
Ipswich Town FC	4-0	3-2	2-1	4-1	4-2		4-0	6-2	3-1	1-0	0-1	3-1	4-1	3-1	2-2	1-1	2-0	0-1	3-3	2-1	4-0	0-3
Leeds United AFC	3-2	1-1	1-0	3-3	1-4	2-5		1-3	7-0	2-2	1-2	4-4	1-0	2-1	0-0	2-0	2-2	1-2	3-0	0-1	2-4	2-2
Leyton Orient FC	2-1	3-2	1-1	2-1	2-0	1-3	0-1		1-2	1-3	2-1	1-1	1-0	1-1	2-1	2-1	1-4	1-1	3-1	0-1	0-1	2-2
Lincoln City FC	2-1	1-2	2-2	3-4	0-0	1-4	2-3	2-0		1-2	1-1	5-2	1-4	3-1	2-3	0-1	0-2	0-5	0-3	1-1	1-2	2-0
Liverpool FC	2-0	3-0	2-1	1-0	3-1	1-1	2-0	5-0	2-0		2-2	3-4	2-1	1-1	3-3	2-1	3-2	4-2	0-1	3-0	1-1	4-0
Luton Town FC	3-1	4-2	4-1	1-1	1-0	3-2	1-1	0-1	3-0	2-1		6-1	0-2	3-2	1-0	2-1	0-0	1-4	4-1	4-1	3-3	2-2
Middlesbrough FC	2-2	1-1	2-2	1-2	2-1	3-1	3-0	2-0	1-1	1-1	2-1		2-0	3-1	3-0	2-2	1-3	3-1	5-0	1-0	1-0	3-1
Norwich City FC	2-2	2-1	4-0	0-2	2-0	0-3	3-2	3-2	5-1	2-1	2-1	4-1		1-0	3-1	3-1	0-1	1-1	5-0	1-0	3-0	0-0
Plymouth Argyle FC	1-2	5-0	6-4	4-2	2-1	1-2	3-1	3-2	1-1	0-4	1-1	3-3	3-0		5-1	3-3	3-1	2-0	1-3	3-1	1-0	1-0
Portsmouth FC	4-0	3-0	1-1	3-2	1-3	1-0	3-1	1-2	3-0	2-2	3-2	0-3	3-0	0-2		2-2	2-2	1-2	1-1	1-0	2-1	1-1
Rotherham United FC	5-2	4-0	2-3	1-1	2-2	1-1	1-3	2-1	2-0	1-0	5-2	1-2	0-2	0-0	1-0		4-0	1-2	1-0	0-0	0-0	3-3
Scunthorpe United FC	2-2	2-1	0-0	1-2	0-1	4-0	3-2	2-2	2-3	2-3	1-0	1-1	2-1	2-0	5-1	1-1		1-1	2-0	1-1	3-3	1-2
Sheffield United FC	2-1	2-3	1-0	3-1	3-1	1-3	3-2	4-1	2-1	1-1	2-1	4-1	1-1	3-0	3-1	3-1	2-0		2-1	4-1	0-1	3-0
Southampton FC	4-2	2-2	1-2	5-1	4-2	1-1	2-4	1-1	2-3	4-1	3-2	2-2	1-1	5-1	3-2	4-2	0-1			0-1	3+2	5-0
Stoke City FC	0-2	2-0	5-3	2-1	2-2	2-4	0-0	1-2	0-0	3-1	3-0	1-1	1-1	9-0	1-0	1-4	2-0	2-0	1-2		0-0	1-3
Sunderland AFC	2-1	2-0	2-2	1-2	1-2	2-0	2-3	4-1	2-2	1-1	7-1	2-0	0-3	2-1	4-1	1-1	0-1	1-1	3-1	4-0		2-1
Swansea Town AFC	2-3	2-1	3-3	2-1	2-0	2-1	3-2	1-0	1-2	2-0	3-1	3-2	4-1	1-2	4-0	2-1	2-2	3-0	4-1	0-0	3-3	

Division 2

		Pd	Wn	Dw	Ls	GF	GA	Pts	
1.	Ipswich Town FC (Ipswich)	42	26	7	9	100	55	59	P
2.	Sheffield United FC (Sheffield)	42	26	6	10	81	51	58	P
3.	Liverpool FC (Liverpool)	42	21	10	11	87	58	52	
4.	Norwich City FC (Norwich)	42	20	9	13	70	53	49	
5.	Middlesbrough FC (Middlesbrough)	42	18	12	12	83	74	48	
6.	Sunderland AFC (Sunderland)	42	17	13	12	75	60	47	
7.	Swansea Town AFC (Swansea)	42	18	11	13	77	73	47	
8.	Southampton FC (Southampton)	42	18	8	16	84	81	44	
9.	Scunthorpe United FC (Scunthorpe)	42	14	15	13	69	64	43	
10.	Charlton Athletic FC (London)	42	16	11	15	97	91	43	
11.	Plymouth Argyle FC (Plymouth)	42	17	8	17	81	82	42	
12.	Derby County FC (Derby)	42	15	10	17	80	80	40	
13.	Luton Town FC (Luton)	42	15	9	18	71	79	39	
14.	Leeds United AFC (Leeds)	42	14	10	18	75	83	38	
15.	Rotherham United FC (Rotherham)	42	12	13	17	65	64	37	
16.	Brighton & Hove Albion FC (Hove)	42	14	9	19	61	75	37	
17.	Bristol Rovers FC (Bristol)	42	15	7	20	73	92	37	
18.	Stoke City FC (Stoke-on-Trent)	42	12	12	18	51	59	36	
19.	Leyton Orient FC (London)	42	14	8	20	55	78	36	
20.	Huddersfield Town AFC (Huddersfield)	42	13	9	20	62	71	35	
21.	Portsmouth FC (Portsmouth)	42	11	11	20	64	91	33	R
22.	Lincoln City FC (Lincoln)	42	8	8	26	48	95	24	R
		924	354	216	354	1609	1609	924	

Football League Division 3 — 1960-61 Season

	Barnsley	Bournemouth	Bradford City	Brentford	Bristol City	Bury	Chesterfield	Colchester United	Coventry City	Grimsby Town	Halifax Town	Hull City	Newport County	Notts County	Port Vale	Q.P.R.	Reading	Shrewsbury Town	Southend United	Swindon Town	Torquay United	Tranmere Rovers	Walsall	Watford
Barnsley FC		2-3	5-2	1-1	2-0	3-1	3-1	3-0	4-1	3-2	1-1	1-0	1-3	5-2	5-1	3-3	1-1	4-2	2-1	2-1	1-0	2-1	2-2	0-1
Bournemouth & Bos.	1-2		2-2	0-1	2-2	0-3	1-0	4-4	2-1	2-1	1-2	2-2	2-2	1-3	1-1	1-0	2-0	2-2	3-2	2-1	1-3	2-1	0-3	0-1
Bradford City AFC	1-4	3-1		3-1	2-0	0-1	3-2	0-1	4-1	1-3	2-2	0-0	1-2	2-2	3-3	1-1	2-1	1-1	2-1	2-1	0-3	1-1	1-2	2-2
Brentford FC	0-0	2-2	2-2		2-0	1-5	2-2	0-0	1-1	0-1	2-0	2-2	2-4	3-0	0-0	2-0	1-4	1-0	1-1	2-1	2-3	4-1	3-1	2-1
Bristol City FC	4-0	1-0	1-2	3-0		1-2	3-0	5-0	2-0	2-1	3-2	1-2	3-0	2-1	3-4	1-1	2-0	0-0	2-0	1-1	2-2	2-0	2-0	4-1
Bury FC	2-1	1-1	2-2	1-0	1-0		3-3	4-0	1-0	2-0	4-1	3-0	4-1	7-0	3-1	1-0	3-0	3-1	2-0	3-0	6-0	3-0	3-4	0-2
Chesterfield FC	5-1	0-1	4-1	1-1	3-0	2-2		2-3	4-1	2-3	3-0	1-2	1-0	3-1	0-0	0-1	2-2	2-3	0-3	1-1	2-0	1-1	1-2	2-0
Colchester United FC	4-2	0-1	2-4	2-4	0-1	0-2	4-3		4-3	1-1	3-1	4-0	1-1	1-2	2-0	0-1	2-1	2-0	3-1	3-3	0-3	0-4		1-4
Coventry City FC	5-2	1-0	2-2	2-0	1-2	1-2	3-1	2-0		0-0	2-0	4-0	4-1	2-2	1-1	4-4	2-1	3-2	3-0	1-1	5-1	4-1	1-2	0-1
Grimsby Town FC	3-2	0-1	1-0	0-0	5-1	2-2	0-0	2-1	2-3		6-1	2-0	2-1	1-1	0-5	3-1	3-1	0-2	1-0	3-2	4-2	4-1	3-1	1-3
Halifax Town AFC	1-0	2-1	3-2	1-0	2-1	0-2	2-1	2-1	2-2	0-0		3-0	2-1	0-1	3-3	1-1	1-0	1-1	6-2	1-1	3-2	5-0	1-0	0-0
Hull City AFC	2-0	2-0	3-0	3-0	3-3	0-1	2-2	1-1	1-1	2-3	4-2		5-1	3-1	2-2	3-1	1-0	3-1	0-1	0-0	2-3	4-2	2-1	3-2
Newport County AFC	2-3	2-0	1-0	4-1	0-0	5-1	3-2	3-3	1-1	1-1	3-1			2-2	2-1	1-3	5-2	1-1	1-2	2-0	2-2	1-0	4-2	5-1
Notts County FC	5-1	3-2	2-1	0-0	3-0	0-3	1-0	4-2	3-0	0-1	1-1	2-1	6-0		2-2	2-1	4-2	1-2	1-0	0-1	4-1	3-1	3-1	
Port Vale FC	2-0	3-0	2-4	3-2	1-1	4-3	7-1	3-0	3-1	3-2	2-3	4-1	3-1	1-3		0-1	1-1	4-0	4-1	0-3	5-0	1-1	3-0	
Queen's Park Rangers	4-2	3-1	1-0	0-0	1-1	3-1	1-2	3-2	2-1	2-1	5-1	2-1	2-0	2-0	1-0		5-2	1-1	2-1	3-1	3-3	9-2	1-0	2-1
Reading FC	0-1	4-3	3-1	4-0	1-1	1-3	2-0	2-1	0-0	3-1	1-1	2-4	2-3	2-0	2-1	3-1		2-1	3-0	1-1	5-1	1-2	3-2	1-1
Shrewsbury Town FC	1-2	2-1	3-1	3-0	4-2	2-1	4-2	2-1	2-1	1-1	1-1	0-0	5-0	1-1	4-1	6-1	2-1		2-2	1-1	2-1	1-1	2-2	2-2
Southend United FC	2-0	0-0	0-0	1-1	1-0	0-3	1-1	2-1	4-1	1-1	2-2	3-1	4-2	3-1	0-0	0-1	1-1	2-2		0-2	3-2	1-2	1-2	6-1
Swindon Town FC	1-0	0-1	4-0	1-1	3-1	4-0	2-0	0-2	1-2	3-0	1-1	1-1	2-0	1-0	6-0	1-0	1-1	2-2	1-1		3-1	1-0	1-0	1-2
Torquay United FC	1-1	0-1	2-1	1-0	0-0	1-1	3-0	1-1	3-0	0-0	1-1	1-2	0-0	2-2	1-1	1-6	4-2	2-0	2-1	1-1		5-2	3-0	2-2
Tranmere Rovers FC	2-1	4-3	1-0	2-0	3-2	1-7	1-1	7-2	2-0	3-6	6-2	1-0	2-4	2-3	3-3	1-2	1-1	4-2	2-1	2-2	2-2		1-4	0-2
Walsall FC	1-0	2-0	4-0	4-0	4-0	1-0	2-1	3-0	1-1	2-1	0-0	1-0	2-2	2-1	6-2	4-3	2-2	3-2	5-1	2-1	3-0	3-1		5-2
Watford FC	1-2	0-1	2-2	6-1	0-1	1-1	3-1	2-2	7-2	2-0	4-3	2-2	4-1	2-2	0-0	0-3	2-0	3-1	3-0	1-0	3-0	2-2	2-0	

		Pd	Wn	Dw	Ls	GF	GA	Pts	
1.	Bury FC (Bury)	46	30	8	8	108	45	68	P
2.	Walsall FC (Walsall)	46	28	6	12	98	60	62	P
3.	Queen's Park Rangers FC (London)	46	25	10	11	93	60	60	
4.	Watford FC (Watford)	46	20	12	14	85	72	52	
5.	Notts County FC (Nottingham)	46	21	9	16	82	77	51	
6.	Grimsby Town FC (Cleethorpes)	46	20	10	16	77	69	50	
7.	Port Vale FC (Stoke-on-Trent)	46	17	15	14	96	79	49	
8.	Barnsley FC (Barnsley)	46	21	7	18	83	80	49	
9.	Halifax Town AFC (Halifax)	46	16	17	13	71	78	49	
10.	Shrewsbury Town FC (Shrewsbury)	46	15	16	15	83	75	46	
11.	Hull City AFC (Kingston-upon-Hull)	46	17	12	17	73	73	46	
12.	Torquay United FC (Torquay)	46	14	17	15	75	83	45	
13.	Newport County AFC (Newport)	46	17	11	18	81	90	45	
14.	Bristol City FC (Bristol)	46	17	10	19	70	68	44	
15.	Coventry City FC (Coventry)	46	16	12	18	80	83	44	
16.	Swindon Town FC (Swindon)	46	14	15	17	62	55	43	
17.	Brentford FC (London)	46	13	17	16	56	70	43	
18.	Reading FC (Reading)	46	14	12	20	72	83	40	
19.	Bournemouth & Boscombe Athletic FC (Bournemouth)	46	15	10	21	58	76	40	
20.	Southend United FC (Southend-on-Sea)	46	14	11	21	60	76	39	
21.	Tranmere Rovers FC (Birkenhead)	46	15	8	23	79	115	38	R
22.	Bradford City AFC (Bradford)	46	11	14	21	65	87	36	R
23.	Colchester United FC (Colchester)	46	11	11	24	68	101	33	R
24.	Chesterfield FC (Chesterfield)	46	10	12	24	67	87	32	R
		1104	411	282	411	1842	1842	1104	

Football League Division 4 — 1960-61 Season

	Accrington Stanley	Aldershot Town	Barrow	Bradford Park Avenue	Carlisle United	Chester	Crewe Alexandra	Crystal Palace	Darlington	Doncaster Rovers	Exeter City	Gillingham	Hartlepools	Mansfield Town	Millwall	Northampton Town	Oldham Athletic	Peterborough United	Rochdale	Southport	Stockport County	Workington	Wrexham	York City
Accrington Stanley		1-0	0-0	1-2	1-0	2-0	1-3	2-3	2-2	2-2	0-1	3-0	3-0	1-4	3-3	3-2	5-1	3-2	2-0	2-1	4-1	1-2	0-3	2-0
Aldershot Town FC	3-1		2-1	3-0	2-1	3-2	5-0	2-1	1-3	5-0	3-1	0-1	4-0	2-0	0-2	2-2	4-0	1-1	3-0	1-0	3-2	0-0	0-0	6-1
Barrow AFC	1-1	2-0		5-0	0-2	3-0	3-4	0-3	1-1	2-1	1-1	0-1	2-1	1-1	2-1	1-0	1-2	2-1	1-0	0-1	3-1	0-4	1-1	1-1
Bradford Park Ave.	2-2	1-0	4-0		0-0	1-0	2-0	3-1	1-0	1-1	5-2	0-0	1-3	2-1	2-1	1-3	5-1	1-0	2-1	1-0	4-2	4-0	3-1	3-3
Carlisle United FC	3-1	2-2	1-0	2-2		3-1	0-1	2-0	4-4	2-2	1-3	2-2	3-1	1-2	2-1	3-0	3-3	1-2	1-0	1-4	2-4	1-0	1-1	
Chester FC	2-3	2-0	0-0	3-1	3-2		0-0	3-0	0-3	1-2	4-4	2-2	1-2	3-3	1-4	0-2	3-1	1-2	3-1	1-0	0-0	2-2	1-0	2-1
Crewe Alexandra FC	0-1	2-1	0-1	1-1	3-0	5-2		1-2	1-1	1-1	2-0	2-1	3-0	1-2	2-2	0-2	2-1	3-1	3-0	0-1	4-1	1-2	2-1	1-5
Crystal Palace FC	9-2	2-1	4-2	4-1	1-1	5-1	0-0		3-2	5-1	0-0	2-0	2-2	4-1	0-2	2-3	2-1	0-2	4-1	5-0	2-1	4-2	3-2	1-0
Darlington FC	3-2	2-2	2-3	0-0	0-0	5-1	0-1	0-1		1-0	3-0	2-2	4-0	3-2	5-2	1-1	0-1	2-2	1-0	1-0	2-0	1-1	1-2	2-1
Doncaster Rovers FC	1-0	3-1	3-0	2-0	1-0	2-1	6-0	1-5	4-0		2-1	2-3	5-3	2-3	3-0	0-2	1-2	3-2	0-1	3-1	3-4	3-1	0-2	
Exeter City FC	2-4	1-0	2-2	4-2	0-0	4-1	0-1	2-3	1-3	2-0		2-0	2-1	0-2	2-3	1-3	3-0	3-4	1-0	2-1	2-1	0-0	1-0	2-1
Gillingham FC	2-1	5-2	2-2	3-4	1-1	3-0	0-0	1-2	0-1	2-0	4-2		5-1	0-0	1-2	0-1	2-3	4-4	0-0	2-0	1-1	4-2	0-3	3-2
Hartlepools United	4-1	3-1	0-2	2-4	0-1	4-4	1-2	2-4	5-0	1-0	0-0	1-0		3-2	2-2	4-2	5-1	2-0	1-5	0-2	4-1	0-0	1-3	
Mansfield Town FC	0-0	2-0	5-1	1-2	1-3	3-1	1-1	1-2	2-1	1-2	2-3	1-0	2-1		5-1	4-2	1-2	1-0	0-2	1-2	2-2	1-1	0-3	1-3
Millwall FC	2-2	2-2	3-0	5-1	4-2	5-1	2-3	0-2	0-1	0-1	2-2	1-2	5-2	3-0		3-1	0-1	4-3	4-1	3-1	3-0	0-3	2-0	3-2
Northampton Town	2-1	2-1	3-0	0-1	0-0	3-2	4-1	1-2	1-1	3-0	3-1	3-1	3-3	1-0	2-2		1-0	0-3	5-1	3-1	4-2	3-2	3-0	3-0
Oldham Athletic AFC	5-2	0-2	3-1	4-0	5-2	4-1	1-0	4-3	3-3	1-1	5-2	1-1	2-1	3-1	2-3	1-2		1-1	0-2	3-2	3-0	3-5	0-2	3-1
Peterborough United	3-0	7-1	6-2	3-1	5-0	6-0	4-1	4-1	5-1	6-2	7-1	2-0	3-2	2-1	4-2	3-3	2-2		4-3	3-4	0-1	2-1	3-0	1-1
Rochdale AFC	3-2	1-1	0-0	2-3	2-1	2-0	3-0	2-2	1-0	2-1	3-1	2-0	4-0	1-2	4-0	1-1	3-0	2-2		0-1	1-1	2-0	2-1	0-0
Southport FC	3-0	1-1	4-1	2-3	3-0	1-2	2-0	3-3	1-4	1-1	2-0	1-2	2-0	2-1	4-1	2-0	2-0	3-3	0-1		1-0	3-0	2-2	2-2
Stockport County FC	0-3	2-0	1-0	2-3	2-0	1-1	0-1	5-2	2-1	1-0	0-0	1-1	1-0	3-1	1-1	0-1	0-6	1-0	2-0			1-0	1-0	2-0
Workington AFC	2-1	0-4	3-1	1-3	2-1	1-0	0-0	1-0	1-3	1-3	3-1	2-0	2-0	1-3	2-2	3-0	1-1	0-3	3-0	3-1	1-0		3-1	2-0
Wrexham AFC	3-0	3-1	1-0	0-1	2-1	1-2	0-1	1-2	3-1	2-2	2-3	0-0	1-0	2-0	0-1	2-2	2-2	0-1	2-0	3-0	1-3	2-1		4-0
York City FC	1-0	4-1	2-0	2-0	4-0	2-0	3-1	0-2	4-1	1-1	6-1	0-0	4-0	3-2	3-2	0-1	1-0	0-1	2-0	2-0	0-0	4-0	2-1	

	Division 4	Pd	Wn	Dw	Ls	GF	GA	Pts	
1.	Peterborough United FC (Peterborough)	46	28	10	8	134	65	66	P
2.	Crystal Palace FC (London)	46	29	6	11	110	69	64	P
3.	Northampton Town FC (Northampton)	46	25	10	11	90	62	60	P
4.	Bradford Park Avenue FC (Bradford)	46	26	8	12	84	74	60	P
5.	York City FC (York)	46	21	9	16	80	60	51	
6.	Millwall FC (London)	46	21	8	17	97	86	50	
7.	Darlington FC (Darlington)	46	18	13	15	78	70	49	
8.	Workington AFC (Workington)	46	21	7	18	74	76	49	
9.	Crewe Alexandra FC (Crewe)	46	20	9	17	61	67	49	
10.	Aldershot FC (Aldershot)	46	18	9	19	79	69	45	
11.	Doncaster Rovers FC (Doncaster)	46	19	7	20	76	78	45	
12.	Oldham Athletic AFC (Oldham)	46	19	7	20	79	88	45	
13.	Stockport County FC (Stockport)	46	18	9	19	57	66	45	
14.	Southport FC (Southport)	46	19	6	21	69	67	44	
15.	Gillingham FC (Gillingham)	46	15	13	18	64	66	43	
16.	Wrexham AFC (Wrexham)	46	17	8	21	62	56	42	
17.	Rochdale AFC (Rochdale)	46	17	8	21	60	66	42	
18.	Accrington Stanley FC (Accrington)	46	16	8	22	74	88	40	
19.	Carlisle United FC (Carlisle)	46	13	13	20	61	79	39	
20.	Mansfield Town FC (Mansfield)	46	16	6	24	71	78	38	
21.	Exeter City FC (Exeter)	46	14	10	22	66	94	38	
22.	Barrow AFC (Barrow-in-Furness)	46	13	11	22	52	79	37	
23.	Hartlepools United FC (Hartlepool)	46	12	8	26	71	103	32	
24.	Chester FC (Chester)	46	11	9	26	61	104	31	
		1104	446	212	446	1810	1810	1104	

F.A. CUP FINAL   (Wembley Stadium, London – 06/05/1961 – 100,000)

TOTTENHAM HOTSPUR FC (LONDON)   2-0   Leicester City FC (Leicester)

Smith, Dyson

Tottenham: Brown, Baker, Henry, Blanchflower, M.Norman, Mackay, Jones, White, Smith, Allen, Dyson.

Leicester: Banks, Chalmers, R.Norman, McLintock, King, Appleton, Riley, Walsh, McIlmoyle, Keyworth, Cheesebrough.

Semi-finals

Burnley FC (Burnley)   0-3   Tottenham Hotspur FC (London)
Leicester City FC (Leicester)   0-0, 0-0, 2-0   Sheffield United FC (Sheffield)

Quarter-finals

Leicester City FC (Leicester)   0-0, 2-1   Barnsley FC (Barnsley)
Newcastle United FC (Newcastle-upon-Tyne)   1-3   Sheffield United FC (Sheffield)
Sheffield Wednesday FC (Sheffield)   0-0, 0-2   Burnley FC (Burnley)
Sunderland AFC (Sunderland)   1-1, 0-5   Tottenham Hotspur FC (London)

Football League Division 1 1961-62 Season	Arsenal	Aston Villa	Birmingham C.	Blackburn R.	Blackpool	Bolton Wands.	Burnley	Cardiff City	Chelsea	Everton	Fulham	Ipswich Town	Leicester City	Man. City	Man. United	Nottingham F.	Sheffield Utd.	Sheffield Wed.	Tottenham H.	W.B.A.	West Ham Utd.	Wolves
Arsenal FC		4-5	1-1	0-0	3-0	1-2	2-2	1-1	0-3	2-3	1-0	0-3	4-4	3-0	5-1	2-1	2-0	1-0	2-1	0-1	2-2	3-1
Aston Villa FC	3-1		1-3	1-0	5-0	3-0	0-2	2-2	3-1	1-1	2-0	3-0	8-3	2-1	1-1	5-1	0-0	1-0	0-0	1-0	2-4	1-0
Birmingham City FC	1-0	0-2		2-1	1-1	2-1	2-6	3-0	3-2	0-0	2-1	3-1	1-5	1-1	1-1	1-1	3-0	1-1	2-3	1-2	4-0	3-6
Blackburn Rovers FC	0-0	4-2	2-0		1-1	2-3	2-1	0-0	3-0	1-1	0-2	2-2	2-1	4-1	3-0	2-1	1-2	0-2	0-1	1-1	1-0	2-1
Blackpool FC	0-1	1-2	1-0	2-1		2-1	1-1	3-0	4-0	1-1	2-1	1-1	2-1	3-1	2-3	1-3	2-4	1-3	1-2	2-2	2-0	7-2
Bolton Wanderers FC	2-1	1-1	3-2	1-1	0-0		0-0	1-1	4-2	1-1	2-3	0-0	1-0	0-2	1-0	6-1	2-0	4-3	1-2	3-2	1-0	1-0
Burnley FC	0-2	3-0	7-1	0-1	2-0	3-1		2-1	1-1	2-1	2-1	4-3	2-0	6-3	1-3	0-0	4-2	4-0	2-2	3-1	6-0	3-3
Cardiff City AFC	1-1	1-0	3-2	1-1	3-2	1-2	1-1		5-2	0-0	0-3	0-3	0-4	0-0	1-2	2-2	1-1	2-1	1-1	2-2	3-0	2-3
Chelsea FC	2-3	1-0	1-1	1-1	1-0	1-0	1-2	2-3		1-1	0-0	2-2	1-3	1-1	2-0	2-2	6-1	1-0	0-2	4-1	0-1	4-5
Everton FC	4-1	2-0	4-1	1-0	2-2	1-0	2-2	8-3	4-0		3-0	5-2	3-2	0-2	5-1	6-0	1-0	0-4	3-0	3-1	3-0	4-0
Fulham FC	5-2	3-1	0-1	2-0	0-1	2-2	3-5	0-1	3-4	2-1		1-2	2-1	3-4	2-0	1-1	5-2	0-2	1-1	1-2	2-0	0-1
Ipswich Town FC	2-2	2-0	4-1	2-1	1-1	2-1	6-2	1-0	5-2	4-2	2-4		1-0	2-4	4-1	1-0	4-0	2-1	3-2	3-0	4-2	3-2
Leicester City FC	0-1	0-2	1-2	2-0	0-2	1-1	2-6	3-0	2-0	2-0	4-1	0-2		2-0	4-3	2-1	4-1	1-0	2-3	1-0	2-2	3-0
Manchester City FC	3-2	1-0	1-4	3-1	2-4	2-1	1-3	1-2	2-2	1-3	2-1	3-0	3-1		0-2	3-0	1-1	3-1	6-2	3-1	3-5	2-2
Manchester United FC	2-3	2-0	0-2	6-1	0-1	0-3	1-4	3-0	3-2	1-1	3-0	5-0	2-2	3-2		6-3	0-1	1-1	1-0	4-1	1-2	0-2
Nottingham Forest FC	0-1	2-0	2-1	1-2	3-4	0-1	3-2	2-1	3-0	2-1	1-1	1-1	0-0	1-2	1-0		2-0	3-1	2-0	4-4	3-0	3-1
Sheffield United FC	2-1	0-2	3-1	0-0	2-1	3-1	2-0	1-0	3-1	1-1	2-2	2-1	3-1	3-1	2-3	2-0		1-0	1-1	1-1	1-4	2-1
Sheffield Wednesday FC	1-1	3-0	5-1	1-0	3-2	4-2	4-0	2-0	5-3	3-1	1-1	1-4	1-2	1-0	3-1	3-0	1-2		0-0	2-1	0-0	3-2
Tottenham Hotspur FC	4-3	1-0	3-1	4-1	5-2	2-2	4-2	3-2	5-2	3-1	4-2	1-3	1-2	2-0	2-2	4-2	3-3	4-0		1-2	2-2	1-0
West Bromwich Albion FC	4-0	1-1	0-0	4-0	7-1	6-2	1-1	5-1	4-0	2-0	2-0	1-3	2-0	2-2	1-1	2-2	3-1	0-2	2-4		0-1	1-1
West Ham United FC	3-3	2-0	2-2	2-3	2-2	1-0	2-1	4-1	2-1	3-1	4-2	2-2	4-1	0-4	1-1	3-2	1-2	2-3	2-1	3-3		4-2
Wolverhampton Wanderers FC	2-3	2-2	2-1	0-2	2-2	5-1	1-1	1-1	1-1	0-3	1-3	2-0	1-1	4-1	2-2	2-1	0-1	3-0	3-1	1-5	3-2	

	Division 1	Pd	Wn	Dw	Ls	GF	GA	Pts	
1.	IPSWICH TOWN FC (IPSWICH)	42	24	8	10	93	67	56	
2.	Burnley FC (Burnley)	42	21	11	10	101	67	53	
3.	Tottenham Hotspur FC (London)	42	21	10	11	88	69	52	
4.	Everton FC (Liverpool)	42	20	11	11	88	54	51	
5.	Sheffield United FC (Sheffield)	42	19	9	14	61	69	47	
6.	Sheffield Wednesday FC (Sheffield)	42	20	6	16	72	58	46	
7.	Aston Villa FC (Birmingham)	42	18	8	16	65	56	44	
8.	West Ham United FC (London)	42	17	10	15	76	82	44	
9.	West Bromwich Albion FC (West Bromwich)	42	15	13	14	83	67	43	
10.	Arsenal FC (London)	42	16	11	15	71	72	43	
11.	Bolton Wanderers FC (Bolton)	42	16	10	16	62	66	42	
12.	Manchester City FC (Manchester)	42	17	7	18	78	81	41	
13.	Blackpool FC (Blackpool)	42	15	11	16	70	75	41	
14.	Leicester City FC (Leicester)	42	17	6	19	72	71	40	
15.	Manchester United FC (Manchester)	42	15	9	18	72	75	39	
16.	Blackburn Rovers FC (Blackburn)	42	14	11	17	50	58	39	
17.	Birmingham City FC (Birmingham)	42	14	10	18	65	81	38	
18.	Wolverhampton Wanderers FC (Wolverhampton)	42	13	10	19	73	86	36	
19.	Nottingham Forest FC (Nottingham)	42	13	10	19	63	79	36	
20.	Fulham FC (London)	42	13	7	22	66	74	33	
21.	Cardiff City AFC (Cardiff)	42	9	14	19	50	81	32	R
22.	Chelsea FC (London)	42	9	10	23	63	94	28	R
		924	356	212	356	1582	1582	924	

Top Goalscorers

1)	Ray CRAWFORD	(Ipswich Town FC)	33
	Derek KEVAN	(West Bromwich Albion FC)	33

Football League Division 2 1961-62 Season	Brighton & Hove Albion	Bristol Rovers	Bury	Charlton Athletic	Derby County	Huddersfield Town	Leeds United	Leyton Orient	Liverpool	Luton Town	Middlesbrough	Newcastle United	Norwich City	Plymouth Argyle	Preston North End	Rotherham United	Scunthorpe United	Southampton	Stoke City	Sunderland	Swansea Town	Walsall
Brighton & Hove Albion FC		1-0	0-2	2-2	1-2	2-2	1-3	0-1	0-0	2-1	2-0	0-4	2-1	3-2	0-0	0-3	0-3	0-0	2-1	1-1	2-2	3-2
Bristol Rovers FC	0-1		0-1	2-2	1-4	1-1	4-0	2-1	0-2	1-0	0-2	2-1	2-1	4-3	2-1	4-2	2-1	1-0	0-2	2-3	4-1	2-2
Bury FC	2-1	2-0		1-2	2-2	1-2	1-1	0-1	0-3	2-1	2-1	2-7	2-3	1-1	2-1	2-1	4-1	0-2	0-2	3-2	1-1	2-1
Charlton Athletic FC	2-3	2-1	1-0		4-0	0-2	3-1	1-2	0-4	0-1	1-0	1-1	2-2	3-1	4-0	0-2	3-3	1-0	2-2	2-0	3-2	3-3
Derby County FC	2-0	4-1	3-0	0-1		1-0	3-3	1-2	2-0	2-0	3-2	1-2	1-1	2-2	3-2	1-1	2-2	1-1	2-0	1-1	6-3	1-3
Huddersfield Town AFC	2-0	4-1	2-0	0-2	4-0		2-1	1-1	1-2	1-2	0-0	2-1	1-1	5-1	2-2	0-3	1-2	1-0	3-0	0-0	3-1	4-2
Leeds United AFC	1-1	0-0	0-0	1-0	0-0	1-0		0-0	1-0	2-1	2-0	0-1	0-1	2-3	1-2	1-3	1-4	1-1	3-1	1-0	2-0	4-1
Leyton Orient FC	4-1	2-3	2-0	2-1	2-0	3-0	0-0		2-2	0-2	2-0	2-0	2-0	1-2	0-2	1-1	0-1	1-3	3-0	1-1	1-0	3-0
Liverpool FC	3-1	2-0	5-0	2-1	4-1	1-1	5-0	3-3		1-1	5-1	2-0	5-4	2-1	4-1	4-1	2-1	2-0	2-1	3-0	5-0	6-1
Luton Town FC	2-1	2-0	4-0	1-6	4-2	3-4	3-2	1-3	1-0		3-2	1-0	1-2	0-2	4-1	4-3	1-2	1-4	0-0	1-2	5-1	2-0
Middlesbrough FC	4-0	5-0	2-1	3-2	3-4	1-0	1-3	2-3	2-0	2-4		3-0	2-1	1-1	1-0	5-1	1-2	1-1	2-2	0-1	1-3	3-0
Newcastle United FC	5-0	5-2	1-2	4-1	3-0	1-0	0-3	0-0	1-2	4-1	3-4		0-0	0-2	0-2	1-0	0-1	3-2	2-0	2-2	2-2	1-0
Norwich City FC	3-0	2-2	3-1	2-2	3-2	1-2	2-0	0-0	1-2	0-4	5-4	0-0		0-2	2-0	0-1	2-2	1-1	1-0	3-1	2-1	3-1
Plymouth Argyle FC	5-0	3-1	1-2	2-1	2-3	4-2	1-1	2-1	2-3	0-3	1-1	1-2	3-1		1-0	2-5	3-1	4-0	3-1	3-2	0-0	2-1
Preston North End FC	3-1	1-0	1-2	2-0	1-0	1-0	1-1	3-2	1-3	2-0	4-3	0-1	2-0	1-1		2-0	4-1	1-1	1-2	0-1	1-1	2-3
Rotherham United FC	2-1	4-0	2-0	3-2	2-2	3-3	2-1	2-1	1-0	1-1	0-1	0-0	3-1	1-3	2-2		0-1	4-2	1-2	0-3	1-2	2-2
Scunthorpe United FC	3-3	2-1	1-2	6-1	0-4	1-3	2-1	0-2	1-1	2-0	1-1	3-2	2-0	5-1	2-1	5-2		5-1	2-2	3-1	2-0	2-1
Southampton FC	6-1	0-2	5-3	1-2	2-1	3-1	4-1	1-2	2-0	3-0	1-3	1-0	2-2	1-2	0-0	2-1	6-4		5-1	2-0	5-1	1-1
Stoke City FC	0-1	2-1	1-3	4-0	1-1	3-0	2-1	0-1	0-0	2-1	2-0	3-1	3-1	2-0	1-1	1-2	1-0	3-2		1-0	0-0	2-1
Sunderland AFC	0-0	6-1	3-0	4-1	2-1	3-1	2-1	1-4	2-2	2-1	3-2	2-0	1-1	0-1	3-1	4-0	4-0	3-0	2-1		7-2	3-0
Swansea Town AFC	3-0	1-1	0-1	1-0	3-1	1-2	2-1	1-3	4-2	3-2	3-3	3-2	0-3	5-0	1-2	2-2	2-1	0-1	1-0	1-1		1-3
Walsall FC	2-2	0-0	3-0	2-2	2-0	2-2	1-1	1-5	1-1	2-0	1-2	1-0	5-0	1-0	2-1	5-0	4-1	0-2	3-1	4-3	0-0	

	Division 2	Pd	Wn	Dw	Ls	GF	GA	Pts	
1.	Liverpool FC (Liverpool)	42	27	8	7	99	43	62	P
2.	Leyton Orient FC (London)	42	22	10	10	69	40	54	P
3.	Sunderland AFC (Sunderland)	42	22	9	11	85	50	53	
4.	Scunthorpe United FC (Scunthorpe)	42	21	7	14	86	71	49	
5.	Plymouth Argyle FC (Plymouth)	42	19	8	15	75	75	46	
6.	Southampton FC (Southampton)	42	18	9	15	77	62	45	
7.	Huddersfield Town AFC (Huddersfield)	42	16	12	14	67	59	44	
8.	Stoke City FC (Stoke-on-Trent)	42	17	8	17	55	57	42	
9.	Rotherham United FC (Rotherham)	42	16	9	17	70	76	41	
10.	Preston North End FC (Preston)	42	15	10	17	55	57	40	
11.	Newcastle United FC (Newcastle-upon-Tyne)	42	15	9	18	64	58	39	
12.	Middlesbrough FC (Middlesbrough)	42	16	7	19	76	72	39	
13.	Luton Town FC (Luton)	42	17	5	20	69	71	39	
14.	Walsall FC (Walsall)	42	14	11	17	70	75	39	
15.	Charlton Athletic FC (London)	42	15	9	18	69	75	39	
16.	Derby County FC (Derby)	42	14	11	17	68	75	39	
17.	Norwich City FC (Norwich)	42	14	11	17	61	70	39	
18.	Bury FC (Bury)	42	17	5	20	52	76	39	
19.	Leeds United AFC (Leeds)	42	12	12	18	50	61	36	
20.	Swansea Town AFC (Swansea)	42	12	12	18	61	83	36	
21.	Bristol Rovers FC (Bristol)	42	13	7	20	53	81	33	R
22.	Brighton & Hove Albion FC (Hove)	42	10	11	21	42	86	31	R
		924	362	200	362	1473	1473	924	

Football League Division 3 1961-62 Season	Barnsley	Bournemouth	Bradford P.A.	Brentford	Bristol City	Coventry City	Crystal Palace	Grimsby Town	Halifax Town	Hull City	Lincoln City	Newport County	Northampton Town	Notts County	Peterborough Utd.	Portsmouth	Port Vale	Q.P.R.	Reading	Shrewsbury Town	Southend United	Swindon Town	Torquay United	Watford
Barnsley FC		2-2	1-2	2-2	7-3	2-1	0-3	0-3	1-2	1-0	0-1	1-1	3-2	2-0	0-3	2-2	2-1	2-4	2-3	1-1	1-1	6-2	4-2	3-0
Bournemouth & Bos.	5-0		2-2	1-1	2-1	1-1	1-0	2-3	2-1	1-1	0-0	2-1	3-2	2-1	1-1	2-0	1-0	3-1	1-0	0-0	3-0	0-0	3-1	4-1
Bradford Park Ave.	3-2	1-2		1-2	2-0	0-0	2-0	0-1	2-0	1-0	2-0	4-1	1-2	3-2	6-2	2-1	2-1	3-3	1-3	1-1	4-0	2-2	3-1	1-1
Brentford FC	1-1	2-2	2-0		0-2	2-1	4-2	0-2	0-2	0-2	1-0	3-1	3-0	0-1	2-0	3-2	1-2	1-4	1-2	4-0	0-0	1-0	0-2	3-1
Bristol City FC	0-0	2-1	6-1	3-0		3-2	2-2	3-0	4-3	1-1	2-0	1-2	1-0	6-0	1-2	0-4	0-1	2-0	5-0	0-1	3-2	5-3	4-1	2-1
Coventry City FC	1-1	0-1	3-0	2-0	1-1		0-2	2-0	3-1	0-2	2-2	3-0	1-0	2-2	1-3	2-0	0-2	2-3	1-0	4-1	3-3	2-1	2-2	1-0
Crystal Palace FC	1-3	0-0	0-0	2-2	2-3	2-2		4-1	4-3	1-2	1-3	2-0	1-4	4-1	5-2	1-2	0-0	2-2	3-4	2-1	2-2	3-1	7-2	1-1
Grimsby Town FC	4-0	3-0	3-2	1-0	1-0	2-0	0-0		3-0	1-0	4-1	1-0	3-2	2-1	2-1	1-0	1-1	1-1	4-0	2-1	3-1	0-1	2-3	5-3
Halifax Town AFC	3-1	3-1	2-3	1-0	3-4	0-2	1-1	3-3		2-1	0-3	0-0	1-3	1-2	2-1	0-1	3-3	1-1	2-1	1-2	0-2	2-0	1-0	2-0
Hull City AFC	4-0	2-1	0-1	3-0	3-2	3-1	2-4	2-1	1-2		1-0	4-0	1-0	2-1	1-1	0-1	3-1	3-1	0-1	3-1	0-0	0-1	4-0	1-0
Lincoln City FC	2-2	0-2	3-2	3-3	1-1	1-2	3-2	1-1	0-1	0-3		3-2	0-0	2-2	1-2	2-2	1-1	0-5	2-3	1-2	2-0	2-2	1-3	0-0
Newport County AFC	0-2	0-1	1-2	6-1	3-1	1-2	2-1	0-2	0-1	0-2	4-0		0-0	2-0	2-3	0-5	1-1	2-4	0-0	3-2	0-3	2-3	2-0	0-0
Northampton Town	3-1	0-3	2-0	5-0	0-1	4-1	1-1	7-0	3-1	2-0	2-2	5-0		1-2	2-2	2-1	1-1	1-1	1-0	3-1	3-1	1-2	1-2	2-0
Notts County FC	0-2	3-2	4-2	3-1	1-0	2-0	0-0	2-0	0-0	3-0	1-0	8-1	1-4		2-2	2-1	2-3	0-0	2-2	3-2	2-0	0-1	2-0	1-0
Peterborough United	4-2	1-2	1-0	6-0	3-4	2-3	4-1	2-1	5-1	3-2	5-4	2-1	0-2	2-0		0-1	1-3	5-1	1-0	0-3	4-1	3-2	2-1	4-3
Portsmouth FC	3-2	1-1	4-2	4-0	5-0	3-2	2-1	0-2	1-1	2-1	0-0	2-2	4-1	0-0	0-3		1-0	4-1	2-0	3-1	1-0	2-2	2-0	2-1
Port Vale FC	2-0	1-0	3-0	3-0	0-2	2-0	0-0	1-1	4-0	3-0	1-1	1-0	0-2	1-1	2-3			2-3	2-1	4-1	0-0	1-1	4-1	3-4
Queen's Park Rangers	3-0	1-1	1-2	3-0	4-1	4-1	1-0	3-2	6-2	1-1	1-3	4-0	2-0	2-0	3-3	0-1	2-1		3-6	3-1	5-3	6-1	6-0	1-2
Reading FC	0-0	0-1	3-1	4-0	2-2	4-0	2-1	1-2	3-2	1-1	4-0	2-1	2-0	4-2	3-2	0-3	0-0	0-2		3-0	3-1	1-1	1-0	3-2
Shrewsbury Town FC	4-1	2-2	4-1	1-3	2-2	1-1	1-5	1-2	0-0	0-0	4-1	1-3	3-0	3-4	0-1	4-2	1-2	4-1			1-1	1-3	1-1	5-1
Southend United FC	1-2	0-0	2-1	0-0	1-0	2-0	2-2	2-0	2-1	2-1	0-0	1-0	1-3	3-2	1-1	2-2	4-1	2-3	0-2	1-1		0-2	2-1	0-1
Swindon Town FC	1-1	1-1	3-2	5-2	0-4	3-3	5-0	0-0	6-0	1-1	4-0	3-0	2-2	1-0	3-2	1-3	1-0	0-0	4-1	1-2	0-0		0-1	3-1
Torquay United FC	6-2	2-1	1-3	3-1	1-3	1-0	1-2	1-2	2-3	4-2	3-4	3-2	1-2	3-3	1-3	0-2	2-0	2-2	0-0	3-1	2-2	3-0		3-4
Watford FC	3-1	0-0	0-2	2-1	1-1	0-1	3-2	2-1	0-0	1-1	3-3	3-1	0-0	3-1	2-3	0-0	3-2	1-1	1-1	1-3	2-0	4-1		

	Division 3	Pd	Wn	Dw	Ls	GF	GA	Pts	
1.	Portsmouth FC (Portsmouth)	46	27	11	8	87	47	65	P
2.	Grimsby Town FC (Cleethorpes)	46	28	6	12	80	56	62	P
3.	Bournemouth & Boscombe Athletic FC (Bournemouth)	46	21	17	8	69	45	59	
4.	Queen's Park Rangers FC (London)	46	24	11	11	111	73	59	
5.	Peterborough United FC (Peterborough)	46	26	6	14	107	82	58	
6.	Bristol City FC (Bristol)	46	23	8	15	94	72	54	
7.	Reading FC (Reading)	46	22	9	15	77	66	53	
8.	Northampton Town FC (Northampton)	46	20	11	15	85	57	51	
9.	Swindon Town FC (Swindon)	46	17	15	14	78	71	49	
10.	Hull City AFC (Kingston-upon-Hull)	46	20	8	18	67	54	48	
11.	Bradford Park Avenue FC (Bradford)	46	20	7	19	80	78	47	
12.	Port Vale FC (Stoke-on-Trent)	46	17	11	18	65	58	45	
13.	Notts County FC (Nottingham)	46	17	9	20	67	74	43	
14.	Coventry City FC (Coventry)	46	16	11	19	64	71	43	
15.	Crystal Palace FC (London)	46	14	14	18	83	80	42	
16.	Southend United FC (Southend-on-Sea)	46	13	16	17	57	69	42	
17.	Watford FC (Watford)	46	14	13	19	63	74	41	
18.	Halifax Town AFC (Halifax)	46	15	10	21	62	84	40	
19.	Shrewsbury Town FC (Shrewsbury)	46	13	12	21	73	84	38	
20.	Barnsley FC (Barnsley)	46	13	12	21	71	95	38	
21.	Torquay United FC (Torquay)	46	15	6	25	76	100	36	R
22.	Lincoln City FC (Lincoln)	46	9	17	20	57	87	35	R
23.	Brentford FC (London)	46	13	8	25	53	93	34	R
24.	Newport County AFC (Newport)	46	7	8	31	46	102	22	R
		1104	424	256	424	1772	1772	1104	

Football League Division 4 1961-62 Season	Accrington Stanley	Aldershot Town	Barrow	Bradford City	Carlisle United	Chester	Chesterfield	Colchester United	Crewe Alexandra	Darlington	Doncaster Rovers	Exeter City	Gillingham	Hartlepools	Mansfield Town	Millwall	Oldham Athletic	Rochdale	Southport	Stockport County	Tranmere Rovers	Workington	Wrexham	York City
Accrington Stanley		0-2	2-2	0-2	1-0	0-1	0-0	0-4	1-0	3-1	---	---	---	---	0-0	0-2	1-0	0-2	---	1-2	1-1	0-4	0-2	--
Aldershot Town FC	2-2		3-1	2-2	0-1	6-2	1-1	1-0	1-0	6-1	3-1	1-1	4-0	1-1	4-2	0-2	3-1	3-0	2-0	4-1	3-1	3-1	3-1	2-0
Barrow AFC	3-1	2-2		1-1	0-3	3-2	1-0	4-0	3-0	3-0	4-1	3-0	7-0	5-1	1-1	2-2	3-1	0-1	1-1	3-1	2-0	1-1	0-2	0-0
Bradford City AFC	0-1	2-1	1-1		3-2	2-0	0-2	4-1	3-3	3-2	2-0	5-1	5-2	5-1	6-1	2-4	1-1	1-0	1-0	1-3	3-1	1-1	5-3	2-2
Carlisle United FC	2-0	2-1	0-0	2-4		2-0	3-1	1-1	3-0	1-0	1-0	2-1	1-2	1-0	1-0	3-2	2-0	2-2	2-1	1-0	0-3	1-2	1-0	3-2
Chester FC	0-0	2-3	2-3	1-2	1-1		4-1	2-2	1-0	2-2	2-3	1-1	1-1	4-4	0-1	2-4	1-0	2-3	2-0	2-0	1-1	1-3	1-1	1-1
Chesterfield FC	---	2-3	2-2	2-1	1-3	4-1		4-1	3-1	1-1	3-0	2-0	3-2	2-0	0-4	2-3	2-3	1-0	3-2	3-2	1-2	0-1	1-5	1-1
Colchester United FC	3-2	3-0	1-1	9-1	2-0	5-2	3-3		5-3	2-0	5-3	2-0	6-0	6-1	2-0	2-2	5-1	1-1	2-0	3-0	3-0	6-1	2-4	3-1
Crewe Alexandra FC	4-0	2-0	1-1	1-2	3-0	1-1	2-1	4-0		5-1	2-0	3-1	5-2	3-0	3-2	2-1	3-5	2-1	3-1	3-2	3-0	2-0	0-3	0-0
Darlington FC	1-1	2-0	1-0	3-3	2-1	2-0	4-4	0-2	2-1		1-0	1-0	1-1	1-2	3-1	1-5	3-0	2-0	1-2	3-0	1-1	1-1	1-0	0-0
Doncaster Rovers FC	1-1	2-1	3-2	2-0	1-2	2-0	0-0	1-4	3-0	1-2		3-1	2-1	2-2	0-1	1-2	0-0	1-2	1-1	1-1	6-1	1-1	0-2	1-2
Exeter City FC	3-0	2-1	3-0	0-1	4-0	5-0	4-1	0-2	2-1	0-1	1-5		1-3	1-1	2-1	1-1	3-3	1-3	1-1	4-3	1-0	3-1	1-1	2-1
Gillingham FC	5-1	0-1	3-2	3-1	4-1	0-0	5-1	2-1	0-1	2-2	2-2	2-2		4-0	2-2	3-1	0-2	4-2	4-0	1-1	0-1	4-2	2-3	1-2
Hartlepools United	---	0-2	2-3	1-3	0-3	1-3	1-2	1-1	2-1	2-0	3-0	0-0	1-3		0-1	2-0	1-1	3-1	4-2	2-2	0-0	0-1	1-4	0-2
Mansfield Town FC	---	4-1	0-1	0-1	5-2	3-0	2-2	4-0	1-1	3-0	4-0	3-1	3-1	3-1		0-0	2-0	0-1	3-1	2-0	1-2	4-1	1-2	3-1
Millwall FC	---	2-1	1-0	1-2	3-0	2-0	2-1	2-0	4-3	4-2	2-0	2-0	0-0	3-2	4-0		2-0	1-1	1-1	1-3	3-0	5-0	0-1	2-1
Oldham Athletic AFC	5-0	2-1	3-2	2-2	5-0	4-1	3-1	2-2	2-0	0-1	3-1	1-1	1-1	5-2	2-3	4-2		2-2	2-1	0-0	2-0	0-2	1-1	1-0
Rochdale AFC	1-0	1-0	0-2	4-1	1-1	3-2	1-1	0-1	3-0	1-3	2-3	3-0	3-1	3-1	3-2	4-1	3-1		2-0	3-3	1-0	1-3	2-1	3-1
Southport FC	---	2-1	0-0	2-1	0-0	1-0	0-2	3-0	2-0	1-4	3-1	1-1	1-1	0-1	2-1	3-1	0-5	3-0		2-1	2-1	1-1	4-2	3-1
Stockport County FC	2-0	3-1	3-0	3-1	1-2	0-1	2-1	1-4	0-1	2-1	2-1	1-1	1-1	1-1	1-1	5-2	1-4				3-0	3-1	1-2	2-1
Tranmere Rovers FC	2-0	1-2	2-1	3-2	0-3	4-1	1-0	5-2	1-6	0-0	3-2	3-4	4-2	3-2	2-0	5-1	3-1	2-0	3-1	1-3		3-2	2-0	2-2
Workington AFC	---	2-1	1-2	5-3	2-1	4-1	2-0	1-2	0-1	2-1	0-0	3-1	5-1	1-1	1-1	2-2	0-2	2-1	3-0	1-1	2-1		1-0	0-0
Wrexham AFC	---	2-1	1-1	2-1	2-2	0-0	4-2	0-0	1-1	5-0	3-1	1-2	3-0	10-1	5-0	2-2	2-1	3-0	2-3	0-1	4-0	2-3		2-1
York City FC	1-0	0-1	5-0	4-0	1-1	5-1	4-0	5-0	4-2	2-1	5-2	2-1	4-0	2-0	2-1	0-1	4-1	2-1	2-2	1-0	1-2	4-0	3-2	

Division 4

		Pd	Wn	Dw	Ls	GF	GA	Pts	
1.	Millwall FC (London)	44	23	10	11	87	62	56	P
2.	Colchester United FC (Colchester)	44	23	9	12	104	71	55	P
3.	Wrexham AFC (Wrexham)	44	22	9	13	96	56	53	P
4.	Carlisle United FC (Carlisle)	44	22	8	14	64	63	52	P
5.	Bradford City AFC (Bradford)	44	21	9	14	94	86	51	
6.	York City FC (York)	44	20	10	14	84	53	50	
7.	Aldershot FC (Aldershot)	44	22	5	17	81	60	49	
8.	Workington AFC (Workington)	44	19	11	14	69	70	49	
9.	Barrow AFC (Barrow-in-Furness)	44	17	14	13	74	58	48	
10.	Crewe Alexandra FC (Crewe)	44	20	6	18	79	70	46	
11.	Oldham Athletic AFC (Oldham)	44	17	12	15	77	70	46	
12.	Rochdale AFC (Rochdale)	44	19	7	18	71	71	45	
13.	Darlington FC (Darlington)	44	18	9	17	61	73	45	
14.	Mansfield Town FC (Mansfield)	44	19	6	19	77	66	44	
15.	Tranmere Rovers FC (Birkenhead)	44	20	4	20	70	81	44	
16.	Stockport County FC (Stockport)	44	17	9	18	70	69	43	
17.	Southport FC (Southport)	44	17	9	18	61	71	43	
18.	Exeter City FC (Exeter)	44	13	11	20	62	77	37	
19.	Chesterfield FC (Chesterfield)	44	14	9	21	70	87	37	
20.	Gillingham FC (Gillingham)	44	13	11	20	73	94	37	
21.	Doncaster Rovers FC (Doncaster)	44	11	7	26	60	85	29	
22.	Hartlepools United FC (Hartlepool)	44	8	11	25	52	101	27	
23.	Chester FC (Chester)	44	7	12	25	54	96	26	
---.	Accrington Stanley FC (Accrington)	33	5	8	20	19	60	18	#
		1012	402	208	402	1690	1690	1012	

61

\# Accrington Stanley FC (Accrington) resigned from the league after only 33 games, their record was expunged and their place was awarded to Oxford United FC (Oxford) for the next season.

F.A. CUP FINAL   (Wembley Stadium, London – 06/05/1961 – 100,000)

TOTTENHAM HOTSPUR FC (LONDON)   3-1   Burnley FC (Burnley)

Greaves, Smith, Blanchflower pen.   *Robson*

Tottenham: Brown, Baker, Henry, Blanchflower, Norman, Mackay, Medwin, White, Smith, Greaves, Jones.

Burnley: Blacklaw, Angus, Elder, Adamson, Cummings, Miller, Connelly, McIlroy, Pointer, Robson, Harris.

Semi-finals

Burnley FC (Burnley)	1-1, 2-1	Fulham FC (London)
Manchester United FC (Manchester)	1-3	Tottenham Hotspur FC (London)

Quarter-finals

Fulham FC (London)	2-2, 1-0	Blackburn Rovers FC (Blackburn)
Preston North End FC (Preston)	0-0, 1-2	Manchester United FC (Manchester)
Sheffield United FC (Sheffield)	0-1	Burnley FC (Burnley)
Tottenham Hotspur FC (London)	2-0	Aston Villa FC (Birmingham)

1962-63

Football League Division 1 — 1962-63 Season

	Arsenal	Aston Villa	Birmingham City	Blackburn Rovers	Blackpool	Bolton Wanderers	Burnley	Everton	Fulham	Ipswich Town	Leicester City	Leyton Orient	Liverpool	Manchester City	Manchester United	Nottingham Forest	Sheffield United	Sheffield Wed.	Tottenham Hotspur	W.B.A.	West Ham United	Wolves
Arsenal FC		1-2	2-0	3-1	2-0	3-2	2-3	4-3	3-0	3-1	1-1	2-0	2-2	2-3	1-3	0-0	1-0	1-2	2-3	3-2	1-1	5-4
Aston Villa FC	3-1		4-0	0-0	1-1	5-0	2-1	0-2	1-2	4-2	3-1	1-0	2-0	3-1	1-2	0-2	1-2	0-2	2-1	2-0	3-1	0-2
Birmingham City FC	2-2	3-2		3-3	3-6	2-2	5-1	0-1	4-1	0-1	3-2	2-2	0-2	2-2	2-1	2-2	0-1	1-1	0-2	0-0	3-2	3-4
Blackburn Rovers FC	5-5	4-1	6-1		3-3	5-0	2-3	3-2	0-1	0-1	2-0	1-1	1-0	4-1	2-2	2-5	1-2	3-0	3-0	3-1	0-4	5-1
Blackpool FC	3-2	4-0	1-1	4-1		3-1	0-0	1-2	0-0	1-0	1-1	3-2	1-2	2-2	2-2	2-1	3-1	2-3	1-2	0-2	0-0	0-2
Bolton Wanderers FC	3-0	4-1	0-0	0-0	3-0		2-2	0-2	1-0	1-3	2-0	0-1	1-0	3-1	3-0	1-0	0-4	1-0	1-2	3-0	3-0	3-0
Burnley FC	2-1	3-1	3-1	1-0	2-0	2-1		1-3	4-0	3-1	1-1	2-0	1-3	0-0	0-1	0-0	5-1	4-0	2-1	2-1	1-1	2-0
Everton FC	1-1	1-1	2-2	0-0	5-0	1-0	3-1		4-1	3-2	3-2	2-2	2-1	3-1	2-0	3-0	4-1	1-0	4-2	1-1	1-1	2-1
Fulham FC	1-3	1-0	3-3	0-0	2-0	2-1	1-1	1-0		1-1	2-1	0-2	0-0	2-4	0-1	3-1	2-2	4-1	0-2	1-2	2-0	0-5
Ipswich Town FC	1-1	1-1	1-5	3-3	5-2	4-1	2-1	0-3	0-1		0-1	1-1	1-2	3-5	1-1	1-1	1-2	0-4	1-1	2-3	2-3	2-3
Leicester City FC	2-0	3-3	3-0	2-0	0-0	4-1	3-3	3-1	2-3	3-0		5-1	3-0	2-0	4-3	2-1	3-1	3-3	2-2	1-0	2-0	1-1
Leyton Orient FC	1-2	0-2	2-2	1-1	0-2	0-1	0-1	3-0	1-1	1-2	0-2		2-1	1-1	1-0	0-1	2-2	2-4	1-5	2-3	2-0	0-4
Liverpool FC	2-1	4-0	5-1	3-1	1-2	1-0	1-2	0-0	2-1	1-0	0-2	5-0		4-1	1-0	0-2	2-0	0-2	5-2	2-2	2-1	4-1
Manchester City FC	2-4	0-2	2-1	0-1	0-3	2-1	2-5	1-1	2-3	2-1	1-1	2-0	2-2		1-1	1-0	1-3	3-2	1-0	1-5	1-6	3-3
Manchester United FC	2-3	2-2	2-0	0-3	1-1	3-0	2-5	0-1	0-2	2-2	3-1	3-3	2-3	2-3		5-1	1-1	1-3	0-2	2-3	3-1	2-1
Nottingham Forest FC	3-0	3-1	0-2	2-0	2-0	1-0	2-1	3-4	3-1	2-1	0-2	1-1	3-1	1-1	3-2		2-1	0-3	1-1	2-2	3-4	2-0
Sheffield United FC	3-3	2-1	0-2	1-1	0-0	4-1	1-0	2-1	2-1	0-0	2-0	0-0	3-1	1-1	3-1	3-1		2-2	3-1	1-0	0-2	1-2
Sheffield Wednesday FC	2-3	0-0	5-0	4-0	0-0	1-1	0-1	2-2	1-0	0-3	3-1	0-2	4-1	1-0	1-3	3-1	3-1		3-1	3-1	1-3	3-1
Tottenham Hotspur FC	4-4	4-2	3-0	4-1	2-0	4-1	1-1	0-0	1-1	5-0	4-0	2-0	7-2	4-2	6-2	9-2	4-2	1-1		2-1	4-4	1-2
West Bromwich Albion FC	1-2	1-0	1-0	2-5	1-2	5-4	1-2	0-4	6-1	6-1	2-1	2-1	1-0	2-1	3-0	1-4	1-2	0-3	1-2		1-0	2-2
West Ham United FC	0-4	1-1	5-0	0-1	2-2	1-2	1-1	1-2	2-2	1-3	2-0	2-0	1-0	6-1	3-1	4-1	1-1	2-0	1-6	2-2		1-4
Wolverhampton Wanderers FC	1-0	3-1	0-2	4-2	2-0	4-0	7-2	0-2	2-1	0-0	1-3	2-1	3-2	8-1	2-3	1-1	0-0	2-2	2-2	7-0	0-0	

Division 1

		Pd	Wn	Dw	Ls	GF	GA	Pts	
1.	EVERTON FC (LIVERPOOL)	42	25	11	6	84	42	61	
2.	Tottenham Hotspur FC (London)	42	23	9	10	111	62	55	
3.	Burnley FC (Burnley)	42	22	10	10	78	57	54	
4.	Leicester City FC (Leicester)	42	20	12	10	79	53	52	
5.	Wolverhampton Wanderers FC (Wolverhampton)	42	20	10	12	93	65	50	
6.	Sheffield Wednesday FC (Sheffield)	42	19	10	13	77	63	48	
7.	Arsenal FC (London)	42	18	10	14	86	77	46	
8.	Liverpool FC (Liverpool)	42	17	10	15	71	59	44	
9.	Nottingham Forest FC (Nottingham)	42	17	10	15	67	69	44	
10.	Sheffield United FC (Sheffield)	42	16	12	14	58	60	44	
11.	Blackburn Rovers FC (Blackburn)	42	15	12	15	79	71	42	
12.	West Ham United FC (London)	42	14	12	16	73	69	40	
13.	Blackpool FC (Blackpool)	42	13	14	15	58	64	40	
14.	West Bromwich Albion FC (West Bromwich)	42	16	7	19	71	79	39	
15.	Aston Villa FC (Birmingham)	42	15	8	19	62	68	38	
16.	Fulham FC (London)	42	14	10	18	50	71	38	
17.	Ipswich Town FC (Ipswich)	42	12	11	19	59	78	35	
18.	Bolton Wanderers FC (Bolton)	42	15	5	22	55	75	35	
19.	Manchester United FC (Manchester)	42	12	10	20	67	81	34	
20.	Birmingham City FC (Birmingham)	42	10	13	19	63	90	33	
21.	Manchester City FC (Manchester)	42	10	11	21	58	102	31	R
22.	Leyton Orient FC (London)	42	6	9	27	37	81	21	R
		924	349	226	349	1536	1536	924	

Top Goalscorer

1) James GREAVES   (Tottenham Hotspur FC)   37

Football League Division 2 1962-63 Season	Bury	Cardiff City	Charlton Athletic	Chelsea	Derby County	Grimsby Town	Huddersfield Town	Leeds United	Luton Town	Middlesbrough	Newcastle United	Norwich City	Plymouth Argyle	Portsmouth	Preston North End	Rotherham United	Scunthorpe United	Southampton	Stoke City	Sunderland	Swansea Town	Walsall
Bury FC	—	1-0	3-1	2-0	3-3	2-0	1-1	3-1	1-0	1-0	0-0	0-3	1-2	2-0	0-0	0-5	0-2	1-1	2-1	3-0	2-0	0-0
Cardiff City AFC	3-1	—	1-2	1-0	1-0	5-3	3-0	0-0	1-0	1-2	4-4	2-4	2-1	1-2	1-1	4-1	4-0	3-1	1-1	5-2	5-2	2-2
Charlton Athletic FC	0-0	2-4	—	1-4	0-0	0-3	1-0	1-2	2-0	3-4	1-2	0-2	6-3	2-0	2-1	2-3	1-0	2-1	0-3	2-2	2-2	3-2
Chelsea FC	2-0	6-0	5-0	—	3-1	2-1	1-2	2-2	3-1	3-2	4-2	2-0	1-1	7-0	2-0	3-0	3-0	2-0	0-1	1-0	2-2	0-1
Derby County FC	0-0	1-2	2-3	1-3	—	2-4	2-1	0-0	1-0	3-3	0-1	3-0	3-2	4-0	1-0	3-2	6-2	3-1	1-1	2-2	0-2	2-0
Grimsby Town FC	5-1	1-2	2-1	0-3	0-0	—	1-1	1-1	3-1	3-4	0-1	0-2	1-1	1-1	2-0	1-2	3-0	4-1	1-1	1-2	1-0	3-1
Huddersfield Town AFC	0-1	1-0	2-0	1-0	3-3	0-0	—	1-1	2-0	0-0	2-1	0-0	4-2	1-3	1-0	1-0	2-0	2-3	3-3	0-3	4-1	4-0
Leeds United AFC	1-2	3-0	4-1	2-0	3-1	3-0	0-1	—	3-0	2-3	1-0	3-0	6-1	3-3	4-1	3-4	1-0	1-1	3-1	1-0	5-0	3-0
Luton Town FC	2-1	2-3	4-1	0-2	1-2	2-2	3-2	2-2	—	4-3	2-3	4-2	3-0	3-3	0-2	2-3	1-0	3-2	0-0	0-3	3-1	4-3
Middlesbrough FC	0-0	3-2	2-1	1-0	5-1	0-1	0-5	2-1	0-2	—	4-2	6-2	3-0	4-2	2-0	2-1	4-3	1-2	2-2	3-3	2-2	2-3
Newcastle United FC	1-3	2-1	3-2	2-0	0-0	0-0	1-1	1-1	3-1	6-1	—	2-1	3-1	1-1	2-2	4-1	1-1	4-1	5-2	1-1	6-0	0-2
Norwich City FC	1-1	0-0	1-4	4-1	2-0	0-0	2-3	3-2	3-3	3-4	1-2	—	2-1	5-3	1-1	4-2	3-3	1-0	6-0	4-2	5-0	2-1
Plymouth Argyle FC	0-0	4-2	6-1	2-1	2-1	2-0	1-1	3-1	3-1	4-5	0-2	1-0	—	2-0	7-1	2-2	2-3	2-1	0-1	1-1	1-0	3-0
Portsmouth FC	2-1	2-0	3-3	0-2	1-0	2-1	1-1	3-0	3-1	1-1	3-1	0-2	1-2	—	1-2	1-2	1-1	0-3	3-1	0-0		4-1
Preston North End FC	0-2	2-6	4-1	1-3	1-0	0-0	2-0	4-1	3-1	0-1	2-1	2-2	0-0	4-2	—	2-2	3-1	1-0	1-1	1-1	6-3	4-2
Rotherham United FC	1-5	2-1	1-2	0-1	2-2	0-0	0-2	2-1	2-1	4-1	3-1	0-3	3-2	0-0	3-1	—	1-0	2-0	1-2	4-2	2-1	1-2
Scunthorpe United FC	1-0	2-2	2-0	3-0	2-1	1-1	2-2	0-2	2-0	1-1	2-1	3-1	2-2	1-2	4-1	1-0	—	2-1	0-0	1-1	1-0	2-0
Southampton FC	0-3	3-5	1-0	2-1	5-0	4-1	3-1	3-1	2-2	6-0	3-0	3-1	1-1	4-2	1-0	1-0	1-1	—	2-0	2-4	3-0	2-0
Stoke City FC	2-0	1-0	6-3	0-0	3-3	4-1	2-1	0-1	2-0	0-1	3-1	3-0	2-2	3-1	3-0	3-1	2-3	3-1	—	2-1	2-0	3-0
Sunderland AFC	0-1	2-1	1-0	0-1	3-0	6-2	1-1	2-1	3-1	3-1	0-0	7-1	1-1	1-0	2-1	2-0	0-0	4-0	0-0	—	3-1	5-0
Swansea Town AFC	3-0	2-1	2-1	2-0	2-0	1-0	1-2	0-2	1-0	1-1	1-0	2-0	2-1	0-0	1-1	2-2	1-0	1-1	2-1	3-4	—	3-0
Walsall FC	3-1	2-1	1-2	1-5	1-3	4-1	1-1	1-1	1-1	1-0	0-6	3-1	2-2	3-5	4-1	1-0	1-1	1-1	0-0	2-3	0-1	—

	Division 2	Pd	Wn	Dw	Ls	GF	GA	Pts	
1.	Stoke City FC (Stoke-on-Trent)	42	20	13	9	73	50	53	P
2.	Chelsea FC (London)	42	24	4	14	81	42	52	P
3.	Sunderland AFC (Sunderland)	42	20	12	10	84	55	52	
4.	Middlesbrough FC (Middlesbrough)	42	20	9	13	86	85	49	
5.	Leeds United AFC (Leeds)	42	19	10	13	79	53	48	
6.	Huddersfield Town AFC (Huddersfield)	42	17	14	11	63	50	48	
7.	Newcastle United FC (Newcastle-upon-Tyne)	42	18	11	13	79	59	47	
8.	Bury FC (Bury)	42	18	11	13	51	47	47	
9.	Scunthorpe United FC (Scunthorpe)	42	16	12	14	57	59	44	
10.	Cardiff City AFC (Cardiff)	42	18	7	17	83	73	43	
11.	Southampton FC (Southampton)	42	17	8	17	72	67	42	
12.	Plymouth Argyle FC (Plymouth)	42	15	12	15	76	73	42	
13.	Norwich City FC (Norwich)	42	17	8	17	80	79	42	
14.	Rotherham United FC (Rotherham)	42	17	6	19	67	74	40	
15.	Swansea Town AFC (Swansea)	42	15	9	18	51	72	39	
16.	Portsmouth FC (Portsmouth)	42	13	11	18	63	79	37	
17.	Preston North End FC (Preston)	42	13	11	18	59	74	37	
18.	Derby County FC (Derby)	42	12	12	18	61	72	36	
19.	Grimsby Town FC (Cleethorpes)	42	11	13	18	55	66	35	
20.	Charlton Athletic FC (London)	42	13	5	24	62	94	31	
21.	Walsall FC (Walsall)	42	11	9	22	53	89	31	R
22.	Luton Town FC (Luton)	42	11	7	24	61	84	29	R
		924	355	214	355	1496	1496	924	

Football League Division 3 — 1962-63 Season

	Barnsley	Bournemouth	Bradford P.A.	Brighton & H.A.	Bristol City	Bristol Rovers	Carlisle United	Colchester United	Coventry City	Crystal Palace	Halifax Town	Hull City	Millwall	Northampton T.	Notts County	Peterborough U.	Port Vale	Q.P.R.	Reading	Shrewsbury T.	Southend United	Swindon Town	Watford	Wrexham
Barnsley FC	■	2-2	1-4	2-0	1-1	4-0	2-0	2-3	2-1	0-4	1-0	1-2	4-1	1-1	3-1	0-2	2-1	0-0	1-0	1-0	2-2	1-1	4-1	2-1
Bournemouth & Bos.	1-1	■	2-2	1-0	1-1	1-1	5-1	1-1	1-1	3-0	1-1	3-0	1-1	3-0	3-1	3-3	2-0	2-1	1-0	0-0	0-0	0-0	1-0	3-1
Bradford Park Ave.	1-1	1-1	■	1-5	2-5	2-2	3-1	1-1	0-0	2-1	1-1	3-1	2-2	2-3	5-0	2-2	2-1	0-3	3-2	2-1	2-2	2-0	1-0	3-1
Brighton & Hove Alb.	2-0	0-1	3-1	■	1-0	1-1	1-0	3-0	2-2	1-2	0-1	2-1	0-2	0-5	1-3	0-3	3-1	2-2	2-4	1-1	0-0	1-1	1-4	1-3
Bristol City FC	5-2	1-0	4-2	1-2	■	4-1	2-2	1-2	1-1	1-1	2-2	3-1	2-2	3-1	1-1	1-1	2-0	2-4	4-2	3-1	6-3	2-2	3-3	0-2
Bristol Rovers FC	3-2	1-2	3-3	4-1	1-2	■	1-1	2-0	2-2	2-0	5-2	2-5	2-0	2-2	1-1	3-1	1-1	0-0	1-0	2-0	1-2	2-0	3-1	1-1
Carlisle United FC	2-1	0-3	3-0	1-0	2-5	4-0	■	3-1	0-1	2-2	1-0	2-1	4-3	1-2	4-2	1-4	1-1	2-5	1-1	2-1	1-2	0-0	2-1	2-1
Colchester United FC	1-1	3-1	1-4	4-1	1-0	1-0	2-1	■	0-0	1-2	2-3	2-5	2-2	2-2	2-0	0-1	4-2	3-2	3-1	0-2	3-2	1-1		
Coventry City FC	2-0	1-2	3-1	1-1	4-2	5-0	3-2	2-2	■	1-0	5-4	2-2	2-0	1-1	2-0	3-3	0-1	4-1	2-1	0-0	3-4	2-0	3-1	3-0
Crystal Palace FC	1-2	1-0	6-0	3-2	2-1	3-0	0-1	0-0	1-0	■	0-0	1-1	3-0	1-2	1-1	0-2	2-1	1-0	2-2	2-3	0-0	0-1	5-0	
Halifax Town AFC	2-0	3-1	4-4		2-5	2-3	2-4	1-2	2-4	2-2	■	0-2	3-0	1-3	2-1	2-0	0-4	1-4	1-2	2-2	0-1	4-3	1-3	2-0
Hull City AFC	0-2	1-1	1-0	2-1	4-0	3-0	3-2	2-2	2-0	0-0	2-0	■	4-1	2-1	1-3	3-2	0-1	4-1	0-1	2-2	1-1	1-1	1-0	1-3
Millwall FC	4-1	1-0	3-1	2-2	4-2	2-1	2-1	3-3	1-1	1-1	5-1	1-3	■	0-2	0-1	0-0	0-0	4-1	1-3	2-1	3-4	6-0	2-4	
Northampton Town	4-2	2-2	2-0	3-0	5-1	2-0	2-1	0-0	3-1	7-1	3-0	1-1		■	2-2	2-3	0-4	0-0	5-0	1-0	5-3	1-1	1-0	8-0
Notts County FC	2-0	2-0	3-2	0-1	3-2	1-3	1-0	6-0	1-1	0-2	5-0	1-1	3-3	2-1	■	2-0	1-0	3-2	1-0	1-5	2-1	2-0	1-3	3-2
Peterborough United	4-2	3-0	2-0	3-1	3-1	1-0	2-2	6-2	0-3	0-0	1-1	1-3	6-0	0-4	0-0	■	3-1	1-2	1-1	2-3	1-3	4-0	1-3	
Port Vale FC	1-0	0-3	2-0	1-2	3-1	2-0	4-2	2-1	1-1	1-0	1-1	3-1	1-1	3-2			■	3-2	2-0	5-1	2-1	1-3	2-2	
Queen's Park Rangers	2-1	1-0	1-2	2-2	3-5	2-2	1-2	1-3	4-1	5-0	4-1	2-3	1-3	0-1	0-0	3-1		■	3-2	0-0	1-0	2-2	2-2	1-2
Reading FC	4-1	2-1	4-1	4-5	0-3	1-0	2-0	4-1	0-1	4-2	2-2	2-0	0-1	4-3	1-1	0-1	4-3	1-1	■	5-0	1-3	1-2	0-0	3-0
Shrewsbury Town FC	1-3	2-1	1-2	2-1	-3	7-2	1-1	1-2	2-1	3-1	1-4	3-3	1-0	2-2	5-4	2-1	0-3	2-1		■	6-0	1-2	3-0	4-2
Southend United FC	0-0	0-1	1-1	1-1	2-2	3-2	2-0	2-3	1-1	1-1	1-1	2-1	5-1	1-2	2-1	2-0	1-3	2-0	3-1	2-0	■	1-1	1-1	2-0
Swindon Town FC	2-1	2-1	2-1	5-1	3-2	3-0	6-1	4-1	1-0	1-1	2-0	1-0	2-3	3-1	2-3	2-3	5-0	1-1	1-0	4-1		■	3-1	3-0
Watford FC	0-0	0-1	3-2	2-0	1-4	0-1	5-1	1-1	6-1	1-4	2-1	4-2	0-2	4-2	4-0	2-3	1-2	2-5	4-0	4-3	3-1	3-3	■	3-1
Wrexham AFC	2-1	1-0	3-1	0-0	2-1	5-1	2-1	4-1	5-1	3-4	3-1	2-0	5-1	1-4	5-1	4-4	0-1	3-1	1-1	2-0	1-1	0-0	0-0	■

	Division 3	Pd	Wn	Dw	Ls	GF	GA	Pts	
1.	Northampton Town FC (Northampton)	46	26	10	10	109	60	62	P
2.	Swindon Town FC (Swindon)	46	22	14	10	87	56	58	P
3.	Port Vale FC (Stoke-on-Trent)	46	23	8	15	72	58	54	
4.	Coventry City FC (Coventry)	46	18	17	11	83	69	53	
5.	Bournemouth & Boscombe Athletic FC (Bournemouth)	46	18	16	12	63	46	52	
6.	Peterborough United FC (Peterborough)	46	20	11	15	93	75	51	
7.	Notts County FC (Nottingham)	46	19	13	14	73	74	51	
8.	Southend United FC (Southend-on-Sea)	46	19	12	15	75	77	50	
9.	Wrexham AFC (Wrexham)	46	20	9	17	84	83	49	
10.	Hull City AFC (Kingston-upon-Hull)	46	19	10	17	74	69	48	
11.	Crystal Palace FC (London)	46	17	13	16	68	58	47	
12.	Colchester United FC (Colchester)	46	18	11	17	73	93	47	
13.	Queen's Park Rangers FC (London)	46	17	11	18	85	76	45	
14.	Bristol City FC (Bristol)	46	16	13	17	100	92	45	
15.	Shrewsbury Town FC (Shrewsbury)	46	16	12	18	83	81	44	
16.	Millwall FC (London)	46	15	13	18	82	87	43	
17.	Watford FC (Watford)	46	17	8	21	82	85	42	
18.	Barnsley FC (Barnsley)	46	15	11	20	63	74	41	
19.	Bristol Rovers FC (Bristol)	46	15	11	20	70	88	41	
20.	Reading FC (Reading)	46	16	8	22	74	78	40	
21.	Bradford Park Avenue FC (Bradford)	46	14	12	20	79	97	40	R
22.	Brighton & Hove Albion FC (Hove)	46	12	12	22	58	84	36	R
23.	Carlisle United FC (Carlisle)	46	13	9	24	61	89	35	R
24.	Halifax Town AFC (Halifax)	46	9	12	25	64	106	30	R
		1104	414	276	414	1855	1855	1104	

Football League Division 4 1962-63 Season	Aldershot Town	Barrow	Bradford City	Brentford	Chester	Chesterfield	Crewe Alexandra	Darlington	Doncaster Rovers	Exeter City	Gillingham	Hartlepools	Lincoln City	Mansfield Town	Newport County	Oldham Athletic	Oxford United	Rochdale	Southport	Stockport County	Torquay United	Tranmere Rovers	Workington	York City
Aldershot Town FC		2-1	3-1	0-0	2-2	1-0	2-2	2-3	3-1	1-1	0-1	3-2	1-2	2-3	2-1	1-1	0-0	2-0	4-2	2-2	1-1	2-3	2-2	4-1
Barrow AFC	1-1		1-1	1-1	4-3	2-0	2-3	4-1	4-0	0-2	1-1	2-0	2-1	3-2	3-0	3-2	3-2	1-1	6-2	1-0	0-0	1-1	5-1	2-1
Bradford City AFC	0-2	3-0		2-1	2-0	1-1	1-0	3-0	2-3	2-3	1-1	1-1	2-2	1-3	3-4	1-3	1-4	1-2	0-2	3-2	2-1	2-1	2-2	1-2
Brentford FC	4-2	2-1	5-2		2-1	2-1	3-1	1-3	1-0	3-1	1-2	4-0	3-2	1-3	3-1	2-1	4-0	1-0	3-3	2-1	2-2	4-0	4-3	2-1
Chester FC	0-2	1-0	2-0	1-2		0-2	1-2	1-2	1-1	3-1	1-0	1-0	3-2	0-2	2-2	1-0	2-1	1-0	6-1	0-1	3-1	0-0	1-1	0-0
Chesterfield FC	3-1	1-1	0-1	1-1	1-1		1-2	6-1	3-1	1-1	0-2	2-2	2-2	4-4	1-2	0-0	1-0	1-3	6-0	1-2	2-0	4-0	1-1	1-1
Crewe Alexandra FC	2-1	2-1	5-0	3-0	3-0	2-0		2-1	3-0	1-0	2-2	4-1	1-1	3-0	4-1	2-3	3-2	1-2	2-2	1-2	1-1	2-0	0-1	1-0
Darlington FC	1-1	2-1	2-1	1-3	2-1	2-1	1-4		5-1	0-1	2-0	0-2	0-0	2-1	4-2	1-1	2-1	3-0	1-3	5-1	1-3	2-3	3-1	2-1
Doncaster Rovers FC	2-1	2-2	1-1	0-2	1-2	0-0	1-1	2-0		1-1	1-0	2-3	3-0	1-1	2-2	1-1	4-2	2-2	0-0	1-2	2-0	2-1	2-0	3-2
Exeter City FC	4-2	0-2	0-2	2-2	2-1	2-2	1-1	1-3	0-1		0-0	3-1	1-1	0-3	1-0	2-1	1-1	0-2	2-1	0-1	0-3	2-1	1-0	2-1
Gillingham FC	1-0	2-3	2-1	1-4	2-1	2-1	4-0	1-0	1-0	4-0		5-1	3-0	0-1	3-1	4-3	2-1	2-1	3-1	1-0	4-2	0-0	2-2	0-0
Hartlepools United	1-2	1-1	2-2	2-1	0-3	1-1	1-5	0-2	1-1	0-2	1-1		3-0	3-4	2-3	0-1	1-2	4-0	4-0	3-0	0-3	0-2	2-2	1-1
Lincoln City FC	2-4	1-2	3-2	1-3	1-3	1-3	1-2	2-1	1-2	4-1	2-1	4-1		2-6	6-3	1-2	1-0	3-0	0-2	0-0	3-0	4-2	3-2	2-4
Mansfield Town FC	2-2	5-0	3-1	1-2	4-0	3-0	2-2	6-0	4-2	1-0	0-0	3-1	2-0		2-1	4-2	3-2	1-0	6-1	0-1	1-2	6-1	0-0	2-0
Newport County AFC	2-2	6-0	2-0	1-4	0-1	2-3	5-1	2-2	2-4	4-0	2-0	2-1	2-1	1-1		0-0	1-0	1-1	1-0	3-1	1-0	1-2	2-2	1-3
Oldham Athletic AFC	2-0	2-1	2-1	2-1	2-0	2-1	2-2	1-0	4-0	1-2	2-1	6-1	4-1	3-2	3-2		2-0	5-1	11-0	2-1	1-1	1-1	2-2	3-2
Oxford United FC	1-1	4-1	2-1	2-1	3-0	0-0	0-0	4-2	3-3	0-3	2-3	6-2	2-1	3-0	5-1	1-1		0-0	0-0	1-1	1-1	2-2	2-1	0-2
Rochdale AFC	1-1	6-0	2-1	3-5	0-0	3-2	2-0	1-1	3-1	3-0	1-1	2-1	1-0	3-1	3-3	1-1	2-1		1-0	1-0	3-0	1-2	3-2	1-0
Southport FC	1-1	3-3	3-3	1-0	4-1	0-2	1-3	4-2	2-1	1-3	0-0	1-1	0-0	3-2	2-1	2-1	4-2	1-1		2-0	4-4	0-0	6-3	2-1
Stockport County FC	3-0	1-3	3-1	2-1	1-0	0-1	1-1	0-1	2-1	4-3	0-0	4-1	1-2	1-1	1-1	2-1	1-1	1-0	0-2		1-2	2-2	2-3	1-0
Torquay United FC	3-1	2-1	4-1	1-1	1-0	2-1	1-2	1-1	2-2	3-0	2-0	0-0	3-3	3-1	2-0	2-2	2-1	5-1	2-2			1-0	2-0	1-0
Tranmere Rovers FC	1-3	2-0	1-1	1-2	3-0	4-1	2-1	3-1	2-3	2-1	2-1	6-1	3-0	5-1	0-0	1-2	3-0	3-2	7-1	3-1	1-1		0-1	2-1
Workington AFC	0-1	3-5	2-3	3-1	3-0	0-0	0-1	2-0	1-0	3-1	5-2	0-0	1-1	3-2	4-0	0-1	0-0	1-0	2-0	4-0	1-2	1-0		3-0
York City FC	0-0	1-1	3-0	1-1	0-0	3-4	2-0	5-1	1-0	3-3	0-3	2-0	3-1	2-1	2-0	5-2	1-2	1-0	1-1	3-1	1-0	1-2	1-2	

Division 4

		Pd	Wn	Dw	Ls	GF	GA	Pts	
1.	Brentford FC (London)	46	27	8	11	98	64	62	P
2.	Oldham Athletic AFC (Oldham)	46	24	11	11	95	60	59	P
3.	Crewe Alexandra FC (Crewe)	46	24	11	11	86	58	59	P
4.	Mansfield Town FC (Mansfield)	46	24	9	13	108	69	57	P
5.	Gillingham FC (Gillingham)	46	22	13	11	71	49	57	
6.	Torquay United FC (Torquay)	46	20	16	10	75	56	56	
7.	Rochdale AFC (Rochdale)	46	20	11	15	67	59	51	
8.	Tranmere Rovers FC (Tranmere)	46	20	10	16	81	67	50	
9.	Barrow AFC (Barrow-in-Furness)	46	19	12	15	82	80	50	
10.	Workington AFC (Workington)	46	17	13	16	76	68	47	
11.	Aldershot FC (Aldershot)	46	15	17	14	73	69	47	
12.	Darlington FC (Darlington)	46	19	6	21	72	87	44	
13.	Southport FC (Southport)	46	15	14	17	72	106	44	
14.	York City FC (York)	46	16	11	19	67	62	43	
15.	Chesterfield FC (Chesterfield)	46	13	16	17	70	64	42	
16.	Doncaster Rovers FC (Doncaster)	46	14	14	18	64	77	42	
17.	Exeter City FC (Exeter)	46	16	10	20	57	77	42	
18.	Oxford United FC (Oxford)	46	13	15	18	70	71	41	
19.	Stockport County FC (Stockport)	46	15	11	20	56	70	41	
20.	Newport County AFC (Newport)	46	14	11	21	76	90	39	
21.	Chester FC (Chester)	46	15	9	22	51	66	39	
22.	Lincoln City FC (Lincoln)	46	13	9	24	68	89	35	
23.	Bradford City AFC (Bradford)	46	11	10	25	64	93	32	
24.	Hartlepools United FC (Hartlepool)	46	7	11	28	56	104	25	
		1104	413	278	413	1755	1755	1104	

F.A. CUP FINAL   (Wembley Stadium, London – 25/05/1963 – 100,000)

MANCHESTER UNITED FC (MANCHESTER)   3-1   Leicester City FC (Leicester)

Law, Herd 2   *Keyworth*

Man. United: Gaskell, Dunne, Cantwell, Crerand, Foulkes, Setters, Giles, Quixall, Herd, Law, R.Charlton.

Leicester: Banks, Sjoberg, Norman, McLintock, King, Appleton, Riley, Cross, Keyworth, Gibson, Stringfellow.

Semi-finals

Leicester City FC (Leicester)	1-0	Liverpool FC (Liverpool)
Southampton FC (Southampton)	0-1	Manchester United FC (Manchester)

Quarter-finals

Coventry City FC (Coventry)	1-3	Manchester United FC (Manchester)
Liverpool FC (Liverpool)	1-0	West Ham United FC (London)
Norwich City FC (Norwich)	0-2	Leicester City FC (Leicester)
Nottingham Forest FC (Nottingham)	1-1, 3-3, 0-5	Southampton FC (Southampton)

1963-64

Football League Division 1 1963-64 Season	Arsenal	Aston Villa	Birmingham City	Blackburn Rovers	Blackpool	Bolton Wanderers	Burnley	Chelsea	Everton	Fulham	Ipswich Town	Leicester City	Liverpool	Manchester United	Nottingham Forest	Sheffield United	Sheffield Wed.	Stoke City	Tottenham Hotspur	W.B.A.	West Ham United	Wolves
Arsenal FC	■	3-0	4-1	0-0	5-3	4-3	3-2	2-4	6-0	2-2	6-0	0-1	1-1	2-1	4-2	1-3	1-1	1-1	4-4	3-2	3-3	1-3
Aston Villa FC	2-1	■	0-3	1-2	3-1	3-0	2-0	2-0	0-1	2-2	0-0	1-3	2-2	4-0	3-0	0-1	2-2	1-3	2-4	1-0	2-2	2-2
Birmingham City FC	1-4	3-3	■	2-2	3-2	2-1	0-0	3-4	0-2	0-0	1-0	2-0	3-1	1-1	3-3	3-0	1-2	0-1	1-2	0-1	2-1	2-2
Blackburn Rovers FC	4-1	2-0	3-0	■	1-2	3-0	1-2	2-2	1-2	2-0	3-1	5-2	1-2	1-3	2-0	2-2	1-1	1-0	7-2	0-2	1-3	1-1
Blackpool FC	0-1	0-4	3-0	3-2	■	2-0	1-1	1-5	1-1	1-0	2-2	3-3	0-1	1-0	1-0	2-2	2-2	1-0	0-2	1-0	0-1	1-2
Bolton Wanderers FC	1-1	1-1	0-2	0-5	1-1	■	2-1	1-0	1-3	2-1	6-0	0-1	1-2	0-1	2-3	3-0	3-0	3-4	1-3	1-2	1-1	0-4
Burnley FC	0-3	2-0	2-1	3-0	1-0	1-1	■	0-0	2-3	4-1	3-1	2-0	0-3	6-1	1-1	1-2	3-1	1-0	7-2	3-2	3-1	1-0
Chelsea FC	3-1	1-0	2-3	1-0	1-0	4-0	2-0	■	1-0	1-2	4-0	1-0	1-3	1-1	1-0	3-2	1-2	3-3	0-3	3-1	0-0	2-3
Everton FC	2-1	4-2	3-0	2-4	3-1	2-0	3-4	1-1	■	3-0	1-1	0-3	3-1	4-0	6-1	4-1	3-2	2-0	1-0	1-1	2-0	3-3
Fulham FC	1-4	2-0	2-1	1-1	1-1	3-1	2-1	0-1	2-2	■	10-1	2-1	1-0	2-2	0-0	3-1	2-0	3-3	1-1	1-1	2-0	4-1
Ipswich Town FC	1-2	4-3	3-2	0-0	4-3	1-3	3-1	1-3	0-0	4-2	■	1-1	1-2	2-7	4-3	1-0	1-4	0-2	2-3	1-2	3-2	1-0
Leicester City FC	7-2	0-0	3-0	4-3	2-3	1-0	0-0	2-4	2-0	0-1	2-1	■	0-2	3-2	1-1	0-1	2-0	2-1	0-1	0-2	2-2	0-1
Liverpool FC	5-0	5-2	2-1	1-2	1-2	2-0	2-0	2-1	2-1	2-0	6-0	0-1	■	3-0	1-2	6-1	3-1	6-1	3-1	1-0	1-2	6-0
Manchester United FC	3-1	1-0	1-2	2-2	3-0	5-0	5-1	1-1	5-1	3-0	2-0	3-1	0-1	■	3-1	2-1	3-1	5-2	4-1	1-0	0-1	2-2
Nottingham Forest FC	2-0	0-1	4-0	1-1	0-1	3-1	1-3	0-1	2-2	2-0	3-1	2-0	0-0	1-2	■	3-3	3-2	0-0	1-2	0-3	3-1	3-0
Sheffield United FC	2-2	1-1	3-0	0-1	1-0	0-1	2-0	1-1	0-0	1-0	3-1	0-1	3-0	1-2	1-2	■	1-1	4-1	3-3	2-1	2-1	4-3
Sheffield Wednesday FC	0-4	1-0	2-1	5-2	1-0	3-0	3-1	3-2	0-3	3-0	3-1	1-2	2-2	3-3	3-1	3-0	■	2-0	2-0	2-2	3-0	5-0
Stoke City FC	1-2	2-2	4-1	3-1	1-2	0-1	4-4	2-0	3-2	1-1	9-1	3-3	3-1	3-1	0-1	0-2	4-4	■	2-1	1-1	3-0	0-2
Tottenham Hotspur FC	3-1	3-1	6-1	4-1	6-1	1-0	3-2	1-2	2-4	1-0	6-3	1-1	1-3	2-3	4-1	0-0	1-1	2-1	■	0-2	3-0	4-3
West Bromwich Albion FC	4-0	4-3	3-1	1-3	2-1	1-1	0-0	1-1	4-2	3-0	2-1	1-1	2-2	1-4	2-3	2-0	1-3	2-3	4-4	■	0-1	3-1
West Ham United FC	1-1	0-1	5-0	2-8	3-1	2-3	1-1	2-2	4-2	1-1	2-2	2-2	1-0	0-2	0-2	2-3	4-3	4-1	4-0	4-2	■	1-1
Wolverhampton Wanderers FC	2-2	3-3	5-1	1-5	1-1	2-2	1-1	4-1	0-0	4-0	2-1	1-2	1-3	2-0	2-3	1-1	1-1	2-1	1-4	0-0	0-2	■

	Division 1	Pd	Wn	Dw	Ls	GF	GA	Pts	
1.	LIVERPOOL FC (LIVERPOOL)	42	26	5	11	92	45	57	
2.	Manchester United FC (Manchester)	42	23	7	12	90	62	53	
3.	Everton FC (Liverpool)	42	21	10	11	84	64	52	
4.	Tottenham Hotspur FC (London)	42	22	7	13	97	81	51	
5.	Chelsea FC (London)	42	20	10	12	72	56	50	
6.	Sheffield Wednesday FC (Sheffield)	42	19	11	12	84	67	49	
7.	Blackburn Rovers FC (Blackburn)	42	18	10	14	89	65	46	
8.	Arsenal FC (London)	42	17	11	14	90	82	45	
9.	Burnley FC (Burnley)	42	17	10	15	71	64	44	
10.	West Bromwich Albion FC (West Bromwich)	42	16	11	15	70	61	43	
11.	Leicester City FC (Leicester)	42	16	11	15	61	58	43	
12.	Sheffield United FC (Sheffield)	42	16	11	15	61	64	43	
13.	Nottingham Forest FC (Nottingham)	42	16	9	17	64	68	41	
14.	West Ham United FC (London)	42	14	12	16	69	74	40	
15.	Fulham FC (London)	42	13	13	16	58	65	39	
16.	Wolverhampton Wanderers FC (Wolverhampton)	42	12	15	15	70	80	39	
17.	Stoke City FC (Stoke-on-Trent)	42	14	10	18	77	78	38	
18.	Blackpool FC (Blackpool)	42	13	9	20	52	73	35	
19.	Aston Villa FC (Birmingham)	42	11	12	19	62	71	34	
20.	Birmingham City FC (Birmingham)	42	11	7	24	54	92	29	
21.	Bolton Wanderers FC (Bolton)	42	10	8	24	48	80	28	R
22.	Ipswich Town FC (Ipswich)	42	9	7	26	56	121	25	R
		924	354	216	354	1571	1571	924	

Top Goalscorer

1) James GREAVES   (Tottenham Hotspur)   35

Football League Division 2 1963-64 Season	Bury	Cardiff City	Charlton Athletic	Derby County	Grimsby Town	Huddersfield Town	Leeds United	Leyton Orient	Manchester City	Middlesbrough	Newcastle United	Northampton Town	Norwich City	Plymouth Argyle	Portsmouth	Preston North End	Rotherham United	Scunthorpe United	Southampton	Sunderland	Swansea Town	Swindon Town
Bury FC	■	4-1	0-2	1-2	1-1	0-2	1-2	1-2	1-1	1-1	1-2	1-1	4-2	2-2	3-2	2-1	4-2	3-2	1-5	0-1	3-2	1-0
Cardiff City AFC	2-1	■	1-1	2-1	0-0	2-1	0-0	2-1	2-2	1-1	2-2	1-0	3-1	3-1	1-2	0-4	2-1	3-1	2-4	0-2	1-1	1-0
Charlton Athletic FC	3-0	5-2	■	2-0	2-1	5-2	0-2	1-2	4-3	2-4	1-2	1-1	3-1	1-0	0-1	3-0	4-3	0-1	2-2	0-0	3-1	2-2
Derby County FC	2-1	2-1	1-1	■	0-0	2-0	1-1	1-0	1-3	2-2	1-2	0-0	2-1	3-1	3-1	1-2	1-4	2-2	3-2	0-3	3-0	3-0
Grimsby Town FC	1-0	0-2	0-2	1-3	■	2-2	0-2	1-1	1-1	3-1	2-1	4-1	3-1	1-1	0-3	0-3	1-3	2-0	2-2	2-2	1-1	1-2
Huddersfield Town AFC	2-1	2-1	2-1	0-0	1-2	■	0-2	2-1	0-2	1-0	3-0	0-1	1-1	4-3	1-1	2-2	0-3	3-2	4-0	0-2	1-0	2-0
Leeds United AFC	3-0	1-1	1-1	2-2	3-1	1-1	■	2-1	1-0	2-0	2-1	0-0	4-2	1-1	3-1	1-1	1-0	1-0	3-1	1-1	2-1	0-0
Leyton Orient FC	1-1	4-0	0-3	3-0	0-0	2-3	0-2	■	0-2	3-2	1-0	0-0	1-1	1-0	3-6	2-2	0-2	2-2	1-0	2-5	4-0	2-1
Manchester City FC	1-1	4-0	1-3	3-2	0-4	5-2	3-2	2-0	■	1-0	3-1	3-0	5-0	1-1	0-2	2-3	6-1	8-1	1-1	0-3	1-0	0-0
Middlesbrough FC	2-0	3-1	2-3	3-0	6-0	1-1	1-3	2-0	2-2	■	3-0	1-0	0-1	5-0	3-1	3-0	2-2	2-0	1-0	2-0	2-1	1-1
Newcastle United FC	0-4	0-4	5-0	3-1	4-0	2-0	0-1	3-0	3-1	2-0	■	2-3	2-0	1-0	1-0	2-4	5-2	3-1	2-2	1-0	4-1	4-1
Northampton Town FC	1-2	2-1	1-2	0-1	1-2	1-0	0-3	1-2	2-1	3-2	2-2	■	3-2	0-0	2-1	0-3	1-3	2-0	2-0	5-1	2-3	4-0
Norwich City FC	0-1	5-1	1-3	3-0	2-0	2-2	2-2	1-2	1-2	1-1	3-1	3-3	■	1-1	3-1	2-1	2-2	2-1	1-1	2-3	3-0	3-2
Plymouth Argyle FC	1-0	1-1	1-1	0-0	3-2	0-0	0-1	2-2	2-1	2-0	3-4	0-3	1-2	■	0-4	0-2	0-0	3-1	1-1	1-1	3-2	2-4
Portsmouth FC	3-3	5-0	4-1	1-1	2-2	2-1	1-1	4-3	2-2	1-0	5-2	3-0	1-1	1-2	■	1-2	2-1	3-4	2-0	2-4	0-0	1-4
Preston North End FC	3-0	4-0	3-1	0-2	1-0	2-1	2-0	0-0	2-0	2-2	3-0	2-1	3-0	0-0	0-0	■	2-2	1-0	2-1	1-1	3-3	1-0
Rotherham United FC	6-2	1-0	5-0	2-0	1-0	3-1	2-2	2-4	1-2	2-1	2-3	1-0	4-0	3-1	4-2	4-2	■	2-1	2-3	2-2	3-0	0-0
Scunthorpe United FC	0-0	1-2	1-1	3-2	2-2	1-0	0-1	0-0	2-4	1-0	2-0	1-2	2-2	1-0	1-1	1-0	4-3	■	1-2	1-1	2-2	3-0
Southampton FC	0-1	3-2	6-1	6-4	6-0	1-1	1-4	3-0	4-2	2-2	2-0	3-1	3-0	1-2	2-3	4-5	6-1	7-2	■	0-0	4-0	5-1
Sunderland AFC	4-1	3-3	2-1	3-0	3-0	3-2	2-0	4-1	2-0	0-1	0-2	1-0	3-0	4-0	2-0	1-0	1-2	1-2	1-2	■	1-0	6-0
Swansea Town AFC	0-2	3-0	1-2	2-1	1-1	1-2	0-3	1-0	3-3	2-1	0-1	1-1	3-1	2-1	1-1	5-1	4-2	4-1	6-0	1-2	■	3-0
Swindon Town FC	2-1	1-2	2-2	0-0	2-1	1-2	2-2	5-0	3-0	2-0	0-0	2-3	2-2	2-1	2-0	1-4	3-1	3-0	1-2	1-0	2-1	■

	Division 2	Pd	Wn	Dw	Ls	GF	GA	Pts	
1.	Leeds United AFC (Leeds)	42	24	15	3	71	34	63	P
2.	Sunderland AFC (Sunderland)	42	25	11	6	81	37	61	P
3.	Preston North End FC (Preston)	42	23	10	9	79	54	56	
4.	Charlton Athletic FC (London)	42	19	10	13	76	70	48	
5.	Southampton FC (Southampton)	42	19	9	14	100	73	47	
6.	Manchester City FC (Manchester)	42	18	10	14	84	66	46	
7.	Rotherham United FC (Rotherham)	42	19	7	16	90	78	45	
8.	Newcastle United FC (Newcastle-upon-Tyne)	42	20	5	17	74	69	45	
9.	Portsmouth FC (Portsmouth)	42	16	11	15	79	70	43	
10.	Middlesbrough FC (Middlesbrough)	42	15	11	16	67	52	41	
11.	Northampton Town FC (Northampton)	42	16	9	17	58	60	41	
12.	Huddersfield Town AFC (Huddersfield)	42	15	10	17	57	64	40	
13.	Derby County FC (Derby)	42	14	11	17	56	67	39	
14.	Swindon Town FC (Swindon)	42	14	10	18	57	69	38	
15.	Cardiff City AFC (Cardiff)	42	14	10	18	56	81	38	
16.	Leyton Orient FC (London)	42	13	10	19	54	72	36	
17.	Norwich City FC (Norwich)	42	11	13	18	64	80	35	
18.	Bury FC (Bury)	42	13	9	20	57	73	35	
19.	Swansea Town AFC (Swansea)	42	12	9	21	63	74	33	
20.	Plymouth Argyle FC (Plymouth)	42	8	16	18	45	67	32	
21.	Grimsby Town FC (Cleethorpes)	42	9	14	19	47	75	32	R
22.	Scunthorpe United FC (Scunthorpe)	42	10	10	22	52	82	30	R
		924	347	230	347	1467	1467	924	

Football League Division 3 1963-64 Season	Barnsley	Bournemouth	Brentford	Bristol City	Bristol Rovers	Colchester United	Coventry City	Crewe Alexandra	Crystal Palace	Hull City	Luton Town	Mansfield Town	Millwall	Notts County	Oldham Athletic	Peterborough Utd.	Port Vale	Q.P.R.	Reading	Shrewsbury Town	Southend United	Walsall	Watford	Wrexham
Barnsley FC	■	2-1	1-1	2-4	1-2	1-1	1-1	1-0	2-0	2-2	3-1	1-1	1-1	2-1	2-2	3-2	0-0	3-1	0-3	2-1	0-1	1-3	0-0	3-0
Bournemouth & Bos.	4-1	■	2-0	0-1	1-0	2-2	2-1	3-0	4-3	1-0	3-1	0-0	4-0	1-1	1-0	3-0	3-0	4-2	1-2	2-0	1-0	1-1	2-0	2-0
Brentford FC	1-1	2-0	■	1-2	2-5	3-1	2-3	2-2	2-1	1-3	2-6	4-0	3-1	4-1	2-0	2-0	1-2	2-2	4-2	0-1	3-0	1-1	1-2	9-0
Bristol City FC	5-2	3-1	3-3	■	3-0	3-1	0-1	1-1	1-1	1-0	5-1	2-3	0-0	2-0	3-1	3-1	0-0	2-1	0-2	2-2	2-2	5-1	2-0	4-0
Bristol Rovers FC	1-1	2-3	3-1	4-0	■	3-1	0-1	1-2	1-3	4-0	1-2	3-2	2-2	4-0	0-1	2-2	4-4	0-0	2-5	7-0	3-1	3-0	1-2	1-1
Colchester United FC	4-1	1-2	1-2	1-1	2-3	■	2-1	4-0	1-1	1-1	1-1	1-1	2-0	4-0	2-3	4-1	1-2	2-0	2-1	1-0	3-3	0-0	1-1	4-1
Coventry City FC	3-1	2-2	2-2	2-1	4-2	1-0	■	5-1	5-1	2-2	3-3	0-3	3-0	2-0	4-1	3-2	1-1	4-2	0-0	8-1	2-5	1-0	2-2	3-0
Crewe Alexandra FC	1-2	1-0	1-1	2-0	4-1	1-1	2-2	■	0-2	1-4	1-0	3-2	1-0	0-1	1-0	0-0	1-0	2-0	2-2	3-2	1-2	0-1	0-1	1-2
Crystal Palace FC	1-2	2-1	1-0	1-0	1-0	0-0	1-1	1-0	■	2-2	1-1	3-1	2-1	2-0	1-3	1-0	2-0	1-0	4-1	3-0	3-0	1-0	2-0	2-1
Hull City AFC	2-2	3-4	0-0	4-4	0-2	0-0	2-1	2-1	1-1	■	2-0	3-1	0-0	4-1	0-1	0-0	4-1	3-0	1-1	4-2	1-0	3-1	2-2	4-2
Luton Town FC	2-3	1-0	0-2	1-4	4-2	3-1	1-3	3-3	0-4	2-1	■	0-2	1-3	2-0	1-2	2-3	1-0	4-4	2-1	2-0	4-1	1-0	2-1	3-1
Mansfield Town FC	2-1	1-1	2-2	4-0	2-0	1-1	3-2	2-1	1-1	2-0	1-1	■	4-1	4-0	1-1	4-1	1-1	1-0	2-1	3-1	4-1	2-1	1-1	3-1
Millwall FC	4-2	3-0	1-3	0-1	0-1	0-1	0-0	1-0	0-1	0-1	3-0	0-1	■	6-1	2-1	0-2	3-1	2-2	2-0	2-2	1-1	2-1	0-3	1-4
Notts County FC	1-1	1-3	2-0	1-1	3-4	3-1	0-3	0-0	1-1	0-1	1-1	1-0	2-0	■	4-2	0-0	2-0	2-2	0-1	0-1	1-1	0-1	1-2	3-0
Oldham Athletic AFC	2-0	2-4	4-1	1-2	2-2	2-2	2-0	3-2	3-1	1-1	0-1	1-0	1-2	2-0	■	4-2	1-0	2-1	3-1	2-4	0-3	2-4	1-0	3-2
Peterborough United	3-2	2-1	3-0	4-2	2-2	4-0	2-0	3-2	1-1	5-1	0-0	1-3	2-3	5-1	0-0	■	1-1	2-1	1-0	2-2	3-0	1-2	0-1	5-2
Port Vale FC	1-0	0-0	3-0	4-1	1-0	0-2	1-1	4-0	1-2	1-0	1-0	1-0	1-0	0-1	1-0	1-2	■	2-0	0-0	1-1	4-1	2-2	0-0	5-0
Queen's Park Rangers	2-2	1-0	2-2	0-2	1-0	0-0	3-6	2-0	3-4	0-2	1-1	2-0	2-0	3-2	3-2	3-0	3-0	■	4-2	3-4	4-5	3-0	1-0	1-0
Reading FC	6-1	2-0	4-3	1-1	3-1	5-3	2-2	2-2	0-0	2-0	1-1	4-3	1-0	3-2	0-1	1-0	1-0	1-2	■	2-0	4-2	0-1	2-0	2-1
Shrewsbury Town FC	3-1	5-2	1-1	2-0	0-1	1-1	0-0	3-0	1-1	5-1	1-0	2-0	0-1	5-2	2-0	0-0	1-0	1-2	2-1	■	2-2	2-1	3-0	1-2
Southend United FC	4-1	1-1	2-1	1-1	3-4	0-0	1-2	1-1	2-1	1-1	0-1	2-1	1-1	3-1	2-2	2-0	1-1	1-3	2-0	7-1	■	1-1	3-0	1-1
Walsall FC	4-4	0-2	2-2	1-1	2-3	1-1	0-3	2-1	2-2	1-1	4-0	3-1	0-2	2-1	1-1	2-0	2-1	0-2	1-1	1-1	2-0	■	1-3	0-2
Watford FC	2-1	3-0	2-2	2-2	3-2	3-1	1-1	4-1	3-1	3-3	2-0	3-0	2-2	2-0	2-1	1-2	1-1	3-1	1-0	2-1	3-1	5-3	■	4-2
Wrexham AFC	7-2	3-4	2-4	1-1	1-2	5-4	1-1	1-1	2-2	3-1	2-0	2-0	3-0	4-0	0-4	2-3	1-2	0-1	0-3	2-3	1-3	4-0	3-1	■

	Division 3	Pd	Wn	Dw	Ls	GF	GA	Pts	
1.	Coventry City FC (Coventry)	46	22	16	9	98	61	60	P
2.	Crystal Palace FC (London)	46	23	14	9	73	51	60	P
3.	Watford FC (Watford)	46	23	12	11	79	59	58	
4.	Bournemouth & Boscombe Athletic FC (Bournemouth)	46	24	8	14	79	58	56	
5.	Bristol City FC (Bristol)	46	20	15	11	84	64	55	
6.	Reading FC (Reading)	46	21	10	15	79	62	52	
7.	Mansfield Town FC (Mansfield)	46	20	11	15	76	62	51	
8.	Hull City AFC (Kingston-upon-Hull)	46	16	17	13	73	68	49	
9.	Oldham Athletic AFC (Oldham)	46	20	8	18	73	70	48	
10.	Peterborough United FC (Peterborough)	46	18	11	17	75	70	47	
11.	Shrewsbury Town FC (Shrewsbury)	46	18	11	17	73	80	47	
12.	Bristol Rovers FC (Bristol)	46	19	8	19	91	79	46	
13.	Port Vale FC (Stoke-on-Trent)	46	16	14	16	53	49	46	
14.	Southend United FC (Southend-on-Sea)	46	15	15	16	77	78	45	
15.	Queen's Park Rangers FC (London)	46	18	9	19	76	78	45	
16.	Brentford FC (London)	46	15	14	17	87	80	44	
17.	Colchester United FC (Colchester)	46	12	19	15	70	68	43	
18.	Luton Town FC (Luton)	46	16	10	20	64	80	42	
19.	Walsall FC (Walsall)	46	13	14	19	59	76	40	
20.	Barnsley FC (Barnsley)	46	12	15	19	68	94	39	
21.	Millwall FC (London)	46	14	10	22	53	67	38	R
22.	Crewe Alexandra FC (Crewe)	46	11	12	23	50	77	34	R
23.	Wrexham AFC (Wrexham)	46	13	6	27	75	107	32	R
24.	Notts County FC (Nottingham)	46	9	9	28	45	92	27	R
		1104	408	288	408	1730	1730	1104	

Football League Division 4 — 1963-64 Season

	Aldershot Town	Barrow	Bradford City	Bradford P.A.	Brighton & H.A.	Carlisle United	Chester	Chesterfield	Darlington	Doncaster Rovers	Exeter City	Gillingham	Halifax Town	Hartlepools	Lincoln City	Newport County	Oxford United	Rochdale	Southport	Stockport County	Torquay United	Tranmere Rovers	Workington	York City
Aldershot Town FC	■	8-2	2-3	0-3	1-0	3-2	2-1	0-2	1-2	4-2	0-1	1-1	0-0	4-1	2-0	2-0	2-0	1-1	3-1	7-0	1-0	5-4	4-0	5-2
Barrow AFC	0-2	■	2-3	2-2	1-1	2-2	2-2	5-2	3-1	0-2	1-1	0-3	0-0	1-2	2-0	1-1	1-1	1-2	1-3	1-2	1-0	1-1	1-1	1-2
Bradford City AFC	3-0	7-1	■	1-0	3-1	2-2	1-1	4-2	1-2	2-1	1-2	0-2	0-0	2-0	4-0	2-1	2-1	2-0	2-0	1-0	2-1	0-3	0-2	3-2
Bradford Park Ave.	2-1	1-0	1-3	■	2-1	1-1	4-0	0-1	4-1	3-1	3-2	1-0	4-4	3-1	0-1	2-5	5-2	2-2	3-0	2-2	1-1	4-2	1-0	1-3
Brighton & Hove Alb.	3-1	2-0	1-2	0-1	■	1-3	0-0	1-1	2-0	4-1	1-2	2-1	3-0	4-1	5-1	1-2	2-1	3-1	1-0	1-2	3-0	1-1	1-2	3-0
Carlisle United FC	4-0	4-1	1-2	4-0	0-1	■	3-1	1-0	3-3	6-0	3-0	3-1	3-0	7-1	5-0	3-3	2-1	1-0	5-2	0-0	0-1	5-2	3-1	4-0
Chester FC	2-0	2-0	3-0	1-0	0-0	4-2	■	4-2	0-1	1-1	2-0	1-0	5-2	2-1	3-1	3-0	0-2	2-0	5-0	2-1	2-1	0-2	2-1	1-1
Chesterfield FC	4-0	1-1	3-2	1-2	1-0	2-0	1-0	■	2-1	3-3	0-1	0-3	2-2	0-2	1-3	0-1	0-0	1-1	1-0	1-1	1-1	1-1	2-2	1-0
Darlington FC	0-1	3-3	1-2	2-2	1-2	1-6	1-0	3-2	■	2-0	1-1	1-1	0-0	1-1	3-1	3-0	3-2	2-2	2-3	2-0	3-5	1-1		4-2
Doncaster Rovers FC	1-1	3-1	2-1	3-2	1-1	1-1	3-2	1-1	10-0	■	1-0	1-2	3-1	2-2	0-0	1-1	1-0	2-0	3-0	4-1	1-0	1-2	2-3	0-0
Exeter City FC	0-0	0-0	4-1	2-3	0-0	1-0	3-0	6-1	1-1	3-1	■	0-0	0-0	2-1	0-0	3-1	3-2	0-1	1-1	2-0	0-0	5-0	2-1	1-0
Gillingham FC	2-0	3-1	0-0	2-0	1-0	2-0	2-1	1-0	2-1	1-1	0-0	■	2-1	1-0	1-1	2-0	1-0	1-1	5-1	0-0	2-2	2-2	3-1	1-0
Halifax Town AFC	3-3	1-0	0-1	2-1	2-2	1-2	1-0	3-2	2-2	0-2	2-0	0-0	■	4-1	0-2	2-0	3-1	3-2	4-1	4-2	5-1	2-0	1-3	0-0
Hartlepools United	1-4	0-0	1-0	4-2	2-2	0-6	2-0	1-0	0-2	2-1	1-1	0-0	1-1	■	1-2	1-1	2-1	1-1	2-3	3-0	1-4	3-2	1-2	0-1
Lincoln City FC	3-3	3-0	1-0	3-0	0-2	0-2	3-2	5-2	3-1	3-1	1-1	0-3	4-0	4-2	■	2-1	3-2	2-0	2-0	1-0	3-2	0-1	0-2	3-2
Newport County AFC	2-1	3-0	3-1	4-0	1-4	0-1	0-1	1-2	1-0	0-1	0-1	4-2	2-1	4-2		■	1-0	1-1	3-0	3-1	0-3	0-2	0-0	0-0
Oxford United FC	1-1	0-0	1-1	2-1	1-3	1-2	2-1	1-2	5-0	0-1	0-2	3-1	2-2	5-1	2-0	2-1	■	1-1	0-0	1-0	1-0	0-2	2-1	4-4
Rochdale AFC	2-2	1-3	1-2	0-1	1-1	1-0	1-0	2-1	2-2	1-3	2-1	4-1	2-0	2-2	0-1	0-0	4-0	■	1-0	1-0	1-1	5-0	2-0	
Southport FC	4-1	3-3	3-3	0-1	3-3	3-0	0-2	0-1	3-1	3-0	1-1	1-1	3-1	2-1	4-2	1-1	2-1		■	2-0	1-0	2-0	0-3	0-3
Stockport County FC	2-2	5-0	2-1	2-1	1-1	0-3	1-1	2-0	1-2	2-0	0-1	0-2	1-0	4-1	1-0	0-0	1-0	1-4		■	0-0	1-1	0-0	2-0
Torquay United FC	3-0	1-1	4-0	6-2	3-0	3-1	5-0	1-1	3-1	1-0	1-1	3-2	4-2	2-2	8-3	0-0	1-0	3-1	4-0		■	1-1	2-1	0-1
Tranmere Rovers FC	3-0	1-1	0-1	3-1	1-2	6-1	3-3	2-1	0-2	3-0	2-1	0-0	2-2	2-3	3-0	2-3	1-3	2-1	2-0	4-2	3-1	■	0-2	1-0
Workington AFC	4-0	4-1	1-0	1-1	1-0	2-2	1-1	1-2	3-0	4-1	0-0	1-0	2-4	2-0	1-1	2-0	3-1	3-0	2-1	1-1	2-1	4-2	■	1-0
York City FC	1-2	1-2	1-0	2-0	2-3	0-0	1-0	2-0	3-1	3-1	1-2	0-1	1-3	0-1	0-0	3-0	0-2	0-3	4-1	2-0	1-1	1-2	0-1	■

Division 4

		Pd	Wn	Dw	Ls	GF	GA	Pts	
1.	Gillingham FC (Gillingham)	46	23	14	9	59	30	60	P
2.	Carlisle United FC (Carlisle)	46	25	10	11	113	58	60	P
3.	Workington AFC (Workington)	46	24	11	11	76	52	59	P
4.	Exeter City FC (Exeter)	46	20	18	8	62	37	58	P
5.	Bradford City AFC (Bradford)	46	25	6	15	76	62	56	
6.	Torquay United FC (Torquay)	46	20	11	15	80	54	51	
7.	Tranmere Rovers FC (Birkenhead)	46	20	11	15	85	73	51	
8.	Brighton & Hove Albion FC (Hove)	46	19	12	15	71	52	50	
9.	Aldershot FC (Aldershot)	46	19	10	17	83	78	48	
10.	Halifax Town AFC (Halifax)	46	17	14	15	77	77	48	
11.	Lincoln City FC (Lincoln)	46	19	9	18	67	75	47	
12.	Chester FC (Chester)	46	19	8	19	65	60	46	
13.	Bradford Park Avenue FC (Bradford)	46	18	9	19	75	81	45	
14.	Doncaster Rovers FC (Doncaster)	46	15	12	19	70	75	42	
15.	Newport County AFC (Newport)	46	17	8	21	64	73	42	
16.	Chesterfield FC (Chesterfield)	46	15	12	19	57	71	42	
17.	Stockport County FC (Stockport)	46	15	12	19	50	68	42	
18.	Oxford United FC (Oxford)	46	14	13	19	59	63	41	
19.	Darlington FC (Darlington)	46	14	12	20	66	93	40	
20.	Rochdale AFC (Rochdale)	46	12	15	19	56	59	39	
21.	Southport FC (Southport)	46	15	9	22	63	88	39	
22.	York City FC (York)	46	14	7	25	52	66	35	
23.	Hartlepools United FC (Hartlepool)	46	12	9	25	54	93	33	
24.	Barrow AFC (Barrow-in-Furness)	46	6	18	22	51	93	30	
		1104	417	270	417	1631	1631	1104	

F.A. CUP FINAL   (Wembley Stadium, London – 25/05/1964 – 100,000)

WEST HAM UNITED FC LONDON)   3-2   Preston North End FC (Preston)

Sissons, Hurst, Boyce   *Holden, Dawson*

West Ham: Standen, Bond, Burkett, Bovington, Brown, Moore, Brabrook, Boyce, Byrne, Hurst, Sissons.

Preston: Kelly, Ross, Lawton, Smith, Singleton, Kendall, Wilson, Ashworth, Dawson, Spavin, Holden.

Semi-finals

Swansea Town AFC (Swansea)	1-2	Preston North End FC (Preston)
West Ham United FC (London)	3-1	Manchester United FC (Manchester)

Quarter-finals

Liverpool FC (Liverpool)	1-2	Swansea Town AFC (Swansea)
Manchester United FC (Manchester)	3-3, 2-2, 5-1	Sunderland AFC (Sunderland)
Oxford United FC (Oxford)	1-2	Preston North End FC (Preston)
West Ham United FC (London)	3-2	Burnley FC (Burnley)

1964-65

Football League Division 1 1964-65 Season	Arsenal	Aston Villa	Birmingham C.	Blackburn R.	Blackpool	Burnley	Chelsea	Everton	Fulham	Leeds United	Leicester City	Liverpool	Manchester U.	Nottingham F.	Sheffield Utd.	Sheffield Wed.	Stoke City	Sunderland	Tottenham H.	W.B.A.	West Ham U.	Wolves
Arsenal FC	■	3-1	3-0	1-1	3-1	3-2	1-3	3-1	2-0	1-2	4-3	0-0	2-3	0-3	1-1	1-1	3-2	3-1	3-1	1-1	0-3	4-1
Aston Villa FC	3-1	■	3-0	0-4	3-2	1-0	2-2	1-2	2-0	1-2	1-0	0-1	2-1	2-1	2-1	2-0	3-0	2-1	1-0	0-1	2-3	3-2
Birmingham City FC	2-3	0-1	■	5-5	3-0	2-1	1-6	3-5	2-2	3-3	2-0	0-0	2-4	1-1	1-1	0-0	1-2	4-3	1-0	1-1	2-1	0-1
Blackburn Rovers FC	1-2	5-1	3-1	■	4-1	1-4	0-3	0-2	2-0	0-2	3-1	3-2	0-5	1-1	4-0	0-1	1-1	3-2	3-1	4-2	4-0	4-1
Blackpool FC	1-1	3-1	3-1	4-2	■	2-4	3-2	1-1	3-0	4-0	1-1	2-3	1-2	0-2	2-2	1-0	1-1	3-1	1-1	3-0	1-2	1-1
Burnley FC	2-1	2-2	2-0	1-1	2-2	■	6-2	1-1	4-0	2-1	1-5	0-0	2-2	3-1	4-1	1-0	0-0	2-2	0-1	3-2	1-1
Chelsea FC	2-1	2-1	3-1	5-1	2-0	0-1	■	5-1	1-0	2-0	4-1	4-0	0-2	0-1	3-0	1-1	4-0	3-1	2-2	0-3	2-1
Everton FC	1-0	3-1	1-1	2-3	0-0	2-1	1-1	■	2-0	0-1	2-2	2-1	3-3	1-0	1-1	1-1	1-1	4-1	3-2	1-1	5-0
Fulham FC	3-4	1-1	3-1	3-2	3-3	0-1	1-2	1-1	■	2-2	5-2	1-1	2-1	4-1	1-2	2-0	1-4	1-0	4-1	3-1	1-2	2-0
Leeds United AFC	3-1	1-0	4-1	1-1	3-0	5-1	2-2	4-1	2-2	■	3-2	4-2	1-0	1-2	4-1	2-3	2-1	3-1	1-0	2-1	3-2
Leicester City FC	2-3	1-1	4-4	2-3	3-2	0-2	1-1	2-1	5-1	2-2	■	2-0	2-2	3-2	0-2	2-2	0-1	0-1	4-2	4-2	1-0	3-2
Liverpool FC	3-2	5-1	4-3	3-2	2-2	1-1	2-0	0-4	3-2	2-1	0-1	■	0-2	2-0	3-1	4-2	3-2	0-0	1-1	0-3	2-2	2-1
Manchester United FC	3-1	7-0	1-1	3-0	2-0	3-2	4-0	2-1	4-1	0-1	1-0	3-0	■	3-0	1-1	1-0	1-1	1-0	4-1	2-2	3-1	3-0
Nottingham Forest FC	3-0	4-2	4-3	2-5	2-1	3-1	2-2	1-2	2-3	0-0	2-1	2-2	2-2	■	0-0	2-2	5-2	1-2	0-0	3-2	0-2
Sheffield United FC	4-0	4-2	3-1	1-1	1-3	2-0	0-2	0-0	1-1	0-3	0-2	3-0	0-2	■	2-3	0-1	3-0	3-3	1-1	2-1	0-2
Sheffield Wednesday FC	2-1	3-1	5-2	1-0	4-1	5-1	2-3	0-1	1-1	3-0	0-0	1-0	1-0	0-0	0-2	■	1-1	2-0	1-0	1-1	2-0	2-0
Stoke City FC	4-1	2-1	2-1	1-1	4-2	2-0	0-2	0-2	3-1	2-3	3-3	1-1	1-2	1-1	0-1	4-1	■	3-1	2-0	2-0	3-1	0-2
Sunderland AFC	0-2	2-2	2-1	1-0	1-0	3-2	3-0	4-0	0-0	3-3	3-3	2-3	1-0	4-0	3-1	3-0	2-2	■	2-1	2-2	3-2	1-2
Tottenham Hotspur FC	3-1	4-0	4-1	5-2	4-1	4-1	1-1	2-2	3-0	0-0	6-2	3-1	4-0	2-0	3-2	1-2	3-0	■	1-0	3-2	7-4
West Bromwich Albion FC	0-0	3-1	0-2	0-0	1-3	1-2	0-2	4-0	2-2	1-2	6-0	1-1	1-2	2-2	0-1	1-0	5-3	4-1	2-0	■	4-2	5-1
West Ham United FC	2-1	3-0	2-1	1-1	2-1	3-2	2-3	0-1	2-1	0-0	2-1	2-3	3-1	1-2	0-1	2-3	3-2	6-1	■	5-0
Wolverhampton Wanderers FC	0-1	0-1	0-2	4-2	1-2	1-2	0-3	2-4	0-0	0-1	1-1	2-4	1-2	1-0	3-1	3-1	3-0	3-1	3-2	4-3	■

	Division 1	Pd	Wn	Dw	Ls	GF	GA	Pts	
1.	MANCHESTER UNITED FC (MANCHESTER)	42	26	9	7	89	39	61	
2.	Leeds United AFC (Leeds)	42	26	9	7	83	52	61	
3.	Chelsea FC (London)	42	24	8	10	89	54	56	
4.	Everton FC (Liverpool)	42	17	15	10	69	60	49	
5.	Nottingham Forest FC (Nottingham)	42	17	13	12	71	67	47	
6.	Tottenham Hotspur FC (London)	42	19	7	16	87	71	45	
7.	Liverpool FC (Liverpool)	42	17	10	15	67	73	44	
8.	Sheffield Wednesday FC (Sheffield)	42	16	11	15	57	55	43	
9.	West Ham United FC (London)	42	19	4	19	82	71	42	
10.	Blackburn Rovers FC (Blackburn)	42	16	10	16	83	79	42	
11.	Stoke City FC (Stoke-on-Trent)	42	16	10	16	67	66	42	
12.	Burnley FC (Burnley)	42	16	10	16	70	70	42	
13.	Arsenal FC (London)	42	17	7	18	69	75	41	
14.	West Bromwich Albion FC (West Bromwich)	42	13	13	16	70	65	39	
15.	Sunderland AFC (Sunderland)	42	14	9	19	64	74	37	
16.	Aston Villa FC (Birmingham)	42	16	5	21	57	82	37	
17.	Blackpool FC (Blackpool)	42	12	11	19	67	78	35	
18.	Leicester City FC (Leicester)	42	11	13	18	69	85	35	
19.	Sheffield United FC (Sheffield)	42	12	11	19	50	64	35	
20.	Fulham FC (London)	42	11	12	19	60	78	34	
21.	Wolverhampton Wanderers FC (Wolverhampton)	42	13	4	25	59	89	30	R
22.	Birmingham City FC (Birmingham)	42	8	11	23	64	96	27	R
		924	356	212	356	1543	1543	924	

Top Goalscorers

1)	James GREAVES	(Tottenham Hotspur FC)	29
	Andrew McEVOY	(Blackburn Rovers FC)	29

Football League Division 2 1964-65 Season	Bolton Wanderers	Bury	Cardiff City	Charlton Athletic	Coventry City	Crystal Palace	Derby County	Huddersfield Town	Ipswich Town	Leyton Orient	Manchester City	Middlesbrough	Newcastle United	Northampton Town	Norwich City	Plymouth Argyle	Portsmouth	Preston North End	Rotherham United	Southampton	Swansea Town	Swindon Town
Bolton Wanderers FC		0-1	1-0	1-1	1-3	3-0	3-1	1-0	0-0	0-0	4-0	4-2	1-1	0-0	5-2	6-1	3-2	5-1	2-0	3-0	2-1	1-1
Bury FC	2-1		1-2	2-0	5-0	3-1	2-1	0-2	0-1	2-1	0-2	3-2	1-2	1-4	1-0	0-2	1-1	1-1	0-1	3-3	2-2	6-1
Cardiff City AFC	1-3	4-0		2-1	3-1	0-0	2-1	1-1	0-0	0-2	2-2	6-1	1-1	0-2	1-3	4-0	1-0	3-3	3-2	2-2	5-0	2-0
Charlton Athletic FC	1-3	1-2	2-2		3-0	1-2	1-3	0-0	4-0	2-0	2-1	0-2	0-1	1-1	2-1	3-2	3-3	2-3	1-1	2-5	1-0	3-2
Coventry City FC	0-0	2-1	0-2	2-0		0-0	0-2	2-3	5-3	1-1	2-2	3-0	5-4	0-1	3-0	2-0	1-2	3-0	3-5	1-1	3-0	3-2
Crystal Palace FC	2-0	0-2	0-0	3-1	2-2		2-3	3-0	1-1	1-0	1-1	3-1	1-1	1-2	2-0	2-1	4-2	1-0	2-1	0-2	3-3	3-1
Derby County FC	2-3	3-1	1-0	4-4	2-1	3-3		2-0	2-3	1-0	2-0	3-3	0-3	2-2	0-1	3-2	4-0	3-1	2-2	2-1	3-4	4-1
Huddersfield Town AFC	1-1	0-2	3-1	0-1	2-1	2-0	3-1		0-0	0-0	1-0	1-0	0-1	2-0	0-0	1-2	2-1	3-0	1-0	0-3	4-0	2-1
Ipswich Town FC	1-4	1-0	1-1	1-1	1-3	3-2	2-1	3-2		1-1	4-1	5-2	3-1	0-0	3-0	2-2	7-0	1-5	4-4	2-0	3-0	0-0
Leyton Orient FC	3-1	1-0	1-3	4-2	1-3	0-1	1-4	1-0	0-0		4-3	1-1	2-1	2-2	2-3	2-0	5-2	2-1	2-1	0-0	2-3	0-3
Manchester City FC	2-4	0-0	2-0	2-1	1-1	0-2	2-0	2-3	4-0	6-0		1-1	3-0	0-2	0-2	2-1	2-0	4-3	2-1	3-1	1-0	1-2
Middlesbrough FC	5-2	3-3	0-0	1-2	2-3	0-0	1-2	0-0	2-4	2-0	0-1		0-2	1-0	2-0	1-3	4-1	1-1	3-5	4-1	4-0	4-1
Newcastle United FC	2-0	2-3	2-0	1-1	2-0	2-0	2-2	2-1	2-2	5-0	0-0	2-1		5-0	2-0	2-1	3-0	5-2	3-1	2-1	3-1	1-0
Northampton Town FC	4-0	2-0	1-0	1-0	1-1	1-1	2-2	3-2	3-2	2-0	2-0	1-1	1-0		0-0	3-1	1-1	2-1	1-0	2-2	2-1	2-1
Norwich City FC	3-2	1-1	2-1	2-0	1-0	1-2	5-2	0-2	2-1	2-0	4-1	2-0	1-1	1-1		3-0	3-1	4-2	3-0	2-2	2-1	3-1
Plymouth Argyle FC	1-3	2-2	3-1	1-5	2-3	1-1	1-1	0-0	1-1	1-1	3-2	1-0	2-1	5-2	1-0		2-1	0-1	1-1	4-0	2-1	2-1
Portsmouth FC	3-0	2-1	1-0	2-3	0-2	1-1	3-1	3-0	0-2	1-1	1-1	2-1	1-2	3-3	4-0	0-1		1-0	2-0	0-3	1-0	5-0
Preston North End FC	2-2	2-2	1-1	2-1	3-2	1-0	2-2	2-0	4-1	3-0	2-5	4-3	2-0	2-2	3-1	1-3	6-1		0-0	0-0	2-2	2-1
Rotherham United FC	0-0	3-0	3-1	3-2	0-2	1-0	1-1	2-3	2-2	3-0	0-0	2-3	1-1	1-1	4-0	4-2	1-0	2-2		1-3	4-2	1-0
Southampton FC	3-2	3-1	1-1	4-0	4-1	0-1	3-3	3-3	1-1	2-2	1-0	0-3	0-1	2-0	1-0	5-0	2-2	3-1	6-1		3-1	2-1
Swansea Town AFC	2-0	2-2	3-2	1-3	1-1	2-1	2-1	2-2	1-1	2-5	3-0	1-2	3-1	1-2	0-0	3-0	0-0	4-0	0-3	3-3		4-0
Swindon Town FC	1-3	2-0	3-3	2-0	4-1	2-0	4-2	4-1	3-1	1-0	0-1	0-1	1-6	4-2	0-1	2-3	0-0	2-2	3-2	2-1	3-0	

	Division 2	Pd	Wn	Dw	Ls	GF	GA	Pts	
1.	Newcastle United FC (Newcastle-upon-Tyne)	42	24	9	9	81	45	57	P
2.	Northampton Town FC (Northampton)	42	20	16	6	66	50	56	P
3.	Bolton Wanderers FC (Bolton)	42	20	10	12	80	58	50	
4.	Southampton FC (Southampton)	42	17	14	11	83	63	48	
5.	Ipswich Town FC (Ipswich)	42	15	17	10	74	67	47	
6.	Norwich City FC (Norwich)	42	20	7	15	61	57	47	
7.	Crystal Palace FC (London)	42	16	13	13	55	51	45	
8.	Huddersfield Town AFC (Huddersfield)	42	17	10	15	53	51	44	
9.	Derby County FC (Derby)	42	16	11	15	84	79	43	
10.	Coventry City FC (Coventry)	42	17	9	16	72	70	43	
11.	Manchester City FC (Manchester)	42	16	9	17	63	62	41	
12.	Preston North End FC (Preston)	42	14	13	15	76	81	41	
13.	Cardiff City AFC (Cardiff)	42	13	14	15	64	57	40	
14.	Rotherham United FC (Rotherham)	42	14	12	16	70	69	40	
15.	Plymouth Argyle FC (Plymouth)	42	16	8	18	63	79	40	
16.	Bury FC (Bury)	42	14	10	18	60	66	38	
17.	Middlesbrough FC (Middlesbrough)	42	13	9	20	70	76	35	
18.	Charlton Athletic FC (London)	42	13	9	20	64	75	35	
19.	Leyton Orient FC (London)	42	12	11	19	50	72	35	
20.	Portsmouth FC (Portsmouth)	42	12	10	20	56	77	34	
21.	Swindon Town FC (Swindon)	42	14	5	23	63	81	33	R
22.	Swansea Town AFC (Swansea)	42	11	10	21	62	84	32	R
		924	344	236	344	1470	1470	924	

Football League Division 3 — 1964-65 Season

	Bar	Bou	Bre	BrC	BrR	Car	Col	Exe	Gil	Gri	Hul	Lut	Man	Old	Pet	PoV	QPR	Rea	Scu	Shr	Sou	Wal	Wat	Wor
Barnsley FC	■	2-2	3-1	1-2	0-2	1-2	1-2	0-0	1-0	1-0	1-1	3-0	2-3	0-1	3-2	0-2	0-0	1-1	2-0	6-2	1-4	0-1	4-0	0-3
Bournemouth & Bos.	1-0	■	0-1	1-2	1-1	0-4	3-1	2-2	1-2	1-2	2-3	4-0	2-0	0-0	0-1	3-0	2-0	3-2	2-1	2-1	2-1	4-0	0-0	4-0
Brentford FC	1-0	2-1	■	2-1	1-1	6-1	1-0	2-1	2-0	2-0	1-3	2-2	1-0	2-2	3-1	4-0	5-2	2-1	4-0	2-0	2-1	0-0	5-1	3-0
Bristol City FC	5-1	0-0	3-2	■	2-1	1-2	1-1	1-1	1-2	4-0	1-2	1-0	1-1	2-0	3-1	3-0	2-0	2-2	3-0	4-0	5-1	1-1	1-1	5-0
Bristol Rovers FC	1-0	4-2	1-2	1-1	■	5-2	2-2	1-1	3-0	5-3	1-1	3-2	4-1	0-0	4-0	4-0	3-1	1-0	2-0	0-0	2-2	0-1	1-0	4-0
Carlisle United FC	4-0	3-4	0-1	1-1	1-2	■	4-1	2-1	3-1	3-1	0-0	1-1	3-0	2-0	2-1	1-1	2-0	1-2	3-1	2-1	4-3	2-1	1-1	1-0
Colchester United FC	4-1	4-3	0-3	2-3	1-1	0-1	■	1-1	2-1	0-1	1-2	0-1	0-1	2-2	0-1	2-0	1-2	2-2	2-1	0-4	3-1	2-1	0-0	1-1
Exeter City FC	3-0	1-3	0-0	0-1	0-1	0-0	2-0	■	1-1	4-1	0-2	5-1	2-3	2-1	4-2	2-1	2-2	2-2	1-3	0-1	1-1	0-1	1-0	0-0
Gillingham FC	1-0	1-1	1-0	2-0	1-3	1-0	2-1	0-1	■	0-0	1-0	5-0	0-0	2-1	2-0	2-0	2-2	2-1	0-0	5-0	1-0	4-0	5-2	5-1
Grimsby Town FC	3-2	2-2	2-1	0-2	1-1	1-1	2-0	2-1	1-1	■	3-0	2-2	1-1	3-1	2-0	2-0	0-0	1-1	3-0	2-2	1-0	2-2	1-0	0-1
Hull City AFC	7-0	2-1	2-1	3-2	3-2	1-0	5-1	3-1	1-1	3-3	■	3-1	1-1	0-2	4-0	3-1	1-0	1-2	1-2	0-0	2-0	1-1	2-2	2-2
Luton Town FC	5-1	0-1	4-2	0-0	0-2	1-1	3-1	1-2	0-2	1-1	1-3	■	1-1	2-0	1-1	1-1	2-0	3-1	1-1	2-7	0-1	1-3	2-4	0-0
Mansfield Town FC	4-3	0-0	4-1	3-0	3-0	2-0	0-1	2-1	3-1	2-2	2-1	2-0	■	4-1	0-0	2-2	8-1	2-1	3-2	1-0	6-1	0-1	3-0	3-5
Oldham Athletic AFC	1-1	1-1	1-2	7-3	1-2	2-3	3-1	2-0	2-0	1-5	2-1	0-2	2-1	■	3-1	0-1	5-3	1-2	2-1	1-3	0-2	1-3	2-0	0-2
Peterborough United	4-1	4-3	3-1	0-1	3-1	1-2	4-1	0-0	1-0	3-1	2-1	2-0	4-5	5-0	■	2-2	6-1	2-2	4-1	4-2	3-2	2-1	0-4	2-1
Port Vale FC	2-0	1-2	1-2	1-2	1-1	1-3	1-2	0-1	0-4	2-3	0-3	1-0	2-2	2-1	0-1	■	0-0	2-0	0-1	1-1	2-2	2-1	2-2	2-0
Queen's Park Rangers	3-2	1-1	1-3	1-0	1-2	1-2	5-0	0-0	3-1	1-1	7-1	2-0	1-1	3-2	3-1	■	0-1	2-1	2-1	1-0	2-2	2-1	2-1	
Reading FC	1-1	1-0	1-1	1-1	1-1	1-2	1-2	2-2	3-0	2-0	3-3	1-2	2-1	1-0	4-2	1-1	5-3	■	2-0	3-1	2-0	0-2	6-2	1-0
Scunthorpe United	2-3	3-1	2-0	5-2	1-1	0-1	0-0	0-0	2-3	2-1	1-1	8-1	0-1	1-1	2-3	0-0	2-1	1-1	■	3-2	2-1	4-0	0-2	1-1
Shrewsbury Town	3-3	1-2	1-0	1-5	2-1	2-2	3-0	1-0	2-0	1-3	0-4	0-2	1-1	1-3	1-1	0-0	3-2	4-0	3-2	■	1-3	3-1	2-2	6-1
Southend United FC	2-0	2-1	0-1	0-4	6-3	1-0	6-3	0-0	3-1	4-0	2-1	5-0	1-4	6-1	2-0	2-1	0-0	2-2	0-1	1-0	■	0-0		3-0
Walsall FC	1-1	0-1	4-3	2-4	2-0	1-0	2-1	2-2	0-1	1-0	3-3	0-1	2-1	1-2	0-1	0-0	4-1	4-1	1-2	1-1	2-3	■	0-4	1-4
Watford FC	1-1	2-0	1-1	2-2	1-1	0-0	3-0	1-0	1-2	1-1	2-1	2-0	3-1	3-2	1-1	1-0	0-2	5-1	5-0	2-2	2-1	3-0	■	3-2
Workington AFC	0-0	2-0	1-1	1-0	2-1	0-1	1-0	0-1	1-1	2-2	1-3	1-0	1-5	0-0	1-0	4-1	0-0	0-2	2-0	2-2	3-1	3-1	2-0	■

Division 3

		Pd	Wn	Dw	Ls	GF	GA	Pts	
1.	Carlisle United FC (Carlisle)	46	25	10	11	76	53	60	P
2.	Bristol City FC (Bristol)	46	24	11	11	92	55	59	P
3.	Mansfield Town FC (Mansfield)	46	24	11	11	95	61	59	
4.	Hull City AFC (Kingston-upon-Hull)	46	23	12	11	91	57	58	
5.	Brentford FC (London)	46	24	9	13	83	55	57	
6.	Bristol Rovers FC (Bristol)	46	20	15	11	82	58	55	
7.	Gillingham FC (Gillingham)	46	23	9	14	70	50	55	
8.	Peterborough United FC (Peterborough)	46	22	7	17	85	74	51	
9.	Watford FC (Watford)	46	17	16	13	71	64	50	
10.	Grimsby Town FC (Cleethorpes)	46	16	17	13	68	67	49	
11.	Bournemouth & Boscombe Athletic FC (Bournemouth)	46	18	11	17	72	63	47	
12.	Southend United FC (Southend-on-Sea)	46	19	8	19	78	71	46	
13.	Reading FC (Reading)	46	16	14	16	70	70	46	
14.	Queen's Park Rangers FC (London)	46	17	12	17	72	80	46	
15.	Workington AFC (Workington)	46	17	12	17	58	69	46	
16.	Shrewsbury Town FC (Shrewsbury)	46	15	12	19	76	84	42	
17.	Exeter City FC (Exeter)	46	12	17	17	51	52	41	
18.	Scunthorpe United FC (Scunthorpe)	46	14	12	20	65	72	40	
19.	Walsall FC (Walsall)	46	15	7	24	55	80	37	
20.	Oldham Athletic AFC (Oldham)	46	13	10	23	61	83	36	
21.	Luton Town FC (Luton)	46	11	11	24	51	94	33	R
22.	Port Vale FC (Stoke-on-Trent)	46	9	14	23	41	76	32	R
23.	Colchester United FC (Colchester)	46	10	10	26	50	89	30	R
24.	Barnsley FC (Barnsley)	46	9	11	26	54	90	29	R
		1104	413	278	413	1667	1667	1104	

Football League Division 4 1964-65 Season	Aldershot Town	Barrow	Bradford City	Bradford P.A.	Brighton & H.A.	Chester	Chesterfield	Crewe Alexandra	Darlington	Doncaster Rovers	Halifax Town	Hartlepools	Lincoln City	Millwall	Newport County	Notts County	Oxford United	Rochdale	Southport	Stockport County	Torquay United	Tranmere Rovers	Wrexham	York City
Aldershot Town FC		2-1	1-1	1-1	0-2	3-1	2-0	5-2	0-1	3-0	2-0	3-0	3-2	0-0	2-1	1-2	4-1	1-2	0-3	2-0	2-5	3-0	5-0	1-0
Barrow AFC	2-0		1-0	2-1	1-4	2-1	1-2	1-2	3-1	1-2	1-0	4-2	2-2	0-5	1-4	2-0	1-1	2-2	1-1	0-1	2-1	0-2	0-2	0-2
Bradford City AFC	2-0	1-3		0-2	4-1	1-3	0-0	5-2	2-3	0-3	3-1	4-0	0-1	1-2	1-0	0-2	2-1	0-2	2-1	1-1	2-3	1-2	4-1	1-2
Bradford Park Ave.	3-1	3-2	3-3		2-0	3-1	1-0	2-3	3-1	5-2	5-1	4-0	3-1	4-0	2-2	2-2	1-0	0-0	0-0	1-0	4-2	1-1	0-0	0-0
Brighton & Hove Alb.	2-0	3-1	3-3	2-2		4-4	5-0	3-1	3-1	1-1	2-1	5-0	4-0	2-0	1-0	6-0	0-0	3-0	3-1	3-1	3-1	2-1	5-1	3-1
Chester FC	6-2	4-1	3-1	3-0	3-1		4-0	2-2	4-5	3-0	1-0	4-0	5-1	3-1	4-3	4-1	2-1	0-1	3-1	4-0	0-1	3-2	6-1	4-1
Chesterfield FC	0-1	2-0	3-1	2-4	1-1	1-3		2-1	3-0	1-0	3-0	3-1	1-0	2-3	2-1	0-0	2-1	1-1	1-2	2-0	2-1	1-0	0-0	1-1
Crewe Alexandra FC	4-1	6-2	2-1	1-1	3-2	5-1	0-2		1-2	4-4	2-2	2-3	5-0	1-1	1-1	2-1	2-2	1-1	4-1	3-2	2-0	1-1	1-0	2-3
Darlington FC	4-1	1-2	3-1	1-2	2-0	2-0	2-2	0-2		2-2	5-1	2-3	3-1	1-3	0-1	5-1	2-0	2-0	3-2	3-2	1-2	2-1	5-1	1-0
Doncaster Rovers FC	1-0	4-2	0-0	1-1	2-1	1-4	2-0	3-1	6-3		4-0	0-1	1-2	4-0	1-0	0-0	2-2	2-2	1-2	3-0	2-0	1-0	1-1	4-3
Halifax Town AFC	3-3	3-2	0-3	2-3	1-1	3-4	2-1	2-0	4-0	2-4		2-1	2-1	1-2	2-0	1-1	1-3	1-2	2-1	0-1	0-1	0-1	2-1	1-1
Hartlepools United	1-1	3-0	2-2	2-0	1-1	1-1	1-1	2-4	4-3	1-1	4-0		3-0	1-0	2-4	2-2	1-1	1-1	2-1	4-3	1-0	2-0	1-0	2-2
Lincoln City FC	3-1	1-0	0-2	2-2	0-1	2-2	0-2	1-2	2-0	0-2	2-3	4-2		2-2	4-3	1-0	0-0	1-1	3-0	6-0	0-1	1-2	0-2	0-1
Millwall FC	5-0	3-1	3-0	1-0	2-0	1-0	4-2	0-0	1-1	1-1	5-1	0-0	2-1		4-0	4-1	2-2	0-0	0-0	1-0	2-2	1-0	2-2	1-1
Newport County AFC	2-1	2-2	4-2	4-3	1-1	0-1	4-1	2-2	2-1	1-0	0-2	2-0	7-0	2-2		3-1	0-3	2-3	5-0	2-0	4-0	1-1	2-0	2-0
Notts County FC	0-0	4-1	1-0	3-3	1-2	1-1	5-1	2-0	4-2	5-2	4-0	1-0	2-1	1-2	1-0		0-0	0-0	0-0	2-0	0-0	2-4	1-3	3-1
Oxford United FC	0-0	7-0	3-1	3-0	2-2	3-2	1-0	4-2	1-0	1-0	3-0	2-0	0-2	4-1	4-0			2-2	1-1	2-0	3-0	1-0	4-0	2-0
Rochdale AFC	3-1	3-0	3-1	4-3	2-2	2-1	1-2	1-0	1-1	2-1	3-0	3-0	2-0	0-2	2-0	1-1	3-3		2-0	4-0	1-0	0-1	2-1	1-2
Southport FC	3-1	0-4	0-4	1-1	1-2	2-2	1-0	2-3	3-3	3-5	5-2	1-1	4-4	0-0	5-3	0-0	0-3	1-0		1-1	0-1	2-2	0-2	0-1
Stockport County FC	2-1	1-0	2-0	0-2	1-4	4-5	0-1	1-1	0-0	2-0	1-0	0-1	3-1	1-4	2-0	0-1	0-0	1-2	2-2		0-2	2-3	3-2	3-1
Torquay United FC	5-2	6-2	2-2	1-1	0-1	3-2	0-2	0-1	2-0	2-4	2-0	2-1	0-2	0-0	2-2	2-1	1-1	2-1	2-0	1-0		2-1	3-4	1-3
Tranmere Rovers FC	3-1	3-0	5-1	0-0	4-2	4-1	4-0	1-0	2-1	3-0	5-2	5-1	4-0	1-0	3-2	4-0	2-4	4-1	3-1	1-1	3-1		6-0	2-1
Wrexham AFC	4-0	3-3	3-2	4-1	1-2	4-2	1-2	3-3	4-2	0-2	1-1	3-0	5-3	0-1	4-2	4-0	1-1	2-3	1-1	4-1	2-3	3-2		2-0
York City FC	1-0	2-0	5-2	0-1	2-1	3-2	7-1	3-1	2-1	4-2	4-0	0-0	3-0	3-1	5-1	2-1	2-1	2-1	3-2	3-0	1-2	4-0	2-1	

Division 4

		Pd	Wn	Dw	Ls	GF	GA	Pts	
1.	Brighton & Hove Albion FC (Hove)	46	26	11	9	102	57	63	P
2.	Millwall FC (London)	46	23	16	7	78	45	62	P
3.	York City FC (York)	46	28	6	12	91	56	62	P
4.	Oxford United FC (Oxford)	46	23	15	8	87	44	61	P
5.	Tranmere Rovers FC (Birkenhead)	46	27	6	13	99	56	60	
6.	Rochdale AFC (Rochdale)	46	22	14	10	74	53	58	
7.	Bradford Park Avenue FC (Bradford)	46	20	17	9	86	62	57	
8.	Chester FC (Chester)	46	25	6	15	119	81	56	
9.	Doncaster Rovers FC (Doncaster)	46	20	11	15	84	72	51	
10.	Crewe Alexandra FC (Crewe)	46	18	13	15	90	81	49	
11.	Torquay United FC (Torquay)	46	21	7	18	70	70	49	
12.	Chesterfield FC (Chesterfield)	46	20	8	18	58	70	48	
13.	Notts County FC (Nottingham)	46	15	14	17	61	73	44	
14.	Wrexham AFC (Wrexham)	46	17	9	20	84	92	43	
15.	Hartlepools United FC (Hartlepool)	46	15	13	18	61	85	43	
16.	Newport County AFC (Newport)	46	17	8	21	85	81	42	
17.	Darlington FC (Darlington)	46	18	6	22	84	87	42	
18.	Aldershot FC (Aldershot)	46	15	7	24	64	84	37	
19.	Bradford City AFC (Bradford)	46	12	8	26	70	88	32	
20.	Southport FC (Southport)	46	8	16	22	58	89	32	
21.	Barrow AFC (Barrow-in-Furness)	46	12	6	28	59	105	30	
22.	Lincoln City FC (Lincoln)	46	11	6	29	58	99	28	
23.	Halifax Town AFC (Halifax)	46	11	6	29	54	103	28	
24.	Stockport County FC (Stockport)	46	10	7	29	44	87	27	
		1104	434	236	434	1820	1820	1104	

F.A. CUP FINAL   (Wembley Stadium, London – 01/05/1965 – 100,000)

LIVERPOOL FC (LIVERPOOL)	2-1 (aet)	Leeds United AFC (Leeds)
Hunt, St. John		*Bremner*

Liverpool: Lawrence, Lawler, Byrne, Strong, Yeats, Stevenson, Callaghan, Hunt, St. John, Smith, Thompson.

Leeds: Sprake, Reaney, Bell, Bremner, J.Charlton, Hunter, Giles, Storrie, Peacock, Collins, Johanneson.

Semi-finals

Liverpool FC (Liverpool)	2-0	Chelsea FC (London)
Manchester United FC (Manchester)	0-0, 0-1	Leeds United AFC (Leeds)

Quarter-finals

Chelsea FC (London)	5-1	Peterborough United FC (Peterborough)
Crystal Palace FC (London)	0-3	Leeds United AFC (Leeds)
Leicester City FC (Leicester)	0-0, 0-1	Liverpool FC (Liverpool)
Wolverhampton Wanderers FC (Wolverhampton)	3-5	Manchester United FC (Manchester)

1965-66

Football League Division 1 1965-66 Season	Arsenal	Aston Villa	Blackburn Rovers	Blackpool	Burnley	Chelsea	Everton	Fulham	Leeds United	Leicester City	Liverpool	Manchester United	Newcastle United	Northampton Town	Nottingham Forest	Sheffield United	Sheffield Wed.	Stoke City	Sunderland	Tottenham Hotspur	W.B.A.	West Ham United
Arsenal FC		3-3	2-2	0-0	1-1	1-3	0-1	2-1	0-3	1-0	0-1	4-2	1-3	1-1	1-0	6-2	5-2	2-1	1-1	1-1	1-1	3-2
Aston Villa FC	3-0		3-1	3-0	2-1	2-4	3-2	2-5	0-2	2-2	0-3	1-1	4-2	1-2	3-0	0-2	2-0	0-1	3-1	3-2	1-1	1-2
Blackburn Rovers FC	2-1	0-2		1-3	0-2	0-1	1-2	3-2	2-3	0-2	1-4	1-4	4-2	6-1	5-0	0-0	1-2	0-1	2-0	0-1	0-1	1-2
Blackpool FC	5-3	0-1	4-2		1-3	1-2	2-0	2-2	1-0	4-0	2-3	1-2	1-1	3-0	0-3	2-1	2-1	1-1	1-2	0-0	1-1	2-1
Burnley FC	2-2	3-1	1-4	3-1		1-2	1-1	1-0	0-1	4-2	2-0	3-0	1-0	4-1	4-1	2-0	2-1	4-1	1-0	1-1	2-0	3-1
Chelsea FC	0-0	0-2	1-0	0-1	1-1		3-1	2-1	1-0	0-2	0-1	2-0	1-1	1-0	1-0	2-0	1-1	1-2	3-2	2-1	2-3	6-2
Everton FC	3-1	2-0	2-2	0-0	1-0	2-1		2-0	0-0	1-0	0-0	1-0	5-2	3-0	1-3	5-1	2-1	2-0	2-1	3-1	2-3	2-1
Fulham FC	1-0	3-6	5-2	0-0	2-5	0-3	3-2		1-3	0-4	2-0	0-1	2-0	1-4	1-1	0-0	4-2	1-1	3-0	0-2	2-1	3-0
Leeds United AFC	2-0	2-0	3-0	1-2	1-1	2-0	4-1	0-1		3-2	0-1	1-1	3-0	6-1	2-1	2-2	3-0	2-2	1-0	2-0	4-0	5-0
Leicester City FC	3-1	2-1	2-0	0-3	0-1	1-1	3-0	5-0	3-3		1-3	0-5	1-2	1-1	2-1	1-0	4-1	1-0	4-1	2-2	2-1	2-1
Liverpool FC	4-2	3-1	5-2	4-1	2-1	2-1	5-0	2-1	0-1	1-0		2-1	2-0	5-0	4-0	0-1	1-0	2-0	4-0	1-0	2-2	1-1
Manchester United FC	2-1	6-1	2-2	2-1	4-2	4-1	3-0	4-1	1-1	1-2	2-0		1-1	6-2	0-0	3-1	1-0	1-1	1-1	5-1	1-1	0-0
Newcastle United FC	0-1	1-0	2-1	2-0	3-2	0-1	0-0	1-1	2-0	1-5	0-0	1-2		2-0	2-2	0-2	2-0	3-1	2-0	0-0	0-1	2-1
Northampton Town FC	1-1	2-1	2-1	2-1	1-2	2-3	0-2	2-4	2-1	2-2	0-0	1-1	3-1		3-3	0-1	0-0	1-0	2-1	0-2	3-4	2-1
Nottingham Forest FC	0-1	1-2	0-3	2-1	1-0	1-2	1-0	1-0	0-4	2-0	1-1	4-2	1-2	1-1		1-0	4-3	0-0	1-0	3-2		5-0
Sheffield United FC	3-0	1-0	2-0	0-1	2-1	1-2	2-0	2-0	1-1	2-2	0-0	3-1	3-2	2-2	1-1		1-0	3-2	2-2	1-3	0-2	5-3
Sheffield Wednesday FC	4-0	2-0	2-1	3-0	0-2	1-1	3-1	1-0	0-0	1-2	0-2	0-0	1-0	3-1	3-1	2-2		4-1	3-1	1-1	1-2	0-0
Stoke City FC	1-3	2-0	3-2	4-1	3-1	2-2	1-1	3-2	1-2	1-0	0-0	2-2	4-0	6-2	1-0	2-0	3-1		1-1	0-1	1-1	1-0
Sunderland AFC	0-2	2-0	1-0	2-1	0-4	2-0	2-0	2-2	2-0	0-3	2-2	2-3	2-0	3-0	3-2	4-1	0-2	2-0		2-0	1-5	2-1
Tottenham Hotspur FC	2-2	5-5	4-0	4-0	0-1	4-2	2-2	4-3	3-2	4-2	2-1	5-1	2-2	1-1	2-3	1-0	2-3	2-2	3-0		2-1	1-4
West Bromwich Albion FC	4-4	2-2	2-1	2-1	1-2	1-2	1-1	6-2	1-2	5-1	3-0	3-3	1-2	1-1	5-3	1-1	4-2	6-2	4-1	2-1		3-0
West Ham United FC	2-1	4-2	4-1	1-1	1-1	2-1	3-0	1-3	2-1	2-5	1-5	3-2	4-3	1-1	0-3	4-0	4-2	0-0	1-1	2-0	4-0	

	Division 1	Pd	Wn	Dw	Ls	GF	GA	Pts	
1.	LIVERPOOL FC (LIVERPOOL)	42	26	9	7	79	34	61	
2.	Leeds United AFC (Leeds)	42	23	9	10	79	38	55	
3.	Burnley FC (Burnley)	42	24	7	11	79	47	55	
4.	Manchester United FC (Manchester)	42	18	15	9	84	59	51	
5.	Chelsea FC (London)	42	22	7	13	65	53	51	
6.	West Bromwich Albion FC (West Bromwich)	42	19	12	11	91	69	50	
7.	Leicester City FC (Leicester)	42	21	7	14	80	65	49	
8.	Tottenham Hotspur FC (London)	42	16	12	14	75	66	44	
9.	Sheffield United FC (Sheffield)	42	16	11	15	56	59	43	
10.	Stoke City FC (Stoke-on-Trent)	42	15	12	15	65	64	42	
11.	Everton FC (Liverpool)	42	15	11	16	56	62	41	
12.	West Ham United FC (London)	42	15	9	18	70	83	39	
13.	Blackpool FC (Blackpool)	42	14	9	19	55	65	37	
14.	Arsenal FC (London)	42	12	13	17	62	75	37	
15.	Newcastle United FC (Newcastle-upon-Tyne)	42	14	9	19	50	63	37	
16.	Aston Villa FC (Birmingham)	42	15	6	21	69	80	36	
17.	Sheffield Wednesday FC (Sheffield)	42	14	8	20	56	66	36	
18.	Nottingham Forest FC (Nottingham)	42	14	8	20	56	72	36	
19.	Sunderland AFC (Sunderland)	42	14	8	20	51	72	36	
20.	Fulham FC (London)	42	14	7	21	67	85	35	
21.	Northampton Town FC (Northampton)	42	10	13	19	55	92	33	R
22.	Blackburn Rovers FC (Blackburn)	42	8	4	30	57	88	20	R
		924	359	206	359	1457	1457	924	

Top Goalscorer

1) Roger HUNT   (Liverpool FC)   30

Football League Division 2 — 1965-66 Season

	BIR	BOL	BRC	BUR	CAR	CRL	CHA	COV	CRY	DER	HUD	IPS	LEY	MNC	MID	NOR	PLY	POR	PRE	ROT	SOU	WOL
Birmingham City FC	■	0-1	1-3	4-0	4-2	2-1	2-2	0-1	2-1	5-5	2-1	4-1	2-2	3-1	1-1	1-0	1-0	1-3	1-1	3-0	0-1	2-2
Bolton Wanderers FC	1-2	■	1-2	2-1	2-1	4-0	4-2	4-2	3-0	0-1	1-1	3-1	2-0	1-0	6-0	1-1	0-1	2-0	1-3	1-3	2-3	1-1
Bristol City FC	2-0	2-2	■	2-1	1-1	2-0	0-0	1-1	1-1	2-1	4-1	2-0	1-1	2-2	0-0	0-0	1-0	1-0	2-1	0-1	0-1	
Bury FC	5-1	1-1	1-2	■	1-1	2-1	3-0	1-1	2-2	4-1	0-4	1-1	3-0	2-1	2-0	2-5	1-0	1-0	5-0	6-1	1-3	1-0
Cardiff City AFC	1-3	1-1	2-1	1-0	■	1-1	3-1	1-2	1-0	2-1	0-1	1-0	3-1	4-3	5-3	0-2	5-1	1-2	1-3	0-0	3-5	1-4
Carlisle United FC	1-0	1-1	5-0	4-1	2-0	■	3-1	2-2	3-1	2-1	2-0	3-1	1-0	1-2	2-1	4-1	1-3	2-1	0-2	1-0	1-0	2-1
Charlton Athletic FC	2-1	0-1	1-4	0-1	5-2	3-2	■	2-0	1-0	2-2	0-2	2-0	3-0	1-0	2-1	1-1	2-2	5-2	2-2	2-2		1-1
Coventry City FC	4-3	2-2	2-2	1-0	3-1	3-2	3-1	■	0-1	3-2	0-3	3-1	1-1	3-3	2-1	2-0	5-1	3-2	5-1	2-2	5-1	2-1
Crystal Palace FC	1-0	1-1	2-1	1-0	0-0	2-0	2-0	0-1	■	1-1	2-1	3-1	2-1	0-2	1-1	0-0	3-1	4-1	1-1	2-2	1-0	0-1
Derby County FC	5-3	2-0	2-1	4-1	1-5	3-1	2-0	1-0	4-0	■	4-1	2-2	1-3	1-2	5-0	3-1	1-2	3-1	1-0	1-3	0-3	2-2
Huddersfield Town AFC	2-0	1-0	3-0	2-0	1-1	2-0	1-1	0-2	1-1	1-3	■	1-0	1-1	0-0	6-0	2-1	2-0	4-0	2-0			1-1
Ipswich Town FC	0-1	2-0	0-0	3-4	2-1	1-0	1-4	2-2	2-2	2-2	1-0	■	3-2	1-1	2-1	2-0	1-0	1-0		3-0		5-2
Leyton Orient FC	2-1	1-0	0-4	2-2	1-1	2-1	1-2	1-1	0-2	0-0	0-2	1-4	■	2-2	2-3	0-0	0-1	0-0	2-2	1-4	1-1	0-3
Manchester City FC	3-1	4-1	2-2	1-0	2-2	2-1	0-0	1-0	3-1	1-0	2-0	2-1	5-0	■	3-1	0-0	1-3	0-0	3-1	0-0		2-1
Middlesbrough FC	1-1	1-1	4-2	1-0	3-4	0-2	2-2	1-1	1-2	0-0	1-3	3-2	2-1	1-1	■	0-1	0-1	5-2	2-1	4-0	0-0	3-1
Norwich City FC	2-2	3-0	0-0	4-0	3-2	2-0	2-0	1-1	2-1	0-1	1-0	2-1	3-3	1-2		■	0-0	1-3	1-1	1-2	3-4	0-3
Plymouth Argyle FC	6-1	1-3	0-2	2-2	2-2	0-0	3-0	1-2	1-2	0-0	0-0	3-0	1-1	1-0	2-2	2-0	■	3-1	0-1	5-2	2-3	2-2
Portsmouth FC	0-1	1-0	2-4	4-0	3-1	4-1	3-1	2-0	1-1	1-1	2-1	1-0	4-1	2-2	4-1	0-3	4-1	■	4-1	1-1	2-5	2-0
Preston North End FC	3-3	0-1	1-1	2-1	9-0	2-1	3-3	0-0	2-0	2-0	1-1	0-1	1-2	0-3	1-1	0-0	2-0	4-1	■	1-1	1-1	2-2
Rotherham United FC	3-4	2-1	1-2	6-4	3-3	0-0	1-1	3-0	0-0	0-0	2-1	0-1	4-1	2-1	4-0	0-0	3-3	6-3		■	1-0	4-3
Southampton FC	0-1	5-1	2-2	6-2	3-2	1-0	1-0	1-0	1-0	3-1	0-1	1-2	1-0	0-1	3-1	2-2	4-1	2-2	5-2	1-1	■	9-3
Wolverhampton Wanderers FC	2-0	3-1	1-1	3-0	2-1	3-0	2-2	0-1	1-0	4-0	2-1	4-1	2-1	2-4	3-0	2-1	0-0	8-2	3-0	4-1	1-1	■

	Division 2	Pd	Wn	Dw	Ls	GF	GA	Pts	
1.	Manchester City FC (Manchester)	42	22	15	5	76	44	59	P
2.	Southampton FC (Southampton)	42	22	10	10	85	56	54	P
3.	Coventry City FC (Coventry)	42	20	13	9	73	53	53	
4.	Huddersfield Town AFC (Huddersfield)	42	19	13	10	62	36	51	
5.	Bristol City FC (Bristol)	42	17	17	8	63	48	51	
6.	Wolverhampton Wanderers FC (Wolverhampton)	42	20	10	12	87	61	50	
7.	Rotherham United FC (Rotherham)	42	16	14	12	75	74	46	
8.	Derby County FC (Derby)	42	16	11	15	71	68	43	
9.	Bolton Wanderers FC (Bolton)	42	16	9	17	62	59	41	
10.	Birmingham City FC (Birmingham)	42	16	9	17	70	75	41	
11.	Crystal Palace FC (London)	42	14	13	15	47	52	41	
12.	Portsmouth FC (Portsmouth)	42	16	8	18	74	78	40	
13.	Norwich City FC (Norwich)	42	12	15	15	52	52	39	
14.	Carlisle United FC (Carlisle)	42	17	5	20	60	63	39	
15.	Ipswich Town FC (Ipswich)	42	15	9	18	58	66	39	
16.	Charlton Athletic FC (London)	42	12	14	16	61	70	38	
17.	Preston North End FC (Preston)	42	11	15	16	62	70	37	
18.	Plymouth Argyle FC (Plymouth)	42	12	13	17	54	63	37	
19.	Bury FC (Bury)	42	14	7	21	62	76	35	
20.	Cardiff City AFC (Cardiff)	42	12	10	20	71	91	34	
21.	Middlesbrough FC (Middlesbrough)	42	10	13	19	58	86	33	R
22.	Leyton Orient FC (London)	42	5	13	24	38	80	23	R
		924	334	256	334	1421	1421	924	

Football League Division 3 1965-66 Season	Bournemouth	Brentford	Brighton & H.A.	Bristol Rovers	Exeter City	Gillingham	Grimsby Town	Hull City	Mansfield Town	Millwall	Oldham Athletic	Oxford United	Peterborough Utd.	Q.P.R.	Reading	Scunthorpe United	Shrewsbury Town	Southend United	Swansea Town	Swindon Town	Walsall	Watford	Workington	York City
Bournemouth & Bos.		0-1	0-1	1-0	0-1	1-1	1-0	1-1	2-2	0-0	1-0	1-1	2-3	1-1	3-2	1-2	2-0	0-0	2-1	1-0	0-1	2-0	1-1	1-0
Brentford FC	1-0		2-0	0-5	1-2	0-2	3-2	2-4	0-3	1-2	0-0	5-1	1-0	6-1	1-1	0-1	4-0	2-0	2-0	0-1	2-2	1-1	0-1	0-1
Brighton & Hove Alb.	1-2	2-0		4-3	2-1	0-1	1-2	1-2	6-4	2-2	3-1	2-0	1-0	0-2	1-1	0-1	1-1	9-1	1-1	1-0	2-1	2-0	3-1	3-1
Bristol Rovers FC	0-0	1-1	0-0		2-0	0-0	2-1	1-2	6-0	1-1	4-0	3-1	1-1	1-0	0-0	2-0	3-2	3-1	2-1	0-1	3-0	1-1	2-2	0-0
Exeter City FC	1-0	5-0	2-0	1-0		3-1	2-0	1-4	2-2	1-2	4-0	1-2	2-5	0-0	1-2	4-0	0-0	1-1	1-1	0-2	1-2	2-1	2-1	0-2
Gillingham FC	2-0	1-0	3-1	2-0	1-1		3-2	0-3	2-0	1-0	3-0	1-2	1-1	3-1	2-4	0-1	0-1	1-0	2-0	1-0	1-0	2-2	1-0	1-0
Grimsby Town FC	2-0	3-2	3-1	1-1	1-1	3-1		1-0	0-1	2-0	3-1	1-1	3-0	4-2	3-3	1-3	2-1	1-0	2-2	2-2	3-1	2-1	1-0	3-1
Hull City AFC	3-0	4-1	1-0	6-1	6-1	1-0	1-1		4-0	1-0	5-1	2-1	2-1	1-3	3-3	3-2	1-0	4-1	1-0	3-2	3-1	6-0	4-0	1-4
Mansfield Town FC	1-0	2-0	3-1	2-0	0-0	0-0	2-1	1-2		1-1	1-0	1-4	1-7	2-1	0-2	2-2	0-3	2-0	3-0	1-5	0-3	2-2	0-1	4-1
Millwall FC	1-0	1-0	3-2	3-3	3-0	2-0	2-1	3-0	2-0		1-0	2-0	4-1	2-1	3-0	2-2	4-2	2-1	1-0	1-1	1-1	0-0	2-0	2-0
Oldham Athletic AFC	2-2	1-1	1-0	2-0	3-1	5-3	1-4	2-2	1-1	0-2		3-0	2-4	0-2	2-2	1-3	0-1	1-0	1-1	1-2	0-1	1-1	1-1	3-0
Oxford United FC	2-1	2-0	0-1	1-0	0-1	0-4	2-0	0-2	4-1	3-1	3-3		1-0	1-3	2-0	0-3	0-1	3-2	2-2	0-3	7-1	1-2	0-2	4-1
Peterborough United	1-0	3-0	2-2	5-2	2-0	1-0	1-1	4-1	3-2	0-2	0-1	2-3		1-1	0-0	3-1	4-0	5-2	2-3	3-1	2-2	1-1	1-1	1-0
Queen's Park Rangers	5-0	1-0	4-1	4-1	1-0	1-3	3-0	3-3	1-2	6-1	1-1	2-3	2-1		0-2	1-0	2-1	6-2	3-2	2-1	1-1	4-1	4-1	7-2
Reading FC	1-0	2-0	0-0	0-1	4-1	2-2	0-0	0-1	2-1	1-1	3-2	0-1	2-1	2-1		2-0	4-1	1-0	2-1	0-2	3-0	1-2	1-1	3-0
Scunthorpe United	3-0	3-2	2-2	3-0	2-1	0-1	2-2	2-4	0-1	4-4	1-1	1-2	1-1	1-2	2-0		1-4	0-0	1-1	2-1	4-2	1-1	4-1	4-1
Shrewsbury Town FC	0-2	0-0	3-1	1-0	4-0	2-1	3-1	2-2	2-1	2-0	3-1	4-0	3-1	0-0	3-3	1-4		3-0	5-0	1-1	1-2	0-0	1-1	4-1
Southend United FC	1-2	1-0	0-0	2-0	4-2	5-2	3-1	1-0	2-0	0-2	0-2	2-1	1-3	2-1	1-0	2-0	2-0		2-0	4-2	5-3	1-0	3-1	2-3
Swansea Town AFC	5-0	1-1	2-2	3-0	1-0	0-3	1-0	4-2	1-2	0-2	4-1	3-2	1-1	4-2	5-4	3-4	4-0	5-0		1-1	1-0	4-2	1-6	7-2
Swindon Town FC	0-0	2-1	3-2	4-3	2-2	0-1	0-0	3-1	6-2	1-0	0-1	0-0	3-0	2-1	5-0	0-0	4-0	2-2	4-0		0-0	0-1	0-1	6-0
Walsall FC	2-1	1-1	2-1	1-1	1-1	6-1	1-0	2-4	2-1	1-4	2-2	1-1	0-1	3-0	3-0	1-1	5-0	3-0	1-1	5-0		3-0	1-1	2-0
Watford FC	1-0	1-1	0-1	2-0	3-0	1-0	1-1	2-1	0-1	4-0	1-1	1-2	1-2	2-1	1-0	4-1	0-1	2-0	0-1	2-2	0-1		1-2	3-2
Workington AFC	2-2	1-1	1-0	0-0	6-1	1-0	1-0	3-0	2-0	0-0	0-1	2-1	1-1	1-1	1-0	1-2	1-3	3-1	7-0	0-3	1-0	1-0		2-1
York City FC	0-2	1-1	0-1	1-5	2-0	1-2	1-1	1-2	2-1	2-1	2-2	1-4	1-1	2-2	1-2	1-3	2-2	0-3	5-1	0-2	0-3	1-0	2-2	

	Division 3	Pd	Wn	Dw	Ls	GF	GA	Pts	
1.	Hull City AFC (Kingston-upon-Hull)	46	31	7	8	109	62	69	P
2.	Millwall FC (London)	46	27	11	8	76	43	65	P
3.	Queen's Park Rangers FC (London)	46	24	9	13	95	65	57	
4.	Scunthorpe United FC (Scunthorpe)	46	21	11	14	80	67	53	
5.	Workington AFC (Workington)	46	19	14	13	67	57	52	
6.	Gillingham FC (Gillingham)	46	22	8	16	62	54	52	
7.	Swindon Town FC (Swindon)	46	19	13	14	74	48	51	
8.	Reading FC (Reading)	46	19	13	14	70	63	51	
9.	Walsall FC (Walsall)	46	20	10	16	77	64	50	
10.	Shrewsbury Town FC (Shrewsbury)	46	19	11	16	73	64	49	
11.	Grimsby Town FC (Cleethorpes)	46	17	13	16	68	62	47	
12.	Watford FC (Watford)	46	17	13	16	55	51	47	
13.	Peterborough United FC (Peterborough)	46	17	12	17	80	66	46	
14.	Oxford United FC (Oxford)	46	19	8	19	70	74	46	
15.	Brighton & Hove Albion FC (Hove)	46	16	11	19	67	65	43	
16.	Bristol Rovers FC (Bristol)	46	14	14	18	64	64	42	
17.	Swansea Town AFC (Swansea)	46	15	11	20	81	96	41	
18.	Bournemouth & Boscombe Athletic FC (Bournemouth)	46	13	12	21	38	56	38	
19.	Mansfield Town FC (Mansfield)	46	15	8	23	59	89	38	
20.	Oldham Athletic AFC (Oldham)	46	12	13	21	55	81	37	
21.	Southend United FC (Southend-on-Sea)	46	16	4	26	54	83	36	R
22.	Exeter City FC (Exeter)	46	12	11	23	53	79	35	R
23.	Brentford FC (London)	46	10	12	24	48	69	32	R
24.	York City FC (York)	46	9	9	28	53	106	27	R
		1104	423	258	423	1628	1628	1104	

Football League Division 4 — 1965-66 Season

Results grid (home team in left column; opponents across the top in the same order):

	Aldershot Town	Barnsley	Barrow	Bradford City	Bradford P.A.	Chester	Chesterfield	Colchester United	Crewe Alexandra	Darlington	Doncaster Rovers	Halifax Town	Hartlepools	Lincoln City	Luton Town	Newport County	Notts County	Port Vale	Rochdale	Southport	Stockport County	Torquay United	Tranmere Rovers	Wrexham
Aldershot Town FC	■	1-1	3-1	5-2	5-1	2-2	1-3	1-3	1-0	0-1	1-1	0-0	5-0	2-0	3-1	2-1	0-0	3-0	2-3	3-0	1-0	3-2	1-3	2-2
Barnsley FC	2-1	■	3-0	4-2	1-1	0-2	0-0	1-1	0-1	3-1	1-5	1-2	2-2	0-1	3-0	2-2	1-1	1-0	5-0	4-0	1-2	1-0	4-0	3-0
Barrow AFC	2-2	1-5	■	2-0	5-2	4-1	3-2	3-0	1-1	1-1	2-1	3-0	2-0	2-2	0-1	2-2	2-1	2-2	0-2	3-3	1-0	2-0	1-1	4-2
Bradford City AFC	1-1	1-0	0-0	■	3-0	1-2	1-1	1-2	0-1	2-0	1-1	0-1	1-3	2-0	2-2	3-2	0-4	2-0	2-1	3-0	1-78	4-1	2-4	4-1
Bradford Park Ave.	5-1	7-2	2-3	5-1	■	0-1	3-1	1-0	2-1	0-2	0-1	2-1	4-1	4-2	1-3	6-1	4-0	1-2	1-2	2-1	3-1	1-1	1-1	4-2
Chester FC	3-2	3-3	0-0	4-0	2-4	■	3-0	2-1	3-0	3-2	1-4	1-0	2-0	4-2	1-1	6-1	1-1	2-0	1-2	1-0	1-0	1-1	3-1	4-2
Chesterfield FC	1-1	3-1	2-2	1-1	0-3	2-2	■	2-4	3-1	1-2	1-1	3-2	1-3	1-0	1-3	1-2	0-1	3-1	4-1	3-2	2-1	1-1	0-0	1-1
Colchester United FC	0-0	4-0	2-2	0-1	6-3	1-1	3-0	■	1-1	2-1	1-0	2-0	3-0	2-2	3-2	4-1	3-0	2-0	0-0	3-2	0-2	2-1	1-1	
Crewe Alexandra FC	2-0	0-1	2-1	7-1	2-5	1-1	1-0	0-2	■	0-1	1-1	3-0	3-1	7-0	2-0	2-2	1-0	0-3	2-1	1-1	2-1	1-2		0-1
Darlington FC	4-3	2-1	1-0	3-0	4-1	0-1	4-1	2-0	1-1	■	3-2	2-0	1-1	0-2	1-0	0-1	2-1	3-1	2-0	3-0	0-0	0-1	2-0	
Doncaster Rovers FC	3-2	2-1	1-1	1-1	6-2	1-1	1-0	2-0	4-1	6-3	■	2-2	4-0	4-0	1-1	1-0	0-3	1-0	2-0	1-1	1-0	2-0	3-1	2-0
Halifax Town AFC	3-4	2-2	3-2	3-2	1-0	2-0	4-1	1-1	1-0	2-2	2-3	■	1-0	2-2	3-0	4-4	0-1	4-1	1-2	0-1	1-2	0-0	2-2	4-2
Hartlepools United	3-0	1-2	3-0	1-1	2-3	2-0	1-2	0-1	4-1	1-1	2-0	1-2	■	3-1	2-0	5-2	2-0	0-0	3-1	2-1	0-2	0-0	4-2	
Lincoln City FC	2-1	4-1	4-0	1-0	1-1	2-2	0-2	0-2	1-1	4-1	0-3	3-3	2-1	■	2-2	1-1	1-2	0-1	2-0	4-0	1-2	1-1	1-0	0-2
Luton Town FC	3-1	5-4	3-2	2-3	3-1	5-2	1-2	1-1	4-0	2-0	4-3	4-1	2-1	0-0	■	2-1	5-1	5-0	4-1	2-0	2-0	3-2	2-1	2-1
Newport County AFC	3-1	1-0	3-2	2-2	3-1	3-2	3-4	2-1	1-0	3-0	4-0	3-1	3-0	0-0	3-1	■	1-2	0-1	1-1	1-1	1-1	3-2	0-0	2-1
Notts County FC	2-0	0-1	0-2	2-1	2-0	3-3	2-0	1-0	0-1	0-0	1-2	1-1	1-0	2-1	1-1	1-1	■	3-1	3-3	1-2	1-1	1-1	1-2	3-1
Port Vale FC	2-1	1-1	0-0	0-0	3-3	5-2	1-1	1-0	2-0	3-1	2-0	0-0	3-0	1-2	3-0	0-1		■	2-1	4-1	2-0	0-0	2-3	1-1
Rochdale AFC	1-0	2-1	4-0	5-1	2-3	3-0	1-1	0-1	2-1	0-1	3-1	0-1	1-2	2-1	0-2	1-0			■	3-0	4-0	2-3	3-5	6-0
Southport FC	0-2	3-1	1-1	4-0	2-1	0-2	1-0	0-1	1-1	1-1	1-0	4-1	1-1	5-1	3-2	1-0	2-1	4-0		■	2-0	3-3	1-1	2-2
Stockport County FC	1-2	1-0	5-2	1-1	2-3	0-1	2-1	1-0	2-0	1-1	3-0	1-2	2-1	4-1	1-3	2-1	1-3	2-2			■	1-0	1-2	2-4
Torquay United FC	5-1	3-0	0-1	4-3	2-1	1-0	2-0	0-1	2-1	0-4	0-0	1-0	2-0	4-1	2-0	1-0	2-0	1-0	4-0	1-1	1-4	■	2-1	3-1
Tranmere Rovers FC	5-2	1-0	1-2	2-2	1-2	1-0	3-2	2-0	3-1	1-2	1-0	5-2	6-1	3-2	2-0	0-1	0-3	1-0	6-2	0-2	6-2	0-1	■	6-3
Wrexham AFC	4-0	6-3	3-1	1-1	3-2	2-1	1-1	2-3	1-4	1-2	4-3	2-2	1-1	0-1	2-0	0-1	1-3	1-0	6-2	3-1	1-4	0-2	1-5	■

Division 4

		Pd	Wn	Dw	Ls	GF	GA	Pts	
1.	Doncaster Rovers FC (Doncaster)	46	24	11	11	85	54	59	P
2.	Darlington FC (Darlington)	46	25	9	12	72	53	59	P
3.	Torquay United FC (Torquay)	46	24	10	12	72	49	58	P
4.	Colchester United FC (Colchester)	46	23	10	13	70	47	56	P
5.	Tranmere Rovers FC (Birkenhead)	46	24	8	14	93	66	56	
6.	Luton Town FC (Luton)	46	24	8	14	90	70	56	
7.	Chester FC (Chester)	46	20	12	14	79	70	52	
8.	Notts County FC (Nottingham)	46	19	12	15	61	53	50	
9.	Newport County AFC (Newport)	46	18	12	16	75	75	48	
10.	Southport FC(Southport)	46	18	12	16	68	69	48	
11.	Bradford Park Avenue FC (Bradford)	46	21	5	20	102	92	47	
12.	Barrow AFC (Barrow-in-Furness)	46	16	15	15	72	76	47	
13.	Stockport County FC (Stockport)	46	18	6	22	71	70	42	
14.	Crewe Alexandra FC (Crewe)	46	16	9	21	61	63	41	
15.	Halifax Town AFC (Halifax)	46	15	11	20	67	75	41	
16.	Barnsley FC (Barnsley)	46	15	10	21	74	78	40	
17.	Aldershot FC (Aldershot)	46	15	10	21	75	84	40	
18.	Hartlepools United FC (Hartlepool)	46	16	8	22	63	75	40	
19.	Port Vale FC (Stoke-on-Trent)	46	15	9	22	48	59	39	
20.	Chesterfield FC (Chesterfield)	46	13	13	20	62	78	39	
21.	Rochdale AFC (Rochdale)	46	16	5	25	71	87	37	
22.	Lincoln City FC (Lincoln)	46	13	11	22	57	82	37	
23.	Bradford City AFC (Bradford)	46	12	13	21	63	94	37	
24.	Wrexham AFC (Wrexham)	46	13	9	24	72	104	35	
		1104	433	238	433	1723	1723	1104	

81

F.A. CUP FINAL   (Wembley Stadium, London – 14/05/1966 – 100,000)

EVERTON FC (LIVERPOOL)   3-2   Sheffield Wednesday FC (Sheffield)
Trebilcock 2, Trevor   *McCalliog, Ford*

Everton: West, Wright, Wilson, Gabriel, Labone, Harris, Scott, Trebilcock, A.Young, Harvey, Temple.
Wednesday: Springett, Smith, Megson, Eustace, Ellis, G.Young, Pugh, Fantham, NcCalliog, Ford, Quinn.

Semi-finals

Chelsea FC (London)	0-2	Sheffield Wednesday FC (Sheffield)
Everton FC (Liverpool)	1-0	Manchester United FC (Manchester)

Quarter-finals

Blackburn Rovers FC (Blackburn)	1-2	Sheffield Wednesday FC (Sheffield)
Chelsea FC (London)	2-2, 3-1	Hull City AFC (Kingston-upon-Hull)
Manchester City FC (Manchester)	0-0, 0-0, 0-2	Everton FC (Liverpool)
Preston North End FC (Preston)	1-1, 1-3	Manchester United FC (Manchester)

1966-67

Football League Division 1 1966-67 Season	Arsenal	Aston Villa	Blackpool	Burnley	Chelsea	Everton	Fulham	Leeds United	Leicester City	Liverpool	Man. City	Man. United	Newcastle United	Nottingham F.	Sheffield United	Sheffield Wed.	Southampton	Stoke City	Sunderland	Tottenham H.	W.B.A.	West Ham United
Arsenal FC	■	1-0	1-1	0-0	2-1	3-1	1-0	0-1	2-4	1-1	1-0	1-1	2-0	1-1	2-0	1-1	4-1	3-1	2-0	0-2	2-3	2-1
Aston Villa FC	0-1	■	3-2	0-1	2-6	2-4	1-1	3-0	0-1	2-3	3-0	2-1	1-1	1-1	0-0	0-1	0-1	2-1	2-1	3-3	3-2	0-2
Blackpool FC	0-3	0-2	■	0-2	0-2	0-1	0-1	0-2	1-1	1-2	0-1	1-2	6-0	1-1	0-1	1-1	2-3	0-1	1-1	2-2	1-3	1-4
Burnley FC	1-4	4-2	1-0	■	1-2	1-1	3-0	1-1	5-2	1-0	2-3	1-1	0-2	0-2	4-0	2-0	4-1	0-2	1-0	2-2	5-1	4-2
Chelsea FC	3-1	3-1	0-2	1-3	■	1-1	0-0	2-2	2-2	1-2	0-0	1-3	2-1	2-1	1-1	0-0	4-1	1-0	1-1	3-0	0-2	5-5
Everton FC	0-0	3-1	0-1	1-1	3-1	■	3-2	2-0	2-0	3-1	1-1	1-2	1-1	0-1	4-1	2-1	0-1	0-1	4-1	0-1	5-4	4-0
Fulham FC	0-0	5-1	2-2	0-0	1-3	0-1	■	2-2	4-2	2-2	4-1	2-2	5-1	2-3	0-1	1-2	3-1	4-1	3-1	3-4	2-2	4-2
Leeds United AFC	3-1	0-2	1-1	3-1	1-0	1-1	3-1	■	3-1	2-1	0-0	3-1	5-0	1-1	2-0	1-0	0-1	3-0	2-1	3-2	2-1	2-1
Leicester City FC	2-1	5-0	3-0	5-1	3-2	2-2	0-2	0-0	■	2-1	2-1	1-2	4-2	3-0	2-2	0-1	1-1	4-2	1-2	0-1	2-1	5-4
Liverpool FC	0-0	1-0	1-3	2-0	2-1	0-0	2-2	5-0	3-2	■	3-2	0-0	3-1	4-0	1-1	1-1	2-1	2-1	2-2	0-0	0-1	2-0
Manchester City FC	1-1	1-1	1-0	1-0	1-4	1-0	3-0	2-1	1-3	2-1	■	1-1	1-1	1-1	1-1	0-0	1-1	3-1	1-0	1-2	2-2	1-4
Manchester United FC	1-0	3-1	4-0	4-1	1-1	3-0	2-1	0-0	5-2	2-2	1-0	■	3-2	1-0	2-0	2-0	3-0	0-0	5-0	1-0	5-3	3-0
Newcastle United FC	2-1	0-3	2-1	1-1	2-2	0-3	1-1	1-2	1-0	0-2	2-0	0-0	■	0-0	1-0	3-1	3-1	3-1	0-3	0-2	1-3	1-0
Nottingham Forest FC	2-1	3-0	2-0	4-1	0-0	1-0	2-1	1-0	1-0	1-1	2-0	4-1	3-0	■	3-1	1-1	3-1	1-2	3-1	1-1	2-1	1-0
Sheffield United FC	1-1	3-3	1-1	1-1	3-0	0-0	4-0	1-4	0-1	1-0	2-1	0-1	1-2	1-2	■	1-0	2-0	2-1	2-0	2-1	4-3	3-1
Sheffield Wednesday FC	1-1	2-0	3-0	7-0	6-1	1-2	1-1	0-0	1-1	0-1	1-0	2-2	0-0	0-2	2-2	■	4-1	1-3	5-0	1-0	1-0	0-2
Southampton FC	2-1	6-2	1-5	4-0	0-3	1-3	4-2	0-2	4-4	1-2	1-1	1-2	2-0	2-1	2-3	4-2	■	3-2	3-1	0-1	2-2	6-2
Stoke City FC	2-2	6-1	2-0	4-3	1-1	2-1	1-2	0-0	3-1	2-0	0-1	3-0	0-1	1-2	3-0	0-2	3-2	■	3-0	2-0	1-1	1-1
Sunderland AFC	1-3	2-1	4-0	4-3	2-0	0-2	3-1	0-2	2-3	2-2	1-0	0-0	3-0	1-0	4-1	2-0	2-1	2-1	■	0-1	2-2	2-4
Tottenham Hotspur FC	3-1	0-1	1-3	2-0	1-1	2-0	4-2	3-1	2-0	2-1	1-1	2-1	4-0	2-1	2-0	2-1	5-3	2-0	1-0	■	0-0	3-4
West Bromwich Albion FC	0-1	2-1	3-1	1-2	0-1	1-0	5-1	2-0	1-0	2-1	0-3	3-4	6-1	1-2	1-2	1-2	3-2	0-1	2-2	3-0	■	3-1
West Ham United FC	2-2	2-1	4-0	3-2	1-2	2-3	6-1	0-1	0-1	1-1	1-1	1-6	3-0	3-1	0-2	3-0	2-2	1-1	2-2	0-2	3-0	■

	Division 1	Pd	Wn	Dw	Ls	GF	GA	Pts	
1.	MANCHESTER UNITED FC (MANCHESTER)	42	24	12	6	84	45	60	
2.	Nottingham Forest FC (Nottingham)	42	23	10	9	64	41	56	
3.	Tottenham Hotspur FC (London)	42	24	8	10	71	48	56	
4.	Leeds United AFC (Leeds)	42	22	11	9	62	42	55	
5.	Liverpool FC (Liverpool)	42	19	13	10	64	47	51	
6.	Everton FC (Liverpool)	42	19	10	13	65	46	48	
7.	Arsenal FC (London)	42	16	14	12	58	47	46	
8.	Leicester City FC (Leicester)	42	18	8	16	78	71	44	
9.	Chelsea FC (London)	42	15	14	13	67	62	44	
10.	Sheffield United FC (Sheffield)	42	16	10	16	52	59	42	
11.	Sheffield Wednesday FC (Sheffield)	42	14	13	15	56	47	41	
12.	Stoke City FC (Stoke-on-Trent)	42	17	7	18	63	58	41	
13.	West Bromwich Albion FC (West Bromwich)	42	16	7	19	77	73	39	
14.	Burnley FC (Burnley)	42	15	9	18	66	76	39	
15.	Manchester City FC (Manchester)	42	12	15	15	43	52	39	
16.	West Ham United FC (London)	42	14	8	20	80	84	36	
17.	Sunderland AFC (Sunderland)	42	14	8	20	58	72	36	
18.	Fulham FC (London)	42	11	12	19	71	83	34	
19.	Southampton FC (Southampton)	42	14	6	22	74	92	34	
20.	Newcastle United FC (Newcastle-upon-Tyne)	42	12	9	21	39	81	33	
21.	Aston Villa FC (Birmingham)	42	11	7	24	54	85	29	R
22.	Blackpool FC (Blackpool)	42	6	9	27	41	76	21	R
		924	352	220	352	1387	1387	924	

Top Goalscorer

1) Ron DAVIES   (Southampton FC)   37

Football League Division 2 1966-67 Season	Birmingham City	Blackburn Rovers	Bolton Wanderers	Bristol City	Bury	Cardiff City	Carlisle United	Charlton Athletic	Coventry City	Crystal Palace	Derby County	Huddersfield Town	Hull City	Ipswich Town	Millwall	Northampton Town	Norwich City	Plymouth Argyle	Portsmouth	Preston North End	Rotherham United	Wolverhampton Wanderers
Birmingham City FC	■	1-1	2-2	4-0	1-3	1-2	1-2	4-0	1-1	3-1	2-0	0-1	2-1	2-2	2-0	3-0	2-1	0-0	3-0	3-1	2-3	3-2
Blackburn Rovers FC	1-0	■	0-0	1-0	2-1	4-1	2-0	2-1	0-1	2-1	0-0	2-0	4-1	1-2	1-0	3-0	0-0	3-0	2-2	2-0	1-1	0-0
Bolton Wanderers FC	3-1	0-1	■	0-0	3-1	3-1	3-0	2-1	1-1	0-0	3-1	1-0	2-1	1-1	5-0	1-2	1-1	1-2	0-1	4-2	2-2	0-0
Bristol City FC	3-1	2-2	1-1	■	3-3	1-2	3-0	4-0	2-2	0-1	4-1	1-1	2-1	1-1	1-1	1-0	1-0	1-0	3-3	2-0	1-2	1-0
Bury FC	0-2	1-2	2-1	2-1	■	2-0	0-2	2-1	0-1	1-1	2-2	0-0	3-2	1-2	0-1	1-2	2-0	1-0	1-3	3-4	5-2	2-1
Cardiff City AFC	3-0	1-1	2-5	5-1	3-0	■	4-2	4-1	1-1	1-2	1-1	1-1	2-4	0-2	1-1	4-2	2-0	4-1	0-0	4-0	0-0	0-3
Carlisle United FC	2-0	1-2	6-1	2-1	2-0	3-0	■	1-0	2-1	3-0	0-0	2-1	2-0	2-1	2-1	2-0	1-0	0-0	5-1	1-1	2-3	1-3
Charlton Athletic FC	1-0	0-0	0-1	5-0	4-0	5-0	1-0	■	1-2	1-1	3-1	1-2	1-3	2-1	0-0	3-0	0-0	1-0	0-2	2-0	2-0	1-3
Coventry City FC	1-1	2-0	1-1	1-0	3-0	3-2	2-1	1-0	■	1-2	2-2	1-0	1-0	5-0	3-1	2-0	2-1	1-0	5-1	2-1	4-2	3-1
Crystal Palace FC	2-1	2-1	3-2	2-1	3-1	3-1	4-2	1-0	1-1	■	2-1	1-1	4-1	0-2	1-2	5-1	0-0	2-1	0-2	1-0	1-1	4-1
Derby County FC	1-2	2-3	2-2	2-0	3-1	1-1	0-1	0-2	1-2	2-0	■	4-3	2-3	2-2	5-1	4-3	1-1	1-1	0-0	5-1	2-0	0-3
Huddersfield Town AFC	3-1	3-1	2-1	2-0	4-2	3-1	1-1	4-1	3-1	0-2	1-0	■	1-0	1-0	2-0	0-2	0-1	1-1	1-1	1-0	3-0	0-1
Hull City AFC	0-2	2-3	1-1	0-2	2-0	1-0	1-2	2-2	2-2	6-1	1-3	2-0	■	1-1	2-0	6-1	5-0	4-2	2-0	2-2	1-0	3-1
Ipswich Town FC	3-2	1-1	2-2	0-0	2-0	0-0	1-2	0-0	1-1	2-0	4-3	3-0	5-4	■	4-1	6-1	0-2	1-1	4-2	0-0	3-2	3-1
Millwall FC	3-1	1-1	2-0	3-2	2-0	1-0	2-1	0-0	1-0	1-1	3-2	1-3	2-1	1-0	■	1-0	2-1	1-2	1-1	2-0	2-0	1-1
Northampton Town FC	2-1	2-1	2-1	2-1	0-0	2-0	3-3	1-1	0-0	1-0	0-2	0-1	2-2	1-1	1-2	■	1-2	2-1	2-4	1-5	3-1	0-4
Norwich City FC	3-3	0-1	1-0	1-0	2-0	3-2	2-0	1-1	1-1	4-3	4-1	0-0	0-2	1-2	1-1	1-0	■	3-1	0-0	1-1	1-0	1-2
Plymouth Argyle FC	1-1	4-0	2-0	1-2	4-1	7-1	1-2	2-1	4-2	1-0	1-2	2-3	3-1	1-1	3-1	1-0	2-2	■	0-0	1-0	1-0	0-1
Portsmouth FC	4-5	1-1	2-1	1-1	1-2	1-2	2-1	1-2	0-2	1-1	0-3	1-1	0-1	4-2	0-1	3-2	3-3	2-1	■	2-0	3-2	2-3
Preston North End FC	3-0	3-0	1-3	2-2	2-2	4-0	2-3	2-1	3-2	1-0	2-0	1-2	4-2	2-0	2-1	2-1	3-1	2-0	1-0	■	1-1	1-2
Rotherham United FC	3-2	2-1	0-1	3-3	3-0	4-1	2-3	2-0	1-1	0-1	0-0	4-2	1-1	0-2	3-1	1-2	2-1	4-2	0-1	2-1	■	2-2
Wolverhampton Wanderers FC	1-2	4-0	5-2	1-1	4-1	7-1	1-1	1-0	1-3	1-1	5-3	1-0	4-0	0-0	2-0	1-0	4-1	2-1	3-1	3-2	2-0	■

	Division 2		Pd	Wn	Dw	Ls	GF	GA	Pts	
1.	Coventry City FC (Coventry)		42	23	13	6	74	43	59	P
2.	Wolverhampton Wanderers FC (Wolverhampton)		42	25	8	9	88	48	58	P
3.	Carlisle United FC (Carlisle)		42	23	6	13	71	54	52	
4.	Blackburn Rovers FC (Blackburn)		42	19	13	10	56	46	51	
5.	Ipswich Town FC (Ipswich)		42	17	16	9	70	54	50	
6.	Huddersfield Town AFC (Huddersfield)		42	20	9	13	58	46	49	
7.	Crystal Palace FC (London)		42	19	10	13	61	55	48	
8.	Millwall FC (London)		42	18	9	15	49	58	45	
9.	Bolton Wanderers FC (Bolton)		42	14	14	14	64	58	42	
10.	Birmingham City FC (Birmingham)		42	16	8	18	70	66	40	
11.	Norwich City FC (Norwich)		42	13	14	15	49	55	40	
12.	Hull City AFC (Kingston-upon-Hull)		42	16	7	19	77	72	39	
13.	Preston North End FC (Preston)		42	16	7	19	65	67	39	
14.	Portsmouth FC (Portsmouth)		42	13	13	16	59	70	39	
15.	Bristol City FC (Bristol)		42	12	14	16	56	62	38	
16.	Plymouth Argyle FC (Plymouth)		42	14	9	19	59	58	37	
17.	Derby County FC (Derby)		42	12	12	18	68	72	36	
18.	Rotherham United FC (Rotherham)		42	13	10	19	61	70	36	
19.	Charlton Athletic FC (London)		42	13	9	20	49	53	35	
20.	Cardiff City AFC (Cardiff)		42	12	9	21	61	87	33	
21.	Northampton Town FC (Northampton)		42	12	6	24	47	84	30	R
22.	Bury FC (Bury)		42	11	6	25	49	83	28	R
			924	351	222	351	1361	1361	924	

84

Football League Division 3 — 1966-67 Season

	Bournemouth	Brighton & H.A.	Bristol Rovers	Colchester U.	Darlington	Doncaster R.	Gillingham	Grimsby Town	Leyton Orient	Mansfield T.	Middlesbrough	Oldham Ath.	Oxford United	Peterborough U.	Q.P.R.	Reading	Scunthorpe U.	Shrewsbury T.	Swansea Town	Swindon Town	Torquay United	Walsall	Watford	Workington
Bournemouth & Bos.	■	2-1	0-0	1-1	1-1	4-1	1-0	0-0	1-0	1-3	1-1	2-1	0-0	1-1	1-3	2-2	0-0	0-3	1-0	1-4	1-0	3-0	0-0	0-2
Brighton & Hove Alb.	0-3	■	3-2	1-1	5-0	0-0	2-2	0-2	1-0	1-0	1-1	2-0	2-0	5-2	2-2	0-1	2-2	2-1	3-2	2-2	0-1	2-3	1-0	0-0
Bristol Rovers FC	1-1	2-2	■	4-1	3-0	4-2	4-1	0-0	1-0	4-4	2-2	2-1	2-1	1-1	2-1	2-1	1-1	1-0	3-3	3-0	1-0	4-2	0-3	0-1
Colchester United FC	2-0	3-2	3-1	■	2-3	5-0	0-0	4-0	2-2	3-0	2-3	3-2	1-2	1-4	1-3	2-0	0-1	3-1	3-1	2-1	1-0	5-1	2-1	2-2
Darlington FC	1-2	3-1	0-3	0-4	■	3-2	1-1	1-0	0-0	1-1	0-3	2-3	1-2	5-0	0-0	0-1	2-1	1-1	1-0	2-1	0-0	1-0	1-0	1-1
Doncaster Rovers FC	1-1	1-1	3-2	1-4	0-4	■	2-3	3-2	2-2	4-6	0-4	1-1	2-1	3-1	1-1	0-2	3-0	2-1	4-1	1-0	2-1	2-1	0-0	2-1
Gillingham FC	0-0	2-0	1-0	2-1	1-2	3-1	■	2-0	0-0	5-2	5-1	1-0	3-1	2-2	2-2	0-2	0-1	1-1	0-0	1-0	0-0	0-0	4-1	1-1
Grimsby Town FC	1-0	2-3	0-0	0-0	4-1	4-1	4-0	■	1-2	1-2	2-1	1-0	1-1	1-1	2-0	7-1	1-1	2-1	3-4	1-0	3-1	0-2		4-1
Leyton Orient FC	1-0	3-2	0-2	3-3	1-2	4-1	1-1	1-1	■	4-2	2-0	2-2	2-1	1-1	0-0	3-2	3-1	2-2	1-0	0-0	0-0	0-2	1-1	2-1
Mansfield Town FC	1-0	2-1	2-0	2-0	2-2	3-1	4-1	4-0	1-1	■	4-5	2-4	1-1	0-0	1-7	4-2	3-1	0-1	1-2	1-3	4-2	4-1	2-1	0-1
Middlesbrough FC	3-1	1-0	1-2	4-0	4-0	2-0	1-1	0-1	3-1	1-0	■	0-2	4-1	2-2	2-2	2-1	1-0	4-1	4-0	4-0	0-2	3-0	3-2	
Oldham Athletic AFC	1-1	4-1	3-0	4-0	1-0	2-1	0-1	3-1	0-0	0-1		■	1-1	0-1	1-3	2-0	4-1	4-1	1-0	5-0	6-2	1-1	3-0	
Oxford United FC	1-1	1-2	4-1	1-1	3-2	6-1	1-1	3-1	0-0	2-1	1-1	3-1	■	0-3	2-1	1-3	2-3	0-0	2-3	0-0	2-1	1-2	0-0	3-0
Peterborough United	2-0	2-1	1-1	2-1	2-0	3-3	2-0	2-1	0-2	3-1	1-2	3-1	2-3	■	0-2	2-1	1-0	0-2	4-4	1-2	0-1	2-1	2-2	3-0
Queen's Park Rangers	4-0	3-0	3-0	2-1	4-0	6-0	5-1	4-1	0-0	4-0	0-1	3-1	0-0		■	2-1	5-1	2-2	4-2	3-1	2-1	0-0	4-1	4-1
Reading FC	0-0	1-1	1-2	2-3	1-0	4-0	2-1	6-0	1-0	2-2	0-0	2-1	1-2	2-2	2-2	■	4-0	2-0	2-0	2-1	3-1	1-1	2-0	
Scunthorpe United	0-1	0-1	1-3	3-1	2-0	2-1	1-2	0-0	2-2	2-1	3-2	1-1	2-2	1-0	0-2	0-2	■	2-0	4-3	1-2	3-1	2-0	1-0	4-1
Shrewsbury Town	4-1	0-0	3-4	2-1	3-0	2-1	3-1	6-1	1-0	1-0	3-1	1-0	1-1	0-0	1-0	4-3		■	2-2	3-1	3-2	1-2	1-1	3-1
Swansea Town AFC	0-1	1-1	2-2	1-0	1-1	6-0	1-1	2-0	2-0	0-1	4-4	3-0	0-1	3-3	1-3	5-2	0-1	5-2	■	2-2	0-0	4-1	2-2	5-2
Swindon Town FC	1-0	1-1	1-1	4-0	0-1	2-0	3-1	5-1	3-1	4-0	6-3	3-0	4-1	1-0	1-1	0-1	2-1	2-2	4-0	■	0-0	1-2	3-0	
Torquay United FC	3-2	5-0	1-1	5-0	2-0	4-0	3-1	1-1	1-2	2-1	1-2	4-0	1-0	1-1	3-0	1-1	0-2	2-4	1-0		■	5-2	1-0	5-1
Walsall FC	3-0	2-1	1-1	1-1	1-1	4-0	3-0	1-1	1-1	1-2	2-1	1-0	2-0	2-1	3-1	2-0	2-2	1-1	1-1	0-1		■	0-1	2-0
Watford FC	3-0	1-1	3-1	0-0	2-0	4-1	1-1	3-1	1-3	0-1	2-0	2-2	2-0	3-1	1-0	1-0	0-1	1-0	1-1	2-0	2-1	2-1	■	2-1
Workington AFC	0-0	2-1	0-2	1-0	1-2	3-1	1-3	2-1	3-1	2-4	1-2	1-1	0-0	1-0	0-2	1-2	2-3	6-3	1-3	1-2	4-0	1-2	4-0	■

	Division 3	**Pd**	**Wn**	**Dw**	**Ls**	**GF**	**GA**	**Pts**	
1.	Queen's Park Rangers FC (London)	46	26	15	5	103	38	67	P
2.	Middlesbrough FC (Middlesbrough)	46	23	9	14	87	64	55	P
3.	Watford FC (Watford)	46	20	14	12	61	46	54	
4.	Reading FC (Reading)	46	22	9	15	76	57	53	
5.	Bristol Rovers FC (Bristol)	46	20	13	13	76	67	53	
6.	Shrewsbury Town FC (Shrewsbury)	46	20	12	14	77	62	52	
7.	Torquay United FC (Torquay)	46	21	9	16	73	54	51	
8.	Swindon Town FC (Swindon)	46	20	10	16	81	59	50	
9.	Mansfield Town FC (Mansfield)	46	20	9	17	84	79	49	
10.	Oldham Athletic AFC (Oldham)	46	19	10	17	80	63	48	
11.	Gillingham FC (Gillingham)	46	15	16	15	58	62	46	
12.	Walsall FC (Walsall)	46	18	10	18	65	72	46	
13.	Colchester United FC (Colchester)	46	17	10	19	76	73	44	
14.	Leyton Orient FC (London)	46	13	18	15	58	68	44	*
15.	Peterborough United FC (Peterborough)	46	14	15	17	66	71	43	
16.	Oxford United FC (Oxford)	46	15	13	16	61	66	43	
17.	Grimsby Town FC (Cleethorpes)	46	17	9	20	61	68	43	
18.	Scunthorpe United FC (Scunthorpe)	46	17	8	21	58	73	42	
19.	Brighton & Hove Albion FC (Hove)	46	13	15	18	61	71	41	
20.	Bournemouth & Boscombe Athletic FC (Bournemouth)	46	12	17	17	39	57	41	
21.	Swansea Town AFC (Swansea)	46	12	15	19	85	89	39	R
22.	Darlington FC (Darlington)	46	13	11	22	47	81	37	R
23.	Doncaster Rovers FC (Doncaster)	46	12	8	26	58	117	32	R
24.	Workington AFC (Workington)	46	12	7	27	55	89	31	R
		1104	411	282	411	1646	1646	1104	

* Leyton Orient FC (London) changed their club name to Orient FC (London) for the next season.

Football League Division 4 — 1966-67 Season

	Aldershot Town	Barnsley	Barrow	Bradford City	Bradford P.A.	Brentford	Chester	Chesterfield	Crewe Alexandra	Exeter City	Halifax Town	Hartlepools	Lincoln City	Luton Town	Newport County	Notts County	Port Vale	Rochdale	Southend United	Southport	Stockport County	Tranmere Rovers	Wrexham	York City
Aldershot Town FC	■	3-2	0-1	0-3	1-2	3-1	3-0	4-0	1-0	1-0	0-1	1-1	1-0	4-1	5-0	4-1	0-1	4-0	5-2	4-1	1-1	1-1	2-0	0-0
Barnsley FC	1-1	■	2-3	1-1	2-0	0-1	1-2	0-3	1-0	2-1	4-1	1-2	2-1	2-1	1-1	0-0	1-0	3-1	1-2	0-0	1-2	2-2	2-2	0-1
Barrow AFC	1-1	2-0	■	0-1	1-0	1-0	1-1	2-1	3-2	5-0	1-0	2-3	2-1	3-0	1-0	0-1	2-2	2-0	1-0	2-2	1-1	0-0	1-1	1-1
Bradford City AFC	4-1	1-1	5-2	■	2-3	2-0	2-3	3-1	0-3	1-1	1-2	3-0	2-1	2-1	1-2	3-1	2-0	4-1	2-1	3-3	0-1	1-0	3-3	1-0
Bradford Park Ave.	1-1	1-3	0-1	2-0	■	2-2	2-3	2-0	1-4	2-2	1-0	1-2	2-1	0-0	3-1	4-1	1-1	0-3	1-2	0-0	0-1	2-3	1-3	1-0
Brentford FC	1-0	3-1	0-3	2-0	1-1	■	4-0	1-0	0-2	3-1	1-0	1-2	2-2	1-0	2-0	4-0	1-1	2-1	2-1	1-1	1-1	1-1	1-1	1-1
Chester FC	0-0	1-0	1-1	1-0	0-3	1-2	■	2-1	0-3	0-2	0-2	1-0	0-1	0-0	4-2	1-2	1-3	3-2	1-1	2-1	1-1	1-3	1-3	3-1
Chesterfield FC	1-1	1-0	1-2	0-1	4-1	3-0	0-2	■	0-0	1-0	1-1	1-0	3-1	0-0	0-1	1-1	2-1	0-0	2-1	2-1	2-1	3-1	4-0	1-0
Crewe Alexandra FC	2-1	2-2	3-2	1-0	1-3	1-0	3-1	2-1	■	2-2	1-1	1-2	3-0	3-1	3-2	4-1	1-0	2-1	1-0	1-1	1-1	1-2	1-2	2-0
Exeter City FC	1-1	0-3	1-1	2-2	4-1	1-0	2-0	1-1	2-0	■	3-2	1-0	1-0	2-1	0-0	1-0	0-0	0-1	0-0	0-3	1-4	4-1	3-1	1-1
Halifax Town AFC	2-2	1-1	1-4	2-2	0-0	3-2	2-1	1-0	1-0	0-0	■	2-1	0-0	1-1	2-2	5-2	2-2	1-1	2-2	2-0	0-1	2-1	3-1	2-1
Hartlepools United	3-2	1-1	2-1	1-0	2-0	2-2	3-2	3-2	1-2	3-1	1-3	■	5-0	2-1	0-1	2-1	2-1	1-2	1-1	1-0	0-2	2-1	4-2	1-0
Lincoln City FC	0-4	0-1	2-1	1-4	2-2	3-	2-3	2-1	1-1	1-1	3-3	3-0	■	8-1	2-2	2-1	0-1	0-2	2-2	0-4	0-1	2-0	1-1	2-2
Luton Town FC	4-0	1-1	3-1	0-0	2-2	3-0	1-0	3-2	2-1	4-0	2-0	0-2	2-1	■	3-1	2-5	1-1	3-1	1-0	0-0	0-3	2-0	3-1	5-1
Newport County AFC	1-2	2-0	0-1	1-1	0-0	1-1	2-3	4-1	2-1	3-2	0-2	0-0	2-0	2-0	■	1-0	1-1	2-2	3-0	0-1	1-1	1-2	1-1	4-2
Notts County FC	3-0	0-3	2-2	1-3	2-1	3-2	3-0	0-2	1-1	0-1	2-1	0-0	2-1	1-2	2-1	■	0-0	2-0	1-0	0-1	2-2	0-0	2-2	2-0
Port Vale FC	0-2	3-1	2-1	3-2	0-0	1-3	1-1	2-3	1-1	2-0	0-1	0-0	2-2	1-0	2-0	0-0	■	5-0	1-3	2-1	0-2	1-1	0-2	4-1
Rochdale AFC	2-1	1-1	1-3	0-1	1-0	1-3	0-1	2-1	0-1	1-0	3-0	3-2	1-0	3-0	2-0	1-1	1-2	■	1-2	1-1	1-0	1-2	1-3	2-2
Southend United FC	4-0	3-0	1-3	2-1	4-0	3-0	5-1	4-1	1-1	1-0	2-0	3-0	2-0	1-0	4-1	0-0	1-0	1-0	■	0-1	0-1	4-1	1-1	2-1
Southport FC	1-0	3-0	4-1	2-1	1-0	1-1	4-3	1-2	4-1	1-1	2-0	3-1	2-1	4-1	1-0	2-1	0-0	1-2	1-0	■	4-0	1-0	1-0	2-0
Stockport County FC	1-0	2-1	2-1	1-0	4-0	1-2	1-1	3-1	1-1	1-0	2-1	2-0	4-5	1-0	0-0	2-0	1-1	2-2	4-1	1-0	■	1-0	1-0	3-1
Tranmere Rovers FC	2-2	3-3	1-2	3-1	2-2	0-0	0-0	1-0	5-0	1-1	2-0	1-0	1-0	2-1	3-0	2-1	3-1	1-2	1-2	3-0	3-0	■	2-1	2-1
Wrexham AFC	2-0	2-2	1-1	1-1	6-0	0-0	3-1	3-2	1-1	0-0	4-0	4-1	0-0	2-0	2-2	3-2	2-1	4-2	2-0	1-1	2-2	0-0	■	1-1
York City FC	1-2	0-3	1-2	4-1	3-1	0-0	1-1	1-1	0-2	2-4	4-3	1-1	3-1	5-1	2-1	4-1	3-1	1-1	2-1	2-0	1-2	0-1	4-0	■

Division 4

		Pd	Wn	Dw	Ls	GF	GA	Pts	
1.	Stockport County FC (Stockport)	46	26	12	8	69	42	64	P
2.	Southport FC (Southport)	46	23	13	10	69	42	59	P
3.	Barrow AFC (Barrow-in-Furness)	46	24	11	11	76	54	59	P
4.	Tranmere Rovers FC (Birkenhead)	46	22	14	10	66	43	58	P
5.	Crewe Alexandra FC (Crewe)	46	21	12	13	70	55	54	
6.	Southend United FC (Southend-on-Sea)	46	22	9	15	70	49	53	
7.	Wrexham AFC (Wrexham)	46	16	20	10	76	62	52	
8.	Hartlepools United FC (Hartlepool)	46	22	7	17	66	64	51	
9.	Brentford FC (London)	46	18	13	15	58	56	49	
10.	Aldershot FC (Aldershot)	46	18	12	16	72	57	48	
11.	Bradford City AFC (Bradford)	46	19	10	17	74	62	48	
12.	Halifax Town AFC (Halifax)	46	15	14	17	59	68	44	
13.	Port Vale FC (Stoke-on-Trent)	46	14	15	17	55	58	43	
14.	Exeter City FC (Exeter)	46	14	15	17	50	60	43	
15.	Chesterfield FC (Chesterfield)	46	17	8	21	60	63	42	
16.	Barnsley FC (Barnsley)	46	13	15	18	60	64	41	
17.	Luton Town FC (Luton)	46	16	9	21	59	73	41	
18.	Newport County AFC (Newport)	46	12	16	18	56	63	40	
19.	Chester FC (Chester)	46	15	10	21	54	78	40	
20.	Notts County FC (Nottingham)	46	13	11	22	53	72	37	
21.	Rochdale AFC (Rochdale)	46	13	11	22	53	75	37	
22.	York City FC (York)	46	12	11	23	65	79	35	
23.	Bradford Park Avenue FC (Bradford)	46	11	13	22	52	79	35	
24.	Lincoln City FC (Lincoln)	46	9	13	24	58	82	31	
		1104	405	294	405	1500	1500	1104	

F.A. CUP FINAL   (Wembley Stadium, London – 20/05/1967 – 100,000)

TOTTENHAM HOTSPUR FC (LONDON)   2-1   Chelsea FC (London)
Robertson, Saul   *Tambling*

Tottenham: Jennings, Kinnear, Knowles, Mullery, England, Mackay, Robertson, Greaves, Gilzean, Venables, Saul.
Chelsea: Bonetti, A.Harris, McCreadie, Hollins, Hinton, R.Harris, Cooke, Baldwin, Hateley, Tambling, Boyle.

Semi-finals

Chelsea FC (London)	1-0	Leeds United AFC (Leeds)
Nottingham Forest FC (Nottingham)	1-2	Tottenham Hotspur FC (London)

Quarter-finals

Birmingham City FC (Birmingham)	0-0, 0-6	Tottenham Hotspur FC (London)
Chelsea FC (London)	1-0	Sheffield Wednesday FC (Sheffield)
Leeds United AFC (Leeds)	1-0	Manchester City FC (Manchester)
Nottingham Forest FC (Nottingham)	3-2	Everton FC (Liverpool)

1967-68

Football League Division 1 1967-68 Season	Arsenal	Burnley	Chelsea	Coventry City	Everton	Fulham	Leeds United	Leicester City	Liverpool	Man. City	Man. United	Newcastle Utd.	Nottingham F.	Sheffield Utd.	Sheffield Wed.	Southampton	Stoke City	Sunderland	Tottenham H.	W.B.A.	West Ham Utd.	Wolves
Arsenal FC	■	2-0	1-1	1-1	2-2	5-3	4-3	2-1	2-0	1-0	0-2	0-0	3-0	1-1	3-2	0-3	2-0	2-1	4-0	2-1	0-0	0-2
Burnley FC	1-0	■	1-1	2-1	2-1	2-0	3-0	1-1	1-1	0-1	2-1	2-0	1-1	0-2	2-1	2-0	4-0	3-0	5-1	0-0	3-3	1-1
Chelsea FC	2-1	2-1	■	1-1	1-1	1-1	0-0	4-1	3-1	1-0	1-1	1-1	1-0	4-2	3-0	2-6	2-2	1-0	2-0	0-3	1-3	1-0
Coventry City FC	1-1	5-1	2-1	■	0-2	0-3	0-1	0-1	1-1	0-3	2-0	1-4	1-3	2-2	3-0	2-1	2-0	2-2	2-3	4-2	1-1	1-0
Everton FC	2-0	2-0	2-1	3-1	■	5-1	0-1	2-1	1-0	1-1	3-1	1-0	1-0	1-0	1-0	4-2	3-0	3-0	0-1	2-1	2-0	4-2
Fulham FC	1-3	4-3	2-2	1-1	2-1	■	0-5	0-1	1-1	2-4	0-4	2-0	2-0	2-2	0-2	3-2	1-2	1-2	0-3	1-3	0-3	1-2
Leeds United AFC	3-1	2-1	7-0	1-1	2-0	2-0	■	3-2	1-2	2-0	1-0	2-0	1-1	3-0	3-2	5-0	2-0	1-1	1-0	3-1	2-1	2-1
Leicester City FC	2-2	0-2	2-2	0-0	0-2	1-2	2-2	■	2-1	1-0	2-2	2-2	4-2	3-1	3-0	4-1	0-0	0-2	2-3	2-3	2-4	3-1
Liverpool FC	2-0	3-2	3-1	1-0	1-0	4-1	2-0	3-1	■	1-1	1-2	6-0	6-1	1-2	1-0	2-0	2-1	2-1	1-1	4-1	3-1	2-1
Manchester City FC	1-1	4-2	1-0	3-1	2-0	5-1	1-0	6-0	0-0	■	1-2	2-0	2-0	5-2	1-0	4-2	4-2	1-0	4-1	0-2	3-0	2-0
Manchester United FC	1-0	2-2	1-3	4-0	3-1	3-0	1-0	1-1	1-2	1-3	■	6-0	3-0	1-0	4-2	3-2	1-0	1-2	3-1	2-1	3-1	4-0
Newcastle United FC	2-1	1-0	5-1	3-2	1-0	2-1	1-1	0-0	1-1	3-4	2-2	■	0-0	1-0	4-0	3-0	1-1	2-1	1-3	2-2	1-0	2-0
Nottingham Forest FC	2-0	1-0	3-0	3-3	1-0	2-2	0-2	2-1	0-1	0-3	3-1	4-0	■	1-0	0-0	2-2	3-0	0-3	0-0	3-2	1-1	3-1
Sheffield United FC	2-4	1-0	1-2	2-0	0-1	2-3	1-0	0-0	1-1	0-3	0-3	2-1	1-3	■	0-1	4-1	1-0	1-2	3-2	1-1	1-2	1-1
Sheffield Wednesday FC	1-2	2-1	2-2	4-0	0-0	4-2	0-1	2-1	1-2	1-1	1-1	1-1	0-0	1-1	■	2-0	1-1	0-1	1-2	2-2	4-1	2-2
Southampton FC	2-0	2-2	3-5	0-0	3-2	2-1	1-1	1-5	1-0	3-2	2-2	0-0	2-1	3-3	2-0	■	1-2	3-2	1-2	4-0	0-0	1-1
Stoke City FC	0-1	0-2	0-1	3-3	1-0	0-1	3-2	3-2	2-1	3-0	2-4	2-1	1-3	1-1	0-1	3-2	■	2-1	2-1	0-0	2-0	0-2
Sunderland AFC	2-0	2-2	2-3	1-1	1-0	3-0	2-2	2-2	1-1	1-0	1-1	3-3	1-0	2-1	0-2	0-3	3-1	■	0-1	0-0	1-5	2-0
Tottenham Hotspur FC	1-0	5-0	2-0	4-2	1-1	2-2	2-1	0-1	1-1	1-3	1-2	1-1	1-1	1-1	2-1	6-1	3-0	3-0	■	0-0	5-1	2-1
West Bromwich Albion FC	1-3	8-1	0-1	0-1	2-6	2-1	2-0	0-0	0-2	3-2	6-3	2-0	2-1	4-1	1-1	0-0	3-0	0-0	2-0	■	3-1	4-1
West Ham United FC	1-1	4-2	0-1	0-0	1-1	7-2	0-0	4-2	1-0	2-3	1-3	5-0	3-0	3-0	2-3	0-1	3-4	1-1	2-1	2-3	■	1-2
Wolverhampton Wanderers FC	3-2	3-2	3-0	2-0	1-3	3-2	2-0	1-3	1-1	0-0	2-3	2-2	6-1	1-3	2-3	2-0	3-4	2-1	2-1	3-3	1-2	■

	Division 1	**Pd**	**Wn**	**Dw**	**Ls**	**GF**	**GA**	**Pts**	
1.	MANCHESTER CITY FC (MANCHESTER)	42	26	6	10	86	43	58	
2.	Manchester United FC (Manchester)	42	24	8	10	89	55	56	
3.	Liverpool FC (Liverpool)	42	22	11	9	71	40	55	
4.	Leeds United AFC (Leeds)	42	22	9	11	71	41	53	
5.	Everton FC (Liverpool)	42	23	6	13	67	40	52	
6.	Chelsea FC (London)	42	18	12	12	62	68	48	
7.	Tottenham Hotspur FC (London)	42	19	9	14	70	59	47	
8.	West Bromwich Albion FC (West Bromwich)	42	17	12	13	75	62	46	
9.	Arsenal FC (London)	42	17	10	15	60	56	44	
10.	Newcastle United FC (Newcastle-upon-Tyne)	42	13	15	14	54	67	41	
11.	Nottingham Forest FC (Nottingham)	42	14	11	17	52	64	39	
12.	West Ham United FC (London)	42	14	10	18	73	69	38	
13.	Leicester City FC (Leicester)	42	13	12	17	64	69	38	
14.	Burnley FC (Burnley)	42	14	10	18	64	71	38	
15.	Sunderland AFC (Sunderland)	42	13	11	18	51	61	37	
16.	Southampton FC (Southampton)	42	13	11	18	66	83	37	
17.	Wolverhampton Wanderers FC (Wolverhampton)	42	14	8	20	66	75	36	
18.	Stoke City FC (Stoke-on-Trent)	42	14	7	21	50	73	35	
19.	Sheffield Wednesday FC (Sheffield)	42	11	12	19	51	63	34	
20.	Coventry City FC (Coventry)	42	9	15	18	51	71	33	
21.	Sheffield United FC (Sheffield)	42	11	10	21	49	70	32	R
22.	Fulham FC (London)	42	10	7	25	56	98	27	R
		924	351	222	351	1398	1398	924	

Top Goalscorers

1)	George BEST	(Manchester United FC)	28
	Ron DAVIES	(Southampton FC)	28

Football League Division 2 1967-68 Season	Aston Villa	Birmingham City	Blackburn Rovers	Blackpool	Bolton Wanderers	Bristol City	Cardiff City	Carlisle United	Charlton Athletic	Crystal Palace	Derby County	Huddersfield Town	Hull City	Ipswich Town	Middlesbrough	Millwall	Norwich City	Plymouth Argyle	Portsmouth	Preston North End	Q.P.R.	Rotherham United
Aston Villa FC	■	2-4	1-2	3-2	1-1	2-4	2-1	1-0	4-1	0-1	2-1	0-0	2-3	2-2	0-1	3-1	4-2	0-1	1-0	1-0	1-2	3-1
Birmingham City FC	2-1	■	1-1	1-2	4-0	4-1	0-0	1-3	4-0	1-0	3-1	6-1	6-2	0-0	6-1	2-3	0-0	2-2	2-2	3-0	2-0	4-1
Blackburn Rovers FC	2-1	1-2	■	2-1	2-1	2-0	1-1	1-0	3-2	2-1	3-0	0-0	2-0	2-1	3-0	2-0	0-0	1-1	2-2	0-1	0-1	3-1
Blackpool FC	1-0	1-0	2-1	■	1-1	1-1	3-1	1-1	2-0	2-0	1-1	2-0	3-1	0-0	3-0	1-4	0-2	2-0	2-0	4-1	0-1	1-1
Bolton Wanderers FC	2-3	1-1	2-1	1-2	■	1-0	1-1	2-3	2-0	2-2	5-3	3-1	6-1	1-2	2-0	1-1	2-0	1-2	1-2	0-0	1-1	0-2
Bristol City FC	0-0	3-1	0-0	2-4	1-1	■	1-1	1-0	0-2	2-1	1-0	2-3	3-3	1-1	0-0	0-2	0-2	2-0	3-0	4-1	0-2	0-1
Cardiff City AFC	3-0	1-3	3-2	1-3	1-3	0-1	■	1-0	0-0	4-2	1-5	0-0	2-3	1-1	3-0	2-2	3-1	1-1	3-0	2-0	1-0	2-2
Carlisle United FC	1-2	1-1	1-0	1-3	3-0	0-0	1-3	■	0-0	3-0	1-1	2-1	1-1	4-1	2-2	1-1	2-2	2-0	1-1	4-1	3-1	4-1
Charlton Athletic FC	3-0	3-1	3-0	0-2	2-0	1-2	1-1	2-2	■	0-1	1-2	4-2	5-1	0-1	2-2	1-0	3-3	1-0	4-1	0-0	3-3	4-1
Crystal Palace FC	0-1	0-0	1-0	3-1	0-3	2-0	2-1	1-1	3-0	■	1-0	0-1	0-1	1-3	1-3	2-2	6-0	5-0	2-2	2-0	1-0	1-0
Derby County FC	3-1	2-2	2-2	1-3	2-1	3-1	3-4	0-1	3-2	1-1	■	1-0	1-2	2-3	2-4	3-3	1-1	1-0	0-1	1-2	4-0	4-1
Huddersfield Town AFC	0-0	2-3	1-3	1-3	1-1	0-3	1-0	1-1	4-1	1-1	3-1	■	2-0	1-4	1-0	1-0	0-1	2-2	1-1	1-0	2-0	2-0
Hull City AFC	3-0	0-1	1-1	0-1	1-2	4-2	1-2	1-0	1-1	1-1	3-0	1-1	■	1-1	0-2	1-1	0-2	0-2	1-1	1-1	2-0	2-1
Ipswich Town FC	2-1	2-1	1-1	1-1	1-1	5-0	4-2	3-1	3-2	2-2	4-0	2-0	2-0	■	1-2	2-1	0-0	1-1	1-2	4-0	2-2	2-0
Middlesbrough FC	1-1	1-1	0-0	0-0	1-2	2-1	2-3	4-0	1-1	3-0	2-2	3-2	2-1	0-2	■	0-1	2-0	5-0	1-0	5-0	3-1	1-1
Millwall FC	1-2	1-1	1-2	1-1	3-0	1-1	3-1	1-0	0-0	5-1	1-1	1-1	1-1	1-1	4-0	■	1-0	3-0	3-2	2-0	1-0	0-0
Norwich City FC	1-0	4-2	1-0	1-2	3-1	3-2	1-0	2-1	1-1	3-2	0-1	2-2	3-4	2-1	5-2	1-1	■	2-0	1-3	1-3	0-0	2-2
Plymouth Argyle FC	2-1	1-2	2-1	2-2	1-2	0-1	0-0	3-1	1-4	2-1	3-4	1-1	2-5	0-1	0-1	2-1	2-2	■	1-2	1-2	0-1	0-1
Portsmouth FC	2-2	1-2	2-1	3-1	3-0	2-0	3-1	2-1	4-0	2-2	3-2	3-1	3-0	1-2	2-0	0-0	3-0	0-0	■	2-1	1-1	1-1
Preston North End FC	2-1	0-0	3-5	0-2	1-1	0-1	3-0	0-2	4-1	0-0	1-1	3-1	1-0	0-1	1-0	2-0	3-1	2-0	1-1	■	0-2	2-2
Queen's Park Rangers FC	3-0	2-0	3-1	2-0	1-0	3-1	1-0	1-0	2-1	2-1	0-1	3-0	1-1	1-0	1-1	3-1	2-0	4-1	2-0	2-0	■	6-0
Rotherham United FC	0-2	1-1	1-0	1-2	2-2	1-0	3-2	1-2	1-1	0-3	1-3	1-0	1-3	1-3	0-1	2-0	1-3	1-0	1-1	1-0	1-3	■

	Division 2	Pd	Wn	Dw	Ls	GF	GA	Pts	
1.	Ipswich Town FC (Ipswich)	42	22	15	5	79	44	59	P
2.	Queen's Park Rangers FC (London)	42	25	8	9	67	36	58	P
3.	Blackpool FC (Blackpool)	42	24	10	8	71	43	58	
4.	Birmingham City FC (Birmingham)	42	19	14	9	83	51	52	
5.	Portsmouth FC (Portsmouth)	42	18	13	11	68	55	49	
6.	Middlesbrough FC (Middlesbrough)	42	17	12	13	60	54	46	
7.	Millwall FC (London)	42	14	17	11	62	50	45	
8.	Blackburn Rovers FC (Blackburn)	42	16	11	15	56	49	43	
9.	Norwich City FC (Norwich)	42	16	11	15	60	65	43	
10.	Carlisle United FC (Carlisle)	42	14	13	15	58	52	41	
11.	Crystal Palace FC (London)	42	14	11	17	56	56	39	
12.	Bolton Wanderers FC (Bolton)	42	13	13	16	60	63	39	
13.	Cardiff City AFC (Cardiff)	42	13	12	17	60	66	38	
14.	Huddersfield Town AFC (Huddersfield)	42	13	12	17	46	61	38	
15.	Charlton Athletic FC (London)	42	12	13	17	63	68	37	
16.	Aston Villa FC (Birmingham)	42	15	7	20	54	64	37	
17.	Hull City AFC (Kingston-upon-Hull)	42	12	13	17	59	73	37	
18.	Derby County FC (Derby)	42	13	10	19	71	78	36	
19.	Bristol City FC (Bristol)	42	13	10	19	48	62	36	
20.	Preston North End FC (Preston)	42	12	11	19	43	65	35	
21.	Rotherham United FC (Rotherham)	42	10	11	21	42	76	31	R
22.	Plymouth Argyle FC (Plymouth)	42	9	9	24	38	72	27	R
		924	334	256	334	1303	1303	924	

89

Football League Division 3 1967-68 Season	Barrow	Bournemouth	Brighton & H.A.	Bristol Rovers	Bury	Colchester U.	Gillingham	Grimsby Town	Mansfield Town	Northampton T.	Oldham Athletic	Orient	Oxford United	Peterborough U.	Reading	Scunthorpe U.	Shrewsbury T.	Southport	Stockport Co.	Swindon Town	Torquay United	Tranmere R.	Walsall	Watford
Barrow AFC		1-1	1-1	1-0	1-1	5-0	0-1	2-0	0-1	4-0	4-1	1-0	3-0	1-2	1-0	2-1	3-0	3-1	3-0	1-1	3-0	2-1	1-1	0-0
Bournemouth & Bos.	3-0		2-2	3-1	1-0	1-2	4-0	1-0	3-0	0-2	0-0	0-0	2-1	3-3	2-0	1-0	1-1	4-1	1-0	2-1	1-1	3-0	1-1	0-1
Brighton & Hove Alb.	1-1	2-3		1-1	1-0	0-0	3-0	3-1	3-0	0-2	0-1	1-1	0-0	1-1	1-1	3-1	3-0	1-0	3-0	0-0	0-1	2-0	1-0	1-0
Bristol Rovers FC	1-0	2-0	3-1		3-1	1-1	1-1	3-0	2-0	2-0	4-3	0-2	1-1	2-1	1-0	4-0	4-1	1-3	0-2	1-2	1-0	3-1	2-3	0-2
Bury FC	1-2	4-0	4-0	4-2		2-0	3-2	2-0	3-1	3-1	3-1	1-0	1-1	4-0	2-0	4-3	2-0	3-2	5-3	1-1	5-1	3-3	2-1	2-0
Colchester United FC	3-2	0-1	0-0	2-0	0-0		2-2	1-3	1-2	2-1	0-1	1-2	1-5	2-5	1-0	0-3	1-1	1-1	2-1	3-5	1-2	2-2	2-1	
Gillingham FC	3-0	0-0	1-1	0-0	2-0	1-0		1-0	2-1	2-0	1-0	2-3	2-1	3-2	3-0	3-1	0-1	1-4	3-1	3-1	1-1	1-1	0-1	0-0
Grimsby Town FC	0-1	2-1	4-2	3-2	3-1	1-2	1-1		0-0	0-0	0-1	0-0	0-1	1-1	1-1	2-1	0-1	2-0	3-1	3-2	1-1	3-0	3-0	1-1
Mansfield Town FC	1-2	1-1	1-3	3-0	1-1	2-1	0-1	1-1		3-2	1-1	0-0	1-0	2-3	2-2	3-0	0-1	4-2	1-0	2-2	2-0	0-3	0-3	1-2
Northampton Town	3-0	1-0	2-2	4-5	0-1	2-2	1-1	3-0	1-1		1-2	2-1	1-1	3-1	1-0	2-2	1-1	4-1	2-0	1-0	0-1	0-1	3-0	1-1
Oldham Athletic AFC	3-1	1-1	3-0	3-5	1-2	2-1	0-1	2-1	1-0	2-0		2-2	3-1	0-2	1-3	3-4	0-0	2-0	4-1	0-2	0-1	2-1	0-3	2-0
Orient FC	4-2	1-0	1-2	2-2	1-0	1-1	0-4	1-0	0-0	1-3	0-2		1-0	3-0	1-0	2-1	1-1	3-0	2-2	0-0	0-2	0-1	2-0	0-1
Oxford United FC	3-1	3-2	2-0	0-2	5-4	3-1	3-0	2-1	2-0	1-0	3-1	2-0		3-1	2-0	2-3	2-2	1-0	2-2	0-0	2-0	1-0	4-0	1-0
Peterborough United	0-1	2-0	2-3	4-1	0-2	3-1	3-0	3-2	2-0	4-0	2-1	3-2	1-1		2-3	1-1	0-1	1-0	2-0	1-1	2-0	1-1	2-1	5-1
Reading FC	3-0	1-0	1-0	2-1	3-4	1-0	3-1	3-0	2-1	0-0	0-1	4-2	1-1	0-1		2-1	0-0	1-3	3-0	2-1	4-0	3-0	2-2	2-0
Scunthorpe United	2-4	1-1	1-3	1-1	3-1	5-1	2-1	0-3	3-3	1-1	2-0	1-1	1-1	2-1	1-2		0-0	1-0	0-2	3-1	2-0	1-1	2-5	1-1
Shrewsbury Town	1-0	1-0	0-0	0-0	1-0	4-0	1-2	3-2	2-1	2-0	4-2	2-2	2-0	1-1	2-1	4-0		3-2	0-0	0-1	5-0	1-1	0-1	3-1
Southport FC	1-0	1-1	1-0	2-1	2-2	2-3	4-1	0-1	1-3	1-0	0-0	1-0	0-1	2-1	1-1	0-0	3-2		4-3	1-1	0-2	2-0	2-0	2-0
Stockport County FC	1-0	3-1	2-0	3-1	4-2	1-0	1-1	1-1	1-0	4-0	0-2	2-0	0-4	2-2	3-0	4-1	4-2	4-3		2-0	0-0	5-2	0-0	2-0
Swindon Town FC	0-1	4-0	2-1	4-1	2-3	1-1	2-2	5-0	1-1	4-0	0-0	4-0	1-1	0-0	5-1	2-0	0-0	3-3	2-0		1-0	3-1	3-0	2-0
Torquay United FC	0-2	2-1	1-1	2-0	3-0	3-0	2-1	1-0	0-2	0-0	2-1	1-1	3-1	2-1	2-1	3-0	2-2	3-0	1-1			1-0	4-1	1-0
Tranmere Rovers FC	0-0	0-0	2-2	3-3	2-0	4-2	2-1	1-2	1-1	2-2	1-0	3-0	1-1	0-1	1-2	2-0	4-1	0-2	2-1	3-2	2-3		2-0	1-2
Walsall FC	4-0	1-1	1-2	2-1	2-1	1-1	3-0	2-0	2-1	4-0	3-1	5-0	0-1	3-2	2-2	0-0	1-2	1-1	0-1	3-2	1-1	5-1		1-1
Watford FC	3-2	0-2	4-0	4-0	1-1	1-1	3-0	7-1	1-2	5-1	1-2	1-1	2-0	4-1	3-0	4-0	2-0	0-1	5-0	2-0	2-1	3-2	1-2	

	Division 3	Pd	Wn	Dw	Ls	GF	GA	Pts	
1.	Oxford United FC (Oxford)	46	22	13	11	69	47	57	P
2.	Bury FC (Bury)	46	24	8	14	91	66	56	P
3.	Shrewsbury Town FC (Shrewsbury)	46	20	15	11	61	49	55	
4.	Torquay United FC (Torquay)	46	21	11	14	60	56	53	
5.	Reading FC (Reading)	46	21	9	16	70	60	51	
6.	Watford FC (Watford)	46	21	8	17	74	50	50	
7.	Walsall FC (Walsall)	46	19	12	15	74	61	50	
8.	Barrow AFC (Barrow-in-Furness)	46	21	8	17	65	54	50	
9.	Swindon Town FC (Swindon)	46	16	17	13	74	51	49	
10.	Brighton & Hove Albion FC (Hove)	46	16	16	14	57	55	48	
11.	Gillingham FC (Gillingham)	46	18	12	16	59	63	48	
12.	Bournemouth & Boscombe Athletic FC (Bournemouth)	46	16	15	15	56	51	47	
13.	Stockport County FC (Stockport)	46	19	9	18	70	75	47	
14.	Southport FC (Southport)	46	17	12	17	65	65	46	
15.	Bristol Rovers FC (Bristol)	46	17	9	20	72	78	43	
16.	Oldham Athletic AFC (Oldham)	46	18	7	21	60	65	43	
17.	Northampton Town FC (Northampton)	46	14	13	19	58	72	41	
18.	Orient FC (London)	46	12	17	17	46	62	41	
19.	Tranmere Rovers FC (Birkenhead)	46	14	12	20	62	74	40	
20.	Mansfield Town FC (Mansfield)	46	12	13	21	51	67	37	
21.	Grimsby Town FC (Cleethorpes)	46	14	9	23	52	69	37	R
22.	Colchester United FC (Colchester)	46	9	15	22	50	87	33	R
23.	Scunthorpe United FC (Scunthorpe)	46	10	12	24	56	87	32	R
24.	Peterborough United FC (Peterborough)	46	20	10	16	79	67	31	R-19
		1104	411	282	411	1531	1531	1085	

Peterborough United FC (Peterborough) had 19 points deducted for offering illegal bonus payments to their players.

	Aldershot Town	Barnsley	Bradford City	Bradford Park Avenue	Brentford	Chester	Chesterfield	Crewe Alexandra	Darlington	Doncaster Rovers	Exeter City	Halifax Town	Hartlepools	Lincoln City	Luton Town	Newport County	Notts County	Port Vale	Rochdale	Southend United	Swansea Town	Workington	Wrexham	York City
Aldershot Town FC		1-1	3-3	1-1	0-0	2-1	3-0	2-0	0-0	2-1	0-0	1-1	2-0	3-2	0-1	0-0	0-0	2-0	2-1	1-3	1-1	5-0	3-1	2-2
Barnsley FC	1-0		1-0	2-0	3-0	2-1	0-0	3-1	1-0	1-0	2-1	0-0	4-0	2-1	2-2	4-2	3-1	2-0	1-1	1-1	3-0	2-1	2-2	1-0
Bradford City AFC	1-3	1-0		1-2	2-3	2-2	3-1	2-1	1-0	1-1	2-1	0-1	1-1	2-1	2-0	3-0	5-1	2-1	0-0	2-1	4-1	1-0	3-1	0-0
Bradford Park Ave.	1-1	1-1	1-2		1-0	0-2	2-1	1-2	1-2	1-1	0-1	0-1	1-5	2-1	0-2	1-4	2-2	0-0	0-1	1-2	1-1	0-1	1-1	1-1
Brentford FC	1-1	0-1	0-1	2-1		3-1	1-1	2-1	2-0	4-2	5-1	0-0	1-3	0-2	3-1	2-1	3-1	4-0	1-2	2-1	2-1	0-0	3-1	3-1
Chester FC	2-5	1-1	2-3	0-0	3-0		3-0	0-4	0-1	2-3	3-1	3-2	0-2	6-0	1-3	2-1	1-3	1-1	0-1	0-0	2-3	1-2	1-1	1-1
Chesterfield FC	1-2	2-3	2-1	2-0	2-1	3-1		4-1	3-1	1-1	1-0	0-0	3-1	2-0	0-0	1-2	4-0	3-0	0-2	3-1	3-1	0-0	3-1	3-1
Crewe Alexandra FC	1-1	3-3	1-1	4-0	2-0	2-0	1-1		1-1	2-2	2-0	5-1	2-1	2-1	1-1	4-0	1-1	1-1	2-1	1-0	3-2	0-0	0-0	0-0
Darlington FC	6-2	0-2	2-2	0-0	2-3	0-2	1-1	0-0		1-1	0-1	0-1	2-3	1-1	1-2	1-0	2-2	2-2	2-0	1-1	2-0	1-1	1-0	3-1
Doncaster Rovers FC	3-0	1-2	2-2	2-0	0-0	1-0	2-2	2-1	2-1		3-1	0-0	0-1	0-0	2-0	1-1	3-1	0-0	2-1	1-2	1-2	2-2	2-0	2-0
Exeter City FC	3-0	2-0	4-1	0-0	0-3	1-0	1-1	1-4	0-0	0-1		0-0	0-0	0-5	2-1	3-3	3-1	3-1	0-2	1-3	1-0	2-2	3-1	3-1
Halifax Town AFC	2-2	1-1	1-1	3-0	2-2	0-2	0-1	2-0	2-3	1-1	1-1		3-0	0-1	4-1	0-0	0-1	1-2	2-2	1-2	0-1	2-2	2-2	2-2
Hartlepools United	1-0	2-1	1-1	2-0	2-0	2-1	1-1	1-0	3-1	0-0	0-0	1-1		1-1	2-1	2-0	3-1	2-2	1-1	2-1	1-0	3-0	1-0	1-0
Lincoln City FC	1-1	0-1	5-1	1-0	3-0	2-2	2-4	1-2	1-1	1-0	1-2	2-3	2-1		2-1	1-0	3-2	4-2	3-0	0-2	1-3	3-0	0-2	1-3
Luton Town FC	3-1	2-0	1-3	2-1	2-1	0-0	1-0	4-0	3-1	5-3	0-0	2-0	1-0	4-2		1-1	2-0	2-0	4-1	3-1	4-0	4-0	2-1	3-1
Newport County AFC	0-2	3-0	0-3	4-0	2-2	1-1	0-3	0-0	1-0	2-1	0-1	2-0	0-1	1-1	1-1		1-0	1-1	1-1	2-0	2-1	1-1	3-2	2-1
Notts County FC	0-1	1-4	2-1	3-0	2-1	1-2	1-0	1-0	0-0	1-0	1-3	0-3	0-0	2-2	3-1	1-1		0-0	4-3	3-2	2-1	1-1	1-1	1-1
Port Vale FC	0-3	2-0	1-2	4-0	4-1	4-4	0-1	0-2	1-0	2-0	2-1	2-3	2-0	4-1	2-0	4-1	1-1		1-1	1-2	4-2	1-1	1-1	1-0
Rochdale AFC	0-2	1-0	3-2	1-1	1-1	1-1	1-4	1-0	2-0	2-2	2-1	1-1	1-2	1-0	4-3	0-0	3-1	0-1		0-1	1-2	1-3	3-0	3-2
Southend United FC	1-1	4-1	1-1	2-1	1-0	5-1	0-0	2-2	1-2	2-2	1-1	2-2	2-1	3-0	2-2	0-1	1-1	3-1	3-1		1-0	7-0	3-1	0-1
Swansea Town AFC	1-0	1-1	0-0	1-1	2-1	1-0	0-1	1-2	0-1	0-2	1-2	2-2	2-2	4-2	2-0	4-2	1-0	2-2	1-0	2-2		5-2	2-0	1-1
Workington AFC	3-2	0-1	0-1	2-2	2-0	1-0	3-1	2-2	0-1	2-1	2-4	0-1	1-1	5-1	0-1	2-2	3-1	1-1	1-1	2-2	3-1		1-2	1-1
Wrexham AFC	2-1	2-0	0-2	3-0	1-2	2-0	3-0	1-1	3-1	0-0	0-0	2-0	6-0	2-1	1-1	0-1	2-0	1-0	2-0	4-1	2-1	5-0		3-1
York City FC	2-3	1-1	0-1	6-2	0-1	4-1	0-2	1-1	1-1	1-2	4-0	1-2	0-2	1-0	1-1	0-1	4-2	5-1	4-1	2-2	2-1	1-1	3-1	

Division 4

		Pd	Wn	Dw	Ls	GF	GA	Pts	
1.	Luton Town FC (Luton)	46	27	12	7	87	44	66	P
2.	Barnsley FC (Barnsley)	46	24	12	9	68	46	61	P
3.	Hartlepools United FC (Hartlepool)	46	25	10	11	60	46	60	P *
4.	Crewe Alexandra FC (Crewe)	46	20	18	8	74	49	58	P
5.	Bradford City AFC (Bradford)	46	23	11	12	72	51	57	
6.	Southend United FC (Southend-on-Sea)	46	20	14	12	77	58	54	
7.	Chesterfield FC (Chesterfield)	46	21	11	14	71	50	53	
8.	Wrexham AFC (Wrexham)	46	20	13	13	72	53	53	
9.	Aldershot FC (Aldershot)	46	18	17	11	70	55	53	
10.	Doncaster Rovers FC (Doncaster)	46	18	15	13	66	56	51	
11.	Halifax Town AFC (Halifax)	46	15	16	15	52	49	46	
12.	Newport County AFC (Newport)	46	16	13	17	58	63	45	
13.	Lincoln City FC (Lincoln)	46	17	9	20	71	68	43	
14.	Brentford FC (London)	46	18	7	21	61	64	43	
15.	Swansea Town AFC (Swansea)	46	16	10	20	63	77	42	
16.	Darlington FC (Darlington)	46	12	17	17	47	53	41	
17.	Notts County FC (Nottingham)	46	15	11	20	53	79	41	
18.	Port Vale FC (Stoke-on-Trent)	46	12	15	19	61	72	39	#
19.	Rochdale AFC (Rochdale)	46	12	14	20	51	72	38	
20.	Exeter City FC (Exeter)	46	11	16	19	45	65	38	
21.	York City FC (York)	46	11	14	21	65	68	36	
22.	Chester FC (Chester)	46	9	14	23	57	78	32	
23.	Workington AFC (Workington)	46	10	11	25	54	87	31	
24.	Bradford Park Avenue FC (Bradford)	46	4	15	27	30	82	23	
		1104	394	316	394	1485	1485	1104	

* Hartlepools United FC (Hartlepool) changed their club name to Hartlepool FC (Hartlepool) for the next season.

Port Vale FC (Stoke-on-Trent) were expelled from the league at the end of the season for making illegal payments to their players but were re-elected immediately to the league for the next season.

F.A. CUP FINAL (Wembley Stadium, London – 18/05/1968 – 100,000)

WEST BROMWICH ALBION FC	1-0	Everton FC (Liverpool)

Astle

West Bromwich: Osborne, Fraser, Williams, Brown, Talbot, Kaye (Clarke), Lovett, Collard, Astle, Hope, Clark.
Everton: West, Wright, Wilson, Kendall, Labone, Harvey, Husband, Ball, Royle, Hurst, Morrissey.

Semi-finals

Birmingham City FC (Birmingham)	0-2	West Bromwich Albion FC (West Bromwich)
Everton FC (Liverpool)	1-0	Leeds United AFC (Leeds)

Quarter-finals

Birmingham City FC (Birmingham)	1-0	Chelsea FC (London)
Everton FC (Liverpool)	3-1	Leicester City FC (Leicester)
Leeds United AFC (Leeds)	1-0	Sheffield United FC (Sheffield)
West Bromwich Albion FC (West Bromwich)	0-0, 1-1, 2-1	Liverpool FC (Liverpool)

Football League Division 1 1968-69 Season	Arsenal	Burnley	Chelsea	Coventry City	Everton	Ipswich Town	Leeds United	Leicester City	Liverpool	Manchester City	Manchester Utd.	Newcastle Utd.	Nottingham F.	Q.P.R.	Sheffield Wed.	Southampton	Stoke City	Sunderland	Tottenham H.	W.B.A.	West Ham Utd.	Wolves
Arsenal FC		2-0	0-1	2-1	3-1	0-2	1-2	3-0	1-1	4-1	3-0	0-0	1-1	2-1	2-0	0-0	1-0	0-0	1-0	2-0	0-0	3-1
Burnley FC	0-1		2-1	1-1	1-2	1-0	5-1	2-1	0-4	2-1	1-0	1-0	3-1	2-2	2-0	3-1	1-1	1-2	2-2	2-2	3-1	1-1
Chelsea FC	2-1	2-3		2-1	1-1	3-1	1-1	3-0	1-2	2-0	3-2	1-1	1-1	2-1	1-0	2-3	1-0	5-1	2-2	3-1	1-1	1-1
Coventry City FC	0-1	4-1	0-1		2-2	0-2	0-1	1-0	0-0	1-1	2-1	2-1	1-1	5-0	3-0	1-1	1-1	3-1	1-2	4-2	1-2	0-1
Everton FC	1-0	3-0	1-2	3-0		2-2	0-0	7-1	0-0	2-0	0-0	1-1	2-1	4-0	3-0	1-0	2-1	2-0	0-2	4-0	1-0	4-0
Ipswich Town FC	1-2	2-0	1-3	0-0	2-2		2-3	2-1	0-2	2-1	1-0	1-4	2-3	3-0	2-0	0-0	3-1	1-0	0-1	4-1	2-2	1-0
Leeds United AFC	2-0	6-1	1-0	3-0	2-0	2-0		2-0	1-0	1-0	2-1	1-0	4-1	2-0	3-2	2-0	1-1	0-0	0-0	2-0	0-0	2-1
Leicester City FC	0-0	0-2	1-4	1-1	1-1	1-3	1-1		1-2	3-0	2-1	2-1	2-2	2-0	1-1	3-1	0-0	2-1	1-0	0-2	1-1	2-0
Liverpool FC	1-1	1-1	2-1	2-0	1-1	4-0	0-0	4-0		2-1	2-0	2-1	0-2	2-0	1-0	1-0	2-1	4-1	1-0	1-0	2-0	1-0
Manchester City FC	1-1	7-0	4-1	4-2	1-3	1-1	3-1	2-0	1-0		0-0	1-0	2-2	3-1	0-1	1-1	3-1	1-0	4-0	5-1	1-1	3-2
Manchester United FC	0-0	2-0	0-4	1-0	2-0	0-0	0-0	3-2	1-0	0-1		3-1	8-1	1-0	1-2	1-0	4-1	3-1	2-1	1-0	1-0	2-0
Newcastle United FC	2-1	1-0	3-2	2-0	0-0	0-1	0-1	0-0	1-1	2-0			1-1	3-2	3-2	4-1	5-0	1-1	2-2	2-3	1-1	4-1
Nottingham Forest FC	0-2	2-2	1-2	0-0	1-0	1-2	0-2	0-0	0-1	1-0	0-1	2-4		1-0	0-0	1-0	3-3	1-0	0-2	3-0	0-1	0-0
Queen's Park Rangers FC	0-1	0-2	0-4	0-1	0-1	0-2	0-1	1-1	1-2	1-1	2-3	1-1	2-1		3-2	1-1	2-1	2-2	1-1	0-4	1-1	0-1
Sheffield Wednesday FC	0-5	1-0	1-1	3-0	2-2	2-0	0-0	1-3	1-2	1-1	5-4	1-1	4-0	0-0		2-1	1-1	0-0	1-0	1-1	1-1	0-2
Southampton FC	1-2	5-1	5-0	1-0	2-5	2-2	1-3	2-1	1-0	2-0	0-0	1-1	3-2	1-1	2-0		1-0	2-1	2-0	2-2	2-1	
Stoke City FC	1-3	1-3	2-0	0-3	0-0	2-1	1-5	1-0	0-0	1-0	0-0	1-0	3-1	1-1	1-1	1-0		2-1	1-1	1-1	0-2	4-1
Sunderland AFC	0-0	2-0	3-2	3-0	1-3	3-0	0-1	2-0	0-2	0-4	1-1	1-1	3-1	0-0	0-0	1-0	4-1		0-0	0-1	2-1	2-0
Tottenham Hotspur FC	1-2	7-0	1-0	2-0	1-1	2-2	0-0	3-2	2-1	1-1	2-2	0-1	2-1	3-2	1-2	2-1	1-1	5-1		1-1	1-0	1-1
West Bromwich Albion FC	1-0	3-2	0-3	6-1	2-2	2-1	1-1	1-0	0-0	2-0	3-1	5-1	2-5	3-1	0-0	1-2	3-0	4-3	3-1		3-1	0-0
West Ham United FC	1-2	5-0	0-0	5-2	1-4	1-3	1-1	4-0	1-1	2-1	0-0	3-1	1-0	4-3	1-1	0-0	0-0	8-0	2-2	4-0		3-1
Wolverhampton Wanderers FC	0-0	1-1	1-1	1-1	1-2	1-1	0-0	1-0	0-6	3-1	2-2	5-0	1-0	3-1	0-3	0-0	1-1	1-1	2-0	0-1	2-0	

	Division 1	Pd	Wn	Dw	Ls	GF	GA	Pts	
1.	LEEDS UNITED AFC (LEEDS)	42	27	13	2	66	26	67	
2.	Liverpool FC (Liverpool)	42	25	11	6	63	24	61	
3.	Everton FC (Liverpool)	42	21	15	6	77	36	57	
4.	Arsenal FC (London)	42	22	12	8	56	27	56	
5.	Chelsea FC (London)	42	20	10	12	73	53	50	
6.	Tottenham Hotspur FC (London)	42	14	17	11	61	51	45	
7.	Southampton FC (Southampton)	42	16	13	13	57	48	45	
8.	West Ham United FC (London)	42	13	18	11	66	50	44	
9.	Newcastle United FC (Newcastle-upon-Tyne)	42	15	14	13	61	55	44	
10.	West Bromwich Albion FC (West Bromwich)	42	16	11	15	64	67	43	
11.	Manchester United FC (Manchester)	42	15	12	15	57	53	42	
12.	Ipswich Town FC (Ipswich)	42	15	11	16	59	60	41	
13.	Manchester City FC (Manchester)	42	15	10	17	64	55	40	
14.	Burnley FC (Burnley)	42	15	9	18	55	82	39	
15.	Sheffield Wednesday FC (Sheffield)	42	10	16	16	41	54	36	
16.	Wolverhampton Wanderers FC (Wolverhampton)	42	10	15	17	41	58	35	
17.	Sunderland AFC (Sunderland)	42	11	12	19	43	67	34	
18.	Nottingham Forest FC (Nottingham)	42	10	13	19	45	57	33	
19.	Stoke City FC (Stoke-on-Trent)	42	9	15	18	40	63	33	
20.	Coventry City FC (Coventry)	42	10	11	21	46	64	31	
21.	Leicester City FC (Leicester)	42	9	12	21	39	68	30	R
22.	Queen's Park Rangers FC (London)	42	4	10	28	39	95	18	R
		924	322	280	322	1213	1213	924	

Top Goalscorer

1) James GREAVES   (Tottenham Hotspur FC)   27

Football League Division 2 1968-69 Season

	Aston Villa	Birmingham City	Blackburn Rovers	Blackpool	Bolton Wanderers	Bristol City	Bury	Cardiff City	Carlisle United	Charlton Athletic	Crystal Palace	Derby County	Fulham	Huddersfield Town	Hull City	Middlesbrough	Millwall	Norwich City	Oxford United	Portsmouth	Preston North End	Sheffield United
Aston Villa FC		1-0	1-1	0-1	1-1	1-0	1-0	2-0	0-0	0-0	1-1	0-1	1-1	1-0	1-1	1-0	1-1	2-1	2-0	2-0	0-1	3-1
Birmingham City FC	4-0		3-1	1-0	5-0	2-0	1-3	2-0	3-0	0-0	0-1	1-1	5-4	5-1	5-2	3-1	1-2	1-2	0-1	5-2	3-1	2-2
Blackburn Rovers FC	2-0	3-2		1-1	2-3	1-3	3-0	1-0	0-2	0-1	1-2	1-1	2-2	0-0	1-1	1-1	2-4	3-0	1-0	3-1	1-0	1-0
Blackpool FC	1-1	2-1	0-1		1-0	2-2	6-0	1-2	1-0	2-3	3-0	2-3	2-2	0-0	2-0	1-1	0-1	2-1	1-0	1-1	1-1	1-1
Bolton Wanderers FC	4-1	0-0	1-1	1-4		1-0	2-0	1-2	0-1	3-0	2-2	1-2	3-2	2-3	1-0	0-0	0-4	1-1	1-1	1-0	0-0	4-2
Bristol City FC	1-0	0-0	1-0	1-1	2-2		2-1	0-3	3-0	2-0	1-1	0-0	6-0	0-1	1-1	3-0	0-0	0-1	2-0	2-2	2-1	1-1
Bury FC	3-2	1-2	1-3	2-0	2-1	1-2		3-3	3-2	2-3	2-1	0-1	5-1	1-1	0-0	2-3	0-0	1-2	3-1	3-2	0-1	0-2
Cardiff City AFC	1-1	4-0	2-1	1-0	0-2	3-0	2-0		2-1	0-1	0-4	1-1	0-2	0-2	3-0	2-0	2-0	3-1	5-0	2-2	1-0	4-1
Carlisle United FC	0-1	2-3	4-1	1-0	1-1	3-0	2-0	1-0		1-1	1-2	1-1	2-0	0-0	1-0	3-0	1-0	0-4	0-2	0-0	1-0	0-1
Charlton Athletic FC	1-1	3-1	4-0	0-0	2-2	0-0	2-2	4-1	1-1		1-1	2-0	5-3	1-0	1-1	2-0	3-4	2-1	1-0	2-1	0-1	2-1
Crystal Palace FC	4-2	3-2	1-0	1-2	2-1	2-1	1-0	3-0	5-0	3-3		1-2	3-2	2-1	2-0	0-0	4-2	2-0	1-1	3-1	1-2	1-1
Derby County FC	3-1	1-0	4-2	1-1	5-1	3-0	2-0	2-0	3-3	2-1	0-1		1-0	1-0	2-2	3-2	1-1	1-1	2-2	2-1	1-0	1-0
Fulham FC	1-1	2-0	1-1	0-0	0-2	1-0	0-0	1-5	0-2	0-1	1-0	0-1		4-3	0-0	0-3	2-0	1-3	0-1	2-2	2-1	2-2
Huddersfield Town AFC	3-1	0-0	2-1	2-1	3-0	4-1	4-1	3-0	2-0	0-0	0-0	2-0	3-0		0-3	3-0	0-2	2-2	2-1	0-0	1-1	1-0
Hull City AFC	1-0	1-2	1-3	2-2	1-0	1-1	3-0	3-3	1-2	5-2	2-0	1-0	4-0	3-0		3-0	2-0	0-1	0-0	2-2	1-1	1-1
Middlesbrough FC	0-0	3-1	2-0	2-1	0-0	4-1	2-3	0-0	1-0	1-0	4-0	0-0	2-0	1-1	5-3		1-1	0-0	2-0	1-0	2-1	3-1
Millwall FC	0-1	1-3	2-2	1-2	3-1	2-2	1-0	2-0	1-1	3-2	0-2	0-1	2-0	5-1	2-3	2-0		3-1	2-1	0-0	0-0	1-0
Norwich City FC	1-1	1-1	3-1	0-1	2-0	1-1	2-2	3-1	2-1	0-1	0-1	1-4	2-0	1-0	1-2	0-2	0-3		1-1	0-1	1-1	2-0
Oxford United FC	1-0	1-2	2-1	0-0	1-1	0-0	2-2	0-2	0-1	0-1	0-2	0-2	1-0	3-0	1-1	2-4	1-0	0-2		3-1	2-1	1-0
Portsmouth FC	2-0	0-0	0-1	1-0	2-2	1-1	1-2	1-3	2-1	4-1	3-3	0-1	3-1	1-2	1-0	3-0	3-0	5-2	3-0		1-1	2-1
Preston North End FC	1-0	4-1	1-1	1-0	1-4	1-0	3-0	0-1	2-2	1-1	0-0	0-0	0-0	1-0	1-0	1-2	0-1	1-3	2-1	0-0		2-2
Sheffield United FC	3-1	2-0	3-0	2-1	5-2	2-1	5-0	2-2	0-1	2-0	1-1	2-0	1-0	0-0	1-1	1-3	1-0	1-0	1-2	2-0	4-0	

	Division 2	Pd	Wn	Dw	Ls	GF	GA	Pts	
1.	Derby County FC (Derby)	42	26	11	5	65	32	63	P
2.	Crystal Palace FC (London)	42	22	12	8	70	47	56	P
3.	Charlton Athletic FC (London)	42	18	14	10	61	52	50	
4.	Middlesbrough FC (Middlesbrough)	42	19	11	12	58	49	49	
5.	Cardiff City AFC (Cardiff)	42	20	7	15	67	54	47	
6.	Huddersfield Town AFC (Huddersfield)	42	17	12	13	53	46	46	
7.	Birmingham City FC (Birmingham)	42	18	8	16	73	59	44	
8.	Blackpool FC (Blackpool)	42	14	15	13	51	41	43	
9.	Sheffield United FC (Sheffield)	42	16	11	15	61	50	43	
10.	Millwall FC (London)	42	17	9	16	57	49	43	
11.	Hull City AFC (Kingston-upon-Hull)	42	13	16	13	59	52	42	
12.	Carlisle United FC (Carlisle)	42	16	10	16	46	49	42	
13.	Norwich City FC (Norwich)	42	15	10	17	53	56	40	
14.	Preston North End FC (Preston)	42	12	15	15	38	44	39	
15.	Portsmouth FC (Portsmouth)	42	12	14	16	58	58	38	
16.	Bristol City FC (Bristol)	42	11	16	15	46	53	38	
17.	Bolton Wanderers FC (Bolton)	42	12	14	16	55	67	38	
18.	Aston Villa FC (Birmingham)	42	12	14	16	37	48	38	
19.	Blackburn Rovers FC (Blackburn)	42	13	11	18	52	63	37	
20.	Oxford United FC (Oxford)	42	12	9	21	34	55	33	
21.	Bury FC (Bury)	42	11	8	23	51	80	30	R
22.	Fulham FC (London)	42	7	11	24	40	81	25	R
		924	333	258	333	1185	1185	924	

Football League Division 3 — 1968-69 Season

	Barnsley	Barrow	Bournemouth	Brighton & H.A.	Bristol Rovers	Crewe Alexandra	Gillingham	Hartlepool	Luton Town	Mansfield Town	Northampton Town	Oldham Athletic	Orient	Plymouth Argyle	Reading	Rotherham United	Shrewsbury Town	Southport	Stockport County	Swindon Town	Torquay United	Tranmere Rovers	Walsall	Watford
Barnsley FC		2-3	1-0	4-0	4-2	2-2	0-1	2-1	3-1	2-0	2-1	0-1	2-2	0-0	1-0	0-1	1-0	2-1	2-0	1-1	1-0	2-2	0-0	3-2
Barrow AFC	0-1		0-2	1-1	3-0	2-0	2-1	1-2	0-0	3-0	0-2	2-1	3-1	1-0	0-0	2-0	2-1	0-0	3-3	0-3	2-0	1-0	1-1	1-4
Bournemouth & Bos.	3-0	1-0		2-0	0-0	4-0	2-0	4-0	0-2	2-1	3-2	3-1	0-1	0-1	1-1	1-0	2-0	2-1	1-0	2-0	3-0	3-4	1-0	1-3
Brighton & Hove Alb.	4-1	4-1	4-1		3-1	3-1	0-2	1-1	1-0	1-2	1-1	6-0	2-0	0-0	2-0	2-2	3-0	4-0	1-1	1-3	1-1	2-2	3-0	0-1
Bristol Rovers FC	4-2	4-2	3-2	1-1		1-0	5-1	2-1	0-0	6-2	2-1	1-0	0-1	1-1	1-3	1-1	1-2	2-1	2-0	2-1	1-1	0-2	0-1	1-1
Crewe Alexandra FC	1-4	1-1	0-2	1-0	6-1		4-2	1-0	2-0	2-1	2-2	3-0	2-0	2-1	1-2	1-0	0-1	3-3	1-1	1-2	2-1	2-3	0-1	2-3
Gillingham FC	1-1	2-0	1-0	5-0	0-2	1-0		2-2	1-3	1-2	2-0	2-2	1-0	2-2	2-0	4-1	0-0	0-0	0-0	0-0	0-0	1-1	4-0	0-5
Hartlepool United FC	2-1	1-4	1-1	2-5	1-0	0-0	1-1		1-0	1-1	3-0	0-2	0-0	1-1	2-0	0-3	0-0	2-2	0-0	0-0	2-2	2-4	1-1	2-1
Luton Town FC	5-1	5-1	1-1	3-0	3-0	2-0	1-1	3-0		4-2	2-1	4-0	2-1	2-0	3-1	2-1	0-0	4-1	2-0	1-0	3-1	1-0	2-1	2-1
Mansfield Town FC	0-0	4-2	3-1	3-2	0-0	2-1	2-0	2-0	1-0		0-2	4-0	0-2	1-1	0-1	1-2	3-1	0-0	2-0	2-1	1-1	2-1	3-0	1-1
Northampton Town FC	3-1	4-0	1-3	1-1	2-2	0-1	0-1	0-0	0-2	0-0		1-1	4-1	4-2	1-0	3-4	1-0	1-1	2-6	1-1	2-1	3-1	2-0	2-0
Oldham Athletic AFC	1-1	0-1	2-0	1-1	2-1	3-0	1-0	1-2	0-1	2-1	1-1		3-1	0-2	1-1	0-0	1-0	5-2	3-1	1-0	2-1	3-1	1-0	0-1
Orient FC	1-1	1-2	3-2	2-1	2-0	1-1	1-0	0-0	1-0	0-0	3-0	1-1		1-2	4-2	3-3	4-0	2-0	2-0	1-0	0-1	0-0	0-0	1-1
Plymouth Argyle FC	0-0	4-1	1-1	1-1	3-1	2-2	1-1	3-0	2-0	1-0	0-1	1-1	2-1		3-1	1-2	1-0	0-4	2-2	2-1	1-2	1-0	1-2	1-2
Reading FC	3-2	0-1	1-1	0-2	3-1	3-2	7-0	1-1	2-1	1-0	4-1	0-1	1-2	1-0		2-4	1-0	4-2	0-1	1-1	1-2	2-2	0-1	0-1
Rotherham United	0-0	3-1	1-1	1-1	3-2	1-1	1-1	2-2	1-0	0-1	1-2	3-1	0-1	4-1	1-0		3-1	4-1	1-0	4-1	0-1	4-1	0-2	0-2
Shrewsbury Town	0-0	1-0	1-1	1-2	1-0	1-1	1-1	3-1	1-0	0-1	1-0	1-0	3-3	1-0	1-0	1-0		5-1	2-1	1-1	1-0	0-1	1-1	1-1
Southport FC	1-0	1-0	2-1	2-3	3-0	4-0	4-2	3-0	1-1	3-2	2-0	3-1	2-2	1-1	0-0	5-0	2-1		5-0	1-1	2-2	2-2	2-1	1-1
Stockport County FC	1-1	4-1	0-1	3-1	0-1	2-1	5-0	1-2	0-1	1-0	2-0	5-2	2-3	2-2	3-1	4-3	3-0	2-1		1-2	1-0	2-2	4-2	4-2
Swindon Town FC	2-0	2-0	3-0	0-2	2-2	1-2	0-0	0-0	5-1	1-0	5-1	1-0	0-0	3-0	5-1	1-0	2-1	1-0	0-1		3-0	5-1	1-0	0-1
Torquay United FC	3-1	3-1	1-0	1-1	1-1	2-0	2-0	2-2	1-1	2-1	2-1	3-0	0-0	1-1	2-0	2-0	3-0	0-1	0-1	1-0		2-5	4-2	2-1
Tranmere Rovers FC	3-1	0-3	2-1	0-2	1-2	0-1	2-0	1-0	0-2	2-1	2-1	6-2	3-0	2-2	2-1	0-0	3-1	1-0	1-1	3-5	0-1		2-1	0-3
Walsall FC	3-0	1-1	0-0	4-0	2-2	1-1	2-1	1-2	2-0	1-1	0-1	2-1	2-1	1-1	2-2	0-0	2-0	3-0	2-0	0-2	0-1	1-1		0-0
Watford FC	1-2	4-0	1-0	1-0	1-0	4-0	2-1	0-0	2-1	0-0	2-1	3-0	0-0	1-0	1-0	5-1	2-0	1-0	0-1	0-0	0-0	3-1	0-0	

Division 3

		Pd	Wn	Dw	Ls	GF	GA	Pts	
1.	Watford FC (Watford)	46	27	10	9	74	34	64	P
2.	Swindon Town FC (Swindon)	46	27	10	9	71	35	64	P
3.	Luton Town FC (Luton)	46	25	11	10	74	38	61	
4.	Bournemouth & Boscombe Athletic FC (Bournemouth)	46	21	9	16	60	45	51	
5.	Plymouth Argyle FC (Plymouth)	46	17	15	14	53	49	49	
6.	Torquay United FC (Torquay)	46	18	12	16	54	46	48	
7.	Tranmere Rovers FC (Birkenhead)	46	19	10	17	70	68	48	
8.	Southport FC (Southport)	46	17	13	16	71	64	47	
9.	Stockport County FC (Stockport)	46	16	14	16	67	68	46	
10.	Barnsley FC (Barnsley)	46	16	14	16	58	63	46	
11.	Rotherham United FC (Rotherham)	46	16	13	17	56	50	45	
12.	Brighton & Hove Albion FC (Hove)	46	16	13	17	72	65	45	
13.	Walsall FC (Walsall)	46	14	16	16	50	49	44	
14.	Reading FC (Reading)	46	15	13	18	67	66	43	
15.	Mansfield Town FC (Mansfield)	46	16	11	19	58	62	43	
16.	Bristol Rovers FC (Bristol)	46	16	11	19	63	71	43	
17.	Shrewsbury Town FC (Shrewsbury)	46	16	11	19	51	67	43	
18.	Orient FC (London)	46	14	14	18	51	58	42	
19.	Barrow AFC (Barrow-in-Furness)	46	17	8	21	56	75	42	
20.	Gillingham FC (Gillingham)	46	13	15	18	54	63	41	
21.	Northampton Town FC (Northampton)	46	14	12	20	54	61	40	R
22.	Hartlepool United FC (Hartlepool)	46	10	19	17	40	70	39	R
23.	Crewe Alexandra FC (Crewe)	46	13	9	24	52	76	35	R
24.	Oldham Athletic AFC (Oldham)	46	13	9	24	50	83	35	R
		1104	406	292	406	1426	1426	1104	

Football League Division 4 1968-69 Season

	Aldershot Town	Bradford City	Bradford P.A.	Brentford	Chester	Chesterfield	Colchester United	Darlington	Doncaster Rovers	Exeter City	Grimsby Town	Halifax Town	Lincoln City	Newport County	Notts County	Peterborough Utd.	Port Vale	Rochdale	Scunthorpe United	Southend United	Swansea Town	Workington	Wrexham	York City
Aldershot Town FC	—	2-1	4-1	1-2	4-0	2-0	1-2	0-0	1-2	2-0	3-1	0-2	0-1	4-0	0-0	1-4	3-0	0-0	3-2	2-1	5-2	0-1	2-1	2-0
Bradford City AFC	1-1	—	1-0	3-0	2-0	2-1	1-1	0-0	1-1	1-0	1-1	1-1	2-0	1-1	1-1	2-1	2-2	1-1	3-0	3-2	1-0	0-1	1-3	5-0
Bradford Park Ave.	0-1	0-0	—	0-2	1-1	0-1	2-1	1-3	2-1	2-1	1-1	0-0	1-1	1-5	1-1	0-2	0-1	1-4	2-2	0-3	1-1	1-0	1-2	1-1
Brentford FC	2-4	2-1	3-0	—	2-1	1-0	4-0	0-1	1-0	0-1	4-2	1-1	2-2	1-1	0-0	2-0	3-1	1-1	2-1	1-1	2-1	0-3	1-1	5-1
Chester FC	3-1	0-0	4-1	2-2	—	2-0	5-1	1-2	2-1	0-1	0-1	2-2	2-0	4-0	3-1	2-3	2-1	0-2	1-2	3-0	0-2	1-1		2-0
Chesterfield FC	1-2	0-1	1-1	1-2	2-0	—	0-2	2-2	0-1	2-0	0-0	2-0	1-1	2-1	0-2	2-0	3-1	1-1	1-2	0-0	2-0	0-1	0-1	1-1
Colchester United FC	2-0	1-1	3-0	2-1	1-1	1-0	—	0-0	1-2	1-0	2-1	0-0	1-1	2-1	1-1	2-2	1-0	0-0	0-4	4-0	0-1	3-0	2-1	1-0
Darlington FC	1-0	1-3	2-0	3-1	2-2	1-3	1-1	—	0-0	1-2	0-0	0-1	5-0	1-0	3-2	3-3	1-0	0-0	0-1	2-3	3-0	6-2	1-0	3-2
Doncaster Rovers FC	7-0	1-1	4-1	5-0	4-3	0-0	1-0	0-1	—	3-1	2-1	0-0	0-2	2-2	0-0	1-0	2-0	2-0	4-3	2-0	0-0	0-0	0-0	2-1
Exeter City FC	0-0	2-3	4-2	2-2	2-2	3-0	1-1	2-0	0-0	—	2-2	2-1	3-0	2-0	0-0	0-1	3-1	2-2	3-1	1-2	0-1	1-0	5-3	5-0
Grimsby Town FC	0-2	1-5	2-0	0-2	0-0	1-2	2-4	1-1	1-3	1-2	—	0-1	1-1	3-0	2-0	2-2	1-1	2-0	0-1	0-0	1-2	0-1	1-1	3-0
Halifax Town AFC	1-0	1-1	3-0	2-0	0-0	0-0	2-1	0-4	4-1	2-1	0-0	—	0-1	3-0	3-1	2-1	1-0	2-0	1-1	2-1	3-0	2-0	0-4	
Lincoln City FC	2-1	2-0	3-2	1-0	2-0	2-2	0-3	2-1	1-1	3-2	3-0	0-0	—	1-0	5-0	1-1	0-1	0-0	1-2	2-1	0-1	4-1	0-0	3-0
Newport County AFC	3-4	1-3	1-0	1-1	2-5	1-2	1-0	0-0	0-0	2-1	2-0	2-0	2-1	—	0-0	4-2	0-0	1-1	1-1	4-1	2-1	0-0	0-2	1-1
Notts County FC	0-2	0-2	5-0	0-2	3-2	2-1	2-0	0-0	1-1	3-1	2-1	1-2	0-0	3-1	—	2-1	0-0	1-1	1-0	2-2	0-3	0-0	5-0	0-0
Peterborough United	2-0	2-2	6-1	2-1	1-2	3-0	0-1	1-1	0-1	1-1	1-1	0-0	0-0	1-1	1-0	—	0-1	0-1	3-2	1-0	2-2	1-1	2-3	2-1
Port Vale FC	0-0	1-1	1-1	4-1	2-1	0-1	0-0	1-0	0-2	1-0	1-0	1-1	1-1	5-0	0-2	1-0	—	1-1	4-1	1-1	1-0	3-1	1-0	2-1
Rochdale AFC	3-0	6-0	6-0	0-0	4-1	0-0	4-0	2-0	0-0	1-1	6-1	1-0	2-1	0-1	0-0	1-1	1-0	—	3-2	3-0	0-1	0-0	2-1	2-1
Scunthorpe United	4-1	1-0	1-0	1-1	2-2	0-1	2-3	0-0	0-2	2-1	1-2	0-1	0-0	1-0	2-1	1-2	0-1	0-0	—	4-1	3-1	0-1	1-0	2-1
Southend United FC	4-2	2-0	5-0	4-0	1-2	2-2	3-1	1-1	2-0	6-1	0-1	2-1	3-0	1-0	4-0	2-1	1-1	1-3	0-3	—	4-0	1-0	1-0	1-2
Swansea Town AFC	2-2	0-2	3-0	2-3	0-5	0-0	2-0	1-1	0-1	2-0	1-1	1-0	5-0	3-2	3-0	0-0	1-0	3-0	2-0	2-2	—	0-0	0-0	2-1
Workington AFC	1-0	0-0	3-1	1-0	0-0	1-1	0-1	1-2	1-1	3-0	2-0	1-1	1-1	3-2	1-1	1-0	0-0	1-2	1-1	0-0	0-3	—	0-0	2-0
Wrexham AFC	2-0	1-1	3-0	2-0	1-1	1-1	0-3	2-1	3-1	2-2	2-0	2-2	0-1	4-0	3-2	0-0	2-0	3-2	0-1	3-3	2-0	1-0	—	2-1
York City FC	2-1	1-1	4-2	2-1	4-2	3-1	2-0	1-1	1-1	0-2	2-5	0-0	1-1	0-0	2-0	2-1	3-1	0-0	2-1	1-1	0-2	2-1	1-0	—

Division 4

		Pd	Wn	Dw	Ls	GF	GA	Pts	
1.	Doncaster Rovers FC (Doncaster)	46	21	17	8	65	38	59	P
2.	Halifax Town AFC (Halifax)	46	20	17	9	53	37	57	P
3.	Rochdale AFC (Rochdale)	46	18	20	8	68	35	56	P
4.	Bradford City AFC (Bradford)	46	18	20	8	65	46	56	P
5.	Darlington FC (Darlington)	46	17	18	11	62	45	52	
6.	Colchester United FC (Colchester)	46	20	12	14	57	53	52	
7.	Southend United FC (Southend-on-Sea)	46	19	13	14	78	61	51	
8.	Lincoln City FC (Lincoln)	46	17	17	12	54	52	51	
9.	Wrexham AFC (Wrexham)	46	18	14	14	61	52	50	
10.	Swansea Town AFC (Swansea)	46	19	11	16	58	54	49	
11.	Brentford FC (London)	46	18	12	16	64	65	48	
12.	Workington AFC (Workington)	46	15	17	14	40	43	47	
13.	Port Vale FC (Stoke-on-Trent)	46	16	14	16	46	46	46	
14.	Chester FC (Chester)	46	16	13	17	76	66	45	
15.	Aldershot FC (Aldershot)	46	19	7	20	66	66	45	
16.	Scunthorpe United FC (Scunthorpe)	46	18	8	20	61	60	44	
17.	Exeter City FC (Exeter)	46	16	11	19	66	65	43	
18.	Peterborough United FC (Peterborough)	46	13	16	17	60	57	42	
19.	Notts County FC (Nottingham)	46	12	18	16	48	57	42	
20.	Chesterfield FC (Chesterfield)	46	13	15	18	43	50	41	
21.	York City FC (York)	46	14	11	21	53	75	39	
22.	Newport County AFC (Newport)	46	11	14	21	49	74	36	
23.	Grimsby Town FC (Cleethorpes)	46	9	15	22	47	69	33	
24.	Bradford Park Avenue FC (Bradford)	46	5	10	31	32	106	20	
		1104	382	340	382	1372	1372	1104	

F.A. CUP FINAL   (Wembley Stadium, London – 26/04/1969 – 100,000)

MANCHESTER CITY FC (MANCHESTER)   1-0   Leicester City FC (Leicester)
Young

Man. City: Dowd, Book, Pardoe, Doyle, Booth, Oakes, Summerbee, Bell, Lee, Young, Coleman.

Leicester: Shilton, Rodrigues, Nish, Roberts, Woollett, Cross, Fern, Gibson, Lochhead, Clarke, Glover (Manley).

Semi-finals

Manchester City FC (Manchester)	1-0	Everton FC (Liverpool)
West Bromwich Albion FC (West Bromwich)	0-1	Leicester City FC (Leicester)

Quarter-finals

Chelsea FC (London)	1-2	West Bromwich Albion FC (West Bromwich)
Manchester City FC (Manchester)	1-0	Tottenham Hotspur FC (London)
Manchester United FC (Manchester)	0-1	Everton FC (Liverpool)
Mansfield Town FC (Mansfield)	0-1	Leicester City FC (Leicester)

1969-70

Football League Division 1 1969-70 Season	Arsenal	Burnley	Chelsea	Coventry City	Crystal Palace	Derby County	Everton	Ipswich Town	Leeds United	Liverpool	Manchester City	Manchester United	Newcastle United	Nottingham Forest	Sheffield Wed.	Southampton	Stoke City	Sunderland	Tottenham Hotspur	W.B.A.	West Ham United	Wolves
Arsenal FC	■	3-2	0-3	0-1	2-0	4-0	0-1	0-0	1-1	2-1	1-1	2-2	0-0	2-1	0-0	2-2	0-0	3-1	2-3	1-1	2-1	2-2
Burnley FC	0-1	■	3-1	0-0	4-2	1-1	1-2	0-1	1-1	1-5	1-1	0-1	5-0	4-2	1-1	1-1	3-0	0-2	2-1	3-2	1-3	
Chelsea FC	3-0	2-0	■	1-0	1-1	2-2	1-1	1-0	2-5	2-1	3-1	2-1	0-0	1-1	3-1	3-1	1-0	3-1	1-0	2-0	0-0	2-2
Coventry City FC	2-0	1-1	0-3	■	2-2	1-1	0-1	3-1	1-2	2-3	3-0	1-2	1-0	3-2	1-1	4-0	0-3	1-1	3-2	3-1	2-2	1-0
Crystal Palace FC	1-5	1-2	1-5	0-3	■	0-1	0-0	1-1	1-1	1-3	1-0	2-2	0-3	1-1	0-2	2-0	3-1	2-0	0-2	1-3	0-0	2-1
Derby County FC	3-2	0-0	2-2	1-3	3-1	■	2-1	3-1	4-1	4-0	0-1	2-0	2-0	0-2	1-0	3-0	0-0	3-0	5-0	2-0	3-0	2-0
Everton FC	2-2	2-1	5-2	0-0	2-1	1-0	■	3-0	3-1	0-3	1-0	3-0	0-0	1-0	2-1	4-2	6-2	3-1	3-2	2-0	2-0	1-0
Ipswich Town FC	2-1	0-1	1-4	0-1	2-0	0-1	0-3	■	3-2	2-2	1-1	0-1	2-0	0-0	1-0	2-0	1-1	2-0	2-0	0-1	1-0	1-1
Leeds United AFC	0-0	2-1	2-0	3-1	2-0	2-0	2-1	4-0	■	1-1	1-3	2-2	1-1	6-1	2-0	1-3	2-1	2-0	3-1	5-1	4-1	3-1
Liverpool FC	0-1	3-3	4-1	2-1	3-0	0-2	0-2	2-0	0-0	■	3-2	1-4	0-0	1-1	3-0	4-1	3-1	2-0	0-0	1-1	2-0	0-0
Manchester City FC	1-1	1-1	0-0	3-1	0-1	0-1	1-1	1-0	1-2	0-2	■	4-0	2-1	1-1	4-1	1-0	0-1	1-1	2-1	1-5	1-0	
Manchester United FC	2-1	3-3	0-1	1-1	1-1	1-0	0-2	2-1	2-2	1-0	1-2	■	0-0	1-1	2-2	1-4	1-1	3-1	3-1	7-0	5-2	0-0
Newcastle United FC	3-1	0-1	0-1	4-0	0-0	0-1	1-2	4-0	2-1	1-0	1-0	5-1	■	3-1	3-1	2-1	3-1	3-0	1-2	1-0	4-1	1-1
Nottingham Forest FC	1-1	1-1	1-1	1-4	0-0	1-3	1-1	1-0	1-4	1-0	2-2	1-2	2-2	■	2-1	2-1	0-0	2-1	2-2	1-0	1-0	4-2
Sheffield Wednesday FC	1-1	2-0	1-3	0-1	0-0	1-0	0-1	2-2	1-2	1-1	1-2	1-3	1-0	2-1	■	1-1	0-2	2-0	1-0	2-0	2-3	2-3
Southampton FC	0-2	1-1	2-2	0-0	1-1	1-1	2-1	4-2	1-1	0-1	0-0	0-3	1-1	1-2	4-0	■	0-0	1-1	2-2	0-1	1-1	2-3
Stoke City FC	0-0	2-1	1-2	2-0	1-0	1-0	0-1	3-3	1-1	0-2	2-0	2-2	0-1	1-1	2-1	2-1	■	4-2	1-1	3-2	2-1	1-1
Sunderland AFC	1-1	0-1	0-0	0-0	0-0	1-1	0-0	2-1	0-0	0-1	1-1	1-1	2-1	1-2	2-2	0-3	2-1	■	2-1	2-2	0-1	2-1
Tottenham Hotspur FC	1-0	4-0	1-1	1-2	2-0	2-1	0-1	3-2	1-1	0-2	0-3	2-1	2-1	4-1	1-0	0-1	1-0	0-1	■	2-0	0-2	0-1
West Bromwich Albion FC	0-1	0-1	3-1	0-1	3-2	0-2	2-0	2-2	1-1	2-2	3-0	2-1	2-2	4-0	3-0	1-0	1-3	3-1	1-1	■	3-1	3-3
West Ham United FC	1-1	3-1	2-0	1-2	2-1	3-0	0-1	0-0	2-2	1-0	0-4	0-0	1-0	1-1	3-0	0-0	3-3	1-1	0-1	1-3	■	3-0
Wolverhampton Wanderers FC	2-0	1-1	3-0	0-1	1-1	1-1	2-3	2-0	1-2	0-1	1-3	0-0	1-1	3-3	2-2	2-1	3-1	1-0	2-2	1-0	1-0	■

	Division 1	Pd	Wn	Dw	Ls	GF	GA	Pts	
1.	EVERTON FC (LIVERPOOL)	42	29	8	5	72	34	66	
2.	Leeds United AFC (Leeds)	42	21	15	6	84	49	57	
3.	Chelsea FC (London)	42	21	13	8	70	50	55	
4.	Derby County FC (Derby)	42	22	9	11	64	37	53	
5.	Liverpool FC (Liverpool)	42	20	11	11	65	42	51	
6.	Coventry City FC (Coventry)	42	19	11	12	58	48	49	
7.	Newcastle United FC (Newcastle-upon-Tyne)	42	17	13	12	57	35	47	
8.	Manchester United FC (Manchester)	42	14	17	11	66	61	45	
9.	Stoke City FC (Stoke-on-Trent)	42	15	15	12	56	52	45	
10.	Manchester City FC (Manchester)	42	16	11	15	55	48	43	
11.	Tottenham Hotspur FC (London)	42	17	9	16	54	55	43	
12.	Arsenal FC (London)	42	12	18	12	51	49	42	
13.	Wolverhampton Wanderers FC (Wolverhampton)	42	12	16	14	55	57	40	
14.	Burnley FC (Burnley)	42	12	15	15	56	61	39	
15.	Nottingham Forest FC (Nottingham)	42	10	18	14	50	71	38	
16.	West Bromwich Albion FC (West Bromwich)	42	14	9	19	58	66	37	
17.	West Ham United FC (London)	42	12	12	18	51	60	36	
18.	Ipswich Town FC (Ipswich)	42	10	11	21	40	63	31	
19.	Southampton FC (Southampton)	42	6	17	19	46	67	29	
20.	Crystal Palace FC (London)	42	6	15	21	34	68	27	
21.	Sunderland AFC (Sunderland)	42	6	14	22	30	68	26	R
22.	Sheffield Wednesday FC (Sheffield)	42	8	9	25	40	71	25	R
		924	319	286	319	1212	1212	924	

Top Goalscorer

1) Jeff ASTLE   (West Bromwich Albion FC)   25

	Aston Villa	Birmingham City	Blackburn Rovers	Blackpool	Bolton Wanderers	Bristol City	Cardiff City	Carlisle United	Charlton Athletic	Huddersfield Town	Hull City	Leicester City	Middlesbrough	Millwall	Norwich City	Oxford United	Portsmouth	Preston North End	Q.P.R.	Sheffield United	Swindon Town	Watford
Aston Villa FC		0-0	1-1	0-0	3-0	0-2	1-1	1-0	1-0	4-1	3-2	0-1	2-0	2-2	0-1	0-0	3-5	0-0	1-1	1-0	0-2	0-2
Birmingham City FC	0-2		3-0	2-3	2-0	2-2	1-1	1-1	3-0	2-2	2-4	0-1	0-0	2-0	3-1	1-3	1-1	1-0	3-0	2-1	2-0	0-0
Blackburn Rovers FC	2-0	1-1		2-1	3-1	3-3	1-0	1-0	3-0	0-2	2-1	3-1	4-0	4-0	3-1	2-0	0-3	4-2	0-1	1-2	2-0	1-0
Blackpool FC	2-1	2-0	0-0		1-1	1-0	3-2	1-1	2-0	2-0	0-1	1-1	1-1	1-1	0-0	1-0	2-1	0-0	1-1	1-0	3-2	0-3
Bolton Wanderers FC	2-1	2-0	1-0	0-2		3-1	0-1	0-0	1-1	1-1	2-1	2-3	2-1	4-1	0-0	1-1	0-1	2-0	6-4	0-0	0-1	2-3
Bristol City FC	1-0	2-0	4-0	2-1	2-2		0-2	0-0	6-0	1-2	3-1	0-0	0-0	1-1	4-0	2-0	3-0	0-0	2-0	0-1	3-3	1-0
Cardiff City AFC	4-0	3-1	0-0	2-2	2-1	1-0		1-1	1-0	0-1	6-0	1-1	1-0	0-0	0-0	2-0	2-1	4-2	3-0	2-2	3-1	1-1
Carlisle United FC	1-1	4-3	0-1	1-2	2-1	2-1	2-3		1-1	0-2	2-1	2-2	1-0	4-0	2-1	1-1	3-3	1-0	3-2	0-1	2-2	5-0
Charlton Athletic FC	1-0	0-1	0-0	0-2	1-1	2-1	0-0	2-1		1-2	1-4	0-5	0-2	2-2	3-0	1-0	2-2	2-1	1-1	3-2	1-1	0-0
Huddersfield Town AFC	2-0	2-0	0-1	2-0	1-0	3-0	1-0	1-0	4-0		2-2	1-1	0-0	0-0	1-1	1-1	4-0	3-2	2-0	2-1	1-1	3-1
Hull City AFC	3-1	0-0	3-0	1-0	4-2	2-0	1-1	2-4	1-1	2-3		4-1	3-2	2-1	1-0	3-3	3-1	1-2	2-3	1-1	1-1	1-1
Leicester City FC	1-0	3-1	1-0	0-0	2-2	1-0	1-2	1-2	2-2	1-1	2-2		2-1	1-0	3-0	1-2	3-0	2-1	2-1	3-0	2-1	3-1
Middlesbrough FC	1-0	4-2	4-1	0-2	4-0	2-0	2-1	0-2	2-0	1-1	1-0	2-1		3-1	0-0	2-0	2-1	1-1	1-0	1-0	0-0	3-1
Millwall FC	2-0	6-2	3-1	1-3	2-0	1-1	1-2	4-2	1-1	1-0	2-1	0-1	1-1		1-0	0-0	2-1	2-0	1-0	3-1	1-0	1-0
Norwich City FC	3-1	6-0	0-1	3-1	1-0	4-1	1-1	1-0	1-1	1-2	2-1	3-0	2-0	2-1		2-0	0-0	1-2	1-0	1-1	1-0	2-1
Oxford United FC	2-2	2-0	1-0	2-0	3-1	2-1	1-1	1-1	1-2	0-0	0-1	1-1	0-0	1-0	0-2		3-1	0-0	0-0	0-0	0-0	2-1
Portsmouth FC	0-0	1-1	2-0	2-3	1-1	0-0	3-0	4-0	5-1	1-3	1-4	2-3	2-3	0-1	1-4	2-1		4-0	1-3	1-5	3-1	3-1
Preston North End FC	1-1	4-1	0-0	0-3	1-3	0-1	1-2	3-1	4-1	1-3	3-3	0-1	1-1	1-1	0-1	1-2	1-2		0-0	2-1	3-1	3-0
Queen's Park Rangers FC	4-2	2-1	2-3	6-1	0-4	2-2	2-1	1-0	4-2	3-0	1-1	4-0	3-2	4-0	1-2	2-0	0-0	2-1		2-0	2-1	2-1
Sheffield United FC	5-0	6-0	2-3	2-3	0-1	2-1	1-0	1-0	2-0	0-0	3-0	1-0	3-0	1-0	5-1	5-0	2-0	2-0	2-1		1-2	1-1
Swindon Town FC	1-1	4-1	1-0	1-1	3-2	1-1	2-1	2-2	5-0	2-1	1-0	1-1	0-3	2-1	2-0	0-0	3-1	1-0	0-0	2-1		1-0
Watford FC	3-0	2-3	0-2	0-1	0-0	2-0	2-1	1-2	1-1	1-1	1-1	2-1	2-3	1-1	1-1	2-0	4-0	0-0	0-1	1-2	0-0	

	Division 2	Pd	Wn	Dw	Ls	GF	GA	Pts	
1.	Huddersfield Town AFC (Huddersfield)	42	24	12	6	68	37	60	P
2.	Blackpool FC (Blackpool)	42	20	13	9	56	45	53	P
3.	Leicester City FC (Leicester)	42	19	13	10	64	50	51	
4.	Middlesbrough FC (Middlesbrough)	42	20	10	12	55	45	50	
5.	Swindon Town FC (Swindon)	42	17	16	9	57	47	50	
6.	Sheffield United FC (Sheffield)	42	22	5	15	73	38	49	
7.	Cardiff City AFC (Cardiff)	42	18	13	11	61	41	49	
8.	Blackburn Rovers FC (Blackburn)	42	20	7	15	54	50	47	
9.	Queen's Park Rangers FC (London)	42	17	11	14	66	57	45	
10.	Millwall FC (London)	42	15	14	13	56	56	44	
11.	Norwich City FC (Norwich)	42	16	11	15	49	46	43	
12.	Carlisle United FC (Carlisle)	42	14	13	15	58	56	41	
13.	Hull City AFC (Kingston-upon-Hull)	42	15	11	16	72	70	41	
14.	Bristol City FC (Bristol)	42	13	13	16	54	50	39	
15.	Oxford United FC (Oxford)	42	12	15	15	35	42	39	
16.	Bolton Wanderers FC (Bolton)	42	12	12	18	54	61	36	
17.	Portsmouth FC (Portsmouth)	42	13	9	20	66	80	35	
18.	Birmingham City FC (Birmingham)	42	11	11	20	51	78	33	
19.	Watford FC (Watford)	42	9	13	20	44	57	31	
20.	Charlton Athletic FC (London)	42	7	17	18	35	76	31	
21.	Aston Villa FC (Birmingham)	42	8	13	21	36	62	29	R
22.	Preston North End FC (Preston)	42	8	12	22	43	63	28	R
		924	330	264	330	1207	1207	924	

Football League Division 3 1969-70 Season	Barnsley	Barrow	Bournemouth	Bradford City	Brighton & H.A.	Bristol Rovers	Bury	Doncaster Rovers	Fulham	Gillingham	Halifax Town	Luton Town	Mansfield Town	Orient	Plymouth Argyle	Reading	Rochdale	Rotherham United	Shrewsbury Town	Southport	Stockport County	Torquay United	Tranmere Rovers	Walsall
Barnsley FC	█	2-1	1-0	3-2	1-2	2-0	3-3	2-1	3-3	5-1	2-0	2-1	1-1	1-2	0-1	4-3	1-0	1-0	1-1	1-1	1-0	3-0	1-1	2-0
Barrow AFC	1-1	█	1-1	0-1	1-1	1-1	3-1	1-1	3-1	1-1	0-1	2-1	0-1	1-1	1-1	2-2	2-0	1-2	2-0	1-0	4-1	0-4	0-3	0-1
Bournemouth & Bos.	3-1	0-0	█	0-0	0-0	2-2	2-0	3-1	2-2	2-1	0-0	0-1	1-0	0-2	1-3	1-2	0-3	1-0	3-3	1-0	1-0	1-2	2-2	2-2
Bradford City AFC	1-1	3-3	8-1	█	1-0	2-4	0-1	3-0	0-0	1-0	2-1	1-1	0-1	0-1	1-0	4-0	0-3	0-1	2-2	1-0	1-0	2-1	1-1	3-0
Brighton & Hove Alb.	2-0	2-0	1-1	2-1	█	0-3	2-0	1-0	2-1	3-1	4-0	1-2	1-2	0-0	2-0	2-1	2-0	2-1	1-0	1-0	1-0	2-2	2-0	1-1
Bristol Rovers FC	3-3	2-1	5-2	1-1	0-2	█	2-1	1-1	3-2	1-2	2-0	3-0	4-1	1-0	3-1	1-1	3-3	3-0	1-3	2-0	1-0	3-1	3-0	3-1
Bury FC	1-2	4-0	1-0	0-2	1-2	2-2	█	1-1	1-0	1-3	1-1	1-3	1-0	0-1	3-1	2-1	2-1	2-1	2-2	4-3	4-1	1-0	8-0	4-2
Doncaster Rovers FC	1-0	3-2	2-1	1-1	2-0	3-1	1-1	█	0-1	1-0	0-1	2-0	2-0	0-1	1-1	2-3	3-1	1-2	2-1	1-0	0-1	1-0	2-1	0-0
Fulham FC	0-0	2-1	1-1	0-0	4-1	3-1	2-4	1-1	█	2-1	2-1	0-1	1-1	4-3	2-1	2-0	3-2	3-1	3-2	1-1	1-1	1-1	1-1	4-0
Gillingham FC	1-3	0-1	0-0	1-1	0-1	1-0	1-0	2-1	2-0	█	2-0	0-2	3-3	0-1	4-0	1-3	2-2	1-1	2-1	2-4	0-2	2-4	0-0	1-3
Halifax Town AFC	0-2	3-0	4-1	0-0	1-0	1-1	2-0	1-1	0-8	1-1	█	0-0	1-2	1-1	2-0	1-1	3-1	4-2	1-0	1-0	1-0	1-1	2-2	0-1
Luton Town FC	1-1	3-0	0-0	5-0	1-1	4-0	0-0	4-0	1-0	1-2	1-1	█	2-2	3-2	0-2	5-0	2-0	2-1	2-2	1-0	2-0	1-1	2-0	3-0
Mansfield Town FC	2-0	4-2	2-0	2-1	1-0	1-1	3-1	1-2	2-3	1-0	3-3	0-0	█	4-1	1-2	2-1	1-2	2-0	2-0	5-0	4-1	2-0	1-2	0-0
Orient FC	4-2	2-0	3-0	2-1	1-1	0-0	3-0	2-0	3-1	1-2	1-0	1-0	1-0	█	4-1	0-1	2-2	1-1	1-0	3-2	3-0	1-1	2-0	2-0
Plymouth Argyle FC	0-0	1-0	0-1	0-1	0-1	2-2	2-2	0-0	2-0	2-2	1-0	1-3	1-0	1-0	█	1-1	2-3	0-3	4-2	1-1	2-0	6-0	2-1	1-0
Reading FC	6-2	6-3	2-0	1-0	1-0	1-5	3-2	1-0	0-4	1-0	4-1	0-1	1-0	3-2	2-1	█	1-0	1-1	3-1	8-0	3-1	1-1	1-1	2-3
Rochdale AFC	1-1	1-0	0-1	1-2	2-1	0-0	3-3	2-0	0-1	0-0	5-0	1-2	2-1	0-3	2-1	3-2	█	4-2	3-0	1-1	2-0	1-1	4-0	1-2
Rotherham United	2-0	5-0	3-0	2-3	2-0	0-0	4-3	0-1	0-0	0-1	1-1	1-1	2-2	0-0	1-0	1-1	3-1	█	1-2	2-0	0-0	2-1	0-1	4-1
Shrewsbury Town	1-1	1-1	2-0	1-0	2-2	0-0	3-3	0-0	1-1	2-2	3-1	5-1	0-0	1-1	3-0	0-0	1-0	1-0	█	1-2	3-1	1-0	2-0	1-1
Southport FC	0-1	1-0	3-0	1-0	2-0	0-0	4-0	2-2	0-2	1-1	1-0	0-3	0-1	1-0	0-0	6-2	0-3	2-1	0-2	█	1-1	4-2	2-0	0-1
Stockport County FC	1-0	2-2	0-2	0-2	0-1	0-1	1-0	3-1	-4	1-0	0-1	1-1	1-3	0-2	0-1	2-2	0-1	1-1	1-1	0-0	█	0-1	0-1	2-2
Torquay United FC	1-1	1-1	2-2	2-1	2-1	1-2	3-0	2-1	1-1	3-2	0-1	1-2	1-1	0-1	1-2	1-1	3-0	0-0	3-0	0-0	3-0	█	5-1	0-0
Tranmere Rovers FC	0-1	5-0	1-5	1-0	2-0	5-2	3-2	1-3	1-0	0-0	1-1	3-2	1-1	1-1	3-1	1-5	0-0	2-2	3-1	0-1	3-0	1-1	█	0-0
Walsall FC	3-2	1-0	2-1	2-0	0-3	2-1	1-1	1-3	1-3	0-1	2-1	1-3	1-0	2-0	2-2	4-1	1-4	0-2	3-2	4-0	0-0	0-1	0-0	█

Division 3

		Pd	Wn	Dw	Ls	GF	GA	Pts	
1.	Orient FC (London)	46	25	12	9	67	36	62	P
2.	Luton Town FC (Luton)	46	23	14	9	77	43	60	P
3.	Bristol Rovers FC (Bristol)	46	20	16	10	80	59	56	
4.	Fulham FC (London)	46	20	15	11	81	55	55	
5.	Brighton & Hove Albion FC (Hove)	46	23	9	14	57	43	55	
6.	Mansfield Town FC (Mansfield)	46	21	11	14	70	49	53	
7.	Barnsley FC (Barnsley)	46	19	15	12	68	59	53	
8.	Reading FC (Reading)	46	21	11	14	87	77	53	
9.	Rochdale AFC (Rochdale)	46	18	10	18	69	60	46	
10.	Bradford City AFC (Bradford)	46	17	12	17	57	50	46	
11.	Doncaster Rovers FC (Doncaster)	46	17	12	17	52	54	46	
12.	Walsall FC (Walsall)	46	17	12	17	54	67	46	
13.	Torquay United FC (Torquay)	46	14	17	15	62	59	45	
14.	Rotherham United FC (Rotherham)	46	15	14	17	62	54	44	
15.	Shrewsbury Town FC (Shrewsbury)	46	13	18	15	62	63	44	
16.	Tranmere Rovers FC (Birkenhead)	46	14	16	16	56	72	44	
17.	Plymouth Argyle FC (Plymouth)	46	16	11	19	56	64	43	
18.	Halifax Town AFC (Halifax)	46	14	15	17	47	63	43	
19.	Bury FC (Bury)	46	15	11	20	75	80	41	
20.	Gillingham FC (Gillingham)	46	13	13	20	52	64	39	
21.	Bournemouth & Boscombe Athletic FC (Bournemouth)	46	12	15	19	48	71	39	R
22.	Southport FC (Southport)	46	14	10	22	48	66	38	R
23.	Barrow AFC (Barrow-in-Furness)	46	8	14	24	46	81	30	R
24.	Stockport County FC (Stockport)	46	6	11	29	27	71	23	R
		1104	395	314	395	1460	1460	1104	

Football League Division 4 1969-70 Season	Aldershot Town	Bradford Park Avenue	Brentford	Chester	Chesterfield	Colchester United	Crewe Alexandra	Darlington	Exeter City	Grimsby Town	Hartlepool	Lincoln City	Newport County	Northampton Town	Notts County	Oldham Athletic	Peterborough United	Port Vale	Scunthorpe United	Southend United	Swansea Town	Workington	Wrexham	York City
Aldershot Town FC	–	4-2	1-2	3-1	1-0	1-1	4-1	4-0	1-0	2-2	4-1	1-1	1-1	5-2	2-0	1-0	1-0	2-0	3-1	2-1	2-2	3-1	0-2	4-1
Bradford Park Ave.	2-0	–	0-1	1-2	1-1	0-1	0-0	0-1	2-1	1-1	3-0	0-3	1-1	1-2	1-3	0-0	2-3	1-2	0-5	1-0	0-2	2-0	2-3	2-0
Brentford FC	0-0	1-1	–	2-0	0-1	2-0	1-1	1-1	2-0	3-0	3-0	2-1	1-0	1-0	1-1	5-2	1-0	3-0	3-1	2-2	1-0	0-0	0-0	0-0
Chester FC	2-1	1-0	1-2	–	1-2	1-0	2-1	1-3	2-0	3-1	2-1	1-2	2-0	2-1	0-1	2-1	2-3	1-1	1-1	2-0	2-2	3-0	2-0	3-0
Chesterfield FC	4-2	4-0	1-0	0-1	–	2-0	1-0	2-0	2-1	1-2	3-0	4-0	4-0	2-1	5-0	3-1	3-1	0-1	2-1	3-0	0-0	4-0	2-0	3-1
Colchester United FC	3-1	2-1	1-1	0-1	4-1	–	1-0	2-1	2-1	3-2	1-1	2-0	1-1	0-3	2-1	3-1	2-1	0-0	1-2	1-1	3-0	2-0	3-0	2-0
Crewe Alexandra FC	1-0	0-0	1-2	3-0	2-1	0-1	–	2-0	1-1	3-0	3-0	3-1	1-1	2-0	1-1	1-1	2-0	0-0	0-2	5-3	0-1	1-0	2-3	3-0
Darlington FC	0-2	1-1	1-2	1-2	0-1	3-2	2-0	–	4-0	0-0	4-0	0-3	0-0	2-2	1-2	1-1	1-2	2-2	2-0	0-2	2-1	1-1	2-1	1-0
Exeter City FC	2-1	3-0	2-2	1-0	1-1	2-1	3-0	1-2	–	0-1	6-0	1-2	1-1	1-1	0-2	1-1	1-2	4-1	3-0	6-0	5-1	1-0	2-1	2-1
Grimsby Town FC	2-2	2-2	2-1	4-1	1-0	5-3	0-2	2-0	2-0	–	2-0	1-2	1-1	2-1	4-1	1-0	0-0	2-0	1-1	2-2	1-1	0-0	0-0	0-0
Hartlepool FC	1-3	5-2	0-0	1-2	0-0	1-1	1-3	2-0	0-1	0-1	–	0-3	0-1	1-1	1-1	4-2	0-2	1-2	2-1	3-0	1-0	1-3	2-2	2-2
Lincoln City FC	1-1	5-2	1-0	2-0	0-2	3-3	2-1	1-0	1-0	2-0	3-0	–	3-0	0-0	2-4	0-1	3-0	0-0	1-2	3-3	1-1	0-0	4-0	4-0
Newport County AFC	3-4	5-1	1-0	3-1	0-2	4-1	0-0	2-1	2-0	1-0	1-1	3-1	–	0-2	1-0	2-1	0-1	1-1	3-0	4-0	1-2	0-1	1-2	1-2
Northampton Town	4-0	3-0	1-1	0-1	1-1	1-1	1-2	1-1	2-0	3-1	0-1	1-1	4-1	–	3-1	0-0	2-2	2-0	2-1	2-0	4-1	3-0	0-1	2-2
Notts County FC	3-0	5-2	3-0	1-1	1-1	1-1	4-1	4-0	2-1	1-0	2-0	4-1	2-0	0-0	–	2-2	1-2	3-1	2-0	0-1	0-3	3-2	3-1	1-1
Oldham Athletic AFC	4-2	0-0	4-1	5-0	1-0	1-2	2-1	1-1	1-1	0-2	1-1	3-0	0-2	5-0	3-0	–	4-2	2-3	1-3	3-0	0-1	1-2	2-3	3-1
Peterborough United	4-1	2-1	0-0	0-0	1-2	1-1	3-0	3-2	1-1	4-0	2-1	4-0	1-0	1-0	8-1	0-0	–	2-2	3-4	1-1	1-1	5-2	3-1	2-1
Port Vale FC	0-0	4-1	0-0	3-0	1-1	2-0	4-0	2-0	1-0	3-0	0-0	1-1	1-1	1-0	0-0	1-2	3-0	–	1-2	3-0	0-0	3-1	0-1	1-0
Scunthorpe United	0-0	2-0	1-1	2-3	1-2	1-1	2-0	0-0	0-0	1-1	3-1	4-0	1-0	2-3	2-1	2-1	2-1	1-0	–	2-0	1-2	1-3	1-1	1-1
Southend United FC	2-2	1-1	2-2	4-2	0-0	2-1	2-0	2-0	1-1	1-3	0-2	2-2	3-2	2-2	2-5	1-0	2-0	1-1	3-0	–	2-1	3-1	1-0	1-0
Swansea Town AFC	1-1	5-0	1-0	2-1	0-0	1-0	3-0	3-1	0-0	2-0	3-0	2-2	1-1	3-2	1-1	4-0	4-1	0-0	2-1	2-0	–	0-0	1-2	2-1
Workington AFC	1-2	1-0	1-2	1-1	1-1	1-1	3-0	1-0	1-2	0-0	1-1	3-0	2-0	0-2	1-0	1-1	3-2	2-2	5-0	0-0	0-0	–	2-0	1-1
Wrexham AFC	1-1	4-0	1-0	2-0	2-1	4-2	2-2	6-2	3-0	3-2	1-0	0-0	3-0	3-0	2-0	1-1	2-1	1-1	2-1	4-0	1-1	4-1	–	4-0
York City FC	2-0	4-1	4-2	0-0	1-1	4-2	0-0	2-1	1-0	1-1	0-0	2-0	2-1	1-1	1-2	0-0	3-0	0-1	3-2	1-0	3-0	1-0	2-1	–

Division 4

		Pd	Wn	Dw	Ls	GF	GA	Pts	
1.	Chesterfield FC (Chesterfield)	46	27	10	9	77	32	64	P
2.	Wrexham AFC (Wrexham)	46	26	9	11	84	49	61	P
3.	Swansea Town AFC (Swansea)	46	21	18	7	66	45	60	P *
4.	Port Vale FC (Stoke-on-Trent)	46	20	19	7	61	33	59	p
5.	Brentford FC (London)	46	20	16	10	58	39	56	
6.	Aldershot FC (Aldershot)	46	20	13	13	78	65	53	
7.	Notts County FC (Nottingham)	46	22	8	16	73	62	52	
8.	Lincoln City FC (Lincoln)	46	17	16	13	66	52	50	
9.	Peterborough United FC (Peterborough)	46	17	14	15	77	69	48	
10.	Colchester United FC (Colchester)	46	17	14	15	64	63	48	
11.	Chester FC (Chester)	46	21	6	19	58	66	48	
12.	Scunthorpe United FC (Scunthorpe)	46	18	10	18	67	65	46	
13.	York City FC (York)	46	16	14	16	55	62	46	
14.	Northampton Town FC (Northampton)	46	16	12	18	64	55	44	
15.	Crewe Alexandra FC (Crewe)	46	16	12	18	51	51	44	
16.	Grimsby Town FC (Cleethorpes)	46	14	15	17	54	58	43	
17.	Southend United FC (Southend-on-Sea)	46	15	10	21	59	85	40	
18.	Exeter City FC (Exeter)	46	14	11	21	57	59	39	
19.	Oldham Athletic AFC (Oldham)	46	13	13	20	60	65	39	
20.	Workington AFC (Workington)	46	12	14	20	46	64	38	
21.	Newport County AFC (Newport)	46	13	11	22	53	74	37	
22.	Darlington FC (Darlington)	46	13	10	23	53	73	36	
23.	Hartlepool FC (Hartlepool)	46	10	10	26	42	82	30	
24.	Bradford Park Avenue FC (Bradford)	46	6	11	29	41	96	23	#
		1104	404	296	404	1464	1464	1104	

Bradford Park Avenue FC (Bradford) were not re-elected to the league for the next season and were replaced in Division 4 by Cambridge United FC (Cambridge).

* Swansea Town AFC (Swansea) changed their club name to Swansea City FC (Swansea) for the next season.

F.A. CUP FINAL   (Wembley Stadium, London – 11/04/1970 – 100,000)

CHELSEA FC (LONDON)   2-2 (aet)   Leeds United AFC (Leeds)

Houseman, Hutchinson   *J.Charlton, Jones*

Chelsea: Bonetti, Webb, McCreadie, Hollins, Dempsey, R.Harris (Hinton), Baldwin, Houseman, Osgood, Hutchinson, Cooke.

Leeds: Sprake, Madeley, Cooper, Bremner, J.Charlton, Hunter, Lorimer, Clarke, Jones, Giles, Gray.

F.A. CUP FINAL REPLAY   (Old Trafford, Manchester – 29/04/1970 – 62,000)

CHELSEA FC (LONDON)   2-1 (aet)   Leeds United AFC (Leeds)

Osgood, Webb   *Jones*

Leeds: Harvey, Madeley, Cooper, Bremner, J.Charlton, Hunter, Lorimer, Clarke, Jones, Giles, Gray.

Chelsea: Bonetti, R.Harris, McCreadie, Hollins, Dempsey, Webb, Baldwin, Cooke, Osgood (Hinton), Hutchinson, Houseman.

3rd Place Play-off

Manchester United FC (Manchester)   2-0   Watford FC (Watford)

Semi-finals

Chelsea FC (London)   5-1   Watford FC (Watford)
Manchester United FC (Manchester)   0-0, 0-0, 0-1   Leeds United AFC (Leeds)

Quarter-finals

Manchester United FC (Manchester)   1-1, 2-1   Middlesbrough FC (Middlesbrough)
Queen's Park Rangers FC (London)   2-4   Chelsea FC (London)
Swindon Town FC (Swindon)   0-2   Leeds United AFC (Leeds)
Watford FC (Watford)   1-0   Liverpool FC (Liverpool)

1970-71

Football League Division 1 1970-71 Season	Arsenal	Blackpool	Burnley	Chelsea	Coventry City	Crystal Palace	Derby County	Everton	Huddersfield T.	Ipswich Town	Leeds United	Liverpool	Man. City	Man. United	Newcastle Utd.	Nottingham F.	Southampton	Stoke City	Tottenham H.	W.B.A.	West Ham Utd.	Wolves
Arsenal FC	■	1-0	1-0	2-0	1-0	1-1	2-0	4-0	1-0	3-2	0-0	2-0	1-0	4-0	1-0	4-0	0-0	1-0	2-0	6-2	2-0	2-1
Blackpool FC	0-1	■	1-1	3-4	1-0	3-1	0-1	0-2	2-2	0-2	1-1	0-0	3-3	1-1	0-1	2-3	0-3	1-1	0-0	3-1	1-1	0-2
Burnley FC	1-2	1-0	■	0-0	0-0	2-1	1-2	2-2	2-3	2-2	0-3	1-2	0-4	0-2	1-1	2-1	0-1	1-1	0-0	1-1	1-0	2-3
Chelsea FC	2-1	2-0	0-1	■	2-1	1-1	2-1	2-2	0-0	2-1	3-1	1-0	1-1	1-2	1-0	2-2	2-1	0-2	4-1	2-1	2-2	3-2
Coventry City FC	1-3	2-0	3-0	0-1	■	2-1	0-0	3-1	0-0	1-0	0-1	1-0	2-1	2-1	2-0	2-0	1-0	1-0	0-0	1-1	0-1	0-1
Crystal Palace FC	0-2	1-0	0-2	0-0	1-2	■	0-0	2-0	0-3	1-0	1-1	1-0	0-1	3-5	1-0	2-0	3-1	3-2	0-3	3-0	1-1	1-1
Derby County FC	2-0	2-0	1-0	1-2	3-4	1-0	■	3-1	3-2	2-0	0-2	0-0	0-0	4-4	1-2	1-2	0-0	2-0	1-1	2-0	2-4	1-2
Everton FC	2-2	0-0	1-1	3-0	3-0	3-1	1-1	■	2-1	2-0	0-0	1-0	3-1	1-0	4-1	2-0	0-0	3-3	0-1	1-2	1-1	1-2
Huddersfield Town AFC	2-1	3-0	0-1	0-1	1-0	0-2	0-0	1-1	■	1-0	0-0	0-0	1-0	1-2	1-1	3-1	0-1	1-1	2-1	1-1	1-2	1-2
Ipswich Town FC	0-1	2-1	3-0	0-0	0-2	1-2	0-1	0-0	2-0	■	2-4	1-0	2-0	4-0	1-0	1-3	2-0	1-2	2-2	2-1	2-3	2-3
Leeds United AFC	1-0	3-1	4-0	1-0	2-0	2-1	1-0	3-2	2-0	0-0	■	0-1	1-0	2-2	3-0	0-0	4-1	1-2	1-2	3-0	0-0	3-0
Liverpool FC	2-0	2-2	2-0	1-0	0-0	1-1	2-0	3-2	4-0	2-1	1-1	■	0-0	1-1	3-0	1-0	0-0	0-0	1-1	1-0	1-0	1-0
Manchester City FC	0-2	2-0	0-0	1-1	1-1	1-0	1-1	3-0	1-1	2-0	0-2	2-2	■	3-4	1-1	1-3	1-1	4-1	0-1	4-1	2-0	0-0
Manchester United FC	1-3	1-1	1-1	0-0	2-0	0-1	1-2	2-0	1-1	3-2	0-1	0-2	1-4	■	1-0	2-0	5-1	2-2	2-1	2-1	1-1	1-0
Newcastle United FC	1-1	1-2	3-1	0-1	0-0	2-0	3-1	2-1	2-1	0-0	1-1	0-0	0-0	1-0	■	1-1	2-2	0-2	1-0	3-0	1-1	3-2
Nottingham Forest FC	0-3	3-1	1-0	1-1	2-0	3-1	2-4	3-2	1-3	0-1	0-0	0-1	0-1	1-2	2-1	■	2-0	0-0	0-1	3-3	1-0	4-1
Southampton FC	1-2	1-1	2-0	0-0	3-0	6-0	4-0	2-1	1-0	0-3	1-0	1-1	1-0	2-0	4-1	1-0	■	2-1	0-0	1-0	1-2	1-2
Stoke City FC	5-0	1-1	0-0	1-2	2-1	0-0	1-0	1-1	3-1	0-0	3-0	0-1	2-0	1-2	3-0	0-0	0-0	■	0-1	2-0	2-1	1-0
Tottenham Hotspur FC	0-1	3-0	4-0	2-1	1-0	2-0	2-1	2-1	1-1	2-0	0-2	1-1	2-0	2-2	1-2	0-1	1-3	3-0	■	2-2	2-2	0-0
West Bromwich Albion FC	2-2	1-1	1-0	2-2	0-0	0-1	3-0	0-0	2-1	1-1	2-2	1-1	4-3	1-2	0-1	1-0	5-2	3-1	1-2	■	2-1	2-4
West Ham United FC	0-0	2-1	3-1	2-2	1-2	0-0	1-4	1-2	2-3	1-2	0-0	2-1	0-2	2-0	1-1	1-0	2-2	2-1	2-2	1-1	■	3-3
Wolverhampton Wanderers FC	0-3	1-0	1-0	1-0	0-0	2-1	2-4	2-0	3-1	0-0	2-3	1-0	3-0	3-2	3-2	4-0	0-1	1-1	0-3	2-1	2-0	■

Division 1

		Pd	Wn	Dw	Ls	GF	GA	Pts	
1.	ARSENAL FC (LONDON)	42	29	7	6	71	29	65	
2.	Leeds United AFC (Leeds)	42	27	10	5	72	30	64	
3.	Tottenham Hotspur FC (London)	42	19	14	9	54	33	52	
4.	Wolverhampton Wanderers FC (Wolverhampton)	42	22	8	12	64	54	52	
5.	Liverpool FC (Liverpool)	42	17	17	8	42	24	51	
6.	Chelsea FC (London)	42	18	15	9	52	42	51	
7.	Southampton FC (Southampton)	42	17	12	13	56	44	46	
8.	Manchester United FC (Manchester)	42	16	11	15	65	66	43	
9.	Derby City FC (Derby)	42	16	10	16	56	54	42	
10.	Coventry City FC (Coventry)	42	16	10	16	37	38	42	
11.	Manchester City FC (Manchester)	42	12	17	13	47	42	41	
12.	Newcastle United FC (Newcastle-upon-Tyne)	42	14	13	15	44	46	41	
13.	Stoke City FC (Stoke-on-Trent)	42	12	13	17	44	48	37	
14.	Everton FC (Liverpool)	42	12	13	17	54	60	37	
15.	Huddersfield Town AFC (Huddersfield)	42	11	14	17	40	49	36	
16.	Nottingham Forest FC (Nottingham)	42	14	8	20	42	61	36	
17.	West Bromwich Albion FC (West Bromwich)	42	10	15	17	58	75	35	
18.	Crystal Palace FC (London)	42	12	11	19	39	57	35	
19.	Ipswich Town FC (Ipswich)	42	12	10	20	42	48	34	
20.	West Ham United FC (London)	42	10	14	18	47	60	34	
21.	Burnley FC (Burnley)	42	7	13	22	29	63	27	R
22.	Blackpool FC (Blackpool)	42	4	15	23	34	66	23	R
		924	327	270	327	1089	1089	924	

Top Goalscorer

1) Tony BROWN   (West Bromwich Albion FC)   28

Football League Division 2 1970-71 Season	Birmingham City	Blackburn Rovers	Bolton Wanderers	Bristol City	Cardiff City	Carlisle United	Charlton Athletic	Hull City	Leicester City	Luton Town	Middlesbrough	Millwall	Norwich City	Orient	Oxford United	Portsmouth	Q.P.R.	Sheffield United	Sheffield Wednesday	Sunderland	Swindon Town	Watford
Birmingham City FC		1-0	4-0	2-0	2-0	1-0	1-1	0-0	0-0	1-1	0-1	3-1	2-2	1-0	1-1	1-1	2-1	0-1	1-0	3-1	2-1	2-0
Blackburn Rovers FC	2-2		0-2	2-2	1-1	0-2	1-0	0-1	2-2	1-0	1-1	0-2	2-1	0-0	0-0	1-1	0-2	1-3	3-2	0-1	1-0	2-3
Bolton Wanderers FC	3-0	1-1		1-0	0-2	0-3	4-0	0-0	0-3	4-2	0-3	1-1	0-1	0-1	0-2	1-1	2-2	2-1	2-1	1-3	0-3	0-1
Bristol City FC	2-1	1-1	1-1		1-0	2-1	2-2	3-3	0-1	3-2	0-2	3-2	0-1	0-0	0-4	2-0	0-0	0-1	1-2	4-3	2-1	3-0
Cardiff City AFC	2-0	4-1	1-0	1-0		4-0	1-1	5-1	2-2	0-0	3-4	2-2	1-1	1-0	1-0	1-0	1-0	1-1	4-0	3-1	1-1	0-1
Carlisle United FC	0-3	1-0	1-0	2-1	1-1		1-1	2-0	0-1	1-0	1-0	3-0	4-2	2-0	3-2	6-0	3-0	1-0	3-0	0-0	2-1	2-1
Charlton Athletic FC	1-1	2-4	4-1	1-1	2-1	1-1		0-1	0-1	1-1	1-0	1-3	2-1	2-0	2-0	2-2	0-3	0-2	2-3	1-1	2-1	1-2
Hull City AFC	0-1	0-0	1-0	1-0	1-1	1-2	2-0		3-0	0-2	1-0	2-0	1-0	5-2	0-1	0-1	1-1	1-1	4-4	4-0	2-0	1-0
Leicester City FC	1-4	1-1	1-0	4-0	0-1	2-2	1-0	0-0		1-0	3-2	2-1	2-1	4-0	0-0	2-0	0-0	0-0	1-0	1-0	3-1	1-1
Luton Town FC	3-2	2-0	2-0	3-0	3-0	3-3	1-1	3-1	1-3		1-0	1-1	0-0	4-0	4-0	2-1	0-0	2-1	2-2	1-2	1-1	1-0
Middlesbrough FC	0-0	1-1	1-0	1-0	1-1	2-1	3-0	1-0	1-0	2-1		1-0	5-0	0-1	0-2	3-2	6-2	1-1	1-0	2-2	3-0	2-2
Millwall FC	2-1	2-0	2-0	2-0	2-1	2-1	2-0	4-0	0-0	4-0	1-0		2-2	0-1	1-2	0-0	3-0	1-2	1-0	0-0	2-2	3-0
Norwich City FC	2-2	2-1	2-1	3-2	1-2	1-1	2-0	0-2	2-2	1-1	1-1	1-0		4-2	1-1	1-1	3-0	1-0	0-0	3-0	1-0	2-1
Orient FC	0-2	1-1	3-1	1-1	0-0	1-1	0-0	0-1	0-1	1-2	0-0	0-0	1-0		0-0	1-1	0-1	3-1	1-1	1-0	1-0	1-1
Oxford United FC	1-0	2-1	1-1	1-0	1-0	1-1	2-1	0-3	1-0	2-1	2-2	2-3	1-1	0-1		1-1	1-3	1-2	1-1	0-0	0-0	2-1
Portsmouth FC	1-0	4-1	4-0	1-1	1-3	1-4	2-0	2-2	1-2	0-1	1-1	0-2	0-2	1-1	1-0		2-0	1-5	2-0	2-1	0-2	5-0
Queen's Park Rangers FC	5-2	2-0	4-0	2-1	0-1	1-1	1-4	1-1	1-3	0-1	1-1	2-0	0-1	5-1	2-0	2-0		2-2	1-0	2-0	4-2	1-1
Sheffield United FC	3-0	5-0	2-2	3-3	5-1	2-2	3-0	1-2	2-1	2-1	1-1	2-0	0-0	3-1	3-0	2-0	1-1		3-2	1-0	2-1	3-0
Sheffield Wednesday FC	3-3	1-1	1-1	2-0	1-2	3-0	1-0	1-1	0-3	1-5	3-2	1-0	2-1	2-1	1-1	3-1	1-0	0-0		1-2	2-2	2-1
Sunderland AFC	2-1	3-2	4-1	1-0	0-4	2-0	3-0	0-1	0-0	0-0	2-2	0-1	2-1	1-0	0-1	0-0	3-1	0-0	3-1		5-2	3-3
Swindon Town FC	1-2	3-0	3-1	2-1	2-2	0-0	1-1	1-1	0-1	0-0	3-0	3-0	3-2	1-1	3-0	2-1	1-0	3-0	3-0	2-0		1-1
Watford FC	2-1	2-1	1-1	0-3	0-1	0-0	1-1	1-2	0-1	0-1	1-0	0-4	2-0	0-0	2-1	0-0	1-2	0-0	3-0	1-1	1-2	

	Division 2	Pd	Wn	Dw	Ls	GF	GA	Pts	
1.	Leicester City FC (Leicester)	42	23	13	6	57	30	59	P
2.	Sheffield United FC (Sheffield)	42	21	14	7	73	39	56	P
3.	Cardiff City AFC (Cardiff)	42	20	13	9	64	41	53	
4.	Carlisle United FC (Carlisle)	42	20	13	9	65	43	53	.
5.	Hull City AFC (Kingston-upon-Hull)	42	19	13	10	54	41	51	
6.	Luton Town FC (Luton)	42	18	13	11	62	43	49	
7.	Middlesbrough FC (Middlesbrough)	42	17	14	11	60	43	48	
8.	Millwall FC (London)	42	19	9	14	59	42	47	
9.	Birmingham City FC (Birmingham)	42	17	12	13	58	48	46	
10.	Norwich City FC (Norwich)	42	15	14	13	54	52	44	
11.	Queen's Park Rangers FC (London)	42	16	11	15	58	53	43	
12.	Swindon Town FC (Swindon)	42	15	12	15	61	51	42	
13.	Sunderland AFC (Sunderland)	42	15	12	15	52	54	42	
14.	Oxford United FC (Oxford)	42	14	14	14	14	48	42	
15.	Sheffield Wednesday FC (Sheffield)	42	12	12	18	51	69	36	
16.	Portsmouth FC (Portsmouth)	42	10	14	18	46	61	34	
17.	Orient FC (London)	42	9	16	17	29	51	34	
18.	Watford FC (Watford)	42	10	13	19	38	60	33	
19.	Bristol City FC (Bristol)	42	10	11	21	46	64	31	
20.	Charlton Athletic FC (London)	42	8	14	20	41	65	30	
21.	Blackburn Rovers FC (Blackburn)	42	6	15	21	37	69	27	R
22.	Bolton Wanderers FC (Bolton)	42	7	10	25	35	74	24	R
		924	321	282	321	1141	1141	924	

Football League Division 3 — 1970-71 Season

	Aston Villa	Barnsley	Bradford City	Brighton & H.A.	Bristol Rovers	Bury	Chesterfield	Doncaster Rovers	Fulham	Gillingham	Halifax Town	Mansfield Town	Plymouth Argyle	Port Vale	Preston North End	Reading	Rochdale	Rotherham United	Shrewsbury Town	Swansea City	Torquay United	Tranmere Rovers	Walsall	Wrexham
Aston Villa FC		0-0	1-0	0-0	1-1	1-0	0-0	3-2	1-0	2-1	1-1	0-1	1-1	1-0	2-0	2-1	1-0	1-0	2-0	3-0	0-1	1-0	0-0	3-4
Barnsley FC	1-1		2-0	1-0	0-4	1-1	1-0	0-1	0-1	3-1	2-2	1-0	2-0	1-0	0-1	3-0	2-2	2-1	2-1	0-0	2-0	0-0	1-2	3-1
Bradford City AFC	1-0	1-0		2-3	1-1	1-3	1-0	3-0	2-3	0-1	0-1	1-1	0-1	1-1	0-2	0-1	3-0	1-1	1-0	0-2	2-0	1-1	0-0	1-3
Brighton & Hove Alb.	1-0	1-2	1-2		0-0	1-0	1-2	3-0	3-2	3-1	0-2	2-0	1-1	0-0	0-0	2-0	1-1	1-1	1-2	2-2	0-0	0-0	2-2	2-0
Bristol Rovers FC	1-2	3-0	4-2	1-3		0-1	3-2	2-0	0-1	2-0	1-0	2-0	1-3	3-0	0-0	4-0	2-2	0-2	2-2	0-0	1-1	0-1	3-0	3-2
Bury FC	3-1	0-0	1-1	0-2	3-0		1-1	2-3	2-0	2-1	1-1	0-0	3-0	2-3	0-1	5-1	0-2	0-1	1-1	1-1	1-0	0-0	1-1	1-2
Chesterfield FC	2-3	4-2	0-1	2-1	2-0	0-0		4-0	0-0	2-0	5-0	2-2	2-0	3-0	0-0	4-0	1-1	1-1	0-0	5-0	2-0	1-1	1-0	
Doncaster Rovers FC	2-1	1-0	3-1	2-0	0-1	2-0	2-1		0-1	2-2	1-2	1-2	0-0	1-2	1-1	2-0	1-2	0-2	1-1	1-2	0-1	2-2	1-2	2-1
Fulham FC	0-2	1-1	5-0	1-0	2-1	2-1	2-0	1-1		1-0	3-1	0-0	1-1	4-1	0-1	1-1	2-0	1-0	0-0	4-1	4-0	2-0	1-0	1-0
Gillingham FC	0-0	2-1	2-1	1-1	1-4	1-2	1-1	0-1	1-3		2-1	2-2	0-2	1-1	2-1	0-0	0-0	2-1	0-2	0-0	1-2	0-0	2-1	1-2
Halifax Town AFC	2-1	4-1	1-2	0-1	0-0	3-0	1-0	4-0	2-1	2-1		0-1	4-1	2-0	1-0	4-0	1-4	1-3	2-2	2-0	4-3	2-1	2-0	
Mansfield Town FC	2-0	1-2	3-5	1-0	4-1	1-0	2-2	2-1	1-0	2-0	3-2		1-5	2-0	3-1	0-0	3-2	1-1	1-1	2-0	0-0	6-2	2-2	1-1
Plymouth Argyle FC	1-1	2-1	1-3	1-1	0-0	3-4	1-1	1-1	1-1	1-1	1-1	0-0		2-1	1-1	4-0	2-2	4-1	4-4	2-3	1-2	0-1	3-1	2-2
Port Vale FC	2-0	1-1	0-0	2-1	2-0	0-0	0-2	1-0	0-1	1-1	0-1	2-0	2-1		1-0	3-1	4-1	1-0	0-1	4-0	0-1	2-2	1-1	0-3
Preston North End	0-0	3-1	1-1	1-1	3-2	2-0	1-0	4-0	1-1	1-0	1-1	2-1	1-0	1-0		4-1	3-1	3-0	2-0	1-1	2-2	1-1	1-0	3-2
Reading FC	3-5	2-0	1-1	0-3	0-2	1-5	1-1	1-0	1-1	3-2	1-1	1-0	0-2	2-1	1-0		1-1	4-2	2-1	3-1	1-1	1-1	1-2	0-0
Rochdale AFC	1-1	1-0	0-0	3-3	1-1	2-0	1-0	1-2	0-1	0-3	1-1	1-1	0-3	1-2	1-2			4-3	1-2	0-0	2-0	0-0		4-1
Rotherham United	1-1	1-0	1-1	0-0	1-1	3-2	1-2	2-0	1-1	0-0	2-2	1-1	2-1	1-1	2-1		5-1		1-1	2-0	3-1	2-0	1-0	1-1
Shrewsbury Town	2-1	1-0	1-1	0-1	1-4	2-0	1-0	0-3	0-1	0-0	2-2	5-2	1-1	7-3	0-1	3-1	0-2	4-2		1-0	1-0	3-1	1-1	1-0
Swansea City FC	1-2	0-2	2-0	1-0	1-3	3-0	1-0	1-1	4-1	1-0	3-1	2-4	0-2	0-2	2-2	5-0	4-2	1-1	5-0		0-1	0-0	1-1	3-0
Torquay United FC	1-1	0-1	1-1	1-0	1-1	2-1	1-1	2-3	3-1	2-3	2-0	0-0	2-1	1-1	0-4	3-0	3-1	1-0	2-1			4-2	1-2	1-2
Tranmere Rovers FC	1-1	2-2	3-1	3-0	0-2	0-0	0-0	1-0	0-3	1-0	0-1	4-1	1-0	1-1	3-3	0-0	0-2	5-0	1-0	0-0	0-0		0-0	1-1
Walsall FC	3-0	1-2	1-2	1-0	1-2	3-0	2-1	1-2	3-2	3-0	0-0	0-1	1-0	3-1	0-1	1-2	0-3	0-1	0-1	0-1	0-1	1-4		3-1
Wrexham AFC	2-3	1-0	2-0	1-1	1-0	3-2	0-3	0-0	2-2	3-4	2-2	4-0	4-0	1-1	1-1	2-0	3-1	1-1	2-1	1-1	1-0	4-1	2-1	

Division 3

		Pd	Wn	Dw	Ls	GF	GA	Pts	
1.	Preston North End FC (Preston)	46	22	17	7	63	39	61	P
2.	Fulham FC (London)	46	24	12	10	68	41	60	P
3.	Halifax Town AFC (Halifax)	46	22	12	12	74	55	56	
4.	Aston Villa FC (Birmingham)	46	19	15	12	54	46	53	
5.	Chesterfield FC (Chesterfield)	46	17	17	12	66	38	51	
6.	Bristol Rovers FC (Bristol)	46	19	13	14	69	50	51	
7.	Mansfield Town FC (Mansfield)	46	18	15	13	64	62	51	
8.	Rotherham United FC (Rotherham)	46	17	16	13	64	60	50	
9.	Wrexham AFC (Wrexham)	46	18	13	15	72	65	49	
10.	Torquay United FC (Torquay)	46	19	11	16	54	57	49	
11.	Swansea City FC (Swansea)	46	15	16	15	59	56	46	
12.	Barnsley FC (Barnsley)	46	17	11	18	49	52	45	
13.	Shrewsbury Town FC (Shrewsbury)	46	16	13	17	58	62	45	
14.	Brighton & Hove Albion FC (Hove)	46	14	16	16	50	47	44	
15.	Plymouth Argyle FC (Plymouth)	46	12	19	15	63	63	43	
16.	Rochdale AFC (Rochdale)	46	14	15	17	61	68	43	
17.	Port Vale FC (Stoke-on-Trent)	46	15	12	19	52	59	42	
18.	Tranmere Rovers FC (Birkenhead)	46	10	22	14	45	55	42	
19.	Bradford City AFC (Bradford)	46	13	14	19	49	62	40	
20.	Walsall FC (Walsall)	46	14	11	21	51	57	39	
21.	Reading FC (Reading)	46	14	11	21	48	85	39	R
22.	Bury FC (Bury)	46	12	13	21	52	60	37	R
23.	Doncaster Rovers FC (Doncaster)	46	13	9	24	45	66	35	R
24.	Gillingham FC (Gillingham)	46	10	13	23	42	67	33	R
		1104	384	336	384	1372	1372	1104	

Football League Division 4 1970-71 Season	Aldershot Town	Barrow	Bournemouth	Brentford	Cambridge United	Chester	Colchester United	Crewe Alexandra	Darlington	Exeter City	Grimsby Town	Hartlepool	Lincoln City	Newport County	Northampton Town	Notts County	Oldham Athletic	Peterborough Utd	Scunthorpe United	Southend United	Southport	Stockport County	Workington	York City
Aldershot Town FC		3-0	2-0	1-0	2-2	1-0	0-1	0-0	2-2	2-2	3-2	1-0	0-2	1-1	1-1	0-1	1-1	2-2	0-1	2-2	2-1	5-0	1-1	0-1
Barrow AFC	1-1		1-2	0-1	2-1	1-4	0-2	0-1	1-1	1-1	0-1	3-0	1-4	3-1	2-1	1-2	1-1	2-3	1-2	2-0	0-2	2-2	0-3	0-2
Bournemouth & Bos.	1-1	0-0		1-0	3-0	3-1	4-1	2-2	1-0	4-1	2-1	3-0	3-0	2-2	4-2	1-1	5-0	1-0	0-2	4-0	0-1	2-0	1-0	4-0
Brentford FC	2-3	2-1	1-2		1-2	1-2	1-0	3-1	1-0	5-0	2-0	1-0	2-1	0-3	3-0	2-2	1-1	1-1	0-1	4-2	0-1	3-0	3-0	6-4
Cambridge United FC	1-1	3-3	0-2	1-0		1-1	2-1	1-0	2-0	2-0	2-3	2-0	1-1	3-2	0-2	2-1	3-1	1-1	1-1	0-3	0-0	1-1	1-2	1-1
Chester FC	1-2	2-1	4-2	1-2	2-1		2-1	1-0	2-1	3-1	5-0	0-1	1-0	2-1	2-2	2-1	0-1	2-0	2-0	2-0	1-0	3-0	1-0	1-1
Colchester United FC	5-2	4-1	1-1	4-0	2-1	0-1		3-0	2-0	1-1	1-0	1-0	1-1	4-2	1-1	2-3	1-2	3-0	2-0	1-1	1-0	1-1	2-1	1-0
Crewe Alexandra FC	0-3	1-0	3-3	5-3	1-2	6-3	0-3		3-0	4-1	4-0	1-0	3-1	2-0	3-0	1-2	0-1	1-3	3-1	1-2	0-2	1-0	2-3	3-4
Darlington FC	1-2	3-1	1-0	2-1	2-0	5-1	0-0	0-1		3-2	5-1	2-0	3-2	2-1	0-0	2-3	3-1	1-0	3-0	0-4	1-1	1-0	0-1	2-0
Exeter City FC	4-1	4-2	0-0	1-0	1-0	3-1	2-2	6-2	2-1		4-0	1-1	0-0	1-1	0-1	0-2	3-2	1-1	2-0	2-1	2-1	0-1	0-2	
Grimsby Town FC	0-2	3-1	1-0	1-5	2-0	2-2	3-1	2-0	1-1	1-2		1-1	1-1	2-0	0-2	2-1	4-1	2-1	1-0	2-0	1-2	1-2	1-0	3-1
Hartlepool FC	1-1	2-1	2-1	0-0	0-0	0-2	1-2	0-2	2-2	3-0	2-2		0-0	2-2	2-2	2-1	0-1	1-2	1-1	0-1	1-2	3-0	1-1	2-1
Lincoln City FC	4-4	0-3	1-2	2-0	0-1	2-0	1-2	2-2	2-1	4-1	3-0	2-0		1-1	1-3	0-1	2-1	2-1	4-1	1-2	3-0	1-1	3-1	4-5
Newport County AFC	1-2	3-2	0-2	0-1	2-0	0-1	1-3	1-3	3-1	0-1	0-1	2-0	2-2		0-1	2-1	1-4	2-0	2-3	3-0	2-2	3-2	2-2	0-3
Northampton Town	2-0	1-0	2-3	1-0	2-1	3-1	2-1	1-1	2-0	2-2	0-4	2-0	2-1	1-0		1-1	1-3	2-0	1-0	0-2	2-1	1-1	5-0	3-2
Notts County FC	3-0	3-1	2-1	0-0	4-1	2-1	4-0	5-1	3-0	1-1	1-0	3-0	0-0	2-0	1-0		2-0	6-0	3-1	2-1	3-1	5-1	2-2	2-1
Oldham Athletic AFC	5-2	2-1	2-2	5-1	4-1	1-1	4-0	5-3	3-1	2-1	1-0	2-0	4-2	4-0	1-1	1-3		3-0	1-1	2-0	2-4	1-1	1-3	1-1
Peterborough United	1-0	4-0	3-1	1-2	2-3	1-0	1-2	3-1	0-1	1-3	1-1	5-0	1-1	2-1	1-0	1-1	2-1		1-2	4-0	5-1	3-1	2-1	
Scunthorpe United	2-1	1-1	1-1	1-1	0-0	0-2	2-0	1-1	0-0	3-0	1-2	2-1	3-1	0-1	2-2	0-1	2-3	5-2		3-0	2-0	1-2	4-0	0-1
Southend United FC	2-2	2-3	1-2	4-3	1-1	1-1	1-1	0-2	0-0	0-0	1-1	2-0	1-1	3-0	1-0	1-0	3-0	1-2	2-2		1-1	2-1	1-1	1-0
Southport FC	3-3	1-0	0-1	2-0	0-1	2-0	2-1	1-0	0-3	0-2	1-0	5-0	1-0	6-1	2-1	0-2	1-4	3-2	5-1	3-0		1-0	1-0	2-2
Stockport County FC	1-0	2-0	1-1	1-0	0-1	0-1	0-0	2-2	1-1	0-3	1-0	2-1	4-3	3-2	1-1	1-0	1-1	0-0	2-0	0-0	3-0		1-0	1-0
Workington AFC	4-0	2-1	1-0	1-1	3-1	1-0	1-1	1-1	0-0	1-0	1-0	0-1	2-1	2-1	2-0	0-1	0-0	2-1	0-0	1-1	2-1	0-1		1-0
York City FC	3-1	4-3	1-1	0-0	3-0	1-1	1-1	1-0	2-0	2-2	4-1	4-0	2-0	1-0	4-1	0-0	0-1	2-1	2-0	3-0	2-0	2-1	1-0	

Division 4

		Pd	Wn	Dw	Ls	GF	GA	Pts	
1.	Notts County FC (Nottingham)	46	30	9	7	89	36	69	P
2.	Bournemouth & Boscombe Athletic FC (Bournemouth)	46	24	12	10	81	46	60	P *
3.	Oldham Athletic AFC (Oldham)	46	24	11	11	88	63	59	P
4.	York City FC (York)	46	23	10	13	78	54	56	P
5.	Chester FC (Chester)	46	24	7	15	69	55	55	
6.	Colchester United FC (Colchester)	46	21	12	13	70	54	54	
7.	Northampton Town FC (Northampton)	46	19	13	14	63	59	51	
8.	Southport FC (Southport)	46	21	6	19	63	57	48	
9.	Exeter City FC (Exeter)	46	17	14	15	67	68	48	
10.	Workington AFC (Workington)	46	18	12	16	48	49	48	
11.	Stockport County FC (Stockport)	46	16	14	16	49	65	46	
12.	Darlington FC (Darlington)	46	17	11	18	58	57	45	
13.	Aldershot FC (Aldershot)	46	14	17	15	66	71	45	
14.	Brentford FC (London)	46	18	8	20	66	62	44	
15.	Crewe Alexandra FC (Crewe)	46	18	8	20	75	76	44	
16.	Peterborough United FC (Peterborough)	46	18	7	21	70	71	43	
17.	Scunthorpe United FC (Scunthorpe)	46	15	13	18	56	61	43	
18.	Southend United FC (Southend-on-Sea)	46	14	15	17	53	66	43	
19.	Grimsby Town FC (Cleethorpes)	46	18	7	21	57	71	43	
20.	Cambridge United FC (Cambridge)	46	15	13	18	51	66	43	
21.	Lincoln City FC (Lincoln)	46	13	13	20	70	71	39	
22.	Newport County AFC (Newport)	46	10	8	28	55	85	28	
23.	Hartlepool FC (Hartlepool)	46	8	12	26	34	74	28	
24.	Barrow AFC (Barrow-in-Furness)	46	7	8	31	51	90	22	
		1104	422	260	422	1527	1527	1104	

* Bournemouth & Boscombe Athletic FC (Bournemouth) changed their name to AFC Bournemouth (Bournemouth) for the next season.

F.A. CUP FINAL   (Wembley Stadium, London – 08/05/1971 – 100,000)

ARSENAL FC (LONDON)   2-1 (aet)   Liverpool FC (Liverpool)
Kelly, George   *Heighway*

Arsenal: Wilson, Rice, McNab, Storey (Kelly), McLintock, Simpson, Armstrong, Graham, Radford, Kennedy, George.

Liverpool: Clemence, Lawler, Lindsay, Smith, Lloyd, Hughes, Callaghan, Evans (Thompson), Heighway, Toshack, Hall.

3rd Place Play-off

Stoke City FC (Stoke-on-Trent)   3-2   Everton FC (Liverpool)

Semi-finals

Arsenal FC (London)   2-2, 2-0   Stoke City FC (Stoke-on-Trent)
Everton FC (Liverpool)   1-2   Liverpool FC (Liverpool)

Quarter-finals

Everton FC (Liverpool)   5-0   Colchester United FC (Colchester)
Hull City AFC (Kingston-upon-Hull)   2-3   Stoke City FC (Stoke-on-Trent)
Leicester City FC (Leicester)   0-0, 0-1   Arsenal FC (London)
Liverpool FC (Liverpool)   0-0, 1-0   Tottenham Hotspur FC (London)

1971-72

Football League Division 1 1971-72 Season	Arsenal	Chelsea	Coventry City	Crystal Palace	Derby County	Everton	Huddersfield Town	Ipswich Town	Leeds United	Leicester City	Liverpool	Manchester City	Manchester United	Newcastle United	Nottingham Forest	Sheffield United	Southampton	Stoke City	Tottenham Hotspur	W.B.A.	West Ham United	Wolves
Arsenal FC	■	3-0	2-0	2-1	2-0	1-1	1-0	2-1	2-0	3-0	0-0	1-2	3-0	4-2	3-0	0-1	1-0	0-1	0-2	2-0	2-1	2-1
Chelsea FC	1-2	■	3-3	2-1	1-1	4-0	2-2	2-0	0-0	2-1	0-0	2-2	2-3	3-3	2-0	2-0	3-0	2-0	1-0	1-0	3-1	3-1
Coventry City FC	0-1	1-1	■	1-1	2-2	4-1	2-1	1-1	3-1	1-1	0-2	1-1	2-3	1-0	1-1	3-2	1-0	1-1	1-0	0-2	1-1	0-0
Crystal Palace FC	2-2	2-3	2-2	■	0-1	2-1	0-0	1-1	1-1	1-1	0-1	1-2	1-3	2-0	1-1	5-1	2-3	2-0	1-1	0-2	0-3	0-2
Derby County FC	2-1	1-0	1-0	3-0	■	2-0	3-0	1-0	2-0	3-0	1-0	3-1	2-2	0-1	4-0	3-0	2-2	4-0	2-2	0-0	2-0	2-1
Everton FC	2-1	2-0	1-2	0-0	0-2	■	2-2	1-1	0-0	1-0	1-2	1-0	1-0	0-1	1-0	8-0	0-0	1-1	2-1	2-1	2-1	2-2
Huddersfield Town AFC	0-1	1-2	0-1	0-1	2-1	0-0	■	1-3	2-1	2-2	0-1	1-1	0-3	0-0	0-0	0-2	0-0	1-1	1-1	1-0	0-1	0-1
Ipswich Town FC	0-1	1-2	3-1	0-2	0-0	0-0	1-0	■	0-2	1-2	0-0	2-1	0-0	0-0	1-1	1-0	1-1	2-1	2-1	2-3	1-0	2-1
Leeds United AFC	3-0	2-0	1-0	2-0	3-0	3-2	3-1	2-2	■	2-1	1-0	3-0	5-1	5-1	6-1	1-0	7-0	1-0	1-1	3-0	0-0	0-0
Leicester City FC	0-0	1-1	1-0	0-0	0-2	0-0	2-0	1-0	0-0	■	1-0	0-0	2-0	3-0	0-1	0-1	2-1	0-1	0-1	2-0	1-2	1-2
Liverpool FC	3-2	0-0	3-1	4-1	3-2	4-0	2-0	2-0	0-2	3-2	■	3-0	2-2	5-0	3-1	2-0	1-0	2-1	0-0	2-0	1-0	3-2
Manchester City FC	2-0	1-0	4-0	4-0	2-0	1-0	1-0	4-0	0-1	1-1	1-1	■	3-3	2-1	2-2	2-1	3-0	1-2	4-0	2-1	3-1	5-2
Manchester United FC	3-1	0-1	2-2	4-0	1-0	0-0	2-0	1-0	0-3	3-2	0-3	1-3	■	0-2	3-2	2-0	3-2	3-0	3-1	3-1	4-2	1-3
Newcastle United FC	2-0	0-0	4-2	1-2	0-1	0-0	0-0	0-1	1-0	2-0	3-2	0-0	0-1	■	2-1	1-2	3-1	0-0	3-1	4-2	2-2	2-0
Nottingham Forest FC	1-1	2-1	4-0	0-1	0-2	1-0	1-2	0-2	0-2	1-2	2-3	2-2	0-0	1-0	■	2-3	2-3	0-0	0-1	4-1	1-0	1-3
Sheffield United FC	0-5	1-0	2-0	1-0	0-4	1-1	3-1	7-0	3-0	1-1	1-1	3-3	1-1	1-0	2-1	■	3-1	2-3	2-2	0-0	3-0	2-2
Southampton FC	0-1	2-2	3-1	1-0	1-2	0-1	1-2	0-0	2-1	1-0	0-1	2-0	2-5	1-2	4-1	3-2	■	3-1	0-0	1-1	3-3	1-2
Stoke City FC	0-0	0-1	1-0	3-1	1-1	1-1	1-0	3-3	0-3	3-1	0-0	1-3	1-1	3-3	0-2	2-2	3-1	■	2-0	1-1	0-0	0-1
Tottenham Hotspur FC	1-1	3-0	1-0	3-0	0-1	3-0	4-1	2-1	1-0	4-3	2-0	1-1	2-0	0-0	6-1	2-0	1-0	2-0	■	3-2	0-1	4-1
West Bromwich Albion FC	0-1	4-0	1-1	1-1	0-0	2-0	1-1	1-2	0-1	0-1	1-0	0-2	2-1	0-3	1-0	2-2	3-2	0-1	1-1	■	0-0	2-3
West Ham United FC	0-0	2-1	4-0	1-1	3-3	1-0	3-0	0-0	2-2	1-1	0-2	0-2	3-0	0-1	4-2	1-2	1-0	2-1	2-0	0-1	■	1-0
Wolverhampton Wanderers FC	5-1	0-2	1-1	1-0	2-1	1-1	2-2	2-2	2-1	0-1	0-0	2-1	1-1	2-0	4-2	1-2	4-2	2-0	2-2	0-1	1-0	■

	Division 1	Pd	Wn	Dw	Ls	GF	GA	Pts	
1.	DERBY COUNTY FC (DERBY)	42	24	10	8	69	33	58	
2.	Leeds United AFC (Leeds)	42	24	9	9	73	31	57	
3.	Liverpool FC (Liverpool)	42	24	9	9	64	30	57	
4.	Manchester City FC (Manchester)	42	23	11	8	77	45	57	
5.	Arsenal FC (London)	42	22	8	12	58	40	52	
6.	Tottenham Hotspur FC (London)	42	19	13	10	63	42	51	
7.	Chelsea FC (London)	42	18	12	12	58	49	48	
8.	Manchester United FC (Manchester)	42	19	10	13	69	61	48	
9.	Wolverhampton Wanderers FC (Wolverhampton)	42	18	11	13	65	57	47	
10.	Sheffield United FC (Sheffield)	42	17	12	13	61	60	46	
11.	Newcastle United FC (Newcastle-upon-Tyne)	42	15	11	16	49	52	41	
12.	Leicester City FC (Leicester)	42	13	13	16	41	46	39	
13.	Ipswich Town FC (Ipswich)	42	11	16	15	39	53	38	
14.	West Ham United FC (London)	42	12	12	18	47	51	36	
15.	Everton FC (Liverpool)	42	9	18	15	37	48	36	
16.	West Bromwich Albion FC (West Bromwich)	42	12	11	19	42	54	35	
17.	Stoke City FC (Stoke-on-Trent)	42	10	15	17	39	56	35	
18.	Coventry City FC (Coventry)	42	9	15	18	44	67	33	
19.	Southampton FC (Southampton)	42	12	7	23	52	80	31	
20.	Crystal Palace FC (London)	42	8	13	21	39	65	29	
21.	Nottingham Forest FC (Nottingham)	42	8	9	25	47	81	25	R
22.	Huddersfield Town AFC (Huddersfield)	42	6	13	23	27	59	25	R
		924	333	258	333	1160	1160	924	

Top Goalscorer

1) Francis LEE   (Manchester City FC)   33

Football League Division 2 1971-72 Season	Birmingham City	Blackpool	Bristol City	Burnley	Cardiff City	Carlisle United	Charlton Athletic	Fulham	Hull City	Luton Town	Middlesbrough	Millwall	Norwich City	Orient	Oxford United	Portsmouth	Preston North End	Q.P.R.	Sheffield Wednesday	Sunderland	Swindon Town	Watford
Birmingham City FC		2-1	1-0	2-0	3-0	3-2	4-1	3-1	2-0	1-0	1-1	1-0	4-0	2-0	0-0	6-3	2-2	0-0	0-0	1-1	4-1	4-1
Blackpool FC	1-1		1-0	4-2	3-0	2-0	5-0	2-1	1-1	0-1	3-1	0-0	1-2	4-1	2-0	1-2	1-1	1-1	1-0	1-1	4-1	5-0
Bristol City FC	1-0	4-0		0-2	2-0	1-4	2-0	1-2	4-0	0-0	2-1	3-3	0-1	5-3	4-2	1-1	4-1	2-0	1-0	3-1	1-0	2-1
Burnley FC	1-1	2-1	1-1		3-0	3-1	3-1	1-1	0-2	2-0	5-2	2-0	1-0	6-1	1-1	1-3	1-0	1-0	5-3	0-1	1-2	3-0
Cardiff City AFC	0-0	3-4	2-3	2-2		3-1	6-1	1-0	1-1	1-1	1-0	1-2	0-0	1-0	1-1	3-2	5-2	0-0	3-2	1-2	0-1	2-0
Carlisle United FC	2-2	2-0	2-0	0-3	2-1		5-2	3-1	2-1	0-0	3-0	3-3	3-0	2-0	2-1	1-0	0-0	1-4	2-2	1-2	0-0	2-0
Charlton Athletic FC	1-1	2-3	2-0	2-0	2-2	1-1		2-2	1-0	2-0	0-2	0-2	0-2	1-2	3-0	1-1	2-1	2-1	2-2	2-2	3-1	2-0
Fulham FC	0-0	2-1	2-0	0-2	4-3	0-1	1-0		1-0	3-1	2-2	0-0	2-1	1-1	1-1	1-1	0-0	0-3	4-0	0-0	2-4	3-0
Hull City AFC	1-0	1-0	1-1	1-2	0-0	2-0	2-3	4-0		0-0	4-3	0-0	1-2	1-1	1-0	1-3	3-2	1-1	1-0	2-3	2-0	4-0
Luton Town FC	0-0	1-4	0-0	1-0	2-2	0-2	1-2	2-0	0-1		3-2	2-1	1-1	2-0	1-2	3-2	1-1	1-1	3-1	1-2	0-0	0-0
Middlesbrough FC	0-0	1-0	1-0	1-0	1-0	2-2	2-2	2-0	3-0	0-0		1-0	1-0	1-0	2-1	2-1	0-1	3-2	2-1	2-0	2-0	2-1
Millwall FC	3-0	1-0	3-1	1-1	1-1	2-1	2-1	4-1	2-1	1-0			2-1	2-1	2-0	1-1	1-1	0-0	1-1	1-1	2-2	3-2
Norwich City FC	2-2	5-1	2-2	3-0	2-1	1-0	3-0	2-1	2-0	3-1	2-0	2-2		0-0	3-2	3-1	1-1	0-0	1-0	1-1	1-0	1-1
Orient FC	0-1	0-1	0-2	1-0	4-1	3-2	1-0	1-0	0-0	1-1	2-2	1-2			1-1	2-1	3-2	2-0	0-3	5-0	0-1	1-0
Oxford United FC	0-1	3-1	0-0	2-1	1-0	3-1	2-1	1-0	2-2	1-1	0-0	1-2	0-2	1-1		2-2	2-0	3-1	1-0	2-0	1-1	0-0
Portsmouth FC	1-0	1-3	1-1	1-2	2-0	1-0	0-0	6-3	0-0	0-3	2-1	1-1	2-1	3-2	2-0		1-1	1-0	1-2	2-2	1-2	2-2
Preston North End FC	0-0	1-4	1-0	1-3	1-2	3-0	2-1	2-0	3-1	0-1	1-0	4-0	0-2	1-1	1-0	4-0		1-1	1-0	1-3	2-2	2-0
Queen's Park Rangers FC	1-0	0-1	3-0	3-1	3-0	3-2	2-0	1-0	1-0	1-0	1-1	1-0	1-1	1-0	4-2	1-1	2-1		3-0	2-1	3-0	3-0
Sheffield Wednesday FC	1-2	1-2	1-5	2-1	2-2	2-1	2-1	4-0	2-2	1-0	1-1	1-1	3-1	0-0	1-1	3-1	1-1	0-0		3-0	1-0	2-1
Sunderland AFC	1-1	0-0	1-1	4-3	1-1	0-3	3-0	2-1	0-1	2-2	4-1	3-3	1-1	2-0	3-0	3-2	4-3	0-1	2-0		1-0	5-0
Swindon Town FC	1-1	1-0	0-1	0-1	3-1	0-0	2-1	4-0	2-1	2-1	0-1	0-2	0-2	4-0	2-2	4-0	3-1	1-1	0-0	1-0		2-0
Watford FC	0-1	1-0	0-2	2-1	2-2	1-2	0-3	1-2	1-2	2-1	0-1	0-1	1-1	0-1	0-1	1-0	1-0	0-2	1-1	1-1	0-0	

Division 2

		Pd	Wn	Dw	Ls	GF	GA	Pts	
1.	Norwich City FC (Norwich)	42	21	15	6	60	36	57	P
2.	Birmingham City FC (Birmingham)	42	19	18	5	60	31	56	P
3.	Millwall FC (London)	42	19	17	6	64	46	55	
4.	Queen's Park Rangers FC (London)	42	20	14	8	57	28	54	
5.	Sunderland AFC (Sunderland)	42	17	16	9	67	57	50	
6.	Blackpool FC (Blackpool)	42	20	7	15	70	50	47	
7.	Burnley FC (Burnley)	42	20	6	16	70	55	46	
8.	Bristol City FC (Bristol)	42	18	10	14	61	49	46	
9.	Middlesbrough FC (Middlesbrough)	42	19	8	15	50	48	46	
10.	Carlisle United FC (Carlisle)	42	17	9	16	61	57	43	
11.	Swindon Town FC (Swindon)	42	15	12	15	47	47	42	
12.	Hull City AFC (Kingston-upon-Hull)	42	14	10	18	49	53	38	
13.	Luton Town FC (Luton)	42	10	18	14	43	48	38	
14.	Sheffield Wednesday FC (Sheffield)	42	13	12	17	51	58	38	
15.	Oxford United FC (Oxford)	42	12	14	16	43	55	38	
16.	Portsmouth FC (Portsmouth)	42	12	13	17	59	68	37	
17.	Orient FC (London)	42	14	9	19	50	61	37	
18.	Preston North End FC (Preston)	42	12	12	18	52	58	36	
19.	Cardiff City AFC (Cardiff)	42	10	14	18	56	69	34	
20.	Fulham FC (London)	42	12	10	20	45	68	34	
21.	Charlton Athletic FC (London)	42	12	9	21	55	77	33	R
22.	Watford FC (Watford)	42	5	9	28	24	75	19	R
		924	331	262	331	1194	1194	924	

Football League Division 3 1971-72 Season	Aston Villa	Barnsley	Blackburn Rovers	Bolton Wanderers	Bournemouth	Bradford City	Brighton & H.A.	Bristol Rovers	Chesterfield	Halifax Town	Mansfield Town	Notts County	Oldham Athletic	Plymouth Argyle	Port Vale	Rochdale	Rotherham United	Shrewsbury Town	Swansea City	Torquay United	Tranmere Rovers	Walsall	Wrexham	York City
Aston Villa FC	■	2-0	4-1	3-2	2-1	3-0	2-0	2-1	1-0	1-0	0-1	1-0	1-0	3-1	2-0	2-0	1-2	3-0	2-0	5-1	2-0	0-0	2-0	1-0
Barnsley FC	0-4	■	0-0	1-0	0-0	0-2	0-1	0-0	1-4	1-2	1-1	2-1	2-1	2-2	0-0	3-3	1-1	1-3	0-1	0-0	0-0	4-2	2-1	2-1
Blackburn Rovers FC	1-1	4-0	■	0-3	2-1	1-0	2-2	1-2	1-0	2-0	1-1	0-2	0-1	3-2	3-1	3-0	2-1	1-0	1-2	1-0	4-1	1-1	2-1	3-0
Bolton Wanderers FC	2-0	0-0	1-0	■	0-0	0-0	1-1	0-0	1-0	1-1	2-0	1-2	2-1	2-1	3-0	2-1	2-2	2-0	0-0	2-0	1-0	0-1	0-2	0-1
AFC Bos. Athletic FC	3-0	0-0	1-0	1-2	■	3-0	1-1	2-0	1-0	3-1	1-1	2-0	2-0	1-0	3-2	4-1	3-1	3-1	2-1	1-0	0-0	0-0	4-0	2-2
Bradford City AFC	0-1	0-2	1-2	0-3	2-2	■	2-1	1-1	2-2	2-1	2-2	2-3	2-2	0-1	0-0	1-1	1-0	2-1	0-2	0-1	1-1	3-0	0-2	3-1
Brighton & Hove Alb.	2-1	0-0	3-0	1-1	2-0	3-1	■	3-1	2-1	2-1	1-0	1-1	0-1	3-0	1-1	1-1	2-1	2-0	1-0	3-1	2-0	1-2	3-2	0-2
Bristol Rovers FC	0-1	3-0	3-0	2-0	1-2	7-1	2-2	■	3-1	1-0	2-1	0-2	1-0	2-2	2-1	5-2	1-2	3-1	2-1	2-0	2-1	2-1	3-1	5-4
Chesterfield FC	0-4	0-0	2-0	2-1	0-0	0-1	0-1	1-3	■	2-1	2-0	1-2	0-1	2-1	2-1	2-0	0-0	1-2	2-0	2-2	1-1	1-0	2-1	
Halifax Town AFC	0-1	2-0	0-1	1-0	1-0	2-1	0-5	2-1	2-0	■	1-1	3-1	0-0	0-0	2-0	2-2	1-1	0-1	0-0	3-2	3-1	4-1	3-1	
Mansfield Town FC	1-1	0-0	1-1	1-0	0-5	1-1	0-3	0-0	2-1	0-0	■	1-1	2-1	2-3	0-1	3-1	0-1	2-2	0-2	0-0	1-1	1-1	0-0	
Notts County FC	0-3	3-0	1-0	1-2	1-1	2-0	1-0	2-3	1-4	3-1	2-0	■	2-0	1-0	2-1	4-0	1-1	5-0	2-1	1-0	3-0	1-0	2-2	
Oldham Athletic AFC	0-6	6-0	1-1	2-2	3-1	0-2	2-4	3-2	1-1	0-0	2-1	0-1	■	0-1	1-0	3-2	5-1	1-4	1-0	1-0	3-1	1-3	0-2	1-0
Plymouth Argyle FC	3-2	2-1	1-0	2-0	1-1	1-4	1-2	2-1	1-0	1-1	3-1	1-1	0-0	■	0-0	4-1	2-1	1-0	4-1	3-1	2-2	3-2	1-2	4-0
Port Vale FC	4-4	1-0	0-0	1-1	1-1	1-0	1-1	0-0	0-2	1-0	1-0	0-3	1-0	0-0	■	1-1	1-2	2-1	3-0	0-0	2-1	1-1	1-0	4-3
Rochdale AFC	1-0	0-2	2-1	2-2	1-1	0-1	1-2	3-1	0-2	3-2	2-1	1-1	1-1	3-2	3-2	■	2-1	0-0	1-1	5-0	2-1	0-0	1-0	1-2
Rotherham United	0-2	3-0	2-1	2-0	0-0	2-0	2-4	0-0	0-1	3-2	3-1	2-2	3-1	4-3	3-0	5-1	■	2-1	4-0	2-2	0-0	1-1	2-2	1-1
Shrewsbury Town	1-1	1-0	7-1	1-0	3-2	3-0	3-5	2-2	3-4	3-0	4-2	1-1	2-4	1-2	4-0	2-1	0-1	■	3-0	2-0	0-0	4-1	2-1	1-0
Swansea City FC	1-2	2-0	0-1	3-2	1-2	2-1	2-1	2-0	1-3	3-0	1-1	1-1	0-0	1-1	0-1	1-0	0-2	1-0	■	0-0	1-1	2-0	0-2	2-1
Torquay United FC	2-1	1-2	3-1	1-1	0-2	2-1	2-2	1-1	3-2	2-0	0-1	1-1	0-2	2-1	3-0	1-1	0-1	2-0	1-4	■	0-1	2-2	2-3	0-1
Tranmere Rovers FC	0-1	0-0	1-3	0-0	1-2	4-1	2-0	0-1	1-2	2-3	2-2	2-1	2-2	3-2	3-2	2-0	0-0	0-4	0-0	2-0	■	3-3	2-1	2-0
Walsall FC	1-1	1-1	0-0	1-1	1-1	3-0	0-1	2-0	1-1	0-0	2-1	1-2	2-3	1-0	2-0	3-0	0-0	4-1	4-0	1-0	4-1	■	2-1	2-1
Wrexham AFC	0-2	2-0	1-1	1-2	1-3	2-1	1-2	1-1	2-0	2-0	1-1	1-1	3-1	0-2	1-2	1-3	0-0	2-1	2-0	1-2	3-0	3-1	■	2-0
York City FC	0-1	1-1	0-1	0-0	0-2	3-1	1-2	0-0	4-1	1-1	1-2	0-2	0-0	2-3	2-1	2-0	2-0	1-1	1-1	3-1	5-0	2-0	1-1	■

	Division 3	Pd	Wn	Dw	Ls	GF	GA	Pts	
1.	Aston Villa FC (Birmingham)	46	32	6	8	85	32	70	P
2.	Brighton & Hove Albion FC (Hove)	46	27	11	8	82	47	65	P
3.	AFC Bournemouth (Bournemouth)	46	23	16	7	73	37	62	
4.	Notts County FC (Nottingham)	46	25	12	9	74	44	62	
5.	Rotherham United FC (Rotherham)	46	20	15	11	69	52	55	
6.	Bristol Rovers FC (Bristol)	46	21	12	13	75	56	54	
7.	Bolton Wanderers FC (Bolton)	46	17	16	13	51	41	50	
8.	Plymouth Argyle FC (Plymouth)	46	20	10	16	74	64	50	
9.	Walsall FC (Walsall)	46	15	18	13	62	57	48	
10.	Blackburn Rovers FC (Blackburn)	46	19	9	18	54	57	47	
11.	Oldham Athletic AFC Oldham	46	17	11	18	59	63	45	
12.	Shrewsbury Town FC (Shrewsbury)	46	17	10	19	73	65	44	
13.	Chesterfield FC (Chesterfield)	46	18	8	20	57	57	44	
14.	Swansea City FC (Swansea)	46	17	10	19	46	59	44	
15.	Port Vale FC (Stoke-on-Trent)	46	13	15	18	43	59	41	
16.	Wrexham AFC (Wrexham)	46	16	8	22	59	63	40	
17.	Halifax Town AFC (Halifax)	46	13	12	21	48	61	38	
18.	Rochdale AFC (Rochdale)	46	12	13	21	57	83	37	
19.	York City FC (York)	46	12	12	22	57	66	36	
20.	Tranmere Rovers FC (Birkenhead)	46	10	16	20	50	71	36	
21.	Mansfield Town FC (Mansfield)	46	8	20	18	41	63	36	R
22.	Barnsley FC (Barnsley)	46	9	18	19	32	64	36	R
23.	Torquay United FC (Torquay)	46	10	12	24	41	69	32	R
24.	Bradford City AFC (Bradford)	46	11	10	25	45	77	32	R
		1104	402	300	402	1407	1407	1104	

Football League Division 4 1971-72 Season

	Aldershot Town	Barrow	Brentford	Bury	Cambridge United	Chester	Colchester United	Crewe Alexandra	Darlington	Doncaster Rovers	Exeter City	Gillingham	Grimsby Town	Hartlepool	Lincoln City	Newport County	Northampton Town	Peterborough Utd.	Reading	Scunthorpe United	Southend United	Southport	Stockport County	Workington
Aldershot Town FC	■	1-1	1-2	2-2	1-1	0-0	0-2	0-0	3-0	3-0	0-0	0-2	1-1	2-0	0-0	3-0	0-2	1-1	1-2	1-1	0-0	1-1	4-0	2-2
Barrow AFC	1-1	■	0-3	1-1	1-1	2-0	2-2	2-1	0-4	1-2	0-0	1-0	0-0	2-0	2-2	1-0	0-1	0-2	0-0	0-1	2-1	0-2	3-2	2-0
Brentford FC	1-1	4-0	■	2-0	2-1	1-1	0-2	1-0	6-2	2-1	1-0	1-3	2-0	6-0	2-0	3-1	6-1	5-1	1-2	0-3	1-2	1-0	2-0	2-0
Bury FC	3-1	4-0	0-2	■	0-1	3-1	3-0	2-0	3-2	3-3	4-3	5-0	1-1	1-1	0-1	3-0	4-2	1-1	2-1	3-1	2-0	2-1	4-0	2-0
Cambridge United FC	1-1	1-0	1-1	0-2	■	2-0	4-2	3-2	6-0	1-1	0-1	2-1	3-1	2-1	0-0	0-1	1-1	2-5	4-1	2-0	1-1	0-0	2-0	0-0
Chester FC	0-0	0-0	0-0	2-0	1-1	■	2-1	0-0	2-1	1-1	1-2	5-1	1-2	4-0	2-1	3-0	3-2	2-0	0-0	1-1	1-1	0-0		2-1
Colchester United FC	1-0	0-1	0-2	0-0	1-1	1-0	■	4-2	4-3	1-2	3-0	2-2	0-1	1-0	5-2	2-3	2-0	1-1	2-1	1-1	1-0	1-1	3-2	0-0
Crewe Alexandra FC	2-1	1-0	2-1	0-0	1-1	3-1	2-4	■	1-1	0-1	0-1	0-1	1-2	3-1	1-2	2-0	2-0	0-2	1-2	2-1	3-1			0-0
Darlington FC	42	0-1	0-0	0-0	2-1	1-1	2-0	1-1	■	4-1	2-1	0-0	3-2	1-2	3-3	0-0	5-2	1-1	1-0	0-1	2-3	0-0	1-2	4-0
Doncaster Rovers FC	2-1	0-1	0-3	4-1	1-1	0-0	2-0	0-0	4-0	■	2-1	1-1	2-1	2-1	2-0	4-2	1-3	1-2	1-1	0-2	0-2	2-1	2-2	0-0
Exeter City FC	1-0	7-1	0-1	3-2	3-4	1-1	3-3	3-1	3-0	1-0	■	1-1	3-4	1-0	1-2	1-0	6-1	3-2	0-0	1-0	0-0	1-3	2-0	0-2
Gillingham FC	0-1	1-1	2-0	2-0	1-0	0-2	2-1	4-2	0-2			■	0-1	1-0	3-3	1-2	1-1	2-1	0-2				3-2	
Grimsby Town FC	3-3	2-0	3-1	4-1	2-1	1-0	3-0	2-3	2-0	3-1	3-0	2-1	■	3-2	2-2	4-2	4-2	3-2	2-0	4-1	4-1	0-1	4-1	1-1
Hartlepool FC	0-1	4-3	1-2	3-1	1-2	2-1	3-2	1-0	2-3	0-0	1-0	3-1	0-1	■	2-1	0-1	2-0	1-0	3-1	1-0	2-2	1-0	5-0	1-3
Lincoln City FC	2-2	3-2	4-1	2-0	3-1	4-0	0-0	0-0	0-1	2-0	4-1	1-1	3-0	2-1	■	3-1	2-0	3-2	1-0	0-0	2-1	2-1	1-0	
Newport County AFC	2-3	2-1	0-0	2-1	3-0	1-0	2-1	2-0	4-0	1-3	0-0	1-2	2-1	0-2	2-0	■	1-1	1-1	2-1	2-2	1-0	0-1		
Northampton Town FC	2-3	2-0	0-0	0-2	1-2	4-2	1-1	4-1	1-2	1-1	1-1	6-1	3-0	2-1	2-3	1-1	■	1-1	5-0	0-2	1-1	0-0	2-0	1-2
Peterborough United FC	0-0	7-0	2-2	2-0	2-0	2-0	4-0	2-0	1-3	2-0	3-3	2-1	0-2	2-2	4-4	3-1	1-0	■	3-2	0-1	2-0	2-0	4-2	1-1
Reading FC	2-0	1-0	1-0	0-2	1-0	1-0	2-4	1-1	2-0	1-1	1-2	1-3	3-0	0-1	4-2	2-1	2-1		■	2-0	1-4	1-1	2-2	0-0
Scunthorpe United FC	1-0	2-1	0-0	3-0	2-1	0-0	2-1	0-0	3-1	0-0	3-0	3-3	1-2	2-1	1-0	0-0	0-0	1-1		■	1-1	1-0	0-2	2-0
Southend United FC	1-0	1-0	3-1	0-0	1-2	4-2	1-4	4-1	3-0	0-0	3-3	1-2	2-0	2-1	3-1	4-1	2-1	4-1	2-3	2-1	■		4-2	2-0
Southport FC	0-0	1-0	0-0	0-1	4-1	4-3	3-0	4-2	2-1	3-0	4-0	1-0	1-0	1-0	1-1	4-2	4-0	2-4	5-2	1-1	0-1	■	1-0	2-2
Stockport County FC	0-0	1-3	0-1	2-2	3-0	0-0	2-2	3-1	2-1	1-2	0-4	2-1	0-2	2-1	4-2	4-4	3-1	0-0	0-1	0-0	2-2	1-1	■	1-1
Workington AFC	5-0	0-1	3-0	1-0	0-1	0-0	1-0	1-0	0-0	0-0	1-1	0-0	0-0	0-0	3-0	2-0	4-1	1-0	5-0	2-1	3-1	0-0	1-1	■

	Division 4	Pd	Wn	Dw	Ls	GF	GA	Pts	
1.	Grimsby Town FC (Cleethorpes)	46	28	7	11	88	56	63	P
2.	Southend United FC (Southend-on-Sea)	46	24	12	10	81	55	60	P
3.	Brentford FC (London)	46	24	11	11	76	44	59	P
4.	Scunthorpe United FC (Scunthorpe)	46	22	13	11	56	37	57	P
5.	Lincoln City FC (Lincoln)	46	21	14	11	77	59	56	
6.	Workington AFC (Workington)	46	16	19	11	50	34	51	
7.	Southport FC (Southport)	46	18	14	14	66	46	50	
8.	Peterborough United FC (Peterborough)	46	17	16	13	82	64	50	
9.	Bury FC (Bury)	46	19	12	15	73	59	50	
10.	Cambridge United FC (Cambridge)	46	17	14	15	62	60	48	
11.	Colchester United FC (Colchester)	46	19	10	17	70	69	48	
12.	Doncaster Rovers FC (Doncaster)	46	16	14	16	56	63	46	
13.	Gillingham FC (Gillingham)	46	16	13	17	61	67	45	
14.	Newport County AFC (Newport)	46	18	8	20	60	72	44	
15.	Exeter City FC (Exeter)	46	16	11	19	61	68	43	
16.	Reading FC (Reading)	46	17	8	21	56	76	42	
17.	Aldershot FC (Aldershot)	46	9	22	15	48	54	40	
18.	Hartlepool FC (Hartlepool)	46	17	6	23	58	69	40	
19.	Darlington FC (Darlington)	46	14	11	21	64	82	39	
20.	Chester FC (Chester)	46	10	18	18	47	56	38	
21.	Northampton Town FC (Northampton)	46	12	13	21	66	79	37	
22.	Barrow AFC (Barrow-in-Furness)	46	13	11	22	40	71	37	#
23.	Stockport County FC (Stockport)	46	9	14	23	55	87	32	
24.	Crewe Alexandra FC (Crewe)	46	10	9	27	43	69	29	
		1104	402	300	402	1496	1496	1104	

F.A. CUP FINAL   (Wembley Stadium, London – 06/05/1972 – 100,000)

LEEDS UNITED AFC (LEEDS)	1-0	Arsenal FC (London)

Clarke

Leeds: Harvey, Reaney, Madeley, Bremner, J.Charlton, Hunter, Lorimer, Clarke, Jones, Giles, Gray.

Arsenal: Barnett, Rice, McNab, Storey, McLintock, Simpson, Armstrong, Ball, George, Radford (Kennedy), Graham.

Semi-finals

Leeds United AFC (Leeds)	3-0	Birmingham City FC (Birmingham)
Stoke City FC (Stoke-on-Trent)	1-1, 1-2	Arsenal FC (London)

Quarter-finals

Birmingham City FC (Birmingham)	3-1	Huddersfield Town AFC (Huddersfield)
Leeds United AFC (Leeds)	2-1	Tottenham Hotspur FC (London)
Manchester United FC (Manchester)	1-1, 1-2	Stoke City FC (Stoke-on-Trent)
Orient FC (London)	0-1	Arsenal FC (London)

1972-73

Football League Division 1 1972-73 Season	Arsenal	Birmingham City	Chelsea	Coventry City	Crystal Palace	Derby County	Everton	Ipswich Town	Leeds United	Leicester City	Liverpool	Manchester City	Manchester United	Newcastle United	Norwich City	Sheffield United	Southampton	Stoke City	Tottenham Hotspur	W.B.A.	West Ham United	Wolves
Arsenal FC	■	2-0	1-1	0-2	1-0	0-1	1-0	1-0	2-1	1-0	0-0	0-0	3-1	2-2	2-0	3-2	1-0	2-0	1-1	2-1	1-0	5-2
Birmingham City FC	1-1	■	2-2	3-0	1-1	2-0	2-1	1-2	2-1	1-1	2-1	4-1	3-1	3-2	4-1	1-2	1-1	3-1	0-0	3-2	0-0	0-1
Chelsea FC	0-1	0-0	■	2-0	0-0	1-1	1-1	2-0	4-0	1-1	1-2	2-1	1-0	1-1	3-1	4-2	2-1	1-3	0-1	3-1	1-3	0-2
Coventry City FC	1-1	0-0	1-3	■	2-0	0-2	1-0	2-1	0-1	3-2	1-2	3-2	1-1	0-3	3-1	3-0	1-1	2-1	0-1	0-0	3-1	0-1
Crystal Palace FC	2-3	0-0	2-0	0-1	■	0-0	1-0	1-1	2-2	0-1	1-1	1-0	5-0	2-1	0-2	0-1	3-0	3-2	0-0	0-2	1-3	1-1
Derby County FC	5-0	1-0	1-2	2-0	2-2	■	3-1	3-0	2-3	2-1	2-1	1-0	3-1	1-1	1-0	2-1	4-0	0-3	2-1	2-0	1-1	3-0
Everton FC	0-0	1-1	1-0	2-0	1-1	1-0	■	2-2	1-2	0-1	0-2	2-3	2-0	3-1	2-2	2-1	0-1	2-0	3-1	1-0	1-2	0-1
Ipswich Town FC	1-2	2-0	3-0	2-0	2-1	3-1	0-1	■	2-2	0-2	1-1	1-1	4-1	1-0	1-2	1-1	2-2	2-0	1-1	2-0	1-1	2-1
Leeds United AFC	6-1	4-0	1-1	1-1	4-0	5-0	2-1	3-3	■	3-1	1-2	3-0	0-1	1-0	2-0	2-1	1-0	1-0	2-0	1-0	1-0	0-0
Leicester City FC	0-1	0-1	1-1	0-0	2-1	0-0	1-2	1-2	2-0	■	3-2	1-1	1-2	0-0	1-2	0-0	1-0	2-0	1-0	3-1	2-1	1-1
Liverpool FC	0-2	4-3	3-1	2-0	1-0	1-1	1-0	2-1	2-0	0-0	■	2-0	3-2	3-1	5-0	3-2	2-1	1-1	1-1	1-0	3-2	4-2
Manchester City FC	1-2	1-0	0-1	1-2	2-3	4-0	0-1	1-1	1-0	1-0	1-1	■	3-0	2-0	3-0	2-1	1-1	2-1	2-1	2-1	4-3	1-1
Manchester United FC	0-0	1-0	0-0	0-1	1-0	0-0	0-0	1-2	1-1	1-1	2-0	0-0	■	2-1	1-0	1-2	2-1	0-2	1-4	2-2	2-2	2-1
Newcastle United FC	2-1	3-0	1-1	1-1	2-0	2-0	0-0	1-2	3-2	2-2	2-1	2-1	2-2	■	3-1	4-1	0-0	1-0	1-1	1-2	2-1	2-1
Norwich City FC	3-2	1-2	1-0	1-1	2-1	1-1	1-1	0-0	1-2	1-1	1-1	0-2	0-1	1-1	■	1-1	0-0	2-0	2-1	2-0	0-1	1-1
Sheffield United FC	1-0	0-1	2-1	3-1	2-0	3-1	0-1	0-0	0-2	2-0	0-3	1-1	1-0	1-2	2-0	■	3-1	0-0	3-2	3-0	0-0	1-2
Southampton FC	2-2	2-0	3-1	2-1	2-0	1-1	0-0	1-2	3-1	0-0	1-1	0-2	1-1	1-0	1-1	1-0	■	1-1	2-1	1-1	0-0	1-1
Stoke City FC	0-0	1-2	1-1	2-1	2-0	4-0	1-1	1-0	2-2	1-0	0-1	5-1	2-2	2-0	2-0	2-2	3-3	■	1-1	2-0	2-0	2-0
Tottenham Hotspur FC	1-2	2-0	2-1	2-1	2-1	1-2	3-0	0-1	0-0	1-1	1-2	2-3	1-1	3-2	3-0	2-0	1-2	4-3	■	1-1	1-0	2-2
West Bromwich Albion FC	1-0	2-2	1-1	1-0	0-4	2-1	4-1	2-0	1-1	1-0	1-1	1-2	2-2	2-3	0-1	0-2	1-1	2-1	0-1	■	0-0	1-0
West Ham United FC	1-2	2-0	3-1	1-0	4-0	1-2	2-0	0-1	1-1	5-2	0-1	2-1	2-2	1-1	4-0	3-1	4-3	3-2	2-2	2-1	■	2-2
Wolverhampton Wanderers FC	1-3	3-2	1-0	3-0	1-1	1-2	4-2	0-1	0-2	2-0	2-1	5-1	2-0	1-1	3-0	1-0	1-1	0-1	5-3	3-2	2-0	■

	Division 1	Pd	Wn	Dw	Ls	GF	GA	Pts	
1.	LIVERPOOL FC (LIVERPOOL)	42	25	10	7	72	42	60	
2.	Arsenal FC (London)	42	23	11	8	57	43	57	
3.	Leeds United AFC (Leeds)	42	21	11	10	71	45	53	
4.	Ipswich Town FC (Ipswich)	42	17	14	11	55	45	48	
5.	Wolverhampton Wanderers FC (Wolverhampton)	42	18	11	13	66	54	47	
6.	West Ham United FC (London)	42	17	12	13	67	53	46	
7.	Derby County FC (Derby)	42	19	8	15	56	54	46	
8.	Tottenham Hotspur FC (London)	42	16	13	13	58	48	45	
9.	Newcastle United FC (Newcastle-upon-Tyne)	42	16	13	13	60	51	45	
10.	Birmingham City FC (Birmingham)	42	15	12	15	53	54	42	
11.	Manchester City FC (Manchester)	42	15	11	16	57	60	41	
12.	Chelsea FC (London)	42	13	14	15	49	51	40	
13.	Southampton FC (Southampton)	42	11	18	13	47	52	40	
14.	Sheffield United FC (Sheffield)	42	15	10	17	51	59	40	
15.	Stoke City FC (Stoke-on-Trent)	42	14	10	18	61	56	38	
16.	Leicester City FC (Leicester)	42	10	17	15	40	46	37	
17.	Everton FC (Liverpool)	42	13	11	18	41	49	37	
18.	Manchester United FC (Manchester)	42	12	13	17	44	60	37	
19.	Coventry City FC (Coventry)	42	13	9	20	40	55	35	
20.	Norwich City FC (Norwich)	42	11	10	21	36	63	32	
21.	Crystal Palace FC (London)	42	9	12	21	41	58	30	R
22.	West Bromwich Albion FC (West Bromwich)	42	9	10	23	38	62	28	R
		924	332	260	332	1160	1160	924	

Top Goalscorer

1) Bryan ROBSON   (West Ham United FC)   28

Football League Division 2 1972-73 Season	Aston Villa	Blackpool	Brighton & Hove Albion	Bristol City	Burnley	Cardiff City	Carlisle United	Fulham	Huddersfield Town	Hull City	Luton Town	Middlesbrough	Millwall	Nottingham Forest	Orient	Oxford United	Portsmouth	Preston North End	Q.P.R.	Sheffield Wednesday	Sunderland	Swindon Town
Aston Villa FC	■	0-0	1-1	1-0	0-3	2-0	1-0	2-3	2-0	2-0	0-2	1-1	1-0	2-2	1-0	2-1	2-0	1-1	0-1	2-1	2-0	2-1
Blackpool FC	1-1	■	6-2	3-0	1-2	1-0	0-0	2-0	1-1	4-3	1-1	0-1	2-1	2-0	1-1	2-1	3-1	2-0	2-0	1-2	0-0	2-0
Brighton & Hove Albion FC	1-3	1-2	■	1-1	0-1	2-2	1-0	2-1	2-1	1-1	2-0	0-2	1-3	2-2	2-1	2-2	1-1	2-0	1-2	3-3	2-2	3-1
Bristol City FC	3-0	3-0	3-1	■	0-1	1-0	4-1	1-1	0-0	2-1	0-1	1-1	2-2	1-1	2-2	0-0	3-1	2-1	1-2	1-2	1-0	3-0
Burnley FC	4-1	4-3	3-0	1-1	■	3-0	2-2	2-2	2-1	4-1	3-0	0-0	2-1	1-0	1-2	1-1	4-0	2-0	1-1	0-1	2-0	2-1
Cardiff City AFC	0-2	1-2	1-1	1-3	0-1	■	1-0	3-1	4-1	0-2	2-1	2-0	1-0	2-1	3-1	2-0	0-2	3-0	0-0	4-1	1-1	1-1
Carlisle United FC	2-2	2-3	5-1	1-2	1-1	4-0	■	2-1	0-0	0-1	2-0	1-1	0-1	1-2	1-0	2-1	1-0	6-1	1-3	1-1	4-3	3-0
Fulham FC	2-0	2-0	5-1	5-1	1-1	1-1	1-0	■	1-1	2-0	0-1	2-1	1-0	3-1	1-1	2-0	0-0	1-3	0-2	1-0	1-2	0-0
Huddersfield Town AFC	1-1	1-0	0-2	0-1	0-2	2-1	1-1	1-0	■	1-3	1-2	1-1	1-0	1-1	1-1	2-0	0-0	2-2	1-0	1-1	1-1	1-1
Hull City AFC	1-2	1-2	2-0	2-0	1-1	1-1	1-1	2-2	0-0	■	4-0	3-1	0-2	0-0	2-0	0-1	5-1	6-2	4-1	1-1	0-2	3-2
Luton Town FC	0-0	2-2	2-1	1-3	2-2	1-1	0-1	1-0	4-1	1-2	■	0-1	2-2	1-0	1-1	0-1	2-2	1-0	2-2	0-0	1-0	0-1
Middlesbrough FC	1-1	2-0	1-1	2-1	3-3	2-0	1-0	1-2	2-1	1-0	0-1	■	1-0	0-0	3-2	1-0	3-0	0-0	0-0	3-0	2-1	0-2
Millwall FC	1-1	1-1	3-0	3-0	1-1	1-1	1-0	1-3	1-0	2-0	3-2	1-0	■	2-1	2-0	3-1	0-2	4-1	0-1	2-1	0-1	1-1
Nottingham Forest FC	1-1	4-0	1-0	1-0	3-0	2-1	2-1	2-1	1-1	1-2	0-1	1-3	3-2	■	2-1	2-1	0-0	0-1	0-0	3-0	1-0	2-2
Orient FC	4-0	2-0	1-0	0-2	1-1	0-0	2-1	3-2	3-1	0-0	0-1	2-0	3-1	3-0	■	1-1	0-1	1-2	2-2	3-2	1-1	1-0
Oxford United FC	2-0	0-1	3-0	0-2	0-2	2-1	1-1	0-0	2-0	5-2	2-1	4-0	2-1	1-0	2-1	■	1-3	0-2	2-0	1-0	5-1	1-0
Portsmouth FC	0-1	1-0	2-0	0-3	0-2	3-1	0-0	1-2	1-2	2-2	2-2	0-0	1-1	2-0	1-0	1-0	■	0-1	0-1	1-0	2-3	1-1
Preston North End FC	0-1	0-3	4-0	3-3	1-1	0-0	1-0	0-3	0-0	1-0	2-0	0-1	1-0	2-1	0-0	0-1	0-5	■	1-1	1-1	1-3	1-1
Queen's Park Rangers FC	1-0	4-0	2-0	1-1	2-0	3-0	4-0	2-0	3-1	1-1	2-0	2-2	1-3	3-0	3-1	0-0	5-0	3-0	■	4-2	3-2	5-0
Sheffield Wednesday FC	2-2	2-0	1-1	3-2	0-1	1-0	0-0	3-0	3-2	4-2	4-0	2-1	2-2	1-2	2-0	0-1	2-1	2-1	3-1	■	1-0	2-1
Sunderland AFC	2-2	1-0	4-0	2-2	0-1	2-1	2-1	0-0	3-0	1-1	0-2	4-0	2-0	4-1	1-0	1-0	2-0	0-0	0-3	1-1	■	3-2
Swindon Town FC	1-3	0-0	2-2	2-1	0-1	3-0	2-0	2-2	1-1	2-1	0-2	1-0	0-0	0-0	3-1	1-3	1-1	3-2	2-2	1-0	1-1	■

Division 2

		Pd	Wn	Dw	Ls	GF	GA	Pts	
1.	Burnley FC (Burnley)	42	24	14	4	72	35	62	P
2.	Queen's Park Rangers FC (London)	42	24	13	5	81	37	61	P
3.	Aston Villa FC (Birmingham)	42	18	14	10	51	47	50	
4.	Middlesbrough FC (Middlesbrough)	42	17	13	12	46	43	47	
5.	Bristol City FC (Bristol)	42	17	12	13	63	51	46	
6.	Sunderland AFC (Sunderland)	42	17	12	13	59	49	46	
7.	Blackpool FC (Blackpool)	42	18	10	14	56	51	46	
8.	Oxford United FC (Oxford)	42	19	7	16	52	43	45	
9.	Fulham FC (London)	42	16	12	14	58	49	44	
10.	Sheffield Wednesday FC (Sheffield)	42	17	10	15	59	55	44	
11.	Millwall FC (London)	42	16	10	16	55	47	42	
12.	Luton Town FC (Luton)	42	15	11	16	44	53	41	
13.	Hull City AFC (Kingston-upon-Hull)	42	14	12	16	64	59	40	
14.	Nottingham Forest FC (Nottingham)	42	14	12	16	47	52	40	
15.	Orient FC (London)	42	12	12	18	49	53	36	
16.	Swindon Town FC (Swindon)	42	10	16	16	46	60	36	
17.	Portsmouth FC (Portsmouth)	42	12	11	19	42	59	35	
18.	Carlisle United FC (Carlisle)	42	11	12	19	50	52	34	
19.	Preston North End FC (Preston)	42	11	12	19	37	64	34	
20.	Cardiff City AFC (Cardiff)	42	11	11	20	43	58	33	
21.	Huddersfield Town AFC (Huddersfield)	42	8	17	17	36	56	33	R
22.	Brighton & Hove Albion FC (Hove)	42	8	13	21	46	83	29	R
		924	329	266	329	1156	1156	924	

Football League Division 3 — 1972-73 Season

(home \ away)	Blackburn Rovers	Bolton Wanderers	Bournemouth	Brentford	Bristol Rovers	Charlton Athletic	Chesterfield	Grimsby Town	Halifax Town	Notts County	Oldham Athletic	Plymouth Argyle	Port Vale	Rochdale	Rotherham United	Scunthorpe United	Shrewsbury Town	Southend United	Swansea City	Tranmere Rovers	Walsall	Watford	Wrexham	York City
Blackburn Rovers FC	■	0-3	2-1	2-1	0-0	3-1	0-1	0-0	3-0	2-0	1-1	3-1	0-1	1-1	2-1	3-0	0-0	2-1	3-0	2-2	2-0	0-0	1-1	2-0
Bolton Wanderers FC	0-1	■	3-0	2-0	2-0	3-0	1-0	2-0	3-0	2-2	2-1	2-0	2-0	2-1	2-1	0-0	2-0	1-1	3-0	2-0	3-1	1-1	1-0	3-0
AFC Bournemouth	3-0	2-0	■	3-2	0-0	3-1	2-2	1-1	1-0	1-1	2-0	0-1	4-0	4-2	4-0	1-1	2-0	2-0	2-0	1-1	0-1	3-0	1-0	2-3
Brentford FC	4-0	2-1	1-1	■	2-1	1-0	3-1	0-1	0-1	1-1	1-1	0-2	5-0	1-0	1-1	1-0	1-2	0-2	2-0	2-0	1-1	1-1	1-0	
Bristol Rovers FC	3-0	1-1	2-0	3-1	■	2-1	2-2	2-1	4-1	1-0	3-3	2-0	4-1	0-0	3-0	5-1	5-1	1-2	3-1	2-0	2-1	2-1	2-0	1-2
Charlton Athletic FC	1-2	2-3	1-1	2-1	3-3	■	2-2	1-1	1-0	6-1	4-2	3-0	2-0	1-0	1-2	2-0	1-2	0-0	6-0	1-1	1-1	2-1	2-1	1-0
Chesterfield FC	3-1	0-1	1-1	3-0	0-1	1-0	■	2-1	2-0	0-2	4-2	1-2	2-1	3-2	2-1	0-2	2-4	1-0	2-0	3-0	0-0	1-2	0-0	
Grimsby Town FC	2-0	2-0	0-1	4-0	2-0	0-2	2-1	■	0-0	3-1	6-2	1-1	0-1	1-0	2-1	1-0	3-2	3-1	2-0	2-0	6-2	2-0	0-1	1-2
Halifax Town AFC	2-2	1-1	2-0	3-2	3-0	3-0	0-1	1-1	■	0-1	0-3	2-1	2-2	0-0	0-1	1-0	0-1	2-1	1-1	2-1	0-1	1-1	2-2	1-0
Notts County FC	0-0	1-0	0-2	1-0	2-0	3-1	2-0	4-0	3-0	■	2-4	2-0	1-1	2-2	2-0	2-0	1-0	2-0	2-0	4-1	1-1	1-0	1-0	1-0
Oldham Athletic AFC	1-2	2-0	1-1	1-1	3-0	0-1	3-0	1-2	1-1	1-1	■	7-1	1-0	1-0	3-0	2-1	1-0	2-0	3-1	2-1	2-1	2-2	1-1	
Plymouth Argyle FC	1-2	1-0	1-0	0-1	3-2	5-0	2-2	3-1	2-1	1-4	1-3	■	2-1	3-2	4-1	3-0	3-0	2-0	3-1	0-1	0-2	1-1	1-1	
Port Vale FC	2-1	2-2	2-1	2-1	2-1	3-1	2-1	3-0	2-1	1-0	1-2	1-1	■	0-0	2-0	1-1	3-1	3-1	0-0	1-2	1-2	0-1	3-2	2-1
Rochdale AFC	0-1	2-2	1-0	0-1	0-0	0-2	1-2	3-2	0-0	4-1	0-0	0-6	0-0	■	0-1	0-2	1-1	3-2	1-1	1-1	1-0	1-0	1-0	1-0
Rotherham United	1-1	1-0	2-7	2-1	1-1	2-1	1-0	2-0	0-1	1-4	2-3	1-0	7-0	0-0	■	2-1	2-0	1-0	0-2	1-2	2-0	1-0	1-1	1-2
Scunthorpe United	1-1	1-1	1-1	1-0	0-2	0-2	0-1	1-2	0-3	1-0	0-1	1-2	2-1			■	1-0	0-0	1-0	1-5	2-1	1-1	1-1	1-0
Shrewsbury Town	2-0	0-2	0-0	2-0	4-2	0-2	2-0	0-0	0-0	2-2	1-1	2-3	3-2	1-1	4-2		■	1-0	2-1	0-0	1-1	0-0	0-0	0-1
Southend United FC	0-1	1-1	2-2	4-0	0-0	1-1	5-1	2-0	1-1	2-1	0-1	3-1	5-0	1-2	1-0	2-0		■	3-1	1-0	2-0	0-0	0-1	3-0
Swansea City FC	2-2	2-3	1-0	2-1	0-2	2-1	2-1	6-2	2-0	3-0	0-0	1-1	2-3	0-1	2-1	0-2	1-1		■	1-1	2-1	2-1	3-1	1-3
Tranmere Rovers FC	1-1	1-1	0-0	6-2	1-1	4-0	1-0	1-1	1-1	0-2	0-1	2-2	2-0	0-1	2-1	2-1	1-0	3-1	1-1	■	3-1	1-0	4-0	1-0
Walsall FC	0-2	3-2	1-0	3-0	4-3	3-2	3-2	1-0	0-1	1-0	3-0	1-3	2-0	1-1	1-1	3-1	1-1	2-0			■	1-3	2-0	0-0
Watford FC	1-3	2-1	3-2	2-2	2-1	1-1	0-0	1-2	2-1	1-0	3-2	1-1	0-0	1-1	5-1	0-1	0-1	1-0	0-1	1-0	1-0	■	0-0	2-2
Wrexham AFC	0-0	1-3	1-1	4-1	2-2	2-2	1-0	3-2	0-0	2-0	1-1	1-2	5-0	3-3	1-0	1-2	0-0	4-2	1-0	0-0	2-1	1-0	■	3-1
York City FC	1-0	0-1	0-0	0-1	1-0	1-1	2-0	0-0	2-1	1-0	0-0	1-2	0-0	1-2	0-1	3-1	2-1	0-0	3-0	4-1	0-0	0-0	1-1	■

Division 3

		Pd	Wn	Dw	Ls	GF	GA	Pts	
1.	Bolton Wanderers FC (Bolton)	46	25	11	10	73	39	61	P
2.	Notts County FC (Nottingham)	46	23	11	12	67	47	57	P
3.	Blackburn Rovers FC (Blackburn)	46	20	15	11	57	47	55	
4.	Oldham Athletic AFC (Oldham)	46	19	16	11	72	54	54	
5.	Bristol Rovers FC (Bristol)	46	20	13	13	77	56	53	
6.	Port Vale FC (Stoke-on-Trent)	46	21	11	14	56	69	53	
7.	AFC Bournemouth (Bournemouth)	46	17	16	13	66	44	50	
8.	Plymouth Argyle FC (Plymouth)	46	20	10	16	74	66	50	
9.	Grimsby Town FC (Cleethorpes)	46	20	8	18	67	61	48	
10.	Tranmere Rovers FC (Birkenhead)	46	15	16	15	56	52	46	
11.	Charlton Athletic FC (London)	46	17	11	18	69	67	45	
12.	Wrexham AFC (Wrexham)	46	14	17	15	55	54	45	
13.	Rochdale AFC (Rochdale)	46	14	17	15	48	54	45	
14.	Southend United FC (Southend-on-Sea)	46	17	10	19	61	54	44	
15.	Shrewsbury Town FC (Shrewsbury)	46	15	14	17	46	54	44	
16.	Chesterfield FC (Chesterfield)	46	17	9	20	57	61	43	
17.	Walsall FC (Walsall)	46	18	7	21	56	66	43	
18.	York City FC (York)	46	13	15	18	42	46	41	
19.	Watford FC (Watford)	46	12	17	17	43	48	41	
20.	Halifax Town AFC (Halifax)	46	13	15	18	43	53	41	
21.	Rotherham United FC (Rotherham)	46	17	7	22	51	65	41	R
22.	Brentford FC (London)	46	15	7	24	51	69	37	R
23.	Swansea City FC (Swansea)	46	14	9	23	51	73	37	R
24.	Scunthorpe United FC (Scunthorpe)	46	10	10	26	33	72	30	R
		1104	406	292	406	1371	1371	1104	

Football League Division 4 — 1972-73 Season

	Ald	Barn	Brad	Bury	Camb	Ches	Colc	Crew	Darl	Donc	Exet	Gill	Hart	Here	Linc	Mans	Newp	Nthn	Pete	Read	Sout	Stoc	Torq	Work
Aldershot Town FC		0-2	2-1	2-0	1-1	1-1	2-0	3-0	3-1	1-0	0-0	0-0	2-1	2-0	0-0	0-1	0-2	3-0	2-1	1-0	2-2	2-0	2-1	2-0
Barnsley FC	0-2		1-2	0-1	3-1	0-0	4-0	2-2	0-2	4-2	1-1	1-1	2-1	0-0	4-1	1-1	2-1	2-0	3-2	0-0	0-1	1-3	0-0	1-0
Bradford City AFC	1-0	3-1		0-0	0-1	0-1	3-0	2-2	7-0	4-3	4-0	3-1	0-2	1-1	3-1	1-1	2-1	2-1	1-4	1-1	0-2	1-0	1-0	2-2
Bury FC	1-2	2-1	0-0		1-1	1-1	4-0	0-1	1-0	5-0	2-1	2-1	1-1	3-0	0-4	1-0	0-0	2-2	3-1	4-0	0-1	1-2	0-0	3-0
Cambridge United FC	2-2	1-1	2-1	2-2		1-0	3-0	1-0	0-3	3-1	1-3	3-1	1-1	1-0	2-1	3-2	3-1	3-1	3-1	1-0	2-2	1-0	0-0	1-0
Chester FC	0-0	0-0	1-1	2-0	1-1		4-0	2-1	5-0	0-1	1-2	0-1	1-0	2-0	2-1	2-2	0-2	3-0	8-2	2-0	0-0	2-0	1-2	1-3
Colchester United FC	2-3	1-2	0-0	2-1	0-1	2-3		5-1	1-0	1-1	1-2	4-0	1-1	1-0	0-2	1-1	1-3	2-2	1-0	2-2	3-1	3-0	1-1	1-1
Crewe Alexandra FC	0-2	1-0	1-2	2-1	1-1	1-1	1-2		0-0	0-1	1-0	1-1	2-1	1-1	0-4	0-0	1-0	0-2	0-0	0-2	0-1	1-1	2-0	
Darlington FC	1-4	0-0	1-0	1-1	3-3	1-1	2-1	3-1		0-1	0-0	2-3	1-2	2-2	1-1	2-3	2-3	0-0	2-2	0-2	0-7	2-0	0-3	2-1
Doncaster Rovers FC	1-0	0-0	1-0	4-1	0-0	0-0	1-0	0-2	2-0		5-1	0-1	2-1	0-0	0-1	1-5	3-0	1-1	0-2	2-0	2-2	1-0	1-1	
Exeter City FC	1-0	2-1	5-1	1-1	3-1	0-0	1-0	0-0	1-1	0-1		3-2	1-1	1-0	2-0	4-2	0-0	4-1	1-1	0-0	0-1	3-0	3-2	4-2
Gillingham FC	1-2	5-1	4-2	2-2	1-2	0-1	2-1	3-2	4-0	3-0	1-0		2-0	2-0	1-1	2-1	0-1	3-1	2-0	1-0	2-0	3-0	1-1	0-2
Hartlepool FC	1-1	1-4	1-0	1-1	0-0	0-1	2-1	1-1	0-0	0-0	0-0	2-0		0-1	1-0	1-1	1-1	2-0	0-1	1-2	0-2	0-0	1-0	1-1
Hereford United FC	1-0	1-2	1-0	1-0	2-1	3-1	4-1	1-0	3-2	1-0	0-0	0-0	2-1		3-1	2-0	3-0	3-0	2-2	1-1	2-1	1-0	2-1	1-1
Lincoln City FC	0-2	1-2	2-1	2-2	2-1	1-0	3-2	1-1	1-0	2-1	2-2	1-0	1-2	4-1		1-1	0-2	1-1	1-0	0-0	3-1	5-3	3-1	1-1
Mansfield Town FC	2-0	3-1	4-1	1-1	3-1	4-1	1-1	5-1	5-0	3-0	2-0	2-0	1-1	0-2			0-0	1-0	4-2	1-1	3-3	1-0	2-1	4-0
Newport County AFC	2-1	1-1	0-0	4-3	0-2	3-2	1-0	0-0	0-0	1-0	2-0	5-1	5-1	0-1	2-2	0-1		1-0	1-1	1-0	3-1	1-0	2-1	1-0
Northampton Town	0-2	2-2	1-2	0-1	2-2	2-2	4-0	1-0	2-2	0-2	1-2	2-1	3-1	0-4	0-0	1-0	0-1		1-3	1-1	0-1	1-1	0-2	1-0
Peterborough United	1-0	6-3	3-0	1-1	1-1	2-2	2-2	4-3	1-1	3-1	0-1	3-0	1-1	2-2	1-0	1-0	1-2			4-2	0-1	2-3	0-1	1-0
Reading FC	0-0	0-0	2-0	0-0	1-0	2-1	1-1	1-1	1-0	1-0	2-0	3-1	1-0	0-1	1-1	2-0	5-0	3-0	2-0		1-1	0-0	3-0	2-1
Southport FC	3-1	1-0	3-1	2-1	1-1	3-2	1-0	2-0	2-1	2-2	0-0	1-1	2-0	1-0	3-1	0-2	1-2	2-1	4-1			1-0	2-1	2-1
Stockport County FC	1-1	2-0	3-1	0-0	2-2	2-1	2-0	0-0	3-1	2-1	1-0	2-3	0-1	1-1	2-1	2-1	1-0	0-0	3-2	2-2	2-0		2-0	3-0
Torquay United FC	1-1	0-0	1-2	0-1	1-2	1-2	0-0	0-0	2-1	1-0	0-2	1-0	0-0	2-0	1-1	2-1	2-1	1-0	2-2	2-0	0-0			3-0
Workington AFC	2-1	3-2	1-1	2-0	5-1	3-1	1-0	1-1	2-1	2-0	3-1	1-1	0-0	2-1	0-3	2-0	3-2	3-0	2-2	0-0	2-0	2-0	2-2	

	Division 4	Pd	Wn	Dw	Ls	GF	GA	Pts	
1.	Southport FC (Southport)	46	26	10	10	71	48	62	P
2.	Hereford United FC (Hereford)	46	23	12	11	56	38	58	P
3.	Cambridge United FC (Cambridge)	46	20	17	9	67	57	57	P
4.	Aldershot FC (Aldershot)	46	22	12	12	60	38	56	P
5.	Newport County AFC (Newport)	46	22	12	12	64	44	56	
6.	Mansfield Town FC (Mansfield)	46	20	14	12	78	51	54	
7.	Reading FC (Reading)	46	17	18	11	51	38	52	
8.	Exeter City FC (Exeter)	46	18	14	14	57	51	50	
9.	Gillingham FC (Gillingham)	46	19	11	16	63	58	49	
10.	Lincoln City FC (Lincoln)	46	16	16	14	64	57	48	
11.	Stockport County FC (Stockport)	46	18	12	16	53	53	48	
12.	Bury FC (Bury)	46	14	18	14	58	51	46	
13.	Workington AFC (Workington)	46	17	12	17	59	61	46	
14.	Barnsley FC (Barnsley)	46	14	16	16	58	60	44	
15.	Chester FC (Chester)	46	14	15	17	61	52	43	
16.	Bradford City AFC (Bradford)	46	16	11	19	61	65	43	
17.	Doncaster Rovers FC (Doncaster)	46	15	12	19	49	58	42	
18.	Torquay United FC (Torquay)	46	12	17	17	44	47	41	
19.	Peterborough United FC (Peterborough)	46	14	13	19	71	76	41	
20.	Hartlepool FC (Hartlepool)	46	12	17	17	34	49	41	
21.	Crewe Alexandra FC (Crewe)	46	9	18	19	38	61	36	
22.	Colchester United FC (Colchester)	46	10	11	25	48	76	31	
23.	Northampton Town FC (Northampton)	46	10	11	25	40	73	31	
24.	Darlington FC (Darlington)	46	7	15	24	42	85	29	
		1104	385	334	385	1347	1347	1104	

F.A. CUP FINAL   (Wembley Stadium, London – 05/05/1973 – 100,000)

SUNDERLAND AFC (SUNDERLAND)   1-0   Leeds United AFC (Leeds)

Porterfield

Sunderland: Montgomery, Malone, Watson, Pitt, Guthrie, Horswill, Kerr, Porterfield, Hughes, Halom, Tueart.

Leeds: Harvey, Reaney, Madeley, Hunter, Cherry, Bremner, Giles, Lorimer, Gray (Yorath), Jones, Clarke.

Semi-finals

Sunderland AFC (Sunderland)   2-1   Arsenal FC (London)
Wolverhampton Wanderers FC (Wolverhampton)   0-1   Leeds United AFC (Leeds)

Quarter-finals

Chelsea FC (London)   2-2, 1-2   Arsenal FC (London)
Derby County FC (Derby)   0-1   Leeds United AFC (Leeds)
Sunderland AFC (Sunderland)   2-0   Luton Town FC (Luton)
Wolverhampton Wanderers FC (Wolverhampton)   2-0   Coventry City FC (Coventry)

1973-74

Football League Division 1 1973-74 Season	Arsenal	Birmingham City	Burnley	Chelsea	Coventry City	Derby County	Everton	Ipswich Town	Leeds United	Leicester City	Liverpool	Manchester City	Manchester United	Newcastle United	Norwich City	Q.P.R.	Sheffield United	Southampton	Stoke City	Tottenham Hotspur	West Ham United	Wolves
Arsenal FC	■	1-0	1-1	0-0	2-2	2-0	1-0	1-1	1-2	0-2	0-2	2-0	3-0	0-1	2-0	1-1	1-0	1-0	2-1	0-1	0-0	2-2
Birmingham City FC	3-1	■	2-2	2-4	1-0	0-0	0-2	0-3	1-1	3-0	1-1	1-1	1-0	1-0	2-1	4-0	1-0	1-1	0-0	1-2	3-1	2-1
Burnley FC	2-1	2-1	■	1-0	2-2	1-1	3-1	0-1	0-0	0-0	2-1	3-0	0-0	1-1	1-0	2-1	1-2	3-0	1-0	2-2	1-1	1-1
Chelsea FC	1-3	3-1	3-0	■	1-0	1-1	3-1	2-3	1-2	3-2	0-1	1-0	1-3	1-0	3-0	3-3	1-2	4-0	0-1	0-0	2-4	2-2
Coventry City FC	3-3	0-1	1-1	2-2	■	1-0	1-2	0-1	0-0	1-2	1-0	2-1	1-0	2-2	1-0	0-1	3-1	2-0	2-0	1-0	0-1	1-0
Derby County FC	1-1	1-1	5-1	1-0	1-0	■	2-1	2-0	0-0	2-1	3-1	1-0	2-2	1-0	1-1	1-2	4-1	6-2	1-1	2-0	1-1	2-0
Everton FC	1-0	4-1	1-0	1-1	1-0	2-1	■	3-0	0-0	1-1	2-0	1-0	1-1	4-1	1-1	1-1	0-3	1-1	1-0	1-1	1-0	2-1
Ipswich Town FC	2-2	3-0	3-2	1-1	3-0	3-0	3-0	■	0-3	1-1	1-1	2-1	2-1	1-3	1-1	1-0	0-1	7-0	1-1	0-0	1-3	2-0
Leeds United AFC	3-1	3-0	1-4	1-1	3-0	2-0	3-1	3-2	■	1-1	1-0	1-0	0-0	1-1	1-0	2-2	0-0	2-1	1-1	1-1	4-1	4-1
Leicester City FC	2-0	3-3	2-0	3-0	0-2	0-1	2-1	5-0	2-2	■	1-1	1-1	1-0	1-0	3-0	2-0	1-1	0-1	1-1	3-0	0-1	2-2
Liverpool FC	0-1	3-2	1-0	1-0	2-1	2-0	0-0	4-2	1-0	1-1	■	4-0	2-0	2-1	1-0	1-0	1-0	0-3	1-0	3-2	1-0	1-0
Manchester City FC	1-2	3-1	2-0	3-2	1-0	1-0	1-1	1-3	0-1	2-0	1-1	■	0-0	2-1	2-1	1-0	0-1	1-1	0-0	0-0	2-1	1-1
Manchester United FC	1-1	1-0	3-3	2-2	2-3	0-1	3-0	2-0	0-2	1-2	0-0	0-1	■	1-0	0-0	2-1	1-2	0-0	1-0	0-1	3-1	0-0
Newcastle United FC	1-1	1-1	1-2	2-0	5-1	0-2	2-1	3-1	0-1	1-1	0-0	1-0	3-2	■	0-0	2-3	1-0	0-1	2-1	0-2	1-1	2-0
Norwich City FC	0-4	2-1	1-0	2-2	0-0	2-4	1-3	2-0	1-0	1-1	1-1	0-2	1-1	■	0-0	2-1	2-0	4-0	1-1	2-2	1-1	
Queen's Park Rangers FC	2-0	2-2	2-1	1-1	3-0	0-0	1-0	0-1	0-1	0-0	2-2	3-0	3-0	3-2	1-2	■	0-0	1-1	3-3	3-1	0-0	0-0
Sheffield United FC	5-0	1-1	0-2	1-2	0-1	3-0	1-1	0-3	0-2	1-1	1-0	1-2	0-1	1-1	1-0	1-1	■	4-2	0-0	2-2	1-0	1-0
Southampton FC	1-1	0-2	2-2	0-0	1-1	1-1	2-0	2-0	1-2	1-0	1-0	0-2	1-1	3-1	2-2	2-2	3-0	■	3-0	1-1	1-1	2-1
Stoke City FC	0-0	5-2	4-0	1-0	3-0	0-0	0-0	1-1	3-2	1-0	1-1	1-0	2-1	2-0	4-1	1-2	4-1	2-0	■	1-0	2-0	2-3
Tottenham Hotspur FC	2-0	4-2	2-3	1-2	2-1	2-0	0-2	1-a	1-0	1-0	0-2	2-1	0-0	0-0	1-2	3-1	2-1		3-1	■	2-0	1-3
West Ham United FC	1-3	0-0	0-1	3-0	2-3	0-0	4-3	3-3	3-1	1-1	2-2	2-1	2-1	1-2	4-2	2-3	2-2	4-1	0-2	0-1	■	0-0
Wolverhampton Wanderers FC	3-1	1-0	0-2	2-0	1-1	4-0	1-1	3-1	0-2	1-0	0-1	0-0	2-1	1-0	3-1	2-4	2-0	2-1	1-1	1-1	0-0	■

Division 1

		Pd	Wn	Dw	Ls	GF	GA	Pts	
1.	LEEDS UNITED AFC (LEEDS)	42	24	14	4	66	31	62	
2.	Liverpool FC (Liverpool)	42	22	13	7	52	31	57	
3.	Derby County FC (Derby)	42	17	14	11	52	42	48	
4.	Ipswich Town FC (Ipswich)	42	18	11	13	67	58	47	
5.	Stoke City FC (Stoke-on-Trent)	42	15	16	11	54	42	46	
6.	Burnley FC (Burnley)	42	16	14	12	56	53	46	
7.	Everton FC (Liverpool)	42	16	12	14	50	48	44	
8.	Queen's Park Rangers FC (London)	42	13	17	12	56	52	43	
9.	Leicester City FC (Leicester)	42	13	16	13	51	41	42	
10.	Arsenal FC (London)	42	14	14	14	49	51	42	
11.	Tottenham Hotspur FC (London)	42	14	14	14	45	50	42	
12.	Wolverhampton Wanderers FC (Wolverhampton)	42	13	15	14	49	49	41	
13.	Sheffield United FC (Sheffield)	42	14	12	16	44	49	40	
14.	Manchester City FC (Manchester)	42	14	12	16	39	46	40	
15.	Newcastle United FC (Newcastle-upon-Tyne)	42	13	12	17	49	48	38	
16.	Coventry City FC (Coventry)	42	14	10	18	43	54	38	
17.	Chelsea FC (London)	42	12	13	17	56	60	37	
18.	West Ham United FC (London)	42	11	15	16	55	60	37	
19.	Birmingham City FC (Birmingham)	42	12	13	17	52	64	37	
20.	Southampton FC (Southampton)	42	11	14	17	47	68	36	R
21.	Manchester United FC (Manchester)	42	10	12	20	38	48	32	R
22.	Norwich City FC (Norwich)	42	7	15	20	37	62	29	R
		924	313	298	313	1107	1107	924	

Top Goalscorer

1) Mick CHANNON   (Southampton FC)   21

Football League Division 2 1973-74 Season	Aston Villa	Blackpool	Bolton Wanderers	Bristol City	Cardiff City	Carlisle United	Crystal Palace	Fulham	Hull City	Luton Town	Middlesbrough	Millwall	Nottingham Forest	Notts County	Orient	Oxford United	Portsmouth	Preston North End	Sheffield Wednesday	Sunderland	Swindon Town	W.B.A.
Aston Villa FC	■	0-1	1-1	2-2	5-0	2-1	2-1	1-1	1-1	0-1	1-1	0-0	3-1	1-1	2-2	2-0	4-1	2-0	1-0	1-2	1-1	1-3
Blackpool FC	2-1	■	0-2	2-2	2-1	4-0	1-0	2-0	1-2	3-0	0-0	1-0	2-2	0-1	1-1	2-0	5-0	3-0	0-0	0-2	2-0	2-3
Bolton Wanderers FC	1-2	1-1	■	2-1	1-1	2-0	2-0	0-0	1-0	1-0	2-1	0-1	1-0	1-3	1-1	2-1	4-0	0-2	4-2	1-0	2-0	1-1
Bristol City FC	0-1	0-1	1-0	■	3-2	2-0	0-1	0-1	3-1	1-3	1-1	5-2	1-0	2-2	0-2	0-0	0-2	0-0	2-0	2-0	1-0	1-1
Cardiff City AFC	0-1	1-0	1-0	0-1	■	2-2	1-1	0-0	1-3	0-0	3-2	1-3	1-1	1-0	1-1	5-0	1-1	2-0	0-1	4-1	2-1	0-1
Carlisle United FC	2-0	2-3	1-0	2-1	1-1	■	1-0	3-0	4-0	2-0	1-1	1-1	2-1	3-0	3-0	2-1	0-2	2-2	2-2	1-0	5-1	0-1
Crystal Palace FC	0-0	1-2	0-0	3-1	3-3	0-1	■	0-2	0-2	1-2	2-3	1-1	0-1	1-4	0-0	0-0	2-0	0-0	3-0	4-2	1-0	1-0
Fulham FC	1-0	0-0	1-1	2-1	0-1	0-2	1-3	■	0-0	2-1	0-4	2-0	2-0	0-3	3-1	0-0	0-0	4-1	0-2	4-1	1-0	0-0
Hull City AFC	1-1	1-0	0-0	2-1	1-1	1-1	3-0	2-0	■	1-3	1-3	1-1	0-0	1-0	1-1	0-0	4-1	1-0	2-1	2-0	2-0	0-1
Luton Town FC	1-0	3-0	2-1	1-0	1-0	6-1	2-1	1-1	2-2	■	0-1	3-0	2-2	1-1	3-1	0-1	3-3	4-2	2-1	3-4	2-1	0-2
Middlesbrough FC	0-0	0-0	0-0	2-0	3-0	1-0	2-0	0-2	1-0	2-1	■	2-1	1-0	4-0	3-2	1-0	3-0	3-0	8-0	2-1	2-1	0-0
Millwall FC	1-1	2-2	2-1	0-2	1-2	1-2	3-2	1-0	3-0	0-1	0-1	■	0-0	1-0	1-1	0-0	0-1	5-1	1-0	3-0	2-0	1-0
Nottingham Forest FC	1-2	2-0	3-2	1-1	2-1	2-0	1-2	3-0	0-0	4-0	5-1	3-0	■	0-0	2-1	1-1	2-0	1-1	2-2	2-2	2-0	1-4
Notts County FC	2-0	0-3	0-0	2-1	0-3	1-3	2-1	3-2	1-1	2-2	3-3	0-1	2-4	■	4-0	2-1	1-5	1-4	0-0	1-1	2-0	1-0
Orient FC	1-1	3-2	3-0	0-1	1-2	0-1	3-0	1-0	1-1	2-0	0-0	1-1	2-1	1-1	■	1-1	2-1	2-2	0-1	2-1	0-0	2-0
Oxford United FC	2-1	2-2	0-2	5-0	4-2	0-1	1-1	0-0	1-1	1-1	0-2	0-3	1-0	2-1	1-1	■	3-0	1-1	1-0	0-1	1-1	1-0
Portsmouth FC	2-0	0-0	0-2	1-0	1-0	2-1	2-2	3-0	3-1	0-0	0-1	0-0	0-2	1-2	0-0	2-1	■	3-0	1-1	1-1	3-1	1-1
Preston North End FC	0-0	1-3	2-1	1-1	2-2	0-1	1-1	2-0	2-2	2-4	2-0	2-1	0-0	2-1	0-2	0-0	2-1	■	0-0	1-0	1-1	3-1
Sheffield Wednesday FC	2-4	0-0	1-0	3-1	5-0	1-0	4-0	0-3	1-1	2-2	2-2	3-2	1-1	0-0	1-2	0-1	1-2	1-0	■	0-1	2-1	3-1
Sunderland AFC	2-0	2-1	3-0	1-2	1-1	2-1	0-0	1-0	1-0	0-1	0-2	4-0	0-0	1-2	1-1	0-0	3-0	2-1	3-1	■	4-1	1-1
Swindon Town FC	1-0	1-0	2-2	0-1	1-1	2-2	0-1	1-1	1-1	0-2	0-1	1-3	0-1	1-4	2-2	2-1	1-0	3-1	3-1	0-2	■	1-0
West Bromwich Albion FC	2-0	1-1	0-0	2-2	2-2	1-1	1-0	2-0	2-3	1-1	0-4	1-1	3-3	2-1	1-0	1-0	1-2	0-2	2-0	1-1	2-0	■

	Division 2	Pd	Wn	Dw	Ls	GF	GA	Pts	
1.	Middlesbrough FC (Middlesbrough)	42	27	11	4	77	30	65	P
2.	Luton Town FC (Luton)	42	19	12	11	64	51	50	P
3.	Carlisle United FC (Carlisle)	42	20	9	13	61	48	49	P
4.	Orient FC (London)	42	15	18	9	55	42	48	
5.	Blackpool FC (Blackpool)	42	17	13	12	57	40	47	
6.	Sunderland AFC (Sunderland)	42	19	9	14	58	44	47	
7.	Nottingham Forest FC (Nottingham)	42	15	15	12	57	43	45	
8.	West Bromwich Albion FC (West Bromwich)	42	14	16	12	48	45	44	
9.	Hull City AFC (Kingston-upon-Hull)	42	13	17	12	46	47	43	
10.	Notts County FC (Nottingham)	42	15	13	14	55	60	43	
11.	Bolton Wanderers FC (Bolton)	42	15	12	15	44	40	42	
12.	Millwall FC (London)	42	14	14	14	51	51	42	
13.	Fulham FC (London)	42	16	10	16	39	43	42	
14.	Aston Villa FC (Birmingham)	42	13	15	16	48	45	41	
15.	Portsmouth FC (Portsmouth)	42	14	12	16	45	62	40	
16.	Bristol City FC (Bristol)	42	14	10	18	47	54	38	
17.	Cardiff City AFC (Cardiff)	42	10	16	16	49	62	36	
18.	Oxford United FC (Oxford)	42	10	16	16	35	46	36	
19.	Sheffield Wednesday FC (Sheffield)	42	12	11	19	51	63	35	
20.	Crystal Palace FC (London)	42	11	12	19	43	56	34	R
21.	Preston North End FC (Preston)	42	9	14	19	40	62	31	R -1
22.	Swindon Town FC (Swindon)	42	7	11	24	36	72	25	R
		924	319	286	319	1106	1106	923	

Note: Preston North End FC (Preston) had 1 point deducted.

Football League Division 3 1973-74 Season	Aldershot Town	Blackburn Rovers	Bournemouth	Brighton & H.A.	Bristol Rovers	Cambridge United	Charlton Athletic	Chesterfield	Grimsby Town	Halifax Town	Hereford United	Huddersfield Town	Oldham Athletic	Plymouth Argyle	Port Vale	Rochdale	Shrewsbury Town	Southend United	Southport	Tranmere Rovers	Walsall	Watford	Wrexham	York City
Aldershot Town AFC	■	4-0	1-3	0-1	2-3	6-0	2-1	2-2	1-0	2-1	1-0	1-0	0-1	3-2	0-0	4-0	2-2	3-3	4-0	0-0	1-0	1-0	5-1	2-2
Blackburn Rovers FC	1-2	■	4-3	3-1	0-2	2-0	1-1	2-1	1-0	1-1	1-2	1-0	0-1	2-0	1-1	3-1	2-0	1-0	2-1	0-0	0-2	5-0	1-2	4-0
AFC Bournemouth	3-0	1-2	■	0-0	0-3	1-0	1-0	0-1	1-1	1-1	3-2	1-0	0-3	0-0	2-2	2-0	1-0	1-3	2-0	2-1	1-0	1-0	0-1	1-3
Brighton & Hove Alb.	0-1	3-0	0-2	■	2-8	4-1	1-2	0-0	1-1	0-1	2-1	1-2	1-2	1-0	2-1	2-1	2-0	0-2	4-0	1-3	2-1	0-1	2-1	0-0
Bristol Rovers FC	2-1	3-0	3-0	1-1	■	1-0	2-1	1-0	1-1	2-0	1-1	2-1	1-2	4-2	1-1	1-1	1-0	4-0	3-1	1-0	0-2	1-0	1-0	0-0
Cambridge United FC	1-2	0-2	2-1	1-1	2-2	■	1-0	1-2	0-1	0-1	2-0	2-2	1-1	3-1	4-2	3-3	2-1	3-2	2-0	1-0	0-0	3-2	2-1	0-0
Charlton Athletic FC	2-0	4-3	0-0	0-4	1-1	2-0	■	3-3	2-1	5-2	2-0	2-1	4-1	2-0	2-0	3-0	3-3	2-1	0-1	1-0	0-1	1-3	0-0	2-4
Chesterfield FC	0-0	3-0	2-1	1-0	0-0	3-0	3-1	■	1-0	1-1	1-1	0-2	1-0	2-1	1-0	0-2	0-0	4-2	1-0	1-0	3-1	2-2	0-2	
Grimsby Town FC	1-0	4-2	1-1	0-0	1-1	1-2	5-0	1-1	■	4-1	1-3	2-1	2-1	3-0	2-0	5-1	2-1	2-1	5-0	1-0	2-2	1-1	1-2	
Halifax Town AFC	0-0	1-1	1-1	2-2	0-0	0-1	2-1	2-0	1-2	■	1-1	0-0	0-0	1-0	1-0	1-0	0-0	1-1	2-1	3-1	0-0	1-2	2-1	
Hereford United FC	0-2	1-0	0-2	3-0	0-0	0-0	2-3	2-1	2-1	3-1	■	0-1	3-4	0-1	2-1	2-1	1-1	1-2	3-0	0-2	3-1	1-1	2-0	0-0
Huddersfield Town	1-0	1-0	1-1	2-2	1-2	2-1	2-0	1-0	1-0	4-0	0-0	■	2-1	2-1	3-0	5-0	0-0	0-1	3-1	0-0	2-2	1-2	2-1	0-1
Oldham Athletic AFC	2-0	2-3	4-2	0-1	1-1	6-1	0-2	0-0	3-1	3-2	1-1	6-0	■	1-0	1-1	3-1	3-0	2-0	6-0	2-2	2-1	0-3	0-0	2-1
Plymouth Argyle FC	2-1	2-1	2-0	0-1	1-0	4-1	1-0	1-1	1-0	1-1	0-1	1-1	0-0	■	2-0	5-0	2-2	1-1	4-1	2-0	2-1	2-0	1-2	0-2
Port Vale FC	0-1	1-2	0-0	2-1	3-1	2-1	3-1	0-1	1-1	1-1	1-3	4-2	3-0	2-1	■	3-1	3-0	0-0	2-1	1-0	1-1	1-2	1-0	2-2
Rochdale AFC	2-2	1-2	3-3	1-1	0-1	0-2	1-1	1-2	1-1	1-1	1-1	1-1	1-3	1-3	1-1	■	3-2	1-1	2-2	0-1	0-1	1-3	0-0	1-3
Shrewsbury Town	0-0	3-0	1-1	1-0	0-2	2-0	3-3	0-1	1-1	0-2	1-1	3-0	0-2	0-0	0-1	2-0	■	1-2	2-0	1-3	0-0	3-2	0-1	0-2
Southend United FC	2-1	1-1	2-2	0-2	0-0	3-1	2-0	1-3	4-1	1-2	2-1	5-2	2-2	2-0	1-0	1-2	2-0	■	0-1	1-1	2-1	2-3	1-1	3-3
Southport FC	3-0	2-2	1-0	1-1	1-0	0-0	1-2	1-1	0-1	1-1	1-1	0-0	0-2	1-1	0-1	0-0	1-0	0-0	■	2-2	1-1	1-1	0-2	1-1
Tranmere Rovers FC	0-1	1-1	1-1	4-1	0-0	5-2	2-0	1-2	0-0	0-0	1-1	0-2	2-0	3-0	1-1	1-0	2-0	1-0	3-1	■	3-0	1-0	0-1	0-0
Walsall FC	3-2	2-0	1-2	0-1	0-0	3-0	4-0	2-0	3-1	2-2	3-1	3-0	1-1	0-4	0-0	0-0	2-0	1-2	2-0	0-1	■	2-2	3-0	0-0
Watford FC	2-1	0-0	1-1	1-0	0-0	3-0	1-3	2-1	1-2	0-0	2-1	1-1	0-1	0-3	2-1	4-0	1-0	1-0	4-0	4-2	1-3	■	2-0	1-1
Wrexham AFC	0-0	2-2	0-1	1-0	1-0	2-1	4-0	2-1	1-1	2-1	5-0	0-0	1-2	5-2	0-0	3-0	3-1	5-1	3-2	0-0	2-0	1-0	■	1-0
York City FC	3-1	1-0	4-1	3-0	2-1	2-0	0-1	0-0	1-1	1-1	0-0	2-1	1-1	1-1	3-1	2-1	0-1	1-0	4-0	2-0	1-1	2-2	1-0	■

Division 3

	Pd	Wn	Dw	Ls	GF	GA	Pts	
1. Oldham Athletic AFC (Oldham)	46	25	12	9	83	47	62	P
2. Bristol Rovers FC (Bristol)	46	22	17	7	65	33	61	P
3. York City FC (York)	46	21	19	6	67	38	61	P
4. Wrexham AFC (Wrexham)	46	22	12	12	63	43	56	
5. Chesterfield FC (Chesterfield)	46	21	14	11	55	42	56	
6. Grimsby Town FC (Cleethorpes)	46	18	15	13	67	50	51	
7. Watford FC (Watford)	46	19	12	15	64	56	50	
8. Aldershot FC (Aldershot)	46	19	11	16	65	52	49	
9. Halifax Town AFC (Halifax)	46	14	21	11	48	51	49	
10. Huddersfield Town AFC (Huddersfield)	46	17	13	16	56	55	47	
11. AFC Bournemouth (Bournemouth)	46	16	15	15	54	58	47	
12. Southend United FC (Southend-on-Sea)	46	16	14	16	62	62	46	
13. Blackburn Rovers FC (Blackburn)	46	18	10	18	62	64	46	
14. Charlton Athletic FC (London)	46	19	8	19	66	73	46	
15. Walsall FC (Walsall)	46	16	13	17	57	48	45	
16. Tranmere Rovers FC (Birkenhead)	46	15	15	16	50	44	45	
17. Plymouth Argyle FC (Plymouth)	46	17	10	19	59	54	44	
18. Hereford United FC (Hereford)	46	14	15	17	53	57	43	
19. Brighton & Hove Albion FC (Hove)	46	16	11	19	52	58	43	
20. Port Vale FC (Stoke-on-Trent)	46	14	14	18	52	58	42	
21. Cambridge United FC (Cambridge)	46	13	9	24	48	81	35	R
22. Shrewsbury Town FC (Shrewsbury)	46	10	11	25	41	62	31	R
23. Southport FC (Southport)	46	6	16	24	35	82	28	R
24. Rochdale AFC (Rochdale)	46	2	17	27	38	94	21	R
	1104	390	324	390	1362	1362	1104	

Football League Division 4 1973-74 Season	Barnsley	Bradford City	Brentford	Bury	Chester	Colchester United	Crewe Alexandra	Darlington	Doncaster Rovers	Exeter City	Gillingham	Hartlepool	Lincoln City	Mansfield Town	Newport County	Northampton Town	Peterborough United	Reading	Rotherham United	Scunthorpe United	Stockport County	Swansea City	Torquay United	Workington
Barnsley FC		2-2	2-1	3-2	1-1	0-1	2-1	1-0	2-0	3-0	3-1	2-0	0-1	1-1	1-1	0-2	0-0	3-2	1-0	5-0	4-0	1-0	1-0	4-0
Bradford City AFC	3-0		1-1	4-2	1-1	1-1	0-1	3-0	1-1	1-0	0-0	2-0	4-0	3-1	3-0	1-1	1-1	4-3	2-1	2-1	0-1	3-1	2-1	3-2
Brentford FC	5-1	2-0		1-2	3-0	0-0	3-0	0-0	2-0	0-1	0-3	1-2	2-1	4-1	1-1	3-1	0-1	0-1	1-1	2-1	0-0	0-2	0-0	1-1
Bury FC	2-0	3-0	3-0		3-1	2-0	2-0	5-1	3-1	0-0	3-2	1-0	2-1	2-0	5-0	3-1	0-2	1-0	3-1	0-0	1-1	0-2	4-0	3-1
Chester FC	3-1	1-0	0-0	1-1		0-4	1-0	1-0	3-0	0-1	2-4	3-1	2-3	1-1	3-0	0-0	2-1	0-0	1-0	2-0	2-1	1-0	1-1	1-0
Colchester United FC	2-0	4-0	2-1	1-1	1-1		3-2	3-0	3-0	1-0	0-2	3-0	4-1	1-0	4-1	1-0	1-1	0-1	2-0	3-1	2-0	2-2	3-0	
Crewe Alexandra FC	0-1	1-0	0-0	1-0	1-0	1-2		1-1	4-0	2-5	1-0	1-3	1-1	4-1	1-0	0-2	2-1	2-1	1-8	1-0	0-0	0-0	1-0	
Darlington FC	4-2	2-1	1-2	0-0	1-2	1-0	3-0		1-0	1-0	1-3	1-1	0-3	1-0	0-1	2-3	2-2	2-1	1-1	3-0	1-1	1-1	0-0	0-0
Doncaster Rovers FC	1-0	2-2	1-2	1-1	1-2	2-0	0-2	0-0		1-0	1-2	2-2	2-0	0-0	2-0	2-1	3-1	0-0	1-2	1-0	1-1	3-1	0-1	5-2
Exeter City FC	6-1	0-0	2-1	0-3	2-1	1-0	2-0	3-0	1-2		2-1	2-0	0-1	1-1	0-1	1-1	1-2	0-1	0-0	4-0	2-1	2-0	4-2	1-1
Gillingham FC	1-1	2-0	1-0	3-0	1-0	4-1	3-0	0-1	5-1	2-1		3-0	2-0	2-2	1-1	3-1	1-0	0-1	1-1	7-2	2-1	1-1	2-1	4-0
Hartlepool FC	1-2	1-0	1-0	1-1	0-0	0-0	1-0	1-0	3-0	1-3	2-1		0-2	4-0	1-0	1-0	0-1	1-2	2-0	3-0	3-0	0-1	0-0	3-0
Lincoln City FC	1-1	0-1	3-2	4-3	2-2	0-1	4-2	2-1	3-3	2-1	2-3	0-1		1-1	3-0	1-1	1-1	0-2	2-1	1-0	1-1	2-2	3-0	2-0
Mansfield Town FC	2-2	0-0	1-1	1-2	3-0	2-2	1-2	1-0	2-0	3-3	2-2	2-0	4-3		2-1	2-0	2-1	1-1	3-0	2-2	5-0	2-1	2-1	2-0
Newport County AFC	1-0	2-2	1-1	1-0	0-2	1-3	4-2	2-0	3-1	3-3	0-0	0-1	2-0			3-1	0-1	0-0	1-0	2-1	3-1	2-1	2-2	4-0
Northampton Town	2-1	3-0	0-0	3-1	3-3	0-0	1-1	5-0	3-1	1-2	0-0	1-0	2-0	1-0			0-1	3-3	3-1	2-0	2-0	2-0	0-0	1-0
Peterborough United	3-0	1-1	1-0	2-2	0-0	2-0	4-0	1-0	5-1	2-0	4-2	2-0	1-0	2-1	2-0	3-0		2-0	2-0	1-0	3-2	3-0	1-1	2-0
Reading FC	1-0	0-0	1-0	2-2	3-0	1-1	2-0	2-0	5-0	4-1	0-1	1-1	0-0	3-1	1-1	1-2	1-1		1-0	0-0	1-1	1-2	4-0	2-0
Rotherham United	2-1	2-1	1-1	1-0	3-2	0-0	1-1	0-1	1-2	4-0	1-1	2-2	2-0	1-1	1-1	1-2	3-1	1-1		1-1	1-2	1-0	1-1	0-1
Scunthorpe United	3-0	2-1	4-1	1-2	2-1	1-0	0-0	2-1	#	1-1	1-1	1-1	5-3	0-2	2-1	3-0	2-1	0-0	0-1					
Stockport County	1-1	0-1	1-1	3-2	0-1	0-3	0-0	1-2	0-0	0-1	2-0	1-1	2-2	1-1	2-2	1-1	0-0	0-1	3-1			0-1	2-1	1-1
Swansea City FC	2-0	0-1	0-0	0-1	2-0	2-0	2-0	0-0	0-0	2-0	0-3	0-0	3-0	2-0	1-1	1-1	0-2	2-1	4-2	1-2	3-0		0-1	1-0
Torquay United FC	1-1	1-0	3-0	1-2	2-2	0-4	2-1	1-0	3-0	0-0	0-1	0-2	2-1	4-0	3-2	1-0	1-2	1-1	3-0	1-1	2-2	3-1		3-0
Workington AFC	1-0	1-0	0-2	0-0	1-1	1-4	0-0	5-2	3-1	3-1	3-3	0-2	1-1	0-0	3-2	1-0	4-1	0-0	0-2	1-2	1-1	1-0	3-1	

	Division 4	Pd	Wn	Dw	Ls	GF	GA	Pts	
1.	Peterborough United FC (Peterborough)	46	27	11	8	75	38	65	P
2.	Gillingham FC (Gillingham)	46	25	12	9	90	49	62	P
3.	Colchester United FC (Colchester)	46	24	12	10	73	36	60	P
4.	Bury FC (Bury)	46	24	11	11	81	49	59	P
5.	Northampton Town FC (Northampton)	46	20	13	13	63	48	53	
6.	Reading FC (Reading)	46	16	19	11	58	37	51	
7.	Chester FC (Chester)	46	17	15	14	54	55	49	
8.	Bradford City AFC (Bradford)	46	17	14	15	58	52	48	
9.	Newport County AFC (Newport)	46	16	14	16	56	65	45	-1
10.	Exeter City FC (Exeter)	45	18	8	19	58	55	44	#
11.	Hartlepool FC (Hartlepool)	46	16	12	18	48	47	44	
12.	Lincoln City FC (Lincoln)	46	16	12	18	63	67	44	
13.	Barnsley FC (Barnsley)	46	17	10	19	58	64	44	
14.	Swansea City FC (Swansea)	46	16	11	19	45	46	43	
15.	Rotherham United FC (Rotherham)	46	15	13	18	56	58	43	
16.	Torquay United FC (Torquay)	46	13	17	16	52	57	43	
17.	Mansfield Town FC (Mansfield)	46	13	17	16	62	69	43	
18.	Scunthorpe United FC (Scunthorpe)	45	14	12	19	47	64	42	#
19.	Brentford FC (London)	46	12	16	18	48	50	40	
20.	Darlington FC (Darlington)	46	13	13	20	40	62	39	
21.	Crewe Alexandra FC (Crewe)	46	14	10	22	43	71	38	
22.	Doncaster Rovers FC (Doncaster)	46	12	11	23	47	80	35	
23.	Workington AFC (Workington)	46	11	13	22	43	74	35	
24.	Stockport County FC (Stockport)	46	7	20	19	44	69	34	
		1102	393	316	393	1362	1362	1103	

\# The Scunthorpe united vs Exeter City match was not played as Exeter City failed to appear for the match. 2 points were awarded to Scunthorpe United.

Newport County AFC had 1 point deducted for fielding an ineligible player.

F.A. CUP FINAL   (Wembley Stadium, London – 04/05/1974 – 100,000)

LIVERPOOL FC (LIVERPOOL)   3-0   Newcastle United FC (Newcastle-upon-Tyne)

Keegan 2, Heighway

Liverpool: Clemence, Smith, Thompson, Hughes, Lindsay, Hall, Callaghan, Cormack, Keegan, Toshack, Heighway.

Newcastle: McFaul, Clark, Howard, Moncur, Kennedy, Smith (Gibb), McDermott, Cassidy, Macdonald, Tudor, Hibbitt.

Semi-finals

Burnley FC (Burnley)	0-2	Newcastle United FC (Newcastle-upon-Tyne)
Liverpool FC (Liverpool)	0-0, 3-1	Leicester City FC (Leicester)

Quarter-finals

Bristol City FC (Bristol)	0-1	Liverpool FC (Liverpool)
Burnley FC (Burnley)	1-0	Wrexham AFC (Wrexham)
Newcastle United FC (Newcastle-upon-Tyne)	4-3, 0-0, 1-0	Nottingham Forest FC (Nottingham)
(A replay was ordered after the pitch was invaded by the crowd during the first game)		
Queen's Park Rangers FC (London)	0-2	Leicester City FC (Leicester)

1974-75

Football League Division 1 1974-75 Season	Arsenal	Birmingham City	Burnley	Carlisle United	Chelsea	Coventry City	Derby County	Everton	Ipswich Town	Leeds United	Leicester City	Liverpool	Luton Town	Manchester City	Middlesbrough	Newcastle United	Q.P.R.	Sheffield United	Stoke City	Tottenham Hotspur	West Ham United	Wolves
Arsenal FC	■	1-1	0-1	2-1	1-2	2-0	3-1	0-2	0-1	1-2	0-0	2-0	2-2	4-0	2-0	3-0	2-2	1-0	1-1	1-0	3-0	0-0
Birmingham City FC	3-1	■	1-1	2-0	2-0	1-2	3-2	0-3	0-1	1-0	3-4	3-1	1-4	4-0	0-3	3-0	4-1	0-0	0-3	1-0	1-1	1-1
Burnley FC	3-3	2-2	■	2-1	1-2	3-0	2-5	1-1	1-0	2-1	2-0	1-1	1-0	2-1	1-1	4-1	3-0	2-1	0-0	3-2	3-5	1-2
Carlisle United FC	2-1	1-0	4-2	■	1-2	0-0	3-0	3-0	2-1	1-2	0-1	0-1	1-2	0-0	0-1	1-2	1-2	0-1	0-2	1-0	0-1	1-0
Chelsea FC	0-0	2-1	3-3	0-2	■	3-3	1-2	1-1	0-0	0-2	0-0	0-3	2-0	0-1	1-2	3-2	0-3	1-1	3-3	1-0	1-1	0-1
Coventry City FC	3-0	1-0	0-3	2-1	1-3	■	1-1	1-1	3-1	1-3	2-2	1-1	2-1	2-2	0-2	2-0	1-1	2-2	2-0	1-1	1-1	2-1
Derby County FC	2-1	2-1	3-2	0-0	4-1	1-1	■	0-1	2-0	0-0	1-0	2-0	5-0	2-3	2-2	5-2	2-0	1-2	3-1	1-0	1-0	
Everton FC	2-1	4-1	1-1	2-3	1-1	1-0	0-0	■	1-1	3-2	3-0	0-0	3-1	2-0	1-1	1-1	2-1	2-3	2-1	1-0	1-1	0-0
Ipswich Town FC	3-0	3-2	2-0	3-1	2-0	4-0	3-0	1-0	■	0-0	2-1	1-0	0-1	1-1	5-4	2-1	0-1	3-1	4-0		4-1	2-0
Leeds United AFC	2-0	1-0	2-2	3-1	2-0	0-0	0-1	0-0	2-1	■	2-2	0-2	1-1	2-2	1-0	0-1	1-1	3-1	2-1	2-1		2-0
Leicester City FC	0-1	1-1	1-0	1-1	1-1	0-1	0-0	0-2	0-1	0-2	■	1-1	0-0	1-0	4-0	3-1	1-1	1-2	3-0	3-2		
Liverpool FC	1-3	1-0	0-1	2-0	2-2	2-1	2-2	0-0	5-2	1-0	2-1	■	2-0	4-1	2-0	4-0	3-0	3-0	5-2	1-1		2-0
Luton Town FC	2-0	1-3	2-3	3-1	1-1	1-3	1-0	2-1	1-4	2-1	3-0	1-2	■	1-1	0-1	1-0	1-1	0-0	1-1	0-0		3-2
Manchester City FC	2-1	3-1	2-0	1-2	1-1	1-0	1-2	1-1	2-1	2-1	4-1	2-0	1-0	■	2-1	5-1	1-0	3-2	1-0	1-0	4-0	
Middlesbrough FC	0-0	3-0	2-0	0-2	1-1	4-4	1-1	2-0	3-0	0-1	3-0	1-0	1-1	3-0	■	0-0	1-3	1-0	2-0	3-0	0-0	2-1
Newcastle United FC	3-1	1-2	3-0	1-0	5-0	3-2	0-2	0-1	1-1	3-0	0-1	4-1	1-0	2-1	2-1	■	2-2	2-2	2-2	2-5	2-0	0-0
Queen's Park Rangers FC	0-0	0-1	0-1	2-1	1-0	2-0	4-1	2-2	2-2	0-1	4-2	0-1	2-1	2-0	0-0	1-2	■	1-0	0-1	0-1	0-2	2-0
Sheffield United FC	1-1	3-2	2-2	2-1	2-1	1-0	1-2	2-2	3-1	1-1	4-0	1-1	1-1	1-0	1-1		1-1	■	2-0	0-1	3-2	1-0
Stoke City FC	0-2			5-2	3-0		1-1	1-2	3-0	1-0	2-0	4-2	1-1	0-0	1-0	0-1	0-0	3-2	■	2-2	2-2	2-2
Tottenham Hotspur FC	2-0	0-0	2-3	1-1	2-0	1-1	2-0	1-1	0-1	4-2	0-3	0-2	2-1	1-2	3-0	1-2	1-3	0-2		■	2-1	3-0
West Ham United FC	1-0	3-0	2-1	2-0	0-1	1-2	2-2	2-3	1-0	2-1	6-2	0-1	2-0	0-0	3-0	0-1	2-2	1-2	2-2	1-1	■	5-2
Wolverhampton Wanderers FC	1-0	0-1	4-2	2-0	7-1	2-0	0-1	2-0	2-1	1-1	1-1	0-0	5-2	1-0	2-0	4-2	1-2	1-1	2-2	2-3	3-1	■

	Division 1	Pd	Wn	Dw	Ls	GF	GA	Pts	
1.	DERBY COUNTY FC (DERBY)	42	21	11	10	67	49	53	
2.	Liverpool FC (Liverpool)	42	20	11	11	60	39	51	
3.	Ipswich Town FC (Ipswich)	42	23	5	14	66	44	51	
4.	Everton FC (Liverpool)	42	16	18	8	56	42	50	
5.	Stoke City FC (Stoke-on-Trent)	42	17	15	10	64	48	49	
6.	Sheffield United FC (Sheffield)	42	18	13	11	58	51	49	
7.	Middlesbrough FC (Middlesbrough)	42	18	12	12	54	40	48	
8.	Manchester City FC (Manchester)	42	18	10	14	54	54	46	
9.	Leeds United AFC (Leeds)	42	16	13	13	57	49	45	
10.	Burnley FC (Burnley)	42	17	11	14	68	67	45	
11.	Queen's Park Rangers FC (London)	42	16	10	16	54	54	42	
12.	Wolverhampton Wanderers FC (Wolverhampton)	42	14	11	17	57	54	39	
13.	West Ham United FC (London)	42	13	13	16	58	59	39	
14.	Coventry City FC (Coventry)	42	12	15	15	51	62	39	
15.	Newcastle United FC (Newcastle-upon-Tyne)	42	15	9	18	59	72	39	
16.	Arsenal FC (London)	42	13	11	18	47	49	37	
17.	Birmingham City FC (Birmingham)	42	14	9	19	53	61	37	
18.	Leicester City FC (Leicester)	42	12	12	18	46	60	36	
19.	Tottenham Hotspur FC (London)	42	13	8	21	52	63	34	
20.	Luton Town FC (Luton)	42	11	11	20	47	65	33	R
21.	Chelsea FC (London)	42	9	15	18	42	72	33	R
22.	Carlisle United FC (Carlisle)	42	12	5	25	43	59	29	R
		924	338	248	338	1213	1213	924	

Top Goalscorer

1) Malcolm McDONALD (Newcastle United FC) 21

Football League Division 2 1974-75 Season	Aston Villa	Blackpool	Bolton Wanderers	Bristol City	Bristol Rovers	Cardiff City	Fulham	Hull City	Manchester United	Millwall	Norwich City	Nottingham Forest	Notts County	Oldham Athletic	Orient	Oxford United	Portsmouth	Sheffield Wednesday	Southampton	Sunderland	W.B.A.	York City
Aston Villa FC	■	1-0	0-0	2-0	1-0	2-0	1-1	6-0	2-0	3-0	1-1	3-0	0-1	5-0	3-1	0-0	2-0	3-1	3-0	2-0	3-1	4-0
Blackpool FC	0-3	■	2-1	2-0	0-0	4-0	1-0	1-2	0-3	1-0	2-1	0-0	3-1	1-0	0-0	0-0	2-2	3-1	3-0	3-2	2-0	1-1
Bolton Wanderers FC	1-0	0-0	■	0-2	5-1	2-1	0-0	1-1	0-1	2-0	0-0	2-0	1-1	1-1	2-0	3-1	3-0	0-1	3-2	0-2	0-1	1-0
Bristol City FC	1-0	0-1	2-1	■	1-1	0-0	3-1	2-0	1-0	2-1	0-1	1-0	3-0	3-1	0-0	3-0	3-1	1-0	2-0	1-1	2-1	0-0
Bristol Rovers FC	2-0	1-3	1-0	1-4	■	1-0	1-2	2-0	1-1	2-0	0-2	4-2	0-0	2-1	0-0	1-0	0-1	1-1	0-1	2-1	2-1	1-3
Cardiff City AFC	3-1	1-1	1-2	0-1	2-2	■	0-0	1-2	0-1	0-1	2-1	2-1	0-0	3-1	0-0	1-1	1-0	0-0	2-2	2-0	0-2	3-2
Fulham FC	3-1	1-0	2-1	1-1	0-0	4-0	■	1-1	1-2	0-0	4-0	0-1	3-0	0-0	0-0	0-0	2-2	2-1	3-2	1-3	1-0	0-2
Hull City AFC	1-1	1-0	2-0	1-0	2-0	1-1	2-1	■	2-0	1-1	0-0	1-3	1-0	1-1	0-0	1-0	0-0	1-0	1-1	3-1	1-0	2-0
Manchester United FC	2-1	4-0	3-0	0-1	2-0	4-0	1-0	2-0	■	4-0	1-1	2-2	1-0	3-2	0-0	4-0	2-1	2-0	1-0	3-2	2-1	2-1
Millwall FC	1-3	0-0	1-1	1-0	1-1	5-1	2-0	2-0	0-1	■	1-1	3-0	3-0	0-0	1-1	0-0	0-0	2-1	4-0	1-4	2-2	1-3
Norwich City FC	1-4	2-1	2-0	3-2	0-1	1-1	1-2	1-0	2-0	2-0	■	3-0	3-0	1-0	2-0	1-0	2-0	1-1	1-0	0-0	3-2	2-3
Nottingham Forest FC	2-3	0-0	2-3	0-0	1-0	0-0	1-1	4-0	1-1	2-1	1-3	■	0-2	1-0	2-2	1-2	1-2	1-0	0-0	1-1	2-1	2-1
Notts County FC	1-3	0-0	1-1	1-2	3-2	0-2	1-1	5-0	2-2	2-1	1-1	2-2	■	1-0	1-1	4-1	1-1	3-3	3-2	0-0	0-0	2-1
Oldham Athletic AFC	1-2	1-0	1-0	2-0	3-4	4-0	1-0	0-1	1-0	1-1	2-2	2-0	1-0	.	0-0	1-1	2-0	2-1	1-1	0-0	0-0	2-3
Orient FC	1-0	0-0	0-0	1-0	1-0	1-1	0-0	0-0	0-2	2-1	0-3	1-1	0-1	3-1	■	1-1	1-1	1-0	2-1	1-1	0-2	1-0
Oxford United FC	1-2	0-0	2-1	2-0	2-1	1-0	2-1	3-1	1-0	3-1	2-1	1-1	1-2	1-0	1-2	■	1-0	1-0	0-4	1-0	1-1	3-1
Portsmouth FC	2-3	0-0	2-0	0-1	3-0	2-2	0-0	1-1	0-0	1-0	0-3	2-0	1-1	1-1	3-0	2-1	■	1-0	1-2	4-2	1-3	1-0
Sheffield Wednesday FC	0-4	0-0	0-2	1-1	1-1	1-2	1-0	2-1	4-4	0-1	0-1	2-3	0-1	1-1	0-1	1-1	0-2	■	0-1	0-2	0-0	3-0
Southampton FC	0-0	1-1	0-1	0-1	3-0	2-0	0-0	3-3	0-1	3-2	1-1	0-1	3-2	1-0	4-2	2-1	2-1	0-1	■	1-1	1-0	2-1
Sunderland AFC	0-0	1-0	0-0	3-0	5-1	3-1	1-2	1-0	0-0	2-0	0-0	0-0	3-0	2-2	3-0	2-0	4-1	3-0	3-1	■	3-0	2-0
West Bromwich Albion FC	2-0	2-0	0-1	1-0	2-2	2-0	0-1	2-2	1-1	2-1	1-1	0-1	4-1	1-0	1-0	3-0	2-1	4-0	0-3	1-0	■	2-0
York City FC	1-1	0-0	1-3	1-0	3-0	1-0	3-2	3-0	0-1	2-1	1-0	1-1	2-2	0-0	0-1	1-1	3-0	3-0	1-1	0-1	1-3	■

Division 2

		Pd	Wn	Dw	Ls	GF	GA	Pts	
1.	Manchester United FC (Manchester)	42	26	9	7	66	30	61	P
2.	Aston Villa FC (Birmingham)	42	25	8	9	79	32	58	P
3.	Norwich City FC (Norwich)	42	20	13	9	58	37	53	P
4.	Sunderland AFC (Sunderland)	42	19	13	10	65	35	51	
5.	Bristol City FC (Bristol)	42	21	8	13	47	33	50	
6.	West Bromwich Albion FC (West Bromwich)	42	18	9	15	54	42	45	
7.	Blackpool FC (Blackpool)	42	14	17	11	38	33	45	
8.	Hull City AFC (Kingston-upon-Hull)	42	15	14	13	40	53	44	
9.	Fulham FC (London)	42	13	16	13	44	39	42	
10.	Bolton Wanderers FC (Bolton)	42	15	12	15	45	41	42	
11.	Oxford United FC (Oxford)	42	15	12	15	41	51	42	
12.	Orient FC (London)	42	11	20	11	28	39	42	
13.	Southampton FC (Southampton)	42	15	11	16	53	54	41	
14.	Notts County FC (Nottingham)	42	12	16	14	49	59	40	
15.	York City FC (York)	42	14	10	18	51	55	38	
16.	Nottingham Forest FC (Nottingham)	42	12	14	16	43	55	38	
17.	Portsmouth FC (Portsmouth)	42	12	13	17	44	54	37	
18.	Oldham Athletic AFC (Oldham)	42	10	15	17	40	48	35	
19.	Bristol Rovers FC (Bristol)	42	12	11	19	42	64	35	
20.	Millwall FC (London)	42	10	12	20	44	56	32	R
21.	Cardiff City AFC (Cardiff)	42	9	14	19	36	62	32	R
22.	Sheffield Wednesday FC (Sheffield)	42	5	11	26	29	64	21	R
		924	323	278	323	1036	1036	924	

Football League Division 3 1974-75 Season	Aldershot Town	Blackburn R.	Bournemouth	Brighton & H.A.	Bury	Charlton Athletic	Chesterfield	Colchester Uttd.	Crystal Palace	Gillingham	Grimsby Town	Halifax Town	Hereford United	Huddersfield T.	Peterborough U.	Plymouth Argyle	Port Vale	Preston N.E.	Southend United	Swindon Town	Tranmere R.	Walsall	Watford	Wrexham
Aldershot Town AFC	■	1-1	1-2	2-1	1-1	3-0	1-0	0-1	2-1	2-1	0-0	3-1	2-2	1-0	5-0	4-3	2-1	1-2	3-0	0-1	2-0	0-0	3-1	1-2
Blackburn Rovers FC	2-0	■	1-0	1-0	1-0	3-1	2-0	3-2	1-1	4-1	1-1	1-0	1-0	1-1	0-1	5-2	2-2	3-0	1-0	2-0	2-1	3-3	0-0	0-0
AFC Bournemouth	1-0	0-0	■	2-0	2-1	1-2	0-0	0-2	4-0	2-0	0-2	0-1	2-1	1-1	2-1	3-7	1-2	1-0	0-0	1-1	0-0	0-1	4-2	0-2
Brighton & Hove Alb.	2-0	0-1	2-1	■	0-0	1-1	2-1	2-0	1-0	4-3	3-1	0-0	2-0	2-2	1-1	0-4	2-0	1-1	3-1	1-0	2-0	1-0		3-3
Bury FC	2-1	1-2	1-0	2-1	■	2-1	1-1	0-0	2-2	0-1	1-1	4-1	3-0	3-0	3-0	0-1	3-1	2-0	0-1	0-0	3-1	2-0	1-0	2-2
Charlton Athletic FC	3-1	2-1	2-3	2-1	0-1	■	3-2	4-1	1-0	2-1	1-1	3-1	2-0	1-0	3-0	0-2	2-2	3-1	2-1	3-3	3-3	4-2	4-1	1-1
Chesterfield FC	0-2	1-2	0-0	2-4	2-0	2-0	■	1-1	2-1	2-0	1-1	4-1	3-0	2-0	1-2	1-0	0-0	1-1	0-1	1-0	2-2	1-0	4-4	3-1
Colchester United FC	0-0	2-0	0-0	2-2	3-2	3-0	1-2	■	1-1	4-2	5-0	1-2	3-2	4-1	1-0	0-0	2-2	1-1	2-0	2-1	1-1	1-1	1-1	1-1
Crystal Palace FC	3-0	1-0	4-1	3-0	2-2	2-1	1-4	2-1	■	4-0	3-0	1-1	2-2	1-1	1-1	3-3	1-1	1-1	1-0	6-2	2-1	1-0	1-0	2-0
Gillingham FC	0-0	1-1	1-0	1-0	1-0	0-1	4-0	2-1	3-1	■	2-0	4-0	2-3	3-2	1-1	2-2	0-0	2-1	3-1	2-3	2-2	2-1	2-1	
Grimsby Town FC	2-0	1-2	0-0	3-2	2-0	1-1	3-2	1-2	2-1	2-1	■	2-1	0-0	1-2	1-2	1-1	3-0	2-1	1-0	0-0	3-2	0-0	2-2	0-0
Halifax Town AFC	1-0	1-1	3-2	1-0	0-1	2-2	1-3	1-1	3-1	1-1	1-1	■	2-2	2-1	2-1	1-1	3-0	1-3	1-0	0-0	1-0	1-0	1-0	1-0
Hereford United FC	2-0	6-3	0-0	1-1	1-1	2-2	5-0	3-1	2-0	1-1	3-2	0-0	■	1-1	2-0	1-5	2-0	1-0	2-1	2-0	2-1	0-1	0-1	1-0
Huddersfield Town	2-2	1-2	2-2	1-0	0-0	1-3	2-0	3-2	0-1	0-2	1-0	1-2	2-1	■	1-2	0-2	3-1	4-1	2-2	3-2	3-1			0-0
Peterborough United	1-1	1-0	3-0	2-0	3-1	1-1	0-2	1-0	1-1	0-1	1-1	1-1	2-1		■	1-0	0-0	0-0	1-0	0-0	1-2	0-0	1-0	2-1
Plymouth Argyle FC	1-0	2-1	1-0	2-2	2-1	1-1	3-0	1-0	0-1	1-1	2-1	2-0	1-0	2-0	2-0	■	1-1	2-1	1-0	4-3	4-1	2-1	1-1	0-3
Port Vale FC	3-1	1-4	0-0	1-0	1-0	1-0	3-2	2-1	2-1	1-0	2-0	1-0	3-0	4-0	1-3	2-0	■	2-1	0-2	1-0	1-1	1-0	0-0	2-0
Preston North End FC	3-1	0-0	5-2	1-0	3-0	2-0	2-1	0-2	1-1	1-0	2-0	1-0	2-2	1-0	1-0	1-0	1-4	■	2-0	1-0		3-2	2-2	3-1
Southend United FC	1-1	2-2	1-0	1-0	2-1	2-1	1-4	1-0	1-1	0-2	2-2	3-0	4-0	0-0	1-0	1-2	2-1	1-3	■	2-0	1-0		0-0	1-1
Swindon Town FC	3-2	2-0	2-1	1-0	0-2	2-0	1-0	4-1	1-1	1-1	3-2	3-1	4-1	1-0	2-0	3-2	1-0	2-0		■	0-0	3-0	2-2	2-1
Tranmere Rovers FC	2-0	1-1	0-1	1-2	0-0	0-1	1-2	2-0	2-0	1-1	3-1	6-1	1-1	1-3	1-0	3-1	2-1	3-0			■	3-0	2-2	0-1
Walsall FC	3-0	1-3	2-0	6-0	3-0	0-1	2-2	5-2	3-0	1-1	2-0	1-1	3-1	2-0	0-1	0-0	0-0	2-0	3-0	2-0	1-0	■	2-0	2-1
Watford FC	1-1	0-0	1-0	1-1	2-1	0-2	2-2	1-2	1-2		3-2	2-2	1-1	1-0	0-3	1-3	3-2	3-2	2-0	1-0	1-0	2-3	■	1-2
Wrexham AFC	4-0	1-1	1-1	2-1	3-1	0-3	0-0	2-1	0-0	2-3	4-0	2-1	3-0	1-2	5-1	2-2	1-1	1-1	1-2	1-0	0-0	5-1		■

	Division 3	Pd	Wn	Dw	Ls	GF	GA	Pts	
1.	Blackburn Rovers FC (Blackburn)	46	22	16	8	68	45	60	P
2.	Plymouth Argyle FC (Plymouth)	46	24	11	11	79	58	59	P
3.	Charlton Athletic FC (London)	46	22	11	13	76	61	55	P
4.	Swindon Town FC (Swindon)	46	21	11	14	64	58	53	
5.	Crystal Palace FC (London)	46	18	15	13	66	57	51	
6.	Port Vale FC (Stoke-on-Trent)	46	18	15	13	61	54	51	
7.	Peterborough United FC (Peterborough)	46	19	12	15	47	53	50	
8.	Walsall FC (Walsall)	46	18	13	15	67	52	49	
9.	Preston North End FC (Preston)	46	19	11	16	63	56	49	
10.	Gillingham FC (Gillingham)	46	17	14	15	65	60	48	
11.	Colchester United FC (Colchester)	46	17	13	16	70	63	47	
12.	Hereford United FC (Hereford)	46	16	14	16	64	66	46	
13.	Wrexham AFC (Wrexham)	46	15	15	16	65	55	45	
14.	Bury FC (Bury)	46	16	12	18	53	50	44	
15.	Chesterfield FC (Chesterfield)	46	16	12	18	62	66	44	
16.	Grimsby Town FC (Cleethorpes)	46	15	13	18	55	64	43	
17.	Halifax Town AFC (Halifax)	46	13	17	16	49	65	43	
18.	Southend United FC (Southend-on-Sea)	46	13	16	17	46	51	42	
19.	Brighton & Hove Albion FC (Hove)	46	16	10	20	56	64	42	
20.	Aldershot FC (Aldershot)	46	14	11	21	53	63	38	-1
21.	AFC Bournemouth (Bournemouth)	46	13	12	21	44	58	38	R
22.	Tranmere Rovers FC (Birkenhead)	46	14	9	23	55	57	37	R
23.	Watford FC (Watford)	46	10	17	19	52	75	37	R
24.	Huddersfield Town AFC (Huddersfield)	46	11	10	25	47	76	32	R
		1104	397	310	397	1427	1427	1103	

Aldershot FC (Aldershot) had 1 point deducted for fielding an ineligible player.

Football League Division 4 1974-75 Season	Barnsley	Bradford City	Brentford	Cambridge United	Chester	Crewe Alexandra	Darlington	Doncaster Rovers	Exeter City	Hartlepool	Lincoln City	Mansfield Town	Newport County	Northampton Town	Reading	Rochdale	Rotherham United	Scunthorpe United	Shrewsbury Town	Southport	Stockport County	Swansea City	Torquay United	Workington
Barnsley FC		2-2	1-1	1-1	0-1	1-1	1-1	0-1	1-0	2-1	0-2	1-3	2-1	5-1	2-0	5-3	1-1	2-2	1-0	3-0	2-0	1-0	0-1	0-1
Bradford City AFC	2-0		1-0	1-1	2-0	1-2	1-1	2-0	0-1	3-0	1-2	1-1	0-1	2-1	1-3	1-0	1-1	3-0	1-2	1-2	2-0	1-2	3-0	1-1
Brentford FC	3-0	0-0		1-0	1-1	1-0	3-0	1-1	2-0	1-0	1-1	2-3	0-0	1-0	1-0	3-0	3-4	2-0	2-1	1-0	3-0	1-0	3-1	2-2
Cambridge United FC	2-0	0-1	2-0		3-0	2-0	1-0	4-1	1-1	3-2	5-0	2-2	1-1	3-4	1-0	1-1	0-0	2-0	0-2	1-0	1-0	2-0	3-1	3-0
Chester FC	2-1	1-0	2-0	1-1		2-0	1-0	3-0	1-1	3-0	4-1	0-0	4-1	4-1	2-0	4-0	0-1	1-0	1-1	3-0	3-1	3-0	3-0	0-0
Crewe Alexandra FC	1-1	0-0	1-1	0-0	0-1		2-1	2-1	2-1	2-0	1-0	0-2	1-2	3-1	1-0	0-1	1-1	0-0	0-0	2-0	2-2	0-1	0-1	2-0
Darlington FC	0-0	0-3	2-1	6-0	1-1	1-0		4-1	2-0	1-2	1-4	2-1	3-0	2-0	0-1	1-2	0-1	3-1	1-2	1-1	0-2	3-2	2-2	2-0
Doncaster Rovers FC	1-1	4-1	2-1	0-1	1-1	2-1	1-3		3-3	3-0	2-2	4-3	0-2	2-0	1-1	4-1	0-0	1-1	1-3	1-1	2-1	3-2	3-0	0-0
Exeter City FC	4-2	1-0	1-0	1-4	1-0	2-0	4-1	2-1		1-0	1-2	0-1	3-1	2-2	0-2	2-1	0-4	0-0	1-0	1-0	4-1	1-2	0-0	1-0
Hartlepool FC	4-3	1-2	3-2	1-1	1-0	1-1	2-0	2-1	0-3		2-0	2-1	2-0	2-0	2-3	5-0	3-2	1-0	1-1	1-1	1-1	0-2	0-0	3-0
Lincoln City FC	3-0	2-1	1-1	0-0	2-1	0-0	1-1	4-0	5-0	2-0		0-0	5-2	2-2	1-1	3-0	1-0	3-0	1-1	2-0	1-3	1-3	1-0	
Mansfield Town FC	2-1	3-0	1-1	0-0	0-0	4-2	5-2	3-2	2-0	3-1	3-0		3-0	1-0	2-0	1-0	7-0	3-1	2-1	1-1	3-0	1-0	3-0	1-0
Newport County AFC	3-4	2-1	1-0	1-2	3-0	1-1	2-1	0-2	1-2	2-0	1-1	2-1		2-1	2-2	3-2	1-1	2-0	2-4	1-0	3-3	3-0	2-1	3-1
Northampton Town FC	2-1	1-2	0-0	1-2	2-0	3-0	3-0	2-0	1-1	3-0	1-0	0-2	3-2		0-3	0-1	11-	3-0	3-3	1-1	4-1	5-1	1-1	3-0
Reading FC	0-3	1-1	1-0	2-0	2-1	3-0	3-0	0-0	3-0	1-1	1-1	3-0	3-2	2-1		1-1	1-1	1-2	4-1	1-3	1-2	1-0	2-1	
Rochdale AFC	3-1	1-1	0-0	0-0	0-1	3-0	2-0	2-0	1-1	3-0	1-1	0-2	2-4	2-2	0-2		1-2	4-2	0-0	3-3	3-0	1-0	1-1	0-0
Rotherham United FC	2-0	4-0	3-0	0-0	1-2	1-1	1-1	1-0	1-1	1-2	2-2	2-1	1-1	1-3	2-1	3-1		3-2	0-0	3-0	3-0	1-0	3-1	1-0
Scunthorpe United FC	1-0	1-2	1-2	2-0	1-3	1-1	1-1	0-0	2-1	1-1	1-1	0-1	4-1	2-1	0-1	2-2	0-3		1-0	3-3	0-0	1-2	0-2	2-1
Shrewsbury Town FC	3-1	3-2	1-0	1-0	2-0	1-0	2-0	7-4	2-2	0-1	0-4	0-1	1-0	6-0	2-0	1-1	3-1	5-0		1-0	2-0	2-0	2-0	2-0
Southport FC	1-0	1-2	3-0	2-2	1-0	1-0	2-1	3-0	0-0	3-2	1-1	1-3	0-0	2-0	1-0	2-0	1-0	1-2			2-1	3-0	1-1	2-2
Stockport County FC	0-3	1-1	1-1	1-0	1-1	1-0	2-1	0-2	3-2	1-1	0-0	3-2	1-1	1-0	1-0	2-3	1-0	3-2	0-3	0-0		2-1	0-0	1-3
Swansea City FC	0-3	1-1	0-1	2-1	0-1	2-1	1-0	3-3	0-2	1-0	2-1	1-2	2-0	1-0	1-2	3-3	0-2	1-0	1-4	2-2	1-0		0-1	0-1
Torquay United FC	1-1	0-1	3-2	1-0	3-0	0-0	0-0	2-0	2-2	2-1	1-3	0-2	0-1	0-1	2-1	3-0	0-3	1-1	1-1	3-2	2-2	0-0		2-1
Workington AFC	1-2	0-0	0-1	1-2	0-0	3-0	1-2	0-3	0-1	1-1	0-2	1-3	3-1	2-2	2-1	2-1	0-2	1-1	0-2	0-1	1-0	2-1	2-1	

	Division 4	Pd	Wn	Dw	Ls	GF	GA	Pts	
1.	Mansfield Town FC (Mansfield)	46	28	12	6	90	40	68	P
2.	Shrewsbury Town FC (Shrewsbury)	46	26	10	10	80	43	62	P
3.	Rotherham United FC (Rotherham)	46	22	15	9	71	41	59	P
4.	Chester FC (Chester)	46	23	11	12	64	38	57	P
5.	Lincoln City FC (Lincoln)	46	21	15	10	79	48	57	
6.	Cambridge United FC (Cambridge)	46	20	14	12	62	44	54	
7.	Reading FC (Reading)	46	21	10	15	63	47	52	
8.	Brentford FC (London)	46	18	13	15	53	45	49	
9.	Exeter City FC (Exeter)	46	19	11	16	60	63	49	
10.	Bradford City AFC (Bradford)	46	17	13	16	56	51	47	
11.	Southport FC (Southport)	46	15	17	14	56	56	47	
12.	Newport County AFC (Newport)	46	19	9	18	68	75	47	
13.	Hartlepool FC (Hartlepool)	46	16	11	19	52	62	43	
14.	Torquay United FC (Torquay)	46	14	14	18	46	61	42	
15.	Barnsley FC (Barnsley)	46	15	11	20	62	65	41	
16.	Northampton Town FC (Northampton)	46	15	11	20	67	73	41	
17.	Doncaster Rovers FC (Doncaster)	46	14	12	20	65	79	40	
18.	Crewe Alexandra FC (Crewe)	46	11	18	17	34	47	40	
19.	Rochdale AFC (Rochdale)	46	13	13	20	59	75	39	
20.	Stockport County FC (Stockport)	46	12	14	20	43	70	38	
21.	Darlington FC (Darlington)	46	13	10	23	54	67	36	
22.	Swansea City FC (Swansea)	46	15	6	25	46	73	36	
23.	Workington AFC (Workington)	46	10	11	25	36	66	31	
24.	Scunthorpe United FC (Scunthorpe)	46	7	15	24	41	78	29	
		1104	404	296	404	1407	1407	1104	

F.A. CUP FINAL   (Wembley Stadium, London – 02/05/1975 – 100,000)

WEST HAM UNITED FC (LONDON)   2-0   Fulham FC (London)

A.Taylor 2

West Ham: Day, McDowell, Lampard, T.Taylor, Lock, Bonds, Paddon, Brooking, A.Taylor, Jennings, Holland.

Fulham: Mellor, Cutbush, Fraser, Lacy, Moore, Mullery, Conway, Slough, Mitchell, Busby, Barrett.

Semi-finals

Birmingham City FC (Birmingham)	1-1, 0-1	Fulham FC (London)
West Ham United FC (London)	0-0, 2-1	Ipswich Town FC (Ipswich)

Quarter-finals

Arsenal FC (London)	0-2	West Ham United FC (London)
Birmingham City FC (Birmingham)	1-0	Middlesbrough FC (Middlesbrough)
Carlisle United FC (Carlisle)	0-1	Fulham FC (London)
Ipswich Town FC (Ipswich)	0-0, 1-1, 0-0, 3-2	Leeds United AFC (Leeds)

Football League Division 1 1975-76 Season	Arsenal	Aston Villa	Birmingham City	Burnley	Coventry City	Derby County	Everton	Ipswich Town	Leeds United	Leicester City	Liverpool	Manchester City	Manchester United	Middlesbrough	Newcastle United	Norwich City	Q.P.R.	Sheffield United	Stoke City	Tottenham Hotspur	West Ham United	Wolves
Arsenal FC	■	0-0	1-0	1-0	5-0	0-1	2-2	1-2	1-2	1-1	1-0	2-3	3-1	2-1	0-0	2-1	2-0	1-0	0-1	0-2	6-1	2-1
Aston Villa FC	2-0	■	2-1	1-1	1-0	1-0	3-1	0-0	1-2	1-1	0-0	1-0	2-1	2-1	1-1	3-2	0-2	5-1	0-0	1-1	4-1	1-1
Birmingham City FC	3-1	3-2	■	4-0	1-1	2-1	0-1	3-0	2-2	2-1	0-1	2-1	0-2	2-1	3-2	1-1	1-1	2-0	1-1	3-1	1-5	0-1
Burnley FC	0-0	2-2	1-0	■	1-3	1-2	1-1	0-1	0-1	1-0	0-0	0-0	0-1	4-1	0-1	4-4	1-0	3-1	0-1	1-2	2-0	1-5
Coventry City FC	1-1	1-1	3-2	1-2	■	1-1	1-2	0-0	0-1	0-2	0-0	2-0	1-1	0-1	1-1	1-0	1-1	1-0	0-3	2-2	2-0	3-1
Derby County FC	2-0	2-0	4-2	3-0	2-0	■	1-3	1-0	3-2	2-2	1-1	1-0	2-1	3-2	3-2	3-1	1-5	3-2	1-1	2-3	2-1	3-2
Everton FC	0-0	2-1	5-2	2-3	1-4	2-0	■	3-3	1-3	1-1	1-1	1-1	3-1	3-0	1-1	0-2	3-0	2-1	1-0	2-0	3-0	
Ipswich Town FC	2-0	3-0	4-2	0-0	1-1	2-6	1-0	■	2-1	1-1	2-0	2-1	3-0	0-3	0-3	2-0	1-1	1-1	1-1	1-2	4-0	3-0
Leeds United AFC	3-0	1-0	3-0	2-1	2-0	1-1	5-2	1-0	■	4-0	0-3	2-1	1-2	0-2	3-0	0-3	2-1	0-1	2-0	1-1	1-1	3-0
Leicester City FC	2-1	2-2	3-3	3-2	0-3	2-1	1-0	0-0	2-1	■	1-1	1-0	2-1	0-0	0-1	1-1	1-1	2-3	3-3	2-0		
Liverpool FC	2-2	3-0	3-1	2-0	1-1	1-1	1-0	3-3	2-0	1-0	■	1-0	0-2	2-0	1-3	2-0	1-0	5-3	3-2	2-2	2-0	
Manchester City FC	3-1	2-1	2-0	0-0	4-2	4-3	3-0	1-1	0-1	1-1	0-3	■	2-2	4-0	4-0	3-0	0-0	4-0	1-0	2-1	3-0	3-2
Manchester United FC	3-1	2-1	3-1	2-1	1-1	1-1	2-1	3-2	0-0	0-0	2-0		■	3-0	1-0	1-0	2-1	5-1	0-1	3-2	4-0	1-0
Middlesbrough FC	0-1	0-0	2-0	1-1	2-0	0-2	1-1	2-0	0-0	0-1	0-1	1-0	0-0	■	3-3	0-1	0-0	3-0	3-0	1-0	3-0	1-0
Newcastle United FC	2-0	3-2	4-0	0-1	4-0	4-3	5-0	1-1	2-3	3-0	1-2	2-1	3-4	1-1	■	5-2	1-2	1-1	2-2	2-1	2-1	5-1
Norwich City FC	3-1	5-3	1-0	3-1	0-3	0-0	4-2	1-1	1-1	2-0	0-1	2-2	1-1	0-1	1-2	■	3-2	1-3	0-1	3-1	1-0	1-1
Queen's Park Rangers FC	2-1	1-1	2-1	1-0	4-1	1-1	5-0	3-1	1-0	2-0	1-0	1-0	1-0	4-2	1-0	2-0	■	1-0	3-2	0-0	1-1	4-2
Sheffield United FC	1-3	2-1	1-1	2-1	0-1	1-1	0-0	1-2	0-2	1-2	0-0	2-2	1-4	1-1	0-1	0-1	0-0	■	0-2	1-2	3-2	1-4
Stoke City FC	2-1	1-1	1-0	4-1	1-0	0-0	3-2	1-0	3-1	1-1	1-0	0-0	1-1	0-1	1-0	1-1	0-2	0-1	■	2-1	1-2	2-2
Tottenham Hotspur FC	0-0	5-2	1-3	2-1	4-1	2-3	2-2	1-1	0-0	1-1	0-4	2-2	1-1	1-0	0-3	2-2	0-3	5-0	1-1	■	1-1	2-1
West Ham United FC	1-0	2-2	1-2	3-2	1-1	1-2	0-1	1-2	1-1	1-1	0-4	1-0	2-1	2-1	2-1	0-1	1-0	2-0	3-1	1-0	■	0-0
Wolverhampton Wanderers FC	0-0	0-0	2-0	3-2	0-1	0-0	1-2	1-0	1-1	2-2	1-3	0-4	0-2	1-2	5-0	1-0	2-2	5-1	2-1	0-1	0-1	■

	Division 1	Pd	Wn	Dw	Ls	GF	GA	Pts	
1.	LIVERPOOL FC (LIVERPOOL)	42	23	14	5	66	31	60	
2.	Queen's Park Rangers FC (London)	42	24	11	7	67	33	59	
3.	Manchester United FC (Manchester)	42	23	10	9	68	42	56	
4.	Derby County FC (Derby)	42	21	11	10	75	58	53	
5.	Leeds United AFC (Leeds)	42	21	9	12	65	46	51	
6.	Ipswich Town FC (Ipswich)	42	16	14	12	54	48	46	
7.	Leicester City FC (Leicester)	42	13	19	10	48	51	45	
8.	Manchester City FC (Manchester)	42	16	11	15	64	46	43	
9.	Tottenham Hotspur FC (London)	42	14	15	13	63	63	43	
10.	Norwich City FC (Norwich)	42	16	10	16	58	58	42	
11.	Everton FC (Liverpool)	42	15	12	15	60	66	42	
12.	Stoke City FC (Stoke-on-Trent)	42	15	11	16	48	50	41	
13.	Middlesbrough FC (Middlesbrough)	42	15	10	17	46	45	40	
14.	Coventry City FC (Coventry)	42	13	14	15	47	57	40	
15.	Newcastle United FC (Newcastle-upon-Tyne)	42	15	9	18	71	62	39	
16.	Aston Villa FC (Birmingham)	42	11	17	14	51	59	39	
17.	Arsenal FC (London)	42	13	10	19	47	53	36	
18.	West Ham United FC (London)	42	13	10	19	48	71	36	
19.	Birmingham City FC (Birmingham)	42	13	7	22	57	75	33	
20.	Wolverhampton Wanderers FC (Wolverhampton)	42	10	10	22	51	68	30	R
21.	Burnley FC (Burnley)	42	9	10	23	43	66	28	R
22.	Sheffield United FC (Sheffield)	42	6	10	26	33	82	22	R
		924	335	254	335	1230	1230	924	

Top Goalscorer

1) Ted MacDOUGALL   (Norwich City FC)   23

Football League — Division 2 — 1975-76 Season

	Blackburn Rovers	Blackpool	Bolton Wanderers	Bristol City	Bristol Rovers	Carlisle United	Charlton Athletic	Chelsea	Fulham	Hull City	Luton Town	Nottingham Forest	Notts County	Oldham Athletic	Orient	Oxford United	Plymouth Argyle	Portsmouth	Southampton	Sunderland	W.B.A.	York City
Blackburn Rovers FC	■	0-2	1-1	1-2	1-2	1-0	2-0	1-1	0-1	1-0	3-0	1-4	2-1	4-1	1-1	0-0	3-1	0-3	1-1	0-1	0-0	4-0
Blackpool FC	1-1	■	1-1	2-1	1-4	2-1	2-1	0-2	1-1	2-2	3-2	1-1	1-0	1-1	1-0	2-0	0-0	0-0	4-3	1-0	0-1	0-0
Bolton Wanderers FC	0-1	1-0	■	1-0	3-1	0-0	5-0	2-1	2-2	1-0	3-0	0-0	2-1	4-0	1-1	0-1	0-0	4-1	3-0	2-1	1-2	1-2
Bristol City FC	1-0	2-0	1-0	■	1-1	0-0	4-0	2-2	0-0	3-0	3-0	0-2	1-2	1-0	0-0	4-1	2-2	1-0	1-1	3-0	0-2	4-1
Bristol Rovers FC	1-1	1-1	2-2	0-0	■	0-1	0-0	1-2	1-0	0-1	0-1	4-2	0-0	1-0	1-1	0-1	0-0	2-0	2-0	1-0	1-1	2-1
Carlisle United FC	0-1	1-0	3-2	0-1	4-2	■	1-1	2-1	2-2	0-0	1-1	1-1	1-2	2-1	1-2	1-1	2-0	2-1	1-0	2-2	1-1	1-0
Charlton Athletic FC	2-1	1-1	0-4	2-2	3-0	4-2	■	1-1	3-2	1-0	1-5	2-2	1-2	3-1	1-1	2-0	1-3	4-1	1-2	2-1		3-2
Chelsea FC	3-1	2-0	0-1	1-1	0-0	3-1	2-3	■	0-0	0-0	2-2	2-0	0-3	0-2	3-1	2-2	2-0	1-1	1-1	1-2		0-0
Fulham FC	1-1	0-0	1-2	1-2	0-2	3-0	1-1	2-0	■	1-1	2-0	0-0	3-2	1-0	1-1	1-1	0-0	0-1	1-0	2-0	4-0	2-0
Hull City AFC	0-1	1-0	2-2	3-1	0-0	2-3	2-2	1-2	1-2	■	1-2	1-0	0-2	3-0	1-0	2-0	4-0	1-0	0-0	1-4	2-1	1-1
Luton Town FC	1-1	3-0	0-2	0-0	3-1	3-0	1-1	3-0	1-0	2-0	■	1-1	1-1	2-3	1-0	3-2	1-1	3-1	1-0	2-0	2-1	4-0
Nottingham Forest FC	1-0	3-0	1-2	1-0	1-0	4-0	1-2	1-3	1-0	1-2	0-0	■	0-1	4-3	1-0	2-0	1-1	3-1	2-1	0-0	2-1	1-0
Notts County FC	3-0	1-2	1-1	1-1	1-1	1-0	2-0	3-2	4-0	1-2	1-0	0-0	■	5-1	2-0	0-1	2-0	0-0	0-0	0-2		4-0
Oldham Athletic AFC	2-1	1-0	2-1	2-4	2-0	2-2	2-0	2-1	2-2	1-0	1-1	0-0	2-2	■	1-1	1-1	3-2	5-2	3-2	1-1	0-1	2-0
Orient FC	1-1	0-1	0-0	0-1	0-0	1-0	0-1	3-1	2-0	1-0	3-0	1-1	1-1	2-0	■	2-1	1-0	2-1	0-2	0-0	0-0	1-0
Oxford United FC	0-0	1-3	2-0	1-1	2-1	0-0	1-0	1-1	1-3	2-3	1-3	0-1	2-1	1-1	2-1	■	2-2	1-0	1-2	1-1	0-1	1-0
Plymouth Argyle FC	2-2	1-2	2-3	0-0	3-0	2-1	0-4	3-0	4-0	1-1	3-0	1-0	1-3	2-1	3-0	2-1	■	3-1	1-0	1-0	1-1	1-1
Portsmouth FC	0-1	2-0	0-1	0-1	1-2	1-0	2-2	1-1	0-1	1-1	0-2	1-1	1-3	1-1	2-1	0-2	2-0	■	0-1	0-0	0-1	0-1
Southampton FC	2-1	3-1	0-0	3-1	3-0	1-1	3-2	4-1	2-1	1-0	3-1	0-3	2-1	3-2	3-0	1-0	4-0		■	4-0	3-0	2-0
Sunderland AFC	3-0	2-0	2-1	1-1	1-1	3-2	4-1	2-1	1-1	3-1	2-0	3-0	4-0	2-0	3-1	1-0	2-1	2-0	3-0	■		2-0
West Bromwich Albion FC	2-2	0-0	2-0	0-1	3-0	1-1	0-0	3-1	1-0	2-0	0-0	1-1	1-1	2-0	1-0	3-1	0-2	0-0			■	2-2
York City FC	2-1	1-1	1-2	1-4	0-0	1-2	1-3	2-2	1-0	1-2	2-3	3-2	1-2	1-0	0-2	2-0	3-1	2-1	2-1	1-4	0-1	■

Division 2	Pd	Wn	Dw	Ls	GF	GA	Pts	
1. Sunderland AFC (Sunderland)	42	24	8	10	67	36	56	P
2. Bristol City FC (Bristol)	42	19	15	8	59	35	53	P
3. West Bromwich Albion FC (West Bromwich)	42	20	13	9	50	33	53	P
4. Bolton Wanderers FC (Bolton)	42	20	12	10	64	38	52	
5. Notts County FC (Nottingham)	42	19	11	12	60	41	49	
6. Southampton FC (Southampton)	42	21	7	14	66	50	49	
7. Luton Town FC (Luton)	42	19	10	13	61	51	48	
8. Nottingham Forest FC (Nottingham)	42	17	12	13	55	40	46	
9. Charlton Athletic FC (London)	42	15	12	15	61	72	42	
10. Blackpool FC (Blackpool)	42	14	14	14	40	49	42	
11. Chelsea FC (London)	42	12	16	14	53	54	40	
12. Fulham FC (London)	42	13	14	15	45	47	40	
13. Orient FC (London)	42	13	14	15	37	39	40	
14. Hull City AFC (Kingston-upon-Hull)	42	14	11	17	45	49	39	
15. Blackburn Rovers FC (Blackburn)	42	12	14	16	45	50	38	
16. Plymouth Argyle FC (Plymouth)	42	13	12	17	48	54	38	
17. Oldham Athletic AFC (Oldham)	42	13	12	17	57	68	38	
18. Bristol Rovers FC (Bristol)	42	11	16	15	38	50	38	
19. Carlisle United FC (Carlisle)	42	12	13	17	45	59	37	
20. Oxford United FC (Oxford)	42	11	11	20	39	59	33	R
21. York City FC (York)	42	10	8	24	39	71	28	R
22. Portsmouth FC (Portsmouth)	42	9	7	26	32	61	25	R
	924	331	262	331	1106	1106	924	

Football League Division 3 1975-76 Season	Aldershot Town	Brighton & H.A.	Bury	Cardiff City	Chester	Chesterfield	Colchester United	Crystal Palace	Gillingham	Grimsby Town	Halifax Town	Hereford United	Mansfield Town	Millwall	Peterborough Utd.	Port Vale	Preston North End	Rotherham United	Sheffield Wed.	Shrewsbury Town	Southend United	Swindon Town	Walsall	Wrexham
Aldershot Town AFC		1-1	1-1	2-1	1-1	3-1	2-2	1-0	3-0	0-3	1-2	0-2	2-1	1-1	1-0	2-0	1-1	3-0	1-1	1-1	2-1	0-1	3-2	2-3
Brighton & Hove Alb.	4-1		2-1	0-1	6-0	3-0	6-0	2-0	1-1	4-2	1-0	4-2	1-0	1-0	5-0	3-0	1-0	3-0	1-1	2-2	2-0	2-0	1-2	3-2
Bury FC	1-1	1-1		0-1	1-0	3-1	0-0	0-1	2-0	1-1	0-0	2-3	2-1	2-0	2-1	1-2	2-0	4-0	0-0	2-1	1-0	5-0	1-1	0-1
Cardiff City AFC	1-0	0-1	1-1		2-0	4-3	2-0	0-1	4-1	2-1	0-0	2-0	1-0	0-0	5-2	1-1	1-0	1-1	2-0	3-0	3-1	0-0	0-0	3-0
Chester FC	1-0	3-0	0-0	1-1		2-1	1-0	2-1	2-2	1-2	2-1	0-1	1-1	3-1	1-1	1-0	3-0	3-1	1-0	1-0	1-1	2-1	1-1	1-3
Chesterfield FC	5-2	2-1	3-2	1-1	1-1		6-1	1-2	0-1	4-3	1-2	2-3	1-2	2-2	1-1	0-1	3-0	1-0	1-0	2-1	1-2	4-0	2-1	1-1
Colchester United FC	2-0	2-0	0-0	3-2	1-0	2-3		0-3	2-2	1-0	0-1	1-4	0-2	0-1	1-1	1-0	1-1	0-0	2-1	1-1	2-1	1-2	2-0	0-2
Crystal Palace FC	0-0	0-1	1-0	0-1	2-0	0-0	3-2		0-1	3-0	1-1	2-2	4-1	0-0	1-1	2-2	2-0	1-1	1-1	1-1	3-3	0-1	1-1	1-1
Gillingham FC	1-1	1-0	2-0	2-2	2-0	2-2	0-1	1-2		3-0	1-1	3-4	3-1	3-1	2-2	2-1	1-0	0-0	0-0	2-1	1-2	3-2	2-3	1-1
Grimsby Town FC	1-0	2-1	0-0	2-0	2-0	3-0	0-1	1-2	2-1		2-2	1-0	4-1	2-1	1-1	1-1	0-0	4-1	1-1	3-2	2-2	1-0	1-2	3-2
Halifax Town AFC	1-3	1-3	0-2	1-1	5-2	1-0	1-1	1-3	1-1	2-1		0-1	1-2	1-2	0-1	1-3	2-1	0-1	0-0	0-0	1-0	0-2	2-1	0-1
Hereford United FC	2-1	1-1	2-0	4-1	5-0	4-2	0-0	1-1	1-1	3-2	1-2		1-0	0-0	2-4	0-0	3-1	3-2	3-1	3-1	2-1	1-0	1-3	2-0
Mansfield Town FC	1-0	1-0	1-1	1-4	1-1	0-1	0-0	1-1	1-1	1-0	1-1	2-2		1-1	1-1	3-1	0-1	1-1	3-1	1-2	3-1	3-1	4-1	0-0
Millwall FC	4-1	3-1	0-0	1-3	1-0	2-0	1-1	2-1	2-2	1-1	1-0	1-0	1-0		2-0	1-0	2-0	3-1	1-0	0-0	2-1	0-0	2-1	2-1
Peterborough United	1-1	1-0	4-0	0-0	3-0	0-1	3-1	2-0	1-1	4-2	1-0	0-3	0-3	1-1		0-0	2-0	1-3	2-2	3-2	3-2	3-1	0-0	2-0
Port Vale FC	0-1	1-1	2-1	2-1	0-1	1-1	3-2	0-0	1-1	4-3	1-1	1-1	2-2	2-0	2-0		1-1	1-0	1-0	0-0	1-1	3-0	1-2	3-1
Preston North End	1-0	1-0	0-0	3-1	1-0	3-1	2-1	0-0	4-0	0-0	2-1	3-4	0-2	2-1	2-1	3-0		3-2	4-2	0-2	5-1	4-2	3-1	0-1
Rotherham United	2-2	1-1	3-3	1-0	0-1	2-0	2-0	4-1	2-0	3-0	0-1	1-1	2-1	1-2	1-1	1-2	1-1		1-0	0-1	2-0	0-2	3-1	2-1
Sheffield Wednesday	3-1	3-3	1-0	1-3	2-0	1-3	1-0	1-0	1-0	4-0	1-1	1-2	0-0	4-1	2-2	0-3	2-2	0-0		1-1	2-1	0-2	2-1	1-0
Shrewsbury Town	5-3	1-2	1-3	3-1	2-0	0-2	1-0	2-4	1-0	1-0	2-0	2-1	1-2	1-0	3-1	1-0	1-0	0-2	0-0		2-1	3-0	1-1	1-2
Southend United FC	0-2	4-0	2-0	0-2	2-0	1-1	2-0	1-2	2-2	5-1	4-1	1-3	2-2	0-0	0-0	3-3	0-2	1-2	2-1	1-3		3-0	2-2	2-1
Swindon Town FC	6-3	3-2	2-1	4-0	2-1	0-1	0-1	1-2	2-2	3-0	3-1	0-1	0-2	0-2	2-1	1-3	1-1	2-1	3-0	0-0	3-0		5-1	2-2
Walsall FC	4-1	2-0	0-1	2-3	1-0	1-0	1-1	1-1	4-0	2-0	2-0	0-0	0-1	1-1	2-2	3-1	3-1	5-1	2-2	2-0	2-3	1-1		2-2
Wrexham AFC	3-1	3-0	2-1	1-1	1-1	1-0	1-1	1-3	2-0	1-0	1-1	2-1	1-0	1-1	3-0	1-0	1-2	3-0	3-0	2-3	2-2	2-0	0-3	

Division 3

		Pd	Wn	Dw	Ls	GF	GA	Pts	
1.	Hereford United FC (Hereford)	46	26	11	9	86	55	63	P
2.	Cardiff City AFC (Cardiff)	46	22	13	11	69	48	57	P
3.	Millwall FC (London)	46	20	16	10	54	43	56	P
4.	Brighton & Hove Albion FC (Hove)	46	22	9	15	78	53	53	
5.	Crystal Palace FC (London)	46	18	17	11	61	46	53	
6.	Wrexham AFC (Wrexham)	46	20	12	14	66	55	52	
7.	Walsall FC (Walsall)	46	18	14	14	74	61	50	
8.	Preston North End FC (Preston)	46	19	10	17	62	57	48	
9.	Shrewsbury Town FC (Shrewsbury)	46	19	10	17	61	59	48	
10.	Peterborough United FC (Peterborough)	46	15	18	13	63	63	48	
11.	Mansfield Town FC (Mansfield)	46	16	15	15	58	52	47	
12.	Port Vale FC (Stoke-on-Trent)	46	15	16	15	55	54	46	
13.	Bury FC (Bury)	46	14	16	16	51	46	44	
14.	Chesterfield FC (Chesterfield)	46	17	9	20	69	69	43	
15.	Gillingham FC (Gillingham)	46	12	19	15	58	68	43	
16.	Rotherham United FC (Rotherham)	46	15	12	19	54	65	42	
17.	Chester FC (Chester)	46	15	12	19	43	62	42	
18.	Grimsby Town FC (Cleethorpes)	46	15	10	21	62	74	40	
19.	Swindon Town FC (Swindon)	46	16	8	22	62	75	40	
20.	Sheffield Wednesday FC (Sheffield)	46	12	16	18	48	59	40	
21.	Aldershot FC (Aldershot)	46	13	13	20	59	75	39	R
22.	Colchester United FC (Colchester)	46	12	14	20	41	65	38	R
23.	Southend United FC (Southend-on-Sea)	46	12	13	21	65	75	37	R
24.	Halifax Town AFC (Halifax)	46	11	13	22	41	61	35	R
		1104	394	316	394	1440	1440	1104	

Football League Division 4 — 1975-76 Season

	Barnsley	Bournemouth	Bradford City	Brentford	Cambridge United	Crewe Alexandra	Darlington	Doncaster Rovers	Exeter City	Hartlepool	Huddersfield Town	Lincoln City	Newport County	Northampton Town	Reading	Rochdale	Scunthorpe United	Southport	Stockport County	Swansea City	Torquay United	Tranmere Rovers	Watford	Workington
Barnsley FC		2-0	1-1	1-1	4-0	1-1	1-0	0-1	0-0	3-1	2-3	0-1	3-1	3-1	4-2	2-1	1-0	2-0	2-2	0-0	0-0	1-0	1-0	0-0
AFC Bournemouth	1-1		2-1	3-0	3-0	1-0	1-2	0-1	1-0	4-2	1-0	1-1	2-0	0-0	0-1	2-1	1-0	3-3	2-0	2-0	0-0	4-2	4-1	1-0
Bradford City AFC	2-1	0-1		1-1	1-2	4-1	2-0	3-4	0-0	1-2	2-2	1-5	3-0	1-2	1-1	3-0	0-0	1-1	1-2	0-0	3-1	3-0	1-0	1-0
Brentford FC	1-0	1-2	2-2		0-0	0-0	3-0	0-1	5-1	1-1	0-0	1-0	1-3	2-1	2-2	3-0	5-2	1-0	2-1	1-0	1-1	0-1	1-0	4-0
Cambridge United FC	1-1	0-1	0-0	2-1		1-1	1-0	3-3	0-1	4-0	0-0	2-4	0-1	0-1	2-2	0-0	2-2	2-2	0-1	3-1	2-1	3-3	4-1	4-1
Crewe Alexandra FC	1-1	1-0	1-3	1-0	1-2		2-0	1-2	0-0	0-0	0-2	2-3	4-0	0-1	3-3	0-0	1-0	4-0	3-1	2-1	6-0	1-0	2-2	1-0
Darlington FC	2-0	2-0	2-2	2-0	1-1	0-0		2-2	0-0	1-2	0-3	0-0	4-0	0-0	1-1	4-0	2-0	0-1	1-1	1-1	2-0	1-0	1-0	1-0
Doncaster Rovers FC	2-2	1-1	1-1	1-1	0-2	3-1	3-2		0-0	3-0	4-1	2-4	5-1	0-4	1-1	1-2	0-1	5-2	3-1	2-1	0-1	3-0	1-2	1-0
Exeter City FC	2-0	1-0	0-0	0-0	1-2	2-2	1-1	1-0		3-1	4-1	0-0	3-0	0-0	4-1	1-0	5-4	2-0	2-0	3-0	0-0	0-2	1-3	1-0
Hartlepool FC	1-0	1-1	2-2	1-0	2-2	1-3	2-3	2-1	2-1		1-1	2-2	4-1	3-0	2-4	3-0	1-2	0-0	1-0	1-0	0-1	1-2	2-1	0-2
Huddersfield Town	1-2	0-0	0-0	2-1	2-0	1-0	1-0	1-2	0-1	2-0		0-1	2-1	1-1	3-0	1-0	1-1	2-2	2-0	2-3	1-0	1-0	1-0	2-0
Lincoln City FC	2-1	1-0	4-2	3-1	3-0	2-0	2-1	5-0	4-1	3-0	0-0		4-1	3-1	3-1	2-0	3-0	6-0	2-0	4-0	4-2	2-2	5-1	4-1
Newport County AFC	1-0	3-1	3-1	1-0	2-0	2-2	4-1	2-3	3-3	0-1	1-2	3-1		1-1	0-0	1-1	2-0	2-2	1-2	0-2	1-5	0-2	1-1	2-3
Northampton Town	5-0	6-0	4-3	4-2	4-2	2-1	3-2	2-1	3-1	5-2	1-1	1-0	3-0		4-1	1-1	2-1	4-0	0-0	2-2	1-1	3-0	2-1	3-0
Reading FC	0-0	2-1	2-1	1-0	2-0	3-1	4-1	0-1	4-3	1-0	2-0	1-1	1-0	1-0		2-0	1-0	5-0	1-0	5-0	3-0	1-0	1-0	3-0
Rochdale AFC	0-0	2-2	0-0	1-2	1-1	0-1	1-0	1-0	0-1	1-1	0-0	0-0	4-3	0-2	0-0		1-1	1-2	2-3	2-1	2-2	4-1	2-1	1-1
Scunthorpe United	1-0	2-0	2-0	2-1	0-1	1-0	2-1	2-1	0-1	5-1	0-1	0-2	1-2	0-2	2-1	1-3		1-2	0-0	1-1	3-1	2-2	0-1	3-0
Southport FC	0-0	0-2	1-2	2-0	2-4	2-2	2-0	1-1	1-0	2-4	1-2	1-2	3-0	0-1	1-2	0-1	1-1		2-0	1-1	1-3	0-0	1-2	2-1
Stockport County FC	1-1	0-0	2-1	2-0	0-1	0-1	0-0	1-2	2-1	2-0	0-1	0-3	1-1	0-1	0-0	1-0	1-3	2-0		3-2	1-0	0-2	2-2	4-1
Swansea City FC	3-1	1-1	3-1	2-2	1-0	4-0	2-0	0-3	3-1	1-2	2-2	1-1	5-1	1-1	2-0	2-0	5-0	2-0	2-0		3-0	1-1	4-2	1-0
Torquay United FC	2-0	2-1	1-0	2-3	0-0	2-1	2-4	2-2	1-0	1-1	1-3	2-2	1-1	0-1	0-0	1-0	1-0	2-1	4-1	0-2		2-1	1-0	1-0
Tranmere Rovers FC	1-0	2-0	3-3	5-1	3-2	2-1	2-0	2-2	1-1	1-2	3-0	2-0	3-1	2-0	0-1	2-1	1-0	5-0	3-0	7-1	5-0		3-0	6-0
Watford FC	1-0	1-1	3-0	3-2	1-0	2-1	2-0	2-1	2-0	2-1	0-2	1-3	3-1	0-1	2-1	3-0	1-0	2-0	1-1	2-1	0-0	2-2		2-0
Workington AFC	1-7	1-3	0-3	1-1	1-0	0-3	0-0	3-1	1-0	1-2	0-2	0-3	1-2	1-0	0-2	0-0	2-3	2-1	1-2	1-1	1-3	0-1	1-3	

	Division 4	Pd	Wn	Dw	Ls	GF	GA	Pts	
1.	Lincoln City FC (Lincoln)	46	32	10	4	111	39	74	P
2.	Northampton Town FC (Northampton)	46	29	10	7	87	40	68	P
3.	Reading FC (Reading)	46	24	12	10	70	51	60	P
4.	Tranmere Rovers FC (Birkenhead)	46	24	10	12	89	55	58	P
5.	Huddersfield Town AFC (Huddersfield)	46	21	14	11	56	41	56	
6.	AFC Bournemouth (Bournemouth)	46	20	12	14	57	48	52	
7.	Exeter City FC (Exeter)	46	18	14	14	56	47	50	
8.	Watford FC (Watford)	46	22	6	18	62	62	50	
9.	Torquay United FC (Torquay)	46	18	14	14	55	63	50	
10.	Doncaster Rovers FC (Doncaster)	46	19	11	16	75	69	49	
11.	Swansea City FC (Swansea)	46	16	15	15	66	57	47	
12.	Barnsley FC (Barnsley)	46	14	16	16	52	48	44	
13.	Cambridge United FC (Cambridge)	46	14	15	17	58	62	43	
14.	Hartlepool FC (Hartlepool)	46	16	10	20	62	78	42	
15.	Rochdale AFC (Rochdale)	46	12	18	16	40	54	42	
16.	Crewe Alexandra FC (Crewe)	46	13	15	18	58	57	41	
17.	Bradford City AFC (Bradford)	46	12	17	17	63	65	41	
18.	Brentford FC (London)	46	14	13	19	56	60	41	
19.	Scunthorpe United FC (Scunthorpe)	46	14	10	22	50	59	38	
20.	Darlington FC (Darlington)	46	14	10	22	48	57	38	
21.	Stockport County FC (Stockport)	46	13	12	21	43	76	38	
22.	Newport County AFC (Newport)	46	13	9	24	57	90	35	
23.	Southport FC (Southport)	46	8	10	28	41	77	26	
24.	Workington AFC (Workington)	46	7	7	32	30	87	21	
		1104	407	290	407	1442	1442	1104	

F.A. CUP FINAL   (Wembley Stadium, London – 01/05/1976 – 100,000)

SOUTHAMPTON FC (SOUTHAMPTON)   1-0   Manchester United FC (Manchester)

Stokes

Southampton: Turner, Rodrigues, Blyth, Steele, Peach, Holmes, Gilchrist, McCalliog, Channon, Osgood, Stokes.
Man. United: Stepney, Forsyth, Greenhoff, Buchan, Houston, Daly, Macari, Coppell, McIlroy, Pearson, Hill
(McCreery).

Semi-finals

Derby County FC (Derby)	0-2	Manchester United FC (Manchester)
Southampton FC (Southampton)	2-0	Crystal Palace FC (London)

Quarter-finals

Bradford City AFC (Bradford)	0-1	Southampton FC (Southampton)
Derby County FC (Derby)	4-2	Newcastle United FC (Newcastle-upon-Tyne)
Manchester United FC (Manchester)	1-1, 3-2	Wolverhampton Wanderers FC (Wolverhampton)
Sunderland AFC (Sunderland)	0-1	Crystal Palace FC (London)

1976-77

Football League Division 1 1976-77 Season	Arsenal	Aston Villa	Birmingham City	Bristol City	Coventry City	Derby County	Everton	Ipswich Town	Leeds United	Leicester City	Liverpool	Man. City	Man. United	Middlesbrough	Newcastle United	Norwich City	Q.P.R.	Stoke City	Sunderland	Tottenham H.	W.B.A.	West Ham United
Arsenal FC	■	3-0	4-0	0-1	2-0	0-0	3-1	1-4	1-1	3-0	1-1	0-0	3-1	1-1	5-3	1-0	3-2	2-0	0-0	1-0	1-2	2-3
Aston Villa FC	5-1	■	1-2	3-1	2-2	4-0	2-0	5-2	2-1	2-0	5-1	1-1	3-2	1-0	2-1	1-0	1-1	1-0	4-1	2-1	4-0	4-0
Birmingham City FC	3-3	2-1	■	3-0	3-1	5-1	1-1	2-4	0-0	1-1	2-1	0-0	2-3	3-1	1-2	3-2	2-1	2-0	2-0	1-2	0-1	0-0
Bristol City FC	2-0	0-0	0-1	■	0-0	2-2	1-2	1-2	1-0	0-1	2-1	1-0	1-1	1-2	1-1	3-1	1-0	1-1	4-1	1-0	1-2	1-1
Coventry City FC	1-2	2-3	2-1	2-2	■	2-0	4-2	1-1	4-2	1-1	0-0	0-1	0-2	1-1	1-1	2-0	2-0	5-2	1-2	1-1	1-1	1-1
Derby County FC	0-0	2-1	0-0	2-0	1-1	■	2-3	0-0	0-1	1-0	2-3	4-0	0-0	0-0	4-2	2-2	2-0	2-0	1-0	8-2	2-2	1-1
Everton FC	2-1	0-2	2-2	2-0	1-1	2-0	■	1-1	0-2	1-2	0-0	2-2	1-2	2-2	2-0	3-1	1-3	3-0	2-0	4-0	1-1	3-2
Ipswich Town FC	3-1	1-0	1-0	1-0	2-1	0-0	2-0	■	1-1	0-0	1-0	1-0	2-1	0-1	2-0	5-0	2-2	0-1	3-1	3-1	7-0	4-1
Leeds United AFC	2-1	1-3	1-0	2-0	1-2	2-0	0-0	2-1	■	2-2	1-1	0-2	0-2	2-1	2-2	3-2	0-1	1-1	1-1	2-1	2-2	1-1
Leicester City FC	4-1	1-1	2-6	0-0	3-1	1-1	1-1	1-0	0-1	■	0-1	2-2	1-1	3-3	1-0	1-1	2-2	1-0	2-0	1-0	0-5	2-0
Liverpool FC	2-0	3-0	4-1	2-1	3-1	3-1	3-1	2-1	3-1	5-1	■	2-1	1-0	1-0	1-0	3-1	1-0	2-0	2-0	1-1		0-0
Manchester City FC	1-0	3-0	4-1	2-1	2-0	3-2	1-1	2-1	2-1	5-0	1-1	■	1-3	1-0	0-0	2-0	0-0	0-0	1-0	5-0	1-1	4-2
Manchester United FC	3-2	2-0	2-2	2-1	2-0	3-1	4-0	0-1	1-0	1-1	0-0	3-1	■	2-0	3-1	2-2	1-0	3-0	3-3	2-3	2-2	0-2
Middlesbrough FC	3-0	3-2	2-2	0-0	1-0	2-0	2-2	0-2	1-0	0-1	0-0	3-0		■	1-0	0-2	0-0	0-0	2-1	1-0	1-0	1-1
Newcastle United FC	0-2	3-2	3-2	0-0	1-0	2-2	4-1	1-1	3-0	0-0	1-0	2-2	2-2	1-0	■	5-1	2-0	1-0	2-2	2-0	2-0	3-0
Norwich City FC	1-3	1-1	1-0	2-1	3-0	0-0	2-1	0-1	1-1	3-2	2-1	0-0	2-1	1-0	3-2	■	2-0	1-1	2-2	1-3	1-0	1-0
Queen's Park Rangers FC	2-1	2-1	2-2	0-1	1-1	1-1	0-4	1-0	0-0	3-2	1-1	0-0	4-0	3-0	1-2	2-3	■	2-0	2-0	2-1	1-0	1-1
Stoke City FC	1-1	1-0	1-0	2-2	2-0	1-0	0-1	2-1	2-1	0-1	0-0	0-2	3-3	3-1	0-0	0-0	1-0	■	0-0	0-0	0-2	2-1
Sunderland AFC	2-2	0-1	1-0	1-0	1-1	1-1	0-1	0-1	0-0	2-0	0-2	2-1	4-0	2-2	0-1	1-0	0-0		■	2-1	6-1	6-0
Tottenham Hotspur FC	2-2	3-1	1-0	0-1	0-1	0-0	3-3	1-0	1-1	2-0	2-1	1-3	0-2	1-3	0-0	0-2	1-0	2-0	1-1	■	0-2	2-1
West Bromwich Albion FC	0-2	1-1	2-1	1-1	1-1	1-0	3-0	4-0	1-2	2-2	0-1	0-2	4-0	2-1	1-1	2-0	1-1	3-1	2-3	4-2	■	3-0
West Ham United FC	0-2	0-1	2-2	2-0	2-0	2-2	2-2	0-2	1-3	0-0	2-0	1-0	4-2	0-1	1-2	1-0	1-0	1-0	1-1	5-3	0-0	■

	Division 1	Pd	Wn	Dw	Ls	GF	GA	Pts	
1.	LIVERPOOL FC (LIVERPOOL)	42	23	11	8	62	33	57	
2.	Manchester City FC (Manchester)	42	21	14	7	60	34	56	
3.	Ipswich Town FC (Ipswich)	42	22	8	12	66	39	52	
4.	Aston Villa FC (Birmingham)	42	22	7	13	76	50	51	
5.	Newcastle United FC (Newcastle-upon-Tyne)	42	18	13	11	64	49	49	
6.	Manchester United FC (Manchester)	42	18	11	13	71	62	47	
7.	West Bromwich Albion FC (West Bromwich)	42	16	13	13	62	56	45	
8.	Arsenal FC (London)	42	16	11	15	64	59	43	
9.	Everton FC (Liverpool)	42	14	14	14	62	64	42	
10.	Leeds United AFC (Leeds)	42	15	12	15	48	51	42	
11.	Leicester City FC (Leicester)	42	12	18	12	47	60	42	
12.	Middlesbrough FC (Middlesbrough)	42	14	13	15	40	45	41	
13.	Birmingham City FC (Birmingham)	42	13	12	17	63	61	38	
14.	Queen's Park Rangers FC (London)	42	13	12	17	47	52	38	
15.	Derby County FC (Derby)	42	9	19	14	50	55	37	
16.	Norwich City FC (Norwich)	42	14	9	19	47	64	37	
17.	West Ham United FC (London)	42	11	14	17	46	65	36	
18.	Bristol City FC (Bristol)	42	11	13	18	38	48	35	
19.	Coventry City FC (Coventry)	42	10	15	17	48	59	35	
20.	Sunderland AFC (Sunderland)	42	11	12	19	46	54	34	R
21.	Stoke City FC (Stoke-on-Trent)	42	10	14	18	28	51	34	R
22.	Tottenham Hotspur FC (London)	42	12	9	21	48	72	33	R
		924	325	274	325	1183	1183	924	

Top Goalscorers

1)	Andrew GRAY	(Aston Villa FC)	25
	Malcolm McDONALD	(Arsenal FC)	25

Football League Division 2 1976-77 Season	Blackburn Rovers	Blackpool	Bolton Wanderers	Bristol Rovers	Burnley	Cardiff City	Carlisle United	Charlton Athletic	Chelsea	Fulham	Hereford United	Hull City	Luton Town	Millwall	Nottingham Forest	Notts County	Oldham Athletic	Orient	Plymouth Argyle	Sheffield United	Southampton	Wolverhampton Wanderers
Blackburn Rovers FC	■	0-1	3-1	0-0	2-2	2-1	1-3	0-0	0-2	1-0	1-0	1-0	1-0	2-0	1-3	6-1	2-0	2-2	2-0	1-0	3-0	0-2
Blackpool FC	1-1	■	1-0	4-0	1-1	1-0	0-0	2-2	0-1	3-2	2-1	0-0	1-0	4-2	1-0	1-1	0-2	3-0	0-2	1-0	1-0	2-2
Bolton Wanderers FC	3-1	0-3	■	1-0	2-1	2-1	3-4	1-0	2-2	2-1	3-1	5-1	2-1	3-1	1-1	4-0	3-0	2-0	3-0	1-2	3-0	0-1
Bristol Rovers FC	0-0	1-4	2-2	■	1-1	1-1	2-1	1-1	2-1	2-1	2-3	3-0	1-0	0-0	1-1	5-1	0-0	1-0	1-1	3-1	2-3	1-5
Burnley FC	3-1	0-0	0-0	1-1	■	0-0	2-0	4-4	1-0	3-1	1-1	0-0	1-2	1-3	0-1	3-1	1-0	3-3	0-2	1-0	2-0	0-0
Cardiff City FC	2-1	2-2	3-2	1-2	0-1	■	1-1	1-1	1-3	3-0	3-1	1-1	4-2	0-0	0-3	2-3	3-1	0-1	0-1	0-2	1-0	2-2
Carlisle United FC	1-1	1-1	0-1	2-3	2-1	4-3	■	4-2	0-1	1-2	2-2	1-1	1-1	0-1	1-1	0-2	1-1	1-0	3-1	4-1	0-6	2-1
Charlton Athletic FC	4-0	1-2	1-1	4-3	5-2	0-2	1-0	■	4-0	1-1	1-1	3-1	4-3	3-2	2-1	1-1	2-1	2-0	3-1	3-2	6-2	1-1
Chelsea FC	3-1	2-2	2-1	2-0	2-1	2-1	2-1	2-1	■	2-0	5-1	4-0	2-0	1-1	2-1	1-1	4-3	1-1	2-2	4-0	3-1	3-3
Fulham FC	2-0	0-0	0-2	1-0	2-2	1-2	2-0	1-1	3-1	■	4-1	0-0	1-2	2-3	2-2	1-5	5-0	6-1	2-0	3-2	1-1	0-0
Hereford United FC	1-0	1-1	3-3	1-1	3-0	2-2	0-0	1-2	2-2	1-0	■	1-0	0-1	3-1	0-1	1-4	0-0	2-3	1-1	2-2	2-0	1-6
Hull City AFC	1-0	2-2	2-2	0-1	4-1	1-2	3-1	0-0	1-1	1-0	1-1	■	3-1	0-0	1-0	0-1	0-1	11-	3-1	1-1	4-0	2-0
Luton Town FC	2-0	0-0	1-1	4-2	2-0	2-1	5-0	2-0	4-0	0-2	2-0	2-1	■	1-2	1-1	4-2	1-0	0-0	1-1	2-0	1-4	2-0
Millwall FC	0-1	1-1	3-0	2-0	2-0	0-2	1-1	1-1	3-0	0-0	4-2	2-1	4-2	■	0-2	2-5	2-1	0-1	3-0	0-1	0-0	1-1
Nottingham Forest FC	3-0	3-0	3-1	4-2	5-2	0-1	5-1	1-1	1-1	3-0	4-3	2-0	1-2	1-0	■	1-2	3-0	3-0	1-1	6-1	2-1	1-3
Notts County FC	0-0	2-0	0-1	2-1	5-1	1-0	2-1	0-1	2-1	0-0	3-2	1-1	0-4	1-2	1-1	■	1-0	0-1	2-0	2-1	3-1	1-1
Oldham Athletic AFC	2-0	1-0	2-2	4-0	3-1	3-2	4-1	1-1	0-0	1-0	3-5	3-0	1-2	2-1	1-0	1-1	■	0-0	2-2	1-2	2-1	0-2
Orient FC	0-1	0-1	2-2	2-0	0-1	3-0	0-0	0-0	0-1	0-0	1-1	1-1	1-0	1-1	0-1	1-0	0-2	■	2-2	0-2	2-3	2-4
Plymouth Argyle FC	4-0	2-0	1-1	1-1	0-1	2-2	0-1	1-0	2-3	2-2	2-1	1-2	1-0	2-2	1-2	1-2	2-2	1-2	■	0-0	1-1	0-0
Sheffield United FC	1-1	1-5	2-3	2-3	1-0	3-0	3-0	3-0	1-0	1-1	1-1	1-1	0-3	1-1	2-0	1-0	2-1	1-1	1-0	■	2-2	2-2
Southampton FC	2-0	3-3	1-3	2-1	2-0	3-2	1-2	2-1	1-1	4-1	1-0	2-2	1-0	0-2	1-1	2-1	4-0	2-2	4-1	1-1	■	1-0
Wolverhampton Wanderers FC	1-2	2-1	1-0	1-0	0-0	4-1	4-0	3-0	1-1	5-1	2-1	2-1	1-2	3-1	2-1	2-2	5-0	1-0	4-0	2-1	2-6	■

	Division 2	Pd	Wn	Dw	Ls	GF	GA	Pts	
1.	Wolverhampton Wanderers FC (Wolverhampton)	42	22	13	7	84	45	57	P
2.	Chelsea FC (London)	42	21	13	8	73	53	55	P
3.	Nottingham Forest FC (Nottingham)	42	21	10	11	77	43	52	P
4.	Bolton Wanderers FC (Bolton)	42	20	11	11	75	54	51	
5.	Blackpool FC (Blackpool)	42	17	17	8	58	42	51	
6.	Luton Town FC (Luton)	42	21	6	15	67	48	48	
7.	Charlton Athletic FC (London)	42	16	16	10	71	58	48	
8.	Notts County FC (Nottingham)	42	19	10	13	65	60	48	
9.	Southampton FC (Southampton)	42	17	10	15	72	67	44	
10.	Millwall FC (London)	42	15	13	14	57	53	43	
11.	Sheffield United FC (Sheffield)	42	14	12	16	54	63	40	
12.	Blackburn Rovers FC (Blackburn)	42	15	9	18	42	54	39	
13.	Oldham Athletic AFC (Oldham)	42	14	10	18	52	64	38	
14.	Hull City AFC (Kingston-upon-Hull)	42	10	17	15	45	53	37	
15.	Bristol Rovers FC (Bristol)	42	12	13	17	53	68	37	
16.	Burnley FC (Burnley)	42	11	14	17	46	64	36	
17.	Fulham FC (London)	42	11	13	18	54	61	35	
18.	Cardiff City AFC (Cardiff)	42	12	10	20	56	67	34	
19.	Orient FC (London)	42	9	16	17	37	55	34	
20.	Carlisle United FC (Carlisle)	42	11	12	19	49	75	34	R
21.	Plymouth Argyle FC (Plymouth)	42	8	16	18	46	65	32	R
22.	Hereford United FC (Hereford)	42	8	15	19	57	78	31	R
		924	324	276	324	1290	1290	924	

Football League Division 3 — 1976-77 Season

	Brighton & H.A.	Bury	Chester	Chesterfield	Crystal Palace	Gillingham	Grimsby Town	Lincoln City	Mansfield Town	Northampton Town	Oxford United	Peterborough Utd.	Portsmouth	Port Vale	Preston North End	Reading	Rotherham United	Sheffield Wed.	Shrewsbury Town	Swindon Town	Tranmere Rovers	Walsall	Wrexham	York City
Brighton & Hove Alb.	■	1-1	3-0	2-1	1-1	2-0	3-0	4-0	3-1	2-0	3-2	1-0	4-0	1-0	2-0	2-0	3-1	3-2	4-0	4-0	1-1	7-0	0-2	7-2
Bury FC	3-0	■	2-0	3-1	0-1	3-1	2-0	3-0	2-0	1-1	2-1	4-1	1-0	3-0	3-2	1-0	1-1	1-3	0-1	0-1	2-1	0-2	0-2	4-2
Chester FC	0-1	1-0	■	1-2	2-1	1-0	2-0	1-0	1-0	2-1	1-3	2-1	1-1	1-1	0-0	3-1	1-3	1-0	1-2	2-1	1-0	1-0	1-2	1-0
Chesterfield FC	1-1	7-0	1-0	■	0-2	1-0	0-1	1-4	0-1	0-0	2-0	0-0	1-2	4-0	1-1	4-0	1-0	2-0	1-1	0-1	0-0	1-1	0-6	2-0
Crystal Palace FC	3-1	2-1	1-2	0-0	■	3-1	2-1	4-1	2-0	1-1	2-2	0-0	2-1	2-0	1-0	1-1	2-1	4-0	2-1	5-0	1-0	3-0	2-1	1-0
Gillingham FC	0-1	1-0	1-0	2-1	0-3	■	1-1	0-1	3-1	1-1	1-1	1-1	2-1	1-1	1-1	2-2	1-2	1-0	2-1	2-2	3-0	1-0	2-0	2-0
Grimsby Town FC	2-0	2-0	0-0	1-2	0-1	1-1	■	1-2	0-1	0-1	1-2	2-2	1-0	2-4	1-0	2-1	1-1	1-1	2-1	2-0	1-0	2-2	3-0	1-0
Lincoln City FC	2-2	2-3	3-3	3-2	3-2	4-0	2-0	■	3-2	5-4	0-1	1-1	2-0	2-0	3-1	2-2	1-1	1-1	0-0	2-2	4-1	1-1	2-0	
Mansfield Town FC	1-1	5-0	1-1	2-1	1-0	2-2	3-0	3-1	■	3-0	3-0	1-1	2-0	2-1	3-1	4-0	3-1	1-0	1-0	1-1	1-1	3-0	2-0	4-1
Northampton Town	0-2	3-0	0-0	2-1	3-0	1-2	0-0	1-0	0-1	■	1-0	2-2	3-1	3-0	0-1	1-2	1-4	0-2	5-3	1-1	3-4	0-1	0-2	3-0
Oxford United FC	1-0	2-2	2-0	3-2	0-1	3-1	5-2	1-2	0-3	1-0	■	2-3	2-1	0-0	2-2	1-0	1-1	4-2	0-0	1-1	0-0	2-2	0-2	
Peterborough United	2-0	0-1	3-2	0-3	0-0	3-1	1-2	2-1	3-1	2-0		■	4-2	1-1	0-0	2-1	0-2	1-2	2-1	1-0	3-5	0-3	1-0	
Portsmouth FC	1-0	1-1	2-1	1-0	0-0	3-2	1-2	1-1	2-2	2-1	1-1	0-0	■	1-1	2-0	0-2	5-1	0-3	2-0	2-1	0-3	1-1	0-1	3-1
Port Vale FC	2-2	0-1	1-0	1-1	4-1	1-2	2-0	1-0	1-4	2-1	2-1	1-1	1-0	■	0-0	1-0	1-4	2-0	1-2	2-2	1-1	1-0	2-3	0-2
Preston North End	1-1	0-1	3-4	2-2	2-1	1-0	2-1	3-0	1-2	3-0	2-1	6-2	0-0	4-0	■	3-0	0-0	4-1	2-1	2-0	1-0	0-1	2-1	4-2
Reading FC	2-3	1-3	2-0	2-0	0-0	1-2	2-0	1-2	1-0	2-4	2-0	1-0	2-0	1-1	0-2	■	0-3	0-1	0-0	4-1	0-0	2-1	2-0	1-1
Rotherham United	0-0	3-0	1-1	1-0	1-1	3-2	1-0	3-0	0-2	1-1	0-0	2-2	1-1	2-0	1-2		■	0-1	1-1	1-1	1-2	1-0	2-0	1-1
Sheffield Wednesday	0-0	1-0	3-0	4-1	1-0	2-0	1-0	0-2	2-1	2-0	4-0	1-1	1-2	1-1	2-1	1-3		■	0-1	3-1	3-1	0-0	3-1	3-2
Shrewsbury Town	1-0	0-1	2-0	3-0	1-1	4-2	2-1	2-1	0-0	3-0	1-0	2-1	4-1	1-1	1-2	2-0	0-0	1-1	■	2-2	2-2	1-2	3-2	2-1
Swindon Town FC	2-1	0-1	2-1	3-0	1-1	2-2	4-1	2-2	0-1	5-1	0-4	4-3	1-0	0-1	2-2	2-4	5-2	1-0		■	1-1	2-2	3-2	5-1
Tranmere Rovers FC	1-3	1-2	0-1	2-1	1-0	2-0	2-0	4-0	1-1	1-0	0-0	3-5	2-0	1-3	1-0	2-0	1-0	2-1	0-1		■	0-0	0-0	4-4
Walsall FC	1-0	3-3	1-0	2-2	0-0	1-2	1-0	1-3	1-2	0-3	2-2	1-1	1-1	3-1	0-1	6-1	0-1	5-1	3-3	2-0	2-0	■	2-3	1-2
Wrexham AFC	0-0	0-0	4-2	3-1	2-4	2-1	3-2	3-0	0-1	3-1	1-1	2-0	2-0	6-2	2-0	3-1	2-1	2-2	1-0	2-2	2-0	1-0	■	1-1
York City FC	0-1	2-2	0-2	2-1	2-1	2-2	1-1	2-2	0-1	1-4	2-1	2-1	1-4	1-0	0-2	1-1	1-0	0-3	4-2	1-0	0-0	0-0		■

Division 3

		Pd	Wn	Dw	Ls	GF	GA	Pts	
1.	Mansfield Town FC (Mansfield)	46	28	8	10	78	33	64	P
2.	Brighton & Hove Albion FC (Hove)	46	25	11	10	83	39	61	P
3.	Crystal Palace FC (London)	46	23	13	10	68	40	59	P
4.	Rotherham United FC (Rotherham)	46	22	15	9	69	44	59	
5.	Wrexham AFC (Wrexham)	46	24	10	12	80	54	58	
6.	Preston North End FC (Preston)	46	21	12	13	64	43	54	
7.	Bury FC (Bury)	46	23	8	15	64	59	54	
8.	Sheffield Wednesday FC (Sheffield)	46	22	9	15	65	55	53	
9.	Lincoln City FC (Lincoln)	46	19	14	13	77	70	52	
10.	Shrewsbury Town FC (Shrewsbury)	46	18	11	17	65	59	47	
11.	Swindon Town FC (Swindon)	46	15	15	16	68	75	45	
12.	Gillingham FC (Gillingham)	46	16	12	18	55	64	44	
13.	Chester FC (Chester)	46	18	8	20	48	58	44	
14.	Tranmere Rovers FC (Birkenhead)	46	13	17	16	51	53	43	
15.	Walsall FC (Walsall)	46	13	15	18	57	65	41	
16.	Peterborough United FC (Peterborough)	46	13	15	18	55	65	41	
17.	Oxford United FC (Oxford)	46	12	15	19	55	65	39	
18.	Chesterfield FC (Chesterfield)	46	14	10	22	56	64	38	
19.	Port Vale FC (Stoke-on-Trent)	46	11	16	19	47	71	38	
20.	Portsmouth FC (Portsmouth)	46	11	14	21	43	70	36	
21.	Reading FC (Reading)	46	13	9	24	49	73	35	R
22.	Northampton Town FC (Northampton)	46	13	8	25	60	75	34	R
23.	Grimsby Town FC (Cleethorpes)	46	12	9	25	45	69	33	R
24.	York City FC (York)	46	10	12	24	50	89	32	R
		1104	409	286	409	1452	1452	1104	

Football League Division 4 — 1976-77 Season

	Aldershot Town	Barnsley	Bournemouth	Bradford City	Brentford	Cambridge United	Colchester United	Crewe Alexandra	Darlington	Doncaster Rovers	Exeter City	Halifax Town	Hartlepool	Huddersfield Town	Newport County	Rochdale	Scunthorpe United	Southend United	Southport	Stockport County	Swansea City	Torquay United	Watford	Workington
Aldershot Town FC	■	0-1	1-0	2-1	1-1	1-3	1-1	1-1	1-2	1-0	2-2	0-0	3-0	1-0	4-0	0-2	1-1	0-0	1-0	2-0	2-2	0-1	2-1	2-0
Barnsley FC	1-0	■	3-1	2-2	2-0	2-1	0-1	2-2	1-1	1-1	3-4	1-0	3-0	2-1	2-0	2-0	5-1	3-1	1-0	1-0	1-0	2-1	1-1	4-0
AFC Bournemouth	4-1	1-0	■	1-1	3-1	0-1	0-0	0-0	0-1	3-1	2-0	3-0	2-0	1-0	1-0	1-1	2-2	2-0	5-0	3-0	1-1	1-1	2-1	1-1
Bradford City AFC	3-1	0-0	1-1	■	3-2	0-0	1-0	1-0	3-1	3-1	1-1	3-0	2-2	3-1	3-1	3-0	4-0	2-0	1-0	3-3	4-1	3-2	0-0	4-1
Brentford FC	0-1	0-1	3-2	4-0	■	0-2	1-4	0-0	0-3	2-2	1-0	2-1	3-1	1-3	1-1	3-2	4-2	1-0	3-0	4-0	4-0	3-2	3-0	5-0
Cambridge United FC	4-1	0-0	2-0	2-1	3-2	■	2-0	2-0	4-0	3-0	1-1	4-0	2-0	1-1	3-1	0-0	1-0	2-3	5-1	2-2	2-3	4-1	4-0	4-1
Colchester United FC	1-0	1-0	1-0	2-1	2-1	0-1	■	3-2	4-0	1-0	3-1	3-0	6-2	3-1	5-0	1-0	1-0	4-1	1-0	1-1	4-0	1-0	1-0	3-1
Crewe Alexandra FC	1-0	1-0	2-1	1-0	3-2	1-0	1-0	■	1-1	1-2	2-0	3-1	3-1	0-0	2-0	1-1	2-1	1-1	0-0	2-1	3-1	2-1	2-0	1-1
Darlington FC	2-1	2-1	4-0	0-0	2-2	0-2	2-0	4-0	■	1-3	2-1	0-0	3-1	2-0	1-0	0-1	5-2	0-0	2-1	0-2	0-4	2-1	0-0	3-2
Doncaster Rovers FC	1-2	2-1	0-0	2-3	5-0	1-1	3-2	3-0	4-0	■	0-3	3-0	2-1	2-0	1-0	2-0	3-0	0-3	3-1	1-0	2-1	0-4	1-0	6-3
Exeter City FC	3-0	1-0	1-1	0-0	3-2	1-1	1-0	3-0	1-0	0-2	■	1-0	3-1	2-0	2-1	2-1	3-1	3-1	2-1	2-0	3-0	2-2	0-0	
Halifax Town AFC	2-0	0-1	2-3	2-1	0-0	0-2	1-2	3-0	2-1	6-0	1-2	■	1-0	0-0		0-0		3-1	1-1	1-0		0-1	1-1	6-1
Hartlepool FC	0-2	0-2	0-1	0-1	2-0	2-2	2-2	3-0	1-1	0-0	2-2	1-0	■	0-1	0-1	2-0	3-0	1-1	1-1	1-1	2-2	4-0	1-0	2-0
Huddersfield Town	2-0	1-0	0-0	3-0	1-0	1-2	0-0	0-1	3-1	2-1	0-1	1-0	4-1	■	3-0	2-1	1-0	1-1	1-0	2-0	2-2	2-1	2-2	2-1
Newport County AFC	2-1	1-1	1-0	2-0	3-1	4-2	1-2	2-1	0-1	1-2	0-3	1-1	1-1	1-1	■	3-0	0-0	3-0	3-1	0-1	0-2	0-0	3-0	1-0
Rochdale AFC	2-1	2-3	0-0	0-1	2-3	2-2	1-0	0-1	2-2	1-0	1-2	4-1	0-1	2-2	0-0	■	5-0	0-0	3-0	1-1	1-0	0-1	3-1	0-3
Scunthorpe United	1-3	1-2	0-0	2-1	2-1	0-2	2-0	4-0	3-0	1-1	4-1	2-1	2-0	0-4	1-0	0-1	■	1-0	1-1	2-2	0-3	0-0	0-0	3-1
Southend United FC	5-0	1-1	2-2	4-1	2-1	0-1	0-0	1-0	0-0	2-1	2-0	1-1	1-0	1-1	1-1	3-0	1-1	■	3-2	0-0	1-2	0-3	2-1	2-0
Southport FC	0-1	1-0	0-0	0-4	1-2	0-0	1-3	0-0	0-0	2-2	1-1	0-0	1-2	2-2	0-1	1-1	2-1	0-0	■	1-0	1-3	1-1	1-3	2-0
Stockport County FC	0-0	2-1	1-0	1-1	2-0	0-0	1-1	1-2	2-2	2-1	0-0	2-3	2-1	0-1	1-0	0-0	2-2			■	3-0	2-1	2-2	1-0
Swansea City FC	4-2	2-1	3-0	2-3	5-3	3-1	2-1	3-0	2-1	1-1	0-1	4-2	2-1	3-1	3-2	2-0	2-0	2-1	4-4		■	4-1	1-4	
Torquay United FC	0-1	1-0	2-1	0-3	1-1	2-2	2-2	5-0	2-0	0-1	3-2	1-0	1-0	1-0	2-0	1-3	0-0	0-0	1-2	2-1		■	3-1	3-1
Watford FC	1-1	1-0	1-1	1-1	0-1	2-0	2-1	3-1	1-1	5-1	4-1	0-0	4-0	2-0	2-0	3-1	2-1	1-1	2-0	1-1	1-2	4-0	■	2-0
Workington AFC	1-1	0-1	1-1	0-1	1-3	0-2	2-4	1-0	2-3	1-1	1-3	1-1	1-1	3-2	0-1	0-2	1-0	0-3	2-2	2-2	1-3	2-4	0-1	■

Division 4

		Pd	Wn	Dw	Ls	GF	GA	Pts	
1.	Cambridge United FC (Cambridge)	46	26	13	7	87	40	65	P
2.	Exeter City FC (Exeter)	46	25	12	9	70	46	62	P
3.	Colchester United FC (Colchester)	46	25	9	12	77	43	59	P
4.	Bradford City AFC (Bradford)	46	23	13	10	78	51	59	P
5.	Swansea City FC (Swansea)	46	25	8	13	92	68	58	
6.	Barnsley FC (Barnsley)	46	23	9	14	62	39	55	
7.	Watford FC (Watford)	46	18	15	13	67	50	51	
8.	Doncaster Rovers FC (Doncaster)	46	21	9	16	71	65	51	
9.	Huddersfield Town AFC (Huddersfield)	46	19	12	15	60	49	50	
10.	Southend United FC (Southend-on-Sea)	46	15	19	12	52	45	49	
11.	Darlington FC (Darlington)	46	18	13	15	59	64	49	
12.	Crewe Alexandra FC (Crewe)	46	19	11	16	47	60	49	
13.	AFC Bournemouth (Bournemouth)	46	15	18	13	54	44	48	
14.	Stockport County FC (Stockport)	46	13	19	14	53	57	45	
15.	Brentford FC (London)	46	18	7	21	77	76	43	
16.	Torquay United FC (Torquay)	46	17	9	20	59	67	43	
17.	Aldershot FC (Aldershot)	46	16	11	19	49	59	43	
18.	Rochdale AFC (Rochdale)	46	13	12	21	50	59	38	
19.	Newport County AFC (Newport)	46	14	10	22	42	58	38	
20.	Scunthorpe United FC (Scunthorpe)	46	13	11	22	49	73	37	
21.	Halifax Town AFC (Halifax)	46	11	14	21	47	58	36	
22.	Hartlepool FC (Hartlepool)	46	10	12	24	47	73	32	*
23.	Southport FC (Southport)	46	3	19	24	33	77	25	
24.	Workington AFC (Workington)	46	4	11	31	41	102	19	#
		1104	404	296	404	1423	1423	1104	

Semi-finals

\# Workington AFC (Workington) were not re-elected to the league and were replaced by Wimbledon FC (London) for the next season.

* Hartlepool FC (Hartlepool) changed their club name to Hartlepool United FC (Hartlepool) for the next season.

F.A. CUP FINAL   (Wembley Stadium, London – 21/05/1977 – 100,000)

MANCHESTER UNITED FC (MANCHESTER)   2-1   Liverpool FC (Liverpool)

Pearson, J.Greenhoff   *Case*

Man. United: Stepney, Nicholl, B.Greenhoff, Buchan, Albiston, McIlroy, Macari, Coppell, Pearson, J.Greenhoff, Hill (McCreery)

Liverpool: Clemence, Neal, Smith, Hughes, Jones, Kennedy, Case, McDermott, Keegan, Johnson (Callaghan), Heighway.

Semi-finals

Everton FC (Liverpool)	2-2, 0-3	Liverpool FC (Liverpool)
Manchester United FC (Manchester)	2-1	Leeds United AFC (Leeds)

Quarter-finals

Everton FC (Liverpool)	2-0	Derby County FC (Derby)
Liverpool FC (Liverpool)	2-0	Middlesbrough FC (Middlesbrough)
Manchester United FC (Manchester)	2-1	Aston Villa FC (Birmingham)
Wolverhampton Wanderers FC (Wolverhampton)	0-1	Leeds United AFC (Leeds)

1977-78

Football League Division 1 1977-78 Season	Arsenal	Aston Villa	Birmingham City	Bristol City	Chelsea	Coventry City	Derby County	Everton	Ipswich Town	Leeds United	Leicester City	Liverpool	Manchester City	Manchester United	Middlesbrough	Newcastle United	Norwich City	Nottingham Forest	Q.P.R.	W.B.A.	West Ham United	Wolves
Arsenal FC	■	0-1	1-1	4-1	3-0	1-1	1-3	1-0	1-0	1-1	2-1	0-0	3-0	3-1	1-0	2-1	0-0	3-0	1-0	4-0	3-0	3-1
Aston Villa FC	1-0	■	0-1	1-0	2-0	1-1	0-0	1-2	6-1	3-1	0-0	0-3	1-4	2-1	0-1	2-0	3-0	0-1	1-1	3-0	4-1	2-0
Birmingham City FC	1-1	1-0	■	3-0	4-5	1-1	3-1	0-0	0-0	2-3	1-1	0-1	1-4	1-4	1-2	3-0	2-1	0-2	2-1	1-2	3-0	2-1
Bristol City FC	0-2	1-1	0-1	■	3-0	1-1	3-1	0-1	2-0	3-2	0-0	1-1	2-2	0-1	4-1	3-1	3-0	1-3	2-2	3-1	3-2	2-3
Chelsea FC	0-0	0-0	2-0	1-0	■	1-2	1-1	0-1	5-3	1-2	0-0	3-1	0-0	2-2	0-0	2-2	1-1	1-0	3-1	2-2	2-1	1-1
Coventry City FC	1-2	2-3	4-0	1-1	5-1	■	3-1	3-2	1-1	2-2	1-0	1-0	4-2	3-0	2-1	0-0	5-4	0-0	4-1	1-2	1-0	4-0
Derby County FC	3-0	0-3	1-3	1-0	1-1	4-2	■	0-1	2-2	4-1	4-2	2-1	0-1	4-1	1-1	2-2	0-0	2-0	0-1	2-1	2-1	3-1
Everton FC	2-0	1-0	2-1	1-0	6-0	6-0	2-1	■	1-0	2-0	2-0	0-1	1-1	2-6	3-0	4-4	3-0	1-3	3-3	3-1	2-1	0-0
Ipswich Town FC	1-0	2-0	5-2	1-0	1-0	1-1	1-2	3-3	■	0-1	1-0	1-1	1-0	1-2	1-1	2-1	4-0	0-2	3-2	2-2	0-2	1-2
Leeds United AFC	1-3	1-1	1-0	0-2	2-0	2-0	2-0	3-1	2-1	■	5-1	1-2	2-0	1-1	5-0	0-2	2-2	1-0	3-0	2-2	1-2	2-1
Leicester City FC	1-1	0-2	1-4	0-0	0-2	1-2	1-1	1-5	2-1	0-0	■	0-4	2-3	0-0	3-0	2-2	0-0	0-1	1-0	1-0	0-1	1-0
Liverpool FC	1-0	1-2	2-3	1-1	2-0	2-0	1-0	0-0	2-2	1-0	3-2	■	4-0	3-1	2-0	2-0	3-0	0-0	1-0	3-0	2-0	1-0
Manchester City FC	2-1	2-0	3-0	2-0	6-2	3-1	1-1	1-0	2-1	2-3	0-0	3-1	■	3-1	2-2	4-0	4-0	0-0	2-1	1-3	3-2	0-2
Manchester United FC	1-2	1-1	1-2	1-1	0-1	2-1	4-0	1-2	0-0	0-1	3-1	2-0	2-2	■	0-0	3-2	1-0	0-4	3-1	1-1	3-0	3-1
Middlesbrough FC	0-1	1-0	1-2	2-0	1-1	3-1	1-0	3-1	1-2	2-1	0-1	1-1	0-2	2-1	■	2-0	2-2	2-2	1-1	1-2	1-0	0-0
Newcastle United FC	1-2	1-1	1-1	1-1	1-0	1-2	1-2	0-2	0-1	3-2	2-0	0-2	2-2	2-2	2-4	■	2-2	0-2	0-3	0-3	2-3	4-0
Norwich City FC	1-0	2-1	1-0	1-0	0-0	1-2	0-0	0-0	1-0	3-0	2-0	2-1	1-3	1-3	1-1	2-1	■	3-3	1-1	1-1	2-2	2-1
Nottingham Forest FC	2-0	2-0	0-0	1-0	3-1	2-1	3-0	1-1	4-0	1-1	1-0	1-1	2-1	2-1	4-0	2-0	1-1	■	1-0	0-0	2-0	2-0
Queen's Park Rangers FC	2-1	1-2	0-0	2-2	1-1	2-1	0-0	1-5	3-3	0-0	3-0	2-0	1-1	2-2	1-0	0-1	2-1	0-2	■	2-1	1-0	1-3
West Bromwich Albion FC	1-3	0-3	3-1	2-1	3-0	3-3	1-0	3-1	1-0	2-0	0-1	0-0	4-0	2-1	2-0	0-0	2-2	2-0	2-0	■	1-0	2-2
West Ham United FC	2-2	2-2	1-0	1-2	3-1	2-1	3-0	1-1	3-0	0-1	3-2	0-2	0-1	2-1	0-2	1-0	1-3	0-0	2-2	3-3	■	1-2
Wolverhampton Wanderers FC	1-1	3-1	0-1	0-0	1-3	1-3	1-2	3-1	0-0	3-1	3-0	1-3	1-1	2-1	0-0	1-0	3-3	2-3	1-0	1-1	2-2	■

	Division 1	Pd	Wn	Dw	Ls	GF	GA	Pts	
1.	NOTTINGHAM FOREST FC (NOTTINGHAM)	42	25	14	3	69	24	64	
2.	Liverpool FC (Liverpool)	42	24	9	9	65	34	57	
3.	Everton FC (Liverpool)	42	22	11	9	76	45	55	
4.	Manchester City FC (Manchester)	42	20	12	10	74	51	52	
5.	Arsenal FC (London)	42	21	10	11	60	37	52	
6.	West Bromwich Albion FC (West Bromwich)	42	18	14	10	62	53	50	
7.	Coventry City FC (Coventry)	42	18	12	12	75	62	48	
8.	Aston Villa FC (Birmingham)	42	18	10	14	57	42	46	
9.	Leeds United AFC (Leeds)	42	18	10	14	63	53	46	
10.	Manchester United FC (Manchester)	42	16	10	16	67	63	42	
11.	Birmingham City FC (Birmingham)	42	16	9	17	55	60	41	
12.	Derby County FC (Derby)	42	14	13	15	54	59	41	
13.	Norwich City FC (Norwich)	42	11	18	13	52	66	40	
14.	Middlesbrough FC (Middlesbrough)	42	12	15	15	42	54	39	
15.	Wolverhampton Wanderers FC (Wolverhampton)	42	12	12	18	51	64	36	
16.	Chelsea FC (London)	42	11	14	17	46	69	36	
17.	Bristol City FC (Bristol)	42	11	13	18	49	53	35	
18.	Ipswich Town FC (Ipswich)	42	11	13	18	47	61	35	
19.	Queen's Park Rangers FC (London)	42	9	15	18	47	64	33	
20.	West Ham United FC (London)	42	12	8	22	52	69	32	R
21.	Newcastle United FC (Newcastle-upon-Tyne)	42	6	10	26	42	78	22	R
22.	Leicester City FC (Leicester)	42	5	12	25	26	70	22	R
		924	330	264	330	1231	1231	924	

Top Goalscorer

1) Robert LATCHFORD (Everton FC) 30

Football League Division 2 — 1977-78 Season

	Blackburn Rovers	Blackpool	Bolton Wanderers	Brighton & Hove Albion	Bristol Rovers	Burnley	Cardiff City	Charlton Athletic	Crystal Palace	Fulham	Hull City	Luton Town	Mansfield Town	Millwall	Notts County	Oldham Athletic	Orient	Sheffield United	Southampton	Stoke City	Sunderland	Tottenham Hotspur
Blackburn Rovers FC		1-2	0-1	0-1	0-1	0-1	3-0	2-1	3-0	4-0	1-1	2-0	3-1	2-1	1-0	4-2	1-0	1-1	2-1	2-1	1-1	0-0
Blackpool FC	5-2		0-2	0-1	3-1	1-1	3-0	5-1	3-1	1-2	3-0	2-1	1-2	2-2	2-2	1-1	0-0	1-1	0-1	1-1	1-1	0-2
Bolton Wanderers FC	4-2	2-1		1-1	3-0	1-2	6-3	2-1	2-0	0-0	1-0	2-1	2-0	2-1	2-0	1-0	2-0	2-1	0-0	1-1	2-0	1-0
Brighton & Hove Albion FC	2-2	2-1	1-2		1-1	2-1	4-0	1-0	1-1	2-0	2-1	3-2	5-1	3-2	2-1	1-1	1-0	2-1	1-1	2-1	2-1	3-1
Bristol Rovers FC	4-1	2-0	0-1	0-4		2-2	3-2	2-2	3-0	0-0	1-1	1-2	3-1	2-0	2-2	0-2	2-1	4-1	0-0	4-1	3-2	2-3
Burnley FC	2-3	0-1	0-1	0-0	3-1		4-2	1-0	1-1	2-0	1-1	2-1	2-0	0-2	3-1	4-1	0-0	4-1	3-3	1-0	0-0	2-1
Cardiff City FC	1-1	2-1	1-0	1-0	1-1	2-1		1-0	2-2	3-1	0-0	1-3	1-1	4-1	2-1	0-1	1-6	1-0	2-0	5-2	0-0	0-0
Charlton Athletic FC	2-2	3-1	2-1	4-3	3-1	3-2	0-0		1-0	0-1	0-1	0-0	2-2	0-2	0-0	2-2	2-1	3-0	1-3	3-2	3-2	4-1
Crystal Palace FC	5-0	2-2	2-1	0-0	1-0	1-1	2-0	1-1		2-3	0-1	3-3	3-1	1-0	2-0	1-0	1-0	1-2	0-1	2-2	1-2	1-2
Fulham FC	0-0	1-1	2-0	2-1	1-1	4-1	1-0	1-1	1-1		2-0	1-0	0-2	0-1	5-1	0-2	1-2	2-0	1-1	3-0	3-3	1-1
Hull City AFC	0-1	2-0	0-0	1-1	0-1	1-3	4-1	0-2	1-0	0-1		1-1	0-2	3-2	1-1	0-1	2-2	2-3	0-3	0-0	3-0	2-0
Luton Town FC	0-0	4-0	2-1	1-0	1-1	1-2	3-1	7-1	1-0	1-1	1-1		1-1	2-0	1-0	4-0	1-2	1-2	1-2	1-2	1-3	1-4
Mansfield Town FC	2-2	1-3	0-1	1-2	3-0	4-1	2-2	0-3	1-3	2-1	1-0	3-1		0-0	1-3	0-2	1-1	1-1	1-2	2-1	1-2	3-3
Millwall FC	1-1	2-0	1-0	0-1	1-3	1-1	1-1	1-1	0-3	0-3	1-1	1-0	1-0		0-0	2-0	2-0	1-1	3-0	0-0	3-1	1-3
Notts County FC	1-1	1-1	1-1	1-0	3-2	3-0	1-1	2-0	2-0	1-1	2-1	2-0	1-0	1-1		3-2	1-1	1-2	2-3	2-0	2-2	3-3
Oldham Athletic AFC	0-2	2-1	2-2	1-1	4-1	2-0	1-1	1-1	2-0	2-1	1-0	0-1	2-2	2-1	1-0		2-1	3-0	1-1	1-1	1-1	1-1
Orient FC	0-0	1-4	1-1	0-1	2-1	3-0	2-1	0-0	0-0	1-2	1-1	0-0	4-2	0-0	0-0	5-3		3-1	1-1	2-0	2-2	1-1
Sheffield United FC	2-0	0-0	1-5	2-0	1-1	2-1	0-1	1-0	0-2	2-1	2-0	4-1	2-0	5-2	4-1	1-0	2-0		3-2	1-2	1-1	2-2
Southampton FC	5-0	2-0	2-2	1-1	3-1	3-0	3-1	4-1	2-0	1-0	0-1	2-3	3-1	2-2	1-0	2-1	1-0	4-2		1-0	4-2	0-0
Stoke City FC	4-2	1-2	0-0	1-0	3-2	2-1	2-0	4-0	2-0	2-0	0-0	1-1	2-1	1-1	2-1	1-1	5-1	4-0	1-0		0-0	1-3
Sunderland AFC	0-1	2-1	0-2	0-2	5-1	3-0	1-1	3-0	0-0	2-2	2-0	1-1	1-0	2-0	3-1	3-1	1-1	5-1	0-0	1-0		1-2
Tottenham Hotspur FC	4-0	2-2	1-0	0-0	9-0	3-0	2-1	2-1	2-2	1-0	1-0	2-0	1-1	3-3	2-1	5-1	1-1	4-2	0-0	3-1	2-3	

	Division 2	Pd	Wn	Dw	Ls	GF	GA	Pts	
1.	Bolton Wanderers FC (Bolton)	42	24	10	8	63	33	58	P
2.	Southampton FC (Southampton)	42	22	13	7	70	39	57	P
3.	Tottenham Hotspur FC (London)	42	20	16	6	83	49	56	P
4.	Brighton & Hove Albion FC (Hove)	42	22	12	8	63	38	56	
5.	Blackburn Rovers FC (Blackburn)	42	16	13	13	56	60	45	
6.	Sunderland AFC (Sunderland)	42	14	16	12	67	59	44	
7.	Stoke City FC (Stoke-on-Trent)	42	16	10	16	53	49	42	
8.	Oldham Athletic AFC (Oldham)	42	13	16	13	54	58	42	
9.	Crystal Palace FC (London)	42	13	15	14	50	47	41	
10.	Fulham FC (London)	42	14	13	15	49	49	41	
11.	Burnley FC (Burnley)	42	15	10	17	56	64	40	
12.	Sheffield United FC (Sheffield)	42	16	8	18	62	73	40	
13.	Luton Town FC (Luton)	42	14	10	18	54	52	38	
14.	Orient FC (London)	42	10	18	14	43	49	38	
15.	Notts County FC (Nottingham)	42	11	16	15	54	62	38	
16.	Millwall FC (London)	42	12	14	16	49	57	38	
17.	Charlton Athletic FC (London)	42	13	12	17	55	68	38	
18.	Bristol Rovers FC (Bristol)	42	13	12	17	61	77	38	
19.	Cardiff City AFC (Cardiff)	42	13	12	17	51	71	38	
20.	Blackpool FC (Blackpool)	42	12	13	17	59	60	37	R
21.	Mansfield Town FC (Mansfield)	42	10	11	21	49	69	31	R
22.	Hull City AFC (Kingston-upon-Hull)	42	8	12	22	34	52	28	R
		924	321	282	321	1235	1235	924	

Football League Division 3 1977-78 Season	Bradford City	Bury	Cambridge	Carlisle United	Chester	Chesterfield	Colchester United	Exeter City	Gillingham	Hereford United	Lincoln City	Oxford United	Peterborough Utd.	Plymouth Argyle	Portsmouth	Port Vale	Preston North End	Rotherham United	Sheffield Wed.	Shrewsbury Town	Swindon Town	Tranmere Rovers	Walsall	Wrexham
Bradford City AFC	■	2-1	4-0	2-2	2-2	1-3	1-2	1-2	2-1	0-0	2-2	2-3	2-1	0-1	1-0	1-1	1-1	3-0	3-2	2-0	2-1	2-0	2-3	2-1
Bury FC	2-2	■	5-2	1-1	1-1	0-0	1-1	5-0	2-2	1-1	1-0	3-2	0-0	1-1	0-0	3-0	1-1	1-1	3-0	0-3	0-0	1-0	0-1	2-3
Cambridge United FC	4-1	3-0	■	2-0	0-0	2-0	2-0	2-1	2-3	2-0	5-0	2-1	1-0	3-0	1-0	2-0	1-1	1-1	3-0	2-0	5-2	1-0	2-1	1-0
Carlisle United FC	1-1	0-3	1-1	■	0-0	2-1	1-3	2-0	1-0	2-0	2-3	2-2	0-0	0-0	3-1	1-1	3-1	2-1	1-0	1-0	2-2	2-2	2-0	1-4
Chester FC	3-2	1-0	0-0	2-2	■	2-1	2-1	2-1	2-2	4-1	2-2	3-1	4-3	1-1	2-0	2-1	1-2	2-1	2-1	1-0	1-0	0-0	1-1	1-1
Chesterfield FC	2-0	2-1	2-1	2-1	1-2	■	0-0	0-0	5-2	2-1	0-0	3-0	2-0	4-1	3-0	2-0	0-1	0-0	2-2	3-1	3-1	1-1	0-1	1-0
Colchester United FC	3-0	1-0	2-1	2-2	2-0	2-0	■	3-1	1-1	0-0	1-1	1-1	3-0	3-1	4-0	2-3	0-0	0-0	1-1	1-2	2-0	0-0	1-1	1-1
Exeter City FC	1-0	2-2	2-4	0-1	1-1	0-0	0-0	■	2-1	1-0	3-0	2-1	1-0	0-0	0-1	4-1	2-0	1-0	2-1	1-1	0-0	4-2	1-1	0-1
Gillingham FC	4-1	1-4	3-1	1-1	1-0	3-0	1-3	1-0	■	4-0	0-0	2-1	0-0	1-1	0-0	1-1	2-1	2-1	2-1	1-2	1-1	3-1	1-1	0-0
Hereford United FC	2-1	1-0	0-0	1-0	2-2	2-1	1-0	4-0	2-0	■	1-1	2-1	0-0	1-3	0-2	1-1	0-0	2-3	0-1	1-1	1-1	0-1	3-2	1-1
Lincoln City FC	3-2	0-0	4-1	2-1	2-1	1-0	0-0	1-2	0-2	0-0	■	1-0	0-1	2-2	1-0	3-0	2-2	3-3	3-1	1-3	3-1	1-1	2-2	0-1
Oxford United FC	3-1	0-0	2-3	0-0	4-1	1-1	3-0	0-0	1-1	3-0	1-0	■	3-3	2-1	0-0	1-1	1-0	2-3	1-0	1-1	3-3	1-0	3-1	2-1
Peterborough United	5-0	2-1	2-0	2-1	0-0	2-0	1-0	1-1	1-1	2-1	0-1	1-0	■	1-0	0-0	1-1	1-0	2-1	2-0	1-0	0-0	0-0	0-0	2-2
Plymouth Argyle FC	6-0	0-1	0-1	0-1	2-2	2-0	1-1	2-2	1-3	2-0	1-2	2-1	1-0	■	3-1	3-2	0-0	1-1	1-1	2-2	0-2	0-1	3-3	0-1
Portsmouth FC	3-1	1-1	2-2	3-3	0-0	3-0	0-0	1-1	1-1	2-0	0-2	0-2	2-2	1-5	■	1-1	0-2	3-3	2-2	2-0	1-2	2-5	1-2	0-1
Port Vale FC	1-0	1-2	1-1	0-1	0-0	1-3	0-3	4-0	2-2	1-0	2-1	1-1	0-0	3-3	2-0	■	0-0	3-0	0-0	1-2	1-0	1-1	2-2	1-1
Preston North End	3-1	4-0	2-0	2-1	2-1	0-0	4-0	0-0	2-0	0-0	4-0	3-2	0-1	5-2	3-1	2-0	■	3-2	2-1	2-2	1-1	2-1	1-0	1-3
Rotherham United	2-1	0-3	1-0	1-1	1-1	1-2	1-0	1-0	2-0	1-0	0-0	1-2	0-0	2-1	0-1	2-0	2-1	■	1-2	0-0	1-3	2-0	3-0	2-2
Sheffield Wednesday	2-0	3-2	0-0	3-1	1-1	1-0	1-2	2-1	0-0	1-0	1-2	2-1	0-1	1-1	3-1	1-0	1-0	1-0	■	0-1	1-1	1-0	0-0	2-1
Shrewsbury Town	4-0	5-3	3-3	0-3	0-0	1-1	1-0	0-2	1-2	3-0	0-1	1-0	0-0	3-1	6-1	3-0	0-0	4-1	0-0	■	2-3	3-1	0-0	2-1
Swindon Town FC	0-1	1-1	0-0	2-2	1-1	2-1	0-0	4-0	3-2	1-0	1-0	3-2	2-0	3-1	1-1	0-2	2-0	2-2	5-0	1-0	■	2-2	2-3	1-2
Tranmere Rovers FC	0-0	0-0	0-1	3-2	5-0	1-1	1-0	2-1	1-1	2-1	3-1	4-1	0-2	1-1	2-0	2-1	1-0	2-2	3-1	2-0	1-1	■	0-1	3-1
Walsall FC	1-1	1-2	0-0	0-0	3-0	2-2	4-2	1-3	2-1	2-0	3-1	2-1	1-0	1-0	2-0	0-0	3-1	1-1	3-0	2-0	0-0	3-0	■	0-1
Wrexham AFC	2-0	3-1	4-1	3-1	1-2	1-1	2-1	2-1	3-3	2-1	1-0	2-2	0-0	2-0	2-0	1-1	0-0	7-1	1-1	0-0	2-1	6-1	1-0	■

Division 3	Pd	Wn	Dw	Ls	GF	GA	Pts	
1. Wrexham AFC (Wrexham)	46	23	15	8	78	45	61	P
2. Cambridge United FC (Cambridge)	46	23	12	11	72	51	58	P
3. Preston North End FC (Preston)	46	20	16	10	63	38	56	P
4. Peterborough United FC (Peterborough)	46	20	16	10	47	33	56	
5. Chester FC (Chester)	46	16	22	8	59	56	54	
6. Walsall FC (Walsall)	46	18	17	11	61	50	53	
7. Gillingham FC (Gillingham)	46	15	20	11	67	60	50	
8. Colchester United FC (Colchester)	46	15	18	13	55	44	48	
9. Chesterfield FC (Chesterfield)	46	17	14	15	58	49	48	
10. Swindon Town FC (Swindon)	46	16	16	14	67	60	48	
11. Shrewsbury Town FC (Shrewsbury)	46	16	15	15	63	57	47	
12. Tranmere Rovers FC (Birkenhead)	46	16	15	15	57	52	47	
13. Carlisle United FC (Carlisle)	46	14	19	13	59	59	47	
14. Sheffield Wednesday FC (Sheffield)	46	15	16	15	50	52	46	
15. Bury FC (Bury)	46	13	19	14	62	56	45	
16. Lincoln City FC (Lincoln)	46	15	15	16	53	61	45	
17. Exeter City FC (Exeter)	46	15	14	17	49	59	44	
18. Oxford United FC (Oxford)	46	13	14	19	64	67	40	
19. Plymouth Argyle FC (Plymouth)	46	11	17	18	61	68	39	
20. Rotherham United FC (Rotherham)	46	13	13	20	51	68	39	
21. Port Vale FC (Stoke-on-Trent)	46	8	20	18	46	67	36	R
22. Bradford City AFC (Bradford)	46	12	10	24	56	86	34	R
23. Hereford United FC (Hereford)	46	9	14	23	34	60	32	R
24. Portsmouth FC (Portsmouth)	46	7	17	22	31	75	31	R
	1104	360	384	360	1373	1373	1104	

Football League Division 4 — 1977-78 Season

	Aldershot Town	Barnsley	Bournemouth	Brentford	Crewe Alexandra	Darlington	Doncaster Rovers	Grimsby Town	Halifax Town	Hartlepool United	Huddersfield Town	Newport County	Northampton Town	Reading	Rochdale	Scunthorpe United	Southend United	Southport	Stockport County	Swansea City	Torquay United	Watford	Wimbledon	York City
Aldershot Town FC	■	0-0	2-0	1-0	2-0	3-2	1-0	4-2	0-0	3-0	3-3	2-2	2-1	1-1	2-0	4-0	3-0	0-0	2-1	2-2	3-0	1-0	3-1	1-1
Barnsley FC	2-0	■	3-0	0-0	4-0	2-1	0-0	1-2	3-2	3-2	1-1	1-0	2-3	4-1	4-0	3-0	1-1	2-1	0-1	0-2	2-0	1-0	3-2	2-1
AFC Bournemouth	0-0	2-2	■	3-2	1-0	2-0	0-1	1-0	0-0	1-0	1-0	4-2	1-1	1-0	1-0	0-3	3-1	1-0	0-1	1-1	1-2	1-2		2-1
Brentford FC	2-0	2-0	1-1	■	5-1	2-0	2-2	3-1	4-1	2-0	1-1	3-3	3-0	1-1	4-2	2-0	1-0	0-0	4-0	0-2	3-0	0-3	4-1	1-0
Crewe Alexandra FC	0-2	2-1	3-1	4-6	■	2-2	2-0	0-2	0-0	1-0	1-1	2-0	3-2	1-1	2-1	1-1	0-2	2-0	1-1	2-1	2-0	2-2	0-0	1-0
Darlington FC	1-1	0-2	1-0	1-3	2-0	■	1-1	1-2	2-1	1-2	2-2	2-1	2-0	2-0	1-0	1-1	2-0	3-0	2-2	1-1	0-0	0-0	3-1	0-2
Doncaster Rovers FC	4-3	2-1	0-0	3-1	2-0	1-2	■	0-1	1-1	2-0	4-3	2-2	4-2	2-2	1-1	1-1	2-1	1-0	1-1	1-0	0-1	0-2	1-1	
Grimsby Town FC	1-0	1-0	0-2	2-1	2-2	2-0	0-0	■	0-0	2-1	1-0	1-0	0-1	2-1	0-0	2-0	2-0	2-1	0-0	2-1	3-1	1-1	3-1	3-2
Halifax Town AFC	2-1	1-1	0-0	1-1	1-1	0-2	0-1	0-0	■	3-0	0-0	3-1	0-1	2-4	3-1	2-2	0-1	2-1	1-1	3-1	0-0	1-1	1-2	2-0
Hartlepool United FC	2-2	1-2	0-1	3-1	1-1	2-1	0-2	3-1	1-1	■	3-2	1-1	0-2	1-0	1-0	2-0	0-4	1-2	1-2	2-0	1-2		2-0	4-2
Huddersfield Town	1-1	2-0	1-0	1-3	3-0	2-1	4-1	1-3	2-2	3-1	■	2-0	0-1	0-2	3-1	4-1	2-0	3-1	0-0	0-0	1-1	1-0	3-0	1-2
Newport County AFC	2-1	3-1	3-2	1-2	1-0	1-1	1-0	3-0	2-0	4-2	2-0	■	5-3	0-0	3-1	1-2	1-0	0-0	2-3	1-0	0-2	0-1		2-1
Northampton Town	1-1	1-1	1-0	2-2	0-0	2-2	0-0	2-1	1-2	5-3	3-1	2-4	■	0-2	3-1	1-2	0-0	1-0	3-1	1-0	0-2	0-3		1-1
Reading FC	1-0	0-0	0-0	0-0	2-0	2-1	3-0	0-0	2-1	2-3	1-0	2-0	0-0	■	4-3	1-0	0-1	3-1	2-1	1-4	3-3	1-3	2-2	1-0
Rochdale AFC	0-0	1-1	1-1	1-2	0-2	2-0	3-1	1-3	3-1	0-0	0-0	0-1	1-1	1-0	■	1-1	1-2	2-1	2-1	1-3	2-3	3-0	1-2	
Scunthorpe United	1-1	1-0	0-0	1-1	3-0	3-0	0-0	2-1	2-0	2-0	1-1	2-2	0-1	1-0		■	1-2	0-2	3-0	1-0	0-1	0-1	3-0	2-1
Southend United FC	3-1	0-0	5-1	2-1	1-2	2-0	4-0	1-1	5-0	1-1	1-3	4-2	0-0	0-2	3-1	2-0	■	4-2	0-2	2-1	4-0	1-0	0-0	
Southport FC	1-1	1-1	0-0	1-3	1-2	1-0	1-1	2-2	1-2	1-1	1-1	3-3	3-1	1-1	3-1	1-1	0-0	■	2-0	0-3	0-0	2-2	0-5	4-1
Stockport County	2-1	3-0	1-1	1-1	1-2	1-1	2-0	1-3	6-0	1-0	0-0	1-2	2-0	2-0	1-1	1-0	2-1	2-0	■	1-3	2-2	1-3	2-1	
Swansea City FC	1-0	2-1	1-0	2-1	5-0	1-2	3-0	2-0	8-0	4-0	2-4	3-0	3-1	0-0	1-1	3-1				■	1-1	3-3	3-0	1-1
Torquay United FC	1-2	3-1	2-1	1-2	1-0	0-0	2-1	4-2	2-2	0-0	2-1	2-1	3-0	3-0	4-2	0-1	2-2	2-0	2-4		■	2-3	1-1	3-0
Watford FC	1-0	0-0	2-1	1-1	5-2	2-1	6-0	1-0	1-1	1-0	2-0	2-0	3-0	1-0	4-1	1-1	3-2	1-0	2-1	1-0		■	2-0	1-3
Wimbledon FC	1-2	0-0	3-1	1-1	0-0	1-1	3-3	2-2	3-3	3-0	2-0	3-0	2-0	1-1	5-1	0-0	1-3	2-2	2-0	1-1	0-1	1-3	■	2-1
York City FC	1-2	1-2	0-0	3-2	1-1	2-1	1-2	1-1	1-0	1-1	2-0	0-3	2-0	2-2	0-2	1-2	2-1	2-1	2-1	1-0	0-4	1-1		■

	Division 4	**Pd**	**Wn**	**Dw**	**Ls**	**GF**	**GA**	**Pts**	
1.	Watford FC (Watford)	46	30	11	5	85	38	71	P
2.	Southend United FC (Southend-on-Sea)	46	25	10	11	66	39	60	P
3.	Swansea City FC (Swansea)	46	23	10	13	87	47	56	P
4.	Brentford FC (London)	46	21	14	11	86	54	56	P
5.	Aldershot FC (Aldershot)	46	19	16	11	67	47	54	
6.	Grimsby Town FC (Cleethorpes)	46	21	11	14	57	51	53	
7.	Barnsley FC (Barnsley)	46	18	14	14	61	49	50	
8.	Reading FC (Reading)	46	18	14	14	55	52	50	
9.	Torquay United FC (Torquay)	46	16	15	15	57	56	47	
10.	Northampton Town FC (Northampton)	46	17	13	16	63	68	47	
11.	Huddersfield Town AFC (Huddersfield)	46	15	15	16	63	55	45	
12.	Doncaster Rovers FC (Doncaster)	46	14	17	15	52	65	45	
13.	Wimbledon FC (London)	46	14	16	16	66	67	44	
14.	Scunthorpe United FC (Scunthorpe)	46	14	16	16	50	55	44	
15.	Crewe Alexandra FC (Crewe)	46	15	14	17	50	69	43	
16.	Newport County AFC (Newport)	46	16	11	19	65	73	43	
17.	AFC Bournemouth (Bournemouth)	46	14	15	17	41	51	43	
18.	Stockport County FC (Stockport)	46	16	10	20	56	56	42	
19.	Darlington FC (Darlington)	46	14	13	19	52	59	41	
20.	Halifax Town AFC (Halifax)	46	10	21	15	52	62	41	
21.	Hartlepool United FC (Hartlepool)	46	15	7	24	51	84	37	
22.	York City FC (York)	46	12	12	22	50	69	36	
23.	Southport FC (Southport)	46	6	19	21	52	76	31	#
24.	Rochdale AFC (Rochdale)	46	8	8	30	43	85	24	
		1104	391	322	391	1427	1427	1104	

\# Southport FC (Southport) were not re-elected to the league and were replaced by Wigan Athletic AFC (Wigan) for the next season.

F.A. CUP FINAL   (Wembley Stadium, London – 06/05/1978 – 100,000)

IPSWICH TOWN FC (IPSWICH)	1-0	Arsenal FC (London)

Osborne

Ipswich: Cooper, Burley, Hunter, Beattie, Mills, Osborne (Lambert), Talbot, Wark, Mariner, Geddis, Woods.
Arsenal: Jennings, Rice, O'Leary, Young, Nelson, Price, Hudson, Brady (Rix), Sunderland. Macdonald, Stapleton.

Semi-finals

Ipswich Town FC (Ipswich)	3-1	West Bromwich Albion FC (West Bromwich)
Orient FC (London)	0-3	Arsenal FC (London)

Quarter-finals

Middlesbrough FC (Middlesbrough)	0-0, 1-2	Orient FC (London)
Millwall FC (London)	1-6	Ipswich Town FC (Ipswich)
West Bromwich Albion FC (West Bromwich)	2-0	Nottingham Forest FC (Nottingham)
Wrexham AFC (Wrexham)	2-3	Arsenal FC (London)

1978-79

Football League Division 1 1978-79 Season	Arsenal	Aston Villa	Birmingham City	Bolton Wanderers	Bristol City	Chelsea	Coventry City	Derby County	Everton	Ipswich Town	Leeds United	Liverpool	Manchester City	Manchester United	Middlesbrough	Norwich City	Nottingham Forest	Q.P.R.	Southampton	Tottenham Hotspur	W.B.A.	Wolves
Arsenal FC		1-1	3-1	1-0	2-0	5-2	1-1	2-0	2-2	4-1	2-2	1-0	1-1	1-1	0-0	1-1	2-1	5-1	1-0	1-0	1-2	0-1
Aston Villa FC	5-1		1-0	3-0	2-0	2-1	1-1	3-3	1-1	2-2	2-2	3-1	1-1	2-2	0-2	1-1	1-2	3-1	1-1	2-3	0-1	1-0
Birmingham City FC	0-0	0-1		3-0	1-1	1-1	0-0	1-1	1-3	1-1	0-1	0-3	1-2	5-1	1-3	1-0	0-2	3-1	2-2	1-0	1-1	1-1
Bolton Wanderers FC	4-2	0-0	2-2		1-2	2-1	0-0	2-1	3-1	2-3	3-1	1-4	2-2	3-0	0-0	3-2	0-1	2-1	2-0	1-3	0-1	3-1
Bristol City FC	1-3	1-0	2-1	4-1		3-1	5-0	1-0	2-2	3-1	0-0	1-0	1-1	1-2	1-1	11-	1-3	2-0	3-1	0-0	1-0	0-1
Chelsea FC	1-1	0-1	2-1	4-3	0-0		1-3	1-1	0-1	0-3	0-3	1-4	0-1	2-1	3-3	1-3	1-2	1-3	1-3	1-3	1-3	1-2
Coventry City FC	1-1	1-1	2-1	2-2	3-2	3-2		4-2	3-2	2-2	0-0	0-0	0-3	4-3	2-1	4-1	0-0	1-0	4-0	1-3	1-3	3-0
Derby County FC	2-0	0-0	2-1	3-0	0-1	1-0	0-2		0-0	0-1	0-1	0-2	1-1	1-3	0-3	1-1	1-2	2-1	2-1	2-2	3-2	4-1
Everton FC	1-0	1-1	1-0	1-0	4-1	3-2	3-3	2-1		0-1	1-1	1-0	1-0	3-0	2-0	2-2	1-1	2-1	0-0	1-1	0-2	2-0
Ipswich Town FC	2-0	0-2	3-0	3-0	0-1	5-1	1-1	2-1	0-1		2-3	0-3	2-1	3-0	1-1	1-1	2-1	1-1	0-0	2-1	3-1	3-1
Leeds United AFC	0-1	1-0	3-0	5-1	1-1	2-1	1-0	4-0	1-0	1-1		0-3	1-1	2-3	3-1	2-2	4-3	4-0	1-2	1-3	1-3	3-0
Liverpool FC	3-0	3-0	1-0	3-0	1-0	2-0	1-0	5-0	1-1	2-0	1-1		1-0	2-0	2-0	6-0	2-0	2-1	2-1	7-0	2-1	2-1
Manchester City FC	1-1	2-3	3-1	2-1	2-0	2-3	1-2	0-0	1-2	3-0	1-4	0-3		0-3	1-0	2-2	3-1	1-2	2-2	2-2	2-2	3-1
Manchester United FC	0-2	1-1	1-0	1-2	1-3	1-1	0-0	0-0	1-1	2-0	4-1	0-3	1-0		3-2	1-0	1-2	2-0	1-0	2-0	3-5	3-2
Middlesbrough FC	2-3	2-0	2-1	1-1	0-0	7-2	1-2	3-1	1-2	0-0	1-0	0-1	2-0	2-2		2-0	1-3	0-2	2-0	1-0	1-1	2-0
Norwich City FC	0-0	1-2	4-0	0-0	3-0	2-0	1-0	3-0	0-1	0-1	2-2	1-4	1-1	2-2	1-0		1-1	1-1	3-1	2-2	1-1	0-0
Nottingham Forest FC	2-1	4-0	1-0	1-1	2-0	6-0	3-0	1-1	1-1	0-0	0-0	0-0	3-1	1-1	2-2	2-1		0-0	1-0	1-1	0-0	3-1
Queen's Park Rangers FC	1-2	1-0	1-3	1-3	1-0	0-0	5-1	2-2	1-1	0-4	1-4	1-3	2-1	1-1	1-1	0-0	0-0		0-1	2-2	2-2	3-3
Southampton FC	2-0	2-0	1-0	2-2	2-0	0-0	4-0	1-2	3-0	1-2	2-2	1-1	1-1	2-1	2-2	0-0	1-1	1-1		3-3	1-1	3-2
Tottenham Hotspur FC	0-5	1-4	1-0	2-0	1-0	2-2	1-1	2-0	1-1	1-2	0-0	0-3	1-1	1-2	0-1	1-3	1-1	0-0	0-0		1-0	1-0
West Bromwich Albion FC	1-1	1-1	1-0	4-0	3-1	1-0	7-1	2-1	1-1	1-2	1-1	4-0	1-0	2-0	2-2	0-1	2-1	1-0	0-1	1-0		1-1
Wolverhampton Wanderers FC	1-0	0-4	2-1	1-1	2-0	0-1	1-1	4-0	1-0	1-3	1-1	0-1	1-1	2-4	1-3	1-0	1-0	2-0	3-2	1-0	0-3	

	Division 1	Pd	Wn	Dw	Ls	GF	GA	Pts	
1.	LIVERPOOL FC (LIVERPOOL)	42	30	8	4	85	16	68	
2.	Nottingham Forest FC (Nottingham)	42	21	18	3	61	26	60	
3.	West Bromwich Albion FC (West Bromwich)	42	24	11	7	72	35	59	
4.	Everton FC (Liverpool)	42	17	17	8	52	40	51	
5.	Leeds United FC (Leeds)	42	18	14	10	70	52	50	
6.	Ipswich Town FC (Ipswich)	42	20	9	13	63	49	49	
7.	Arsenal FC (London)	42	17	14	11	61	48	48	
8.	Aston Villa FC (Birmingham)	42	15	16	11	59	49	46	
9.	Manchester United FC (Manchester)	42	15	15	12	60	63	45	
10.	Coventry City FC (Coventry)	42	14	16	12	58	68	44	
11.	Tottenham Hotspur FC (London)	42	13	15	14	48	61	41	
12.	Middlesbrough FC (Middlesbrough)	42	15	10	17	57	50	40	
13.	Bristol City FC (Bristol)	42	15	10	17	47	51	40	
14.	Southampton FC (Southampton)	42	12	16	14	47	53	40	
15.	Manchester City FC (Manchester)	42	13	13	16	58	56	39	
16.	Norwich City FC (Norwich)	42	7	23	12	51	57	37	
17.	Bolton Wanderers FC (Bolton)	42	12	11	19	54	75	35	
18.	Wolverhampton Wanderers FC (Wolverhampton)	42	13	8	21	44	68	34	
19.	Derby County FC (Derby)	42	10	11	21	44	71	31	
20.	Queen's Park Rangers FC (London)	42	6	13	23	45	73	25	R
21.	Birmingham City FC (Birmingham)	42	6	10	26	37	64	22	R
22.	Chelsea FC (London)	42	5	10	27	44	92	20	R
		924	318	288	318	1217	1217	924	

Top Goalscorer

1)   Frank WORTHINGTON   (Bolton Wanderers FC)   24

Football League Division 2 1978-79 Season	Blackburn Rovers	Brighton & Hove Albion	Bristol Rovers	Burnley	Cambridge	Cardiff City	Charlton Athletic	Crystal Palace	Fulham	Leicester City	Luton Town	Millwall	Newcastle United	Notts County	Oldham Athletic	Orient	Preston North End	Sheffield United	Stoke City	Sunderland	West Ham United	Wrexham
Blackburn Rovers FC		1-1	0-2	1-2	1-0	1-4	1-2	1-1	2-1	1-1	0-0	1-1	1-3	3-4	0-2	3-0	0-1	2-0	2-2	1-1	1-0	1-1
Brighton & Hove Albion FC	2-1		3-0	2-1	0-2	5-0	2-0	0-0	3-0	3-1	3-1	3-0	2-0	0-0	1-0	2-0	5-1	2-0	1-1	2-0	1-2	2-1
Bristol Rovers FC	4-1	1-2		2-0	2-0	4-2	5-5	0-1	3-1	1-1	2-0	0-3	2-0	2-2	0-0	2-1	0-1	2-1	0-0	0-0	0-1	2-1
Burnley FC	2-1	3-0	2-0		1-1	0-0	2-1	2-1	5-3	2-2	2-1	0-1	1-0	2-1	1-0	0-1	1-1	1-1	0-3	1-2	3-2	0-0
Cambridge United FC	0-1	0-0	1-1	2-2		5-0	1-1	0-0	1-0	1-1	0-0	2-1	0-0	0-1	3-3	3-1	1-0	1-0	0-1	0-2	0-0	1-0
Cardiff City FC	2-0	3-1	2-0	1-1	1-0		1-4	2-2	2-0	1-0	2-1	2-1	2-3	1-3	1-0	2-2	4-0	1-3	1-1	0-0	1-0	
Charlton Athletic FC	2-0	0-3	3-0	1-1	2-3	1-1		1-1	0-0	1-0	1-2	2-4	4-1	1-1	2-0	0-2	1-1	3-1	1-4	1-2	0-0	1-1
Crystal Palace FC	3-0	3-1	0-1	2-0	1-1	2-0	1-0		0-1	3-1	3-1	0-0	1-0	2-0	1-1	1-0	1-1	0-0	3-1	1-1	1-1	1-1
Fulham FC	1-2	0-1	3-0	0-0	5-1	2-2	3-1	0-0		3-0	1-0	1-0	1-3	1-1	1-0	2-2	5-3	2-0	2-0	2-2	0-0	0-1
Leicester City FC	1-1	4-1	0-0	2-1	1-1	1-2	0-3	1-1	1-0		3-0	0-0	2-1	0-1	2-0	5-3	1-1	0-1	1-1	1-2	1-2	1-1
Luton Town FC	2-1	1-1	3-2	4-1	1-1	7-1	3-0	0-1	2-0	0-1		2-2	2-0	6-0	6-1	2-1	1-2	1-1	0-0	0-3	1-4	2-1
Millwall FC	1-1	1-4	0-3	0-2	2-0	2-0	0-2	0-3	0-0	2-0	0-2		2-1	0-1	2-3	2-0	0-1	1-1	3-0	0-1	2-1	2-2
Newcastle United FC	3-1	1-3	3-0	3-1	1-0	3-0	5-3	1-0	0-0	1-0	1-0	1-0		1-2	1-1	0-0	4-3	1-3	2-0	1-4	0-3	2-0
Notts County FC	2-1	1-0	2-1	1-1	1-1	1-0	1-1	0-0	1-1	0-1	3-1	1-1	1-2		0-0	1-0	0-0	4-1	0-1	1-1	1-0	1-1
Oldham Athletic AFC	5-0	1-3	3-1	2-0	4-1	2-1	0-3	0-0	0-2	2-1	2-0	4-1	1-3	3-3		0-0	2-0	1-1	1-1	0-0	2-2	1-0
Orient FC	2-0	3-3	1-1	2-1	3-0	2-2	2-1	0-1	1-0	0-1	3-2	2-1	2-0	3-0	0-0		2-0	1-1	0-1	3-0	0-2	1-0
Preston North End FC	4-1	1-0	1-1	2-2	0-2	2-1	6-1	2-3	2-2	4-0	2-2	0-0	0-0	1-1	1-1	1-1		2-2	0-1	3-1	0-0	2-1
Sheffield United FC	0-1	0-1	1-0	4-0	3-3	2-1	2-1	0-2	1-1	2-2	1-1	0-2	1-0	5-1	4-2	1-2	0-1		0-0	3-2	3-0	1-1
Stoke City FC	1-2	2-2	2-0	3-1	1-3	2-0	2-2	1-1	2-0	0-0	0-0	2-0	0-0	2-0	4-0	3-1	1-1	2-1		0-1	2-0	3-0
Sunderland AFC	0-1	2-1	5-0	3-1	0-2	1-2	1-0	1-2	1-1	1-1	3-2	1-1	3-0	3-0	1-0	3-1	6-2	0-1			2-1	1-0
West Ham United FC	4-0	1-1	2-0	3-1	5-0	1-1	2-0	1-1	0-1	1-1	1-0	3-0	5-0	5-2	3-0	0-2	3-1	2-0	1-1	3-3		1-1
Wrexham AFC	2-1	0-0	0-1	0-1	2-0	1-2	1-1	0-0	1-1	0-0	2-0	3-0	0-0	3-1	2-0	3-1	2-1	1-1	4-0	0-1	1-2	

	Division 2	Pd	Wn	Dw	Ls	GF	GA	Pts	
1.	Crystal Palace FC (London)	42	19	19	4	51	24	57	P
2.	Brighton & Hove Albion FC (Hove)	42	23	10	9	72	39	56	P
3.	Stoke City FC (Stoke-on-Trent)	42	20	16	6	58	31	56	P
4.	Sunderland AFC (Sunderland)	42	22	11	9	70	44	55	
5.	West Ham United FC (London)	42	18	14	10	70	39	50	
6.	Notts County FC (Nottingham)	42	14	16	12	48	60	44	
7.	Preston North End FC (Preston)	42	12	18	12	59	57	42	
8.	Newcastle United FC (Newcastle-upon-Tyne)	42	17	8	17	51	55	42	
9.	Cardiff City AFC (Cardiff)	42	16	10	16	56	70	42	
10.	Fulham FC (London)	42	13	15	14	50	47	41	
11.	Orient FC (London)	42	15	10	17	51	51	40	
12.	Cambridge United FC (Cambridge)	42	12	16	14	44	52	40	
13.	Burnley FC (Burnley)	42	14	12	16	51	62	40	
14.	Oldham Athletic AFC (Oldham)	42	13	13	16	52	61	39	
15.	Wrexham AFC (Wrexham)	42	12	14	16	45	42	38	
16.	Bristol Rovers FC (Bristol)	42	14	10	18	48	60	38	
17.	Leicester City FC (Leicester)	42	10	17	15	43	52	37	
18.	Luton Town FC (Luton)	42	13	10	19	60	57	36	
19.	Charlton Athletic FC (London)	42	11	13	18	60	69	35	
20.	Sheffield United FC (Sheffield)	42	11	12	19	52	69	34	R
21.	Millwall FC (London)	42	11	10	21	42	61	32	R
22.	Blackburn Rovers FC (Blackburn)	42	10	10	22	41	72	30	R
		924	320	284	320	1174	1174	924	

Football League Division 3 — 1978-79 Season

Results grid (home team in left column, away team across top). Diagonal cells (team vs itself) are shaded.

Home \ Away	Blackpool	Brentford	Bury	Carlisle United	Chester	Chesterfield	Colchester United	Exeter City	Gillingham	Hull City	Lincoln City	Mansfield Town	Oxford United	Peterborough Utd.	Plymouth Argyle	Rotherham United	Sheffield Wed.	Shrewsbury Town	Southend United	Swansea City	Swindon Town	Tranmere Rovers	Walsall	Watford
Blackpool FC		0-1	1-2	3-1	3-0	0-0	2-1	1-1	2-0	3-1	2-0	2-0	1-0	0-0	0-0	1-2	0-1	5-0	1-2	1-3	5-2	2-0	2-1	1-1
Brentford FC	3-2		0-1	0-0	6-0	0-3	1-0	0-0	0-2	1-0	2-1	1-0	3-0	0-0	2-1	1-0	2-1	2-3	3-0	1-0	1-2	2-0	1-0	3-3
Bury FC	1-3	2-3		2-2	1-1	3-1	2-2	4-2	2-2	1-1	1-2	0-0	1-1	1-0	1-2	3-2	0-0	3-0	3-3	0-1	0-1	1-0	1-1	1-2
Carlisle United FC	1-1	1-0	1-2		1-1	1-1	4-0	1-1	1-0	2-2	2-0	1-0	0-1	4-1	1-1	1-1	0-1	1-1	0-0	2-0	2-0	2-0	1-0	1-0
Chester FC	4-2	3-1	1-1	1-2		3-0	2-2	3-0	1-1	2-1	5-1	1-1	4-1	1-1	0-0	0-1	2-2	0-0	0-1	2-0	2-0	1-1	2-1	2-1
Chesterfield FC	1-3	0-0	2-1	2-3	3-1		2-1	0-1	0-2	1-2	1-3	1-0	1-1	3-1	1-3	1-0	3-3	2-1	3-2	2-1	1-1	5-2	0-0	0-2
Colchester United FC	3-1	1-1	0-0	2-1	2-1	0-0		2-2	2-2	2-1	2-0	1-0	1-1	4-2	2-1	0-0	1-0	1-0	1-1	2-2	3-2	1-0	2-0	0-1
Exeter City FC	3-0	2-2	2-1	3-2	0-1	3-1	2-1		0-0	3-1	3-2	0-0	2-0	1-0	2-0	2-2	0-1	0-0	2-1	1-2	3-0	3-1	0-0	0-0
Gillingham FC	2-0	0-0	3-3	0-0	1-0	2-1	3-0	2-0		2-0	4-2	0-1	1-0	2-0	0-0	0-0	2-0	1-0	2-0	2-0	3-2	3-1	2-0	2-3
Hull City AFC	0-0	1-0	4-1	1-1	3-0	1-1	1-0	1-0	0-1		0-0	3-0	0-1	1-1	1-0	1-1	1-1	2-0	2-2	1-1	2-1	4-1	2-1	4-0
Lincoln City FC	1-2	1-0	1-4	1-1	0-0	0-1	0-0	0-1	2-4	4-2		0-1	2-2	0-1	3-3	3-0	1-2	1-2	1-1	2-1	0-3	2-1	1-1	0-5
Mansfield Town FC	1-1	2-1	3-0	1-0	2-0	2-1	1-1	1-1	1-1	0-2	2-0		1-1	1-1	5-0	0-1	1-1	1-2	1-1	2-2	0-1	0-0	1-3	0-3
Oxford United FC	1-0	0-1	2-1	5-0	0-1	1-1	2-0	3-2	1-1	1-0	2-1	3-2		0-2	3-2	1-0	1-1	0-1	0-0	0-2	1-0	2-1	2-1	1-1
Peterborough United	1-2	3-1	2-2	0-0	2-1	0-0	1-2	1-1	1-1	3-0	0-1	1-2	1-1		2-1	1-1	2-0	0-2	0-1	2-0	2-1	1-0	0-3	0-1
Plymouth Argyle FC	0-0	2-1	3-0	2-0	2-2	1-1	1-1	4-2	2-1	3-4	2-1	1-4	0-1	3-2		2-0	2-0	1-1	1-1	2-2	2-0	2-2	1-0	1-1
Rotherham United	2-1	1-0	2-1	1-3	0-1	1-0	1-0	2-1	1-1	2-0	2-0	2-0	0-0	1-1	1-0		0-1	1-2	2-1	0-1	1-3	3-2	4-1	2-1
Sheffield Wednesday	2-0	1-0	0-0	0-0	0-0	4-0	0-0	2-1	2-1	2-3	0-0	1-2	1-1	3-0	2-3	2-1		0-0	3-2	0-0	2-1	1-2	0-2	2-3
Shrewsbury Town	2-0	1-0	1-0	1-0	1-1	1-0	2-0	4-1	1-1	1-0	2-0	2-0	0-0	2-0	3-1	2-2	2-0		3-0	0-0	2-1	1-1	1-1	1-0
Southend United FC	4-0	1-1	1-1	0-1	0-1	2-0	1-1	0-1	3-0	2-0	1-1	2-0	0-0	2-1	2-1	0-1	2-1	2-1		0-2	5-3	0-1	1-0	1-0
Swansea City FC	1-0	2-1	1-0	0-0	2-2	2-1	4-1	1-0	3-1	5-3	3-0	3-2	1-1	4-1	2-1	4-4	4-2	1-1	3-2		1-2	4-3	2-2	3-2
Swindon Town FC	0-1	2-0	0-0	0-0	2-0	1-0	1-2	1-1	3-1	2-0	6-0	1-1	2-0	3-1	1-3	1-0	3-0	2-1	1-0	0-1		4-1	4-1	2-0
Tranmere Rovers FC	0-2	0-1	0-0	1-1	6-2	1-1	1-5	2-2	1-1	3-0	1-0	1-0	0-1	2-1	1-1	1-1	2-2	1-2	1-2	1-1	1-1		0-0	1-1
Walsall FC	2-1	2-3	0-1	1-2	2-1	0-1	2-2	2-2	0-1	1-2	4-1	1-1	0-1	4-1	1-1	0-1	0-2	1-1	1-1	1-1	4-1	2-0		2-4
Watford FC	5-1	2-0	3-3	2-1	1-0	2-0	0-3	1-0	1-0	4-0	2-0	1-1	4-2	1-2	2-2	2-2	1-0	2-2	2-0	0-2	2-0	4-0	3-1	

Division 3

#	Club	Pd	Wn	Dw	Ls	GF	GA	Pts	
1.	Shrewsbury Town FC (Shrewsbury)	46	21	19	6	61	41	61	P
2.	Watford FC (Watford)	46	24	12	10	83	52	60	P
3.	Swansea City FC (Swansea)	46	24	12	10	83	61	60	P
4.	Gillingham FC (Gillingham)	46	21	17	8	65	42	59	
5.	Swindon Town FC (Swindon)	46	25	7	14	74	52	57	
6.	Carlisle United FC (Carlisle)	46	15	22	9	53	42	52	
7.	Colchester United FC (Colchester)	46	17	17	12	60	55	51	
8.	Hull City AFC (Kingston-upon-Hull)	46	19	11	16	66	61	49	
9.	Exeter City FC (Exeter)	46	17	15	14	61	56	49	
10.	Brentford FC (London)	46	19	9	18	53	49	47	
11.	Oxford United FC (Oxford)	46	14	18	14	44	50	46	
12.	Blackpool FC (Blackpool)	46	18	9	19	61	59	45	
13.	Southend United FC (Southend-on-Sea)	46	15	15	16	51	49	45	
14.	Sheffield Wednesday FC (Sheffield)	46	13	19	14	53	53	45	
15.	Plymouth Argyle FC (Plymouth)	46	15	14	17	67	68	44	
16.	Chester FC (Chester)	46	14	16	16	57	61	44	
17.	Rotherham United FC (Rotherham)	46	17	10	19	49	55	44	
18.	Mansfield Town FC (Mansfield)	46	12	19	15	51	52	43	
19.	Bury FC (Bury)	46	11	20	15	59	65	42	
20.	Chesterfield FC (Chesterfield)	46	13	14	19	51	65	40	
21.	Peterborough United FC (Peterborough)	46	11	14	21	44	63	36	R
22.	Walsall FC (Walsall)	46	10	12	24	56	71	32	R
23.	Tranmere Rovers FC (Birkenhead)	46	6	16	24	45	78	28	R
24.	Lincoln City FC (Lincoln)	46	7	11	28	41	88	25	R
		1104	378	348	378	1388	1388	1104	

Football League Division 4 — 1978-79 Season

	Aldershot Town	Barnsley	Bournemouth	Bradford City	Crewe Alexandra	Darlington	Doncaster Rovers	Grimsby Town	Halifax Town	Hartlepool	Hereford United	Huddersfield Town	Newport County	Northampton Town	Portsmouth	Port Vale	Reading	Rochdale	Scunthorpe United	Stockport County	Torquay United	Wigan Ath.	Wimbledon	York City
Aldershot Town FC	■	1-0	1-0	6-0	3-0	1-1	2-1	2-0	1-0	1-1	2-0	1-0	2-3	2-0	0-2	1-1	2-2	1-0	2-0	3-2	1-0	1-0	1-1	1-0
Barnsley FC	2-0	■	1-0	0-1	3-1	1-1	3-0	2-1	4-2	1-0	2-1	1-0	1-0	1-1	1-1	6-2	3-1	0-3	4-1	4-4	1-2	0-0	3-1	3-0
AFC Bournemouth	0-1	0-2	■	1-0	0-1	2-2	7-1	0-0	1-0	0-1	1-1	2-0	3-1	0-0	3-1	3-1	0-0	3-1	0-0	3-1	1-0	2-1	1-2	1-2
Bradford City AFC	0-2	1-2	2-1	■	6-0	0-0	1-0	1-3	3-0	1-2	2-1	1-1	1-3	3-0	2-0	2-3	2-3	1-1	11-	3-1	1-1	1-0	2-1	2-1
Crewe Alexandra FC	1-1	0-2	1-0	1-2	■	1-1	2-4	0-3	1-0	0-1	0-0	3-3	0-1	2-4	0-0	1-5	0-2	1-2	0-2	2-2	6-2	1-1	1-2	0-1
Darlington FC	2-1	0-0	0-0	1-1	1-1	■	3-2	0-1	2-1	0-1	2-1	1-0	1-0	0-0	2-0	4-0	1-2	0-2	2-2	0-1	1-2	1-1	1-1	0-1
Doncaster Rovers FC	1-1	2-2	1-1	2-0	2-0	2-3	■	0-1	1-1	0-0	1-0	0-2	0-0	2-0	2-3	1-3	2-2	1-0	0-0	2-0	1-0	0-1	1-0	1-2
Grimsby Town FC	0-0	2-0	1-0	5-1	2-2	7-2	3-4	■	2-1	0-1	1-1	2-1	1-0	4-3	1-0	1-0	4-0	1-1	2-1	3-0	3-1	2-2	3-0	
Halifax Town AFC	1-1	0-2	0-2	2-0	0-0	0-2	0-0	1-2	■	2-4	1-0	2-3	1-2	2-2	2-0	0-3	0-0	2-1	2-3	2-1	1-0	1-2	2-1	0-1
Hartlepool United FC	2-2	1-1	0-0	2-2	2-2	0-2	3-4	1-0	3-1	■	2-1	2-0	0-0	2-0	1-1	1-2	0-0	5-1	1-1	1-3	3-2	1-1	1-1	1-1
Hereford United FC	1-1	1-1	0-0	3-1	6-1	1-0	2-0	0-1	2-2	1-0	■	3-0	0-3	4-3	0-1	1-0	0-0	2-2	3-1	1-0	3-1	0-0	0-0	1-1
Huddersfield Town	0-0	1-0	2-1	0-0	0-0	2-2	2-1	2-0	2-0	2-0	2-3	■	0-1	1-0	2-0	3-2	1-1	3-2	0-0	1-1	1-1	3-0	1-1	
Newport County AFC	1-2	1-1	2-0	2-4	1-2	2-1	3-0	1-1	2-0	3-2	4-1	2-1	■	2-1	1-2	1-0	3-2	0-0	2-0	1-2	1-1	2-1	1-3	1-1
Northampton Town	2-3	0-1	4-2	1-0	3-1	4-1	3-0	1-2	2-1	1-1	2-1	2-3	3-1	■	0-2	1-0	2-2	1-0	1-0	2-2	1-2	2-4	1-1	1-1
Portsmouth FC	1-1	0-1	1-1	0-1	3-0	3-0	4-0	1-3	3-1	3-0	1-0	2-0	1-0	2-1	■	2-0	4-0	1-1	0-0	1-1	1-0	1-0	0-0	1-1
Port Vale FC	1-1	3-2	1-2	2-1	2-2	2-1	1-3	1-1	0-1	2-0	1-1	1-0	1-1	2-2	0-0	■	0-3	1-1	2-2	2-1	1-2	2-1	1-0	0-0
Reading FC	4-0	1-0	1-0	3-0	3-0	1-0	3-0	4-0	1-0	3-1	3-0	1-1	2-1	5-1	2-0	0-0	■	2-0	0-1	3-3	1-0	2-0	1-0	3-0
Rochdale AFC	1-1	0-3	2-1	1-0	2-1	2-1	2-0	2-5	1-1	1-1	0-2	0-2	1-0	4-1	0-2	0-1	1-0	■	1-0	2-0	1-0	0-2	0-0	1-2
Scunthorpe United	2-0	0-1	1-0	3-2	0-1	1-0	0-0	2-1	1-0	3-1	4-2	3-1	2-3	0-3	2-2	2-0	0-3	0-4	■	1-0	2-2	0-1	2-0	2-3
Stockport County	2-2	0-0	1-0	1-0	4-3	3-0	0-1	2-1	1-2	4-0	0-2	3-1	1-1	2-1	4-2	0-0	0-0	3-0	0-2	■	0-1	0-1	0-1	2-0
Torquay United FC	2-1	3-2	0-1	1-2	3-0	1-0	2-1	3-1	2-0	4-1	2-1	2-0	0-1	2-1	2-2	1-1	1-1	0-1	1-0	■	1-1	1-6	3-0	
Wigan Athletic AFC	3-2	1-1	1-0	1-3	1-0	2-2	1-0	0-3	1-0	2-2	0-0	2-1	2-3	2-0	2-0	5-3	3-0	3-0	1-0	2-0	3-1	■	1-1	1-1
Wimbledon FC	3-1	1-1	4-0	2-1	1-1	2-0	3-2	0-1	2-1	3-1	2-0	2-1	0-0	4-1	1-0	1-0	3-2	3-1	2-0	5-0	2-1		■	2-1
York City FC	1-1	0-1	2-1	2-2	1-0	5-2	1-1	0-0	2-0	1-1	1-0	1-3	1-2	1-0	5-3	4-0	0-1	2-1	1-0	1-0	0-0	0-1	1-4	■

	Division 4	Pd	Wn	Dw	Ls	GF	GA	Pts	
1.	Reading FC (Reading)	46	26	13	7	76	35	65	P
2.	Grimsby Town FC (Cleethorpes)	46	26	9	11	82	49	61	P
3.	Wimbledon FC (London)	46	25	11	10	78	46	61	P
4.	Barnsley FC (Barnsley)	46	24	13	9	73	42	61	P
5.	Aldershot FC (Aldershot)	46	20	17	9	63	47	57	
6.	Wigan Athletic AFC (Wigan)	46	21	13	12	63	48	55	
7.	Portsmouth FC (Portsmouth)	46	20	12	14	62	48	52	
8.	Newport County AFC (Newport)	46	21	10	15	66	55	52	
9.	Huddersfield Town AFC (Huddersfield)	46	18	11	17	57	53	47	
10.	York City FC (York)	46	18	11	17	51	55	47	
11.	Torquay United FC (Torquay)	46	19	8	19	58	65	46	
12.	Scunthorpe United FC (Scunthorpe)	46	17	11	18	54	60	45	
13.	Hartlepool United FC (Hartlepool)	46	13	18	15	57	66	44	
14.	Hereford United FC (Hereford)	46	15	13	18	53	53	43	
15.	Bradford City AFC (Bradford)	46	17	9	20	62	68	43	
16.	Port Vale FC (Stoke-on-Trent)	46	14	14	18	57	70	42	
17.	Stockport County FC (Stockport)	46	14	12	20	58	60	40	
18.	AFC Bournemouth (Bournemouth)	46	14	11	21	47	48	39	
19.	Northampton Town FC (Northampton)	46	15	9	22	64	76	39	
20.	Rochdale AFC (Rochdale)	46	15	9	22	47	64	39	
21.	Darlington FC (Darlington)	46	11	15	20	49	66	37	
22.	Doncaster Rovers FC (Doncaster)	46	13	11	22	50	73	37	
23.	Halifax Town AFC (Halifax)	46	9	8	29	39	72	26	
24.	Crewe Alexandra FC (Crewe)	46	6	14	26	43	90	26	
		1104	411	282	411	1409	1409	1104	

F.A. CUP FINAL   (Wembley Stadium, London – 12/05/1979)

ARSENAL FC (LONDON)   3-2   Manchester United FC (Manchester)
Talbot, Stapleton, Sunderland   *(H.T. 2-0)*   *McQueen, McIlroy*

Arsenal: Jennings, Rice, Nelson, Talbot, O'Leary, Young, Brady, Sunderland, Stapleton, Price (Walford), Rix.

Man. United: Bailey, Nicholl, Albiston, McIlroy, McQueen, Buchan, Coppell, J.Greenhoff, Jordan, Macari, Thomas.

Semi-finals

Arsenal FC (London)   2-0   Wolverhampton Wanderers FC (Wolverhampton)
Liverpool FC (Liverpool)   2-2, 0-1   Manchester United FC (Manchester)

Quarter-finals

Ipswich Town FC (Ipswich)   0-1   Liverpool FC (Liverpool)
Southampton FC (Southampton)   1-1, 0-2   Arsenal FC (London)
Tottenham Hotspur FC (London)   1-1, 0-2   Manchester United FC (Manchester)
Wolverhampton Wanderers FC (Wolverhampton) 1-1, 3-1   Shrewsbury Town FC (Shrewsbury)

1979-80

Football League Division 1 1979-80 Season	Arsenal	Aston Villa	Bolton Wanderers	Brighton & H.A.	Bristol City	Coventry City	Crystal Palace	Derby County	Everton	Ipswich Town	Leeds United	Liverpool	Manchester City	Manchester United	Middlesbrough	Norwich City	Nottingham Forest	Southampton	Stoke City	Tottenham Hotspur	W.B.A.	Wolves
Arsenal FC		3-1	2-0	3-0	0-0	3-1	1-1	2-0	2-0	0-2	0-1	0-0	0-0	0-0	2-0	1-1	0-0	1-1	0-0	1-0	1-1	2-3
Aston Villa FC	0-0		3-1	2-1	0-2	3-0	2-0	1-0	2-1	1-1	0-0	1-3	2-2	0-3	0-2	2-0	3-2	3-0	2-1	1-0	0-0	1-3
Bolton Wanderers FC	0-0	1-1		0-2	1-1	1-1	1-1	1-2	1-1	0-1	1-1	1-1	0-1	1-3	2-2	1-0	1-0	2-1	2-1	2-1	0-0	0-0
Brighton & Hove Albion FC	0-4	1-1	3-1		0-1	1-1	3-0	2-0	0-0	2-0	0-0	1-4	4-1	0-0	2-1	2-4	1-0	0-0	0-0	0-2	0-0	3-0
Bristol City FC	0-1	1-3	2-1	2-2		1-0	0-2	0-2	2-1	0-3	2-2	1-3	1-0	1-1	3-1	2-3	1-1	0-1	0-0	1-3	0-0	2-0
Coventry City FC	0-1	1-2	3-1	2-1	3-1		2-1	2-1	2-1	4-1	3-0	1-0	0-0	1-2	2-0	2-0	0-3	3-0	1-3	1-1	0-2	1-3
Crystal Palace FC	1-0	2-0	3-1	1-1	1-1	0-0		4-0	1-1	4-1	1-0	0-0	0-2	1-2	0-0	1-0	0-0	1-0	0-0	1-1	2-2	1-0
Derby County FC	3-2	1-3	4-0	3-0	3-3	1-2	1-2		0-1	0-1	2-0	1-3	3-1	1-3	1-0	0-0	4-1	2-2	2-2	2-1	2-1	0-1
Everton FC	0-1	1-1	3-1	2-0	0-0	1-1	3-1	1-1		0-4	5-1	1-2	1-2	0-0	0-2	2-4	1-0	2-0	2-0	1-1	0-0	2-3
Ipswich Town FC	1-2	0-0	1-0	1-1	1-0	3-0	3-0	1-1	1-1		1-0	1-2	4-0	6-0	1-0	4-2	0-1	3-1	3-1	3-1	4-0	1-0
Leeds United AFC	1-1	0-0	2-2	1-1	1-3	0-0	1-0	1-0	2-0	2-1		1-1	1-2	2-0	2-0	2-2	1-2	2-0	3-0	1-2	1-0	3-0
Liverpool FC	1-1	4-1	0-0	1-0	4-0	4-0	3-0	3-0	2-2	1-1	3-0		2-0	2-0	4-0	0-0	2-0	1-1	1-0	2-1	3-1	3-0
Manchester City FC	0-3	1-1	2-2	3-2	3-1	3-0	0-0	3-0	1-1	2-1	1-1	0-4		2-0	1-0	0-0	1-0	0-1	1-1	1-1	1-3	2-3
Manchester United FC	3-0	2-1	2-0	2-0	4-0	2-1	1-1	1-0	0-0	1-0	1-1	2-1	1-0		2-1	5-0	3-0	1-0	4-0	4-1	2-0	0-1
Middlesbrough FC	5-0	0-0	3-1	1-1	1-0	1-2	1-1	2-1	1-1	3-1	1-0	3-0	1-1	1-1		1-0	0-0	0-1	1-3	0-0	2-1	1-0
Norwich City FC	2-1	1-1	2-1	2-2	2-0	1-0	2-1	4-2	0-0	3-3	2-1	3-5	2-2	0-2	0-0		3-1	2-1	2-2	4-0	1-1	0-4
Nottingham Forest FC	1-1	2-1	5-2	0-1	0-0	4-1	4-0	1-0	1-0	2-0	0-0	1-0	4-0	2-0	2-2	2-0		2-0	1-0	4-0	3-1	3-2
Southampton FC	0-1	2-0	2-0	5-1	5-2	2-3	4-1	4-0	1-0	0-1	1-2	3-2	4-1	1-1	4-1	2-0	4-1		3-1	5-2	1-1	0-3
Stoke City FC	2-3	2-0	1-0	1-0	1-0	3-2	1-2	3-2	2-3	0-1	0-2	0-2	0-0	0-0	2-1	1-1	1-2	1-1		3-1	3-2	0-1
Tottenham Hotspur FC	1-2	1-2	2-0	2-1	0-0	4-3	0-0	1-0	3-0	0-2	2-1	2-0	2-1	1-2	1-3	3-2	1-0	0-0	1-0		1-1	2-2
West Bromwich Albion FC	2-2	1-2	4-4	2-2	3-0	4-1	3-0	0-0	1-1	0-0	2-1	0-2	4-0	2-0	0-0	2-1	1-5	4-0	0-1	2-1		0-0
Wolverhampton Wanderers FC	1-2	1-1	3-1	1-3	3-0	0-3	1-1	0-0	0-0	3-0	3-1	1-0	1-2	3-1	0-2	1-0	3-1	0-0	3-0	1-2	0-0	

	Division 1	Pd	Wn	Dw	Ls	GF	GA	Pts	
1.	LIVERPOOL FC (LIVERPOOL)	42	25	10	7	81	30	60	
2.	Manchester United FC (Manchester)	42	24	10	8	65	35	58	
3.	Ipswich Town FC (Ipswich)	42	22	9	11	68	39	53	
4.	Arsenal FC (London)	42	18	16	8	52	36	52	
5.	Nottingham Forest FC (Nottingham)	42	20	8	14	63	43	48	
6.	Wolverhampton Wanderers FC (Wolverhampton)	42	19	9	14	58	47	47	
7.	Aston Villa FC (Birmingham)	42	16	14	12	51	50	46	
8.	Southampton FC (Southampton)	42	18	9	15	65	53	45	
9.	Middlesbrough FC (Middlesbrough)	42	16	12	14	50	44	44	
10.	West Bromwich Albion FC (West Bromwich)	42	11	19	12	54	50	41	
11.	Leeds United AFC (Leeds)	42	13	14	15	46	50	40	
12.	Norwich City FC (Norwich)	42	13	14	15	58	66	40	
13.	Crystal Palace FC (London)	42	12	16	14	41	50	40	
14.	Tottenham Hotspur FC (London)	42	15	10	17	52	62	40	
15.	Coventry City FC (Coventry)	42	16	7	19	56	66	39	
16.	Brighton & Hove Albion FC (Hove)	42	11	15	16	47	57	37	
17.	Manchester City FC (Manchester)	42	12	13	17	43	66	37	
18.	Stoke City FC (Stoke-on-Trent)	42	13	10	19	44	58	36	
19.	Everton FC (Liverpool)	42	9	17	16	43	51	35	
20.	Bristol City FC (Bristol)	42	9	13	20	37	66	31	R
21.	Derby County FC (Derby)	42	11	8	23	47	67	30	R
22.	Bolton Wanderers FC (Bolton)	42	5	15	22	38	73	25	R
		924	328	268	328	1159	1159	924	

Top Goalscorer

1) Phil BOYER   (Southampton FC)   23

Football League Division 2 — 1979-80 Season

	Birmingham City	Bristol Rovers	Burnley	Cambridge	Cardiff City	Charlton Athletic	Chelsea	Fulham	Leicester City	Luton Town	Newcastle United	Notts County	Oldham Athletic	Orient	Preston North End	Q.P.R.	Shrewsbury Town	Sunderland	Swansea City	Watford	West Ham United	Wrexham
Birmingham City FC	■	1-1	2-0	1-0	2-1	1-0	5-1	3-4	1-2	1-0	0-0	3-3	2-0	3-1	2-2	2-1	1-0	1-0	2-0	2-0	0-0	2-0
Bristol Rovers FC	1-0	■	0-0	0-0	1-1	3-0	3-0	1-0	1-1	3-2	1-1	2-3	2-0	1-2	3-3	1-3	2-1	2-2	4-1	1-1	0-2	1-0
Burnley FC	0-0	1-1	■	5-3	0-2	1-1	0-1	2-1	1-2	0-0	3-2	0-1	1-1	1-2	1-1	0-3	0-0	1-1	0-0	1-0	0-1	1-0
Cambridge United FC	2-1	4-1	3-1	■	2-0	1-0	0-1	4-0	1-1	1-2	0-0	2-3	3-3	1-1	3-2	2-1	2-0	3-3	0-1	2-2	2-0	2-0
Cardiff City FC	1-2	0-1	2-1	0-0	■	3-1	1-2	1-0	0-1	2-1	1-1	3-2	1-0	0-0	0-2	1-0	1-0	1-1	1-0	1-0	0-1	1-0
Charlton Athletic FC	0-1	4-0	3-3	1-1	3-2	■	1-2	0-1	2-0	1-4	1-1	0-0	2-1	0-1	0-3	2-2	2-1	0-4	1-2	0-0	1-0	1-2
Chelsea FC	1-2	1-0	2-1	1-1	1-0	3-1	■	0-2	1-1	4-0	1-1	3-0	1-0	2-0	0-2	2-4	0-0	3-0	2-0	2-1		3-1
Fulham FC	2-4	1-1	3-1	1-2	2-1	1-0	1-2	■	0-0	1-3	1-0	1-3	0-1	0-0	1-0	0-2	2-1	0-1	1-2	0-0	1-2	0-2
Leicester City FC	2-1	3-0	1-1	2-1	0-0	2-1	1-0	3-3	■	1-3	1-0	1-0	0-1	2-2	1-2	2-0	2-0	2-1	1-1	1-2	1-2	2-0
Luton Town FC	2-3	3-1	1-1	1-1	1-2	3-0	3-3	4-0	0-0	■	1-1	2-1	0-0	2-1	1-1	1-1	0-0	2-0	5-0	1-0	1-1	2-0
Newcastle United FC	0-0	3-1	1-1	2-0	1-0	2-1	2-1	2-0	3-2	2-2	■	2-2	3-2	0-0	4-2	1-0	3-1	1-3	0-2	0-0		1-0
Notts County FC	1-1	0-0	2-3	0-0	4-1	0-0	2-3	1-1	0-0	2-2		■	1-1	1-2	2-1	1-0	5-2	0-1	0-0		1-1	1-1
Oldham Athletic AFC	1-0	2-1	2-1	1-1	0-3	4-3	1-0	0-1	1-1	2-1	1-0	1-0	■	1-0	3-2	0-0	0-2	3-0	4-1	1-1	0-0	2-3
Orient FC	2-2	2-1	2-2	2-0	1-1	1-1	3-7	1-0	0-0	2-2	1-4	1-0	1-1	■	2-2	1-1	0-1	2-1	0-0	1-0	0-4	4-0
Preston North End FC	0-0	3-2	3-2	2-2	2-0	1-1	1-1	3-2	1-1	1-1	2-0	0-1	2-2		■	0-3	3-0	2-1	1-1	1-2	1-1	0-0
Queen's Park Rangers FC	1-1	2-0	7-0	2-2	3-0	4-0	2-2	1-4	2-2	2-1	1-3	4-3	0-0	1-1		■	2-1	0-0	3-2	1-1	3-0	2-2
Shrewsbury Town FC	1-0	3-1	3-1	1-2	1-2	3-1	3-0	5-2	2-2	1-2	3-1	1-1	0-1	1-0	1-3	3-0	■	1-2	2-2	1-0		3-1
Sunderland AFC	2-0	3-2	5-0	2-0	2-1	4-0	2-1	2-1	0-0	1-0	1-0	3-1	4-2	1-1	1-1	3-0	2-1	■	1-1	5-0	2-0	1-1
Swansea City FC	0-1	2-0	2-1	2-4	1-0	1-1	4-1	1-0	2-0	2-0	2-3	0-0	0-1	1-0	1-2	2-0	3-1		■	1-0	2-1	1-0
Watford FC	1-0	0-0	4-0	0-0	1-1	2-1	2-3	4-0	1-3	0-1	2-0	2-0	1-0	0-3	0-0	0-1	1-1	0-0		■	2-0	3-1
West Ham United FC	1-2	2-1	2-1	3-1	3-0	4-1	0-1	2-3	3-1	1-0	1-1	1-2	1-0	2-0	2-1	1-3	2-0	2-0	1-1		■	1-0
Wrexham AFC	1-0	1-2	1-0	1-0	0-1	3-2	2-0	1-1	0-1	3-1	1-0	1-0	1-1	2-1	2-0	1-3	0-1	0-1	1-0	3-0	1-0	■

	Division 2	Pd	Wn	Dw	Ls	GF	GA	Pts	
1.	Leicester City FC (Leicester)	42	21	13	8	58	38	55	P
2.	Sunderland AFC (Sunderland)	42	21	12	9	69	42	54	P
3.	Birmingham City FC (Birmingham)	42	21	11	10	58	38	53	P
4.	Chelsea FC (London)	42	23	7	12	66	52	53	
5.	Queen's Park Rangers FC (London)	42	18	13	11	75	53	49	
6.	Luton Town FC (Luton)	42	16	17	9	66	45	49	
7.	West Ham United FC (London)	42	20	7	15	54	43	47	
8.	Cambridge United FC (Cambridge)	42	14	16	12	61	53	44	
9.	Newcastle United FC (Newcastle-upon-Tyne)	42	15	14	13	53	49	44	
10.	Preston North End FC (Preston)	42	12	19	11	56	52	43	
11.	Oldham Athletic AFC (Oldham)	42	16	11	15	49	53	43	
12.	Swansea City FC (Swansea)	42	17	9	16	48	53	43	
13.	Shrewsbury Town FC (Shrewsbury)	42	18	5	19	60	53	41	
14.	Orient FC (London)	42	12	17	13	48	54	41	
15.	Cardiff City AFC (Cardiff)	42	16	8	18	41	48	40	
16.	Wrexham AFC (Wrexham)	42	16	6	20	40	49	38	
17.	Notts County FC (Nottingham)	42	11	15	16	51	52	37	
18.	Watford FC (Watford)	42	12	13	17	39	46	37	
19.	Bristol Rovers FC (Bristol)	42	11	13	18	50	64	35	
20.	Fulham FC (London)	42	11	7	24	42	74	29	R
21.	Burnley FC (Burnley)	42	6	15	21	39	73	27	R
22.	Charlton Athletic FC (London)	42	6	10	26	39	78	22	R
		924	333	258	333	1162	1162	924	

Football League Division 3 1979-80 Season	Barnsley	Blackburn Rovers	Blackpool	Brentford	Bury	Carlisle United	Chester	Chesterfield	Colchester United	Exeter City	Gillingham	Grimsby Town	Hull City	Mansfield Town	Millwall	Oxford United	Plymouth Argyle	Reading	Rotherham United	Sheffield United	Sheffield Wed.	Southend United	Swindon Town	Wimbledon
Barnsley FC		1-1	2-1	1-0	2-1	1-1	1-1	0-1	1-2	2-2	2-0	0-1	3-1	1-0	2-1	2-0	0-0	2-0	0-0	0-0	0-3	1-2	1-2	4-0
Blackburn Rovers FC	0-1		2-0	3-0	1-2	1-2	2-0	1-0	3-0	1-1	3-1	0-0	1-0	0-0	1-1	2-1	1-0	4-2	0-3	1-0	1-2	1-1	2-0	3-0
Blackpool FC	1-1	2-1		5-4	1-2	2-1	0-0	2-2	1-0	1-0	2-1	0-3	2-2	1-1	2-2	1-2	1-3	5-2	3-2	2-3	1-1	1-0	0-1	3-0
Brentford FC	3-1	2-0	2-1		0-0	0-3	2-2	3-1	1-0	0-2	0-2	1-0	7-2	2-0	1-0	1-1	0-0	2-2	0-1	1-2	2-2	2-0	1-3	0-1
Bury FC	2-2	1-2	3-0	4-2		0-2	2-0	2-0	0-1	3-0	0-2	1-1	0-1	0-2	3-0	1-2	2-1	1-0	1-0	1-2	1-0	1-1	0-0	1-2
Carlisle United FC	3-1	1-1	2-0	3-1	1-0		2-2	0-2	2-0	4-1	1-2	0-2	3-2	1-1	4-0	2-2	2-1	3-3	3-1	1-0	0-2	4-0	2-1	1-1
Chester FC	0-0	0-0	1-0	1-1	1-0	1-0		1-0	2-1	1-3	0-2	3-1	2-1	1-0	1-1	1-0	0-2	3-1	1-1	2-2	2-1	1-0	3-1
Chesterfield FC	2-0	0-1	0-0	1-0	2-0	3-2	2-0		3-0	3-0	1-1	2-3	1-1	2-0	3-2	2-2	3-1	7-1	3-0	2-1	2-1	1-0	2-1	0-0
Colchester United FC	0-0	0-1	3-1	6-1	2-1	1-1	1-1	0-1		0-0	2-2	2-1	1-1	2-1	0-0	3-0	5-2	1-1	1-1	1-0	0-0	2-1	2-3	4-0
Exeter City FC	2-1	2-0	1-0	0-1	1-0	1-2	1-0	1-2	3-1		3-1	1-2	2-2	2-1	2-1	0-0	2-2	1-0	1-1	3-1	1-0	4-2	4-1	0-2
Gillingham FC	1-1	1-2	1-1	0-1	2-1	1-1	2-2	0-1	2-2	1-0		0-1	1-0	2-0	1-1	4-0	0-1	1-1	0-1	3-0	1-1	1-0	0-0	1-0
Grimsby Town FC	3-0	1-2	4-3	5-1	1-0	2-0	0-2	1-1	1-2	4-1	1-0		1-1	2-0	2-0	1-0	2-1	2-0	4-0	3-1	1-0	2-0	1-0	
Hull City AFC	0-2	0-1	3-1	2-1	0-1	2-0	1-0	2-1	0-2	2-2	0-0	2-2		3-1	1-0	2-2	1-0	0-1	1-1	3-1	1-1	1-0	1-0	1-1
Mansfield Town FC	1-4	0-1	1-1	1-0	1-0	2-1	2-1	3-2	0-1	0-1	2-0	0-0	1-1		1-0	1-0	2-2	5-1	3-4	1-1	3-1	1-1	1-1	
Millwall FC	2-2	1-0	2-0	3-1	0-1	1-0	3-1	2-0	1-2	5-1	2-0	2-0	3-2	2-2		3-0	2-1	2-0	0-0	1-1	3-3	1-2	6-2	2-2
Oxford United FC	1-0	0-1	0-2	0-2	3-1	1-0	0-1	1-2	0-2	2-0	1-1	0-1	3-0	3-1	1-2		1-1	4-0	5-1	1-1	0-2	1-0	2-2	4-1
Plymouth Argyle FC	2-1	0-1	2-2	0-1	2-0	4-2	1-0	1-0	2-0	2-0	2-2	1-1	5-1	0-0	1-1	1-1		2-0	1-0	4-1	1-3	0-0	2-0	3-0
Reading FC	7-0	1-1	0-1	2-2	3-1	2-1	2-1	2-2	2-0	2-1	1-3	1-1	3-0	1-0	2-0	2-0	1-0		1-1	2-1	2-1	1-2	2-1	3-0
Rotherham United	1-1	1-3	0-2	4-2	0-2	4-1	2-0	2-0	3-0	2-0	2-1	0-0	2-1	2-1	2-1	0-2	3-1	1-1		1-2	1-2	2-1	3-0	0-0
Sheffield United FC	2-0	2-1	3-1	0-2	0-0	0-2	1-1	0-2	1-2	3-1	4-0	1-1	1-1	1-0	0-1	3-1	3-2	2-0	1-0		1-1	2-0	2-1	2-1
Sheffield Wednesday	0-2	0-3	4-1	0-2	5-1	0-0	3-0	3-3	3-0	0-1	1-0	2-0	0-0	0-0	2-0	2-2	0-1	1-1	5-0	4-0		2-0	4-2	3-1
Southend United FC	2-1	0-1	1-2	3-2	0-0	1-0	4-1	0-0	0-1	4-0	0-3	1-0	3-0	1-1	1-0	1-1	4-1	2-2	0-2	2-1	1-1		1-0	1-3
Swindon Town FC	0-1	2-0	2-1	4-0	8-0	0-0	3-1	2-1	2-3	2-3	3-0	3-0	0-0	2-1	1-0	1-1	2-1	0-0	6-2	3-2	1-2	1-0		2-1
Wimbledon FC	1-2	1-0	1-2	0-0	0-1	0-0	2-3	1-1	3-3	2-2	1-0	3-6	3-2	3-2	2-2	1-3	3-1	1-1	0-1	1-1	3-4	0-1	2-0	

	Division 3	Pd	Wn	Dw	Ls	GF	GA	Pts	
1.	Grimsby Town FC (Cleethorpes)	46	26	10	10	73	42	62	P
2.	Blackburn Rovers FC (Blackburn)	46	25	9	12	58	36	59	P
3.	Sheffield Wednesday FC (Sheffield)	46	21	16	9	81	47	58	P
4.	Chesterfield FC (Chesterfield)	46	23	11	12	71	46	57	
5.	Colchester United FC (Colchester)	46	20	12	14	64	56	52	
6.	Carlisle United FC (Carlisle)	46	18	12	16	66	56	48	
7.	Reading FC (Reading)	46	16	16	14	66	65	48	
8.	Exeter City FC (Exeter)	46	19	10	17	60	68	48	
9.	Chester FC (Chester)	46	17	13	16	49	57	47	
10.	Swindon Town FC (Swindon)	46	19	8	19	71	63	46	
11.	Barnsley FC (Barnsley)	46	16	14	16	53	56	46	
12.	Sheffield United FC (Sheffield)	46	18	10	18	60	66	46	
13.	Rotherham United FC (Rotherham)	46	18	10	18	58	66	46	
14.	Millwall FC (London)	46	16	13	17	65	59	45	
15.	Plymouth Argyle FC (Plymouth)	46	16	12	18	59	55	44	
16.	Gillingham FC (Gillingham)	46	14	14	18	49	51	42	
17.	Oxford United FC (Oxford)	46	14	13	19	57	62	41	
18.	Blackpool FC (Blackpool)	46	15	11	20	62	74	41	
19.	Brentford FC (London)	46	15	11	20	59	73	41	
20.	Hull City AFC (Kingston-upon-Hull)	46	12	16	18	51	69	40	
21.	Bury FC (Bury)	46	16	7	23	45	59	39	R
22.	Southend United FC (Southend-on-Sea)	46	14	10	22	47	58	38	R
23.	Mansfield Town FC (Mansfield)	46	10	16	20	47	58	36	R
24.	Wimbledon FC (London)	46	10	14	22	52	81	34	R
		1104	408	288	408	1423	1423	1104	

Football League Division 4 — 1979-80 Season

	Aldershot Town	Bournemouth	Bradford City	Crewe Alexandra	Darlington	Doncaster Rovers	Halifax Town	Hartlepool	Hereford United	Huddersfield Town	Lincoln City	Newport County	Northampton Town	Peterborough United	Portsmouth	Port Vale	Rochdale	Scunthorpe United	Stockport County	Torquay United	Tranmere Rovers	Walsall	Wigan Ath.	York City
Aldershot Town FC		0-1	3-1	3-0	1-1	1-1	3-1	0-2	3-3	0-2	2-0	0-1	2-0	2-0	1-2	3-1	3-0	2-0	2-0	1-1	0-0	1-1	0-3	2-2
AFC Bournemouth	3-1		1-1	0-1	1-0	0-0	0-1	2-1	2-2	1-3	0-0	3-2	2-2	0-0	0-1	3-1	4-0	3-3	2-0	1-2	2-1	1-1	1-2	0-0
Bradford City AFC	2-0	2-2		4-0	3-0	3-1	2-0	2-0	1-0	0-0	1-1	3-0	3-1	1-1	0-0	2-0	1-2	2-0	6-1	1-1	2-0	0-1	2-1	1-2
Crewe Alexandra FC	1-0	0-0	2-0		0-0	1-2	2-1	2-1	1-0	1-3	0-2	0-3	2-1	1-4	1-1	0-2	2-1	1-1	1-0	2-2	0-0	1-2	2-1	2-0
Darlington FC	0-0	0-1	3-4	0-0		2-1	1-1	0-1	1-1	2-3	1-1	1-1	0-0	1-1	1-1	3-1	3-1	3-0	2-0	3-1	1-3	2-2		2-1
Doncaster Rovers FC	1-1	1-0	0-3	1-1	0-1		2-1	0-2	1-0	1-2	1-1	1-3	2-1	2-1	2-0	2-3	5-0	1-1	5-3	1-1	1-1	3-1	1-1	
Halifax Town AFC	1-0	2-0	0-1	3-1	1-1	1-1		1-0	2-1	0-0	1-2	0-0	2-1	2-0	0-2	1-3	3-3	0-0					0-0	1-1
Hartlepool United FC	1-0	3-1	0-1	3-1	3-1	1-2	1-2		3-0	1-1	0-0	0-0	2-1	1-2	0-3	2-1	11-	3-2	1-2	2-2	2-1	2-2	1-1	3-1
Hereford United FC	0-1	2-1	0-2	2-0	1-0	2-2	2-0	2-1		1-3	0-0	0-2	0-1	0-0	4-1	1-1	1-1	2-0	0-0	1-2	0-1	2-1		2-1
Huddersfield Town	2-0	2-0	0-0	3-0	2-1	3-0	5-0	2-1	0-1		3-2	2-1	5-0	0-0	1-3	7-1	5-1	2-1	5-0	4-2	1-1	1-1	4-0	2-2
Lincoln City FC	1-1	1-1	1-0	2-1	2-1	1-1	4-0	3-3	2-0	2-0		2-1	0-0	1-1	3-0	0-0	4-0	1-0	2-0	3-0	2-2	4-0		1-1
Newport County AFC	4-2	2-0	1-2	4-0	2-1	5-2	1-0	1-0	2-2	1-1	2-1		1-1	4-3	2-1	1-2	3-1	3-0	2-0	3-1	3-0	0-0	3-2	2-0
Northampton Town	2-1	0-1	1-0	2-0	1-0	0-0	2-1	2-0	4-2	0-0	3-2			1-0	0-2	3-1	2-0	3-1	1-0	2-1	1-2	1-1	1-1	2-2
Peterborough United	1-3	2-0	1-0	3-0	3-0	3-2	2-1	2-0	1-3	3-1	0-1	0-0			0-0	3-0	2-0	3-1	1-1	2-1	1-2	1-3	1-2	2-1
Portsmouth FC	1-3	4-0	4-1	1-1	4-3	2-0	3-1	0-0	4-1	0-0	4-0	0-2	6-1	4-0		2-2	3-0	6-0	1-0	3-0	1-1	1-1		5-2
Port Vale FC	0-2	1-1	1-2	2-0	2-0	3-0	1-0	1-1	0-1	1-1	1-2	2-0	5-0	0-1	2-3		5-1	1-0	1-2	1-1	0-1	2-2	1-1	1-2
Rochdale AFC	2-1	0-2	1-2	0-0	2-2	3-2	2-2	1-0	0-2	1-2	2-0	3-2	0-0	1-2	0-2			0-1	0-1	0-0	2-0	1-1	0-2	0-2
Scunthorpe United	1-1	2-1	3-3	1-1	3-0	0-0	1-0	1-3	1-0	1-3	1-3	3-0	1-0	1-0	1-0	2-0			1-1	1-1	2-2	2-2	1-3	6-1
Stockport County FC	0-4	1-1	2-1	2-1	1-1	4-1	0-3	2-1	1-2	0-5	2-0	2-2	2-0	1-1	0-2	1-1	1-2			4-0	2-1	1-0	1-2	2-1
Torquay United FC	2-1	0-0	2-3	1-1	4-0	2-2	3-0	3-1	1-1	3-1	2-5	2-0	2-2	2-1	1-1	3-0	1-1	0-0			3-1	2-2		4-3
Tranmere Rovers FC	1-2	0-5	4-0	2-0	1-2	1-0	2-0	1-0	0-0	0-0	1-0	0-2	1-1	3-0	4-1	1-1	5-1	1-2	0-1	2-0		0-1	1-3	1-2
Walsall FC	1-1	0-0	0-1	1-0	1-1	3-1	2-0	3-1	3-2	1-1	2-4	5-1	2-3	1-1	2-1	2-0	1-1	2-1	1-1	2-0			1-1	3-1
Wigan Athletic AFC	2-1	2-1	4-1	2-0	4-1	0-0	3-1	1-2	1-0	0-1	0-0	2-1	1-2	0-1	3-1	1-1	4-1	1-3	0-3	0-0	3-0			2-5
York City FC	1-1	1-1	2-2	2-2	3-1	1-3	2-2	2-1	3-1	0-4	0-2	2-1	1-2	0-2	1-0	5-1	3-2	2-0	2-2	1-0	0-1	0-1	1-2	

	Division 4	Pd	Wn	Dw	Ls	GF	GA	Pts	
1.	Huddersfield Town AFC (Huddersfield)	46	27	12	7	101	48	66	P
2.	Walsall FC (Walsall)	46	23	18	5	75	47	64	P
3.	Newport County AFC (Newport)	46	27	7	12	83	50	61	P
4.	Portsmouth FC (Portsmouth)	46	24	12	10	91	49	60	P
5.	Bradford City AFC (Bradford)	46	24	12	10	77	50	60	
6.	Wigan Athletic AFC (Wigan)	46	21	13	12	76	61	55	
7.	Lincoln City FC (Lincoln)	46	18	17	11	64	42	53	
8.	Peterborough United FC (Peterborough)	46	21	10	15	58	47	52	
9.	Torquay United FC (Torquay)	46	15	17	14	70	69	47	
10.	Aldershot FC (Aldershot)	46	16	13	17	62	53	45	
11.	AFC Bournemouth (Bournemouth)	46	13	18	15	52	51	44	
12.	Doncaster Rovers FC (Doncaster)	46	15	14	17	62	63	44	
13.	Northampton Town FC (Northampton)	46	16	12	18	51	66	44	
14.	Scunthorpe United FC (Scunthorpe)	46	14	15	17	58	75	43	
15.	Tranmere Rovers FC (Birkenhead)	46	14	13	19	50	56	41	
16.	Stockport County FC (Stockport)	46	14	12	20	48	72	40	
17.	York City FC (York)	46	14	11	21	65	82	39	
18.	Halifax Town AFC (Halifax)	46	13	13	20	46	72	39	
19.	Hartlepool United FC (Hartlepool)	46	14	10	22	59	64	38	
20.	Port Vale FC (Stoke-on-Trent)	46	12	12	22	56	70	36	
21.	Hereford United FC (Hereford)	46	11	14	21	38	52	36	
22.	Darlington FC (Darlington)	46	9	17	20	50	74	35	
23.	Crewe Alexandra FC (Crewe)	46	11	13	22	35	68	35	
24.	Rochdale AFC (Rochdale)	46	7	13	26	33	79	27	
		1104	393	318	393	1460	1460	1104	

F.A. CUP FINAL   (Wembley Stadium, London – 10/05/1980 – 100,000)

WEST HAM UNITED FC (LONDON)   1-0   Arsenal FC (London)

Brooking

West Ham: Parkes, Stewart, Lampard, Bonds, Martin, Devonshire, Pike, Brooking, Cross, Pearson, Allen.
Arsenal: Jennings, Rice, Devine (Nelson), Talbot, O'Leary, Young, Price, Rix, Brady, Stapleton, Sunderland.

Semi-finals

Arsenal FC (London)	0-0, 1-1, 1-1, 1-0	Liverpool FC (Liverpool)
Everton FC (Liverpool)	1-1, 1-2	West Ham United FC (London)

Quarter-finals

Everton FC (Liverpool)	2-1	Ipswich Town FC (Ipswich)
Tottenham Hotspur FC (London)	0-1	Liverpool FC (Liverpool)
Watford FC (Watford)	1-2	Arsenal FC (London)
West Ham United FC (London)	1-0	Aston Villa FC (Birmingham)

1980-81

Football League Division 1 1980-81 Season	Arsenal	Aston Villa	Birmingham City	Brighton & H.A.	Coventry City	Crystal Palace	Everton	Ipswich Town	Leeds United	Leicester City	Liverpool	Man. City	Man. United	Middlesbrough	Norwich City	Nottingham F.	Southampton	Stoke City	Sunderland	Tottenham H.	W.B.A.	Wolves
Arsenal FC	■	2-0	2-1	2-0	2-2	3-2	2-1	1-1	0-0	1-0	1-0	2-0	2-1	2-2	3-1	1-0	1-1	2-0	2-2	2-0	2-2	1-1
Aston Villa FC	1-1	■	3-0	4-1	1-0	2-1	0-2	1-2	1-1	2-0	2-0	1-0	3-3	3-0	1-0	2-0	2-1	1-0	4-0	3-0	1-0	2-1
Birmingham City FC	3-1	1-2	■	2-1	3-1	1-0	1-1	1-3	0-2	1-2	1-1	2-0	0-0	2-1	4-0	2-0	0-3	1-1	3-2	2-1	1-1	1-0
Brighton & Hove Albion FC	0-1	1-0	2-2	■	4-1	3-2	1-3	1-0	2-0	2-1	2-2	1-2	1-4	0-1	2-0	0-1	2-0	1-1	2-1	0-2	1-2	2-0
Coventry City FC	3-1	1-2	2-1	3-3	■	3-1	0-5	0-4	2-1	4-1	0-0	1-1	0-2	1-0	0-1	1-1	1-0	2-2	2-1	0-1	3-0	2-2
Crystal Palace FC	2-2	0-1	3-1	0-3	0-3	■	2-3	1-2	0-1	2-1	2-2	2-3	1-0	5-1	4-1	1-3	3-2	1-1	0-1	3-4	0-1	0-0
Everton FC	1-2	1-3	1-1	4-3	3-0	5-0	■	0-0	1-2	1-0	2-2	0-2	0-1	4-1	1-0	2-1	0-1	2-1	2-2	1-1	1-1	2-0
Ipswich Town FC	0-2	1-0	5-1	2-0	3-2	4-0	1-0	■	3-1	1-1	1-1	1-0	2-0	2-0	2-3	4-0	4-1	3-0	2-0	1-1	4-0	3-1
Leeds United AFC	0-5	1-2	0-0	1-0	3-0	1-0	1-0	3-0	■	1-2	0-0	1-0	0-0	2-1	1-0	1-0	0-3	1-3	1-0	0-0	0-0	1-3
Leicester City FC	1-0	2-4	1-0	0-1	1-3	1-1	0-1	0-1	0-1	■	2-0	1-1	1-0	1-0	1-2	1-1	2-2	1-1	0-1	2-1	0-2	2-0
Liverpool FC	1-1	2-1	2-2	4-1	2-1	3-0	1-0	1-1	0-0	1-2	■	1-0	0-1	4-2	4-1	0-0	2-0	3-0	0-1	4-1	1-0	1-0
Manchester City FC	1-1	2-2	0-1	1-1	3-0	1-1	3-1	1-1	3-3	3-1	0-3	■	1-0	3-2	1-0	3-0	1-2	0-4	3-1	1-0	0-1	2-0
Manchester United FC	0-0	3-3	2-0	2-1	0-0	2-0	2-1	2-1	0-1	5-0	0-0	2-2	■	3-0	1-0	1-1	1-1	2-2	1-1	0-0	1-0	0-0
Middlesbrough FC	2-1	2-1	1-2	1-0	0-1	2-0	1-0	3-0	1-0	1-2	2-2	1-1	2-2	■	6-1	0-0	1-1	3-1	1-0	4-1	2-1	2-0
Norwich City FC	1-1	1-3	2-2	3-1	2-0	1-1	2-1	1-0	2-3	2-3	0-1	2-0	2-2	2-0	■	1-1	1-0	5-1	1-0	2-2	0-2	1-1
Nottingham Forest FC	3-1	2-2	2-1	4-1	1-1	3-0	1-0	1-2	5-0	0-0	3-2	1-2	1-0	2-1	3-1	■	2-1	5-0	3-1	0-3	2-1	1-0
Southampton FC	3-1	2-2	3-1	3-1	1-0	4-2	3-3	3-3	4-0	2-2	2-0	1-0	2-1	2-0	3-2	1-0	■	1-2	2-1	1-1	2-2	4-2
Stoke City FC	1-1	1-1	0-0	0-0	2-2	1-0	2-2	2-2	3-0	1-0	0-2	2-1	1-2	1-0	3-1	1-2	1-2	■	2-0	2-3	0-0	3-2
Sunderland AFC	2-0	1-2	3-0	1-2	3-0	1-0	3-1	0-2	4-1	0-1	0-2	2-4	2-0	2-0	0-1	3-0	2-2	1-2	■	1-1	0-0	0-1
Tottenham Hotspur FC	2-0	2-0	1-0	2-2	4-1	4-2	2-2	5-3	1-1	1-2	1-1	2-1	0-0	3-2	2-3	0-3	4-4	2-2	0-0	■	2-3	2-2
West Bromwich Albion FC	0-1	0-0	2-2	2-0	1-0	1-0	3-1	1-2	3-1	2-0	3-1	3-1	3-0	3-0	2-1	2-1	0-0	2-1	4-2	2-3	■	1-1
Wolverhampton Wanderers FC	1-2	0-1	1-0	0-2	0-1	2-0	0-0	0-2	2-1	0-1	4-1	1-3	1-0	3-0	3-0	1-4	1-1	1-0	2-1	1-0	2-0	■

Division 1

		Pd	Wn	Dw	Ls	GF	GA	Pts	
1.	ASTON VILLA FC (BIRMINGHAM)	42	26	8	8	72	40	60	
2.	Ipswich Town FC (Ipswich)	42	23	10	9	77	43	56	
3.	Arsenal FC (London)	42	19	15	8	61	45	53	
4.	West Bromwich Albion FC (West Bromwich)	42	20	12	10	60	42	52	
5.	Liverpool FC (Liverpool)	42	17	17	8	62	42	51	
6.	Southampton FC (Southampton)	42	20	10	12	76	56	50	
7.	Nottingham Forest FC (Nottingham)	42	19	12	11	62	44	50	
8.	Manchester United FC (Manchester)	42	15	18	9	51	36	48	
9.	Leeds United AFC (Leeds)	42	17	10	15	39	47	44	
10.	Tottenham Hotspur FC (London)	42	14	15	13	70	68	43	
11.	Stoke City FC (Stoke-on-Trent)	42	12	18	12	51	60	42	
12.	Manchester City FC (Manchester)	42	14	11	17	56	59	39	
13.	Birmingham City FC (Birmingham)	42	13	12	17	50	61	38	
14.	Middlesbrough FC (Middlesbrough)	42	16	5	21	53	61	37	
15.	Everton FC (Liverpool)	42	13	10	19	55	58	36	
16.	Coventry City FC (Coventry)	42	13	10	19	48	68	36	
17.	Sunderland AFC (Sunderland)	42	14	7	21	52	53	35	
18.	Wolverhampton Wanderers FC (Wolverhampton)	42	13	9	20	43	55	35	
19.	Brighton & Hove Albion FC (Hove)	42	14	7	21	54	67	35	
20.	Norwich City FC (Norwich)	42	13	7	22	49	73	33	R
21.	Leicester City FC (Leicester)	42	13	6	23	40	67	32	R
22.	Crystal Palace FC (London)	42	6	7	29	47	83	19	R
		924	344	236	344	1288	1288	924	

Top Goalscorer

1)	Steve ARCHIBALD	(Tottenham Hotspur FC)	20
	Peter WITHE	(Aston Villa FC)	20

Football League Division 2 1980-81 Season	Blackburn Rovers	Bolton Wanderers	Bristol City	Bristol Rovers	Cambridge	Cardiff City	Chelsea	Derby County	Grimsby Town	Luton Town	Newcastle United	Notts County	Oldham Athletic	Orient	Preston North End	Q.P.R.	Sheffield Wednesday	Shrewsbury Town	Swansea City	Watford	West Ham United	Wrexham
Blackburn Rovers FC	■	0-0	1-0	2-0	2-0	2-3	1-1	1-0	2-0	3-0	3-0	0-0	1-0	2-0	0-0	2-1	3-1	2-0	0-0	0-0	0-0	1-1
Bolton Wanderers FC	1-2	■	1-1	2-0	6-1	4-2	2-3	3-1	1-1	0-3	4-0	3-0	2-0	3-1	2-1	1-2	0-0	0-2	1-4	2-1	1-1	1-1
Bristol City FC	2-0	3-1	■	0-0	0-1	0-0	0-0	2-2	1-1	2-1	2-0	0-1	1-1	3-1	0-0	0-1	1-0	1-1	0-1	0-0	1-1	0-2
Bristol Rovers FC	0-1	2-1	0-0	■	0-1	0-1	1-0	1-1	2-2	2-4	0-0	1-1	0-0	1-1	2-0	1-2	3-3	1-1	1-2	3-1	0-1	0-1
Cambridge United FC	0-0	2-3	2-1	1-3	■	2-0	0-1	3-0	5-1	1-3	2-1	1-2	3-1	1-0	1-0	1-0	0-2	3-1	3-1	3-1	1-2	1-0
Cardiff City FC	1-2	1-1	2-3	2-1	1-2	■	0-1	0-0	1-1	1-0	1-0	0-1	0-2	4-2	1-3	1-0	0-0	2-2	3-3	1-0	0-0	1-0
Chelsea FC	0-0	2-0	0-0	2-0	3-0	0-1	■	1-3	2-0	0-2	6-0	0-2	1-0	0-1	1-1	1-1	1-1	3-0	0-0	0-1	0-1	2-2
Derby County FC	2-2	1-0	1-0	2-1	0-3	1-1	3-2	■	2-1	2-2	2-0	2-2	4-1	1-1	1-2	3-3	3-1	1-1	0-1	1-1	2-0	0-1
Grimsby Town FC	0-0	4-0	1-0	2-0	3-1	0-1	2-0	0-1	■	0-0	0-0	2-1	0-0	2-0	0-0	0-0	0-0	1-0	1-0	1-1	1-5	1-0
Luton Town FC	3-1	2-2	3-1	1-0	0-0	2-2	2-0	1-2	0-2	■	0-1	0-1	1-2	2-1	4-2	3-0	3-0	1-1	2-2	1-0	3-2	1-1
Newcastle United FC	0-0	1-1	0-0	0-0	2-1	2-1	1-0	0-2	1-1	2-1	■	1-1	0-0	3-1	2-0	1-0	1-0	1-0	1-2	2-1	0-0	1-1
Notts County FC	2-0	2-1	2-1	3-1	2-0	4-2	1-1	0-0	0-0	1-0	0-0	■	0-2	1-0	0-0	2-1	2-0	0-0	2-1	1-2	1-1	1-1
Oldham Athletic AFC	1-0	1-1	2-0	1-0	2-2	2-0	0-0	0-2	1-2	0-0	0-0	0-1	■	0-1	1-1	1-0	2-0	0-0	2-2	2-1	0-0	1-3
Orient FC	1-1	2-2	3-1	2-2	3-0	2-2	0-1	1-0	2-0	0-0	1-1	0-2	2-3	■	4-0	4-0	2-0	1-0	1-1	1-1	0-2	2-1
Preston North End FC	0-0	1-2	1-1	0-0	2-0	3-1	1-0	0-3	2-4	1-0	2-3	2-2	1-2	3-0	■	3-2	2-1	0-0	1-3	2-1	0-0	1-1
Queen's Park Rangers FC	1-1	3-1	4-0	4-0	5-0	2-0	1-0	3-1	1-0	3-2	1-2	1-1	2-0	0-0	1-1	■	1-2	0-0	0-0	0-0	3-0	0-1
Sheffield Wednesday FC	2-1	2-0	2-1	4-1	4-1	2-0	0-0	0-0	1-2	3-1	2-0	1-2	3-0	2-2	3-0	1-0	■	1-1	2-0	1-0	0-1	2-1
Shrewsbury Town FC	1-1	1-2	4-0	3-1	2-1	2-0	2-2	1-0	1-1	0-1	1-0	1-1	2-2	1-2	3-0	3-3	2-0	■	0-0	2-1	0-2	1-2
Swansea City FC	2-0	3-0	0-0	2-1	1-1	1-1	3-0	3-1	1-0	2-2	4-0	1-1	3-0	0-2	3-0	1-2	2-3	2-1	■	1-0	1-3	3-1
Watford FC	1-1	3-1	1-0	3-1	0-0	4-2	2-3	1-1	3-1	0-1	0-0	2-0	2-1	2-0	2-1	1-1	2-1	1-0	2-1	■	1-2	1-0
West Ham United FC	2-0	2-1	5-0	2-0	4-2	1-0	4-0	3-1	2-1	1-2	1-0	4-0	1-1	2-1	5-0	3-0	2-1	3-0	2-0	3-2	■	1-0
Wrexham AFC	0-1	0-1	1-0	3-1	0-0	0-1	0-4	2-2	0-2	0-0	0-0	1-1	3-2	3-1	0-1	1-1	4-0	1-2	1-1	0-1	2-2	■

	Division 2	Pd	Wn	Dw	Ls	GF	GA	Pts	
1.	West Ham United FC (London)	42	28	10	4	79	29	66	P
2.	Notts County FC (Nottingham)	42	18	17	7	49	38	53	P
3.	Swansea City FC (Swansea)	42	18	14	10	64	44	50	P
4.	Blackburn Rovers FC (Blackburn)	42	16	18	8	42	29	50	
5.	Luton Town FC (Luton)	42	18	12	12	61	46	48	
6.	Derby County FC (Derby)	42	15	15	12	57	52	45	
7.	Grimsby Town FC (Cleethorpes)	42	15	15	12	44	42	45	
8.	Queen's Park Rangers FC (London)	42	15	13	14	56	46	43	
9.	Watford FC (Watford)	42	16	11	15	50	45	43	
10.	Sheffield Wednesday FC (Sheffield)	42	17	8	17	53	51	42	
11.	Newcastle United FC (Newcastle-upon-Tyne)	42	14	14	14	30	45	42	
12.	Chelsea FC (London)	42	14	12	16	46	41	40	
13.	Cambridge United FC (Cambridge)	42	17	6	19	53	65	40	
14.	Shrewsbury Town FC (Shrewsbury)	42	11	17	14	46	47	39	
15.	Oldham Athletic AFC (Oldham)	42	12	15	15	39	48	39	
16.	Wrexham AFC (Wrexham)	42	12	14	16	43	45	38	
17.	Orient FC (London)	42	13	12	17	52	56	38	
18.	Bolton Wanderers FC (Bolton)	42	14	10	18	61	66	38	
19.	Cardiff City AFC (Cardiff)	42	12	12	18	44	60	36	
20.	Preston North End FC (Preston)	42	11	14	17	41	62	36	R
21.	Bristol City FC (Bristol)	42	7	16	19	29	51	30	R
22.	Bristol Rovers FC (Bristol)	42	5	13	24	34	65	23	R
		924	318	288	318	1073	1073	924	

	Barnsley	Blackpool	Brentford	Burnley	Carlisle United	Charlton Athletic	Chester	Chesterfield	Colchester United	Exeter City	Fulham	Gillingham	Huddersfield Town	Hull City	Millwall	Newport County	Oxford United	Plymouth Argyle	Portsmouth	Reading	Rotherham United	Sheffield United	Swindon Town	Walsall
Barnsley FC	■	2-0	0-1	3-2	3-1	0-0	2-0	1-1	3-0	1-0	2-2	3-3	1-0	5-0	2-0	4-1	1-1	2-1	1-2	2-3	1-0	2-1	2-0	3-0
Blackpool FC	1-0	■	0-3	0-0	0-1	0-2	2-3	0-3	1-1	0-0	0-2	4-0	1-2	2-2	0-0	2-4	1-1	1-0	0-2	0-0	0-0	2-1	1-1	1-0
Brentford FC	1-1	2-0	■	0-0	1-1	0-1	0-1	3-2	2-1	0-1	1-3	3-3	0-0	2-2	1-0	0-1	3-0	0-1	2-2	1-2	2-1	1-1	1-1	4-0
Burnley FC	0-1	4-1	2-0	■	0-3	0-1	1-0	1-0	1-0	3-0	3-2	4-2	2-0	5-0	1-1	1-1	2-1	1-3	1-2	1-1	3-2	0-0	0-0	0-0
Carlisle United FC	2-2	2-0	1-2	3-2	■	1-2	3-0	2-6	4-0	1-1	2-2	0-0	1-1	2-0	2-1	1-4	0-0	2-0	0-0	0-0	0-1	0-3	2-1	1-1
Charlton Athletic FC	1-1	2-1	3-1	2-0	2-1	■	1-0	1-0	1-2	1-0	1-1	2-1	1-2	3-2	0-0	3-0	0-0	1-1	1-2	4-2	2-0	2-0	0-0	2-0
Chester FC	2-2	2-1	0-0	0-0	1-0	4-0	■	2-1	0-0	0-0	1-2	0-2	4-1	0-1	1-1	0-1	1-0	0-1	1-0	0-1	3-2	1-0	1-0	1-0
Chesterfield FC	0-0	3-2	2-1	3-0	1-0	0-1	2-0	■	3-0	1-0	0-0	2-0	2-1	1-0	3-0	3-2	2-2	3-0	3-2	2-2	1-0	2-2	2-2	1-2
Colchester United FC	2-2	3-2	0-2	2-1	1-0	2-0	1-1	1-1	■	1-2	3-2	2-1	1-2	2-0	3-0	1-0	3-0	2-2	1-0	1-2	0-0	1-1	1-0	1-1
Exeter City FC	0-1	0-0	0-0	0-0	2-0	4-3	2-2	2-2	4-0	■	1-0	2-1	1-4	1-3	2-0	2-2	1-1	1-1	2-0	3-1	2-1	1-1	3-4	0-3
Fulham FC	2-3	1-2	1-1	0-2	2-3	1-0	0-1	1-1	1-0	0-2	■	3-2	2-2	0-0	1-1	2-1	0-4	0-0	3-0	1-2	1-1	2-1	2-0	2-1
Gillingham FC	1-1	3-1	2-0	0-0	0-1	0-1	2-1	1-0	0-0	1-5	1-0	■	0-0	2-0	1-2	3-2	1-1	0-1	0-0	2-0	1-1	1-1	0-2	1-1
Huddersfield Town	1-0	1-1	3-0	0-0	1-1	0-1	0-0	0-0	2-0	5-0	4-2	1-0	■	5-0	0-1	4-1	2-0	2-0	0-0	4-1	1-0	1-0	0-2	1-1
Hull City AFC	1-2	2-1	0-0	0-0	0-1	0-2	0-0	0-0	0-1	3-3	0-1	2-2	2-1	■	3-1	3-1	0-1	1-0	2-1	2-0	1-2	1-1	0-0	0-1
Millwall FC	1-1	0-0	2-2	2-2	3-0	2-0	1-0	0-2	3-1	1-0	3-1	0-0	2-1	1-1	■	0-0	2-1	1-1	0-0	2-1	0-1	1-4	3-1	0-1
Newport County AFC	0-0	3-1	1-1	1-2	4-0	1-2	1-1	5-1	1-0	2-1	2-1	1-1	3-2	4-0	2-1	■	0-1	0-2	2-1	1-1	0-0	4-0	0-2	1-1
Oxford United FC	1-1	0-2	1-1	0-2	1-2	1-0	0-3	2-1	1-2	2-0	1-1	0-2	1-1	1-0	0-1	0-1	■	0-0	1-2	2-1	1-1	2-0	0-0	1-1
Plymouth Argyle FC	1-3	0-2	0-1	2-1	4-1	1-1	2-0	1-0	1-1	0-2	2-1	4-1	0-0	0-0	2-0	3-2	3-0	■	1-0	2-1	3-1	1-0	0-0	2-0
Portsmouth FC	0-1	3-3	0-2	4-2	2-1	1-0	2-0	1-0	2-1	5-0	1-0	0-0	1-2	2-1	0-0	1-1	1-3	1-2	■	0-0	3-1	1-0	1-0	2-0
Reading FC	3-2	3-0	0-0	1-3	3-1	1-3	3-0	2-3	1-0	2-1	0-0	2-1	4-1	1-1	0-1	1-1	2-1	1-0	2-1	■	1-1	1-0	4-1	2-0
Rotherham United	2-0	4-0	4-1	1-0	3-0	3-0	0-0	0-0	2-0	3-1	2-0	0-0	1-1	3-0	2-0	2-1	3-0	2-0	3-0	1-1	■	2-1	1-0	2-1
Sheffield United FC	1-1	4-2	0-0	0-0	2-2	3-2	2-0	2-0	3-0	3-1	1-2	0-1	2-2	3-1	2-3	2-0	1-0	0-0	1-0	2-0	1-2	■	3-0	0-1
Swindon Town FC	2-0	1-2	0-0	0-3	1-1	0-3	1-2	0-1	3-0	2-2	3-4	0-0	1-0	3-1	0-0	1-1	1-0	3-0	0-2	3-1	2-1	5-2	■	3-1
Walsall FC	1-1	2-2	2-3	3-1	4-3	2-2	2-1	4-3	3-1	1-3	1-2	3-3	2-2	1-1	0-0	1-0	0-3	1-3	2-0	2-2	0-2	4-4	2-1	■

Division 3

		Pd	Wn	Dw	Ls	GF	GA	Pts	
1.	Rotherham United FC (Rotherham)	46	24	13	9	62	32	61	P
2.	Barnsley FC (Barnsley)	46	21	17	8	72	45	59	P
3.	Charlton Athletic FC (London)	46	25	9	12	63	44	59	P
4.	Huddersfield Town AFC (Huddersfield)	46	21	14	11	71	40	56	
5.	Chesterfield FC (Chesterfield)	46	23	10	15	72	48	56	
6.	Portsmouth FC (Portsmouth)	46	22	9	15	55	47	53	
7.	Plymouth Argyle FC (Plymouth)	46	19	14	13	56	44	52	
8.	Burnley FC (Burnley)	46	18	14	14	60	48	50	
9.	Brentford FC (London)	46	14	19	13	52	49	47	
10.	Reading FC (Reading)	46	18	10	18	62	62	46	
11.	Exeter City FC (Exeter)	46	16	13	17	62	66	45	
12.	Newport County AFC (Newport)	46	15	13	18	64	61	43	
13.	Fulham FC (London)	46	15	13	18	57	64	43	
14.	Oxford United FC (Oxford)	46	13	17	16	39	47	43	
15.	Gillingham FC (Gillingham)	46	12	18	16	48	58	42	
16.	Millwall FC (London)	46	14	14	18	43	60	42	
17.	Swindon Town FC (Swindon)	46	13	15	18	51	56	41	
18.	Chester FC (Chester)	46	15	11	20	38	48	41	
19.	Carlisle United FC (Carlisle)	46	14	13	19	56	70	41	
20.	Walsall FC (Walsall)	46	13	15	18	59	74	41	
21.	Sheffield United FC (Sheffield)	46	14	12	20	65	63	40	R
22.	Colchester United FC (Colchester)	46	14	11	21	45	65	39	R
23.	Blackpool FC (Blackpool)	46	9	14	23	45	75	32	R
24.	Hull City AFC (Kingston-upon-Hull)	46	8	16	22	40	71	32	R
		1104	390	324	390	1337	1337	1104	

Football League Division 4 — 1980-81 Season

	Aldershot Town	Bournemouth	Bradford City	Bury	Crewe Alexandra	Darlington	Doncaster Rovers	Halifax Town	Hartlepool	Hereford United	Lincoln City	Mansfield Town	Northampton Town	Peterborough United	Port Vale	Rochdale	Scunthorpe United	Southend United	Stockport County	Torquay United	Tranmere Rovers	Wigan Ath.	Wimbledon	York City
Aldershot Town FC		0-0	1-1	1-0	2-0	2-1	1-0	2-1	2-1	4-0	0-0	1-0	0-0	0-0	0-0	0-0	0-0	1-2	3-0	2-1	3-2	0-1	2-0	1-1
AFC Bournemouth	0-2		4-0	2-2	0-0	3-3	1-2	2-1	1-0	1-0	0-1	0-1	0-0	4-1	0-0	2-1	2-2	2-1	0-1	1-1	1-0	3-0	0-1	1-1
Bradford City AFC	1-0	1-1		0-2	2-2	3-0	1-1	0-0	2-0	0-1	1-2	0-2	3-1	1-1	2-1	2-1	0-0	2-1	1-1	2-0	0-3	3-3	2-0	1-1
Bury FC	0-0	3-0	2-2		1-3	1-2	2-0	0-0	0-0	2-1	1-1	4-1	1-2	1-1	2-1	3-1	6-1	0-1	3-0	2-2	0-0	1-0	2-0	
Crewe Alexandra FC	0-0	0-2	1-0	2-2		1-1	0-0	2-1	2-0	5-0	0-3	1-2	3-1	1-0	0-0	1-0	1-0	1-1	2-0	0-1	3-0	1-2	0-3	1-1
Darlington FC	1-2	1-2	2-1	2-1	2-1		5-0	3-1	3-0	2-1	0-0	2-2	1-0	2-0	1-1	4-4	0-1	0-2	2-2	1-0	2-0	3-1	4-1	0-0
Doncaster Rovers FC	3-1	2-1	2-0	1-0	1-1	2-0		0-0	1-2	5-1	0-1	2-1	1-1	0-4	2-0	1-2	1-0	1-0	2-1	2-0	1-0	1-1	2-1	3-2
Halifax Town AFC	1-0	1-2	2-0	4-2	1-0	1-2	0-3		1-2	0-0	1-3	0-2	0-1	2-3	2-2	2-0	1-0	1-5	2-0	2-1	1-1	0-1	0-1	3-1
Hartlepool United FC	1-0	1-0	2-2	1-2	6-2	2-0	1-0	3-0		2-0	2-0	0-1	2-3	1-1	3-0	2-2	2-0	1-3	1-0	0-2	3-0	3-1	2-3	1-0
Hereford United FC	0-0	1-0	4-0	0-1	0-0	0-1	1-3	0-1	3-0		0-2	2-1	4-1	1-1	2-3	3-0	2-1	0-0	2-0	0-1	1-1	1-1	1-1	1-1
Lincoln City FC	0-1	2-0	1-1	2-1	2-1	1-0	1-1	3-0	2-0	1-0		1-1	8-0	1-1	1-0	3-0	3-2	2-1	1-0	5-0	2-0	2-0	0-0	1-1
Mansfield Town FC	1-2	1-1	2-0	1-0	4-1	1-0	0-1	0-1	4-0	1-0			2-0	2-1	5-0	2-2	1-0	1-0	1-1	1-1	1-1	1-0		0-1
Northampton Town	2-0	0-1	0-1	5-3	4-1	2-2	0-2	2-1	3-1	0-0	1-1	0-1		2-2	5-1	3-2	3-3	2-0	0-1	1-0	3-1	1-1	1-1	2-0
Peterborough United	0-0	1-0	2-2	2-0	2-1	1-0	0-1	2-2	1-1	3-0	1-0	1-0	3-0		1-1	2-2	0-2	5-2	1-2	1-3	4-1	0-0	1-1	3-0
Port Vale FC	0-1	0-2	2-1	1-3	2-2	4-2	3-0	0-0	1-1	4-0	0-0	1-1	1-1			1-1	2-2	1-0	2-0	3-1	5-1	3-0	2-3	2-0
Rochdale AFC	0-2	0-0	2-1	2-0	0-0	2-2	1-1	1-1	0-0	1-1	1-4	0-1	2-3	2-1			4-0	0-2	2-1	3-1	3-0	2-0	3-2	
Scunthorpe United	2-2	1-1	1-0	2-2	1-1	3-0	1-1	2-2	3-3	3-1	2-2	2-0	0-2	1-1	1-1	1-1		2-1	2-0	0-2	2-0	4-4	1-2	3-2
Southend United FC	3-0	2-1	3-1	1-0	3-0	1-0	0-0	5-1	4-0	2-0	0-0	2-0	0-0	1-0	5-1	1-1	2-0		2-0	3-1	2-0	1-0	1-0	
Stockport County FC	1-0	2-1	1-2	1-2	1-3	0-1	2-1	1-1	0-2	0-0	0-0	2-1	1-2	3-4	2-1	2-2	2-0	1-0		4-1	1-0	0-1	0-0	1-2
Torquay United FC	2-0	2-0	2-0	3-1	1-0	2-3	1-0	2-1	0-1	1-2	1-1	3-3	2-0	4-0	2-0	2-1	0-3	1-2			2-1	2-0	2-3	1-2
Tranmere Rovers FC	3-1	0-1	1-1	3-1	0-1	3-1	1-1	2-0	2-2	2-1	0-0	1-0	3-2	1-2	1-2	3-1	1-2	2-2	1-0	1-0		2-3	3-0	5-0
Wigan Athletic AFC	1-0	0-1	0-1	2-1	0-0	3-1	3-0	4-1	0-3	1-0	0-2	2-0	3-0	1-1	1-0	0-1	1-1	0-1	2-1	2-0	1-1		1-0	1-0
Wimbledon FC	4-0	2-0	2-2	2-4	2-0	1-1	1-0	3-0	5-0	0-0	2-1	1-0	2-1	1-0	4-1	2-2	1-0	1-2	1-0	2-1	1-0			3-0
York City FC	4-1	4-0	0-3	0-1	2-0	1-2	0-1	1-1	0-1	1-2	1-0	2-0	1-2	1-2	4-1	1-2	1-0	0-1	1-0	0-0	4-1	2-1	0-1	

	Division 4	Pd	Wn	Dw	Ls	GF	GA	Pts	
1.	Southend United FC (Southend-on-Sea)	46	30	7	9	79	31	67	P
2.	Lincoln City FC (Lincoln)	46	25	15	6	66	25	65	P
3.	Doncaster Rovers FC (Doncaster)	46	22	12	12	59	49	56	P
4.	Wimbledon FC (London)	46	23	9	14	64	46	55	P
5.	Peterborough United FC (Peterborough)	46	17	18	11	68	54	52	
6.	Aldershot FC (Aldershot)	46	18	14	14	43	41	50	
7.	Mansfield Town FC (Mansfield)	46	20	9	17	58	44	49	
8.	Darlington FC (Darlington)	46	19	11	16	65	59	49	
9.	Hartlepool United FC (Hartlepool)	46	20	9	17	64	61	49	
10.	Northampton Town FC (Northampton)	46	18	13	15	65	67	49	
11.	Wigan Athletic AFC (Wigan)	46	18	11	17	51	55	47	
12.	Bury FC (Bury)	46	17	11	18	70	62	45	
13.	AFC Bournemouth (Bournemouth)	46	16	13	17	47	48	45	
14.	Bradford City AFC (Bradford)	46	14	16	16	53	60	44	
15.	Rochdale AFC (Rochdale)	46	14	15	17	60	70	43	
16.	Scunthorpe United FC (Scunthorpe)	46	11	20	15	60	69	42	
17.	Torquay United FC (Torquay)	46	18	5	23	55	63	41	
18.	Crewe Alexandra FC (Crewe)	46	13	14	19	48	61	40	
19.	Port Vale FC (Stoke-on-Trent)	46	12	15	19	57	70	39	
20.	Stockport County FC (Stockport)	46	16	7	23	44	57	39	
21.	Tranmere Rovers FC (Birkenhead)	46	13	10	23	59	73	36	
22.	Hereford United FC (Hereford)	46	11	13	22	38	62	35	
23.	Halifax Town AFC (Halifax)	46	11	12	23	44	71	34	
24.	York City FC (York)	46	12	9	25	47	66	33	
		1104	408	288	408	1364	1364	1104	

F.A. CUP FINAL   (Wembley Stadium, London – 09/05/1981 – 99,500)

TOTTENHAM HOTSPUR FC (LONDON)   1-1 (aet)   Manchester City FC (Manchester)

Hutchison o.g.   *Hutchison*

Tottenham: Aleksic, Hughton, Miller, Roberts, Perryman, Villa (Brooks), Ardiles, Archibald, Galvin, Hoddle, Crooks.

Man. City: Corrigan, Ranson, McDonald, Reid, Power, Caton, Bennett, Gow, MacKenzie, Hutchison (Henry), Reeves.

F.A. CUP FINAL REPLAY   (Wembley Stadium, London – 14/05/1981 – 92,000)

TOTTENHAM HOTSPUR FC (LONDON)   3-2   Manchester City FC (Manchester)

Villa 2, Crooks   *MacKenzie, Reeves pen.*

Man. City: Corrigan, Ranson, McDonald (Tueart), Caton, Reid, Gow, Power, MacKenzie, Reeves, Bennett, Hutchison.

Tottenham: Aleksic, Hughton, Miller, Roberts, Perryman, Villa, Ardiles, Archibald, Galvin, Hoddle, Crooks.

Semi-finals

Manchester City FC (Manchester)	1-0	Ipswich Town FC (Ipswich)
Tottenham Hotspur FC (London)	2-2, 3-0	Wolverhampton Wanderers FC (Wolverhampton)

Quarter-finals

Everton FC (Liverpool)	2-2, 1-3	Manchester City FC (Manchester)
Middlesbrough FC (Middlesbrough)	1-1, 1-3	Wolverhampton Wanderers FC (Wolverhampton)
Nottingham Forest FC (Nottingham)	3-3, 0-1	Ipswich Town FC (Ipswich)
Tottenham Hotspur FC (London)	2-0	Exeter City FC (Exeter)

1981-82

Football League Division 1 — 1981-82 Season

	Arsenal	Aston Villa	Birmingham City	Brighton & H.A.	Coventry City	Everton	Ipswich Town	Leeds United	Liverpool	Manchester City	Manchester United	Middlesbrough	Nottingham Forest	Notts County	Southampton	Stoke City	Sunderland	Swansea City	Tottenham Hotspur	W.B.A.	West Ham United	Wolves
Arsenal FC		4-3	1-0	0-0	1-0	1-0	1-0	1-0	1-1	1-0	0-0	1-0	2-0	1-0	4-1	0-1	1-1	0-2	1-3	2-2	2-0	2-1
Aston Villa FC	0-2		0-0	3-0	2-1	1-2	0-1	1-4	0-3	0-0	1-1	1-0	3-1	0-1	1-1	2-2	1-0	3-0	1-1	2-1	3-2	3-1
Birmingham City FC	0-1	0-1		1-0	3-3	0-2	1-1	0-1	0-1	3-0	0-1	0-0	4-3	2-1	4-0	2-1	2-0	2-1	0-0	3-3	3-3	0-3
Brighton & Hove Albion FC	2-1	0-1	1-1		2-2	3-1	0-1	1-0	3-3	4-1	0-1	2-0	0-1	2-2	1-1	0-0	2-1	1-2	1-3	2-2	1-0	2-0
Coventry City FC	1-0	1-1	0-1	0-1		1-0	2-4	4-0	1-2	0-1	2-1	1-1	0-1	1-5	4-2	3-0	6-1	3-1	0-0	0-2	1-0	0-0
Everton FC	2-1	2-0	3-1	1-1	3-2		2-1	1-0	1-3	0-1	3-3	2-0	2-1	3-1	0-0	1-2	3-1	1-1	1-0	1-0	0-0	1-1
Ipswich Town FC	2-1	3-1	3-2	3-1	1-0	3-0		2-1	2-0	2-0	2-1	3-1	1-3	1-3	5-2	2-0	3-3	2-3	2-1	1-0	3-2	1-0
Leeds United AFC	0-0	1-1	3-3	2-1	0-0	1-1	0-2		0-2	0-1	0-0	1-1	1-1	1-0	1-3	0-1	2-0	0-0	3-1	3-3	3-3	3-0
Liverpool FC	2-0	0-0	3-1	0-1	4-0	3-1	4-0	3-0		1-3	1-2	1-1	2-0	1-0	0-1	2-0	1-0	2-2	3-1	1-0	3-0	2-1
Manchester City FC	0-0	1-0	4-2	4-0	1-3	1-1	1-1	4-0	0-5		0-0	3-2	0-0	1-0	1-1	2-3	4-0	0-1	2-1	0-1	2-1	2-1
Manchester United FC	0-0	4-1	1-1	2-0	0-1	1-1	1-2	1-0	0-1	1-1		1-0	0-0	2-1	1-0	2-0	1-0	2-0	1-0	1-0	1-0	5-0
Middlesbrough FC	1-3	3-3	2-1	2-1	0-0	0-2	0-1	0-0	0-0	0-0	0-2		1-1	3-0	0-1	3-2	0-0	1-1	1-3	0-0	2-3	0-0
Nottingham Forest FC	1-2	1-1	2-1	2-1	2-1	1-1	1-1	2-1	0-2	1-1	0-1	1-1		0-2	2-1	0-0	2-0	0-2	2-0	0-0	0-0	0-1
Notts County FC	2-1	1-0	1-4	4-1	2-1	2-2	1-4	2-0	0-4	1-1	1-3	0-1	1-2		1-1	3-1	2-0	0-1	2-2	1-2	1-1	4-0
Southampton FC	3-1	0-3	3-1	0-2	5-5	1-0	4-3	4-0	2-3	2-1	3-2	2-0	2-0	3-1		4-3	1-0	3-1	1-2	2-0	2-1	4-1
Stoke City FC	0-1	1-0	1-0	0-0	4-0	3-1	2-0	1-2	1-5	1-3	0-3	2-0	1-2	2-2	0-2		0-1	1-2	0-2	3-0	2-1	2-1
Sunderland AFC	0-0	2-1	2-0	3-0	0-0	3-1	1-1	0-1	0-2	1-0	1-5	0-2	2-3	1-1	2-0	0-2		0-1	0-2	1-2	0-2	0-0
Swansea City FC	2-0	2-1	1-0	2-0	0-0	1-3	1-2	5-1	2-0	2-0	2-0	1-2	1-2	3-2	1-0	3-0	2-0		2-1	3-1	0-1	0-0
Tottenham Hotspur FC	2-2	1-3	1-1	0-1	1-2	3-0	1-0	2-1	2-2	2-1	3-1	1-0	3-0	3-1	3-2	2-0	2-2	2-1		1-2	0-4	6-1
West Bromwich Albion FC	0-2	2-1	1-1	0-0	1-2	0-0	1-2	2-0	1-0	0-1	0-3	2-0	2-1	2-4	1-1	1-2	2-3	4-1	1-0		0-0	3-0
West Ham United FC	1-2	2-2	2-2	1-1	5-2	1-1	2-0	4-3	1-1	1-1	1-1	3-2	0-1	1-0	4-2	3-2	1-1	1-1	2-2	3-1		3-1
Wolverhampton Wanderers FC	1-1	0-3	1-1	0-1	1-0	0-3	2-1	1-0	1-0	4-1	0-1	0-0	0-0	3-2	0-0	2-0	0-1	0-1	0-1	1-2	2-1	

	Division 1	Pd	Wn	Dw	Ls	GF	GA	Pts	
1.	LIVERPOOL FC (LIVERPOOL)	42	26	9	7	80	32	87	
2.	Ipswich Town FC (Ipswich)	42	26	5	11	75	53	83	
3.	Manchester United FC (Manchester)	42	22	12	8	59	29	78	
4.	Tottenham Hotspur FC (London)	42	20	11	11	67	48	71	
5.	Arsenal FC (London)	42	20	11	11	48	37	71	
6.	Swansea City FC (Swansea)	42	21	6	15	58	51	69	
7.	Southampton FC (Southampton)	42	19	9	14	72	67	66	
8.	Everton FC (Liverpool)	42	17	13	12	56	50	64	
9.	West Ham United FC (London)	42	14	16	12	66	57	58	
10.	Manchester City FC (Manchester)	42	15	13	14	49	50	58	
11.	Aston Villa FC (Birmingham)	42	15	12	15	55	53	57	
12.	Nottingham Forest FC (Nottingham)	42	15	12	15	42	48	57	
13.	Brighton & Hove Albion FC (Hove)	42	13	13	16	43	52	52	
14.	Coventry City FC (Coventry)	42	13	11	18	56	62	50	
15.	Notts County FC (Nottingham)	42	13	8	21	61	69	47	
16.	Birmingham City FC (Birmingham)	42	10	14	18	53	61	44	
17.	West Bromwich Albion FC (West Bromwich)	42	11	11	20	46	57	44	
18.	Stoke City FC (Stoke-on-Trent)	42	12	8	22	44	63	44	
19.	Sunderland AFC (Sunderland)	42	11	11	20	38	58	44	
20.	Leeds United AFC (Leeds)	42	10	12	20	39	61	42	R
21.	Wolverhampton Wanderers FC (Wolverhampton)	42	10	10	22	32	63	40	R
22.	Middlesbrough FC (Middlesbrough)	42	8	15	19	34	52	39	R
		924	341	242	341	1173	1173	1265	

Top Goalscorer

1) Kevin KEEGAN (Southampton FC) 26

Football League Division 2 1981-82 Season	Barnsley	Blackburn Rovers	Bolton Wanderers	Cambridge	Cardiff City	Charlton Athletic	Chelsea	Crystal Palace	Derby County	Grimsby Town	Leicester City	Luton Town	Newcastle United	Norwich City	Oldham Athletic	Orient	Q.P.R.	Rotherham United	Sheffield Wednesday	Shrewsbury Town	Watford	Wrexham
Barnsley FC	■	0-1	3-0	0-0	0-1	1-0	2-1	2-0	0-0	3-2	0-2	4-3	1-0	0-1	3-1	1-0	3-0	3-0	1-0	4-0	0-0	2-2
Blackburn Rovers FC	2-1	■	0-2	1-0	1-0	0-2	1-1	1-0	4-1	2-0	0-2	0-1	4-1	3-0	0-0	2-0	2-1	2-0	0-1	0-0	1-2	0-0
Bolton Wanderers FC	2-1	2-2	■	3-4	1-0	2-0	2-2	0-0	3-2	1-2	0-3	1-2	1-0	0-1	0-2	1-0	1-0	0-1	3-1	1-1	2-0	2-0
Cambridge United FC	2-1	1-0	2-1	■	2-1	4-0	1-0	0-0	1-2	2-2	1-2	1-1	1-0	1-2	0-0	2-0	1-0	3-0	1-2	2-0	1-2	2-3
Cardiff City FC	0-0	1-3	2-1	5-4	■	0-1	1-2	0-1	1-0	2-1	3-1	2-3	0-4	1-0	0-1	2-1	1-2	1-2	0-2	1-1	2-0	3-2
Charlton Athletic FC	2-1	2-0	1-0	0-0	2-2	■	3-4	2-1	2-1	2-0	1-4	0-0	0-1	0-0	3-1	5-2	1-2	1-2	3-0	1-0	1-1	1-0
Chelsea FC	1-2	1-1	2-0	4-1	1-0	2-2	■	1-2	0-2	1-1	4-1	1-2	2-1	2-1	2-2	2-2	2-1	1-4	2-1	3-1	1-3	2-0
Crystal Palace FC	1-2	1-2	1-0	2-1	1-0	2-0	0-1	■	0-1	0-3	0-2	3-3	1-2	2-1	4-0	1-0	0-0	3-1	1-2	0-1	0-3	2-1
Derby County FC	0-1	1-1	0-2	2-1	0-0	1-1	1-1	4-1	■	1-1	3-1	0-0	2-2	0-2	1-0	1-2	3-1	3-1	3-1	1-1	3-2	2-1
Grimsby Town FC	3-2	1-1	1-1	1-2	0-1	3-3	3-3	0-1	1-0	■	2-2	0-1	1-1	1-2	2-1	1-2	1-2	0-1	5-1	0-2		1-1
Leicester City FC	1-0	1-0	1-0	4-1	3-1	3-1	1-1	1-1	2-1	1-2	■	1-2	3-0	1-4	2-1	0-1	3-2	1-0	0-0	0-0	1-1	1-0
Luton Town FC	1-1	2-0	2-0	1-0	2-3	3-0	2-2	1-0	3-2	6-0	2-1	■	3-2	2-0	2-0	2-0	3-2	3-1	0-3	4-1	4-1	0-0
Newcastle United FC	1-0	0-0	2-0	1-0	2-1	4-1	1-0	0-0	3-0	0-1	0-0	3-2	■	2-1	2-0	1-0	0-4	1-1	1-0	2-0	0-1	4-2
Norwich City FC	1-1	2-0	2-0	2-1	5-0	2-1	1-0	4-1	2-1	1-1	0-0	1-3	2-1	■	1-2	2-0	0-1	2-0	2-3	4-2	4-0	
Oldham Athletic AFC	1-1	0-3	1-1	2-0	2-2	1-0	1-0	0-0	1-1	3-1	1-1	1-1	3-1	2-0	■	3-2	2-0	0-3	0-3	1-1	1-1	2-1
Orient FC	1-3	0-0	3-0	0-0	1-1	1-1	0-2	0-0	3-2	1-2	q3-0	0-3	1-0	1-1	0-3	■	1-1	1-2	3-0	2-0	1-3	0-0
Queen's Park Rangers FC	1-0	2-0	7-1	2-1	4-0	0-2	1-0	3-0	1-0	2-0	1-2	3-0	2-0	0-0	3-0		■	1-1	2-0	2-1	0-0	1-1
Rotherham United FC	2-4	4-1	2-0	1-0	1-0	2-1	6-0	2-1	2-1	2-2	1-1	2-2	0-0	4-1	1-2	0-0	1-0	■	2-2	3-0	1-2	2-0
Sheffield Wednesday FC	2-2	2-2	0-1	2-1	2-1	1-1	0-0	1-1	1-1	1-1	2-0	3-3	2-1	2-1	1-3	2-0			■	0-0	3-1	0-3
Shrewsbury Town FC	0-2	1-2	2-0	1-0	1-1	1-1	1-0	1-0	4-1	2-0	1-1	2-0	0-2	2-1	2-0	2-1	2-1	0-1		■	0-2	1-1
Watford FC	3-1	3-2	3-0	0-0	0-0	2-2	1-0	1-1	6-1	0-2	3-1	1-1	2-3	3-0	1-1	3-0	4-0	1-0	4-0	3-1	■	2-0
Wrexham AFC	0-0	1-0	2-1	0-0	3-1	1-0	1-0	0-1	1-1	2-0	0-0	0-2	4-2	2-3	0-3	0-1	1-3	3-2	0-1	1-0	0-1	■

	Division 2	Pd	Wn	Dw	Ls	GF	GA	Pts	
1.	Luton Town FC (Luton)	42	25	13	4	86	46	88	P
2.	Watford FC (Watford)	42	23	11	8	76	42	80	P
3.	Norwich City FC (Norwich)	42	22	5	15	64	50	71	P
4.	Sheffield Wednesday FC (Sheffield)	42	20	10	12	55	51	70	
5.	Queen's Park Rangers FC (London)	42	21	6	15	65	43	69	
6.	Barnsley FC (Barnsley)	42	19	10	13	59	41	67	
7.	Rotherham United FC (Rotherham)	42	20	7	15	66	54	67	
8.	Leicester City FC (Leicester)	42	18	12	12	56	48	66	
9.	Newcastle United FC (Newcastle-upon-Tyne)	42	18	8	16	52	50	62	
10.	Blackburn Rovers FC (Blackburn)	42	16	11	15	47	43	59	
11.	Oldham Athletic AFC (Oldham)	42	15	14	13	50	51	59	
12.	Chelsea FC (London)	42	15	12	15	60	60	57	
13.	Charlton Athletic FC (London)	42	13	12	17	50	65	51	
14.	Cambridge United FC (Cambridge)	42	13	9	20	48	53	48	
15.	Crystal Palace FC (London)	42	13	9	20	34	45	48	
16.	Derby County FC (Derby)	42	12	12	18	53	68	48	
17.	Grimsby Town FC (Cleethorpes)	42	11	13	18	53	65	46	
18.	Shrewsbury Town FC (Shrewsbury)	42	11	13	18	37	57	46	
19.	Bolton Wanderers FC (Bolton)	42	13	7	22	39	61	46	
20.	Cardiff City AFC (Cardiff)	42	12	8	22	45	61	44	R
21.	Wrexham AFC (Wrexham)	42	11	11	20	40	56	44	R
22.	Orient FC (London)	42	10	9	23	36	61	39	R
		924	351	222	351	1171	1171	1275	

Football League Division 3 1981-82 Season	Brentford	Bristol City	Bristol Rovers	Burnley	Carlisle United	Chester	Chesterfield	Doncaster R.	Exeter City	Fulham	Gillingham	Huddersfield T.	Lincoln City	Millwall	Newport County	Oxford United	Plymouth Argyle	Portsmouth	Preston N.E.	Reading	Southend United	Swindon Town	Walsall	Wimbledon
Brentford FC		0-1	1-0	0-0	1-2	1-0	2-0	2-2	2-0	0-1	0-1	0-1	3-1	4-1	2-0	1-2	0-0	2-2	0-0	1-2	0-1	4-2	0-0	2-3
Bristol City FC	0-1		1-2	2-3	1-1	1-0	0-0	2-2	3-2	0-0	2-1	0-0	0-1	4-1	2-1	0-2	3-2	0-1	0-0	2-0	0-2	0-3	0-1	1-3
Bristol Rovers FC	1-2	1-0		2-1	0-1	2-2	1-0	3-0	3-2	1-2	2-0	3-2	0-2	0-1	2-0	1-0	2-3	1-1	2-0	1-1	2-1	1-4	2-1	2-2
Burnley FC	0-0	2-0	4-0		1-0	1-0	1-1	0-1	3-3	2-2	1-0	0-0	1-0	1-1	2-1	2-1	1-0	3-0	2-0	3-0	3-5	0-2	2-1	2-2
Carlisle United FC	1-0	2-2	1-2	1-0		3-0	3-0	2-0	3-2	1-2	2-0	2-2	1-0	2-1	2-2	2-1	3-1	2-0	1-0	2-1	3-2	1-1	2-1	2-1
Chester FC	1-2	0-0	1-1	0-1	0-1		0-2	1-1	0-2	0-2	0-0	3-1	1-2	0-0	0-2	2-2	0-3	3-2	0-1	2-3	1-1	0-0	0-0	1-1
Chesterfield FC	0-2	1-0	2-0	1-2	1-0	3-5		3-1	2-1	3-0	1-3	1-0	0-2	0-1	1-0	2-2	2-2	2-2	0-0	2-1	1-2	2-1	1-0	2-0
Doncaster Rovers FC	1-0	2-2	4-2	0-1	1-1	4-3	0-0		3-0	2-1	1-1	1-2	4-1	1-0	0-2	1-1	2-2	0-0	1-0	0-1	1-1	0-0	1-0	1-3
Exeter City FC	3-1	4-0	1-3	2-1	2-1	0-3	0-1	2-1		1-0	1-1	1-0	1-2	5-4	1-0	1-2	1-1	3-3	4-3	4-3	1-1	1-2	2-0	2-1
Fulham FC	1-2	2-1	4-2	1-1	4-1	2-0	1-0	3-1	4-1		0-0	2-2	1-1	0-0	3-1	0-0	1-3	1-1	3-0	2-2	2-1	2-0	1-1	4-1
Gillingham FC	1-1	1-1	2-0	3-1	0-0	0-1	3-2	3-0	2-3	2-0		3-2	1-0	1-1	2-1	3-2	4-2	0-2	2-1	2-0	1-0	1-4	6-1	
Huddersfield Town	1-1	5-0	0-2	1-2	2-1	1-2	1-1	1-2	1-1	1-0	2-0		0-2	1-2	2-0	2-0	0-0	0-1	2-3	6-1	3-2	3-0	2-1	1-1
Lincoln City FC	1-0	1-2	1-0	1-1	0-0	3-0	2-1	5-0	2-0	1-1	2-0	2-0		0-1	2-2	2-1	2-0	1-1	1-2	2-1	1-1	2-0	1-1	5-1
Millwall FC	0-1	2-0	0-0	4-3	1-2	2-1	3-2	0-2	5-1	4-3	1-2	1-3	1-1		1-0	1-2	2-1	1-0	2-1	0-1	1-1	0-0	2-0	2-1
Newport County AFC	0-1	1-1	1-1	0-0	2-0	0-1	1-0	1-0	1-1	1-3	4-2	1-0	0-0	1-1		3-2	0-1	1-1	1-1	3-1	3-2	1-0	2-2	0-0
Oxford United FC	1-2	1-0	1-1	0-0	2-1	3-1	1-1	3-1	0-0	2-0	1-1	1-0	1-1	0-0	1-1		1-0	0-2	3-0	1-0	0-2	5-0	0-1	0-3
Plymouth Argyle FC	1-0	2-1	4-0	1-1	1-0	5-1	0-2	4-2	2-1	3-1	1-2	1-1	0-2	2-1	1-2	0-1		0-0	0-3	1-1	0-0	2-1	4-1	2-0
Portsmouth FC	2-2	2-0	0-0	1-2	1-2	2-0	5-1	0-0	2-0	1-1	2-1	1-1	2-2	0-0	1-1	1-0	1-0		1-1	3-0	0-0	3-0	1-0	1-0
Preston North End	1-3	1-3	0-1	1-1	0-1	0-1	2-0	3-1	1-0	1-3	1-1	1-1	1-1	1-0	2-1	2-2	1-0	1-0		0-0	1-0	0-0	1-0	3-2
Reading FC	4-1	3-1	0-3	1-1	2-2	4-1	0-2	3-3	4-0	0-3	3-2	1-2	3-2	4-0	2-1	0-3	2-2	2-1	2-1		0-2	1-1	0-0	1-2
Southend United FC	1-1	3-0	1-0	1-4	1-1	2-0	0-2	1-1	2-1	0-0	3-0	4-0	0-2	2-2	0-4	0-1	3-0	2-0	2-2	2-0		0-0	3-2	2-0
Swindon Town FC	0-3	0-0	5-2	1-2	2-1	3-0	1-2	2-2	3-2	1-4	0-1	1-5	1-0	1-2	1-1	3-2	0-2	2-0	4-0	0-2	0-0		2-2	4-1
Walsall FC	3-0	0-1	2-1	1-1	1-1	2-1	1-1	0-0	2-1	1-1	1-0	1-1	2-1	1-1	3-1	1-3	0-1	3-1	0-3	1-2	0-1	5-0		1-0
Wimbledon FC	1-2	0-0	1-0	0-0	3-1	1-0	3-1	0-1	1-1	1-3	0-2	2-0	1-1	1-3	2-3	2-3	2-1	3-2	3-2	0-0	3-0	1-1	2-0	

	Division 3	Pd	Wn	Dw	Ls	GF	GA	Pts	
1.	Burnley FC (Burnley)	46	21	17	8	66	45	80	P
2.	Carlisle United FC (Carlisle)	46	23	11	12	65	50	80	P
3.	Fulham FC (London)	46	21	15	10	77	51	78	P
4.	Lincoln City FC (Lincoln)	46	21	14	11	66	40	77	
5.	Oxford United FC (Oxford)	46	19	14	13	63	49	71	
6.	Gillingham FC (Gillingham)	46	20	11	15	64	56	71	
7.	Southend United FC (Southend-on-Sea)	46	18	15	13	63	51	69	
8.	Brentford FC (London)	46	19	11	16	56	47	68	
9.	Millwall FC (London)	46	18	13	15	62	62	67	
10.	Plymouth Argyle FC (Plymouth)	46	18	11	17	64	56	65	
11.	Chesterfield FC (Chesterfield)	46	18	10	18	57	58	64	
12.	Reading FC (Reading)	46	17	11	18	67	75	62	
13.	Portsmouth FC (Portsmouth)	46	14	19	13	56	51	61	
14.	Preston North End FC (Preston)	46	16	13	17	50	56	61	
15.	Bristol Rovers FC (Bristol)	46	18	9	19	58	65	61	-2
16.	Newport County AFC (Newport)	46	14	16	16	54	54	58	
17.	Huddersfield Town AFC (Huddersfield)	46	15	12	19	64	59	57	
18.	Exeter City FC (Exeter)	46	16	9	21	71	84	57	
19.	Doncaster Rovers FC (Doncaster)	46	13	17	16	55	68	56	
20.	Walsall FC (Walsall)	46	13	14	19	51	55	53	
21.	Wimbledon FC (London)	46	14	11	21	61	75	53	R
22.	Swindon Town FC (Swindon)	46	13	13	20	55	71	52	R
23.	Bristol City FC (Bristol)	46	11	13	22	40	65	46	R
24.	Chester FC (Chester)	46	7	11	28	36	78	32	R
		1104	397	310	397	1421	1421	1499	

Note: Bristol Rovers FC (Bristol) had 2 points deducted for fielding an ineligible player.

Football League Division 4 — 1981-82 Season

	Aldershot Town	Blackpool	Bournemouth	Bradford City	Bury	Colchester Utd.	Crewe Alexandra	Darlington	Halifax Town	Hartlepool	Hereford United	Hull City	Mansfield Town	Northampton T.	Peterborough U.	Port Vale	Rochdale	Scunthorpe Utd.	Sheffield United	Stockport Co.	Torquay United	Tranmere R.	Wigan Athletic	York City
Aldershot Town FC		3-2	2-0	0-2	1-2	1-1	3-0	0-0	3-1	1-2	2-2	0-3	2-3	2-1	0-1	1-2	2-2	4-0	1-1	1-1	1-1	2-1	2-0	0-1
Blackpool FC	0-2		0-3	1-0	1-1	0-0	5-0	1-0	7-1	2-2	1-0	3-1	2-3	1-0	2-2	2-3	1-1	2-0	0-1	2-0	2-1	1-2	1-2	3-1
AFC Bournemouth	2-2	1-0		0-2	3-2	1-1	2-0	2-0	1-1	5-1	1-1	1-0	1-0	1-1	1-1	1-0	2-0	0-0	1-0	4-0	1-1	0-0		5-1
Bradford City AFC	4-1	1-0	2-2		1-1	2-1	4-1	3-0	5-2	1-0	0-0	1-1	3-4	2-1	2-0	1-0	2-0	0-0	0-2	5-1	3-0	1-1	3-3	6-2
Bury FC	1-1	0-1	2-2	1-1		4-3	2-1	2-0	1-1	1-1	0-2	3-2	7-1	3-1	3-2	3-0	4-0	1-1	2-0	0-1	4-0	5-3		3-1
Colchester United FC	1-1	2-1	1-2	1-2	1-1		1-1	1-0	1-1	3-3	4-0	2-0	0-1	5-1	1-1	3-2	2-1	5-2	0-1	3-0	4-0	1-2		4-0
Crewe Alexandra FC	2-3	1-1	0-1	1-2	1-3	1-3		1-0	0-1	1-2	1-1	0-2	2-2	0-2	1-2	3-0	2-3	0-2	0-1	1-1	0-1	1-1		
Darlington FC	0-1	2-2	0-1	1-5	2-3	1-2	1-0		1-1	5-2	0-1	2-1	1-0	3-0	0-0	1-1	2-0	4-1	0-2	2-0	1-1	1-2	3-1	3-1
Halifax Town AFC	2-2	0-0	1-1	0-0	2-1	0-2	2-1	3-3		2-0	1-2	2-2	2-1	1-1	1-1	0-0	1-2	1-5	4-1	1-2	0-2	0-0		0-0
Hartlepool United FC	2-2	2-2	0-2	0-2	1-0	1-3	1-2	1-2	3-2		2-1	3-2	3-0	3-1	0-1	3-1	1-1	3-3	2-3	2-2	0-0	0-0		2-1
Hereford United FC	0-1	2-1	1-2	3-0	2-2	4-1	1-1	2-2	1-1	2-1		2-2	3-1	2-1	1-0	0-0	1-1	0-0	0-3	1-3	3-0	2-1		
Hull City AFC	1-2	1-0	0-0	2-1	3-2	2-3	1-0	1-3	2-0	5-2	2-1		2-0	0-1	1-3	2-1	3-1	0-0	1-0	1-2	0-2	2-0		2-0
Mansfield Town FC	1-0	2-2	1-0	0-2	1-1	1-3	0-1	2-3	3-2	3-2	2-1	3-3		4-1	1-2	1-3	4-3	1-1	1-1	1-2	2-3	3-1	3-0	0-2
Northampton Town FC	0-0	0-1	1-1	0-2	1-0	1-2	3-0	0-1	0-1	2-1	2-3	1-1	1-1		1-0	3-5	2-1	1-1	1-2	1-2	0-2	3-2	2-3	5-0
Peterborough United FC	7-1	3-1	1-1	0-2	2-2	2-0	3-1	0-0	4-4	3-0	1-0	1-0	1-0	1-0		5-1	0-4	2-0	1-0	0-3	2-0	1-0	1-0	0-1
Port Vale FC	1-0	2-0	1-1	1-1	0-0	2-1	0-0	2-2	0-0	5-2	1-1	2-1	0-0	1-0	1-3		1-1	0-2	1-0	2-0	0-0	1-1		0-0
Rochdale AFC	0-0	0-0	0-1	1-1	1-1	1-2	1-0	3-2	0-1		0-1	0-1	1-1	5-3	1-1	1-2		1-1	0-1	4-1	1-1	0-0	1-1	2-0
Scunthorpe United FC	1-1	1-1	0-2	1-3	2-2	2-1	0-1	1-1	0-0	2-2	4-4	1-0	0-1	0-1	0-0	1-0	2-1		0-0	0-2	2-1	2-7		0-3
Sheffield United FC	2-0	3-1	0-0	1-1	1-1	4-0	0-0	2-2	1-1	2-2	1-2	0-0	4-1	7-3	4-0	2-1	3-1	1-0		4-0	4-1	2-0	1-0	
Stockport County FC	4-2	2-3	2-2	2-3	2-1	0-0	2-0	2-1	0-2	0-2	1-2	3-0	0-0	3-0	1-2	0-4	1-1	1-0			2-1	0-1	0-1	4-1
Torquay United FC	2-1	1-1	1-2	2-0	1-1	1-0	1-1	1-2	2-2	1-1	1-2	2-1	2-0	2-2	1-2	0-1	2-1	1-0	1-1	1-0		1-2	0-0	3-2
Tranmere Rovers FC	1-0	3-1	0-1	1-1	1-3	2-1	3-0	1-1	1-1	1-0	0-0	2-2	2-2	0-2	1-2	1-2	0-1	2-2	2-0	1-1			0-0	0-2
Wigan Athletic AFC	1-0	2-1	0-0	4-1	3-2	3-2	3-0	2-1	2-0	1-1	1-1	3-1	5-0	2-1	0-1	2-1	1-0	2-1	1-0	0-0		0-0		4-2
York City FC	4-0	0-4	0-1	0-3	0-0	3-0	6-0	2-2	4-0	1-2	3-4	1-3	2-1	2-1	4-3	2-0	1-2	3-1	3-4	2-2	1-1	1-3	0-0	

Division 4

		Pd	Wn	Dw	Ls	GF	GA	Pts	
1.	Sheffield United FC (Sheffield)	46	27	15	4	94	41	96	P
2.	Bradford City AFC (Bradford)	46	26	13	7	88	45	91	P
3.	Wigan Athletic AFC (Wigan)	46	26	13	7	80	46	91	P
4.	AFC Bournemouth (Bournemouth)	46	23	19	4	62	30	88	P
5.	Peterborough United FC (Peterborough)	46	24	10	12	71	57	82	
6.	Colchester United FC (Colchester)	46	20	12	14	82	57	72	
7.	Port Vale FC (Stoke-on-Trent)	46	18	16	12	56	49	70	
8.	Hull City AFC (Kingston-upon-Hull)	46	19	12	15	70	61	69	
9.	Bury FC (Bury)	46	17	17	12	80	59	68	
10.	Hereford United FC (Hereford)	46	16	19	11	64	58	67	
11.	Tranmere Rovers FC (Birkenhead)	46	14	18	14	51	56	60	
12.	Blackpool FC (Blackpool)	46	15	13	18	66	60	58	
13.	Darlington FC (Darlington)	46	15	13	18	61	62	58	
14.	Hartlepool United FC (Hartlepool)	46	13	16	17	73	84	55	
15.	Torquay United FC (Torquay)	46	14	13	19	47	59	55	
16.	Aldershot FC (Aldershot)	46	13	15	18	57	68	54	
17.	York City FC (York)	46	14	8	24	69	91	50	
18.	Stockport County FC (Stockport)	46	12	13	21	48	67	49	
19.	Halifax Town AFC (Halifax)	46	9	22	15	51	72	49	
20.	Mansfield Town FC (Mansfield)	46	13	10	23	63	81	47	-2
21.	Rochdale AFC (Rochdale)	46	10	16	20	50	62	46	
22.	Northampton Town FC (Northampton)	46	11	9	26	57	84	42	
23.	Scunthorpe United FC (Scunthorpe)	46	9	15	22	43	79	42	
24.	Crewe Alexandria FC (Crewe)	46	6	9	31	29	84	27	
		1104	384	336	384	1512	1512	1486	

Note: Mansfield Town FC (Mansfield) had 2 points deducted.

F.A. CUP FINAL   (Wembley Stadium, London – 22/05/1982 – 100,000)

TOTTENHAM HOTSPUR FC (LONDON)   1-1 (aet)   Queen's Park Rangers FC (London)

Hoddle   *(H.T. 0-0)*   *Fenwick*

Tottenham: Clemence, Hughton, Miller, Price, Hazard (Brooke), Perryman, Roberts, Archibald, Galvin, Hoddle, Crooks.

Q.P.R.: Hucker, Fenwick, Gillard, Waddock, Hazell, Roeder, Currie, Flanagan, Allen (Micklewhite), Stainrod, Gregory.

F.A. CUP FINAL REPLAY   (Wembley Stadium, London – 27/05/1982 – 90,000)

TOTTENHAM HOTSPUR FC (LONDON)   1-0   Queen's Park Rangers FC (London)

Hoddle pen.   *(H.T. 1-0)*

Q.P.R.: Hucker, Fenwick, Gillard, Waddock, Hazell, Neill, Currie, Flanagan, Micklewhite (Burke), Stainrod, Gregory.

Tottenham: Clemence, Hughton, Miller, Price, Hazard (Brooks), Perryman, Roberts, Archibald, Galvin, Hoddle, Crooks.

Semi-finals

Queen's Park Rangers FC (London)	1-0	West Bromwich Albion FC (West Bromwich)
Tottenham Hotspur FC (London)	2-0	Leicester City FC (Leicester)

Quarter-finals

Chelsea FC (London)	2-3	Tottenham Hotspur FC (London)
Leicester City FC (Leicester)	5-2	Shrewsbury Town FC (Shrewsbury)
Queen's Park Rangers FC (London)	1-0	Crystal Palace FC (London)
West Bromwich Albion FC (West Bromwich)	2-0	Coventry City FC (Coventry)

1982-83

Football League Division 1 1982-83 Season	Arsenal	Aston Villa	Birmingham City	Brighton & H.A.	Coventry City	Everton	Ipswich Town	Liverpool	Luton Town	Manchester City	Manchester United	Norwich City	Nottingham Forest	Notts County	Southampton	Stoke City	Sunderland	Swansea City	Tottenham Hotspur	Watford	W.B.A.	West Ham United
Arsenal FC	■	2-1	0-0	3-1	2-1	1-1	2-2	0-2	4-1	3-0	3-0	1-1	0-0	2-0	0-0	3-0	0-1	2-1	2-0	2-4	2-0	2-3
Aston Villa FC	2-1	■	1-0	1-0	4-0	2-0	1-1	2-4	4-1	1-1	2-1	3-2	4-1	2-0	2-0	4-0	1-3	2-0	4-0	3-0	1-0	1-0
Birmingham City FC	2-1	3-0	■	1-1	1-0	1-0	0-0	0-0	2-3	2-2	1-2	0-4	1-1	3-0	0-2	1-4	2-1	1-1	2-0	1-1	2-1	3-0
Brighton & Hove Albion FC	1-0	0-0	1-0	■	1-0	1-2	1-1	2-2	2-4	0-1	1-0	3-0	1-1	0-2	0-1	1-2	3-2	1-1	2-1	1-1	0-0	3-1
Coventry City FC	0-2	0-0	0-1	2-0	■	4-2	1-1	0-0	4-2	4-0	3-0	2-0	1-2	1-0	1-0	2-0	1-0	0-0	1-1	0-1	0-1	2-4
Everton FC	2-3	5-0	0-0	2-2	1-0	■	1-1	0-5	5-0	2-1	2-0	1-1	3-1	3-0	2-0	3-1	3-1	2-2	3-1	1-0	0-0	2-0
Ipswich Town FC	0-1	1-2	3-1	2-0	1-1	0-2	■	1-0	3-0	1-0	1-1	2-3	2-0	0-0	2-1	2-3	4-1	3-1	1-2	3-1	6-1	1-2
Liverpool FC	3-1	1-1	1-0	3-1	4-0	0-0	1-0	■	3-3	5-2	0-0	0-2	4-3	5-1	5-0	5-1	1-0	3-0	3-0	3-1	2-0	3-0
Luton Town FC	2-2	2-1	3-1	5-0	1-2	1-5	1-1	1-3	■	3-1	1-1	0-1	0-2	5-3	3-3	0-0	1-3	3-1	1-1	1-0	0-0	0-2
Manchester City FC	2-1	0-1	0-0	1-1	3-2	0-0	0-1	0-4	0-1	■	1-2	4-1	1-2	0-1	2-0	2-2	2-1	2-2	1-1	2-1	2-0	1-0
Manchester United FC	0-0	3-1	3-0	1-1	3-0	2-1	3-1	1-1	3-0	2-2	■	3-0	2-0	4-0	1-1	1-0	0-0	2-1	1-0	2-0	0-0	2-1
Norwich City FC	3-1	1-0	5-1	2-1	1-1	0-0	0-0	1-0	1-0	1-2	1-1	■	0-1	1-2	1-1	4-2	2-0	1-0	0-0	3-0	1-3	1-1
Nottingham Forest FC	3-0	1-2	1-1	4-0	4-2	2-0	2-1	1-0	0-1	3-0	0-3	2-2	■	2-1	1-2	1-0	2-1	2-2	2-0	0-0	1-0	1-0
Notts County FC	1-0	4-1	0-0	1-0	5-1	1-0	0-6	1-2	1-1	1-0	3-2	2-2	3-2	■	1-2	4-0	0-1	0-0	3-0	3-2	2-1	1-2
Southampton FC	2-2	1-0	0-1	0-0	1-1	3-2	0-1	3-2	2-2	4-1	0-1	4-0	1-1	1-0	■	1-0	2-0	2-1	1-2	1-4	4-1	3-0
Stoke City FC	2-1	0-3	1-1	3-0	0-3	1-0	1-0	1-1	4-4	1-0	1-0	1-0	1-0	1-1	1-0	■	0-1	4-1	2-0	4-0	0-3	5-2
Sunderland AFC	3-0	2-0	1-2	1-1	2-1	2-1	2-3	0-0	1-1	3-2	0-0	4-1	0-1	1-1	1-1	2-2	■	1-1	0-1	2-2	1-1	1-0
Swansea City FC	1-2	2-1	0-0	1-2	2-1	0-3	1-1	0-3	2-0	4-1	0-0	4-0	0-3	2-0	3-2	1-1	3-0	■	2-0	1-3	2-1	1-5
Tottenham Hotspur FC	5-0	2-0	2-1	2-0	4-0	2-1	3-1	2-0	2-2	1-2	2-0	4-1	4-2	6-0	4-1	1-1	1-0	2-0	■	0-1	1-1	2-1
Watford FC	2-1	2-1	2-1	4-1	0-0	2-0	2-1	2-1	5-2	2-0	0-1	2-2	1-3	5-3	2-0	1-0	8-0	2-1	0-1	■	3-0	2-1
West Bromwich Albion FC	0-0	0-1	2-0	5-0	2-0	2-2	4-1	0-1	1-0	0-2	3-1	1-0	2-1	2-2	1-0	1-1	3-0	3-3	0-1	1-3	■	1-2
West Ham United FC	1-3	2-0	5-0	2-1	0-3	2-0	1-1	3-1	2-3	4-1	3-1	1-0	1-2	2-0	1-1	1-1	2-1	3-2	3-0	2-1	0-1	■

	Division 1	Pd	Wn	Dw	Ls	GF	GA	Pts	
1.	LIVERPOOL FC (LIVERPOOL)	42	24	10	8	87	37	82	
2.	Watford FC (Watford)	42	22	5	15	74	57	71	
3.	Manchester United FC (Manchester)	42	19	13	10	56	38	70	
4.	Tottenham Hotspur FC (London)	42	20	9	13	65	50	69	
5.	Nottingham Forest FC (Nottingham)	42	20	9	13	62	50	69	
6.	Aston Villa FC (Birmingham)	42	21	5	16	62	50	68	
7.	Everton FC (Liverpool)	42	18	10	14	66	48	64	
8.	West Ham United FC (London)	42	20	4	18	68	62	64	
9.	Ipswich Town FC (Ipswich)	42	15	13	14	64	50	58	
10.	Arsenal FC (London)	42	16	10	16	58	56	58	
11.	West Bromwich Albion FC (West Bromwich)	42	15	12	15	51	49	57	
12.	Southampton FC (Southampton)	42	15	12	15	54	58	57	
13.	Stoke City FC (Stoke-on-Trent)	42	16	9	17	53	64	57	
14.	Norwich City FC (Norwich)	42	14	12	16	52	58	54	
15.	Notts County FC (Nottingham)	42	15	7	20	55	71	52	
16.	Sunderland AFC (Sunderland)	42	12	14	16	48	61	50	
17.	Birmingham City FC (Birmingham)	42	12	14	16	40	55	50	
18.	Luton Town FC (Luton)	42	12	13	17	65	84	49	
19.	Coventry City FC (Coventry)	42	13	9	20	48	59	48	
20.	Manchester City FC (Manchester)	42	13	8	21	47	70	47	R
21.	Swansea City FC (Swansea)	42	10	11	21	51	69	41	R
22.	Brighton & Hove Albion FC (Hove)	42	9	13	20	38	68	40	R
		924	351	222	351	1264	1264	1275	

Top Goalscorer

1) Luther BLISSETT   (Watford FC)   27

Football League Division 2 — 1982-83 Season

	Barnsley	Blackburn Rovers	Bolton Wanderers	Burnley	Cambridge	Carlisle United	Charlton Athletic	Chelsea	Crystal Palace	Derby County	Fulham	Grimsby Town	Leeds United	Leicester City	Middlesbrough	Newcastle United	Oldham Athletic	Q.P.R.	Rotherham United	Sheffield Wednesday	Shrewsbury Town	Wolverhampton Wanderers
Barnsley FC	■	2-2	3-1	3-0	2-3	2-2	0-0	1-1	3-1	1-1	4-3	4-0	2-1	1-2	2-0	0-5	1-1	0-1	2-1	0-0	2-2	2-1
Blackburn Rovers FC	1-1	■	1-1	2-1	3-1	3-2	2-0	3-0	3-0	2-0	0-0	2-1	0-0	3-1	1-1	1-2	2-2	1-3	3-0	2-3	1-0	2-2
Bolton Wanderers FC	0-2	1-0	■	3-0	2-0	1-0	4-1	0-1	1-0	0-2	0-1	0-0	1-2	3-1	3-1	3-1	2-3	3-2	2-2	0-2	1-4	0-1
Burnley FC	3-1	0-1	0-0	■	2-1	4-1	7-1	3-0	2-1	1-1	1-0	1-1	1-2	2-4	1-1	1-0	1-2	2-1	1-2	4-1	1-2	0-1
Cambridge United FC	1-1	2-0	0-0	2-0	■	1-1	3-2	0-1	1-0	0-0	1-0	1-0	0-0	3-1	2-0	1-0	1-4	1-4	2-0	2-2	0-0	2-1
Carlisle United FC	1-1	3-1	5-0	1-1	2-2	■	4-1	2-1	4-1	3-0	3-2	2-3	2-2	0-1	1-3	2-0	0-0	1-0	2-2	4-2	2-3	0-2
Charlton Athletic FC	3-2	3-0	4-1	2-1	2-1	0-0	■	5-2	2-1	1-1	3-0	0-1	0-1	2-1	2-3	2-0	4-1	1-3	1-5	0-3	0-1	3-3
Chelsea FC	0-3	2-0	2-1	2-1	6-0	4-2	3-1	■	0-0	1-3	0-0	5-2	0-0	1-1	0-0	0-2	2-0	0-2	1-1	11-	1-2	0-0
Crystal Palace FC	1-1	2-0	3-0	1-0	0-0	2-1	1-1	0-0	■	4-1	1-1	2-0	1-1	1-0	3-0	0-2	1-0	0-3	1-1	2-0	2-1	3-4
Derby County FC	1-1	1-2	0-0	2-0	1-1	0-3	1-1	1-0	1-1	■	1-0	2-0	3-3	0-4	1-1	2-1	2-2	2-0	3-0	0-0	2-3	1-1
Fulham FC	1-0	3-1	4-0	3-1	1-1	2-0	2-1	1-1	1-0	2-1	■	4-0	3-2	0-1	1-0	2-2	0-3	1-1	1-1	1-0	2-1	1-3
Grimsby Town FC	1-2	5-0	1-0	3-2	1-0	2-1	1-1	2-1	4-1	1-1	0-4	■	1-1	2-0	0-3	2-2	0-1	1-1	1-2	1-1	2-0	1-1
Leeds United AFC	0-0	2-1	1-1	3-1	2-1	1-1	1-2	3-3	2-1	2-1	1-1	1-0	■	2-2	0-0	3-1	0-0	0-1	2-2	1-2	1-1	0-0
Leicester City FC	1-0	0-1	0-0	0-0	4-0	6-0	1-2	3-0	0-1	1-1	2-0	2-0	0-1	■	1-0	2-2	2-1	0-1	3-1	0-2	3-2	5-0
Middlesbrough FC	2-0	1-5	1-0	1-4	0-1	1-0	3-0	3-1	2-0	2-3	1-4	1-4	0-0	1-1	■	1-1	1-1	2-1	1-1	1-1	2-1	0-0
Newcastle United FC	1-2	3-2	2-2	3-0	2-0	2-2	4-2	1-1	1-0	1-0	1-4	4-0	2-1	2-2	1-1	■	1-0	1-0	4-0	2-1	4-0	1-1
Oldham Athletic AFC	1-1	0-0	2-3	3-0	3-0	4-3	2-2	2-2	2-0	2-2	1-0	1-1	2-2	1-2	3-0	2-2	■	0-1	1-1	1-1	1-0	4-1
Queen's Park Rangers FC	3-0	2-2	1-0	3-2	2-1	1-0	5-1	1-2	0-0	4-1	3-1	4-0	1-0	2-2	6-1	2-0	1-0	■	4-0	0-2	4-0	2-1
Rotherham United FC	1-0	3-1	1-1	1-1	2-0	1-2	1-0	1-0	2-2	1-1	0-1	3-0	0-1	1-3	1-1	1-5	1-3	0-0	■	0-3	0-3	1-1
Sheffield Wednesday FC	0-1	0-0	3-1	1-1	3-1	1-1	5-4	3-2	2-1	2-0	2-1	2-3	2-2	3-1	1-1	1-1	0-1	0-1	0-1	■	0-0	0-0
Shrewsbury Town FC	3-1	0-0	1-0	1-2	2-1	2-1	0-0	2-0	1-1	1-1	0-1	0-0	0-0	0-2	2-2	2-1	0-0	0-0	2-0	1-0	■	0-2
Wolverhampton Wanderers FC	2-0	2-1	0-0	2-0	1-1	2-1	5-0	2-1	1-0	2-1	2-4	3-0	3-0	0-3	4-0	2-2	0-0	4-0	2-0	1-0	2-2	■

	Division 2	Pd	Wn	Dw	Ls	GF	GA	Pts	
1.	Queen's Park Rangers FC (London)	42	26	7	9	77	36	85	P
2.	Wolverhampton Wanderers FC (Wolverhampton)	42	20	15	7	68	44	75	P
3.	Leicester City FC (Leicester)	42	20	10	12	72	44	70	P
4.	Fulham FC (London)	42	20	9	13	64	47	69	
5.	Newcastle United FC (Newcastle-upon-Tyne)	42	18	13	11	75	53	67	
6.	Sheffield Wednesday FC (Sheffield)	42	16	15	11	60	47	63	
7.	Oldham Athletic AFC (Oldham)	42	14	19	9	64	47	61	
8.	Leeds United AFC (Leeds)	42	13	21	8	51	46	60	
9.	Shrewsbury Town FC (Shrewsbury)	42	15	14	13	48	48	59	
10.	Barnsley FC (Barnsley)	42	14	15	13	57	55	57	
11.	Blackburn Rovers FC (Blackburn)	42	15	12	15	58	58	57	
12.	Cambridge United FC (Cambridge)	42	13	12	17	42	60	51	
13.	Derby County FC (Derby)	42	10	19	13	49	58	49	
14.	Carlisle United FC (Carlisle)	42	12	12	18	68	70	48	
15.	Crystal Palace FC (London)	42	12	12	18	43	52	48	
16.	Middlesbrough FC (Middlesbrough)	42	11	15	16	46	67	48	
17.	Charlton Athletic FC (London)	42	13	9	20	63	86	48	
18.	Chelsea FC (London)	42	11	14	17	51	61	47	
19.	Grimsby Town FC (Cleethorpes)	42	12	11	19	45	70	47	
20.	Rotherham United FC (Rotherham)	42	10	15	17	45	68	45	R
21.	Burnley FC (Burnley)	42	12	8	22	56	66	44	R
22.	Bolton Wanderers FC (Bolton)	42	11	11	20	42	61	44	R
		924	318	288	318	1244	1244	1242	

Football League Division 3 1982-83 Season — Results Grid

	Bournemouth	Bradford C	Brentford	Bristol Rovers	Cardiff City	Chesterfield	Doncaster Rovers	Exeter City	Gillingham	Huddersfield Town	Lincoln City	Millwall	Newport County	Orient	Oxford United	Plymouth Argyle	Portsmouth	Preston North End	Reading	Sheffield United	Southend United	Walsall	Wigan Athletic	Wrexham
AFC Bournemouth	■	2-2	4-3	0-0	3-1	2-1	2-2	2-0	0-1	0-1	1-0	3-0	0-1	2-0	2-0	1-0	0-2	4-0	1-1	0-0	0-2	3-0	2-2	1-1
Bradford City AFC	2-3	■	0-1	2-0	4-2	1-0	1-0	3-3	1-1	3-1	1-1	0-0	4-2	2-3	3-2	4-0	2-2	1-2	3-2	2-0	1-0	1-1	0-1	0-0
Brentford FC	2-1	0-2	■	5-1	1-3	4-2	1-0	4-0	1-1	1-0	2-0	1-1	2-0	5-2	1-1	2-0	1-1	3-1	1-2	2-1	4-2	2-3	1-3	4-1
Bristol Rovers FC	1-1	4-1	2-0	■	1-1	3-0	2-0	4-4	2-1	1-0	1-2	4-0	1-3	2-1	0-1	2-0	5-1	3-2	3-0	2-1	2-2	2-2	4-0	4-0
Cardiff City AFC	1-1	1-0	3-1	3-1	■	1-1	3-0	1-0	1-0	1-1	1-0	3-0	3-2	2-0	3-0	0-0	1-0	3-1	0-0	2-0	4-1	3-1	3-2	1-2
Chesterfield FC	0-0	3-0	2-1	0-0	0-1	■	3-3	1-3	1-2	0-1	1-3	0-1	3-1	1-2	1-2	1-2	1-1	1-1	0-0	3-1	0-2	0-0	2-0	5-1
Doncaster Rovers FC	2-1	1-2	4-4	1-2	2-2	0-0	■	6-1	0-2	0-4	2-2	2-1	0-0	0-3	0-1	2-2	2-2	2-0	7-5	2-0	0-0	1-3	3-6	1-1
Exeter City FC	4-2	2-1	1-7	0-1	0-2	2-3	3-0	■	2-2	3-4	3-1	2-1	2-0	3-1	1-0	1-1	5-1	2-2	0-3	4-3	4-3	2-1	3-3	
Gillingham FC	2-5	3-0	2-2	1-0	2-3	3-1	1-1	4-4	■	1-3	0-2	1-0	2-0	4-0	0-1	2-1	1-0	2-1	1-0	0-2	1-0	3-0	0-2	1-1
Huddersfield Town	0-0	6-3	2-0	3-1	4-0	3-1	3-0	1-1	3-2	■	1-1	5-1	1-0	6-0	2-0	2-0	1-1	1-1	3-1	0-0	2-1	2-2	1-1	4-1
Lincoln City FC	9-0	1-0	2-1	2-1	2-1	2-0	5-1	4-1	3-1	1-2	■	3-1	1-4	2-0	1-1	1-2	0-3	3-0	4-0	3-0	0-1	2-1	2-1	2-0
Millwall FC	2-0	1-1	1-0	1-1	0-4	1-1	3-0	5-2	4-1	3-0	2-1	■	3-0	0-1	2-1	2-2	2-0	1-0	1-1	1-2	3-1	2-2	2-1	1-1
Newport County AFC	5-1	1-1	0-0	2-1	1-0	1-0	1-2	2-1	2-1	1-0	2-2	2-2	■	4-1	1-2	2-2	0-3	3-0	1-0	3-1	1-1	1-1	1-0	4-0
Orient FC	5-0	0-1	3-3	1-5	4-0	2-0	1-0	5-1	2-0	1-3	1-1	2-3	1-5	■	1-5	0-2	2-1	2-1	3-3	4-1	1-1	2-1	1-1	0-0
Oxford United FC	2-0	5-1	2-2	4-2	2-2	1-0	3-0	1-1	1-1	1-1	1-0	1-0	0-3	2-2	■	1-1	1-3	1-2	0-0	1-0	4-2	2-0	2-0	
Plymouth Argyle FC	2-0	3-1	1-2	0-4	3-2	2-0	1-2	1-0	2-0	0-2	3-1	2-4	2-0	2-1	0-1	■	1-1	3-0	3-1	1-0	0-0	0-2	2-0	
Portsmouth FC	0-2	0-1	2-1	1-0	0-0	4-0	2-1	3-2	1-0	1-2	4-1	0-2	1-2	2-0	2-1	0-1	■	3-2	2-1	4-1	1-0	0-0	3-0	
Preston North End	0-1	0-0	3-0	2-2	2-1	1-1	4-1	2-2	0-0	0-0	1-0	3-2	0-0	1-2	1-2	2-2	0-0	■	2-0	1-0	1-1	1-0	4-1	3-0
Reading FC	2-1	2-1	1-1	1-2	1-2	0-0	2-0	3-1	0-0	1-1	3-3	4-2	3-0	0-3	3-2	1-2	2-3		■	2-0	1-1	1-1	2-1	1-0
Sheffield United FC	2-2	2-1	1-2	2-1	2-0	3-1	3-1	3-0	0-2	2-0	0-1	1-1	2-0	3-2	3-1	2-1	2-1	1-1		■	0-1	3-1	2-0	2-0
Southend United FC	0-0	1-1	4-2	1-0	1-2	2-0	3-2	1-1	1-1	0-1	2-0	1-4	0-1	2-1	4-0	2-3	4-2	3-1			■	1-1	2-0	2-2
Walsall FC	3-1	1-1	2-1	5-0	1-2	0-1	1-0	3-2	0-0	2-0	1-1	4-0	2-1	2-0	2-0	0-3	2-1	2-1	0-0	1-3		■	2-0	1-1
Wigan Athletic AFC	1-2	3-2	3-2	0-5	0-0	2-2	0-3	1-0	2-2	2-0	2-1	3-1	0-1	0-1	0-1	3-0	0-1	0-1	2-2	3-2	4-0	1-3	■	3-1
Wrexham AFC	1-0	0-4	3-4	0-0	0-0	0-0	5-0	1-2	1-0	1-1	0-1	4-3	1-0	1-1	2-3	0-2	3-1	4-0	4-1	3-2	4-0	1-1		■

Division 3

		Pd	Wn	Dw	Ls	GF	GA	Pts	
1.	Portsmouth FC (Portsmouth)	46	27	10	9	74	41	91	P
2.	Cardiff City AFC (Cardiff)	46	25	11	10	76	50	86	P
3.	Huddersfield Town AFC (Huddersfield)	46	23	13	10	84	49	82	P
4.	Newport County AFC (Newport)	46	23	9	14	76	54	78	
5.	Oxford United FC (Oxford)	46	22	12	12	71	53	78	
6.	Lincoln City FC (Lincoln)	46	23	7	16	77	51	76	
7.	Bristol Rovers FC (Bristol)	46	22	9	15	84	58	75	
8.	Plymouth Argyle FC (Plymouth)	46	19	8	19	61	66	65	
9.	Brentford FC (London)	46	18	10	18	88	77	64	
10.	Walsall FC (Walsall)	46	17	13	16	64	63	64	
11.	Sheffield United FC (Sheffield)	46	19	7	20	62	64	64	
12.	Bradford City AFC (Bradford)	46	16	13	17	68	69	61	
13.	Gillingham FC (Gillingham)	46	16	13	17	58	59	61	
14.	AFC Bournemouth (Bournemouth)	46	16	13	17	59	68	61	
15.	Southend United FC (Southend-on-Sea)	46	15	14	17	66	65	59	
16.	Preston North End FC (Preston)	46	15	13	18	60	69	58	
17.	Millwall FC (London)	46	14	13	19	64	77	55	
18.	Wigan Athletic AFC (Wigan)	46	15	9	22	60	72	54	
19.	Exeter City FC (Exeter)	46	14	12	20	81	104	54	
20.	Orient FC (London)	46	15	9	22	64	88	54	
21.	Reading FC (Reading)	46	12	17	17	64	79	53	R
22.	Wrexham AFC (Wrexham)	46	12	15	19	56	76	51	R
23.	Doncaster Rovers FC (Doncaster)	46	9	11	26	57	97	38	R
24.	Chesterfield FC (Chesterfield)	46	8	13	25	43	68	37	R
		1104	415	274	415	1617	1617	1519	

165

Football League Division 4 1982-83 Season	Aldershot Town	Blackpool	Bristol City	Bury	Chester	Colchester United	Crewe Alexandra	Darlington	Halifax Town	Hartlepool	Hereford United	Hull City	Mansfield Town	Northampton Town	Peterborough United	Port Vale	Rochdale	Scunthorpe United	Stockport County	Swindon Town	Torquay United	Tranmere Rovers	Wimbledon	York City
Aldershot Town FC	■	2-1	0-0	1-1	1-2	0-1	2-1	1-6	6-1	0-2	2-1	1-2	2-1	3-0	2-0	1-4	6-4	1-1	2-1	1-1	2-1	1-0	1-1	2-3
Blackpool FC	4-1	■	1-4	1-1	1-1	1-2	2-0	2-0	0-0	1-2	5-1	1-1	2-1	0-0	0-3	2-0	1-0	3-1	0-0	2-1	1-0	0-2	1-1	1-1
Bristol City FC	2-0	0-0	■	2-1	0-0	0-2	2-1	2-2	3-0	2-0	1-1	2-1	3-1	1-3	1-0	1-3	0-0	0-2	2-2	1-1	0-1	1-0	4-2	2-2
Bury FC	3-1	4-1	2-2	■	3-2	1-0	0-1	3-0	2-0	4-0	3-2	2-3	1-0	1-1	1-0	0-1	0-0	1-0	3-2	0-0	3-0	3-0	1-3	2-1
Chester FC	1-1	1-2	1-0	0-1	■	1-1	1-0	2-3	2-0	2-1	5-0	0-0	1-3	2-1	1-1	1-0	5-2	1-2	0-2	0-1	0-0	0-0	1-2	0-1
Colchester United FC	0-0	4-1	3-1	2-1	1-0	■	4-3	2-2	1-0	4-1	3-2	0-0	2-0	3-1	1-0	1-2	4-1	5-1	3-0	1-0	1-0	3-3	3-0	0-0
Crewe Alexandra FC	0-0	3-1	4-1	3-3	3-2	0-1	■	2-5	1-1	3-0	3-1	0-3	1-2	1-0	0-3	1-2	1-1	0-1	3-0	3-0	1-1	0-1	0-2	2-1
Darlington FC	1-1	0-1	2-2	1-2	0-2	1-3	1-1	■	1-2	2-1	2-1	1-2	0-0	2-0	4-3	0-0	3-0	3-1	3-1	1-0	0-2	1-0	0-2	1-3
Halifax Town AFC	1-3	2-0	2-2	1-0	0-0	4-0	0-3	2-0	■	1-1	2-2	1-2	0-0	2-0	1-2	0-2	0-0	3-1	1-0	1-0	3-0	1-2	1-1	2-2
Hartlepool United FC	1-1	2-1	3-1	0-1	1-0	1-4	1-0	2-0	1-2	■	0-1	0-0	0-4	2-1	0-0	2-2	3-0	0-0	3-2	1-2	0-2	4-0	1-0	2-0
Hereford United FC	2-1	0-0	1-3	0-2	5-2	0-0	1-0	0-0	2-0	1-0	■	2-0	0-2	1-1	0-1	0-2	1-0	0-2	0-0	1-2	0-1	1-0	1-4	0-0
Hull City AFC	2-2	3-1	1-0	2-1	2-0	3-0	1-0	0-0	1-1	1-1	2-0	■	2-2	4-0	4-1	1-0	2-1	1-1	7-0	0-0	4-1	0-1	1-1	4-0
Mansfield Town FC	4-1	2-1	1-1	1-4	2-1	1-1	1-0	0-2	1-2	3-0	0-1	3-1	■	2-0	0-0	0-2	2-1	0-2	1-0	1-0	2-1	1-1	2-2	2-2
Northampton Town	1-1	2-1	7-1	0-3	1-1	2-1	4-0	3-3	3-1	3-1	2-1	1-2	1-2	■	0-0	2-2	1-1	2-1	2-3	0-1	2-0	1-0	2-2	1-1
Peterborough United	0-0	3-1	3-0	1-1	0-1	2-1	2-1	1-1	2-1	2-1	4-0	1-1	3-2	2-0	■	0-0	1-0	0-1	1-0	4-3	1-3	3-0	0-3	2-2
Port Vale FC	2-1	1-0	1-1	0-0	2-1	0-0	1-1	2-1	2-1	3-0	1-0	1-0	4-1	1-2	2-1	■	4-0	0-2	2-3	3-0	1-0	0-1	1-0	2-1
Rochdale AFC	3-1	3-1	1-0	0-0	0-1	2-1	2-0	1-1	2-2	2-0	4-1	1-3	2-2	2-0	1-1	3-3	■	0-1	1-0	1-1	2-2	4-2	0-2	1-0
Scunthorpe United	1-1	4-3	1-1	0-1	2-0	2-1	2-0	2-2	2-0	3-0	1-2	0-1	2-2	5-1	3-0	1-0	1-1	■	3-0	2-0	2-0	2-1	0-0	0-0
Stockport County	2-1	3-0	2-2	2-1	3-3	3-0	3-2	2-1	4-2	1-1	2-1	1-1	1-1	0-1	1-1	0-2	2-2	1-1	■	1-2	1-0	3-2	1-3	2-1
Swindon Town FC	2-0	3-3	2-0	1-1	2-3	3-0	1-0	1-2	0-1	3-0	3-2	0-1	4-0	1-5	1-0	1-0	4-1	2-2	2-0	■	2-1	4-2	0-1	3-2
Torquay United FC	4-2	1-3	0-2	2-3	0-1	2-0	2-1	1-0	1-3	3-2	2-1	0-0	3-1	3-1	2-1	0-1	3-2	1-1	3-0	1-1	■	3-0	0-1	1-3
Tranmere Rovers FC	1-1	1-1	2-2	1-1	2-4	2-4	1-1	2-0	1-2	1-1	2-1	0-1	3-0	2-1	1-0	0-2	0-0	0-4	1-1	2-0	2-0	■	0-2	3-0
Wimbledon FC	6-1	5-0	2-1	2-1	4-0	2-1	3-2	3-1	2-4	2-0	1-0	1-2	1-1	1-1	2-1	1-0	3-0	2-2	2-1	0-0	4-1	4-0	■	4-3
York City FC	4-0	2-0	3-0	3-1	1-0	3-0	2-0	5-2	3-2	5-1	5-1	1-0	6-1	5-2	1-1	0-0	1-0	2-1	3-1	0-0	1-1	2-1	1-4	■

Division 4

		Pd	Wn	Dw	Ls	GF	GA	Pts	
1.	Wimbledon FC (London)	46	29	11	6	96	45	98	P
2.	Hull City AFC (Kingston-upon-Hull)	46	25	15	6	75	34	90	P
3.	Port Vale FC (Stoke-on-Trent)	46	26	10	10	67	34	88	P
4.	Scunthorpe United FC (Scunthorpe)	46	23	14	9	71	42	83	P
5.	Bury FC (Bury)	46	23	12	11	74	46	81	
6.	Colchester United FC (Colchester)	46	24	9	13	75	55	81	
7.	York City FC (York)	46	22	13	11	88	58	79	
8.	Swindon Town FC (Swindon)	46	19	11	16	61	54	68	
9.	Peterborough United FC (Peterborough)	46	17	13	16	58	52	64	
10.	Mansfield Town FC (Mansfield)	46	16	13	17	61	70	61	
11.	Halifax Town AFC (Halifax)	46	16	12	18	59	66	60	
12.	Torquay United FC (Torquay)	46	17	7	22	56	65	58	
13.	Chester FC (Chester)	46	15	11	20	55	60	56	*
14.	Bristol City FC (Bristol)	46	13	17	16	59	70	56	
15.	Northampton Town FC (Northampton)	46	14	12	20	65	75	54	
16.	Stockport County FC (Stockport)	46	14	12	20	60	79	54	
17.	Darlington FC (Darlington)	46	13	13	20	61	71	52	
18.	Aldershot FC (Aldershot)	46	12	15	19	61	82	51	
19.	Tranmere Rovers FC (Birkenhead)	46	13	11	22	49	71	50	
20.	Rochdale AFC (Rochdale)	46	11	16	19	55	73	49	
21.	Blackpool FC (Blackpool)	46	13	12	21	55	74	49	-2
22.	Hartlepool United FC (Hartlepool)	46	13	9	24	46	76	48	
23.	Crewe Alexandra FC (Crewe)	46	11	8	27	53	71	41	
24.	Hereford United FC (Hereford)	46	11	8	27	42	79	41	
		1104	410	284	410	1502	1502	1512	

Note: Blackpool FC (Blackpool) had 2 points deducted for fielding an ineligible player.

* Chester FC (Chester) changed their club name to Chester City FC (Chester) for the next season.

F.A. CUP FINAL   (Wembley Stadium, London – 21/05/1983 – 100,000)

MANCHESTER UNITED FC (MANCHESTER)   2-2   Brighton & Hove Albion FC (Hove)

Stapleton 55', Wilkins 73'   *Smith 14', Stevens 87'*

Man. United: Bailey, Duxbury, Moran, McQueen, Albiston, Davies, Wilkins, Robson, Muhren, Stapleton, Whiteside.

Brighton: Moseley, Ramsey (Ryan), Stevens, Gatting, Pearce, Smillie, Case, Grealish, Howlett, Robinson, Smith.

F.A. CUP FINAL REPLAY   (Wembley Stadium, London – 26/05/83 – 100,000)

MANCHESTER UNITED FC (MANCHESTER)   4-0   Brighton & Hove Albion FC (Hove)

Robson 23', 44', Whiteside 25', Muhren 62' pen.

Man. United: Bailey, Duxbury, Moran, McQueen, Albiston, Davies, Wilkins, Robson, Muhren, Stapleton, Whiteside.

Brighton: Moseley, Foster, Stevens, Gatting, Pearce, Smillie, Case, Grealish, Howlett, Robinson, Smith.

Semi-finals

Brighton & Hove Albion FC (Hove)	2-1	Sheffield Wednesday FC (Sheffield)
Manchester United FC (Manchester)	2-1	Arsenal FC (London)

Quarter-finals

Arsenal FC (London)	2-0	Aston Villa FC (Birmingham)
Brighton & Hove Albion FC (Hove)	1-0	Norwich City FC (Norwich)
Burnley FC (Burnley)	1-1, 0-5	Sheffield Wednesday FC (Sheffield)
Manchester United FC (Manchester)	1-0	Everton FC (Liverpool)

1983-84

Football League Division 1 1983-84 Season	Arsenal	Aston Villa	Birmingham City	Coventry City	Everton	Ipswich Town	Leicester City	Liverpool	Luton Town	Manchester United	Norwich City	Nottingham Forest	Notts County	Q.P.R.	Southampton	Stoke City	Sunderland	Tottenham Hotspur	Watford	W.B.A.	West Ham United	Wolves
Arsenal FC	■	1-1	1-1	0-1	2-1	4-1	2-1	0-2	2-1	2-3	3-0	4-1	1-1	0-2	2-2	3-1	1-2	3-2	3-1	0-1	3-3	4-1
Aston Villa FC	2-6	■	1-0	2-0	0-2	4-0	3-1	1-3	0-0	0-3	1-0	3-1	2-1	1-0	1-1	1-0	0-0	2-1	4-3	1-0	1-0	4-0
Birmingham City FC	1-1	2-1	■	1-2	0-2	1-0	2-1	0-0	1-1	2-2	0-1	1-2	0-0	0-2	0-0	1-0	0-1	0-1	2-0	2-1	3-0	0-0
Coventry City FC	1-4	3-3	0-1	■	1-1	1-2	2-1	4-0	2-2	1-1	2-1	2-1	2-1	1-0	0-0	2-3	2-1	2-4	1-2	1-2	1-2	2-1
Everton FC	0-0	1-1	1-1	0-0	■	1-0	1-1	1-1	0-1	1-1	0-2	1-0	4-1	3-1	1-0	1-0	0-0	2-1	1-0	0-0	0-1	2-0
Ipswich Town FC	1-0	2-1	1-2	3-1	3-0	■	0-0	1-1	3-0	0-2	2-0	2-2	1-0	0-2	0-3	5-0	1-0	3-1	0-0	3-4	0-3	3-1
Leicester City FC	3-0	2-0	2-3	1-1	2-0	2-0	■	3-3	0-3	1-1	2-1	2-1	0-4	2-1	2-1	2-2	0-2	0-3	4-1	1-1	4-1	5-1
Liverpool FC	2-1	2-1	1-0	5-0	3-0	2-2	2-2	■	6-0	1-1	1-1	1-0	5-0	2-0	1-1	1-0	0-1	3-1	3-0	3-0	6-0	0-1
Luton Town FC	1-2	1-0	1-1	2-4	0-3	2-1	0-0	0-0	■	0-5	2-2	2-3	3-2	0-0	3-1	0-1	4-1	2-4	1-2	2-0	0-1	4-0
Manchester United FC	4-0	1-2	1-0	4-0	0-1	1-2	2-0	1-0	2-0	■	0-0	1-2	3-3	3-1	3-2	1-0	2-1	4-2	4-1	3-0	0-0	3-0
Norwich City FC	1-1	3-1	1-1	0-0	1-1	0-0	3-1	0-1	0-0	3-3	■	2-3	0-1	0-3	1-0	2-2	3-0	2-1	6-1	2-0	1-0	3-0
Nottingham Forest FC	0-1	2-2	5-1	3-0	1-0	2-1	3-2	0-1	1-0	2-0	3-0	■	3-1	3-2	0-1	0-0	1-1	2-2	5-1	3-1	3-0	5-0
Notts County FC	0-4	5-2	2-1	2-1	0-1	0-2	2-5	0-0	0-3	1-0	1-1	0-0	■	0-3	1-3	1-1	6-1	0-0	3-5	1-1	2-2	4-0
Queen's Park Rangers FC	2-0	2-1	2-1	2-1	2-0	1-0	0-1	0-1	1-1	1-1	2-0	0-1	1-0	■	4-0	6-0	3-0	2-1	1-1	1-1	1-1	2-1
Southampton FC	1-0	2-2	2-1	8-2	3-1	3-2	2-2	2-0	3-0	2-1	0-1	0-2	0-0	0-0	■	3-1	1-1	5-0	1-0	1-0	2-0	1-0
Stoke City FC	1-0	1-0	2-1	1-3	1-1	1-0	0-1	2-0	2-4	0-1	2-0	1-1	1-0	1-2	1-1	■	2-1	1-1	0-4	3-1	3-1	4-0
Sunderland AFC	2-2	0-1	2-1	1-0	2-1	1-1	1-1	0-0	2-0	0-1	1-1	1-1	0-0	1-0	0-2	2-2	■	1-1	3-0	3-0	0-1	3-2
Tottenham Hotspur FC	2-4	2-1	0-1	1-1	1-2	2-0	3-2	2-2	2-1	1-1	2-0	2-1	1-0	3-2	0-0	1-0	3-0	■	2-3	0-1	0-2	1-0
Watford FC	2-1	3-2	1-0	2-3	4-4	2-2	3-3	0-2	1-2	0-0	1-3	3-2	3-1	1-0	1-1	2-0	2-1	2-3	■	3-1	0-0	0-0
West Bromwich Albion FC	1-3	3-1	1-2	1-1	1-1	2-1	1-0	1-2	3-0	2-0	0-0	0-5	2-0	1-2	0-2	3-0	3-1	1-1	2-0	■	1-0	1-3
West Ham United FC	3-1	0-1	4-0	5-2	0-1	2-1	3-1	1-3	3-1	1-1	0-0	1-2	3-0	2-2	0-1	3-0	0-1	4-1	2-4	1-0	■	1-1
Wolverhampton Wanderers FC	1-2	1-1	1-1	0-0	3-0	0-3	1-0	1-1	1-2	1-1	2-0	1-0	0-1	0-4	0-1	0-0	0-0	2-3	0-5	0-0	0-3	■

	Division 1	Pd	Wn	Dw	Ls	GF	GA	Pts	
1.	LIVERPOOL FC (LIVERPOOL)	42	22	14	6	73	32	80	
2.	Southampton FC (Southampton)	42	22	11	9	66	38	77	
3.	Nottingham Forest FC (Nottingham)	42	22	8	12	76	45	74	
4.	Manchester United FC (Manchester)	42	20	14	8	71	41	74	
5.	Queen's Park Rangers FC (London)	42	22	7	13	67	37	73	
6.	Arsenal FC (London)	42	18	9	15	74	60	63	
7.	Everton FC (Liverpool)	42	16	14	12	44	42	62	
8.	Tottenham Hotspur FC (London)	42	17	10	15	64	65	61	
9.	West Ham United FC (London)	42	17	9	16	60	55	60	
10.	Aston Villa FC (Birmingham)	42	17	9	16	59	61	60	
11.	Watford FC (Watford)	42	16	9	17	68	77	57	
12.	Ipswich Town FC (Ipswich)	42	15	8	19	55	57	53	
13.	Sunderland AFC (Sunderland)	42	13	13	16	42	53	52	
14.	Norwich City FC (Norwich)	42	12	15	15	48	49	51	
15.	Leicester City FC (Leicester)	42	13	12	17	65	68	51	
16.	Luton Town FC (Luton)	42	14	9	19	53	66	51	
17.	West Bromwich Albion FC (West Bromwich)	42	14	9	19	48	62	51	
18.	Stoke City FC (Stoke-on-Trent)	42	13	11	18	44	63	50	
19.	Coventry City FC (Coventry)	42	13	11	18	57	77	50	
20.	Birmingham City FC (Birmingham)	42	12	12	18	39	50	48	R
21.	Notts County FC (Nottingham)	42	10	11	21	50	72	41	R
22.	Wolverhampton Wanderers FC (Wolverhampton)	42	6	11	25	27	80	29	R
		924	344	236	344	1250	1250	1268	

Top Goalscorer

1) Ian RUSH   (Liverpool FC)   32

Football League Division 2 — 1983-84 Season

	Barnsley	Blackburn Rovers	Brighton & Hove Albion	Cambridge	Cardiff City	Carlisle United	Charlton Athletic	Chelsea	Crystal Palace	Derby County	Fulham	Grimsby Town	Huddersfield Town	Leeds United	Manchester City	Middlesbrough	Newcastle United	Oldham Athletic	Portsmouth	Sheffield Wednesday	Shrewsbury Town	Swansea City
Barnsley FC		0-0	3-1	2-0	2-3	2-1	2-0	0-0	1-1	5-1	3-0	3-1	2-2	0-2	1-1	0-2	1-1	0-1	0-3	0-1	3-0	3-2
Blackburn Rovers FC	1-1		2-2	1-0	1-1	4-1	1-1	0-0	2-1	5-1	0-1	1-1	2-2	1-1	2-1	1-0	1-1	3-1	2-1	0-0	1-1	4-1
Brighton & Hove Albion FC	1-0	1-1		3-0	3-1	1-1	7-0	1-2	3-1	1-0	1-1	2-0	3-1	3-0	1-1	3-0	0-1	4-0	0-1	1-3	2-2	1-1
Cambridge United FC	0-3	2-0	3-4		0-2	0-2	2-2	0-1	1-3	0-1	1-1	2-2	0-3	2-2	0-0	0-0	1-0	2-1	1-3	1-2	1-0	1-1
Cardiff City AFC	0-3	0-1	2-2	5-0		2-0	2-1	3-3	0-2	1-0	0-4	3-1	3-1	0-1	2-1	2-1	0-2	2-0	0-0	0-2	2-0	3-2
Carlisle United FC	4-2	0-1	1-2	0-0	1-1		3-0	0-0	2-2	2-1	2-0	1-1	0-0	1-0	2-0	1-1	3-1	2-0	0-0	1-1	1-0	2-0
Charlton Athletic FC	3-2	2-0	2-0	5-2	2-0	1-0		1-1	1-0	1-0	3-4	3-3	1-2	2-0	1-0	1-3	2-1	2-1	1-1	2-4	2-2	
Chelsea FC	3-1	2-1	1-0	2-1	2-0	0-0	3-2		2-2	5-0	4-0	2-3	3-1	5-0	0-1	4-0	3-0	2-2	3-2	3-0	6-1	
Crystal Palace FC	0-1	0-2	0-2	1-1	1-0	1-2	2-0	0-1		0-1	1-1	0-1	0-0	0-0	0-2	3-1	2-1	2-1	1-0	1-1	2-0	
Derby County FC	0-2	1-1	0-3	1-0	2-3	1-4	0-1	1-2	3-0		1-0	1-2	1-1	1-1	1-0	3-2	2-2	2-0	1-1	1-0	2-1	
Fulham FC	1-0	0-1	3-1	1-0	0-2	0-0	0-1	3-5	1-1	2-2		1-1	0-2	2-1	5-1	2-1	2-2	3-0	0-2	1-1	3-0	5-0
Grimsby Town FC	1-0	3-2	5-0	0-0	1-0	1-1	1-2	0-1	2-0	2-1	2-1		2-1	1-0	0-0	1-1	1-3	3-4	1-0	1-1	3-0	
Huddersfield Town AFC	0-1	0-2	0-1	3-0	4-0	0-0	0-0	2-3	2-1	3-0	2-0	0-0		2-2	1-3	2-2	2-2	0-1	2-1	1-1	1-0	1-0
Leeds United AFC	1-2	1-0	3-2	3-1	1-0	3-0	1-0	1-1	1-1	0-0	1-0	2-1	1-2		1-2	4-1	0-1	2-0	2-1	1-1	3-0	1-0
Manchester City FC	3-2	6-0	4-0	5-0	2-1	3-1	0-1	0-2	3-1	1-1	0-0	2-1	2-3	1-1		2-1	1-2	2-0	2-1	1-2	0-1	2-1
Middlesbrough FC	2-1	1-2	0-0	1-1	2-0	0-1	1-0	1-3	0-0	0-2	1-1	0-0	2-2	0-0			3-2	3-2	0-0	2-0	4-0	1-0
Newcastle United FC	1-0	1-1	3-1	2-1	3-1	5-1	2-1	1-1	3-1	4-0	3-2	0-1	5-2	1-0	5-0	3-1		3-0	4-2	0-1	0-1	2-0
Oldham Athletic AFC	1-0	0-0	1-0	0-0	2-1	2-3	0-0	1-1	3-2	3-0	3-0	2-1	0-3	3-2	2-2	2-1	1-2		3-2	1-3	0-1	3-3
Portsmouth FC	2-1	2-4	5-1	5-0	1-1	0-1	4-0	2-2	2-0	3-0	1-4	4-0	1-1	2-3	1-2	0-1	1-4	3-4		0-1	4-1	5-0
Sheffield Wednesday FC	2-0	4-2	2-1	1-0	5-2	2-0	4-1	2-1	1-0	3-1	1-1	1-0	0-0	3-0	0-2	4-2	2-0	2-0			1-1	6-1
Shrewsbury Town FC	3-2	1-0	2-1	1-0	1-0	0-0	1-1	2-4	1-1	3-0	0-0	1-2	1-0	5-1	1-3	1-0	2-2	2-0	2-0	2-1		2-0
Swansea City FC	1-0	0-1	1-3	2-1	3-2	0-0	1-0	1-3	1-0	2-0	0-3	0-1	2-2	2-2	0-2	2-1	1-2	0-0	1-2	0-1	0-2	

	Division 2	Pd	Wn	Dw	Ls	GF	GA	Pts	
1.	Chelsea FC (London)	42	25	13	4	90	40	88	P
2.	Sheffield Wednesday FC (Sheffield)	42	26	10	6	72	34	88	P
3.	Newcastle United FC (Newcastle-upon-Tyne)	42	24	8	10	85	53	80	P
4.	Manchester City FC (Manchester)	42	20	10	12	66	48	70	
5.	Grimsby Town FC (Cleethorpes)	42	19	13	10	60	47	70	
6.	Blackburn Rovers FC (Blackburn)	42	17	16	9	57	46	67	
7.	Carlisle United FC (Carlisle)	42	16	16	10	48	41	64	
8.	Shrewsbury Town FC (Shrewsbury)	42	17	10	15	49	53	61	
9.	Brighton & Hove Albion FC (Hove)	42	17	9	16	69	60	60	
10.	Leeds United AFC (Leeds)	42	16	12	14	55	56	60	
11.	Fulham FC (London)	42	15	12	15	60	53	57	
12.	Huddersfield Town AFC (Huddersfield)	42	14	15	13	56	49	57	
13.	Charlton Athletic FC (London)	42	16	9	17	53	64	57	
14.	Barnsley FC (Barnsley)	42	15	7	20	57	53	52	
15.	Cardiff City AFC (Cardiff)	42	15	6	21	53	66	51	
16.	Portsmouth FC (Portsmouth)	42	14	7	21	73	64	49	
17.	Middlesbrough FC (Middlesbrough)	42	12	13	17	41	47	49	
18.	Crystal Palace FC (London)	42	12	11	19	42	52	47	
19.	Oldham Athletic AFC (Oldham)	42	13	8	21	47	73	47	
20.	Derby County FC (Derby)	42	11	9	22	36	72	42	R
21.	Swansea City FC (Swansea)	42	7	8	27	36	85	29	R
22.	Cambridge United FC (Cambridge)	42	4	12	26	28	77	24	R
		924	345	234	345	1233	1233	1269	

	Bolton Wanderers	Bournemouth	Bradford C	Brentford	Bristol Rovers	Burnley	Exeter City	Gillingham	Hull City	Lincoln City	Millwall	Newport County	Orient	Oxford United	Plymouth Argyle	Port Vale	Preston North End	Rotherham United	Scunthorpe United	Sheffield United	Southend United	Walsall	Wigan Athletic	Wimbledon
Bolton Wanderers FC	■	0-1	0-2	1-0	3-0	0-0	1-0	0-1	0-0	0-2	2-0	2-3	3-2	1-0	2-1	2-0	2-2	2-0	0-0	3-1	2-0	8-1	0-1	2-0
AFC Bournemouth	2-2	■	4-1	0-3	0-1	1-0	3-1	2-0	2-3	3-0	1-1	1-1	3-2	2-1	2-1	1-1	0-1	4-2	1-1	0-1	1-0	3-0	0-1	2-3
Bradford City AFC	0-2	5-2	■	1-1	0-1	2-1	1-3	3-2	0-0	0-0	3-3	1-0	4-1	2-2	2-0	2-2	3-2	1-0	2-2	2-1	1-1	0-0	6-2	5-2
Brentford FC	3-0	1-1	1-4	■	2-2	0-0	3-0	2-3	1-1	3-0	2-2	2-0	1-1	1-2	2-2	3-1	4-1	2-1	3-0	1-3	0-0	1-1	0-1	3-4
Bristol Rovers FC	2-1	1-3	1-0	3-1	■	2-1	2-0	3-0	1-3	3-1	3-2	4-0	0-0	1-1	2-0	0-0	3-1	2-0	4-1	1-1	2-1	4-2	2-1	1-1
Burnley FC	2-2	5-1	1-2	2-2	0-0	■	4-0	2-3	0-2	4-0	1-0	2-0	2-3	1-1	2-1	7-0	2-1	2-2	5-0	2-1	3-0	0-2	3-0	0-2
Exeter City FC	2-2	0-2	0-2	1-2	1-2	1-1	■	0-0	2-1	0-3	3-2	1-2	3-4	3-1	1-1	1-1	2-1	0-1	1-1	1-2	3-3	0-1	1-1	0-3
Gillingham FC	2-0	2-1	0-0	4-2	1-2	0-1	3-1	■	1-2	2-0	3-3	4-1	3-1	2-3	2-1	1-1	2-0	4-2	1-1	4-2	5-1	1-3	3-0	0-1
Hull City AFC	1-1	3-1	1-0	2-0	0-0	4-1	1-0	0-0	■	2-0	5-0	0-0	2-1	0-1	1-2	1-0	3-0	5-0	1-0	4-1	2-2	1-0	1-0	
Lincoln City FC	0-0	3-0	2-3	2-0	4-0	3-1	1-1	4-0	1-3	■	2-2	2-3	2-0	2-2	3-1	3-2	2-1	0-1	2-1	0-2	1-2	2-1	0-1	1-2
Millwall FC	3-0	3-1	0-0	1-2	1-0	2-0	3-0	2-2	1-0	0-2	■	1-1	4-3	2-1	1-0	3-2	1-0	2-0	2-1	1-2	4-0	2-0	2-0	1-1
Newport County AFC	2-3	2-1	4-3	1-1	2-1	1-0	1-0	1-0	1-1	1-0	1-1	■	0-0	1-1	2-0	2-1	1-1	1-4	1-1	0-2	1-1	3-1	5-3	1-1
Orient FC	2-1	2-0	2-0	2-0	0-1	1-2	2-2	1-1	3-1	1-1	5-3	2-2	■	1-2	3-2	3-0	2-1	2-1	1-0	2-0	1-0	0-1	0-0	2-6
Oxford United FC	5-0	3-2	2-0	2-1	3-2	2-2	1-1	0-1	1-1	3-0	4-2	2-0	5-2	■	5-0	2-0	2-0	3-2	1-0	2-2	2-1	6-3	0-0	2-0
Plymouth Argyle FC	2-0	1-0	3-0	1-1	1-1	1-1	2-2	1-1	2-0	2-2	0-1	0-1	3-1	2-1	■	3-0	1-0	1-1	4-0	0-1	4-0	3-1	0-0	1-2
Port Vale FC	1-2	2-1	1-2	4-3	2-0	2-3	2-2	0-1	1-0	0-1	1-0	4-2	2-0	1-3	0-1	■	1-1	2-3	0-0	2-0	2-1	0-2	1-1	2-0
Preston North End	2-1	2-0	1-2	3-3	1-0	4-2	2-1	2-2	0-0	1-2	0-0	2-0	3-1	1-2	2-1	4-0	■	1-0	1-0	2-2	4-1	0-1	2-3	2-3
Rotherham United	1-1	1-0	4-0	2-2	1-1	1-0	3-0	0-1	1-1	1-0	0-1	0-1	1-2	2-0	2-1	0-1		■	3-0	0-1	0-0	4-1		1-2
Scunthorpe United	1-0	1-2	2-1	4-4	2-2	4-0	3-1	2-0	2-0	0-1	3-3	3-1	0-0	3-0	1-1	1-5	1-2		■	1-1	1-6	0-0	0-0	5-1
Sheffield United FC	5-0	2-0	2-0	0-0	4-0	0-0	2-2	4-0	2-2	0-0	2-0	2-0	6-3	1-2	2-0	3-1	1-1	3-0	5-3	■	5-0	2-0	2-2	1-2
Southend United FC	0-1	0-0	2-1	6-0	1-2	2-2	0-3	3-1	2-2	2-0	3-2	3-1	3-0	0-1	1-1	1-2	1-1	2-2	0-0	0-1	■	0-0	1-0	1-1
Walsall FC	1-0	3-1	1-2	1-0	2-1	1-1	4-1	3-1	2-1	0-1	1-1	3-2	0-1	0-1	3-2	2-0	2-1	2-2	1-1	1-2	4-0	■	3-0	4-0
Wigan Athletic AFC	0-1	1-3	0-1	2-1	0-0	1-0	1-1	1-2	1-1	2-0	0-0	1-0	0-1	0-2	1-1	3-0	1-0	2-1	2-0	3-0	1-0	0-1	■	3-2
Wimbledon FC	4-0	3-2	4-1	2-1	1-1	1-4	2-1	1-3	1-4	3-1	4-3	6-0	2-2	3-1	1-0	4-2	2-2	3-1	1-1	3-1	3-2	2-0	2-2	■

	Division 3	Pd	Wn	Dw	Ls	GF	GA	Pts	
1.	Oxford United FC (Oxford)	46	28	11	7	91	50	95	P
2.	Wimbledon FC (London)	46	26	9	11	97	76	87	P
3.	Sheffield United FC (Sheffield)	46	24	11	11	86	53	83	P
4.	Hull City AFC (Kingston-upon-Hull)	46	23	14	9	71	38	83	
5.	Bristol Rovers FC (Bristol)	46	22	13	11	68	54	79	
6.	Walsall FC (Walsall)	46	22	9	15	68	61	75	
7.	Bradford City AFC (Bradford)	46	20	11	15	73	65	71	
8.	Gillingham FC (Gillingham)	46	20	10	16	74	69	70	
9.	Millwall FC (London)	46	18	13	15	71	65	67	
10.	Bolton Wanderers FC (Bolton)	46	18	10	18	56	60	64	
11.	Orient FC (London)	46	18	9	19	71	81	63	
12.	Burnley FC (Burnley)	46	16	14	16	76	61	62	
13.	Newport County AFC (Newport)	46	16	14	16	58	75	62	
14.	Lincoln City FC (Lincoln)	46	17	10	19	59	62	61	
15.	Wigan Athletic AFC (Wigan)	46	16	13	17	46	56	61	
16.	Preston North End FC (Preston)	46	15	11	20	66	66	56	
17.	AFC Bournemouth (Bournemouth)	46	16	7	23	63	73	55	
18.	Rotherham United FC (Rotherham)	46	15	9	22	57	64	54	
19.	Plymouth Argyle FC (Plymouth)	46	13	12	21	56	62	51	
20.	Brentford FC (London)	46	11	16	19	69	79	49	
21.	Scunthorpe United FC (Scunthorpe)	46	9	19	18	54	73	46	R
22.	Southend United FC (Southend-on-Sea)	46	10	14	22	55	76	44	R
23.	Port Vale FC (Stoke-on-Trent)	46	11	10	25	51	83	43	R
24.	Exeter City FC (Exeter)	46	6	15	25	50	84	33	R
		1104	410	284	410	1586	1586	1514	

Football League Division 4 1983-84 Season	Aldershot Town	Blackpool	Bristol City	Bury	Chester City	Chesterfield	Colchester United	Crewe Alexandra	Darlington	Doncaster Rovers	Halifax Town	Hartlepool	Hereford United	Mansfield Town	Northampton Town	Peterborough United	Reading	Rochdale	Stockport County	Swindon Town	Torquay United	Tranmere Rovers	Wrexham	York City
Aldershot Town FC		3-2	1-0	1-2	5-2	2-1	5-1	0-0	0-0	2-1	5-2	2-1	1-4	7-1	1-0	3-2	0-0	2-1	1-1	2-1	3-1	1-1	1-1	1-4
Blackpool FC	5-0		1-0	1-1	3-3	1-0	3-2	3-0	3-1	3-1	4-0	1-0	3-1	2-0	2-3	1-2	1-0	0-2	1-1	1-1	1-0	0-2	4-0	3-0
Bristol City FC	2-1	1-1		3-2	4-2	2-0	4-1	2-1	1-0	1-2	3-0	2-0	1-0	4-0	4-1	0-1	3-1	1-1	3-1	1-0	5-0	1-1	2-1	1-0
Bury FC	0-3	0-0	2-1		2-1	2-0	1-1	1-1	0-3	2-3	3-0	3-0	-4	2-2	1-2	2-2	2-3	3-1	2-1	2-1	0-0	0-0	2-0	1-3
Chester City FC	1-2	0-2	1-2	2-1		0-2	1-4	0-1	2-1	1-0	1-1	4-1	0-1	0-4	1-1	1-1	2-1	1-0	2-4	0-3	1-2	0-0	1-0	1-1
Chesterfield FC	3-1	1-1	1-1	1-5	1-1		1-1	1-3	1-1	0-0	0-0	4-1	0-0	0-0	2-1	1-0	2-1	3-0	2-0	1-0	3-2	2-3	1-1	2-1
Colchester United FC	4-1	2-1	0-0	1-0	1-0	2-0		2-0	2-1	1-1	4-1	6-0	3-0	1-0	2-2	1-1	3-0	4-0	1-1	0-0	1-1	1-1	1-1	1-3
Crewe Alexandra FC	0-0	2-1	2-2	2-1	1-1	2-1	1-1		2-1	1-1	6-1	2-0	1-1	1-3	3-2	0-1	1-1	0-1	0-3	2-0	2-1	3-0	1-1	0-3
Darlington FC	0-1	2-0	0-1	1-2	2-1	2-1	0-2	2-0		1-2	3-2	2-0	0-0	3-0	5-3	1-0	1-1	1-0	1-0	1-0	0-1	1-0	2-2	0-0
Doncaster Rovers FC	3-1	2-1	1-0	3-1	0-0	2-1	3-3	1-0	3-2		3-2	0-1	3-0	3-1	1-0	1-1	2-3	3-0	2-1	3-0	1-1	1-1	3-0	2-2
Halifax Town AFC	1-0	1-0	1-2	0-0	2-2	2-1	4-1	1-0	0-2	1-2		3-2	2-1	0-2	2-1	0-1	5-0	2-0	2-1	2-2	1-2	1-1	1-1	1-2
Hartlepool United FC	0-1	0-1	2-2	1-3	1-1	2-2	0-0	2-1	2-1	1-0	3-0		0-0	4-1	2-0	1-1	3-3	1-2	1-2	0-1	2-1	1-1	1-1	2-3
Hereford United FC	2-1	1-2	2-1	1-2	2-1	3-1	1-1	0-1	1-0	0-3	0-0	5-0		0-0	0-0	2-1	1-1	2-1	2-0	2-1	1-1	0-1	3-0	2-1
Mansfield Town FC	5-2	1-1	0-1	1-1	3-1	0-1	0-0	3-3	1-0	1-2	7-1	5-0	1-1		3-1	0-0	2-0	3-0	1-2	2-2	1-3	1-0	3-4	0-1
Northampton Town	1-4	1-5	1-0	1-0	2-1	1-1	3-1	2-0	2-0	1-4	1-1	1-1	0-3	2-1		2-1	2-2	1-1	0-0	2-0	2-1	0-0	3-3	1-2
Peterborough United	1-2	4-0	4-1	2-1	1-0	2-0	2-0	1-0	0-2	1-1	4-0	3-1	1-1	3-0	6-0		3-3	2-0	2-0	1-1	5-0	2-0	0-1	0-2
Reading FC	1-0	2-0	2-0	1-1	1-0	1-1	1-1	5-0	1-0	3-2	1-0	5-1	3-1	4-0	3-0	1-1		0-0	6-2	2-2	2-2	1-0	4-1	1-0
Rochdale AFC	3-1	1-0	0-1	0-2	1-1	2-4	0-0	1-0	2-0	3-3	1-1	2-0	3-3	0-0	1-1	2-1	4-1		2-2	3-3	1-0	2-3	1-2	0-2
Stockport County	2-2	1-2	0-0	1-1	2-1	0-2	2-3	2-0	0-2	4-0	1-0	0-4	1-0	4-1	3-0	2-1	3-0	2-1		1-3	2-1	2-1	1-1	0-2
Swindon Town FC	0-2	0-0	1-1	0-0	4-0	1-2	0-1	1-0	2-1	0-2	1-2	2-3	3-2	3-0	1-1	0-2	1-1	2-1	2-1		2-3	1-1	0-1	3-2
Torquay United FC	0-1	1-0	1-0	2-0	1-0	1-1	3-1	0-1	4-1	1-1	0-0	1-1	1-0	2-1	1-0	2-2	4-2	1-1	1-0	2-1		1-1	1-0	1-3
Tranmere Rovers FC	3-0	3-2	2-0	1-1	2-2	0-3	2-1	2-3	0-1	1-1	3-2	0-1	0-1	1-0	1-0	0-0	2-3	2-2	1-0	2-1	3-0		2-1	0-1
Wrexham AFC	1-1	0-1	3-1	3-0	2-0	4-2	0-2	0-1	1-1	1-2	1-0	1-4	0-0	2-3	0-1	2-2	0-3	5-1	1-2	0-3	2-2	5-1		0-0
York City FC	2-0	4-0	1-1	3-0	4-1	1-0	3-0	5-2	2-0	1-1	4-1	2-0	4-0	2-1	3-0	2-0	2-2	2-0	3-1	2-0	2-3	1-1	3-2	

	Division 4	Pd	Wn	Dw	Ls	GF	GA	Pts	
1.	York City FC (York)	46	31	8	7	96	39	101	P
2.	Doncaster Rovers FC (Doncaster)	46	24	13	9	82	54	85	P
3.	Reading FC (Reading)	46	22	16	8	84	56	82	P
4.	Bristol City FC (Bristol)	46	24	10	12	70	44	82	P
5.	Aldershot FC (Aldershot)	46	22	9	15	76	69	75	
6.	Blackpool FC (Blackpool)	46	21	9	16	70	52	72	
7.	Peterborough United FC (Peterborough)	46	18	14	14	72	48	68	
8.	Colchester United FC (Colchester)	46	17	16	13	69	53	67	
9.	Torquay United FC (Torquay)	46	18	13	15	59	64	67	
10.	Tranmere Rovers FC (Birkenhead)	46	17	15	14	53	53	66	
11.	Hereford United FC (Hereford)	46	16	15	15	54	53	63	
12.	Stockport County FC (Stockport)	46	17	11	18	60	64	62	
13.	Chesterfield FC (Chesterfield)	46	15	15	16	59	61	60	
14.	Darlington FC (Darlington)	46	17	8	21	49	50	59	
15.	Bury FC (Bury)	46	15	14	17	61	64	59	
16.	Crewe Alexandra FC (Crewe)	46	16	11	19	56	67	59	
17.	Swindon Town FC (Swindon)	46	15	13	18	58	56	58	
18.	Northampton Town FC (Northampton)	46	13	14	19	53	78	53	
19.	Mansfield Town FC (Mansfield)	46	13	13	20	66	70	52	
20.	Wrexham AFC (Wrexham)	46	11	15	20	59	74	48	
21.	Halifax Town AFC (Halifax)	46	12	12	22	55	89	48	
22.	Rochdale AFC (Rochdale)	46	11	13	22	52	80	46	
23.	Hartlepool United FC (Hartlepool)	46	10	10	26	47	85	40	
24.	Chester City FC (Chester)	46	7	13	26	45	82	34	
		1104	402	300	402	1505	1505	1104	

F.A. CUP FINAL   (Wembley Stadium, London – 19/05/1984 – 100,000)

EVERTON FC (LIVERPOOL)	2-0	Watford FC (Watford)
Sharp, Gray	*(H.T. 1-0)*	

Everton: Southall, Stevens, Bailey, Ratcliffe, Mountfield, Reid, Steven, Heath, Sharp, Gray, Richardson.

Watford: Sherwood, Bardsley, Price (Atkinson), Taylor, Terry, Sinnott, Callaghan, Johnston, Reilly, Jackett, Barnes.

Semi-finals

Plymouth Argyle FC (Plymouth)	0-1	Watford FC (Watford)
Southampton FC (Southampton)	0-1	Everton FC (Liverpool)

Quarter-finals

Birmingham City FC (Birmingham)	1-3	Watford FC (Watford)
Notts County FC (Nottingham)	1-2	Everton FC (Liverpool)
Plymouth Argyle FC (Plymouth)	0-0, 1-0	Derby County FC (Derby)
Sheffield Wednesday FC (Sheffield)	0-0, 1-5	Southampton FC (Southampton)

172

Football League Division 1 1984-85 Season	Arsenal	Aston Villa	Chelsea	Coventry City	Everton	Ipswich Town	Leicester City	Liverpool	Luton Town	Man. United	Newcastle Utd.	Norwich City	Nottingham F.	Q.P.R.	Sheffield Wed.	Southampton	Stoke City	Sunderland	Tottenham H.	Watford	W.B.A.	West Ham Utd.
Arsenal FC		1-1	1-1	2-1	1-0	1-1	2-0	3-1	3-1	0-1	2-0	2-0	1-1	1-0	1-0	1-0	4-0	3-2	1-2	1-1	4-0	2-1
Aston Villa FC	0-0		4-2	1-0	1-1	2-1	0-1	0-0	0-1	3-0	4-0	2-2	0-5	5-2	3-0	2-2	2-0	1-0	0-1	1-1	3-1	0-0
Chelsea FC	1-1	3-1		6-2	0-1	2-0	3-0	3-1	2-0	1-3	1-0	1-2	1-0	1-0	2-1	0-2	1-1	1-0	1-1	2-3	3-1	3-0
Coventry City FC	1-2	0-3	1-0		4-1	1-0	2-0	0-2	1-0	0-3	1-1	0-0	1-3	3-0	1-0	2-1	4-0	0-1	1-1	3-1	2-1	1-2
Everton FC	2-0	2-1	3-4	2-1		1-1	3-0	1-0	2-1	5-0	4-0	3-0	5-0	2-0	1-1	2-2	4-0	4-1	1-4	4-0	4-1	3-0
Ipswich Town FC	2-1	3-0	2-0	0-0	0-2		2-0	0-0	1-1	1-1	1-1	2-0	1-0	1-1	1-2	0-1	5-1	0-2	0-3	3-3	2-0	0-1
Leicester City FC	1-4	5-0	1-1	5-1	1-2	2-1		0-1	2-2	2-3	2-3	2-0	1-0	4-0	3-1	1-2	0-0	2-0	1-2	1-1	2-1	1-0
Liverpool FC	3-0	2-1	4-3	3-1	0-1	2-0	1-2		1-0	0-1	3-1	4-0	1-0	1-1	0-2	1-1	2-0	1-1	0-1	4-3	0-0	3-0
Luton Town FC	3-1	1-0	0-0	2-0	2-0	3-1	4-0	1-2		2-1	2-2	3-1	1-2	2-0	1-2	1-1	2-0	2-1	2-2	3-2	1-2	2-2
Manchester United FC	4-2	4-0	1-1	0-1	1-1	3-0	2-1	1-1	2-0		5-0	2-0	3-0	1-2	0-0	5-0	2-2	1-0	1-1	2-0	5-1	
Newcastle United FC	1-3	3-0	2-1	0-1	2-3	3-0	1-4	0-2	1-0	1-1		1-1	1-1	1-0	2-1	2-1	2-1	3-1	2-3	3-1	1-0	1-1
Norwich City FC	1-0	2-2	0-0	2-1	4-2	0-2	1-3	3-3	3-0	0-1	0-0		0-1	2-0	1-1	1-0	0-0	1-3	1-2	3-2	2-1	1-0
Nottingham Forest FC	2-0	3-2	2-0	2-0	1-0	2-0	2-1	0-2	3-1	3-2	0-0	3-1		2-0	0-0	2-0	1-1	3-1	1-2	1-1	1-2	1-2
Queen's Park Rangers FC	1-0	2-2	2-2	2-1	0-0	3-0	4-3	2-3	2-3	1-3	5-5	2-2	3-0		0-0	4-0	2-1	2-0	2-2	2-0	3-1	4-2
Sheffield Wednesday FC	2-1	1-1	1-1	1-0	0-1	2-2	5-0	1-1	1-1	1-0	4-2	1-2	3-1	3-1		2-1	2-2	2-1	1-1	1-1	2-0	2-1
Southampton FC	1-0	2-0	1-0	2-1	1-2	3-0	3-1	1-1	1-0	0-0	1-0	2-1	1-0	1-1	0-3		0-0	1-0	1-0	1-2	4-3	2-3
Stoke City FC	2-0	1-3	0-1	0-1	0-2	0-2	2-2	0-4	2-1	0-1	2-3	1-4	0-2	2-1	1-3		2-2	0-1	1-3	0-0	2-4	
Sunderland AFC	0-0	0-4	0-2	0-0	1-2	1-2	0-4	0-3	3-0	3-2	0-2	0-2	1-0	3-0	0-0	3-0	1-0		1-0	1-1	1-1	0-1
Tottenham Hotspur FC	0-2	0-2	1-1	4-2	1-2	2-3	2-2	1-0	4-2	1-2	3-1	3-1	1-0	5-0	2-0	5-1	4-2	2-0		1-5	2-3	2-2
Watford FC	3-4	3-3	1-3	0-1	4-5	3-1	4-1	1-1	3-0	5-1	3-3	2-0	2-0	1-1	1-0	1-1	2-0	3-1	1-2		0-2	5-0
West Bromwich Albion FC	2-2	1-0	0-1	5-2	2-1	1-2	2-0	0-5	4-0	1-2	2-1	0-1	4-1	0-0	2-2	0-0	2-0	1-0	0-1	2-1		5-1
West Ham United FC	3-1	1-2	1-1	3-1	0-1	0-0	3-1	0-3	0-0	2-2	1-1	1-0	0-0	1-3	0-0	2-3	5-1	1-0	1-1	2-0	0-2	

Division 1

		Pd	Wn	Dw	Ls	GF	GA	Pts	
1.	EVERTON FC (LIVERPOOL)	42	28	6	8	88	43	90	
2.	Liverpool FC (Liverpool)	42	22	11	9	68	35	77	
3.	Tottenham Hotspur FC (London)	42	23	8	11	78	51	77	
4.	Manchester United FC (Manchester)	42	22	10	10	77	47	76	
5.	Southampton FC (Southampton)	42	19	11	12	56	47	68	
6.	Chelsea FC (London)	42	18	12	12	63	48	66	
7.	Arsenal FC (London)	42	19	9	14	61	49	66	
8.	Sheffield Wednesday FC (Sheffield)	42	17	14	11	58	45	65	
9.	Nottingham Forest FC (Nottingham)	42	19	7	16	56	48	64	
10.	Aston Villa FC (Birmingham)	42	15	11	16	60	60	56	
11.	Watford FC (Watford)	42	14	13	15	81	71	55	
12.	West Bromwich Albion FC (West Bromwich)	42	16	7	19	58	62	55	
13.	Luton Town FC (Luton)	42	15	9	18	57	61	54	
14.	Newcastle United FC (Newcastle-upon-Tyne)	42	13	13	16	55	70	52	
15.	Leicester City FC (Leicester)	42	15	6	21	65	73	51	
16.	West Ham United FC (London)	42	13	12	17	51	68	51	
17.	Ipswich Town FC (Ipswich)	42	13	11	18	46	57	50	
18.	Coventry City FC (Coventry)	42	15	5	22	47	64	50	
19.	Queen's Park Rangers FC (London)	42	13	11	18	53	72	50	
20.	Norwich City FC (Norwich)	42	13	10	19	46	64	49	R
21.	Sunderland AFC (Sunderland)	42	10	10	22	40	62	40	R
22.	Stoke City FC (Stoke-on-Trent)	42	3	8	31	24	91	17	R
		924	355	214	355	1288	1288	1279	

Top Goalscorers

1)	Kerry DIXON	(Chelsea FC)	24
	Gary LINEKER	(Leicester City FC)	24

	Barnsley	Birmingham City	Blackburn Rovers	Brighton & Hove Albion	Cardiff City	Carlisle United	Charlton Athletic	Crystal Palace	Fulham	Grimsby Town	Huddersfield Town	Leeds United	Manchester City	Middlesbrough	Notts County	Oldham Athletic	Oxford United	Portsmouth	Sheffield United	Shrewsbury Town	Wimbledon	Wolverhampton Wanderers
Barnsley FC	■	0-1	1-1	0-0	2-0	1-3	1-0	3-1	1-0	0-0	2-1	1-0	0-0	1-0	0-0	0-1	3-0	2-2	1-0	3-1	0-0	5-1
Birmingham City FC	0-0	■	0-2	1-1	2-0	2-0	2-1	3-0	2-2	2-1	1-0	1-0	0-0	3-2	2-1	0-1	0-0	0-1	4-1	0-0	4-2	1-0
Blackburn Rovers FC	0-0	2-1	■	2-0	2-1	4-0	3-0	0-1	2-1	3-1	1-3	2-1	0-1	3-0	1-0	1-1	1-1	0-1	3-1	3-1	2-0	3-0
Brighton & Hove Albion FC	0-0	2-0	3-1	■	1-0	4-1	2-1	1-0	2-0	0-0	0-1	1-1	0-0	1-2	2-1	2-0	0-0	1-1	1-0	1-0	2-1	5-1
Cardiff City AFC	3-0	1-2	1-2	2-4	■	2-1	0-3	0-3	0-2	2-4	3-0	2-1	0-3	2-1	1-4	2-2	0-2	1-2	1-3	0-0	1-3	0-0
Carlisle United FC	2-0	2-1	0-1	0-3	0-1	■	1-1	1-0	3-0	1-1	0-1	2-2	0-0	0-3	1-0	2-5	0-1	3-0	1-1	2-0	6-1	0-1
Charlton Athletic FC	5-3	2-1	1-0	0-1	1-4	1-1	■	1-1	1-2	4-1	2-2	2-3	1-3	1-0	3-0	2-1	3-3	2-2	0-0	1-1	0-1	1-0
Crystal Palace FC	0-1	0-2	1-1	1-1	1-1	2-1	2-1	■	2-2	0-2	1-1	3-1	1-2	1-0	1-0	3-0	1-0	2-1	1-3	2-2	0-5	0-0
Fulham FC	1-1	0-1	3-2	2-0	3-2	3-2	0-0	2-2	■	2-1	2-1	0-2	3-2	2-1	1-0	3-1	1-0	1-3	1-0	1-2	3-1	1-2
Grimsby Town FC	1-0	1-0	1-1	2-4	6-3	1-0	2-1	1-3	2-4	■	5-1	0-2	4-1	3-1	2-0	4-1	1-2	2-3	0-2	2-1	2-1	5-1
Huddersfield Town AFC	1-1	0-1	1-1	1-2	2-1	2-0	2-1	2-0	2-2	0-0	■	1-0	0-2	3-1	1-2	2-1	0-3	0-2	2-2	1-5	2-1	3-1
Leeds United AFC	2-0	0-1	0-0	1-0	1-1	1-1	1-0	4-1	2-0	0-0	0-0	■	1-1	2-0	5-0	6-0	1-0	0-1	1-1	1-0	5-2	3-2
Manchester City FC	1-1	1-0	2-1	2-0	2-2	1-3	5-1	2-1	2-3	3-0	1-0	1-2	■	1-0	2-0	0-0	1-0	2-2	2-0	4-0	3-0	4-0
Middlesbrough FC	0-0	0-0	1-2	2-1	3-2	1-2	1-0	1-1	2-0	1-5	2-2	0-0	2-1	■	0-1	1-2	0-1	0-0	1-0	1-1	2-4	1-1
Notts County FC	0-2	1-3	0-3	1-2	0-2	3-0	0-0	0-0	2-1	1-1	0-2	1-2	3-2	3-2	■	0-0	2-0	1-3	0-0	1-3	2-3	4-1
Oldham Athletic AFC	2-1	0-1	2-0	1-0	0-1	2-3	2-1	1-0	2-1	2-0	2-2	1-1	0-2	2-0	3-2	■	0-0	0-2	2-2	0-1	0-1	3-2
Oxford United FC	4-0	0-3	2-1	2-1	4-0	4-0	5-0	5-0	3-2	1-0	3-0	5-2	3-0	1-0	1-1	5-2	■	1-1	5-1	1-0	4-0	3-1
Portsmouth FC	0-0	1-3	2-2	1-1	0-0	3-1	0-1	1-1	4-4	3-2	3-2	3-1	1-2	1-0	3-1	5-1	2-1	■	2-1	3-0	1-0	0-1
Sheffield United FC	3-1	3-4	1-3	1-1	2-1	0-0	1-1	1-2	0-1	2-3	0-2	2-1	0-0	0-3	3-0	2-0	1-1	4-1	■	0-1	3-0	2-2
Shrewsbury Town FC	2-0	1-0	3-0	0-0	0-0	4-2	1-1	4-1	3-1	4-1	5-1	2-3	1-0	0-2	4-2	3-0	2-2	0-0	3-3	■	1-2	2-1
Wimbledon FC	3-3	1-2	1-1	1-0	2-1	3-0	1-3	3-2	1-1	1-1	0-1	2-2	2-2	1-1	3-2	1-0	1-3	3-2	5-0	4-1	■	1-1
Wolverhampton Wanderers FC	0-1	0-2	0-3	0-1	3-0	0-2	1-0	2-1	0-4	0-1	2-1	0-2	2-0	0-0	2-3	0-3	1-2	0-0	2-2	0-1	3-3	■

	Division 2	Pd	Wn	Dw	Ls	GF	GA	Pts	
1.	Oxford United FC (Oxford)	42	25	9	8	84	36	84	P
2.	Birmingham City FC (Birmingham)	42	25	7	10	59	33	82	P
3.	Manchester City FC (Manchester)	42	21	11	10	66	40	74	P
4.	Portsmouth FC (Portsmouth)	42	20	14	8	69	50	74	
5.	Blackburn Rovers FC (Blackburn)	42	21	10	11	66	41	73	
6.	Brighton & Hove Albion FC (Hove)	42	20	12	10	54	34	72	
7.	Leeds United AFC (Leeds)	42	19	12	11	66	43	69	
8.	Shrewsbury Town FC (Shrewsbury)	42	18	11	13	66	53	65	
9.	Fulham FC (London)	42	19	8	15	68	64	65	
10.	Grimsby Town FC (Cleethorpes)	42	18	8	16	72	64	62	
11.	Barnsley FC (Barnsley)	42	14	16	12	42	42	58	
12.	Wimbledon FC (London)	42	16	10	16	71	75	58	
13.	Huddersfield Town AFC (Huddersfield)	42	15	10	17	52	64	55	
14.	Oldham Athletic AFC (Oldham)	42	15	8	19	49	67	53	
15.	Crystal Palace FC (London)	42	12	12	18	46	65	48	
16.	Carlisle United FC (Carlisle)	42	13	8	21	50	67	47	
17.	Charlton Athletic FC (London)	42	11	12	19	51	63	45	
18.	Sheffield United FC (Sheffield)	42	10	14	18	54	66	44	
19.	Middlesbrough FC (Middlesbrough)	42	10	10	22	41	57	40	
20.	Notts County FC (Nottingham)	42	10	7	25	45	73	37	R
21.	Cardiff City AFC (Cardiff)	42	9	8	25	47	79	35	R
22.	Wolverhampton Wanderers FC (Wolverhampton)	42	8	9	25	37	79	33	R
		924	349	226	349	1255	1255	1273	

Football League Division 3 1984-85 Season

	BW	Bmth	BradC	Bren	BriC	BriR	Burn	Camb	Derby	Donc	Gill	Hull	Linc	Mill	Newp	Ori	Ply	PNE	Read	Roth	Swan	Wals	Wig	York
Bolton Wanderers FC	■	2-1	0-2	1-1	1-4	0-1	1-3	0-0	3-0	3-1	1-2	0-0	1-0	2-0	3-1	0-0	7-2	4-0	1-2	2-0	0-0	3-1	1-0	2-1
AFC Bournemouth	4-0	■	4-1	1-0	2-1	1-0	1-1	0-0	1-0	1-3	2-0	1-1	3-1	1-2	3-0	1-0	1-0	2-0	0-3	3-0	1-2	4-1	1-0	4-0
Bradford City AFC	2-1	1-0	■	5-4	1-1	2-0	3-2	2-0	3-1	0-1	1-1	2-0	0-0	3-1	1-0	4-1	1-0	3-0	2-5	1-1	1-1	1-1	4-2	1-0
Brentford FC	2-1	0-0	0-1	■	1-2	0-3	2-1	2-0	1-1	1-1	5-2	2-1	2-2	1-1	2-5	0-1	3-1	3-1	2-1	3-0	3-0	3-1	2-0	2-1
Bristol City FC	3-2	2-0	2-0	1-1	■	3-0	1-0	3-0	3-0	1-0	2-0	2-0	0-1	2-1	3-2	4-3	4-0	2-3	0-1	2-2	1-2	2-0	2-0	1-0
Bristol Rovers FC	1-2	1-0	2-0	3-0	1-0	■	4-0	2-1	2-1	1-1	3-2	1-1	0-0	1-1	2-0	0-1	1-1	3-0	1-0	4-2	0-0	2-0	1-1	1-1
Burnley FC	3-2	1-1	1-2	3-1	0-1	0-0	■	2-0	0-1	2-1	1-1	1-2	1-1	1-1	1-2	0-2	7-0	1-1	1-2	1-2	1-1	1-1	1-2	1-1
Cambridge United FC	2-3	1-0	0-4	1-2	2-3	0-2	2-3	■	0-2	1-1	1-2	1-3	2-1	1-0	1-2	2-3	1-0	0-3	0-2	0-2	0-1	1-1	1-1	0-4
Derby County FC	3-2	2-3	1-0	1-0	0-0	2-2	1-0	3-1	■	3-1	1-0	3-1	2-0	1-2	3-3	1-0	3-1	2-0	4-1	1-1	1-1	2-0	2-2	1-0
Doncaster Rovers FC	2-0	3-0	0-3	2-2	1-1	2-2	2-0	3-2	2-1	■	0-1	1-2	3-2	0-1	3-2	1-1	4-3	1-2	0-4	0-1	4-1	4-1	1-1	3-0
Gillingham FC	2-3	3-2	2-2	2-0	1-3	4-1	1-1	3-0	3-2	2-1	■	1-0	3-2	1-4	1-1	2-0	3-2	4-0	4-1	2-1	1-3	5-1	1-0	1-0
Hull City AFC	2-2	3-0	2-0	4-0	2-1	2-0	2-0	2-1	3-2	3-2	2-0	■	1-0	2-1	2-0	5-1	1-2	0-0	4-1	1-0	0-0	3-1	3-1	0-2
Lincoln City FC	2-0	0-0	0-1	1-1	1-2	3-1	1-1	0-0	0-2	2-0	0-0	0-1	■	1-2	2-0	2-2	4-1	5-1	3-3	1-0	0-1	1-0	2-1	1-0
Millwall FC	5-2	2-1	4-0	2-0	1-1	1-0	2-1	2-1	2-1	2-1	2-1	2-2	2-0	■	2-0	1-0	2-0	3-0	0-0	0-0	2-0	4-1	1-0	1-0
Newport County AFC	3-2	1-1	0-1	2-0	0-0	1-1	2-1	1-2	1-3	0-3	0-1	2-1	3-2	0-1	■	2-0	1-0	3-3	1-2	0-2	2-1	1-2	1-1	1-1
Orient FC	4-3	0-0	0-0	0-1	0-1	1-4	0-2	2-2	2-2	1-1	2-4	4-5	1-0	1-1	1-1	■	3-0	0-0	4-0	4-2	0-3	1-1	1-3	0-3
Plymouth Argyle FC	2-0	0-0	0-0	1-1	1-0	3-2	2-2	2-0	1-1	1-1	1-1	0-1	2-0	3-1	1-0	1-1	■	6-4	1-2	1-0	4-1	1-0	1-1	2-0
Preston North End FC	2-0	2-1	1-4	3-2	2-2	3-3	3-1	2-1	2-0	0-0	1-4	0-1	2-1	1-0	0-1	1-2	0-1	■	0-2	0-3	3-2	1-0	2-5	2-4
Reading FC	3-1	0-2	0-3	0-0	1-0	3-2	5-1	3-1	0-0	1-4	0-2	4-2	1-1	2-2	0-1	1-1	1-1	3-0	■	1-0	0-1	1-1	0-1	1-1
Rotherham United	3-1	1-0	1-0	1-2	2-1	3-3	3-2	0-1	2-0	2-0	1-1	1-1	2-1	0-2	2-1	0-2	3-0	3-0	3-0	■	0-1	0-1	3-3	4-1
Swansea City FC	2-1	0-0	3-2	0-0	3-2	0-1	2-2	1-5	3-1	0-2	2-2	1-2	0-3	3-1	0-2	4-1	1-0	1-0	0-2	2-2	■	1-2	2-2	1-3
Walsall FC	1-0	0-0	0-0	0-1	4-1	1-2	2-3	5-0	0-0	1-0	0-1	0-0	3-3	1-1	4-2	0-3	2-1	3-1	0-2	3-0	3-0	■	0-0	3-0
Wigan Athletic AFC	1-0	1-2	1-0	1-1	2-2	1-0	2-0	3-3	2-0	5-2	0-1	1-1	1-0	0-1	1-1	4-2	1-0	2-0	1-1	2-1	2-0	1-2	■	1-2
York City FC	0-3	4-1	1-2	1-0	0-2	1-0	4-0	3-2	1-1	3-1	7-1	1-2	2-1	1-1	2-0	2-1	0-0	0-1	2-2	3-0	1-0	1-1	2-0	■

	Division 3	Pd	Wn	Dw	Ls	GF	GA	Pts	
1.	Bradford City AFC (Bradford)	46	28	10	8	77	45	94	P
2.	Millwall FC (London)	46	26	12	8	73	42	90	P
3.	Hull City AFC (Kingston-upon-Hull)	46	25	12	9	78	49	87	P
4.	Gillingham FC (Gillingham)	46	25	8	13	80	62	83	
5.	Bristol City FC (Bristol)	46	24	9	13	74	47	81	
6.	Bristol Rovers FC (Bristol)	46	21	12	13	66	48	75	
7.	Derby County FC (Derby)	46	19	13	14	65	54	70	
8.	York City FC (York)	46	20	9	17	70	57	69	
9.	Reading FC (Reading)	46	19	12	15	68	62	69	
10.	AFC Bournemouth (Bournemouth)	46	19	11	16	57	46	68	
11.	Walsall FC (Walsall)	46	18	13	15	58	52	67	
12.	Rotherham United FC (Rotherham)	46	18	11	17	55	55	65	
13.	Brentford FC (London)	46	16	14	16	62	64	62	
14.	Doncaster Rovers FC (Doncaster)	46	17	8	21	72	74	59	
15.	Plymouth Argyle FC (Plymouth)	46	15	14	17	62	65	59	
16.	Wigan Athletic AFC (Wigan)	46	15	14	17	60	64	59	
17.	Bolton Wanderers FC (Bolton)	46	16	6	24	69	75	54	
18.	Newport County AFC (Newport)	46	13	13	20	55	67	52	
19.	Lincoln City FC (Lincoln)	46	11	18	17	50	51	51	
20.	Swansea City FC (Swansea)	46	12	11	23	53	80	47	
21.	Burnley FC (Burnley)	46	11	13	22	60	73	46	R
22.	Orient FC (London)	46	11	13	22	51	76	46	R
23.	Preston North End FC (Preston)	46	13	7	26	51	100	46	R
24.	Cambridge United FC (Cambridge)	46	4	9	33	37	95	21	R
		1104	416	272	416	1503	1503	1520	

Football League Division 4 — 1984-85 Season

	Aldershot Town	Blackpool	Bury	Chester City	Chesterfield	Colchester United	Crewe Alexandra	Darlington	Exeter City	Halifax Town	Hartlepool	Hereford United	Mansfield Town	Northampton Town	Peterborough United	Port Vale	Rochdale	Scunthorpe United	Southend United	Stockport County	Swindon Town	Torquay United	Tranmere Rovers	Wrexham
Aldershot Town FC		1-0	0-1	1-2	1-1	1-0	1-1	3-4	1-1	2-0	1-0	0-1	0-0	0-0	0-0	1-0	5-0	1-2	6-2	2-1	0-1	1-0	3-2	2-1
Blackpool FC	1-0		0-0	3-1	1-0	1-1	6-1	0-0	3-0	1-1	2-1	2-0	1-0	2-1	4-2	1-1	3-0	1-0	1-0	4-1	1-0	3-3	1-2	0-0
Bury FC	2-1	1-0		4-1	0-0	4-3	2-2	1-0	2-2	3-0	1-0	2-1	0-0	3-1	1-1	4-0	2-2	0-1	2-0	2-1	2-0	3-1	3-0	2-1
Chester City FC	2-0	0-0	2-3		1-1	1-2	0-2	5-2	1-3	2-0	1-0	0-3	1-0	1-3	2-0	0-1	1-1	5-1	2-1	1-0	0-1	2-4	2-1	
Chesterfield FC	2-1	2-1	0-1	3-1		1-1	3-1	0-0	5-1	3-0	0-0	3-1	0-0	2-1	2-0	0-0	0-0	1-0	2-1	3-0	1-0	1-0	4-2	2-1
Colchester United FC	2-0	1-1	1-0	1-1	3-1		4-1	1-2	3-4	1-3	1-0	2-2	2-1	4-1	3-1	3-2	1-1	1-1	3-3	3-0	1-1	2-1	2-1	4-1
Crewe Alexandra FC	1-1	0-2	1-0	2-0	1-1	1-4		2-2	0-0	0-1	2-0	0-3	1-1	3-2	2-1	0-0	3-1	1-1	0-2	2-1	3-2	3-0	1-3	3-0
Darlington FC	1-1	0-4	1-1	2-1	1-3	4-0	2-1		2-1	2-0	0-1	1-1	3-1	2-1	1-1	1-0	2-1	3-1	3-1	1-0	1-0	2-1		
Exeter City FC	3-0	1-1	0-2	1-1	0-1	1-5	0-2	1-1		1-0	3-2	0-0	0-0	5-0	0-1	2-1	1-1	2-1	2-1	0-2	1-1	4-3	0-1	2-0
Halifax Town AFC	1-2	0-2	4-1	0-4	1-3	0-0	1-1	0-1	2-3		2-3	2-1	1-0	1-0	0-0	2-1	0-2	1-2	1-0	2-1	2-1	0-1	2-1	1-2
Hartlepool United FC	1-0	0-2	0-1	2-1	1-0	2-1	3-0	1-2	1-1	0-1		2-2	0-0	0-0	0-3	2-2	3-2	2-1	5-1	2-2	3-1	2-4	2-0	
Hereford United FC	2-1	2-1	5-3	0-0	0-1	3-2	0-1	1-2	3-0	2-1			3-0	1-1	1-0	1-0	1-2	1-0	3-0	2-0	0-3	1-0	2-1	
Mansfield Town FC	1-2	1-1	0-2	2-0	0-0	0-1	0-2	2-0	2-2	2-1	2-0	1-1		2-0	0-0	1-1	5-1	0-1	1-0	1-0	0-0	1-0	0-0	1-0
Northampton Town	4-0	0-1	0-1	0-2	1-3	1-3	1-3	2-1	5-2	0-1	2-0	0-3	1-0		0-3	1-0	0-0	0-2	1-2	4-0	4-0	3-1	2-0	0-4
Peterborough United	1-2	2-0	1-4	3-1	0-0	0-1	2-1	1-1	0-0	2-0	3-1	1-1	1-0	0-0		0-0	1-1	3-1	1-4	3-1	0-1	1-0	1-0	2-1
Port Vale FC	1-2	1-1	0-0	0-0	0-0	3-2	2-0	0-2	5-1	3-1	1-1	3-1	0-1	0-3	3-1		3-1	1-1	4-1	3-2	2-0	2-2	2-1	0-0
Rochdale AFC	1-2	1-1	1-1	1-2	3-1	1-1	1-3	1-2	2-0	4-3	0-1	2-1	3-0	2-1	1-2			3-3	2-2	0-0	1-1	2-0	2-1	0-2
Scunthorpe United	2-1	1-1	2-2	2-1	2-4	2-2	2-3	0-1	7-1	4-0	2-0	1-1	2-2	2-1	2-1	3-3	4-2		2-1	1-0	6-2	2-0	5-2	5-2
Southend United FC	1-0	1-4	3-3	1-1	0-1	2-5	3-1	1-1	1-0	1-1	1-1	0-0	1-3	2-1	2-1	1-1	0-2	1-1		1-1	3-2	1-0	2-3	0-1
Stockport County FC	6-0	1-3	2-0	5-1	0-1	1-0	0-1	0-0	1-0	0-3	4-1	2-1	4-2	1-1	3-1	1-1	2-0	1-2			2-1	1-2	0-2	2-2
Swindon Town FC	2-1	4-1	1-0	4-4	4-0	2-1	1-1	1-0	2-0	2-1	0-3	1-0	2-0	1-1	0-1	2-1	0-0	2-0	4-0			1-3	2-1	2-1
Torquay United FC	1-3	0-2	0-2	2-0	0-1	1-1	0-0	1-1	1-1	1-1	0-1	1-0	1-0	0-2	0-0	1-3	1-0	0-0	2-2	0-0	0-0		1-1	4-3
Tranmere Rovers FC	4-3	3-0	3-2	1-0	0-1	3-1	3-1	3-0	3-2	1-0	1-2	0-1	0-0	1-2	4-0	4-1	3-1	2-0	2-0	3-0	0-2	3-1		3-1
Wrexham AFC	1-0	1-2	3-0	2-0	2-0	2-2	1-3	1-1	2-0	0-1	1-1	1-1	2-2	0-3	1-3	1-1	2-0	2-1	1-2	3-4	4-0	2-0	4-0	

Division 4

		Pd	Wn	Dw	Ls	GF	GA	Pts	
1.	Chesterfield FC (Chesterfield)	46	26	13	7	64	35	91	P
2.	Blackpool FC (Blackpool)	46	24	14	8	73	39	86	P
3.	Darlington FC (Darlington)	46	24	13	9	66	49	85	P
4.	Bury FC (Bury)	46	24	12	10	76	50	84	P
5.	Hereford United FC (Hereford)	46	22	11	13	65	47	77	
6.	Tranmere Rovers FC (Birkenhead)	46	24	3	19	83	66	75	
7.	Colchester United FC (Colchester)	46	20	14	12	87	65	74	
8.	Swindon Town FC (Swindon)	46	21	9	16	62	58	72	
9.	Scunthorpe United FC (Scunthorpe)	46	19	14	13	83	62	71	
10.	Crewe Alexandra FC (Crewe)	46	18	12	16	65	69	66	
11.	Peterborough United FC (Peterborough)	46	16	14	16	54	53	62	
12.	Port Vale FC (Stoke-on-Trent)	46	14	18	14	61	59	60	
13.	Aldershot FC (Aldershot)	46	17	8	21	56	63	59	
14.	Mansfield Town FC (Mansfield)	46	13	18	15	41	38	57	
15.	Wrexham AFC (Wrexham)	46	15	9	22	67	70	54	
16.	Chester City FC (Chester)	46	15	9	22	60	72	54	
17.	Rochdale AFC (Rochdale)	46	13	14	19	55	69	53	
18.	Exeter City FC (Exeter)	46	13	14	19	57	79	53	
19.	Hartlepool United FC (Hartlepool)	46	14	10	22	54	67	52	
20.	Southend United FC (Southend-on-Sea)	46	13	11	22	58	83	50	
21.	Halifax Town AFC (Halifax)	46	15	5	26	42	69	50	
22.	Stockport County FC (Stockport)	46	13	8	25	58	79	47	
23.	Northampton Town FC (Northampton)	46	14	5	27	53	74	47	
24.	Torquay United FC (Torquay)	46	9	14	23	38	63	41	
		1104	416	272	416	1478	1478	1520	

F.A. CUP FINAL   (Wembley Stadium, London – 18/05/1985 – 100,000)

MANCHESTER UNITED FC	1-0 (aet)	Everton FC (Liverpool)
Whiteside	*(H.T. 0-0)*	

Man. United: Bailey, Gidman, Albiston (Duxbury), Whiteside, McGrath, Moran, Robson, Strachan, Hughes, Stapleton, Olsen.

Everton: Southall, Stevens, van den Hauwe, Ratcliffe, Maountfield, Reid, Sreven, Gray, Sharp, Bracewell, Sheedy.

Semi-finals

Everton FC (Liverpool)	2-1	Luton Town FC (Luton)
Liverpool FC (Liverpool)	2-2 (aet), 1-2	Manchester United FC (Manchester)

Quarter-finals

Barnsley FC (Barnsley)	0-4	Liverpool FC (Liverpool)
Everton FC (Liverpool)	2-2, 1-0	Ipswich Town FC (Ipswich)
Luton Town FC (Luton)	1-0	Millwall FC (London)
Manchester United FC (Manchester)	4-2	West Ham United FC (London)

1985-86

Football League Division 1 1985-86 Season	Arsenal	Aston Villa	Birmingham City	Chelsea	Coventry City	Everton	Ipswich Town	Leicester City	Liverpool	Luton Town	Manchester City	Manchester United	Newcastle United	Nottingham Forest	Oxford United	Q.P.R.	Sheffield Wed.	Southampton	Tottenham Hotspur	Watford	W.B.A.	West Ham United
Arsenal FC	■	3-2	0-0	2-0	3-0	0-1	1-0	1-0	2-0	2-1	1-0	1-2	0-0	1-1	2-1	3-1	1-0	3-2	0-0	0-2	2-2	1-0
Aston Villa FC	1-4	■	0-3	3-1	1-1	0-0	1-0	1-0	2-2	3-1	0-1	1-3	1-2	1-2	3-0	1-2	1-1	0-0	1-2	4-1	1-1	2-1
Birmingham City FC	0-1	0-0	■	1-2	0-1	0-2	0-1	2-1	0-2	0-2	1-0	1-1	0-1	0-1	3-1	2-0	0-2	0-2	1-2	1-2	0-1	1-0
Chelsea FC	2-1	2-1	2-0	■	1-0	2-1	1-1	2-2	0-1	1-0	1-0	1-2	1-1	4-2	1-4	1-1	2-1	2-0	2-0	1-5	3-0	0-4
Coventry City FC	0-2	3-3	4-4	1-1	■	1-3	0-1	3-0	0-3	1-0	1-1	1-3	1-2	0-0	5-2	2-1	0-1	3-2	2-3	0-2	3-0	0-1
Everton FC	6-1	2-0	4-1	1-1	1-1	■	1-0	1-2	2-3	2-0	4-0	3-1	1-0	1-1	2-0	4-3	3-1	6-1	1-0	4-1	2-0	3-1
Ipswich Town FC	1-2	0-3	0-1	0-2	1-0	3-4	■	0-2	2-1	1-1	0-0	0-1	2-2	1-0	3-2	1-0	2-1	1-1	1-0	0-0	1-0	0-1
Leicester City FC	2-2	3-1	4-2	0-0	2-1	3-1	1-0	■	0-2	0-0	1-1	3-0	2-0	0-3	4-4	1-4	2-3	2-2	1-4	2-2	2-2	1-1
Liverpool FC	2-0	3-0	5-0	1-1	5-0	0-2	5-0	1-0	■	3-2	2-0	1-1	1-1	2-0	6-0	4-1	2-2	1-0	4-1	3-1	4-1	3-1
Luton Town FC	2-2	2-0	2-0	1-1	0-1	2-1	1-0	3-1	0-1	■	2-1	1-1	2-0	1-1	1-2	2-0	1-0	7-0	1-1	3-2	3-0	0-0
Manchester City FC	0-1	2-2	1-1	0-1	5-1	1-1	1-1	1-1	1-0	1-1	■	0-3	1-0	1-2	0-3	2-0	1-3	1-0	2-1	0-1	2-1	2-2
Manchester United FC	0-1	4-0	1-0	1-2	2-0	0-0	1-0	4-0	1-1	2-0	2-2	■	3-0	2-3	3-0	0-2	1-0	0-1	0-0	1-1	3-0	2-0
Newcastle United FC	1-0	2-2	4-1	1-3	3-2	2-2	3-1	2-1	1-0	2-2	3-1	2-4	■	0-3	3-0	3-1	4-1	2-1	2-2	1-1	4-1	1-2
Nottingham Forest FC	3-2	1-1	3-0	0-0	5-2	0-0	3-1	4-3	1-1	2-0	0-2	1-3	1-2	■	1-1	4-0	2-1	0-1	3-2	2-1	2-1	2-1
Oxford United FC	3-0	1-1	0-1	2-1	0-1	1-0	4-3	5-0	2-2	1-1	1-0	1-3	1-2	1-2	■	3-3	0-1	3-0	1-1	1-1	2-2	1-2
Queen's Park Rangers FC	0-1	0-1	3-1	6-0	0-2	3-0	1-0	2-0	2-1	1-1	0-0	1-0	3-1	2-1	3-1	■	1-1	0-2	2-5	2-1	1-0	0-1
Sheffield Wednesday FC	2-0	2-0	5-1	1-1	2-2	1-5	1-0	0-0	3-2	3-2	1-0	2-2	2-1	2-1	2-1	0-0	■	2-1	1-2	2-1	1-0	2-2
Southampton FC	3-0	0-0	1-0	0-1	1-1	2-3	1-0	0-0	1-2	1-2	3-0	1-0	1-1	3-1	1-1	3-0	2-3	■	1-0	3-1	3-1	1-1
Tottenham Hotspur FC	1-0	4-2	2-0	4-1	0-1	0-1	2-0	1-3	1-2	1-3	0-2	0-0	5-1	0-3	5-1	1-1	5-1	5-3	■	4-0	5-0	1-0
Watford FC	3-0	1-1	3-0	3-1	3-0	0-2	0-0	2-1	2-3	1-2	3-2	1-1	4-1	1-1	2-2	2-1	2-1	1-1	1-0	■	5-1	0-2
West Bromwich Albion FC	0-0	0-3	2-1	0-3	0-0	0-3	1-2	2-2	1-2	1-2	2-3	1-5	1-1	1-1	0-1	1-1	1-0	1-1	1-1	3-1	■	2-3
West Ham United FC	0-0	4-1	2-0	1-2	1-0	2-1	2-1	3-0	2-2	0-1	1-0	2-1	8-1	4-2	3-1	3-1	1-0	1-0	2-1	2-1	4-0	■

	Division 1	Pd	Wn	Dw	Ls	GF	GA	Pts	
1.	LIVERPOOL FC (LIVERPOOL)	42	26	10	6	89	37	88	
2.	Everton FC (Liverpool)	42	26	8	8	87	41	86	
3.	West Ham United FC (London)	42	26	6	10	74	40	84	
4.	Manchester United FC (Manchester)	42	22	10	10	70	36	76	
5.	Sheffield Wednesday FC (Sheffield)	42	21	10	11	63	54	73	
6.	Chelsea FC (London)	42	20	11	11	57	56	71	
7.	Arsenal FC (London)	42	20	9	13	49	47	69	
8.	Nottingham Forest FC (Nottingham)	42	19	11	12	69	53	68	
9.	Luton Town FC (Luton)	42	18	12	12	61	44	66	
10.	Tottenham Hotspur FC (London)	42	19	8	15	74	52	65	
11.	Newcastle United FC (Newcastle-upon-Tyne)	42	17	12	13	67	72	63	
12.	Watford FC (Watford)	42	16	11	15	69	62	59	
13.	Queen's Park Rangers FC (London)	42	15	7	20	53	64	52	
14.	Southampton FC (Southampton)	42	12	10	20	51	62	46	
15.	Manchester City FC (Manchester)	42	11	12	19	43	57	45	
16.	Aston Villa FC (Birmingham)	42	10	14	18	51	67	44	
17.	Coventry City FC (Coventry)	42	11	10	21	48	71	43	
18.	Oxford United FC (Oxford)	42	10	12	20	62	80	42	
19.	Leicester City FC (Leicester)	42	10	12	20	54	76	42	
20.	Ipswich Town FC (Ipswich)	42	11	8	23	32	55	41	R
21.	Birmingham City FC (Birmingham)	42	8	5	29	30	73	29	R
22.	West Bromwich Albion FC (West Bromwich)	42	4	12	26	35	89	24	R
		924	352	220	352	1288	1288	1276	

Top Goalscorer

1)	Gary LINEKER	(Everton FC)	30

Football League Division 2 1985-86 Season	Barnsley	Blackburn Rovers	Bradford City	Brighton & Hove Albion	Carlisle United	Charlton Athletic	Crystal Palace	Fulham	Grimsby Town	Huddersfield Town	Hull City	Leeds United	Middlesbrough	Millwall	Norwich City	Oldham Athletic	Portsmouth	Sheffield United	Shrewsbury Town	Stoke City	Sunderland	Wimbledon
Barnsley FC	■	1-1	2-2	3-2	1-2	2-1	2-4	2-0	1-0	1-3	1-4	3-0	0-0	2-1	2-2	1-0	0-1	2-1	2-0	0-0	1-1	0-1
Blackburn Rovers FC	0-3	■	3-0	1-4	2-0	0-0	1-2	1-0	3-1	0-1	2-2	2-0	0-1	1-2	2-1	0-0	1-0	6-1	1-1	0-1	2-0	2-0
Bradford City AFC	2-0	3-2	■	3-2	1-0	1-2	1-0	3-1	0-1	3-0	4-2	0-1	2-1	0-2	0-2	1-0	2-1	1-4	3-1	3-1	2-0	1-1
Brighton & Hove Albion FC	0-1	3-1	2-1	■	6-1	3-5	2-0	2-3	2-2	4-3	3-1	0-1	3-3	1-0	1-1	1-1	2-3	0-0	0-2	2-0	3-1	2-0
Carlisle United FC	1-1	2-1	1-2	2-0	■	2-3	2-2	2-1	1-2	2-0	2-1	1-2	1-0	1-0	0-4	3-1	0-1	1-0	0-2	3-0	1-2	2-3
Charlton Athletic FC	2-1	3-0	1-1	2-2	3-0	■	3-1	2-0	2-0	3-0	1-2	4-0	2-0	3-3	1-0	1-1	1-2	2-0	4-1	2-0	2-1	0-0
Crystal Palace FC	1-0	2-0	2-1	1-0	1-1	2-1	■	0-0	2-1	2-3	0-2	3-0	2-1	2-1	1-2	3-2	2-1	1-1	0-1	0-1	1-0	1-3
Fulham FC	2-0	3-3	4-1	1-0	0-1	0-3	2-3	■	2-1	2-1	1-1	3-1	0-3	1-2	0-1	2-2	0-1	2-3	2-1	1-0	1-2	0-2
Grimsby Town FC	1-2	5-2	2-0	0-2	1-0	2-2	3-0	1-0	■	1-1	0-1	1-0	3-2	5-1	1-0	1-4	1-0	0-1	3-1	3-3	1-1	0-1
Huddersfield Town AFC	1-1	0-0	2-0	1-0	3-3	0-2	0-0	1-3	2-2	■	2-1	3-1	0-3	4-3	0-0	0-0	1-2	3-1	1-0	2-0	2-0	0-1
Hull City AFC	0-1	2-2	1-0	2-0	4-0	1-1	1-2	5-0	2-0	3-1	■	2-1	0-0	3-0	1-0	4-2	2-2	0-0	4-3	0-2	1-1	1-1
Leeds United AFC	0-2	1-1	2-3	2-0	1-2	1-3	1-0	1-1	2-0	1-1	1-0	■	0-2	3-1	1-1	1-1	1-1	4-0	1-1	4-0	1-1	0-0
Middlesbrough FC	0-0	0-0	1-1	0-1	1-3	1-3	0-2	1-0	3-1	0-1	1-2	2-2	■	3-0	1-1	3-2	1-0	1-2	3-1	1-1	2-0	1-0
Millwall FC	2-2	0-1	2-1	0-1	3-1	2-2	3-2	1-1	1-0	2-1	5-0	3-1	3-0	■	4-2	0-1	0-4	3-0	2-0	2-3	1-0	0-1
Norwich City FC	1-1	3-0	0-0	3-0	2-1	3-1	4-3	2-1	3-2	4-1	2-0	4-0	2-0	6-1	■	1-0	2-0	4-0	3-1	1-1	0-0	1-2
Oldham Athletic AFC	1-1	3-1	0-1	4-0	2-1	2-1	2-0	2-1	1-1	3-1	3-1	1-0	0-0	1-3	1-0	■	2-0	1-5	4-3	2-4	2-2	2-1
Portsmouth FC	1-1	3-0	4-0	1-2	4-0	1-0	1-0	1-1	3-1	4-1	1-1	2-3	1-0	2-1	2-0	1-2	■	0-3	4-0	3-0	3-0	1-1
Sheffield United FC	3-1	3-3	3-1	3-0	1-0	1-1	0-0	2-1	1-1	1-1	3-1	3-2	0-1	1-3	2-5	2-0	0-0	■	1-1	1-2	1-0	4-0
Shrewsbury Town FC	3-0	2-0	2-0	2-1	0-0	2-1	0-2	0-2	3-0	0-0	1-3	2-1	1-1	0-3	2-0	1-1	3-1	3-1	■	1-0	1-2	1-1
Stoke City FC	0-0	2-2	3-1	1-1	0-0	0-0	0-0	1-0	1-1	3-0	6-2	3-2	0-0	1-1	2-0	2-0	1-3	2-2	1-2	■	1-0	0-0
Sunderland AFC	2-0	0-2	1-1	2-1	2-2	1-2	1-1	4-2	3-3	1-0	1-1	4-2	1-0	1-2	0-2	0-3	1-3	2-1	2-1	2-0	■	2-1
Wimbledon FC	1-0	1-1	1-0	0-0	4-1	3-1	1-1	1-0	3-0	2-2	3-1	0-3	3-0	1-1	2-1	0-0	1-3	5-0	2-1	1-0	3-0	■

	Division 2	Pd	Wn	Dw	Ls	GF	GA	Pts	
1.	Norwich City FC (Norwich)	42	25	9	8	84	37	84	P
2.	Charlton Athletic FC (London)	42	22	11	9	78	45	77	P
3.	Wimbledon FC (London)	42	21	13	8	58	37	76	P
4.	Portsmouth FC (Portsmouth)	42	22	7	13	69	41	73	
5.	Crystal Palace FC (London)	42	19	9	14	57	52	66	
6.	Hull City AFC (Kingston-upon-Hull)	42	17	13	12	65	55	64	
7.	Sheffield United FC (Sheffield)	42	17	11	14	64	63	62	
8.	Oldham Athletic AFC (Oldham)	42	17	9	16	62	61	60	
9.	Millwall FC (London)	42	17	8	17	64	65	59	
10.	Stoke City FC (Stoke-on-Trent)	42	14	15	13	48	50	57	
11.	Brighton & Hove Albion FC (Hove)	42	16	8	18	64	64	56	
12.	Barnsley FC (Barnsley)	42	14	14	14	47	50	56	
13.	Bradford City AFC (Bradford)	42	16	6	20	51	63	54	
14.	Leeds United AFC (Leeds)	42	15	8	19	56	72	53	
15.	Grimsby Town FC (Cleethorpes)	42	14	10	18	58	62	52	
16.	Huddersfield Town AFC (Huddersfield)	42	14	10	18	51	67	52	
17.	Shrewsbury Town FC (Shrewsbury)	42	14	9	19	52	64	51	
18.	Sunderland AFC (Sunderland)	42	13	11	18	47	61	50	
19.	Blackburn Rovers FC (Blackburn)	42	12	13	17	53	62	49	
20.	Carlisle United FC (Carlisle)	42	13	7	22	47	71	46	R
21.	Middlesbrough FC (Middlesbrough)	42	12	9	21	44	53	45	R
22.	Fulham FC (London)	42	10	6	26	45	69	36	R
		924	354	216	354	1264	1264	1278	

Football League Division 3 — 1985-86 Season

Results grid (home team in left column; columns in same order as rows):

	Blk	Bol	Bou	Bre	BrC	BrR	Bur	Car	Che	Dar	Der	Don	Gil	Lin	New	Not	Ply	Rea	Rot	Swa	Wal	Wig	Wol	Yor
Blackpool FC		1-1	2-0	4-0	2-1	4-2	5-0	3-0	0-1	0-0	0-1	4-0	2-2	2-0	0-0	1-3	1-1	0-0	2-1	2-0	2-1	1-2	0-1	0-2
Bolton Wanderers FC	1-3		1-0	1-2	0-4	0-2	1-4	5-0	2-1	0-3	0-1	2-0	0-1	1-1	4-0	1-0	3-1	2-0	1-1	1-1	3-1	1-2	4-1	1-1
AFC Bournemouth	1-4	2-1		0-0	5-0	6-1	2-1	1-1	3-2	4-2	1-1	1-1	2-3	2-2	0-1	0-0	1-3	0-1	1-2	4-0	0-1	0-2	3-2	2-0
Brentford FC	1-1	1-1	1-0		1-2	1-0	1-0	3-0	1-0	2-1	3-3	1-3	1-2	0-1	0-0	1-1	1-1	1-2	1-1	1-0	1-3	1-3	2-1	3-1
Bristol City FC	2-1	2-0	1-3	0-0		2-0	4-1	2-1	0-0	1-0	1-1	4-1	1-2	1-1	3-1	3-0	2-0	3-0	3-1	0-1	2-3	1-0	3-0	2-2
Bristol Rovers FC	1-0	2-1	2-3	0-1	1-1		2-1	2-1	1-1	3-1	0-0	1-0	1-0	0-0	2-0	1-1	1-2	0-2	5-2	0-0	0-1	1-1	1-1	0-1
Bury FC	4-1	2-1	3-0	0-0	6-3	1-1		3-0	1-1	0-1	1-1	1-2	1-2	4-0	1-1	2-4	0-1	3-1	2-0	2-2	2-1	0-0	3-1	4-2
Cardiff City AFC	1-0	0-1	0-1	1-0	1-3	2-0	0-0		0-2	0-1	0-2	0-1	1-1	2-1	1-1	1-3	1-2	2-3	1-0	1-1	3-1	1-1	2-1	2-1
Chesterfield FC	1-2	3-0	0-1	1-3	0-0	2-0	4-3	3-4		1-0	1-0	0-0	1-1	2-2	3-1	2-2	1-2	3-4	2-0	4-1	2-3	1-1	3-0	1-0
Darlington FC	2-1	0-1	0-0	3-5	1-1	3-3	1-1	4-1	2-1		2-1	0-2	3-2	1-0	3-2	2-3	0-2	2-2	6-0	0-3	1-1	2-1	2-1	1-0
Derby County FC	1-2	2-1	3-0	1-1	2-0	0-2	1-1	2-1	0-0	1-1		1-1	2-0	7-0	1-1	2-0	1-2	1-1	2-1	5-1	3-1	1-0	4-2	2-1
Doncaster Rovers FC	0-0	1-1	1-1	1-0	1-1	0-2	1-0	0-2	2-0	2-0	0-3		2-3	1-1	1-1	2-1	1-0	0-0	0-0	1-0	2-2	0-1	2-2	1-1
Gillingham FC	2-2	2-1	2-0	1-2	1-1	2-0	1-0	2-0	1-1	1-1	1-2	4-0		2-0	0-1	4-0	1-1	3-0	5-1	5-2	2-0	2-0	2-0	1-2
Lincoln City FC	0-3	1-1	3-2	3-0	1-1	2-2	2-0	0-4	2-1	1-1	0-1	3-3	1-0		1-1	0-2	1-1	0-0	4-1	3-2	0-0	2-3	2-2	3-4
Newport County AFC	1-1	0-1	2-1	1-2	1-1	3-0	1-0	1-2	3-3	3-0	1-1	2-2	1-1	1-2		1-2	3-1	0-2	0-0	2-0	1-5	3-4	3-1	1-1
Notts County FC	1-2	1-0	3-1	0-4	4-0	0-0	2-2	1-4	2-1	5-0	0-3	1-1	1-1	3-2	1-2		2-0	1-0	3-0	3-1	1-1	4-0	4-0	3-1
Plymouth Argyle FC	3-1	4-1	2-1	2-0	4-0	4-2	3-0	4-4	0-0	4-2	4-1	0-1	3-0	2-1	2-0	0-1		0-1	4-0	2-0	2-0	2-1	3-1	2-2
Reading FC	1-0	1-0	1-2	3-1	1-0	3-2	2-0	1-1	4-2	0-2	1-0	0-2	0-2	3-1	4-3	2-0	3-2		2-1	2-0	2-1	1-0	2-2	0-0
Rotherham United	4-1	4-0	4-1	1-2	2-0	2-0	2-0	3-0	1-2	1-2	2-1	1-1	1-0	0-0	1-0	1-1	1-2	1-2		4-1	3-0	0-0	1-2	4-1
Swansea City FC	2-0	3-1	1-1	2-0	1-3	0-1	1-0	2-0	1-1	2-2	0-3	0-2	2-2	3-1	1-1	0-0	0-2	2-3	1-0		2-1	0-1	0-2	1-0
Walsall FC	1-1	2-0	4-2	1-2	2-1	6-0	3-2	6-3	3-0	0-0	1-1	1-0	4-1	2-1	2-0	0-0	2-2	6-0	3-1	3-1		3-3	1-1	3-1
Wigan Athletic AFC	1-1	1-3	3-0	4-0	1-1	4-0	1-0	2-0	2-0	5-1	2-1	0-1	3-3	3-2	0-0	3-1	1-0	2-0	5-0	2-0	5-0		5-3	1-0
Wolverhampton W.	2-1	0-2	0-3	1-4	2-1	3-4	1-1	3-1	1-0	2-1	0-4	1-2	1-3	1-1	1-2	2-2	0-3	2-3	0-0	1-5	0-0	2-2		3-2
York City FC	3-0	3-0	2-1	1-0	1-1	4-0	0-0	1-1	2-0	7-0	1-3	0-1	2-0	2-1	3-1	2-2	3-1	0-1	2-1	3-1	1-0	4-1	2-1	

	Division 3	Pd	Wn	Dw	Ls	GF	GA	Pts	
1.	Reading FC (Reading)	46	29	7	10	67	51	94	P
2.	Plymouth Argyle FC (Plymouth)	46	26	9	11	88	53	87	P
3.	Derby County FC (Derby)	46	23	15	8	80	41	84	P
4.	Wigan Athletic AFC (Wigan)	46	23	14	9	82	48	83	
5.	Gillingham FC (Gillingham)	46	22	13	11	81	54	79	
6.	Walsall FC (Walsall)	46	22	9	15	90	64	75	
7.	York City FC (York)	46	20	11	15	77	58	71	
8.	Notts County FC (Nottingham)	46	19	14	13	71	60	71	
9.	Bristol City FC (Bristol)	46	18	14	14	69	60	68	
10.	Brentford FC (London)	46	18	12	16	58	61	66	
11.	Doncaster Rovers FC (Doncaster)	46	16	16	14	45	52	64	
12.	Blackpool FC (Blackpool)	46	17	12	17	66	55	63	
13.	Darlington FC (Darlington)	46	15	13	18	61	78	58	
14.	Rotherham United FC (Rotherham)	46	15	12	19	61	59	57	
15.	AFC Bournemouth (Bournemouth)	46	15	9	22	65	72	54	
16.	Bristol Rovers FC (Bristol)	46	14	12	20	51	75	54	
17.	Chesterfield FC (Chesterfield)	46	13	14	19	61	64	53	
18.	Bolton Wanderers FC (Bolton)	46	15	8	23	54	68	53	
19.	Newport County AFC (Newport)	46	11	18	17	52	65	51	
20.	Bury FC (Bury)	46	12	13	21	63	67	49	
21.	Lincoln City FC (Lincoln)	46	10	16	20	55	77	46	R
22.	Cardiff City AFC (Cardiff)	46	12	9	25	53	83	45	R
23.	Wolverhampton Wanderers FC (Wolverhampton)	46	11	10	25	57	98	43	R
24.	Swansea City FC (Swansea)	46	11	10	25	43	87	43	R
		1104	407	290	407	1550	1550	1511	

Football League Division 4 1985-86 Season

	Aldershot Town	Burnley	Cambridge	Chester City	Colchester United	Crewe Alexandra	Exeter City	Halifax Town	Hartlepool	Hereford United	Mansfield Town	Northampton Town	Orient	Peterborough United	Port Vale	Preston North End	Rochdale	Scunthorpe United	Southend United	Stockport County	Swindon Town	Torquay United	Tranmere Rovers	Wrexham
Aldershot Town FC		0-2	2-1	1-1	1-1	3-2	4-0	1-2	0-1	2-0	1-2	1-0	1-1	1-0	0-0	4-0	2-1	2-1	1-3	6-1	2-4	1-1	3-1	6-0
Burnley FC	1-2		1-1	1-0	0-2	0-1	3-1	1-3	2-0	3-2	2-1	3-2	1-0	1-1	1-2	1-1	1-0	1-2	1-3	0-1	0-2	3-0	3-1	5-2
Cambridge United FC	0-2	0-4		3-2	1-3	1-0	1-1	4-0	4-2	4-0	4-2	2-5	1-2	3-1	1-3	2-0	1-0	0-1	1-2	1-2	1-1	3-0	3-2	4-3
Chester City FC	1-0	4-0	1-1		4-0	4-0	2-1	1-1	1-1	1-0	1-0	2-3	3-0	2-1	4-1	2-0	1-1	1-1	2-0	1-2	0-1	3-1	1-0	2-1
Colchester United FC	4-0	2-2	4-1	2-3		1-2	1-1	3-1	3-1	4-1	0-0	0-2	4-0	5-0	1-0	4-0	0-1	1-1	2-0	3-1	1-1	0-0	1-2	5-2
Crewe Alexandra FC	2-0	3-1	0-1	2-2	0-2		0-1	2-2	0-0	2-0	2-1	0-1	1-3	1-1	0-1	3-3	4-2	4-0	1-1	0-1	2-0	1-0	2-1	3-2
Exeter City FC	2-0	0-2	0-0	1-3	2-2	1-2		1-0	1-2	3-2		1-2	1-1	1-0	3-0	2-0	2-0	0-2	1-0	0-3	2-2	1-0		0-1
Halifax Town AFC	1-1	2-2	1-1	1-2	2-2	1-0	1-0		3-2	1-0	1-2	2-0	2-1	1-2	2-0	2-1	1-1	2-1	2-3	0-0	1-3	0-0	1-2	5-2
Hartlepool United FC	2-1	3-1	1-0	1-1	4-1	4-1	0-0	3-0		2-1	1-1	2-1	1-2	1-1	1-0	0-1	3-2	1-1	1-0	1-0	1-0	1-0	1-0	3-3
Hereford United FC	4-1	2-2	1-0	0-2	2-0	4-1	4-1	2-1	2-2			4-2	3-0	3-2	1-1	1-1	2-2	1-1	2-1	3-2	4-1	4-1	1-4	3-1
Mansfield Town FC	1-2	0-0	2-0	0-0	2-2	2-1	2-1	4-0	4-0			1-0	1-1	0-1	2-3	3-2	1-1	3-0	4-2	1-1	4-0	0-0	1-1	
Northampton Town	2-3	2-0	0-2	2-2	1-0	0-1	2-2	4-0	3-0	1-3	1-0		2-3	2-2	2-2	6-0	1-0	2-2	0-0	3-1	0-1	5-1	2-2	1-2
Orient FC	1-1	3-0	3-1	0-0	1-2	0-1	2-2	1-0	1-1	2-2	0-1	0-1		2-2	1-0	2-0	5-0	3-0	3-0	0-1	1-0	4-2	3-1	1-3
Peterborough United	3-0	0-0	2-0	3-0	1-2	1-1	1-1	3-1	0-0	4-2	0-5	2-2			1-0		1-1	1-0	1-1	2-0	3-0	2-0	0-1	1-1
Port Vale FC	3-1	1-1	4-1	1-1	1-1	3-0	0-0	3-2	4-0	1-0	2-0	2-0				0-1	1-1	3-1	4-0	1-1	3-0	1-1	0-0	1-0
Preston North End	1-3	1-0	1-2	3-6	3-2	1-2	2-2	0-1	2-1	2-0	0-1	1-1	1-3	2-4	0-1		1-1	0-1	3-2	1-2	0-3	4-0	2-2	1-0
Rochdale AFC	2-0	1-0	2-1	1-2	3-3	1-0	1-1	1-0	0-2	1-1	1-1	3-2	1-4	20-1	2-2	1-1		1-0	2-1	4-1	1-2	5-0	1-1	3-2
Scunthorpe United	1-0	1-1	0-0	2-0	1-1	3-1	1-0	3-3	1-0	0-3	0-0	2-2	0-0	1-3	3-1				2-0	2-3	0-2	4-0	1-1	0-1
Southend United FC	2-0	2-3	1-1	1-1	2-4	0-1	2-1	2-3	3-2	3-1	0-4	5-1	0-1	2-1	2-1	5-0				0-0	0-0	1-2	2-2	3-0
Stockport County FC	3-2	1-1	3-1	2-1	1-1	3-0	1-1	2-1	1-3	1-1	0-0	2-3	2-2	1-2	2-1	3-0	0-0	2-1			0-2	1-1	1-1	2-0
Swindon Town FC	4-1	3-1	1-0	4-2	2-1	1-0	2-1	3-2	3-1	1-0	2-1	3-2	4-1	3-0	0-0	4-1	4-0	1-1	2-1	1-0		2-1	2-1	0-1
Torquay United FC	1-2	2-0	1-1	0-3	2-1	0-0	1-2	2-0	1-3	2-1	1-2	1-1	2-2	1-0	1-2	1-0	2-2	4-3	0-1				1-2	1-3
Tranmere Rovers FC	3-0	2-1	6-2	2-3	3-4	0-1	0-1	0-3	4-2	1-2	1-2	1-3	0-3	7-0	1-2	2-3	2-1	1-1	2-3	3-1	2-0			1-3
Wrexham AFC	4-1	0-1	6-2	1-1	2-1	2-1	1-1	2-1	1-0	0-1	1-2	1-0	1-3	0-1	1-3	1-1	2-0	1-0	0-0	3-0	0-1	3-2	1-1	

	Division 4	Pd	Wn	Dw	Ls	GF	GA	Pts	
1.	Swindon Town FC (Swindon)	46	32	6	8	82	43	102	P
2.	Chester City FC (Chester)	46	23	15	8	83	50	84	P
3.	Mansfield Town FC (Mansfield)	46	23	12	11	74	47	81	P
4.	Port Vale FC (Stoke-on-Trent)	46	21	16	9	67	37	79	P
5.	Orient FC (London)	46	20	12	14	79	64	72	
6.	Colchester United FC (Colchester)	46	19	13	14	88	63	70	
7.	Hartlepool United FC (Hartlepool)	46	20	10	16	68	67	70	
8.	Northampton Town FC (Northampton)	46	18	10	18	79	58	64	
9.	Southend United FC (Southend-on-Sea)	46	18	10	18	69	67	64	
10.	Hereford United FC (Hereford)	46	18	10	18	74	73	64	
11.	Stockport County FC (Stockport)	46	17	13	16	63	71	64	
12.	Crewe Alexandra FC (Crewe)	46	18	9	19	54	61	63	
13.	Wrexham AFC (Wrexham)	46	17	9	20	68	80	60	
14.	Burnley FC (Burnley)	46	16	11	19	60	65	59	
15.	Scunthorpe United FC (Scunthorpe)	46	15	14	17	50	55	59	
16.	Aldershot FC (Aldershot)	46	17	7	22	66	74	58	
17.	Peterborough United FC (Peterborough)	46	13	17	16	52	64	56	
18.	Rochdale AFC (Rochdale)	46	14	13	19	57	77	55	
19.	Tranmere Rovers FC (Birkenhead)	46	15	9	22	74	73	54	
20.	Halifax Town AFC (Halifax)	46	14	12	20	60	71	54	
21.	Exeter City FC(Exeter)	46	13	15	18	47	59	54	
22.	Cambridge United FC(Cambridge)	46	15	9	22	65	80	54	
23.	Preston North End FC (Preston)	46	11	10	25	54	89	43	
24.	Torquay United FC (Torquay)	46	9	10	27	43	88	37	
		1104	416	272	416	1576	1576	1520	

F.A. CUP FINAL   (Wembley Stadium, London – 10/05/1986 – 98,000)

LIVERPOOL FC (LIVERPOOL)	3-1	Everton FC (Liverpool)
Rush 2, Johnston	*(H.T. 1-0)*	*Lineker*

Liverpool: Grobbelaar, Lawrenson, Beglin, Nicol, Whelan, Hansen, Dalglish, Johnston, Rush, Molby, MacDonald.
Everton: Mimms, Stevens (Heath), van den Hauwe, Ratcliffe, Mountfield, Reid, Steven, Lineker, Sharp, Bracewell, Sheedy.

Semi-finals

Everton FC (Liverpool)	2-1	Sheffield Wednesday FC (Sheffield)
Liverpool FC (Liverpool)	2-0	Southampton FC (Southampton)

Quarter-finals

Brighton & Hove Albion FC (Hove)	0-2	Southampton FC (Southampton)
Liverpool FC (Liverpool)	0-0, 2-1	Watford FC (Watford)
Luton Town FC (Luton)	2-2, 0-1	Everton FC (Liverpool)
Sheffield Wednesday FC (Sheffield)	2-1	West Ham United FC (London)

1986-87

Football League Division 1 1986-87 Season	Arsenal	Aston Villa	Charlton Ath.	Chelsea	Coventry City	Everton	Leicester City	Liverpool	Luton Town	Manchester C.	Man. United	Newcastle Utd.	Norwich City	Nottingham F.	Oxford United	Q.P.R.	Sheffield Wed.	Southampton	Tottenham H.	Watford	West Ham Utd.	Wimbledon
Arsenal FC	■	2-1	2-1	3-1	0-0	0-1	4-1	0-1	3-0	3-0	1-0	0-1	1-2	0-0	0-0	3-1	2-0	1-0	0-0	3-1	0-0	3-1
Aston Villa FC	0-4	■	2-0	0-0	1-0	0-1	2-0	2-2	2-1	0-0	3-3	2-0	1-4	0-0	1-2	0-1	1-2	3-1	0-3	1-1	4-0	0-0
Charlton Athletic FC	0-2	3-0	■	0-0	1-1	3-2	2-0	0-0	0-1	5-0	0-0	1-1	1-2	0-1	0-0	2-1	1-1	1-3	0-2	4-3	2-1	0-1
Chelsea FC	1-0	4-1	0-1	■	0-0	1-2	3-1	3-3	1-3	2-1	1-1	1-3	0-0	2-6	4-0	3-1	2-0	1-1	0-2	0-0	1-0	0-4
Coventry City FC	2-1	0-1	2-1	3-0	■	1-1	1-0	1-0	0-1	2-2	1-1	3-0	2-1	1-0	3-0	4-1	1-0	1-1	4-3	1-0	1-3	1-0
Everton FC	0-1	3-0	2-1	2-2	3-1	■	5-1	0-0	3-1	0-0	3-1	3-0	4-0	2-0	3-1	0-0	2-2	3-0	1-0	3-2	4-0	3-0
Leicester City FC	1-1	1-1	1-0	2-2	1-1	0-2	■	2-1	1-1	4-0	1-1	1-1	0-2	3-1	2-0	4-1	6-1	2-3	1-2	1-2	2-0	3-1
Liverpool FC	2-1	3-3	2-0	3-0	2-0	3-1	4-3	■	2-0	0-1	2-0	6-2	3-0	4-0	1-1	1-0	0-1	1-0	1-0	1-0		1-2
Luton Town FC	0-0	2-1	1-0	1-0	2-0	1-0	1-0	4-1	■	1-0	2-1	0-0	0-0	4-2	2-3	1-0	0-0	2-1	3-1	0-2	2-1	0-0
Manchester City FC	3-0	3-1	1-2	1-2	0-1	1-3	1-2	0-1	1-1	■	1-1	0-0	2-2	1-0	1-0	0-0	2-4	1-1	1-2	3-1	3-1	3-1
Manchester United FC	2-0	3-1	0-1	0-1	1-1	0-0	2-0	1-0	1-0	2-0	■	4-1	2-0	3-2	1-0	3-1	5-1	3-3	3-1	2-3	0-1	
Newcastle United FC	1-2	1-1	0-3	1-0	1-2	0-4	2-0	0-2	2-2	3-1	2-1	■	4-1	3-2	0-0	0-2	2-3	2-0	1-1	2-2	4-0	1-0
Norwich City FC	1-1	1-1	1-1	2-2	0-1	0-1	2-1	0-0	1-1	0-0	2-0	2-0	■	2-1	2-1	1-0	4-3	2-1	1-3	1-1	1-1	
Nottingham Forest FC	1-0	6-0	4-0	0-1	0-0	1-0	1-1	1-1	2-2	1-1	2-1	1-1		■	2-0	1-0	3-2	0-0	2-0	1-1	1-1	3-2
Oxford United FC	0-0	2-2	3-2	1-1	2-0	1-1	0-0	1-3	4-2	0-0	2-0	1-1	0-1	2-1	■	0-1	2-1	3-1	2-4	1-3	0-0	3-1
Queen's Park Rangers FC	1-4	1-0	0-0	1-1	3-1	0-1	0-1	1-2		2-1		1-1		3-1	1-1	■	2-2	2-1	2-0	3-2	2-3	2-1
Sheffield Wednesday FC	1-1	2-1	1-1	2-0	2-2	2-2	2-2	1-0	2-1	2-0	1-1	2-3		6-1	7-1		■	3-1	0-1	0-1	2-2	0-2
Southampton FC	0-4	5-0	2-2	1-2	0-2	4-0	2-1	1-4	1-2	1-0	3-0	5-1	1-1					■	2-0	3-1	2-2	
Tottenham Hotspur FC	1-2	3-0	0-1	1-3	1-0	2-0	5-0	1-0	4-0	1-1	3-0	2-3	3-1	1-0	1-1	2-0			■	2-1	4-0	1-2
Watford FC	2-0	4-2	4-1	3-1	2-3	2-1	5-1	1-0	1-0	2-1	1-0	1-1	1-1	1-1	3-0	0-3	0-1	1-1	1-0	■	2-2	0-1
West Ham United FC	3-1	1-1	1-3	5-3	1-0	1-0	4-1	2-5	2-0	0-0	1-1	0-2	1-2	0-1	1-0	0-2	3-1	2-1	1-0		■	2-3
Wimbledon FC	1-2	3-2	2-0	2-1	2-1	1-0	1-3	0-1	0-0	1-0	3-1	2-0	2-1	1-1	1-1	3-0	2-2	2-2	2-1	0-1		■

Division 1

	Division 1	Pd	Wn	Dw	Ls	GF	GA	Pts	
1.	EVERTON FC (LIVERPOOL)	42	26	8	8	76	31	86	
2.	Liverpool FC (Liverpool)	42	23	8	11	72	42	77	
3.	Tottenham Hotspur FC (London)	42	21	8	13	68	43	71	
4.	Arsenal FC (London)	42	20	10	12	58	35	70	
5.	Norwich City FC (Norwich)	42	17	17	8	53	51	68	
6.	Wimbledon FC (London)	42	19	9	14	57	50	66	
7.	Luton Town FC (Luton)	42	18	12	12	47	45	66	
8.	Nottingham Forest FC (Nottingham)	42	18	11	13	64	51	65	
9.	Watford FC (Watford)	42	18	9	15	67	54	63	
10.	Coventry City FC (Coventry)	42	17	12	13	50	45	63	
11.	Manchester United FC (Manchester)	42	14	14	14	52	45	56	
12.	Southampton FC (Southampton)	42	14	10	18	69	68	52	
13.	Sheffield Wednesday FC (Sheffield)	42	13	13	16	58	59	52	
14.	Chelsea FC (London)	42	13	13	16	53	64	52	
15.	West Ham United FC (London)	42	14	10	18	52	67	52	
16.	Queen's Park Rangers FC (London)	42	13	11	18	48	64	50	
17.	Newcastle United FC (Newcastle-upon-Tyne)	42	12	11	19	47	65	47	
18.	Oxford United FC (Oxford)	42	11	13	18	44	69	46	
19.	Charlton Athletic FC (London)	42	11	11	20	45	55	44	PO
20.	Leicester City FC (Leicester)	42	11	9	22	54	76	42	R
21.	Manchester City FC (Manchester)	42	8	15	19	36	57	39	R
22.	Aston Villa FC (Birmingham)	42	8	12	22	45	79	36	R
		924	339	246	339	1215	1215	1263	

Top Goalscorers

1)	Clive ALLEN	(Tottenham Hotspur FC)	33
2)	Ian RUSH	(Liverpool FC)	30
3)	Tony COTTEE	(West Ham United FC)	22

Promotion/Relegation Play-offs

Charlton Athletic FC (London)	1-0, 0-1, 2-1 (aet)	Leeds United AFC (Leeds)
Ipswich Town FC (Ipswich)	0-0, 1-2	Charlton Athletic FC (London)
Leeds United AFC (Leeds)	1-0, 1-2	Oldham Athletic AFC (Oldham)

(Leeds United FC won on the away goals rule.)

Football League Division 2 — 1986-87 Season

	Barnsley	Birmingham C.	Blackburn R.	Bradford City	Brighton & H.A.	Crystal Palace	Derby County	Grimsby Town	Huddersfield T.	Hull City	Ipswich Town	Leeds United	Millwall	Oldham Ath.	Plymouth A.	Portsmouth	Reading	Sheffield United	Shrewsbury T.	Stoke City	Sunderland	W.B.A.
Barnsley FC		2-2	1-1	2-0	3-1	2-3	0-1	1-0	0-1	1-1	2-1	0-1	1-0	1-1	1-1	0-2	2-0	2-2	2-1	0-2	1-0	2-2
Birmingham City FC	1-1		1-1	2-1	2-0	4-1	1-1	1-0	1-1	0-0	2-2	2-1	1-1	1-3	3-2	0-1	1-1	2-1	0-2	0-0	2-0	0-1
Blackburn Rovers FC	4-2	1-0		2-1	1-1	0-2	3-1	2-2	1-2	0-2	0-0	2-1	1-0	1-0	1-2	1-0	0-0	0-2	2-1	2-1	6-1	0-1
Bradford City AFC	0-0	0-0	2-0		2-0	1-2	0-1	4-2	4-3	2-0	3-4	2-0	4-0	0-3	2-2	1-0	3-0	1-1	0-0	1-4	3-2	1-3
Brighton & Hove Albion FC	1-1	2-0	0-2	2-2		2-0	0-1	0-1	1-1	2-1	1-2	0-1	0-1	1-2	1-1	0-0	1-1	2-0	3-0	1-0	0-3	2-0
Crystal Palace FC	0-1	6-0	2-0	1-1	2-0		1-0	0-3	1-0	5-1	3-3	1-0	2-1	2-1	0-0	1-0	1-3	1-2	2-3	1-0	2-0	1-1
Derby County FC	3-2	2-2	3-2	1-0	4-1	1-0		4-0	2-0	1-1	2-1	2-1	1-1	0-1	4-2	0-0	3-0	2-0	3-1	0-0	3-2	1-1
Grimsby Town FC	0-1	0-1	1-0	0-0	1-2	0-1	0-1		0-1	2-2	1-1	0-0	1-0	2-2	1-1	0-2	3-2	1-0	0-1	1-1	1-1	3-1
Huddersfield Town AFC	2-2	2-2	1-2	5-2	2-1	1-2	2-0	0-0		1-3	1-2	1-1	3-0	5-4	1-2	2-0	2-0	1-1	2-1	2-2	0-2	2-1
Hull City AFC	3-4	3-2	0-0	2-1	1-0	3-0	1-1	1-1	0-0		2-1	0-0	2-1	1-0	0-3	0-2	0-2	0-0	3-0	0-4	1-0	2-0
Ipswich Town FC	1-0	3-0	3-1	1-0	1-0	3-0	0-2	1-1	3-0	0-0		2-0	0-0	3-0	0-1	1-1	2-2	1-0	2-0	1-1	1-0	1-0
Leeds United AFC	2-2	4-0	0-0	1-0	3-1	3-0	2-0	2-0	1-1	3-0	3-2		2-0	0-2	4-0	3-1	3-2	0-1	1-0	2-1	1-1	3-2
Millwall FC	1-0	0-2	2-2	1-2	3-1	0-1	0-1	1-0	4-0	0-1	1-0	1-2		0-0	3-1	1-1	2-1	1-0	4-0	1-1	1-1	0-1
Oldham Athletic AFC	2-0	2-2	3-0	2-1	1-1	1-0	1-4	4-1	2-0	0-0	2-1	0-1	2-1		2-1	0-0	4-0	3-1	3-0	2-0	1-1	2-1
Plymouth Argyle FC	2-0	0-0	1-1	3-2	2-2	3-1	1-1	5-0	1-1	4-0	2-0	1-1	1-0	3-2		2-3	1-0	1-0	3-2	1-3	2-4	1-0
Portsmouth FC	2-1	2-0	1-0	2-1	1-0	2-0	3-1	2-1	1-0	1-0	1-1	1-1	2-0	3-0	0-1		1-0	1-2	3-0	3-0	3-1	2-1
Reading FC	0-0	2-2	4-0	0-1	2-1	1-0	2-0	2-3	3-2	1-0	1-4	2-1	0-1	2-3	2-0	2-2		2-0	3-1	0-1	1-0	1-1
Sheffield United FC	1-0	1-1	4-1	2-2	0-1	1-0	0-1	1-2	0-0	4-2	0-0	0-0	2-1	2-0	2-1	1-0	3-3		1-1	3-1	2-1	1-1
Shrewsbury Town FC	1-0	1-0	0-1	0-1	1-0	0-0	0-1	4-1	1-2	3-0	2-1	0-2	1-2	2-0	1-1	1-0	0-0	1-0		4-1	0-1	1-0
Stoke City FC	1-2	0-2	1-0	2-3	1-1	3-1	0-2	5-1	2-0	1-1	0-0	7-2	2-0	0-2	1-0	1-1	3-0	5-2	1-0		3-0	1-1
Sunderland AFC	2-3	2-0	3-0	2-3	1-1	1-0	1-2	0-1	2-1	1-0	1-0	1-1	1-1	0-2	2-1	0-0	1-1	1-2	1-1	2-0		0-3
West Bromwich Albion FC	0-1	3-2	0-1	2-2	0-0	1-2	2-0	1-1	1-0	1-1	3-4	3-0	0-1	2-0	0-0	1-0	1-2	1-0	1-2	4-1	2-2	

	Division 2	Pd	Wn	Dw	Ls	GF	GA	Pts	
1.	Derby County FC (Derby)	42	25	9	8	64	38	84	P
2.	Portsmouth FC (Portsmouth)	42	23	9	10	53	28	78	P
3.	Oldham Athletic AFC (Oldham)	42	22	9	11	65	44	75	PO
4.	Leeds United AFC (Leeds)	42	19	11	12	58	44	68	PO
5.	Ipswich Town FC (Ipswich)	42	17	13	12	59	43	64	PO
6.	Crystal Palace FC (London)	42	19	5	18	51	53	62	
7.	Plymouth Argyle FC (Plymouth)	42	16	13	13	62	57	61	
8.	Stoke City FC (Stoke-on-Trent)	42	16	10	16	63	53	58	
9.	Sheffield United FC (Sheffield)	42	15	13	14	50	49	58	
10.	Bradford City AFC (Bradford)	42	15	10	17	62	62	55	
11.	Barnsley FC (Barnsley)	42	14	13	15	49	52	55	
12.	Blackburn Rovers FC (Blackburn)	42	15	10	17	45	55	55	
13.	Reading FC (Reading)	42	14	11	17	52	59	53	
14.	Hull City AFC (Kingston-upon-Hull)	42	13	14	15	41	55	53	
15.	West Bromwich Albion FC (West Bromwich)	42	13	12	17	51	49	51	
16.	Millwall FC (London)	42	14	9	19	39	45	51	
17.	Huddersfield Town AFC (Huddersfield)	42	13	12	17	54	61	51	
18.	Shrewsbury Town FC (Shrewsbury)	42	15	6	21	41	53	51	
19.	Birmingham City FC (Birmingham)	42	11	17	14	47	59	50	
20.	Sunderland AFC (Sunderland)	42	12	12	18	49	59	48	POR
21.	Grimsby Town FC (Cleethorpes)	42	10	14	18	39	59	44	R
22.	Brighton & Hove Albion FC (Hove)	42	9	12	21	37	54	39	R
		924	340	244	340	1131	1131	1264	

Promotion/Relegation Play-offs

Gillingham FC (Gillingham)	1-0, 1-2, 0-2	Swindon Town FC (Swindon)
Gillingham FC (Gillingham)	3-2, 3-4	Sunderland AFC (Sunderland)
	(Gillingham FC won on the away goals rule)	
Wigan Athletic AFC (Wigan)	2-3, 0-0	Swindon Town FC (Swindon)

Football League Division 3 — 1986-87 Season

	Blackpool	Bolton Wanderers	Bournemouth	Brentford	Bristol City	Bristol Rovers	Bury	Carlisle United	Chester City	Chesterfield	Darlington	Doncaster Rovers	Fulham	Gillingham	Mansfield Town	Middlesbrough	Newport County	Notts County	Port Vale	Rotherham United	Swindon Town	Walsall	Wigan Athletic	York City
Blackpool FC		1-1	1-3	2-0	1-0	6-1	1-1	1-2	1-0	0-0	2-1	1-1	1-0	0-1	1-2	0-1	1-1	3-1	2-0	1-0	1-1	1-1	5-1	2-1
Bolton Wanderers FC	1-0		0-1	0-2	0-0	2-2	2-3	2-0	1-1	1-2	4-3	0-1	3-2	3-0	0-1	0-1	0-1	1-1	3-0	0-0	1-2	1-0	1-2	3-1
AFC Bournemouth	1-1	2-1		1-1	2-0	2-0	1-0	2-1	2-0	2-0	1-0	3-2	3-2	0-2	4-1	3-1	2-1	3-0	0-0	2-0	1-0	1-0	3-1	3-0
Brentford FC	1-1	1-2	1-1		1-1	1-2	0-2	3-1	3-1	2-2	5-3	1-1	3-3	3-2	3-1	0-1	2-0	1-0	0-2	2-0	1-1	0-1	2-3	3-1
Bristol City FC	3-1	4-1	2-0	0-2		0-1	2-2	3-0	1-0	1-0	1-1	5-0	0-0	2-0	0-0	2-2	4-0	3-1	1-0	0-1	1-1	2-1	2-1	3-0
Bristol Rovers FC	2-2	1-0	0-3	0-1	0-0		1-1	4-0	3-2	3-2	2-1	2-3	0-0	0-1	0-0	1-2	2-2	0-0	0-0	0-2	3-4	0-3	1-0	1-0
Bury FC	4-1	0-0	0-1	1-1	1-2	1-0		0-0	1-1	1-1	2-0	2-0	2-1	1-0	1-1	0-3	4-3	0-2	2-2	0-2	1-2	4-0	1-3	1-0
Carlisle United FC	3-1	0-0	0-0	0-0	1-2	2-0	2-1		0-2	3-0	1-0	1-0	1-3	2-4	1-2	0-1	2-2	0-2	2-0	3-5	0-3	0-3	0-2	2-2
Chester City FC	1-4	0-0	2-2	1-1	0-3	3-1	0-1	2-2		1-1	6-0	1-0	2-2	1-1	1-1	1-2	2-0	1-2	1-2	1-0	2-0	0-0	1-2	2-1
Chesterfield FC	1-1	0-0	1-1	1-2	0-3	1-1	1-1	3-2	0-1		1-0	4-1	3-1	0-1	2-1	3-2	1-2	2-4	2-1	1-3	3-2	4-3	1-0	
Darlington FC	1-1	0-1	0-3	1-1	0-0	1-1	4-1	0-1	1-0	1-1		2-2	0-1	1-1	2-1	0-1	1-3	2-1	3-2	1-1	0-0	1-3	1-0	2-2
Doncaster Rovers FC	2-2	3-0	0-3	2-0	1-0	2-0	0-0	2-0	1-1	1-1	0-0		2-1	2-0	1-0	0-2	0-1	1-2	2-1	3-0	2-2	2-2	2-2	3-1
Fulham FC	0-1	4-2	1-3	1-3	0-3	2-2	2-1	3-0	0-5	3-1	3-1	0-0		2-2	1-1	2-2	2-0	3-1	0-6	1-1	0-2	2-2	2-2	1-0
Gillingham FC	2-1	1-0	2-1	2-0	1-1	4-1	1-0	1-0	1-2	3-0	4-1	2-1	4-1		2-0	0-0	1-1	3-1	0-0	1-0	1-3	4-0	0-0	2-0
Mansfield Town FC	1-1	2-2	1-1	1-0	2-0	5-0	1-3	2-0	2-3	1-1	1-0	2-1	1-1	1-0		1-1	1-0	1-2	0-1	0-0	0-0	2-0	1-5	1-1
Middlesbrough FC	1-3	0-0	4-0	2-0	1-0	1-0	3-1	1-0	1-2	2-0	1-1	1-0	3-0	3-0	1-0		2-0	2-0	2-2	0-0	1-0	3-1	0-0	3-1
Newport County AFC	1-1	2-1	0-1	2-2	0-1	0-1	2-2	1-1	2-2	1-0	3-0	3-2	0-0	1-2	0-3	0-1		1-1	0-2	1-2	2-2	2-4	1-2	1-1
Notts County FC	3-2	0-0	1-1	1-1	2-0	3-0	1-2	2-1	1-1	2-1	2-2	2-3	3-1	0-0	1-0	5-2			4-1	5-0	2-3	2-1	2-0	5-1
Port Vale FC	1-6	1-1	1-2	4-1	0-0	4-1	2-0	0-1	2-1	2-2	1-2	4-2	0-1	1-2	3-2	0-0	6-1	1-1		1-1	3-4	4-1	0-1	2-3
Rotherham United	1-0	1-0	4-2	2-3	0-1	2-1	2-1	3-0	0-1	0-0	2-0	0-0	0-1	2-2	1-4	3-1	1-1	1-1	1-1		1-2	1-0	0-2	0-0
Swindon Town FC	2-6	2-0	1-1	2-0	1-2	1-2	1-0	2-0	1-1	2-1	1-0	1-1	1-1	3-0	1-0	3-0	1-2	1-0	2-0			0-0	3-1	3-1
Walsall FC	2-1	3-3	2-0	5-2	1-1	0-3	3-1	3-0	1-0	2-1	4-2	1-3	1-1	1-0	2-0	1-0	2-0	1-2	5-2	4-1	1-0		2-3	3-2
Wigan Athletic AFC	4-1	2-1	0-2	1-1	3-1	4-3	1-0	2-0	2-2	1-1	1-1	1-1	2-0	3-1	3-0	0-2	1-2	1-0	2-1	2-1	3-2	5-1		3-2
York City FC	1-1	2-1	2-0	2-1	1-1	1-0	1-0	2-0	1-1	1-1	3-1	1-1	1-1	2-1	1-3	3-1	3-0	1-1	1-4	2-1	0-3	1-5	1-1	

Division 3		Pd	Wn	Dw	Ls	GF	GA	Pts	
1.	AFC Bournemouth (Bournemouth)	46	29	10	7	76	40	97	P
2.	Middlesbrough FC (Middlesbrough)	46	28	10	8	67	30	94	P
3.	Swindon Town FC (Swindon)	46	25	12	9	77	47	87	POP
4.	Wigan Athletic AFC (Wigan)	46	25	10	11	83	60	85	PO
5.	Gillingham FC (Gillingham)	46	23	9	14	65	48	78	PO
6.	Bristol City FC (Bristol)	46	21	14	11	63	36	77	
7.	Notts County FC (Nottingham)	46	21	13	12	77	56	76	
8.	Walsall FC (Walsall)	46	22	9	15	80	67	75	
9.	Blackpool FC (Blackpool)	46	16	16	14	74	59	64	
10.	Mansfield Town FC (Mansfield)	46	15	16	15	52	55	61	
11.	Brentford FC (London)	46	15	15	16	64	66	60	
12.	Port Vale FC (Stoke-on-Trent)	46	15	12	19	76	70	57	
13.	Doncaster Rovers FC (Doncaster)	46	14	15	17	56	62	57	
14.	Rotherham United FC (Rotherham)	46	15	12	19	48	57	57	
15.	Chester City FC (Chester)	46	13	17	16	61	59	56	
16.	Bury FC (Bury)	46	14	13	19	54	60	55	
17.	Chesterfield FC (Chesterfield)	46	13	15	18	56	69	54	
18.	Fulham FC (London)	46	12	17	17	59	77	53	
19.	Bristol Rovers FC (Bristol)	46	13	12	21	49	75	51	
20.	York City FC (York)	46	12	13	21	55	79	49	
21.	Bolton Wanderers FC (Bolton)	46	10	15	21	46	58	45	POR
22.	Carlisle United FC (Carlisle)	46	10	8	28	39	78	38	R
23.	Darlington FC (Darlington)	46	7	16	23	45	77	37	R
24.	Newport County AFC (Newport)	46	8	13	25	49	86	37	R
		1104	396	312	396	1471	1471	1500	

Promotion/Relegation Play-offs

Aldershot FC (Aldershot)	2-0, 1-0	Wolverhampton Wanderers FC (Wolverhampton)
Aldershot FC (Aldershot)	1-0, 2-2	Bolton Wanderers FC (Bolton)
Colchester United FC (Colchester)	0-2, 0-0	Wolverhampton Wanderers FC (Wolverhampton)

Football League Division 4 — 1986-87 Season

	Ald	Bur	Cam	Car	Col	Cre	Exe	Hal	Har	Her	Lin	Nor	Ori	Pet	Pre	Roc	Scu	Sou	Sto	Swa	Tor	Tra	Wol	Wre
Aldershot Town FC		2-0	4-1	1-2	1-0	1-0	2-1	4-1	1-1	1-0	4-0	3-3	1-2	1-1	0-0	2-1	2-1	0-1	3-1	4-1	1-1	0-2	1-2	1-0
Burnley FC	0-1		0-2	1-3	2-1	4-0	0-0	3-0	1-1	0-6	3-1	2-1	2-1	0-0	1-4	0-3	1-0	2-1	2-0	1-1	2-2	2-2	2-5	0-0
Cambridge United FC	0-3	3-1		2-1	0-1	0-3	2-2	1-0	3-0	2-1	1-1	2-3	2-0	1-1	2-0	3-0	1-1	1-2	5-0	1-0	3-3	1-1	0-0	1-0
Cardiff City AFC	2-0	1-0	3-0		0-2	1-1	0-0	0-0	4-0	4-1	1-1	1-1	0-1	1-1	0-0	1-0	0-2	1-1	0-0	3-1	0-2	0-2	0-0	0-0
Colchester United FC	0-1	1-0	1-2	3-1		2-1	1-1	3-1	2-1	2-0	2-0	3-1	0-0	1-3	0-2	2-0	1-0	1-2	5-1	2-1	3-0	1-1	3-0	2-1
Crewe Alexandra FC	1-3	1-0	0-0	1-2	1-1		2-2	2-2	1-0	1-2	1-2	0-5	3-2	1-3	2-2	5-1	2-2	2-1	5-0	1-1	1-0	3-2	1-1	1-1
Exeter City FC	4-0	3-0	1-1	0-0	2-0	1-0		2-2	2-0	1-0	2-0	1-1	1-0	1-2	1-1	0-0	0-0	4-0	2-2	2-2	1-0	1-3	1-1	4-2
Halifax Town AFC	1-0	2-2	1-0	1-1	0-0	0-3	2-0		1-0	2-1	1-2	3-6	4-0	1-0	1-3	3-1	1-1	0-2	1-0	2-4	1-0	3-4	2-1	2-1
Hartlepool United FC	1-1	2-2	2-2	1-1	1-1	0-5	1-0	0-0		0-0	2-1	3-3	1-3	1-2	2-2	1-1	0-2	1-0	1-0	1-1	2-1	1-1	0-1	0-1
Hereford United FC	1-0	2-0	2-3	0-2	2-3	2-0	1-1	1-0	4-0		0-0	3-2	1-1	2-0	2-3	0-1	2-1	0-1	1-2	2-0	2-2	1-0	2-0	0-0
Lincoln City FC	0-2	2-1	0-3	0-1	3-1	2-1	1-1	0-0	1-4	0-0		3-1	2-0	1-2	1-1	1-1	1-3	0-0	4-0	1-1	3-1	3-0	0-1	0-1
Northampton Town	4-2	4-2	3-0	4-1	3-2	2-1	4-0	1-0	1-1	3-2	3-1		2-0	2-1	3-1	5-0	2-1	2-1	1-0	1-0	2-0	2-1	2-2	2-0
Orient FC	1-3	2-0	3-0	2-0	1-0	1-1	2-0	1-3	2-0	2-0	2-1	0-1		1-0	1-2	3-0	3-1	1-0	1-0	1-4	3-2	2-2	3-1	2-4
Peterborough United	1-1	1-1	2-1	1-2	2-0	1-2	2-2	2-0	3-1	2-1	0-1	0-1	0-1		2-1	1-1	2-0	0-0	1-1	2-1	2-1	0-1	1-0	1-0
Preston North End	1-2	2-1	1-0	1-1	1-0	2-1	3-2	0-0	3-2	3-0	1-0	1-0	0-0	1-0		2-4	2-1	2-0	3-0	2-1	1-1	1-0	2-2	1-0
Rochdale AFC	3-1	0-2	2-0	0-0	0-1	1-1	0-0	5-3	0-2	2-0	1-1	1-2	0-0	3-2	0-2		1-1	1-2	2-1	2-0	3-3	0-1	0-3	3-3
Scunthorpe United	2-0	2-1	1-1	1-3	5-2	2-1	3-1	1-2	3-1	2-1	2-2	0-2	2-0	4-0	2-0	2-0		3-0	1-2	3-2	2-0	6-0	0-2	3-3
Southend United FC	2-0	2-1	3-1	2-0	1-1	3-1	2-3	1-1	2-0	1-0	0-4	2-1	2-2	1-2	5-3	3-1	3-1		0-0	1-2	4-0	3-0	1-0	0-3
Stockport County FC	0-0	0-1	3-2	2-0	1-1	2-1	0-0	2-0	0-2	1-2	1-0	0-3	2-2	3-1	1-3	1-1	1-0	0-2		3-1	0-0	0-2	0-2	2-1
Swansea City FC	2-1	2-2	2-0	0-2	1-2	1-1	1-0	0-3	2-0	1-1	1-3	2-0	4-1	0-1	1-1	1-0	0-1	1-2	1-0		0-1	2-0	1-0	0-3
Torquay United FC	2-2	1-1	1-0	1-0	3-1	2-2	1-0	1-1	1-1	0-1	1-1	0-1	2-2	1-1	2-2	2-1	1-0	3-5	3-1	3-0		0-2	1-2	2-1
Tranmere Rovers FC	1-1	2-1	1-1	2-1	3-4	3-2	1-0	3-4	1-1	3-3	1-1	1-1	1-1	1-0	1-3	0-3	1-1	2-2	0-3	1-1	2-2		0-1	0-2
Wolverhampton W	3-0	0-1	1-2	0-1	2-0	2-3	2-2	1-2	4-1	1-0	3-0	1-1	3-1	0-3	1-0	0-0	1-0	1-2	3-1	4-0	1-0	2-1		0-3
Wrexham AFC	3-0	2-2	2-1	5-1	0-1	2-1	0-0	3-1	1-1	2-2	1-1	1-3	4-3	1-1	2-2	1-1	4-0	0-0	0-0	2-1	1-1	0-0	1-1	

	Division 4	Pd	Wn	Dw	Ls	GF	GA	Pts	
1.	Northampton Town FC (Northampton)	46	30	9	7	103	53	99	P
2.	Preston North End FC (Preston)	46	26	12	8	72	47	90	P
3.	Southend United FC (Southend-on-Sea)	46	25	5	16	68	55	80	P
4.	Wolverhampton Wanderers FC (Wolverhampton)	46	24	7	15	69	50	70	PO
5.	Colchester United FC (Colchester)	46	21	7	18	64	56	70	PO
6.	Aldershot FC (Aldershot)	46	20	10	16	64	57	70	POP
7.	Orient FC (London)	46	20	9	17	64	61	69	*
8.	Scunthorpe United FC (Scunthorpe)	46	18	12	16	73	57	66	
9.	Wrexham AFC (Wrexham)	46	15	20	11	70	51	65	
10.	Peterborough United FC (Peterborough)	46	17	14	15	57	50	65	
11.	Cambridge United FC (Cambridge)	46	17	11	18	60	62	62	
12.	Swansea City FC (Swansea)	46	17	11	18	56	61	62	
13.	Cardiff City AFC (Cardiff)	46	15	16	15	48	50	61	
14.	Exeter City FC (Exeter)	46	11	23	12	53	49	56	
15.	Halifax Town AFC (Halifax)	46	15	10	21	59	74	55	
16.	Hereford United FC (Hereford)	46	14	11	21	60	61	53	
17.	Crewe Alexandra FC (Crewe)	46	13	14	19	70	72	53	
18.	Hartlepool United FC (Hartlepool)	46	11	18	17	44	65	51	
19.	Stockport County FC (Stockport)	46	13	12	21	40	69	51	
20.	Tranmere Rovers FC (Birkenhead)	46	11	17	18	54	72	50	
21.	Rochdale AFC (Rochdale)	46	11	17	18	54	73	50	
22.	Burnley FC (Burnley)	46	12	13	21	53	74	49	
23.	Torquay United FC (Torquay)	46	10	18	18	56	72	48	
24.	Lincoln City FC (Lincoln)	46	12	12	22	45	65	48	R
		1104	398	308	398	1456	1456	1502	

Promoted to Division 4: Scarborough FC (Scarborough)

* Orient FC (London) changed their club name to Leyton Orient FC (London) for the next season.

F.A. CUP FINAL   (Wembley Stadium, London – 16/05/1987 – 98,000)

COVENTRY CITY FC (COVENTRY)	3-2 (aet)	Tottenham Hotspur FC (London)
Bennett, Houchen, Mabbutt o.g.	*(H.T. 1-2)*	*C.Allen, Kilcline o.g.*

Coventry: Ogrizovic, Phillips, Downs, McGrath, Kilcline (Rodger), Peake, Bennett, Gynn, Regis, Houchen, Pickering.

Tottenham: Clemence, Hughton (Claesen), M.Thomas, Hodge, Gough, Mabbutt, C.Allen, P.Allen, Waddle, Hoddle, Ardiles (Stevens).

Semi-finals

Coventry City FC (Coventry)	3-2	Leeds United AFC (Leeds)
Tottenham Hotspur FC (London)	4-1	Watford FC (Watford)

Quarter-finals

Arsenal FC (London)	1-3	Watford FC (Watford)
Sheffield Wednesday FC (Sheffield)	0-3	Coventry City FC (Coventry)
Wigan Athletic AFC (Wigan)	0-2	Leeds United AFC (Leeds)
Wimbledon FC (London)	0-2	Tottenham Hotspur FC (London)

1987-88

Football League Division 1 1987-88 Season	Arsenal	Charlton Athletic	Chelsea	Coventry City	Derby County	Everton	Liverpool	Luton Town	Manchester United	Newcastle United	Norwich City	Nottingham Forest	Oxford United	Portsmouth	Q.P.R.	Sheffield Wednesday	Southampton	Tottenham Hotspur	Watford	West Ham United	Wimbledon
Arsenal FC	■	4-0	3-1	1-1	2-1	1-1	1-2	2-1	1-2	1-1	2-0	0-2	2-0	6-0	0-0	3-1	0-1	2-1	0-1	1-0	3-0
Charlton Athletic FC	0-3	■	2-2	2-2	0-1	0-0	0-2	1-0	1-3	2-0	2-0	1-2	0-0	2-1	0-1	3-1	1-1	1-1	1-0	3-0	1-1
Chelsea FC	1-1	1-1	■	1-0	1-0	0-0	1-1	3-0	1-2	2-2	1-0	4-3	2-1	0-0	1-1	2-1	0-1	0-0	1-1	1-1	1-1
Coventry City FC	0-0	0-0	3-3	■	0-3	1-2	1-4	4-0	0-0	1-3	0-0	0-3	1-0	1-0	0-0	3-0	2-3	2-1	1-0	0-0	3-3
Derby County FC	0-0	1-1	2-0	2-0	■	0-0	1-1	1-2	2-1	1-2	0-1	0-1	0-0	0-2	2-2	2-0	1-2	1-1	1-0	0-1	
Everton FC	1-2	1-1	4-1	1-2	3-0	■	1-0	2-0	2-1	1-0	1-0	1-0	0-0	2-1	2-0	4-0	1-0	0-0	2-0	3-1	2-2
Liverpool FC	2-0	3-2	2-1	4-0	4-0	2-0	■	1-1	3-3	4-0	0-0	5-0	2-0	4-0	4-0	1-0	1-1	1-0	4-0	0-0	2-1
Luton Town FC	1-1	1-0	3-0	0-1	1-0	2-1	0-1	■	1-1	4-0	1-2	1-1	7-4	4-1	2-1	2-2	2-2	2-0	2-1	2-2	2-0
Manchester United FC	0-0	0-0	3-1	1-0	4-1	2-1	1-1	3-0	■	2-2	2-1	2-2	3-1	4-1	2-1	4-1	0-2	1-0	2-0	3-1	2-1
Newcastle United FC	0-1	2-1	3-1	2-2	0-0	1-1	1-4	4-0	1-0	■	1-3	0-1	3-1	1-1	1-1	2-2	2-1	2-0	3-0	2-1	1-2
Norwich City FC	2-4	2-0	3-0	3-1	1-2	0-3	0-0	2-2	1-0	1-1	■	0-2	4-2	0-1	1-1	0-3	0-1	2-1	0-0	4-1	0-1
Nottingham Forest FC	0-1	2-2	3-2	4-1	2-1	0-0	2-1	1-1	0-0	0-2	2-0	■	5-3	5-0	4-0	3-3	3-0	1-0	0-0	0-0	
Oxford United FC	0-0	2-1	4-4	1-0	0-0	1-1	0-3	2-5	0-2	1-3	3-0	0-2	■	4-2	2-0	0-3	0-0	0-0	1-1	1-2	2-5
Portsmouth FC	1-1	1-1	0-3	0-0	2-1	0-1	0-2	3-1	1-2	1-2	2-2	0-1	2-2	■	0-1	1-2	2-2	0-0	1-1	2-1	2-1
Queen's Park Rangers FC	2-0	2-0	3-1	1-2	1-1	1-0	0-1	2-0	0-2	1-1	3-0	2-1	3-2	2-1	■	1-1	3-0	2-0	0-0	0-1	1-0
Sheffield Wednesday FC	3-3	2-0	3-0	0-3	2-1	1-0	1-5	0-2	2-4	0-1	1-0	0-1	1-1	1-0	3-1	■	2-1	0-3	2-3	2-1	1-0
Southampton FC	4-2	0-1	3-0	1-2	1-2	0-4	2-2	1-1	2-2	1-1	0-0	1-0	3-0	0-2	0-1	1-1	■	2-1	1-0	2-1	2-2
Tottenham Hotspur FC	1-2	0-1	1-0	2-2	0-0	2-1	0-2	1-1	1-1	3-1	1-3	3-0	0-1	1-1	2-0	2-1		■	2-1	2-1	0-3
Watford FC	2-0	2-1	0-3	0-1	1-1	1-2	1-4	0-1	0-1	1-1	0-1	0-0	3-0	0-0	0-1	1-3	0-1	1-1	■	1-2	1-0
West Ham United FC	0-1	1-1	4-1	1-1	1-1	0-0	1-1	1-1	1-1	2-0	3-2	1-1	0-3	0-1	0-1	0-1	1-0			■	1-2
Wimbledon FC	3-1	4-1	2-2	1-2	2-1	1-1	1-1	2-0	2-1	0-0	1-0	1-1	1-1	2-2	1-2	1-1	2-0	3-0	1-2	1-1	■

	Division 1	Pd	Wn	Dw	Ls	GF	GA	Pts	
1.	LIVERPOOL FC (LIVERPOOL)	40	26	12	2	87	24	90	
2.	Manchester United FC (Manchester)	40	23	12	5	71	38	81	
3.	Nottingham Forest FC (Nottingham)	40	20	13	7	67	39	73	
4.	Everton FC (Liverpool)	40	19	13	8	53	27	70	
5.	Queen's Park Rangers FC (London)	40	19	10	11	48	38	67	
6.	Arsenal FC (London)	40	18	12	10	58	39	66	
7.	Wimbledon FC (London)	40	14	15	11	58	47	57	
8.	Newcastle United FC (Newcastle-upon-Tyne)	40	14	14	12	55	53	56	
9.	Luton Town FC (Luton)	40	14	11	15	57	58	53	
10.	Coventry City FC (Coventry)	40	13	14	13	46	53	53	
11.	Sheffield Wednesday FC (Sheffield)	40	15	8	17	52	66	53	
12.	Southampton FC (Southampton)	40	12	14	14	49	53	50	
13.	Tottenham Hotspur FC (London)	40	12	11	17	38	48	47	
14.	Norwich City FC (Norwich)	40	12	9	19	40	52	45	
15.	Derby County FC (Derby)	40	10	13	17	35	45	43	
16.	West Ham United FC (London)	40	9	15	16	40	52	42	
17.	Charlton Athletic FC (London)	40	9	15	16	38	52	42	
18.	Chelsea FC (London)	40	9	15	16	50	68	42	POR
19.	Portsmouth FC (Portsmouth)	40	7	14	19	36	66	35	R
20.	Watford FC (Watford)	40	7	11	22	27	51	32	R
21.	Oxford United FC (Oxford)	40	6	13	21	44	80	31	R
		840	288	264	288	1049	1049	1128	

Top Goalscorers

1)	John ALDRIDGE	(Liverpool FC)	26
2)	Brian McCLAIR	(Manchester United FC)	24
3)	Nigel CLOUGH	(Nottingham Forest FC)	20

Promotion/Relegation Play-offs

Middlesbrough FC (Middlesbrough)	2-0, 0-1	Chelsea FC (London)
Blackburn Rovers FC (Blackburn)	0-2, 1-4	Chelsea FC (London)
Bradford City AFC (Bradford)	2-1, 0-2 (aet)	Middlesbrough FC (Middlesbrough)

Football League Division 2 — 1987-88 Season

	Aston Villa	Barnsley	Birmingham	Blackburn R.	Bournemouth	Bradford City	Crystal Palace	Huddersfield T.	Hull City	Ipswich Town	Leeds United	Leicester City	Man. City	Middlesbro'	Millwall	Oldham Ath.	Plymouth A.	Reading	Sheffield U.	Shrewsbury T.	Stoke City	Swindon Town	W.B.A.
Aston Villa FC	■	0-0	0-2	1-1	1-1	1-0	4-1	1-1	5-0	1-0	1-2	2-1	1-1	0-1	1-2	1-2	5-2	2-1	1-1	1-0	0-1	2-1	0-0
Barnsley FC	1-3	■	2-2	0-1	2-1	3-0	2-1	1-0	1-3	2-3	1-1	1-1	3-1	0-3	4-1	1-1	2-1	5-2	1-2	2-1	5-2	0-1	3-1
Birmingham City FC	1-2	2-0	■	1-0	1-1	1-1	0-6	2-0	1-1	1-0	0-0	2-2	0-3	0-0	1-0	1-3	0-1	2-2	1-0	0-0	2-0	1-1	0-1
Blackburn Rovers FC	3-2	0-1	2-0	■	3-1	1-1	2-0	2-2	2-1	1-0	1-1	3-3	2-1	0-2	2-1	1-0	1-1	1-1	4-1	2-2	2-0	0-0	3-1
AFC Bournemouth	1-2	1-2	4-2	1-1	■	2-0	2-3	0-2	6-2	1-1	0-0	2-3	0-2	0-0	1-2	2-2	2-2	3-0	1-2	2-0	0-0	2-0	3-2
Bradford City AFC	2-4	1-1	4-0	2-1	2-0	■	2-0	0-1	2-0	2-3	0-0	4-1	2-4	2-0	3-1	5-3	3-1	3-0	2-0	1-1	1-4	2-0	4-1
Crystal Palace FC	1-1	3-2	3-0	2-0	3-0	1-1	■	2-1	2-2	1-2	3-0	2-1	2-0	3-1	1-0	3-1	5-1	2-3	2-1	1-2	2-0	2-1	4-1
Huddersfield Town AFC	0-1	2-2	2-2	1-2	1-2	1-2	2-2	■	0-2	1-2	0-0	1-0	1-4	2-1	2-2	2-1	0-2	0-2	1-1	0-0	0-3	0-3	1-3
Hull City AFC	2-1	1-2	2-0	2-2	2-1	0-0	2-1	4-0	■	1-0	3-1	2-2	3-1	0-0	0-1	1-0	1-2	1-1	2-1	1-0	0-0	1-4	1-0
Ipswich Town FC	1-1	1-0	1-0	0-2	1-2	4-0	2-3	3-0	2-0	■	1-0	0-2	3-0	4-0	1-1	2-0	1-2	2-1	1-0	2-0	2-0	3-2	1-1
Leeds United AFC	1-3	0-2	4-1	2-2	3-2	2-0	1-0	3-0	0-2	1-0	■	1-0	2-0	2-0	1-2	1-1	1-0	0-0	5-0	2-1	0-0	4-2	1-0
Leicester City FC	0-2	0-0	2-0	1-2	0-1	0-2	4-4	3-0	2-1	1-1	3-2	■	1-0	0-0	1-0	4-1	4-0	1-0	1-1	1-3	3-2	3-0	
Manchester City FC	0-2	1-1	3-0	1-2	2-0	2-2	1-3	10-1	2-0	2-0	1-2	4-2	■	1-1	4-0	1-2	2-1	2-0	2-3	1-3	3-0	1-1	4-2
Middlesbrough FC	2-1	2-0	1-1	1-1	3-0	1-2	2-1	2-0	1-0	3-1	2-0	1-2	2-1	■	1-1	1-0	3-1	0-0	6-0	4-1	2-0	2-3	2-1
Millwall FC	2-1	3-1	3-1	1-4	1-2	0-1	1-1	4-1	2-0	2-1	3-1	1-0	0-1	2-1	■	1-1	3-2	3-0	3-1	4-1	2-0	2-2	2-0
Oldham Athletic AFC	0-1	1-0	1-2	4-2	2-0	0-2	1-0	3-2	1-2	3-1	1-1	2-0	1-1	3-1	0-0	■	0-1	4-2	2-2	5-1	4-3	2-1	
Plymouth Argyle FC	1-3	0-0	1-1	3-0	1-2	2-1	1-3	6-1	3-1	0-0	6-3	4-0	3-2	0-1	1-2	1-0	■	1-3	1-0	2-0	3-0	1-0	3-3
Reading FC	0-2	2-1	1-1	0-0	0-0	1-1	2-3	3-2	0-0	1-1	0-1	1-2	0-2	0-0	2-3	3-0	0-1	■	2-1	1-1	0-1	0-1	1-2
Sheffield United FC	1-1	1-0	0-2	3-1	0-1	1-2	1-1	2-2	2-1	4-1	2-2	2-1	1-2	0-2	1-2	0-5	1-0	4-1	■	0-1	0-0	1-0	0-0
Shrewsbury Town FC	1-2	1-1	0-0	1-2	2-1	2-2	2-0	3-1	2-2	0-0	1-0	1-0	0-0	0-0	2-3	2-1	0-1	2-0		■	0-3	2-1	0-1
Stoke City FC	0-0	3-1	3-1	2-1	1-0	1-2	1-1	1-1	1-1	1-2	2-1	2-1	1-3	1-0	2-2	1-0	4-2	1-0	1-1		■	1-0	3-0
Swindon Town FC	0-0	3-0	0-2	1-2	4-2	2-2	2-2	4-1	0-0	4-2	1-2	3-2	3-4	1-1	0-1	2-0	1-1	4-0	2-0	1-1	3-0	■	2-0
West Bromwich Albion FC	0-2	2-2	3-1	0-1	3-0	0-1	1-0	3-2	1-1	2-2	1-4	1-1	1-1	0-0	1-4	0-0	1-0	0-1	4-0	2-1	2-0	1-2	■

#	Division 2	Pd	Wn	Dw	Ls	GF	GA	Pts	
1.	Millwall FC (London)	44	25	7	12	72	52	82	P
2.	Aston Villa FC (Birmingham)	44	22	12	10	68	41	78	P
3.	Middlesbrough FC (Middlesbrough)	44	22	12	10	63	36	78	POP
4.	Bradford City AFC (Bradford)	44	22	11	11	74	54	77	PO
5.	Blackburn Rovers FC (Blackburn)	44	21	14	9	68	52	77	PO
6.	Crystal Palace FC (London)	44	22	9	13	86	59	75	
7.	Leeds United AFC (Leeds)	44	19	12	14	61	51	69	
8.	Ipswich Town FC (Ipswich)	44	19	9	16	61	52	66	
9.	Manchester City FC (Manchester)	44	19	8	17	80	60	65	
10.	Oldham Athletic AFC (Oldham)	44	18	11	15	72	64	65	
11.	Stoke City FC (Stoke-on-Trent)	44	17	11	16	50	57	62	
12.	Swindon Town FC (Swindon)	44	16	11	17	73	60	59	
13.	Leicester City FC (Leicester)	44	16	11	17	62	61	59	
14.	Barnsley FC (Barnsley)	44	15	12	17	61	62	57	
15.	Hull City AFC (Kingston-upon-Hull)	44	14	15	15	54	60	57	
16.	Plymouth Argyle FC (Plymouth)	44	16	8	20	65	67	56	
17.	AFC Bournemouth (Bournemouth)	44	13	10	21	56	68	49	
18.	Shrewsbury Town FC (Shrewsbury)	44	11	16	17	42	54	49	
19.	Birmingham City FC (Birmingham)	44	11	15	18	41	66	48	
20.	West Bromwich Albion FC (West Bromwich)	44	12	11	21	50	69	47	
21.	Sheffield United FC (Sheffield)	44	13	7	24	45	74	46	POR
22.	Reading FC (Reading)	44	10	12	22	44	70	42	R
23.	Huddersfield Town AFC (Huddersfield)	44	6	10	28	41	100	28	R
		1012	379	254	379	1389	1389	1391	

Promotion/Relegation Play-offs

Bristol City FC (Bristol)	1-3, 2-0, 0-4	Walsall FC (Walsall)
Bristol City FC (Bristol)	1-0, 1-1	Sheffield United FC (Sheffield)
Notts County FC (Nottingham)	1-3, 1-1	Walsall FC (Walsall)

Football League Division 3 1987-88 Season

Team	Aldershot Town	Blackpool	Brentford	Brighton & Hove Albion	Bristol City	Bristol Rovers	Bury	Chester City	Chesterfield	Doncaster Rovers	Fulham	Gillingham	Grimsby Town	Mansfield Town	Northampton Town	Notts County	Port Vale	Preston North End	Rotherham United	Southend United	Sunderland	Walsall	Wigan Athletic	York City
Aldershot Town FC	■	0-0	4-1	1-4	2-1	3-0	0-2	4-1	2-0	2-1	0-3	6-0	3-2	3-0	4-4	0-2	3-0	0-0	1-3	0-1	3-2	0-1	3-2	1-2
Blackpool FC	3-2	■	0-1	1-3	4-2	2-1	5-1	0-1	1-0	4-2	2-1	3-3	3-0	2-0	3-1	1-1	1-2	3-0	3-0	1-1	0-2	1-2	0-0	2-1
Brentford FC	3-0	2-1	■	1-1	0-1	1-1	0-3	1-1	2-0	1-1	3-1	2-2	0-2	2-2	0-1	1-0	1-0	2-0	1-1	1-0	0-1	0-0	2-1	1-2
Brighton & Hove Alb.	1-1	1-3	2-1	■	3-2	2-1	2-1	1-0	2-2	2-0	2-0	2-0	0-0	3-1	3-0	1-1	2-0	0-0	1-1	0-0	3-1	2-1	1-0	1-0
Bristol City FC	2-0	2-1	2-3	5-2	■	3-3	3-2	2-2	2-1	1-0	4-0	3-3	1-1	1-2	2-2	2-1	0-1	3-1	2-0	3-2	0-1	0-0	4-1	3-2
Bristol Rovers FC	3-1	2-0	0-0	1-2	1-0	■	0-0	2-2	2-0	4-0	3-1	2-0	4-2	2-1	0-2	1-1	1-0	1-2	3-1	0-0	4-0	3-0	2-3	2-1
Bury FC	1-0	3-1	2-2	2-1	1-1	4-1	■	0-1	2-0	2-1	1-1	2-1	0-2	1-0	0-0	0-1	0-1	4-0	2-2	2-2	2-3	2-2	0-2	0-1
Chester City FC	4-1	1-1	1-1	2-2	1-0	0-3	4-4	■	1-1	1-2	3-1	1-0	0-2	0-5	1-2	1-0	1-0	1-1	1-2	1-1	1-0	1-0	1-0	1-0
Chesterfield FC	1-0	1-1	2-1	0-0	1-4	0-1	1-0	0-0	■	0-1	1-0	1-4	0-3	3-1	0-2	2-0	1-3	0-0	3-2	3-1	1-1	2-1	0-1	2-1
Doncaster Rovers FC	0-0	2-1	0-1	0-2	1-2	0-1	1-2	2-2	1-0	■	2-2	4-2	1-0	0-2	0-1	1-1	3-2	2-2	0-1	0-2	0-4	3-4	2-0	2-0
Fulham FC	1-2	3-1	2-2	1-2	0-0	3-1	0-1	1-0	1-3	4-0	■	0-2	5-0	0-0	0-0	0-0	1-2	0-1	3-1	3-1	0-2	2-0	3-2	3-1
Gillingham FC	2-1	0-0	1-1	1-1	1-1	3-0	3-3	0-1	10-0	3-1	2-2	■	1-1	0-0	1-2	3-1	0-0	4-0	0-2	8-1	0-0	0-1	0-1	3-1
Grimsby Town FC	1-1	1-1	0-1	0-1	1-4	0-0	2-0	2-1	1-1	0-0	2-0	2-0	■	2-3	2-2	0-0	3-1	0-1	2-1	1-3	0-1	0-2	0-2	5-1
Mansfield Town FC	1-0	0-0	2-1	1-1	2-0	1-0	0-0	1-2	0-1	2-0	0-2	2-2	1-0	■	3-1	1-1	4-0	0-0	0-1	1-0	0-4	1-3	0-1	2-1
Northampton Town	1-1	3-3	2-1	1-1	3-0	2-1	0-0	2-0	4-0	1-0	3-2	2-1	2-1	2-0	■	0-1	1-0	0-1	0-0	4-0	0-2	2-2	1-1	0-0
Notts County FC	2-1	2-3	3-0	1-2	0-1	1-1	3-0	1-0	2-0	2-0	5-1	0-1	0-0	1-1	3-1	■	1-2	4-2	4-0	6-2	2-1	3-1	4-4	3-0
Port Vale FC	4-2	0-0	1-0	2-0	1-1	2-1	1-0	1-1	0-1	5-0	1-1	0-0	2-0	1-1	1-1	1-3	■	3-2	0-0	4-1	0-1	2-1	2-1	2-1
Preston North End	0-2	2-1	1-2	3-0	2-0	3-1	1-0	0-1	1-2	2-1	1-1	1-3	1-0	0-0	1-2	3-2	1-2	■	0-0	1-1	2-2	1-0	0-1	3-0
Rotherham United	1-0	0-1	2-0	1-0	4-1	1-1	0-1	5-2	1-1	1-0	0-2	1-2	0-0	2-1	2-2	1-1	1-0	2-2	■	1-1	1-4	0-1	1-1	0-1
Southend United FC	0-1	4-0	2-3	2-1	2-0	4-2	1-0	2-2	3-0	4-1	0-2	1-3	0-0	1-1	1-1	1-2	3-3	1-2	1-1	■	1-4	1-1	3-2	3-1
Sunderland AFC	3-1	2-2	2-0	1-0	0-1	1-1	1-1	0-2	3-2	3-1	2-0	2-1	1-1	4-1	3-1	1-1	2-1	1-1	3-0	7-0	■	1-1	4-1	4-2
Walsall FC	2-0	3-2	4-2	1-1	0-0	2-1	1-0	0-0	2-1	0-1	0-0	3-2	2-1	1-0	2-1	2-1	1-0	5-2	2-1	2-2	1-1	■	1-2	2-1
Wigan Athletic AFC	4-0	0-0	1-1	3-3	1-1	1-0	0-2	1-0	1-2	2-1	1-3	1-1	0-1	2-1	2-2	2-1	2-0	2-0	3-0	1-0	2-2	3-1	■	1-1
York City FC	2-2	1-3	1-1	0-2	0-1	0-4	1-1	2-0	1-0	1-1	1-3	0-2	2-2	2-2	3-5	2-3	1-1	1-2	0-3	2-1	1-3	3-1	3-1	■

	Division 3	Pd	Wn	Dw	Ls	GF	GA	Pts	
1.	Sunderland AFC (Sunderland)	46	27	12	7	92	48	93	P
2.	Brighton & Hove Albion FC (Hove)	46	23	15	8	69	47	84	P
3.	Walsall FC (Walsall)	46	23	13	10	68	50	82	POP
4.	Notts County FC (Nottingham)	46	23	12	11	82	49	81	PO
5.	Bristol City FC (Bristol)	46	21	12	13	77	62	75	PO
6.	Northampton Town FC (Northampton)	46	18	19	9	70	51	73	
7.	Wigan Athletic AFC (Wigan)	46	20	12	14	70	61	72	
8.	Bristol Rovers FC (Bristol)	46	18	12	16	68	56	66	
9.	Fulham FC (London)	46	19	9	18	69	60	66	
10.	Blackpool FC (Blackpool)	46	17	14	15	71	62	65	
11.	Port Vale FC (Stoke-on-Trent)	46	18	11	17	58	56	65	
12.	Brentford FC (London)	46	16	14	16	53	59	62	
13.	Gillingham FC (Gillingham)	46	14	17	15	77	61	59	
14.	Bury FC (Bury)	46	15	14	17	58	57	59	
15.	Chester City FC (Chester)	46	14	16	16	51	62	58	
16.	Preston North End FC (Preston)	46	15	13	18	48	59	58	
17.	Southend United FC (Southend-on-Sea)	46	14	13	19	65	83	55	
18.	Chesterfield FC (Chesterfield)	46	15	10	21	41	70	55	
19.	Mansfield Town FC (Mansfield)	46	14	12	20	48	59	54	
20.	Aldershot FC (Aldershot)	46	15	8	23	64	74	53	
21.	Rotherham United FC (Rotherham)	46	12	16	18	50	66	52	POR
22.	Grimsby Town FC (Cleethorpes)	46	12	14	20	48	58	50	R
23.	York City FC (York)	46	8	9	29	48	91	33	R
24.	Doncaster Rovers FC (Doncaster)	46	8	9	29	40	84	33	R
		1104	399	306	399	1485	1485	1503	

Promotion/Relegation Play-offs

Swansea City FC (Swansea)	2-1, 3-3	Torquay United FC (Torquay)
Swansea City FC (Swansea)	1-0, 1-1	Rotherham United FC (Rotherham)
Torquay United FC (Torquay)	2-1, 1-1	Scunthorpe United FC (Scunthorpe)

Football League Division 4 1987-88 Season

	Bolton Wanderers	Burnley	Cambridge	Cardiff City	Carlisle United	Colchester United	Crewe Alexandra	Darlington	Exeter City	Halifax Town	Hartlepool	Hereford United	Leyton Orient	Newport County	Peterborough Utd.	Rochdale	Scarborough	Scunthorpe United	Stockport County	Swansea City	Torquay United	Tranmere Rovers	Wolves	Wrexham
Bolton Wanderers FC		2-1	2-2	1-0	5-0	4-0	1-1	1-1	1-0	2-0	1-2	1-0	1-0	6-0	2-0	0-0	3-1	0-0	2-1	1-1	1-2	2-0	1-0	2-0
Burnley FC	2-1		0-2	1-2	4-3	0-3	0-0	2-1	3-0	3-1	1-0	0-0	2-0	2-0	1-2	4-0	0-1	1-1	1-1	1-0	1-0	1-1	0-3	1-0
Cambridge United FC	2-2	2-0		0-0	1-2	0-1	4-1	1-0	2-1	2-1	1-1	0-1	2-0	4-0	1-3	1-2	3-3	2-0	0-3	1-0	1-1	1-1	1-1	0-1
Cardiff City AFC	1-0	2-1	4-0		4-2	1-0	2-0	3-1	3-2	0-0	1-1	0-1	1-1	4-0	0-0	1-0	0-1	0-0	1-0	2-1	3-0	3-2	1-1	1-1
Carlisle United FC	0-2	3-4	2-1	0-0		4-0	0-1	3-3	0-0	1-1	1-3	3-1	1-2	3-1	0-2	2-0	4-0	3-1	2-0	0-1	3-3	3-2	0-1	0-4
Colchester United FC	3-0	0-1	0-0	2-1	1-0		1-4	2-1	0-2	2-1	0-0	1-0	0-0	0-0	4-1	1-0	1-3	0-3	2-0	2-1	0-1	0-0	0-1	1-2
Crewe Alexandra FC	2-1	0-1	0-0	0-0	4-1	0-0		3-1	0-0	0-0	0-0	0-0	3-3	2-1	0-1	0-1	1-0	2-2	3-1	2-2	0-1	0-0	0-2	2-0
Darlington FC	1-0	4-2	0-1	0-0	2-1	2-0	1-0		4-1	4-1	1-1	3-1	2-2	0-2	2-1	2-1	1-4	1-2	2-0	1-1	0-0	2-2	2-2	1-1
Exeter City FC	1-1	1-2	3-0	0-1	1-1	0-2	3-1	4-1		1-2	1-0	2-2	2-3	3-0	0-1	1-1	1-0	2-1	3-1	0-1	0-1	2-4	1-4	1-1
Halifax Town AFC	0-0	2-1	1-1	1-1	1-1	1-2	1-2	2-2	2-0		3-1	2-1	1-0	3-1	0-1	1-2	2-2	2-2	2-0	3-1	2-3	2-1	2-1	2-0
Hartlepool United FC	0-0	2-1	2-1	0-1	0-0	3-1	2-1	2-5	3-1	2-1		1-2	2-2	0-0	0-1	1-1	1-0	1-3	0-2	0-0	1-2	0-0	0-2	1-0
Hereford United FC	0-3	2-1	1-0	1-2	2-0	1-0	1-1	1-0	1-1	2-1	4-2		0-3	4-2	0-0	0-0	2-3	0-1	0-0	3-0	0-0	1-1	1-2	0-2
Leyton Orient FC	1-2	4-1	0-2	4-1	4-1	0-0	1-1	4-3	2-3	4-1	0-2	4-0		4-1	2-0	8-0	3-1	1-1	1-1	3-0	0-2	3-1	1-1	2-1
Newport County FC	0-1	0-1	1-0	1-2	1-2	1-2	1-2	2-1	1-1	1-0	2-3	0-0	0-0		0-4	0-1	0-4	1-1	1-2	1-2	3-1	0-3	1-3	2-0
Peterborough United	0-4	5-0		4-3	1-0	2-0	0-4	1-2	2-1	1-1	0-1	1-2	1-2	3-0		1-1	0-0	1-1	0-0	0-1	0-2	2-1	1-1	1-0
Rochdale AFC	2-2	2-1	2-1	2-2	1-2	1-4	2-2	1-3	0-0	0-0	0-2	3-1	1-3	3-0	1-1		1-1	2-1	0-1	2-3	1-1	0-0	0-1	1-2
Scarborough FC	4-0	1-0	1-0	1-1	3-1	3-1	2-0	0-1	3-1	1-1	1-1	2-1	3-1	3-1	1-1	2-1		0-0	1-1	2-0	1-2	2-0	2-2	0-2
Scunthorpe United	1-1	1-1	3-2	1-0		2-2	1-0	1-1	1-0	3-0	3-2	3-1	0-1	5-0	1-0	0-1	2-1		0-0	1-2	2-3	3-0	0-1	3-1
Stockport County FC	1-2	2-0	0-2		3-0	1-1	1-1	2-1	1-1	1-0	0-2	1-2	5-1	0-1	1-1	1-1	1-1			0-2	1-2	0-2		1-1
Swansea City FC	1-0	0-0	1-1	2-2	3-1	1-2	2-4	3-0	0-2		3-0	0-0	1-2	2-1	0-3	3-0	1-1	1-1			1-1	1-2		1-2
Torquay United FC	2-1	1-3	0-1	2-0	1-0	0-0	1-0	0-0	1-1	2-1	1-1	1-0	6-1	0-0	5-0	1-2	3-0	0-1				1-0	0-0	6-1
Tranmere Rovers FC	2-0	0-1	0-1	0-1	3-0	0-2	2-2	2-1	2-1	2-0	3-1	0-1	2-1	4-0	3-1	1-0	1-3	4-0	1-2	1-1			3-0	1-0
Wolverhampton W.	4-0	3-0	3-0	1-4	3-1	2-0	2-2	5-3	3-0	0-1	2-0	2-0	2-1	0-1	2-0	0-0	4-1	1-1	2-0	1-2	3-0			0-2
Wrexham AFC	0-1	1-3	3-0	3-0	4-0	0-1	2-1	0-1	3-0	2-2	2-1	0-0	2-2	4-1	3-1	1-0	2-1	2-1	1-2	2-3	3-0	1-0	4-2	

Division 4

		Pd	Wn	Dw	Ls	GF	GA	Pts	
1.	Wolverhampton Wanderers FC (Wolverhampton)	46	27	9	10	82	43	90	P
2.	Cardiff City AFC (Cardiff)	46	24	13	9	66	41	85	P
3.	Bolton Wanderers FC (Bolton)	46	22	12	12	66	42	78	P
4.	Scunthorpe United FC (Scunthorpe)	46	20	17	9	76	51	77	PO
5.	Torquay United FC (Torquay)	46	21	14	11	66	41	77	PO
6.	Swansea City FC (Swansea)	46	20	10	16	62	56	70	POP
7.	Peterborough United FC (Peterborough)	46	20	10	16	52	53	70	
8.	Leyton Orient FC (London)	46	19	12	15	85	63	69	
9.	Colchester United FC (Colchester)	46	19	10	17	47	51	67	
10.	Burnley FC (Burnley)	46	20	7	19	57	62	67	
11.	Wrexham AFC (Wrexham)	46	20	6	20	69	58	66	
12.	Scarborough FC (Scarborough)	46	17	14	15	56	48	65	
13.	Darlington FC (Darlington)	46	18	11	17	71	69	65	
14.	Tranmere Rovers FC (Birkenhead)	46	19	9	18	61	53	64	-2
15.	Cambridge United FC (Cambridge)	46	16	13	17	50	52	61	
16.	Hartlepool United FC (Hartlepool)	46	15	14	17	50	57	59	
17.	Crewe Alexandra FC (Crewe)	46	13	19	14	57	53	58	
18.	Halifax Town AFC (Halifax)	46	14	14	18	54	59	55	
19.	Hereford United FC (Hereford)	46	14	12	20	41	59	54	-1
20.	Stockport County FC (Stockport)	46	12	15	19	44	58	51	
21.	Rochdale AFC (Rochdale)	46	11	15	20	47	76	48	
22.	Exeter City FC (Exeter)	46	11	13	22	53	68	46	
23.	Carlisle United FC (Carlisle)	46	12	8	26	57	86	44	
24.	Newport County AFC (Newport)	46	6	7	33	35	105	25	R
		1104	410	284	410	1404	1404	1511	

Promoted to Division 4: Lincoln City FC (Lincoln)

Note: Halifax Town AFC (Halifax) had 1 point deducted for fielding an unregistered player. Tranmere Rovers FC (Birkenhead) had 2 points deducted for failing to meet a fixture on a set date.

F.A. CUP FINAL (Wembley Stadium, London – 14/05/1988 – 98,203)

WIMBLEDON FC (LONDON)	1-0	Liverpool FC (Liverpool)

Sanchez 36'

Wimbledon: Beasant, Goodyear, Phelan, Jones, Young, Thorn, Gibson (Soales 64'), Cork (Cunningham 55'), Fashanu, Sanchez, Wise.

Liverpool: Grobbelaar, Gillespie, Ablett, Nicol, Spackman (Mølby 72'), Hansen, Beardsley, Aldridge (Johnston 64'), Houghton, Barnes, McMahon.

Semi-finals

Liverpool FC (Liverpool)	2-1	Nottingham Forest FC (Nottingham)
Luton Town FC (Luton)	1-2	Wimbledon FC (London)

Quarter-finals

Arsenal FC (London)	1-2	Nottingham Forest FC (Nottingham)
Luton Town FC (Luton)	3-1	Portsmouth FC (Portsmouth)
Manchester City FC (Manchester)	0-4	Liverpool FC (Liverpool)
Wimbledon FC (London)	2-1	Watford FC (Watford)

1988-89

Football League Division 1 1988-89 Season	Arsenal	Aston Villa	Charlton Athletic	Coventry City	Derby County	Everton	Liverpool	Luton Town	Manchester United	Middlesbrough	Millwall	Newcastle United	Norwich City	Nottingham Forest	Q.P.R.	Sheffield Wednesday	Southampton	Tottenham Hotspur	West Ham United	Wimbledon
Arsenal FC	■	2-3	2-2	2-0	1-2	2-0	1-1	2-0	2-1	3-0	0-0	1-0	5-0	1-3	2-1	1-1	2-2	2-0	2-1	2-2
Aston Villa FC	0-3	■	1-2	1-1	1-2	2-0	1-1	2-1	0-0	1-1	2-2	3-1	3-1	1-1	2-1	2-0	1-2	2-1	0-1	0-1
Charlton Athletic FC	2-3	2-2	■	0-0	3-0	1-2	0-3	3-0	1-0	2-0	0-3	2-2	1-2	0-1	1-1	2-1	2-2	2-2	0-0	1-0
Coventry City FC	1-0	2-1	3-0	■	0-2	0-1	1-3	1-0	1-0	3-4	0-0	1-2	2-1	2-2	0-3	5-0	2-1	1-1	1-1	2-1
Derby County FC	2-1	2-1	0-0	1-0	■	3-2	0-1	0-1	2-2	1-0	0-1	2-0	0-1	0-2	0-1	1-0	3-1	1-1	1-2	4-1
Everton FC	1-3	1-1	3-2	3-1	1-0	■	0-0	0-2	1-1	2-1	1-1	4-0	1-1	1-1	4-1	1-0	4-1	1-0	3-1	1-1
Liverpool FC	0-2	1-0	2-0	0-0	1-0	1-1	■	5-0	1-0	3-0	1-1	1-2	0-1	1-0	2-0	5-1	2-0	1-1	5-1	1-1
Luton Town FC	1-1	1-1	5-2	2-2	3-0	1-0	1-0	■	0-2	1-0	1-2	0-0	1-0	2-3	0-0	0-1	6-1	1-3	4-1	2-2
Manchester United FC	1-1	1-1	3-0	0-1	0-2	1-2	3-1	2-0	■	1-0	3-0	2-0	1-2	2-0	0-0	1-1	2-2	1-0	2-0	1-0
Middlesbrough FC	0-1	3-3	0-0	1-1	0-1	3-3	0-4	2-1	1-0	■	4-2	1-1	2-3	3-4	1-0	0-1	3-3	2-2	1-0	1-0
Millwall FC	1-2	2-0	1-0	1-0	1-0	2-1	1-2	3-1	0-0	2-0	■	4-0	2-3	2-2	3-2	1-0	1-1	0-5	0-1	0-1
Newcastle United FC	0-1	1-2	0-2	0-3	0-1	2-0	2-2	0-0	0-0	3-0	1-1	■	0-2	0-1	1-2	1-3	3-3	2-2	1-2	2-1
Norwich City FC	0-0	2-2	1-3	1-2	1-0	1-0	0-1	2-2	2-1	0-0	2-2	0-2	■	2-1	1-0	1-1	1-1	3-1	2-1	1-0
Nottingham Forest FC	1-4	4-0	4-0	0-0	1-1	2-0	2-1	0-0	2-0	2-2	4-1	1-1	2-0	■	0-0	1-1	3-0	1-2	1-2	0-1
Queen's Park Rangers FC	0-0	1-0	1-0	2-1	0-1	0-0	0-1	1-1	3-2	0-0	1-2	3-0	1-1	1-2	■	2-0	0-1	1-0	2-1	4-3
Sheffield Wednesday FC	2-1	1-0	3-1	1-2	1-1	1-1	2-2	1-0	0-2	1-0	3-0	1-2	2-2	0-3	0-2	■	1-1	0-2	0-2	1-1
Southampton FC	1-3	3-1	2-0	2-2	0-0	1-1	1-3	2-1	2-1	1-3	2-2	1-0	0-0	1-1	1-4	1-2	■	0-2	4-0	0-0
Tottenham Hotspur FC	2-3	2-0	1-1	1-1	1-3	2-1	1-2	0-0	2-2	3-2	2-0	2-0	2-1	1-2	2-2	0-0	1-2	■	3-0	3-2
West Ham United FC	1-4	2-2	1-3	1-1	1-1	0-1	0-2	1-0	1-3	1-2	3-0	2-0	0-2	3-3	0-0	0-0	1-2	0-2	■	1-2
Wimbledon FC	1-5	1-0	1-1	0-1	4-0	2-1	1-2	4-0	1-1	1-1	1-0	4-0	0-2	4-1	1-0	1-0	2-1	1-2	0-1	■

Division 1

		Pd	Wn	Dw	Ls	GF	GA	Pts	
1.	ARSENAL FC (LONDON)	38	22	10	6	73	36	76	
2.	Liverpool FC (Liverpool)	38	22	10	6	65	28	76	
3.	Nottingham Forest FC (Nottingham)	38	17	13	8	64	43	64	
4.	Norwich City FC (Norwich)	38	17	11	10	48	45	62	
5.	Derby County FC (Derby)	38	17	7	14	40	38	58	
6.	Tottenham Hotspur FC (London)	38	15	12	11	60	46	57	
7.	Coventry City FC (Coventry)	38	14	13	11	47	42	55	
8.	Everton FC (Liverpool)	38	14	12	12	50	45	54	
9.	Queen's Park Rangers FC (London)	38	14	11	13	43	37	53	
10.	Millwall FC (London)	38	14	11	13	47	52	53	
11.	Manchester United FC (Manchester)	38	13	12	13	45	35	51	
12.	Wimbledon FC (London)	38	14	9	15	50	46	51	
13.	Southampton FC (Southampton)	38	10	15	13	52	66	45	
14.	Charlton Athletic FC (London)	38	10	12	16	44	58	42	
15.	Sheffield Wednesday FC (Sheffield)	38	10	12	16	34	51	42	
16.	Luton Town FC (Luton)	38	10	11	17	42	52	41	
17.	Aston Villa FC (Birmingham)	38	9	13	16	45	56	40	
18.	Middlesbrough FC (Middlesbrough)	38	9	12	17	44	61	39	R
19.	West Ham United FC (London)	38	10	8	20	37	62	38	R
20.	Newcastle United FC (Newcastle-upon-Tyne)	38	7	10	21	32	63	31	R
		760	268	224	268	962	962	1028	

Top Goalscorers

1)	Alan SMITH	(Arsenal FC)	23
2)	John ALDRIDGE	(Liverpool FC)	21
3)	Bernard SLAVEN	(Middlesbrough FC)	15

	Barnsley	Birmingham City	Blackburn Rovers	Bournemouth	Bradford City	Brighton & H.A.	Chelsea	Crystal Palace	Hull City	Ipswich Town	Leeds United	Leicester City	Manchester City	Oldham Athletic	Oxford United	Plymouth Argyle	Portsmouth	Shrewsbury Town	Stoke City	Sunderland	Swindon Town	Walsall	Watford	W.B.A.
Barnsley FC	■	0-0	0-1	5-2	0-0	2-2	1-1	1-1	0-2	2-0	2-2	3-0	1-2	4-3	1-0	3-1	1-0	1-0	1-0	3-0	1-1	1-0	2-2	2-1
Birmingham City FC	3-5	■	2-0	0-1	1-0	1-2	1-4	0-1	1-0	1-0	0-0	2-3	0-2	0-0	0-0	0-1	0-0	1-2	0-1	3-2	1-2	1-0	2-3	1-4
Blackburn Rovers FC	2-1	3-0	■	2-0	2-1	2-1	1-1	5-4	4-0	1-0	2-0	0-0	4-0	3-1	3-1	1-2	3-1	0-1	4-3	2-2	0-0	3-0	2-1	1-2
AFC Bournemouth	3-2	0-1	2-1	■	3-0	2-1	1-0	2-0	5-1	1-0	0-0	2-1	0-1	2-2	2-1	0-0	1-0	0-1	0-1	0-1	2-3	2-1	0-1	2-1
Bradford City AFC	1-2	2-2	1-1	0-1	■	0-1	2-2	0-1	1-1	2-2	1-1	2-1	1-1	2-0	0-0	1-1	2-1	1-0	0-0	1-0	2-2	3-1	2-1	2-0
Brighton & Hove Alb.	0-1	4-0	3-0	1-2	1-3	■	0-1	3-1	1-1	0-1	2-1	1-1	2-1	2-0	2-1	2-2	2-1	3-1	1-1	3-0	0-2	2-2	1-0	0-1
Chelsea FC	5-3	3-1	1-2	2-0	3-1	2-0	■	1-0	2-1	3-0	1-0	2-1	1-3	2-2	1-1	5-0	3-3	2-0	2-1	1-1	3-2	2-0	2-2	1-1
Crystal Palace FC	1-1	4-1	2-2	2-3	2-0	2-1	1-1	■	3-1	2-0	0-0	4-2	0-0	2-0	1-0	4-1	2-0	1-1	1-0	1-0	2-1	4-0	0-2	1-0
Hull City AFC	0-0	1-1	1-3	4-0	1-1	5-2	3-0	0-1	■	1-1	1-2	2-2	1-0	1-1	1-2	3-0	1-1	3-0	1-4	0-0	1-0	0-0	0-3	0-1
Ipswich Town FC	2-0	4-0	2-0	3-1	1-1	2-3	0-1	1-2	1-1	■	0-1	2-0	1-0	2-1	1-2	2-2	0-1	2-0	5-1	2-0	1-2	3-1	3-2	2-1
Leeds United AFC	2-0	1-0	2-0	3-0	3-3	1-0	0-2	1-2	2-1	2-4	■	1-1	1-1	0-0	1-1	2-0	1-0	2-3	4-0	2-0	1-0	1-0	0-1	1-1
Leicester City FC	0-1	2-0	4-0	0-1	1-0	1-0	2-0	2-2	0-2	0-1	1-2	■	0-0	1-2	1-0	1-0	2-1	1-1	2-0	3-1	3-3	1-0	2-2	1-1
Manchester City FC	1-2	0-0	1-0	3-3	4-0	2-1	2-3	1-1	4-1	4-0	0-0	4-2	■	1-4	2-1	2-0	4-1	2-2	2-1	1-1	2-1	2-2	3-1	1-1
Oldham Athletic AFC	1-1	4-0	1-1	2-0	1-1	2-1	1-4	2-3	2-2	4-0	2-2	1-1	0-1	■	3-0	2-2	5-3	3-0	2-2	2-2	2-2	3-0	3-1	1-3
Oxford United FC	2-0	3-0	1-1	3-1	3-4	3-2	2-3	1-0	1-0	1-1	3-2	1-1	2-4	1-1	■	0-1	1-0	4-1	3-2	2-4	1-1	1-0	0-4	1-1
Plymouth Argyle FC	1-2	0-1	4-3	1-1	3-1	3-0	0-1	0-2	2-0	0-1	1-0	1-1	0-1	3-0	3-1	■	0-1	0-0	4-0	1-4	4-1	2-0	1-0	1-1
Portsmouth FC	3-0	1-0	1-2	2-1	1-2	2-0	2-3	1-1	1-3	0-1	4-0	3-0	0-1	1-1	2-1	2-0	■	2-0	0-0	2-0	0-2	1-1	2-2	0-0
Shrewsbury Town	2-3	0-0	1-1	1-0	1-3	1-1	1-1	2-1	1-3	1-5	3-3	3-0	0-1	0-0	2-2	2-0	1-2	■	1-2	0-0	0-1	1-0	1-1	1-1
Stoke City FC	1-1	1-0	0-1	2-1	2-1	2-2	0-3	2-1	4-0	1-1	2-3	2-2	3-1	0-0	1-0	2-2	2-2	0-0	■	2-0	2-1	0-3	2-0	0-0
Sunderland AFC	1-0	2-2	2-0	1-1	0-0	1-0	1-2	1-1	2-0	4-0	2-1	2-2	2-4	3-2	1-0	2-1	4-0	2-1	1-1	■	4-0	0-3	1-1	1-1
Swindon Town FC	0-0	2-1	1-1	3-1	1-0	3-0	1-1	1-0	1-0	2-3	0-0	2-1	1-2	2-2	3-0	1-0	1-1	1-0	3-0	4-1	■	1-0	1-1	0-0
Walsall FC	1-3	5-0	1-2	1-1	0-1	1-0	0-7	0-0	1-1	2-4	0-3	0-1	3-3	2-2	1-5	2-2	1-1	1-1	1-2	2-0	2-2	■	0-1	0-0
Watford FC	4-0	1-0	2-2	1-0	2-0	1-1	1-2	0-1	2-0	3-2	1-1	2-1	1-0	3-1	1-1	3-0	1-0	0-0	3-2	0-1	2-3	5-0	■	2-0
West Bromwich Alb.	1-1	0-0	2-0	0-0	1-0	1-0	2-3	5-3	2-0	1-2	2-1	1-1	1-0	3-1	3-2	2-2	3-0	4-0	6-0	0-0	3-1	0-0	0-1	■

Division 2

		Pd	Wn	Dw	Ls	GF	GA	Pts	
1.	Chelsea FC (London)	46	29	12	5	96	50	99	P
2.	Manchester City FC (Manchester)	46	23	13	10	77	53	82	P
3.	Crystal Palace FC (London)	46	23	12	11	71	49	81	POP
4.	Watford FC (Watford)	46	22	12	12	74	48	78	PO
5.	Blackburn Rovers FC (Blackburn)	46	22	11	13	74	59	77	PO
6.	Swindon Town FC (Swindon)	46	20	16	10	68	53	76	PO
7.	Barnsley FC (Barnsley)	46	20	14	12	66	58	74	
8.	Ipswich Town FC (Ipswich)	46	22	7	17	71	61	73	
9.	West Bromwich Albion FC (West Bromwich)	46	18	18	10	65	41	72	
10.	Leeds United AFC (Leeds)	46	17	16	13	59	50	67	
11.	Sunderland AFC (Sunderland)	46	16	15	15	60	60	63	
12.	AFC Bournemouth (Bournemouth)	46	18	8	20	53	62	62	
13.	Stoke City FC (Stoke-on-Trent)	46	15	14	17	57	72	59	
14.	Bradford City AFC (Bradford)	46	13	17	16	52	59	56	
15.	Leicester City FC (Leicester)	46	13	16	17	56	63	55	
16.	Oldham Athletic AFC (Oldham)	46	11	21	14	75	72	54	
17.	Oxford United FC (Oxford)	46	14	12	20	62	70	54	
18.	Plymouth Argyle FC (Plymouth)	46	14	12	20	55	66	54	
19.	Brighton & Hove Albion FC (Hove)	46	14	9	23	57	66	51	
20.	Portsmouth FC (Portsmouth)	46	13	12	21	53	62	51	
21.	Hull City AFC (Kingston-upon-Hull)	46	11	14	21	52	68	47	
22.	Shrewsbury Town FC (Shrewsbury)	46	8	18	20	40	67	42	R
23.	Birmingham City FC (Birmingham)	46	8	11	27	31	76	35	R
24.	Walsall FC (Walsall)	46	5	16	25	41	80	31	R
		1104	389	326	389	1465	1465	1493	

Promotion Play-offs

Blackburn Rovers FC (Blackburn)   3-1, 0-3 (aet)   Crystal Palace FC (London)
Blackburn Rovers FC (Blackburn)   0-0, 1-1   Watford FC (Watford)
(Blackburn Rovers FC won on the away goals rule)
Swindon Town FC (Swindon)   1-0, 0-2   Crystal Palace FC (London)

Football League Division 3 1988-89 Season

	Aldershot Town	Blackpool	Bolton Wanderers	Brentford	Bristol City	Bristol Rovers	Bury	Cardiff City	Chester City	Chesterfield	Fulham	Gillingham	Huddersfield Town	Mansfield Town	Northampton Town	Notts County	Port Vale	Preston North End	Reading	Sheffield United	Southend United	Swansea City	Wigan Athletic	Wolverhampton Wanderers
Aldershot Town FC	■	1-0	0-3	0-0	0-1	1-3	4-1	0-1	1-1	2-0	1-2	0-2	0-1	0-0	5-1	2-3	2-2	2-1	1-1	1-0	2-2	0-1	3-1	1-2
Blackpool FC	4-0	■	2-0	0-3	2-2	1-1	2-2	1-0	1-1	1-2	0-1	4-1	2-1	1-1	3-1	0-1	3-2	1-0	2-4	1-2	3-2	0-0	2-0	0-2
Bolton Wanderers FC	1-0	2-2	■	4-2	2-0	1-1	2-4	4-0	0-1	5-0	3-2	2-1	3-1	0-0	2-1	3-3	1-1	1-0	1-1	2-0	0-0	1-0	1-1	1-2
Brentford FC	2-1	1-0	3-0	■	3-0	2-1	2-2	1-1	0-1	0-1	1-0	1-0	2-0	2-1	2-1	0-2	3-2	1-4	4-0	1-1	1-1	2-2		
Bristol City FC	1-1	1-2	1-1	0-1	■	0-1	3-0	2-0	0-1	4-0	1-5	1-0	6-1	2-0	3-1	0-4	0-1	1-1	2-1	2-0	0-2	2-0	0-1	0-1
Bristol Rovers FC	2-2	1-0	2-0	1-2	1-1	■	1-3	0-1	4-1	2-1	0-0	2-0	5-1	0-0	1-1	2-0	2-2	1-0	1-1	1-1	1-1	1-1	3-2	0-0
Bury FC	0-1	0-0	0-0	3-1	2-1	0-0	■	1-0	2-1	2-1	3-1	1-0	0-6	0-1	0-1	1-1	0-0	1-1	2-1	1-2	3-1	1-0	1-1	3-1
Cardiff City AFC	3-2	0-0	1-0	1-1	2-2	3-0	3-0	■	2-0	0-1	1-2	0-0	1-0	0-0	1-0	1-2	0-0	2-0				2-2	2-2	1-1
Chester City FC	1-1	1-1	0-0	3-2	2-0	0-2	2-0	0-0	■	3-1	7-0	2-0	3-0	0-0	2-1	1-0	1-2	0-1	3-0	0-1	2-4	3-1	1-0	1-1
Chesterfield FC	2-1	0-2	1-1	2-2	1-0	0-3	1-2	4-0	1-2	■	4-1	3-1	0-0	1-3	1-1	3-0	1-2	0-3	2-4	2-1	2-1	2-0	1-1	0-3
Fulham FC	5-1	1-1	1-1	3-3	3-1	0-2	1-0	2-0	4-1	2-1	■	1-2	1-2	1-1	3-2	2-1	2-1	2-1	2-2	1-0	1-0	1-1		2-2
Gillingham FC	1-1	1-0	0-1	0-0	0-1	2-3	3-4	1-2	0-2	0-1	0-1	■	1-2	3-0	1-2	0-1	1-0	1-3	0-1	2-1	1-1	2-3	2-1	0-0
Huddersfield Town	2-1	1-1	0-1	1-2	0-1	2-3	3-2	1-0	3-1	1-1	2-0	1-1	■	2-0	1-2	3-1	0-0	2-0	2-2	3-2	3-2	1-1	1-1	0-0
Mansfield Town FC	1-1	0-1	1-1	1-0	2-2	2-1	1-1	2-2	2-0	3-1	3-1	2-1	1-0	■	1-1	1-1	0-3	2-1	0-1	4-0	0-0	0-1	3-1	
Northampton Town	6-0	4-2	2-3	1-0	1-3	1-2	2-0	3-0	0-2	3-0	2-1	1-2	1-3	2-1	■	1-3	1-3	1-0	1-3	1-2	2-2	1-1	1-1	3-1
Notts County FC	4-1	1-1	2-0	3-0	0-0	3-0	3-0	2-2	4-0	0-1	1-2	3-0	0-1			■	1-4	0-0	3-3	1-4	1-1	1-0	1-0	1-1
Port Vale FC	3-0	1-0	2-1	3-2	0-1	1-0	1-3	6-1	1-2	5-0	3-0	2-1	2-0	1-2	1-2	1-0	■	1-1	3-0	3-3	2-0	2-1	2-1	0-0
Preston North End	2-2	1-0	3-1	5-3	2-0	1-1	1-0	3-3	3-3	6-0	1-4	5-0	1-0	2-0	3-2	3-0	1-3	■	2-1	2-0	3-2	1-1	2-2	3-3
Reading FC	3-1	2-1	2-2	2-2	1-2	3-1	1-1	3-1	3-1	0-0	0-1	1-2	2-1	1-0	1-1	1-3	3-0	2-2	■	1-3	4-0	2-0	0-3	0-2
Sheffield United FC	1-0	4-1	4-0	2-2	3-0	4-1	2-1	0-1	6-1	1-3	1-0	4-2	5-2	1-2	4-0	1-1	3-1	1-0		■	1-2	5-1	2-1	2-0
Southend United FC	1-1	2-1	2-0	1-1	1-2	2-2	1-1	0-0	1-0	3-1	0-0	2-1	2-4	1-2	1-1	1-1	2-1	2-1			■	0-2	1-2	3-1
Swansea City FC	1-0	1-2	1-0	1-1	1-1	1-2	1-1	1-1	1-1	2-0	2-0	3-2	1-0	3-1	1-0	2-0	0-0	1-1	2-0	2-2	2-0	■	1-2	2-5
Wigan Athletic AFC	2-1	2-1	1-1	1-1	0-1	3-0	1-0	1-0	3-0	0-2	3-0	0-2	1-3	0-1	0-2	1-1	3-0	1-2	3-0	1-2	3-0	1-2	■	1-1
Wolverhampton W.	1-0	2-1	1-0	2-0	2-0	0-1	4-0	2-0	3-1	1-0	5-2	6-1	4-1	6-2	3-2	0-0	3-3	6-0	2-1	2-2	3-0	1-1	2-1	■

	Division 3	Pd	Wn	Dw	Ls	GF	GA	Pts	
1.	Wolverhampton Wanderers FC (Wolverhampton)	46	26	14	6	96	49	92	P
2.	Sheffield United FC (Sheffield)	46	25	9	12	93	54	84	P
3.	Port Vale FC (Stoke-on-Trent)	46	24	12	10	78	48	84	POP
4.	Fulham FC (London)	46	22	9	15	69	67	75	PO
5.	Bristol Rovers FC (Bristol)	46	19	17	10	67	51	74	PO
6.	Preston North End FC (Preston)	46	19	15	12	79	60	72	PO
7.	Brentford FC (London)	46	18	14	14	66	61	68	
8.	Chester City FC (Chester)	46	19	11	16	64	61	68	
9.	Notts County FC (Nottingham)	46	18	13	15	64	54	67	
10.	Bolton Wanderers FC (Bolton)	46	16	16	14	58	54	64	
11.	Bristol City FC (Bristol)	46	18	9	19	53	55	63	
12.	Swansea City FC (Swansea)	46	15	16	15	51	53	61	
13.	Bury FC (Bury)	46	16	13	17	55	67	61	
14.	Huddersfield Town AFC (Huddersfield)	46	17	9	20	63	73	60	
15.	Mansfield Town FC (Mansfield)	46	14	17	15	48	52	59	
16.	Cardiff City AFC (Cardiff)	46	14	15	17	44	56	57	
17.	Wigan Athletic AFC (Wigan)	46	14	14	18	55	53	56	
18.	Reading FC (Reading)	46	15	11	20	68	72	56	
19.	Blackpool FC (Blackpool)	46	14	13	19	56	59	55	
20.	Northampton Town FC (Northampton)	46	16	6	24	66	76	54	
21.	Southend United FC (Southend-on-Sea)	46	13	15	18	56	75	54	R
22.	Chesterfield FC (Chesterfield)	46	14	7	25	51	86	49	R
23.	Gillingham FC (Gillingham)	46	12	4	30	47	81	40	R
24.	Aldershot FC (Aldershot)	46	8	13	25	48	78	37	R
		1104	406	292	406	1495	1495	1510	

Promotion Play-offs

Bristol Rovers FC (Bristol)	1-1, 0-1	Port Vale FC (Stoke-on-Trent)
Bristol Rovers FC (Bristol)	1-0, 4-0	Fulham FC (London)
Preston North End FC (Preston)	1-1, 1-3	Port Vale FC (Stoke-on-Trent)

Football League Division 4 — 1988-89 Season

	Burnley	Cambridge	Carlisle United	Colchester United	Crewe Alexandra	Darlington	Doncaster Rovers	Exeter City	Grimsby Town	Halifax Town	Hartlepool	Hereford United	Leyton Orient	Lincoln City	Peterborough Utd.	Rochdale	Rotherham United	Scarborough	Scunthorpe United	Stockport County	Torquay United	Tranmere Rovers	Wrexham	York City
Burnley FC		2-0	0-0	2-0	1-0	0-1	3-0	3-0	1-0	2-1	0-0	3-3	2-2	1-4	1-1	2-1	1-0	0-1	0-1	1-0	1-0	2-2	1-3	6-0
Cambridge United FC	2-1		3-2	3-1	1-1	1-3	0-0	2-0	4-1	2-1	6-0	2-1	2-2	2-3	2-1	2-0	1-1	2-2	0-3	1-0	3-0	1-1	2-0	1-1
Carlisle United FC	0-0	1-1		1-2	0-1	1-2	0-1	1-0	2-1	3-1	2-1	3-0	2-1	2-1	2-2	1-0	0-2	0-1	0-3	1-1	2-1	1-1	1-2	0-0
Colchester United FC	2-2	1-2	1-1		2-1	1-2	0-1	4-0	0-0	3-2	1-2	1-1	1-0	1-3	1-2	3-0	1-1	3-1	1-2	1-2	2-2	2-3	2-1	1-0
Crewe Alexandra FC	4-0	2-0	1-0	3-1		2-0	0-2	2-1	2-2	2-2	3-0	2-1	2-1	2-0	1-1	3-1	1-3	1-1	3-2	1-1	0-0	2-2	2-2	1-2
Darlington FC	1-1	1-1	2-3	1-2	1-1		1-3	2-2	1-1	0-2	0-0	0-0	1-3	2-1	2-2	1-2	1-1	2-1	3-3	1-4	0-0	1-2	2-1	2-2
Doncaster Rovers FC	1-0	1-1	1-3	3-1	0-1	1-0		2-1	2-3	1-4	1-0	3-2	1-0	0-1	2-3	1-1	0-1	3-1	2-2	2-2	1-2	0-0	2-2	1-2
Exeter City FC	3-0	0-3	3-0	4-2	1-2	2-1	3-0		2-1	4-1	2-1	3-1	1-1	0-1	3-1	5-1	0-0	1-0	2-2	2-2	3-0	0-1	0-2	2-0
Grimsby Town FC	1-0	4-0	0-0	2-2	0-0	0-0	5-0	2-1		3-2	3-0	1-1	2-2	1-0	0-0	1-3	0-4	2-1	1-1	2-0	1-0	0-0	0-1	2-0
Halifax Town AFC	1-2	0-0	3-3	3-2	0-1	1-0	2-0	0-3	2-1		1-0	2-2	2-2	0-1	5-0	4-1	1-1	0-2	5-1	2-2	2-0	2-3	4-0	0-0
Hartlepool United FC	2-2	3-2	2-1	2-1	0-3	2-1	2-1	2-2	2-1	2-0		1-1	1-0	3-2	2-1	0-1	1-0	0-2	2-2	0-1	2-2	2-2	1-3	0-1
Hereford United FC	0-0	4-2	2-1	1-1	0-1	1-1	3-1	1-0	2-1	3-1	2-0		1-1	3-2	4-0	4-4	1-3	1-2	1-1	1-2	1-1	2-1	0-0	1-2
Leyton Orient FC	3-0	1-1	2-0	8-0	0-0	1-0	4-0	5-0	2-0	4-3	1-3	1-3		3-1	1-2	3-0	3-1	2-3	4-1	1-2	3-1	2-0	0-1	4-0
Lincoln City FC	2-3	3-0	0-2	1-1	2-2	3-2	3-1	2-0	2-2	2-1	0-1	2-0	0-1		1-1	4-1	0-1	2-2	1-0	0-0	1-0	2-1	4-3	2-1
Peterborough United	3-0	1-5	1-4	3-0	3-2	1-1	2-0	0-1	1-2	0-1	2-1	0-1	1-1	1-1		1-0	0-3	1-4	1-2	1-0	3-1	1-1	1-0	0-1
Rochdale AFC	2-1	2-1	0-0	1-1	2-2	2-2	2-1	0-2	1-1	2-0	0-2	2-0	0-3	2-2	0-0		0-2	2-1	1-0	1-1	2-1	3-1	3-3	2-0
Rotherham United	3-1	0-0	2-1	2-0	1-2	1-2	3-0	0-1	1-0	2-0	4-0	6-0	3-1	3-1	3-1	2-0		1-1	3-3	2-1	1-0	2-2	0-2	0-1
Scarborough FC	1-0	2-1	0-1	0-0	2-1	3-2	2-1	2-1	2-3	3-1	2-0	0-2	0-0	2-1	1-2	1-0	1-1		1-0	1-1	5-2	2-0	0-3	0-0
Scunthorpe United	2-1	1-0	1-1	2-3	2-2	5-1	2-1	2-0	1-1	0-0	1-1	3-1	2-2	0-0	3-0	4-0	0-0	0-3		1-1	1-0	0-1	3-1	4-2
Stockport County	0-0	0-0	1-1	1-0	0-0	0-0	2-0	4-0	3-1	1-2	3-0	1-0	1-2	3-0	1-3	2-2	1-2	1-2	0-3		0-0	1-1	2-2	3-2
Torquay United FC	2-0	3-1	1-0	1-3	2-1	1-0	3-2	0-4	2-2	0-2	2-0	1-0	3-0	1-0	1-0	1-0	0-2	2-1	1-0	2-0		3-2	0-0	2-1
Tranmere Rovers FC	2-1	1-2	0-0	0-0	1-1	2-0	2-2	0-1	3-2	2-0	2-1	1-1	3-0	1-0	1-0	2-0	0-0	1-1	2-1	1-0	3-0		2-1	0-1
Wrexham AFC	4-2	3-1	2-1	2-2	0-0	3-3	1-1	3-0	1-2	3-0	4-3	1-1	0-1	3-0	1-1	2-1	1-4	0-1	2-0	2-0	1-0	3-3		2-1
York City FC	0-0	1-2	0-0	1-2	3-0	4-1	1-1	3-1	0-3	5-3	2-3	4-1	1-1	2-1	5-1	3-3	1-1	0-0	1-2	2-0	1-1	0-1	1-0	

Division 4

		Pd	Wn	Dw	Ls	GF	GA	Pts	
1.	Rotherham United FC (Rotherham)	46	22	16	8	76	35	82	P
2.	Tranmere Rovers FC (Birkenhead)	46	21	17	8	62	43	80	P
3.	Crewe Alexandra FC (Crewe)	46	21	15	10	67	48	78	P
4.	Scunthorpe United FC (Scunthorpe)	46	21	14	11	77	57	77	PO
5.	Scarborough FC (Scarborough)	46	21	14	11	67	52	77	PO
6.	Leyton Orient FC (London)	46	21	12	13	86	50	75	POP
7.	Wrexham AFC (Wrexham)	46	19	14	13	77	63	71	PO
8.	Cambridge United FC (Cambridge)	46	18	14	14	71	62	68	
9.	Grimsby Town FC (Cleethorpes)	46	17	15	14	65	59	66	
10.	Lincoln City FC (Lincoln)	46	18	10	18	64	60	64	
11.	York City FC (York)	46	17	13	16	62	63	64	
12.	Carlisle United FC (Carlisle)	46	15	15	16	53	52	60	
13.	Exeter City FC (Exeter)	46	18	6	22	65	68	60	
14.	Torquay United FC (Torquay)	46	17	8	21	45	60	59	
15.	Hereford United FC (Hereford)	46	14	16	16	66	72	58	
16.	Burnley FC (Burnley)	46	14	13	19	52	61	55	
17.	Peterborough United FC (Peterborough)	46	14	12	20	52	74	54	
18.	Rochdale AFC (Rochdale)	46	13	14	19	56	82	53	
19.	Hartlepool United FC (Hartlepool)	46	14	10	22	50	78	52	
20.	Stockport County FC (Stockport)	46	10	21	15	54	52	51	
21.	Halifax Town AFC (Halifax)	46	13	11	22	69	75	50	
22.	Colchester United FC (Colchester)	46	12	14	20	60	78	50	
23.	Doncaster Rovers FC (Doncaster)	46	13	10	23	49	78	49	
24.	Darlington FC (Darlington)	46	8	18	20	53	76	42	R
		1104	391	322	391	1498	1498	1495	

Promotion Play-offs

Wrexham AFC (Wrexham)	0-0, 1-2	Scunthorpe United FC (Scunthorpe)
Leyton Orient FC (London)	2-0, 0-1	Scarborough FC (Scarborough)
Wrexham AFC (Wrexham)	3-1, 2-0	Scunthorpe United FC (Scunthorpe)

Promoted to Division 4: Maidstone United FC (Maidstone).

F.A. CUP FINAL   (Wembley Stadium, London – 20/05/1989 – 82,800)

LIVERPOOL FC (LIVERPOOL)	3-2 (aet)	Everton FC (Liverpool)
Aldridge, Rush 2	*(H.T. 0-1)*	*McCall 2*

Liverpool: Grobbelaar, Ablett, Staunton (Venison), Nicol, Whelan, Hansen, Beardsley, Aldridge (Rush), Houghton, Barnes, McMahon.

Everton: Southall, McDonald, van der Hauwe, Ratcliffe, Watson, Bracewell (McCall), Nevin, Steven, Sharp, Cottee, Sheedy (Wilson).

Semi-finals

Everton FC (Liverpool)	1-0	Norwich City FC (Norwich)
Liverpool FC (Liverpool)	0-0, 3-1	Nottingham Forest FC (Nottingham)

(The first match was played at Hillsborough and was abandoned after 6 minutes when 94 Liverpool fans died after being crushed behind a safety fence)

Quarter-finals

Everton FC (Liverpool)	1-0	Wimbledon FC (London)
Liverpool FC (Liverpool)	4-0	Brentford FC (London)
Manchester United FC (Manchester)	0-1	Nottingham Forest FC (Nottingham)
West Ham United FC (London)	0-0, 1-3	Norwich City FC (Norwich)

1989-90

Football League Division 1 — 1989-90 Season	Arsenal	Aston Villa	Charlton Athletic	Chelsea	Coventry City	Crystal Palace	Derby County	Everton	Liverpool	Luton Town	Manchester City	Manchester United	Millwall	Norwich City	Nottingham Forest	Q.P.R.	Sheffield Wednesday	Southampton	Tottenham Hotspur	Wimbledon
Arsenal FC	■	0-1	1-0	0-1	2-0	4-1	1-1	1-0	1-1	3-2	4-0	1-0	2-0	4-3	3-0	3-0	5-0	2-1	1-0	0-0
Aston Villa FC	2-1	■	1-1	1-0	4-1	2-1	1-0	6-2	1-1	2-0	1-2	3-0	1-0	3-3	2-1	1-3	1-0	2-1	2-0	0-3
Charlton Athletic FC	0-0	0-2	■	3-0	1-1	1-2	0-0	0-1	0-4	2-0	1-1	2-0	1-1	0-1	1-1	1-0	1-2	2-4	1-3	1-2
Chelsea FC	0-0	0-3	3-1	■	1-0	3-0	1-1	2-1	2-5	1-0	1-1	1-0	4-0	0-0	2-2	1-1	4-0	2-2	1-2	2-5
Coventry City FC	0-1	2-0	1-2	3-2	■	1-0	1-0	2-0	1-6	1-0	2-1	1-4	3-1	1-0	0-2	1-1	1-4	1-0	0-0	2-1
Crystal Palace FC	1-1	1-0	2-0	2-2	0-1	■	1-1	2-1	0-2	1-1	2-2	1-1	4-3	1-0	1-0	0-3	1-1	3-1	2-3	2-0
Derby County FC	1-3	0-1	2-0	0-1	4-1	3-1	■	0-1	0-3	2-3	6-0	2-0	2-0	0-2	0-2	2-0	2-0	0-1	2-1	1-1
Everton FC	3-0	3-3	2-1	0-1	2-0	4-0	2-1	■	1-3	2-1	0-0	3-2	2-1	3-1	4-0	1-0	2-0	3-0	2-1	1-1
Liverpool FC	2-1	1-1	1-0	4-1	0-1	9-0	1-0	2-1	■	2-2	3-1	0-0	1-0	0-0	2-2	2-1	2-1	3-2	1-0	2-1
Luton Town FC	2-0	0-1	1-0	0-3	3-2	1-0	1-0	2-2	0-0	■	1-1	1-3	2-1	4-1	1-1	1-1	2-0	1-1	0-0	1-1
Manchester City FC	1-1	0-2	1-2	1-1	1-0	3-0	0-1	1-0	1-4	3-1	■	5-1	2-0	1-0	0-3	1-0	2-1	1-2	1-1	1-1
Manchester United FC	4-1	2-0	1-0	0-0	3-0	1-2	1-2	0-0	1-2	4-1	1-1	■	5-1	0-2	1-0	0-0	2-1	0-1	0-0	0-0
Millwall FC	1-2	2-0	2-2	1-3	4-1	1-2	1-1	1-2	1-2	1-1	1-1	1-2	■	0-1	1-0	1-2	2-0	2-2	0-1	0-0
Norwich City FC	2-2	2-0	0-0	2-0	0-0	2-0	1-0	1-1	0-0	2-0	0-1	2-0	1-1	■	1-1	0-0	2-1	4-4	2-2	0-1
Nottingham Forest FC	1-2	1-1	2-0	1-1	2-4	3-1	2-1	0-2	2-2	3-0	1-0	4-0	3-1	0-1	■	2-2	0-1	2-0	1-3	0-1
Queen's Park Rangers FC	2-0	1-1	0-1	4-2	1-1	2-0	1-1	3-2	0-0	1-3	1-2	0-0	2-1	2-0	2-0	■	1-0	1-4	3-1	2-3
Sheffield Wednesday FC	1-0	1-0	3-0	1-1	0-0	2-2	1-0	2-0	1-1	2-0	1-0	1-1	0-2	0-3	2-0	0-2	■	0-1	2-4	0-1
Southampton FC	1-0	2-1	3-2	2-3	3-0	1-1	2-1	2-2	4-1	6-3	2-1	0-1	1-2	4-1	2-0	0-2	2-2	■	1-1	2-2
Tottenham Hotspur FC	2-1	0-2	3-0	1-4	3-2	0-1	1-2	1-0	2-1	1-0	2-1	3-1	4-0	2-3	3-2	3-0	2-1	1-1	■	0-1
Wimbledon FC	1-0	0-2	3-1	0-1	0-0	0-1	1-1	3-1	1-2	1-2	1-0	2-2	2-2	1-1	1-3	0-0	1-1	3-3	1-0	■

Division 1

#	Club	Pd	Wn	Dw	Ls	GF	GA	Pts	
1.	LIVERPOOL FC (LIVERPOOL)	38	23	10	5	78	37	79	
2.	Aston Villa FC (Birmingham)	38	21	7	10	57	38	70	
3.	Tottenham Hotspur FC (London)	38	19	6	13	59	47	63	
4.	Arsenal FC (London)	38	18	8	12	54	38	62	
5.	Chelsea FC (London)	38	16	12	10	58	50	60	
6.	Everton FC (Liverpool)	38	17	8	13	57	46	59	
7.	Southampton FC (Southampton)	38	15	10	13	71	63	55	
8.	Wimbledon FC (London)	38	13	16	9	47	40	55	
9.	Nottingham Forest FC (Nottingham)	38	15	9	14	55	47	54	
10.	Norwich City FC (Norwich)	38	13	14	11	44	42	53	
11.	Queen's Park Rangers FC (London)	38	13	1	14	45	44	50	
12.	Coventry City FC (Coventry)	38	14	7	17	39	59	49	
13.	Manchester United FC (Manchester)	38	13	9	16	46	47	48	
14.	Manchester City FC (Manchester)	38	12	12	14	43	52	48	
15.	Crystal Palace FC (London)	38	13	9	16	42	66	48	
16.	Derby County FC (Derby)	38	13	7	18	43	40	46	
17.	Luton Town FC (Luton)	38	10	13	15	43	57	43	
18.	Sheffield Wednesday FC (Sheffield)	38	11	10	17	35	51	43	R
19.	Charlton Athletic FC (London)	38	7	9	22	31	57	30	R
20.	Millwall FC (London)	38	5	11	22	39	65	26	R
		760	281	198	281	986	986	1041	

Top Goalscorers

1)	Gary LINEKER	(Tottenham Hotspur FC)	24
2)	John BARNES	(Liverpool FC)	22
3)	Kerry DIXON	(Chelsea FC)	20
	Matthew LE TISSIER	(Southampton FC)	20

Football League Division 2 1989-90 Season	Barnsley	Blackburn Rovers	Bournemouth	Bradford City	Brighton & H.A.	Hull City	Ipswich Town	Leeds United	Leicester City	Middlesbrough	Newcastle United	Oldham Athletic	Oxford United	Plymouth Argyle	Portsmouth	Port Vale	Sheffield United	Stoke City	Sunderland	Swindon Town	Watford	W.B.A.	West Ham United	Wolves
Barnsley FC	■	0-0	0-1	2-0	1-0	1-1	0-1	1-0	2-2	1-1	1-1	1-0	1-0	1-1	0-1	0-3	1-2	3-2	1-0	0-1	0-1	2-2	1-1	2-2
Blackburn Rovers FC	5-0	■	1-1	2-2	1-1	0-0	2-2	1-2	2-4	2-4	2-0	1-0	2-2	2-0	2-0	1-0	0-0	3-0	1-1	2-1	2-2	2-1	5-4	2-3
AFC Bournemouth	2-1	2-4	■	1-0	0-2	5-4	3-1	0-1	2-3	2-2	2-1	2-0	0-1	2-2	0-1	1-0	0-1	2-1	0-1	1-2	0-0	1-1	1-1	1-1
Bradford City AFC	0-0	0-1	1-0	■	2-0	2-3	1-0	0-1	2-0	0-1	3-2	1-1	1-2	0-1	1-1	2-2	1-4	1-0	0-1	1-1	2-1	2-0	2-1	1-1
Brighton & Hove Alb.	1-1	1-2	2-1	2-1	■	2-0	1-0	2-2	1-0	1-0	0-3	1-1	0-1	2-1	0-0	2-0	2-2	1-4	1-2	1-2	1-0	0-3	3-0	1-1
Hull City AFC	1-2	2-0	1-4	2-1	0-2	■	4-3	0-1	1-1	0-0	1-3	0-0	1-1	3-3	1-2	2-1	0-0	3-2	2-3	0-0	0-0	1-1	2-0	2-0
Ipswich Town FC	3-1	3-1	1-1	1-0	2-1	0-1	■	2-2	2-2	3-0	2-1	1-1	1-0	3-0	0-1	3-2	1-1	2-2	1-1	1-0	1-0	3-1	1-0	1-3
Leeds United AFC	1-2	1-1	3-0	1-1	3-0	4-3	1-1	■	2-1	2-1	1-0	1-1	2-1	2-1	2-0	0-0	4-0	2-0	2-0	4-0	2-1	2-2	3-2	1-0
Leicester City FC	2-2	0-1	2-1	1-1	1-0	2-1	0-1	4-3	■	2-1	2-2	3-0	0-0	1-1	1-1	2-0	2-5	2-1	2-3	2-1	1-1	1-3	1-0	0-0
Middlesbrough FC	0-1	0-3	4-0	2-0	2-2	1-2	0-2	4-1	2-1	■	4-1	1-0	0-2	2-0	2-3	3-3	3-1	0-1	3-0	0-2	1-2	0-0	0-1	4-2
Newcastle United FC	4-1	2-1	3-0	1-0	2-0	2-0	2-1	5-2	5-4	2-2	■	2-1	2-3	3-1	1-0	2-2	2-0	3-0	1-1	0-0	2-1	2-1	2-1	1-4
Oldham Athletic AFC	2-0	2-0	4-0	2-2	1-1	3-2	4-1	3-1	1-0	2-0	1-1	■	4-1	3-2	3-3	2-1	0-2	2-0	2-1	2-2	1-1	2-1	3-0	1-1
Oxford United FC	2-3	1-1	1-2	2-1	0-1	0-0	2-2	2-4	4-2	3-1	2-1	0-1	■	3-2	2-1	0-0	3-0	0-1	1-1	0-2	1-1	0-2	2-2	2-0
Plymouth Argyle FC	2-1	2-2	1-0	1-1	2-1	1-2	1-0	1-1	3-1	1-1	2-0	2-0	0-2	■	1-2	0-0	3-0	3-0	0-3	0-0	2-2	1-1	0-1	1-0
Portsmouth FC	2-1	1-1	2-1	3-0	3-0	2-2	2-3	3-3	2-3	3-1	1-1	2-1	2-1	0-3	■	2-0	3-2	0-0	3-3	1-1	1-2	1-1	0-1	1-3
Port Vale FC	2-1	0-0	3-1	3-2	2-1	1-1	5-0	0-0	2-1	1-1	1-2	2-0	1-2	3-0	1-1	■	1-1	0-0	1-2	2-0	1-0	2-1	2-2	3-1
Sheffield United FC	1-2	1-2	4-2	1-1	5-4	0-0	2-0	2-2	1-1	1-0	1-1	2-1	2-1	1-0	2-1	2-1	■	2-1	1-3	2-0	4-1	3-1	0-2	3-0
Stoke City FC	0-1	0-1	0-0	1-1	3-2	1-1	0-0	1-1	0-1	1-1	0-1	1-2	1-2	0-0	1-2	1-1	0-1	■	0-2	1-1	2-2	2-1	1-1	2-0
Sunderland AFC	4-2	0-1	3-2	1-0	2-1	0-1	2-4	1-1	2-2	2-1	0-0	2-3	1-0	3-1	2-2	2-2	1-1	2-1	■	2-2	4-0	1-1	4-3	1-1
Swindon Town FC	0-0	4-3	2-3	3-1	1-2	1-3	3-0	3-2	1-1	1-1	3-2	3-0	3-0	2-2	3-0	0-2	6-0	0-2	2-0	■	2-0	2-2	2-2	3-1
Watford FC	2-2	3-1	2-2	7-2	4-2	3-1	3-3	1-0	3-1	1-0	0-0	3-0	0-1	1-2	1-0	1-0	1-3	1-1	1-1	0-2	■	0-2	0-1	3-1
West Bromwich Alb.	7-0	2-2	2-2	2-0	3-0	1-1	1-3	2-1	0-1	1-5	2-2	3-2	0-3	0-0	2-3	0-3	1-1	1-2	2-0	2-0	1-1	■	1-3	1-2
West Ham United FC	4-2	1-1	4-1	2-0	3-1	1-2	2-0	0-1	3-1	2-0	0-0	0-2	3-2	2-1	2-2	5-0	0-0	5-0	1-1	1-0	2-3	2-1	■	4-0
Wolverhampton W.	1-1	1-2	3-1	1-1	2-4	1-2	2-1	1-0	5-0	2-0	0-1	1-1	2-0	1-0	5-0	2-0	1-2	0-0	0-1	2-1	1-1	2-1	1-0	■

Division 2

	Team	Pd	Wn	Dw	Ls	GF	GA	Pts	
1.	Leeds United AFC (Leeds)	46	24	13	9	79	52	85	P
2.	Sheffield United FC (Sheffield)	46	24	13	9	78	58	85	P
3.	Newcastle United FC (Newcastle-upon-Tyne)	46	22	14	10	80	55	80	PO
4.	Swindon Town FC (Swindon)	46	20	14	12	79	59	74	PO*
5.	Blackburn Rovers FC (Blackburn)	46	19	17	10	74	59	74	PO
6.	Sunderland AFC (Sunderland)	46	20	14	12	70	64	74	POP
7.	West Ham United FC (London)	46	20	12	14	80	57	72	
8.	Oldham Athletic AFC (Oldham)	46	19	14	13	70	57	71	
9.	Ipswich Town FC (Ipswich)	46	19	12	15	67	66	69	
10.	Wolverhampton Wanderers FC (Wolverhampton)	46	18	13	15	67	60	67	
11.	Port Vale FC (Stoke-on-Trent)	46	15	16	15	62	57	61	
12.	Portsmouth FC (Portsmouth)	46	15	16	15	62	65	61	
13.	Leicester City FC (Leicester)	46	15	14	17	67	79	59	
14.	Hull City AFC (Kingston-upon-Hull)	46	14	16	16	58	65	58	
15.	Watford FC (Watford)	46	14	15	17	58	60	57	
16.	Plymouth Argyle FC (Plymouth)	46	14	13	19	58	63	55	
17.	Oxford United FC (Oxford)	46	15	9	22	57	66	54	
18.	Brighton & Hove Albion FC (Hove)	46	15	9	22	56	72	54	
19.	Barnsley FC (Barnsley)	46	13	15	18	49	71	54	
20.	West Bromwich Albion FC (West Bromwich)	46	12	15	19	67	71	51	
21.	Middlesbrough FC (Middlesbrough)	46	13	11	22	52	63	50	
22.	AFC Bournemouth (Bournemouth)	46	12	12	22	57	76	48	R
23.	Bradford City AFC (Bradford)	46	9	14	23	44	68	41	R
24.	Stoke City FC (Stoke-on-Trent)	46	6	19	21	35	63	37	R
		1104	387	330	387	1526	1526	1491	

Promotion Play-offs

Swindon Town FC (Swindon)	1-0	Sunderland AFC (Sunderland)
Blackburn Rovers FC (Blackburn)	1-2, 1-2	Swindon Town FC (Swindon)
Sunderland AFC (Sunderland)	0-0, 2-0	Newcastle United FC (Newcastle-upon-Tyne)

Note: Swindon Town FC (Swindon) were found guilty of making illegal payments to players and were initially relegated to Division 3. On appeal they were allowed to remain in Division 2 with Sunderland AFC (Sunderland) being promoted to Division 1.

Football League Division 3 — 1989-90 Season

	Birmingham City	Blackpool	Bolton Wanderers	Brentford	Bristol City	Bristol Rovers	Bury	Cardiff City	Chester City	Crewe Alexandra	Fulham	Huddersfield Town	Leyton Orient	Mansfield Town	Northampton Town	Notts County	Preston North End	Reading	Rotherham United	Shrewsbury Town	Swansea City	Tranmere Rovers	Walsall	Wigan Athletic
Birmingham City FC		3-1	1-0	0-1	0-4	2-2	0-0	1-1	0-0	3-0	1-1	0-1	0-0	4-1	4-0	1-2	3-1	0-1	4-1	0-1	2-0	2-1	2-0	0-0
Blackpool FC	3-2		2-1	4-0	1-3	0-3	0-1	1-0	1-3	1-3	0-1	2-2	1-0	3-1	1-0	0-0	2-2	0-0	1-2	0-1	2-2	0-3	4-3	0-0
Bolton Wanderers FC	3-1	2-0		0-1	1-0	1-0	3-1	3-1	1-0	0-0	0-0	2-2	2-1	1-1	0-3	3-0	2-1	3-0	0-2	0-1	0-0	1-1	1-1	3-2
Brentford FC	0-1	5-0	1-2		0-2	2-1	0-1	0-1	1-1	0-2	2-0	2-1	4-3	2-1	3-2	0-1	2-2	1-1	4-2	1-1	2-1	2-4	4-0	3-1
Bristol City FC	1-0	2-0	1-1	2-0		0-0	1-0	1-0	1-0	4-1	5-1	1-1	2-1	1-1	3-1	2-0	2-1	0-1	0-0	2-1	1-3	1-3	4-0	3-0
Bristol Rovers FC	0-0	1-1	1-1	1-0	3-0		2-1	2-1	2-1	1-1	2-0	2-2	0-0	1-1	4-2	3-2	3-0	0-0	2-0	1-0	2-0	2-0	2-0	6-1
Bury FC	0-0	2-0	2-0	0-2	1-1	0-0		2-0	1-0	0-3	0-0	6-0	2-0	3-0	1-0	3-2	1-2	4-0	1-1	0-0	3-2	1-2	0-2	2-2
Cardiff City AFC	0-1	2-2	0-2	2-2	0-3	1-1	3-1		1-1	0-0	3-3	1-5	1-1	1-0	2-3	1-3	3-0	3-2	2-0	0-1	0-2	0-0	3-1	1-1
Chester City FC	4-0	2-0	2-0	1-1	0-3	0-0	1-4	1-0		2-1	0-2	2-1	1-0	0-2	0-1	3-3	3-1	1-1	2-0	1-0	1-0	2-2	1-1	0-0
Crewe Alexandra FC	0-2	2-0	2-2	2-3	0-1	1-0	2-1	1-1	0-0		2-3	3-0	0-1	2-1	1-0	1-0	1-1	0-0	1-1	1-1	2-2	3-1	3-2	
Fulham FC	1-2	0-0	2-2	1-0	0-1	1-2	2-2	2-5	1-0	1-1		0-0	1-2	1-0	1-1	5-2	3-1	1-2	1-1	2-1	2-0	1-2	0-0	4-0
Huddersfield Town	1-2	2-2	1-1	1-0	2-1	1-1	2-1	2-3	4-1	0-1	0-1		2-0	1-0	2-2	1-2	0-2	0-1	2-1	1-1	1-0	1-0	1-0	2-0
Leyton Orient FC	1-2	2-0	0-0	0-1	1-1	0-1	2-3	3-1	0-3	2-1	1-1	1-0		3-1	1-1	0-1	3-1	4-1	1-1	1-0	0-2	0-1	1-1	1-0
Mansfield Town FC	5-2	0-3	0-1	2-3	1-0	0-1	1-0	1-0	1-0	2-1	3-0	1-2	1-0		1-2	1-3	2-2	1-1	3-1	2-1	4-0	1-0	0-2	1-0
Northampton Town	2-2	4-2	0-2	0-2	2-0	1-2	0-1	1-1	1-0	3-1	2-2	1-0	0-1	1-2		0-0	1-2	2-1	1-2	2-1	1-1	0-4	1-1	1-1
Notts County FC	3-2	0-1	2-1	3-1	0-0	3-1	0-4	2-1	0-0	2-0	2-0	1-0	1-0	4-2	3-2		2-1	0-0	2-0	4-0	2-1	1-0	2-0	1-1
Preston North End	2-2	2-1	1-4	4-2	2-2	0-1	2-3	4-0	5-0	0-0	1-0	3-3	0-3	4-0	0-0	2-4		1-0	0-1	2-1	2-0	2-2	2-0	1-1
Reading FC	0-2	1-1	2-0	1-0	1-1	0-1	1-0	0-1	1-1	1-1	3-2	0-0	1-1	1-0	3-2	1-1	6-0		3-2	3-3	1-1	1-0	0-1	2-0
Rotherham United	5-1	1-1	1-0	2-1	1-2	3-2	1-3	4-0	5-0	1-3	2-1	0-0	5-2	0-0	2-0	1-2	3-1	1-1		4-2	3-2	0-0	2-2	1-2
Shrewsbury Town	2-0	1-1	3-3	1-0	0-1	2-3	3-1	0-0	2-0	0-0	2-0	3-3	4-2	0-1	2-0	2-2	2-0	1-1	1-1		1-1	3-1	2-0	1-3
Swansea City FC	1-1	0-0	0-0	2-1	0-5	0-0	0-1	0-1	2-1	3-2	4-2	1-3	0-1	1-0	1-1	0-0	2-1	1-6	1-0	0-1		1-0	2-0	3-0
Tranmere Rovers FC	5-1	4-2	1-3	2-2	6-0	1-2	2-4	3-0	0-0	1-1	2-1	4-0	3-0	1-1	0-0	2-0	2-1	3-1	2-1	3-1	3-0		2-1	2-0
Walsall FC	0-1	1-1	2-1	2-1	0-2	1-2	2-2	0-2	1-1	1-1	0-0	2-3	1-3	1-0	1-0	2-2	1-0	1-1	1-1	0-2	0-1	2-1		1-2
Wigan Athletic AFC	1-0	1-1	2-0	2-1	2-3	1-2	0-0	1-1	1-0	1-0	2-1	1-2	0-2	4-0	0-0	1-1	0-1	3-1	0-3	0-0	2-0	1-3	3-0	

	Division 3	Pd	Wn	Dw	Ls	GF	GA	Pts	
1.	Bristol Rovers FC (Bristol)	46	26	15	5	71	35	93	P
2.	Bristol City FC (Bristol)	46	27	10	9	76	40	91	P
3.	Notts County FC (Nottingham)	46	25	12	9	73	53	87	POP
4.	Tranmere Rovers FC (Birkenhead)	46	23	11	12	86	49	80	PO
5.	Bury FC (Bury)	46	21	11	14	70	49	74	PO
6.	Bolton Wanderers FC (Bolton)	46	18	15	13	59	48	69	PO
7.	Birmingham City FC (Birmingham)	46	18	12	16	60	59	66	
8.	Huddersfield Town AFC (Huddersfield)	46	17	14	15	61	62	65	
9.	Rotherham United FC (Rotherham)	46	17	13	16	71	62	64	
10.	Reading FC (Reading)	46	15	19	12	56	52	64	
11.	Shrewsbury Town FC (Shrewsbury)	46	16	15	15	59	54	63	
12.	Crewe Alexandra FC (Crewe)	46	15	17	14	56	53	62	
13.	Brentford FC (London)	46	18	7	21	66	66	61	
14.	Leyton Orient FC (London)	46	16	10	20	52	56	58	
15.	Mansfield Town FC (Mansfield)	46	16	7	23	50	65	55	
16.	Chester City FC (Chester)	46	13	15	18	43	55	54	
17.	Swansea City FC (Swansea)	46	14	12	20	44	62	54	
18.	Wigan Athletic AFC (Wigan)	46	13	14	19	48	64	53	
19.	Preston North End FC (Preston)	46	14	10	22	65	79	52	
20.	Fulham FC (London)	46	12	15	19	55	66	51	
21.	Cardiff City AFC (Cardiff)	46	12	14	20	51	70	50	R
22.	Northampton Town FC (Northampton)	46	11	14	21	51	68	47	R
23.	Blackpool FC (Blackpool)	46	10	16	20	49	73	46	R
24.	Walsall FC (Walsall)	46	9	14	23	40	72	41	R
		1104	396	312	396	1412	1412	1500	

Promotion Play-offs

Notts County FC (Nottingham)	2-0	Tranmere Rovers FC (Birkenhead)
Bolton Wanderers FC (Bolton)	1-1, 0-2	Notts County FC (Nottingham)
Bury FC (Bury)	0-0, 0-2	Tranmere Rovers FC (Birkenhead)

Football League Division 4 — 1989-90 Season

	Aldershot Town	Burnley	Cambridge	Carlisle United	Chesterfield	Colchester United	Doncaster Rovers	Exeter City	Gillingham	Grimsby Town	Halifax Town	Hartlepool	Hereford United	Lincoln City	Maidstone	Peterborough Utd.	Rochdale	Scarborough	Scunthorpe United	Southend United	Stockport County	Torquay United	Wrexham	York City
Aldershot Town FC	■	1-1	0-2	1-0	0-0	4-0	1-1	0-1	1-0	0-0	2-0	6-1	0-2	0-1	0-2	0-1	1-1	1-1	4-2	0-5	2-1	1-2	1-0	2-2
Burnley FC	0-0	■	1-3	2-1	0-0	0-0	0-1	1-0	1-2	1-1	1-0	0-0	3-1	0-0	1-1	1-2	0-1	3-0	0-1	0-0	0-0	1-0	2-3	1-1
Cambridge United FC	2-2	0-1	■	1-2	0-1	4-0	1-0	3-2	2-1	2-0	1-0	2-1	0-1	2-1	2-0	3-2	0-3	5-2	5-3	2-1	0-2	5-2	1-1	2-2
Carlisle United FC	1-3	1-1	3-1	■	4-3	1-0	1-0	0-0	3-0	1-1	1-1	1-0	2-1	1-2	3-2	0-0	3-1	0-1	3-0	3-1	2-0	1-0	2-1	
Chesterfield FC	2-0	0-1	1-1	3-0	■	1-1	0-1	2-1	2-0	4-3	3-1	0-0	3-1	1-1	2-1	2-2	1-1	1-1	1-1	5-1	3-0			0-0
Colchester United FC	1-0	1-2	1-2	4-0	1-0	■	2-0	0-1	2-0	1-0	2-2	3-1	1-1	0-1	4-1	0-1	1-2	0-0	1-0	0-2	0-1	0-3	1-3	0-2
Doncaster Rovers FC	0-1	2-3	2-1	1-1	1-0	2-0	■	2-1	0-0	0-0	3-4	2-2	0-1	0-1	1-1	0-3	4-0	1-1	1-2	0-1	2-1	2-1	2-2	1-2
Exeter City FC	2-0	2-1	3-2	0-0	2-1	2-1	1-0	■	3-1	2-1	2-0	3-1	3-0	2-0	2-0	5-0	3-2	1-0	2-1	1-1	3-0	1-1	3-1	
Gillingham FC	0-0	0-0	1-0	2-1	3-0	3-3	3-1	1-1	■	1-2	3-1	0-0	1-1	1-2	0-0	1-0	0-3	5-0	0-3	0-2	1-0	0-0		
Grimsby Town FC	2-1	4-2	1-0	0-1	4-1	2-1	1-0	2-0		■	1-1	0-0	0-2	1-0	2-3	1-2	1-2	3-0	2-1	2-0	4-2	0-0	5-1	3-0
Halifax Town AFC	4-1	0-0	0-0	1-1	1-1	1-1	0-2	1-2	0-1	2-2	■	4-0	1-1	1-2	2-2	1-1	1-2	1-1	1-2	3-1	4-2	2-2		
Hartlepool United FC	2-0	3-0	1-2	1-0	3-1	0-2	0-6	0-3	1-2	4-2	2-0	■	1-2	1-1	4-2	2-2	2-1	4-1	3-2	1-1	5-0	1-1	3-0	1-2
Hereford United FC	4-1	0-1	0-2	2-2	3-2	2-0	2-1	2-1	1-2	1-2	0-1	4-1	■	2-2	3-0	1-2	1-3	0-2	1-2	0-3	1-2	0-0	1-2	
Lincoln City FC	0-1	1-0	4-3	1-3	1-1	2-1	2-1	1-5	1-3	1-1	2-1	4-1	1-0	■	1-2	1-0	1-0	2-0	0-0	2-2	1-0	0-0		
Maidstone United FC	5-1	1-2	2-2	5-2	0-1	4-1	1-0	1-0	0-1	2-2	1-2	4-2	2-0	2-0	■	1-1	2-0	4-1	1-1	3-0	0-1	5-1	2-0	1-0
Peterborough United	1-1	4-1	1-2	3-0	1-1	1-0	2-1	4-3	1-1	1-1	3-0	0-2	1-1	1-0	1-0	■	0-1	1-2	1-1	1-2	2-0	1-1	3-1	1-1
Rochdale AFC	2-0	2-1	2-0	1-2	1-0	2-2	1-3	1-0	1-0	0-2	0-0	5-2	1-0	3-2	1-2	■		1-0	3-0	0-1	1-1	0-0	0-3	0-1
Scarborough FC	1-0	4-2	1-1	2-1	2-3	2-2	1-2	1-2	0-1	3-1	2-3	4-1	0-1	2-0	0-1	2-1	2-1	■	0-0	1-1	2-0	0-0	2-1	1-3
Scunthorpe United	3-2	3-0	1-1	2-3	0-1	4-0	4-1	5-4	0-0	2-2	1-0	0-1	3-3	1-1	1-0	0-0	0-1	0-1	■	1-1	5-0	2-0	3-1	1-1
Southend United	5-0	3-2	0-0	2-0	0-2	0-2	2-0	1-0	2-0	0-2	3-0	2-0	1-1	0-0		0-2	3-2	1-0	0-0	■	2-0	1-0	2-1	1-1
Stockport County	1-1	3-1	3-1	3-1	3-1	1-1	3-1	2-1	1-0	2-4	0-1	6-0	2-1	1-1	1-2	0-0	3-2	4-2	1-0		■	1-1	0-2	2-2
Torquay United	1-2	0-1	3-2	1-2	1-0	4-1	2-0	0-2	0-2	0-3	1-0	4-3	1-1	0-3	2-1	2-1	1-0	3-2	0-3	3-0	3-0	■	0-1	1-1
Wrexham AFC	2-2	1-0	2-3	1-0	0-2	3-2	0-0	1-1	2-1	0-1	2-1	1-2	0-0	0-2	4-2	2-1	1-1	0-2	0-0	3-3	0-1	1-1	■	2-0
York City FC	2-2	1-3	4-2	0-1	4-0	3-1	2-1	3-0	1-0	0-1	0-2	1-1	1-2	0-0	0-0	1-0	1-0	1-2	0-1	2-1	0-3	1-1	1-0	■

	Division 4	Pd	Wn	Dw	Ls	GF	GA	Pts	
1.	Exeter City FC (Exeter)	46	28	5	13	83	48	89	P
2.	Grimsby Town FC (Cleethorpes)	46	22	13	11	70	47	79	P
3.	Southend United FC (Southend-on-Sea)	46	22	9	15	61	48	75	P
4.	Stockport County FC (Stockport)	46	21	11	14	67	61	74	PO
5.	Maidstone United FC (Maidstone)	46	22	7	17	77	61	73	PO
6.	Cambridge United FC (Cambridge)	46	21	10	15	76	66	73	POP
7.	Chesterfield FC (Chesterfield)	46	19	14	13	63	50	71	PO
8.	Carlisle United FC (Carlisle)	46	21	8	17	61	60	71	
9.	Peterborough United FC (Peterborough)	46	17	17	12	59	46	68	
10.	Lincoln City FC (Lincoln)	46	18	14	14	48	48	68	
11.	Scunthorpe United FC (Scunthorpe)	46	17	15	14	69	54	66	
12.	Rochdale AFC (Rochdale)	46	20	6	20	51	54	66	
13.	York City FC (York)	46	16	16	14	55	53	64	
14.	Gillingham FC (Gillingham)	46	17	11	18	46	48	62	
15.	Torquay United FC (Torquay)	46	15	12	19	53	66	57	
16.	Burnley FC (Burnley)	46	14	14	18	45	55	56	
17.	Hereford United FC (Hereford)	46	15	10	21	56	62	55	
18.	Scarborough FC (Scarborough)	46	15	10	21	60	73	55	
19.	Hartlepool United FC (Hartlepool)	46	15	10	21	66	88	55	
20.	Doncaster Rovers FC (Doncaster)	46	14	9	23	53	60	51	
21.	Wrexham AFC (Wrexham)	46	13	12	21	51	67	51	
22.	Aldershot FC (Aldershot)	46	12	14	20	49	69	50	
23.	Halifax Town AFC (Halifax)	46	12	13	21	57	65	49	
24.	Colchester United FC (Colchester)	46	11	10	25	48	75	43	R
		1104	417	270	417	1424	1424	1521	

Promotion Play-offs

Cambridge United FC (Cambridge)	1-0	Chesterfield FC (Chesterfield)
Cambridge United FC (Cambridge)	1-1, 2-0 (aet)	Maidstone United FC (Maidstone)
Chesterfield FC (Chesterfield)	4-0, 2-0	Stockport County FC (Stockport)

Promoted to Division 4: Darlington FC (Darlington)

F.A. CUP FINAL   (Wembley Stadium, London – 12/05/1990 – 80,000)

MANCHESTER UNITED FC	3-3 (aet)	Crystal Palace FC (London)
Robson 35', Hughes 62', 113'		*O'Reilly 19', Wright 72', 92'*

Man. United: Leighton, Ince, Martin (Blackmore 88'), Bruce, Phelan, Pallister (Robins 63'), Robson, Webb, McClair, Hughes, Wallace.

Crystal Palace: Martyn, Pemberton, Shaw, Gray (Madden 118'), O'Reilly, Thorn, Barber (Wright 69'), Thomas, Bright, Salako, Pardew.

F.A. CUP FINAL REPLAY   (Wembley Stadium, London – 17/05/1990 – 80,000)

MANCHESTER UNITED FC (MANCHESTER)	1-0	Crystal Palace FC (London)
Martin 61'		

Crystal Palace: Martyn, Pemberton, Shaw, Gray, O'Reilly, Thorn, Barber (Wright 64'), Thomas, Bright, Salako (Madden 79'), Pardew.

Man. United: Sealey, Ince, Martin, Bruce, Phelan, Pallister, Robson, Webb, McClair, Hughes, Wallace.

Semi-finals

Crystal Palace FC (London)	4-3 (aet)	Liverpool FC (Liverpool)
Manchester United FC (Manchester)	3-3 (aet), 2-1 (aet)	Oldham Athletic AFC (Oldham)

Quarter-finals

Cambridge United FC (Cambridge)	0-1	Crystal Palace FC (London)
Oldham Athletic AFC (Oldham)	3-0	Aston Villa FC (Birmingham)
Queen's Park Rangers FC (London)	2-2, 0-1	Liverpool FC (Liverpool)
Sheffield United FC (Sheffield)	0-1	Manchester United FC (Manchester)

1990-91

Football League Division 1 1990-91 Season	Arsenal	Aston Villa	Chelsea	Coventry City	Crystal Palace	Derby County	Everton	Leeds United	Liverpool	Luton Town	Man. City	Man. United	Norwich City	Nottingham F.	Q.P.R.	Sheffield United	Southampton	Sunderland	Tottenham H.	Wimbledon
Arsenal FC		5-0	4-1	6-1	4-0	3-0	1-0	2-0	3-0	2-1	2-2	3-1	2-0	1-1	2-0	4-1	4-0	1-0	0-0	2-2
Aston Villa FC	0-0		2-2	2-1	2-0	3-2	2-2	0-0	0-0	1-2	1-5	1-1	2-1	1-1	2-2	2-1	1-1	3-0	3-2	1-2
Chelsea FC	2-1	1-0		2-1	2-1	2-1	1-2	1-2	4-2	3-3	1-1	3-2	1-1	0-0	2-0	2-2	0-2	3-2	3-2	0-0
Coventry City FC	0-2	2-1	1-0		3-1	3-0	3-1	1-1	0-1	2-1	3-1	2-2	2-0	2-2	3-1	0-0	1-2	0-0	2-0	0-0
Crystal Palace FC	0-0	0-0	2-1	2-1		2-1	0-0	1-1	1-0	1-0	1-3	3-0	1-3	2-2	0-0	1-0	2-1	2-1	1-0	4-3
Derby County FC	0-2	0-2	4-6	1-1	0-2		2-3	0-1	1-7	2-1	1-1	0-0	0-0	2-1	1-1	1-1	6-2	3-3	0-1	1-1
Everton FC	1-1	1-0	2-2	1-0	0-0	2-0		2-3	2-3	1-0	2-0	0-1	1-0	0-0	3-0	1-2	3-0	2-0	1-1	1-2
Leeds United AFC	2-2	5-2	4-1	2-0	1-2	3-0	2-0		4-5	2-1	1-2	0-0	3-0	3-1	2-3	2-1	2-1	5-0	0-2	3-0
Liverpool FC	0-1	2-1	2-0	1-1	3-0	2-0	3-1	3-0		4-0	2-2	4-0	3-0	2-0	1-3	2-0	3-2	2-1	2-0	1-1
Luton Town FC	1-1	2-0	2-0	1-0	1-1	2-0	1-1	1-0	3-1		2-2	0-1	0-1	1-0	1-2	0-1	3-4	1-2	0-0	0-1
Manchester City FC	0-1	2-1	2-1	2-0	0-2	2-1	1-0	2-3	0-3	3-0		3-3	2-1	3-1	2-1	2-0	3-3	3-2	2-1	1-1
Manchester United FC	0-1	1-1	2-3	2-0	2-0	3-1	0-2	1-1	1-1	4-1	1-0		3-0	0-1	3-1	2-0	3-2	3-0	1-1	2-1
Norwich City FC	0-0	2-0	1-3	2-2	0-3	2-1	1-0	2-0	1-1	1-3	1-2	0-3		2-6	1-0	3-0	3-1	3-2	2-1	0-4
Nottingham Forest FC	0-2	2-2	7-0	3-0	0-1	1-0	3-1	4-3	2-1	2-2	1-3	1-1	5-0		1-1	2-0	3-1	2-0	1-2	2-1
Queen's Park Rangers FC	1-3	2-1	1-0	1-0	1-2	1-1	1-1	2-0	1-1	6-1	1-0	1-1	1-3	1-2		1-2	2-1	3-2	0-0	0-1
Sheffield United FC	0-2	2-1	1-0	0-1	0-1	1-0	0-0	0-2	1-3	2-1	1-1	2-1	2-1	3-2	1-0		4-1	0-2	2-2	1-2
Southampton FC	1-1	1-1	3-3	2-1	2-3	0-1	3-4	2-0	1-0	1-2	2-1	1-1	1-0	1-1	3-1	2-0		3-1	3-0	1-1
Sunderland AFC	0-0	1-3	1-0	0-0	2-1	1-2	2-2	0-1	0-1	2-0	1-1	2-1	1-2	1-0	0-1	0-1	1-0		0-0	0-0
Tottenham Hotspur FC	0-0	2-1	1-1	2-2	1-1	3-0	3-3	0-0	1-3	2-1	3-1	1-2	2-1	1-1	0-0	4-0	2-0	3-3		4-2
Wimbledon FC	0-3	0-0	2-1	1-0	0-3	3-1	2-1	0-1	1-2	2-0	1-1	1-3	0-0	3-1	3-0	1-1	1-1	2-2	5-1	

	Division 1	Pd	Wn	Dw	Ls	GF	GA	Pts	
1.	ARSENAL FC (LONDON)	38	24	13	1	74	18	83	-2
2.	Liverpool FC (Liverpool)	38	23	7	8	77	40	76	
3.	Crystal Palace FC (London)	38	20	9	9	50	41	69	
4.	Leeds United AFC (Leeds)	38	19	7	12	65	47	64	
5.	Manchester City FC (Manchester)	38	17	11	10	64	53	62	
6.	Manchester United FC (Manchester)	38	16	12	10	58	45	59	-1
7.	Wimbledon FC (London)	38	14	14	10	53	46	56	
8.	Nottingham Forest FC (Nottingham)	38	14	12	12	65	50	54	
9.	Everton FC (Liverpool)	38	13	12	13	50	46	51	
10.	Tottenham Hotspur FC (London)	38	11	16	11	51	50	49	
11.	Chelsea FC (London)	38	13	10	15	58	69	49	
12.	Queen's Park Rangers FC (London)	38	12	10	16	44	53	46	
13.	Sheffield United FC (Sheffield)	38	13	7	18	36	55	46	
14.	Southampton FC (Southampton)	38	12	9	17	58	69	45	
15.	Norwich City FC (Norwich)	38	13	6	19	41	64	45	
16.	Coventry City FC (Coventry)	38	11	11	16	42	49	44	
17.	Aston Villa FC (Birmingham)	38	9	14	15	46	58	41	
18.	Luton Town FC (Luton)	38	10	7	21	42	61	37	
19.	Sunderland AFC (Sunderland)	38	8	10	20	38	60	34	R
20.	Derby County FC (Derby)	38	5	9	24	37	75	24	R
		760	277	206	277	1049	1049	1034	

Note: Arsenal FC were deducted 2 points and Manchester United deducted 1 point after players of each club were involved in a mass brawl during the league match at Old Trafford, Manchester on 20th October 1990.

Top Goalscorers

1)	Alan SMITH	(Arsenal FC)	22
2)	Lee CHAPMAN	(Leeds United AFC)	21
3)	John FASHANU	(Wimbledon FC)	20
	Niall QUINN	(Manchester City FC)	20

Football League Division 2 1990-91 Season	Barnsley	Blackburn Rovers	Brighton & H.A.	Bristol City	Bristol Rovers	Charlton Athletic	Hull City	Ipswich Town	Leicester City	Middlesbrough	Millwall	Newcastle United	Notts County	Oldham Athletic	Oxford United	Plymouth Argyle	Portsmouth	Port Vale	Sheffield Wednesday	Swindon Town	Watford	W.B.A.	West Ham United	Wolves
Barnsley FC	■	0-1	2-1	2-0	1-0	1-1	3-1	5-1	1-1	1-0	1-2	1-1	1-0	0-1	3-0	1-0	4-0	1-1	1-1	5-1	2-1	1-1	1-0	1-1
Blackburn Rovers FC	1-2	■	1-2	0-1	2-2	2-2	2-1	0-1	4-1	1-0	1-0	0-1	0-1	2-0	1-3	0-0	1-1	1-1	1-0	2-1	0-2	0-3	3-1	1-1
Brighton & Hove Alb.	1-0	1-0	■	0-1	0-1	3-2	3-1	2-1	3-0	2-4	0-0	4-2	0-0	1-2	0-3	3-2	3-2	1-2	0-4	3-3	3-0	2-0	1-0	1-1
Bristol City FC	1-0	4-2	3-1	■	1-0	0-1	4-1	4-2	1-0	3-0	1-4	1-0	3-2	1-2	3-1	1-1	4-1	1-1	1-1	0-4	3-2	2-0	1-1	1-1
Bristol Rovers FC	2-1	1-2	1-3	3-2	■	2-1	1-1	1-0	0-0	2-0	1-1	1-1	2-0	1-0	0-0	1-2	2-0	0-1	2-1	3-1	1-1	0-1	1-1	
Charlton Athletic FC	2-1	0-0	1-2	2-1	2-2	■	2-1	1-1	1-2	0-1	0-0	1-0	3-1	1-1	3-3	0-1	2-1	0-1	0-1	1-2	1-2	2-0	1-1	1-0
Hull City AFC	1-2	3-1	0-1	1-2	2-0	2-2	■	3-3	5-2	0-0	1-1	2-1	1-2	2-2	3-3	2-0	0-2	3-2	0-1	1-1	1-1	1-1	0-0	1-2
Ipswich Town FC	2-0	2-1	1-3	1-1	2-1	4-4	2-0	■	3-2	0-1	0-3	2-1	0-0	1-2	1-1	3-1	2-2	3-0	0-2	1-1	1-1	1-0	0-0	
Leicester City FC	2-1	1-3	3-0	3-0	3-2	1-2	0-1	1-2	■	4-3	1-2	5-4	2-1	0-0	1-0	3-1	2-1	1-1	2-4	2-2	0-0	2-1	1-2	1-0
Middlesbrough FC	1-0	0-1	2-0	2-1	1-2	1-2	3-0	1-1	6-0	■	2-1	3-0	1-0	0-1	0-0	0-0	1-2	4-0	0-2	2-0	1-2	3-2	0-0	2-0
Millwall FC	4-1	2-1	3-0	1-2	1-1	3-1	3-3	1-1	2-1	2-2	■	0-1	1-2	0-0	1-2	4-1	2-0	1-2	4-2	1-0	0-2	4-1	1-1	2-1
Newcastle United FC	0-0	1-0	0-0	0-0	0-2	1-3	1-2	2-2	2-1	0-0	1-2	■	0-2	3-2	2-2	2-0	2-1	2-0	1-0	1-1	1-0	1-1	1-1	0-0
Notts County FC	2-3	4-1	2-1	3-2	3-2	2-2	2-1	3-1	0-2	3-2	0-1	3-0	■	2-0	3-1	4-0	2-1	1-1	0-2	0-0	1-0	4-3	0-1	1-1
Oldham Athletic AFC	2-0	1-1	6-1	2-1	2-0	1-1	1-2	2-0	2-0	2-0	1-1	1-1	2-1	■	3-0	5-3	3-1	2-0	3-2	3-2	4-1	2-1	1-1	4-1
Oxford United FC	2-0	0-0	3-0	3-1	3-1	1-1	1-0	2-1	2-2	2-5	0-0	0-0	3-3	5-1	■	0-0	1-0	5-2	2-2	2-4	0-1	1-3	2-1	1-1
Plymouth Argyle FC	1-1	4-1	2-0	1-0	2-2	2-0	4-1	0-0	2-0	1-1	3-2	0-1	0-0	1-2	2-2	■	1-1	2-0	1-1	3-3	1-1	2-0	0-1	1-0
Portsmouth FC	0-0	3-2	1-0	4-1	3-1	0-1	5-1	1-1	3-1	0-3	0-0	2-1	1-4	1-1	3-1		■	2-4	2-0	2-1	0-1	1-1	1-1	0-0
Port Vale FC	0-1	3-0	0-1	3-2	3-2	1-1	0-0	1-2	2-0	0-1	0-1	0-1	1-0	0-1	5-1	3-2		■	1-1	3-1	0-1	0-2	1-1	1-2
Sheffield Wednesday	3-1	3-1	1-1	3-1	2-1	0-0	5-1	2-2	0-0	2-0	2-1	2-2	2-2	2-2	0-2	3-0	2-1	1-1	■	2-1	2-0	1-0	1-1	2-2
Swindon Town FC	1-2	1-1	1-3	0-1	0-2	2-1	0-1	1-0	5-2	1-3	0-0	3-2	1-2	2-2	0-0	1-1	3-0	1-2	2-1	■	1-2	2-1	1-0	1-0
Watford FC	0-0	0-3	0-1	2-3	1-1	2-1	0-1	1-1	1-0	0-3	1-2	1-2	1-3	1-1	1-1	2-0	0-1	2-1	2-2	2-2	■	1-1	0-1	3-1
West Bromwich Alb.	1-1	2-0	1-1	2-1	3-1	1-0	1-1	1-2	2-1	1-0	1-1	1-1	2-2	0-0	2-0	1-2	0-0	1-1	1-2	2-1	1-1	■	0-0	1-1
West Ham United FC	3-2	1-0	2-1	1-0	1-0	2-1	7-1	3-1	1-0	0-0	3-1	1-1	1-2	2-0	2-0	2-2	1-1	0-0	1-3	2-0	1-0	3-1	■	1-1
Wolverhampton W.	0-5	2-3	2-3	4-0	1-1	3-0	0-0	2-2	2-1	1-0	4-1	2-1	0-2	2-3	3-3	3-1	3-1	3-2	1-2	0-0	2-2	2-1		■

Division 2

		Pd	Wn	Dw	Ls	GF	GA	Pts	
1.	Oldham Athletic AFC (Oldham)	46	25	13	8	83	53	88	P
2.	West Ham United FC (London)	46	24	15	7	60	34	87	P
3.	Sheffield Wednesday FC (Sheffield)	46	22	16	8	80	51	82	P
4.	Notts County FC (Nottingham)	46	23	11	12	76	55	80	POP
5.	Millwall FC (London)	46	20	13	13	70	51	73	PO
6.	Brighton & Hove Albion FC (Hove)	46	21	7	18	63	69	70	PO
7.	Middlesbrough FC (Middlesbrough)	46	20	9	17	66	47	69	PO
8.	Barnsley FC (Barnsley)	46	19	12	15	63	48	69	
9.	Bristol City FC (Bristol)	46	20	7	19	68	71	67	
10.	Oxford United FC (Oxford)	46	14	19	13	69	66	61	
11.	Newcastle United FC (Newcastle-upon-Tyne)	46	14	17	15	49	56	59	
12.	Wolverhampton Wanderers FC (Wolverhampton)	46	13	19	14	63	63	58	
13.	Bristol Rovers FC (Bristol)	46	15	13	18	56	59	58	
14.	Ipswich Town FC (Ipswich)	46	13	18	15	60	68	57	
15.	Port Vale FC (Stoke-on-Trent)	46	15	12	19	56	64	57	
16.	Charlton Athletic FC (London)	46	13	17	16	57	61	56	
17.	Portsmouth FC (Portsmouth)	46	14	11	21	58	70	53	
18.	Plymouth Argyle FC (Plymouth)	46	12	17	17	54	68	53	
19.	Blackburn Rovers FC (Blackburn)	46	14	10	22	51	66	52	
20.	Watford FC (Watford)	46	12	15	19	45	59	51	
21.	Swindon Town FC (Swindon)	46	12	14	20	65	73	50	
22.	Leicester City FC (Leicester)	46	14	8	24	60	83	50	
23.	West Bromwich Albion FC (West Bromwich)	46	10	18	18	52	61	48	R
24.	Hull City AFC (Kingston-upon-Hull)	46	10	15	21	57	85	45	R
		1104	389	326	389	1481	1481	1493	

Promotion Play-offs

Notts County FC (Nottingham)	3-1	Brighton & Hove Albion FC (Hove)
Brighton & Hove Albion FC (Hove)	4-1, 2-1	Millwall FC (London)
Middlesbrough FC (Middlesbrough)	1-1, 0-1	Notts County FC (Nottingham)

Football League Division 3 1990-91 Season

	Birmingham City	Bolton Wanderers	Bournemouth	Bradford City	Brentford	Bury	Cambridge United	Chester City	Crewe Alexandra	Exeter City	Fulham	Grimsby Town	Huddersfield Town	Leyton Orient	Mansfield Town	Preston North End	Reading	Rotherham United	Shrewsbury Town	Southend United	Stoke City	Swansea City	Tranmere Rovers	Wigan Athletic
Birmingham City FC	■	1-3	0-0	1-1	0-2	1-0	0-3	1-0	0-2	1-1	2-0	0-0	1-2	3-1	0-0	1-1	1-1	2-1	0-1	1-1	2-1	2-0	1-0	0-0
Bolton Wanderers FC	3-1	■	4-1	0-1	1-0	1-3	2-2	1-0	3-2	1-0	3-0	0-0	1-1	1-0	1-1	1-2	3-1	0-0	1-0	1-0	0-1	1-0	2-1	2-1
AFC Bournemouth	1-2	1-0	■	3-1	2-0	1-1	0-1	1-0	1-1	2-1	3-0	2-1	3-1	2-2	0-0	0-0	2-0	4-2	3-2	3-1	1-1	1-0	1-0	0-3
Bradford City AFC	2-0	1-1	3-0	■	0-1	3-1	0-1	2-1	2-0	3-0	0-0	0-2	2-2	4-0	1-0	2-1	1-0	2-4	2-1	1-0	1-2	0-1	1-2	2-1
Brentford FC	2-2	4-2	0-0	6-1	■	2-2	0-3	0-1	1-0	1-0	1-2	1-0	1-0	1-0	0-0	2-0	1-0	1-2	3-0	0-1	0-4	2-0	0-2	1-0
Bury FC	0-1	2-2	2-4	0-0	1-1	■	3-1	2-1	1-3	3-1	1-1	3-2	2-1	1-0	1-0	3-1	2-1	3-1	2-1	0-1	1-1	1-0	3-0	2-2
Cambridge United FC	0-1	2-1	4-0	2-1	0-0	2-2	■	1-1	3-4	1-0	1-0	0-0	1-0	2-1	1-1	3-0	4-1	3-1	1-4	3-0	2-0	3-1		2-3
Chester City FC	0-1	0-2	0-0	4-2	1-2	1-0	0-2	■	3-1	1-2	1-0	1-2	1-2	2-0	1-0	1-1	1-0	1-2	3-2	1-0	1-1	2-1	0-2	1-2
Crewe Alexandra FC	1-1	1-3	0-0	0-0	3-3	2-2	3-1	1-3	■	1-1	1-1	1-2	1-1	3-3	3-0	2-2	3-1	1-2	0-2	1-2	3-0	2-3		1-0
Exeter City FC	0-2	2-1	2-0	2-2	1-1	2-0	0-1	1-1	3-0	■	0-1	0-0	2-2	2-0	2-0	4-0	1-3	2-0	3-0	1-2	2-0	2-0	0-0	1-0
Fulham FC	2-2	0-1	1-1	0-0	0-1	2-0	0-2	4-1	2-1	3-2	■	0-0	0-0	1-1	1-0	1-0	1-1	2-0	4-0	0-3	0-1	1-1	1-2	1-2
Grimsby Town FC	0-0	0-1	5-0	1-1	2-0	0-1	1-0	2-0	0-1	2-1	3-0	■	4-0	2-2	2-0	4-1	3-0	2-1	1-0	1-0	2-0	1-0	0-1	4-3
Huddersfield Town	0-1	4-0	1-3	1-2	1-2	2-1	3-1	1-1	3-1	1-0	1-0	1-1	■	1-0	2-2	1-0	0-2	4-0	2-1	1-2	3-0	1-2	2-1	1-0
Leyton Orient FC	1-1	0-1	2-0	2-1	1-2	1-0	0-3	1-0	3-2	1-0	1-0	0-2	1-0	■	2-1	1-0	4-0	3-0	3-2	0-1	0-2	3-0	4-0	1-1
Mansfield Town FC	1-2	4-0	1-1	0-1	0-2	0-1	2-2	1-0	1-3	0-2	1-1	1-1	0-0	3-3	■	0-1	2-0	1-2	2-1	0-1	0-0	2-0	0-2	1-1
Preston North End	2-0	1-2	0-0	0-3	1-1	1-1	0-2	0-0	5-1	1-0	1-0	1-3	1-1	2-1	3-1	■	1-2	1-2	4-3	2-1	2-0	2-0	0-4	2-1
Reading FC	2-2	0-1	2-1	1-2	1-2	1-0	2-2	2-2	2-1	1-0	1-0	2-0	1-2	1-2	2-1	3-3	■	2-0	1-2	2-4	1-0	0-0	1-0	3-1
Rotherham United	1-1	2-2	1-1	0-2	2-2	0-3	3-2	2-1	1-1	2-4	3-1	1-4	1-3	0-0	1-1	1-0	0-2	■	2-2	0-1	0-0	2-3	1-1	5-1
Shrewsbury Town	4-1	0-1	3-1	1-0	1-1	1-1	1-2	1-0	1-0	2-2	2-2	1-2	0-0	3-0	0-3	0-1	5-1	0-0	■	0-1	2-0	1-2	0-1	0-0
Southend United	2-1	1-1	2-1	1-1	0-1	2-1	0-0	1-1	3-2	2-1	1-1	2-0	1-1	2-1	3-2	1-2	2-1	2-1		■	1-0	4-1	1-0	0-2
Stoke City FC	0-1	2-2	1-3	2-1	2-2	2-2	1-1	2-3	1-0	2-1	2-1	0-0	2-0	1-2	3-1	0-1	0-1	3-1	1-3	4-0	■	2-2	1-1	2-0
Swansea City FC	2-0	1-2	1-2	0-2	2-2	1-2	0-0	1-0	3-1	0-3	2-2	0-0	1-0	0-0	1-2	3-1	3-1	5-0	0-1	1-4	2-1	■	1-1	1-6
Tranmere Rovers FC	1-0	1-1	1-0	2-1	2-1	1-2	2-0	1-2	2-0	1-0	1-1	1-2	2-0	3-0	6-2	2-1	0-0	1-2	1-1	3-1	1-2	2-1	■	1-1
Wigan Athletic AFC	1-1	2-1	2-0	3-0	1-0	1-2	0-1	2-0	1-0	4-1	2-0	2-0	1-1	1-2	0-2	2-1	1-0	2-0	2-2	4-1	4-0	2-4	0-1	■

Division 3	Pd	Wn	Dw	Ls	GF	GA	Pts	
1. Cambridge United FC (Cambridge)	46	25	11	10	75	45	86	P
2. Southend United FC (Southend-on-Sea)	46	26	7	13	67	51	85	P
3. Grimsby Town FC (Cleethorpes)	46	24	11	11	66	34	83	P
4. Bolton Wanderers FC (Bolton)	46	24	11	11	64	50	83	PO
5. Tranmere Rovers FC (Birkenhead)	46	23	9	14	64	46	78	POP
6. Brentford FC (London)	46	21	13	12	59	47	76	PO
7. Bury FC (Bury)	46	20	13	13	67	56	73	PO
8. Bradford City AFC (Bradford)	46	20	10	16	62	54	70	
9. AFC Bournemouth (Bournemouth)	46	19	13	14	58	58	70	
10. Wigan Athletic AFC (Wigan)	46	20	9	17	71	54	69	
11. Huddersfield Town AFC (Huddersfield)	46	18	13	15	57	51	67	
12. Birmingham City FC (Birmingham)	46	16	17	13	45	49	65	
13. Leyton Orient FC (London)	46	18	10	18	55	58	64	
14. Stoke City FC (Stoke-on-Trent)	46	16	12	18	55	59	60	
15. Reading FC (Reading)	46	17	8	21	53	66	59	
16. Exeter City FC (Exeter)	46	16	9	21	58	52	57	
17. Preston North End FC (Preston)	46	15	11	20	54	67	56	
18. Shrewsbury Town FC (Shrewsbury)	46	14	10	22	61	68	52	
19. Chester City FC (Chester)	46	14	9	23	46	58	51	
20. Swansea City FC (Swansea)	46	13	9	24	49	72	48	
21. Fulham FC (London)	46	10	16	20	41	56	46	
22. Crewe Alexandra FC (Crewe)	46	11	11	24	62	80	44	R
23. Rotherham United FC (Rotherham)	46	10	12	24	50	87	42	R
24. Mansfield Town FC (Mansfield)	46	8	14	24	42	63	38	R
	1104	418	268	418	1381	1381	1522	

Promotion Play-offs

Tranmere Rovers FC (Birkenhead)	1-0 (aet)	Bolton Wanderers FC (Bolton)
Brentford FC (London)	2-2, 0-1	Tranmere Rovers FC (Birkenhead)
Bury FC (Bury)	1-1, 0-1	Bolton Wanderers FC (Bolton)

Football League Division 4 1990-91 Season	Aldershot Town	Blackpool	Burnley	Cardiff City	Carlisle United	Colchester United	Darlington	Doncaster Rovers	Gillingham	Halifax Town	Hartlepool	Hereford United	Lincoln City	Maidstone	Northampton Town	Peterborough United	Rochdale	Scarborough	Scunthorpe United	Stockport County	Torquay United	Walsall	Wrexham	York City
Aldershot Town FC		1-4	1-2	0-0	3-0	1-0	0-2	1-1	1-0	2-2	1-5	1-0	0-3	4-3	3-3	5-0	2-2	2-2	3-2	2-2	2-3	0-4	3-2	0-1
Blackpool FC	4-2		1-2	3-0	6-0	3-0	1-2	2-0	2-0	2-0	2-0	3-0	5-0	2-2	2-1	1-1	0-0	3-1	3-1	3-2	1-0	1-2	4-1	1-0
Burnley FC	3-0	2-0		2-0	2-1	0-1	3-1	1-0	2-2	2-1	4-0	2-1	2-2	2-1	3-0	4-1	1-0	2-1	1-1	3-2	1-1	2-0	2-0	0-0
Cardiff City AFC	1-3	1-1	3-0		3-1	2-1	0-1	0-2	2-0	1-0	1-0	0-2	0-1	0-0	1-0	1-1	0-1	0-0	1-0	3-3	3-3	0-2	1-0	2-1
Carlisle United FC	1-2	1-0	1-1	3-2		1-0	0-2	2-3	0-4	0-3	1-0	0-1	0-0	1-0	4-1	3-2	1-1	4-1	0-3	1-0	3-1	0-3	2-0	1-0
Chesterfield FC	1-0	2-2	2-1	0-0	4-1		2-2	2-1	1-1	2-2	2-3	1-0	1-1	1-2	0-0	2-2	1-1	0-1	1-1	1-1	2-2	2-1	2-2	
Darlington FC	3-1	1-1	3-1	4-1	3-1	1-0		1-1	1-1	3-0	0-1	1-1	3-1	1-1	1-1	0-1	2-0	0-0	1-0	1-0	0-0			
Doncaster Rovers FC	3-0	1-0	2-1	1-1	4-0	0-1	0-1		1-1	1-2	2-2	3-1	1-0	3-0	2-1	0-2	1-0	0-2	2-3	1-0	1-1	2-0	3-1	2-2
Gillingham FC	1-1	2-2	3-2	4-0	2-1	0-1	1-0	2-0		1-0	3-0	2-1	2-2	0-2	0-0	2-3	2-2	1-1	1-1	1-3	2-2	1-0	2-3	2-1
Halifax Town AFC	3-0	5-3	1-2	1-2	1-1	2-1	0-0	0-1	1-2		1-2	0-4	1-1	3-2	2-1	1-1	2-0	1-2	0-0	0-1	5-2	2-0	2-1	
Hartlepool United FC	1-0	1-2	0-0	0-2	4-1	2-0	0-0	1-1	1-0	2-1		2-1	1-0	3-1	0-2	1-0	2-0	2-2	3-1	1-0	2-1	2-1	0-1	
Hereford United FC	1-0	1-1	3-0	1-1	4-2	2-3	1-1	1-1	1-1	1-3		0-1	4-0	1-2	0-0	2-0	3-3	2-0	0-1	1-0	2-0			
Lincoln City FC	2-2	0-1	0-0	0-0	6-2	1-1	0-3	0-0	1-1	1-0	3-1	1-1		2-1	3-1	0-2	1-2	2-0	1-2	0-3	3-2	2-1	0-0	2-1
Maidstone United FC	1-1	1-1	2-1	3-0	0-0	1-0	2-3	0-1	3-1	5-1	1-4	1-1	4-1		1-3	2-0	0-1	6-1	2-3	2-2	1-3	0-2	5-4	
Northampton Town	2-1	1-0	0-0	0-0	1-2	0-3	0-0	2-1	1-0	3-2	3-0	1-1	2-0		1-2	3-2	0-2	1-1	2-0	2-1	1-0	5-0	1-0	
Peterborough United	3-2	2-0	3-2	1-1	2-1	2-1	2-2	1-1	2-0	2-0	1-1	3-0	2-0	2-0	1-0		1-1	2-0	0-0	0-0	1-2	0-0	2-2	2-0
Rochdale AFC	4-0	2-1	0-0	0-0	0-1	3-0	1-1	0-3	1-3	1-1	0-0	2-1	0-0	3-2	1-1	0-3		1-1	2-1	1-0	0-0	3-2	2-0	2-1
Scarborough FC	2-0	0-1	0-1	1-2	1-1	1-0	1-1	2-1	2-1	1-1	2-0	1-1	3-0	0-2	1-1	3-1	0-0		3-1	0-2	1-0	1-1	4-2	2-2
Scunthorpe United	6-2	2-0	1-3	0-2	2-0	2-1	1-1	1-0	4-4	2-1	3-0	1-1	2-2	3-0	1-2	2-1	3-0		3-0	3-0	1-0	2-0	2-0	
Stockport County	3-2	0-0	2-2	1-1	3-1	3-1	3-1	0-0	1-1	5-1	1-3	4-2	4-0	1-2	2-1	3-0	2-2	5-0		2-1	3-0	2-0	2-0	
Torquay United FC	5-0	2-1	2-0	2-1	3-0	2-0	2-1	1-0	3-1	3-1	1-5	1-1	0-1	1-1	0-0	3-1	2-0	1-1	1-1		0-0	1-0	2-1	
Walsall FC	2-2	2-0	1-0	0-0	1-1	3-0	2-2	1-0	0-0	3-1	0-1	0-0	0-0	3-3	0-1	0-0	3-0	0-2	2-2		1-0		1-1	
Wrexham AFC	4-2	0-1	2-4	1-0	3-0	1-1	1-1	2-1	3-0	1-2	2-2	1-2	2-2	2-2	0-2	0-0	2-1	1-2	1-0	1-3	2-1	1-1		0-4
York City FC	2-0	0-1	2-0	1-2	2-0	0-2	0-1	3-1	1-1	3-3	0-0	1-0	1-0	0-1	0-1	0-4	0-2	2-0	2-2	2-0	0-2	0-0	1-0	

	Division 4	Pd	Wn	Dw	Ls	GF	GA	Pts	
1.	Darlington FC (Darlington)	46	22	17	7	68	38	83	P
2.	Stockport County FC (Stockport)	46	23	13	10	84	47	82	P
3.	Hartlepool United FC (Hartlepool)	46	24	10	12	67	48	82	P
4.	Peterborough United FC (Peterborough)	46	21	17	8	67	45	80	P
5.	Blackpool FC (Blackpool)	46	23	10	13	78	47	79	PO
6.	Burnley FC (Burnley)	46	23	10	13	70	51	79	PO
7.	Torquay United FC (Torquay)	46	18	18	10	64	47	72	POP
8.	Scunthorpe United FC (Scunthorpe)	46	20	11	15	71	62	71	PO
9.	Scarborough FC (Scarborough)	46	19	12	15	59	56	69	
10.	Northampton Town FC (Northampton)	46	18	13	15	57	58	67	
11.	Doncaster Rovers FC (Doncaster)	46	17	14	15	56	46	65	
12.	Rochdale AFC (Rochdale)	46	15	17	14	50	53	62	
13.	Cardiff City AFC (Cardiff)	46	15	15	16	43	54	60	
14.	Lincoln City FC (Lincoln)	46	14	17	15	50	61	59	
15.	Gillingham FC (Gillingham)	46	12	18	16	57	60	54	
16.	Walsall FC (Walsall)	46	12	17	17	48	51	53	
17.	Hereford United FC (Hereford)	46	13	14	19	53	58	53	
18.	Chesterfield FC (Chesterfield)	46	13	14	19	47	62	53	
19.	Maidstone United FC (Maidstone)	46	13	12	21	66	71	51	
20.	Carlisle United FC (Carlisle)	46	13	9	24	47	89	48	
21.	York City FC (York)	46	11	13	22	45	57	46	
22.	Halifax Town AFC (Halifax)	46	12	10	24	59	79	46	
23.	Aldershot FC (Aldershot)	46	10	11	25	61	101	41	
24.	Wrexham AFC (Wrexham)	46	10	10	26	48	74	40	*
		1104	391	322	391	1415	1415	1495	

Promotion Play-offs

Torquay United FC (Torquay)	2-2 (aet)	Blackpool FC (Blackpool)
	(Torquay United won 5-4 on penalties)	
Scunthorpe United FC (Scunthorpe)	1-1, 1-2	Blackpool FC (Blackpool)
Torquay United FC (Torquay)	2-0, 0-1	Burnley FC (Burnley)

Promoted to Division 4: Barnet FC (London)

* Wrexham AFC were saved from relegation to non-league status due to the expansion of the Football League from 92 to 93 clubs. As a result Division 1 was extended to 22 clubs and Division 4 was reduced to 23 clubs.

F.A. CUP FINAL   (Wembley Stadium, London – 18/05/1991 – 80,000)

TOTTENHAM HOTSPUR FC (LONDON)   2-1 (aet)   Nottingham Forest FC (Nottingham)

Stewart 54', Walker 93' o.g.   *Pearce 15'*

Tottenham: Thorstvedt, Edinburgh, van den Hauwe, Sedgley, Howells, Mabbutt, Stewart, Gascoigne (Nayim 17'), Samways (Walsh 81'), Lineker, Allen.

Forest: Crossley, Charles, Pearce, Walker, Chettle, Keane, Crosby, Parker, Clough, Glover (Laws 107'), Woan (Hodge 61').

Semi-finals

Nottingham Forest FC (Nottingham)	4-0	West Ham United FC (London)
Tottenham Hotspur FC (London)	3-1	Arsenal FC (London)

Quarter-finals

Arsenal FC (London)	2-1	Cambridge United FC (Cambridge)
Norwich City FC (Norwich)	0-1	Nottingham Forest FC (Nottingham)
Tottenham Hotspur FC (London)	2-1	Notts County FC (Nottingham)
West Ham United FC (London)	2-1	Everton FC (Liverpool)

1991-92

Football League Division 1 1991-92 Season	Arsenal	Aston Villa	Chelsea	Coventry City	Crystal Palace	Everton	Leeds United	Liverpool	Luton Town	Man. City	Man. United	Norwich City	Nottingham F.	Notts County	Oldham Athletic	Q.P.R.	Sheffield United	Sheffield Wed.	Southampton	Tottenham H.	West Ham Utd.	Wimbledon
Arsenal FC	■	0-0	3-2	1-2	4-1	4-2	1-1	4-0	2-0	2-1	1-1	1-1	3-3	2-0	2-1	1-1	5-2	7-1	5-1	2-0	0-1	1-1
Aston Villa FC	3-1	■	3-1	2-0	0-1	0-0	1-4	1-0	4-0	3-1	0-1	1-0	3-1	1-0	1-0	0-1	1-1	0-1	2-1	0-0	3-1	2-1
Chelsea FC	1-1	2-0	■	0-1	1-1	2-2	0-1	2-2	4-1	1-1	1-3	0-3	1-0	2-2	4-2	2-1	1-2	0-3	1-1	2-0	2-1	2-2
Coventry City FC	0-1	1-0	0-1	■	1-2	0-1	0-0	0-0	5-0	0-1	0-0	0-0	0-2	1-0	1-1	2-2	3-1	0-0	2-0	1-2	1-0	0-1
Crystal Palace FC	1-4	0-0	0-0	0-1	■	2-0	1-0	1-0	1-1	1-1	1-3	3-4	0-0	1-1	0-0	2-2	2-1	1-1	1-0	1-2	2-3	3-2
Everton FC	3-1	0-2	2-1	3-0	2-2	■	1-1	1-1	1-1	1-2	0-0	1-1	1-0	1-1	2-2	0-1	2-1	1-6	3-1	4-0	2-0	0-0
Leeds United AFC	2-2	0-0	3-0	2-0	1-1	1-0	■	1-0	3-0	1-1	1-0	1-0	3-0	1-0	2-0	4-3	1-1	3-3	1-1	0-0	1-1	5-1
Liverpool FC	2-0	1-1	1-2	1-0	1-2	3-1	0-0	■	2-1	2-2	2-0	2-1	2-0	4-0	2-1	2-1	1-1	2-0	2-1	1-0	0-0	2-3
Luton Town FC	1-0	2-0	2-0	1-0	1-1	1-0	0-2	0-0	■	2-2	1-1	2-0	2-1	1-1	2-1	0-1	2-1	2-2	2-1	0-0	0-1	2-1
Manchester City FC	1-0	2-0	0-0	1-0	3-2	0-1	4-0	2-1	4-0	■	0-0	2-1	2-1	0-0	1-2	3-2	1-0	0-1	1-0	2-0	0-0	0-0
Manchester United FC	1-1	1-0	1-1	4-0	2-0	1-0	1-1	0-0	5-0	1-1	■	3-0	1-2	2-0	1-0	1-4	2-0	1-1	1-0	3-1	2-2	0-0
Norwich City FC	1-3	2-1	0-1	3-2	3-3	4-3	2-2	3-0	1-0	0-0	1-3	■	0-0	0-1	1-2	0-2	1-0	2-1	0-1	2-1	1-1	1-1
Nottingham Forest FC	3-2	1-1	1-1	1-0	5-1	4-1	0-1	1-1	1-1	2-0	1-0	2-0	■	1-1	3-1	1-2	5-0	0-2	1-3	1-3	2-2	4-2
Notts County FC	0-1	0-0	2-0	1-0	2-3	0-0	2-4	1-2	2-1	1-3	2-2	0-4	0-1	■	2-0	0-1	1-3	2-1	1-0	0-2	3-0	1-1
Oldham Athletic AFC	1-1	3-2	3-0	2-1	2-3	2-2	1-1	2-3	5-1	2-5	3-6	2-2	2-1	4-3	■	2-1	2-1	3-0	1-1	1-0	2-2	0-1
Queen's Park Rangers FC	0-0	0-1	2-2	1-1	1-0	3-1	4-1	0-0	4-0	0-0	0-2	0-2	1-1	1-3	1-0	■	1-0	1-1	2-2	1-2	0-0	1-1
Sheffield United FC	1-1	2-0	0-1	0-3	1-1	2-1	2-3	2-0	1-1	4-2	1-2	1-0	4-2	1-3	2-0	0-0	■	2-0	0-2	1-1	1-1	0-0
Sheffield Wednesday FC	1-1	2-3	3-0	1-1	4-1	2-1	1-6	0-0	3-2	2-0	3-2	2-0	1-0	1-1	4-1	1-3	1-0	■	2-0	0-0	2-1	2-0
Southampton FC	0-4	1-1	1-1	0-0	1-0	1-2	0-4	1-1	2-1	0-1	0-0	0-1	1-0	2-1	1-0	1-0	2-1	0-1	■	2-3	0-1	1-0
Tottenham Hotspur FC	1-1	2-5	1-3	4-3	0-1	3-3	1-3	1-2	4-1	0-1	1-2	3-0	1-2	2-1	0-0	2-0	1-1	0-2	1-2	■	3-0	3-2
West Ham United FC	0-2	3-1	1-1	0-1	0-2	0-2	1-3	0-0	0-0	1-2	1-0	4-0	3-0	0-2	1-0	2-2	1-1	1-2	0-1	2-1	■	1-1
Wimbledon FC	1-3	2-0	1-2	1-1	1-1	0-0	0-0	0-0	3-0	1-2	3-1	3-0	2-0	2-1	0-1	3-0	2-1	0-1	3-5	2-0	0-1	■

	Division 1	Pd	Wn	Dw	Ls	GF	GA	Pts	
1.	LEEDS UNITED AFC (LEEDS)	42	22	16	4	74	37	82	
2.	Manchester United FC (Manchester)	42	21	15	6	63	33	78	
3.	Sheffield Wednesday FC (Sheffield)	42	21	12	9	62	49	75	
4.	Arsenal FC (London)	42	19	15	8	81	46	72	
5.	Manchester City FC (Manchester)	42	20	10	12	61	48	70	
6.	Liverpool FC (Liverpool)	42	16	16	10	47	40	64	
7.	Aston Villa FC (Birmingham)	42	17	9	16	48	44	60	
8.	Nottingham Forest FC (Nottingham)	42	16	11	15	60	58	59	
9.	Sheffield United FC (Sheffield)	42	16	9	17	65	63	57	
10.	Crystal Palace FC (London)	42	14	15	13	53	61	57	
11.	Queen's Park Rangers FC (London)	42	12	18	12	48	47	54	
12.	Everton FC (Liverpool)	42	13	14	15	52	51	53	
13.	Wimbledon FC (London)	42	13	14	15	53	53	53	
14.	Chelsea FC (London)	42	13	14	15	50	60	53	
15.	Tottenham Hotspur FC (London)	42	15	7	20	58	63	52	
16.	Southampton FC (Southampton)	42	14	10	18	39	55	52	
17.	Oldham Athletic AFC (Oldham)	42	14	9	19	63	67	51	
18.	Norwich City FC (Norwich)	42	11	12	19	47	63	45	
19.	Coventry City FC (Coventry)	42	11	11	20	35	44	44	
20.	Luton Town FC (Luton)	42	10	12	20	38	71	42	R
21.	Notts County FC (Nottingham)	42	10	10	22	40	62	40	R
22.	West Ham United FC (London)	42	9	11	22	37	59	38	R
		924	327	270	327	1174	1174	1251	

The Football Association took over administration of Division 1 which was changed to "F.A. Premiership" for the next season. The "Football League" retained control of the lower divisions (2, 3, 4) whose names were changed to Divisions 1, 2, 3 respectively.

Top Goalscorers

1)	Ian WRIGHT	(Crystal Palace/Arsenal)	29	(including 5 for Crystal Palace)
2)	Gary LINEKER	(Tottenham Hotspur FC)	28	

Football League Division 2 — 1991-92 Season

Results grid (home team in left column, away team across top):

Home \ Away	Barnsley	Blackburn	Brighton&HA	Bristol City	Bristol Rovers	Cambridge	Charlton	Derby	Grimsby	Ipswich	Leicester	Middlesbrough	Millwall	Newcastle	Oxford	Plymouth	Portsmouth	Port Vale	Southend	Sunderland	Swindon	Tranmere	Watford	Wolves
Barnsley FC	■	2-1	1-2	1-2	0-1	0-0	1-0	0-3	4-1	1-0	3-1	2-1	0-2	3-0	1-0	1-3	2-0	0-0	1-0	0-3	1-1	1-1	0-3	2-0
Blackburn Rovers FC	3-0	■	1-0	4-0	3-0	2-1	0-2	2-0	2-1	1-2	0-1	2-1	2-1	3-1	1-1	5-2	1-1	1-0	2-2	2-2	2-1	0-0	1-0	1-2
Brighton & Hove Alb.	3-1	0-3	■	0-0	3-1	1-1	1-2	1-2	3-0	2-2	1-2	1-1	3-4	2-2	1-2	1-0	2-1	3-1	3-2	2-2	0-2	0-2	0-1	3-3
Bristol City FC	0-2	1-0	2-1	■	1-0	1-2	0-2	1-2	1-1	2-1	2-1	1-1	2-2	1-1	1-1	2-0	0-2	3-0	2-2	1-0	1-1	2-2	1-0	2-0
Bristol Rovers FC	0-0	3-0	4-1	3-2	■	2-2	1-0	2-3	2-3	3-3	1-1	2-1	3-2	1-2	2-1	0-0	1-0	3-3	4-1	2-1	1-1	1-0	1-1	1-1
Cambridge United FC	2-1	2-1	0-0	0-0	6-1	■	1-0	0-0	0-1	1-1	5-1	0-0	1-0	0-2	1-1	1-1	2-2	4-2	0-1	3-0	3-2	0-0	0-1	2-1
Charlton Athletic FC	1-1	0-2	2-0	2-1	1-0	1-2	■	0-2	1-3	1-1	0-0	1-0	2-1	2-2	0-0	3-0	2-0	2-0	1-4	0-0	0-1	1-1	1-1	1-1
Derby County FC	1-1	0-2	3-1	4-1	1-0	0-0	1-2	■	0-0	1-0	1-2	2-0	0-2	4-1	2-2	2-0	3-1	1-2	1-2	2-1	0-1	3-1	1-2	1-2
Grimsby Town FC	0-1	2-3	0-1	3-1	0-1	3-4	1-0	0-1	■	1-2	0-1	1-0	1-1	1-1	1-0	2-1	1-1	1-2	3-2	2-0	0-0	2-2	0-1	0-2
Ipswich Town FC	2-0	2-1	3-1	4-2	1-0	1-2	2-0	2-1	0-0	■	0-0	2-1	1-0	3-2	2-1	2-0	5-2	2-1	1-0	0-1	1-4	4-0	1-2	2-1
Leicester City FC	3-1	3-0	2-1	1-1	2-1	1-1	0-2	1-2	2-0	2-2	■	2-1	1-1	1-2	2-1	2-0	2-0	0-1	2-0	3-2	3-1	1-1	1-2	3-0
Middlesbrough FC	0-1	0-0	4-0	3-1	2-1	1-1	2-1	1-1	2-0	1-0	3-0	■	1-0	3-0	2-1	2-1	1-0	1-1	2-1	2-2	1-1	1-2	1-0	0-0
Millwall FC	1-1	1-3	1-2	2-3	0-1	1-2	1-0	1-2	1-1	2-3	2-0	2-0	■	2-1	2-1	2-1	1-1	1-0	2-0	4-1	1-1	0-3	0-4	2-1
Newcastle United FC	1-1	0-0	0-1	3-0	2-1	1-1	3-4	2-2	2-0	1-1	2-0	0-1	0-1	■	4-3	2-2	1-0	2-2	3-2	1-0	3-1	2-3	2-2	1-2
Oxford United FC	0-1	1-3	3-1	1-1	2-2	1-0	1-2	2-0	1-2	1-1	1-2	1-2	2-2	5-2	■	3-2	2-1	2-0	2-1	3-0	5-3	1-0	0-0	0-0
Plymouth Argyle FC	2-1	1-3	1-1	1-0	0-0	0-1	0-2	1-1	1-2	1-0	2-2	1-1	3-2	2-0	3-1	■	3-2	1-0	0-2	1-0	0-4	1-0	0-1	1-0
Portsmouth FC	2-0	2-2	0-0	1-0	2-0	3-0	1-2	0-1	2-0	1-1	1-0	4-0	6-1	3-1	2-1	4-1	■	1-0	1-1	1-0	1-1	2-0	0-0	0-0
Port Vale FC	0-0	2-0	2-1	1-1	0-1	1-1	1-1	1-0	0-1	1-2	1-2	1-2	0-2	0-1	2-1	1-0	0-2	■	0-0	3-3	2-2	1-1	2-1	1-1
Southend United FC	2-1	3-0	2-1	1-1	2-2	1-1	1-1	1-0	3-1	1-2	1-2	2-3	4-0	2-3	2-1	2-3	0-0	1-0	■	2-0	3-2	1-1	1-0	0-2
Sunderland AFC	2-0	1-1	4-2	1-3	1-1	2-2	1-2	1-1	1-2	3-0	1-0	6-2	1-1	2-0	0-1	1-0	1-1	1-2	0-0	■	0-0	1-1	3-1	2-1
Swindon Town FC	3-1	2-1	2-1	2-0	1-0	0-2	1-2	1-2	1-1	0-0	0-0	0-1	3-1	2-1	2-1	1-0	2-3	1-0	3-1	5-3	■	2-0	3-1	1-0
Tranmere Rovers FC	2-1	2-2	1-1	2-2	2-2	1-2	2-2	4-3	1-1	0-1	1-2	1-2	2-1	3-2	1-2	1-0	2-0	2-1	1-1	1-0	0-0	■	1-1	4-3
Watford FC	1-1	2-1	0-1	5-2	1-0	1-3	2-0	1-2	2-0	0-1	0-1	1-2	0-2	2-2	2-0	1-0	2-1	0-0	1-2	1-0	0-0	0-0	■	0-2
Wolverhampton W.	1-2	0-0	2-0	1-1	2-3	2-1	1-1	2-3	2-1	1-2	0-1	1-2	0-0	6-2	3-1	1-0	0-0	0-2	3-1	1-0	2-1	1-1	3-0	■

	Division 2	Pd	Wn	Dw	Ls	GF	GA	Pts	
1.	Ipswich Town FC (Ipswich)	46	24	12	10	70	50	84	P
2.	Middlesbrough FC (Middlesbrough)	46	23	11	12	58	41	80	P
3.	Derby County FC (Derby)	46	23	9	14	69	51	78	PO
4.	Leicester City FC (Leicester)	46	23	8	15	62	55	77	PO
5.	Cambridge United FC (Cambridge)	46	19	17	10	65	47	74	PO
6.	Blackburn Rovers FC (Blackburn)	46	21	11	14	70	53	74	POP
7.	Charlton Athletic FC (London)	46	20	11	15	54	48	71	
8.	Swindon Town FC (Swindon)	46	18	15	13	69	55	69	
9.	Portsmouth FC (Portsmouth)	46	19	12	15	65	51	69	
10.	Watford FC (Watford)	46	18	11	17	51	48	65	
11.	Wolverhampton Wanderers FC (Wolverhampton)	46	18	10	18	61	54	64	
12.	Southend United FC (Southend-on-Sea)	46	17	11	18	63	63	62	
13.	Bristol Rovers FC (Bristol)	46	16	14	16	60	63	62	
14.	Tranmere Rovers FC (Birkenhead)	46	14	19	13	56	56	61	
15.	Millwall FC (London)	46	17	10	19	64	71	61	
16.	Barnsley FC (Barnsley)	46	16	11	19	46	57	59	
17.	Bristol City FC (Bristol)	46	13	15	18	55	71	54	
18.	Sunderland AFC (Sunderland)	46	14	11	21	61	65	53	
19.	Grimsby Town FC (Cleethorpes)	46	14	11	21	47	62	53	
20.	Newcastle United FC (Newcastle-upon-Tyne)	46	13	13	20	66	84	52	
21.	Oxford United FC (Oxford)	46	13	11	22	66	73	50	
22.	Plymouth Argyle FC (Plymouth)	46	13	9	24	42	64	48	R
23.	Brighton & Hove Albion FC (Hove)	46	12	11	23	56	77	47	R
24.	Port Vale FC (Stoke-on-Trent)	46	10	15	21	42	59	45	R
		1104	408	288	408	1418	1418	1412	

Promotion Play-offs

Blackburn Rovers FC (Blackburn)	1-0	Leicester City FC (Leicester)
Blackburn Rovers FC (Blackburn)	4-2, 1-2	Derby County FC (Derby)
Cambridge United FC (Cambridge)	1-1, 0-5	Leicester City FC (Leicester)

Football League Division 3 — 1991-92 Season

	Birmingham City	Bolton Wanderers	Bournemouth	Bradford City	Brentford	Bury	Chester City	Darlington	Exeter City	Fulham	Hartlepool	Huddersfield Town	Hull City	Leyton Orient	Peterborough United	Preston North End	Reading	Shrewsbury Town	Stockport County	Stoke City	Swansea City	Torquay United	W.B.A.	Wigan Athletic
Birmingham City FC		2-1	0-1	2-0	1-0	3-2	3-2	1-0	1-0	3-1	2-1	2-0	2-2	2-2	1-1	3-1	2-0	1-0	3-0	1-1	1-1	3-0	0-3	3-3
Bolton Wanderers FC	1-1		0-2	1-1	1-2	2-1	0-0	2-0	1-2	0-3	2-2	1-1	1-0	1-0	2-1	1-0	1-1	1-0	0-0	3-1	0-0	1-0	3-0	1-1
AFC Bournemouth	2-1	1-2		1-3	0-0	4-0	2-0	1-2	1-0	0-0	2-0	1-1	0-0	0-1	1-2	1-0	3-2	1-0	1-0	1-2	3-0	2-1	2-1	3-0
Bradford City AFC	1-2	4-4	3-1		0-1	1-1	1-1	0-1	1-1	3-4	1-1	1-1	2-1	1-1	2-1	1-1	1-0	3-0	1-0	1-0	4-6	2-0	1-1	1-1
Brentford FC	2-2	3-2	2-2	3-4		0-3	2-0	4-1	3-0	4-0	1-0	2-3	4-1	4-3	2-1	1-0	1-0	2-0	2-1	2-0	3-2	3-2	1-2	4-0
Bury FC	1-0	1-1	0-1	0-1	0-3		1-2	1-0	3-1	3-1	1-1	4-4	3-2	4-2	3-0	2-3	0-1	0-0	0-0	1-3	1-0	0-0	1-1	1-4
Chester City FC	0-1	0-1	0-1	0-0	1-1	3-1		2-5	5-2	2-0	2-0	0-0	1-1	1-0	2-4	3-2	2-2	1-4	3-2	0-0	2-0	2-0	1-2	1-0
Darlington FC	1-1	3-2	0-0	1-3	1-2	0-2	1-1		5-2	3-1	4-0	1-3	0-1	0-1	1-2	0-2	2-4	3-3	1-3	0-1	1-1	3-2	0-1	0-1
Exeter City FC	2-1	2-2	0-3	1-0	1-2	5-2	0-0	4-1		1-1	1-1	0-1	0-3	2-0	2-2	4-1	2-1	1-0	2-1	0-0	2-1	1-0	1-1	0-1
Fulham FC	0-1	1-1	2-0	2-1	0-1	4-2	2-2	4-0	0-0		1-0	1-0	2-1	0-1	1-0	1-0	0-1	1-2	1-1	3-0	2-1	0-0	1-1	
Hartlepool United FC	1-0	0-4	1-0	1-0	1-0	0-0	1-0	2-0	3-1	2-0		0-0	2-3	2-3	0-1	2-0	2-0	4-2	0-1	1-1	0-1	1-1	0-0	4-3
Huddersfield Town	3-2	1-0	0-0	1-0	2-1	3-0	2-0	2-1	0-0	3-1	1-0		1-1	1-0	0-0	1-2	1-2	2-1	0-1	1-2	1-0	4-0	3-0	3-1
Hull City AFC	1-2	2-0	0-1	0-0	0-3	0-1	1-0	5-2	1-2	0-0	0-2	1-0		1-0	1-2	2-2	0-1	4-0	0-2	0-1	3-0	4-1	1-0	1-1
Leyton Orient FC	0-0	2-1	1-1	1-1	4-2	4-0	1-0	2-1	1-0	4-0	1-0	1-0			1-2	0-0	1-1	2-0	3-3	0-1	1-2	2-0	1-1	3-1
Peterborough United	2-3	1-0	2-0	2-1	1-0	0-0	2-0	1-1	1-1	4-1	3-2	2-0	3-0	0-2		1-0	5-3	3-2	1-1	3-1	1-1	0-0		0-0
Preston North End	3-2	2-1	2-2	1-1	3-2	2-0	0-3	2-1	1-3	1-2	1-4	1-0	3-1	2-1	1-1		1-1	2-2	3-2	2-2	1-1	3-0	2-0	3-0
Reading FC	1-1	1-0	0-0	1-2	0-0	3-2	0-0	2-2	1-0	0-2	0-1	1-0	0-1	3-2	1-1	2-2		2-1	1-1	3-4	1-0	6-1	1-2	3-2
Shrewsbury Town	1-1	1-3	1-2	3-2	1-0	1-1	2-2	0-2	6-1	0-0	1-4	1-1	2-3	0-1	2-0	2-0	1-2		0-1	1-0	0-0	2-2	1-3	1-0
Stockport County	2-0	2-2	5-0	4-1	2-1	2-0	0-4	2-0	4-1	2-0	0-1	1-1	1-0	3-0	2-0	1-0	1-4	0-1		0-0	5-0	2-1	3-0	3-3
Stoke City FC	2-1	2-0	1-1	0-0	2-1	1-2	0-1	3-0	5-2	2-2	3-2	0-2	2-3	2-0	3-3	2-1	3-0	1-0	2-2		2-1	3-0	1-0	3-0
Swansea City FC	0-2	1-1	3-1	2-2	1-1	2-1	3-0	4-2	1-0	2-2	1-1	0-1	0-0	2-2	1-0	2-2	1-2	1-2	2-1	2-1		1-0	0-0	3-0
Torquay United FC	1-2	2-0	1-0	1-1	1-1	0-2	3-2	3-0	1-0	0-1	3-1	0-1	2-1	1-0	2-2	1-0	1-2	1-2	2-0	1-0	1-0		1-0	0-1
West Bromwich Alb.	0-1	2-2	4-0	1-1	2-0	1-1	1-1	3-1	6-3	2-3	1-2	2-1	1-0	1-3	4-0	3-0	2-0	2-0	1-0	2-2	2-3	1-0		1-1
Wigan Athletic AFC	3-0	1-1	2-0	2-1	2-1	2-0	2-1	1-2	4-1	0-2	1-1	1-3	0-1	1-1	3-0	3-0	1-1	1-1	1-3	1-0	1-0	0-0	0-1	

	Division 3	Pd	Wn	Dw	Ls	GF	GA	Pts	
1.	Brentford FC (London)	46	25	7	14	81	55	82	P
2.	Birmingham City FC (Birmingham)	46	23	12	11	69	52	81	P
3.	Huddersfield Town AFC (Huddersfield)	46	22	12	12	59	38	78	PO
4.	Stoke City FC (Stoke-on-Trent)	46	21	14	11	69	49	77	PO
5.	Stockport County FC (Stockport)	46	22	10	14	75	51	76	PO
6.	Peterborough United FC (Peterborough)	46	20	14	12	65	58	74	POP
7.	West Bromwich Albion FC (West Bromwich)	46	19	14	13	64	49	71	
8.	AFC Bournemouth (Bournemouth)	46	20	11	15	52	48	71	
9.	Fulham FC (London)	46	19	13	14	57	53	70	
10.	Leyton Orient FC (London)	46	18	11	17	62	52	65	
11.	Hartlepool United FC (Hartlepool)	46	18	11	17	57	57	65	
12.	Reading FC (Reading)	46	16	13	17	59	62	61	
13.	Bolton Wanderers FC (Bolton)	46	14	17	15	57	56	59	
14.	Hull City AFC (Kingston-upon-Hull)	46	16	11	19	54	54	59	
15.	Wigan Athletic AFC (Wigan)	46	15	14	17	58	64	59	
16.	Bradford City AFC (Bradford)	46	13	19	14	62	61	58	
17.	Preston North End FC (Preston)	46	15	12	19	61	72	57	
18.	Chester City FC (Chester)	46	14	14	18	56	59	56	
19.	Swansea City FC (Swansea)	46	14	14	18	55	65	56	
20.	Exeter City FC (Exeter)	46	14	11	21	57	80	53	
21.	Bury FC (Bury)	46	13	12	21	55	74	51	R
22.	Shrewsbury Town FC (Shrewsbury)	46	12	11	23	53	68	47	R
23.	Torquay United FC (Torquay)	46	13	8	25	42	68	47	R
24.	Darlington FC (Darlington)	46	10	7	29	56	90	37	R
		1104	406	292	406	1435	1435	1510	

Promotion Play-offs

Peterborough United FC (Peterborough)	2-1	Stockport County FC (Stockport)
Peterborough United FC (Peterborough)	2-2, 2-1	Huddersfield Town AFC (Huddersfield)
Stockport County FC (Stockport)	1-0, 1-1	Stoke City FC (Stoke-on-Trent)

Football League Division 4 1991-92 Season

	Aldershot Town	Barnet	Blackpool	Burnley	Cardiff City	Carlisle United	Chesterfield	Crewe Alexandra	Doncaster R.	Gillingham	Halifax Town	Hereford United	Lincoln City	Maidstone	Mansfield Town	Northampton T.	Rochdale	Rotherham Utd.	Scarborough	Scunthorpe Utd.	Walsall	Wrexham	York City
Aldershot Town FC	■	0-1	2-5	1-2	1-2	2-2	---	0-2	0-0	0-0	1-3	---	0-3	3-0	1-3	1-4	1-1	0-1	---	0-0	1-1	---	---
Barnet FC	5-0	■	3-0	0-0	3-1	4-2	1-2	4-7	1-0	2-0	3-0	1-0	1-0	3-2	2-0	3-0	3-0	2-5	5-1	3-2	0-1	2-0	2-0
Blackpool FC	1-0	4-2	■	5-2	1-1	1-0	3-1	0-2	1-0	2-0	3-0	2-0	3-0	1-1	2-1	1-0	3-0	3-0	1-1	2-1	3-0	4-0	3-1
Burnley FC	2-0	3-0	1-1	■	3-1	2-0	3-0	1-1	2-1	4-1	1-0	2-0	1-0	2-1	3-2	5-0	0-1	1-2	1-1	1-1	2-0	1-2	3-1
Cardiff City AFC	2-0	3-1	1-1	0-2	■	1-0	4-0	1-1	2-1	2-3	4-0	1-0	1-2	0-5	3-2	3-2	1-2	1-0	2-1	2-2	2-1	5-0	3-0
Carlisle United FC	---	1-3	1-2	1-1	2-2	■	1-2	2-1	1-0	0-0	1-1	1-0	0-2	3-0	1-2	2-1	0-0	1-3	2-2	0-0	3-3	0-1	1-1
Chesterfield FC	2-1	3-2	1-1	0-2	2-2	0-0	■	2-1	0-0	3-3	4-0	2-0	1-5	2-0	2-1	1-0	1-1	1-1	1-0	0-1	1-1	1-3	1-1
Crewe Alexandra FC	4-0	3-0	1-0	1-0	1-1	2-1	3-1	■	1-0	2-1	3-2	4-2	1-0	1-1	1-2	1-1	1-1	0-1	3-3	1-1	0-1	2-1	1-0
Doncaster Rovers FC	1-0	1-0	0-2	1-4	1-2	0-3	0-1	1-3	■	1-1	0-2	2-0	1-5	3-0	0-1	0-3	2-0	1-1	3-2	1-2	0-1	3-1	0-1
Gillingham FC	3-1	3-3	3-2	3-0	0-0	1-2	0-1	0-1	2-1	■	2-0	2-1	1-3	1-1	2-0	3-1	0-0	5-1	2-0	4-0	4-0	2-1	1-1
Halifax Town AFC	---	3-1	1-2	0-2	1-1	3-2	2-0	2-1	0-0	0-3	■	0-2	1-4	1-1	1-3	0-1	1-1	0-4	1-0	1-4	1-0	4-3	0-0
Hereford United FC	1-0	2-2	1-2	2-0	2-2	1-0	1-0	1-2	0-1	2-0	0-2	■	3-0	2-2	0-1	1-2	1-1	1-0	4-1	1-2	1-2	3-1	2-1
Lincoln City FC	0-0	0-6	2-0	0-3	0-0	1-0	1-2	2-2	2-0	1-0	0-0	3-0	■	1-0	2-0	1-2	0-3	0-2	0-2	4-2	1-0	0-0	0-0
Maidstone United FC	1-2	1-1	0-0	0-1	1-1	5-1	0-1	2-0	2-2	1-1	0-1	3-2	0-2	■	0-0	1-1	1-1	0-0	2-1	0-1	2-1	2-4	1-0
Mansfield Town FC	3-0	1-2	1-1	0-1	3-0	2-1	2-1	4-3	2-2	4-3	3-2	1-1	0-0	2-0	■	2-0	2-1	1-0	1-2	1-3	3-1	3-0	5-2
Northampton Town FC	1-0	1-1	1-1	1-2	0-0	2-2	1-1	0-1	3-1	0-0	4-0	0-1	1-0	1-0	1-2	■	2-2	1-2	3-2	0-1	0-1	1-1	2-2
Rochdale AFC	---	1-0	4-2	1-3	2-0	3-1	3-3	1-0	1-1	2-1	1-0	3-1	1-0	1-2	0-2	1-0	■	1-1	2-2	2-0	1-1	2-1	1-1
Rotherham United FC	2-0	3-0	2-0	2-1	1-2	1-0	1-1	1-2	3-1	1-1	1-1	0-0	1-1	3-3	1-1	1-0	2-0	■	0-2	5-0	2-1	3-0	4-0
Scarborough FC	0-2	0-4	1-2	3-1	2-2	2-2	3-2	2-1	1-0	2-1	3-0	1-1	1-2	2-0	0-0	2-1	3-2	0-3	■	4-1	2-3	4-1	1-0
Scunthorpe United FC	1-0	1-1	2-1	2-2	1-0	4-0	2-0	1-0	3-2	1-0	1-1	1-0	0-2	2-0	1-4	3-0	6-2	1-0	1-1	■	1-1	3-1	1-0
Walsall FC	3-1	2-0	4-2	2-2	0-0	0-0	2-2	2-3	1-3	0-1	3-0	3-0	0-0	1-1	3-3	1-2	1-3	0-2	0-0	2-1	■	0-0	1-1
Wrexham AFC	0-0	1-0	1-1	2-6	0-3	3-0	0-1	1-0	1-2	2-0	0-1	1-1	0-0	3-2	2-2	2-1	0-3	2-0	4-0	2-1	2-1	■	2-1
York City FC	1-0	1-4	1-0	1-2	1-3	2-0	0-1	1-1	1-1	1-1	1-1	1-0	1-1	1-1	1-2	0-0	0-1	1-1	4-1	3-0	2-0	2-2	■

Division 4

		Pd	Wn	Dw	Ls	GF	GA	Pts	
1.	Burnley FC (Burnley)	42	25	8	9	79	43	83	P
2.	Rotherham United FC (Rotherham)	42	22	11	9	70	37	77	P
3.	Mansfield Town FC (Mansfield)	42	23	8	11	75	53	77	P
4.	Blackpool FC (Blackpool)	42	22	10	10	71	45	76	POP
5.	Scunthorpe United FC (Scunthorpe)	42	21	9	12	64	59	72	PO
6.	Crewe Alexandra FC (Crewe)	42	20	10	12	66	51	70	PO
7.	Barnet FC (London)	42	21	6	15	81	61	69	PO
8.	Rochdale AFC (Rochdale)	42	18	13	11	57	53	67	
9.	Cardiff City AFC (Cardiff)	42	17	15	10	66	53	66	
10.	Lincoln City FC (Lincoln)	42	17	11	14	50	44	62	
11.	Gillingham FC (Gillingham)	42	15	12	15	63	53	57	
12.	Scarborough FC (Scarborough)	42	15	12	15	64	68	57	
13.	Chesterfield FC (Chesterfield)	42	14	11	17	49	61	53	
14.	Wrexham AFC (Wrexham)	42	14	9	19	52	73	51	
15.	Walsall FC (Walsall)	42	12	13	17	48	58	49	
16.	Northampton Town FC (Northampton)	42	11	13	18	46	57	46	
17.	Hereford United FC (Hereford)	42	12	8	22	44	57	44	
18.	Maidstone United FC (Maidstone)	42	8	18	16	45	56	42	
19.	York City FC (York)	42	8	16	18	42	58	40	
20.	Halifax Town AFC (Halifax)	42	10	8	24	34	75	38	
21.	Doncaster Rovers FC (Doncaster)	42	9	8	25	40	65	35	
22.	Carlisle United FC (Carlisle)	42	7	13	22	41	67	34	
---.	Aldershot FC (Aldershot)	36	3	8	25	21	63	17	#
		924	341	242	341	1247	1247	1265	

Aldershot FC resigned from the league on 26th March 1992 after being declared bankrupt, their playing record was deleted.

Promoted to Division 4: Colchester United FC (Colchester)

F.A. CUP FINAL   (Wembley Stadium, London – 09/05/1992 – 79,544)

LIVERPOOL FC (LIVERPOOL)   2-0   Sunderland AFC (Sunderland)

Thomas 46', Rush 69'

Liverpool: Grobbelaar, Jones, Burrows, Nicol, Mølby, Wright, Saunders, Houghton, I.Rush, McManaman, Thomas.

Sunderland: Norman, Owers, Rogan, Bennett, Ball, D.Rush (Hardyman 70'), Bracewell, Davenport, Armstrong (Hawke 79'), Byrne, Atkinson.

Semi-finals

Liverpool FC (Liverpool)   1-1 (aet), 0-0 (aet)   Portsmouth FC (Portsmouth)
Liverpool won 3-1 on penalties.
Sunderland AFC (Sunderland)   1-0   Norwich City FC (Norwich)

Quarter-finals

Chelsea FC (London)   1-1, 1-2   Sunderland AFC (Sunderland)
Liverpool FC (Liverpool)   1-0   Aston Villa FC (Birmingham)
Portsmouth FC (Portsmouth)   1-0   Nottingham Forest FC (Nottingham)
Southampton FC (Southampton)   0-0, 1-2   Norwich City FC (Norwich)

1992-93

F.A. Premiership 1992-93 Season	Arsenal	Aston Villa	Blackburn R.	Chelsea	Coventry City	Crystal Palace	Everton	Ipswich Town	Leeds United	Liverpool	Man. City	Man. United	Middlesbrough	Norwich City	Nottingham F.	Oldham Athletic	Q.P.R.	Sheffield United	Sheffield Wed.	Southampton	Tottenham H.	Wimbledon
Arsenal FC	■	0-1	0-1	2-1	3-0	3-0	2-0	0-0	0-0	0-1	1-0	0-1	1-1	2-4	1-0	2-0	0-0	1-1	2-1	4-3	1-3	0-1
Aston Villa FC	1-0	■	0-0	1-3	0-0	3-0	2-1	2-0	1-1	4-2	3-1	1-0	5-1	2-3	2-1	0-1	2-0	3-1	2-0	1-1	0-0	1-0
Blackburn Rovers FC	1-0	3-0	■	2-0	2-5	1-2	2-3	2-1	3-1	4-1	1-0	0-0	1-1	7-1	4-1	2-0	1-0	1-0	1-0	0-0	0-2	0-0
Chelsea FC	0-0	0-1	0-0	■	2-1	3-1	2-1	2-1	1-0	0-0	2-4	1-1	4-0	2-3	0-0	1-1	1-0	1-2	0-2	1-1	1-1	4-2
Coventry City FC	0-2	3-0	0-2	1-2	■	2-2	0-1	2-2	3-3	5-1	2-3	0-1	2-1	1-1	0-1	3-0	0-1	1-3	1-0	2-0	1-0	0-2
Crystal Palace FC	1-2	1-0	3-3	1-1	0-0	■	0-2	3-1	1-0	1-1	0-0	0-2	4-1	1-2	1-1	2-2	1-1	2-0	1-1	1-2	1-3	2-0
Everton FC	0-0	1-0	2-1	0-1	1-1	0-2	■	3-0	2-0	2-1	1-3	0-2	2-2	0-1	3-0	2-3	5-0	0-2	1-1	2-1	1-2	0-0
Ipswich Town FC	1-2	1-1	2-1	1-1	0-0	2-2	1-0	■	4-2	2-2	3-1	2-1	0-1	3-1	2-1	1-2	1-1	0-1	0-1	0-0	1-1	2-1
Leeds United AFC	3-0	1-1	5-2	1-1	2-2	0-0	2-0	1-0	■	2-2	1-0	0-0	3-0	0-0	1-4	2-0	1-1	3-1	3-1	2-1	5-0	2-1
Liverpool FC	0-2	1-2	2-1	2-1	4-0	5-0	1-0	0-0	2-0	■	1-1	1-2	4-1	4-1	0-0	1-0	1-0	2-1	1-0	1-1	6-2	2-3
Manchester City FC	0-1	1-1	3-2	0-1	1-0	0-0	2-5	3-1	4-0	1-1	■	1-1	0-1	3-1	2-2	3-3	1-1	2-0	1-2	1-0	0-1	1-1
Manchester United FC	0-0	1-1	3-1	3-0	5-0	1-0	0-3	1-1	2-0	2-2	2-1	■	3-0	1-0	2-0	3-0	0-0	2-1	2-1	2-1	4-1	0-1
Middlesbrough FC	1-0	2-3	3-2	0-0	0-2	0-1	1-2	2-2	4-1	1-2	2-0	1-1	■	3-3	1-2	2-3	1-0	2-0	1-1	2-1	3-0	2-0
Norwich City FC	1-1	1-0	0-0	2-1	1-1	4-2	1-1	0-2	4-2	1-0	2-1	1-3	1-1	■	3-1	1-0	2-1	2-1	1-0	1-0	0-0	2-1
Nottingham Forest FC	0-1	0-1	1-3	3-0	1-1	1-1	0-1	0-1	1-1	1-0	0-2	0-2	1-0	0-3	■	2-0	1-0	0-2	1-2	1-2	2-1	1-1
Oldham Athletic AFC	0-1	1-1	0-1	3-1	0-1	1-1	1-0	4-2	2-2	3-2	0-1	1-0	4-1	2-3	5-3	■	2-2	1-1	1-1	4-3	2-1	6-2
Queen's Park Rangers FC	0-0	2-1	0-3	1-1	2-0	1-3	4-2	0-0	0-1	0-1	1-1	1-3	3-3	3-1	4-3	3-2	■	3-2	3-1	3-1	4-1	1-2
Sheffield United FC	1-1	0-2	1-3	4-2	1-1	0-1	1-0	3-0	2-1	1-0	1-1	2-1	2-0	0-1	0-0	2-1	1-2	■	1-1	2-0	6-0	2-2
Sheffield Wednesday FC	1-0	1-2	0-0	3-3	1-2	2-1	3-1	1-1	1-1	1-0	0-3	3-3	2-3	1-0	2-0	2-1	1-0	1-1	■	5-2	2-0	1-1
Southampton FC	2-0	2-0	1-1	1-0	2-2	1-0	0-0	4-3	1-1	2-1	0-1	0-1	3-0	1-2	1-0	2-1	3-2	1-2	2-1	■	0-0	2-2
Tottenham Hotspur FC	1-0	0-0	1-2	1-2	0-2	2-2	2-1	0-2	2-0	2-0	1-1	2-2	5-1	2-1	4-1	3-2	2-0	0-2	4-2	4-2	■	1-1
Wimbledon FC	3-2	2-3	1-1	0-0	1-2	4-0	1-3	0-1	1-0	2-0	0-1	1-2	2-0	3-0	1-0	5-2	0-2	2-0	1-1	1-2	1-1	■

	F.A. Premiership	Pd	Wn	Dw	Ls	GF	GA	Pts	
1.	MANCHESTER UNITED FC (MANCHESTER)	42	24	12	6	67	31	84	
2.	Aston Villa FC (Birmingham)	42	21	11	10	57	40	74	
3.	Norwich City FC (Norwich)	42	21	9	12	61	65	72	
4.	Blackburn Rovers FC (Blackburn)	42	20	11	11	68	46	71	
5.	Queen's Park Rangers FC (London)	42	17	12	13	63	55	63	
6.	Liverpool FC (Liverpool)	42	16	11	15	62	55	59	
7.	Sheffield Wednesday FC (Sheffield)	42	15	14	13	55	51	59	
8.	Tottenham Hotspur FC (London)	42	16	11	15	60	66	59	
9.	Manchester City FC (Manchester)	42	15	12	15	56	51	57	
10.	Arsenal FC (London)	42	15	11	16	40	38	56	
11.	Chelsea FC (London)	42	14	14	14	51	54	56	
12.	Wimbledon FC (London)	42	14	12	16	56	55	54	
13.	Everton FC (Liverpool)	42	15	8	19	53	55	53	
14.	Sheffield United FC (Sheffield)	42	14	10	18	54	53	52	
15.	Coventry City FC (Coventry)	42	13	13	16	52	57	52	
16.	Ipswich Town FC (Ipswich)	42	12	16	14	50	55	52	
17.	Leeds United AFC (Leeds)	42	12	15	15	57	62	51	
18.	Southampton FC (Southampton)	42	13	11	18	54	61	50	
19.	Oldham Athletic AFC (Oldham)	42	13	10	19	63	74	49	
20.	Crystal Palace FC (London)	42	11	16	15	48	61	49	R
21.	Middlesbrough FC (Middlesbrough)	42	11	11	20	54	75	44	R
22.	Nottingham Forest FC (Nottingham)	42	10	10	22	41	62	40	R
		924	332	260	332	1222	1222	1256	

Top Goalscorers

1) Teddy SHERINGHAM (Nottm.Forest/Tottenham Hotspur) 22 (1 for Nottingham Forest)
2) Les FERDINAND (Queen's Park Rangers FC) 20
3) Dean HOLDSWORTH (Wimbledon FC) 19

Football League Division 1 1992-93 Season	Barnsley	Birmingham City	Brentford	Bristol City	Bristol Rovers	Cambridge	Charlton Athletic	Derby County	Grimsby Town	Leicester City	Luton Town	Millwall	Newcastle United	Notts County	Oxford United	Peterborough Utd.	Portsmouth	Southend United	Sunderland	Swindon Town	Tranmere Rovers	Watford	West Ham United	Wolves
Barnsley FC		1-0	3-2	2-1	2-1	2-0	1-0	1-1	0-2	2-3	3-0	0-0	1-0	0-0	0-1	1-2	1-1	3-1	2-0	1-0	3-1	0-1	0-1	0-1
Birmingham City FC	3-0		1-3	0-1	2-1	0-2	1-0	1-1	2-1	0-2	2-1	0-0	2-3	1-0	1-0	2-0	2-3	2-0	1-0	4-6	0-0	2-2	1-2	0-4
Brentford FC	3-1	0-2		5-1	0-3	0-1	2-0	2-1	1-3	1-3	1-2	1-1	1-2	2-2	1-0	0-1	4-1	2-1	1-1	0-0	0-1	1-1	0-0	0-2
Bristol City FC	2-1	3-0	4-1		2-1	0-0	2-1	0-0	1-0	2-1	0-0	0-1	1-2	1-0	1-1	0-1	3-3	0-1	0-0	2-2	1-3	2-1	1-5	1-0
Bristol Rovers FC	1-5	3-3	2-1	4-0		1-1	0-2	1-2	0-3	0-0	2-0	1-0	1-2	3-3	0-1	3-1	1-2	0-2	2-2	3-4	1-0	0-3	0-4	1-1
Cambridge United FC	1-2	0-3	1-0	2-1	0-1		1-3	2-0	1-3	3-3	1-1	0-3	3-0	2-2	2-2	0-1	3-1	2-1	1-0	0-1	1-1	2-1	1-1	1-1
Charlton Athletic FC	0-0	0-0	1-0	2-1	4-1	0-0		2-1	3-1	2-0	0-0	0-2	1-3	2-1	1-1	0-1	1-0	1-1	0-1	2-0	2-2	3-1	1-1	0-1
Derby County FC	3-0	3-1	3-2	3-4	3-1	0-0	4-3		2-1	2-0	1-1	1-2	1-2	2-0	0-1	2-3	2-4	2-0	0-1	2-1	1-2	1-2	0-2	2-0
Grimsby Town FC	4-2	1-1	0-1	2-1	2-0	1-1	1-0	0-2		1-3	3-1	1-0	0-2	3-3	1-1	1-3	3-0	1-0	1-0	2-1	0-0	3-2	1-1	1-0
Leicester City FC	2-1	2-1	0-0	0-0	0-1	2-2	3-1	3-2	3-0		2-1	3-0	2-1	1-1	2-1	0-2	1-0	4-1	3-2	4-2	0-1	5-2	1-2	1-0
Luton Town FC	2-2	1-1	0-0	0-3	1-1	2-0	1-0	1-3	1-4	2-0		1-1	0-0	0-0	3-1	0-0	1-4	2-2	0-0	0-0	3-3	2-0	2-0	1-1
Millwall FC	0-4	0-0	6-1	4-1	0-3	2-2	1-0	1-0	2-1	2-0	1-0		1-2	6-0	3-1	4-0	1-1	1-1	0-0	2-1	0-0	5-2	2-1	2-0
Newcastle United FC	6-0	2-2	5-1	5-0	0-0	4-1	2-2	1-1	0-1	7-1	2-0	1-1		4-0	2-1	3-0	3-1	3-2	1-0	1-0	2-0	2-0	2-1	
Notts County FC	1-3	3-1	1-1	0-0	3-0	1-2	0-0	2-0	1-0	1-1	0-0	1-2	0-2		1-1	1-0	4-0	3-1	1-1	5-1	1-2	1-0	0-1	
Oxford United FC	0-0	0-0	0-2	2-0	2-1	3-0	0-1	0-1	0-1	0-0	4-0	3-0	4-2	1-1		2-1	5-5	0-1	0-1	0-1	1-2	1-1	1-0	0-0
Peterborough United FC	1-1	2-1	0-0	1-1	1-1	1-0	1-1	1-0	1-0	3-0	2-3	0-0	0-1	1-3	1-1		1-1	1-0	5-2	3-3	1-1	0-0	1-3	2-3
Portsmouth FC	1-0	4-0	1-0	2-3	4-1	3-0	1-0	3-0	2-1	1-1	2-1	1-0	2-0	0-0	3-0	4-0		2-0	2-0	3-1	4-0	1-0	0-1	2-0
Southend United FC	3-0	4-0	3-0	1-1	3-0	1-1	0-2	0-0	1-0	2-1	3-3	1-1	3-1	0-3	0-1	0-0		0-1	1-1	1-2	1-2	1-0	1-1	
Sunderland AFC	2-1	1-2	1-3	0-0	1-1	3-3	0-2	1-0	2-0	1-2	2-2	2-0	1-2	2-2	2-0	3-0	4-1	2-4		0-1	1-0	1-2	0-0	2-0
Swindon Town FC	1-0	0-0	0-2	2-1	2-2	4-1	2-2	2-4	1-0	1-1	1-0	3-0	2-1	5-1	2-2	1-0	1-0	3-2	1-0		2-0	3-1	1-3	1-0
Tranmere Rovers FC	2-1	4-0	3-2	3-0	2-1	2-0	0-0	2-1	1-1	2-3	0-2	1-1	0-3	3-1	4-0	1-1	0-2	3-0	2-1	3-1		2-1	5-2	3-0
Watford FC	1-2	1-0	1-0	0-0	4-2	2-2	1-1	0-0	2-3	0-3	0-0	3-1	1-0	1-3	0-1	1-2	0-0	0-0	2-1	0-4	3-2		1-2	3-1
West Ham United FC	1-1	3-1	4-0	2-0	2-1	2-0	0-1	1-1	2-1	3-0	2-2	2-2	0-0	2-0	5-3	2-1	2-0	2-0	6-0	0-1	2-0	2-1		3-1
Wolverhampton W.	1-0	2-1	1-2	0-0	5-1	1-2	2-1	0-2	2-1	3-0	1-2	3-1	1-0	3-0	0-1	4-3	1-1	1-1	2-1	2-2	0-2	2-2	0-0	

	Football League Division 1	**Pd**	**Wn**	**Dw**	**Ls**	**GF**	**GA**	**Pts**	
1.	Newcastle United FC (Newcastle-upon-Tyne)	46	29	9	8	92	38	96	P
2.	West Ham United FC (London)	46	26	10	10	81	41	88	P
3.	Portsmouth FC (Portsmouth)	46	26	10	10	80	46	88	PO
4.	Tranmere Rovers FC (Birkenhead)	46	23	10	13	72	56	79	PO
5.	Swindon Town FC (Swindon)	46	21	13	12	74	59	76	POP
6.	Leicester City FC (Leicester)	46	22	10	14	71	64	76	PO
7.	Millwall FC (London)	46	18	16	12	65	53	70	
8.	Derby County FC (Derby)	46	19	9	18	68	57	66	
9.	Grimsby Town FC (Cleethorpes)	46	19	7	20	58	57	64	
10.	Peterborough United FC (Peterborough)	46	16	14	16	55	63	62	
11.	Wolverhampton Wanderers FC (Wolverhampton)	46	16	13	17	57	56	61	
12.	Charlton Athletic FC (London)	46	16	13	17	49	46	61	
13.	Barnsley FC (Barnsley)	46	17	9	20	56	60	60	
14.	Oxford United FC (Oxford)	46	14	14	18	53	56	56	
15.	Bristol City FC (Bristol)	46	14	14	18	49	67	56	
16.	Watford FC (Watford)	46	14	13	19	57	71	55	
17.	Notts County FC (Nottingham)	46	12	16	18	55	70	52	
18.	Southend United FC (Southend-on-Sea)	46	13	13	20	54	64	52	
19.	Birmingham City FC (Birmingham)	46	13	12	21	50	72	51	
20.	Luton Town FC (Luton)	46	10	21	15	48	62	51	
21.	Sunderland AFC (Sunderland)	46	13	11	22	50	64	50	
22.	Brentford FC (London)	46	13	10	23	52	71	49	R
23.	Cambridge United FC (Cambridge)	46	11	16	19	48	69	49	R
24.	Bristol Rovers FC (Bristol)	46	10	11	25	55	87	41	R
		1104	405	294	405	1449	1449	1509	

Promotion Play-offs

Swindon Town FC (Swindon)	4-3	Leicester City FC (Leicester)
Leicester City FC (Leicester)	1-0, 2-2	Portsmouth FC (Portsmouth)
Swindon Town FC (Swindon)	3-1, 2-3	Tranmere Rovers FC (Birkenhead)

Football League Division 2 1992-93 Season

	Blackpool	Bolton Wanderers	Bournemouth	Bradford City	Brighton & Hove Albion	Burnley	Chester City	Exeter City	Fulham	Hartlepool	Huddersfield Town	Hull City	Leyton Orient	Mansfield Town	Plymouth Argyle	Port Vale	Preston North End	Reading	Rotherham United	Stockport County	Stoke City	Swansea City	W.B.A.	Wigan Athletic
Blackpool FC		1-1	2-0	3-3	2-2	1-3	2-0	2-0	1-1	1-1	2-2	5-1	3-1	1-1	1-1	2-4	2-3	0-1	2-0	2-0	1-3	0-0	2-1	2-1
Bolton Wanderers FC	3-0		1-1	5-0	0-1	4-0	5-0	4-1	1-0	1-2	2-0	2-0	1-0	2-1	3-1	1-1	1-0	2-1	2-0	2-1	1-0	3-1	0-2	2-1
AFC Bournemouth	5-1	1-2		1-1	1-1	1-1	0-0	1-3	2-1	0-2	1-1	0-0	3-0	4-1	1-3	2-1	2-1	1-1	0-0	1-0	1-1	0-2	0-1	0-0
Bradford City AFC	2-0	2-1	0-1		1-1	1-0	3-1	3-1	3-2	0-2	0-1	1-2	1-0	0-0	0-0	3-2	4-0	3-0	0-3	2-3	3-1	0-0	2-2	2-1
Brighton & Hove Alb.	1-1	2-1	1-0	1-1		3-0	3-2	3-0	0-2	1-1	2-1	2-0	1-3	3-1	2-1	0-2	2-0	0-1	1-2	2-0	2-2	0-2	3-1	1-0
Burnley FC	2-2	0-1	1-1	2-2	1-3		5-0	3-1	5-2	3-0	2-1	2-0	2-0	1-0	0-0	1-1	2-0	1-1	1-1	1-1	0-2	1-0	2-1	0-1
Chester City FC	1-2	2-2	1-0	2-5	2-1	3-0		0-3	2-3	1-0	0-2	3-0	1-3	1-2	1-2	2-4	0-3	1-2	0-3	1-1	3-2	1-3	1-2	
Exeter City FC	0-1	1-3	1-1	0-1	2-3	2-2	2-0		1-2	3-1	1-2	1-1	1-0	2-0	2-0	1-1	0-1	0-0	0-2	2-2	2-2	0-2	2-3	0-0
Fulham FC	1-0	1-4	1-1	1-1	2-0	4-0	1-0	1-1		1-3	0-1	3-3	1-0	0-0	3-1	1-2	2-1	0-1	2-1	0-0	1-1	1-1	1-0	
Hartlepool United FC	1-0	0-2	0-1	2-0	2-0	0-0	2-0	1-3	0-3		1-0	1-0	0-2	1-0	1-1	0-0	1-1	0-2	3-2	1-2	0-1	2-2	0-0	
Huddersfield Town	5-2	1-1	0-1	1-2	1-2	1-1	0-2	0-0	1-0	3-0		3-0	1-1	2-1	2-1	1-2	1-0	0-0	1-1	2-1	1-0	0-1	0-1	2-1
Hull City AFC	3-2	1-2	3-0	0-2	1-0	0-2	1-1	4-0	1-1	3-2	2-3		0-0	1-0	2-0	0-1	2-4	1-1	0-1	0-2	1-0	1-0	1-2	0-0
Leyton Orient FC	1-0	1-0	1-0	4-2	3-2	3-2	4-3	5-0	0-0	0-0	4-1	0-0		5-1	2-0	0-1	3-1	1-2	1-1	3-0	1-0	4-2	2-0	1-2
Mansfield Town FC	2-2	1-1	0-2	5-2	1-3	1-1	2-0	0-0	2-3	2-0	1-2	3-1	3-0		0-0	2-2	1-1	1-3	2-0	0-4	3-3	0-3	2-0	
Plymouth Argyle FC	2-1	2-1	2-1	3-0	3-2	1-2	2-0	0-3	1-1	2-2	1-3	0-0	2-0	3-2		0-1	4-0	2-2	2-1	3-4	1-1	0-1	0-0	2-0
Port Vale FC	2-1	0-0	3-0	1-2	3-1	3-0	2-0	2-2	0-0	2-0	1-0	1-1	2-0	3-0	4-0		2-2	3-1	4-2	0-0	0-2	2-0	2-1	2-2
Preston North End	3-3	2-2	1-1	3-2	1-0	2-0	4-3	2-2	1-2	0-2	2-1	1-2	1-4	1-5	1-2	2-5		2-0	5-2	2-3	1-2	1-3	1-1	2-0
Reading FC	0-0	1-2	3-2	1-1	3-0	1-0	1-0	2-3	3-0	2-1	2-1	1-2	1-1	3-1	3-0	1-0	4-0		3-1	2-4	0-1	2-0	1-1	4-0
Rotherham United	3-2	2-1	1-2	2-0	0-1	3-3	1-1	1-1	0-0	0-1	1-1	2-0	2-2	4-1	1-0	3-2	0-2	0-2		0-2	0-2	0-0	0-2	2-3
Stockport County	0-0	2-0	0-0	2-2	0-0	2-1	2-0	2-2	0-0	4-1	5-0	5-3	1-1	0-1	3-0	2-0	3-0	2-2	2-2		1-1	1-1	5-1	3-0
Stoke City FC	0-1	0-0	2-0	1-0	1-1	1-1	4-0	1-1	1-0	3-0	3-0	2-1	4-0	1-0	2-1	1-0	2-0	2-0	2-1	2-1		2-1	4-3	2-1
Swansea City FC	3-0	1-2	2-1	1-1	0-1	1-1	4-2	0-0	2-2	3-0	3-0	1-0	0-1	4-0	0-0	2-0	2-0	2-1	1-2	2-0	1-2		0-0	2-1
West Bromwich Alb.	3-1	3-1	2-1	1-1	3-1	2-0	2-0	2-0	4-0	3-1	2-2	3-1	2-0	2-0	2-5	0-1	3-2	3-0	2-2	3-0	1-2	3-0		5-1
Wigan Athletic AFC	2-1	0-2	0-0	1-2	1-2	1-1	1-2	0-1	1-3	2-2	1-0	2-0	3-1	2-0	0-2	0-4	2-3	1-1	1-1	1-2	1-1	2-3	1-0	

Football League Division 2	Pd	Wn	Dw	Ls	GF	GA	Pts	
1. Stoke City FC (Stoke-on-Trent)	46	27	12	7	73	34	93	P
2. Bolton Wanderers FC (Bolton)	46	27	9	10	80	41	90	P
3. Port Vale FC (Stoke-on-Trent)	46	26	11	9	79	44	89	PO
4. West Bromwich Albion FC (West Bromwich)	46	25	10	11	88	54	85	POP
5. Swansea City FC (Swansea)	46	20	13	13	65	47	73	PO
6. Stockport County FC (Stockport)	46	19	15	12	81	57	72	PO
7. Leyton Orient FC (London)	46	21	9	16	69	53	72	
8. Reading FC (Reading)	46	18	15	13	66	51	69	
9. Brighton & Hove Albion FC (Hove)	46	20	9	17	63	59	69	
10. Bradford City AFC (Bradford)	46	18	14	14	69	67	68	
11. Rotherham United FC (Rotherham)	46	17	14	15	60	60	65	
12. Fulham FC (London)	46	16	17	13	57	55	65	
13. Burnley FC (Burnley)	46	15	16	15	57	59	61	
14. Plymouth Argyle FC (Plymouth)	46	16	12	18	59	64	60	
15. Huddersfield Town AFC (Huddersfield)	46	17	9	20	54	61	60	
16. Hartlepool United FC (Hartlepool)	46	14	12	20	42	60	54	
17. AFC Bournemouth (Bournemouth)	46	12	17	17	45	52	53	
18. Blackpool FC (Blackpool)	46	12	15	19	63	75	51	
19. Exeter City FC (Exeter)	46	11	17	18	54	69	50	
20. Hull City AFC (Kingston-upon-Hull)	46	13	11	22	46	69	50	
21. Preston North End FC (Preston)	46	13	8	25	65	94	47	R
22. Mansfield Town FC (Mansfield)	46	11	11	24	52	80	44	R
23. Wigan Athletic AFC (Wigan)	46	10	11	25	43	72	41	R
24. Chester City FC (Chester)	46	8	5	33	49	102	29	R
	1104	406	292	406	1479	1479	1510	

Promotion Play-offs

West Bromwich Albion FC (West Bromwich)	3-0	Port Vale FC (Stoke-on-Trent)
Stockport County FC (Stockport)	1-1, 0-1	Port Vale FC (Stoke-on-Trent)
Swansea City FC (Swansea)	2-1, 0-2	West Bromwich Albion FC (West Bromwich)

Football League Division 3 1992-93 Season	Barnet	Bury	Cardiff City	Carlisle United	Chesterfield	Colchester United	Crewe Alexandra	Darlington	Doncaster Rovers	Gillingham	Halifax Town	Hereford United	Lincoln City	Northampton Town	Rochdale	Scarborough	Scunthorpe United	Shrewsbury Town	Torquay United	Walsall	Wrexham	York City
Barnet FC		1-0	2-1	2-0	2-1	3-1	3-2	0-0	2-0	2-0	0-0	2-0	1-1	3-0	2-0	3-1	3-0	2-2	5-5	3-0	3-1	1-5
Bury FC	0-0		1-0	6-0	3-0	3-2	1-2	1-1	3-0	1-0	1-2	2-0	1-2	3-3	2-2	0-2	0-0	0-0	2-0	2-1	3-1	1-1
Cardiff City AFC	1-1	3-0		2-2	2-1	3-1	1-1	0-0	1-1	3-1	2-1	2-1	3-1	2-1	1-1	1-0	3-0	2-1	4-0	2-1	1-2	3-3
Carlisle United FC	0-1	5-1	1-2		3-1	0-2	1-3	2-2	1-1	1-0	1-1	0-0	2-0	2-0	3-0	2-2	0-2	1-0	0-1	3-4	0-2	1-2
Chesterfield FC	1-2	2-1	2-1	1-0		4-0	2-1	2-0	0-0	1-1	2-1	1-0	2-1	1-3	2-3	0-3	1-2	2-4	1-0	2-1	2-3	1-1
Colchester United FC	1-2	0-0	2-4	2-1	3-0		3-2	0-3	2-0	3-0	2-1	3-2	2-1	2-0	4-4	1-0	1-0	0-2	2-0	3-1	2-4	0-0
Crewe Alexandra FC	4-1	2-1	2-0	4-0	0-2	7-1		1-0	4-0	3-1	2-1	1-1	1-2	3-2	1-1	2-3	2-2	4-2	0-1	0-1	3-1	
Darlington FC	1-0	0-0	0-2	1-1	1-1	1-0	3-0		1-2	1-1	0-3	0-1	1-3	3-1	0-4	2-3	2-2	0-2	4-1	1-2	1-1	0-1
Doncaster Rovers FC	2-1	2-3	0-1	1-2	2-1	1-0	1-1	0-1		1-0	0-1	2-1	0-0	2-2	1-1	4-3	0-1	0-1	2-3	0-3	1-1	0-1
Gillingham FC	1-1	1-4	0-1	1-0	0-0	0-1	1-2	3-1	1-1		2-0	3-1	3-1	2-3	4-2	3-0	1-1	1-0	0-2	0-1	4-1	1-4
Halifax Town AFC	1-2	0-1	0-1	0-2	1-1	2-4	1-2	1-0	2-2	2-0		0-1	2-1	2-2	2-3	3-4	0-0	1-1	0-2	0-4	0-1	0-1
Hereford United FC	1-1	3-1	1-1	1-0	1-3	3-1	0-1	1-1	0-2	3-1	3-0		0-2	3-2	1-1	1-1	2-2	1-1	3-1	1-3	1-1	1-1
Lincoln City FC	4-1	1-2	3-2	2-1	1-1	1-1	1-1	2-0	1-1	1-1	2-1	2-0		2-0	1-2	3-0	1-0	0-1	2-2	0-2	0-0	0-1
Northampton Town FC	1-1	1-0	1-2	2-0	0-1	1-0	0-2	1-2	0-1	2-2	2-5	1-1	0-2		1-0	1-3	1-0	0-0	0-1	0-0	0-2	4-3
Rochdale AFC	0-1	1-2	1-2	2-2	2-1	5-2	0-1	3-1	1-1	1-2	2-3	1-3	5-1	0-3		3-0	2-0	2-0	1-0	4-3	1-2	1-0
Scarborough FC	2-2	1-3	1-3	2-2	2-2	0-1	1-0	0-3	1-1	1-1	2-0	2-0	0-1	4-2	1-1		1-0	1-2	1-0	4-1	1-1	4-2
Scunthorpe United FC	2-0	2-0	0-3	0-0	0-1	3-1	3-3	1-3	0-1	2-2	4-1	3-1	1-1	5-0	5-1	1-2		1-1	2-2	2-0	0-0	1-2
Shrewsbury Town FC	1-0	2-0	3-2	2-3	2-2	4-3	4-1	1-2	2-1	1-0	1-1	3-2	2-3	1-2	2-0	2-1			0-1	0-3	0-1	1-1
Torquay United FC	0-1	0-1	2-1	0-2	1-2	1-2	0-2	1-2	0-2	2-0	0-1	1-1	0-1	1-0	1-3	0-1	1-0	1-0		0-1	2-0	1-0
Walsall FC	2-0	4-3	2-3	2-1	3-2	1-3	1-0	2-2	3-1	1-1	1-2	1-1	1-2	2-0	3-1	3-2	3-2	1-1	2-2		1-1	3-1
Wrexham AFC	2-3	4-2	0-2	3-1	5-4	4-3	2-0	1-1	1-1	2-0	1-1	2-0	2-0	0-1	3-1	4-1	0-2	2-0	4-2	3-1		3-0
York City FC	2-0	1-2	3-1	2-2	0-0	2-0	3-1	0-0	1-1	1-1	1-1	4-2	2-0	2-1	3-0	1-0	5-1	2-0	2-1	0-1	4-0	

	Football League Division 3	**Pd**	**Wn**	**Dw**	**Ls**	**GF**	**GA**	**Pts**	
1.	Cardiff City AFC (Cardiff)	42	25	8	9	77	47	83	P
2.	Wrexham AFC (Wrexham)	42	23	11	8	75	52	80	P
3.	Barnet FC (London)	42	23	10	9	66	48	79	P
4.	York City FC (York)	42	21	12	9	72	45	75	POP
5.	Walsall FC (Walsall)	42	22	7	13	76	61	73	PO
6.	Crewe Alexandra FC (Crewe)	42	21	7	14	75	56	70	PO
7.	Bury FC (Bury)	42	18	9	15	63	55	63	PO
8.	Lincoln City FC (Lincoln)	42	18	9	15	57	53	63	
9.	Shrewsbury Town FC (Shrewsbury)	42	17	11	14	57	52	62	
10.	Colchester United FC (Colchester)	42	18	5	19	67	76	59	
11.	Rochdale AFC (Rochdale)	42	16	10	16	70	70	58	
12.	Chesterfield FC (Chesterfield)	42	15	11	16	59	63	56	
13.	Scarborough FC (Scarborough)	42	15	9	18	66	71	54	
14.	Scunthorpe United FC (Scunthorpe)	42	14	12	16	57	54	54	
15.	Darlington FC (Darlington)	42	12	14	16	48	53	50	
16.	Doncaster Rovers FC (Doncaster)	42	11	14	17	42	57	47	
17.	Hereford United FC (Hereford)	42	10	15	17	47	60	45	
18.	Carlisle United FC (Carlisle)	42	11	11	20	51	65	44	
19.	Torquay United FC (Torquay)	42	12	7	23	45	67	43	
20.	Northampton Town FC (Northampton)	42	11	8	23	44	74	41	
21.	Gillingham FC (Gillingham)	42	9	13	20	48	64	40	
22.	Halifax Town AFC (Halifax)	42	9	9	24	45	68	36	R
		924	351	222	351	1311	1311	1275	

Note: Maidstone United FC (Maidstone) resigned from the league on 17th August 1992 and their full fixture list was cancelled.

Promotion Play-offs

York City FC (York)	1-1 (aet)	Crewe Alexandra FC (Crewe)
	(York City won 5-3 on penalties)	
Bury FC (Bury)	0-0, 0-1	York City FC (York)
Crewe Alexandra FC (Crewe)	5-1, 4-2	Walsall FC (Walsall)

Promoted to Division 3: Wycombe Wanderers FC (High Wycombe)

F.A. CUP FINAL   (Wembley Stadium, London – 15/05/1993 – 79,347)

ARSENAL FC (LONDON)	1-1 (aet)	Sheffield Wednesday FC (Sheffield)
Wright 21'		*Hirst 61'*

Arsenal: Seaman, Dixon, Winterburn, Davis, Linighan, Adams, Jensen, Wright (O'Leary 90'), Campbell, Merson, Parlour (Smith 65').

Wednesday: Woods, Nilsson, Worthington, Palmer, Anderson (Hyde 85'), Warhurst, Harkes, Waddle (Bart-William 111'), Hirst, Bright, Sheridan.

F.A. CUP FINAL REPLAY   (Wembley Stadium, London – 20/05/1993 – 62,267)

ARSENAL FC (LONDON)	2-1 (aet)	Sheffield Wednesday FC (Sheffield)
Wright 34', Linighan 120'		*Waddle 68'*

Wednesday: Woods, Nilsson (Bart-Williams 116'), Worthington, Harkes, Palmer, Warhurst, Wilson (Hyde 63'), Waddle, Hirst, Bright, Sheridan.

Arsenal: Seaman, Dixon, Winterburn, Davis, Linighan, Adams, Jensen, Wright (O'Leary 91'), Smith, Merson, Campbell.

Semi-finals

Arsenal FC (London)	1-0	Tottenham Hotspur FC (London)
Sheffield United FC (Sheffield)	1-2	Sheffield Wednesday FC (Sheffield)

Quarter-finals

Blackburn Rovers FC (Blackburn)	0-0, 2-2 (aet)	Sheffield United FC (Sheffield)
Sheffield United won 5-3 on penalties.		
Derby County FC (Derby)	3-3, 0-1	Sheffield Wednesday FC (Sheffield)
Ipswich Town FC (Ipswich)	2-4	Arsenal FC (London)
Manchester City FC (Manchester)	2-4	Tottenham Hotspur FC (London)

1993-94

F.A. Premiership 1993-94 Season	Arsenal	Aston Villa	Blackburn R.	Chelsea	Coventry City	Everton	Ipswich Town	Leeds United	Liverpool	Man. City	Man. United	Newcastle Utd.	Norwich City	Oldham Athletic	Q.P.R.	Sheffield United	Sheffield Wed.	Southampton	Swindon Town	Tottenham H.	West Ham Utd.	Wimbledon
Arsenal FC	■	1-2	1-0	1-0	0-3	2-0	4-0	2-1	1-0	0-0	2-2	2-1	0-0	1-1	0-0	3-0	1-0	1-0	1-1	1-1	0-2	1-1
Aston Villa FC	1-2	■	0-1	1-0	0-0	0-0	0-1	1-0	2-1	0-0	1-2	0-2	0-0	1-2	4-1	1-0	2-2	0-2	5-0	1-0	3-1	0-1
Blackburn Rovers FC	1-1	1-0	■	2-0	2-1	2-0	0-0	2-1	2-0	2-0	2-0	1-0	2-3	1-0	1-1	0-0	1-1	2-0	3-1	1-0	0-2	3-0
Chelsea FC	0-2	1-1	1-2	■	1-2	4-2	1-1	1-1	1-0	0-0	1-0	1-0	1-2	0-1	2-0	3-2	1-1	2-0	2-0	4-3	2-0	2-0
Coventry City FC	1-0	0-1	2-1	1-1	■	2-1	1-0	0-2	1-0	4-0	0-1	2-1	2-1	1-1	0-1	1-1	1-1	1-0	1-1	1-0	1-1	1-2
Everton FC	1-1	0-1	0-3	4-2	0-0	■	0-0	1-1	2-0	1-0	0-1	0-2	1-5	2-1	0-3	4-2	0-2	1-0	6-2	0-1	0-1	3-2
Ipswich Town FC	1-5	1-2	1-0	1-0	0-2	0-2	■	0-0	1-2	2-2	1-2	1-1	2-1	0-0	1-3	3-2	1-4	1-0	1-1	2-2	1-1	0-0
Leeds United AFC	2-1	2-0	3-3	4-1	1-0	3-0	0-0	■	2-0	3-2	0-2	1-1	0-4	1-0	1-1	2-1	2-2	0-0	3-0	2-0	1-0	4-0
Liverpool FC	0-0	2-1	0-1	2-1	1-0	2-1	1-0	2-0	■	2-1	3-3	0-2	0-1	2-1	3-2	1-2	2-0	4-2	2-2	1-2	2-0	1-1
Manchester City FC	0-0	3-0	0-2	2-2	1-1	1-0	2-1	1-1	1-1	■	2-3	2-1	1-1	1-1	3-0	1-0	1-3	1-1	2-1	0-2	0-0	0-1
Manchester United FC	1-0	3-1	1-1	0-1	0-0	1-0	0-0	0-0	1-0	2-0	■	1-1	2-2	3-2	2-1	3-0	5-0	2-0	4-2	1-0	3-0	3-1
Newcastle United FC	2-0	5-1	1-1	0-0	4-0	1-0	2-1	1-1	3-0	2-0	1-1	■	3-0	3-2	1-2	4-0	4-2	1-2	7-1	0-1	2-0	4-0
Norwich City FC	1-1	1-2	2-2	1-1	3-0	1-0	2-2	2-1	1-1	0-2	1-2	1-2	■	1-1	3-4	2-1	1-1	4-5	0-0	1-1	0-0	0-1
Oldham Athletic AFC	0-0	1-1	1-2	2-1	3-3	0-1	0-3	1-1	0-3	0-0	2-5	1-3	2-1	■	4-1	1-1	0-0	2-1	2-1	0-2	1-2	1-1
Queen's Park Rangers FC	1-1	2-2	1-0	1-1	5-1	2-1	3-0	0-4	1-1	1-1	2-3	1-2	2-2	2-0	■	2-1	1-2	2-1	1-3	1-1	0-0	1-0
Sheffield United FC	1-1	1-2	1-2	1-0	0-0	0-0	1-1	3-2	0-0	0-3	2-0	1-2	2-1	1-1	1-1	■	1-1	0-0	3-1	2-2	3-2	2-1
Sheffield Wednesday FC	0-1	0-0	1-2	3-1	0-0	5-1	5-0	3-3	3-1	1-1	2-3	0-1	3-3	3-0	3-1	3-1	■	2-0	3-3	1-0	5-0	2-2
Southampton FC	0-4	4-1	3-1	3-1	1-0	0-2	1-0	0-2	4-2	1-0	1-3	2-1	0-1	1-3	0-1	3-3	1-1	■	5-1	1-0	0-2	1-0
Swindon Town FC	0-4	1-2	1-3	1-3	3-1	1-1	2-2	0-5	0-5	1-3	2-2	2-2	3-3	0-1	1-0	0-3	0-1	2-1	■	2-1	1-1	2-4
Tottenham Hotspur FC	0-1	1-1	0-2	1-1	1-2	3-2	1-1	1-1	3-3	0-1	1-2	1-3	5-0	1-2	1-3	1-1	1-0	1-1	1-1	■	1-4	1-1
West Ham United FC	0-0	0-0	1-2	1-0	3-2	0-1	2-1	0-1	1-2	3-1	2-2	2-4	3-3	2-0	0-4	0-0	3-3	0-0	1-3	1-3	■	0-2
Wimbledon FC	0-3	2-2	4-1	1-1	1-2	1-1	0-2	1-0	1-1	1-0	1-0	4-2	3-1	3-0	1-1	2-0	2-1	1-0	3-0	2-1	1-2	■

F.A. Premiership

		Pd	Wn	Dw	Ls	GF	GA	Pts	
1.	MANCHESTER UNITED FC (MANCHESTER)	42	27	11	4	80	38	92	
2.	Blackburn Rovers FC (Blackburn)	42	25	9	8	63	36	84	
3.	Newcastle United FC (Newcastle-upon-Tyne)	42	23	8	11	82	41	77	
4.	Arsenal FC (London)	42	18	17	7	53	28	71	
5.	Leeds United AFC (Leeds)	42	18	16	8	65	39	70	
6.	Wimbledon FC (London)	42	18	11	13	56	53	65	
7.	Sheffield Wednesday FC (Sheffield)	42	16	16	10	76	54	64	
8.	Liverpool FC (Liverpool)	42	17	9	16	59	55	60	
9.	Queen's Park Rangers FC (London)	42	16	12	14	62	61	60	
10.	Aston Villa FC (Birmingham)	42	15	12	15	46	50	57	
11.	Coventry City FC (Coventry)	42	14	14	14	43	45	56	
12.	Norwich City FC (Norwich)	42	12	17	13	65	61	53	
13.	West Ham United FC (London)	42	13	13	16	47	58	52	
14.	Chelsea FC (London)	42	13	12	17	49	53	51	
15.	Tottenham Hotspur FC (London)	42	11	12	19	54	59	45	
16.	Manchester City FC (Manchester)	42	9	18	15	38	49	45	
17.	Everton FC (Liverpool)	42	12	8	22	42	63	44	
18.	Southampton FC (Southampton)	42	12	7	23	49	66	43	
19.	Ipswich Town FC (Ipswich)	42	9	16	17	35	58	43	
20.	Sheffield United FC (Sheffield)	42	8	18	16	42	60	42	R
21.	Oldham Athletic AFC (Oldham)	42	9	13	20	42	68	40	R
22.	Swindon Town FC (Swindon)	42	5	15	22	47	100	30	R
		924	320	284	320	1195	1195	1244	

Top Goalscorers

1)	Andrew COLE	(Newcastle United FC)	34
2)	Alan SHEARER	(Blackburn Rovers FC)	31
3)	Matthew LE TISSIER	(Southampton FC)	25
	Chris SUTTON	(Norwich City FC)	25

Football League Division 1 1993-94 Season	Barnsley	Birmingham City	Bolton Wanderers	Bristol City	Charlton Athletic	Crystal Palace	Derby County	Grimsby Town	Leicester City	Luton Town	Middlesbrough	Millwall	Nottingham Forest	Notts County	Oxford United	Peterborough Utd.	Portsmouth	Southend United	Stoke City	Sunderland	Tranmere Rovers	Watford	W.B.A.	Wolves
Barnsley FC	■	2-3	1-1	1-1	0-1	1-3	0-1	1-2	0-1	1-0	1-4	0-1	1-0	0-3	1-0	1-0	2-0	1-3	3-0	4-0	1-0	0-1	1-1	2-0
Birmingham City FC	0-2	■	2-1	2-2	1-0	2-4	3-0	1-1	0-3	1-1	1-0	1-0	0-3	2-3	1-1	0-0	0-1	3-1	3-1	0-0	0-3	1-0	2-0	2-2
Bolton Wanderers FC	2-3	1-1	■	2-2	3-2	1-0	0-2	1-1	1-2	2-1	4-1	4-0	4-3	4-2	1-0	1-1	1-1	0-2	1-1	0-0	2-1	3-1	1-1	1-3
Bristol City FC	0-2	3-0	2-0	■	0-0	2-0	0-0	1-0	1-3	1-0	0-0	2-2	1-4	0-2	0-1	4-1	1-0	2-1	0-0	2-0	2-0	1-1	0-0	2-1
Charlton Athletic FC	2-1	1-0	3-0	3-1	■	0-0	1-2	0-1	2-1	1-0	2-5	0-0	0-1	5-1	1-0	5-1	0-1	4-3	2-0	0-0	3-1	2-1	2-1	0-1
Crystal Palace FC	1-0	2-1	1-1	4-1	2-0	■	1-1	1-0	2-1	3-2	0-1	1-0	2-0	1-2	2-1	3-2	5-1	1-0	4-1	1-0	0-0	0-2	1-0	1-1
Derby County FC	2-0	1-1	2-0	1-0	2-0	3-1	■	2-1	3-2	2-1	0-1	0-0	0-2	1-1	2-1	2-0	1-0	1-3	4-2	5-0	4-0	1-2	5-3	0-4
Grimsby Town FC	2-2	1-0	0-0	1-1	0-1	1-1	1-1	■	0-0	2-0	1-1	0-0	2-2	1-0	3-2	1-1	4-0	0-0	0-1	1-0	0-0	2-2	2-2	2-0
Leicester City FC	0-1	1-1	1-1	3-0	2-1	1-1	3-3	1-1	■	2-1	2-0	4-0	1-0	3-2	2-3	2-1	0-3	3-0	1-1	2-1	1-1	4-4	4-2	2-2
Luton Town FC	5-0	1-1	0-2	0-2	1-0	0-1	2-1	2-1	0-2	■	1-1	1-1	1-2	1-0	3-0	2-0	4-1	1-1	6-2	1-0	2-1	0-2	3-2	0-2
Middlesbrough FC	5-0	2-2	0-1	0-1	2-0	2-3	3-0	1-0	2-0	0-0	■	3-2	2-2	3-0	2-1	1-1	0-2	1-0	1-2	4-1	0-0	1-1	3-0	1-0
Millwall FC	2-0	2-1	1-0	0-0	2-1	3-0	0-0	1-0	0-0	2-2	1-1	■	2-2	2-0	2-2	1-0	0-0	1-4	2-0	2-1	3-1	4-1	2-1	1-0
Nottingham Forest	2-1	1-0	3-2	0-0	1-1	1-1	1-1	5-3	4-0	2-0	1-1	1-3	■	1-0	0-0	2-0	1-1	2-0	2-3	2-2	2-1	2-1	2-1	0-0
Notts County FC	3-1	2-1	2-1	2-0	3-3	3-2	4-1	2-1	4-1	1-2	2-3	1-3	2-1	■	2-1	2-1	1-1	2-0	1-0	0-0	1-0	0-1	1-0	0-1
Oxford United FC	1-1	2-0	0-2	4-2	0-4	1-3	2-0	2-2	2-2	0-1	1-1	0-2	1-0	2-1	■	1-2	3-2	2-1	1-0	0-3	1-0	2-3	1-1	4-0
Peterborough United	4-1	1-0	2-3	0-2	0-1	1-1	2-2	1-2	1-1	0-0	1-0	0-0	2-3	1-1	3-1	■	2-2	3-1	1-1	1-3	0-0	3-4	2-0	0-1
Portsmouth FC	2-1	0-2	0-0	0-0	1-2	0-1	3-2	3-1	0-1	1-0	2-0	2-2	2-1	0-0	1-1	0-2	■	2-1	3-3	0-1	2-0	2-0	0-1	3-0
Southend United FC	0-3	3-1	0-2	1-1	4-2	1-2	4-3	1-2	0-0	2-1	1-0	1-1	1-1	1-0	6-1	3-0	2-1	■	0-0	0-1	1-2	2-0	0-3	1-0
Stoke City FC	5-4	2-1	2-0	3-0	1-0	0-2	2-1	1-0	1-0	2-2	3-1	1-2	0-1	3-0	0-1	3-0	2-0	0-1	■	1-0	1-2	2-0	1-0	1-1
Sunderland AFC	1-0	1-0	2-0	0-0	4-0	1-0	1-0	2-2	2-3	2-0	2-1	2-1	2-3	2-0	2-3	2-0	1-2	0-2	0-1	■	3-2	2-0	1-0	0-2
Tranmere Rovers FC	0-3	1-2	2-1	2-2	2-0	0-1	4-0	1-2	1-0	4-1	4-0	3-2	1-2	3-1	2-0	2-1	3-1	1-1	2-0	4-1	■	2-1	3-0	1-1
Watford FC	0-2	5-2	4-3	1-1	2-2	1-3	3-4	0-3	1-1	2-2	2-0	2-0	3-1	2-1	2-1	1-0	3-0	1-3	1-1	1-2		■	0-1	1-0
West Bromwich Alb.	1-1	2-4	2-2	0-1	2-0	1-4	1-2	1-0	1-2	1-1	1-1	0-0	0-2	3-0	3-1	3-0	4-1	2-2	0-0	2-1	1-3	4-1	■	3-2
Wolverhampton W.	1-1	3-0	1-0	3-1	1-1	2-0	2-2	0-0	1-1	1-0	2-3	2-0	1-1	3-0	2-1	1-1	1-1	0-1	1-1	1-1	2-1	2-0	1-2	■

	Football League Division 1	**Pd**	**Wn**	**Dw**	**Ls**	**GF**	**GA**	**Pts**	
1.	Crystal Palace FC (London)	46	27	9	10	73	46	90	P
2.	Nottingham Forest FC (Nottingham)	46	23	14	9	74	49	83	P
3.	Millwall FC (London)	46	19	17	10	58	49	74	PO
4.	Leicester City FC (Leicester)	46	19	16	11	72	59	73	POP
5.	Tranmere Rovers FC (Birkenhead)	46	21	9	16	69	53	72	PO
6.	Derby County FC (Derby)	46	20	11	15	73	68	71	PO
7.	Notts County FC (Nottingham)	46	20	8	18	65	69	68	
8.	Wolverhampton Wanderers FC (Wolverhampton)	46	17	17	12	60	47	68	
9.	Middlesbrough FC (Middlesbrough)	46	18	13	15	66	54	67	
10.	Stoke City FC (Stoke-on-Trent)	46	18	13	15	57	59	67	
11.	Charlton Athletic FC (London)	46	19	8	19	61	58	65	
12.	Sunderland AFC (Sunderland)	46	19	8	19	54	57	65	
13.	Bristol City FC (Bristol)	46	16	16	14	47	50	64	
14.	Bolton Wanderers FC (Bolton)	46	15	14	17	63	64	59	
15.	Southend United FC (Southend-on-Sea)	46	17	8	21	63	67	59	
16.	Grimsby Town FC (Cleethorpes)	46	13	20	13	52	47	59	
17.	Portsmouth FC (Portsmouth)	46	15	13	18	52	58	58	
18.	Barnsley FC (Barnsley)	46	16	7	23	55	67	55	
19.	Watford FC (Watford)	46	15	9	22	66	80	54	
20.	Luton Town FC (Luton)	46	14	11	21	56	60	53	
21.	West Bromwich Albion FC (West Bromwich)	46	13	12	21	60	69	51	
22.	Birmingham City FC (Birmingham)	46	13	12	21	52	69	51	R
23.	Oxford United FC (Oxford)	46	13	10	23	54	75	49	R
24.	Peterborough United FC (Peterborough)	46	8	13	25	48	76	37	R
		1104	408	288	408	1450	1450	1512	

Promotion Play-offs

Leicester City FC (Leicester)	2-1	Derby County FC (Derby)
Derby County FC (Derby)	2-0, 3-1	Millwall FC (London)
Tranmere Rovers FC (Birkenhead)	0-0, 1-2	Leicester City FC (Leicester)

Football League Division 2 — 1993-94 Season

	Barnet	Blackpool	Bournemouth	Bradford City	Brentford	Brighton & Hove Albion	Bristol Rovers	Burnley	Cambridge	Cardiff City	Exeter City	Fulham	Hartlepool	Huddersfield Town	Hull City	Leyton Orient	Plymouth Argyle	Port Vale	Reading	Rotherham United	Stockport County	Swansea City	Wrexham	York City
Barnet FC		0-1	1-2	1-2	0-0	1-1	1-2	1-1	2-3	0-0	2-1	0-2	3-2	0-1	1-2	3-1	0-0	2-3	0-1	2-1	0-0	0-1	1-2	1-3
Blackpool FC	3-1		2-1	1-3	1-1	2-0	0-1	1-2	2-3	1-0	1-0	2-3	2-1	2-1	6-2	4-1	2-1	1-3	0-4	1-2	2-0	1-1	4-1	0-5
AFC Bournemouth	1-1	1-0		1-1	0-3	2-1	3-0	1-0	1-2	3-2	1-1	1-3	0-0	1-2	0-2	1-1	0-1	2-1	2-1	0-0	1-1	0-1	1-2	3-1
Bradford City AFC	2-1	2-1	0-0		1-0	2-0	0-1	0-1	2-0	2-0	6-0	0-0	2-1	3-0	1-1	0-0	1-5	2-1	2-4	2-1	1-2	2-1	1-0	0-0
Brentford FC	1-0	3-0	1-1	2-0		1-1	3-4	0-0	3-3	1-1	2-1	1-2	1-0	1-2	0-3	0-1	1-1	1-2	1-0	2-2	1-1	1-1	2-1	1-1
Brighton & Hove Alb.	1-0	3-2	3-3	0-1	2-1		0-2	1-1	4-1	3-5	0-0	2-0	1-1	2-2	3-0	2-0	2-1	1-3	0-1	0-2	1-1	4-1	1-1	2-0
Bristol Rovers FC	5-2	1-0	0-1	4-3	1-4	1-0		3-1	2-1	2-1	1-1	2-1	1-1	0-0	1-1	1-1	0-0	2-0	1-1	0-2	1-1	1-2	3-1	0-1
Burnley FC	5-0	3-1	4-0	0-1	4-1	3-0	3-1		3-0	2-0	3-2	3-1	2-0	1-1	3-1	4-1	4-2	2-1	0-0	1-1	1-1	1-1	2-1	2-1
Cambridge United FC	1-1	3-2	3-2	2-1	1-1	2-1	1-3	0-1		1-1	3-0	3-0	1-0	4-5	3-4	3-1	2-0	1-0	0-1	0-1	0-0	2-0	2-2	0-2
Cardiff City AFC	0-0	0-2	2-1	1-1	1-1	2-2	1-2	2-1	2-7		2-0	1-0	2-2	2-2	3-4	2-0	2-3	1-3	3-0	1-0	3-1	1-0	5-1	0-0
Exeter City	0-0	1-0	0-2	0-0	2-2	1-1	1-0	4-1	0-5	2-2		6-4	2-1	2-3	0-1	1-0	2-3	1-1	4-6	1-1	1-2	1-0	5-0	1-2
Fulham FC	3-0	1-0	0-2	1-1	0-0	0-1	0-1	3-2	0-2	1-3	0-2		2-0	1-1	0-1	2-3	1-1	0-0	1-0	1-0	3-1	0-0	0-1
Hartlepool United FC	2-1	2-0	1-1	1-2	0-1	2-2	2-1	4-1	0-2	3-0	1-2	0-1		1-4	0-1	1-1	1-8	1-4	1-4	2-0	1-0	1-0	1-2	0-2
Huddersfield Town	1-2	2-1	1-1	1-1	1-3	1-3	1-0	1-1	1-1	2-0	0-1	1-0	1-1		0-2	1-0	1-0	1-1	0-3	2-1	1-1	1-1	3-0	3-2
Hull City AFC	4-4	0-0	1-1	3-1	1-0	0-0	3-0	1-2	2-0	1-0	5-1	1-1	1-0	2-1		0-1	2-2	0-0	1-2	4-1	0-1	0-1	0-0	1-1
Leyton Orient FC	4-2	2-0	0-0	2-1	1-1	1-3	1-0	3-1	2-1	2-2	1-1	2-2	1-2	1-0	3-1		2-1	2-3	1-1	1-1	0-0	2-1	2-2	2-0
Plymouth Argyle FC	3-2	2-1	2-0	3-1	1-1	1-1	3-3	3-2	0-3	1-2	1-0	3-1	2-0	2-0	2-1	3-1		2-0	3-1	4-2	2-3	2-1	1-1	2-1
Port Vale FC	6-0	2-0	2-1	0-0	1-0	4-0	2-0	1-1	2-2	2-2	3-0	2-2	1-0	1-0	2-1	2-1	2-1		0-4	2-1	1-1	3-0	3-0	2-1
Reading FC	4-1	1-1	3-0	1-1	2-1	2-0	2-0	2-1	3-1	1-1	1-0	1-0	4-0	0-0	1-1	2-1	3-2	1-2		0-0	2-0	2-1	0-1	2-1
Rotherham United	1-1	0-2	1-2	2-1	2-0	0-1	1-1	3-2	3-0	5-2	3-0	1-2	7-0	2-3	1-0	2-1	0-3	0-2	2-2		1-2	1-1	2-1	2-1
Stockport County	2-1	1-0	0-2	4-1	3-1	3-0	0-2	2-1	3-1	2-2	4-0	2-4	5-0	3-0	0-0	3-0	2-3	2-1	1-1	2-0		4-0	1-0	1-2
Swansea City FC	2-0	4-4	1-1	2-0	1-1	3-0	2-0	3-1	4-2	1-0	2-0	2-1	1-1	1-0	1-0	1-1	0-1	0-1	1-1	0-0	1-2		3-1	1-2
Wrexham AFC	4-0	2-3	2-1	0-3	1-2	1-3	3-2	1-0	1-1	3-1	1-1	2-0	2-0	3-1	3-0	4-2	0-3	2-1	3-2	3-3	0-1	3-2		1-1
York City FC	1-1	2-1	2-0	1-1	0-2	3-1	0-1	0-0	2-0	5-0	3-0	2-0	3-0	0-2	0-0	3-0	0-0	1-0	1-0	0-0	1-2	2-1	1-1	

Football League Division 2	Pd	Wn	Dw	Ls	GF	GA	Pts	
1. Reading FC (Reading)	46	26	11	9	81	44	89	P
2. Port Vale FC (Stoke-on-Trent)	46	26	10	10	79	46	88	P
3. Plymouth Argyle FC (Plymouth)	46	25	10	11	88	56	85	PO
4. Stockport County FC (Stockport)	46	24	13	9	74	44	85	PO
5. York City FC (York)	46	21	12	13	64	40	75	PO
6. Burnley FC (Burnley)	46	21	10	15	79	58	73	POP
7. Bradford City AFC (Bradford)	46	19	13	14	61	53	70	
8. Bristol Rovers FC (Bristol)	46	20	10	16	60	59	70	
9. Hull City AFC (Kingston-upon-Hull)	46	18	14	14	62	54	68	
10. Cambridge United FC (Cambridge)	46	19	9	18	79	73	66	
11. Huddersfield Town AFC (Huddersfield)	46	17	14	15	58	61	65	
12. Wrexham AFC (Wrexham)	46	17	11	18	66	77	62	
13. Swansea City FC (Swansea)	46	16	12	18	56	58	60	
14. Brighton & Hove Albion FC (Hove)	46	15	14	17	60	67	59	
15. Rotherham United FC (Rotherham)	46	15	13	18	63	60	58	
16. Brentford FC (London)	46	13	19	14	57	55	58	
17. AFC Bournemouth (Bournemouth)	46	14	15	17	51	59	57	
18. Leyton Orient FC (London)	46	14	14	18	57	71	56	
19. Cardiff City AFC (Cardiff)	46	13	15	18	66	79	54	
20. Blackpool FC (Blackpool)	46	16	5	25	63	75	53	
21. Fulham FC (London)	46	14	10	22	50	63	52	R
22. Exeter City FC (Exeter)	46	11	12	23	52	83	45	R
23. Hartlepool United FC (Hartlepool)	46	9	9	28	41	87	36	R
24. Barnet FC (London)	46	5	13	28	41	86	28	R
	1104	408	288	408	1508	1508	1512	

Promotion Play-offs

Burnley FC (Burnley)	2-1	Stockport County FC (Stockport)
Burnley FC (Burnley)	0-0, 3-1	Plymouth Argyle FC (Plymouth)
York City FC (York)	0-0, 0-1	Stockport County FC (Stockport)

Football League Division 3 1993-94 Season	Bury	Carlisle United	Chester City	Chesterfield	Colchester United	Crewe Alexandra	Darlington	Doncaster Rovers	Gillingham	Hereford United	Lincoln City	Mansfield Town	Northampton Town	Preston North End	Rochdale	Scarborough	Scunthorpe United	Shrewsbury Town	Torquay United	Walsall	Wigan Athletic	Wycombe W.
Bury FC		2-1	1-1	2-1	0-1	1-0	5-1	4-0	0-0	5-3	1-0	2-2	0-0	1-1	0-1	0-2	1-0	2-3	1-1	1-2	3-0	1-2
Carlisle United FC	1-2		1-0	3-0	2-0	1-2	2-0	4-2	1-2	1-2	3-3	1-1	0-1	0-1	0-1	2-0	3-1	2-1	1-1	2-1	3-0	2-2
Chester City FC	3-0	0-0		3-1	2-1	1-2	0-0	0-1	1-0	3-1	1-1	1-1	1-0	3-2	3-1	4-1	0-2	1-0	1-1	2-1	2-1	3-1
Chesterfield FC	1-1	3-0	1-2		0-0	2-0	1-1	1-3	3-2	3-1	2-2	0-2	4-0	1-1	1-1	1-0	1-1	1-2	3-1	0-1	1-0	2-3
Colchester United FC	4-1	2-1	0-0	0-2		2-4	1-2	3-1	1-2	1-0	1-0	0-0	3-2	1-1	2-5	1-2	2-1	3-3	1-2	0-1	3-1	0-2
Crewe Alexandra FC	2-4	2-3	2-1	0-1	2-1		2-1	2-0	1-0	6-0	2-2	2-1	3-1	4-3	2-1	1-1	3-3	0-0	2-3	1-2	4-1	2-1
Darlington FC	1-0	1-3	1-2	0-0	7-3	1-0		1-3	2-1	1-3	3-2	2-0	0-1	0-2	1-1	0-2	2-1	0-2	1-2	0-0	0-0	0-0
Doncaster Rovers FC	1-3	0-0	3-4	0-0	2-1	0-0	1-3		0-0	1-0	1-0	0-1	2-1	1-1	2-1	0-4	3-1	0-0	0-2	4-0	3-1	0-3
Gillingham FC	1-0	2-0	2-2	0-2	3-0	1-3	2-1	0-0		2-0	1-1	1-0	2-2	1-2	2-2	1-0	0-2	2-2	1-1	2-2	2-1	0-1
Hereford United FC	3-0	0-0	0-5	0-3	5-0	1-2	1-1	2-1	2-0		1-2	2-3	1-1	2-3	5-1	0-1	1-2	0-1	2-2	0-1	3-0	3-4
Lincoln City FC	2-2	0-0	0-3	1-2	2-0	1-2	1-1	2-1	3-1	3-1		1-2	4-3	0-2	1-1	0-1	2-0	0-1	1-0	1-2	0-1	1-3
Mansfield Town FC	2-2	0-1	0-4	1-2	1-1	1-2	0-3	2-1	2-1	2-1	1-0		1-0	2-2	0-1	4-2	0-1	1-0	2-1	1-2	2-3	3-0
Northampton Town FC	0-1	1-1	1-0	2-2	1-1	2-2	1-0	0-0	1-2	0-1	0-0	5-1		2-0	1-2	3-2	4-0	0-3	0-1	0-1	0-2	1-1
Preston North End FC	3-1	0-3	1-1	4-1	1-0	0-2	3-2	3-1	0-0	3-0	2-0	3-1	1-1		2-1	2-2	2-2	6-1	3-1	2-0	3-0	2-3
Rochdale AFC	2-1	0-1	2-0	5-1	1-1	2-1	0-0	0-1	3-0	2-0	0-1	1-1	6-2	2-1		2-1	2-3	1-2	4-1	0-0	1-2	2-2
Scarborough FC	1-0	0-3	0-1	1-1	0-2	1-2	3-0	2-0	1-1	0-1	2-2	1-1	2-1	3-4	2-1		0-1	1-3	1-2	1-0	4-1	3-1
Scunthorpe United FC	1-1	2-1	1-1	2-2	1-2	1-2	3-0	1-3	1-1	1-2	2-0	2-3	7-0	3-1	2-1	1-1		1-4	1-3	5-0	1-0	0-0
Shrewsbury Town FC	1-0	1-0	3-0	0-0	2-1	2-2	1-1	1-2	2-2	2-0	1-2	2-2	2-1	1-0	1-1	2-0	0-0		3-2	1-2	0-0	1-0
Torquay United FC	0-0	1-1	1-3	1-0	3-3	3-3	2-1	2-1	0-1	1-1	3-2	1-0	2-0	4-3	1-1	2-0	1-1	0-0		0-1	1-1	1-1
Walsall FC	0-1	0-1	1-1	0-1	1-2	2-2	3-0	1-2	1-0	3-3	5-2	0-2	1-3	2-0	1-0	1-0	0-0	0-1	1-2		1-1	4-2
Wigan Athletic AFC	3-1	0-2	6-3	1-0	0-1	2-2	2-0	0-0	2-0	3-4	0-1	4-1	1-1	2-2	0-0	1-2	0-2	2-5	1-3	2-2		1-1
Wycombe Wanderers FC	2-1	2-0	1-0	0-1	2-5	3-1	2-0	1-0	1-1	3-2	2-3	1-0	1-0	1-1	1-1	4-0	2-2	1-1	1-1	3-0	0-1	

	Football League Division 3	**Pd**	**Wn**	**Dw**	**Ls**	**GF**	**GA**	**Pts**	
1.	Shrewsbury Town FC (Shrewsbury)	42	22	13	7	63	39	79	P
2.	Chester City FC (Chester)	42	21	11	10	69	46	74	P
3.	Crewe Alexandra FC (Crewe)	42	21	10	11	80	61	73	P
4.	Wycombe Wanderers FC (High Wycombe)	42	19	13	10	67	53	70	POP
5.	Preston North End FC (Preston)	42	18	13	11	79	60	67	PO
6.	Torquay United FC (Torquay)	42	17	16	9	64	56	67	PO
7.	Carlisle United FC (Carlisle)	42	18	10	14	57	42	64	PO
8.	Chesterfield FC (Chesterfield)	42	16	14	12	55	48	62	
9.	Rochdale AFC (Rochdale)	42	16	12	14	63	51	60	
10.	Walsall FC (Walsall)	42	17	9	16	48	53	60	
11.	Scunthorpe United FC (Scunthorpe)	42	15	14	13	64	56	59	
12.	Mansfield Town FC (Mansfield)	42	15	10	17	53	62	55	
13.	Bury FC (Bury)	42	14	11	17	55	56	53	
14.	Scarborough FC (Scarborough)	42	15	8	19	55	61	53	
15.	Doncaster Rovers FC (Doncaster)	42	14	10	18	44	57	52	
16.	Gillingham FC (Gillingham)	42	12	15	15	44	51	51	
17.	Colchester United FC (Colchester)	42	13	10	19	56	71	49	
18.	Lincoln City FC (Lincoln)	42	12	11	19	52	63	47	
19.	Wigan Athletic AFC (Wigan)	42	11	12	19	51	70	45	
20.	Hereford United FC (Hereford)	42	12	6	24	60	79	42	
21.	Darlington FC (Darlington)	42	10	11	21	42	64	41	
22.	Northampton Town FC (Northampton)	42	9	11	22	44	66	38	#
		924	337	250	337	1265	1265	1261	

GM Vauxhall Conference champions Kidderminster Harriers FC (Kidderminster) were refused promotion to Football League Division 3 as ground improvements to Football League standards could not be completed prior to the start of 1994-95 season. As a result of this decision Northampton Town FC (Northampton) retained their Football League status.

F.A. CUP FINAL   (Wembley Stadium, London – 14/05/1994 – 79,634)

MANCHESTER UNITED FC (MANCHESTER)   4-0   Chelsea FC (London)

Cantona 60' pen., 66' pen., Hughes 69, McClair 90'

Man. United: Schmeichel, Parker, Irwin (Sharpe 85'), Bruce, Kanchelskis (McClair 85'), Pallister, Cantona, Ince, Keane, Hughes, Giggs.

Chelsea: Kharine, Clarke, Sinclair, Kjeldbjerg, Johnsen, Burley (Hoddle 67'), Spencer, Newton, Stein (Cascarino 79'), Peacock, Wise.

Semi-finals

Chelsea FC (London)	2-0	Luton Town FC
Manchester United FC (Manchester)	1-1, 4-1	Oldham Athletic AFC (Oldham)

Quarter-finals

Bolton Wanderers FC (Bolton)	0-1	Oldham Athletic AFC (Oldham)
Chelsea FC (London)	1-0	Wolverhampton Wanderers FC (Wolverhampton)
Manchester United FC (Manchester)	3-1	Charlton Athletic FC (London)
West Ham United FC (London)	0-0, 2-3	Luton Town FC (Luton)

1994-95

F.A. Premiership 1994-95 Season	Arsenal	Aston Villa	Blackburn R.	Chelsea	Coventry City	Crystal Palace	Everton	Ipswich Town	Leeds United	Leicester City	Liverpool	Man. City	Man. United	Newcastle Utd.	Norwich City	Nottingham F.	Q.P.R.	Sheffield Wed.	Southampton	Tottenham H.	West Ham Utd	Wimbledon
Arsenal FC		0-0	0-0	3-1	2-1	1-2	1-1	4-1	1-3	1-1	0-1	3-0	0-0	2-3	5-1	1-0	1-3	0-0	1-1	1-1	0-1	0-0
Aston Villa FC	0-4		0-1	3-0	0-0	1-1	0-0	2-0	0-0	4-4	2-0	1-1	1-2	0-2	1-1	0-2	2-1	1-1	1-1	1-0	0-2	7-1
Blackburn Rovers FC	3-1	3-1		2-1	4-0	2-1	3-0	4-1	1-1	3-0	3-2	2-3	2-4	1-0	0-0	3-0	4-0	3-1	3-2	2-0	4-2	2-1
Chelsea FC	2-1	1-0	1-2		2-2	0-0	0-1	2-0	0-3	4-0	0-0	3-0	2-3	1-1	2-0	0-2	1-0	1-1	0-2	1-1	1-2	1-1
Coventry City FC	0-1	0-1	1-1	2-2		1-4	0-0	2-0	2-1	4-2	1-1	2-3	0-0	1-0	0-0	0-1	2-0	1-3	0-4	2-0	1-1	
Crystal Palace FC	0-3	0-0	0-1	0-1	0-2		1-0	3-0	1-2	2-0	1-6	2-1	1-1	0-1	0-1	1-2	0-0	2-1	0-0	1-1	1-0	0-0
Everton FC	1-1	2-2	1-2	3-3	0-2	3-1		4-1	3-0	1-1	2-0	1-1	1-0	2-0	2-1	1-2	2-2	1-4	0-0	0-0	1-0	0-0
Ipswich Town FC	0-2	0-1	1-3	2-2	2-0	0-2	0-1		2-0	4-1	1-3	1-2	3-2	0-2	1-2	0-1	0-1	1-2	2-1	1-3	1-1	2-2
Leeds United AFC	1-0	1-0	1-1	2-3	3-0	3-1	1-0	4-0		2-1	0-2	2-0	2-1	0-0	2-1	1-0	4-0	0-1	0-0	1-1	2-2	3-1
Leicester City FC	3-1	1-1	0-0	1-1	2-2	0-1	2-2	2-0	1-3		1-2	0-1	0-4	1-3	1-0	2-4	1-1	0-1	4-3	3-1	1-2	3-4
Liverpool FC	3-0	3-2	2-1	3-1	2-3	0-0	0-0	0-1	0-1	2-0		2-0	2-0	2-0	4-0	1-0	1-1	4-1	3-1	1-1	0-0	3-0
Manchester City FC	1-2	2-2	1-3	1-2	0-0	1-1	4-0	2-0	0-0	0-1	2-1		0-3	0-0	2-0	3-3	2-3	3-2	3-3	5-2	3-0	2-0
Manchester United FC	3-0	1-0	1-0	0-0	2-0	3-0	2-0	9-0	0-0	1-1	2-0	5-0		2-0	1-0	1-2	2-0	1-0	2-1	0-0	1-0	3-0
Newcastle United FC	1-0	3-1	1-1	4-2	4-0	3-2	2-0	1-1	1-2	3-1	1-1	0-1	1-1		3-0	2-1	2-1	5-1	3-3	2-0	2-1	
Norwich City FC	0-0	1-1	2-1	3-0	2-2	2-0	0-0	3-0	2-1	1-2	1-1	1-1	0-2	2-1		0-1	4-2	0-0	2-2	0-2	1-0	1-2
Nottingham Forest FC	2-2	1-2	0-2	0-1	2-0	1-0	2-1	4-1	3-0	1-0	1-1	1-0	1-1	0-0	1-0		3-2	4-1	3-0	2-2	1-1	3-1
Queen's Park Rangers FC	3-1	2-0	0-1	1-0	2-2	0-1	2-3	1-2	3-2	2-0	2-1	1-2	2-3	3-0	2-0	1-1		3-2	2-2	2-1	2-1	0-1
Sheffield Wednesday FC	3-1	1-2	0-1	1-1	5-1	1-0	1-4	1-0	0-1	0-0	1-1	1-0	0-0	0-0	1-7	0-0			1-1	3-4		
Southampton FC	1-0	2-1	0-1	0-1	0-0	3-1	2-0	3-1	1-3	2-2	0-2	2-2	2-2	3-1	1-1	1-1	2-1	0-0		4-3	1-1	2-3
Tottenham Hotspur FC	1-0	3-4	3-1	0-0	1-3	0-0	2-1	3-0	1-0	0-0	0-0	2-1	0-1	4-2	1-0	1-4	1-1	3-1	1-2		3-1	1-2
West Ham United FC	0-2	1-0	2-0	1-2	0-1	1-0	2-2	1-1	0-0	1-0	3-0	3-0	1-1	1-3	2-2	3-1	0-0	0-2	2-0	1-2		3-0
Wimbledon FC	1-3	4-3	0-3	1-1	2-0	2-0	2-1	1-1	0-0	2-1	0-0	2-0	0-1	3-2	1-0	2-2	1-3	0-1	0-2	1-2	1-0	

	F.A. Premiership	**Pd**	**Wn**	**Dw**	**Ls**	**GF**	**GA**	**Pts**	
1.	BLACKBURN ROVERS FC (BLACKBURN)	42	27	8	7	80	39	89	
2.	Manchester United FC (Manchester)	42	26	10	6	77	28	88	
3.	Nottingham Forest FC (Nottingham)	42	22	11	9	72	43	77	
4.	Liverpool FC (Liverpool)	42	21	11	10	65	37	74	
5.	Leeds United AFC (Leeds)	42	20	13	9	59	38	73	
6.	Newcastle United FC (Newcastle-upon-Tyne)	42	20	12	10	67	47	72	
7.	Tottenham Hotspur FC (London)	42	16	14	12	66	58	62	
8.	Queen's Park Rangers FC (London)	42	17	9	16	61	59	60	
9.	Wimbledon FC (London)	42	15	11	16	48	65	56	
10.	Southampton FC (Southampton)	42	12	18	12	61	63	54	
11.	Chelsea FC (London)	42	13	15	14	50	55	54	
12.	Arsenal FC (London)	42	13	12	17	52	49	51	
13.	Sheffield Wednesday FC (Sheffield)	42	13	12	17	49	57	51	
14.	West Ham United FC (London)	42	13	11	18	44	48	50	
15.	Everton FC (Liverpool)	42	11	17	14	44	51	50	
16.	Coventry City FC (Coventry)	42	12	14	16	44	62	50	
17.	Manchester City FC (Manchester)	42	12	13	17	53	64	49	
18.	Aston Villa FC (Birmingham)	42	11	15	16	51	56	48	
19.	Crystal Palace FC (London)	42	11	12	19	34	49	45	R
20.	Norwich City FC (Norwich)	42	10	13	19	37	54	43	R
21.	Leicester City FC (Leicester)	42	6	11	25	45	80	29	R
22.	Ipswich Town FC (Ipswich)	42	7	6	29	36	93	27	R
		924	328	268	328	1195	1195	1252	

The F.A. Premiership was reduced to 20 clubs for the next season

Top Goalscorers

1)	Alan SHEARER	(Blackburn Rovers FC)	34
2)	Robbie FOWLER	(Liverpool FC)	25

Football League Division 1 1994-95 Season	Barnsley	Bolton Wanderers	Bristol City	Burnley	Charlton Athletic	Derby County	Grimsby Town	Luton Town	Middlesbrough	Millwall	Notts County	Oldham Athletic	Portsmouth	Port Vale	Reading	Sheffield United	Southend United	Stoke City	Sunderland	Swindon Town	Tranmere Rovers	Watford	W.B.A.	Wolves
Barnsley FC		3-0	2-1	2-0	2-1	2-1	4-1	3-1	1-1	4-1	1-1	1-1	1-0	3-1	0-2	2-1	0-0	2-0	2-0	2-1	2-2	0-0	2-0	1-3
Bolton Wanderers FC	2-1		0-2	1-1	5-1	1-0	3-3	0-0	1-0	1-0	2-0	2-2	1-1	1-0	1-0	1-1	3-0	4-0	1-0	3-0	1-0	3-0	1-0	5-1
Bristol City FC	3-2	0-1		1-1	2-1	0-2	1-2	2-2	0-1	1-0	2-1	2-2	1-1	0-0	1-2	2-1	0-0	3-1	0-0	3-2	0-1	0-0	1-0	1-5
Burnley FC	0-1	2-2	1-1		2-0	3-1	0-2	2-1	0-3	1-2	2-1	2-1	1-2	4-3	1-2	4-2	5-1	1-1	1-1	1-2	1-1	1-1	1-1	0-1
Charlton Athletic FC	2-2	1-2	3-2	1-2		3-4	2-1	1-0	0-2	1-1	1-0	2-0	1-0	1-1	1-2	1-1	3-1	0-0	1-0	1-0	0-1	3-0	1-1	3-2
Derby County FC	1-0	2-1	3-1	4-0	2-2		2-1	0-0	0-1	3-2	0-0	2-1	3-0	2-0	1-2	2-3	1-2	3-0	0-1	3-1	5-0	1-1	1-1	3-3
Grimsby Town FC	1-0	3-3	1-0	2-2	0-1	0-1		5-0	2-1	1-0	2-1	1-3	2-0	4-1	1-0	0-0	4-1	0-0	3-1	1-1	3-1	0-0	0-2	0-0
Luton Town FC	0-1	0-3	0-1	0-1	0-1	0-0	1-2		5-1	1-1	2-0	2-0	2-0	2-1	0-1	3-6	2-2	2-3	3-0	3-0	2-0	1-1	1-1	3-3
Middlesbrough FC	1-1	1-0	3-0	2-0	1-0	2-4	1-1	2-1		3-0	2-1	2-1	4-0	3-0	0-1	1-1	1-2	2-1	2-2	3-1	0-1	2-0	1-1	1-0
Millwall FC	0-1	0-1	1-1	0-0	3-1	4-1	2-0	0-0	0-0		0-0	1-1	2-2	1-3	2-0	2-1	3-1	1-1	2-0	3-1	2-1	2-1	2-2	1-0
Notts County FC	1-3	1-1	1-1	3-0	3-3	0-0	0-2	0-1	1-1	0-1		1-3	0-1	2-2	1-0	2-1	2-2	0-2	3-2	0-1	1-0	1-0	2-0	1-1
Oldham Athletic AFC	1-0	3-1	2-0	3-0	5-2	1-0	1-0	0-0	1-0	0-1	1-1		3-2	3-2	1-3	3-3	0-2	0-0	0-0	1-1	0-0	0-2	1-0	4-1
Portsmouth FC	3-0	1-1	0-0	2-0	1-1	0-1	2-1	3-2	0-0	3-2	2-1	1-1		0-2	1-1	1-0	1-1	0-1	1-4	4-3	0-0	2-1	1-2	1-2
Port Vale FC	2-1	1-1	1-0	1-0	0-2	1-0	1-2	0-1	2-1	2-1	1-1	3-1	1-0		0-2	0-2	5-0	1-1	0-0	2-2	2-0	0-1	1-0	2-4
Reading FC	0-3	2-1	1-0	0-0	2-1	1-0	1-1	0-0	1-1	0-0	2-0	2-1	0-0	3-3		1-0	2-0	4-0	0-2	3-0	1-3	4-1	0-2	4-2
Sheffield United FC	0-0	3-1	3-0	2-0	2-1	2-1	3-1	1-3	1-1	1-1	1-3	2-0	3-1	1-1	1-1		2-0	1-1	0-0	2-2	2-0	3-0	2-0	3-3
Southend United FC	3-1	2-1	2-1	2-1	2-1	1-0	0-0	3-0	0-2	0-1	1-0	1-0	1-2	4-1	1-3			4-2	0-1	2-0	0-0	0-4	2-1	0-1
Stoke City FC	0-0	1-1	2-1	2-0	2-0	0-0	3-0	1-2	1-1	4-3	2-1	0-1	0-2	0-1	1-1	4-1			0-1	0-0	1-0	1-0	4-1	1-1
Sunderland AFC	2-0	1-1	2-0	0-0	1-1	1-1	2-2	1-0	0-1	1-1	1-1	0-0	2-2	2-1	1-0	0-1	1-0	1-0		1-0	0-1	1-3	2-2	1-1
Swindon Town FC	0-0	0-1	0-3	1-1	0-1	1-1	3-2	1-2	2-1	1-2	3-0	3-1	0-2	2-0	0-0	1-3	2-2	0-1	1-0		2-2	1-0	0-0	3-2
Tranmere Rovers FC	6-1	1-0	2-0	4-1	1-1	3-1	2-0	4-2	1-1	3-1	3-2	3-1	4-2	1-1	1-0	2-1	0-2	0-1	1-0	3-2		2-1	3-1	1-1
Watford FC	3-2	0-0	1-0	2-0	2-0	2-1	0-0	2-4	1-1	3-1	1-2	2-0	3-2	2-2	0-0	1-0	0-0	0-1	2-0	2-0			1-0	2-1
West Bromwich Alb.	2-1	1-0	1-0	1-0	0-1	0-0	1-1	1-0	1-3	3-0	3-2	3-1	0-2	0-0	2-0	1-0	2-0	1-3	1-3	2-5	5-1	0-1		2-0
Wolverhampton W.	0-0	3-1	2-0	2-0	2-0	0-2	2-1	2-3	0-2	3-3	1-0	2-1	1-0	2-1	1-0	2-2	5-0	2-0	1-0	1-1	2-0	1-1	2-0	

	Football League Division 1	Pd	Wn	Dw	Ls	GF	GA	Pts	
1.	Middlesbrough FC (Middlesbrough)	46	23	13	10	67	40	82	P
2.	Reading FC (Reading)	46	23	10	13	58	44	79	PO
3.	Bolton Wanderers FC (Bolton)	46	21	14	11	67	45	77	POP
4.	Wolverhampton Wanderers FC (Wolverhampton)	46	21	13	12	77	61	76	PO
5.	Tranmere Rover FC (Birkenhead)	46	22	10	14	67	58	76	PO
6.	Barnsley FC (Barnsley)	46	20	12	14	63	52	72	
7.	Watford FC (Watford)	46	19	13	14	52	46	70	
8.	Sheffield United FC (Sheffield)	46	17	17	12	74	55	68	
9.	Derby County FC (Derby)	46	18	12	16	66	51	66	
10.	Grimsby Town FC (Cleethorpes)	46	17	14	15	62	56	65	
11.	Stoke City FC (Stoke-on-Trent)	46	16	15	15	50	53	63	
12.	Millwall FC (London)	46	16	14	16	60	60	62	
13.	Southend United FC (Southend-on-Sea)	46	18	8	20	54	73	62	
14.	Oldham Athletic AFC (Oldham)	46	16	13	17	60	60	61	
15.	Charlton Athletic FC (London)	46	16	11	19	58	66	59	
16.	Luton Town FC (Luton)	46	15	13	18	61	64	58	
17.	Port Vale FC (Stoke-on-Trent)	46	15	13	18	58	64	58	
18.	West Bromwich Albion FC (West Bromwich)	46	16	10	20	51	57	58	
19.	Portsmouth FC (Portsmouth)	46	15	13	18	53	63	58	
20.	Sunderland AFC (Sunderland)	46	12	18	16	41	45	54	
21.	Swindon Town FC (Swindon)	46	12	12	22	54	73	48	R
22.	Burnley FC (Burnley)	46	11	13	22	49	74	46	R
23.	Bristol City FC (Bristol)	46	11	12	23	42	63	45	R
24.	Notts County FC (Nottingham)	46	9	13	24	45	66	40	R
		1104	399	306	399	1389	1389	1503	

Promotion Play-offs

Bolton Wanderers FC (Bolton)	4-3 (aet)	Reading FC (Reading)
Tranmere Rovers FC (Birkenhead)	1-3, 0-0	Reading FC (Reading)
Wolverhampton Wanderers FC	2-1, 0-2 (aet)	Bolton Wanderers FC (Bolton)

Football League Division 2 — 1994-95 Season

	Birmingham City	Blackpool	Bournemouth	Bradford City	Brentford	Brighton & Hove Albion	Bristol Rovers	Cambridge	Cardiff City	Chester City	Crewe Alexandra	Huddersfield Town	Hull City	Leyton Orient	Oxford United	Peterborough United	Plymouth Argyle	Rotherham United	Shrewsbury Town	Stockport County	Swansea City	Wrexham	Wycombe Wanderers	York City
Birmingham City FC		7-1	0-0	0-0	2-0	3-3	2-0	1-1	2-1	1-0	5-0	1-1	2-2	2-0	3-0	4-0	4-2	2-1	2-0	1-0	0-1	5-2	0-1	4-2
Blackpool FC	1-1		3-1	2-0	1-2	2-2	0-2	2-3	2-1	3-1	0-0	1-4	1-2	2-1	2-1	4-0	5-2	2-2	2-1	1-2	2-1	2-1	0-1	0-5
AFC Bournemouth	2-1	1-2		2-3	0-1	0-3	2-0	1-0	3-2	1-1	1-1	0-2	2-3	2-0	0-2	0-3	0-0	1-1	3-0	2-0	3-2	1-3	2-0	1-4
Bradford City AFC	1-1	0-1	1-2		1-0	2-1	2-1	1-1	2-3	1-1	0-2	3-4	1-0	2-0	0-2	4-2	2-0	0-3	1-1	1-2	1-3	1-1	2-1	0-0
Brentford FC	1-2	3-2	1-2	4-3		2-1	3-0	6-0	2-0	1-1	2-0	0-0	0-1	3-0	2-0	0-1	7-0	2-0	1-0	1-0	0-0	0-2	0-0	3-0
Brighton & Hove Alb.	0-1	2-2	0-0	1-0	1-1		1-2	2-0	0-0	1-0	0-1	0-0	1-0	1-0	1-1	1-2	1-1	1-1	2-1	2-0	1-1	4-0	1-1	1-0
Bristol Rovers FC	1-1	0-0	2-1	4-0	2-2	3-0		2-1	2-2	3-0	2-2	1-1	0-2	1-1	3-2	3-1	2-0	2-0	4-0	2-2	1-0	4-2	1-0	3-1
Cambridge United FC	1-0	0-0	2-2	4-1	0-0	0-2	1-1		2-0	2-1	1-2	1-1	2-2	1-0	2-0	1-1	2-1	3-1	3-4	1-3	1-2	2-2		1-0
Cardiff City AFC	0-1	0-1	1-1	2-4	2-3	3-0	0-1	3-1		2-1	1-2	0-0	0-2	2-1	1-3	1-2	0-1	1-1	1-2	1-1	1-1	0-0	2-0	1-2
Chester City FC	0-4	2-0	1-1	1-4	1-4	1-2	0-0	1-3	0-2		0-1	1-2	1-2	1-0	2-0	1-1	1-0	4-4	1-3	1-0	2-2	1-1	0-2	0-4
Crewe Alexandra FC	2-1	4-3	2-0	0-1	0-2	4-0	2-1	4-2	0-0	2-1		3-3	3-2	3-0	3-2	1-3	2-2	3-1	1-0	2-1	1-2	1-3	1-2	1-4
Huddersfield Town	1-2	1-1	3-0	0-0	1-0	3-0	1-1	3-1	5-1	5-1	1-2		1-1	2-1	3-3	1-2	2-0	1-0	2-1	2-0	2-1	3-0		
Hull City AFC	0-0	1-0	3-1	2-0	1-2	2-2	0-2	1-0	4-0	2-0	7-1	1-0		2-0	3-1	1-1	2-0	0-2	2-2	0-0	0-2	3-2	0-0	3-0
Leyton Orient FC	2-1	0-1	3-2	0-0	0-2	0-3	1-2	1-1	2-0	1-4	0-2	1-1			1-1	4-1	1-0	2-0	0-0	0-1	0-1	1-1	0-1	0-1
Oxford United FC	1-1	3-2	0-3	1-0	1-1	0-0	0-0	1-0	1-0	2-1	3-1	4-0	3-2			1-0	1-0	2-1	0-0	4-0	1-2	0-0	0-1	1-1
Peterborough United	1-1	1-0	0-0	0-0	2-2	2-1	2-0	2-2	2-1	1-5	2-2	2-1	0-0	1-4			1-2	2-2	1-0	0-1	1-0	1-0	1-3	1-1
Plymouth Argyle FC	1-3	0-2	0-1	1-5	1-5	0-3	1-1	0-0	0-0	1-0	3-2	0-3	2-1	1-0	1-1	0-1		0-0	1-0	0-2	2-1	4-1	2-2	1-2
Rotherham United	1-1	0-2	4-0	3-1	0-2	4-3	0-3	1-0	2-0	2-2	1-1	2-0	2-0	1-1	0-0	3-1			0-4	1-0	3-3	0-1	2-0	2-1
Shrewsbury Town	0-2	0-0	3-0	1-2	2-1	1-1	1-0	1-1	0-1	1-0	2-1	2-3	3-0	1-1	2-2	3-2	1-0			1-1	3-3	2-2	2-2	1-0
Stockport County	0-1	3-2	1-0	1-2	2-0	2-1	2-1	4-1	2-2	3-1	1-2	4-0	0-2	1-1	2-4	1-0	2-1				0-1	1-1	4-1	2-3
Swansea City FC	0-2	1-0	1-0	0-0	0-2	1-1	0-0	1-0	4-1	0-1	0-1	1-1	2-0	2-0	1-3	2-0	3-0	0-0	2-0			0-0	1-1	0-0
Wrexham AFC	1-1	0-1	2-0	0-1	0-0	2-1	1-1	0-1	0-3	2-2	1-2	2-2	4-1	3-2	3-3	3-1	3-1	0-1	1-0	4-1			4-1	1-1
Wycombe Wanderers	0-3	1-1	1-1	3-1	4-3	0-0	0-0	3-0	3-1	3-1	0-0	2-1	1-2	2-1	1-0	3-1	1-2	1-0	1-1	1-0	3-0			0-0
York City FC	2-0	4-0	1-0	0-0	2-1	1-0	0-3	2-0	1-0	2-0	1-2	3-0	3-1	4-1	0-2	1-1	1-0	2-0	3-0	2-4	2-4	0-1	0-0	

	Football League Division 2	Pd	Wn	Dw	Ls	GF	GA	Pts	
1.	Birmingham City FC (Birmingham)	46	25	14	7	84	37	89	P
2.	Brentford FC (London)	46	25	10	11	81	39	85	PO
3.	Crewe Alexandra FC (Crewe)	46	25	8	13	80	68	83	PO
4.	Bristol Rovers FC (Bristol)	46	22	16	8	70	40	82	PO
5.	Huddersfield Town AFC (Huddersfield)	46	22	15	9	79	49	81	POP
6.	Wycombe Wanderers FC (High Wycombe)	46	21	15	10	60	46	78	
7.	Oxford United FC (Oxford)	46	21	12	13	66	52	75	
8.	Hull City AFC (Kingston-upon-Hull)	46	21	11	14	70	57	74	
9.	York City FC (York)	46	21	9	16	67	51	72	
10.	Swansea City FC (Swansea)	46	19	14	13	57	45	71	
11.	Stockport County FC (Stockport)	46	19	8	19	63	60	65	
12.	Blackpool FC (Blackpool)	46	18	10	18	64	70	64	
13.	Wrexham AFC (Wrexham)	46	16	16	16	65	64	63	
14.	Bradford City AFC (Bradford)	46	16	12	18	57	64	60	
15.	Peterborough United FC (Peterborough)	46	14	18	14	54	69	60	
16.	Brighton & Hove Albion FC (Hove)	46	14	17	15	54	53	59	
17.	Rotherham United FC (Rotherham)	46	14	14	18	57	61	56	
18.	Shrewsbury Town FC (Shrewsbury)	46	13	14	19	54	62	53	
19.	AFC Bournemouth (Bournemouth)	46	13	11	22	49	69	50	
20.	Cambridge United FC (Cambridge)	46	11	15	20	52	69	48	R
21.	Plymouth Argyle FC (Plymouth)	46	12	10	24	45	83	46	R
22.	Cardiff City AFC (Cardiff)	46	9	11	26	46	74	38	R
23.	Chester City FC (Chester)	46	6	11	29	37	84	29	R
24.	Leyton Orient FC (London)	46	6	8	32	30	75	26	R
		1104	403	298	403	1441	1441	1507	

Promotion Play-offs

Huddersfield Town AFC (Huddersfield)	2-1	Bristol Rovers FC (Bristol)
Bristol Rovers FC (Bristol)	0-0, 1-1 (aet)	Crewe Alexandra FC (Crewe)

(Bristol Rovers won on the away goals rule)

Huddersfield Town AFC (Huddersfield)	1-1, 1-1 (aet)	Brentford FC (London)

(Huddersfield Town won 4-3 on penalties)

Football League Division 3 1994-95 Season	Barnet	Bury	Carlisle United	Chesterfield	Colchester United	Darlington	Doncaster Rovers	Exeter City	Fulham	Gillingham	Hartlepool United	Hereford United	Lincoln City	Mansfield Town	Northampton Town	Preston North End	Rochdale	Scarborough	Scunthorpe United	Torquay United	Walsall	Wigan Athletic
Barnet FC	■	1-1	0-2	4-1	0-1	2-3	0-0	1-1	0-0	1-0	4-0	2-2	2-1	2-2	2-3	2-1	6-2	3-1	1-2	2-0	1-3	1-1
Bury FC	3-0	■	2-0	2-1	4-1	2-1	2-0	0-0	0-0	3-2	2-0	1-1	2-0	2-2	5-0	0-0	0-1	1-0	2-0	3-1	0-0	3-3
Carlisle United FC	4-0	3-0	■	1-1	0-0	2-1	1-1	1-0	1-1	2-0	0-1	1-0	1-3	2-1	2-1	0-0	4-1	2-0	2-1	1-0	2-1	2-1
Chesterfield FC	2-0	0-0	1-2	■	2-2	0-0	2-0	2-0	1-1	2-0	2-0	1-0	1-0	0-1	3-0	1-0	2-2	0-1	3-1	1-0	0-0	0-0
Colchester United FC	1-1	1-0	0-1	0-3	■	1-0	0-3	3-1	5-2	2-2	1-0	2-2	1-2	1-1	0-1	3-1	0-0	0-2	4-2	1-3	3-2	0-1
Darlington FC	0-1	0-2	0-2	0-1	2-3	■	0-2	2-0	0-0	2-0	1-2	3-1	0-0	0-0	4-1	0-0	4-0	1-0	1-3	2-1	2-2	1-3
Doncaster Rovers FC	1-1	1-2	0-0	1-3	1-2	0-0	■	1-0	0-0	1-2	3-0	3-0	0-2	1-0	2-1	0-1	1-0	1-1	1-1	3-0	0-2	5-3
Exeter City FC	1-2	0-4	1-1	1-2	1-0	0-2	1-5	■	0-1	3-0	2-1	1-1	1-0	2-3	0-0	0-1	0-0	5-2	2-2	1-2	1-3	2-4
Fulham FC	4-0	1-0	1-3	1-1	1-2	3-1	0-2	4-0	■	1-0	1-0	1-1	1-1	4-2	4-4	0-1	5-0	1-2	1-0	2-1	1-1	2-0
Gillingham FC	2-1	1-1	0-1	1-1	1-3	2-1	4-2	3-0	4-1	■	0-0	0-0	0-0	0-2	3-1	2-3	1-1	3-1	2-2	1-0	1-3	0-1
Hartlepool United FC	0-1	3-1	1-5	0-2	3-1	1-0	2-1	2-2	1-2	2-0	■	4-0	0-3	3-2	1-1	3-1	1-0	3-3	1-4	1-1	1-1	0-1
Hereford United FC	3-2	1-0	0-2	0-2	3-0	0-0	0-0	3-0	1-1	2-1	1-0	■	0-3	0-0	2-1	0-2	0-0	2-1	2-1	1-1	0-0	1-2
Lincoln City FC	1-2	0-3	1-1	0-1	2-0	3-1	1-0	2-0	2-0	1-1	3-0	2-0	■	3-2	2-2	1-1	2-2	2-0	3-3	1-2	1-1	1-0
Mansfield Town FC	3-0	0-2	1-2	4-2	2-0	0-1	0-1	1-1	1-1	4-0	2-0	7-1	6-2	■	1-1	1-2	1-1	3-2	1-0	2-2	1-3	4-3
Northampton Town FC	1-1	0-5	2-1	2-3	1-1	2-1	0-0	2-1	0-1	2-0	1-1	1-3	3-1	0-1	■	2-1	1-2	0-3	0-1	2-0	2-2	1-0
Preston North End FC	1-0	5-0	1-0	0-0	2-1	1-3	2-2	0-1	3-2	1-1	3-0	4-2	4-0	2-1	2-0	■	3-0	1-0	0-1	0-1	1-2	1-0
Rochdale AFC	2-2	0-3	1-1	4-1	0-0	2-0	2-0	0-1	1-2	2-1	1-0	1-3	1-0	3-3	0-0	0-1	■	1-1	1-2	2-0	0-2	1-0
Scarborough FC	0-1	1-2	1-2	0-1	0-1	3-1	2-2	0-2	3-1	0-0	2-2	3-1	1-1	2-5	0-0	1-1	2-4	■	3-0	1-1	1-2	0-1
Scunthorpe United FC	1-0	3-2	2-3	0-1	3-4	2-1	0-5	3-0	1-0	3-0	0-0	1-0	2-0	3-4	1-1	2-1	4-1	3-1	■	3-2	0-1	3-1
Torquay United FC	1-2	2-2	1-1	3-3	3-3	1-0	1-0	0-0	2-1	3-1	2-2	0-1	2-1	2-1	1-0	4-1	2-1	1-1	1-1	■	3-2	0-0
Walsall FC	4-0	0-1	1-2	1-3	2-0	2-0	1-0	1-0	5-1	2-1	4-1	4-3	2-1	1-0	1-1	2-2	0-0	4-1	2-1	1-0	■	2-0
Wigan Athletic AFC	1-2	0-3	0-2	2-3	1-2	4-1	3-2	3-1	1-1	0-3	2-0	1-1	0-1	0-4	2-1	1-1	4-0	1-1	0-0	1-1	1-0	■

Football League Division 3

		Pd	Wn	Dw	Ls	GF	GA	Pts	
1.	Carlisle United FC (Carlisle)	42	27	10	5	67	31	91	P
2.	Walsall FC (Walsall)	42	24	11	7	75	40	83	P
3.	Chesterfield FC (Chesterfield)	42	23	12	7	62	37	81	POP
4.	Bury FC (Bury)	42	23	11	8	73	36	80	PO
5.	Preston North End FC (Preston)	42	19	10	13	58	41	67	PO
6.	Mansfield Town FC (Mansfield)	42	18	11	13	84	59	65	PO
7.	Scunthorpe United FC (Scunthorpe)	42	18	8	16	68	63	62	
8.	Fulham FC (London)	42	16	14	12	60	54	62	
9.	Doncaster Rovers FC (Doncaster)	42	17	10	15	58	43	61	
10.	Colchester United FC (Colchester)	42	16	10	16	56	64	58	
11.	Barnet FC (London)	42	15	11	16	56	63	56	
12.	Lincoln City FC (Lincoln)	42	15	11	16	54	55	56	
13.	Torquay United FC (Torquay)	42	14	13	15	54	57	55	
14.	Wigan Athletic AFC (Wigan)	42	14	10	18	53	60	52	
15.	Rochdale AFC (Rochdale)	42	12	14	16	44	67	50	
16.	Hereford United FC (Hereford)	42	12	13	17	45	62	49	
17.	Northampton Town FC (Northampton)	42	10	14	18	45	67	44	
18.	Hartlepool United FC (Hartlepool)	42	11	10	21	43	69	43	
19.	Gillingham FC (Gillingham)	42	10	11	21	46	64	41	
20.	Darlington FC (Darlington)	42	11	8	23	43	57	41	
21.	Scarborough FC (Scarborough)	42	8	10	24	49	70	34	
22.	Exeter City FC (Exeter)	42	8	10	24	36	70	34	#
		924	341	242	341	1229	1229	1265	

\# Macclesfield Town FC (Macclesfield) were refused promotion as their ground did not meet Football League standards. As a result of this Exeter City FC (Exeter) retained their Football League Division 3 status.

Promotion Play-offs

Chesterfield FC (Chesterfield)	2-9	Bury FC (Bury)
Mansfield Town FC (Mansfield)	1-1, 2-5 (aet)	Chesterfield FC (Chesterfield)
Preston North End FC (Preston)	0-1, 0-1	Bury FC (Bury)

F.A. CUP FINAL (Wembley Stadium, London – 20/05/1995 – 79,592)

EVERTON FC (LIVERPOOL)	1-0	Manchester United FC (Manchester)

Rideout 30'

Everton: Southall, Jackson, Watson, Unsworth, Ablett, Limpar (Amokachi 69'), Parkinson, Horne, Hinchcliffe, Stuart, Rideout (Ferguson 51').

Man. United: Schmeichel, G.Neville, Bruce (Giggs 46'), Pallister, Irwin, Butt, Keane, Ince, Sharpe (Scholes 72'), Hughes, McClair.

Semi-finals

Crystal Palace FC (London)	2-2 (aet), 0-2	Manchester United FC (Manchester)
Everton FC (Liverpool)	4-1	Tottenham Hotspur FC (London)

Quarter-finals

Crystal Palace FC (London)	1-1, 4-1	Wolverhampton Wanderers FC (Wolverhampton)
Everton FC (Liverpool)	1-0	Newcastle United FC (Newcastle-upon-Tyne)
Liverpool FC (Liverpool)	1-2	Tottenham Hotspur FC (London)
Manchester United FC (Manchester)	2-0	Queen's Park Rangers FC (London)

F.A. Premiership 1995-96 Season — results grid (home team in rows, away team in columns)

Column key: Ars = Arsenal, AV = Aston Villa, Bla = Blackburn Rovers, Bol = Bolton Wanderers, Che = Chelsea, Cov = Coventry City, Eve = Everton, Lee = Leeds United, Liv = Liverpool, MC = Manchester City, MU = Manchester United, Mid = Middlesbrough, New = Newcastle United, NF = Nottingham Forest, QPR = Q.P.R., SW = Sheffield Wednesday, Sou = Southampton, Tot = Tottenham Hotspur, WH = West Ham United, Wim = Wimbledon

	Ars	AV	Bla	Bol	Che	Cov	Eve	Lee	Liv	MC	MU	Mid	New	NF	QPR	SW	Sou	Tot	WH	Wim
Arsenal FC		2-0	0-0	2-1	1-1	1-1	1-2	2-1	0-0	3-1	1-0	1-1	2-0	1-1	3-0	4-2	4-2	0-0	1-0	1-3
Aston Villa FC	1-1		2-0	1-0	0-1	4-1	1-0	3-0	0-2	0-1	3-1	0-0	1-1	1-1	4-2	3-2	3-0	2-1	1-1	2-0
Blackburn Rovers FC	1-1	1-1		3-1	3-0	5-1	0-3	1-0	2-3	2-0	1-2	1-0	2-1	7-0	1-0	3-0	2-1	2-1	4-2	3-2
Bolton Wanderers FC	1-0	0-2	2-1		2-1	1-2	1-1	0-2	0-1	1-1	0-6	1-1	1-3	1-1	0-1	2-1	0-1	2-3	0-3	1-0
Chelsea FC	1-0	1-2	2-3	3-2		2-2	0-0	4-1	2-2	1-1	1-4	5-0	1-0	1-1	0-0	3-0	0-0	0-0	1-2	1-2
Coventry City FC	0-0	0-3	5-0	0-2	1-0		2-1	0-0	1-0	2-1	0-4	0-0	0-1	1-1	1-0	0-1	1-1	2-3	2-2	3-3
Everton FC	0-2	1-0	1-0	3-0	1-1	2-2		2-0	1-1	2-0	2-3	4-0	1-3	3-0	2-0	2-2	2-0	1-1	3-0	2-4
Leeds United AFC	0-3	2-0	0-0	0-1	1-0	3-1	2-2		1-0	0-1	3-1	0-1	0-1	1-3	1-3	2-0	1-0	1-3	2-0	1-1
Liverpool FC	3-1	3-0	3-0	5-2	2-0	0-0	1-2	5-0		6-0	2-0	1-0	4-3	4-2	1-0	1-0	1-1	0-0	2-0	2-2
Manchester City FC	0-1	1-0	1-1	1-0	0-1	1-1	0-2	0-0	2-2		2-3	0-1	3-3	1-1	2-0	1-0	2-1	1-1	2-1	1-0
Manchester United FC	1-0	0-0	1-0	3-0	1-1	1-0	2-0	1-0	2-2	1-0		2-0	2-0	5-0	2-1	2-2	4-1	1-0	2-1	3-1
Middlesbrough FC	2-3	0-2	2-0	1-4	2-0	2-1	0-2	1-1	2-1	4-1	0-3		1-2	1-1	1-0	3-1	0-0	0-1	4-2	1-2
Newcastle United FC	2-0	1-0	1-0	2-1	2-0	1-0	1-0	2-1	2-1	3-1	0-1	1-0		3-1	2-1	2-0	1-0	1-1	3-0	6-1
Nottingham Forest FC	0-1	1-1	1-5	3-2	0-0	0-0	3-2	2-1	1-0	3-0	1-1	1-0	1-1		3-0	1-0	1-0	2-1	1-1	4-1
Queen's Park Rangers FC	1-1	1-0	0-1	2-1	1-2	1-1	3-1	1-2	1-2	1-0	1-1	1-1	2-3	1-1		0-3	3-0	2-3	3-0	0-3
Sheffield Wednesday FC	1-0	2-0	2-1	4-2	0-0	4-3	2-5	6-2	1-1	1-1	0-0	0-1	0-2	1-3	1-3		2-2	1-3	0-1	2-1
Southampton FC	0-0	0-1	1-0	1-0	2-3	1-0	2-2	1-1	1-3	1-1	3-1	2-1	1-0	3-4	2-0	0-1		0-0	0-0	0-0
Tottenham Hotspur FC	2-1	0-1	2-3	2-2	1-1	3-1	0-0	1-1	1-3	4-1	1-1	1-1	0-1	1-0	1-0	1-0	0-0		0-1	3-1
West Ham United FC	0-1	1-4	1-1	1-0	1-3	3-2	2-1	1-2	0-0	4-2	0-1	2-0	2-0	1-0	1-0	1-1	2-1	1-1		1-1
Wimbledon FC	0-3	3-3	1-1	3-2	1-1	0-2	2-3	2-4	1-0	3-0	2-4	0-0	3-3	1-0	2-1	2-2	1-2	0-1	0-1	

F.A. Premiership

		Pd	Wn	Dw	Ls	GF	GA	Pts	
1.	MANCHESTER UNITED FC (MANCHESTER)	38	25	7	6	73	35	82	
2.	Newcastle United FC (Newcastle-upon-Tyne)	38	24	6	8	66	37	78	
3.	Liverpool FC (Liverpool)	38	20	11	7	70	34	71	
4.	Aston Villa FC (Birmingham)	38	18	9	11	52	35	63	
5.	Arsenal FC (London)	38	17	12	9	49	32	63	
6.	Everton FC (Liverpool)	38	17	10	11	64	44	61	
7.	Blackburn Rovers FC (Blackburn)	38	18	7	13	61	47	61	
8.	Tottenham Hotspur FC (London)	38	16	13	9	50	38	61	
9.	Nottingham Forest FC (Nottingham)	38	15	13	10	50	54	58	
10.	West Ham United FC (London)	38	14	9	15	43	52	51	
11.	Chelsea FC (London)	38	12	14	12	46	44	50	
12.	Middlesbrough FC (Middlesbrough)	38	11	10	17	35	50	43	
13.	Leeds United AFC (Leeds)	38	12	7	19	40	57	43	
14.	Wimbledon FC (Wimbledon)	38	10	11	17	55	70	41	
15.	Sheffield Wednesday FC (Sheffield)	38	10	10	18	48	61	40	
16.	Coventry City FC (Coventry)	38	8	14	16	42	60	38	
17.	Southampton FC (Southampton)	38	9	11	8	34	52	38	
18.	Manchester City FC (Manchester)	38	9	11	18	33	58	38	R
19.	Queen's Park Rangers FC (London)	38	9	6	23	38	57	33	R
20.	Bolton Wanderers FC (Bolton)	38	8	5	25	39	71	29	R
		760	282	196	282	988	988	1042	

Top Goalscorers

1)	Alan SHEARER	(Blackburn Rovers FC)	31
2)	Robbie FOWLER	(Liverpool FC)	28
3)	Les FERDINAND	(Newcastle United FC)	25

Football League Division 1 1995-96 Season	Barnsley	Birmingham City	Charlton Athletic	Crystal Palace	Derby County	Grimsby Town	Huddersfield Town	Ipswich Town	Leicester City	Luton Town	Millwall	Norwich City	Oldham Athletic	Portsmouth	Port Vale	Reading	Sheffield United	Southend United	Stoke City	Sunderland	Tranmere Rovers	Watford	W.B.A.	Wolves
Barnsley FC		0-5	1-1	1-1	2-0	1-1	3-0	3-3	2-2	1-0	3-1	2-2	2-1	0-0	1-1	0-1	2-2	1-1	3-1	0-1	2-1	2-1	1-1	1-0
Birmingham City FC	0-0		3-4	0-0	1-4	3-1	2-0	3-1	2-2	4-0	2-2	3-1	0-0	2-0	3-1	1-2	0-1	2-0	1-1	0-2	1-0	1-0	1-1	2-0
Charlton Athletic FC	1-1	3-1		0-0	0-0	0-1	2-1	0-2	0-1	1-1	2-0	1-1	1-1	2-1	2-2	2-1	1-1	0-3	2-1	1-1	0-0	2-1	4-1	1-1
Crystal Palace FC	4-3	3-2	1-1		0-0	5-0	0-0	1-1	0-1	2-0	1-2	0-1	2-2	0-0	2-2	0-2	0-0	2-0	1-1	0-1	2-1	4-0	1-0	3-2
Derby County FC	4-1	1-1	2-0	2-1		1-1	3-2	1-1	0-1	1-1	2-2	2-1	2-1	3-2	0-0	3-0	4-2	1-0	3-1	3-1	6-2	1-1	3-0	0-0
Grimsby Town FC	3-1	2-1	1-2	0-2	1-1		1-1	3-1	2-2	0-0	1-2	2-2	1-1	2-1	1-0	0-0	0-2	1-1	1-0	0-4	1-1	0-0	1-0	3-0
Huddersfield Town	3-0	4-2	2-2	3-0	0-1	1-3		2-1	3-1	1-0	3-0	3-2	0-0	0-1	0-2	3-1	1-2	3-1	1-1	1-1	1-0	1-0	4-1	2-1
Ipswich Town FC	2-2	2-0	1-5	1-0	1-0	2-2	2-1		4-2	0-1	0-0	2-1	2-1	3-2	5-1	1-2	1-1	1-1	4-1	3-1	1-2	4-2	2-1	1-2
Leicester City FC	2-2	3-0	1-1	2-3	0-0	2-1	2-1	0-2		1-1	2-1	3-2	2-0	1-1	1-1	0-2	1-3	2-3	0-0	0-1	1-0	1-0	1-2	1-0
Luton Town FC	1-3	0-0	0-1	0-0	1-2	3-2	2-2	1-2	1-1		1-0	1-3	1-1	3-1	3-2	1-2	1-0	3-1	1-2	0-2	3-2	0-0	1-2	2-3
Millwall FC	0-1	2-0	0-2	1-4	0-1	2-1	0-0	2-1	1-1	1-0		2-1	0-1	1-1	1-2	1-1	1-0	0-0	2-3	1-2	2-2	1-2	2-1	0-1
Norwich City FC	3-1	3-1	1-0	1-0	1-0	2-2	2-0	2-1	0-1	0-1	0-0		2-1	1-1	2-1	3-3	0-0	0-1	0-1	0-0	1-1	1-2	2-2	2-3
Oldham Athletic AFC	0-1	4-0	1-1	3-1	0-1	1-0	3-0	1-1	3-1	1-0	2-2	2-0		1-1	2-2	2-1	2-1	0-1	2-0	1-2	1-2	0-0	1-2	0-0
Portsmouth FC	0-0	0-1	2-1	2-3	2-2	3-1	1-1	0-1	2-1	4-0	0-1	1-0	2-1		1-2	0-0	1-2	4-2	3-3	2-2	0-2	4-2	0-2	0-2
Port Vale FC	3-0	1-2	1-3	1-2	1-1	1-0	1-0	2-1	0-2	1-0	0-1	1-0	1-3	0-2		3-2	2-3	2-1	1-0	1-1	1-1	1-1	3-1	2-2
Reading FC	0-0	0-1	0-0	0-2	3-2	0-2	3-1	1-4	1-1	3-1	1-2	0-3	2-0	0-1	2-2		0-3	3-3	1-0	1-1	1-0	0-0	3-1	3-0
Sheffield United FC	1-0	1-1	2-0	2-3	0-2	1-2	0-2	2-2	1-3	1-0	2-0	2-1	2-1	4-1	1-1	0-0		3-0	0-0	0-0	0-2	1-1	1-2	2-1
Southend United FC	0-0	3-1	1-1	1-1	1-2	1-0	0-0	2-1	2-1	0-1	2-0	1-1	1-1	2-1	2-1	0-0	2-1		2-4	0-2	2-0	1-1	2-1	2-1
Stoke City FC	2-0	1-0	1-0	1-2	1-1	1-2	1-1	3-1	1-0	5-0	1-0	1-1	0-1	2-1	0-1	1-1	2-2	1-0		1-0	0-0	2-0	2-1	2-0
Sunderland AFC	2-1	3-0	0-0	1-0	3-0	1-0	3-2	1-0	1-2	6-0	0-1	0-1	1-1	0-0	2-2	2-0	1-0	0-0	0-0		0-0	1-1	0-0	2-0
Tranmere Rovers FC	1-3	2-2	0-0	2-3	5-1	0-1	3-1	5-2	1-1	1-0	2-2	1-1	2-0	1-2	2-1	2-1	1-1	3-0	0-0	2-0		2-3	2-2	2-2
Watford FC	2-3	1-1	1-2	0-0	0-0	6-3	0-1	2-3	0-1	1-1	0-1	0-2	2-1	1-2	5-2	4-2	2-1	2-2	3-0	3-3	3-0		1-1	1-1
West Bromwich Alb.	2-1	1-0	1-0	2-3	3-2	3-1	1-2	0-0	2-3	0-2	1-0	1-4	1-0	2-1	1-1	2-0	3-1	3-1	0-1	0-1	1-1	4-4		0-0
Wolverhampton W.	2-2	3-2	0-0	0-2	3-0	4-1	0-0	2-2	2-3	0-0	1-1	0-2	1-3	2-2	0-1	1-1	1-0	2-0	1-4	3-0	2-1	3-0	1-1	

Football League Division 1

		Pd	Wn	Dw	Ls	GF	GA	Pts	
1.	Sunderland AFC (Sunderland)	46	22	17	7	59	33	83	P
2.	Derby County FC (Derby)	46	21	16	9	71	51	79	P
3.	Crystal Palace FC (London)	46	20	15	11	67	48	75	PO
4.	Stoke City FC (Stoke-on-Trent)	46	20	13	13	60	49	73	PO
5.	Leicester City FC (Leicester)	46	19	14	13	66	60	71	POP
6.	Charlton Athletic FC (London)	46	17	20	9	57	45	71	PO
7.	Ipswich Town FC (Ipswich)	46	19	12	15	79	69	69	
8.	Huddersfield Town AFC (Huddersfield)	46	17	12	17	61	58	63	
9.	Sheffield United FC (Sheffield)	46	16	14	16	57	54	62	
10.	Barnsley FC (Barnsley)	46	14	18	14	60	66	60	
11.	West Bromwich Albion FC (West Bromwich)	46	16	12	18	60	68	60	
12.	Port Vale FC (Stoke -on Trent)	46	15	15	16	59	66	60	
13.	Tranmere Rovers FC (Birkenhead)	46	14	17	15	64	60	59	
14.	Southend United FC (Southend-on-Sea)	46	15	14	17	52	61	59	
15.	Birmingham City FC (Birmingham)	46	15	13	18	61	64	58	
16.	Norwich City FC (Norwich)	46	14	15	17	59	55	57	
17.	Grimsby Town FC (Cleethorpes)	46	14	14	18	55	69	56	
18.	Oldham Athletic AFC (Oldham)	46	14	14	18	54	50	56	
19.	Reading FC (Reading)	46	13	17	16	54	63	56	
20.	Wolverhampton Wanderers FC (Wolverhampton)	46	13	16	17	56	62	55	
21.	Portsmouth FC (Portsmouth)	46	13	13	20	61	69	52	
22.	Millwall FC (London)	46	13	13	20	43	63	52	R
23.	Watford FC (Watford)	46	10	18	18	62	70	48	R
24.	Luton Town FC (Luton)	46	11	12	23	40	64	45	R
		1104	375	354	375	1417	1417	1479	

Promotion Play-offs

Leicester City FC (Leicester)	2-1 (aet)	Crystal Palace FC (London)
Charlton Athletic FC (London)	1-2, 0-1	Crystal Palace FC (London)
Leicester City FC (Leicester)	0-0, 1-0	Stoke City FC (Stoke-on-Trent)

Football League Division 2 — 1995-96 Season

	Blackpool	Bournemouth	Bradford City	Brentford	Brighton & Hove Albion	Bristol City	Bristol Rovers	Burnley	Carlisle United	Chesterfield	Crewe Alexandra	Hull City	Notts County	Oxford United	Peterborough United	Rotherham United	Shrewsbury Town	Stockport County	Swansea City	Swindon Town	Walsall	Wrexham	Wycombe Wanderers	York City
Blackpool FC	■	2-1	4-1	1-0	2-1	3-0	3-0	3-1	3-1	0-0	2-1	1-1	2-0	1-1	2-0	1-2	2-1	0-1	4-0	1-1	1-2	2-0	1-1	1-3
AFC Bournemouth	1-0	■	3-1	1-0	3-1	1-1	2-1	0-2	2-0	2-0	0-4	2-0	0-2	0-1	3-0	2-1	0-2	3-2	3-1	0-0	0-0	1-1	2-3	2-2
Bradford City AFC	2-1	1-0	■	2-1	1-3	3-0	2-3	2-2	3-1	2-1	2-1	1-1	1-0	1-0	2-1	2-0	3-1	0-1	5-1	1-1	1-0	2-0	0-4	2-2
Brentford FC	1-2	2-0	2-1	■	0-1	2-2	0-0	1-0	1-1	1-2	2-1	1-0	0-0	1-0	3-0	1-1	0-2	1-0	0-0	0-2	1-0	1-0	1-0	2-0
Brighton & Hove Alb.	1-2	2-0	0-0	0-0	■	0-2	2-0	1-0	1-0	0-2	2-2	4-0	1-0	1-2	1-2	1-1	2-2	1-1	0-2	1-3	0-3	2-2	1-2	1-3
Bristol City FC	1-1	3-0	2-1	0-0	0-1	■	0-2	0-1	1-1	2-1	3-2	4-0	0-2	0-2	0-1	4-3	2-0	1-0	1-0	0-0	0-2	3-1	0-0	1-1
Bristol Rovers FC	1-1	0-2	1-0	2-0	1-0	2-4	■	1-0	1-1	1-0	1-2	2-1	0-3	2-0	1-1	1-0	2-1	1-3	2-2	1-4	2-0	1-2	2-1	1-0
Burnley FC	0-1	0-0	2-3	1-0	3-0	0-0	0-1	■	2-0	2-2	0-1	2-1	3-4	0-2	2-1	2-1	4-3	3-0	0-0	1-1	2-2	1-1		3-3
Carlisle United FC	1-2	4-0	2-2	2-1	1-0	2-1	1-2	2-0	■	1-1	1-0	2-0	0-0	1-2	1-1	2-0	1-1	0-1	3-0	0-1	1-1	1-2	4-2	2-0
Chesterfield FC	1-0	3-0	2-1	2-2	1-0	1-1	2-1	4-2	3-0	■	1-2	0-0	1-0	1-0	1-1	3-0	1-0	1-2	3-2	1-3	1-1	1-1	3-1	2-1
Crewe Alexandra FC	1-2	2-0	1-2	3-1	3-1	4-2	1-2	3-1	2-1	3-0	■	1-0	2-2	1-2	2-1	0-2	3-0	0-1	4-1	0-2	1-0	0-0	2-0	1-1
Hull City AFC	2-1	1-1	2-3	0-1	0-0	2-3	1-3	3-0	2-5	0-0	1-2	■	0-0	2-3	1-4	2-3	1-1	0-0	0-1	1-1	4-2	0-3		
Notts County FC	1-1	2-0	0-2	4-0	2-1	2-2	4-2	1-1	3-1	4-1	0-1	1-0	■	1-1	1-0	2-1	1-1	1-0	1-3	2-1	1-0	2-0		2-2
Oxford United FC	1-0	2-0	2-0	2-1	1-1	2-0	1-2	5-0	4-0	1-0	1-0	2-0	1-1	■	4-0	1-1	6-0	2-1	5-1	3-0	3-2	0-0	1-4	2-0
Peterborough United	0-0	4-5	3-1	0-1	3-1	1-1	0-0	0-2	6-1	0-1	3-1	3-1	0-1	1-1	■	1-0	2-2	0-1	1-1	0-2	2-3	1-1	3-0	6-1
Rotherham United	2-1	1-0	2-0	1-0	1-0	2-3	1-0	2-2	0-1	2-2	1-1	2-0	1-0	5-1		■	2-2	2-0	1-1	0-2	0-1	0-0	0-1	
Shrewsbury Town	0-2	1-2	1-1	2-1	4-1	1-1	3-0	1-1	0-0	2-3	1-1	0-1	2-0	1-1	3-1		■	1-2	1-2	1-2	0-2	2-2	1-1	2-1
Stockport County	1-1	3-1	1-2	1-1	3-1	0-0	2-0	0-0	2-0	0-1	1-1	0-0	2-0	4-2	0-1	1-1	0-2	■	2-0	1-1	0-1	2-3	1-1	3-0
Swansea City FC	0-2	1-1	2-0	2-1	2-1	2-1	2-2	2-4	1-1	3-2	0-0	0-0	1-1	0-0	0-0	3-1	0-3		■	0-1	2-1	1-3	1-2	0-1
Swindon Town FC	1-1	2-2	4-1	2-2	3-2	2-0	2-1	0-0	2-1	1-1	3-0	1-0	1-1	2-0	1-0	0-1	0-0	2-0		■	1-1	1-1	1-0	3-0
Walsall FC	1-1	0-0	2-1	0-1	2-1	2-1	1-1	3-1	2-1	3-0	3-2	3-0	0-0	2-2	1-1	3-1	3-0	0-2	4-1	0-0	■	1-2	0-1	2-0
Wrexham AFC	1-1	5-0	1-2	2-2	1-1	0-0	3-2	0-2	3-2	3-0	5-0	1-1	2-1	1-0	7-0	1-1	2-3	1-0	4-3	3-0	1-0	■	1-0	2-3
Wycombe Wanderers	0-1	1-2	5-2	2-1	0-2	1-1	1-1	4-1	4-0	1-0	1-1	1-2	2-1	1-0	1-3	1-1	1-1	2-0	4-1	0-1	1-2	1-0	■	2-1
York City FC	0-2	3-1	0-3	2-2	3-1	0-1	0-1	1-1	0-1	2-3	0-1	1-3	1-0	3-1	2-2	1-2	2-2	0-0	2-0	1-0	1-0	2-1		■

	Football League Division 2	Pd	Wn	Dw	Ls	GF	GA	Pts	
1.	Swindon Town FC (Swindon)	46	25	17	4	71	34	92	P
2.	Oxford United FC (Oxford)	46	24	11	11	76	39	83	P
3.	Blackpool FC (Blackpool)	46	23	13	10	67	40	82	PO
4.	Notts County FC (Nottingham)	46	21	15	10	63	39	78	PO
5.	Crewe Alexandra FC (Crewe)	46	22	7	17	77	60	73	PO
6.	Bradford City AFC (Bradford)	46	22	7	17	71	69	73	POP
7.	Chesterfield FC (Chesterfield)	46	20	12	14	56	51	72	
8.	Wrexham AFC (Wrexham)	46	18	16	12	76	55	70	
9.	Stockport County FC (Stockport)	46	19	13	14	61	47	70	
10.	Bristol Rovers FC (Bristol)	46	20	10	16	57	60	70	
11.	Walsall FC (Walsall)	46	19	12	15	60	45	69	
12.	Wycombe Wanderers FC (High Wycombe)	46	15	15	16	63	59	60	
13.	Bristol City FC (Bristol)	46	15	15	16	55	60	60	
14.	AFC Bournemouth (Bournemouth)	46	16	10	20	51	70	58	
15.	Brentford FC (London)	46	15	13	18	43	49	58	
16.	Rotherham United FC (Rotherham)	46	14	14	18	54	62	56	
17.	Burnley FC (Burnley)	46	14	13	19	56	68	55	
18.	Shrewsbury Town FC (Shrewsbury)	46	13	14	19	58	70	53	
19.	Peterborough United FC (Peterborough)	46	13	13	20	59	66	52	
20.	York City FC (York)	46	13	13	20	58	73	52	
21.	Carlisle United FC (Carlisle)	46	12	13	21	57	72	49	R
22.	Swansea City FC (Swansea)	46	11	14	21	43	79	47	R
23.	Brighton & Hove Albion FC (Hove)	46	10	10	26	46	69	40	R
24.	Hull City AFC (Kingston-upon-Hull)	46	5	16	25	36	78	31	R
		1104	399	306	399	1414	1414	1503	

Promotion Play-offs

Bradford City AFC (Bradford)	2-0	Notts County FC (Nottingham)
Bradford City AFC (Bradford)	0-2, 3-0	Blackpool FC (Blackpool)
Crewe Alexandra FC (Crewe)	2-2, 0-1	Notts County FC (Nottingham)

Football League Division 3 1995-96 Season	Barnet	Bury	Cambridge	Cardiff City	Chester City	Colchester U.	Darlington	Doncaster R.	Exeter City	Fulham	Gillingham	Hartlepool	Hereford United	Leyton Orient	Lincoln City	Mansfield Town	Northampton T.	Plymouth Arg.	Preston N.E.	Rochdale	Scarborough	Scunthorpe U.	Torquay United	Wigan Athletic
Barnet FC	■	0-0	2-0	1-0	1-1	1-1	1-1	1-1	3-2	3-0	0-2	5-1	1-3	3-0	3-1	0-0	2-0	1-2	1-0	0-4	1-0	1-0	4-0	5-0
Bury FC	0-0	■	1-2	3-0	1-1	0-0	0-0	4-1	2-0	3-0	1-0	0-3	2-0	2-1	7-1	0-2	0-1	0-5	0-0	1-1	0-2	3-0	1-0	2-1
Cambridge United FC	1-1	2-4	■	4-2	1-1	3-1	0-1	2-2	1-0	0-0	0-1	2-2	2-0	2-1	0-2	0-1	2-3	2-1	2-1	4-1	1-2	1-1	2-1	2-1
Cardiff City AFC	1-1	0-1	1-1	■	0-0	1-2	0-2	3-2	0-1	1-4	2-0	2-0	3-2	0-0	1-1	3-0	0-1	0-1	1-0	2-1	0-1	0-0	0-0	3-0
Chester City FC	0-2	1-1	1-1	4-0	■	1-1	4-1	0-3	2-2	1-1	1-1	2-0	2-1	1-1	5-1	2-1	1-0	3-1	1-1	1-2	5-0	3-0	4-1	0-0
Colchester United FC	3-2	1-0	2-1	1-0	1-2	■	1-1	1-0	1-1	2-2	1-1	4-1	2-0	0-0	3-0	1-3	1-0	2-0	2-2	1-0	1-1	2-1	3-1	1-2
Darlington FC	1-1	4-0	0-0	0-1	3-1	2-2	■	1-2	1-0	1-1	1-0	1-0	1-0	2-0	3-2	1-1	1-2	2-0	1-2	0-1	1-2	0-0	1-2	2-1
Doncaster Rovers FC	1-0	0-1	2-1	0-0	1-2	3-2	1-2	■	2-0	0-2		1-0	1-0	4-1	1-1	0-0	1-0		0-0	2-2	0-3	1-0	2-0	1-0
Exeter City FC	1-0	1-1	1-0	2-0	2-2	2-2	0-1	1-0	■	2-1	1-0	0-2	2-2	1-1	2-2	1-2	1-1	1-1	2-0	1-1	0-0		0-0	0-4
Fulham FC	1-1	0-0	0-2	4-2	2-0	1-1	2-2	3-1	2-1	■	0-0	2-2	0-0	2-1	1-2	4-2	1-3	4-0	2-2	1-1	1-0	1-3	4-0	1-0
Gillingham FC	1-0	4-0	3-0	1-0	3-1	0-1	0-0	4-0	1-0	1-0	■	2-0	1-1	1-0	2-0	2-0	0-0	1-1	1-0	1-0	0-0	2-0	2-1	
Hartlepool United FC	0-0	1-2	1-2	2-1	2-1	2-1	1-1	0-1	0-0	1-1	1-1	■	0-1	4-1	3-0	1-1	2-2	2-2	1-1	1-1	1-2	0-0	2-2	1-2
Hereford United FC	4-1	3-4	5-2	1-3	1-0	1-1	1-0	1-2	0-0	2-2	1-0	4-1	■	3-2	1-0	0-1	1-0	3-0	0-0	2-0	0-0	3-0	2-1	2-2
Leyton Orient FC	3-3	0-2	3-1	4-1	0-2	0-1	1-1	3-1	0-3	1-0	0-1	4-1	0-1	■	2-0	1-0	2-0	0-1	0-2	2-0	1-0	0-0	1-0	1-1
Lincoln City FC	1-2	2-2	1-3	0-1	0-0	0-0	0-2	4-0	0-1	4-0	0-3	1-1	2-1	1-0	■	2-1	1-0	0-0	0-0	1-2	3-1	2-2	5-0	2-4
Mansfield Town FC	2-1	1-5	2-1	1-1	3-4	1-2	2-2	0-0	1-1	1-1	0-3	1-2	0-0	1-2		■	0-0	1-1	0-0	2-2	2-0	1-1	2-0	1-0
Northampton Town FC	0-2	4-1	3-0	1-0	1-0	2-1	1-1	3-3	0-0	2-0	1-1	0-1	1-1	1-2	1-1	3-3	■	1-0	1-2	2-1	1-0	1-2	1-1	0-0
Plymouth Argyle FC	1-1	1-0	1-0	0-0	4-2	1-1	1-1	3-1	2-2	3-0	1-0	3-0	0-1	1-1	3-0	1-0	1-0	■	0-2	2-0	5-1	1-3	4-3	3-1
Preston North End FC	0-1	0-0	3-3	5-0	2-0	2-0	1-1	1-0	2-0	1-1	0-0	3-0	2-2	4-0	1-2	6-0	0-3	3-2	■	1-2	3-2	2-2	1-0	1-1
Rochdale AFC	0-4	1-1	3-1	3-3	1-3	1-1	1-1	4-2	1-1	2-0	4-0	0-0	3-3	1-1	1-2	0-1	0-3			■	0-2	1-1	3-0	0-2
Scarborough FC	1-1	0-3	2-0	1-0	0-0	0-0	1-2	0-2	0-0	2-2	0-2	1-2	2-2	2-1	0-0	1-1	2-1	1-2	1-1		■	1-4	2-1	0-0
Scunthorpe United	2-0	1-2	1-2	1-1	0-2	1-0	3-3	2-2	4-0	3-1	1-1	2-1	0-1	2-0	2-3	1-1	0-0	1-1	1-2	1-3	3-3	■	1-0	3-1
Torquay United FC	1-1	0-2	0-3	0-0	1-1	2-3	0-1	1-2	0-2	2-1	0-0	0-0	1-1	2-1	0-2	1-1	3-0	0-2	0-4	1-0	0-0	1-8	■	1-1
Wigan Athletic AFC	1-0	1-2	3-1	3-1	2-1	2-0	1-1	2-0	1-0	1-1	2-1	1-0	2-1	1-0	1-1	2-6	1-2	0-1	0-1	2-0	2-0	2-1	3-0	■

	Football League Division 3	Pd	Wn	Dw	Ls	GF	GA	Pts	
1.	Preston North End FC (Preston)	46	23	17	6	78	38	86	P
2.	Gillingham FC (Gillingham)	46	22	17	7	49	20	83	P
3.	Bury FC (Bury)	46	22	13	11	66	48	79	P
4.	Plymouth Argyle FC (Plymouth)	46	22	12	12	68	49	78	POP
5.	Darlington FC (Darlington)	46	20	18	8	60	42	78	PO
6.	Hereford United FC (Hereford)	46	20	14	12	65	47	74	PO
7.	Colchester United FC (Colchester)	46	18	18	10	61	51	72	PO
8.	Chester City FC (Chester)	46	18	16	12	72	53	70	
9.	Barnet FC (London)	46	18	16	12	65	45	70	
10.	Wigan Athletic AFC (Wigan)	46	20	10	16	62	56	70	
11.	Northampton Town FC (Northampton)	46	18	13	15	51	44	67	
12.	Scunthorpe United FC (Scunthorpe)	46	15	15	16	67	61	60	
13.	Doncaster Rovers FC (Doncaster)	46	16	11	19	49	60	59	
14.	Exeter City FC (Exeter)	46	13	18	15	46	53	57	
15.	Rochdale AFC (Rochdale)	46	14	13	19	57	61	55	
16.	Cambridge United FC (Cambridge)	46	14	12	20	61	71	54	
17.	Fulham FC (London)	46	12	17	17	57	63	53	
18.	Lincoln City FC (Lincoln)	46	13	14	19	57	73	53	
19.	Mansfield Town FC (Mansfield)	46	11	20	15	54	64	53	
20.	Hartlepool United FC (Hartlepool)	46	12	13	21	47	67	49	
21.	Leyton Orient FC (London)	46	12	11	23	44	63	47	
22.	Cardiff City AFC (Cardiff)	46	11	12	23	41	64	45	
23.	Scarborough FC (Scarborough)	46	8	16	22	39	69	40	
24.	Torquay United FC (Torquay)	46	5	14	27	30	84	29	#
		1104	377	350	377	1346	1346	1481	

Stevenage Borough FC (Stevenage) were refused promotion to Division 3 as their ground did not meet Football League standards. As a result of this Torquay United FC (Torquay) retained their Football League Division 3 status.

Promotion Play-offs

Plymouth Argyle FC (Plymouth)	1-0	Darlington FC (Darlington)
Colchester United FC (Colchester)	1-0, 1-3	Plymouth Argyle FC (Plymouth)
Hereford United FC (Hereford)	1-2, 1-2	Darlington FC (Darlington)

F.A. CUP FINAL   (Wembley Stadium, London – 11/05/1996 – 79,007)

MANCHESTER UNITED FC (MANCHESTER)   1-0   Liverpool FC (Liverpool)

Cantona 85'

Man. United: Schmeichel, Irwin, May, Pallister, P.Neville, Beckham (G.Neville 89'), Butt, Keane, Giggs, Cantona, Cole (Scholes 63').

Liverpool: James, Babb, Wright, Scales, McAteer, Barnes, Redknapp, McManaman, Jones (Thomas 85'), Collymore (Rush 74'), Fowler.

Semi-finals

Aston Villa FC (Birmingham)	0-3	Liverpool FC (Liverpool)
Chelsea FC (London)	1-2	Manchester United FC (Manchester)

Quarter-finals

Chelsea FC (London)	2-2, 3-1	Wimbledon FC (London)
Leeds United AFC (Leeds)	0-0, 0-3	Liverpool FC (Liverpool)
Manchester United FC (Manchester)	2-0	Southampton FC (Southampton)
Nottingham Forest FC (Nottingham)	0-1	Aston Villa FC (Birmingham)

1996-97

F.A. Premiership 1996-97 Season	Arsenal	Aston Villa	Blackburn R.	Chelsea	Coventry City	Derby County	Everton	Leeds United	Leicester City	Liverpool	Man. United	Middlesbrough	Newcastle Utd	Nottingham F.	Sheffield Wed.	Southampton	Sunderland	Tottenham H.	West Ham Utd.	Wimbledon
Arsenal FC	■	2-2	1-1	3-3	0-0	2-2	3-1	3-0	2-0	1-2	1-2	2-0	0-1	2-0	4-1	3-1	2-0	3-1	2-0	0-1
Aston Villa FC	2-2	■	1-0	0-2	2-1	2-0	3-1	2-0	1-3	1-0	0-0	1-0	2-2	2-0	0-1	1-0	1-0	1-1	0-0	5-0
Blackburn Rovers FC	0-2	0-2	■	1-1	4-0	1-2	0-2	0-1	2-4	3-0	2-3	0-0	1-0	1-1	4-1	2-1	1-0	0-2	2-1	3-1
Chelsea FC	0-3	1-1	1-1	■	2-0	3-1	2-2	0-0	2-1	1-0	1-1	1-0	1-1	1-1	2-2	1-0	6-2	3-1	3-1	2-4
Coventry City FC	1-1	1-2	0-0	3-1	■	1-2	0-0	2-1	0-0	0-1	0-2	3-0	2-1	0-3	0-0	1-1	2-2	1-2	1-3	1-1
Derby County FC	1-3	2-1	0-0	3-2	2-1	■	0-1	3-3	2-0	0-1	1-1	2-1	0-1	0-0	2-2	1-1	1-0	4-2	1-0	0-2
Everton FC	0-2	0-1	0-2	1-2	1-1	1-0	■	0-0	1-1	1-1	0-2	1-2	2-0	2-0	2-0	7-1	1-3	1-0	2-1	1-3
Leeds United AFC	0-0	0-0	0-0	2-0	1-3	0-0	1-0	■	3-0	0-2	0-4	1-1	0-1	2-0	0-2	0-0	3-0	0-0	1-0	1-0
Leicester City FC	0-2	1-0	1-1	1-3	0-2	4-2	1-2	1-0	■	0-3	2-2	1-3	2-0	2-2	1-0	2-1	1-1	1-1	0-1	1-1
Liverpool FC	2-0	3-0	0-0	5-1	1-2	2-1	1-1	4-0	1-1	■	1-3	5-1	4-3	4-2	0-1	2-1	0-0	2-1	0-0	1-1
Manchester United FC	1-0	0-0	2-2	1-2	3-1	2-3	2-2	1-0	3-1	1-0	■	3-3	0-0	4-1	2-0	2-1	5-0	2-0	2-0	2-1
Middlesbrough FC	0-2	3-2	2-1	1-0	4-0	6-1	4-2	0-0	0-2	3-3	2-2	■	0-1	1-1	4-2	0-1	0-1	0-3	4-1	0-0
Newcastle United FC	1-2	4-3	2-1	3-1	4-0	3-1	4-1	3-0	4-3	1-1	5-0	3-1	■	5-0	1-2	0-1	1-1	7-1	1-1	2-0
Nottingham Forest FC	2-1	0-0	2-2	2-0	0-1	1-1	0-1	1-1	0-1	0-4	1-1	0-0		■	0-3	1-3	1-4	2-1	0-2	1-1
Sheffield Wednesday FC	0-0	2-1	1-1	0-2	0-0	0-0	2-1	2-2	2-1	1-1	1-1	3-1	1-1	2-0	■	1-1	2-0	2-1	0-0	3-1
Southampton FC	0-2	0-1	2-0	0-0	2-2	3-1	2-2	0-2	2-2	0-1	6-3	4-0	2-2	2-2	2-3	■	3-0	0-1	2-0	0-0
Sunderland AFC	1-0	1-0	0-0	3-0	1-0	2-0	3-0	0-1	0-0	1-2	2-1	2-2	1-2	1-1	1-1	0-0	■	0-4	0-0	1-3
Tottenham Hotspur FC	0-0	1-0	2-1	1-2	1-2	1-1	0-0	1-0	1-2	0-2	1-2	1-0	0-1	0-1	1-1	3-1	2-0	■	1-0	1-0
West Ham United FC	1-2	0-2	2-1	3-2	1-1	1-1	2-2	0-2	1-0	1-2	2-2	0-0	0-0	0-1	5-1	2-1	2-0	4-3	■	0-2
Wimbledon FC	2-2	0-2	1-0	0-1	2-2	1-1	4-0	2-0	1-3	2-1	0-3	1-1	1-1	1-0	4-2	3-1	1-0	1-0	1-1	■

F.A. Premiership

		Pd	Wn	Dw	Ls	GF	GA	Pts	
1.	MANCHESTER UNITED FC (MANCHESTER)	38	21	12	5	76	44	75	
2.	Newcastle United FC (Newcastle-upon-Tyne)	38	19	11	8	73	40	68	
3.	Arsenal FC (London)	38	19	11	8	62	32	68	
4.	Liverpool FC (Liverpool)	38	19	11	8	62	37	68	
5.	Aston Villa FC (Birmingham)	38	17	10	11	47	34	61	
6.	Chelsea FC (London)	38	16	11	11	58	55	59	
7.	Sheffield Wednesday FC (Sheffield)	38	14	15	9	50	51	57	
8.	Wimbledon FC (London)	38	15	11	12	49	46	56	
9.	Leicester City FC (Leicester)	38	12	11	15	46	54	47	
10.	Tottenham Hotspur FC (London)	38	13	7	18	44	51	46	
11.	Leeds United AFC (Leeds)	38	11	13	14	28	38	46	
12.	Derby County FC (Derby)	38	11	13	14	45	58	46	
13.	Blackburn Rovers FC (Blackburn)	38	9	15	14	42	43	42	
14.	West Ham United FC (London)	38	10	12	16	39	48	42	
15.	Everton FC (Liverpool)	38	10	12	16	44	57	42	
16.	Southampton FC (Southampton)	38	10	11	17	50	56	41	
17.	Coventry City FC (Coventry)	38	9	14	15	38	54	41	
18.	Sunderland AFC (Sunderland)	38	10	10	18	35	53	40	R
19.	Middlesbrough FC (Middlesbrough)	38	10	12	16	51	60	39	R -3
20.	Nottingham Forest FC (Nottingham)	38	6	16	16	31	59	34	R
		760	261	238	261	970	970	1018	

Note: Middlesbrough FC (Middlesbrough) had 3 points deducted for failing to appear for the away match versus Blackburn Rovers FC (Blackburn) claiming that they could not field a full team due to illness. The match was played at a later date.

Top Goalscorers

1)	Alan SHEARER	(Newcastle United FC)	25
2)	Ian WRIGHT	(Arsenal FC)	23
3)	Robbie FOWLER	(Liverpool FC)	18
	Ole Gunnar SOLKSJÆR	(Manchester United FC)	18

Football League Division 1 1996-97 Season	Barnsley	Birmingham City	Bolton Wanderers	Bradford City	Charlton Athletic	Crystal Palace	Grimsby Town	Huddersfield Town	Ipswich Town	Manchester City	Norwich City	Oldham Athletic	Oxford United	Portsmouth	Port Vale	Q.P.R.	Reading	Sheffield United	Southend United	Stoke City	Swindon Town	Tranmere Rovers	W.B.A.	Wolves
Barnsley FC	■	0-1	2-2	2-0	4-0	0-0	1-3	3-1	1-2	2-0	3-1	2-0	0-0	3-2	1-0	1-3	3-0	2-0	3-0	3-0	1-1	3-0	2-0	1-3
Birmingham City FC	0-0	■	3-1	3-0	0-0	1-0	0-0	1-0	1-0	2-0	2-3	0-0	2-0	0-3	1-2	0-0	4-1	1-1	2-1	3-1	1-0	0-0	2-3	1-2
Bolton Wanderers FC	2-2	2-1	■	2-1	4-1	2-2	6-1	2-0	1-2	1-0	3-1	3-1	4-0	2-0	4-2	2-1	2-1	2-2	3-1	1-1	7-0	1-0	1-0	3-0
Bradford City AFC	2-2	0-2	2-4	■	1-0	0-4	3-4	1-1	2-1	1-3	0-2	0-3	2-0	3-1	1-0	3-0	0-0	1-2	0-0	1-0	2-1	1-0	1-1	2-1
Charlton Athletic FC	2-2	2-1	3-3	0-2	■	2-1	1-3	2-1	1-1	1-1	4-4	1-0	2-0	2-1	1-3	2-1	1-0	0-0	2-0	1-2	2-0	3-1	1-1	0-0
Crystal Palace FC	1-1	0-1	1-1	3-1	1-0	■	3-0	1-1	0-0	3-1	2-0	3-1	2-2	1-1	1-1	3-0	3-2	0-1	6-1	2-0	1-2	0-1	0-0	2-3
Grimsby Town FC	2-3	1-2	1-2	1-1	2-0	2-1	■	2-2	2-1	1-1	1-4	0-3	0-2	0-1	1-1	2-0	2-0	2-4	4-0	1-1	2-1	0-0	1-1	1-3
Huddersfield Town FC	0-0	3-0	1-2	3-3	2-0	1-1	2-0	■	2-0	1-1	2-0	3-2	1-0	1-3	0-1	1-2	1-0	2-1	0-0	2-1	0-0	0-1	0-0	0-2
Ipswich Town FC	1-1	1-1	0-1	3-2	2-1	3-1	1-1	1-3	■	1-0	2-0	4-0	2-1	1-1	2-1	2-0	5-2	3-1	1-1	1-1	3-2	0-2	5-0	0-0
Manchester City FC	1-2	1-0	1-2	3-2	2-1	1-1	3-1	0-0	1-0	■	2-1	1-0	2-3	1-1	0-1	0-3	3-2	0-0	3-0	2-0	3-0	1-2	3-2	0-1
Norwich City FC	1-1	0-1	0-1	2-0	1-2	1-1	2-1	2-0	3-1	0-0	■	2-0	1-1	1-0	1-1	1-1	1-1	1-1	0-0	2-0	2-0	1-1	2-4	1-0
Oldham Athletic AFC	0-1	2-2	0-0	1-2	1-1	0-1	0-3	1-2	3-3	2-1	3-0	■	2-1	0-0	3-0	0-2	1-1	0-0	1-2	5-1	1-2	1-1	3-2	
Oxford United FC	5-1	0-0	0-0	2-0	0-2	1-4	3-2	1-0	3-1	1-4	0-1	3-1	■	2-0	0-2	2-3	2-1	4-1	5-0	4-1	2-0	2-1	1-0	1-1
Portsmouth FC	4-2	1-1	0-3	3-1	2-0	2-2	1-0	3-1	0-1	2-1	0-1	1-0	2-1	■	1-1	1-2	1-0	1-1	1-0	1-0	0-1	1-3	4-0	0-2
Port Vale FC	1-3	3-0	1-1	1-1	2-0	0-2	1-1	0-0	2-2	0-2	6-1	3-2	2-0	0-2	■	4-4	1-0	0-0	2-1	1-1	1-0	2-1	2-2	1-2
Queen's Park Rangers	3-1	1-1	1-2	1-0	1-1	0-1	3-0	2-0	0-1	2-2	3-2	0-1	2-1	2-1	1-2	■	0-2	1-0	4-0	1-1	1-1	2-0	0-2	2-2
Reading FC	1-2	0-0	3-2	0-0	2-2	1-6	1-1	4-1	1-0	2-0	2-1	2-0	2-0	0-0	0-1	2-1	■	1-0	3-2	2-2	2-0	2-0	2-2	2-1
Sheffield United FC	0-1	4-4	1-1	3-0	3-0	3-0	3-1	3-1	1-3	2-0	2-3	2-2	3-1	1-0	3-0	1-1	2-0	■	3-0	1-0	2-0	0-0	1-2	2-3
Southend United FC	1-2	1-1	5-2	1-1	0-2	2-1	1-0	1-2	0-0	2-3	1-1	1-1	2-2	2-1	0-0	0-1	2-1	3-2	■	2-1	1-3	1-1	2-3	1-1
Stoke City FC	1-0	1-0	1-2	1-0	1-0	2-2	2-1	3-2	0-1	1-2	2-1	2-1	3-1	2-0	0-0	1-1	0-4	1-2		■	2-0	2-0	2-1	1-0
Swindon Town FC	3-0	3-1	2-2	1-1	1-0	0-2	3-3	6-0	0-4	2-0	0-3	1-0	1-0	0-1	1-1	1-1	3-1	2-1	0-0	1-0	■	2-1	2-3	1-2
Tranmere Rovers FC	1-1	1-0	2-2	3-0	4-0	1-3	3-2	1-1	3-0	1-1	3-1	1-1	0-0	4-3	2-0	2-3	2-2	1-1	3-0	0-0	2-1	■	2-3	0-2
West Bromwich Alb.	1-2	2-0	2-2	0-0	1-2	1-0	2-0	1-1	0-0	1-3	5-1	1-1	3-3	0-2	1-1	4-1	3-2	1-2	4-0	0-2	1-2	1-1	■	2-4
Wolverhampton W.	3-3	1-2	1-2	1-0	1-0	0-3	1-1	0-0	0-0	3-0	3-2	0-1	3-1	0-1	0-1	1-1	0-1	1-2	4-1	2-0	1-0	3-2	2-0	■

Football League Division 1

		Pd	Wn	Dw	Ls	GF	GA	Pts	
1.	Bolton Wanderers FC (Bolton)	46	28	14	4	100	53	98	P
2.	Barnsley FC (Barnsley)	46	22	14	10	76	55	80	P
3.	Wolverhampton Wanderers FC (Wolverhampton)	46	22	10	14	68	51	76	PO
4.	Ipswich Town FC (Ipswich)	46	20	14	12	68	50	74	PO
5.	Sheffield United FC (Sheffield)	46	20	13	13	75	52	73	PO
6.	Crystal Palace FC (London)	46	19	14	13	78	48	71	POP
7.	Portsmouth FC (Portsmouth)	46	20	8	18	59	53	68	
8.	Port Vale FC (Stoke-on-Trent)	46	17	16	13	58	55	67	
9.	Queen's Park Rangers FC (London)	46	18	12	16	64	60	66	
10.	Birmingham City FC (Birmingham)	46	17	15	14	52	48	66	
11.	Tranmere Rovers FC (Birkenhead)	46	17	14	15	63	56	65	
12.	Stoke City FC (Stoke-on-Trent)	46	18	10	18	51	57	64	
13.	Norwich City FC (Norwich)	46	17	12	17	63	68	63	
14.	Manchester City FC (Manchester)	46	17	10	19	59	60	61	
15.	Charlton Athletic FC (London)	46	16	11	19	52	66	59	
16.	West Bromwich Albion FC (West Bromwich)	46	14	15	17	68	72	57	
17.	Oxford United FC (Oxford)	46	16	9	21	64	68	57	
18.	Reading FC (Reading)	46	15	12	19	58	67	57	
19.	Swindon Town FC (Swindon)	46	15	9	22	52	71	54	
20.	Huddersfield Town AFC (Huddersfield)	46	13	15	18	48	61	54	
21.	Bradford City AFC (Bradford)	46	12	12	22	47	72	48	
22.	Grimsby Town FC (Cleethorpes)	46	11	13	22	60	81	46	R
23.	Oldham Athletic AFC (Oldham)	46	10	13	23	51	66	43	R
24.	Southend United FC (Southend-on-Sea)	46	8	15	23	42	86	39	R
		1104	402	300	402	1476	1476	1506	

Promotion Play-offs

Crystal Palace FC (London)   1-0   Sheffield United FC (Sheffield)

Crystal Palace FC (London)   3-1, 1-2   Wolverhampton Wanderers FC (Wolverhampton)

Sheffield United FC (Sheffield)   1-1, 2-2   Ipswich Town FC (Ipswich)

Football League Division 2 — 1996-97 Season

	Blackpool	Bournemouth	Brentford	Bristol City	Bristol Rovers	Burnley	Bury	Chesterfield	Crewe Alexandra	Gillingham	Luton Town	Millwall	Notts County	Peterborough United	Plymouth Argyle	Preston North End	Rotherham United	Shrewsbury Town	Stockport County	Walsall	Watford	Wrexham	Wycombe Wanderers	York City
Blackpool FC	■	1-1	1-0	1-0	3-2	1-3	2-0	0-1	1-2	2-0	0-0	3-0	1-0	5-1	2-2	2-1	4-1	1-1	2-1	2-1	1-1	3-3	0-0	3-0
AFC Bournemouth	0-0	■	2-1	0-2	1-0	0-0	1-1	3-0	0-1	2-2	3-2	1-1	0-1	1-2	1-0	2-0	1-1	0-0	0-0	0-1	1-2	2-1	2-1	1-1
Brentford FC	1-1	1-0	■	0-0	0-0	0-3	0-2	1-0	0-2	2-0	3-2	0-0	2-0	0-1	3-2	0-0	4-2	0-0	2-2	1-1	1-1	2-0	0-0	3-3
Bristol City FC	0-1	0-1	1-2	■	1-1	2-1	1-0	2-0	3-0	0-1	5-0	1-1	4-0	2-0	3-1	2-1	0-2	3-2	1-1	4-1	1-1	2-1	3-0	2-0
Bristol Rovers FC	0-0	3-2	2-1	1-2	■	1-2	4-3	2-0	2-0	0-0	3-2	1-0	1-0	1-0	2-0	1-0	1-2	2-0	1-1	0-1	0-1	2-0	3-4	1-1
Burnley FC	2-0	1-0	1-2	2-3	2-2	■	3-1	0-0	2-0	5-1	0-2	1-0	1-0	5-0	2-1	1-2	3-3	1-3	5-2	2-1	4-1	2-0	2-1	1-2
Bury FC	1-0	2-1	1-1	4-0	2-1	1-0	■	1-0	1-0	3-0	0-0	2-0	2-0	1-0	1-0	3-0	3-1	2-0	0-0	2-1	1-1	0-0	2-0	4-1
Chesterfield FC	0-0	1-1	0-2	1-1	1-0	0-0	1-2	■	1-0	2-2	1-1	1-0	1-0	2-1	1-2	2-1	1-1	2-1	0-1	1-0	0-0	0-0	4-2	2-0
Crewe Alexandra FC	3-2	2-0	2-0	1-2	1-0	1-1	2-0	1-2	■	3-2	0-0	0-0	3-0	1-1	3-0	1-0	1-0	5-1	1-0	1-0	0-2	3-1	3-0	0-1
Gillingham FC	2-3	1-1	1-2	3-2	1-0	1-0	2-2	0-1	2-1	■	1-2	2-3	1-0	4-1	1-1	3-1	2-0	1-0	2-0	3-1	1-2	1-0	0-1	2-0
Luton Town FC	1-0	2-0	1-0	2-2	2-1	1-2	0-0	0-1	6-0	2-1	■	0-2	2-0	3-0	2-2	5-1	1-0	2-0	1-1	3-1	0-0	0-0	0-0	2-0
Millwall FC	2-1	0-1	0-0	0-2	2-0	2-1	1-0	2-1	2-0	0-2	0-1	■	1-0	0-2	0-0	3-2	2-0	2-1	3-4	1-0	0-1	1-1	2-1	1-1
Notts County FC	1-1	0-2	1-1	2-0	1-1	1-1	0-1	0-0	0-1	1-1	1-2	1-2	■	0-0	2-1	2-1	0-0	1-2	1-2	2-0	2-3	0-0	1-2	0-1
Peterborough United	0-0	3-1	0-1	3-1	1-2	3-2	1-2	1-1	2-2	0-1	0-1	3-3	1-3	■	0-0	2-0	6-2	2-2	0-2	0-1	2-1	0-1	6-3	2-2
Plymouth Argyle FC	0-1	0-0	1-4	0-0	0-1	0-0	2-0	0-3	1-0	2-0	3-3	0-0	0-0	1-1	■	2-1	1-0	0-2	0-0	2-0	0-0	0-1	0-0	2-1
Preston North End	3-0	0-1	1-0	0-2	0-0	1-1	3-1	0-1	2-1	1-0	3-2	2-1	2-0	3-4	1-1	■	0-0	2-1	1-0	2-0	1-1	2-1	2-1	1-0
Rotherham United	1-2	1-0	0-1	2-2	0-0	1-0	1-1	0-1	1-4	1-2	0-3	0-0	2-2	2-0	1-2	0-1	■	1-2	0-1	1-2	0-0	0-0	2-1	0-2
Shrewsbury Town	1-3	1-1	0-3	1-0	2-0	2-1	1-1	2-0	0-1	1-2	0-3	1-1	2-1	2-2	2-3	0-2	0-2	■	3-2	2-2	1-0	0-1	1-1	2-0
Stockport County	1-0	0-1	1-2	1-1	1-0	1-0	2-1	1-0	1-0	2-1	1-1	5-1	0-0	0-0	3-1	1-0	0-0	3-1	■	2-0	1-0	0-2	2-1	2-1
Walsall FC	1-1	2-1	1-0	2-0	1-0	1-3	3-1	1-1	1-0	1-0	3-2	2-1	3-1	4-0	0-1	1-0	1-1	2-2	1-1	■	1-1	0-1	2-2	1-1
Watford FC	2-2	0-1	2-0	3-0	1-0	2-2	0-0	0-2	0-1	0-0	1-1	0-2	0-0	0-0	0-2	1-0	2-0	2-0	1-0	1-0	■	1-1	1-0	4-0
Wrexham AFC	2-1	2-0	0-2	2-1	1-0	0-0	1-1	3-2	1-1	1-1	2-1	3-3	3-3	1-1	4-4	1-0	1-0	2-1	2-3	1-2	3-1	■	1-0	0-0
Wycombe Wanderers	1-0	1-1	0-1	2-0	2-0	5-0	0-1	1-0	2-0	1-1	0-1	1-0	1-0	2-0	2-1	0-1	4-2	3-0	0-2	0-2	0-0	0-0	■	3-1
York City FC	1-0	1-2	2-4	0-3	2-2	1-0	0-2	0-0	1-1	2-3	1-1	3-2	1-2	1-0	1-1	3-1	2-1	0-0	1-2	0-2	1-2	1-0	2-0	■

Football League Division 2	Pd	Wn	Dw	Ls	GF	GA	Pts	
1. Bury FC (Bury)	46	24	12	10	62	38	84	P
2. Stockport County FC (Stockport)	46	23	13	10	59	41	82	P
3. Luton Town FC (Luton)	46	21	15	10	71	45	78	PO
4. Brentford FC (London)	46	20	14	12	56	43	74	PO
5. Bristol City FC (Bristol)	46	21	10	15	69	51	73	PO
6. Crewe Alexandra FC (Crewe)	46	22	7	17	56	47	73	POP
7. Blackpool FC (Blackpool)	46	18	15	13	60	47	69	
8. Wrexham AFC (Wrexham)	46	17	18	11	54	50	69	
9. Burnley FC (Burnley)	46	19	11	16	71	55	68	
10. Chesterfield FC (Chesterfield)	46	18	14	14	42	39	68	
11. Gillingham FC (Gillingham)	46	19	10	17	60	59	67	
12. Walsall FC (Walsall)	46	19	10	17	54	53	67	
13. Watford FC (Watford)	46	16	19	11	45	38	67	
14. Millwall FC (London)	46	16	13	17	50	55	61	
15. Preston North End FC (Preston)	46	18	7	21	49	55	61	
16. AFC Bournemouth (Bournemouth)	46	15	15	16	43	45	60	
17. Bristol Rovers FC (Bristol)	46	15	11	20	47	50	56	
18. Wycombe Wanderers FC (High Wycombe)	46	15	10	21	51	56	55	
19. Plymouth Argyle FC (Plymouth)	46	12	18	16	47	58	54	
20. York City FC (York)	46	13	13	20	47	68	52	
21. Peterborough United FC (Peterborough)	46	11	14	21	55	73	47	R
22. Shrewsbury Town FC (Shrewsbury)	46	11	13	22	49	74	46	R
23. Rotherham United FC (Rotherham)	46	7	14	25	39	70	35	R
24. Notts County FC (Nottingham)	46	7	14	25	25	59	35	R
	1104	397	310	397	1269	1269	1501	

Promotion Play-offs

Crewe Alexandra FC (Crewe)	1-0	Brentford FC (London)
Bristol City FC (Bristol)	1-2, 1-2	Brentford FC (London)
Crewe Alexandra FC (Crewe)	2-1, 2-2	Luton Town FC (Luton)

Football League Division 3 1996-97 Season	Barnet	Brighton & H.A.	Cambridge	Cardiff City	Carlisle United	Chester City	Colchester Utd.	Darlington	Doncaster R.	Exeter City	Fulham	Hartlepool	Hereford United	Hull City	Leyton Orient	Lincoln City	Mansfield Town	Northampton T.	Rochdale	Scarborough	Scunthorpe Utd.	Swansea City	Torquay United	Wigan Athletic
Barnet FC		3-0	2-1	3-1	0-0	1-2	2-4	0-0	3-0	3-0	2-2	1-0	2-3	1-0	0-0	1-0	1-1	1-1	3-2	1-3	1-1	0-1	0-0	1-1
Brighton & Hove Alb.	1-0		1-2	2-0	1-3	2-1	1-1	2-3	1-0	1-0	0-0	5-0	0-1	3-0	4-4	1-3	1-1	2-1	3-0	3-2	1-1	3-2	2-2	1-0
Cambridge United FC	1-0	1-1		0-2	1-3	2-2	1-0	5-2	0-1	3-2	0-1	1-0	0-1	1-0	2-0	1-3	2-1	0-0	2-2	2-1	0-2	2-1	2-1	1-1
Cardiff City AFC	1-2	1-0	0-0		2-0	1-0	1-2	2-0	0-2	2-1	1-2	2-0	2-0	2-0	3-0	1-3	1-2	2-2	2-1	1-1	0-0	1-3	2-0	0-2
Carlisle United FC	2-1	2-1	3-0	0-2		3-1	3-0	1-0	0-0	2-1	1-2	1-0	2-3	0-0	1-0	1-1	2-1	3-2	1-0	3-2	4-1	5-1	0-3	
Chester City FC	1-0	2-1	1-1	0-1	1-1		1-2	2-1	6-0	2-1	1-1	0-0	1-3	0-0	0-1	4-1	1-0	2-1	0-0	1-0	1-0	2-0	0-0	1-1
Colchester United FC	1-0	2-0	1-1	1-1	1-1	0-0		0-3	2-2	1-0	2-1	0-2	1-1	1-1	2-1	7-1	1-1	0-0	1-0	1-3	3-1	2-0	3-1	
Darlington FC	0-1	2-0	2-0	2-1	2-1	1-1	1-1		0-3	0-1	0-2	1-2	1-0	1-0	1-1	5-2	2-4	3-1	1-1	2-0	4-1	2-3	3-1	
Doncaster Rovers FC	1-1	3-0	2-1	3-3	0-1	0-1	0-0	3-2		1-2	0-1	1-0	2-0	0-1	1-3	0-1	1-0	1-2	3-0	1-0	1-2	2-1	2-0	
Exeter City FC	1-1	2-1	0-1	2-0	2-1	1-5	0-3	3-2	1-1		0-1	2-0	1-1	0-0	3-2	3-3	0-0	0-1	0-0	2-2	0-1	1-2	1-1	0-1
Fulham FC	2-0	2-0	3-0	1-4	1-0	1-1	3-1	6-0	3-1	1-1		1-0	1-0	2-0	1-2	1-2	0-1	1-1	4-0	2-1	2-1	1-2	1-1	
Hartlepool United FC	4-0	2-3	0-2	2-3	1-2	2-0	1-0	1-2	2-4	1-1	2-1		2-1	1-1	3-1	2-1	2-2	0-2	1-2	1-0	1-1	1-1	1-1	3-1
Hereford United FC	1-1	1-1	0-1	1-1	2-3	1-2	1-1	1-1	1-0	1-0	0-0	0-1		0-1	2-0	1-1	1-2	0-3	2-2	3-2	0-1	1-1	3-1	
Hull City AFC	0-0	3-0	1-3	1-1	0-1	1-0	1-2	3-2	3-1	2-0	0-3	1-0	1-1		3-2	2-1	1-1	1-1	1-1	0-2	0-2	1-1	2-0	1-1
Leyton Orient FC	0-1	2-0	1-1	3-0	2-1	0-0	1-1	0-0	2-1	1-1	0-2	2-0	2-1	1-1		2-3	2-1	2-1	2-1	0-1	0-1	1-0	1-0	1-2
Lincoln City FC	1-0	2-1	1-1	1-1	1-1	0-0	3-2	2-0	3-2	2-3	2-0	2-1	3-3	0-1	1-1		0-0	1-1	0-2	1-1	2-0	4-0	1-2	1-3
Mansfield Town FC	0-0	1-1	1-1	1-3	0-0	0-2	1-1	2-1	2-0	1-0	3-1	1-0	0-2	2-2	1-0	1-0		0-0	2-1	2-2	0-1	0-0	1-2	0-1
Northampton Town FC	2-0	3-0	1-1	4-0	0-1	5-1	2-1	3-0	2-0	4-1	0-1	3-0	1-0	2-1	0-1	1-1	3-0		2-2	1-0	1-0	1-2	1-1	0-1
Rochdale AFC	1-1	3-0	3-0	1-0	2-2	0-1	0-0	2-0	2-1	2-0	1-2	1-3	0-0	1-2	1-0	2-0	0-1	1-1		3-3	1-2	2-3	2-1	3-1
Scarborough FC	1-1	1-1	1-0	0-1	1-1	0-0	4-1	2-1	3-4	0-2	2-4	1-1	3-2	2-1	0-2	2-1	1-1	2-2			3-2	0-1	3-1	3-1
Scunthorpe United FC	1-2	1-0	3-2	0-1	0-0	0-2	2-1	3-2	1-2	4-1	1-4	2-1	5-1	2-2	1-2	2-0	0-2	2-1	2-2	0-1		1-0	1-0	2-3
Swansea City FC	3-0	1-0	3-1	0-1	0-1	2-1	1-1	1-1	2-0	3-1	1-2	2-2	4-0	0-1	1-2	3-2	1-0	3-0	1-2	1-1			2-0	2-1
Torquay United FC	1-2	2-1	0-1	2-0	1-2	0-0	0-2	1-1	1-0	2-0	3-1	0-1	2-1	1-1	0-0	2-1	1-2	1-2	0-1	1-0	1-2	2-0		0-3
Wigan Athletic AFC	2-0	1-0	1-1	0-1	1-0	4-2	1-0	3-2	4-1	2-0	1-1	2-2	4-1	1-2	5-1	1-0	2-0	2-1	0-1	7-1	3-0	3-2	3-2	

Football League Division 3

		Pd	Wn	Dw	Ls	GF	GA	Pts	
1.	Wigan Athletic AFC (Wigan)	46	26	9	11	84	51	87	P
2.	Fulham FC (London)	46	25	12	9	72	38	87	P
3.	Carlisle United FC (Carlisle)	46	24	12	10	67	44	84	P
4.	Northampton Town FC (Northampton)	46	20	12	14	67	44	72	POP
5.	Swansea City FC (Swansea)	46	21	8	17	62	58	71	PO
6.	Chester City FC (Chester)	46	18	16	12	55	43	70	PO
7.	Cardiff City AFC (Cardiff)	46	20	9	17	56	54	69	PO
8.	Colchester United FC (Colchester)	46	17	17	12	62	51	68	
9.	Lincoln City FC (Lincoln)	46	18	12	16	70	69	66	
10.	Cambridge United FC (Cambridge)	46	18	11	17	53	59	65	
11.	Mansfield Town FC (Mansfield)	46	16	16	14	47	45	64	
12.	Scarborough FC (Scarborough)	46	16	15	15	65	68	63	
13.	Scunthorpe United FC (Scunthorpe)	46	18	9	19	59	62	63	
14.	Rochdale AFC (Rochdale)	46	14	16	16	58	58	58	
15.	Barnet FC (London)	46	14	16	16	46	51	58	
16.	Leyton Orient FC (London)	46	15	12	19	50	58	57	
17.	Hull City AFC (Kingston-upon-Hull)	46	13	18	15	44	57	57	
18.	Darlington FC (Darlington)	46	14	10	22	64	78	52	
19.	Doncaster Rovers FC (Doncaster)	46	14	10	22	52	66	52	
20.	Hartlepool United FC (Hartlepool)	46	14	9	23	53	66	51	
21.	Torquay United FC (Torquay)	46	13	11	22	46	62	50	
22.	Exeter City FC (Exeter)	46	12	12	22	48	73	48	
23.	Brighton & Hove Albion FC (Hove)	46	13	10	23	53	70	47	-2
24.	Hereford United FC (Hereford)	46	11	14	21	50	65	47	R
		1104	404	296	404	1383	1383	1506	

Note: Brighton & Hove Albion FC had 2 points deducted after fans invaded the pitch during the match versus Lincoln City FC.

Promotion Play-offs

Northampton Town FC (Northampton)	1-0	Swansea City AFC (Swansea)
Cardiff City AFC (Cardiff)	0-1, 2-3	Northampton Town FC (Northampton)
Chester City FC (Chester)	0-0, 0-3	Swansea City FC (Swansea)

F.A. CUP FINAL   (Wembley Stadium, London – 17/05/1997 – 79,160)

CHELSEA FC (LONDON)	2-0	Middlesbrough FC (Middlesbrough)

Di Matteo 01', Newton 82'

Chelsea: Grodas, Petrescu, Minto, Sinclair, Leboeuf, Clarke, Zola (Vialli 88'), Di Matteo, Newton, Hughes, Wise.

Middlesbrough: Roberts, Blackmore, Fleming, Stamp, Pearson, Festa, Emerson, Mustoe (Vickers 28'), Ravanelli (Beck 23'), Juninho, Hignett (Kinder 74').

Semi-finals

Middlesbrough FC (Middlesbrough)	3-3, 3-0	Chesterfield FC (Chesterfield)
Wimbledon FC (London)	0-3	Chelsea FC (London)

Quarter-finals

Chesterfield FC (Chesterfield)	1-0	Wrexham AFC (Wrexham)
Derby County FC (Derby)	0-2	Middlesbrough FC (Middlesbrough)
Portsmouth FC (Portsmouth)	1-4	Chelsea FC (London)
Sheffield Wednesday FC (Sheffield)	0-2	Wimbledon FC (London)

1997-98

F.A. Premiership 1997-98 Season

	Arsenal	Aston Villa	Barnsley	Blackburn Rovers	Bolton Wanderers	Chelsea	Coventry City	Crystal Palace	Derby County	Everton	Leeds United	Leicester City	Liverpool	Manchester United	Newcastle United	Sheffield Wednesday	Southampton	Tottenham Hotspur	West Ham United	Wimbledon
Arsenal FC	■	0-0	5-0	1-3	4-1	2-0	2-0	1-0	1-0	4-0	2-1	2-1	0-1	3-2	3-1	1-0	3-0	0-0	4-0	5-0
Aston Villa FC	1-0	■	0-1	0-4	1-3	0-2	3-0	3-1	2-1	2-1	1-0	1-1	2-1	0-2	0-1	2-2	1-1	4-1	2-0	1-2
Barnsley FC	0-2	0-3	■	1-1	2-1	0-6	2-0	1-0	1-0	2-2	2-3	0-2	2-3	0-2	2-2	2-1	4-3	1-1	1-2	2-1
Blackburn Rovers FC	1-4	5-0	2-1	■	3-1	1-0	0-0	2-2	1-0	3-2	3-4	5-3	1-1	1-3	1-0	7-2	1-0	0-3	3-0	0-0
Bolton Wanderers FC	0-1	0-1	1-1	2-1	■	1-0	1-5	5-2	3-3	0-0	2-3	2-0	1-1	0-0	1-0	3-2	0-0	1-1	1-1	1-0
Chelsea FC	2-3	0-1	2-0	0-1	2-0	■	3-1	6-2	4-0	2-0	0-0	1-0	4-1	0-1	1-0	1-0	4-2	2-0	2-1	1-1
Coventry City FC	2-2	1-2	1-0	2-0	2-2	3-2	■	1-1	1-0	0-0	0-0	0-2	1-1	3-2	2-2	1-0	1-0	4-0	1-1	0-0
Crystal Palace FC	0-0	1-1	0-1	1-2	2-2	0-3	0-3	■	3-1	1-3	0-2	0-3	0-3	0-3	1-2	1-0	1-1	1-3	3-3	0-3
Derby County FC	3-0	0-1	1-0	3-1	4-0	0-1	3-1	0-0	■	3-1	0-5	0-4	1-0	2-2	1-0	3-0	4-0	2-1	2-0	1-1
Everton FC	2-2	1-4	4-2	1-0	3-2	3-1	1-1	1-2	1-2	■	2-0	1-1	2-0	0-2	0-0	1-3	0-2	0-2	2-1	0-0
Leeds United AFC	1-1	1-1	2-1	4-0	2-0	3-1	3-3	0-2	4-3	0-0	■	0-1	0-2	1-0	4-1	1-2	0-1	1-0	3-1	1-1
Leicester City FC	3-3	1-0	1-0	1-1	0-0	2-0	1-1	1-1	1-2	0-1	1-0	■	0-0	0-0	0-0	1-1	3-3	3-0	2-1	1-0
Liverpool FC	4-0	3-0	0-1	0-0	2-1	4-2	1-0	2-1	4-0	1-1	3-1	1-2	■	1-3	1-0	2-1	2-3	4-0	5-0	2-0
Manchester United FC	0-1	1-0	7-0	4-0	1-1	2-2	3-0	2-0	2-0	2-0	3-0	0-1	1-1	■	1-1	6-1	1-0	2-0	2-1	2-0
Newcastle United FC	0-1	1-0	2-1	1-1	2-1	3-1	0-0		0-0	1-0	1-1	3-3	1-2	0-1	■	2-1	2-1	1-0	0-1	1-3
Sheffield Wednesday FC	2-0	1-3	2-1	0-0	5-0	1-4	0-0	1-3	2-5	3-1	1-3	1-0	3-3	2-0	2-1	■	1-0	1-0	1-1	1-1
Southampton FC	1-3	1-2	4-1	3-0	0-1	1-0	1-2	1-0	0-2	2-1	0-2	2-1	1-1	1-0	2-1	2-3	■	3-2	3-0	0-1
Tottenham Hotspur FC	1-1	3-2	3-0	0-0	1-0	1-6	1-1	0-1	1-0	1-1	0-1	1-1	3-3	0-2	2-0	3-2	1-1	■	1-0	0-0
West Ham United FC	0-0	2-1	6-0	2-1	3-0	2-1	1-0	4-1	0-0	2-2	3-0	4-3	2-1	1-1	0-1	1-0	2-4	2-1	■	3-1
Wimbledon FC	0-1	2-1	4-1	0-1	0-0	0-2	1-2	0-1	0-0	0-0	1-0	2-1	1-1	2-5	0-0	1-1	1-0	2-6	1-2	■

	F.A. Premiership	Pd	Wn	Dw	Ls	GF	GA	Pts	
1.	ARSENAL FC (LONDON)	38	23	9	6	68	33	78	
2.	Manchester United FC (Manchester)	38	23	8	7	73	26	77	
3.	Liverpool FC (Liverpool)	38	18	11	9	68	42	65	
4.	Chelsea FC (London)	38	20	3	15	71	43	63	
5.	Leeds United AFC (Leeds)	38	17	8	13	57	46	59	
6.	Blackburn Rovers FC (Blackburn)	38	16	10	12	57	52	58	
7.	Aston Villa FC (Birmingham)	38	17	6	15	49	48	57	
8.	West Ham United FC (London)	38	16	8	14	56	57	56	
9.	Derby County FC (Derby)	38	16	7	15	52	49	55	
10.	Leicester City FC (Leicester)	38	13	14	11	51	41	53	
11.	Coventry City FC (Coventry)	38	12	16	10	46	44	52	
12.	Southampton FC (Southampton)	38	14	6	18	50	55	48	
13.	Newcastle United FC (Newcastle-upon-Tyne)	38	11	11	16	35	44	44	
14.	Tottenham Hotspur FC (London)	38	11	11	16	44	56	44	
15.	Wimbledon FC (London)	38	10	14	14	34	46	44	
16.	Sheffield Wednesday FC (Sheffield)	38	12	8	18	52	67	44	
17.	Everton FC (Liverpool)	38	9	13	16	41	56	40	
18.	Bolton Wanderers FC (Bolton)	38	9	13	16	41	61	40	R
19.	Barnsley FC (Barnsley)	38	10	5	23	37	82	35	R
20.	Crystal Palace FC (London)	38	8	9	21	37	71	33	R
		760	285	190	285	1019	1019	1045	

Top Goalscorers

1)	Dion DUBLIN	(Coventry City FC)	18
	Michael OWEN	(Liverpool FC)	18
	Chris SUTTON	(Blackburn Rovers FC)	18

Football League Division 1 — 1997-98 Season

	Birmingham City	Bradford City	Bury	Charlton Athletic	Crewe Alexandra	Huddersfield Town	Ipswich Town	Manchester City	Middlesbrough	Norwich City	Nottingham Forest	Oxford United	Portsmouth	Port Vale	Q.P.R.	Reading	Sheffield United	Stockport County	Stoke City	Sunderland	Swindon Town	Tranmere Rovers	W.B.A.	Wolves
Birmingham City FC		0-0	1-3	0-0	0-1	0-0	1-1	2-1	1-1	1-2	1-2	0-0	2-1	1-1	1-0	3-0	2-0	4-1	2-0	0-1	3-0	0-0	1-0	1-0
Bradford City AFC	0-0		1-0	1-0	1-0	1-1	2-1	2-1	2-2	2-1	0-3	0-0	1-3	2-1	1-1	4-1	1-1	2-1	0-0	0-4	1-1	0-1	0-0	2-0
Bury FC	2-1	2-0		0-0	1-1	2-2	0-1	1-1	0-1	1-0	2-0	1-0	0-2	2-2	1-1	1-1	1-0	0-1	0-0	1-1	1-0	1-0	1-3	1-3
Charlton Athletic FC	1-1	4-1	0-0		3-2	1-0	3-0	2-1	3-0	2-1	4-2	3-2	1-0	1-0	1-1	3-0	2-1	1-3	1-1	1-1	3-0	2-0	5-0	1-0
Crewe Alexandra FC	0-2	5-0	1-2	0-3		2-5	0-0	1-0	1-1	1-0	1-4	2-1	3-1	0-1	2-3	1-0	2-1	0-1	2-0	0-3	2-0	2-1	2-3	0-2
Huddersfield Town	0-1	1-2	2-0	0-3	2-0		2-2	1-3	0-1	1-3	0-2	5-1	1-1	0-4	1-1	1-0	0-0	1-0	3-1	2-3	0-0	3-0	1-0	1-0
Ipswich Town FC	0-1	2-1	2-0	3-1	3-2	5-1		1-0	1-1	5-0	0-1	5-2	2-0	5-1	0-0	2-2	0-2	2-3	2-0	2-1	0-0	1-1	3-0	
Manchester City FC	0-1	1-0	0-1	2-2	1-0	0-1	1-2		2-0	1-2	2-3	0-2	2-2	2-3	2-2	0-0	0-0	4-1	0-1	0-1	6-0	1-1	1-0	0-1
Middlesbrough FC	3-1	1-0	4-0	2-1	1-0	3-0	1-1	1-0		3-0	0-0	4-1	1-1	2-1	3-0	4-0	1-2	3-1	0-1	3-1	6-0	3-0	1-0	1-1
Norwich City FC	3-3	2-3	2-2	0-4	0-2	5-0	2-1	0-0	1-3		1-0	2-1	2-0	1-0	0-0	0-0	2-1	1-1	0-0	2-1	5-0	0-2	1-1	0-2
Nottingham Forest FC	1-0	2-2	3-0	5-2	3-1	2-1	1-3	4-0	4-1	4-1		1-3	1-0	2-1	4-0	1-0	3-0	2-1	1-0	0-3	3-0	2-2	1-0	3-0
Oxford United FC	0-2	0-0	1-1	1-2	0-0	2-0	0-0	1-4	2-0	0-1			1-0	2-0	3-1	3-0	2-4	3-0	5-1	1-1	2-1	1-1	2-1	3-0
Portsmouth FC	1-1	1-1	1-1	0-2	2-3	3-0	0-1	0-3	0-0	1-1	0-1	2-1		3-1	3-1	0-2	1-1	1-0	2-0	1-4	0-1	1-0	2-3	3-2
Port Vale FC	0-1	0-0	1-1	0-1	2-3	4-1	1-3	2-1	0-1	2-2	0-1	3-0	2-1		2-0	0-0	3-1	0-1	0-1	1-2	1-2	2-1		
Queen's Park Rangers	1-1	1-0	0-1	2-4	3-2	2-1	0-0	2-0	5-0	1-1	0-1	1-1	1-0	0-1		1-1	2-2	2-1	1-1	0-1	1-2	0-0	2-0	0-0
Reading FC	2-0	0-3	1-1	2-0	3-3	0-2	0-4	3-0	0-1	0-1	3-3	2-1	0-1	0-3	1-2		0-1	1-0	2-0	4-0	0-1	1-3	2-1	1-0
Sheffield United FC	0-0	2-1	3-0	4-1	1-0	1-1	0-1	1-1	1-0	2-2	1-0	1-0	2-1	2-1	2-2	4-0		5-1	3-2	2-0	2-1	2-1	2-4	1-0
Stockport County FC	2-2	1-2	0-0	3-0	0-1	3-0	0-1	3-1	1-1	2-2	2-2	3-1	3-0	2-0	5-1	1-0			1-0	1-1	4-2	3-1	2-1	1-0
Stoke City FC	0-7	2-1	3-2	1-2	0-2	1-2	1-1	2-5	1-2	2-0	1-1	0-0	2-1	2-1	2-1	1-2	2-2	2-1		1-2	1-2	0-3	0-0	0-1
Sunderland AFC	1-1	2-1	2-1	0-0	2-1	3-1	2-1	3-1	1-1	3-1	0-1	4-2	2-4	4-2	4-1	4-2	4-1	3-0			0-0	3-0	2-0	1-1
Swindon Town FC	1-1	1-0	3-1	0-1	2-0	1-1	0-2	1-3	1-2	1-0	0-0	4-1	0-1	4-2	3-1	0-2	1-1	1-1	1-0	1-2		2-1	0-2	0-0
Tranmere Rovers FC	0-3	3-1	0-0	2-2	0-3	1-0	1-1	0-0	0-2	2-0	0-0	0-2	2-2	1-2	2-1	6-0	3-3	3-0	3-1	0-2	3-0		0-0	2-1
West Bromwich Alb.	1-0	1-1	1-1	1-0	0-1	0-2	2-3	0-1	2-1	1-0	1-1	1-2	0-3	2-2	1-1	1-0	2-0	3-2	1-1	3-3	0-0	2-1		1-0
Wolverhampton W.	1-3	2-1	4-2	3-1	1-0	1-1	1-1	2-2	1-0	5-0	2-1	1-0	2-0	1-1	3-2	3-1	0-0	3-4	1-1	0-1	3-1	1-1	0-1	

Football League Division 1

		Pd	Wn	Dw	Ls	GF	GA	Pts	
1.	Nottingham Forest FC (Nottingham)	46	28	10	8	82	42	94	P
2.	Middlesbrough FC (Middlesbrough)	46	27	10	9	77	41	91	P
3.	Sunderland AFC (Sunderland)	46	26	12	8	86	50	90	PO
4.	Charlton Athletic FC (London)	46	26	10	10	80	49	88	POP
5.	Ipswich Town FC (Ipswich)	46	23	14	9	77	43	83	PO
6.	Sheffield United FC (Sheffield)	46	19	17	10	69	54	74	PO
7.	Birmingham City FC (Birmingham)	46	19	17	10	60	35	74	
8.	Stockport County FC (Stockport)	46	19	8	19	71	69	65	
9.	Wolverhampton Wanderers FC (Wolverhampton)	46	18	11	17	57	53	65	
10.	West Bromwich Albion FC (West Bromwich)	46	16	13	17	50	56	61	
11.	Crewe Alexandra FC (Crewe)	46	18	5	23	58	65	59	
12.	Oxford United FC (Oxford)	46	16	10	20	60	64	58	
13.	Bradford City AFC (Bradford)	46	14	15	17	46	59	57	
14.	Tranmere Rovers FC (Birkenhead)	46	14	14	18	54	57	56	
15.	Norwich City FC (Norwich)	46	14	13	19	52	69	55	
16.	Huddersfield Town FC (Huddersfield)	46	14	11	21	50	72	53	
17.	Bury FC (Bury)	46	11	19	16	42	58	52	
18.	Swindon Town FC (Swindon)	46	14	10	22	42	73	52	
19.	Port Vale FC (Stoke-on-Trent)	46	13	10	23	56	66	49	
20.	Portsmouth FC (Portsmouth)	46	13	10	23	51	63	49	
21.	Queen's Park Rangers FC (London)	46	10	19	17	51	63	49	
22.	Manchester City FC (Manchester)	46	12	12	22	56	57	48	R
23.	Stoke City FC (Stoke-on-Trent)	46	11	13	22	44	74	46	R
24.	Reading FC (Reading)	46	11	9	26	39	78	42	R
		1104	406	292	406	1410	1410	1510	

Promotion Play-offs

Charlton Athletic FC (London)	4-4 (aet)	Sunderland AFC (Sunderland)
	(Charlton Athletic won 7-6 on penalties)	
Ipswich Town FC (Ipswich)	0-1, 0-1	Charlton Athletic FC (London)
Sheffield United FC (Sheffield)	2-1, 0-2	Sunderland AFC (Sunderland)

Football League Division 2 1997-98 Season	Blackpool	Bournemouth	Brentford	Bristol City	Bristol Rovers	Burnley	Carlisle United	Chesterfield	Fulham	Gillingham	Grimsby Town	Luton Town	Millwall	Northampton Town	Oldham Athletic	Plymouth Argyle	Preston North End	Southend United	Walsall	Watford	Wigan Athletic	Wrexham	Wycombe Wanderers	York City
Blackpool FC		1-0	1-2	2-2	1-0	2-1	2-1	2-1	2-1	2-1	2-2	1-0	3-0	1-1	2-2	0-0	2-1	3-0	1-0	1-1	0-2	1-2	2-4	1-0
AFC Bournemouth	2-0		0-0	1-0	1-1	2-1	3-2	2-0	2-1	4-0	0-1	1-1	0-0	3-0	0-0	3-3	0-2	2-1	1-0	0-1	1-0	0-1	0-0	0-0
Brentford FC	3-1	3-2		1-4	2-3	2-1	0-1	0-0	0-2	2-0	3-1	2-2	2-1	0-0	2-1	3-1	0-0	1-1	3-0	1-2	0-2	1-1	1-1	1-2
Bristol City FC	2-0	1-1	2-2		2-0	3-1	1-0	1-0	0-2	0-2	4-1	3-0	4-1	0-0	1-0	2-1	2-1	1-0	2-1	1-1	3-0	1-1	3-1	2-1
Bristol Rovers FC	0-3	5-3	2-1	1-2		1-0	3-1	3-1	2-3	1-2	0-4	2-1	2-1	0-2	3-1	1-1	2-2	2-0	2-0	1-2	5-0	1-0	3-1	1-2
Burnley FC	1-2	2-2	1-1	1-0	0-0		3-1	0-0	2-1	0-0	2-1	1-1	1-2	2-1	0-0	2-1	1-1	1-0	2-1	2-0	0-2	1-2	2-2	7-2
Carlisle United FC	1-1	0-1	1-2	0-3	3-1	2-1		0-2	2-0	2-1	0-1	0-1	1-0	0-2	3-1	2-2	0-2	5-0	1-1	0-2	1-0	2-2	0-0	1-1
Chesterfield FC	1-1	1-1	0-0	1-0	0-0	1-0	2-1		0-2	1-1	0-0	3-1	2-1	2-1	3-2	1-0	3-1	0-1	2-3	1-0	1-1			
Fulham FC	1-0	0-1	1-1	1-0	1-0	1-0	5-0	1-1		3-0	0-2	0-0	1-2	1-1	3-1	2-0	2-1	2-0	1-1	1-2	2-0	1-0	0-0	1-1
Gillingham FC	1-1	2-1	3-1	2-0	1-1	2-0	1-0	1-0	2-0		0-2	2-1	1-3	1-0	2-1	2-1	0-0	1-2	2-1	2-2	0-0	1-1	1-0	0-0
Grimsby Town FC	1-0	2-1	4-0	1-1	1-2	4-1	1-0	0-0	1-1	0-0		0-1	0-1	1-0	0-2	1-0	3-1	5-1	3-0	0-1	2-1	0-0	0-0	0-0
Luton Town FC	3-0	1-2	2-0	0-0	2-4	2-3	3-2	3-0	1-4	2-2	2-2		0-2	2-2	1-1	3-0	1-3	2-1	1-0	0-4	1-1	2-5	1-0	3-0
Millwall FC	2-1	1-2	3-0	0-2	1-1	1-0	1-1	1-1	1-1	1-0	0-1	0-2		0-0	2-1	1-1	0-1	3-1	0-1	1-1	1-1	0-1	1-0	2-3
Northampton Town	2-0	0-2	4-0	2-1	1-1	0-1	2-1	0-0	1-0	2-1	2-1	1-0	2-0		0-0	2-1	2-2	3-1	3-2	0-1	1-0	0-1	2-0	1-1
Oldham Athletic AFC	0-1	2-1	1-1	1-2	4-4	3-3	3-1	2-0	1-0	3-1	2-0	2-1	1-1	2-2		2-0	1-0	2-0	0-0	2-2	3-1	3-0	0-1	3-1
Plymouth Argyle FC	3-1	3-0	0-0	2-0	1-2	2-2	1-1	1-1	1-4	0-2	3-0	1-3	0-2				2-0	2-3	2-1	0-1	3-2	2-0	4-2	0-0
Preston North End	3-3	0-1	2-1	2-1	1-2	2-3	0-3	0-0	3-1	1-3	2-0	1-0	2-1	1-0	1-1	0-1		1-0	0-0	2-0	1-1	0-1	1-1	3-2
Southend United FC	2-1	5-3	3-1	0-2	1-1	1-0	1-1	0-2	1-0	0-0	0-1	1-2	0-0	0-0	1-1	3-0	3-2		0-1	0-3	1-0	1-3	1-2	4-4
Walsall FC	2-1	2-1	0-0	0-0	0-1	0-0	3-1	3-2	1-1	1-0	0-0	2-3	2-0	0-2	0-0	0-1	1-1	3-1		0-0	1-0	3-0	0-1	2-0
Watford FC	4-1	2-1	3-1	1-1	3-2	1-0	2-1	2-1	2-0	0-2	0-1	1-1	2-1	1-1	3-1	1-1	1-2				2-1	1-0	2-1	1-1
Wigan Athletic AFC	3-0	1-0	4-0	0-3	3-0	5-1	0-2	2-1	2-1	1-4	0-2	1-0	1-1	0-0	1-1	1-0	1-1	1-4	1-3	2-0		3-2	5-2	1-1
Wrexham AFC	3-4	2-1	2-2	2-1	1-0	0-0	2-2	0-0	0-3	0-0	0-0	2-1	1-0	3-1	1-1	0-0	3-1	2-1	1-1	2-2			2-0	1-2
Wycombe Wanderers	2-1	1-1	0-0	1-2	1-0	2-1	1-4	1-1	2-0	1-0	1-1	2-2	0-0	0-0	2-1	5-1	0-0	4-1	4-2	0-0	1-2	0-0		1-0
York City FC	1-1	0-1	3-1	0-1	0-1	3-1	4-3	0-1	0-1	2-1	0-0	1-2	2-3	0-0	0-0	1-0	1-0	1-1	1-0	1-1	2-2	1-0	2-0	

	Football League Division 2	Pd	Wn	Dw	Ls	GF	GA	Pts	
1.	Watford FC (Watford)	46	24	16	6	67	41	88	P
2.	Bristol City FC (Bristol)	46	25	10	11	69	39	85	P
3.	Grimsby Town FC (Cleethorpes)	46	19	15	12	55	37	72	POP
4.	Northampton Town FC (Northampton)	46	18	17	11	52	37	71	PO
5.	Bristol Rovers FC (Bristol)	46	20	10	16	70	64	70	PO
6.	Fulham FC (London)	46	20	10	16	60	43	70	PO
7.	Wrexham AFC (Wrexham)	46	18	16	12	55	51	70	
8.	Gillingham FC (Gillingham)	46	19	13	14	52	47	70	
9.	AFC Bournemouth (Bournemouth)	46	18	12	16	57	52	66	
10.	Chesterfield FC (Chesterfield)	46	16	17	13	46	44	65	
11.	Wigan Athletic AFC (Wigan)	46	17	11	18	64	66	62	
12.	Blackpool FC (Blackpool)	46	17	11	18	59	67	62	
13.	Oldham Athletic AFC (Oldham)	46	15	16	15	62	54	61	
14.	Wycombe Wanderers FC (High Wycombe)	46	14	18	14	51	53	60	
15.	Preston North End FC (Preston)	46	15	14	17	56	56	59	
16.	York City FC (York)	46	14	17	15	52	58	59	
17.	Luton Town FC (Luton)	46	14	15	17	60	64	57	
18.	Millwall FC (London)	46	14	13	19	43	54	55	
19.	Walsall FC (Walsall)	46	14	12	20	43	52	54	
20.	Burnley FC (Burnley)	46	13	13	20	55	65	52	
21.	Brentford FC (London)	46	11	17	18	50	71	50	R
22.	Plymouth Argyle FC (Plymouth)	46	12	13	21	55	70	49	R
23.	Carlisle United FC (Carlisle)	46	12	8	26	57	73	44	R
24.	Southend United FC (Southend-on-Sea)	46	11	10	25	47	79	43	R
		1104	390	324	390	1337	1337	1494	

Promotion Play-offs

Grimsby Town FC (Cleethorpes)	1-0	Northampton Town FC (Northampton)
Bristol Rovers FC (Bristol)	3-1, 0-3	Northampton Town FC (Northampton)
Fulham FC (London)	1-1, 0-1	Grimsby Town FC (Cleethorpes)

Football League Division 3 — 1997-98 Season

	Barnet	Brighton & H.A.	Cambridge	Cardiff City	Chester City	Colchester Utd.	Darlington	Doncaster R.	Exeter City	Hartlepool	Hull City	Leyton Orient	Lincoln City	Macclesfield T.	Mansfield Town	Notts County	Peterborough U.	Rochdale	Rotherham U.	Scarborough	Scunthorpe U.	Shrewsbury T.	Swansea City	Torquay United
Barnet FC	■	2-0	2-0	2-2	2-1	3-2	2-0	1-1	1-2	1-1	2-0	1-2	0-0	3-1	0-1	1-2	2-0	3-1	0-0	1-1	0-1	1-1	2-0	3-3
Brighton & Hove Alb.	0-3	■	0-2	0-1	3-2	4-4	0-0	0-0	1-3	0-0	2-2	0-1	0-1	1-1	1-1	0-1	2-2	2-1	1-2	1-1	2-1	0-0	0-1	1-4
Cambridge United FC	1-3	1-1	■	2-2	1-2	4-1	1-0	2-1	2-1	2-0	0-1	1-0	1-1	0-0	2-0	2-2	1-0	1-1	2-1	2-3	2-2	4-3	4-1	1-1
Cardiff City AFC	1-1	0-0	0-0	■	0-2	0-2	0-0	7-1	1-1	1-1	2-1	1-0	0-1	1-2	4-1	1-1	0-0	2-1	2-2	1-1	0-0	2-2	0-1	1-1
Chester City FC	0-1	2-0	1-1	0-0	■	3-1	2-1	1-1	3-1	1-0	1-1	2-0	1-1	0-1	0-1	4-0	4-0	1-1	2-1	0-0	2-0	2-0	1-3	
Colchester United FC	1-1	3-1	3-2	2-1	2-0	■	2-1	2-1	1-2	1-2	4-3	1-1	0-1	5-1	2-0	2-0	1-0	0-0	2-1	1-0	3-3	1-1	1-2	1-0
Darlington FC	2-3	1-0	1-1	0-0	1-0	4-2	■	5-1	3-2	1-1	4-3	1-0	2-2	4-2	0-0	0-2	3-1	1-0	1-1	1-2	1-0	3-1	3-2	1-2
Doncaster Rovers FC	0-2	1-3	0-0	1-1	2-1	0-1	0-2	■	0-1	2-2	1-4	2-4	0-3	0-3	1-2	0-5	0-3	0-3	1-2	1-2	1-0	0-3	0-1	
Exeter City FC	0-0	2-1	1-0	1-1	5-0	0-1	1-0	5-1	■	1-1	3-0	2-2	1-2	1-1	2-5	0-0	3-1	1-1	2-3	2-2	1-0	1-1		
Hartlepool United FC	2-0	0-0	3-3	2-0	0-0	3-2	2-2	3-1	1-1	■	2-2	2-2	1-1	0-0	2-2	1-1	2-1	2-0	0-0	3-0	0-1	4-2	3-0	
Hull City AFC	0-2	0-0	1-0	0-1	1-2	3-1	1-1	3-0	3-2	2-1	■	3-2	0-2	0-0	0-3	3-1	0-2	0-0	3-0	2-1	1-4	7-4	3-3	
Leyton Orient FC	2-0	3-1	1-0	1-0	1-0	2-0	8-0	1-0	2-1	2-1		■	1-0	1-1	2-1	1-1	0-0	1-1	3-1	1-0	2-3	2-2	1-1	
Lincoln City FC	2-0	2-1	1-0	1-3	0-1	3-1	2-1	2-1	1-1	1-1	1-1	1-0	■	0-2	3-5	1-0	1-1	0-3	3-3	1-1	1-1	1-1	1-1	
Macclesfield Town	1-0	1-0	3-1	1-0	3-2	0-0	2-1	3-0	2-2	2-1	2-0	1-0	1-0	■	1-0	2-0	1-1	1-0	0-3	1-0	3-0	2-1		
Mansfield Town FC	1-2	1-1	3-2	1-2	4-1	1-1	4-0	1-1	3-2	2-2	2-0	0-0	2-2	1-0	■	0-2	2-0	3-0	3-3	3-2	1-1	1-1	1-0	2-2
Notts County FC	2-0	2-2	2-1	3-1	1-2	0-0	1-1	5-1	1-1	2-1	1-1	1-2	1-1	1-0		■	2-2	2-1	5-2	1-0	2-1	1-1	2-1	3-0
Peterborough United	5-1	1-2	1-2	2-0	2-0	3-2	1-1	0-1	1-1	2-0	2-0	5-1	1-1	1-0			■	3-1	1-0	0-0	1-1	3-1	3-1	2-0
Rochdale AFC	2-1	2-0	1-1	1-2	2-1	5-0	4-1	3-0	1-2	0-2	0-0	2-0	1-2	1-2				■	4-0	2-0	1-3	3-0	0-1	
Rotherham United	2-3	0-0	2-2	1-1	4-2	3-2	3-0	3-0	1-0	5-4	2-1	3-1	1-0	2-2	1-1	2-2	2-2		■	0-0	1-3	1-1	0-1	
Scarborough FC	1-0	2-1	1-0	4-1	1-3	4-1	3-0	4-1	1-1	2-0	2-2	2-2	1-2	1-3	1-0	1-2	1-2	1-0	1-2	■	0-0	3-2	4-1	
Scunthorpe United	1-1	0-2	3-3	3-3	2-1	1-0	1-1	1-1	2-1	1-1	2-0	1-2	1-3	2-0	1-1	1-3	2-0	1-3			■	1-1	1-0	2-0
Shrewsbury Town	2-0	2-1	1-1	3-2	1-1	0-2	3-0	1-1	1-1	0-0	1-2	0-2	4-3	3-2	1-2	4-1	1-0	2-1	0-1	0-2		■	0-1	1-2
Swansea City FC	0-2	1-0	1-1	1-1	2-0	0-1	4-0	0-0	2-1	0-2	2-0	1-1	0-0	0-1	1-2	0-1	3-0	1-1	0-0	2-0	0-1		■	2-0
Torquay United FC	0-0	3-0	0-3	1-0	3-1	1-1	2-1	2-0	1-2	1-0	5-1	1-1	3-2	2-1	2-1	0-2	3-1	0-0	1-2	1-0	2-4	3-0	2-0	■

Football League Division 3

		Pd	Wn	Dw	Ls	GF	GA	Pts	
1.	Notts County FC (Nottingham)	46	29	12	5	82	43	99	P
2.	Macclesfield Town FC (Macclesfield)	46	23	13	10	63	44	82	P
3.	Lincoln City FC (Lincoln)	46	20	15	11	60	51	75	P
4.	Colchester United FC (Colchester)	46	21	11	14	72	60	74	POP
5.	Torquay United FC (Torquay)	46	21	11	14	68	59	74	PO
6.	Scarborough FC (Scarborough)	46	19	15	12	67	58	72	PO
7.	Barnet FC (London)	46	19	13	14	61	51	70	PO
8.	Scunthorpe United FC (Scunthorpe)	46	19	12	15	56	52	69	
9.	Rotherham United FC (Rotherham)	46	16	19	11	67	61	67	
10.	Peterborough United FC (Peterborough)	46	18	13	15	63	51	67	
11.	Leyton Orient FC (London)	46	19	12	15	62	47	66	-3
12.	Mansfield Town FC (Mansfield)	46	16	17	13	64	55	65	
13.	Shrewsbury Town FC (Shrewsbury)	46	16	13	17	61	62	61	
14.	Chester City FC (Chester)	46	17	10	19	60	61	61	
15.	Exeter City FC (Exeter)	46	15	15	16	68	63	60	
16.	Cambridge United FC (Cambridge)	46	14	18	14	63	57	60	
17.	Hartlepool United FC (Hartlepool)	46	12	23	11	61	53	59	
18.	Rochdale AFC (Rochdale)	46	17	7	22	56	55	58	
19.	Darlington FC (Darlington)	46	14	12	20	56	72	54	
20.	Swansea City FC (Swansea)	46	13	11	22	49	62	50	
21.	Cardiff City AFC (Cardiff)	46	9	23	14	48	52	50	
22.	Hull City AFC (Kingston-upon-Hull)	46	11	8	27	56	83	41	
23.	Brighton & Hove Albion FC (Brighton)	46	6	17	23	38	66	35	
24.	Doncaster Rovers FC (Doncaster)	46	4	8	34	30	113	20	R
		1104	388	328	388	1431	1431	1489	

Note: Leyton Orient FC had 3 points deducted. Brighton & Hove Albion FC moved to a different stadium also in Brighton.

Promotion Play-offs

Colchester United FC (Colchester)	1-0	Torquay United FC (Torquay)
Barnet FC (London)	1-0, 1-3	Colchester United FC (Colchester)
Scarborough FC (Scarborough)	1-3, 1-4	Torquay United FC (Torquay)

Promoted to Division 3: Halifax Town AFC (Halifax)

F.A. CUP FINAL   (Wembley Stadium, London – 16/05/1998 – 79,183)

| ARSENAL FC (LONDON) | 2-0 | Newcastle United FC (Newcastle-upon-Tyne) |

Overmars 23', Anelka 69'

Arsenal: Seaman, Dixon, Adams, Keown, Winterburn, Parlour, Vieira, Petit, Overmars, Anelka, Wreh (Platt 62').

Newcastle: Given, Pistone, Dabizas, Howey, Pearce (Anderson 73'), Barton (Watson 76'), Lee, Batty, Ketsbaia (Barnes 86'), Speed, Shearer.

Semi-finals

| Arsenal FC (London) | 1-0 | Wolverhampton Wanderers FC (Wolverhampton) |
| Sheffield United FC (Sheffield) | 0-1 | Newcastle United FC (Newcastle-upon-Tyne) |

Quarter-finals

Arsenal FC (London)	1-1, 1-1 (aet)	West Ham United FC (London)
Arsenal won 4-3 on penalties.		
Coventry City FC (Coventry)	1-1, 1-1 (aet)	Sheffield United FC (Sheffield)
Sheffield United won 3-1 on penalties.		
Leeds United AFC (Leeds)	0-1	Wolverhampton Wanderers FC (Wolverhampton)
Newcastle United FC (Newcastle-upon-Tyne)	3-1	Barnsley FC (Barnsley)

1998-99

F.A. Premiership 1998-99 Season	Arsenal	Aston Villa	Blackburn Rovers	Charlton Athletic	Chelsea	Coventry City	Derby County	Everton	Leeds United	Leicester City	Liverpool	Manchester United	Middlesbrough	Newcastle United	Nottingham Forest	Sheffield Wednesday	Southampton	Tottenham Hotspur	West Ham United	Wimbledon
Arsenal FC	■	1-0	1-0	0-0	1-0	2-0	1-0	1-0	3-1	5-0	0-0	3-0	1-1	3-0	2-1	3-0	1-1	0-1	1-0	5-1
Aston Villa FC	3-2	■	1-3	3-4	0-3	1-4	1-0	3-0	1-2	1-1	2-4	1-1	3-1	1-0	2-0	2-1	3-0	3-2	0-0	2-0
Blackburn Rovers FC	1-2	2-1	■	1-0	3-4	1-2	0-0	1-2	1-0	1-0	1-3	0-1	0-0	0-0	1-2	1-4	0-2	1-1	3-0	3-1
Charlton Athletic FC	0-1	0-1	0-0	■	0-1	1-1	1-2	1-2	1-1	0-0	1-0	0-1	1-1	2-2	0-0	0-1	5-0	1-4	4-2	2-0
Chelsea FC	0-0	2-1	1-1	2-1	■	2-1	2-1	3-1	1-0	2-2	2-1	0-0	2-0	1-1	2-1	1-1	1-0	2-0	0-1	3-0
Coventry City FC	0-1	1-2	1-1	2-1	2-1	■	1-1	3-0	2-2	1-1	2-1	0-1	1-2	1-5	4-0	1-0	1-0	1-1	0-0	2-1
Derby County FC	0-0	2-1	1-0	0-2	2-2	0-0	■	2-1	2-2	2-0	3-2	1-1	2-1	3-4	1-0	1-0	0-0	0-1	0-2	0-0
Everton FC	0-2	0-0	0-0	4-1	0-0	2-0	0-0	■	0-0	0-0	0-0	1-4	5-0	1-0	1-0	1-2	1-0	0-1	6-0	1-1
Leeds United AFC	1-0	0-0	1-0	4-1	0-0	2-1	4-1	1-0	■	0-1	0-0	1-1	2-0	0-1	3-1	2-1	3-0	2-0	4-0	2-2
Leicester City FC	1-1	2-2	1-1	1-1	2-4	1-0	1-2	2-0	1-2	■	1-0	2-6	0-1	2-0	3-1	0-2	2-0	2-1	0-0	1-1
Liverpool FC	0-0	0-1	2-0	3-3	1-1	2-0	1-2	3-2	1-3	0-1	■	2-2	3-1	4-2	5-1	2-0	7-1	3-2	2-2	3-0
Manchester United FC	1-1	2-1	3-2	4-1	1-1	2-0	1-0	3-1	3-2	2-2	2-0	■	2-3	0-0	3-0	3-0	2-1	2-1	4-1	5-1
Middlesbrough FC	1-6	0-0	2-1	2-0	0-0	2-0	1-1	2-2	0-0	0-0	1-3	0-1	■	2-2	1-1	4-0	3-0	0-0	1-0	3-1
Newcastle United FC	1-1	2-1	1-1	0-0	0-1	4-1	2-1	1-3	0-3	1-0	1-4	1-2	1-1	■	2-0	1-1	4-0	1-1	0-3	3-1
Nottingham Forest FC	0-1	2-2	2-2	0-1	1-3	1-0	2-2	0-2	1-1	0-1	2-2	1-8	1-2	1-2	■	2-0	1-1	0-1	0-0	0-1
Sheffield Wednesday FC	1-0	0-1	3-0	3-0	0-0	1-2	0-1	0-0	0-2	0-1	1-0	3-1	3-1	1-1	3-2	■	0-0	0-0	0-1	1-2
Southampton FC	0-0	1-4	3-3	3-1	0-2	2-1	0-1	2-0	3-0	2-1	1-2	0-3	3-3	2-1	1-2	1-0	■	1-1	1-0	3-1
Tottenham Hotspur FC	1-3	1-0	2-1	2-2	2-2	0-0	1-1	4-1	3-3	0-2	2-2	2-2	0-3	2-0	2-0	0-3	3-0	■	1-2	0-0
West Ham United FC	0-4	0-0	2-0	0-1	1-1	2-0	5-1	2-1	1-5	3-2	2-1	0-0	4-0	2-0	2-1	0-4	1-0	2-1	■	3-4
Wimbledon FC	1-0	0-0	1-1	2-1	1-2	2-1	2-1	1-2	1-1	0-1	1-0	1-1	2-2	1-1	1-3	2-1	0-2	3-1	0-0	■

F.A. Premiership

		Pd	Wn	Dw	Ls	GF	GA	Pts	
1.	MANCHESTER UNITED FC (MANCHESTER)	38	22	13	3	80	37	79	
2.	Arsenal FC (London)	38	22	12	4	59	17	78	
3.	Chelsea FC (London)	38	20	15	3	57	30	75	
4.	Leeds United AFC (Leeds)	38	18	13	7	62	34	67	
5.	West Ham United FC (London)	38	16	9	13	46	53	57	
6.	Aston Villa FC (Birmingham)	38	15	10	13	51	46	55	
7.	Liverpool FC (Liverpool)	38	15	9	14	68	49	54	
8.	Derby County FC (Derby)	38	13	13	12	40	45	52	
9.	Middlesbrough FC (Middlesbrough)	38	12	15	11	48	54	51	
10.	Leicester City FC (Leicester)	38	12	13	13	40	46	49	
11.	Tottenham Hotspur FC (London)	38	11	14	13	47	50	47	
12.	Sheffield Wednesday FC (Sheffield)	38	13	7	18	41	42	46	
13.	Newcastle United FC (Newcastle-upon-Tyne)	38	11	13	14	48	54	46	
14.	Everton FC (Liverpool)	38	11	10	17	42	47	43	
15.	Coventry City FC (Coventry)	38	11	9	18	39	51	42	
16.	Wimbledon FC (London)	38	10	12	16	40	63	42	
17.	Southampton FC (Southampton)	38	11	8	19	37	64	41	
18.	Charlton Athletic FC (London)	38	8	12	18	41	56	36	R
19.	Blackburn Rovers FC (Blackburn)	38	7	14	17	38	52	35	R
20.	Nottingham Forest FC (Nottingham)	38	7	9	22	35	69	30	R
		760	265	230	265	959	959	1025	

Top Goalscorers

1)	Jimmy Floyd HASSELBAINK	(Leeds United AFC)	18
	Michael OWEN	(Liverpool FC)	18
	Dwight YORKE	(Manchester United FC)	18

Football League Division 1 1998-99 Season	Barnsley	Birmingham City	Bolton Wanderers	Bradford City	Bristol City	Bury	Crewe Alexandra	Crystal Palace	Grimsby Town	Huddersfield Town	Ipswich Town	Norwich City	Oxford United	Portsmouth	Port Vale	Q.P.R.	Sheffield United	Stockport County	Sunderland	Swindon Town	Tranmere Rovers	Watford	W.B.A.	Wolves
Barnsley FC	■	0-0	2-2	0-1	2-0	1-1	2-2	4-0	0-0	7-1	0-1	1-3	1-0	2-1	0-2	1-0	2-1	1-1	1-3	1-3	1-1	2-2	2-2	2-3
Birmingham City FC	0-0	■	0-0	2-1	4-1	1-0	3-1	3-1	0-1	1-1	1-0	0-0	0-1	4-1	1-0	1-0	1-0	2-0	0-0	1-1	2-2	1-2	4-0	0-1
Bolton Wanderers FC	3-3	3-1	■	0-0	1-0	4-0	1-3	3-0	2-0	3-0	2-0	2-0	1-1	3-1	3-1	2-1	2-2	1-2	0-3	2-1	2-2	1-2	2-1	1-1
Bradford City AFC	2-1	2-1	2-2	■	5-0	3-0	4-1	2-1	3-0	2-3	0-0	4-1	0-0	2-1	4-0	0-3	2-2	1-2	0-1	3-0	2-0	2-0	1-0	2-1
Bristol City FC	1-1	1-2	2-1	2-3	■	1-1	5-2	1-1	4-1	1-2	0-1	1-0	2-2	2-2	2-0	0-0	2-0	1-1	0-1	3-1	1-1	1-4	1-3	1-6
Bury FC	0-0	2-4	2-1	0-2	0-1	■	1-0	0-0	1-0	0-3	0-2	1-0	2-1	1-0	1-1	3-3	1-1	2-5	3-0	0-0	1-3	2-0	0-0	
Crewe Alexandra FC	3-1	0-0	4-4	2-1	1-0	3-1	■	0-1	0-0	1-2	0-3	3-2	3-1	3-1	0-0	0-2	1-2	0-2	1-4	0-2	1-4	0-1	1-1	0-0
Crystal Palace FC	1-0	1-1	2-2	1-0	2-1	4-2	1-1	■	3-1	2-2	3-2	5-1	2-0	4-1	0-1	1-1	1-0	2-2	1-1	0-1	1-1	2-2	1-1	3-2
Grimsby Town FC	1-2	0-3	0-1	2-0	2-1	0-0	1-1	2-0	■	1-0	0-0	0-1	1-0	1-1	2-2	1-0	1-0	0-2	1-0	1-0	2-1	1-0	5-1	0-0
Huddersfield Town	0-1	1-1	3-2	2-1	2-2	2-2	0-0	4-0	2-0	■	2-2	1-1	2-0	3-3	2-0	1-0	3-0	1-1	1-2	0-0	2-0	0-3	2-1	
Ipswich Town FC	0-2	1-0	0-1	3-0	3-1	0-0	1-2	3-0	0-1	3-0	■	0-1	2-1	3-0	1-0	3-1	4-1	1-0	0-2	1-0	1-0	3-2	2-0	2-0
Norwich City FC	0-0	2-0	2-2	2-2	2-1	0-0	2-1	0-1	3-1	4-1	0-0	■	1-3	0-0	3-4	4-2	1-1	0-2	2-2	2-1	2-2	1-1	1-1	
Oxford United FC	1-0	1-7	0-0	0-1	0-0	0-1	1-1	1-3	0-0	2-2	3-3	2-4	■	3-0	2-1	4-1	0-2	5-0	0-0	2-0	1-2	0-0	3-0	0-2
Portsmouth FC	1-3	0-1	0-2	2-4	0-1	2-1	2-1	1-0	1-1	0-1	1-2	2-0		■	4-0	3-0	1-0	3-1	1-1	5-2	1-1	1-2	2-1	1-0
Port Vale FC	1-0	0-2	0-2	1-1	3-2	1-0	1-0	1-0	0-1	0-3	1-0	1-0	0-2		■	2-0	2-3	1-1	0-2	0-1	2-2	1-2	0-3	2-1
Queen's Park Rangers	2-1	0-1	2-0	1-3	1-1	0-0	0-1	6-0	1-2	1-1	1-1	2-0	1-0	1-1	3-2	■	1-2	2-0	2-2	4-0	0-0	1-2	2-1	0-1
Sheffield United FC	1-1	0-2	1-2	2-2	3-1	3-1	3-1	1-1	3-2	2-1	1-2	2-1	1-2	2-1	3-0	2-0	■	1-1	0-4	2-1	2-2	3-0	3-0	1-1
Stockport County	0-1	1-0	0-1	1-2	2-2	0-0	1-1	1-2	0-1	0-2	2-0	2-0	4-2	0-0	1-0			■	0-1	2-1	0-0	1-1	2-2	1-2
Sunderland AFC	2-3	2-1	3-1	0-0	1-1	1-0	2-0	2-0	3-1	2-0	2-1	1-0	7-0	2-0	2-0	1-0	0-0	1-0	■	2-0	5-0	4-1	3-0	2-1
Swindon Town FC	1-3	0-1	3-3	1-4	3-2	1-1	1-2	2-0	2-0	3-0	0-6	1-1	4-1	3-3	1-1	3-1	2-2	2-3	1-1	■	2-3	1-4	2-2	1-0
Tranmere Rovers FC	3-0	0-1	1-1	0-1	1-1	4-0	3-0	3-1	1-2	2-3	0-2	1-3	2-2	1-1	1-1	3-2	2-3	1-1	1-0	0-0	■	3-2	3-1	1-2
Watford FC	0-0	1-1	2-0	1-0	1-0	0-0	4-2	2-1	1-0	1-1	1-0	2-0	0-0	2-2	2-1	1-1	4-2	2-1	0-1	2-1		■	0-2	0-2
West Bromwich Alb.	2-0	1-3	2-3	0-2	2-2	1-0	1-5	3-2	1-1	3-1	0-1	2-0	2-0	2-2	3-2	2-0	4-1	3-1	2-3	1-1	0-2	4-1	■	2-0
Wolverhampton W.	1-1	3-1	1-1	2-3	3-0	1-0	3-0	0-0	2-0	2-2	1-0	2-2	1-1	2-0	3-1	1-2	2-1	2-2	1-1	1-0	2-0	0-0	1-1	■

Football League Division 1		Pd	Wn	Dw	Ls	GF	GA	Pts	
1.	Sunderland AFC (Sunderland)	46	31	12	3	91	28	105	P
2.	Bradford City AFC (Bradford)	46	26	9	11	82	47	87	P
3.	Ipswich Town FC (Ipswich)	46	26	8	12	69	32	86	PO
4.	Birmingham City FC (Birmingham)	46	23	12	11	66	37	81	PO
5.	Watford FC (Watford)	46	21	14	11	65	56	77	POP
6.	Bolton Wanderers FC (Bolton)	46	20	16	10	78	59	76	PO
7.	Wolverhampton Wanderers FC (Wolverhampton)	46	19	16	11	64	43	73	
8.	Sheffield United FC (Sheffield)	46	18	13	15	71	66	67	
9.	Norwich City FC (Norwich)	46	15	17	14	62	61	62	
10.	Huddersfield Town AFC (Huddersfield)	46	15	16	15	62	71	61	
11.	Grimsby Town FC (Cleethorpes)	46	17	10	19	40	52	61	
12.	West Bromwich Albion FC (West Bromwich)	46	16	11	19	69	76	59	
13.	Barnsley FC (Barnsley)	46	14	17	15	59	56	59	
14.	Crystal Palace FC (London)	46	14	16	16	58	71	58	
15.	Tranmere Rovers FC (Birkenhead)	46	12	20	14	63	61	56	
16.	Stockport County FC (Stockport)	46	12	17	17	49	60	53	
17.	Swindon Town FC (Swindon)	46	13	11	22	59	81	50	
18.	Crewe Alexandra FC (Crewe)	46	12	12	22	54	78	48	
19.	Portsmouth FC (Portsmouth)	46	11	14	21	57	73	47	
20.	Queen's Park Rangers FC (London)	46	12	11	23	52	61	47	
21.	Port Vale FC (Stoke-on-Trent)	46	13	8	25	45	75	47	
22.	Bury FC (Bury)	46	10	17	19	35	60	47	R
23.	Oxford United FC (Oxford)	46	10	14	22	48	71	44	R
24.	Bristol City FC (Bristol)	46	9	15	22	57	80	42	R
		1104	389	326	389	1455	1455	1497	

Promotion Play-offs

Watford FC (Watford)	2-0	Bolton Wanderers FC (Bolton)
Bolton Wanderers FC (Bolton)	1-0, 3-4 (aet)	Ipswich Town FC (Ipswich)
	(Bolton Wanderers won on the away goals rule)	
Watford FC (Watford)	1-0, 0-1 (aet)	Birmingham City FC (Birmingham)
	(Watford won 7-6 on penalties)	

Football League Division 2 1998-99 Season	Blackpool	Bournemouth	Bristol Rovers	Burnley	Chesterfield	Colchester United	Fulham	Gillingham	Lincoln City	Luton Town	Macclesfield Town	Manchester City	Millwall	Northampton Town	Notts County	Oldham Athletic	Preston North End	Reading	Stoke City	Walsall	Wigan Athletic	Wrexham	Wycombe Wanderers	York City
Blackpool FC	■	0-0	1-2	0-1	1-1	2-1	2-3	2-2	0-1	1-0	2-1	0-0	2-3	2-1	1-0	3-0	0-0	2-0	0-1	0-2	1-1	1-1	0-0	1-2
AFC Bournemouth	1-1	■	1-0	5-1	0-0	2-1	1-1	3-3	2-0	1-0	1-0	0-0	3-0	1-1	2-0	2-0	3-1	0-1	4-0	0-1	1-0	0-0	2-0	2-1
Bristol Rovers FC	0-2	1-0	■	3-4	0-0	1-1	2-3	0-1	3-0	1-0	0-0	2-2	3-0	1-1	1-1	2-2	2-2	4-1	1-0	3-4	3-2	0-0	0-2	2-0
Burnley FC	1-0	0-0	2-1	■	1-2	3-1	1-0	0-5	1-1	1-2	4-3	0-6	2-1	0-2	1-1	1-0	0-1	1-1	0-2	0-0	1-1	2-1	1-1	0-1
Chesterfield FC	1-2	3-1	0-0	1-0	■	3-1	1-0	1-0	3-0	3-1	2-0	1-1	2-1	0-0	3-0	1-3	0-1	1-0	1-1	0-1	1-1	2-1	2-0	2-1
Colchester United FC	2-2	2-1	0-3	0-4	1-0	■	0-1	1-1	1-3	2-2	1-1	0-1	0-0	1-0	2-1	2-2	1-0	1-1	0-1	1-0	2-1	1-3	2-1	2-1
Fulham FC	4-0	0-0	1-0	4-0	2-1	2-0	■	3-0	1-0	1-3	1-0	3-0	4-1	2-0	2-1	1-0	3-0	3-1	1-0	4-1	2-0	1-1	2-0	3-3
Gillingham FC	1-0	2-1	0-0	2-1	3-1	1-1	1-0	■	4-0	1-0	2-2	0-2	1-1	2-3	4-0	2-1	1-1	2-1	4-0	0-1	4-0	3-0	3-1	
Lincoln City FC	1-2	2-1	1-0	1-1	2-0	0-0	1-2	1-2	■	2-2	1-0	2-1	2-0	1-0	0-1	1-3	3-4	2-2	1-2	0-1	1-0	1-0	0-1	1-2
Luton Town FC	1-0	2-2	2-0	1-0	1-0	2-0	0-4	1-0	0-1	■	1-2	1-1	1-2	1-0	0-1	2-0	1-1	1-1	1-2	0-1	0-4	1-2	3-1	2-1
Macclesfield Town	0-1	2-2	3-4	2-1	2-0	2-0	0-1	1-0	0-0	2-2	■	0-1	0-2	0-1	0-1	1-0	3-2	2-1	1-2	1-1	0-1	0-2	1-3	1-2
Manchester City FC	3-0	2-1	0-0	2-2	1-1	2-1	3-0	0-0	4-0	2-0	2-0	■	3-0	0-0	2-1	0-1	2-1	3-1	1-0	0-1	1-0	1-2	4-0	
Millwall FC	1-0	1-2	1-1	1-2	0-0	2-0	0-1	3-3	2-0	0-1	0-0	1-1	■	2-1	1-3	1-1	2-2	1-1	2-0	1-2	3-1	3-0	2-1	3-1
Northampton Town	0-0	2-1	3-1	2-2	1-0	3-3	1-1	0-1	0-0	1-0	0-2	2-2	1-2	■	1-1	1-1	1-1	0-1	1-3	0-1	3-3	0-2	1-1	2-2
Notts County FC	0-1	1-2	1-1	0-0	2-0	1-3	1-0	0-1	2-3	1-2	1-1	1-1	3-1	3-1	■	0-1	2-3	1-1	1-0	2-1	0-1	1-1	1-0	4-2
Oldham Athletic AFC	3-0	2-3	2-1	1-1	2-0	1-0	1-1	1-4	2-0	1-1	1-2	0-3	0-1	0-1	1-3	■	0-1	2-0	1-0	0-2	2-3	3-2	0-0	0-2
Preston North End	1-2	0-1	2-2	4-1	2-0	2-0	0-1	1-1	5-0	2-1	2-2	1-1	0-1	3-0	1-1	2-1	■	4-0	3-4	1-0	2-2	3-1	2-1	3-0
Reading FC	1-1	3-3	0-6	1-1	1-2	1-1	0-1	0-0	2-1	3-0	1-0	1-3	2-0	0-1	1-0	1-1	2-1	■	2-1	0-1	0-1	4-0	2-1	1-0
Stoke City FC	1-3	2-0	1-4	1-4	0-0	3-3	0-1	0-0	2-0	3-1	0-1	1-0	3-1	2-3	2-0	0-1	0-4	■	2-0	2-1	1-3	2-2	2-0	
Walsall FC	1-0	1-0	3-3	3-1	1-1	1-1	2-2	2-1	1-0	2-1	3-0	0-0	3-2	0-1	1-0	0-2	1-0	■	1-2	1-0	2-2	2-3		
Wigan Athletic AFC	3-0	2-1	1-0	0-0	3-1	1-1	2-0	4-1	3-1	1-3	2-0	0-1	1-0	3-0	2-0	2-2	4-1	2-3	2-0	■	1-1	0-0	5-0	
Wrexham AFC	1-1	0-1	1-0	1-1	0-0	2-4	0-2	2-1	2-1	1-1	2-1	0-0	1-0	1-0	1-2	0-5	3-0	0-1	2-1	0-2	■	0-2	1-1	
Wycombe Wanderers	2-2	0-2	1-1	2-0	1-0	2-2	1-1	0-2	4-1	0-1	3-0	1-0	0-1	1-2	1-1	3-0	0-1	2-3	0-1	1-2	2-1	3-0	■	1-2
York City FC	1-0	0-1	1-0	3-3	1-2	1-2	0-3	1-1	2-1	3-3	0-2	2-1	2-1	1-1	1-1	0-1	0-1	1-1	2-2	1-2	1-3	1-1	3-0	■

Football League Division 2	Pd	Wn	Dw	Ls	GF	GA	Pts	
1. Fulham FC (London)	46	31	8	7	79	32	101	P
2. Walsall FC (Walsall)	46	26	9	11	63	47	87	P
3. Manchester City FC (Manchester)	46	22	16	8	69	33	82	POP
4. Gillingham FC (Gillingham)	46	22	14	10	75	44	80	PO
5. Preston North End FC (Preston)	46	22	13	11	78	50	79	PO
6. Wigan Athletic AFC (Wigan)	46	22	10	14	75	48	76	PO
7. AFC Bournemouth (Bournemouth)	46	21	13	12	63	41	76	
8. Stoke City FC (Stoke-on-Trent)	46	21	6	19	59	63	69	
9. Chesterfield FC (Chesterfield)	46	17	13	16	46	44	64	
10. Millwall FC (London)	46	17	11	18	52	59	62	
11. Reading FC (Reading)	46	16	13	17	54	63	61	
12. Luton Town FC (Luton)	46	16	10	20	51	60	58	
13. Bristol Rovers FC (Bristol)	46	13	17	16	65	56	56	
14. Blackpool FC (Blackpool)	46	14	14	18	44	54	56	
15. Burnley FC (Burnley)	46	13	16	17	54	73	55	
16. Notts County FC (Nottingham)	46	14	12	20	52	61	54	
17. Wrexham AFC (Wrexham)	46	13	14	19	43	62	53	
18. Colchester United FC (Colchester)	46	12	16	18	52	70	52	
19. Wycombe Wanderers FC (High Wycombe)	46	13	12	21	52	58	51	
20. Oldham Athletic AFC (Oldham)	46	14	9	23	48	66	51	
21. York City FC (York)	46	13	11	22	56	80	50	R
22. Northampton Town FC (Northampton)	46	10	18	18	43	57	48	R
23. Lincoln City FC (Lincoln)	46	13	7	26	42	74	46	R
24. Macclesfield Town FC (Macclesfield)	46	11	10	25	43	63	43	R
	1104	406	292	406	1358	1358	1510	

Promotion Play-offs

Manchester City FC (Manchester)	2-2 (aet)	Gillingham FC (Gillingham)
	(Manchester City won 3-1 on penalties)	
Preston North End FC (Preston)	1-1, 0-1	Gillingham FC (Gillingham)
Wigan Athletic AFC (Wigan)	1-1, 0-1	Manchester City FC (Manchester)

Football League Division 3 — 1998-99 Season

	Barnet	Brentford	Brighton & H.A.	Cambridge	Cardiff City	Carlisle United	Chester City	Darlington	Exeter City	Halifax Town	Hartlepool	Hull City	Leyton Orient	Mansfield Town	Peterborough Utd.	Plymouth Argyle	Rochdale	Rotherham United	Scarborough	Scunthorpe United	Shrewsbury Town	Southend United	Swansea City	Torquay United
Barnet FC	■	0-3	0-1	3-0	1-0	1-0	0-0	3-0	0-1	2-2	0-2	4-1	3-2	0-0	1-9	1-1	0-1	4-2	1-0	1-0	2-2	0-2	0-1	3-1
Brentford FC	3-2	■	2-0	1-0	1-0	1-1	2-1	3-0	3-0	1-1	3-1	0-2	0-0	3-0	3-0	3-1	2-1	0-3	1-1	2-1	0-0	4-1	4-1	3-2
Brighton & Hove Alb.	0-1	3-1	■	1-3	0-2	1-3	2-2	0-4	0-1	0-1	3-2	0-0	1-2	1-3	1-0	1-3	1-1	4-1	1-0	1-3	1-0	0-2	1-0	2-0
Cambridge United	3-2	0-1	2-3	■	0-0	1-0	2-1	2-1	1-1	4-0	1-2	2-0	1-0	7-2	1-1	1-0	1-1	3-2	2-3	0-0	0-0	3-0	2-1	2-0
Cardiff City AFC	1-0	4-1	2-0	0-1	■	2-1	0-0	3-2	1-0	1-1	4-1	1-1	0-0	4-2	1-3	1-0	2-1	0-1	1-0	0-0	3-0	2-0	0-0	2-2
Carlisle United FC	2-1	0-1	1-0	1-1	0-1	■	1-1	3-3	1-3	0-1	2-1	0-0	1-1	0-0	1-1	2-1	0-1	0-0	1-0	0-1	2-1	3-0	1-2	3-0
Chester City FC	3-0	1-3	1-1	0-3	2-2	2-1	■	1-0	0-0	2-2	1-1	2-2	0-2	1-1	1-1	3-2	1-1	1-1	1-3	0-2	1-1	1-1	1-1	2-0
Darlington FC	0-2	2-2	1-2	0-0	3-0	1-1	1-2	■	4-0	2-2	2-0	0-1	1-0	5-1	3-0	1-2	3-0	1-2	3-0	3-1	1-0	2-1	2-2	0-2
Exeter City FC	1-0	0-1	1-0	0-3	0-2	2-0	0-1	0-0	■	2-1	2-1	3-0	1-1	2-1	2-0	1-1	2-1	3-0	1-0	2-2	0-1	2-1	4-0	1-1
Halifax Town AFC	1-1	1-0	3-3	1-2	1-0	3-2	0-0	1-1		■	2-1	0-1	1-2	2-2	2-2	2-0	0-0	2-4	1-2	1-0	2-0	3-1	2-0	1-1
Hartlepool United FC	2-2	0-1	0-0	2-2	1-1	0-0	2-0	2-3	4-3	2-0	■	1-0	1-0	2-1	2-0	0-1	0-0	3-0	1-2	1-1	2-4	1-2		4-1
Hull City AFC	1-1	2-3	0-2	0-3	1-2	1-0	1-2	1-2	2-1	1-2	4-0	■	0-1	1-0	1-0	2-1	1-0	1-1	2-3	1-1	1-0	1-1	0-2	1-0
Leyton Orient FC	2-2	2-1	1-0	2-0	0-1	2-1	2-2	3-2	2-0	1-0	1-1	1-2	■	1-1	1-2	4-3	3-0	1-4	0-3	1-0	6-1	0-3	1-1	2-0
Mansfield Town FC	5-0	3-1	2-0	1-3	3-0	1-1	3-0	0-1	0-1	0-1	2-0	2-0	1-2	■	1-0	2-0	3-1	0-3	3-2	2-1	1-0	0-0	1-0	2-1
Peterborough United	5-2	2-4	3-2	2-1	2-1	0-1	3-0	0-1	4-1	0-2	1-1	3-0	1-0		■	0-2	2-0	2-4	2-3	1-2	1-1	1-0	0-1	4-0
Plymouth Argyle FC	2-0	3-0	1-2	2-2	1-2	2-0	2-0	1-2	1-0	1-0	0-0	0-0	2-4	3-0	0-2	■	2-1	1-0	0-0	5-0	2-0	0-3	1-2	0-0
Rochdale AFC	0-0	2-0	2-1	0-2	1-1	1-1	3-1	0-0	1-1	1-0	0-1	3-0	2-1	1-0	0-3	1-1	■	0-0	0-1	2-2	1-0	1-0	0-3	0-2
Rotherham United	1-1	2-4	2-4	2-0	1-0	3-1	2-4	3-1	0-0	3-1	3-0	3-1	0-0	2-2	0-2	2-2	2-2	■	4-0	0-0	0-1	2-2	1-0	2-2
Scarborough FC	0-0	3-1	1-2	1-5	3-0	0-2	1-0	0-2	1-0	1-2	1-2	2-3	1-1	3-0	1-1	0-4			■	1-4	3-0	1-1	2-1	1-1
Scunthorpe United	3-1	0-0	3-1	3-2	2-1	3-1	2-1	1-0	2-0	0-4	2-0	3-2	0-1	3-2	2-1	1-0	0-2	0-1	4-3	■	3-0	1-1	1-2	2-0
Shrewsbury Town	0-2	2-0	1-3	1-1	0-3	1-1	2-0	3-0	1-1	2-2	1-0	3-2	1-1	1-0	1-1	2-1	3-2	2-3	3-1	2-1	■	3-1	1-0	1-2
Southend United FC	2-3	1-4	3-0	0-1	0-1	0-1	0-1	2-1	0-0	0-0	1-1	0-1	2-2	1-2	2-0	1-0	1-1	3-0	1-0	0-1	2-1	■	2-0	0-0
Swansea City FC	2-1	2-1	2-2	2-0	2-1	1-1	1-1	2-0	2-0	1-2	1-0	2-0	1-1	0-0	2-3	1-1	1-1	2-0	1-2	1-1	3-1		■	0-0
Torquay United FC	1-1	3-1	1-1	0-1	0-0	2-2	0-3	2-2	1-0	4-0	3-0	2-0	1-1	0-0	0-1	1-1	2-1	2-0	0-1	1-0	0-3	2-0	1-1	■

Football League Division 3

		Pd	Wn	Dw	Ls	GF	GA	Pts	
1.	Brentford FC (London)	46	26	7	13	79	56	85	P
2.	Cambridge United FC (Cambridge)	46	23	12	11	78	48	81	P
3.	Cardiff City AFC (Cardiff)	46	22	14	10	60	39	80	P
4.	Scunthorpe United FC (Scunthorpe)	46	22	8	16	69	58	74	POP
5.	Rotherham United FC (Rotherham)	46	20	13	13	79	61	73	PO
6.	Leyton Orient FC (London)	46	19	15	12	68	59	72	PO
7.	Swansea City FC (Swansea)	46	19	14	13	56	48	71	PO
8.	Mansfield Town FC (Mansfield)	46	19	10	17	60	58	67	
9.	Peterborough United FC (Peterborough)	46	18	12	16	72	56	66	
10.	Halifax Town AFC (Halifax)	46	17	15	14	58	56	66	
11.	Darlington FC (Darlington)	46	18	11	17	69	58	65	
12.	Exeter City FC (Exeter)	46	17	12	17	47	50	63	
13.	Plymouth Argyle FC (Plymouth)	46	17	10	19	58	54	63	
14.	Chester City FC (Chester)	46	13	18	15	57	66	57	
15.	Shrewsbury Town FC (Shrewsbury)	46	14	14	18	52	63	56	
16.	Barnet FC (London)	46	14	13	19	54	71	55	
17.	Brighton & Hove Albion FC (Brighton)	46	16	7	23	49	66	55	
18.	Southend United FC (Southend-on-Sea)	46	14	12	20	52	58	54	
19.	Rochdale AFC (Rochdale)	46	13	15	18	42	55	54	
20.	Torquay United FC (Torquay)	46	12	17	17	47	58	53	
21.	Hull City AFC (Kingston-upon-Hull)	46	14	11	21	44	62	53	
22.	Hartlepool United FC (Hartlepool)	46	13	12	21	52	65	51	
23.	Carlisle United FC (Carlisle)	46	11	16	19	43	53	49	
24.	Scarborough FC (Scarborough)	46	14	6	26	50	77	48	R
		1104	405	294	405	1395	1395	1509	

Promotion Play-offs

Scunthorpe United FC (Scunthorpe)	1-0	Leyton Orient FC (London)
Leyton Orient FC (London)	0-0, 0-0 (aet)	Rotherham United FC (Rotherham)
	(Leyton Orient won 4-2 on penalties)	
Swansea City FC (Swansea)	1-0, 1-3	Scunthorpe United FC (Scunthorpe)

Promoted to Division 3: Cheltenham Town FC (Cheltenham)

F.A. CUP FINAL   (Wembley Stadium, London – 22/05/1999 – 79,101)

MANCHESTER UNITED FC (MANCHESTER)   2-0   Newcastle United FC (Newcastle-upon-Tyne)

Sheringham 11', Scholes 53'

Man. United: Schmeichel, G.Neville, May, Johnson, P.Neville, Beckham, Keane (Sheringham 09'), Scholes (Stam 78'), Giggs, Solskjær, Cole (Yorke 60').

Newcastle: Harper, Griffin, Charvet, Dabizas, Domi, Lee, Hamann (Ferguson 46'), Speed, Solano (Maric 68'), Shearer, Ketsbaia, (Glass 79').

Semi-finals

Manchester United FC (Manchester)	0-0 (aet), 2-1	Arsenal FC (London)
Newcastle United FC (Newcastle-upon-Tyne)	2-0	Tottenham Hotspur FC (London)

Quarter-finals

Arsenal FC (London)	1-0	Derby County FC (Derby)
Barnsley FC (Barnsley)	0-1	Tottenham Hotspur FC (London)
Manchester United FC (Manchester)	0-0, 2-0	Chelsea FC (London)
Newcastle United FC (Newcastle-upon-Tyne)	4-1	Everton FC (Liverpool)

1999-2000

F.A. Premiership 1999-2000 Season	Arsenal	Aston Villa	Bradford City	Chelsea	Coventry City	Derby County	Everton	Leeds United	Leicester City	Liverpool	Manchester United	Middlesbrough	Newcastle United	Sheffield Wednesday	Southampton	Sunderland	Tottenham Hotspur	Watford	West Ham United	Wimbledon
Arsenal FC		3-1	2-0	2-1	3-0	2-1	4-1	2-0	2-1	0-1	1-2	5-1	0-0	3-3	3-1	4-1	2-1	1-0	2-1	1-1
Aston Villa FC	1-1		1-0	0-0	1-0	2-0	3-0	1-0	2-2	0-0	0-1	1-0	0-1	2-1	0-1	1-1	1-1	4-0	2-2	1-1
Bradford City AFC	2-1	1-1		1-1	1-1	4-4	0-0	1-2	3-1	1-0	0-4	1-1	2-0	1-1	1-2	0-4	1-1	3-2	0-3	3-0
Chelsea FC	2-3	1-0	1-0		2-1	4-0	1-1	0-2	1-1	2-0	5-0	1-1	1-0	3-0	1-1	4-0	1-0	2-1	0-0	3-1
Coventry City FC	3-2	2-1	4-0	2-2		2-0	1-0	3-4	0-1	0-3	1-2	2-1	4-1	4-1	0-1	3-2	0-1	4-0	1-0	2-0
Derby County FC	1-2	0-2	0-1	3-1	0-0		1-0	0-1	3-0	0-2	1-2	1-3	0-0	3-3	2-0	0-5	0-1	2-0	1-2	4-0
Everton FC	0-1	0-0	4-0	1-1	1-1	2-1		4-4	2-2	0-0	1-1	0-2	0-2	1-1	4-1	5-0	2-2	4-2	1-0	4-0
Leeds United AFC	0-4	1-2	2-1	0-1	3-0	0-0	1-1		2-1	1-2	0-1	2-0	3-2	2-0	1-0	2-1	1-0	3-1	1-0	4-1
Leicester City FC	0-3	3-1	3-0	2-2	1-0	0-1	1-1	2-1		2-2	0-2	2-1	1-2	3-0	2-1	5-2	0-1	1-0	1-3	2-1
Liverpool FC	2-0	0-0	3-1	1-0	2-0	2-0	0-1	3-1	0-2		2-3	0-0	2-1	4-1	0-0	1-1	2-0	0-1	1-0	3-1
Manchester United FC	1-1	3-0	4-0	3-2	3-2	3-1	5-1	2-0	2-0	1-1		1-0	5-1	4-0	3-3	4-0	3-1	4-1	7-1	1-1
Middlesbrough FC	2-1	0-4	0-1	0-1	2-0	1-4	2-1	0-0	0-3	1-0	3-4		2-2	1-0	3-2	1-1	2-1	1-1	2-0	0-0
Newcastle United FC	4-2	0-1	2-0	0-1	2-0	2-0	1-1	2-2	0-2	2-2	3-0	2-1		8-0	5-0	1-2	2-1	1-0	2-2	3-3
Sheffield Wednesday FC	1-1	0-1	2-0	1-0	0-0	0-2	0-2	0-3	4-0	1-2	0-1	1-0	0-2		0-1	0-2	1-2	2-2	3-1	5-1
Southampton FC	0-1	2-0	1-0	1-2	0-0	3-2	2-0	0-3	1-2	1-1	0-3	1-1	4-2	2-0		1-2	0-1	2-0	2-1	2-0
Sunderland AFC	0-0	2-1	0-1	4-1	1-1	1-1	2-1	1-2	2-0	0-2	2-2	1-1	2-2	1-0	2-0		2-1	2-0	1-0	2-1
Tottenham Hotspur FC	2-1	2-4	1-1	0-1	3-2	1-1	3-2	1-2	2-3	1-0	3-1	2-3	3-1	0-1	7-2	3-1		4-0	0-0	2-0
Watford FC	2-3	0-1	1-0	1-0	1-0	0-0	1-3	1-2	1-1	2-3	2-3	1-3	1-1	1-0	3-2	2-3	1-1		1-2	2-3
West Ham United FC	2-1	1-1	5-4	0-0	5-0	1-1	0-4	0-0	2-1	1-0	2-4	0-1	2-1	4-3	2-0	1-1	1-0	1-0		2-1
Wimbledon FC	1-3	2-2	3-2	0-1	1-1	2-2	0-3	2-0	2-1	1-2	2-2	2-3	2-0	0-2	1-1	1-0	1-1	5-0	2-2	

F.A. Premiership

		Pd	Wn	Dw	Ls	GF	GA	Pts	
1.	MANCHESTER UNITED FC (MANCHESTER)	38	28	7	3	97	45	91	
2.	Arsenal FC (London)	38	22	7	9	73	43	73	
3.	Leeds United AFC (Leeds)	38	21	6	11	58	43	69	
4.	Liverpool FC (Liverpool)	38	19	10	9	51	30	67	
5.	Chelsea FC (London)	38	17	11	9	53	34	65	
6.	Aston Villa FC (Birmingham)	38	15	13	10	46	35	58	
7.	Sunderland AFC (Sunderland)	38	16	10	12	57	56	58	
8.	Leicester City FC (Leicester)	38	16	7	15	55	55	55	
9.	West Ham United FC (London)	38	15	10	13	52	53	55	
10.	Tottenham Hotspur FC (London)	38	15	8	15	57	49	53	
11.	Newcastle United FC (Newcastle-upon-Tyne)	38	14	10	14	63	54	52	
12.	Middlesbrough FC (Middlesbrough)	38	14	10	14	46	52	52	
13.	Everton FC (Liverpool)	38	12	14	12	59	49	50	
14.	Coventry City FC (Coventry)	38	12	8	18	47	54	44	
15.	Southampton FC (Southampton)	38	12	8	18	45	62	44	
16.	Derby County FC (Derby)	38	9	11	18	44	57	38	
17.	Bradford City AFC (Bradford)	38	9	9	20	38	68	36	
18.	Wimbledon FC (London)	38	7	12	19	46	74	33	R
19.	Sheffield Wednesday FC (Sheffield)	38	8	7	23	38	70	31	R
20.	Watford FC (Watford)	38	6	6	26	35	77	24	R
		760	288	184	288	1060	1060	1048	

Top Goalscorers

1)	Kevin PHILLIPS	(Sunderland AFC)	30
2)	Alan SHEARER	(Newcastle United FC)	23
3)	Dwight YORKE	(Manchester United FC)	20

Football League Division 1 1999-2000 Season	Barnsley	Birmingham City	Blackburn Rovers	Bolton Wanderers	Charlton Athletic	Crewe Alexandra	Crystal Palace	Fulham	Grimsby Town	Huddersfield Town	Ipswich Town	Manchester City	Norwich City	Nottingham Forest	Portsmouth	Port Vale	Q.P.R.	Sheffield United	Stockport County	Swindon Town	Tranmere Rovers	Walsall	W.B.A.	Wolves
Barnsley FC	■	2-1	5-1	1-1	1-1	0-2	2-3	1-0	3-0	4-2	0-2	2-1	2-1	1-0	6-0	3-1	1-1	2-0	2-1	1-0	3-0	3-2	2-2	1-2
Birmingham City FC	3-1	■	1-0	2-1	1-0	5-1	2-0	2-2	0-0	1-0	1-1	0-1	2-0	0-1	1-0	4-2	2-0	0-2	2-1	1-1	3-1	2-0	1-1	1-0
Blackburn Rovers FC	1-2	1-0	■	3-1	1-1	0-1	1-1	2-0	1-1	2-0	2-2	1-4	1-1	2-1	0-1	0-0	0-2	5-0	2-0	0-0	2-0	2-0	2-1	1-1
Bolton Wanderers FC	2-2	3-3	3-1	■	0-2	2-2	2-0	3-1	3-0	1-0	1-1	0-1	1-0	3-2	3-0	2-1	2-1	2-0	0-1	2-0	2-3	4-3	1-1	2-1
Charlton Athletic FC	3-1	1-0	1-2	2-1	■	1-0	2-1	1-0	4-0	0-1	1-3	0-1	1-0	3-0	1-1	2-2	2-1	1-0	4-0	0-1	3-2	2-1	0-0	2-0
Crewe Alexandra FC	0-1	2-3	0-0	1-3	0-2	■	2-0	1-1	1-1	1-1	1-2	1-1	1-0	0-3	1-3	2-1	2-1	1-0	3-2	2-1	0-2	2-3	2-0	1-0
Crystal Palace FC	0-2	0-2	2-1	0-0	0-1	1-1	■	0-0	3-0	2-2	2-2	1-1	1-0	2-0	4-0	1-1	3-0	1-1	3-3	1-2	2-2	3-2	0-2	1-1
Fulham FC	1-3	0-0	2-2	1-1	2-1	3-0	1-0	■	0-1	3-0	0-0	0-0	1-1	1-1	1-0	3-1	1-0	4-0	4-1	1-0	1-0	2-0	1-0	0-1
Grimsby Town FC	0-3	1-1	0-0	0-1	2-5	1-1	1-0	1-1	■	0-0	2-1	1-1	2-1	4-3	1-0	2-0	2-1	2-2	0-1	1-0	1-2	1-0	1-1	1-0
Huddersfield Town	2-1	0-0	3-2	0-3	1-2	3-0	7-1	1-1	3-1	■	3-1	1-4	1-0	0-1	2-2	1-0	4-0	0-2	4-0	1-1	1-1	1-0	1-0	2-0
Ipswich Town FC	6-1	0-1	0-0	1-0	4-2	2-1	1-0	1-0	2-0	2-1	■	2-1	0-2	3-1	0-1	3-0	1-4	1-1	1-0	3-0	0-0	2-0	3-1	1-0
Manchester City FC	3-1	1-0	2-0	2-0	1-1	4-0	2-1	4-0	2-1	0-1	1-0	■	3-1	1-0	4-2	2-1	1-3	6-0	1-2	3-0	2-0	1-1	2-1	0-1
Norwich City FC	2-2	0-1	0-2	2-1	0-3	2-1	0-1	1-2	3-0	1-1	0-0	1-0	■	1-0	2-1	0-0	2-1	2-0	0-2	1-1	1-1	2-1	1-0	
Nottingham Forest	3-0	1-0	0-1	1-1	1-1	1-0	2-0	0-0	2-1	1-3	0-1	1-3	1-1	■	2-0	2-0	1-1	0-1	3-1	1-1	4-1	0-0	1-1	
Portsmouth FC	3-0	2-2	1-2	0-0	0-2	0-2	3-1	0-1	1-2	0-0	1-1	2-2	2-1	2-1	■	0-0	1-3	2-0	2-0	4-1	1-2	5-1	2-0	2-3
Port Vale FC	2-2	3-1	0-0	0-1	2-2	1-0	2-2	0-2	3-1	1-2	1-2	1-2	0-1	0-2	2-0	■	1-1	2-3	1-1	2-0	1-0	1-2	1-2	0-1
Queen's Park Rangers	2-2	2-2	0-0	0-1	0-0	1-1	0-1	0-0	1-0	3-1	3-1	1-1	2-2	1-1	0-0	3-2	■	3-1	1-1	2-1	2-1	2-1	0-0	1-1
Sheffield United FC	3-3	1-2	2-1	1-2	1-2	1-1	3-1	0-0	0-1	2-2	1-0	0-0	2-1	1-0	1-3	1-1	1-0	■	2-2	3-1	1-1	6-0	3-0	
Stockport County FC	1-3	2-0	0-1	0-0	1-3	2-1	1-2	2-1	2-1	1-1	0-1	2-2	2-2	2-3	1-1	1-0	3-3	1-1	■	3-0	2-1	1-1	0-1	3-2
Swindon Town FC	1-2	1-4	2-1	0-4	1-2	0-1	2-4	1-0	0-1	2-0	1-4	0-2	0-0	0-0	1-1	2-1	0-1	2-2	1-1	■	3-1	1-1	1-2	1-1
Tranmere Rovers FC	2-2	2-1	2-1	0-0	2-2	2-0	1-2	1-1	3-2	1-0	0-2	1-1	1-2	3-0	2-4	2-1	1-1	1-3	0-0	3-1	■	1-1	3-0	1-0
Walsall FC	1-4	1-0	1-1	2-0	2-4	1-4	2-2	1-3	1-0	2-0	0-1	0-1	2-2	0-2	1-0	0-0	2-3	2-1	1-2	0-0	1-2	■	2-1	1-1
West Bromwich Alb.	0-2	0-3	2-2	4-4	2-0	1-0	0-0	0-0	2-1	0-1	1-1	0-2	1-1	1-1	3-2	0-0	0-1	2-2	2-0	1-1	2-0	0-1	■	1-1
Wolverhampton W.	2-0	2-1	2-1	1-0	2-3	2-0	2-1	3-0	3-0	0-1	2-1	4-1	1-0	3-0	1-1	2-2	3-2	1-0	2-2	1-1	4-0	1-2	1-1	■

	Football League Division 1	**Pd**	**Wn**	**Dw**	**Ls**	**GF**	**GA**	**Pts**	
1.	Charlton Athletic FC (London)	46	27	10	9	79	45	91	P
2.	Manchester City FC (Manchester)	46	26	11	9	78	40	89	P
3.	Ipswich Town FC (Ipswich)	46	25	12	9	71	42	87	POP
4.	Barnsley FC (Barnsley)	46	24	10	12	88	67	82	PO
5.	Birmingham City FC (Birmingham)	46	22	11	13	65	44	77	PO
6.	Bolton Wanderers FC (Bolton)	46	21	13	12	69	50	76	PO
7.	Wolverhampton Wanderers FC (Wolverhampton)	46	21	11	14	64	48	74	
8.	Huddersfield Town AFC (Huddersfield)	46	21	11	14	62	49	74	
9.	Fulham FC (London)	46	17	16	13	49	41	67	
10.	Queen's Park Rangers FC (London)	46	16	18	12	62	53	66	
11.	Blackburn Rovers FC (Blackburn)	46	15	17	14	55	51	62	
12.	Norwich City FC (Norwich)	46	14	15	17	45	50	57	
13.	Tranmere Rovers FC (Birkenhead)	46	15	12	19	57	68	57	
14.	Nottingham Forest FC (Nottingham)	46	14	14	18	53	55	56	
15.	Crystal Palace FC (London)	46	13	15	18	57	67	54	
16.	Sheffield United FC (Sheffield)	46	13	15	18	59	71	54	
17.	Stockport County FC (Stockport)	46	13	15	18	55	67	54	
18.	Portsmouth FC (Portsmouth)	46	13	12	21	55	66	51	
19.	Crewe Alexandra FC (Crewe)	46	14	9	23	46	67	51	
20.	Grimsby Town FC (Cleethorpes)	46	13	12	21	41	67	51	
21.	West Bromwich Albion FC (West Bromwich)	46	10	19	17	43	60	49	
22.	Walsall FC (Walsall)	46	11	13	22	52	77	46	R
23.	Port Vale FC (Stoke-on-Trent)	46	7	15	24	48	69	36	R
24.	Swindon Town FC (Swindon)	46	8	12	26	38	77	36	R
		1104	393	318	393	1391	1391	1497	

Promotion Play-offs

Ipswich Town FC (Ipswich)	4-2	Barnsley FC (Barnsley)
Birmingham City FC (Birmingham)	0-4, 2-1	Barnsley FC (Barnsley)
Bolton Wanderers FC (Bolton)	2-2, 3-5 (aet)	Ipswich Town FC (Ipswich)

Football League Division 2 1999-2000 Season	Blackpool	Bournemouth	Brentford	Bristol City	Bristol Rovers	Burnley	Bury	Cambridge United	Cardiff City	Chesterfield	Colchester United	Gillingham	Luton Town	Millwall	Notts County	Oldham Athletic	Oxford United	Preston North End	Reading	Scunthorpe United	Stoke City	Wigan Athletic	Wrexham	Wycombe Wanderers
Blackpool FC		0-0	0-1	1-2	2-1	1-1	0-5	2-1	2-2	2-2	1-1	1-1	3-3	1-2	2-1	1-2	1-1	0-0	0-2	0-2	1-2	2-2	2-1	1-2
AFC Bournemouth	2-0		4-1	2-3	0-1	0-1	1-1	2-1	1-0	1-1	4-0	0-1	1-0	1-2	1-1	3-0	4-0	0-1	3-1	1-1	1-1	2-2	1-0	2-0
Brentford FC	2-0	0-2		2-1	0-3	2-3	2-1	1-1	2-1	1-1	0-0	1-2	2-0	1-3	0-2	2-0	2-0	2-2	1-1	4-3	0-1	0-2	0-2	0-0
Bristol City FC	5-2	3-1	1-0		0-0	0-0	1-1	1-1	0-0	3-0	1-1	0-1	0-0	0-0	2-2	1-1	2-2	0-2	3-1	2-1	2-2	0-0	4-0	0-0
Bristol Rovers FC	3-1	2-2	0-0	2-0		1-0	0-0	1-0	1-1	3-1	2-1	2-1	3-0	1-0	0-1	3-2	1-0	0-2	0-1	1-1	3-3	1-1	3-1	1-0
Burnley FC	1-0	2-1	2-2	2-0	1-0		2-2	2-0	2-1	2-1	3-0	0-3	0-2	4-3	2-1	3-0	3-2	0-3	3-0	1-2	1-0	0-0	5-0	1-0
Bury FC	3-2	2-2	2-2	0-0	0-0	4-2		0-2	3-2	1-1	5-2	2-1	1-0	2-2	1-3	2-2	1-2	1-3	1-1	3-0	0-0	2-2	0-2	2-0
Cambridge United FC	0-2	0-2	2-2	3-0	1-1	0-1	3-0		0-0	2-0	5-2	2-2	3-1	0-2	1-1	2-3	2-0	2-0	3-1	1-3	1-3	1-1	3-4	1-2
Cardiff City FC	1-1	1-2	1-1	0-0	1-0	1-2	0-2	0-4		2-1	3-2	1-2	1-3	11-	2-1	1-1	1-1	0-4	1-0	1-1	1-2	0-0	1-1	2-2
Chesterfield FC	0-0	0-1	1-0	0-2	0-1	1-1	0-1	4-2	1-1		0-1	0-0	1-3	2-0	2-1	0-1	0-0	2-1	2-0	1-1	0-2	1-1	0-3	1-2
Colchester United FC	1-1	3-1	0-3	3-4	5-4	1-2	1-3	3-1	0-3	1-0		2-1	3-0	1-2	0-3	0-1	1-2	2-2	3-2	0-1	1-0	2-2	2-2	1-0
Gillingham FC	1-3	4-1	2-0	3-0	0-1	2-2	1-0	2-1	4-1	1-0	2-1		2-0	2-0	0-1	2-1	1-0	0-2	2-2	3-1	3-0	2-1	5-1	2-2
Luton Town FC	3-2	1-2	1-2	1-2	1-4	2-1	1-1	2-2	1-0	1-1	3-2	3-1		0-2	2-2	1-1	4-2	0-2	3-1	4-1	2-1	1-1	3-1	1-1
Millwall FC	1-1	3-1	3-2	4-1	3-0	1-1	3-0	2-1	2-0	1-1	1-0	2-2	1-0		1-0	1-0	0-2	5-0	1-2	1-0	3-3	0-0	1-1	
Notts County FC	2-1	5-1	0-1	4-4	0-2	2-0	2-2	2-3	2-1	1-0	1-2	1-1	0-0	1-1		0-1	0-1	1-0	1-2	3-0	0-0	0-2	2-1	2-1
Oldham Athletic AFC	1-1	1-0	3-0	1-1	1-4	0-1	2-0	1-0	1-2	1-2	1-2	1-3	2-1	2-1	1-2		2-0	0-1	1-2	1-1	0-1	2-1	0-0	2-2
Oxford United FC	0-1	1-0	1-1	3-0	0-5	1-2	1-1	1-0	2-3	2-1	1-1	1-2	0-1	1-3	2-3	1-0		0-4	1-3	2-0	1-1	1-2	1-4	0-0
Preston North End	3-0	3-0	2-1	1-0	2-1	0-0	1-1	2-1	0-0	0-2	2-3	0-2	1-0	3-2	2-0	2-0	3-1		2-2	1-0	2-1	1-4	1-0	3-2
Reading FC	1-1	2-0	1-0	2-1	2-0	0-0	2-0	0-0	0-1	1-0	1-0	2-2	1-2	2-0	0-0	1-1	1-2	2-2		1-1	1-0	0-2	2-2	2-1
Scunthorpe United	1-0	3-1	0-0	1-2	0-2	1-2	0-2	0-3	0-0	0-0	0-0	1-4	1-2	1-4	1-0	1-2	1-0	1-1	2-2		0-2	1-2	0-2	0-1
Stoke City FC	3-0	1-0	1-0	1-1	1-2	2-2	3-0	1-0	2-1	5-1	1-1	1-1	2-1	3-1	0-1	0-0	1-2	2-1	2-1	1-0		1-1	2-0	1-1
Wigan Athletic AFC	5-1	3-1	1-0	2-1	3-1	1-1	1-0	1-1	2-0	3-0	0-1	2-0	1-0	1-1	2-0	0-1	2-0	0-1	1-0	3-0	1-2		0-1	2-1
Wrexham AFC	1-1	1-0	0-1	0-1	2-1	0-1	1-0	1-1	2-1	1-1	1-0	1-0	1-0	1-1	2-3	0-3	1-0	0-0	0-1	3-1	2-3	1-1		1-3
Wycombe Wanderers	0-2	2-1	2-0	1-2	1-1	1-1	3-0	1-0	3-1	3-0	3-0	1-0	0-1	1-2	2-0	0-0	0-1	1-1	5-3	2-1	0-4	0-2	0-1	

Football League Division 2	Pd	Wn	Dw	Ls	GF	GA	Pts	
1. Preston North End FC (Preston)	46	28	11	7	74	37	95	P
2. Burnley FC (Burnley)	46	25	13	8	69	47	88	P
3. Gillingham FC (Gillingham)	46	25	10	11	79	48	85	POP
4. Wigan Athletic AFC (Wigan)	46	22	17	7	72	38	83	PO
5. Millwall FC (London)	46	23	13	10	76	50	82	PO
6. Stoke City FC (Stoke-on-Trent)	46	23	13	10	68	42	82	PO
7. Bristol Rovers FC (Bristol)	46	23	11	12	69	45	80	
8. Notts County FC (Nottingham)	46	18	11	17	61	55	65	
9. Bristol City FC (Bristol)	46	15	19	12	59	57	64	
10. Reading FC (Reading)	46	16	14	16	57	63	62	
11. Wrexham AFC (Wrexham)	46	17	11	18	52	61	62	
12. Wycombe Wanderers FC (High Wycombe)	46	16	13	17	56	53	61	
13. Luton Town FC (Luton)	46	17	10	19	61	65	61	
14. Oldham Athletic AFC (Oldham)	46	16	12	18	50	55	60	
15. Bury FC (Bury)	46	13	18	15	61	64	57	
16. AFC Bournemouth (Bournemouth)	46	16	9	21	59	62	57	
17. Brentford FC (London)	46	13	13	20	47	61	52	
18. Colchester United FC (Colchester)	46	14	10	22	59	82	52	
19. Cambridge United FC (Cambridge)	46	12	12	22	64	65	48	
20. Oxford United FC (Oxford)	46	12	9	25	43	73	45	
21. Cardiff City AFC (Cardiff)	46	9	17	20	45	67	44	R
22. Blackpool FC (Blackpool)	46	8	17	21	49	77	41	R
23. Scunthorpe United FC (Scunthorpe)	46	9	12	25	40	74	39	R
24. Chesterfield FC (Chesterfield)	46	7	15	24	34	63	36	R
	1104	397	310	397	1404	1404	1501	

Promotion Play-offs

Gillingham FC (Gillingham)	3-2 (aet)	Wigan Athletic AFC (Wigan)
Millwall FC (London)	0-0, 0-1	Wigan Athletic AFC (Wigan)
Stoke City FC (Stoke-on-Trent)	3-2, 0-3	Gillingham FC (Gillingham)

Football League Division 3 1999-2000 Season	Barnet	Brighton & H.A.	Carlisle United	Cheltenham Town	Chester City	Darlington	Exeter City	Halifax Town	Hartlepool	Hull City	Leyton Orient	Lincoln City	Macclesfield Town	Mansfield Town	Northampton Town	Peterborough Utd.	Plymouth Argyle	Rochdale	Rotherham United	Shrewsbury Town	Southend United	Swansea City	Torquay United	York City
Barnet FC	■	0-1	3-0	3-2	2-0	1-0	2-2	0-1	1-1	0-0	2-2	5-3	2-1	0-0	2-1	0-2	1-0	1-0	2-2	1-1	2-1	0-1	1-2	6-3
Brighton & Hove Alb.	1-1	■	1-0	1-0	2-3	1-1	4-2	2-1	1-0	3-0	0-1	2-2	5-2	6-0	1-3	0-0	1-1	3-4	1-0	1-1	1-0	1-1	0-1	0-1
Carlisle United FC	3-1	0-1	■	1-1	4-1	1-1	0-0	1-1	0-3	0-4	2-1	1-0	0-1	0-2	0-1	1-1	4-2	1-2	1-1	1-1	1-1	2-0	0-0	0-1
Cheltenham Town	1-2	0-0	3-1	■	1-0	0-0	3-1	3-0	2-1	1-1	2-0	1-1	1-0	2-1	2-0	0-2	0-1	0-1	2-1	1-1	2-1	0-0	2-0	0-1
Chester City FC	0-2	1-7	0-1	2-1	■	1-2	1-1	2-1	1-1	0-0	1-5	1-3	1-2	5-0	0-2	0-1	0-1	0-2	0-0	0-0	0-0	0-1	2-1	2-0
Darlington FC	4-0	1-1	3-1	1-0	3-1	■	1-0	4-0	1-1	0-0	3-1	2-0	3-0	0-0	0-1	2-0	2-0	4-1	0-2	2-2	1-0	1-1	1-1	2-2
Exeter City FC	0-0	0-0	1-1	1-2	0-2	1-4	■	1-0	1-2	1-3	3-0	0-3	1-0	1-2	2-2	1-1	2-0	3-1	1-2	0-1	1-1	3-2	2-1	
Halifax Town AFC	1-2	2-1	5-2	1-1	0-1	0-1	1-0	■	1-1	0-1	0-2	3-0	0-1	2-2	2-1	1-0	0-0	2-1	0-0	0-1	1-0	2-0	1-0	2-1
Hartlepool United FC	3-0	0-0	1-0	0-1	1-0	2-0	2-1	0-2	■	2-0	1-0	2-0	1-4	1-0	2-1	1-0	3-0	3-2	1-2	1-0	1-2	2-0	2-1	
Hull City AFC	1-3	2-0	2-1	1-1	2-1	0-1	4-0	0-1	0-3	■	2-0	1-1	2-3	2-0	0-1	2-3	0-1	2-2	0-0	0-0	0-0	2-0	0-0	1-1
Leyton Orient FC	0-0	1-2	2-1	0-1	1-2	2-1	4-1	1-0	2-1	0-0	■	2-3	0-0	1-3	0-0	1-1	3-0	0-0	0-1	1-2	0-1	2-0	0-0	
Lincoln City FC	0-0	1-3	5-0	1-2	4-1	1-0	1-1	1-1	1-2	2-1	0-0	■	1-1	3-0	1-1	2-0	1-3	1-1	2-1	0-1	2-1	0-1	2-1	4-2
Macclesfield Town	2-0	1-1	1-1	2-1	2-1	1-0	0-2	3-3	0-2	1-0	1-1		■	5-2	1-0	1-1	4-1	1-2	1-1	4-2	1-2	1-2	1-2	1-1
Mansfield Town FC	0-1	1-0	1-1	0-1	2-1	1-2	1-1	0-2	2-3	0-1	1-1	5-2	1-0	■	0-0	3-1	2-2	0-0	1-2	4-0	3-1	0-4	4-3	1-0
Northampton Town	1-0	1-0	0-0	3-2	3-1	0-3	2-1	3-4	2-1	1-0	2-1	1-0	2-0	1-0	■	0-1	1-1	0-1	3-0	2-0	2-1	3-0	3-0	
Peterborough United	1-2	0-0	0-2	1-0	2-1	4-2	3-1	2-1	2-1	2-1	2-1	2-2	1-0	1-0	0-1	■	2-0	3-3	0-5	4-1	1-0	2-3	0-2	2-0
Plymouth Argyle FC	4-1	3-3	4-2	0-0	0-0	1-1	1-1	1-1	1-1		5-0	1-1	3-2	2-1	2-1	2-1	■	1-1	1-1	0-0	3-1	1-0	2-2	2-0
Rochdale AFC	1-1	1-0	3-2	0-0	2-1	0-0	0-2	1-1	2-0	0-2	1-4	1-1	0-1	0-3	1-2	0-0		■	0-1	2-1	0-0	1-1	2-1	
Rotherham United	2-0	1-3	4-2	2-0	4-0	2-1	5-0	0-1	3-0	3-0	1-1	2-1	2-3	3-0	1-1	1-1	0-1		■	4-0	0-0	1-1	1-0	1-0
Shrewsbury Town	1-1	1-2	4-1	0-2	0-1	0-1	1-4	0-0	0-0	3-0	1-1	1-2	1-0	0-1	0-0	0-1	0-0	2-4	0-0	■	2-1	1-1	1-2	
Southend United FC	1-3	2-1	2-0	2-1	3-1	1-2	4-1	1-2	1-2	1-1	2-0	1-0	2-0	2-1	0-1	2-1	3-3	1-2	3-2		■	2-1	0-2	0-0
Swansea City FC	1-2	2-0	1-0	0-0	2-1	0-0	3-0	3-1	2-1	0-0	2-1	1-0	0-1	4-1	0-0	1-0	1-0	2-0	1-1	3-1		■	2-1	1-0
Torquay United FC	0-1	0-0	4-1	1-1	2-2	1-0	1-0	4-0	0-0	0-1	0-0	5-2	3-2	4-0	1-2	2-1	0-4	2-1	3-1	0-1	1-0		■	0-0
York City FC	1-0	0-0	1-1	1-2	2-2	0-0	0-0	2-0	2-1	1-1	2-1	2-0	0-2	0-1	0-1	0-0	0-0	0-3	1-2	1-0	2-2	1-0	2-2	■

Football League Division 3

		Pd	Wn	Dw	Ls	GF	GA	Pts	
1.	Swansea City FC (Swansea)	46	24	13	9	51	30	85	P
2.	Rotherham United (Rotherham)	46	24	12	10	72	36	84	P
3.	Northampton Town FC (Northampton)	46	25	7	14	63	45	82	P
4.	Darlington FC (Darlington)	46	21	16	9	66	36	79	PO
5.	Peterborough United FC (Peterborough)	46	22	12	12	63	54	78	POP
6.	Barnet FC (London)	46	21	12	13	59	53	75	PO
7.	Hartlepool United FC (Hartlepool)	46	21	9	16	60	49	72	PO
8.	Cheltenham Town FC (Cheltenham)	46	20	10	16	50	42	70	
9.	Torquay United FC (Torquay)	46	19	12	15	62	52	69	
10.	Rochdale AFC (Rochdale)	46	18	14	14	57	54	68	
11.	Brighton & Hove Albion FC (Brighton)	46	17	16	13	64	46	67	
12.	Plymouth Argyle FC (Plymouth)	46	16	18	12	55	51	66	
13.	Macclesfield Town FC (Macclesfield)	46	18	11	17	66	61	65	
14.	Hull City AFC (Kingston-upon-Hull)	46	15	14	17	43	43	59	
15.	Lincoln City FC (Lincoln)	46	15	14	17	67	69	59	
16.	Southend United FC (Southend-on-Sea)	46	15	11	20	53	61	56	
17.	Mansfield Town FC (Mansfield)	46	16	8	22	50	65	56	
18.	Halifax Town AFC (Halifax)	46	15	9	22	44	58	54	
19.	Leyton Orient FC (London)	46	13	13	20	47	52	52	
20.	York City FC (York)	46	12	16	18	39	53	52	
21.	Exeter City FC (Exeter)	46	11	11	24	46	72	44	
22.	Shrewsbury Town FC (Shrewsbury)	46	9	13	24	40	67	40	
23.	Carlisle United FC (Carlisle)	46	9	12	25	42	75	39	
24.	Chester City FC (Chester)	46	10	9	27	44	79	39	R
		1104	406	292	406	1303	1303	1510	

Promotion Play-offs

Peterborough United FC (Peterborough)	1-0	Darlington FC (Darlington)
Barnet FC (London)	1-2, 0-3	Peterborough United FC (Peterborough)
Hartlepool United FC (Hartlepool)	0-2, 0-1	Darlington FC (Darlington)

Promoted to Division 3: Kidderminster Harriers FC (Kidderminster)

F.A. CUP FINAL (Wembley Stadium, London – 20/05/2000 – 78,217)

CHELSEA FC (LONDON)	1-0	Aston Villa FC (Birmingham)

Di Matteo 73'

Chelsea: de Goey, Babayaro, Leboeuf, Desailly, Melchiot, Deschamps, Di Matteo, Poyet, Wise, Zola (Morris 90'), Weah (Flo 88').

Aston Villa: James, Barry, Southgate, Ehiogu, Wright (Hendrie 88'), Boateng, Taylor (Stone 79'), Merson, Delaney, Dublin, Carbone (Joachim 79').

Semi-finals

Bolton Wanderers FC (Bolton)	0-0 (aet)	Aston Villa FC (Birmingham)
Aston Villa won 4-1 on penalties.		
Newcastle United FC (Newcastle-upon-Tyne)	1-2	Chelsea FC (London)

Quarter-finals

Bolton Wanderers FC (Bolton)	1-0	Charlton Athletic FC (London)
Chelsea FC (London)	5-0	Gillingham FC (Gillingham)
Everton FC (Liverpool)	1-2	Aston Villa FC (Birmingham)
Tranmere Rovers FC (Birkenhead)	2-3	Newcastle United FC (Newcastle-upon-Tyne)

2000-01

F.A. Premiership 2000-01 Season	Arsenal	Aston Villa	Bradford City	Charlton Athletic	Chelsea	Coventry City	Derby County	Everton	Ipswich Town	Leeds United	Leicester City	Liverpool	Manchester City	Manchester United	Middlesbrough	Newcastle United	Southampton	Sunderland	Tottenham Hotspur	West Ham United
Arsenal FC	■	1-0	2-0	5-3	1-1	2-1	0-0	4-1	1-0	2-1	6-1	2-0	5-0	1-0	0-3	5-0	1-0	2-2	2-0	3-0
Aston Villa FC	0-0	■	2-0	2-1	1-1	3-2	4-1	2-1	2-1	1-2	2-1	0-3	2-2	0-1	1-1	1-1	0-0	0-0	2-0	2-2
Bradford City AFC	1-1	0-3	■	2-0	2-0	2-1	2-0	0-1	0-2	1-1	0-0	0-2	2-2	0-3	1-1	2-2	0-1	1-4	3-3	1-2
Charlton Athletic FC	1-0	3-3	2-0	■	2-0	2-2	2-1	1-0	2-1	1-2	2-0	0-4	4-0	3-3	1-0	2-0	1-1	0-1	1-0	1-1
Chelsea FC	2-2	1-0	3-0	0-1	■	6-1	4-1	2-1	4-1	1-1	0-2	3-0	2-1	1-1	2-1	3-1	1-0	2-4	3-0	4-2
Coventry City FC	0-1	1-1	0-0	2-2	0-0	■	2-0	1-3	0-1	0-0	1-0	0-2	1-1	1-2	1-3	0-2	1-1	1-0	2-1	0-3
Derby County FC	1-2	1-0	2-0	2-2	0-4	1-0	■	1-0	1-1	1-1	2-0	0-4	1-1	0-3	3-3	2-0	2-2	1-0	2-1	0-0
Everton FC	2-0	0-1	2-1	3-0	2-1	1-2	2-2	■	0-3	2-2	2-1	2-3	3-1	1-3	2-2	1-1	1-1	2-2	0-0	1-1
Ipswich Town FC	1-1	1-2	3-1	2-0	2-2	2-0	0-1	2-0	■	1-2	2-0	1-1	2-1	1-1	2-1	1-0	3-1	1-0	3-0	1-1
Leeds United AFC	1-0	1-2	6-1	3-1	2-0	1-0	0-0	2-0	1-2	■	3-1	4-3	1-2	1-1	1-1	1-3	2-0	2-0	4-3	0-1
Leicester City FC	0-0	0-0	1-2	3-1	2-1	1-3	2-1	1-1	2-1	3-1	■	2-0	1-2	0-3	0-3	1-1	1-0	2-0	4-2	2-1
Liverpool FC	4-0	3-1	1-0	3-0	2-2	4-1	1-1	3-1	0-1	1-2	1-0	■	3-2	2-0	0-0	3-0	2-1	1-1	3-1	3-0
Manchester City FC	0-4	1-3	2-0	1-4	1-2	1-2	0-0	5-0	2-3	0-4	0-1	1-1	■	0-1	1-1	0-1	0-1	4-2	0-1	1-0
Manchester United FC	6-1	2-0	6-0	2-1	3-3	4-2	0-1	1-0	2-0	3-0	2-0	0-1	1-1	■	2-1	2-0	5-0	3-0	2-0	3-1
Middlesbrough FC	0-1	1-1	2-2	0-0	1-0	1-1	4-0	1-2	1-2	1-2	0-3	1-0	1-1	0-2	■	1-3	0-1	0-0	1-1	2-1
Newcastle United FC	0-0	3-0	2-1	0-1	0-0	3-1	3-2	0-1	2-1	2-1	1-0	2-1	0-1	1-1	1-2	■	1-1	1-2	2-0	2-1
Southampton FC	3-2	2-0	2-0	0-0	3-2	1-2	1-0	1-0	0-3	1-0	3-3	0-2	2-1	1-3	2-0		■	0-1	2-0	2-3
Sunderland AFC	1-0	1-1	0-0	3-2	1-0	1-0	2-1	2-0	4-1	0-2	0-0	1-1	1-0	0-1	1-0	1-1	2-2	■	2-3	1-1
Tottenham Hotspur FC	1-1	0-0	2-1	0-0	0-3	3-0	3-1	3-2	3-1	1-2	3-0	2-1	0-0	3-1	0-0	4-2	0-0	2-1	■	1-0
West Ham United FC	1-2	1-1	1-1	5-0	0-2	1-1	3-1	0-2	0-1	0-2	0-1	1-1	4-1	2-2	1-0	1-0	3-0	0-2	0-0	■

	F.A. Premiership	Pd	Wn	Dw	Ls	GF	GA	Pts	
1.	MANCHESTER UNITED FC (MANCHESTER)	38	24	8	6	79	31	80	
2.	Arsenal FC (London)	38	20	10	8	63	38	70	
3.	Liverpool FC (Liverpool)	38	20	9	9	71	39	69	
4.	Leeds United AFC (Leeds)	38	20	8	10	64	43	68	
5.	Ipswich Town FC (Ipswich)	38	20	6	12	57	42	66	
6.	Chelsea FC (London)	38	17	10	11	68	45	61	
7.	Sunderland AFC (Sunderland)	38	15	12	11	46	41	57	
8.	Aston Villa FC (Birmingham)	38	13	15	10	46	43	54	
9.	Charlton Athletic FC (London)	38	14	10	14	50	57	52	
10.	Southampton FC (Southampton)	38	14	10	14	40	48	52	
11.	Newcastle United FC (Newcastle-upon-Tyne)	38	14	9	15	44	50	51	
12.	Tottenham Hotspur FC (London)	38	13	10	15	47	54	49	
13.	Leicester City FC (Leicester)	38	14	6	18	39	51	48	
14.	Middlesbrough FC (Middlesbrough)	38	9	15	14	44	44	42	
15.	West Ham United FC (London)	38	10	12	16	45	50	42	
16.	Everton FC (Liverpool)	38	11	9	18	45	59	42	
17.	Derby County FC (Derby)	38	10	12	16	37	59	42	
18.	Manchester City FC (Manchester)	38	8	10	20	41	65	34	R
19.	Coventry City FC (Coventry)	38	8	10	20	36	63	34	R
20.	Bradford City AFC (Bradford)	38	5	11	22	30	70	26	R
		760	279	202	279	992	992	1039	

Top Goalscorers

1)	Jimmy Floyd HASSELBAINK	(Chelsea FC)	23
2)	Marcus STEWART	(Ipswich Town FC)	19
3)	Thierry HENRY	(Arsenal FC)	17
	Mark VIDUKA	(Leeds United AFC)	17

Football League Division 1 2000-01 Season	Barnsley	Birmingham City	Blackburn Rovers	Bolton Wanderers	Burnley	Crewe Alexandra	Crystal Palace	Fulham	Gillingham	Grimsby Town	Huddersfield Town	Norwich City	Nottingham Forest	Portsmouth	Preston North End	Q.P.R.	Sheffield United	Sheffield Wed.	Stockport County	Tranmere Rovers	Watford	W.B.A.	Wimbledon	Wolves
Barnsley FC		2-3	1-2	0-1	1-0	3-0	1-0	0-0	3-1	2-0	3-1	1-0	3-4	1-0	0-4	4-2	0-0	1-0	0-2	1-1	0-1	4-1	0-1	1-2
Birmingham City FC	4-1		0-2	1-1	3-2	2-0	2-1	1-3	1-0	1-0	2-1	2-1	0-2	0-0	3-1	0-0	1-0	1-2	4-0	2-0	2-0	2-1	0-3	0-1
Blackburn Rovers FC	0-0	2-1		1-1	5-0	1-0	2-0	1-2	1-2	2-0	2-0	3-2	3-0	3-1	3-2	0-0	1-1	2-0	2-1	3-2	3-4	1-0	1-1	2-0
Bolton Wanderers FC	2-0	2-2	1-4		1-1	4-1	3-3	0-2	3-3	2-2	2-2	1-0	0-0	2-0	2-0	3-1	1-1	2-0	1-1	2-0	2-1	0-1	2-2	2-1
Burnley FC	2-1	0-0	0-2	0-2		1-0	1-2	2-1	1-1	1-1	1-0	2-0	1-0	1-1	3-0	2-1	2-0	1-0	2-1	2-0	1-1	1-0	1-2	
Crewe Alexandra FC	2-2	0-2	0-0	2-1	4-1		1-1	1-2	2-1	2-0	1-0	0-0	1-0	1-0	1-3	2-2	1-0	1-0	1-2	3-1	2-0	0-1	0-4	2-0
Crystal Palace FC	1-0	1-2	2-3	0-2	0-1	1-0		0-2	2-2	0-1	0-0	1-1	2-3	2-3	0-2	1-1	0-1	4-1	2-2	3-2	1-0	2-2	3-1	0-2
Fulham FC	5-1	0-1	2-1	1-1	3-1	2-0	3-1		3-0	2-1	3-0	2-0	1-0	3-1	0-1	2-0	1-1	1-1	4-1	3-1	5-0	0-0	1-1	2-0
Gillingham FC	0-0	1-2	1-1	2-2	0-0	0-1	4-1	0-2		1-0	2-1	4-3	1-3	1-1	4-0	0-1	4-1	2-0	1-3	2-1	0-3	1-2	0-0	1-0
Grimsby Town FC	0-2	1-1	1-4	0-1	1-0	1-3	2-2	1-0	1-0		1-0	2-0	0-2	2-1	1-2	3-1	0-1	0-1	1-1	3-1	2-1	2-0	1-1	0-2
Huddersfield Town	1-1	1-2	0-1	2-3	0-1	3-1	1-2	1-2	2-3	0-0		2-0	1-1	4-1	0-0	2-1	2-1	0-0	0-0	3-0	1-2	0-2	0-2	3-0
Norwich City FC	0-0	1-0	1-1	0-2	2-3	1-1	0-0	0-1	1-0	2-1	1-1		0-0	0-0	1-2	1-0	4-2	1-0	4-0	1-0	2-1	0-1	1-2	1-0
Nottingham Forest	1-0	1-2	2-1	0-2	5-0	1-0	0-3	0-3	0-1	3-1	1-3	0-0		2-0	3-1	1-1	2-0	0-1	1-0	3-0	1-0	0-2	1-0	0-0
Portsmouth FC	3-0	1-1	2-2	1-2	2-0	2-1	2-4	1-1	0-0	1-1	1-1	2-0	0-2		0-1	1-1	0-0	2-1	2-1	2-0	1-3	0-1	2-1	3-1
Preston North End	1-2	0-2	0-1	0-2	2-1	2-1	2-0	1-1	0-0	1-2	0-0	1-0	1-1	1-0		5-0	3-0	2-0	1-1	1-0	3-2	2-1	1-1	2-0
Queen's Park Rangers	2-0	0-0	1-3	1-1	0-1	1-0	1-1	0-2	2-2	0-1	1-1	2-3	1-0	1-1	0-0		1-3	1-2	0-3	2-0	1-1	2-0	2-1	2-2
Sheffield United FC	1-2	3-1	2-0	1-0	1-0	1-0	1-1	1-1	1-2	3-2	3-0	1-1	1-3	2-0	3-2	1-1		1-1	1-0	2-0	0-1	2-0	0-1	1-0
Sheffield Wednesday	2-1	1-0	1-1	0-3	2-0	0-0	4-1	3-3	2-1	1-0	2-3	3-2	0-1	0-0	1-3	5-2	1-2		2-4	1-0	2-3	1-2	0-5	0-1
Stockport County	2-0	2-0	0-0	4-3	0-0	3-0	0-1	2-0	2-2	1-1	0-0	1-3	1-2	1-1	0-1	2-2	0-2	2-1		1-1	2-3	0-0	2-2	1-1
Tranmere Rovers	2-3	1-0	1-1	0-1	2-3	1-3	1-1	1-4	3-2	2-0	2-0	0-1	2-2	1-1	1-1	1-1	1-0	2-0	2-1		2-0	2-2	0-4	0-2
Watford FC	1-0	2-0	0-1	1-0	0-1	3-0	2-2	1-3	0-0	4-0	1-2	4-1	3-0	2-2	2-3	3-1	4-1	1-3	2-2	1-1		3-3	3-1	3-2
West Bromwich Alb.	1-0	1-1	1-0	0-2	1-1	2-2	1-0	1-3	3-1	0-1	1-1	2-3	3-0	2-0	3-1	2-1	2-1	1-2	1-1	2-1	3-0		3-1	1-0
Wimbledon FC	1-1	3-1	0-2	0-1	0-2	3-3	1-0	0-3	4-4	2-2	1-1	0-0	2-1	1-1	3-1	5-0	0-0	4-1	2-0	0-0	0-0	0-1		1-1
Wolverhampton W.	2-0	0-1	0-0	0-2	1-0	0-0	1-3	0-0	1-1	2-0	0-1	4-0	2-0	1-1	0-1	1-1	0-0	1-1	3-2	1-2	2-2	3-1	0-1	

Football League Division 1

		Pd	Wn	Dw	Ls	GF	GA	Pts	
1.	Fulham FC (London)	46	30	11	5	90	32	101	P
2.	Blackburn Rovers FC (Blackburn)	46	25	13	7	76	39	91	P
3.	Bolton Wanderers FC (Bolton)	46	24	15	7	76	45	87	POP
4.	Preston North End FC (Preston)	46	23	9	14	64	52	78	PO
5.	Birmingham City FC (Birmingham)	46	23	9	14	59	48	78	PO
6.	West Bromwich Albion FC (West Bromwich)	46	21	11	14	60	52	74	PO
7.	Burnley FC (Burnley)	46	21	9	16	50	54	72	
8.	Wimbledon FC (London)	46	17	18	11	71	50	69	
9.	Watford FC (Watford)	46	20	9	17	76	67	69	
10.	Sheffield United FC (Sheffield)	46	19	11	16	52	49	68	
11.	Nottingham Forest FC (Nottingham)	46	20	8	18	55	53	68	
12.	Wolverhampton Wanderers FC (Wolverhampton)	46	14	13	19	45	48	55	
13.	Gillingham FC (Gillingham)	46	13	16	17	61	66	55	
14.	Crewe Alexandra FC (Crewe)	46	15	10	21	47	62	55	
15.	Norwich City FC (Norwich)	46	14	12	20	46	58	54	
16.	Barnsley FC (Barnsley)	46	15	9	22	49	62	54	
17.	Sheffield Wednesday FC (Sheffield)	46	15	8	23	52	71	53	
18.	Grimsby Town FC (Cleethorpes)	46	14	10	22	43	62	52	
19.	Stockport County FC (Stockport)	46	11	18	17	58	65	51	
20.	Portsmouth FC (Portsmouth)	46	10	19	17	47	59	49	
21.	Crystal Palace FC (London)	46	12	13	21	57	70	49	
22.	Huddersfield Town AFC (Huddersfield)	46	11	15	20	48	57	48	R
23.	Queen's Park Rangers FC (London)	46	7	19	20	45	75	40	R
24.	Tranmere Rovers FC (Birkenhead)	46	9	11	26	46	77	38	R
		1104	404	296	404	1373	1373	1508	

Promotion Play-offs

Bolton Wanderers FC (Bolton)	3-0	Preston North End FC (Preston)
Birmingham City FC (Birmingham)	1-0, 1-2 (aet)	Preston North End FC (Preston)
	(Preston North End won 4-2 on penalties)	
West Bromwich Albion FC (West Bromwich)	2-2, 0-3	Bolton Wanderers FC (Bolton)

Football League Division 2 2000-01 Season

	Bournemouth	Brentford	Bristol City	Bristol Rovers	Bury	Cambridge United	Colchester United	Luton Town	Millwall	Northampton Town	Notts County	Oldham Athletic	Oxford United	Peterborough United	Port Vale	Reading	Rotherham United	Stoke City	Swansea City	Swindon Town	Walsall	Wigan Athletic	Wrexham	Wycombe Wanderers
AFC Bournemouth		2-0	4-0	1-2	1-0	1-1	2-2	3-2	1-2	2-0	0-1	1-1	4-3	2-1	1-1	1-2	0-1	1-0	2-0	3-0	2-2	0-0	1-2	2-0
Brentford FC	3-2		2-1	2-6	3-1	2-2	1-0	2-2	1-1	1-1	3-1	1-1	3-0	1-0	1-1	1-2	0-3	2-2	0-0	0-1	2-1	2-2	1-0	0-0
Bristol City FC	3-3	1-2		3-2	4-1	6-2	1-1	3-1	2-1	2-0	4-0	2-2	0-0	2-1	1-1	4-0	0-1	1-2	3-1	0-1	1-3	1-1	2-1	1-2
Bristol Rovers FC	1-1	0-0	1-1		2-0	2-1	2-0	3-3	1-2	0-1	0-0	0-2	6-2	1-2	0-3	2-2	1-1	0-3	1-0	0-0	0-0	0-0	4-0	1-2
Bury FC	2-5	0-1	0-1	1-0		0-1	0-0	1-1	2-1	1-0	1-1	1-1	3-1	2-1	2-0	0-2	0-0	1-0	3-0	1-0	2-0	0-1	1-4	1-1
Cambridge United	0-2	1-1	1-0	0-3	0-1		2-1	2-1	1-5	1-2	2-2	2-0	1-0	0-0	4-0	1-1	6-1	1-1	3-3	0-1	1-1	1-2	2-3	1-0
Colchester United	3-1	3-1	4-0	2-1	1-1	2-0		3-1	0-1	0-2	2-0	1-1	3-2	2-2	0-1	2-1	0-1	0-1	3-0	0-1	0-2	0-2	1-1	0-0
Luton Town FC	1-0	3-1	0-3	0-0	1-2	1-0	0-3		0-1	0-2	0-1	0-0	1-1	3-2	1-1	1-1	0-1	1-2	5-3	2-3	0-0	0-2	3-4	1-2
Millwall FC	0-1	1-0	1-1	3-0	4-0	3-1	6-1	1-0		0-1	2-3	5-0	5-0	0-0	1-0	2-0	4-0	2-0	1-0	1-0	2-0	3-1	1-0	1-2
Northampton Town	0-3	1-1	2-0	2-1	2-1	0-2	2-0	0-1	3-3		1-0	2-1	0-1	0-0	0-2	2-0	2-2	2-1	0-1	0-3	1-0	2-2	2-2	
Notts County FC	0-2	2-2	2-1	1-1	1-0	0-1	2-2	1-3	3-4	2-0		1-0	2-1	3-3	0-1	3-2	4-1	2-2	2-0	3-2	2-2	2-2	1-0	0-2
Oldham Athletic AFC	2-1	3-0	0-0	1-0	1-1	1-3	1-1	2-0	0-1	2-1	0-1		3-2	1-4	4-1	0-2	2-3	1-2	1-1	1-0	0-0	2-1	5-1	2-0
Oxford United FC	1-2	0-1	0-1	0-1	1-0	1-1	0-1	0-0	0-2	3-1	2-3	0-1		0-1	1-1	0-2	4-3	1-1	3-1	0-2	2-1	0-2	3-4	1-2
Peterborough United	1-2	1-1	2-1	2-2	1-1	4-1	3-1	1-1	1-4	1-2	1-0	0-0	4-2		2-0	1-0	1-1	0-4	0-2	4-0	2-0	1-0	3-2	
Port Vale FC	2-1	1-1	1-2	1-0	1-1	4-2	3-1	3-0	1-1	2-2	2-3	0-0	3-0	5-0		0-1	0-2	1-1	1-0	3-0	0-2	0-0	1-1	0-1
Reading FC	3-3	4-0	1-3	1-0	4-1	3-0	0-1	4-1	3-4	1-1	2-1	5-0	4-3	1-1	1-0		2-0	3-3	5-1	2-0	2-2	1-0	4-1	2-0
Rotherham United	3-1	2-1	1-1	3-0	1-2	3-0	3-2	1-1	3-2	1-0	0-0	3-0	3-1	3-0	3-2	1-3		2-1	4-2	4-3	2-3	1-1	2-0	1-0
Stoke City FC	2-1	1-0	1-0	4-1	2-1	2-3	3-1	1-3	3-2	1-1	0-1	0-1	4-0	3-0	1-1	0-0	1-1		1-2	4-1	0-0	2-0	3-1	0-0
Swansea City FC	0-3	6-0	2-2	0-0	0-2	1-1	0-2	4-0	0-0	1-1	0-1	1-2	1-2	2-2	0-1	0-1	0-0	2-1		0-0	3-1	0-0	0-1	3-1
Swindon Town FC	1-1	2-3	1-1	1-3	3-0	3-1	0-0	1-3	0-2	1-1	1-2	3-0	2-1	2-1	0-1	0-1	2-1	0-3	1-1		1-4	2-2	2-2	1-1
Walsall FC	1-1	3-2	0-0	2-1	1-2	3-1	0-1	3-1	0-0	3-0	5-1	3-2	3-2	1-1	2-1	2-1	1-1	3-0	5-1	1-0		2-0	2-3	5-1
Wigan Athletic AFC	1-1	1-3	0-0	0-0	1-0	2-1	3-1	2-1	1-0	2-1	1-1	3-1	3-2	1-0	1-0	1-1	0-1	1-1	2-0	0-0	1-1		0-0	2-1
Wrexham AFC	2-2	2-1	0-2	1-0	0-1	2-2	1-1	3-1	1-1	3-0	1-1	5-3	2-1	1-0	1-2	1-3	1-2	1-0	1-1	0-1	1-3			0-0
Wycombe Wanderers	0-3	0-0	1-2	0-1	2-1	0-2	1-1	1-1	0-0	1-0	3-1	2-1	3-1	2-0	0-1	1-1	0-1	0-1	2-1	0-0	3-1	1-2	1-1	

Football League Division 2	Pd	Wn	Dw	Ls	GF	GA	Pts	
1. Millwall FC (London)	46	28	9	9	89	38	93	P
2. Rotherham United FC (Rotherham)	46	27	10	9	79	55	91	P
3. Reading FC (Reading)	46	25	11	10	86	52	86	PO
4. Walsall FC (Walsall)	46	23	12	11	79	50	81	POP
5. Stoke City FC (Stoke-on-Trent)	46	21	14	11	74	49	77	PO
6. Wigan Athletic AFC (Wigan)	46	19	18	9	53	42	75	PO
7. AFC Bournemouth (Bournemouth)	46	20	13	13	79	55	73	
8. Notts County FC (Nottingham)	46	19	12	15	62	66	69	
9. Bristol City FC (Bristol)	46	18	14	14	70	56	68	
10. Wrexham AFC (Wrexham)	46	17	12	17	65	71	63	
11. Port Vale FC (Stoke-on-Trent)	46	16	14	16	55	49	62	
12. Peterborough United FC (Peterborough)	46	15	14	17	61	66	59	
13. Wycombe Wanderers FC (High Wycombe)	46	15	14	17	46	53	59	
14. Brentford FC (London)	46	14	17	15	56	70	59	
15. Oldham Athletic AFC (Oldham)	46	15	13	18	53	65	58	
16. Bury FC (Bury)	46	16	10	20	45	59	58	
17. Colchester United FC (Colchester)	46	15	12	19	55	59	57	
18. Northampton Town FC (Northampton)	46	15	12	19	46	59	57	
19. Cambridge United FC (Cambridge)	46	14	11	21	61	77	53	
20. Swindon Town FC (Swindon)	46	13	13	20	47	65	52	
21. Bristol Rovers FC (Bristol)	46	12	15	19	53	57	51	R
22. Luton Town FC (Luton)	46	9	13	24	52	80	40	R
23. Swansea City FC (Swansea)	46	8	13	25	47	73	37	R
24. Oxford United FC (Oxford)	46	7	6	33	53	100	27	R
	1104	401	302	401	1466	1466	1505	

Promotion Play-offs

Walsall FC (Walsall)	3-2	Reading FC (Reading)
Stoke City FC (Stoke-on-Trent)	0-0, 2-4	Walsall FC (Walsall)
Wigan Athletic AFC (Wigan)	0-0, 1-2	Reading FC (Reading)

Football League Division 3 — 2000-01 Season

	Barnet	Blackpool	Brighton & H.A.	Cardiff City	Carlisle United	Cheltenham T.	Chesterfield	Darlington	Exeter City	Halifax Town	Hartlepool	Hull City	Kidderminster H.	Leyton Orient	Lincoln City	Macclesfield T.	Mansfield Town	Plymouth Argyle	Rochdale	Scunthorpe Utd.	Shrewsbury T.	Southend United	Torquay United	York City
Barnet FC	■	7-0	0-1	2-2	0-1	2-2	1-1	3-0	1-1	1-0	1-3	1-1	0-0	1-2	4-3	0-2	3-3	1-1	3-0	4-2	3-0	2-1	2-3	2-0
Blackpool FC	3-2	■	0-2	1-0	3-2	2-2	1-3	2-1	3-0	0-1	1-2	3-1	5-1	2-2	2-0	2-1	2-2	1-0	3-1	6-0	0-1	2-2	5-0	1-0
Brighton & Hove Alb.	4-1	1-0	■	1-0	4-1	3-0	1-0	2-0	2-0	2-1	4-2	3-0	0-2	2-0	2-0	4-1	2-0	2-0	2-1	0-0	4-0	0-2	6-2	1-1
Cardiff City AFC	1-0	3-1	1-1	■	4-1	3-1	3-3	2-0	6-1	4-2	3-2	2-0	0-0	1-1	3-2	2-0	2-0	4-1	0-0	3-0	3-1	2-2	2-1	4-0
Carlisle United FC	0-2	1-0	0-0	2-2	■	1-1	2-4	0-2	0-1	2-2	2-3	0-0	2-0	1-0	1-1	1-0	2-1	1-1	1-2	1-2	1-0	3-1	1-0	1-1
Cheltenham Town	4-3	0-1	3-1	3-1	1-0	■	0-1	1-0	1-0	4-2	1-2	0-1	1-3	1-1	2-1	1-1	2-2	5-2	0-2	1-0	1-1	2-1	2-0	1-1
Chesterfield FC	1-2	2-1	1-0	2-2	1-1	2-0	■	2-0	2-0	3-0	0-0	1-0	1-0	4-1	1-2	4-1	4-0	2-1	1-1	1-0	3-0	1-1	3-0	4-1
Darlington FC	1-0	1-3	1-2	2-0	1-0	1-0	0-3	■	1-1	0-1	1-1	0-2	1-2	1-1	3-0	1-1	1-0	1-2	2-1	3-0	1-1	2-0	1-1	2-0
Exeter City FC	1-0	2-0	1-0	1-2	1-0	0-2	1-1	1-1	■	0-0	1-1	0-1	2-1	2-3	0-0	0-0	0-0	0-2	0-1	2-1	1-0	2-2	1-1	3-1
Halifax Town AFC	3-0	1-2	0-3	1-2	0-0	1-2	2-2	1-0	3-1	■	0-1	0-2	3-2	2-2	1-1	3-0	3-4	2-0	1-2	3-4	0-0	0-1	2-1	1-3
Hartlepool United FC	6-1	3-1	2-2	3-1	2-2	0-0	1-2	2-1	2-0	1-1	■	0-1	3-1	1-0	2-2	1-1	1-1	1-1	1-0	1-3	1-0	3-1	1-0	1-0
Hull City AFC	2-1	0-1	0-2	2-0	2-1	0-2	3-1	2-0	2-1	1-0	0-0	■	0-0	1-0	1-1	1-1	3-2	1-1	0-0	1-1	1-1	1-2	0-0	1-0
Kidderminster Harr.	2-1	1-4	0-2	2-4	0-1	1-1	0-2	1-0	0-0	2-1	0-1	2-2	■	2-1	1-3	2-1	1-0	3-0	0-0	0-0	3-1	2-1	2-0	3-1
Leyton Orient FC	3-1	1-0	2-1	1-0	0-0	2-0	1-0	2-1	3-0	3-1	2-2	0-0	2-0	■	1-0	2-1	1-1	1-1	1-1	2-0	0-2	0-2	1-1	1-1
Lincoln City FC	2-1	1-1	2-0	2-0	1-1	1-0	1-1	2-2	3-1	1-1	0-2	2-0	3-3	2-3	■	1-2	0-2	2-1	1-1	1-1	2-2	3-0	1-2	2-1
Macclesfield Town	3-0	2-1	0-0	2-5	1-0	2-1	1-2	1-1	0-2	0-1	0-1	1-0	0-2	2-0	0-1	■	3-1	0-0	1-1	2-2	1-0	2-1	2-1	0-1
Mansfield Town FC	4-1	0-1	2-0	3-1	1-2	0-1	3-2	1-1	5-1	4-3	1-1	2-1	2-0	2-3	4-4	2-0	■	0-0	1-0	1-0	1-0	1-0	0-0	1-3
Plymouth Argyle FC	2-3	2-0	0-2	2-1	2-0	0-0	3-0	1-1	1-0	1-0	2-1	4-0	1-0	1-0	0-1	2-0	2-0	■	0-0	1-0	3-1	3-3	3-1	1-0
Rochdale AFC	0-0	1-0	1-1	1-1	6-0	1-1	2-2	1-1	3-0	1-0	2-1	1-0	0-0	3-1	3-1	2-2	1-0	2-1	■	3-2	1-7	1-0	2-1	1-0
Scunthorpe United	2-1	1-0	2-1	0-2	3-0	1-1	1-1	1-1	0-2	1-0	3-0	0-1	2-1	1-2	1-1	2-2	6-0	4-1	0-0	■	2-0	1-1	3-0	4-0
Shrewsbury Town	3-2	1-0	3-0	0-4	0-1	1-0	0-0	1-0	2-0	2-1	1-1	1-1	0-1	1-0	2-2	2-1	4-1	0-4	0-2	1-0	■	0-1	1-1	2-0
Southend United FC	2-0	0-3	2-0	1-1	1-1	0-1	3-2	0-2	1-1	0-3	2-1	1-1	1-1	0-1	1-0	3-1	3-1	2-2	3-0	1-0	0-0	■	1-1	1-0
Torquay United FC	2-1	3-2	0-1	1-4	4-2	1-2	0-0	2-1	2-1	1-2	1-0	1-1	1-1	1-2	1-1	2-0	2-2	1-1	1-0	0-2	0-0	1-1	■	2-2
York City FC	1-0	0-2	0-1	3-3	0-0	0-2	0-1	2-0	0-3	2-1	1-1	0-0	1-0	1-1	0-0	1-3	2-1	1-2	0-2	2-0	2-1	1-0	3-2	■

Football League Division 3

		Pd	Wn	Dw	Ls	GF	GA	Pts	
1.	Brighton & Hove Albion FC (Brighton)	46	28	8	10	73	35	92	P
2.	Cardiff City AFC (Cardiff)	46	23	13	10	95	58	82	P
3.	Chesterfield FC (Chesterfield)	46	25	14	7	79	42	80	P -9
4.	Hartlepool United FC (Hartlepool)	46	21	14	11	71	54	77	PO
5.	Leyton Orient FC (London)	46	20	15	11	59	51	75	PO
6.	Hull City AFC (Kingston-upon-Hull)	46	19	17	10	47	39	74	PO
7.	Blackpool FC (Blackpool)	46	22	6	18	74	58	72	POP
8.	Rochdale AFC (Rochdale)	46	18	17	11	59	48	71	
9.	Cheltenham Town FC (Cheltenham)	46	18	14	14	59	52	68	
10.	Scunthorpe United FC (Scunthorpe)	46	18	11	17	62	52	65	
11.	Southend United FC (Southend-on-Sea)	46	15	18	13	55	53	63	
12.	Mansfield Town FC (Mansfield)	46	15	13	18	64	72	58	
13.	Plymouth Argyle FC (Plymouth)	46	15	13	18	54	61	58	
14.	Macclesfield Town FC (Macclesfield)	46	14	14	18	51	62	56	
15.	Shrewsbury Town FC (Shrewsbury)	46	15	10	21	49	65	55	
16.	Kidderminster Harriers FC (Kidderminster)	46	13	14	19	47	61	53	
17.	York City FC (York)	46	13	13	20	42	63	52	
18.	Lincoln City FC (Lincoln)	46	12	15	19	58	66	51	
19.	Exeter City FC (Exeter)	46	12	14	20	40	58	50	
20.	Darlington FC (Darlington)	46	12	13	21	44	56	49	
21.	Torquay United FC (Torquay)	46	12	13	21	52	77	49	
22.	Carlisle United FC (Carlisle)	46	11	15	20	42	65	48	
23.	Halifax Town AFC (Halifax)	46	12	11	23	54	68	47	
24.	Barnet FC (London)	46	12	9	25	67	81	45	R
		1104	395	314	395	1397	1397	1490	

Note: Chesterfield FC had 9 points deducted for "financial irregularities".

Promotion Play-offs

Blackpool FC (Blackpool)	4-2	Leyton Orient FC (London)
Blackpool FC (Blackpool)	2-0, 3-1	Hartlepool United FC (Hartlepool)
Hull City AFC (Kingston-upon-Hull)	1-0, 0-2	Leyton Orient FC (London)

Promoted to Division 3: Rushden & Diamonds FC (Irthlingborough)

F.A. CUP FINAL   (Millennium Stadium, Cardiff – 12/05/2001 – 74,200)

LIVERPOOL FC (LIVERPOOL)	2-1	Arsenal FC (London)
Owen 83', 88'		*Ljungberg 72'*

Liverpool: Westerveld, Babbel, Henchoz, Hyypia, Carragher, Murphy (Berger 77'), Gerrard, Hamann (McAllister 60'), Smicer (Fowler 77'), Heskey, Owen.

Arsenal: Seaman, Dixon (Bergkamp 90'), Keown, Adams, Pires, Grimandi, Vieira, Ljungberg (Kanu 85'), Wiltord (Parlour 76'), Henry.

Semi-finals

Arsenal FC (London)	2-1	Tottenham Hotspur FC (London)
Wycombe Wanderers FC (High Wycombe)	1-2	Liverpool FC (Liverpool)

Quarter-finals

Arsenal FC (London)	3-0	Blackburn Rovers FC (Blackburn)
Leicester City FC (Leicester)	1-2	Wycombe Wanderers FC (High Wycombe)
Tranmere Rovers FC (Birkenhead)	2-4	Liverpool FC (Liverpool)
West Ham United FC (London)	2-3	Tottenham Hotspur FC (London)

2001-02

F.A. Premiership 2001-02 Season	Arsenal	Aston Villa	Blackburn Rovers	Bolton Wanderers	Charlton Athletic	Chelsea	Derby County	Everton	Fulham	Ipswich Town	Leeds United	Leicester City	Liverpool	Manchester United	Middlesbrough	Newcastle United	Southampton	Sunderland	Tottenham Hotspur	West Ham United
Arsenal FC	■	3-2	3-3	1-1	2-4	2-1	1-0	4-3	4-1	2-0	1-2	4-0	1-1	3-1	2-1	1-3	1-1	3-0	2-1	2-0
Aston Villa FC	1-2	■	2-0	3-2	1-0	1-1	2-1	0-0	2-0	2-1	0-1	0-2	1-2	1-1	0-0	1-1	2-1	0-0	1-1	2-1
Blackburn Rovers FC	2-3	3-0	■	1-1	4-1	0-0	0-1	1-0	3-0	2-1	1-2	0-0	1-1	2-2	0-1	2-2	2-0	0-3	2-1	7-1
Bolton Wanderers FC	0-2	3-2	1-1	■	0-0	2-2	1-3	2-2	0-0	4-1	0-3	2-2	2-1	0-4	1-0	0-4	0-1	0-2	1-1	1-0
Charlton Athletic FC	0-3	1-2	0-2	1-2	■	2-1	1-0	1-2	1-1	3-2	0-2	2-0	0-2	0-2	0-0	1-1	1-1	2-2	3-1	4-4
Chelsea FC	1-1	1-3	0-0	5-1	0-1	■	2-1	3-0	3-2	2-1	2-0	2-0	4-0	0-3	2-2	1-1	2-4	4-0	4-0	5-1
Derby County FC	0-2	3-1	2-1	1-0	1-1	1-1	■	3-4	0-1	1-3	0-1	2-3	0-1	2-2	0-1	2-3	1-0	0-1	1-0	0-0
Everton FC	0-1	3-2	1-2	3-1	0-3	0-0	1-0	■	2-1	1-2	0-0	2-2	1-3	0-2	2-0	1-3	2-0	1-0	1-1	5-0
Fulham FC	1-3	0-0	2-0	3-0	0-0	1-1	0-0	2-0	■	1-1	0-0	0-0	0-2	2-3	2-1	3-1	2-1	2-0	0-2	0-1
Ipswich Town FC	0-2	0-0	1-1	1-2	0-1	0-0	3-1	0-0	1-0	■	1-2	2-0	0-6	0-1	1-0	0-1	1-3	5-0	2-1	2-3
Leeds United AFC	1-1	1-1	3-1	0-0	0-0	0-0	3-0	3-2	0-1	2-0	■	2-2	0-4	3-4	1-0	3-4	2-0	2-0	2-1	3-0
Leicester City FC	1-3	2-2	2-1	0-5	1-1	2-3	0-3	0-0	0-0	1-1	0-2	■	1-4	0-1	1-2	0-0	0-4	1-0	2-1	1-1
Liverpool FC	1-2	1-3	4-3	1-1	2-0	1-0	2-0	1-1	0-0	5-0	1-1	1-0	■	3-1	2-0	3-0	1-1	1-0	1-0	2-1
Manchester United FC	0-1	1-0	2-1	1-2	0-0	0-3	5-0	4-1	3-2	4-0	1-1	2-0	0-1	■	0-1	3-1	6-1	4-1	4-0	0-1
Middlesbrough FC	0-4	2-1	1-3	1-1	0-0	0-2	5-1	1-0	2-1	0-0	2-2	1-0	1-2	0-1	■	1-4	1-3	2-0	1-1	2-0
Newcastle United FC	0-2	3-0	2-1	3-2	3-0	1-2	1-0	6-2	1-1	2-2	3-1	1-0	0-2	4-3	3-0	■	3-1	1-1	0-2	3-1
Southampton FC	0-2	1-3	1-2	0-0	1-0	0-2	2-0	0-1	1-1	3-3	0-1	2-2	2-0	1-3	1-1	3-1	■	2-0	1-0	2-0
Sunderland AFC	1-1	1-1	1-0	1-0	2-2	0-0	1-1	1-0	1-1	1-0	2-0	2-1	0-1	1-3	0-1	0-1	1-1	■	1-2	1-0
Tottenham Hotspur FC	1-1	0-0	1-0	3-2	0-1	2-3	3-1	1-1	4-0	1-2	2-1	2-1	1-0	3-5	2-1	1-3	2-0	2-1	■	1-1
West Ham United FC	1-1	1-1	2-0	2-1	2-0	2-1	4-0	1-0	0-2	3-1	0-0	1-0	1-1	3-5	1-0	3-0	2-0	3-0	0-1	■

	F.A. Premiership	Pd	Wn	Dw	Ls	GF	GA	Pts	
1.	ARSENAL FC (LONDON)	38	26	9	3	79	36	87	
2.	Liverpool FC (Liverpool)	38	24	8	6	67	30	80	
3.	Manchester United FC (Manchester)	38	24	5	9	87	45	77	
4.	Newcastle United FC (Newcastle-upon-Tyne)	38	21	8	9	74	52	71	
5.	Leeds United AFC (Leeds)	38	18	12	8	53	37	66	
6.	Chelsea FC (London)	38	17	13	8	66	38	64	
7.	West Ham United FC (London)	38	15	8	15	48	57	53	
8.	Aston Villa FC (Birmingham)	38	12	14	12	46	47	50	
9.	Tottenham Hotspur FC (London)	38	14	8	16	49	53	50	
10.	Blackburn Rovers FC (Blackburn)	38	12	10	16	55	51	46	
11.	Southampton FC (Southampton)	38	12	9	17	46	54	45	
12.	Middlesbrough FC (Middlesbrough)	38	12	9	17	35	47	45	
13.	Fulham FC (London)	38	10	14	14	36	44	44	
14.	Charlton Athletic FC (London)	38	10	14	14	38	49	44	
15.	Everton FC (Liverpool)	38	11	10	17	45	57	43	
16.	Bolton Wanderers FC (Bolton)	38	9	13	16	44	62	40	
17.	Sunderland AFC (Sunderland)	38	10	10	18	29	51	40	
18.	Ipswich Town FC (Ipswich)	38	9	9	20	41	64	36	R
19.	Derby County FC (Derby)	38	8	6	24	33	63	30	R
20.	Leicester City FC (Leicester)	38	5	13	20	30	64	28	R
		760	279	202	279	1001	1001	1039	

Top Goalscorers

1)	Thierry HENRY	(Arsenal FC)	24
2)	Jimmy Floyd HASSELBAINK	(Chelsea FC)	23
	Alan SHEARER	(Newcastle United FC)	23
	Ruud VAN NISTELROOY	(Manchester United FC)	23

Football League Division 1 2001-02 Season	Barnsley	Birmingham City	Bradford City	Burnley	Coventry City	Crewe Alexandra	Crystal Palace	Gillingham	Grimsby Town	Manchester City	Millwall	Norwich City	Nottingham Forest	Portsmouth	Preston North End	Rotherham United	Sheffield United	Sheffield Wed.	Stockport County	Walsall	Watford	W.B.A.	Wimbledon	Wolves
Barnsley FC		1-3	3-3	1-1	1-1	2-0	1-4	4-1	0-0	0-3	1-1	0-2	2-1	1-4	2-1	1-1	1-1	3-0	2-2	4-1	2-0	3-2	1-1	1-0
Birmingham City FC	1-0		4-0	2-3	2-0	3-1	1-0	2-1	4-0	1-2	4-0	4-0	1-1	1-1	0-1	2-2	2-0	2-0	2-1	1-0	3-2	0-1	0-2	2-2
Bradford City AFC	4-0	1-3		2-3	2-1	2-0	1-2	5-1	3-2	0-2	1-2	0-1	2-1	3-1	0-1	3-1	1-2	0-2	2-4	2-0	4-3	0-1	3-3	0-3
Burnley FC	3-3	0-1	1-1		1-0	3-3	1-0	2-0	1-0	2-4	0-0	1-1	1-1	2-1	3-0	2-0	1-2	3-2	5-2	1-0	0-2	3-2	0-0	2-3
Coventry City FC	4-0	1-1	4-0	0-2		1-0	2-0	1-2	0-1	4-3	0-1	2-1	0-0	2-0	2-2	2-0	1-0	2-0	0-0	2-1	0-2	0-1	3-1	0-1
Crewe Alexandra FC	2-0	0-0	2-2	1-2	1-6		0-0	0-0	2-0	1-3	1-0	1-0	0-3	1-1	2-1	2-0	2-2	0-0	0-0	1-1	1-1	0-4	1-4	1-4
Crystal Palace FC	1-0	0-0	2-0	1-2	1-3	4-1		3-1	5-0	2-1	1-3	3-2	1-1	0-0	2-0	2-0	0-1	4-1	4-1	2-0	0-2	0-1	4-0	0-2
Gillingham FC	3-0	1-1	0-4	2-2	1-2	1-0	3-0		2-1	1-3	1-0	0-2	3-1	2-0	5-0	2-1	0-1	2-1	3-3	2-0	0-0	2-1	0-0	2-3
Grimsby Town FC	1-0	3-1	0-1	3-1	0-1	1-0	5-2	1-2		0-2	2-2	0-2	3-1	2-2	0-2	1-0	0-0	3-1	2-2	0-3	0-0	6-2	1-1	1-1
Manchester City FC	5-1	3-0	3-1	5-1	4-2	5-2	1-0	4-1	4-0		2-0	3-1	3-0	3-1	3-2	2-1	0-0	4-0	2-2	3-0	3-0	0-0	0-4	1-0
Millwall FC	3-1	1-1	3-1	0-2	3-2	2-0	3-0	1-2	3-1	2-3		4-0	3-3	1-0	2-1	1-0	2-0	1-2	3-0	2-2	1-0	1-0	0-1	1-0
Norwich City FC	2-1	0-1	1-4	2-1	2-0	2-2	2-1	2-1	1-1	2-0	0-0		1-0	0-0	3-0	0-0	2-1	2-0	2-0	1-1	3-1	2-0	2-1	2-0
Nottingham Forest	0-0	0-0	1-0	1-0	2-1	2-2	4-2	2-2	0-0	1-1	1-2	2-0		0-1	1-1	2-0	0-1	2-1	2-3	0-0	0-1	0-0	2-2	2-2
Portsmouth FC	4-4	1-1	0-1	1-1	1-0	2-4	4-2	2-1	4-2	2-1	3-0	1-2	3-2		0-1	0-0	1-0	0-0	2-0	1-1	0-1	1-2	1-2	1-2
Preston North End	2-2	1-0	1-1	2-3	4-0	2-2	2-1	0-2	0-0	2-1	1-0	4-0	2-1	2-0		2-1	3-0	4-2	6-0	1-1	1-2	1-0	1-1	1-2
Rotherham United	1-1	2-2	1-1	1-1	0-0	2-2	2-3	3-2	1-1	1-1	0-0	1-1	1-2	2-1	1-0		1-1	1-1	3-2	2-0	1-1	2-1	3-2	0-3
Sheffield United FC	1-1	4-0	2-2	3-0	0-1	1-0	1-3	0-0	3-1	1-3	3-2	2-1	0-0	4-3	2-2	2-2		0-0	3-0	0-1	0-2	0-3	0-1	2-2
Sheffield Wednesday	3-1	0-1	1-1	0-2	2-1	1-0	1-3	0-0	0-0	2-6	1-1	0-5	0-2	1-2	1-2	1-0	0-0		5-0	2-1	2-1	1-1	1-2	1-2
Stockport County	1-3	0-3	1-0	0-2	0-2	0-1	0-1	0-2	3-3	2-1	0-4	2-1	1-3	0-1	1-2	0-1	1-2	3-1		0-2	2-1	1-2	1-2	1-4
Walsall FC	2-1	1-2	2-2	1-0	0-1	2-1	2-2	1-1	4-0	0-0	0-0	2-0	2-0	0-0	1-2	3-2	1-2	0-3	1-0		0-3	2-1	2-1	0-3
Watford FC	3-0	3-3	0-0	1-2	3-0	0-1	1-0	2-3	2-0	1-2	1-4	2-1	1-2	3-0	1-1	3-2	0-3	3-1	1-1	2-1		1-2	3-0	1-1
West Bromwich Alb.	3-1	1-0	1-0	1-0	1-0	4-1	2-0	1-0	0-1	4-0	0-2	1-0	1-0	5-0	2-0	1-1	0-1	1-1	4-0	1-0	1-1		0-1	1-1
Wimbledon FC	0-1	3-1	1-2	0-0	0-1	2-0	1-1	3-1	2-1	2-1	2-2	0-1	1-0	3-3	2-0	1-0	1-1	1-1	3-1	2-2	0-0	0-1		0-1
Wolverhampton W.	4-1	2-1	3-1	3-0	3-1	0-1	0-1	2-0	0-1	0-2	1-0	0-0	1-0	2-2	2-3	2-1	1-0	0-0	2-2	3-0	1-0	0-1	1-0	

	Football League Division 1	Pd	Wn	Dw	Ls	GF	GA	Pts	
1.	Manchester City FC (Manchester)	46	31	6	9	108	52	99	P
2.	West Bromwich Albion FC (West Bromwich)	46	27	8	11	61	29	89	P
3.	Wolverhampton Wanderers FC (Wolverhampton)	46	25	11	10	76	43	86	PO
4.	Millwall FC (London)	46	22	11	13	69	48	77	PO
5.	Birmingham City FC (Birmingham)	46	21	13	12	70	49	76	POP
6.	Norwich City FC (Norwich)	46	22	9	15	60	51	75	PO
7.	Burnley FC (Burnley)	46	21	12	13	70	62	75	
8.	Preston North End FC (Preston)	46	20	12	14	71	59	72	
9.	Wimbledon FC (London)	46	18	13	15	63	57	67	
10.	Crystal Palace FC (London)	46	20	6	20	70	62	66	
11.	Coventry City FC (Coventry)	46	20	6	20	59	53	66	
12.	Gillingham FC (Gillingham)	46	18	10	18	64	67	64	
13.	Sheffield United FC (Sheffield)	46	15	15	16	53	54	60	
14.	Watford FC (Watford)	46	16	11	19	62	56	59	
15.	Bradford City AFC (Bradford)	46	15	10	21	69	76	55	
16.	Nottingham Forest FC (Nottingham)	46	12	18	16	50	51	54	
17.	Portsmouth FC (Portsmouth)	46	13	14	19	60	72	53	
18.	Walsall FC (Walsall)	46	13	12	21	51	71	51	
19.	Grimsby Town FC (Cleethorpes)	46	12	14	20	50	72	50	
20.	Sheffield Wednesday FC (Sheffield)	46	12	14	20	49	71	50	
21.	Rotherham United FC (Rotherham)	46	10	19	17	52	66	49	
22.	Crewe Alexandra FC (Crewe)	46	12	13	21	47	76	49	R
23.	Barnsley FC (Barnsley)	46	11	15	20	59	86	48	R
24.	Stockport County FC (Stockport)	46	6	8	32	42	102	26	R
		1104	412	280	412	1485	1485	1516	

Promotion Play-offs

Birmingham City FC (Birmingham)   1-1 (aet)   Norwich City FC (Norwich)
(Birmingham City won 4-2 on penalties)

Birmingham City FC (Birmingham)   1-1, 1-0   Millwall FC (London)

Norwich City FC (Norwich)   3-1, 0-1   Wolverhampton Wanderers FC (Wolverhampton)

Football League Division 2 2001-02 Season	Blackpool	Bournemouth	Brentford	Brighton & Hove Albion	Bristol City	Bury	Cambridge United	Cardiff City	Chesterfield	Colchester United	Huddersfield Town	Northampton Town	Notts County	Oldham Athletic	Peterborough United	Port Vale	Q.P.R.	Reading	Stoke City	Swindon Town	Tranmere Rovers	Wigan Athletic	Wrexham	Wycombe Wanderers
Blackpool FC		4-3	1-3	2-2	5-1	0-1	1-1	1-1	1-0	2-1	1-2	1-2	0-0	0-2	2-2	4-0	2-2	0-2	2-2	1-0	1-1	3-1	3-0	2-2
AFC Bournemouth	0-1		0-2	1-1	1-3	3-2	2-2	1-3	3-1	0-1	2-3	5-1	4-2	3-2	0-2	0-0	1-2	1-0	3-1	0-0	0-2	2-0	3-0	1-2
Brentford FC	2-0	1-0		4-0	2-2	5-1	2-1	2-1	0-0	4-1	3-0	3-0	2-1	2-2	2-1	2-0	0-0	1-1	1-0	2-0	4-0	0-1	3-0	1-0
Brighton & Hove Alb.	4-0	2-1	1-2		2-1	2-1	4-3	1-0	2-2	1-0	1-0	2-0	2-2	3-0	1-1	1-0	2-1	3-1	1-0	0-0	1-0	2-1	0-0	4-0
Bristol City FC	2-1	1-0	0-2	0-1		2-0	2-0	1-1	3-0	3-1	1-1	1-3	3-2	3-0	1-0	1-1	2-0	3-3	1-1	3-1	2-0	2-2	1-0	0-1
Bury FC	1-1	2-1	2-0	0-2	2-2		2-2	3-0	2-1	1-3	0-0	2-1	0-4	1-1	2-0	1-1	1-2	1-1	0-1	0-3	0-1	0-2	2-2	1-1
Cambridge United FC	0-3	2-2	2-1	0-0	0-3	3-1		2-1	4-1	1-2	0-1	3-3	0-2	1-1	0-0	0-1	2-1	2-2	0-2	1-2	2-1	2-2	0-2	2-0
Cardiff City AFC	2-2	2-2	3-1	1-1	1-3	1-0	2-0		2-1	1-1	1-2	2-0	2-1	3-1	0-2	1-0	1-1	2-2	2-0	3-0	1-1	2-2	3-2	1-0
Chesterfield FC	2-1	2-1	0-1	1-2	2-1	2-0	2-0	0-2		3-6	1-1	4-2	2-1	4-2	0-1	1-1	2-3	0-2	1-2	4-0	0-2	1-2	3-2	0-1
Colchester United FC	1-1	1-2	1-1	1-4	0-0	0-1	3-1	0-1	1-2		3-3	3-1	0-1	2-1	2-1	2-0	3-1	2-0	1-3	1-3	2-1	2-2	2-1	2-2
Huddersfield Town	2-4	1-0	1-1	1-2	1-0	2-0	2-1	2-2	0-0	2-1		2-0	2-2	0-0	3-1	2-1	1-0	0-1	0-0	2-0	1-0	0-0	5-1	2-1
Northampton Town	1-3	1-0	1-0	2-0	0-3	1-0	2-2	1-2	0-2	2-3	0-3		0-2	0-1	2-1	1-0	2-2	0-2	1-1	1-1	4-1	0-2	4-1	4-1
Notts County FC	1-0	2-0	0-0	2-2	0-1	1-2	2-1	0-0	1-1	1-1	2-1	0-3		0-2	1-0	1-3	0-2	3-4	0-0	3-1	3-0	1-3	2-2	0-1
Oldham Athletic AFC	2-1	3-3	3-2	2-0	0-1	4-0	2-2	1-7	1-1	4-1	1-1	4-2	4-1		2-0	2-0	1-0	0-1	2-1	2-0	1-1	1-1	3-1	2-0
Peterborough United	3-2	6-0	1-1	0-1	4-1	2-1	1-0	1-1	1-1	3-1	1-2	2-0	0-1	2-2		3-0	4-1	1-2	1-2	1-1	5-0	0-2	2-3	2-1
Port Vale FC	1-1	0-0	2-1	0-1	1-0	1-0	5-0	0-2	4-1	3-1	1-1	0-1	4-2	3-2	4-1		1-0	0-2	1-1	0-2	1-1	1-0	1-3	1-1
Queen's Park Rangers	2-0	1-1	0-0	0-0	3-0	0-0	2-1	0-0	2-2	3-2	0-1	3-2	1-1	1-0	4-1			0-0	1-0	4-0	1-2	1-1	2-1	4-3
Reading FC	3-0	2-2	1-2	0-0	3-2	1-1	1-0	1-2	0-1	3-0	1-0	0-0	2-1	2-2	2-2	2-0	1-0		1-0	1-3	4-1	1-1	2-0	2-0
Stoke City FC	2-0	2-0	3-2	3-1	1-0	4-0	5-0	1-1	1-0	3-0	1-1	2-0	1-0	0-0	1-0	0-1	0-1	2-0		2-0	1-2	2-2	1-0	5-1
Swindon Town FC	1-0	0-0	2-0	1-1	1-2	3-1	0-3	2-1	1-0	0-1	2-1	1-0	0-2	0-0	3-0	0-1	0-0	0-3			2-2	1-1	3-1	1-1
Tranmere Rovers FC	4-0	0-0	1-1	0-0	1-2	1-2	6-1	0-1	0-0	0-0	1-1	0-2	4-2	2-2	1-0	3-1	2-3	2-2	2-2	0-0		1-2	5-0	1-1
Wigan Athletic AFC	0-1	0-0	1-1	3-0	1-2	1-1	4-1	4-0	1-1	2-3	1-0	3-0	1-1	1-0	2-1	0-1	1-2	0-2	6-1	1-0	1-2		2-3	0-0
Wrexham AFC	1-1	2-1	0-3	1-2	0-2	1-0	5-0	1-3	0-1	1-1	1-1	3-2	2-1	3-3	1-2	1-3	1-0	0-1	2-2	1-1	2-0			0-0
Wycombe Wanderers	1-4	1-1	5-3	1-1	2-1	0-2	2-0	0-1	0-0	0-0	2-4	2-1	3-0	2-1	3-0	3-1	1-0	0-2	1-0	1-1	2-1	1-0	5-2	

	Football League Division 2	Pd	Wn	Dw	Ls	GF	GA	Pts	
1.	Brighton & Hove Albion FC (Brighton)	46	25	15	6	66	42	90	P
2.	Reading FC (Reading)	46	23	15	8	70	43	84	P
3.	Brentford FC (London)	46	24	11	11	77	43	83	PO
4.	Cardiff City AFC (Cardiff)	46	23	14	9	75	50	83	PO
5.	Stoke City FC (Stoke-on-Trent)	46	23	11	12	67	40	80	POP
6.	Huddersfield Town AFC (Huddersfield)	46	21	15	10	65	47	78	PO
7.	Bristol City FC (Bristol)	46	21	10	15	68	53	73	
8.	Queen's Park Rangers FC (London)	46	19	14	13	60	49	71	
9.	Oldham Athletic AFC (Oldham)	46	18	16	12	77	65	70	
10.	Wigan Athletic AFC (Wigan)	46	16	16	14	66	51	64	
11.	Wycombe Wanderers FC (High Wycombe)	46	17	13	16	58	64	64	
12.	Tranmere Rovers FC (Birkenhead)	46	16	15	15	63	60	63	
13.	Swindon Town FC (Swindon)	46	15	14	17	46	56	59	
14.	Port Vale FC (Stoke-on-Trent)	46	16	10	20	51	62	58	
15.	Colchester United FC (Colchester)	46	15	12	19	65	76	57	
16.	Blackpool FC (Blackpool)	46	14	14	18	66	69	56	
17.	Peterborough United FC (Peterborough)	46	15	10	21	64	59	55	
18.	Chesterfield FC (Chesterfield)	46	13	13	20	53	65	52	
19.	Notts County FC (Nottingham)	46	13	11	22	59	71	50	
20.	Northampton Town FC (Northampton)	46	14	7	25	54	79	49	
21.	AFC Bournemouth (Bournemouth)	46	10	14	22	56	71	44	R
22.	Bury FC (Bury)	46	11	11	24	43	75	44	R
23.	Wrexham AFC (Wrexham)	46	11	10	25	56	89	43	R
24.	Cambridge United FC (Cambridge)	46	7	13	26	47	93	34	R
		1104	400	304	400	1472	1472	1504	

Promotion Play-offs

Stoke City FC (Stoke-on-Trent)	2-0	Brentford FC (London)
Huddersfield Town AFC (Huddersfield)	0-0, 1-2	Brentford FC (London)
Stoke City FC (Stoke-on-Trent)	1-2, 2-0 (aet)	Cardiff City AFC (Cardiff)

Football League Division 3 — 2001-02 Season

Home \ Away	Bristol Rovers	Carlisle United	Cheltenham Town	Darlington	Exeter City	Halifax Town	Hartlepool	Hull City	Kidderminster H.	Leyton Orient	Lincoln City	Luton Town	Macclesfield Town	Mansfield Town	Oxford United	Plymouth Argyle	Rochdale	Rushden & Diam.	Scunthorpe United	Shrewsbury Town	Southend United	Swansea City	Torquay United	York City
Bristol Rovers FC	■	0-0	1-2	1-0	0-0	2-0	0-1	1-1	2-1	5-3	1-2	3-2	0-2	0-1	1-1	1-2	0-2	0-3	1-1	0-0	2-1	4-1	1-0	2-2
Carlisle United FC	1-0	■	0-0	1-3	1-0	0-0	0-2	0-0	1-0	6-1	2-2	0-2	3-2	0-1	2-1	0-2	1-2	3-0	3-0	0-1	0-0	3-0	2-0	2-1
Cheltenham Town	0-0	2-0	■	0-0	3-1	2-1	3-0	1-0	2-1	1-1	2-1	1-1	4-1	2-3	2-0	0-0	1-1	1-1	3-3	1-0	1-1	2-2	2-2	4-0
Darlington FC	1-0	2-2	0-2	■	4-0	5-0	1-1	0-1	2-0	3-0	2-1	3-2	0-1	1-0	1-4	1-0	0-0	2-1	3-3	2-2	0-0	1-3	2-1	3-1
Exeter City FC	1-0	1-0	0-2	4-2	■	0-0	0-2	1-3	2-1	0-0	1-1	2-2	0-0	1-3	3-2	2-3	1-1	1-1	0-4	2-2	2-1	0-3	0-0	2-1
Halifax Town AFC	0-0	2-2	4-1	2-2	1-1	■	0-2	0-1	1-0	0-0	3-0	2-4	0-0	1-0	0-2	0-2	1-2	2-4	0-0	1-2	1-1	0-1	2-0	1-1
Hartlepool United FC	1-1	3-1	0-1	1-2	2-0	3-0	■	4-0	1-1	3-1	1-1	1-2	1-2	1-1	1-0	1-0	1-1	5-1	3-2	2-2	5-1	7-1	4-1	3-0
Hull City AFC	0-0	0-1	5-1	1-2	2-0	3-0	1-1	■	2-1	1-1	1-1	0-4	0-1	4-1	3-0	1-2	2-1	0-1	3-0	0-0	2-1	1-0	1-0	4-0
Kidderminster Harr.	2-0	2-2	0-0	1-0	3-1	2-0	3-2	0-1	■	0-1	1-1	1-4	0-1	1-1	0-0	4-1	3-0	1-0	1-0	2-0	0-2	1-0	4-1	1-0
Leyton Orient FC	3-1	0-0	0-2	0-0	1-1	3-1	2-0	0-0	1-3	■	5-0	1-3	2-0	2-0	3-0	0-0	4-2	2-1	0-0	2-4	2-1	2-2	1-2	1-2
Lincoln City FC	0-1	3-1	0-1	1-1	0-0	1-2	2-0	2-1	0-1	2-0	■	0-1	1-0	1-4	1-0	0-1	1-1	1-2	4-3	1-2	0-1	3-0	0-0	1-3
Luton Town FC	3-0	1-1	2-1	5-2	3-0	5-0	2-1	1-0	3-0	1-1	0-0	■	5-3	1-1	2-0	0-1	1-0	2-3	1-0	2-0	3-0	5-1	2-1	3-0
Macclesfield Town	2-1	1-1	1-0	1-1	1-2	1-1	0-0	0-1	2-1	0-1	4-1	0-1	■	0-1	1-1	0-1	0-0	4-3	2-1	0-0	1-3	0-2	2-1	2-1
Mansfield Town FC	2-0	2-0	2-1	4-2	2-1	3-0	4-2	1-1	3-2	2-1	4-1	4-0	4-0	■	2-1	0-3	3-1	1-4	2-1	2-1	0-0	3-0	2-0	1-1
Oxford United FC	0-0	1-1	3-0	1-2	1-2	6-1	1-2	1-0	1-1	1-2	2-1	1-2	0-2	3-2	■	1-1	1-2	3-2	0-1	0-1	2-0	2-1	1-1	2-2
Plymouth Argyle FC	1-0	3-0	2-0	1-0	3-0	3-0	2-0	2-0	2-0	2-1	2-0	1-0	2-1	2-0	4-2	■	1-2	1-0	0-0	3-1	2-2	1-0	2-0	1-0
Rochdale AFC	2-1	1-1	2-2	3-1	2-0	2-0	0-0	3-2	2-0	3-2	1-0	1-1	3-1	1-1	1-3	0-2	■	0-0	2-2	1-0	0-1	0-0	2-1	5-4
Rushden & Diamonds	3-1	3-1	1-0	2-1	2-1	2-1	3-3	0-2	1-0	1-2	2-0	3-1	2-1	2-3	1-1	2-0	1-1	■	0-0	3-0	0-1	4-0	0-0	3-0
Scunthorpe United	1-2	2-1	1-2	7-1	3-4	4-0	1-0	2-1	1-0	4-1	1-1	0-2	1-1	0-1	1-0	2-1	2-1	1-1	■	3-1	2-0	2-2	1-0	1-0
Shrewsbury Town	0-1	1-0	2-1	3-0	1-0	3-0	1-1	4-0	1-0	0-0	3-1	1-0	0-2	2-2	3-1	1-0	0-2	2-2	1-1	■	2-0	3-0	0-1	3-2
Southend United	2-1	3-2	0-1	1-0	3-1	4-1	0-0	2-0	1-0	1-2	3-0	1-0	2-2	0-1	0-0	4-2	2-0	0-2	1-1	2-0	■	4-2	1-1	0-1
Swansea City FC	2-1	0-0	2-2	2-0	4-2	0-2	0-1	1-0	2-1	0-1	0-0	1-3	0-1	2-0	0-0	0-1	0-0	2-2	3-3	3-2	1-1	■	2-2	0-1
Torquay United FC	2-1	2-1	0-1	2-1	0-2	2-4	1-0	1-1	1-4	1-1	2-0	0-1	1-2	0-0	3-3	0-1	3-0	1-1	0-0	2-1	2-1	1-2	■	0-3
York City FC	3-0	0-0	1-3	2-0	2-3	1-0	0-1	2-1	0-1	2-1	2-0	1-2	3-1	1-0	0-0	0-0	0-1	0-2	1-1	2-1	0-2	1-1	0-2	■

Football League Division 3

	Team	Pd	Wn	Dw	Ls	GF	GA	Pts	
1.	Plymouth Argyle FC (Plymouth)	46	31	9	6	71	28	102	P
2.	Luton Town FC (Luton)	46	30	7	9	96	48	97	P
3.	Mansfield Town FC (Mansfield)	46	24	7	15	72	60	79	P
4.	Cheltenham Town FC (Cheltenham)	46	21	15	10	66	49	78	POP
5.	Rochdale AFC (Rochdale)	46	21	15	10	65	52	78	PO
6.	Rushden & Diamonds FC (Irthlingborough)	46	20	13	13	69	53	73	PO
7.	Hartlepool United FC (Hartlepool)	46	20	11	15	74	48	71	PO
8.	Scunthorpe United FC (Scunthorpe)	46	19	14	13	74	56	71	
9.	Shrewsbury Town FC (Shrewsbury)	46	20	10	16	64	53	70	
10.	Kidderminster Harriers FC (Kidderminster)	46	19	9	18	56	47	66	
11.	Hull City AFC (Kingston-upon-Hull)	46	16	13	17	57	51	61	
12.	Southend United FC (Southend-on-Sea)	46	15	13	18	51	54	58	
13.	Macclesfield Town FC (Macclesfield)	46	15	13	18	41	52	58	
14.	York City FC (York)	46	16	9	21	54	67	57	
15.	Darlington FC (Darlington)	46	15	11	20	60	71	56	
16.	Exeter City FC (Exeter)	46	14	13	19	48	73	55	
17.	Carlisle United FC (Carlisle)	46	12	16	18	49	56	52	
18.	Leyton Orient FC (London)	46	13	13	20	55	71	52	
19.	Torquay United FC (Torquay)	46	12	15	19	46	63	51	
20.	Swansea City FC (Swansea)	46	13	12	21	53	77	51	
21.	Oxford United FC (Oxford)	46	11	14	21	53	62	47	
22.	Lincoln City FC (Lincoln)	46	10	16	20	44	62	46	
23.	Bristol Rovers FC (Bristol)	46	11	12	23	40	60	45	
24.	Halifax Town AFC (Halifax)	46	8	12	26	39	84	36	R
		1104	406	262	406	1397	1397	1510	

Promotion Play-offs

Cheltenham Town FC (Cheltenham)	3-1	Rushden & Diamonds FC (Irthlingborough)
Hartlepool United FC (Hartlepool)	1-1, 1-1 (aet)	Cheltenham Town FC (Cheltenham)
	(Cheltenham Town won 5-4 on penalties)	
Rushden & Diamonds FC (Irthlingborough)	2-2, 2-1	Rochdale AFC (Rochdale)

Promoted to Division 3: Boston United FC (Boston)

F.A. CUP FINAL   (Millennium Stadium, Cardiff – 04/05/2002 – 73,963)

ARSENAL FC (LONDON)	2-0	Chelsea FC (London)

Parlour 70', Ljungberg 80'

Arsenal: Seaman, Lauren, Campbell, Adams, Cole, Wiltord (Keown 90'), Parlour, Vieira, Ljungberg, Bergkamp (Edu 72'), Henry (Kanu 81').

Chelsea: Cudicini, Melchiot (Zenden 76'), Gallas, Desailly, Babayaro (Terry 45'), Gronkjaer, Lampard, Petit, Le Saux, Gudjohnsen, Hasselbaink (Zola 68').

Semi-finals

Fulham FC (London)	0-1	Chelsea FC (London)
Middlesbrough FC (Middlesbrough)	0-1	Arsenal FC (London)

Quarter-finals

Middlesbrough FC (Middlesbrough)	3-0	Everton FC (Liverpool)
Newcastle United FC (Newcastle-upon-Tyne)	1-1, 0-3	Arsenal FC (London)
Tottenham Hotspur FC (London)	0-4	Chelsea FC (London)
West Bromwich Albion FC (West Bromwich)	0-1	Fulham FC (London)

2002-03

F.A. Premiership 2002-03 Season	Arsenal	Aston Villa	Birmingham City	Blackburn Rovers	Bolton Wanderers	Charlton Athletic	Chelsea	Everton	Fulham	Leeds United	Liverpool	Manchester City	Manchester United	Middlesbrough	Newcastle United	Southampton	Sunderland	Tottenham Hotspur	W.B.A.	West Ham United
Arsenal FC	■	3-1	2-0	1-2	2-1	2-0	3-2	2-1	2-1	2-3	1-1	2-1	2-2	2-0	1-0	6-1	3-1	3-0	5-2	3-1
Aston Villa FC	1-1	■	0-2	3-0	2-0	2-0	2-1	3-2	3-1	0-0	0-1	1-0	0-1	1-0	0-1	0-1	1-0	0-1	2-1	4-1
Birmingham City FC	0-4	3-0	■	0-1	3-1	1-1	1-3	1-1	0-0	2-1	2-1	0-2	0-1	3-0	0-2	3-2	2-0	1-1	1-0	2-2
Blackburn Rovers FC	2-0	0-0	1-1	■	0-0	1-0	2-3	0-1	2-1	1-0	2-2	1-0	1-0	1-0	5-2	1-0	0-0	1-2	1-1	2-2
Bolton Wanderers FC	2-2	1-0	4-2	1-1	■	1-2	1-1	1-2	0-0	0-3	2-3	2-0	1-1	2-1	4-3	1-1	1-1	1-0	1-1	1-0
Charlton Athletic FC	0-3	3-0	0-2	3-1	1-1	■	2-3	2-1	0-1	1-6	2-0	2-2	1-3	1-0	0-2	2-1	1-1	0-1	1-0	4-2
Chelsea FC	1-1	2-0	3-0	1-2	1-0	4-1	■	4-1	1-1	3-2	2-1	5-0	2-2	1-0	3-0	0-0	3-0	1-1	2-0	2-3
Everton FC	2-1	2-1	1-1	2-1	0-0	1-0	1-3	■	2-0	2-0	1-2	2-2	1-2	2-1	2-1	2-1	2-1	2-2	1-0	0-0
Fulham FC	0-1	2-1	0-1	0-4	4-1	1-0	0-0	2-0	■	1-0	3-2	0-1	1-1	1-0	2-1	2-2	1-0	3-2	3-0	0-1
Leeds United AFC	1-4	3-1	2-0	2-3	2-4	1-2	2-0	0-1	2-0	■	0-1	3-0	1-0	2-3	0-3	1-1	0-1	2-2	0-0	1-0
Liverpool FC	2-2	1-1	2-2	1-1	2-0	2-1	1-0	0-0	2-0	3-1	■	1-2	1-2	1-1	2-2	3-0	0-0	2-1	2-0	2-0
Manchester City FC	1-5	3-1	1-0	2-2	2-0	0-1	0-3	3-1	4-1	2-1	0-3	■	3-1	0-0	1-0	0-1	3-0	2-3	1-2	0-1
Manchester United FC	2-0	1-1	2-0	3-1	0-1	4-1	2-1	3-0	3-0	2-1	4-0	1-1	■	1-0	5-3	2-1	2-1	1-0	1-0	3-0
Middlesbrough FC	0-2	2-5	1-0	1-0	2-0	1-1	1-1	1-1	2-2	22-	1-0	3-1	3-1	■	1-0	2-2	3-0	5-1	3-0	2-2
Newcastle United FC	1-1	1-1	1-0	5-1	1-0	2-1	2-1	2-0	0-2	1-0	2-0	2-6	2-0	2-0	■	2-1	2-0	2-1	2-1	4-0
Southampton FC	3-2	2-2	2-0	1-1	0-0	0-0	1-1	1-0	4-2	3-2	0-1	2-0	0-2	0-0	1-1	■	2-1	1-0	1-1	1-1
Sunderland AFC	0-4	1-0	0-1	0-0	0-2	1-3	1-2	0-1	0-3	1-2	2-1	0-3	1-1	1-3	0-1	0-1	■	2-0	1-2	0-1
Tottenham Hotspur FC	1-1	1-0	2-1	0-4	3-1	2-2	0-0	4-3	1-1	2-0	2-3	0-2	0-2	0-3	0-1	2-1	4-1	■	3-1	3-2
West Bromwich Albion FC	1-2	0-0	1-1	0-2	1-1	0-1	0-2	1-2	1-0	1-3	0-6	1-2	1-3	1-0	2-2	1-0	2-2	2-3	■	1-2
West Ham United FC	2-2	2-2	1-2	2-1	1-1	2-1	1-0	0-1	1-1	3-4	0-3	1-1	1-0	2-2	0-1	2-0	2-0	0-1	2-0	■

F.A. Premiership

		Pd	Wn	Dw	Ls	GF	GA	Pts	
1.	MANCHESTER UNITED FC (MANCHESTER)	38	25	8	5	74	34	83	
2.	Arsenal FC (London)	38	23	9	6	85	42	78	
3.	Newcastle United FC (Newcastle-upon-Tyne)	38	21	6	11	63	48	69	
4.	Chelsea FC (London)	38	19	10	9	68	38	67	
5.	Liverpool FC (Liverpool)	38	18	10	10	61	41	64	
6.	Blackburn Rovers FC (Blackburn)	38	16	12	10	52	43	60	
7.	Everton FC (Liverpool)	38	17	8	13	48	49	59	
8.	Southampton FC (Southampton)	38	13	13	12	43	46	52	
9.	Manchester City FC (Manchester)	38	15	6	17	47	54	51	
10.	Tottenham Hotspur FC (London)	38	14	8	16	51	62	50	
11.	Middlesbrough FC (Middlesbrough)	38	13	10	15	48	44	49	
12.	Charlton Athletic FC (London)	38	14	7	17	45	56	49	
13.	Birmingham City FC (Birmingham)	38	13	9	16	41	49	48	
14.	Fulham FC (London)	38	13	9	16	41	50	48	
15.	Leeds United AFC (Leeds)	38	14	5	19	58	57	47	
16.	Aston Villa FC (Birmingham)	38	12	9	17	42	47	45	
17.	Bolton Wanderers FC (Bolton)	38	10	14	14	41	51	44	
18.	West Ham United FC (London)	38	10	12	16	42	59	42	R
19.	West Bromwich Albion FC (West Bromwich)	38	6	8	24	29	65	26	R
20.	Sunderland AFC (Sunderland)	38	4	7	27	21	65	19	R
		760	290	180	290	1000	1000	1050	

Top Goalscorers

1)	Ruud Van NISTELROOY	(Manchester United FC)	25
2)	Thierry HENRY	(Arsenal FC)	24
3)	James BEATTIE	(Southampton FC)	23

Football League Division 1 — 2002-03 Season

	Bradford City	Brighton & H.A.	Burnley	Coventry City	Crystal Palace	Derby County	Gillingham	Grimsby Town	Ipswich Town	Leicester City	Millwall	Norwich City	Nottingham Forest	Portsmouth	Preston North End	Reading	Rotherham United	Sheffield United	Sheffield Wed.	Stoke City	Walsall	Watford	Wimbledon	Wolves
Bradford City AFC		0-1	2-2	1-1	2-1	0-0	1-3	0-0	2-0	0-0	0-1	2-1	1-0	0-5	1-1	0-1	4-2	0-5	1-1	4-2	1-2	2-1	3-5	0-0
Brighton & Hove Alb.	3-2		2-2	0-0	0-0	1-0	2-4	1-2	1-1	0-1	1-0	0-2	1-0	1-1	0-2	0-1	2-0	2-4	1-1	1-2	0-2	4-0	2-3	4-1
Burnley FC	0-2	1-3		3-1	0-0	2-0	2-0	1-1	1-1	1-2	2-2	2-0	1-0	0-3	2-0	2-5	2-6	0-1	2-7	2-1	2-1	4-7	1-0	2-1
Coventry City FC	0-2	0-0	0-1		1-0	3-0	0-0	3-2	2-4	1-2	2-3	1-1	0-1	0-4	1-2	2-0	2-1	2-1	1-1	0-1	0-0	0-1	2-2	0-2
Crystal Palace FC	1-1	5-0	1-1	1-1		0-1	2-2	2-0	1-1	0-0	1-0	2-0	0-0	2-3	2-0	0-1	0-0	2-2	0-0	1-0	2-0	0-1	0-1	4-2
Derby County FC	1-2	1-0	1-2	1-0	0-1		1-1	1-3	1-4	1-1	1-2	2-1	0-0	1-2	0-1	3-0	3-0	2-1	2-2	2-0	2-2	3-0	3-2	1-4
Gillingham FC	1-0	3-0	4-2	0-2	2-1	1-0		3-0	1-3	3-2	1-0	1-4	1-3	0-1	1-1	1-1	1-1	1-1	0-1	3-0	3-0	3-3	1-1	0-4
Grimsby Town FC	1-2	2-2	6-5	0-2	1-4	1-2	1-1		3-0	1-2	0-2	1-1	0-3	0-1	3-3	0-3	0-0	1-4	2-0	2-0	0-1	1-0	0-0	0-1
Ipswich Town FC	1-2	2-2	2-2	2-1	1-2	0-1	0-1	2-2		6-1	4-1	1-1	3-4	3-0	3-0	3-1	1-2	3-2	2-1	0-0	3-2	4-2	1-5	2-4
Leicester City FC	4-0	2-0	0-1	2-1	1-0	3-1	2-0	2-0	1-2		4-1	1-1	1-0	1-1	2-1	2-1	0-0	1-1	0-0	2-0	2-0	4-0	1-0	1-0
Millwall FC	1-0	1-0	1-1	2-0	3-2	3-0	2-2	2-0	1-1	2-2		0-2	1-2	0-5	1-0	0-2	0-6	1-0	3-0	3-1	0-3	4-0	1-1	1-1
Norwich City FC	3-2	0-1	2-0	2-0	2-0	1-0	1-0	4-0	0-2	0-0	3-1		0-0	1-0	2-0	0-1	1-1	2-3	3-0	2-2	2-1	4-0	1-0	0-1
Nottingham Forest	3-0	3-2	2-0	1-1	2-1	3-0	4-1	2-2	2-1	2-2	3-3	4-0		1-2	2-2	2-0	3-2	3-0	4-0	6-0	1-1	0-1	2-0	2-2
Portsmouth FC	3-0	4-2	1-0	1-1	1-1	6-2	1-0	3-0	1-1	0-2	1-0	3-2	2-0		3-2	3-0	1-2	1-2	3-0	3-2	3-0	4-1	1-0	1-0
Preston North End	1-0	2-2	3-1	2-2	1-2	4-2	3-0	3-0	0-0	2-0	2-1	1-2	1-1	1-1		1-0	0-2	2-2	4-3	5-0	1-1	3-5	0-2	0-2
Reading FC	1-0	1-2	3-0	1-2	2-1	2-1	2-1	2-1	3-1	1-3	2-0	0-2	1-0	0-0	5-1		3-0	0-2	2-1	1-1	0-0	1-0	0-1	0-1
Rotherham United	3-2	1-0	0-0	1-0	1-3	2-1	1-1	0-1	2-1	1-1	1-3	1-1	2-2	2-3	0-0	0-0		1-2	0-2	4-0	0-0	2-1	2-1	0-0
Sheffield United FC	3-0	2-1	4-2	0-0	2-1	2-0	2-2	2-1	0-0	2-1	3-1	0-1	1-0	1-1	1-0	1-3	1-0		3-1	2-1	1-1	1-2	1-1	3-3
Sheffield Wednesday	2-1	1-1	1-3	5-1	0-0	1-3	0-2	0-0	0-1	0-0	0-1	2-2	2-0	1-3	0-2	3-2	1-2	2-0		0-0	2-1	2-2	4-2	0-4
Stoke City FC	2-1	1-0	0-1	1-2	1-1	1-3	0-0	1-2	2-1	0-0	0-1	1-1	2-2	1-1	2-1	1-0	2-0	0-0	3-2		1-0	1-2	2-1	0-2
Walsall FC	0-1	1-0	3-2	0-0	3-4	3-2	1-0	3-1	0-2	1-4	1-2	0-0	2-1	1-2	3-3	0-2	3-4	0-1	1-0	4-2		2-0	2-0	0-1
Watford FC	1-0	1-0	2-1	5-2	3-3	2-0	0-1	2-0	0-2	1-2	0-0	2-1	1-1	2-2	0-1	0-3	1-2	2-0	1-0	1-2	2-0		3-2	1-1
Wimbledon FC	2-2	1-0	2-1	0-1	2-2	0-2	0-1	3-3	0-1	2-3	2-0	4-2	2-3	2-1	2-0	2-0	2-1	1-0	3-0	1-1	3-2	0-0		3-2
Wolverhampton W.	1-2	1-1	3-0	0-2	4-0	1-1	6-0	4-1	1-1	1-1	3-0	1-0	2-1	1-1	4-0	0-1	0-0	1-3	2-2	0-0	3-2	0-0	1-1	

	Football League Division 1	Pd	Wn	Dw	Ls	GF	GA	Pts	
1.	Portsmouth FC (Portsmouth)	46	29	11	6	97	45	98	P
2.	Leicester City FC (Leicester)	46	26	14	6	73	40	92	P
3.	Sheffield United FC (Sheffield)	46	23	11	12	72	52	80	PO
4.	Reading FC (Reading)	46	25	4	17	61	46	79	PO
5.	Wolverhampton Wanderers FC (Wolverhampton)	46	20	16	10	81	44	76	POP
6.	Nottingham Forest FC (Nottingham)	46	20	14	12	82	50	74	PO
7.	Ipswich Town FC (Ipswich)	46	19	13	14	80	64	70	
8.	Norwich City FC (Norwich)	46	19	12	15	60	49	69	
9.	Millwall FC (London)	46	19	9	18	59	69	66	
10.	Wimbledon FC (London)	46	18	11	17	76	73	65	
11.	Gillingham FC (Gillingham)	46	16	14	16	56	65	62	
12.	Preston North End FC (Preston)	46	16	13	17	68	70	61	
13.	Watford FC (Watford)	46	17	9	20	54	70	60	
14.	Crystal Palace FC (London)	46	14	17	15	59	52	59	
15.	Rotherham United FC (Rotherham)	46	15	14	17	62	62	59	
16.	Burnley FC (Burnley)	46	15	10	21	65	89	55	
17.	Walsall FC (Walsall)	46	15	9	22	57	69	54	
18.	Derby County FC (Derby)	46	15	7	24	55	74	52	
19.	Bradford City AFC (Bradford)	46	14	10	22	51	73	52	
20.	Coventry City FC (Coventry)	46	12	14	20	46	62	50	
21.	Stoke City FC (Stoke-on-Trent)	46	12	14	20	45	69	50	
22.	Sheffield Wednesday FC (Sheffield)	46	10	16	20	56	73	46	R
23.	Brighton & Hove Albion FC (Brighton)	46	11	12	23	49	67	45	R
24.	Grimsby Town FC (Cleethorpes)	46	9	12	25	48	85	39	R
		1104	409	286	409	1512	1512	1513	

Promotion Play-offs

Wolverhampton Wanderers FC	3-0	Sheffield United FC (Sheffield)
Nottingham Forest FC (Nottingham)	1-1, 3-4 (aet)	Sheffield United FC (Sheffield)
Wolverhampton Wanderers FC	2-1, 1-0	Reading FC (Reading)

Football League Division 2 — 2002-03 Season

	Barnsley	Blackpool	Brentford	Bristol City	Cardiff City	Cheltenham Town	Chesterfield	Colchester United	Crewe Alexandra	Huddersfield Town	Luton Town	Mansfield Town	Northampton Town	Notts County	Oldham Athletic	Peterborough United	Plymouth Argyle	Port Vale	Q.P.R.	Stockport County	Swindon Town	Tranmere Rovers	Wigan Athletic	Wycombe Wanderers
Barnsley FC	■	2-1	1-0	1-4	3-2	1-1	2-1	1-1	1-2	0-1	2-3	0-1	1-2	0-0	2-2	1-2	1-1	2-1	1-0	1-0	1-1	1-1	1-3	1-1
Blackpool FC	1-2	■	1-0	0-0	1-0	3-1	1-1	3-1	0-1	1-1	5-2	3-3	2-1	1-1	0-0	3-0	1-1	3-2	1-3	1-3	0-0	3-0	0-2	1-0
Brentford FC	1-2	5-0	■	1-0	0-2	2-2	2-1	1-1	1-2	1-0	0-0	1-0	3-0	1-1	0-0	1-1	0-0	1-1	1-2	1-2	3-1	1-2	0-1	1-0
Bristol City FC	2-0	2-0	0-0	■	2-0	3-1	4-0	1-2	2-2	1-0	1-1	5-2	3-0	3-2	2-0	1-0	0-0	2-0	1-3	1-1	2-0	2-0	0-1	3-0
Cardiff City AFC	1-1	2-1	2-0	0-2	■	2-1	1-0	0-3	3-1	4-0	0-0	1-0	1-2	0-2	1-1	3-0	1-1	3-1	1-2	2-1	1-1	4-0	0-0	1-0
Cheltenham Town	1-3	3-0	1-0	2-3	1-1	■	0-0	1-1	0-4	1-0	2-2	3-1	1-1	1-4	1-1	1-2	0-1	1-1	0-2	2-0	3-1	0-2	0-0	
Chesterfield FC	1-0	1-0	0-2	2-0	0-3	2-2	■	0-4	0-2	1-0	2-1	1-2	4-0	0-0	0-1	0-0	3-2	2-1	2-4	1-0	2-4	1-0	0-0	4-0
Colchester United FC	1-1	0-2	0-1	2-2	1-2	1-1	2-0	■	1-2	2-0	0-5	1-0	2-0	1-1	0-1	1-1	0-0	4-1	0-1	1-0	1-0	2-2	1-0	0-1
Crewe Alexandra FC	2-0	3-0	2-1	1-1	1-1	1-0	0-0	2-0	■	1-0	0-1	2-0	3-3	0-3	1-2	0-1	0-1	1-1	2-0	1-0	0-1	2-0	0-1	4-2
Huddersfield Town	1-0	0-0	0-2	1-2	1-0	3-3	4-0	1-1	1-1	■	0-1	1-1	2-0	3-0	1-1	0-1	1-0	2-2	0-3	2-1	2-3	1-2	0-0	0-0
Luton Town FC	2-3	1-3	0-1	2-2	2-0	2-1	3-0	1-2	0-4	3-0	■	2-3	3-2	2-2	0-0	2-3	1-0	0-0	0-0	1-1	3-0	0-0	1-1	1-0
Mansfield Town FC	0-1	4-0	0-0	4-5	0-1	0-2	0-2	4-2	0-5	0-2	3-2	■	2-1	3-2	0-1	1-5	4-3	0-1	0-4	4-2	2-1	6-1	1-2	0-0
Northampton Town	1-0	0-1	1-2	1-2	0-1	1-2	0-1	4-1	1-1	0-0	3-0	2-0	■	2-0	0-2	0-1	2-2	3-0	1-1	0-3	1-0	0-4	0-2	0-5
Notts County FC	3-2	3-1	2-2	2-0	0-1	1-0	1-1	2-3	2-2	3-2	2-1	2-2	2-1	■	1-3	2-2	0-2	1-0	3-0	3-2	1-1	0-1	0-2	1-1
Oldham Athletic AFC	2-1	1-1	2-1	1-0	1-2	0-0	4-0	2-0	1-3	4-0	1-2	6-1	4-0	1-1	■	0-0	0-1	1-1	0-0	2-0	4-2	2-0	0-2	0-2
Peterborough United	1-3	1-0	5-1	1-3	2-0	4-1	1-0	0-1	0-0	1-1	0-0	0-0	1-0	0-1	0-1	■	2-0	1-2	0-2	2-0	1-1	0-0	1-1	1-2
Plymouth Argyle FC	1-1	1-3	3-0	2-0	2-2	3-1	0-1	0-0	1-3	2-1	2-1	3-1	0-0	1-0	2-2	6-1	■	3-0	0-1	4-1	1-1	0-1	1-3	1-0
Port Vale FC	0-0	1-0	1-0	2-3	0-2	1-2	5-2	1-0	5-1	1-2	4-2	3-2	3-2	1-1	1-0	1-2	1-2	■	0-0	0-1	1-1	1-4	0-1	1-1
Queen's Park Rangers	1-0	2-1	1-1	1-0	0-4	4-1	3-1	2-0	0-0	3-0	2-0	2-2	0-1	2-0	1-2	2-0	2-2	4-0	■	1-0	2-0	1-2	0-1	2-1
Stockport County	4-1	2-2	2-3	1-4	1-1	1-1	2-1	1-1	1-4	2-1	2-3	2-0	4-0	0-0	1-2	2-1	2-1	1-1	1-1	■	2-5	2-3	1-1	2-1
Swindon Town FC	3-1	1-1	2-1	1-1	0-1	0-3	3-0	2-2	1-3	0-1	2-1	2-1	2-0	5-0	0-1	1-1	2-0	1-2	3-1	0-1	■	1-1	2-1	0-3
Tranmere Rovers FC	1-0	2-1	3-1	1-3	3-3	1-0	2-1	1-1	2-1	1-3	3-1	4-0	2-2	1-2	1-1	2-1	1-1	3-0	1-0	0-1	0-1	■	0-2	1-0
Wigan Athletic AFC	1-0	1-1	2-0	2-0	2-2	0-0	3-1	2-1	2-0	1-0	1-1	3-2	1-0	3-1	3-1	2-2	0-1	0-1	1-1	2-1	2-0	0-0	■	3-0
Wycombe Wanderers	2-2	1-2	4-0	2-1	0-4	1-1	2-0	0-0	1-2	0-0	1-2	3-3	1-1	3-1	2-2	3-2	2-1	3-1	4-1	1-4	2-3	1-3	0-2	■

Football League Division 2	Pd	Wn	Dw	Ls	GF	GA	Pts	
1. Wigan Athletic AFC (Wigan)	46	29	13	4	68	25	100	P
2. Crewe Alexandra FC (Crewe)	46	25	11	10	76	40	86	P
3. Bristol City FC (Bristol)	46	24	11	11	79	48	83	PO
4. Queen's Park Rangers FC (London)	46	24	11	11	69	45	83	PO
5. Oldham Athletic AFC (Oldham)	46	22	16	8	68	38	82	PO
6. Cardiff City AFC (Cardiff)	46	23	12	11	68	43	81	POP
7. Tranmere Rovers FC (Birkenhead)	46	23	11	12	66	57	80	
8. Plymouth Argyle FC (Plymouth)	46	17	14	15	63	52	65	
9. Luton Town FC (Luton)	46	17	14	15	67	62	65	
10. Swindon Town FC (Swindon)	46	16	12	18	59	63	60	
11. Peterborough United FC (Peterborough)	46	14	16	16	51	54	58	
12. Colchester United FC (Colchester)	46	14	16	16	52	56	58	
13. Blackpool FC (Blackpool)	46	15	13	18	56	64	58	
14. Stockport County FC (Stockport)	46	15	10	21	65	70	55	
15. Notts County FC (Nottingham)	46	13	16	17	62	70	55	
16. Brentford FC (London)	46	14	12	20	47	56	54	
17. Port Vale FC (Stoke-on-Trent)	46	14	11	21	54	70	53	
18. Wycombe Wanderers FC (High Wycombe)	46	13	13	20	59	66	52	
19. Barnsley FC (Barnsley)	46	13	13	20	51	64	52	
20. Chesterfield FC (Chesterfield)	46	14	8	24	43	73	50	
21. Cheltenham Town FC (Cheltenham)	46	10	18	18	53	68	48	R
22. Huddersfield Town AFC (Huddersfield)	46	11	12	23	39	61	45	R
23. Mansfield Town FC (Mansfield)	46	12	8	26	66	97	44	R
24. Northampton Town FC (Northampton)	46	10	9	27	40	79	39	R
	1104	402	300	402	1421	1421	1506	

Promotion Play-offs

Cardiff City AFC (Cardiff)	1-0 (aet)	Queen's Park Rangers FC (London)
Cardiff City AFC (Cardiff)	1-0, 0-0	Bristol City FC (Bristol)
Oldham Athletic AFC (Oldham)	1-1, 0-1	Queen's Park Rangers FC (London)

Football League Division 3 2002-03 Season	Boston United	Bournemouth	Bristol Rovers	Bury	Cambridge Utd.	Carlisle United	Darlington	Exeter City	Hartlepool	Hull City	Kidderminster H.	Leyton Orient	Lincoln City	Macclesfield T.	Oxford United	Rochdale	Rushden & D.	Scunthorpe Utd.	Shrewsbury T.	Southend United	Swansea City	Torquay United	Wrexham	York City
Boston United FC	■	2-2	0-0	1-1	1-3	0-0	1-0	0-3	0-1	0-1	3-0	0-1	2-0	2-1	1-3	3-1	1-1	1-0	6-0	1-0	1-0	2-1	3-3	3-0
AFC Bournemouth	2-1	■	1-0	1-2	1-1	3-1	2-0	2-0	2-1	0-0	0-0	3-1	0-1	2-2	1-1	3-3	3-1	2-1	2-1	1-0	3-0	1-1	2-0	1-0
Bristol Rovers FC	1-1	0-0	■	2-1	3-1	1-2	2-1	1-1	1-0	1-1	1-2	1-2	2-0	1-1	0-2	1-2	1-2	2-1	0-0	0-1	3-1	1-1	0-3	0-1
Bury FC	0-0	2-1	0-1	■	0-1	1-1	2-2	1-0	1-1	1-0	1-1	2-0	2-1	1-1	1-1	0-1	0-0	4-3	1-3	3-2	0-1	0-3	2-1	
Cambridge United	1-2	2-1	3-1	1-2	■	2-1	1-2	2-1	0-0	1-2	0-2	2-1	0-0	3-1	1-1	2-2	4-1	1-1	5-0	1-1	1-0	1-1	2-2	3-0
Carlisle United FC	4-2	0-2	0-0	1-2	0-1	■	2-2	0-2	1-3	1-5	2-2	3-0	1-4	1-0	1-0	0-2	1-2	1-2	1-2	1-0	2-2	1-2	1-2	1-1
Darlington FC	2-3	2-2	1-0	3-1	1-2	2-0	■	2-2	2-2	2-0	2-1	2-2	0-0	0-1	0-1	2-2	11-	5-1	2-1	2-1	1-1	0-1	2-1	
Exeter City FC	0-2	1-3	0-2	1-2	1-2	1-0	0-4	■	1-2	3-1	2-5	1-0	2-0	1-1	2-2	1-1	1-1	1-1	1-0	1-0	1-2	1-0	0-1	
Hartlepool United	2-0	0-0	2-0	0-0	3-0	2-1	4-1	2-1	■	2-0	2-1	4-1	2-1	0-2	3-0	2-2	1-2	2-2	3-0	2-1	4-0	3-2	4-3	0-0
Hull City AFC	1-0	3-1	1-0	1-1	1-1	4-0	0-1	2-2	2-0	■	4-1	1-1	0-1	1-3	0-0	3-0	1-1	2-0	2-0	2-2	1-1	1-1	1-2	0-0
Kidderminster Harr.	0-0	1-0	1-1	3-2	2-1	1-2	1-1	4-3	2-2	1-0	■	3-2	1-1	0-2	1-3	0-0	1-3	2-2	1-0	2-2	2-0	2-0	0-2	1-2
Leyton Orient FC	3-2	0-0	1-2	1-2	1-1	2-1	1-1	1-2	1-2	2-0	0-0	■	1-1	3-2	0-2	0-2	2-1	3-1	2-0	2-1	1-0	0-1	0-1	
Lincoln City FC	1-1	1-2	2-1	1-2	1-2	2-1	0-1	1-0	2-0	1-1	1-0	1-1	■	3-0	0-1	2-0	1-0	1-1	1-0	1-1	1-0	1-1	1-1	1-0
Macclesfield Town	2-0	0-1	2-1	0-0	1-1	2-2	1-0	1-1	0-1	0-1	2-0	3-1	0-1	■	2-1	3-2	0-1	2-3	1-2	2-1	1-3	3-3	0-1	1-1
Oxford United FC	2-1	3-0	0-1	2-1	1-1	0-0	1-1	2-2	0-1	0-0	2-1	0-2	1-0	0-1	■	2-0	3-0	0-1	2-2	0-1	1-0	2-2	0-2	2-0
Rochdale AFC	1-0	1-1	1-1	1-2	4-3	0-1	1-1	3-3	4-0	2-1	0-1	3-1	1-1	1-1	1-2	■	0-1	1-1	1-2	1-0	2-2	2-2	0-0	
Rushden & Diamonds	1-0	2-1	2-1	0-1	4-1	1-1	2-0	1-1	1-1	4-2	3-1	2-0	1-0	3-0	0-2	3-3	■	2-0	5-1	3-0	1-1	3-0	2-2	2-1
Scunthorpe United	2-0	0-2	2-2	0-1	1-2	3-1	0-1	1-1	4-0	3-1	1-1	2-1	0-0	1-1	2-0	3-1	0-0	■	1-1	4-1	2-0	5-1	1-1	2-1
Shrewsbury Town	1-2	0-0	2-5	4-1	3-1	2-3	2-2	1-0	0-1	1-1	1-2	1-2	3-1	1-2	■	0-1	0-0	2-3	1-2	2-2				
Southend United	4-2	0-1	2-1	1-2	2-1	0-1	0-0	0-1	3-0	0-1	1-0	2-1	1-0	2-1	1-2	2-3	■	0-2	3-0	0-1	1-0			
Swansea City FC	0-0	2-0	0-1	2-3	2-0	1-2	1-0	2-2	4-2	0-4	0-1	2-0	1-0	3-1	2-2	1-1	6-0	1-0	■	0-1	0-0	1-2		
Torquay United FC	1-1	4-0	2-1	1-1	3-2	2-3	3-1	1-0	1-1	1-4	2-2	2-2	0-0	2-2	2-3	2-2	1-1	1-1	2-1	3-1	0-0	■	2-1	3-1
Wrexham AFC	1-1	3-2	3-2	2-2	5-0	6-1	0-0	4-0	2-0	0-0	0-2	0-1	1-3	1-0	2-5	3-0	2-1	3-3	3-0	4-0	2-1	■	1-1	
York City FC	2-0	1-0	2-2	1-1	3-1	1-0	0-2	0-0	1-1	0-0	3-2	1-1	0-1	2-0	0-0	1-3	2-1	2-0	3-1	4-3	1-1	■		

Football League Division 3

		Pd	Wn	Dw	Ls	GF	GA	Pts	
1.	Rushden & Diamonds FC (Irthlingborough)	46	24	15	7	73	47	87	P
2.	Hartlepool United FC (Hartlepool)	46	24	13	9	71	51	85	P
3.	Wrexham AFC (Wrexham)	46	23	15	8	84	50	84	P
4.	AFC Bournemouth (Bournemouth)	46	20	14	12	60	48	74	POP
5.	Scunthorpe United FC (Scunthorpe)	46	19	15	12	68	49	72	PO
6.	Lincoln City FC (Lincoln)	46	18	16	12	46	37	70	PO
7.	Bury FC (Bury)	46	18	16	12	57	56	70	PO
8.	Oxford United FC (Oxford)	46	19	12	15	57	47	69	
9.	Torquay United FC (Torquay)	46	16	18	12	71	71	66	
10.	York City FC (York)	46	17	15	14	52	53	66	
11.	Kidderminster Harriers FC (Kidderminster)	46	16	15	15	62	63	63	
12.	Cambridge United FC (Cambridge)	46	16	13	17	67	70	61	
13.	Hull City AFC (Kingston-upon-Hull)	46	14	17	15	58	53	59	
14.	Darlington FC (Darlington)	46	12	18	16	58	59	54	
15.	Boston United FC (Boston)	46	15	13	18	55	56	54	-4
16.	Macclesfield Town FC (Macclesfield)	46	14	12	20	57	63	54	
17.	Southend United FC (Southend-on-Sea)	46	17	3	26	47	59	54	
18.	Leyton Orient FC (London)	46	14	11	21	51	61	53	
19.	Rochdale AFC (Rochdale)	46	12	16	18	63	70	52	
20.	Bristol Rovers FC (Bristol)	46	12	15	19	50	57	51	
21.	Swansea City FC (Swansea)	46	12	13	21	48	65	49	
22.	Carlisle United FC (Carlisle)	46	13	10	23	52	78	49	
23.	Exeter City FC (Exeter)	46	11	15	20	50	64	48	R
24.	Shrewsbury Town FC (Shrewsbury)	46	9	14	23	62	92	41	R
		1104	385	334	385	1419	1419	1485	

Note: Boston United FC had 4 points deducted.

Promotion Play-offs

AFC Bournemouth (Bournemouth)	5-2	Lincoln City FC (Lincoln)
Bury FC (Bury)	0-0, 1-3	AFC Bournemouth (Bournemouth)
Lincoln City FC (Lincoln)	5-3, 1-0	Scunthorpe United FC (Scunthorpe)

Promoted to Division 3: Doncaster Rovers FC (Doncaster), Yeovil Town FC (Yeovil)

F.A. CUP FINAL   (Millennium Stadium, Cardiff – 17/05/2003 – 73,726)

ARSENAL FC (LONDON)	1-0	Southampton FC (Southampton)

Pires 38'

Arsenal: Seaman, Lauren, Keown, Luzhny, Cole, Pires, Parlour, Silva, Ljungberg, Henry, Bergkamp (Wiltord 77').

Southampton: Niemi (Jones 66'), Baird (Fernandes 86'), Lundekvam, M.Svensson, Bridge, Telfer, Oakley, A.Svensson (Tessem 75'), Marsden, Ormerod, Beattie.

Semi-finals

Arsenal FC (London)	1-0	Sheffield United FC (Sheffield)
Watford FC (Watford)	1-2	Southampton FC (Southampton)

Quarter-finals

Arsenal FC (London)	2-2, 3-1	Chelsea FC (London)
Sheffield United FC (Sheffield)	1-0	Leeds United AFC (Leeds)
Southampton FC (Southampton)	2-0	Wolverhampton Wanderers FC (Wolverhampton)
Watford FC (Watford)	2-0	Burnley FC (Burnley)

2003-04

F.A. Premiership 2003-04 Season	Arsenal	Aston Villa	Birmingham City	Blackburn Rovers	Bolton Wanderers	Charlton Athletic	Chelsea	Everton	Fulham	Leeds United	Leicester City	Liverpool	Manchester City	Manchester United	Middlesbrough	Newcastle United	Portsmouth	Southampton	Tottenham Hotspur	Wolves
Arsenal FC	■	2-0	0-0	1-0	2-1	2-1	2-1	2-1	0-0	5-0	2-1	4-2	2-1	1-1	4-1	3-2	1-1	2-0	2-1	3-0
Aston Villa FC	0-2	■	2-2	0-2	1-1	2-1	3-2	0-0	3-0	2-0	3-1	0-0	1-1	0-2	0-2	0-0	2-1	1-0	1-0	3-2
Birmingham City FC	0-3	0-0	■	0-4	2-0	1-2	0-0	3-0	2-2	4-1	0-1	0-3	2-1	1-2	3-1	1-1	2-0	2-1	1-0	2-2
Blackburn Rovers FC	0-2	0-2	1-1	■	3-4	0-1	2-3	2-1	0-2	1-2	1-0	1-3	2-3	1-0	2-2	1-1	1-2	1-1	1-0	5-1
Bolton Wanderers FC	1-1	2-2	0-1	2-2	■	0-0	0-2	2-0	0-2	4-1	2-2	2-2	1-3	1-2	2-0	1-0	1-0	0-0	2-0	1-1
Charlton Athletic FC	1-1	2-1	1-1	3-2	1-2	■	4-2	2-2	3-1	0-1	2-2	3-2	0-3	0-2	1-0	0-0	1-1	2-1	2-4	2-0
Chelsea FC	1-2	1-0	0-0	2-2	1-2	1-0	■	0-0	2-1	1-0	2-1	0-1	1-0	1-0	0-0	5-0	3-0	4-0	4-2	5-2
Everton FC	1-1	2-0	1-0	0-1	1-2	0-1	0-1	■	3-1	4-0	3-2	0-3	0-0	3-4	1-1	2-2	1-0	0-0	3-1	2-0
Fulham FC	0-1	1-2	0-0	3-4	2-1	2-0	0-1	2-1	■	2-0	2-0	1-2	2-2	1-1	3-2	2-3	2-0	2-0	2-1	0-0
Leeds United AFC	1-4	0-0	0-2	2-1	0-2	3-3	1-1	1-1	3-2	■	3-2	2-2	2-1	0-1	0-3	2-2	1-2	0-0	0-1	4-1
Leicester City FC	1-1	0-5	0-2	2-0	1-1	1-1	0-4	1-1	0-2	4-0	■	0-0	1-1	1-4	0-0	1-1	3-1	2-2	1-2	0-0
Liverpool FC	1-2	1-0	3-1	4-0	3-1	0-1	1-2	0-0	0-0	3-1	2-1	■	2-1	1-2	2-0	1-1	3-0	1-2	0-0	1-0
Manchester City FC	1-2	4-1	0-0	1-1	6-1	1-1	0-1	5-1	0-0	1-1	0-3	2-2	■	4-1	0-1	1-0	1-1	1-3	0-3	3-3
Manchester United FC	0-0	4-0	3-0	2-1	4-0	2-0	1-1	3-2	1-3	1-1	1-0	0-1	3-1	■	2-3	0-0	3-0	3-2	3-0	1-0
Middlesbrough FC	0-4	1-2	5-3	0-1	2-0	0-0	1-2	1-0	2-1	2-3	3-3	0-0	2-1	0-1	■	0-1	0-0	3-1	1-0	2-0
Newcastle United FC	0-0	1-1	0-1	0-1	0-0	3-1	2-1	4-2	3-1	1-0	3-1	1-1	3-0	1-2	2-1	■	3-0	1-0	4-0	1-1
Portsmouth FC	1-1	2-1	3-1	1-2	4-0	1-2	0-2	1-2	1-1	6-1	0-2	1-0	4-2	1-0	5-1	1-1	■	1-0	2-0	0-0
Southampton FC	0-1	1-1	0-0	2-0	1-2	3-2	0-1	3-3	0-0	2-1	0-0	2-0	1-0	0-1	3-3	3-0		■	1-0	2-0
Tottenham Hotspur FC	2-2	2-1	4-1	1-0	0-1	0-1	0-1	3-0	0-3	2-1	4-4	2-1	1-1	1-2	0-0	1-0	4-3	1-3	■	5-2
Wolverhampton Wanderers FC	1-3	0-4	1-1	2-2	1-2	0-4	0-5	2-1	2-1	4-3	1-1	1-0	1-0	2-0	1-1	0-0	1-4	0-2		■

F.A. Premiership

		Pd	Wn	Dw	Ls	GF	GA	Pts	
1.	ARSENAL FC (LONDON)	38	26	12	-	73	26	90	
2.	Chelsea FC (London)	38	24	7	7	67	30	79	
3.	Manchester United FC (Manchester)	38	23	6	9	64	35	75	
4.	Liverpool FC (Liverpool)	38	16	12	10	55	37	60	
5.	Newcastle United FC (Newcastle-upon-Tyne)	38	13	17	8	52	40	56	
6.	Aston Villa FC (Birmingham)	38	15	11	12	48	44	56	
7.	Charlton Athletic FC (London)	38	14	11	13	51	51	53	
8.	Bolton Wanderers FC (Bolton)	38	14	11	13	48	56	53	
9.	Fulham FC (London)	38	14	10	14	52	46	52	
10.	Birmingham City FC (Birmingham)	38	12	14	12	43	48	50	
11.	Middlesbrough FC (Middlesbrough)	38	13	9	16	44	52	48	
12.	Southampton FC (Southampton)	38	12	11	15	44	45	47	
13.	Portsmouth FC (Portsmouth)	38	12	9	17	47	54	45	
14.	Tottenham Hotspur Fc(London)	38	13	6	19	47	57	45	
15.	Blackburn Rovers FC (Blackburn)	38	12	8	18	51	59	44	
16.	Manchester City FC (Manchester)	38	9	14	15	55	54	41	
17.	Everton FC (Liverpool)	38	9	12	17	45	57	39	
18.	Leicester City FC (Leicester)	38	6	15	17	48	65	33	R
19.	Leeds United AFC (Leeds)	38	8	9	21	40	79	33	R
20.	Wolverhampton Wanderers FC (Wolverhampton)	38	7	12	19	38	77	33	R
		760	272	216	272	1012	1012	1032	

Top Goalscorers

1)	Thierry HENRY	(Arsenal FC)	30
2)	Alan SHEARER	(Newcastle United FC)	22
3)	Louis SAHA	(Fulham/Manchester Utd.)	20
	Ruud VAN NISTELROOY	(Manchester United FC)	20

Football League Division 1 2003-04 Season	Bradford City	Burnley	Cardiff City	Coventry City	Crewe Alexandra	Crystal Palace	Derby County	Gillingham	Ipswich Town	Millwall	Norwich City	Nottingham Forest	Preston North End	Reading	Rotherham United	Sheffield United	Stoke City	Sunderland	Walsall	Watford	W.B.A.	West Ham United	Wigan Athletic	Wimbledon
Bradford City AFC	■	1-2	0-1	1-0	2-1	1-2	1-2	0-1	0-1	3-2	2-2	1-2	2-1	2-1	0-2	1-2	0-2	0-4	1-1	5-1	0-1	1-2	0-0	2-3
Burnley FC	4-0	■	1-1	1-2	1-0	2-3	1-0	1-0	4-2	1-1	3-5	0-3	1-1	3-0	1-1	3-2	0-1	1-2	3-1	2-3	1-1	1-1	0-2	2-0
Cardiff City AFC	0-2	2-0	■	0-1	3-0	0-2	4-1	5-0	2-3	1-3	2-1	0-0	2-2	2-3	3-2	2-1	3-1	4-0	0-1	3-0	1-1	0-0	0-0	1-1
Coventry City FC	0-0	4-0	1-3	■	2-0	2-1	2-0	2-2	1-1	4-0	0-2	1-3	4-1	1-2	1-1	0-1	4-2	1-1	0-0	0-0	1-0	1-1	1-1	1-1
Crewe Alexandra FC	2-2	3-1	0-1	3-1	■	2-3	3-0	1-1	1-0	1-2	1-3	3-1	2-1	1-0	0-0	0-1	2-0	3-0	1-0	0-1	1-2	0-3	2-3	1-0
Crystal Palace FC	0-1	0-0	2-1	1-1	1-3	■	1-1	1-0	3-4	0-1	1-0	1-0	1-1	2-2	1-1	1-2	6-3	3-0	1-0	1-0	2-2	1-0	1-1	3-1
Derby County FC	3-2	2-0	2-2	1-3	0-0	2-1	■	2-1	2-2	2-0	0-4	4-2	5-1	2-3	1-0	2-0	0-3	1-1	0-1	3-2	0-1	0-1	2-2	3-1
Gillingham FC	1-0	0-3	1-2	2-5	2-0	1-0	0-0	■	1-2	4-3	1-2	2-1	0-1	0-1	2-0	0-3	3-1	1-3	3-0	1-0	0-2	2-0	0-3	1-2
Ipswich Town FC	3-1	6-1	1-1	1-1	6-4	1-3	2-1	3-4	■	1-3	0-2	1-2	2-0	1-1	2-1	3-0	1-0	1-0	2-1	4-1	2-3	1-2	1-3	4-1
Millwall FC	1-0	2-0	0-0	2-1	1-1	1-1	0-0	1-2	0-0	■	0-0	1-0	0-1	0-1	2-1	2-0	1-1	2-1	2-1	1-2	1-1	4-1	2-0	2-0
Norwich City	0-1	2-0	41	1-1	1-0	2-1	2-1	3-0	3-1	3-1	■	1-0	3-2	2-1	2-0	1-0	1-0	1-0	5-0	1-2	0-0	1-1	2-0	3-2
Nottingham Forest	2-1	1-1	1-2	0-1	2-0	3-2	1-1	0-0	1-1	2-2	2-0	■	0-1	0-1	2-2	3-1	0-0	2-0	3-3	1-1	0-3	0-2	1-0	6-0
Preston North End	1-0	5-3	2-2	4-2	0-0	4-1	3-0	0-0	1-1	1-2	0-0	2-2	■	2-1	4-1	3-3	1-0	0-2	1-2	2-1	3-0	1-2	2-4	1-0
Reading FC	2-2	2-2	2-1	1-2	1-1	0-3	3-1	2-1	1-1	1-0	0-1	3-0	3-2	■	0-0	2-1	0-0	0-2	0-1	2-1	1-0	2-0	1-0	0-3
Rotherham United	1-2	3-0	0-0	2-0	0-2	1-2	0-0	1-1	1-3	0-0	4-4	1-1	1-0	5-1	■	1-1	3-0	2-0	1-1	0-3	1-0	0-3	0-3	3-1
Sheffield United FC	2-0	1-0	5-3	2-1	2-0	0-3	1-1	0-0	1-1	1-1	1-0	1-2	2-0	1-2	5-0	■	0-1	0-1	2-0	2-2	1-2	3-3	1-1	2-1
Stoke City FC	1-0	1-2	2-3	1-0	1-1	0-1	2-1	0-0	2-0	0-0	1-1	2-1	1-1	3-0	0-2	2-2	■	3-1	3-2	3-1	4-1	0-2	1-1	2-1
Sunderland AFC	3-0	1-1	0-0	0-0	1-1	2-1	2-1	2-1	3-2	0-1	1-0	3-3	2-0	0-0	3-0	1-1		■	1-0	2-0	0-1	2-0	1-1	2-1
Walsall FC	1-0	0-1	1-1	1-6	1-1	0-0	2-1	1-3	1-1	1-3	4-1	2-1	1-1	3-2	0-1	1-1	1-3		■	0-1	4-1	1-1	2-0	1-0
Watford FC	1-0	1-1	2-1	1-1	2-1	1-5	2-1	2-2	1-2	3-1	1-2	1-1	2-0	1-0	0-2	1-3	2-2	1-1		■	0-1	0-0	1-1	4-0
West Bromwich Alb.	2-0	4-1	2-1	3-0	2-2	2-0	1-1	1-0	4-1	2-1	1-0	0-2	1-0	0-0	0-1	0-2	1-0	0-0	2-0	3-1	■	1-1	2-1	0-1
West Ham United FC	1-0	2-2	1-0	2-0	4-2	3-0	0-0	2-1	1-2	1-1	1-1	1-2	1-0	2-1	0-0	0-1	3-2	0-0	4-0	3-4		■	4-0	2-0
Wigan Athletic AFC	1-0	0-0	3-0	2-1	2-3	5-0	2-0	1-0	1-0	0-0	1-1	2-2	1-1	0-2	1-2	1-1	2-1	2-0	1-0	1-0	1-0	1-1	■	0-1
Wimbledon FC	2-1	2-2	0-1	0-3	3-1	1-3	1-0	1-2	1-2	0-1	0-1	0-1	3-3	0-3	1-2	1-2	0-1	1-2	0-1	1-3	0-0	1-1	2-4	■

	Football League Division 1	**Pd**	**Wn**	**Dw**	**Ls**	**GF**	**GA**	**Pts**	
1.	Norwich City FC (Norwich)	46	28	10	8	79	39	94	P
2.	West Bromwich Albion FC (West Bromwich)	46	25	11	10	64	42	86	P
3.	Sunderland AFC (Sunderland)	46	22	13	11	62	45	79	PO
4.	West Ham United FC (London)	46	19	17	10	67	45	74	PO
5.	Ipswich Town FC (Ipswich)	46	21	10	15	84	72	73	PO
6.	Crystal Palace FC (London)	46	21	10	15	72	61	73	POP
7.	Wigan Athletic AFC (Wigan)	46	18	17	11	60	45	71	
8.	Sheffield United FC (Sheffield)	46	20	11	15	65	56	71	
9.	Reading FC (Reading)	46	20	10	16	55	57	70	
10.	Millwall FC (London)	46	18	15	13	55	48	69	
11.	Stoke City FC (Stoke-on-Trent)	46	18	12	16	58	55	66	
12.	Coventry City FC (Coventry)	46	17	14	15	67	54	65	
13.	Cardiff City AFC (Cardiff)	46	17	14	15	68	58	65	
14.	Nottingham Forest FC (Nottingham)	46	15	15	16	61	58	60	
15.	Preston North End FC (Preston)	46	15	14	17	69	71	59	
16.	Watford FC (Watford)	46	15	12	19	54	68	57	
17.	Rotherham United FC (Rotherham)	46	13	15	18	53	61	54	
18.	Crewe Alexandra FC (Crewe)	46	14	11	21	57	66	53	
19.	Burnley FC (Burnley)	46	13	14	19	60	77	53	
20.	Derby County FC (Derby)	46	13	13	20	53	67	52	
21.	Gillingham FC (Gillingham)	46	14	9	23	48	67	51	
22.	Walsall FC (Walsall)	46	13	12	21	45	65	51	R
23.	Bradford City AFC (Bradford)	46	10	6	30	38	69	36	R
24.	Wimbledon FC (Milton Keynes)	46	8	5	33	41	89	29	R
		1104	407	290	407	1435	1435	1511	

Promotion Play-offs

Crystal Palace FC (London)	1-0	West Ham United FC (London)
Crystal Palace FC (London)	3-2, 1-2 (aet)	Sunderland AFC (Sunderland)
	(Crystal Palace won 5-4 on penalties)	
Ipswich Town FC (Ipswich)	1-0, 0-2	West Ham United FC (London)

Football League Division 2 — 2003-04 Season

Club	Barnsley	Blackpool	Bournemouth	Brentford	Brighton & Hove Albion	Bristol City	Chesterfield	Colchester United	Grimsby Town	Hartlepool	Luton Town	Notts County	Oldham Athletic	Peterborough United	Plymouth Argyle	Port Vale	Q.P.R.	Rushden & Diamonds	Sheffield Wednesday	Stockport County	Swindon Town	Tranmere Rovers	Wrexham	Wycombe Wanderers
Barnsley FC		3-0	1-1	0-2	1-0	0-1	0-1	1-0	0-0	2-2	0-0	1-1	1-1	0-1	1-0	0-0	3-3	2-0	1-1	3-3	0-1	2-0	2-1	0-0
Blackpool FC	0-2		1-2	1-1	3-1	1-0	1-0	0-0	0-1	4-0	0-1	2-1	1-1	1-4	0-1	2-1	0-1	2-3	4-1	1-1	2-2	2-1	0-1	3-2
AFC Bournemouth	2-2	1-2		1-0	1-0	0-0	2-2	1-1	0-0	2-2	6-3	1-0	1-0	1-2	0-2	2-1	1-0	2-1	1-0	0-0	2-2	1-5	6-0	1-0
Brentford FC	2-1	0-0	1-0		4-0	1-2	1-1	3-2	1-3	2-1	4-2	2-3	2-1	0-3	1-3	3-2	1-1	3-2	0-3	0-2	0-2	2-2	0-1	1-1
Brighton & Hove Alb.	1-0	3-0	3-0	1-0		1-4	1-0	2-1	3-0	2-0	2-1	1-0	0-0	1-0	2-1	1-1	2-1	0-0	2-0	0-1	2-2	3-0	2-0	4-0
Bristol City FC	2-1	2-1	2-0	3-1	0-0		4-0	1-0	1-0	1-1	1-1	5-0	0-2	1-1	1-0	0-1	1-0	1-0	1-1	1-0	2-1	2-0	1-0	1-1
Chesterfield FC	0-2	1-0	1-1	1-2	0-2	1-1		1-2	4-4	1-2	1-0	0-1	1-1	2-1	1-1	1-0	4-2	2-0	3-1	0-3	3-0	2-2	2-1	2-2
Colchester United FC	1-1	1-1	1-0	1-1	1-0	2-1	1-0		2-0	1-2	1-1	4-1	2-1	0-0	0-2	1-4	2-2	2-3	2-1	3-1	2-1	1-1	3-1	1-1
Grimsby Town FC	6-1	0-2	1-1	1-0	2-1	1-2	4-0	2-0		0-2	3-2	2-0	3-3	1-1	0-0	1-2	0-1	1-0	2-0	1-1	1-2	0-1	3-1	3-1
Hartlepool United FC	1-2	1-1	2-1	1-2	0-0	1-2	2-0	0-0	8-1		4-3	4-0	0-0	1-3	2-0	1-4	2-1	1-1	2-2	2-0	0-0	2-0	1-1	
Luton Town FC	0-1	3-2	1-1	4-1	2-0	3-2	1-1	1-0	1-2	3-2		2-0	1-1	1-1	1-1	2-0	1-1	3-1	3-2	2-2	0-3	3-1	3-2	3-1
Notts County FC	1-1	4-1	0-1	2-0	1-2	1-2	1-1	3-0	3-1	1-0	1-1		1-1	0-0	1-2	3-3	1-3	0-0	4-1	1-3	2-2	2-2	1-1	1-1
Oldham Athletic AFC	0-0	2-3	1-1	1-1	1-3	1-1	2-0	0-0	6-0	0-2	3-0	0-1		1-1	4-1	2-1	2-1	3-2	1-0	2-0	0-1	1-1	1-1	2-3
Peterborough United	2-3	0-1	0-1	0-0	2-2	0-1	0-2	1-2	0-0	3-4	1-2	5-2	2-2		2-2	3-1	0-0	3-1	0-1	1-2	4-2	0-0	6-1	1-1
Plymouth Argyle FC	2-0	1-0	0-0	2-0	3-3	0-1	7-0	2-0	2-2	2-0	2-1	3-0	2-2	2-0		2-1	2-0	3-0	2-0	3-1	2-1	6-0	0-0	2-1
Port Vale FC	3-1	2-1	2-1	1-0	1-1	2-1	1-1	4-3	5-1	2-5	1-0	1-0	3-0	1-5		2-0	1-1	3-0	2-2	3-3	2-1	1-0	1-1	
Queen's Park Rangers	4-0	5-0	1-0	1-0	1-1	1-1	3-0	2-0	3-0	4-1	1-1	3-2	1-1	1-1	3-0	3-2		1-0	3-0	1-1	1-0	1-1	2-0	0-0
Rushden & Diamonds	2-3	0-0	0-3	0-1	1-3	1-1	2-1	4-0	3-1	0-2	2-2	2-1	4-1	0-1	2-1	0-2	3-3		1-2	2-2	2-0	2-1	2-3	2-0
Sheffield Wednesday	2-1	0-1	0-2	1-1	2-1	1-0	0-0	0-1	0-0	1-0	0-0	2-1	2-2	2-0	1-3	2-3	1-3	0-0		2-2	1-1	2-0	2-3	1-1
Stockport County FC	2-3	1-3	3-2	1-1	1-1	2-0	0-0	1-3	2-1	1-2	1-2	2-1	2-2	0-2	2-2	1-2	2-1	1-0		2-4	1-1	0-1	2-0
Swindon Town FC	1-1	2-2	2-1	2-1	1-1	1-1	2-0	2-0	1-1	2-2	4-0	1-2	2-0	2-3	0-0	1-1	4-2	2-3	1-2		2-0	1-0	2-0
Tranmere Rovers FC	2-0	1-1	1-1	4-1	1-0	1-0	2-3	1-1	2-1	0-0	1-0	4-0	2-1	0-0	3-0	1-0	0-0	1-2	2-2	3-2	1-0		1-2	2-1
Wrexham AFC	1-0	4-2	0-1	1-0	0-2	0-0	0-0	0-1	3-0	1-2	0-1	4-0	2-2	2-1	0-2	1-1	1-2	0-0	3-2	0-1				0-0
Wycombe Wanderers	1-2	0-3	2-0	1-2	1-1	3-0	3-3	1-2	4-1	3-4	0-0	1-1	2-5	1-2	0-0	2-1	2-2	0-2	1-2	1-0	0-3	1-2	1-1	

287

	Football League Division 2	Pd	Wn	Dw	Ls	GF	GA	Pts	
1.	Plymouth Argyle FC (Plymouth)	46	26	12	8	85	41	90	P
2.	Queen's Park Rangers FC (London)	46	22	17	7	80	45	83	P
3.	Bristol City FC (Bristol)	46	23	13	10	58	37	82	PO
4.	Brighton & Hove Albion FC (Brighton)	46	22	11	13	64	43	77	POP
5.	Swindon Town FC (Swindon)	46	20	13	13	76	58	73	PO
6.	Hartlepool United FC (Hartlepool)	46	20	13	13	76	61	73	PO
7.	Port Vale FC (Stoke-on-Trent)	46	21	10	15	73	63	73	
8.	Tranmere Rovers FC (Birkenhead)	46	17	16	13	59	56	67	
9.	AFC Bournemouth (Bournemouth)	46	17	15	14	56	51	66	
10.	Luton Town FC (Luton)	46	17	15	14	69	66	66	
11.	Colchester United FC (Colchester)	46	17	13	16	52	56	64	
12.	Barnsley FC (Barnsley)	46	15	17	14	54	58	62	
13.	Wrexham AFC (Wrexham)	46	17	9	20	50	60	60	
14.	Blackpool FC (Blackpool)	46	16	11	19	58	65	59	
15.	Oldham Athletic AFC (Oldham)	46	12	21	13	66	60	57	
16.	Sheffield Wednesday FC (Sheffield)	46	13	14	19	48	64	53	
17.	Brentford FC (London)	46	14	11	21	52	69	53	
18.	Peterborough United FC (Peterborough)	46	12	16	18	58	58	52	
19.	Stockport County FC (Stockport)	46	11	19	16	62	70	52	
20.	Chesterfield FC (Chesterfield)	46	12	15	19	49	71	51	
21.	Grimsby Town FC (Cleethorpes)	46	13	11	22	55	81	50	R
22.	Rushden & Diamonds FC (Irthlingborough)	46	13	9	24	60	74	48	R
23.	Notts County FC (Nottingham)	46	10	12	24	50	78	42	R
24.	Wycombe Wanderers FC (High Wycombe)	46	6	19	21	50	75	37	R
		1104	386	332	386	1460	1460	1490	

Promotion Play-offs

Brighton & Hove Albion FC (Brighton)	1-0	Bristol City FC (Bristol)
Hartlepool United FC (Hartlepool)	1-1, 1-2	Bristol City FC (Bristol)
Swindon Town FC (Swindon)	0-1, 2-1 (aet)	Brighton & Hove Albion FC (Brighton)

(Brighton & Hove Albion won 4-3 on penalties)

Home \ Away	Boston United	Bristol Rovers	Bury	Cambridge United	Carlisle United	Cheltenham Town	Darlington	Doncaster Rovers	Huddersfield Town	Hull City	Kidderminster Harriers	Leyton Orient	Lincoln City	Macclesfield Town	Mansfield Town	Northampton Town	Oxford United	Rochdale	Scunthorpe United	Southend United	Swansea City	Torquay United	Yeovil Town	York City
Boston United FC	■	1-0	1-0	1-2	1-0	3-1	1-0	0-0	2-2	1-2	2-2	3-0	0-1	3-0	1-2	1-1	1-1	2-0	1-1	0-2	1-1	4-0	3-2	2-0
Bristol Rovers FC	2-0	■	1-2	0-2	1-0	2-0	0-3	1-2	1-1	2-1	1-0	1-1	3-1	2-2	1-3	1-2	1-1	0-0	1-0	1-1	2-1	2-2	0-1	3-0
Bury FC	1-3	0-0	■	1-0	1-3	1-1	1-1	1-3	2-1	0-0	0-0	1-1	2-1	2-0	3-0	1-0	0-4	1-2	2-3	1-1	2-0	2-1	2-1	2-0
Cambridge United	0-1	3-1	1-2	■	2-2	2-1	1-0	3-3	1-2	0-2	0-0	1-4	0-0	3-1	1-2	0-1	1-1	0-0	3-2	0-1	0-1	1-1	1-4	2-0
Carlisle United FC	2-1	0-2	2-1	0-0	■	1-1	1-1	0-1	1-0	1-1	1-0	0-1	0-2	0-1	0-2	1-1	2-0	3-2	1-4	1-2	1-2	2-0	2-0	1-2
Cheltenham Town	1-0	1-2	1-2	0-3	2-1	■	2-1	1-3	1-1	2-1	1-0	3-2	3-2	4-2	4-3	0-0	0-2	2-1	1-1	3-4	1-3	3-1	1-1	1-1
Darlington FC	3-0	0-4	1-3	3-4	2-0	2-1	■	2-1	0-1	0-1	0-2	2-1	0-1	1-0	1-0	1-0	0-1	4-2	0-0	2-0	2-0	1-1	3-2	3-0
Doncaster Rovers	3-0	5-1	3-1	2-0	1-0	1-1	1-1	■	1-1	0-0	5-0	5-0	0-2	1-0	4-2	1-0	2-0	2-1	1-0	2-0	3-1	1-0	0-1	3-1
Huddersfield Town	2-0	1-2	1-0	2-2	2-1	0-0	0-2	3-1	■	3-1	1-0	3-0	2-1	4-0	1-3	3-0	1-1	1-1	3-2	1-0	3-0	1-0	3-1	0-1
Hull City AFC	2-1	3-0	2-0	2-0	2-1	3-3	4-1	3-1	0-0	■	6-1	3-0	3-0	2-2	0-1	2-3	4-2	1-0	2-1	3-2	1-0	0-1	0-0	2-1
Kidderminster Harr.	2-0	1-0	0-2	2-2	1-1	0-0	1-1	0-2	2-1	1-1	■	2-1	1-2	1-4	2-1	2-1	1-0	0-2	1-2	0-1	2-1	0-1	0-1	4-1
Leyton Orient FC	1-3	1-1	2-0	0-1	1-1	1-45	1-0	1-3	1-1	1-1	1-1	■	0-2	2-0	3-1	1-1	2-1	1-1	2-1	1-2	0-0	2-0	2-0	2-2
Lincoln City FC	1-1	3-1	2-1	2-2	2-0	0-0	1-1	0-0	3-1	2-0	1-1	0-0	■	3-2	4-1	0-0	0-1	1-1	1-1	2-2	2-1	1-3	2-3	3-0
Macclesfield Town	0-0	2-1	1-0	0-1	1-1	1-2	0-1	1-3	4-0	1-1	1-1	1-0	0-0	■	1-1	0-4	2-1	2-2	1-2	2-1	1-1	1-1	4-1	0-0
Mansfield Town FC	2-1	0-0	5-3	1-1	2-3	4-0	3-1	1-2	3-3	1-0	1-0	1-1	1-2	3-2	■	1-2	3-1	1-0	5-0	1-1	2-1	0-1	2-1	2-0
Northampton Town	2-1	2-0	3-2	1-2	2-0	1-0	1-0	0-1	1-5	0-1	1-0	1-1	0-0	0-3	1-1	■	2-1	3-1	1-1	2-2	2-1	0-1	2-0	2-1
Oxford United FC	0-0	0-0	1-1	2-2	2-1	1-0	3-1	0-0	0-1	2-1	2-1	2-1	0-0	3-1	1-1	3-0	■	2-0	3-2	2-0	3-0	1-0	1-0	0-0
Rochdale AFC	1-0	2-2	0-0	2-2	2-0	0-0	4-2	1-1	1-1	0-2	1-1	3-0	0-3	1-2	3-0	1-1	1-2	■	2-0	1-1	0-1	1-0	1-3	1-2
Scunthorpe United	0-1	1-2	0-0	4-0	2-3	5-2	0-1	2-2	6-2	1-1	0-2	1-1	1-3	0-0	1-0	1-1	2-2	1-2	■	1-1	2-2	2-1	3-0	1-0
Southend United FC	0-2	0-1	1-0	2-2	2-0	2-0	1-0	1-2	2-2	3-0	1-2	0-2	1-0	0-1	0-1	4-0	4-2	0-0	0-1	■	1-1	2-0	0-2	1-0
Swansea City FC	3-0	0-0	4-2	0-2	1-2	0-0	1-0	1-1	2-0	2-3	0-0	2-1	2-2	3-0	4-1	0-2	0-0	1-1	4-2	2-3	■	1-2	3-2	0-0
Torquay United FC	2-0	2-1	3-1	3-0	4-1	3-1	2-2	1-0	0-1	1-1	11-	2-1	1-0	4-1	1-0	3-1	3-0	1-3	1-0	3-0	0-0	■	2-2	1-1
Yeovil Town FC	2-0	4-0	2-1	4-1	3-0	0-0	1-0	0-1	2-1	1-2	1-2	1-2	3-1	2-2	1-0	0-2	1-0	2-1	4-0	2-0	0-2	1-1	■	3-0
York City FC	1-1	2-1	1-1	2-0	2-0	0-2	1-1	1-0	0-2	0-2	1-0	1-2	1-4	0-2	1-2	1-0	2-2	1-2	1-3	2-0	0-0	0-0	1-2	■

Football League Division 3

		Pd	Wn	Dw	Ls	GF	GA	Pts	
1.	Doncaster Rovers FC (Doncaster)	46	27	11	8	79	37	92	P
2.	Hull City AFC (Kingston-upon-Hull)	46	25	13	8	82	44	88	P
3.	Torquay United FC (Torquay)	46	23	12	11	68	44	81	P
4.	Huddersfield Town AFC (Huddersfield)	46	23	12	11	68	52	81	POP
5.	Mansfield Town FC (Mansfield)	46	22	9	15	76	62	75	PO
6.	Northampton Town FC (Northampton)	46	22	9	15	58	51	75	PO
7.	Lincoln City FC (Lincoln)	46	19	17	10	68	47	74	PO
8.	Yeovil Town FC (Yeovil)	46	23	5	18	70	57	74	
9.	Oxford United FC (Oxford)	46	18	17	11	55	44	71	
10.	Swansea City FC (Swansea)	46	15	14	17	58	61	59	
11.	Boston United FC (Boston)	46	16	11	19	50	54	59	
12.	Bury FC (Bury)	46	15	11	20	54	64	56	
13.	Cambridge United FC (Cambridge)	46	14	14	18	55	67	56	
14.	Cheltenham Town FC (Cheltenham)	46	14	14	18	57	71	56	
15.	Bristol Rovers FC (Bristol)	46	14	13	19	50	61	55	
16.	Kidderminster Harriers FC (Kidderminster)	46	14	13	19	45	59	55	
17.	Southend United FC (Southend-on-Sea)	46	14	12	20	51	63	54	
18.	Darlington FC (Darlington)	46	14	11	21	53	61	53	
19.	Leyton Orient FC (London)	46	13	14	19	48	65	53	
20.	Macclesfield Town FC (Macclesfield)	46	13	13	20	54	69	52	
21.	Rochdale AFC (Rochdale)	46	12	14	20	49	58	50	
22.	Scunthorpe United FC (Scunthorpe)	46	11	16	19	69	72	49	
23.	Carlisle United FC (Carlisle)	46	12	9	25	46	69	45	R
24.	York City FC (York)	46	10	14	22	35	66	44	R
		1104	403	298	403	1398	1398	1507	

Promotion Play-offs

Huddersfield Town AFC (Huddersfield)	0-0 (aet)	Mansfield Town FC (Mansfield)

(Huddersfield Town won 4-1 on penalties)

Lincoln City FC (Lincoln)	1-2, 2-2	Huddersfield Town AFC (Huddersfield)
Northampton Town FC (Northampton)	0-2, 3-1 (aet)	Mansfield Town FC (Mansfield)

(Mansfield Town won 5-4 on penalties)

Promoted to League 2: Chester City FC (Chester), Shrewsbury Town FC (Shrewsbury)

Note: From the next season the names of Football League Divisions 1, 2 and 3 were changed to "The Championship", "League 1" and "League 2" respectively.

F.A. CUP FINAL   (Millennium Stadium, Cardiff – 22/05/2004 – 72,350)

MANCHESTER UNITED FC (MANCHESTER)	3-0	Millwall FC (London)

Ronaldo 42', van Nistelrooy 64' pen., 80'

Man. United: Howard (Carroll 83'), G.Neville, O'Shea, Brown, Keane, Silvestre, Ronaldo (Solskjær 85'), Fletcher (Butt 85'), Van Nistelrooy, Scholes, Giggs.

Millwall: Marshall, Elliott, Ryan (Cogan 75'), Cahill, Lawrence, Ward, Ifill, Wise (Weston 89'), Harris (McCammon 75'), Livermore, Sweeney.

Semi-finals

Arsenal FC (London)	0-1	Manchester United FC (Manchester)
Sunderland AFC (Sunderland)	0-1	Millwall FC (London)

Quarter-finals

Manchester United FC (Manchester)	2-1	Fulham FC (London)
Millwall FC (London)	0-0, 2-1	Tranmere Rovers FC (Birkenhead)
Portsmouth FC (Portsmouth)	1-5	Arsenal FC (London)
Sunderland AFC (Sunderland)	1-0	Sheffield United FC (Sheffield)

2004-05

F.A. Premiership 2004-05 Season	Arsenal	Aston Villa	Birmingham City	Blackburn Rovers	Bolton Wanderers	Charlton Athletic	Chelsea	Crystal Palace	Everton	Fulham	Liverpool	Manchester City	Manchester United	Middlesbrough	Newcastle United	Norwich City	Portsmouth	Southampton	Tottenham Hotspur	West Bromwich Alb.
Arsenal FC	■	3-1	3-0	3-0	2-2	4-0	2-2	5-1	7-0	2-0	3-1	1-1	2-4	5-3	1-0	4-1	3-0	2-2	1-0	1-1
Aston Villa FC	1-3	■	1-2	1-0	1-1	0-0	0-0	1-1	1-3	2-0	1-1	1-2	0-1	2-0	4-2	3-0	3-0	2-0	1-0	1-1
Birmingham City FC	2-1	2-0	■	2-1	1-2	1-1	0-1	0-1	0-1	1-2	2-0	1-0	0-0	2-0	2-2	1-1	0-0	2-1	1-1	4-0
Blackburn Rovers FC	0-1	2-2	3-3	■	0-1	1-0	0-1	1-0	0-0	1-3	2-2	0-0	1-1	0-4	2-2	3-0	1-0	3-0	0-1	1-1
Bolton Wanderers FC	1-0	1-2	1-1	0-1	■	4-1	0-2	1-0	3-2	3-1	1-0	0-1	2-2	0-0	2-1	1-0	0-1	1-1	3-1	1-1
Charlton Athletic FC	1-3	3-0	3-1	1-0	1-2	■	0-4	2-2	2-0	2-1	1-2	2-2	0-4	1-2	1-1	4-0	2-1	0-0	2-0	1-4
Chelsea FC	0-0	1-0	1-1	4-0	2-2	1-0	■	4-1	1-0	3-1	1-0	0-0	1-0	2-0	4-0	4-0	3-0	2-1	0-0	1-0
Crystal Palace FC	1-1	2-0	2-0	0-0	0-1	0-1	0-2	■	1-3	2-0	1-0	1-2	0-0	0-1	0-2	3-3	0-1	2-2	3-0	3-0
Everton FC	1-4	1-1	1-1	0-1	3-2	0-1	0-1	4-0	■	1-0	1-0	2-1	1-0	1-0	2-0	2-1	1-0	0-1		2-1
Fulham FC	0-3	1-1	2-3	0-2	2-0	0-0	1-4	3-1	2-0	■	2-4	1-1	1-1	0-2	1-3	6-0	3-1	1-0	1-0	1-0
Liverpool FC	2-1	2-1	0-1	0-0	1-0	2-0	1-0	3-2	2-1	3-1	■	2-1	0-1	1-1	3-0	1-1	1-0	2-2		3-0
Manchester City FC	0-1	2-0	3-0	1-1	0-1	4-0	1-0	3-1	0-1	1-1	1-0	■	0-2	1-1	1-1	2-0	2-1	0-1		1-1
Manchester United FC	2-0	3-1	2-0	0-0	2-0	2-1	1-3	5-2	0-0	1-0	2-1	0-0	■	1-1	2-1	2-1	2-1	3-0	0-0	1-1
Middlesbrough FC	0-1	3-0	2-1	1-0	1-1	2-2	0-1	2-1	1-1	1-1	2-0	3-2	0-2	■	2-2	2-0	1-1	1-3	1-0	4-0
Newcastle United FC	0-1	0-3	2-1	3-0	2-1	1-1	1-1	0-0	1-1	1-4	1-0	4-3	1-3	0-0	■	2-2	1-1	2-1	0-1	3-1
Norwich City FC	1-4	0-0	1-0	1-1	3-2	1-0	1-3	1-1	2-3	0-1	1-2	2-3	2-0	4-4	2-1	■	2-2	2-1	0-2	3-2
Portsmouth FC	0-1	1-2	1-1	0-1	1-1	4-2	0-2	0-1	4-3	1-2	1-3	2-0	2-1	1-1	1-1		■	4-1	1-0	3-2
Southampton FC	1-1	2-3	0-0	3-2	1-2	0-0	1-3	2-2	2-2	3-3	2-0	0-0	1-2	2-2	1-2	4-3	2-1	■	1-0	2-2
Tottenham Hotspur FC	4-5	5-1	1-0	0-0	1-2	2-3	0-2	1-1	5-2	2-0	1-1	2-1	0-1	2-0	1-0	0-0	3-1	5-1	■	1-1
West Bromwich Albion FC	0-2	1-1	2-0	1-1	2-1	0-1	1-4	2-2	1-0	1-1	0-5	2-0	0-3	1-2	0-0	2-0	0-0	2-0	1-1	■

	F.A. Premiership	Pd	Wn	Dw	Ls	GF	GA	Pts	
1.	CHELSEA FC (LONDON)	38	29	8	1	72	15	95	
2.	Arsenal FC (London)	38	25	8	5	87	36	83	
3.	Manchester United FC (Manchester)	38	22	11	5	58	26	77	
4.	Everton FC (Liverpool)	38	18	7	13	45	46	61	
5.	Liverpool FC (Liverpool)	38	17	7	14	52	41	58	
6.	Bolton Wanderers FC (Bolton)	38	16	10	12	49	44	58	
7.	Middlesbrough FC (Middlesbrough)	38	14	13	11	53	46	55	
8.	Manchester City FC (Manchester)	38	13	13	12	47	39	52	
9.	Tottenham Hotspur FC (London)	38	14	10	14	47	41	52	
10.	Aston Villa FC (Birmingham)	38	12	11	15	45	52	47	
11.	Charlton Athletic FC (London)	38	12	10	16	42	58	46	
12.	Birmingham City FC (Birmingham)	38	11	12	15	40	46	45	
13.	Fulham FC (London)	38	12	8	18	52	60	44	
14.	Newcastle United FC (Newcastle-upon-Tyne)	38	10	14	14	47	57	44	
15.	Blackburn Rovers FC (Blackburn)	38	9	15	14	32	43	42	
16.	Portsmouth FC (Portsmouth)	38	10	9	19	43	59	39	
17.	West Bromwich Albion FC (West Bromwich)	38	6	16	16	36	61	34	
18.	Crystal Palace FC (London)	38	7	12	19	41	62	33	R
19.	Norwich City FC (Norwich)	38	7	12	19	42	77	33	R
20.	Southampton FC (Southampton)	38	6	14	18	45	66	32	R
		760	270	220	270	975	975	1030	

Top Goalscorers

1)	Thierry HENRY	(Arsenal FC)	25
2)	Andy JOHNSON	(Crystal Palace FC)	21

Football League The Championship 2004-05 Season	Brighton & H.A.	Burnley	Cardiff City	Coventry City	Crewe A.	Derby Co.	Gillingham	Ipswich T.	Leeds Utd.	Leicester C.	Millwall	Not. Forest	Plymouth A.	Preston NE	Q.P.R.	Reading	Rotherham	Sheff. Utd.	Stoke C.	Sunderland	Watford	West Ham	Wigan A.	Wolves
Brighton & H. Albion	■	0-1	1-1	1-1	1-3	2-3	2-1	1-1	1-0	1-1	1-0	0-0	0-2	1-0	2-3	0-1	1-0	1-1	0-1	2-1	2-1	2-2	2-4	0-1
Burnley FC	1-1	■	1-0	2-2	3-0	0-2	1-2	0-2	0-1	0-0	1-0	1-0	2-0	2-0	0-0	2-1	1-1	2-2	0-2	3-1	0-1	1-0	1-1	1-1
Cardiff City AFC	2-0	2-0	■	2-1	1-1	0-2	3-1	0-1	0-0	0-0	0-1	3-0	0-1	0-1	1-0	2-0	2-0	1-0	0-1	0-2	0-3	4-1	0-2	1-1
Coventry City FC	2-1	0-2	1-1	■	0-1	6-2	2-2	1-2	1-2	1-1	0-1	2-0	2-1	1-1	1-2	3-2	0-0	1-2	0-0	2-0	1-0	2-1	1-2	2-2
Crewe Alexandra FC	3-1	1-1	2-2	2-1	■	1-2	4-1	2-2	2-2	2-2	2-1	1-1	3-0	1-2	0-2	1-1	1-1	2-3	0-2	0-1	3-0	2-3	1-3	1-4
Derby County FC	3-0	1-1	0-1	2-2	2-4	■	2-0	3-2	2-0	1-2	0-3	3-0	1-0	3-1	0-0	2-1	3-2	0-1	3-1	0-2	2-2	1-1	1-1	3-3
Gillingham FC	0-1	1-0	1-1	3-1	1-1	0-2	■	0-0	2-1	0-0	2-0	2-1	1-0	0-1	0-0	3-1	1-3	2-1	0-4	0-0	0-1	2-1	1-0	1-0
Ipswich Town FC	1-0	1-1	3-1	3-2	5-1	3-2	2-1	■	1-0	2-1	2-0	6-0	3-2	3-0	0-2	1-1	4-3	5-1	1-0	2-2	1-2	0-2	2-1	2-1
Leeds United AFC	1-1	1-2	1-1	3-0	0-2	1-0	1-1	1-1	■	0-2	1-1	1-1	2-1	1-0	6-1	3-1	0-0	0-4	0-0	0-1	2-2	2-1	0-2	1-1
Leicester City FC	0-1	0-0	1-1	3-0	1-1	1-0	2-0	2-2	2-0	■	3-1	0-1	2-1	1-1	1-0	0-2	0-1	3-2	1-1	0-1	0-1	0-0	0-2	1-1
Millwall FC	2-0	0-0	2-2	1-1	4-3	3-1	2-1	3-1	1-1	2-0	■	1-0	3-0	2-1	0-0	1-0	1-2	1-2	0-1	2-0	0-2	1-0	0-2	1-2
Nottingham Forest FC	0-1	1-0	0-0	1-4	2-2	2-2	2-2	1-1	0-0	1-1	1-2	■	0-3	2-0	2-1	1-0	2-2	1-1	1-0	1-2	1-2	2-1	1-1	1-0
Plymouth Argyle FC	5-1	1-0	1-1	1-1	3-0	0-2	2-1	1-2	0-1	0-0	0-0	3-2	■	0-2	2-1	2-2	1-1	3-0	0-0	2-1	1-0	1-1	1-2	1-2
Preston North End FC	3-0	1-0	3-0	3-2	1-0	3-0	1-1	1-1	2-4	1-1	1-1	3-2	1-1	■	2-1	3-0	2-0	0-1	3-0	3-2	2-1	2-1	1-1	2-2
Queen's Park Rangers	0-0	3-0	1-0	4-1	1-2	0-2	1-1	2-4	1-1	3-2	1-1	2-1	3-2	1-2	■	0-0	1-1	0-1	1-0	1-3	3-1	1-0	1-0	1-2
Reading FC	3-2	0-0	2-1	1-2	4-0	0-1	3-1	1-1	1-1	0-0	2-1	1-0	0-0	3-1	1-0	■	1-0	0-0	1-0	1-0	3-0	3-1	1-1	1-2
Rotherham United FC	0-1	0-0	2-2	1-2	2-3	1-3	1-3	0-2	1-0	0-2	1-1	0-0	0-1	1-2	0-1	1-0	■	2-2	1-1	0-1	0-1	2-2	0-2	1-2
Sheffield United FC	1-2	2-1	2-1	1-1	4-0	0-1	0-0	0-2	2-0	2-0	0-1	1-1	2-1	1-1	3-2	0-1	1-0	■	0-0	1-0	1-1	1-2	0-2	3-3
Stoke City FC	2-0	0-1	1-3	1-0	1-0	1-0	2-0	3-2	0-1	3-2	1-0	0-0	2-0	0-0	0-1	0-1	1-2	2-0	■	0-1	0-1	0-1	0-1	2-1
Sunderland AFC	2-0	2-1	2-1	1-0	3-1	0-0	1-1	2-0	2-3	2-1	1-0	2-0	5-1	3-1	2-2	1-2	4-1	1-0	1-0	■	4-2	0-2	1-1	3-1
Watford FC	1-1	0-1	0-0	2-3	3-1	2-2	2-0	2-2	1-2	2-2	1-0	0-2	3-1	0-2	3-0	0-1	0-0	0-0	0-1	1-1	■	1-2	0-0	1-1
West Ham United FC	0-1	1-0	1-0	3-0	1-1	1-2	3-1	1-1	1-1	2-2	1-1	3-2	5-0	1-2	2-1	1-0	1-0	0-2	2-0	1-2	3-2	■	1-3	1-0
Wigan Athletic AFC	3-0	0-0	2-1	4-1	4-1	1-2	2-0	1-0	3-0	0-0	2-0	1-1	0-2	5-0	0-0	3-1	2-0	4-0	0-1	0-1	2-2	1-2	■	2-0
Wolverhampton W.	1-1	2-0	2-3	0-1	1-1	2-0	2-2	2-0	0-0	1-1	1-2	2-1	1-1	2-2	2-1	4-1	2-0	4-2	1-1	1-1	0-0	4-2	3-3	■

Football League "The Championship"

#	Club	Pd	Wn	Dw	Ls	GF	GA	Pts	
1.	Sunderland AFC (Sunderland)	46	29	7	10	76	41	94	P
2.	Wigan Athletic AFC (Wigan)	46	25	12	9	79	35	87	P
3.	Ipswich Town FC (Ipswich)	46	24	13	9	85	56	85	PO
4.	Derby County FC (Derby)	46	22	10	14	71	60	76	PO
5.	Preston North End FC (Preston)	46	21	12	13	67	58	75	PO
6.	West Ham United FC (London)	46	21	10	15	66	56	73	PO
7.	Reading FC (Reading)	46	19	13	14	51	44	70	
8.	Sheffield United FC (Sheffield)	46	18	13	15	57	56	67	
9.	Wolverhampton Wanderers FC (Wolverhampton)	46	15	21	10	72	59	66	
10.	Millwall FC (London)	46	18	12	16	51	45	66	
11.	Queen's Park Rangers FC (London)	46	17	11	18	54	58	62	
12.	Stoke City FC (Stoke-on-Trent)	46	17	10	19	36	38	61	
13.	Burnley FC (Burnley)	46	15	15	16	38	39	60	
14.	Leeds United AFC (Leeds)	46	14	18	14	49	52	60	
15.	Leicester City FC (Leicester)	46	12	21	13	49	46	57	
16.	Cardiff City AFC (Cardiff)	46	13	15	18	48	51	54	
17.	Plymouth Argyle FC (Plymouth)	46	14	11	21	52	64	53	
18.	Watford FC (Watford)	46	12	16	18	52	59	52	
19.	Coventry City FC (Coventry)	46	13	13	20	61	73	52	
20.	Brighton & Hove Albion FC (Brighton)	46	13	12	21	40	65	51	
21.	Crewe Alexandra FC (Crewe)	46	12	14	20	66	86	50	
22.	Gillingham FC (Gillingham)	46	12	14	20	45	66	50	R
23.	Nottingham Forest FC (Nottingham)	46	9	17	20	42	66	44	R
24.	Rotherham United FC (Rotherham)	46	5	14	27	35	69	29	R
		1104	390	324	390	1342	1342	1494	

Promotion Play-Offs

West Ham United FC (London)	1-0	Preston North End FC (Preston)
Preston North End FC (Preston)	2-0, 0-0	Derby County FC (Derby)
West Ham United FC (London)	2-2, 2-0	Ipswich Town FC (Ipswich)

Football League — League 1 — 2004-05 Season

2004-05 Season	Barnsley	Blackpool	Bournemouth	Bradford C.	Brentford	Bristol C.	Chesterfield	Colchester	Doncaster	Hartlepool	Huddersfield	Hull City	Luton T.	Milton K.	Oldham A.	Peterborough	Port Vale	Sheff. Wed.	Stockport	Swindon T.	Torquay U.	Tranmere R.	Walsall	Wrexham
Barnsley FC		1-0	0-1	2-2	0-0	2-1	1-0	1-1	1-3	0-0	4-2	1-2	3-4	1-1	2-2	4-0	1-2	0-0	3-3	2-2	4-1	0-0	3-2	2-2
Blackpool FC	0-2		3-3	2-1	2-1	1-1	1-0	1-1	1-1	2-2	1-1	0-2	1-3	1-0	2-0	0-1	0-2	1-2	0-4	1-1	4-0	0-1	2-0	2-1
AFC Bournemouth	1-3	2-3		2-0	3-2	2-2	0-0	1-3	5-0	2-2	2-2	0-4	0-1	0-1	4-0	0-1	4-0	1-1	2-1	2-1	3-0	1-1	2-2	1-0
Bradford City AFC	1-0	2-1	4-2		4-1	4-1	2-3	2-2	2-0	1-2	2-0	0-2	0-1	1-4	1-3	2-2	0-2	3-1	3-1	1-2	2-2	1-1	1-1	1-1
Brentford FC	1-1	0-3	2-1	1-2		1-0	2-2	1-0	4-3	2-1	0-1	2-1	2-0	1-0	2-0	0-0	1-0	3-3	3-0	2-1	1-3	1-0	1-0	1-0
Bristol City FC	0-0	1-1	0-2	0-0	4-1		2-3	0-0	2-2	0-0	3-3	3-1	1-2	4-1	5-1	2-0	2-0	1-4	5-0	1-2	1-1	4-0	0-1	1-0
Chesterfield FC	2-2	1-0	2-3	0-0	3-1	2-2		2-1	0-0	0-1	2-1	1-1	0-1	2-2	1-0	1-3	1-0	1-3	4-0	1-0	1-1	2-2	1-0	2-4
Colchester United	0-2	0-1	3-1	0-0	0-1	0-2	1-0		4-1	1-1	0-0	1-2	0-0	0-0	2-1	2-1	1-1	3-2	0-1	2-1	1-2	5-0		1-2
Doncaster Rovers	4-0	2-0	1-1	1-1	0-0	1-1	0-1	1-1		2-0	2-1	1-0	3-3	3-0	1-1	2-1	2-0	0-4	3-1	1-1	2-2	0-0	3-1	0-0
Hartlepool United	1-1	1-1	3-2	2-1	3-1	2-1	3-2	2-1	2-1		0-1	2-0	2-3	5-0	2-1	2-2	1-0	3-0	3-1	3-0	4-1	0-1	1-3	4-6
Huddersfield Town	0-2	1-0	3-2	0-1	1-1	2-2	0-0	2-2	3-1	0-2		4-0	1-1	3-1	2-1	2-1	2-1	1-0	5-3	4-0	1-1	1-3	3-1	1-2
Hull City AFC	2-1	2-1	1-0	0-1	2-0	1-1	1-0	2-0	2-1	1-0	2-1		3-0	3-2	2-0	2-2	2-2	1-2	0-0	0-0	2-0	6-1	3-1	2-1
Luton Town FC	1-3	1-0	1-0	4-0	4-2	5-0	1-0	2-2	1-1	3-0	1-2	1-0		1-0	2-1	2-1	1-0	1-1	3-0	3-1	1-0	1-1	1-0	5-1
Milton Keynes Dons	1-1	3-1	1-3	1-2	0-0	1-2	1-1	2-0	0-1	4-2	2-1	1-1	1-4		1-1	1-1	1-1	2-2	2-1	1-1	1-0	2-1	1-1	3-0
Oldham Athletic	3-2	1-2	1-2	2-1	0-2	0-0	4-1	1-1	1-2	3-2	1-0	2-2	3-0			2-1	3-0	1-1	1-2	1-2	1-2	2-2	5-3	2-3
Peterborough United	1-3	0-0	0-1	2-2	3-0	0-1	1-2	0-3	0-2	3-0	1-2	2-3	2-2	0-3	1-2		4-0	1-1	0-2	1-1	1-0	0-2	2-2	
Port Vale FC	5-0	0-3	2-1	0-1	0-1	3-0	1-0	0-0	2-0	0-1	0-3	3-2	3-1	3-2	3-1	1-0		0-2	0-0	1-0	1-2	3-1	2-0	0-2
Sheffield Wed.	1-0	3-2	0-1	1-2	1-2	2-3	2-2	0-3	2-0	2-0	1-0	2-4	0-0	1-1	1-1	2-1	1-0		0-0	2-0	2-2	1-2	3-2	4-0
Stockport County	2-2	0-1	2-2	0-1	1-2	1-2	1-2	1-2	2-4	1-0	2-3	1-3	3-1	1-2	1-0	1-2	0-3			3-3	0-2	1-1	0-1	1-4
Swindon Town FC	2-1	2-2	0-3	1-0	3-0	0-0	1-1	0-3	1-1	3-0	4-2	2-3	2-1	1-0	0-1	1-0	3-2	3-0			3-3	2-1	1-2	4-2
Torquay United FC	0-1	2-0	1-2	0-0	2-2	0-4	2-2	1-3	2-1	1-2	2-1	0-3	1-4	1-0	2-0	1-0	2-4	1-2	2-2			1-2	0-0	1-0
Tranmere Rovers	1-1	0-0	2-0	4-5	1-0	0-1	1-0	1-1	2-4	2-1	3-0	1-3	1-1	2-0	2-0	5-0	1-0	4-2	1-0	2-1	4-1		2-1	1-1
Walsall FC	2-2	3-2	1-2	1-1	0-1	1-2	3-0	2-1	1-1	2-1	4-3	3-0	2-0	0-0	0-1	2-1	3-2	1-1	3-0	3-2	1-1	0-2		2-2
Wrexham AFC	2-1	1-2	1-2	1-0	1-2	1-3	3-1	2-2	0-0	1-5	0-1	2-2	1-2	0-0	1-0	1-1	1-1	0-3	2-1	2-1	1-1	1-5	1-1	

	Football League "League 1"	Pd	Wn	Dw	Ls	GF	GA	Pts	
1.	Luton Town FC (Luton)	46	29	11	6	87	48	98	P
2.	Hull City AFC (Kingston-upon-Hull)	46	26	8	12	80	53	86	P
3.	Tranmere Rovers FC (Birkenhead)	46	22	13	11	73	55	79	PO
4.	Brentford FC (London)	46	22	9	15	57	60	75	PO
5.	Sheffield Wednesday FC (Sheffield)	46	19	15	12	77	59	72	PO
6.	Hartlepool United FC (Hartlepool)	46	21	8	17	76	66	71	PO
7.	Bristol City FC (Bristol)	46	18	16	12	74	57	70	
8.	AFC Bournemouth (Bournemouth)	46	20	10	16	77	64	70	
9.	Huddersfield Town AFC (Huddersfield)	46	20	10	16	74	65	70	
10.	Doncaster Rovers FC (Doncaster)	46	16	18	12	65	60	66	
11.	Bradford City AFC (Bradford)	46	17	14	15	64	62	65	
12.	Swindon Town FC (Swindon)	46	17	12	17	66	68	63	
13.	Barnsley FC (Barnsley)	46	14	19	13	69	64	61	
14.	Walsall FC (Walsall)	46	16	12	18	65	69	60	
15.	Colchester United FC (Colchester)	46	14	17	15	60	50	59	
16.	Blackpool FC (Blackpool)	46	15	12	19	54	59	57	
17.	Chesterfield FC (Chesterfield)	46	14	15	17	55	62	57	
18.	Port Vale FC (Stoke-on-Trent)	46	17	5	24	49	59	56	
19.	Oldham Athletic AFC (Oldham)	46	14	10	22	60	73	52	
20.	Milton Keynes Dons FC (Milton Keynes)	46	12	15	19	54	68	51	
21.	Torquay United FC (Torquay)	46	12	15	19	55	79	51	R
22.	Wrexham AFC (Wrexham)	46	13	14	19	62	80	43	R-10
23.	Peterborough United FC (Peterborough)	46	9	12	25	49	73	39	R
24.	Stockport County FC (Stockport)	46	6	8	32	49	98	26	R
		1104	407	298	407	1551	1551	1497	

Note: Wrexham AFC (Wrexham) had 10 points deducted for entering administration.

Promotion Play-Offs

Sheffield Wednesday FC (Sheffield)	4-2 (aet)	Hartlepool United FC (Hartlepool)
Hartlepool United FC (Hartlepool)	2-0, 0-2 (aet)	Tranmere Rovers FC (Birkenhead)
	(Hartlepool United won 6-5 on penalties)	
Sheffield Wednesday FC (Sheffield)	1-0, 2-1	Brentford FC (London)

Football League — League 2 — 2004-05 Season

Home \ Away	Boston United	Bristol Rovers	Bury	Cambridge Utd.	Cheltenham T.	Chester City	Darlington	Grimsby Town	Kidderminster H.	Leyton Orient	Lincoln City	Macclesfield	Mansfield Town	Northampton	Notts County	Oxford United	Rochdale	Rushden & Diam.	Scunthorpe United	Shrewsbury	Southend United	Swansea City	Wycombe Wands.	Yeovil Town
Boston United FC	■	2-2	2-2	2-1	2-1	3-1	3-1	1-1	3-0	2-2	0-2	1-1	0-0	0-1	4-0	1-0	1-1	1-0	2-1	2-2	2-0	2-3	2-0	1-2
Bristol Rovers FC	1-1	■	2-2	1-1	1-1	4-1	3-3	3-0	2-0	1-1	0-0	0-0	4-4	3-1	2-1	2-0	0-0	3-0	0-3	0-0	2-1	2-0	1-0	2-2
Bury FC	1-1	1-1	■	2-1	3-1	1-1	0-1	3-1	4-0	0-0	0-1	2-1	0-2	2-0	1-0	0-0	0-1	0-1	0-0	0-1	0-1	0-1	2-2	3-1
Cambridge United	0-1	1-0	1-1	■	1-0	0-0	3-1	0-2	1-3	1-1	0-1	1-1	2-2	0-1	0-0	2-1	0-0	3-1	1-2	1-0	0-2	0-1	2-1	3-5
Cheltenham Town	1-0	1-1	1-0	2-1	■	0-0	0-2	2-3	2-0	1-2	1-0	3-0	1-0	0-2	2-0	4-1	0-2	1-1	0-3	1-2	1-1	1-2	1-1	1-1
Chester City FC	2-1	2-2	2-1	0-0	0-3	■	0-3	2-1	3-0	1-1	1-0	1-0	0-3	0-2	3-2	1-3	0-0	3-1	1-1	1-1	2-2	1-1	0-2	0-2
Darlington FC	1-0	0-1	1-2	1-1	3-1	1-0	■	1-0	0-2	3-0	0-3	3-1	2-1	1-1	1-2	1-1	0-3	2-0	0-0	3-0	4-0	2-1	1-0	2-1
Grimsby Town FC	1-1	0-0	5-1	3-0	1-1	1-0	0-1	■	2-1	2-0	2-4	0-0	2-1	3-2	1-1	0-1	0-0	0-0	1-1	1-1	1-1	1-1	0-0	0-0
Kidderminster Harr.	0-4	1-1	2-2	1-1	1-0	0-1	1-0	1-4	■	1-2	1-1	1-3	0-2	0-0	1-3	2-1	0-0	3-2	0-1	1-3	1-5	0-2	1-1	1-1
Leyton Orient FC	0-0	4-2	1-1	1-1	2-3	2-0	1-0	1-2	2-1	■	1-1	1-3	2-1	3-2	2-0	0-0	2-1	2-2	1-1	4-1	2-2	3-1	1-2	2-3
Lincoln City FC	2-2	1-1	1-0	2-1	0-0	1-1	0-0	0-0	3-0	3-4	■	2-0	2-0	3-2	1-2	3-0	1-1	1-3	2-0	2-0	1-1	1-0	2-3	3-1
Macclesfield Town	1-1	2-1	1-1	1-1	0-2	1-2	1-0	3-1	2-0	3-1	2-1	■	3-1	1-3	1-2	1-0	3-0	1-0	2-1	2-1	1-2	1-0	2-1	3-1
Mansfield Town FC	3-2	0-2	0-0	0-0	1-2	0-0	1-1	2-0	2-1	0-1	2-2	0-1	■	4-1	3-1	1-3	1-0	0-0	1-1	1-1	1-1	1-4	1-1	4-1
Northampton Town	2-1	2-1	2-1	2-2	1-1	1-1	1-1	3-0	2-2	1-0	1-0	2-1	2-1	■	0-0	1-0	5-1	1-2	2-0	2-2	1-1	1-1	1-1	1-1
Notts County FC	2-1	1-2	0-1	2-1	0-0	1-1	1-1	2-2	1-3	1-2	1-0	0-5	0-1	0-0	■	0-1	0-0	1-1	2-0	3-0	1-2	1-0	0-1	1-2
Oxford United FC	2-0	3-2	3-1	2-1	1-0	0-1	1-2	1-2	0-2	2-2	0-1	1-1	1-0	1-2	2-1	■	0-1	0-0	1-1	2-0	0-1	2-1	2-1	2-1
Rochdale AFC	2-0	0-0	0-3	2-1	1-2	2-2	1-1	2-0	1-1	2-0	3-1	3-0	1-1	1-0	0-3	5-1	■	2-0	0-0	1-1	0-0	1-2	1-1	2-1
Rushden/Diamonds	4-2	0-0	3-0	1-1	0-0	2-0	1-1	0-0	2-0	1-4	0-2	0-0	3-2	5-1	3-3	0-0	1-3	■	0-0	1-4	0-0	1-2	2-0	2-0
Scunthorpe United	1-1	4-0	3-2	4-0	4-1	1-2	0-1	2-0	2-1	1-0	3-2	0-0	1-1	2-0	0-0	1-1	3-1	1-0	■	3-1	3-2	1-0	2-0	1-0
Shrewsbury Town	0-0	2-0	2-2	0-0	2-0	5-0	4-0	1-1	4-2	4-1	1-1	2-1	3-0	0-1	0-0	0-1	0-0	1-3	0-0	■	1-1	2-0	0-1	1-1
Southend United FC	2-1	2-0	1-0	2-1	0-2	1-0	2-0	1-1	1-0	0-1	2-1	0-1	2-1	1-0	2-1	4-0	3-0	0-0	1-0	1-0	■	4-2	1-2	0-1
Swansea City FC	3-1	1-0	1-3	3-0	1-1	3-0	2-1	0-0	3-0	1-0	1-0	2-0	1-0	0-2	4-0	1-0	2-2	1-0	2-1	1-0	1-1	■	2-2	0-2
Wycombe Wanderers	1-2	1-0	1-2	2-1	1-1	4-2	1-1	2-0	3-0	3-2	1-0	1-1	1-1	0-1	1-2	1-1	0-3	1-1	2-1	1-1	0-1	0-1	■	0-1
Yeovil Town FC	2-0	4-2	0-1	2-1	4-1	4-1	1-1	2-1	2-1	1-0	3-0	1-2	5-2	1-1	1-3	6-1	0-3	3-1	4-3	4-2	3-1	1-0	1-1	■

Football League "League 2"

		Pd	Wn	Dw	Ls	GF	GA	Pts	
1.	Yeovil Town FC (Yeovil)	46	25	8	13	90	65	83	P
2.	Scunthorpe United FC (Scunthorpe)	46	22	14	10	69	42	80	P
3.	Swansea City FC (Swansea)	46	24	8	14	62	43	80	P
4.	Southend United FC (Southend-on-Sea)	46	22	12	12	65	46	78	PO
5.	Macclesfield Town FC (Macclesfield)	46	22	9	15	60	49	75	PO
6.	Lincoln City FC (Lincoln)	46	20	12	14	64	47	72	PO
7.	Northampton Town FC (Northampton)	46	20	12	14	62	51	72	PO
8.	Darlington FC (Darlington)	46	20	12	14	57	49	72	
9.	Rochdale FC (Rochdale)	46	16	18	12	54	48	66	
10.	Wycombe Wanderers FC (High Wycombe)	46	17	14	15	58	52	65	
11.	Leyton Orient FC (London)	46	16	15	15	65	67	63	
12.	Bristol Rovers FC (Bristol)	46	13	21	12	60	57	60	
13.	Mansfield Town FC (Mansfield)	46	15	15	16	56	56	60	
14.	Cheltenham Town FC (Cheltenham)	46	16	12	18	51	54	60	
15.	Oxford United FC (Oxford)	46	16	11	19	50	63	59	
16.	Boston United FC (Boston)	46	14	16	16	62	58	58	
17.	Bury FC (Bury)	46	14	16	16	54	54	58	
18.	Grimsby Town FC (Cleethorpes)	46	14	16	16	51	52	58	
19.	Notts County FC (Nottingham)	46	13	13	20	46	62	52	
20.	Chester City FC (Chester)	46	12	16	18	43	69	52	
21.	Shrewsbury Town FC (Shrewsbury)	46	11	16	19	48	53	49	
22.	Rushden & Diamonds FC (Irthlingborough)	46	10	14	22	42	63	44	
23.	Kidderminster Harriers FC (Kidderminster)	46	10	8	28	39	85	38	R
24.	Cambridge United FC (Cambridge)	46	8	16	22	39	62	30	R-10
		1104	390	324	390	1347	1347	1484	

Note: Cambridge United FC (Cambridge) had 10 points deducted for entering administration.

Promotion Play-Offs

Southend United FC (Southend-on-Sea)	2-0 (aet)	Lincoln City FC (Lincoln)
Lincoln City FC (Lincoln)	1-0, 1-1	Macclesfield Town FC (Macclesfield)
Northampton Town FC (Northampton)	0-0, 0-1	Southend United FC (Southend-on-Sea)

Promoted to League 2: Barnet FC (London) and Carlisle United FC (Carlisle)

F.A. CUP FINAL   (Millennium Stadium, Cardiff – 21/05/2005 – 71,876)

ARSENAL FC (LONDON)	0-0 (aet)	Manchester United FC (Manchester)

(Arsenal won 5-4 on penalties)

Arsenal: Lehmann, Lauren, Touré, Senderos, Cole, Gilberto, Fabregas (van Persie 86'), Vieira, Pires (Edu 106'), Bergkamp (Ljungberg 64'), Reyes.

Man. United: Carroll, Brown, Ferdinand, Silvestre, O'Shea (Fortune 76'), Fletcher (Giggs 91'), Keane, Scholes, Ronaldo, van Nistelrooy, Rooney.

Semi-finals

Arsenal FC (London)	3-0	Blackburn Rovers FC (Blackburn)
Newcastle United FC (Newcastle-upon-Tyne)	1-4	Manchester United FC (Manchester)

Quarter-finals

Blackburn Rovers FC (Blackburn)	1-0	Leicester City FC (Leicester)
Bolton Wanderers FC (Bolton)	0-1	Arsenal FC (London)
Newcastle United FC (Newcastle-upon-Tyne)	1-0	Tottenham Hotspur FC (London)
Southampton FC (Southampton)	0-4	Manchester United FC (Manchester)